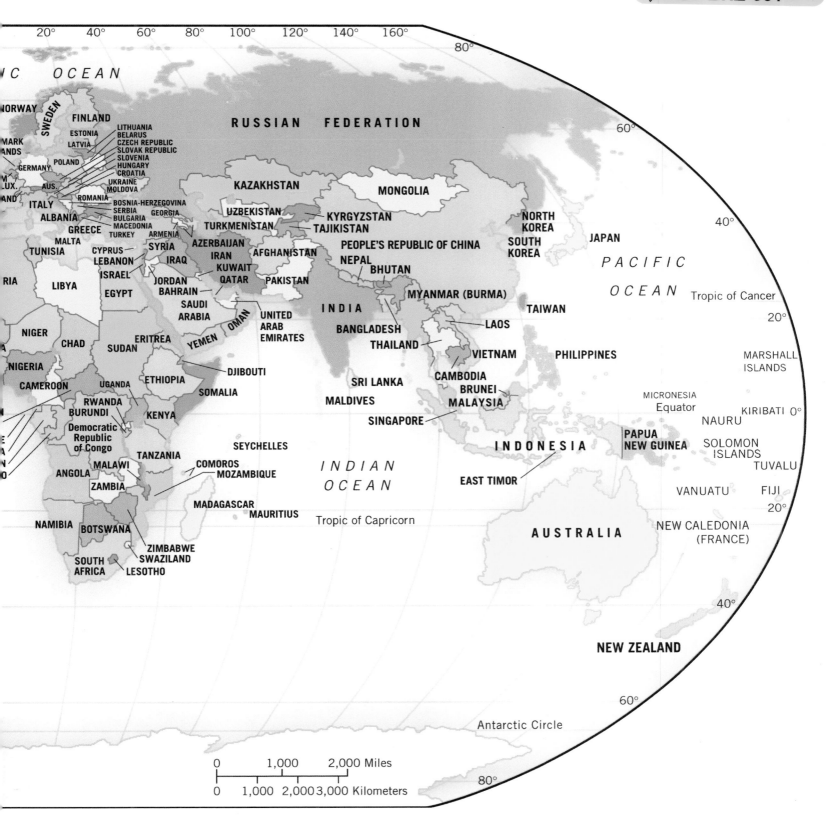

20° 40° 60° 80° 100° 120° 140° 160° 80°

OCEAN

60°

NORWAY SWEDEN FINLAND **RUSSIAN FEDERATION**

ESTONIA LITHUANIA
LATVIA BELARUS
CZECH REPUBLIC
SLOVAK REPUBLIC
SLOVENIA
HUNGARY
CROATIA
UKRAINE
MOLDOVA

MARK
ANDS

GERMANY
LUX.
AND AUS.
POLAND

ITALY ROMANIA
ALBANIA BOSNIA-HERZEGOVINA
SERBIA
BULGARIA GEORGIA
GREECE MACEDONIA
TURKEY ARMENIA

KAZAKHSTAN MONGOLIA

40°

UZBEKISTAN KYRGYZSTAN
TURKMENISTAN TAJIKISTAN

NORTH
KOREA
SOUTH
KOREA

JAPAN

MALTA
TUNISIA CYPRUS
LEBANON SYRIA
ISRAEL IRAQ
AZERBAIJAN
IRAN
KUWAIT
QATAR
AFGHANISTAN
NEPAL
BHUTAN

PEOPLE'S REPUBLIC OF CHINA

PACIFIC

OCEAN Tropic of Cancer

20°

LIBYA EGYPT
JORDAN
BAHRAIN
SAUDI
ARABIA
PAKISTAN

MYANMAR (BURMA)

TAIWAN

NIGER CHAD SUDAN
ERITREA
YEMEN OMAN
UNITED
ARAB
EMIRATES

INDIA

BANGLADESH

LAOS

MARSHALL
ISLANDS

NIGERIA
CAMEROON UGANDA
ETHIOPIA
DJIBOUTI

THAILAND

VIETNAM

PHILIPPINES

RWANDA
BURUNDI
Democratic
Republic
of Congo
SOMALIA
KENYA

SRI LANKA
MALDIVES

CAMBODIA
BRUNEI
MALAYSIA

MICRONESIA
Equator

KIRIBATI 0°

NAURU

SINGAPORE

ANGOLA MALAWI
ZAMBIA
TANZANIA

SEYCHELLES

COMOROS
MOZAMBIQUE

INDIAN
OCEAN

INDONESIA

PAPUA
NEW GUINEA

SOLOMON
ISLANDS
TUVALU

EAST TIMOR

VANUATU FIJI

MADAGASCAR
MAURITIUS Tropic of Capricorn

20°

NAMIBIA BOTSWANA

ZIMBABWE
SWAZILAND

NEW CALEDONIA
(FRANCE)

AUSTRALIA

SOUTH
AFRICA LESOTHO

40°

NEW ZEALAND

60°

Antarctic Circle

80°

0	1,000	2,000 Miles

0	1,000	2,000	3,000 Kilometers

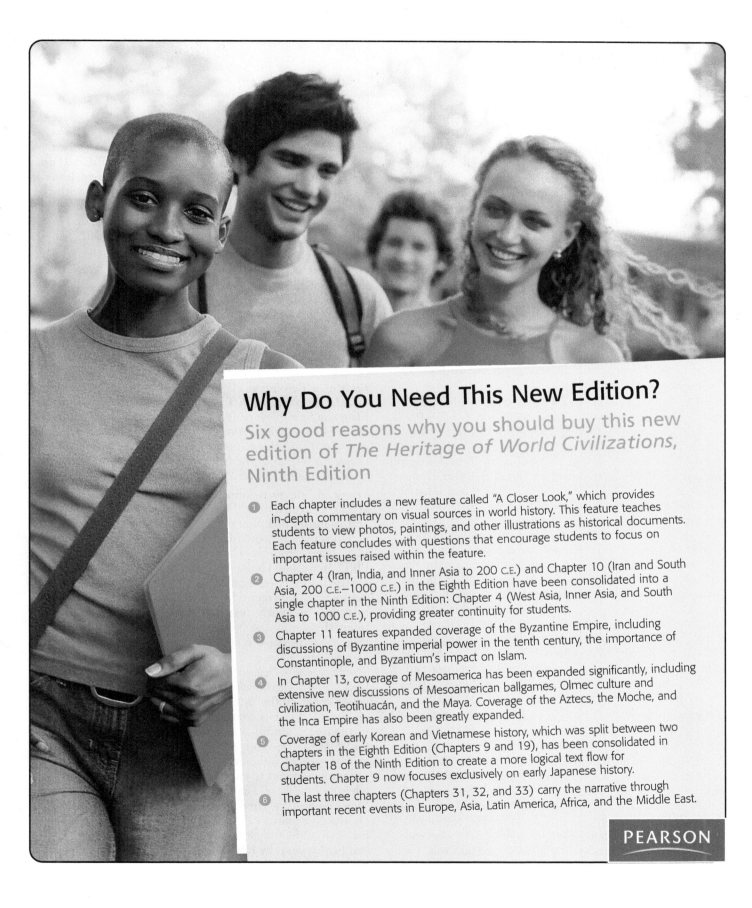

Why Do You Need This New Edition?

Six good reasons why you should buy this new edition of *The Heritage of World Civilizations*, Ninth Edition

1. Each chapter includes a new feature called "A Closer Look," which provides in-depth commentary on visual sources in world history. This feature teaches students to view photos, paintings, and other illustrations as historical documents. Each feature concludes with questions that encourage students to focus on important issues raised within the feature.

2. Chapter 4 (Iran, India, and Inner Asia to 200 C.E.) and Chapter 10 (Iran and South Asia, 200 C.E.–1000 C.E.) in the Eighth Edition have been consolidated into a single chapter in the Ninth Edition: Chapter 4 (West Asia, Inner Asia, and South Asia to 1000 C.E.), providing greater continuity for students.

3. Chapter 11 features expanded coverage of the Byzantine Empire, including discussions of Byzantine imperial power in the tenth century, the importance of Constantinople, and Byzantium's impact on Islam.

4. In Chapter 13, coverage of Mesoamerica has been expanded significantly, including extensive new discussions of Mesoamerican ballgames, Olmec culture and civilization, Teotihuacán, and the Maya. Coverage of the Aztecs, the Moche, and the Inca Empire has also been greatly expanded.

5. Coverage of early Korean and Vietnamese history, which was split between two chapters in the Eighth Edition (Chapters 9 and 19), has been consolidated in Chapter 18 of the Ninth Edition to create a more logical text flow for students. Chapter 9 now focuses exclusively on early Japanese history.

6. The last three chapters (Chapters 31, 32, and 33) carry the narrative through important recent events in Europe, Asia, Latin America, Africa, and the Middle East.

PEARSON

About the Authors

Albert M. Craig is the Harvard-Yenching Research Professor of History Emeritus at Harvard University, where he has taught since 1959. A graduate of Northwestern University, he received his Ph.D. at Harvard University. He has studied at Strasbourg University and at Kyoto, Keio, and Tokyo universities in Japan. He is the author of *Choshu in the Meiji Restoration* (1961), *The Heritage of Chinese Civilization,* Third Edition (2011), *Civilization and Enlightenment: The Early Thought of Fukuzawa Yukichi* (2009), *The Heritage of Japanese Civilization*, Second Edition (2011), and, with others, of *East Asia, Tradition and Transformation* (1989). He is the editor of *Japan, A Comparative View* (1973) and co-editor of *Personality in Japanese History* (1970). For eleven years (1976–1987) he was the director of the Harvard-Yenching Institute. He has also been a visiting professor at Kyoto and Tokyo universities. He has received Guggenheim, Fulbright, and Japan Foundation Fellowships. In 1988 he was awarded the Order of the Rising Sun by the Japanese government.

William A. Graham is Albertson Professor of Middle Eastern Studies in the Faculty of Arts and Sciences and O'Brian Professor and Dean of the Faculty of Divinity at Harvard University, where he has taught since 1973. He has directed the Center for Middle Eastern Studies and chaired Near Eastern Languages and Civilizations and the Study of Religion. He received his B.A. from the University of North Carolina, Chapel Hill and the A.M. and Ph.D. from Harvard. He also studied in Göttingen, Tübingen, Lebanon, and London. He has chaired the (North American) Council on Graduate Studies in Religion. In 2000 he received the quinquennial Award for Excellence in Research in Islamic History and Culture from the Research Centre for Islamic History, Art and Culture of the Organisation of the Islamic Conference. He has held Guggenheim and von Humboldt research fellowships and is a fellow of the American Academy of Arts and Sciences. He is the author of *Divine Word and Prophetic Word in Early Islam* (1977—ACLS History of Religions Prize, 1978), *Beyond the Written Word: Oral Aspects of Scripture in the History of Religion* (1987), *Islamic and Comparative Religious Studies* (2010), and, with others, of *Three Faiths, One God* (2003).

Donald Kagan is Sterling Professor of History and Classics at Yale University, where he has taught since 1969. He received the A.B. degree in history from Brooklyn College, the M.A. in classics from Brown University, and the Ph.D. in history from Ohio State University. During 1958–1959 he studied at the American School of Classical Studies as a Fulbright Scholar. He has received three awards for undergraduate teaching at Cornell and Yale. He is the author of a history of Greek political thought, *The Great Dialogue* (1965); a four-volume history of the Peloponnesian war, *The Origins of the Peloponnesian War* (1969); *The Archidamian War* (1974); *The Peace of Nicias and the Sicilian Expedition* (1981); *The Fall of the Athenian Empire* (1987); a biography of Pericles, *Pericles of Athens and the Birth of Democracy* (1991); *On the Origins of War* (1995); and *The Peloponnesian War* (2003). He is coauthor, with Frederick W. Kagan, of *While America Sleeps* (2000). With Brian Tierney and L. Pearce Williams, he is the editor of *Great Issues in Western Civilization*, a collection of readings. And with Gregory F. Viggiano, he is the editor of *Problems in the History of Ancient Greece: Sources and Interpretation* (2010). He was awarded the National Humanities Medal for 2002.

Steven Ozment is McLean Professor of Ancient and Modern History at Harvard University. He has taught Western Civilization at Yale, Stanford, and Harvard. He is the author of nine books. *The Age of Reform,* 1250–1550 (1980), won the Schaff Prize, and was nominated for the 1981 National Book Award. Five of his books have been selections of the History Book Club: *Magdalena and Balthasar: An Intimate Portrait of Life in Sixteenth Century Europe* (1986), *Three Behaim Boys: Growing Up in Early Modern Germany* (1990), *Protestants: The Birth of a Revolution* (1992), *The Burgermeister's Daughter: Scandal in a Sixteenth Century German Town* (1996), and *Flesh and Spirit: Private Life in Early Modern Germany* (1999). Recent books include *Ancestors: The Loving Family of Old Europe* (2001), *A Mighty Fortress: A New History of the German People* (2004), and *The Serpent and the Lamb: When Lucas Cranach, the Elder Met Martin Luther* (2012).

Frank M. Turner is John Hay Whitney Professor of History at Yale University and Director of the Beinecke Rare Book and Manuscript Library at Yale University, where he served as University Provost from 1988 to 1992. He received his B.A. degree from the College of William and Mary and his Ph.D. from Yale. He has received the Yale College Award for Distinguished Undergraduate Teaching. He has directed a National Endowment for the Humanities Summer Institute. His scholarly research has received the support of fellowships from the National Endowment for the Humanities, the Guggenheim Foundation, and the Woodrow Wilson Center. He is the author of *Between Science and Religion: The Reaction to Scientific Naturalism in Late Victorian England* (1974), *The Greek Heritage in Victorian Britain* (1981), which received the British Council Prize of the Conference on British Studies and the Yale Press Governors Award, *Contesting Cultural Authority: Essays in Victorian Intellectual Life* (1993), and *John Henry Newman: The Challenge to Evangelical Religion* (2002). He has also contributed numerous articles to journals and has served on the editorial advisory boards of *The Journal of Modern History, Isis*, and *Victorian Studies*. He edited *The Idea of a University*, by John Henry Newman (1996), *Reflections on the Revolution in France by Edmund Burke* (2003), and *Apologia Pro Vita Sua and Six Sermons* by John Henry Newman (2008). He served as a Trustee of Connecticut College from 1996–2006. In 2003, Professor Turner was appointed Director of the Beinecke Rare Book and Manuscript Library at Yale University.

VOLUME 2: Since 1500

The Heritage of World Civilizations

Ninth Edition

ALBERT M. CRAIG
Harvard University

WILLIAM A. GRAHAM
Harvard University

DONALD KAGAN
Yale University

STEVEN OZMENT
Harvard University

FRANK M. TURNER
Yale University

Prentice Hall
Boston   Columbus   Indianapolis   New York   San Francisco   Upper Saddle River
Amsterdam   Cape Town   Dubai   London   Madrid   Milan   Munich   Paris   Montreal   Toronto   Delhi
Mexico City   Sao Paulo   Sydney   Hong Kong   Seoul   Singapore   Taipei   Tokyo

Editorial Director: Craig Campanella
Executive Editor: Jeff Lasser
Editorial Project Manager: Rob DeGeorge
Editorial Assistant: Julia Feltus
Supplements Editor: Emsal Hassan
Senior Manufacturing and Operations Manager for Arts
 & Sciences: Nick Sklitsis
Operations Specialist: Christina Amato
Director of Marketing: Brandy Dawson
Senior Marketing Manager: Maureen E. Prado Roberts
Senior Managing Editor: Ann Marie McCarthy
Project Manager: Cheryl Keenan
Manager, Visual Research and Permissions: Beth Brenzel
Media Director: Brian Hyland

Media Project Manager: Tina Rudowski
Media Editor: Alison Lorber
Senior Art Director: Maria Lange
Text and Cover Designer: Brian Salisbury
Cover Art: Snark/Art Resource, NY/The transformation of a
 Chinese mountain village. Painted by peasants from Houhsien
 (after 1958).
AV Project Manager: Mirella Signoretto
Composition and Full-Service Project Management: Frank
 Weihenig/Prepare, Inc.
Printer/Binder: Courier Corporation
Cover Printer: Courier Corporation
Text Font: 10.5/13 Fairfield Light

Credits and acknowledgments borrowed from other sources and reproduced, with permission, in this textbook appear on appropriate page within text and on page C-1.

Library of Congress Cataloging-in-Publication Data
The heritage of world civilizations / Albert M. Craig ... [et al.]. -- 9th
ed., combined volume.
    p. cm.
 Includes bibliographical references and index.
 ISBN-13: 978-0-205-80350-7 (comb. vol.: alk. paper)
 ISBN-10: 0-205-80350-4 (comb. vol.: alk. paper)
 ISBN-13: 978-0-205-80348-4 (v. 1: alk. paper)
 ISBN-10: 0-205-80348-2 (v. 1: alk. paper)
 1. Civilization–History–Textbooks. I. Craig, Albert M.
 CB69.H45 2011
 909–dc22   2010044112
10 9 8 7 6 5 4 3 2 V092 13 14 15

Combined Volume
ISBN-10: 0-205-80350-4
ISBN-13: 978-0-205-80350-7

Examination Edition
ISBN-10: 0-205-80766-6
ISBN-13: 978-0-205-80766-6

Volume 1
ISBN-10: 0-205-80348-2
ISBN-13: 978-0-205-80348-4

Volume 1 a la Carte
ISBN-10: 0-205-83903-7
ISBN-13: 978-0-205-83903-2

Volume 2
ISBN-10: 0-205-80347-4
ISBN-13: 978-0-205-80347-7

Volume 2 a la Carte
ISBN: 0-205-00306-0
ISBN: 978-0-205-00306-8

Prentice Hall
is an imprint of

PEARSON   www.pearsonhighered.com

Brief Contents

Part 3
Consolidation and Interaction of World Civilizations, 500 C.E. to 1500 C.E.

14 Africa, ca. 1000–1700   401

15 Europe to the Early 1500s: Revival, Decline, and Renaissance   424

Part 4
The World in Transition, 1500 to 1850

16 Europe 1500–1650: Expansion, Reformation, and Religious Wars   460

17 Conquest and Exploitation: The Development of the Transatlantic Economy   496

18 East Asia in the Late Traditional Era   529

19 State Building and Society in Early Modern Europe   575

20 The Last Great Islamic Empires, 1500–1800   612

Part 5
Enlightenment and Revolution in the Atlantic World, 1700–1850

21 The Age of European Enlightenment   637

22 Revolutions in the Transatlantic World   667

23 Political Consolidation in Nineteenth-Century Europe and North America   699

Part 6
Into the Modern World, 1815–1949

24 Northern Transatlantic Economy and Society, 1815–1914   731

25 Latin America from Independence to the 1940s   766

26 India, the Islamic Heartlands, and Africa, 1800–1945   792

27 Modern East Asia   824

Part 7
Global Conflict and Change, 1900–Present

28 Imperialism and World War I   863

29 Depression, European Dictators, and the American New Deal   895

30 World War II   923

31 The West Since World War II   951

32 East Asia: The Recent Decades   989

33 Postcolonialism and Beyond: Latin America, Africa, Asia, and the Middle East   1019

Contents

DOCUMENTS xiv

MAPS xvi

PREFACE xvii

Part 3
Consolidation and Interaction of World Civilizations, 500 C.E. to 1500 C.E.

CHAPTER 14
Africa ca. 1000–1700 401

North Africa and Egypt 402

The Spread of Islam South of the Sahara 402

Global Perspective: Africa, 1000–1700 402

Sahelian Empires of the Western and Central Sudan 404
  Ghana 404
  Mali 405
  Songhai 408
  Kanem and Kanem-Bornu 410

The Eastern Sudan 412

The Forestlands—Coastal West and
  Central Africa 412
  West African Forest Kingdoms: The Example
    of Benin 412

A Closer Look: Benin Bronze Plaque with Chief
and Two Attendants 413
  European Arrivals on the Coastlands 414
  Central Africa 415

East Africa 417
  Swahili Culture and Commerce 417
  The Portuguese and the Omanis of Zanzibar 419

Southern Africa 419
  Southeastern Africa: "Great Zimbabwe" 419
  The Portuguese in Southeastern Africa 420
  South Africa: The Cape Colony 421

Summary 422

Key Terms 422

Review Questions 422

CHAPTER 15
**Europe to the Early 1500s: Revival, Decline,
and Renaissance 424**

Revival of Empire, Church, and Towns 425

Otto I and the Revival of the Empire 425
  The Reviving Catholic Church 425
  The Crusades 426

Global Perspective: The High Middle Ages
in Western Europe 426

A Closer Look: European Embrace
of a Black Saint 431
  Towns and Townspeople 432

Society 436
  The Order of Life 436
  Medieval Women 439

Growth of National Monarchies 440
  England and France: Hastings (1066) to Bouvines
    (1214) 440
  France in the Thirteenth Century: Reign of
    Louis IX 441
  The Hohenstaufen Empire (1152–1272) 442

Political and Social Breakdown 444
  Hundred Years' War 444
  The Black Death 444
  New Conflicts and Opportunities 447

Ecclesiastical Breakdown and Revival:
  The Late Medieval Church 447
  Boniface VIII and Philip the Fair 447
  The Great Schism (1378–1417) and the Conciliar
    Movement to 1449 448

The Renaissance in Italy (1375–1527) 448
  The Italian City-State: Social Conflict and Despotism 449
  Humanism 449
  Renaissance Art in and beyond Italy 451
  Italy's Political Decline: The French Invasions
    (1494–1527) 452
  Niccolò Machiavelli 453

Revival of Monarchy: Nation Building
  in the Fifteenth Century 454
  Medieval Russia 455
  France 455
  Spain 455
  England 457

Summary 457

Key Terms 458

Review Questions 458

Part 4
The World in Transition, 1500 to 1850

CHAPTER 16
Europe, 1500–1650: Expansion, Reformation, and Religious Wars   460

The Discovery of a New World   461
The Portuguese Chart the Course   461
The Spanish Voyages of Christopher Columbus   462
Global Perspective: European Expansion   462
Impact on Europe and America   463
The Reformation   463
Religion and Society   465
Popular Movements and Criticism of the Church   465
Secular Control over Religious Life   466
The Northern Renaissance   466
Martin Luther and German Reformation to 1525   467
Zwingli and the Swiss Reformation   472
Anabaptists and Radical Protestants   472
John Calvin and the Genevan Reformation   472
Political Consolidation of the Lutheran Reformation   473
The English Reformation to 1553   474
Catholic Reform and Counter-Reformation   475
The Reformation's Achievements   476
Religion in Fifteenth-Century Life   477
Religion in Sixteenth-Century Life   478
Family Life in Early Modern Europe   478
A Closer Look: A Contemporary Commentary on the Sexes   479
The Wars of Religion   480
French Wars of Religion (1562–1598)   481
Imperial Spain and the Reign of Philip II (1556–1598)   483
England and Spain (1558–1603)   484
The Thirty Years' War (1618–1648)   485
Superstition and Enlightenment: The Battle Within   487
Witch Hunts and Panic   487
Writers and Philosophers   488
Summary   492
Key Terms   492
Review Questions   492
Religions of the World: Christianity   494

CHAPTER 17
Conquest and Exploitation: The Development of the Transatlantic Economy   496

Periods of European Overseas Expansion   497
Mercantilist Theory of Economic Exploitation   498
Global Perspective: The Atlantic World   498
Establishment of the Spanish Empire in America   500

Conquest of the Aztecs and the Incas   500
The Roman Catholic Church in Spanish America   501
Economies of Exploitation in the Spanish Empire   503
Varieties of Economic Activity   503
Commercial Regulation and the Flota System   505
Colonial Brazil   507
French and British Colonies in North America   509
The Columbian Exchange: Disease, Animals, and Agriculture   510
Diseases Enter the Americas   511
Animals and Agriculture   513
Slavery in the Americas   515
The Background of Slavery   515
Establishment of Slavery   516
The Plantation Economy and Transatlantic Trade   517
Slavery on the Plantations   517
Africa and the Transatlantic Slave Trade   518
Slavery and Slaving in Africa   519
The African Side of the Transatlantic Trade   520
The Extent of the Slave Trade   522
Consequences of the Slave Trade for Africa   522
A Closer Look: The Slave Ship *Brookes*   525
Summary   526
Key Terms   527
Review Questions   527

CHAPTER 18
East Asia in the Late Traditional Era   529

Global Perspective: East Asia in the Late Traditional Era   530
LATE IMPERIAL CHINA   531
Ming (1368–1644) and Qing (1644–1911) Dynasties   531
Land and People   531
China's Third Commercial Revolution   532
Political System   534
Ming–Qing Foreign Relations   540
Ming–Qing Culture   544
JAPAN   547
Warring States Era (1467–1600)   547
War of All against All   547
Foot Soldier Revolution   547
Foreign Relations and Trade   549
Tokugawa Era (1600–1868)   550
Political Engineering and Economic Growth during the Seventeenth Century   550
Eighteenth and Early Nineteenth Centuries   555
A Closer Look: Bridal Procession   558
Languages of East Asia   559
Tokugawa Culture   559
KOREA AND VIETNAM   564

Korea   565
 Early History   565
 Choson Dynasty   567
Vietnam   569
 Vietnam in Southeast Asia   569
 Vietnamese Origins   569
 A Millennium of Chinese Rule: 111 B.C.E.–939 C.E.   570
 An Independent Vietnam   571
 The March South   571
Summary   573
Key Terms   573
Review Questions   573

CHAPTER 19
State Building and Society in Early Modern Europe   575

European Political Consolidation   576
 Two Models of European Political Development   576
Global Perspective: Early Modern Europe   576
 Toward Parliamentary Government in England   577
 The "Glorious Revolution"   578
 Rise of Absolute Monarchy in France: The World of Louis XIV   580
 Years of Personal Rule   581
A Closer Look: Versailles   582
 Russia Enters the European Political Arena   583
 Birth of the Romanov Dynasty   583
 Peter the Great   583
 The Habsburg Empire and the Pragmatic Sanction   586
 The Rise of Prussia   587
European Warfare: From Continental to World Conflict   588
 The Wars of Louis XIV   588
 The Eighteenth-Century Colonial Arena   590
 War of Jenkins's Ear   590
 The War of the Austrian Succession (1740–1748)   590
 The Seven Years' War (1756–1763)   591
The Old Regime   592
 Hierarchy and Privilege   592
 Aristocracy   592
 The Land and Its Tillers   594
 Peasants and Serfs   594
Family Structures and the Family Economy   595
 The Family Economy   595
 Women and the Family Economy   597
The Revolution in Agriculture   597
 New Crops and New Methods   599
 Population Expansion   600
The Eighteenth-Century Industrial Revolution: An Event in World History   601
 Industrial Leadership of Great Britain   602

European Cities   605
 Patterns of Preindustrial Urbanization   605
 Urban Classes   605
The Jewish Population: Age of the Ghetto   607
Summary   608
Key Terms   609
Review Questions   610

CHAPTER 20
The Last Great Islamic Empires, 1500–1800   612

The Ottoman Empire and the Eastern Mediterranean World   614
 Origins and Development of the Ottoman State before 1600   614
Global Perspective: The Last Great Islamic Empires   614
 The "Classical" Ottoman Order   616
 After Süleyman: Challenges and Change   618
 The Decline of Ottoman Military and Political Power   621
The Safavid Empire and the West Asian World   622
 Origins   622
 Shah Abbas I   623
 Safavid Decline   624
 Culture and Learning   625
The Mughals   626
 Origins   626
 Akbar's Reign   626
 The Last Great Mughals   626
 Sikhs and Marathas   627
 Political Decline   627
A Closer Look: The Mughal Emperor Jahangir Honoring a Muslim Saint over Kings and Emperors   628
 Religious Developments   629
Central Asia: Islamization in the Post-Timur Era   630
 Uzbeks and Chaghatays   630
 Consequences of the Shi'ite Rift   630
Power Shifts in the Southern Oceans   632
 Southern-Oceans Trade   632
 Control of the Southern Seas   632
 The East Indies: Acheh   634
Summary   635
Key Terms   635
Review Questions   635

Part 5
Enlightenment and Revolution in the Atlantic World, 1700–1850

CHAPTER 21
The Age of European Enlightenment   637

The Scientific Revolution   638

Global Perspective: The European Enlightenment   638

   Nicolaus Copernicus Rejects an Earth-Centered Universe   639
   Tycho Brahe and Johannes Kepler   640
   Galileo Galilei   641
   Francis Bacon: The Empirical Method   642
   Isaac Newton Discovers the Laws of Gravitation   643
   Women in the World of the Scientific Revolution   644
   John Locke   645

The Enlightenment   646
   Voltaire   647
   The Encyclopedia   647

The Enlightenment and Religion   649
   Deism   649
   Toleration   650
   Islam in Enlightenment Thought   651

The Enlightenment and Society   653
   Montesquieu and the Spirit of the Laws   653
   Adam Smith on Economic Growth and Social Progress   654
   Rousseau   654
   Enlightened Critics of European Empire   655
   Women in the Thought and Practice of the Enlightenment   657

Enlightened Absolutism   659
   Joseph II of Austria   659

A Closer Look: An Eighteenth-Century Artist Appeals to the Ancient World   661
   Catherine the Great of Russia   662
   The Partition of Poland   664

Summary   664
Key Terms   665
Review Questions   665

CHAPTER 22
Revolutions in the Transatlantic World   667

Revolution in the British Colonies in North America   668
   Resistance to the Imperial Search for Revenue   668

Global Perspective: The Transatlantic Revolutions   668
   American Political Ideas   669
   Crisis and Independence   669

Revolution in France   672
   Revolutions of 1789   672

A Closer Look: Challenging the French Political Order   674
   Reconstruction of France   675

   A Second Revolution   678
   The Reign of Terror and Its Aftermath   679
   The Napoleonic Era   682
   The Congress of Vienna and the European Settlement   686

Wars of Independence in Latin America   689
   Eighteenth-Century Developments   689
   Revolution in Haiti   689
   First Movements towards Independence on the South American Continent   690
   Eighteenth-Century Developments in the Spanish Empire   690
   San Martín in Río de la Plata   691
   Simón Bolívar's Liberation of Venezuela   691
   Independence in New Spain   692
   Brazilian Independence   693

Toward the Abolition of Slavery in the Transatlantic Economy   693

Summary   696
Key Terms   697
Review Questions   697

CHAPTER 23
Political Consolidation in Nineteenth-Century Europe and North America   699

The Emergence of Nationalism in Europe   700

Global Perspective: European and North American Political Consolidation   700
   Creating Nations   701
   Meaning of Nationhood   701
   Regions of Nationalistic Pressure in Europe   703

Early Nineteenth-Century Political Liberalism   704
   Politics   704
   Economics   704
   Relationship of Nationalism and Liberalism   705
   Liberalism and Nationalism in Modern World History   705

Efforts to Liberalize Early Nineteenth-Century European Political Structures   705
   Russia: The Decembrist Revolt of 1825 and the Autocracy of Nicholas I   705
   Revolution in France (1830)   706
   The Great Reform Bill in Britain (1832)   708
   1848: Year of Revolutions in Europe   709

Testing the New American Republic   711
   Toward Sectional Conflict   711
   The Abolitionist Movement   714

The Canadian Experience   717
   Road to Self-Government   717
   Keeping a Distinctive Culture   718

Midcentury Political Consolidation in Europe   718

The Crimean War   718
Italian Unification   718

A Closer Look: The Crimean War Recalled   720
German Unification   722
The Franco-Prussian War and the German Empire   722

Unrest of Nationalities in Eastern Europe   723

Racial Theory and Anti-Semitism   725
Anti-Semitism and the Birth of Zionism   726

Summary   728

Key Terms   729

Review Questions   729

Part 6
Into the Modern World, 1815–1949

CHAPTER 24
Northern Transatlantic Economy and Society, 1815–1914   731

Global Perspective: The Building of Northern Transatlantic Supremacy   732

European Factory Workers and Urban Artisans   733

Nineteenth-Century European Women   735
Women in the Early Industrial Revolution   735
Social Disabilities Confronted by All Women   736
New Employment Patterns for Women   738
Late Nineteenth-Century Working-Class Women   739
The Rise of Political Feminism   740

Jewish Emancipation   742
Early Steps to Equal Citizenship   742
Broadened Opportunities   742

European Labor, Socialism, and Politics to World War I   743
The Working Classes in the Late Nineteenth Century   743
Marxist Critique of the Industrial Order   744
Germany: Social Democrats and Revisionism   745
Great Britain: The Labour Party and Fabianism   747
Russia: Industrial Development and the Birth of Bolshevism   748

A Closer Look: Bloody Sunday, Saint Petersburg 1905   750
European Socialism in World History   751

North America and the New Industrial Economy   751
European Immigration to the United States   752
Unions: Organization of Labor   754
The Progressives   755
Social Reform   755
The Progressive Presidency   756

The Emergence of Modern European Thought   758
Darwin's Theory of Natural Selection   758

The Revolution in Physics   760
Friedrich Nietzsche and the Revolt against Reason   761
The Birth of Psychoanalysis   761

Islam and Late Nineteenth-Century European Thought   763

Summary   763

Key Terms   764

Review Questions   764

CHAPTER 25
Latin America from Independence to the 1940s   766

Independence without Revolution   767
Immediate Consequences of Latin American Independence   767
Absence of Social Change   767
Control of the Land   767

Global Perspective: Latin American History   768
Submissive Political Philosophies   769

Economy of Dependence   773
New Exploitation of Resources   773
Increased Foreign Ownership and Influence   774
Economic Crises and New Directions   775

Search for Political Stability   775

Three National Histories   776
Argentina   776
Mexico   779

A Closer Look: Benito Juárez   781
Brazil   785

Summary   789

Key Terms   790

Review Questions   790

CHAPTER 26
India, the Islamic Heartlands, and Africa, 1800–1945   792

THE INDIAN EXPERIENCE   793

British Dominance and Colonial Rule   793
Building the Empire: The First Half of the Nineteenth Century   793

Global Perspective: The Challenge of Modernity: India, Islam, and Africa   794
British-Indian Relations   795

From British Crown Raj to Independence   798
The Burden of Crown Rule   798
Indian Resistance   798
Hindu-Muslim Friction on the Road to Independence   800

A Closer Look: Gandhi and His Spinning Wheel   801

THE ISLAMIC EXPERIENCE   802

Islamic Responses to Declining Power and Independence 802

Western Political and Economic Encroachment 803

The Western Impact 805

Islamic Responses to Foreign Encroachment 805

Emulation of the West 805

Integration of Western and Islamic Ideas 807

Women and Reform in the Middle East 808

Purification and Revival of Islam 808

Nationalism 809

THE AFRICAN EXPERIENCE 810

New States and Power Centers 810

Southern Africa 810

East and Central Africa 811

West Africa 811

Islamic Reform Movements 811

Increasing European Involvement: Exploration and Colonization 813

Explorers 814

Christian Missions 814

The Colonial "Scramble for Africa" 814

Patterns in European Colonial Rule and African Resistance 817

The Rise of African Nationalism 818

Summary 819

Key Terms 820

Review Questions 820

Religions of the World: Islam 822

CHAPTER 27
Modern East Asia 824

Global Perspective: Modern East Asia 826

MODERN JAPAN (1853–1945) 825

Overthrow of the Tokugawa Bakufu (1853–1868) 825

A Closer Look: East Meets the West 828

Building the Meiji State (1868–1890) 827

Centralization of Power 829

Political Parties 831

The Constitution 831

Growth of a Modern Economy 832

First Phase: Model Industries 833

Second Phase: 1880s–1890s 833

Third Phase: 1905–1929 834

Fourth Phase: Depression and Recovery 836

The Politics of Imperial Japan (1890–1945) 836

From Confrontation to the Founding of the Seiyūkai (1890–1900) 836

The Golden Years of Meiji 837

Rise of the Parties to Power 838

Militarism and War (1927–1945) 840

Japanese Militarism and German Nazism 843

MODERN CHINA (1839–1949) 844

Close of Manchu Rule 844

The Opium War 844

Rebellions against the Manchu 846

Self-Strengthening and Decline (1874–1895) 848

The Borderlands: The Northwest, Vietnam, and Korea 850

From Dynasty to Warlordism (1895–1926) 852

Cultural and Ideological Ferment: The May Fourth Movement 854

Nationalist China 855

Guomindang Unification of China and the Nanjing Decade (1927–1937) 855

War and Revolution (1937–1949) 858

Summary 860

Key Terms 861

Review Questions 861

Part 7
Global Conflict and Change, 1900–Present

CHAPTER 28
Imperialism and World War I 863

Expansion of European Power and the "New Imperialism" 864

Global Perspective: Imperialism and the Great War 864

The New Imperialism 865

Motives for the New Imperialism 865

The "Scramble for Africa" 867

Emergence of the German Empire 872

Formation of the Triple Alliance (1873–1890) 872

Bismarck's Leadership (1873–1890) 873

Forging the Triple Entente (1890–1907) 874

World War I 877

The Road to War (1908–1914) 877

Sarajevo and the Outbreak of War (June–August 1914) 878

Strategies and Stalemate (1914–1917) 00

A Closer Look: The Development of the Armored Tank 882

The Russian Revolution 884

End of World War I 886

Military Resolution 886

Settlement at Paris 887

Evaluation of the Peace 891

Summary   892

Key Terms   893

Review Questions   893

CHAPTER 29
Depression, European Dictators, and the
American New Deal   895

After Versailles: Demands for Revision and
Enforcement   896

Toward the Great Depression in Europe   896

Global Perspective: The Interwar Period in Europe
and the United States   896
Problems in Agricultural Commodities   897

The Soviet Experiment   898
War Communism   899
The New Economic Policy   899
Stalin versus Trotsky   900
Decision for Rapid Industrialization   900
The Purges   903

The Fascist Experiment in Italy   904
Rise of Mussolini   905
The Fascists in Power   906

German Democracy and Dictatorship   907
The Weimar Republic   907
Depression and Political Deadlock   912
Hitler Comes to Power   912
Hitler's Consolidation of Power   913
The Police State   914
Women in Nazi Germany   915

A Closer Look: The Nazi Party Rally   917

The Great Depression and the New Deal
in the United States   916
Economic Collapse   918
New Role for Government   919

Summary   920

Key Terms   921

Review Questions   921

CHAPTER 30
World War II   923

Again the Road to War (1933–1939)   924
Hitler's Goals   924
Destruction of Versailles   924

Global Perspective: World War II   924
Italy Attacks Ethiopia   925
Remilitarization of the Rhineland   925
The Spanish Civil War   926
Austria and Czechoslovakia   928
Munich   928
The Nazi–Soviet Pact   930

World War II (1939–1945)   931
German Conquest of Europe   931
Battle of Britain   932
German Attack on Russia   933
Hitler's Europe   934
Racism and the Holocaust   934
The Road to Pearl Harbor   935
America's Entry into the War   937
The Tide Turns   937
Defeat of Nazi Germany   939
Fall of the Japanese Empire   940
The Cost of War   941

The Domestic Fronts   941
Germany: From Apparent Victory to Defeat   941
France: Defeat, Collaboration, and Resistance   943
Great Britain: Organization for Victory   943
*The United States: American Women and African Americans
in the War Effort*   944
The Soviet Union: "The Great Patriotic War"   944

A Closer Look: The Vichy Regime in France   945

Preparations for Peace   946
The Atlantic Charter   947
Tehran   947
Yalta   947
Potsdam   948

Summary   949

Key Terms   949

Review Questions   949

CHAPTER 31
The West since World War II   951

The Cold War Era   951
Areas of Early Cold War Conflict   951

Global Perspective: The West since 1945   951
NATO and the Warsaw Pact   955
Crises of 1956   956
The Cold War Intensified   957
Détente and Afterward   958

Toward Western European Unification   959

European Society in the Second Half of the Twentieth
Century and Beyond   961
Toward a Welfare State Society   961
Resistance to the Expansion of the Welfare State   962
The Movement of Peoples   963
The New Muslim Population   966
New Patterns in the Work and Expectations of Women   967

American Domestic Scene since World War II   968
Truman and Eisenhower Administrations   968
Civil Rights   969
New Social Programs   970

The Vietnam War and Domestic Turmoil   970
The Watergate Scandal   970
The Triumph of Political Conservatism   971

The Soviet Union to 1989   972
The Khrushchev Years   972
Brezhnev   973
Communism and Solidarity in Poland   973
Gorbachev Attempts to Redirect the Soviet Union   974

1989: Year of Revolutions in Eastern Europe   974
Solidarity Reemerges in Poland   975
Hungary Moves toward Independence   975
The Breach of the Berlin Wall and German Reunification   975
The Velvet Revolution in Czechoslovakia   975

A Closer Look: Collapse of the Berlin Wall   976
Violent Revolution in Romania   977

The Collapse of the Soviet Union   977
Renunciation of Communist Political Monopoly   977
The August 1991 Coup   978
The Yeltsin Years   979

The Collapse of Yugoslavia and Civil War   981

Challenges to the Atlantic Alliance
Challenges on the International Security Front   983
Strains over Environmental Policy   984

Summary   986
Key Terms   987
Review Questions   987

CHAPTER 32
East Asia: The Recent Decades   989

Japan   990

Global Perspective: Modern East Asia   990
The Occupation   991
Parliamentary Politics   993
Economic Growth   996
Society and Culture   998
Japan and the World   1000

China   1000
Soviet Period (1950–1960)   1001

A Closer Look: Trial of a Landlord   1002
The Great Proletarian Cultural Revolution (1965–1976)   1003
China after Mao   1004

Taiwan   1008

Korea   1010
Korea as a Japanese Colony   1010
North and South   1010
The Korean War and U.S. Involvement   1011
South Korea: Growth and Democracy   1012
North Korea   1013

Vietnam   1013
The Colonial Backdrop   1013

The Anticolonial War   1014
The Vietnam War   1014
War with Cambodia   1015
Recent Developments   1016

Summary   1017
Key Terms   1017
Review Questions   1017

CHAPTER 33
Postcolonialism and Beyond: Latin America, Africa, Asia, and the Middle East   1019

Beyond the Postcolonial Era   1020

Global Perspective: Democratization, Globalization, and Terrorism   1020

Latin America since 1945   1023
Revolutionary Challenges   1026
Pursuit of Stability under the Threat of Revolution   1028
Continuity and Change in Recent Latin American History   1030

A Closer Look: Mexican Farmers Protest the North American Free Trade Agreement   1031

Postcolonial Africa   1030
The Transition to Independence   1032
The African Future   1036
Trade and Development   1038

The Islamic Heartlands, from North Africa to Indonesia   1038
Turkey   1039
Iran and Its Islamic Revolution   1040
Afghanistan and the Former Soviet Republics   1041
India   1042
Pakistan and Bangladesh   1043
Indonesia and Malaysia   1044

The Postcolonial Middle East   1044
Postcolonial Nations in the Middle East   1044
The Arab-Israeli Conflict   1046
Middle Eastern Oil   1050
The Rise of Militant Islamism   1050
The Modern Middle Eastern Background   1051
Iraq: Intervention and Occupation   1052

Summary   1054
Key Terms   1055
Review Questions   1055

GLOSSARY   G-1
SUGGESTED READINGS   S-1
CREDITS   C-1
INDEX   I-1

Documents

Chapter 14

Ghana and Its People in the Mid-Eleventh Century   405
Muslim Reform in Songhai   410
Affonso I of Kongo Writes to the King of Portugal   416
Visiting Mogadishu (1331)   418

Chapter 15

Pope Gregory VII Asserts the Power of the Pope   429
Pope Urban II (r. 1088–1099) Preaches the First Crusade   430
Student Life at the University of Paris   436
Pico della Mirandola States the Renaissance Image of Man   452

Chapter 16

German Peasants Protest Rising Feudal Exactions   471
Ignatius of Loyola's "Rules for Thinking with the Church"   477
Theodore Beza Defends the Right to Resist Tyranny   483
John Locke Explains the Sources of Human Knowledge   491

Chapter 17

A Spaniard Describes the Glory of the Aztec Capital   502
A Contemporary Describes Forced Indian Labor at Potosí   504
Visitors Describe the Portobello Fair   508
A Slave Trader Describes the Atlantic Passage   524

Chapter 18

The Thin Horse Market   535
The Seven Transformations of an Examination Candidate   537
Qianlong's Edict to King George III of England   544
A Star in Heaven   546
The Virtuous Wife   556
A Tokugawa Skeptic   562
On Husband-Sharing   572

Chapter 19

John Locke Denounces the Idea of Absolute Monarchy   579
Bishop Bossuet Defends the Divine Right of Kings   581
Russian Serfs Lament Their Condition   596
Priscilla Wakefield Demands More Occupations Be Opened to
    Women   598
Belorussian Jews Petition Catherine the Great   607

Chapter 20

The Distinctiveness of Ottoman Identity and Culture   620
Guru Arjun's Faith   629

Chapter 21

Galileo Discusses the Relationship of Science to the Bible   642
The *Encyclopedia* Praises Mechanical Arts and Artisans   648
Denis Diderot Condemns European Empires   656
Rousseau Argues for Separate Spheres for Men and Women   658
Mary Wollstonecraft Criticizes Rousseau's View of Women   659

Chapter 22

The Stamp Act Congress Addresses George III   671
Olympe de Gouges Issues a Declaration of the Rights of Woman   676
A Free Person of Color from St. Domingue Demands Recognition of
    His Status   677
The Paris Jacobin Club Alerts the Nations to Internal Enemies of the
    Revolution   679
Bolívar Denounces Spanish Rule in Latin America   692

Chapter 23

Mazzini Defines Nationality   703
Parnell Calls for Home Rule for Ireland   711
Daniel A. Payne Denounces American Slavery   715
Lord Acton Condemns Nationalism   726
Herzl Calls for the Establishment of a Jewish State   727

Chapter 24

English Women Industrial Workers Explain Their
    Economic Situation   737
Karl Marx and Friedrich Engels Describe the Class Struggle   746
Lenin Argues for the Necessity of a Secret and Elite Party of
    Professional Revolutionaries   749
Theodore Roosevelt States His Progressive Creed   757
Darwin Defends a Mechanistic View of Nature   759

Chapter 25

A Peruvian Commentator Decries Racial Thinking   772
Eva Perón Explains the Sources of Her Popularity   779
Emiliano Zapata Issues the Plan of Ayala   783
A Brazilian Liberal Denounces Slavery   786

Chapter 26

Macaulay Writes on Indian Education   797
Gandhi on Passive Resistance and *Svarāj*   800
Tâhâ Hussein, "The Future of Culture in Egypt"   809
Usman Dan Fodio on Evil and Good Government   812
Oginga Odinga on European Influences   819

Chapter 27

A Japanese View of the Inventiveness of the West   829
On Wives and Concubines   830
Natsume Sôseki on the Costs of Rapid Modernization   835
Commissioner Lin Urges Morality on Queen Victoria   845
Liang Qichao Urges the Chinese to Reform (1896)   853
Chen Duxiu's "Call to Youth" in 1915   855

Chapter 28

Social Darwinism and Imperialism   868
Bismarck Explains His Foreign Policy   875

Chapter 29

Stalin Calls for the Liquidation of the *Kulaks* as a Class   902
Mussolini Heaps Contempt on Political Liberalism   906
Hitler Denounces the Versailles Treaty   909

The Nazis Pass Their Racial Legislation   915

Chapter 30

Hitler States His Plans for Russia   926

Winston Churchill Warns of the Effects of the Munich Agreement   929

Mass Murder at Belsen   936

Chapter 31

The United States National Security Council Proposes to Contain the Soviet Union   956

Pope Benedict XVI Calls for the Recognition of Religious Freedom as a Human Right   962

Tony Blair Seeks to Redefine the British Welfare State   964

Simone de Beauvoir Urges Economic Freedom for Women   968

Vladimir Putin Outlines a Vision of the Russian Future   980

Chapter 32

Two Views of the "Symbol Emperor"   994

U.S. Foreign Policy: A Chinese Dissident's View   1007

Chapter 33

Lourdes Arizpe Discusses the Silence of Peasant Women   1025

The Pan-African Congress Demands Independence   1032

A Modernist Muslim Poet's Eulogy for His Mother   1039

The King-Crane Commission Report, August 28, 1919   1047

Jihad against Jews and Crusaders: World Islamic Front Statement, 1998   1052

Maps

14–1 Africa ca. 900–1500 406

14–2 Africa ca. 1500–1700 409

15–1 The Early Crusades 428

15–2 Medieval Trade Routes and Regional Products 433

15–3 Germany and Italy in the Middle Ages 443

15–4 Spread of the Black Death 446

15–5 Renaissance Italy 449

15–6 Russia, ca. 1500 456

16–1 European Voyages of Discovery and the Colonial Claims of Spain and Portugal in the Fifteenth and Sixteenth Centuries 464

16–2 Martin Behaim's "Globe Apple" 465

16–3 The Empire of Charles V 469

16–4 The Holy Roman Empire ca. 1618 486

16–5 Religious Division ca. 1600 487

17–1 European Explorations and Conquests, ca. 1550 501

17–2 The Americas, ca. 1750 506

17–3 Biological Exchanges 512

17–4 The Slave Trade, 1400–1860 515

17–5 Origins of African Slaves Sent to the Americas 521

18–1 The Ming Empire and the Voyages of Zheng He 540

18–2 The Qing Empire at Its Peak 542

18–3 Tokugawa Japan and the Korean Peninsula 552

18–4 Early Korean States 565

18–5 Korea during the Choson Era 567

18–6 Vietnam and Neighboring Southeast Asia 570

19–1 The Austrian Habsburg Empire, 1521–1772 586

19–2 Prussian Expansions 1748–1795 588

19–3 Europe in 1714 589

19–4 The Colonial Arena 593

19–5 The Industrial Revolution in Britain 602

20–1 The Islamic Heartlands, ca. 1700 613

20–2 The Ottoman Empire at Its Zenith 616

20–3 The Safavid Empire 622

20–4 India under the Mughals 626

20–5 The Spread of Islam in Southeast Asia, 1300–1900 632

20–6 European Commercial Penetration of Southeast Asia 633

21–1 Subscriptions to Diderot's *Encyclopedia* throughout Europe 650

21–2 Expansion of Russia, 1689–1796 664

22–1 North America in 1763 670

22–2 Napoleonic Europe in Late 1812 686

22–3 Europe 1815, after the Congress of Vienna 688

22–4 The Independence Campaigns of San Martín and Bolívar 691

22–5 The Haitian Revolution 695

23–1 Languages of Europe 702

23–2 Centers of Revolution in 1848–1849 710

23–3 The United States, 1776–1850 713

23–4 The Unification of Italy 719

23–5 The Unification of Germany 723

23–6 Nationalities within the Habsburg Empire 724

24–1 Patterns of Global Migration, 1840–1900 753

25–1 Latin America in 1830 770

26–1 British India, 1820 and 1856 796

26–2 West Asia, Central Asia, and the Mediterranean, ca. 1850 803

26–3 Islamic Reform Movements in Africa and Arabia in the Nineteenth Century 813

26–4 Partition of Africa, 1880–1914 816

27–1 Formation of the Japanese Empire 838

27–2 The Taiping, Nian, and Muslim Rebellions 847

27–3 The Northern Expeditions of the Guomindang 857

27–4 The Long March, 1934–1935 859

28–1 Asia, 1880–1914 866

28–2 The Colonial Economy of Africa, 1885–1939 869

28–3 The American Domain, ca. 1900 872

28–4 The Balkans, 1912–1913 878

28–5 The Schlieffen Plan of 1905 880

28–6 World War I in Europe 883

28–7 World War I Peace Settlement in Europe and the Middle East 890

30–1 The Spanish Civil War, 1936–1939 927

30–2 Partitions of Czechoslovakia and Poland, 1938–1939 930

30–3 Axis Europe 1941 933

30–4 The Holocaust 935

30–5 The War in the Pacific 938

30–6 North African Campaigns, 1942–1945 939

30–7 Defeat of the Axis in Europe, 1942–1945 940

30–8 Territorial Changes in Europe after World War II 948

31–1 Major Cold War European Alliance Systems 955

31–2 The Growth of the European Union 961

31–3 Displaced Peoples in East and Central Europe, 1945–1950 965

31–4 The Commonwealth of Independent States 978

31–5 Ethnic Composition in the Former Yugoslavia 982

32–1 Contemporary East Asia 992

32–2 The Korean War, 1950–1953 1011

32–3 Vietnam and Its Southeast Asian Neighbors 1015

33–1 Decolonizaton since World War II 1022

33–2 Contemporary Central and South America 1023

33–3 Distribution of HIV Infection Rates in Africa 1037

33–4 The Modern Middle East and the Distribution of Major Religious Communities 1045

The global financial crisis that commenced in 2008 has sparked for this generation a new sense of the connectedness of international economic events and financial forces. The banking crisis in the United States, the burgeoning Chinese economy, the debt upheaval within the European Union, the rise and fall of commodity prices, and the entanglement of the flows of capital from one part of the developed world to another have painfully demonstrated how events and decisions in one nation or on one continent can impact millions of people living far from the centers of those decisions. The economic crisis has followed fast upon a decade during which the military forces of the United States and Europe have invaded nations of the Middle East in response to terrorist attacks. Environmental crises whether in the form of oceanic oil spills or volcanic eruption can interfere with trade, commerce, and tourism, as can changes in the price and availability of oil on which the United States, Europe, Japan, China, and India, to mention only the largest industrial economies, are dependent from sources outside their borders and regions.

Economic and military interaction and environmental crises on the global scene are the most dramatic and disruptive signs of the impact of globalization. However, more quietly but not less dramatically for the past two decades the steady growth of the Internet has created a sense of worldwide cultural and commercial interconnectedness. Whereas once undergraduates in American universities might have gone to a larger newspaper room in their college or university library to read newspapers from other countries several days or even weeks after they had been published, today's students can follow the press of countries around the world from smart phones, computers, and other electronic reading devices. The Internet permits students to view museum collections located on every continent. Books of great rarity and value once reserved for students in a few elite universities are now available electronically in all parts of the world. United States colleges and universities to an extent previously unimagined are establishing branches far beyond North America. Whereas as recently as the 1970s American students found almost half the world closed to travel, they can now travel globally with almost no barriers.

Today, the interconnectedness of cultures and peoples as well as of economies is inescapable. We dwell in an era in which no active citizen or educated person can escape the necessity of understanding the past in global terms. Both the historical experience and the moral, political, and religious values of the different world civilizations now demand our attention and our understanding. It is our hope that in these new, challenging times *The Heritage of World Civilizations* will provide one path to such knowledge.

The Roots of Globalization

Globalization—that is, the increasing interaction and interdependency of the various regions of the world—has resulted from two major historical developments: the closing of the European era of world history and the rise of technology.

From approximately 1500 C.E. to the middle of the twentieth century, Europe, followed later by the United States, gradually came to dominate the world through colonization (most particularly in North and South America), state-building, economic productivity, and military power. That era of European dominance ended during the third quarter of the twentieth century after Europe had brought unprecedented destruction on itself during World War II; as the United States eventually confronted limitations in its postwar influence; and as the nations of Asia, the Near East, and Africa achieved new positions on the world scene. Their new political independence, their control over strategic natural resources, the expansion of their economies (especially those of the nations of the Pacific rim of Asia), and in some cases their access to nuclear weapons have changed the shape of world affairs.

Further changing the world political and social situation has been a growing discrepancy in the economic development of different regions, which is often portrayed as a problem between the northern and southern hemispheres. Beyond the emergence of this economic disparity has been the remarkable advance of radical political Islamism during the past forty years. In the midst of all these developments, as a result of the political collapse of the former Soviet Union, the United States has emerged as the single major world power, though its position has been increasingly challenged by China, whose economic might now rivals that of the United States and whose military has embarked on a rapid buildup of its forces in Asia.

The second historical development that continues to fuel the pace of globalization is the advance of technology, associated most importantly with transportation, military weapons, and electronic communication. The advances in transportation over the past two centuries, including ships, railways, and airplanes, have made more parts of the world and its resources accessible to more people in ever shorter spans of time. Over the past century and a half, military weapons of increasingly destructive power enabled Europeans and then later the United States to dominate other regions of the globe. Now, the spread of these weapons means that any nation with sophisticated military technology can threaten other nations, no matter how far away. Furthermore, technologies that originated in the West from the early twentieth century to the present have been turned against the West. More recently, as already noted, the electronic revolution associated with computer technology and most particularly the Internet has sparked unprecedented speed and complexity in global communications. It is astonishing to recall that personal computers have been generally available for less than twenty-five years and that the rapid personal communication associated with them has existed for less than fifteen years.

Why not, then, focus only on new factors in the modern world, such as the impact of technology and the end of the European era? To do so would ignore the very deep roots that these developments have in the past. More important, the events of recent years demonstrate, as the authors of this book have long contended, that the major religious traditions continue to shape and drive the modern world as well as the world of the past. The religious traditions link today's civilizations to their most ancient roots. We believe this emphasis on the great religious traditions recognizes not only a factor that has shaped the past, but one that is profoundly and dynamically alive in our world today.

Strengths of the Text

Balanced and Flexible Presentation In this edition, as in past editions, we have sought to present world history fairly, accurately, and in a way that does justice to its great variety. History has many facets, no one of which can account for the others. Any attempt to tell the story of civilization from a single perspective, no matter how timely, is bound to neglect or suppress some important part of that story.

Historians have recently brought a vast array of new tools and concepts to bear on the study of history. Our coverage introduces students to various aspects of social and intellectual history as well as to the more traditional political, diplomatic, and military coverage. We firmly believe that only through an appreciation of all pathways to understanding the past can the real heritage of world civilizations be claimed.

The Heritage of World Civilizations, Ninth Edition, is designed to accommodate a variety of approaches to a course in world history, allowing teachers to stress what is most important to them. Some teachers will ask students to read all the chapters. Others will select among them to reinforce assigned readings and lectures.

Clarity and Accessibility Good narrative history requires clear, vigorous prose. Our goal has been to make our presentation fully accessible to students without compromising on vocabulary or conceptual level. We hope this effort will benefit both teachers and students.

Current Scholarship As in previous editions, changes in this edition reflect our determination to incorporate the most recent developments in historical scholarship and the expanding concerns of professional historians. To better highlight the dynamic processes of world history, significant new and expanded coverage of the Byzantine Empire and the early civilizations of the Americas—particularly the civilizations of Mesoamerica and the Andes during the precolonial period—has been added to the Ninth Edition.

Content and Organization The many changes in content and organization in this edition of *The Heritage of World Civilizations* reflect our ongoing effort to present a truly global survey of world civilizations that at the same time gives a rich picture of the history of individual regions:

- **Global Approach.** The Ninth Edition continues to explicitly highlight the connections and parallels in global history among regions of the world. Each chapter begins with a "Global Perspective" essay that succinctly places in a wider, global framework the regions and topics that are to be discussed, with an emphasis on the connections, parallels, and comparisons between and among different cultures.

- **Improved Organization.** Some chapters have been reorganized to improve narrative flow and to highlight important topics more clearly. At the suggestion of reviewers, Chapter 4 (Iran, India, and Inner Asia to 200 C.E.) and Chapter 10 (Iran and South Asia, 200 C.E.–1000 C.E.) in the Eighth Edition have been consolidated into a single chapter in the Ninth Edition: Chapter 4 (West Asia, Inner Asia, and South Asia to 1000 C.E.). Coverage of early Korean and Vietnamese history has been moved from Chapter 9 to Chapter 18, leaving Chapter 9 solely devoted to early Japan. Coverage of Korea and Vietnam has been consolidated in Chapter 18 with a far greater sense of continuity and a more effective and concise presentation.

- **New Design and Photo Program.** The entire text has been set in a crisp and engaging new design. Each of the 33 chapters also includes photos new to this edition of the text.

Pedagogical Features

This edition retains many of the pedagogical features of previous editions, while providing increased assessment opportunities.

- **Global Perspective Essays** introduce the key problems of each chapter and place them in a global and historical context. Focus Questions prompt students to consider the causes, connections, and consequences of the topics they will encounter in the main narrative.

- **Religions of the World** essays examine the historical impact of each of the world's great religious traditions: Judaism, Christianity, Islam, Buddhism, and Hinduism.

- **Chapter Outlines** open each chapter and help students easily access important topics for study and review.

- **Overview Tables** summarize key concepts and reinforce material presented in the main narrative.

- **Chronologies** within each chapter help students situate key events in time.

- **Documents**, including selections from sacred books, poems, philosophical tracts, political manifestos, letters, and travel accounts, expose students to the raw material of history, providing an intimate contact with peoples of the past. Questions accompanying the source documents direct students to important, thought-provoking issues and help them relate the documents to the main narrative.

- **Key Terms** are boldfaced in the text, listed (with page reference) at the end of each chapter, along with phonetic spellings when appropriate, and are defined in the book's glossary.

- **Interactive Maps**, usually one per chapter, prompt students to explore the relationship between geography and history in a dynamic fashion.

- **Chapter Summaries** conclude each chapter, organized by subtopic, and recap important points.

- **Chapter Review Questions** help students interpret the broad themes of each chapter. These questions can be used for class discussion and essay topics.

New to This Edition

There is a new feature in the Ninth Edition:

A Closer Look – *Each* chapter includes a new feature called "A Closer Look," which provides in-depth commentary on visual sources in world history. This feature teaches students to view photos, paintings, and other illustrations as historical documents. Each feature concludes with questions that encourage students to focus on important issues raised within the feature. See the Contents on page vi for the title of each of these new features.

Here are just some of the changes that can be found in the Ninth Edition of *The Heritage of World Civilizations*:

Chapter 17, Conquest and Exploitation: The Development of the Transatlantic Economy

- A new document has been added: "Visitors Describe the Portobello Fair."
- There is new coverage of the Indian Wars in the seventeenth-century North American British colonies.
- There is new coverage of the alleged slave conspiracy in 1741 in New York City.

Chapter 18, East Asia in the Late Traditional Era

- Coverage of Korea and Vietnam has been consolidated in Chapter 18 with a far greater sense of continuity and a more effective and concise presentation.
- The introduction to the Vietnam section contains a new overview of Southeast Asia.
- Coverage of the Choson Dynasty in the Korean section has been revised and greatly improved.

Chapter 19, State Building and Society in Early Modern Europe

- A new document has been added titled "John Locke Denounces the Idea of Absolute Monarchy."
- New coverage has been added on the Revolution of 1688.

Chapter 21, The Age of European Enlightenment

- A new document has been added emphasizing the Enlightenment interest in technology and the mechanical arts.
- Coverage of technology has been emphasized to a greater extent throughout the chapter.
- A brief new commentary has been introduced on why the Enlightenment is unpopular in some Islamic circles.

Chapter 22, Revolutions in the Transatlantic World

- A substantial new section has been added on the Haitian Revolution.
- Two new documents have been added: "Olympe de Gouges Issues a Declaration of the Rights of Woman" and "A Free Person of Color from St. Domingue Demands Recognition of His Status."

Chapter 23, Political Consolidation in Nineteenth-Century Europe and North America

- A new document has been added: "Parnell Calls for Home Rule for Ireland."
- Coverage of race and Social Darwinism has been expanded.

Chapter 24, Northern Transatlantic Economy and Society, 1815–1914

- Two new documents—one from *The Communist Manifesto* and another by Lenin on elite professional parties—have been added.
- There is new coverage of child labor.

Chapter 25, Latin America from Independence to the 1940s

- A new document has been added: "A Peruvian Commentator Decries Racial Thinking."

Chapter 26, India, the Islamic Heartlands, and Africa, 1800–1945

- The chapter has been updated to include coverage of the British Zulu War.

Chapter 28, Imperialism and World War I

- A new document has been added: "Social Darwinism and Imperialism."

Chaper 29, Depression, European Dictators, and the American New Deal

- The following new documents have been added: "Stalin Calls for the Liquidation of the *Kulaks* as a Class" and "Mussolini Heaps Contempt on Political Liberalism."
- There is new coverage of forced starvation in the Ukraine by Stalin.
- New coverage has been added on FDR's failure to support antilynching legislation.

Chapter 30, World War II

- A new document has been added: "Hitler States His Plans for Russia."

Chapter 31, The West Since World War II

■ The following new documents have been introduced: "The United States National Security Council Proposes to Contain the Soviet Union," "Pope Benedict XVI Calls for the Recognition of Religious Freedom as a Human Right," "Tony Blair Seeks to Redefine the British Welfare State," and "Vladimir Putin Outlines a Vision of the Russian Future."

■ The section on recent events in Russia has been significantly updated.

Chapter 32, East Asia: The Recent Decades

■ Coverage of China and Japan has been updated to reflect recent events.

Chapter 33, Postcolonialism and Beyond: Latin America, Africa, Asia, and the Middle East

■ Coverage of Latin America, Africa, Asia, and the Middle East has been updated to reflect recent events.

A Note on Dates and Transliteration

We have used B.C.E. (before the common era) and C.E. (common era) instead of B.C. (before Christ) and A.D. (anno domini, the year of our Lord) to designate dates.

Until recently, most scholarship on China used the Wade-Giles system of romanization for Chinese names and terms. China, today, however, uses another system known as Pinyin. Virtually all Western newspapers have adopted it. In order that students may move easily from the present text to the existing body of advanced scholarship on Chinese history, we now use the Pinyin system throughout the text.

Also, we have followed the currently accepted English transliterations of Arabic words. For example, today Koran is being replaced by the more accurate Qur'an; similarly Muhammad is preferable to Mohammed and Muslim to Moslem. We have not tried to distinguish the letters *'ayn* and *hamza*; both are rendered by a simple apostrophe (') as in Shi'ite. With regard to Sanskritic transliteration, we have not distinguished linguals and dentals, and both palatal and lingual *s* are rendered *sh*, as in Shiva and Upanishad.

MyHistoryLab (www.myhistorylab.com) *Save Time. Improve Results*. MyHistoryLab is a dynamic website that provides a wealth of resources geared to meet the diverse teaching and learning needs of today's instructors and students. MyHistoryLab's many accessible tools will encourage students to read their text and help them improve their grade in their course.

The Instructor's Resource Manual with Test Bank
Available for download at the Instructor's Resource Center, at **www.pearsonhighered.com/irc**, the Instructor's Resource Manual with Test Bank includes chapter outlines, overviews, key concepts, discussion questions, suggestions for useful audiovisual resources, and approximately 1,500 test items (essay, multiple choice, true/false, and matching).

The Instructor's Resource Center
(www.pearsonhighered.com/irc) Text-specific materials, such as the Instructor's Resource Manual with Test Bank, map files, and PowerPoint™ presentations, are available for downloading by adopters.

MyTest Available at **www.pearsonmytest.com**, MyTest is a powerful assessment generation program that helps instructors easily create and print quizzes and exams. Questions and tests can be authored online, allowing instructors ultimate flexibility and the ability to efficiently manage assessment anytime, anywhere! Instructors can easily access existing questions and can edit, create, and store using simple drag-and-drop and Word-like controls.

MyHistoryLab (www.myhistorylab.com) *Save Time. Improve Results*. MyHistoryLab is a dynamic website that provides a wealth of resources geared to meet the diverse teaching and learning needs of today's instructors and students. MyHistoryLab's many accessible tools will encourage you to read your text and help you improve your grade in your course.

CourseSmart (www.coursesmart.com) CourseSmart eTextbooks offer the same content as the printed text in a convenient online format—with highlighting, online search, and printing capabilities. You **save 60 percent over the list price** of the traditional book.

Books à la Carte Books à la Carte editions feature the exact same content as the traditional printed text in a convenient, three-hole-punched, loose-leaf version at a discounted price—allowing you to take only what you need to class. You'll **save 35 percent over the net price** of the traditional book.

Primary Source: Documents in Global History **DVD** is an immense collection of textual and visual documents in world history and an indispensable tool for working with sources. Extensively developed with the guidance of historians and teachers, the DVD includes over 800 sources in world history—from cave art to satellite images of the Earth from space. More sources from Africa, Latin America, and Southeast Asia have been added to the latest version of the DVD. All sources are accompanied by head notes, focus questions, and are searchable by topic, region, or time period. The DVD can be bundled with *The Heritage of World Civilizations*, Ninth Edition, at no charge. Please contact your Pearson representative for ordering information. (ISBN 0-13-178938-4)

 Titles from the renowned *Penguin Classics* series can be bundled with *The Heritage of World Civilizations*, Ninth Edition, for a nominal charge. Please contact your Pearson sales representative for details.

Library of World Biography Series
www.pearsonhighered.com/educator/series/Library-of-World-Biography/10492.page Each interpretive biography in the Library of World Biography Series focuses on a person whose actions and ideas either significantly influenced world events or whose life reflects important themes and developments in global history. Titles from the series can be bundled with *The Heritage of World Civilizations*, Ninth Edition, for a nominal charge. Please contact your Pearson sales representative for details.

 The Prentice Hall Atlas of World History, Second Edition Produced in collaboration with Dorling Kindersley, the leader in cartographic publishing, the updated second edition of *The Prentice Hall Atlas of World History* applies the most innovative cartographic techniques to present world history in all of its complexity and diversity. Copies of the atlas can be bundled with *The Heritage of World Civilizations*, Ninth Edition, for a nominal charge. Contact your Pearson sales representative for details. (ISBN 0-13-604247-3)

Longman Atlas of World History This atlas features carefully selected historical maps that provide comprehensive coverage of the major historical periods. Contact your Pearson sales representative for details. (ISBN 0-321-20998-2)

A Guide to Your History Course: What Every Student Needs to Know Written by Vincent A. Clark, this concise, spiral-bound guidebook orients students to the issues and problems they will face in the history classroom. Available at a discount when bundled with *The Heritage of World Civilizations*, Ninth Edition. (ISBN 0-13-185087-3)

A Short Guide to Writing about History, Seventh Edition Written by Richard Marius, late of Harvard University, and Melvin E. Page, Eastern Tennessee State University, this engaging and practical text helps students get beyond merely compiling dates and facts. Covering both brief essays and the documented resource paper, the text explores the writing and researching processes, identifies different modes of historical writing, including argument, and concludes with guidelines for improving style. (ISBN 0-13-205-67370-8)

MyHistoryLab (www.myhistorylab.com)

Save TIME. Improve Results. MyHistoryLab is a dynamic website that provides a wealth of resources geared to meet the diverse teaching and learning needs of today's instructors and students. MyHistoryLab's many accessible tools will encourage students to read their text and help them improve their grade in their course .

Here are some of the features that will help you and your students save time and improve results:

- Pearson eText—Just like the printed text, students can highlight and add their own notes. Students save time and improve results by having access to their book online.

- Gradebook—Students can follow their own progress and instructors can monitor the work of the entire class. Automated grading of quizzes and assignments helps both instructors and students save time and monitor their results throughout the course.

- History Bookshelf—Students may read, download, or print 100 of the most commonly assigned history works, like Homer's *The Iliad* or Machiavelli's *The Prince*.

- Audio Files—Full audio of the entire book is included to suit the varied learning styles of today's students.

New Read/View/See/Watch/Hear/Study and Review Icons integrated in the text lead to Web-based expansions on topics, allowing instructors and students access to extra information, videos, and simulations. The icons draw attention to the most high-interest material available, although many more resources may be accessed at **www.myhistorylab.com.**

Read the Document

Points students to primary and secondary source documents related to the chapter.

View the Image

Identifies primary and secondary source images, including photographs, fine art, and artifacts to provide students with a visual perspective on history.

See the Map

Directs students to atlas and interactive maps that present both broad overviews and detailed examinations of historical developments.

Watch the Video

Notes pertinent archival videos and videos by Pearson history authors that probe various topics.

Hear the Audio

Marks audio clips from historically significant songs and speeches that enrich students' engagement with history.

Study and Review

Alerts students to study resources for each chapter of the textbook available online through **www.myhistorylab.com**. These resources include practice tests and flashcards.

Acknowledgments

We are grateful to the many scholars and teachers whose thoughtful and often detailed comments helped shape this as well as previous editions of *The Heritage of World Civilizations*. The advice and guidance provided by Katie Janssen on the coverage of African history and Thomas M. Ricks on the coverage of Islam and the Middle East is especially appreciated. Steven Ozment would like to thank Ammanuel Gashaw Gebeyehu and Ece G. Turnator for their contributions to Chapter 11. Much of the coverage of the Byzantine Empire that is new to the Ninth Edition was written by these two fine scholars.

Reviewers of the Ninth Edition
Wayne Ackerson, *Salisbury University*
Heather Barry, *St. Joseph's College*
Eric Martin, *Lewis-Clark State College*
Gary Paul Ritter, *Central Piedmont Community College*
Anthony R. Santoro, *Christopher Newport University*
Gilmar Visoni, *Queensborough Community College*
Kristen Post Walton, *Salisbury University*
William Zogby, *Mohawk Valley Community College*

Reviewers of Previous Editions
W. Nathan Alexander, *Troy University*
Jack Martin Balcer, *Ohio State University*
Charmarie J. Blaisdell, *Northeastern University*
Gayle K. Brunelle, *California State University, Fullerton*
Deborah Buffton, *University of Wisconsin at La Crosse*
Loretta Burns, *Mankato State University*
Douglas Chambers, *University of Southern Mississippi*
Chun-shu Chang, *University of Michigan, Ann Arbor*
Mark Chavalas, *University of Wisconsin at La Crosse*
Anthony Cheeseboro, *Southern Illinois University at Edwardsville*
William J. Courteney, *University of Wisconsin*
Samuel Willard Crompton, *Holyoke Community College*

James B. Crowley, *Yale University*
Bruce Cummings, *The University of Chicago*
Stephen F. Dale, *Ohio State University, Columbus*
Clarence B. Davis, *Marian College*
Raymond Van Dam, *University of Michigan, Ann Arbor*
Bill Donovan, *Loyola University of Maryland*
Wayne Farris, *University of Tennessee*
Anita Fisher, *Clark College*
Suzanne Gay, *Oberlin College*
Katrina A. Glass, *United States Military Academy*
Robert Gerlich, *Loyola University*
Samuel Robert Goldberger, *Capital Community-Technical College*
Andrew Gow, *University of Alberta*
Katheryn L. Green, *University of Wisconsin, Madison*
David Griffiths, *University of North Carolina, Chapel Hill*
Louis Haas, *Duquesne University*
Joseph T. Hapak, *Moraine Valley Community College*
Hue-Tam Ho Tai, *Harvard University*
David Kieft, *University of Minnesota*
Don Knox, *Wayland Baptist University*
Frederick Krome, *Northern Kentucky University*
Lisa M. Lane, *Mira Costa College*
Richard Law, *Washington State University*
David Lelyveld, *Columbia University*
Jan Lewis, *Rutgers University, Newark*
James C. Livingston, *College of William and Mary*
Garth Montgomery, *Radford University*
Richard L. Moore Jr., *St. Augustine's College*
Beth Nachison, *Southern Connecticut State University*
Robin S. Oggins, *Binghamton University*
George S. Pabis, *Georgia Perimeter College*
Louis A. Perez Jr., *University of South Florida*
Jonathan Perry, *University of South Florida*
Cora Ann Presley, *Tulane University*
Norman Raiford, *Greenville Technical College*
Norman Ravitch, *University of California, Riverside*
Thomas M. Ricks, *University of Pennsylvania*
Philip F. Riley, *James Madison University*
Thomas Robisheaux, *Duke University*
William S. Rodner, *Tidewater Community College*

David Ruffley, *United States Air Force Academy*
Dankwart A. Rustow, *The City University of New York*
James J. Sack, *University of Illinois at Chicago*
William Schell, *Murray State University*
Daniel Scavone, *University of Southern Indiana*
Linda B. Scherr, *Mercer County Community College*
Roger Schlesinger, *Washington State University*
Marvin Slind, *Washington State University*
Charles C. Stewart, *University of Illinois*
Nancy L. Stockdale, *University of Central Florida*
Carson Tavenner, *United States Air Force Academy*
Truong-bu Lam, *University of Hawaii*
Deborah Vess, *Georgia College and State University*
Harry L. Watson, *Loyola College of Maryland*
William B. Whisenhunt, *College of DuPage*
Paul Varley, *Columbia University*

Finally, we would like to thank the dedicated people who helped produce this revision: our editor, Jeff Lasser; editorial project manager Rob DeGeorge; Brian Salisbury and Maria Lange, who created the handsome new design for this edition; Cheryl Keenan, our project manager; Christina Amato, our operations specialist; and Frank Weihenig, our production editor.

A.M.C

W.A.G

D.K

S.O

F.M.T

14 | Africa ca. 1000–1700

- North Africa and Egypt
- The Spread of Islam South of the Sahara
- Sahelian Empires of the Western and Central Sudan
- The Eastern Sudan
- The Forestlands—Coastal West and Central Africa
- East Africa
- Southern Africa

THE HISTORY OF AFRICA IN THE FIRST HALF OF THE second millennium C.E. varied considerably in different regions. Many parts of Africa had substantial interactions with the Islamic and European worlds; others were engaged in trade and cultural exchanges within the continent.

The Atlantic slave trade affected almost all of Africa between the fifteenth and nineteenth centuries and is treated in Chapter 17. However, here we cannot overlook its importance in disrupting and reconfiguring African economies, social organization, and politics.

We begin with Africa above the equator, where Islam's influence increased and substantial kingdoms and empires flourished. Then we discuss West, East, central, and southern Africa and the effects of Arab-Islamic and then European influence in these regions. ■

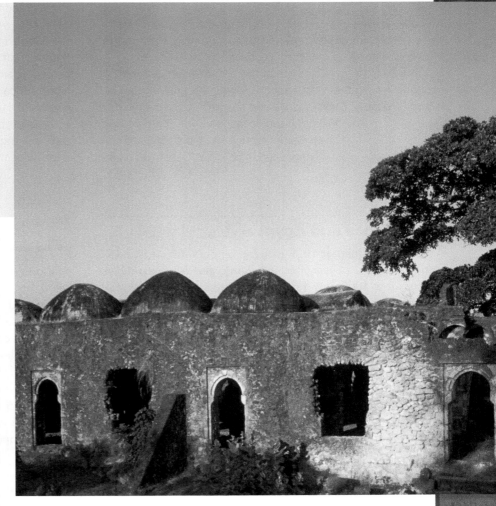

The Great Mosque at Kilwa, ca. 1100 C.E. The Swahili city of Kilwa, on the coast of present-day Tanzania, was likely founded by Muslim traders with strong links to the Indian Ocean world. The insides of its domes were lined with Chinese porcelain. Now in ruins, this large congregational mosque was probably in its day the largest fully enclosed structure in sub-Saharan Africa. *blickwinkel/Alamy*

Africa, 1000–1700

Africa

Long-distance trade—the supply-and-demand-driven movement of goods, people, and cultural attitudes and practices—typically stimulates historical change. This was as true in Africa in the early second millennium as in the Americas, Europe, or Asia. Different African regions were oriented differently vis-à-vis trade routes and trading partners and consequently developed in markedly different ways in these centuries.

The North African coast and the Sahel lay amidst trading networks linking the Mediterranean world, the growing **Dar-al-Islam** ("House of Submission"—the Islamic realm), and the rich West African kingdoms. The East African coast was integrated into the trading and cultural networks of the Indian Ocean basin and

See the Map
Trade Routes in Africa
at **MyHistoryLab.com**

firmly engaged with the Islamic world. The rest of sub-Saharan Africa was culturally diverse; people here engaged primarily in intra-African trade with cultures occupying different ecological niches. Africa is home to many societies with different histories, languages, religions, and cultures. In this it is similar to, but much larger and more ethnically and culturally diverse than, Europe.

In Mediterranean Africa, the major new reality in these centuries was Ottoman imperial expansion into Egypt and the **Maghreb**. Ottoman hegemony altered the political configuration of the Mediterranean. Merchants and missionaries carried Islam and Arabian culture across the Sahara from North Africa and the Middle East to the western, central, and Nilotic Sudan (see Map 14–2 on page 409), where Muslim conversion played a growing social and political role, especially among ruling elites who profited most from brokering trade with the Islamic north. Islam provided a shared arena

North Africa and Egypt

As we saw in Chapter 12, Egypt and other North African societies played a central role in Islamic and Mediterranean history after 1000 C.E. From Tunisia to Egypt, Sunni religious and political leaders and their Shi'ite, especially Isma'ili, counterparts struggled for the minds of the masses. By the thirteenth century, however, the Shi'ites had become a small minority of the Muslims in Mediterranean Africa. In Egypt a Sunni revival confirmed the Sunni character of Egyptian religiosity and legal interpretation. In general, a feisty regionalism characterized states, city-states, and tribal groups north of the Sahara and along the lower Nile. No single power controlled them for long. Regionalism persisted even after 1500, when most of North Africa came under the influence—and often, direct control—of the Ottoman Empire centered in Istanbul and felt the pressure of Ottoman-European naval rivalry.

By 1800 the nominally Ottoman domains from Egypt to Algeria were effectively independent. In Egypt the Ottomans had established direct rule after defeating the Mamluks in 1517, but by the seventeenth and eighteenth centuries, power had passed to Egyptian governors descended from the earlier Mamluks. These governors survived until the rise of Muhammad Ali in the wake of the French invasion of 1800 (see Chapter 26). The Mediterranean coastlands between Egypt and Morocco were offi-

Watch the Video
Piracy
at **MyHistoryLab.com**

cially Ottoman provinces, or regencies. By the 1700s, however, Algiers was a locally run principality with an economy based on piracy. Tripoli (in modern Libya) was ruled by a family of hereditary, effectively independent rulers, and Tunisia was virtually independent of its nominal Ottoman overlords.

Morocco, ruled by a succession of **Sharifs** (leaders claiming descent from the Prophet's family), was the only North African sultanate to remain fully independent after 1700. The most important *Sharifian* dynasty was that of the Sa'dis (1554–1659). Morocco's independence was largely due to the uniting of its Arab and Berber populations after 1500 to oppose Portuguese and Spanish threats.

The Spread of Islam South of the Sahara

Islamic influence in sub-Saharan Africa began as early as the eighth century and by 1800 affected most of the Sudanic belt and the East African coast as far south as modern Zimbabwe. Islam's spread was mostly peaceful, gradual, and partial. Conversion to Islam was rare beyond the ruling or commercial classes, and Islamic faith tended to coexist or blend with indigenous traditions. Nevertheless, agents of Islam brought not only the Qur'an, new religious practices, and literate culture, but

See the Map
Discovery: The Maghrib and West Africa, Fourteenth Century
at **MyHistoryLab.com**

of expression for at least some social groups and classes over a vast area from Egypt to Senegambia. In Africa as elsewhere, new converts adapted Islam to local circumstances. Distinctively African Islamic forms resulted, faithful to basic Muslim tenets but differing from "classical" Arabo-Persian forms, especially in attitudes toward women and relationships between the sexes.

South of the Sahara, dynamic state-building and trade were principal motors of cultural change. In sub-Saharan Africa, except on the east coast and in the West African forests, older African traditions held sway, and there was little or no Islamic presence beyond individual Muslims involved in trade. On the east coast, however, Islam influenced the development of Swahili culture and language, a unique blend of African, Indian, and Arabian traditions, and Muslim traders linked this region to India, China, and the Indies. In West Africa, Islamic states became important centers of Muslim culture and faith. Throughout sub-Saharan Africa, the spread of Islam occurred almost entirely by peaceful means.

Along the Atlantic and Indian Ocean coasts of Africa, the key fifteenth-century development was the shipboard arrival of

Hear the Audio
Influences in Africa 2
at **MyHistoryLab.com**

traders and missionaries from Christian Europe. The strength of African societies and the biological dangers to Europeans in the African interior meant that most of the Europeans' trade with the interior on both coasts remained for generations under African control. Well before Europeans reached the interior, however, the trade in slaves, weapons, and gold that they fostered greatly altered African political and social structures both along the coasts and in regions untouched by outsiders. The European voyages of discovery of the 1400s and 1500s presaged Africa's involvement in a new, expanding and, by the 1700s, European-dominated global trading system. This system generally exploited rather than bolstered African development, as the Atlantic slave trade (see Chapter 17) and the South African experience illustrate.

Focus Questions

■ Where in Africa was Islamic influence concentrated? How did Islam spread? What does this reveal about the relationship between commerce and cultural diffusion?

■ Why did different regions in Africa develop in different ways between 1000 and 1700?

also commercial and political changes, which substantially affected subsequent history. Many innovations, from architecture and technology to intellectual life and administrative practice, depended on writing and literacy, two major bases for developing large-scale societies and cultures.

Comparison of the spread of Islam in West and central Africa with that in East Africa is instructive. In East Africa, Muslim traders moving down the coastline with the ancient monsoon trade routes had begun to "Islamize" ports

See the Map
East African Coast to 1600
at **MyHistoryLab.com**

and coastal regions even before 800 C.E. From the thirteenth century on, Islamic trading communities and city-states developed along the coast from Mogadishu to Kilwa. By contrast, in western and central Africa, Islam was introduced into the Sudan by overland routes, primarily through traders from North Africa and the Nile valley. Berbers who, as early as the eighth century, plied the desert routes (see Chapter 5) to trading towns such as Awdaghast on the edge of the Sahel were Islam's chief agents. From there Islam spread south to centers such as Kumbi Saleh, southeast across the Niger, and west into Senegambia. Another source of Islam's penetration into the central and western Sudan was migration from Egypt and the Nilotic Sudan. In particular, migrating Arab tribal groups in search of new land came west to settle in the central sub-Saharan Sahel.

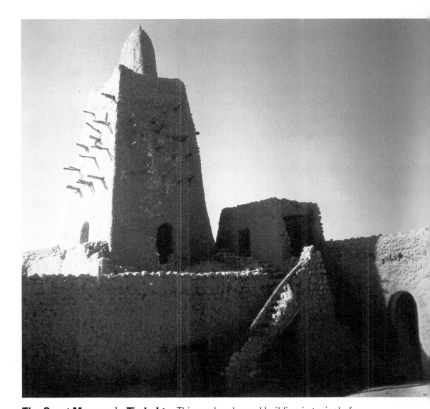

The Great Mosque in Timbuktu. This mud and wood building is typical of western Sudanese mosques. The distinctive tower of the mosque was a symbol of Islam, which came to places like Timbuktu in central and West Africa by way of overland trade routes. *Werner Forman, Art Resource, N.Y.*

Some early Muslim conversion took place in the western and central Sudan, again almost exclusively through the agency of Muslim traders. In 985, for the first time, a West African royal court—that of the kingdom of Gao, east of the Niger bend—became officially Muslim (see Chapter 5). The Gao rulers did not, however, try to convert their subjects. By contrast, as we shall see, the rulers of the later kingdom of Ghana long maintained their indigenous traditions even though they traded with Muslims and had Muslim advisers.

From the 1030s zealous militants known as Almoravids (see Chapter 12) began a conversion campaign extending to the western Sahel and Sahara. This movement eventually swept into Ghana's territory, taking Awdaghast and later, in 1076, Kumbi Saleh. Thereafter, the forcibly converted Soninke ruling elite of Ghana spread Islam among their own peoples. They also converted Mande-speaking traders farther south in the savannah, and these traders carried Islam into the forestlands. Farther west, the Fulbe rulers of Takrur along the Senegal became Muslim in the 1030s and propagated their new faith among their subjects. The Fulbe, or Fulani, remained important carriers of Islam over the next eight centuries as they migrated gradually into new regions as far east as Lake Chad, where some rulers were Muslim as early as 1100. Major groups in West Africa strongly resisted Islamization, especially the Mossi kingdoms founded in the Volta region at Wagadugu around 1050 and Yatenga about 1170.

Sahelian Empires of the Western and Central Sudan

As we noted in Chapter 5, substantial states had risen in the first millennium C.E. in the Sahel just south of the Sahara proper.[1] From about 1000 to 1600, four of these states developed into relatively long-lived empires: Ghana, Mali, and Songhai in the western Sudan, and Kanem-Bornu in the central Sudan.

Ghana

Ghana established the model for later Sahelian empires in the western Sudan. Well north of modern Ghana (and unrelated to it except by name), it lay between the inland Niger Delta and the upper Senegal. A Ghanaian kingdom existed as early as 400–600 C.E., but Ghana emerged as a regional power only near the end of the first millennium to flourish

for about two centuries. Its capital, Kumbi (or Kumbi Saleh), on the desert's edge, was well sited for the Saharan and Sahelian trade networks. Ghana's major population group was the Soninke. (*Ghana* is the Soninke term for "ruler.")

Ghanaian rulers were descended matrilineally (through the previous king's sister) and ruled through a council of ministers. Contemporaneous reports, especially from the eleventh-century Muslim writer al-Bakri (see Document, "Ghana and Its People in the Mid-Eleventh Century" on page 405), indicate that the king was supreme judge and held court regularly to hear grievances. The royal ceremonies reportedly held in Kumbi Saleh were embellished with the full trappings of wealth and power befitting a king held to be divinely blessed, if not semidivine.

In Ghana's hierarchical society, slaves were at the bottom; farmers and draftsmen above them; merchants above them; and the king, his court, and the nobility on top. Ghana's power had a solid economic base. Tribute from the empire's many chieftaincies and taxes on royal lands and crops supplemented levies on all external trade. This trade, north–south between the Sahara and the savannah and especially east–west through the Sahel between Senegambia and trading towns like Gao on the Niger Bend, involved a variety of goods. Imported salt, cloth, and metal goods such as copper from the north were apparently exchanged for gold and perhaps kola nuts from the south. The regime also controlled the gold (and, presumably, the slave) trade originating in the savannah to the south and west, in the Bambuk and Galam regions of the middle Senegal and its southern tributary, the Faleme, and in the Boure region of the upper Niger and its tributaries.

Although the Ghanaian king and court did not convert to Islam, they made elaborate arrangements to accommodate Muslim traders and government servants in a separate settlement a few miles from Khumbi's royal preserve. Muslim traders were prominent at court, literate Muslims administered the government, and Muslim legists advised the ruler.

A huge, well-trained army secured royal control, enabling the kings to extend their sway in the late tenth century to the Atlantic shore and to the south (see Map 14–1 on page 406). In 992, Ghanaian troops wrested Awdaghast, the southern terminus of the trans-Saharan trade route with Morocco, from the Berbers. The empire was, however, vulnerable to attack from the desert, as Almoravid Berber forces proved in 1054 when they took Awdaghast in a single raid.

Ghana's empire was probably destroyed in the late twelfth century by a Malinke clan from the mountains southeast of Kumbi Saleh, the anti-Muslim Soso, who had

---

[1] S. K. and R. J. McIntosh, *Prehistoric Investigations in the Region of Jenne, Mali* (Oxford: B.A. R., 1980), pp. 41–59, 434–461; R. Oliver, *The African Experience* (New York: HarperCollins, 1991), pp. 90–101.

Document

Ghana and Its People in the Mid-Eleventh Century

The Spanish Muslim geographer al-Bakri (d. 1094) seems never to have visited West Africa himself. Nonetheless, his writings were considered authoritative. Here he describes customs of the ruler and people of the Ghanaian capital based on information from other Arabic sources and travelers.

■ *How did the ruler of Ghana deal with the differing religious groups in his capital?*

Ghana is a title given to their kings; the name of the region is Awkar, and their king today, namely in the year 460 [1067–8 C.E.], is Tanka Manin. . . . This Tanka Manin is powerful, rules an enormous kingdom, and possesses great authority.

The city of Ghana consists of two towns situated on a plain. One of these towns, which is inhabited by Muslims, is large and possesses twelve mosques, in one of which they assemble for the Friday prayer. There are salaried imams and muezzins, as well as jurists and scholars. In the environs are wells with sweet water, from which they drink and with which they grow vegetables. The king's town is six miles distant from this one and bears the name of Al-Ghaba. Between these two towns there are continuous habitations. The houses of the inhabitants are of stone and acacia wood. The king has a palace and a number of domed dwellings all surrounded with an enclosure like a city wall. In the king's town, and not far from his court of justice, is a mosque where the Muslims who arrive at his court . . . pray. Around the king's town are domed buildings and groves and thickets where the sorcerers of these people, men in charge of the religious cult, live. In them too are their idols and the tombs of their kings. . . .

All of them shave their beards, and women shave their heads. The king adorns himself like a woman [wearing necklaces] round his neck and [bracelets] on his forearms,

and he puts on a high cap (*tartur*) decorated with gold and wrapped in a turban of fine cotton. He sits in audience or to hear grievances against officials (*mazalim*) in a domed pavilion around which stand ten horses covered with gold-embroidered materials. Behind the king stand ten pages holding shields and swords decorated with gold, and on his right are the sons of the [vassal] kings of his country wearing splendid garments and their hair plaited with gold. The governor of the city sits on the ground before the king and around him are ministers seated likewise. . . . When the people who profess the same religion as the king approach him they fall on their knees and sprinkle dust on their heads, for this is their way of greeting him. As for the Muslims, they greet him only by clapping their hands.

Their religion is paganism and the worship of idols (*dakakir*). When their king dies they construct over the place where his tomb will be an enormous dome of saj wood. Then they bring him on a bed covered with a few carpets and cushions and place him beside the dome. At his side they place his ornaments, his weapons, and the vessels from which he used to eat and drink, filled with various kinds of food and beverages.

Excerpt from *Corpus of Early Arabic Sources for West African History* by N. Levitzon and J.F.P. Hopkins. Copyright © 1981 Reprinted with the permission of Cambridge University Press.

---

long belonged to the Ghanaian Empire. The brief Soso ascendancy (1180–1230) apparently spelled the end of the once great transregional power centered at Kumbi.[2]

Mali

With Ghana's collapse and the Almoravids' failure at empire-building below the Sahara (largely because of their focus on North Africa), the western Sudan fragmented into smaller

kingdoms. The former Ghanaian provinces of Mande and Takrur were already independent before 1076, and in the early twelfth century Takrur's control of the Senegal valley and the gold-producing region of Galam made it briefly the strongest state in the western Sudan. Like Ghana, however, it was soon eclipsed, first by the brief Soso ascendancy and then by the rise of Mali.

In the mid-thirteenth century the Keita ruling clan of a Ghanaian successor kingdom, Mali, forged a new and lasting empire. This empire seems to have developed on the same economic base as had Ghana and Takrur earlier: monopolization of the lucrative north–south gold trade. The

---

[2] D. Conrad and H. Fisher, "The Conquest That Never Was: Ghana and the Almoravids, 1076," *History in Africa* 9 (1982): 1–59; 10 (1983): 53–78.

Map 14–1. Africa ca. 900–1500. Shown are major cities and states referred to in the text. The main map shows the region of West Africa occupied by the empire of Ghana from ca. 990 to ca. 1180. The inset shows the region occupied by Mali between 1230 and 1450.

Keita kings dominated sufficient Sahelian territory to control the flow of West African gold from the Senegal and forest regions south of the Niger to the trans-Saharan trade routes, and the influx of copper and salt in exchange. Because they were farther south than their Ghanaian predecessors had been, in the fertile land along the Niger, they were better placed to control upper-Niger trade and to add also the Gambia and Senegal trade to the west. They used captives for plantation labor in the Niger inland delta to produce surplus food for trade.

Agriculture and cattle farming were Mali's primary occupations and, together with the gold trade, its economic mainstays. Rice was grown in the river valleys and millet in drier parts of the Sahel. Together with beans, yams, and

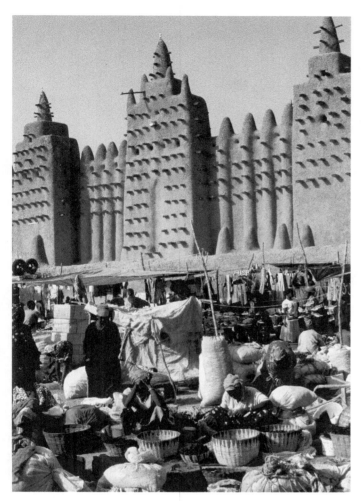

The Great Mosque at Jenne. Jenne was one of the important commercial centers controlled by the empire of Mali in the thirteenth and fourteenth centuries. The thriving market in front of the mosque reflects the enduring vitality of trade and commerce in the region.

other agricultural produce, this ensured a plentiful food supply. Fishing flourished along the Niger and elsewhere. Cattle, sheep, and goats were abundant. The chief craft specialties were iron and gold metalworking and weaving of cotton grown within the empire.

The Malinke, a southern Mande-speaking people of the upper Niger region, formed the core population of the new state. They apparently lived in walled urban settlements typical of the western savannah. Each town was surrounded by its own agricultural land, held perhaps 1,000 to 15,000 people, and presumably had enough arable land within its walls to deal with siege. Each was linked to neighboring cities by trade and possibly intermarriage.

The Keita dynasty had converted early to Islam, around 1100 C.E. Keita's rulers even claimed descent from Muhammad's famous *muezzin*, Bilal ibn Ribah, a

former black Abyssinian slave whose son was said to have settled in Mande-speaking territory. During Mali's heyday in the 1200s and 1300s, its kings often made the pilgrimage to Mecca. From their travel in the central Islamic lands, they brought back not only military aids, such as Barbary war horses, but also new ideas about political and military organization. Through Muslim traders' networks, Islam also connected Mali to other areas of Africa, especially to the east.

Mali's imperial power was built largely by the Keita King Sundiata (or Sunjaata, r. 1230–1255). Sundiata and his successors exploited their agricultural resources, significant population growth, and Malinke commercial skills to build an empire even more powerful than Ghana's. Sundiata extended his imperium west to the Atlantic and east beyond Timbuktu. By controlling the commercial entrepôts of Gao, Walata, and Jenne, he dominated the Saharan as well as the Niger trade. He built his capital, Niani, into a major city. Niani was located on a tributary of the Niger in the savannah at the edge of the forest in a gold- and iron-rich region. It had access to the forest trade products of gold, kola nuts, and palm oil; it was easily defended because of its surrounding hills; and it was readily reached by river.

Read the Document
Excerpts from Sundiata: An Epic of Old Mali, 1235
at **MyHistoryLab.com**

The empire that Sundiata and his successors built ultimately encompassed three major regions and language groups of Sudanic West Africa: (1) the Senegal region (including Takrur), populated by speakers of the West Atlantic Niger-Kongo language group (including Fulbe, Tukulor, Wolof, Serer); (2) the central Mande states between Senegal and Niger, occupied by the Niger-Kongo-speaking Soninke and Mandinke; and (3) the peoples of the Niger in the Gao region who spoke Songhai, the only Nilo-Saharan language west of the Lake Chad basin. Mali was less a centralized bureaucratic state than the center of a vast sphere of influence that included provinces and tribute-paying kingdoms. Many individual chieftaincies were independent but recognized the sovereignty of the supreme, sacred *mansa*, or "emperor," of the Malian realms.

Read the Document
The Travels of Ibn Battuta "Ibn Battuta in Mali"
at **MyHistoryLab.com**

The greatest Keita king was Mansa Musa (r. 1312–1337), famous for his pilgrimage through Mamluk Cairo to Mecca in 1324. He spent or gave away so much gold in Cairo alone that he started a massive inflation that lasted over a decade. He brought many Muslim scholars, artists, and architects back to Mali, where he consolidated his power, securing peace for most of his reign throughout his vast dominions. The devout ruler fostered the spread of Islam in the empire and

Read the Document
Al-Umari describes Mansa Musa of Mali
at **MyHistoryLab.com**

Mansa Musa, King of Mali. The fourteenth-century Catalan Atlas shows King Mansa Musa of Mali, seated on a throne holding a nugget of gold. A camel rider approaches him.

beyond. Under Musa's rule, Timbuktu became famous for its *madrasa*s and libraries, poets, scientists, and architects, making it the leading intellectual center of sub-Saharan Islam and a major trading city of the Sahel—roles it retained long after Mali's empire declined.[3] After Musa, rivalries for the throne diminished Mali's dominance. The empire slowly withered until a new Songhai power supplanted it after about 1450.

Songhai

Evidence suggests that as early as the eleventh or twelfth century there was a Songhai kingdom around Gao, on the eastern arc of the great bend of the Niger. In 1325 Mansa Musa brought this kingdom and the Gao region under the control of Mali and the Malinke. Mali's domination ended with the rise of the Sonni dynasty in Gao in the mid-1300s. The kingdom became an empire under the greatest Sunni ruler, Sonni Ali (r. 1462–1492). For more than a century thereafter, the Songhai Empire was arguably Africa's most powerful state (see Map 14–2 on page 409). With a strong military built around a riverboat flotilla and cavalry, Sonni Ali took Jenne and Timbuktu. He pushed the Tuareg Berbers into the northern Sahel and Sahara and stifled threats from the southern forestlands.

His successor, Askia Muhammad al-Turi (r. 1493–1528), continued Sonni Ali's expansionist policies. Between them, these two rulers built an empire that stretched west nearly to the Atlantic, northwest into the Sahara, and east into the central Sudan. Taking advantage of their control of access to gold and other desirable West African commodities, they emulated their Ghanaian predecessors in taking advantage of the ancient caravan trade across the Sahara to the Libyan and Tunisian coasts. This was their major source of wealth.

Unlike Sonni Ali, who maintained his people's traditional African religious faith, Askia Muhammad and his Askia successors were emphatically Muslim. At-Turi modeled the Songhai state on the Islamic empire of Mali. (See Document, "Muslim Reform in Songhai." on page 410) In his reign, many Muslim scholars came to Gao, Timbuktu, and Jenne. He appointed Muslim judges (*qadi*s) throughout the empire and made Timbuktu a major intellectual and legal training center for the whole Sudan. He replaced native Songhais with Arab Muslim immigrants as government officials to strengthen his

[3] For more on Mali, especially its wealth and Timbuktu's role as a center of scholarship, see E. Gilbert and J. T. Reynolds, *Africa in World History: From Prehistory to the Present* (Upper Saddle River, NJ: Prentice Hall, 2004), pp. 91–93.

See the Map
African Empires in the Western Sudan at **MyHistoryLab.com**

Map Exploration

To explore this map further, go to **http://www.myhistorylab.com**

Map 14–2. **Africa ca. 1500–1700.** Important towns, regions, peoples, and states. The inset shows the empire of Songhai at its greatest extent in the early sixteenth century.

centralized power. Like Mansa Musa before him, Muhammad made a triumphal pilgrimage to Mecca, where he was hailed as "Caliph of the western Sahara." From his vast royal treasury he supported the poor and Sufi leaders, or **marabouts**, and built mosques throughout the realm. Nevertheless, he failed to Islamize the empire or to ensure a strong central state for his successors.

The last powerful Askia leader was Askia Dawud (r. 1549–1583), under whom Songhai prosperity and intellectual life reached its apogee. The trans-Saharan trade reached new heights, and royal patronage of the arts rose to new levels. Still, difficulties mounted. The last Askias battled the Mossi to the south and Berbers from the north. Civil war broke out over the royal succession in

Document Muslim Reform in Songhai

Around 1500 Askia Muhammad al-Turi, the first Muslim Songhai ruler, wrote to the North African Muslim theologian Muhammad al-Maghili (d. 1504) about proper Muslim practices. In these excerpts from al-Turi's seventh question, we glimpse the new convert's zeal for conformity to traditional religious norms, as well as the king's desire to better the social order and his concern for justice. The answers from al-Maliki reflect the puritanical "official line" of the conservative *ulama* who did not want to allow syncretism to emerge among newly converted groups.

■ *What are the problems and corresponding solutions described in the letters? Which problem did al-Maghili find most serious? Why? Which do you think would have been most serious? Why?*

FROM ASKIA MUHAMMAD AL-TURI'S SEVENTH QUESTION

Among the people [of the Songhay Empire], there are some who claim knowledge of the supernatural through sand divining and the like, or through the disposition of the stars . . . [while] some assert that they can write (talismans) to bring good fortune . . . or to ward off bad fortune. . . . Some defraud in weights and measures. . . .

One of their evil practices is the free mixing of men and women in the markets and streets and the failure of women to veil themselves . . . [while] among the people of Djenné [Jenne] it is an established custom for a girl not to cover any part of her body as long as she remains a virgin . . . and all the most beautiful girls walk about naked. . . .

So give us legal ruling concerning these people and their ilk, and may God Most High reward you!

FROM MUHAMMAD AL-MAGHILI'S ANSWER

The answer—and God it is who directs to the right course—is that everything you have mentioned concerning people's behavior in some parts of this country is gross error. It is the bounden duty of the commander of the Muslims and all other believers who have the power to change every one of these evil practices.

As for any who claims knowledge of the supernatural in the ways you have mentioned . . . he is a liar and an unbeliever. . . . Such people must be forced to renounce it by the sword. Then whoever renounces such deeds should be left in peace, but whoever persists should be killed with the sword as an unbeliever; his body should not be washed or shrouded, and he should not be buried in a Muslim graveyard. . . .

As for defrauding in weights and measures it is forbidden (*haram*) according to the Qur'an, the Sunna and the consensus of opinion of the learned men of the Muslim community. It is the bounden duty of the commander of the Muslims to appoint a trustworthy man in charge of the markets, and to safeguard people's means of subsistence. He should standardize all the scales in each province. . . . Similarly, all measures both large and small must be rectified so that they conform to a uniform standard. . . .

Now, what you mentioned about the free mixing of men and women and leaving the pudenda uncovered is one of the greatest abominations. The commander of the Muslims must exert himself to prevent all these things. . . He should appoint trustworthy men to watch over this by day and night, in secret and in the open. This is not to be considered as spying on the Muslims; it is only a way of caring for them and curbing evildoers, especially when corruption becomes widespread in the land as it has done in Timbuktu and Djenné. . . .

1586, dividing the empire. In 1591 an expedition sent by the Moroccan Sa'dis used superior gunpowder weapons and help from disaffected Songhai princes to defeat the last Askia of Gao at Tondibi, and the empire collapsed.

Kanem and Kanem-Bornu

A fourth sizable Sahelian empire, Kanem, arose in the central Sudan after 1100. Kanem began as a southern Saharan confederation of nomadic tribes, the Zaghawah, who were spread over much of the south-central and southeastern Sahara. By

Chronology

Sahelian Empires of the Western Sudan

ca. 990–ca. 1180?	Empire of Ghana
1076	Ghana loses Awdaghast to Almoravids
1180–1230	Soso clan controls old Ghanaian territories
ca. 1230–1450	Empire of Mali, founded by Sundiata
1230–1255	Reign of Sundiata
1312–1337	Reign of Mansa Musa
1340–1370s	Independent Songhai state emerges in Gao after throwing off Malian rule
ca. 1450–1591	Songhai Empire at Gao
1462–1492	Reign of Sonni Ali
1493–1591	Askia dynasty rules Songhai Empire
1493–1528	Reign of Askia Muhammad al-Turi
1549–1583	Reign of Askia Dawud

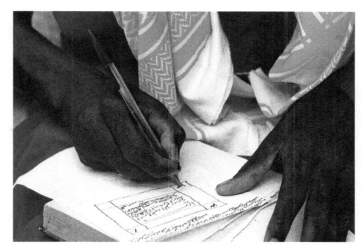

A Marabout Creates a *Grigri*. A verse from the Qur'an is copied onto a piece of paper, which will be folded and put in a leather pouch. The pouch is worn as an amulet, to protect the wearer from sickness, harm, or evil.

the twelfth century a Zaghawah group known as the Kanuri had settled in Kanem, and from there they began a military campaign of expansion in the thirteenth century. Their key leader in this campaign, Mai Dunama Dibbalemi (r. ca. 1221–1259), was a contemporary of Mali's Sundiata, and, like him, a Muslim. During his reign, Islam appears to have become entrenched among the Kanuri ruling class. Dibbalemi used it to sanction his rule, which had otherwise familiar African trappings of sacred kingship. Islam also provided a rationale for expansion through *jihad*, or holy "struggle" against polytheists.

Dibbalemi and his successors extended Kanuri power north into the desert across the Fezzan in modern Libya and northeast along the Sahelian-Saharan fringe toward Nilotic Africa. In both directions they controlled important trade routes—north to Libya and east to the Nile. The next two centuries saw the mixing of Kanuri and local Kanembu peoples. There was a corresponding transformation of the Kanuri leader from nomadic **shaykh** to Sudanic king and of Kanem from a nomadic to a largely sedentary, quasi-feudal kingdom. Like Mali to the west, Kanem's dominion was of two kinds: direct rule over and taxation of core territories, and indirect control over and collection of tribute from a wider region of vassal chieftaincies. Islamic acculturation progressed most rapidly in the core territories.

Civil strife, largely over royal succession, weakened the Kanuri state in the later fourteenth and fifteenth centuries. After 1400 the locus of power shifted from Kanem proper westward, to Bornu, southwest of Lake Chad. Here, in the 1490s, a new Kanuri Empire arose almost simultaneously with the collapse of the Askia dynasty of the Songhai Empire at Gao. Firearms and Turkish military instructors acquired after a pilgrimage to Mecca enabled the Kanuri leader Idris Alawma (r. ca. 1575–1610) to unify Kanem and Bornu. He set up an avowedly Islamic state and extended his rule as far as Hausaland, between Bornu and the Niger. The center of trading activity as well as political power now shifted from the Niger Bend east to Kanuri-controlled territory.

Deriving its prosperity from the trans-Saharan trade, Idris Alawma's regional empire survived for over a century. It was finally broken up by a long famine, repeated Tuareg attacks, weak leadership, and loss of control over trade to

Chronology

Central Sudanic Empires

ca. 1100–1500	Kanuri Empire of Kanem
ca. 1220s–1400	Height of Empire of Kanem
ca. 1221–1259	Reign of Mai Dunama Dibbalemi
ca. 1575–1610	Reign of Idris Alawma, major architect of the Kanem-Bornu state
ca. 1575–late 1600s (1846)	Kanuri Empire of Kanem-Bornu

smaller, better-organized Hausa states. The ruling dynasty held out until 1846, but by 1700 its power had been sharply reduced by the growing Hausa states to the west in what is now northern Nigeria. Their power peaked in the nineteenth century with their unification under the Fulani sultanate of Sokoto (see Chapter 26).

The Eastern Sudan

The Christian states of Maqurra and Alwa in the Nilotic Sudan, or Nubia, lasted more than 600 years from their early-seventh-century beginnings and maintained political, religious, and commercial contact with Egypt, the Red Sea world, and much of the Sudan.

After 1000 C.E. Maqurra and Alwa continued treaty relations with their more powerful northern Egyptian neighbors. However, the Mamluks intervened repeatedly in Nubian affairs, and Arab nomads constantly threatened the Nubian states. From late Fatimid times, both Maqurra and Alwa were increasingly subject to immigrating Muslim Arab tribesmen, traders, and growing Muslim minorities. The result was a long-term intermingling of Arab and Nubian cultures and the creation of a new Nilotic Sudanese culture.

A significant factor in the gradual disappearance of Christianity in Nubia was its elite status there and its association with the foreign Egyptian Coptic Christianity. Maqurra became officially Muslim in the early fourteenth century, although Christianity survived until late in the same century. The Islamization of Alwa came somewhat later, most effectively under the long-lived Funj sultanate that replaced the Alwa state.

The Funj state flourished between the Blue and White Niles and to the north along the main Nile from just after 1500 until 1762. The Funj were originally cattle nomads who apparently adopted Islam soon after establishing their kingdom. In the late sixteenth and the seventeenth centuries, the Funj developed an Islamic society whose Arabized character was unique in sub-Saharan Africa. A much-reduced Funj state held out until an Ottoman Egyptian invasion in 1821.

The Forestlands—Coastal West and Central Africa

West African Forest Kingdoms: The Example of Benin

Many states with distinct political, religious, and cultural traditions had developed in southern and coastal regions of West Africa before 1400. Even those states like Asante or the Yoruba kingdoms of Oyo and Ife, which reached their height only after 1500, had much earlier origins. Benin, the best known of these forest kingdoms, reflects the sophistication of West African culture before 1500; its art, in particular, is renowned for enduring beauty.

Benin State and Society The Edo speakers of Benin have occupied the southern Nigerian region between Yorubaland and the Ibo peoples east of the lower Niger for millennia. Traditional Edo society is organized according to a patrilineal system of primogeniture. The village is the fundamental political unit; authority rests on organization of males into age-grade units.[4]

((•─Hear the Audio
Influences in Africa 2
at **MyHistoryLab.com**

According to archaeological evidence, the local Edo cultural traditions of Benin were closely linked to those of Ife, one of the most prominent Yoruba states northwest of Benin. Some kind of distinct kingdom of Benin likely existed as early as the twelfth century, and traditional accounts of both Ife and Edo agree that an Ife prince was sent to rule Benin around 1300. There are indications that the power of the **oba**, or king, at this time was sharply limited by the Edo leaders who invited the foreign ruler. These leaders were known as the **uzama**, an order of hereditary indigenous chiefs. According to tradition, the fourth oba managed to wrest more control from these chiefs and instituted something of the ceremonial authority of absolute monarchy. However, only under King Ewuare (r. 1440–1475), did Benin become a royal autocracy and a large state of major regional importance.

Ewuare rebuilt the capital—known today as Benin City—and named it and his kingdom Edo. He apparently established a government in which he had sweeping authority, although he exercised it in light of the deliberations of a royal council. Ewuare formed this council from not only the palace *uzama*, but also townspeople. He gave each chief specific administrative responsibilities and rank in the government hierarchy. Ewuare and his successors developed a tradition of military kingship and undertook major wars of expansion, both west into Yorubaland and east into Ibo country, across the Niger River. They also claimed for the office of *oba* an increasing ritual authority that presaged more radical development of the king's role.

In the seventeenth century the *oba* was transformed from a military leader into a religious figure with supernatural powers. Human sacrifice, specifically of slaves, seems to have accompanied the cult of deceased kings and became

---

[4] A. F. C. Ryder, *Benin and the Europeans, 1485–1897* (New York: Longman, 1969), p. 1. Ryder's work is a basic reference for the following brief summary about Benin.

A Closer Look

Benin Bronze Plaque with Chief and Two Attendants

BENIN ARTISTS AND ARTISANS produced spectacular sculptures from the late thirteenth century until the coming of the British in 1897. Their figures typically have the head-to-body proportions of this example, about one to four—perhaps emphasizing the head's importance as a marker of identity and behavior and a symbol of life. The details of the clothing might have been "readable" as to the wearer's rank and family. The stylized faces are typical of Benin bronzes (often actually of brass); dating the piece is hard, but given the two small European figures depicted in the upper field and the sophisticated detail, it is most likely sixteenth or seventeenth century.

Two European figures, possibly Portuguese, are shown from the waist up; both have long moustaches, club-like weapons, plumed helmets, neck ruffs, and armor.

The royal figure here has an elaborate headdress with two feathers on top and pendant plumes behind; two bead necklaces, one with leopard teeth mixed in; armlets and anklets; a loincloth; a leopard skin with fringe; a quadrangular bell on a double necklace; a spear with leaf-shaped blade; and an ornamented shield.

The two royal attendants are carrying round fans, wearing helmets, and adorned like the king with bracelets.

*Benin Plaque. Brass. Lost wax. W. Africa 16th–17th century c.e. Hillel Burger/
Peabody Museum, Harvard University © President and Fellows of Harvard College.
All rights reserved.*

Questions

1. The sophisticated Benin bronze artistry allowed for highly detailed sculpture that, for all their stylization, captured its subjects vividly and in great detail. What do you make of the differences between the depictions of the Benin Africans and the two European figures?

2. It has been speculated that this was a piece of court art and the depiction of the royal figure and attendants was intended to exalt royal power and prestige. Do you see evidence of this? What?

myhist**o**ry**lab**   To examine this image in an interactive fashion, please go to **www.myhistorylab.com**

Ife figure, ca. twelfth–fifteenth centuries C.E. The serene classicism of Ife art is equaled only by that of ancient Greece or Buddhist Asia.

Chronology

Benin	
ca. 1100–1897	Benin state
ca. 1300	First Ife king of Benin state
1440–1475	Reign of Ewuare

changes connected with trade in West African gold and other commodities and with the importation and spread in West and central Africa of food crops such as maize, peanuts, squash, sweet potatoes, cocoa, and cassava (manioc) from the Americas. The gradual involvement of Africa in the emerging global economy paved the way for eventual colonial domination of the continent, especially its coastal regions, by Europeans. The European names for segments of the coastline—the Grain (or Pepper) Coast, the Ivory Coast, the Gold Coast, and the Slave Coast—identify the main exports that could be extracted by ship.

even more frequent in the nineteenth century. Succession by primogeniture was discontinued, and the *uzama* chose *obas* from any branch of the royal family.

Benin Art The global significance of Benin, however, lies in its court art, especially its famous sculptures. The splendid terra-cotta, ivory, and brass statuary sculptures of Ife-Benin are among the glories of human creativity. Some scholars trace the artistic and technical lineage of these masterpieces to the sculptures of the Nok culture of ancient West Africa (see Chapter 5).

The best sculptures are cast bronze plaques depicting legendary and historical scenes. These were displayed in the royal palace in Benin City before the sixteenth century. There are also brass heads, apparently of royalty, that resemble many life-size terra-cotta and brass heads found at Ife. The heads at Ife are held to represent the Oni, or religious chief of ancient Ife, or particular ancestors cherished by their descendants.

Similar sculptures have been found both to the north and in the Niger Delta. Recent excavations east of the Niger at Igbo-Ukwu have unearthed stunning terra cottas and bronzes that belong to the same general artistic culture and dated as early as the ninth century. These artifacts testify to the high cultural levels of traditional African societies.

European Arrivals on the Coastlands

The coasts of West and central Africa witnessed many important changes between 1500 and 1800. Those changes wrought by the burgeoning Atlantic slave trade are the most notorious (see Chapter 17). Of comparable importance are

Benin Bronze Plaque. From the palace of the *obas* of Benin, this dates to the Edo period of Benin culture, 1575–1625. It depicts two Portuguese males, perhaps father and son, holding hands. The figures may portray traders or government officials who came to the African coasts in increasing numbers from the end of the fifteenth century.

Senegambia In West Africa, Senegambia—which takes its name from the Senegal and Gambia rivers—was a region early affected by European trade. Its interior had long been involved in both trans-Saharan trade and east–west trade in the Sahel and savannah, especially in the imperial heydays of Ghana, Mali, and Songhai. Senegambia's maritime trade with Europe, like the older overland trade, was primarily in gold and products such as salt, cotton goods, hides, and copper. For roughly a century Senegambian states also provided slaves for European purchase; indeed, perhaps a third of all African slaves exported during the sixteenth century came from Senegambia. Thereafter, however, the focus of the slave trade shifted south and east along the coast (see Chapter 17). Over time, Portuguese-African mulattos and the British came to control the Gambia River trade, while the French won the Senegal River markets.

The Gold Coast The Gold Coast, like Senegambia, was one of the West African coastal districts most affected by the arrival of international maritime trade. The name derives from the region's importance after 1500 as the outlet for the more southern gold fields of West Africa in the forestland of Akan. Here, beginning with the Portuguese at Elmina in 1481, but primarily after 1600, European states and companies built coastal forts to protect their trade and serve as depots for inland goods. The trade in gold, kola nuts, and other commodities seems to have encouraged the growth of larger states in the region, perhaps because they could better handle and control the overland commerce.

The intensive Gold Coast involvement with Europeans also led to the importation and spread of American crops, notably maize and cassava. The success of these crops in West and central Africa likely contributed to substantial population growth in the sixteenth and seventeenth centuries.

The Gold Coast escaped the ravages of the slave trade for some decades; it even was an importer of slaves until long after 1500. Slaves, however, became big business here in the late seventeenth century, especially in the Accra region. The economy was so disrupted by the slave trade that gold mining declined sharply. Eventually more gold came to the Gold Coast from slave sales than went out from its mines (see Chapter 17).

Central Africa

The continent's vast center is bounded by swamps in the north, coastal rain forests to the west, highlands to the east, and deserts in the south. Before 1500 these natural barriers impeded international contact and trade with the interior. They also shaped the two-pronged route by which Bantu peoples and languages moved, over many centuries, from western and west-central Africa south into the Zaire basin and east around the equatorial forest into the lakes of highland East

Africa. In the tropical central area, regional interaction in movements of peoples and in trade and culture had always been the norm. Here as elsewhere in Africa were large as well as small political, economic, and social units. Peoples such as the Lunda and the Luba, on the southern savannah below the rain forest, carved out sizable kingdoms before 1500 and expanded their control over neighboring areas into the 1800s.

The Portuguese came to the western coasts looking for gold and silver but found none. Ultimately, their main export was slaves. These slaves were taken first for gang labor to Portuguese sugar plantations on Sao Thomé island in the Gulf of Guinea and then, in vast numbers, to perform similar plantation labor in Brazil. In the 1640s the Dutch briefly succeeded the Portuguese as the major suppliers of African slaves to English and French plantations in the Caribbean.

The Kongo Kingdom Kongo was the major state with which the Portuguese dealt after coming to central Africa in 1483. Dating from probably the fourteenth century, the Kongo kingdom was located on a fertile, well-watered plateau south of the lower Zaïre River valley, between the coast and the Kwango River in the east. Here, astride the border between forest and grassland, the Kongo kings had built a central government based on a pyramid structure of tax or tribute collection. The king's authority was tied to acceptance of him as a spiritual spokesman of the gods or ancestors. By 1600 Kongo was half the size of England and boasted a high state of specialization in weaving and pottery, salt production, fishing, and metalworking.

The Portuguese brought Mediterranean goods, preeminently luxury textiles from North Africa, to trade for central African goods. Such luxuries enhanced the prestige and wealth of the ruler and his elites. Slaves became the primary export that could be traded for foreign luxuries. Meanwhile,

Queen Nzinga of Ndongo, who ruled from 1615 to 1660. This contemporary engraving shows her negotiating a treaty with the Portuguese. She is seated on the back of a slave.

Document

Affonso I of Kongo Writes to the King of Portugal

In 1526 Affonso, the Christian king of Kongo, wrote to the Portuguese monarch ostensibly to complain about the effects of slaving on Kongo's people and economy. But the real issue was that the Portuguese were circumventing Affonso's royal monopoly on the inland slave trade. One of the insidious effects of the massive demand of the Atlantic slave trade was the increased engagement in it of African monarchs, chieftains, and merchants.

■ *How did the presence of Portuguese merchants and European goods upset the social and political situation in Kongo? How were Affonso's subjects tempted into the slave trade? How did Affonso wish to change the relationship of his people to Portugal? Was the king more worried about human rights or his economic losses?*

Sir, Your Highness [of Portugal] should know how our Kingdom is being lost in so many ways that it is convenient to provide for the necessary remedy, since this is caused by the excessive freedom given by your factors and officials to the men and merchants who are allowed to come to this Kingdom to set up shops with goods and many things which have been prohibited by us, and which they spread throughout our Kingdoms and Domains in such an abundance that many of our vassals, whom we had in obedience, do not comply because they have the things in greater abundance than we ourselves; and it was with these things that we had them content and subjected under our vassalage and jurisdiction, so it is doing a great harm not only to the service of God, but the security and peace of our Kingdoms and State as well.

And we cannot reckon how great the damage is, since the mentioned merchants are taking every day our natives, sons of the land and the sons of our noblemen and vassals and our relatives, because the thieves and men of bad conscience grab them wishing to have the things and wares of this Kingdom which they are ambitious of; they grab them and get them to be sold; and so great, Sir, is

the corruption and licentiousness that our country is being completely depopulated, and Your Highness should not agree with this nor accept it as in your service. And to avoid it we need from those [your] Kingdoms no more than some priests and a few people to teach in schools, and no other goods except wine and flour for the holy sacrament. That is why we beg of Your Highness to help and assist us in this matter, commanding your factors that they should not send here either merchants or wares, because it is *our will that in these Kingdoms there should not be any trade of slaves nor outlet for them* [emphasis in the original].

Concerning what is referred above, again we beg of Your Highness to agree with it, since otherwise we cannot . . . remedy such an obvious damage. Pray Our Lord in His mercy to have Your Highness under His guard and let you do for ever the things of His service. I kiss your hands many times. . . .

From *The African Past*, trans. by J. O. Hunwick, reprinted in Basil Davidson (Grosset and Dunlap, The Universal Library), pp. 191–193. Reprinted by permission of Curtis Brown Ltd. Copyright © 1964 by Basil Davidson.

Read the Document
Voyage from Lisbon
at **MyHistoryLab.com**
imports such as fine clothing, tobacco, and alcohol did nothing to replace the labor pool lost to slavery.

At first the Portuguese put resources into education and Christian proselytizing, but the demand for slaves eventually eclipsed these concerns. Regional rulers procured slaves from neighboring kingdoms, as did Portuguese traders who went inland themselves. As demand grew, local rulers increasingly attacked neighbors to capture slaves for Portuguese traders (see Chapter 17).

The Kongo ruler Affonso I (r. ca. 1506–1543), a Christian convert, at first welcomed Jesuit missionaries and sup-

ported conversion. But he eventually broke with the Jesuits and encouraged traditional practices, despite remaining a Christian himself. Affonso had difficulty curbing the more exploitative slaving practices and independent-minded provincial governors, who often dealt directly with the Portuguese, undermining royal authority. (See Document, "Affonso I of Kongo Writes to the King of Portugal.") Affonso's successor finally restricted Portuguese activity to Mpinda harbor and the Kongo capital of Mbanza Kongo (São Salvador). A few years later, Portuguese attempts to name the Kongo royal successor caused a bloody uprising against them that led in turn to a Portuguese trade boycott of the kingdom.

Chronology

Central Africa

1300s	Kongo kingdom founded
1483	Portuguese come to central African coast
ca. 1506–1543	Reign of Affonso I as king of Kongo
1571	Angola becomes Portuguese proprietary colony

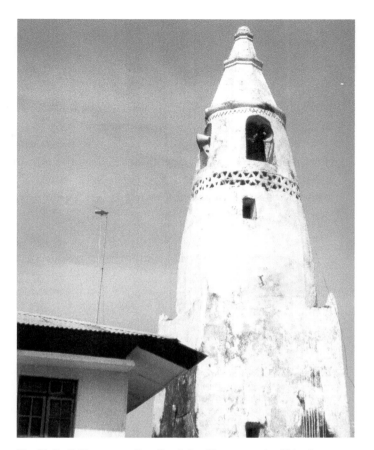

The Malindi Mosque on Zanzibar Island is an example of Islamic influence in Swahili culture.

View the Image
Loango, the Capital of the Kingdom of the Congo at **MyHistoryLab.com**

Thereafter, disastrous internal wars shattered the Kongo state. Slavery apparently contributed significantly to provincial unrest. Independent Portuguese traders and adventurers soon did their business outside government channels and tried to manipulate the Kongo kings.

Kongo, however, enjoyed renewed vigor in the seventeenth century. The Kongo kings, descendants of Affonso, were divine-right monarchs at the apex of a sociopolitical pyramid that rose from district headmen through provincial governors to the court nobility and king. Royal power came to depend on a guard of musket-armed hired soldiers. The kingdom was financially dependent on tribute from officials and taxes and tolls on commerce. Christianity, the state religion, was accommodated to the traditional ancestor cult, magic, and sorcery. Iron and copper technology, sculpture, dance, and music flourished.

Angola To the south, in Portuguese Angola, the experience was even worse than in Kongo. The Ndongo kingdom flourished among the Mbundu people during the sixteenth century, though the Portuguese controlled parts of Angola as a proprietary colony (the first white colonial enterprise in black Africa). By 1600 Angola was exporting thousands of slaves annually through the port of Luanda. In less than a century the hinterland had been depopulated. New internal trade in salt and the spread of American food crops such as maize and cassava (which became part of the staple diet of the populace) produced some positive changes in the interior, but in the coastal region the Portuguese brought only catastrophe.

East Africa

Swahili Culture and Commerce

The participation of East African port towns in the lucrative South Seas trade was ancient. Arabs, Indonesians, and even Indians had trafficked there for centuries. Many had been absorbed into what had become, during the first millennium C.E., from Somalia south, a predominantly Bantu-speaking

Read the Document
Descriptions of the cities of Zanj at **MyHistoryLab.com**

population. From the eighth century, Islam traveled with Arab and Persian sailors and merchants to these trading centers of what the Arabs called the land of the *Zanj*, or "Blacks" (hence "Zanzibar"). Conversion to Islam, however, occurred only along the coast. In the thirteenth century Arab and Persian Muslims began to dominate the coastal trade from Mogadishu to Kilwa. By 1331 the traveler Ibn Battuta describes Mogadishu as a thoroughly Islamic port and Kilwa's ruler and inhabitants as Muslims. He also notes that coastal towns had mosques for the faithful.[5] (See Document, "Visiting Mogadishu [1331]." on page 418)

By this time a common language called **Swahili**, or *Kiswahili* (from the Arabic plural *sawahil*, "coastlands"), had developed from the interaction of Bantu and Arabic speakers along the coast. Its structure is Bantu, its script Arabic, and its vocabulary largely Bantu, but incorporating many words from Arabic.

---

[5] *Travels in Asia and Africa, 1325–1354*, trans. and selected by H. A. R. Gibb (New York: Robert M. McBride, 1929), pp. 110–113.

Document Visiting Mogadishu (1331)

Ibn Battuta (d. 1369 or 1377) of Tangier became one of history's most famous travelers through his voluminous, entertaining writings about his years of journeying from Africa to India and China. In the following excerpt from his description of his 1331 trip down the East African coast, he depicts first the proceedings at the grievance and petitions court convened by the sultan of Mogadishu. The East Africans referred to their sultan as "Shaikh." A *qadi* is a judge; a *faqih*, a jurisconsult or legal scholar; a *wazir*, a government minister; an *amir*, a military commander; and a *sharif*, a descendant of the Prophet Muhammad (conferring special social status).

■ *What Muslim values and practices does the report describe? As an Arab Muslim outsider, does Ibn Battuta seem to approve or disapprove of what he reports?*

MOGADISHU

When it is Saturday, the people come to the door of the shaikh (the local term for the Sultan), and they sit in covered halls outside the house. The *qadi*, the *faqihs*, the *sharifs*, the men of piety, the shaikhs and the men who have performed the pilgrimage enter the second council room. They sit on wooden platforms prepared for the purpose. The *qadi* is on a platform by himself and each group on a platform reserved for them which nobody shares with them. Then the shaikh sits in his council and sends for the *qadi* who sits on his left. Then enter the *faqihs* and their leaders sit in front of him while the rest of them salute and go away. Then the *sharifs* enter, their leaders sit before him, the rest of them salute and go away. If they are guests, they sit on his right. Then enter the shaikhs and those who have performed the pilgrimage, and their great ones sit and the rest salute and go away. Then enter the *wazirs* and *amirs*; the heads of the soldiers, rank upon rank, they salute and go. Food is brought and the *qadi*, the *sharifs* and whoever is sitting in that session eat with the shaikh and the shaikh eats with them. If he wishes to honour one of the leaders of his *amirs*, he sends for him that he should eat with them. The rest of the people eat in the dining hall and their eating is according to precedence in the manner of their entrance before the shaikh. Then the shaikh goes into his house and the *qadi*, the *wazirs*, the private secretary, and four of the leading *amirs* sit for hearing litigation between the members of the public and hearing the cases of people with complaints. In a matter connected with the rules of the *shari'a* [religious law] the *qadi* passes judgement; in a matter other than that, the members of the council pass judgement, that is, the ministers and the *amirs*. In a matter where there is need of consultation with the sultan, they write about it to him and he sends out the reply to them immediately on the back of the note in accordance with his view. And such is always their custom.

From Said Hamdun and Noël King, ed. and trans., *Ibn Battuta in Black Africa* (Princeton, NJ: Markus Wiener, rev. ed., 1994), pp. 20–21. Reprinted by permission of Markus Wiener Publishers, Inc.

Current theory suggests that, like the language, Swahili culture is basically African with a large contribution by Arab, Persian, and other extra-African elements. This admixture created a new consciousness and identity. Today, the many coastal peoples who speak Swahili join African to Persian, Indian, Arab, and other ancestries.

Swahili language and culture probably developed first in the northern towns of Manda, Lamu, and Mombasa, then farther south along the coast to Kilwa. They remained localized largely along the coast until recently. Likewise, the spread of Islam was largely limited to the coast, with the possible exception of the Zambezi valley, where Muslim traders penetrated upriver. This contrasts with the Horn of Africa, where Islamic kingdoms developed both in the Somali hinterland and on the coast.

Swahili civilization reached its apogee in the fourteenth and fifteenth centuries. The harbor trading towns were administrative centers of local Swahili states, and most of them were sited on coastal islands or easily defended peninsulas. To these ports came merchants from abroad and from the African hinterlands. These towns were impressive. Stone mosques, fortress-palaces, harbor fortifications, fancy residences, and commercial buildings have a distinctive combination of African and Arabo-Persian elements.

The Swahili states' ruling dynasties were probably African in origin, though elite families often included Arab or Persian members. Swahili coastal centers boasted an advanced, cosmopolitan culture. By comparison, most of the populace in the small villages lived in mud or sometimes stone houses and earned their living farming or

Chronology

East and Southeast Africa

900–1500	"Great Zimbabwe" civilization
ca. 1200–1400	Development of Bantu Kiswahili language
ca. 1300–1600	Height of Swahili culture
1698	Omani forces take Mombasa, oust Portuguese from East Africa north of the port of Mozambique
1741–1856	United sultanate of Oman and Zanzibar

fishing. Society seems to have consisted of three principal groups: the local nobility, the commoners, and resident foreigners engaged in commerce. Slaves constituted a fourth class, although their local extent (as opposed to their sale) is disputed.

The flourishing trade of the coastal centers was fed mainly by export of inland ivory. Other exports included gold, slaves, turtle shells, ambergris, leopard skins, pearls, fish, sandalwood, ebony, and cotton cloth. The chief imports were cloth, porcelain, glassware, glass beads, and glazed pottery. Certain exports tended to dominate particular ports: cloth, sandalwood, ebony, and ivory at Mogadishu, ivory at Manda, and gold at Kilwa (brought up the coast from Sofala, still farther south). Cowrie shells were a common currency in the inland trade, but coins minted at Mogadishu and Kilwa from the fourteenth century on were increasingly used in the major trading centers.

The Portuguese and the Omanis of Zanzibar

Swahili civilization declined in the sixteenth century. The trade that had originally made everything possible waned with the arrival of the Portuguese and their destruction of both the old oceanic trade (and the Islamic commercial monopoly) and the main Islamic city-states along the eastern coast. Decreases in rainfall or invasions by inland Zimba peoples may also have contributed to the decline.

Nevertheless, the Portuguese undoubtedly wanted control of the South Seas trade (see Chapter 17). In Africa, as everywhere, they saw the **Moors** (the Spanish and Portuguese term for Muslims) as implacable enemies and the struggle to wrest African and Asian commerce and spheres of influence from the Muslims as a Christian crusade.

Initial Portuguese victories along the African coast brought the submission of many small Islamic ports and states. Still, there was no concerted effort to spread Chris-

tianity beyond the fortified settlements established in places like Sofala, Zanzibar, Mozambique, and Mombasa. Thus the long-term cultural and religious consequences of Portuguese presence were slight.

The Portuguese did, however, cause widespread economic decline on the east coast. When inland Africans refused to cooperate, the formerly heavy gold trade up the Zambezi from Sofala dried up. The militant Portuguese presence also sharply reduced Muslim coastal shipping from India and Arabia. The Ottomans failed in the late sixteenth century to defeat the Portuguese, but after 1660 the strong Arabian state of Oman raided the African coast with impunity. In 1698 the Omanis took Mombasa and ejected the Portuguese everywhere north of Mozambique.

Under the Omanis, Zanzibar became a new, major East African power center. Its control of the coastal ivory and slave trade seems to have fueled a substantial recovery of prosperity by the late eighteenth century. Zanzibar benefited from the introduction of clove cultivation in the 1830s, and cloves became its staple export. (The clove plantations also became the chief market for a new, devastating internal slave trade in East Africa lasting into the late nineteenth century, even as the external slave trade was crushed.) Omani African sultans dominated the east coast until 1856. Thereafter, Zanzibar and its coastal holdings became independent under a branch of the ruling family in Oman. Zanzibar passed eventually to the British when they, the Germans, and the Italians divided East Africa in the late 1880s. Still, the Islamic imprint on the whole coast survives today.

Southern Africa

Southeastern Africa: "Great Zimbabwe"

About the same time that east coast trading centers were beginning to flourish, a different civilization was enjoying its heyday farther south, in the rocky, savannah-woodland watershed between the Limpopo and Zambezi rivers, in modern southern Zimbabwe. This civilization was sited far enough inland never to have felt the impact of Islam. It was founded in the tenth or eleventh century by a Bantu-speaking Shona people, who still inhabit the same general area today. It seems to have become a large and prosperous state between the late thirteenth and the late fifteenth centuries. We know it only through archaeological remains of an estimated 150 settlements in the Zambezi-Limpopo region.

See the Map
African Climate Zones and Bantu Migration Routes, ca. 3000 BCE at **MyHistoryLab.com**

The most impressive of these ruins, and the apparent capital of this ancient Shona state, is known today as "Great Zimbabwe"—a huge, 60-odd-acre site encompassing

Great Zimbabwe. Ruins of the Conical Tower inside the Great Enclosure at Great Zimbabwe.

two major building complexes. One—the so-called acropolis—is a series of stone enclosures on a high hill. It overlooks another, much larger enclosure with many ruins and a circular tower, surrounded by a massive wall some 32 feet high and up to 17 feet thick. The acropolis may have contained a shrine, whereas the larger enclosure was apparently the royal palace and fort. The stonework suggests a wealthy and sophisticated society. Artifacts from the site include gold and copper ornaments, soapstone carvings, and imported beads, as well as glass and porcelain of Chinese, Syrian, and Persian origins.

The state itself seems to have had partial control of the increasing gold trade between inland areas and the port of Sofala. Its territory lay east and south of substantial gold-mining enterprises. We can speculate that this large settlement was the capital city of a prosperous empire and home to its ruling elite. Its wider realm consisted mostly of smaller settlements whose inhabitants lived by subsistence agriculture and cattle raising and whose culture differed from that of the capital.

We are not sure why the Great Zimbabwe civilization flourished. The evidence suggests first general population growth and increasing prosperity in the Zambezi-Limpopo region before 1500 C.E. Even earlier Iron Age sites farther south indicate that other large states may have preceded Great Zimbabwe. The specific impetus for Great Zimbabwe may have been a significant immigration around 1000 C.E. of Late Iron Age Shona speakers who brought mining tech-

niques and farming innovations along with their ancestor cults. Improved farming and animal husbandry could have enabled substantial population growth. The Sofala gold trade with inland mining areas may also have expanded, with Great Zimbabwe the chief beneficiary of this trade. This hypothesis links Zimbabwe's flourishing to that of the East African coast from about the thirteenth century.

Without new sources, we may never know precisely why this impressive civilization developed and dominated regionally for nearly 200 years. The reasons for its demise are also obscure. It appears that the northern and southern sectors of the state split up, and people moved away from Great Zimbabwe, probably because their farming and grazing land was exhausted. The southern successor kingdom, known as Changamire, was powerful from the late 1600s until about 1830. The northern successor state, stretched along the middle and lower course of the Zambezi, was known to the first Portuguese sources as the kingdom of the Mwene Mutapa, or "Master Pillager," the title of its sixteenth-century ruler, Mutota, and his successors.

The Portuguese in Southeastern Africa

The Portuguese destroyed Swahili control of both the inland gold trade and the multifaceted overseas trade. Their chief object was obtaining gold from the upper Zambezi region. However, because the entire regional gold production was small and they encountered repeated difficulties trying to control it, the Portuguese derived little lasting profit from the enterprise. When they failed to sustain the Zambezi gold trade by simply trying to

Carving from Great Zimbabwe. This soapstone carving of a bird comprises the top portion of a monolith from Great Zimbabwe, c. 1200–1400 C.E. [H: Bird—14 1/2″ (36.8 cm); H: Monolith—5′ 4 1/2″ (1.64 m).] Stone-carved birds are national emblems in Zimbabwe and were commonly found on walls and monoliths dating back to Great Zimbabwe in the eleventh century.

supplant Swahili merchants on the coast, they established fortified posts up the Zambezi and meddled in Shona regional politics. This tactic led to ongoing conflicts with the Shona kingdoms. In the 1690s the Changamire Shona dynasty conquered the northern Shona territory and finally pushed the Portuguese out of gold country.

All along the Zambezi, however, a lasting, destabilizing consequence of Portuguese intrusion was the creation of quasi-tribal chiefdoms. These were led by mixed-blood Portuguese landholders, or **prazeros**, descended from the first Portuguese estate holders along the Zambezi, who had built up huge estates. Their descendants eventually formed a few clanlike groups of mixed-blood members (from unions with Africans, Indian immigrants, or other estate families). By 1800, they held vast land tracts, commanded armies (often largely of slaves), and were a disruptive force in the region because they were too strong for either the Portuguese or regional African rulers to control. They remind us of how diverse the peoples of modern Africa are.

South Africa: The Cape Colony

In South Africa the Dutch planted the first European colonials almost inadvertently, yet the consequences of this were to be as grave and far-reaching as any European incursion into Africa. The first Cape settlement was built in 1652 by the Dutch East India Company as a resupply and way station for Dutch vessels on their voyages between the Netherlands and the East Indies. This station grew gradually to become by 1700 a large settler colony. Its population in 1662, including slaves, was 392; by 1714 it was 3,878.[6] These settlers were the forebears of the Afrikaners of modern South Africa.

Many of the Khoikhoi people of the region were gradually incorporated into the new colonial economy. The local Khoikhoi (see Chapter 5) were almost exclusively pastoralists; they had neither traditions of strong political organization nor an economic base beyond their herds. At first they bartered livestock freely to Dutch ships and then to the Company settlement for iron, copper, and tobacco. However, when settlers began to displace the Khoikhoi in the southwestern Cape, conflicts ensued. The results were the consolidation of European landholdings and a breakdown of Khoikhoi society. Dutch military success brought even greater Dutch control of the Khoikhoi by the 1670s. Treated as free persons, they became the chief source of colonial wage labor—labor in increasing demand as the colony grew.

Early European View of Khoikhoi. This seventeenth-century illustration of Khoikhoi reflects a European view of daily life near the Cape of Good Hope.

The colony also imported slaves from along the South Seas trade routes, including India, East Africa, and Madagascar. Slavery set the tone for relations between the emergent, and ostensibly "white," Afrikaner population and the "coloreds" of other races. Free or not, the latter were eventually all too easily seen as slave peoples.

After the first settlers spread out around the Company station, nomadic white livestock farmers, or **Trekboers**, moved more widely afield, leaving the richer, but limited, farming lands of the coast for the drier interior tableland. There they contested wider groups of Khoikhoi cattle herders for the best grazing lands. To this end, they developed military techniques—notably the "commando," a collective civilian punitive raid—to secure their way of life by force where necessary. Again the Khoikhoi were victims. By 1700 they were stripped of almost all of their pasturages, and their way of life was destroyed. Ever more Khoikhoi took up employment in the colonial economy, among Trekboers as well as settled colonists. Others moved north to join other refugees from Cape society (slaves, mixed bloods, and some freedmen) in raiding bands operating along the frontiers of Trekboer territory close to the Orange River. The disintegration of Khoikhoi society continued in the 1700s, accelerated sharply by smallpox—a European import against which this previously isolated group had no immunity.

---

[6] R. Elphick and H. Giliomee, *The Shaping of South African Society, 1652–1820* (Cape Town: Longman, 1979), p. 4.

Chronology

Southern Africa

1652	First Cape Colony settlement of Dutch East India Company
1795	British replace Dutch as masters of Cape Colony

The Cape society in this period was thus a diverse one. The Dutch Company officials (including Dutch Reformed ministers), emerging Afrikaners (both settled colonists and Trekboers), the Khoikhoi, and slaves played differing roles in the developing new society radiating from Capetown. Intermarriage and cohabitation of masters and slaves increased the social complexity, despite laws against such mixing. Accommodation of nonwhite minorities within Cape society continued; the slow emergence of **Afrikaans** as the vernacular of the colonials, shows that the Dutch immigrants were also subject to acculturative processes. By the time of English domination after 1795, the sociopolitical foundations of twentieth-century **Apartheid** South Africa were firmly laid.

Summary

North Africa. From 1000 to 1700 in North Africa, the key new factor was the Ottoman Empire's expansion as far west as Morocco. But the development of independent regional rulers soon rendered Ottoman authority in North Africa largely nominal.

Empires of the Sudan. Several substantial states arose south of the Sahara: Ghana, Mali, Songhai, and Kanem. The ruling elites of these states converted to or were heavily influenced by Islam, although most of their populations practiced local religions. Much of these states' wealth was tied to their control of the trans-Saharan trade routes. Farther south, in the coastal forestlands of central Africa, another substantial kingdom arose in Benin, famous for its brass sculptures.

East Africa. On the east coast, Islam influenced the development of the distinctive Swahili culture and language, and Islamic traders linked the region to India and East Asia.

The Coming of the Europeans. The key development of the fifteenth century was the arrival of European traders, missionaries, and warships. The Portuguese and later Europeans came in search of commerce, Christian con-

verts, and spheres of influence. Their arrival disrupted indigenous African culture and political relations and presaged Africa's involvement in and exploitation by a new, expanding global trading system dominated by Europeans.

Key Terms

Afrikaans (p. 422)	**oba** (p. 412)
Apartheid (p. 422)	**prazeros** (p. 421)
Dar-al-Islam (p. 402)	**Sharifs** (p. 402)
Maghreb (p. 402)	**shaykh** (p. 411)
mansa (p. 407)	**Swahili** (p. 417)
marabouts (p. 409)	**Trekboers** (p. 421)
Moors (p. 419)	**uzama** (p. 412)
muezzin (p. 407)	

Review Questions

1. Why did Islam succeed in sub-Saharan and East Africa? What role did warfare play? Trade?

2. What is the world-historical importance of the empires of Ghana, Mali, and Songhai? Why was control of the trans-Saharan trade crucial for these kingdoms? What was the importance of Islamic culture to them? Why did each empire break up?

3. What was the impact of the Portuguese on East Africa? on central Africa? How did European coastal activities affect the African interior?

4. Why did Ottoman influence decline in northern Africa in the eighteenth century?

5. How did the Portuguese and Dutch differ from or resemble the Arabs and other Muslims who came as outsiders to sub-Saharan Africa?

6. Discuss the diversity of Cape society in South Africa before 1700. Who were the Trekboers, and what was their conflict with the Khoikhoi? How was the basis for apartheid formed in this period?

Note: *To learn more about the topics in this chapter, please turn to the Suggested Readings at the end of the book. For additional sources related to this chapter, please see My-HistoryLab.com*

myhistorylab Connections

Reinforce what you learned in this chapter by studying the many documents, images, maps, review tools, and videos available at **www.myhistorylab.com**.

Read and Review

✓● Study and Review **Chapter 14**

●●● Read the Document *Excerpts from Sundiata: An Epic of Old Mali, 1235, p. 407*

The Travels of Ibn Battuta "Ibn Battuta in Mali", p. 407

Al-Umari describes Mansa Musa of Mali, p. 407

Voyage from Lisbon, p. 416

Descriptions of the cities of Zanj, p. 417

👁● See the Map *Trade Routes in Africa, p. 402*

The Maghrib and West Africa, Fourteenth Century, p. 403

East African Coast to 1600, p. 403

African Empires in the Western Sudan, p. 408

African Climate Zones and Bantu Migration Routes, ca. 3000 BCE, p. 419

((●● Hear the Audio *Influences in Africa 2, p. 403*

Influences in Africa 2, p. 412

●● View the Image *Loango, the Capital of the Kingdom of the Congo, p. 417*

Research and Explore

●● Watch the Video *Piracy, p. 402*

●● Watch the Video *West African States*

((●● **Hear** the **Audio**

Hear the audio file for Chapter 14 at
www.myhistorylab.com.

15 Europe to the Early 1500s: Revival, Decline, and Renaissance

The Medieval Universe. In medieval Europe, the traditional geocentric or earth-centered universe was usually depicted by concentric circles. In this popular German work on natural history, medicine, and science, Konrad von Megenberg (1309–1374) depicted the universe in a most unusual but effective manner. The seven known planets are contained within straight horizontal bands that separate the earth below from heaven, populated by the saints, above.

- Revival of Empire, Church, and Towns
- Society
- Growth of National Monarchies
- Political and Social Breakdown
- Ecclesiastical Breakdown and Revival: The Late Medieval Church
- The Renaissance in Italy (1375–1527)
- Revival of Monarchy: Nation Building in the Fifteenth Century

THE HIGH MIDDLE AGES (FROM THE ELEVENTH through the thirteenth centuries) was a period of political expansion and consolidation and of intellectual flowering and synthesis. The Latin, or Western, church established itself as a spiritual authority independent of secular monarchies, which became more powerful and self-aggrandizing. The parliaments and popular assemblies that accompanied the rise of these monarchies laid the foundations of modern representative institutions. ■

The High Middle Ages saw a revolution in agriculture that increased food supplies and populations. Trade and commerce revived, towns expanded, protomodern forms of banking and credit developed, and a "new rich" merchant class became ascendant in Europe's cities. Universities sprouted. Contact with the Arab world made possible the discovery of antiquity in the writings of the ancient Greek philosophers. Those sources in turn stimulated the great expansion of Western education and culture during the Late Middle Ages and the Renaissance.

The Late Middle Ages and the Renaissance, roughly 1300–1500, were years of both unprecedented calamity and bold new beginnings in Europe. France and England grappled with each other in a bitter conflict known as the Hundred Years' War (1337–1453). Bubonic plague, which contemporaries called the Black Death, killed as much as one third of the population in many regions between 1348 and 1350. Thereafter a schism occurred in the church (1378–1417). If that were not calamity enough, in 1453 the Turks captured Constantinople and seemed to be taking dead aim at western Europe.

The Late Middle Ages also witnessed a rebirth that would continue into the seventeenth century. Scholars began to criticize medieval assumptions about the nature of God, humankind, and society. Italian and northern humanists made a full recovery of classical knowledge and languages and ignited new cultural fires that would burn bright throughout Europe. The "divine art" of printing was invented. The **vernacular**, the local language, took its place alongside Latin. In the independent nation-states of Europe, patriotism and incipient nationalism became major forces.

Revival of Empire, Church, and Towns

Otto I and the Revival of the Empire

The fortunes of both the old empire and the papacy began to revive when the Saxon Henry I ("the Fowler"; d. 936) became the first non-Frankish king of Germany in 918. Henry rebuilt royal power and left his son and successor Otto I (r. 936–973) in a strong position. Otto maneuvered his own kin into power in Bavaria, Swabia, and Franconia and then invaded Italy and proclaimed himself its king in 951. In 955 he defeated the Hungarians at Lechfeld, securing the German borders against new barbarian attacks and earning himself the title "the Great."

As part of a royal rebuilding program, Otto enlisted the strong hands of the church. Bishops and abbots, men who possessed a sense of universal empire, yet did not marry and found competitive dynasties, were made royal princes and agents of the king. On February 2, 962, Otto, who had long aspired to the imperial crown, gained it from Pope John XII (955–964) after having rescued the pope from his Italian enemies in the previous year. Thereafter, the church came more than ever under royal control and increasingly determined to be free of it.

The Reviving Catholic Church

With the royal focus shifted from Germany to Italy, Otto's successors, transfixed by their Italian possessions, allowed their German base to deteriorate. As the German empire began to crumble in the eleventh century, the church, long unhappy with imperial domination, declared its independence by embracing a reform movement that had erupted in a monastic order.

The Cluny Reform Movement In a great monastery at Cluny, founded in 910 in east-central France, a reform movement, aimed at freeing the church from secular political influence and control, was born. The reformers of Cluny were aided in their efforts by popular respect for the church that found expression in both religious fervor among laypersons and generous baronial patronage of religious houses. People admired clerics and monks because the church was medieval society's most open institution as far as lay participation was concerned. In the Middle Ages any man could theoretically become pope, since the pope was supposed to be elected by the people and the clergy of Rome. All people were candidates for the church's grace and salvation. The church promised a better life to come to the great mass of ordinary people, who found their present existence brutish and without hope.

The Cluny reformers uncompromisingly condemned the state's contemporary mixing of religious and secular institutions and the clergy's subservience to royal authority. They taught that the pope in Rome alone commanded the clergy, and they demanded a clear demarcation between ecclesiastical and secular authority. They further denounced the transgression of ascetic piety by "secular" parish clergy, who lived openly with concubines in a relationship akin to marriage. Although in narrow religious guise, both the celibacy of the clergy and the separation of church and state found precedents in this powerful monastic reform movement. From Cluny, reformers were dispatched throughout France and Italy in the late eleventh century to save the clergy from wives and the church from the state. In both cases, the pope embraced their reforms.

The High Middle Ages in Western Europe

Europe

With its borders finally secured, western Europe during the High Middle Ages was able to concentrate on its political institutions and cultural development, which had been ignored during the Early Middle Ages. For western Europe, the High Middle Ages was a period of clearer self-definition during which individual lands gained much of the geographic shape we recognize today. Europe also began to escape its relative isolation from the rest of the world, which had prevailed since the Early Middle Ages. Two factors contributed to this increased engagement: the Crusades and renewed trade along the Silk Road linking China and Europe, made possible by the Mongol conquests in Asia.

Under the Song Dynasty (960–1279), before Mongol rule, China continued its technological advance. In addition to the printing press, the Chinese invented the abacus and gunpowder. They also enjoyed a money economy unknown in the West. But culturally, these centuries between 1000 and 1300 were closed and narrow by comparison with those of the Tang Dynasty. Politically, the Song were far more autocratic. This was also an era of expansion for Chinese trade, and one of the few periods in Chinese history in which merchants as a group were able to advance in wealth and status. Although the imperial reach of the Song was limited, Chinese culture in this period was more open to outside influences than in any previous era.

In the late twelfth century Japan shifted from civilian to military rule; the Kamakura *bakufu* governed by mounted warriors who were paid with rights to income from land in exchange for their military services. This rise of a military aristocracy marked the beginning of Japan's "medieval," as dis-

Investiture Struggle: Gregory VII and Henry IV In 1075 Pope Gregory VII (r. 1073–1085), a fierce advocate of church reform, condemned under penalty of excommunication lay investiture of the clergy in their religious offices at any level. He had in mind primarily the emperor's well-established custom of installing favored bishops to administer his royal estates. This installation involved presenting the bishops with the ring and staff of episcopal office at the very same time they received their new secular titles and endowments. Henry IV considered Gregory's action a direct challenge to his ability to administer his realm, while Gregory believed the emperor was usurping the keys to his kingdom. Perceiving that Gregory's measure would weaken royal power vis-à-vis their own, the German princes eagerly supported the pope's edict. (See Document, "Pope Gregory VII Asserts the Power of the Pope" on page 429)

The lines of battle were quickly drawn. Henry assembled his loyal German bishops at Worms in January 1076 and had them proclaim their independence from Gregory. Gregory promptly excommunicated Henry and absolved all Henry's subjects from loyalty to him. The German princes were delighted, and Henry now faced a general revolt. He had no choice but to come to terms with Gregory. In a famous scene, he prostrated himself outside the pope's castle retreat at Canossa in northern Italy on January 25, 1077.

There he reportedly stood barefoot in the snow off and on for three days before the pope gave him absolution. Papal power had reached a pinnacle.

The Investiture Controversy was finally settled in 1122 with the Concordat of Worms. There, the new emperor Henry V (r. 1106–1125) formally renounced his power to invest bishops with ring and staff. In exchange, the new Pope Calixtus II (r. 1119–1124) recognized the emperor's right to be present and to invest bishops with fiefs before or after their investment with ring and staff by the church. The emperor also effectively retained the right to nominate, or veto, candidates. Despite the continuing cooperation between church and state, which was desirable for both sides, distinctive spheres of ecclesiastical and secular authority had been stipulated to by both sides. In settling the Investiture Controversy in this way, pope and emperor had also set the stage for greater conflicts and division between church and state.

The Crusades

If an index of popular piety and support for the pope in the High Middle Ages is needed, the **Crusades** amply provide it. What the Cluny reform was to the clergy, the Crusades to the Holy Land were to the laity: an outlet for the heightened religiosity of the late eleventh and twelfth centuries.

tinct from its "classical," period. Three Mongol invasions in the thirteenth century also fostered a strong military to resist them. With a civilian court also in existence, Japan actually had a dual government (that is, two emperors and two courts) until the fourteenth century. However, this situation differed greatly from the deep and permanent national divisions developing at this time among the emerging states and autonomous principalities of western Europe.

Within the many developing autonomous Islamic lands at this time, the teachings of Muhammad created an international culture. Religious identity enabled Muslims to transcend their new and often very deep regional divisions. Similarly, Christianity allowed Englishmen, Frenchmen, Germans, and Italians to think of themselves as one people and to unite in the Crusades to the Holy Land. As these Crusades got under way in the late eleventh century, Islam too was on the march, penetrating Anatolia and Afghanistan and impinging upon India, where it met a new challenge in Hinduism.

The legacy of the Crusades was mixed. They accomplished few of the goals that originally motivated the European Crusaders; the Holy Land remained under Islamic control, the Crusader kingdoms there collapsed within a few genera-

tions of their founding, and the animosity toward Christians fostered by the Crusades resonates even today in the Middle East. Still, the Crusades brought Europeans into more direct and frequent contact with the non- European world than they had known since the heyday of the Roman Empire. Crusaders sampled and sent home products from the Middle East, Asia, and North Africa, creating new tastes in food, art, and even fashion. The resulting growth in demand for these products impelled rising numbers of European merchants to seek these products beyond Europe. Eventually Europeans sought to bypass the Islamic world entirely and secure supplies of Eastern products, especially spices, by going directly to the sources in India and East Asia. Through such development European isolation came to an end.

Focus Questions

■ How did the High Middle Ages in Europe differ from the Early Middle Ages?

■ What was the legacy of the Crusades for Europe? In what ways did they signal the start of new relationships between Europe and the wider world?

Late in the eleventh century, the Byzantine Empire was under severe pressure from the Seljuk Turks, and the Eastern emperor, Alexius I Comnenus, appealed for Western aid. At the Council of Clermont in 1095, Pope Urban II responded positively to that appeal, setting the First Crusade in motion. (See Document, "Pope Urban II (r. 1088–1099) Preaches the First Crusade" on page 430) This event has puzzled some historians, because the First Crusade was a very risky venture. But the pope, the nobility, and Western society at large had much to gain by removing large numbers of nobility temporarily from Europe. Too many idle, restless noble youths spent too great a part of their lives feuding with each other and raiding other people's lands. The pope saw that peace and tranquility might more easily be gained at home by sending these factious aristocrats abroad, 100,000 of whom marched off with the First Crusade (see Map 15–1 on page 428). The nobility, in turn, saw that fortunes could be made in foreign wars. That was especially true for the younger sons of noblemen, who, in an age of growing population and shrinking landed wealth, found in crusading the opportunity to become landowners. Pope Urban may well have also believed that the Crusade would reconcile and reunite Western and Eastern Christianity.

Religion was not the only motive inspiring the Crusaders; hot blood and greed were no less strong. But unlike the later

Crusades, which were undertaken for mercenary reasons, the early Crusades were inspired by genuine religious piety and were carefully orchestrated by a revived papacy. Popes promised the first Crusaders a plenary indulgence should they die in battle. That was a complete remission of the temporal punishment due them for unrepented mortal sins, and hence a release from suffering for them in purgatory. In addition to this spiritual reward, the prospect of Holy War against the Muslim infidel also propelled the Crusaders. The Crusade to the Holy

✔— Study and Review at MyHistoryLab.com

Land was also a romantic pilgrimage. All these motives combined to make the First Crusade a Christian success.

En route, the Crusaders began a general cleansing of Christendom that would intensify during the thirteenth-century papacy of Pope Innocent III. Accompanied by the new mendicant orders of Dominicans and Franciscans, Christian knights attempted to rid Europe of Jews as well as Muslims.

•◦— Read the Document Expulsion Jews from France 12th Century at MyHistoryLab.com

Along the Crusaders' routes, especially in the Rhineland, Jewish communities were subjected to pogroms.

The First Victory The Eastern emperor welcomed Western aid against advancing Islamic armies. However, the Crusaders had not assembled merely to defend Europe's outermost borders against Muslim aggression. Their goal

Map 15–1. The Early Crusades. Routes and several leaders of the Crusades during the first century of the movement are shown. The names on this map do not exhaust the list of great nobles who went on the First Crusade. The even showier array of monarchs of the Second and Third Crusades still left the Crusades, on balance, ineffective in achieving their goals.

was to rescue the holy city of Jerusalem, which had been in the hands of the Seljuk Turks since the seventh century. To this end, three great armies—tens of thousands of Crusaders—gathered in France, Germany, and Italy and taking different routes reassembled in Constantinople in 1097.

See the Map
The Crusades
at MyHistoryLab.com

The convergence of these spirited soldiers on the Eastern capital was a cultural shock that deepened antipathy toward the West. The Eastern emperor suspected their motives, and the common people, whose villages they plundered and suppressed, did not consider them to be Christian brothers in a common cause. Nonetheless, the Crusaders accomplished what no Byzantine army had been able to do. They soundly defeated one Seljuk army after another in a steady advance toward Jerusalem, which they captured on July 15, 1099. The Crusaders owed their victory to superior military discipline and weaponry and were also helped by the deep political divisions within the Islamic world that prevented a unified Muslim resistance.

Study and Review
at MyHistoryLab.com

The victorious Crusaders divided conquered territories into the feudal states of Jerusalem, Edessa, and Antioch, which were apportioned to them as fiefs from the pope. Godfrey of Bouillon, leader of the French-German army, and after him his brother Baldwin, ruled over the kingdom of Jerusalem. The Crusaders, however, remained small islands within a great sea of Muslims, who looked on the Western invaders as savages to be slain or driven out. Once settled in the Holy Land, the Crusaders found themselves increasingly on the defensive. Now an occupying rather than a conquering army, they became obsessed with fortification, building castles and forts throughout the Holy Land, the ruins of which can still be seen today.

Read the Document
Arab-Syrian Gentleman
Discusses Franks
at MyHistoryLab.com

Once secure within their new enclaves, the Crusaders ceased to live off the land as they had done since departing Europe and increasingly relied on imports from home. As they developed the economic resources of their new posses-

Document
Pope Gregory VII Asserts the Power of the Pope

In the Investiture Controversy between Emperor Henry IV and Pope Gregory VII, the pope's assertion of the powers of his office drew a line in the sand between church and state. Although Gregory's statement bore the modest title, DICTATUS PAPAE ("Dictates of the Pope"), it was dynamite in the history of church-state relations.

■ *In defining his powers as pope, on what authority does Pope Gregory base his power? How many of his assertions are historically verifiable by actual events in church history?*

That the Roman Church was founded by God alone.

That the Roman Pontiff alone is rightly to be called universal.

That the Pope may depose the absent.

That for him alone it is lawful to enact new laws according to the needs of the time, to assemble together new congregations, to make an abbey of a canonry; and . . . to divide a rich bishopric and unite the poor ones.

That he alone may use the imperial insignia.

That the Pope is the only one whose feet are to be kissed by all princes.

That his name alone is to be recited in churches.

That his title is unique in the world.

That he may depose emperors.

That he may transfer bishops, if necessary, from one See to another.

That no synod may be called a general one without his order.

That no chapter or book may be regarded as canonical without his authority.

That no sentence of his may be retracted by any one; and that he, alone of all, can retract it.

That he himself may be judged by no one.

That the Roman Church has never erred, nor ever, by the witness of Scripture, shall err to all eternity.

That the Pope may absolve subjects of unjust men from their featly.

Source: Church and State through the Centuries: A Collection of Historic Documents with Commentaries by Ehler and Morrall. Copyright © 1967 Biblio-Moser. Reproduced with permission of Biblio-Moser in the formats Text and Other Book via Copyright Clearance Center.

---

sions, the once fierce warriors were transformed into international traders and businessmen. The Knights Templar, originally a military-religious order, remade themselves into castle stewards and escorts for Western pilgrims going to and from the Holy Land. Through such endeavors, they became very rich, ending up as wealthy bankers and moneylenders.

The Second and Third Crusades Native resistance broke the Crusaders' resolve around midcentury, and the forty-year-plus Latin presence in the East began to crumble. Edessa fell to Islamic armies in 1144. A Second Crusade, preached by Christendom's most eminent religious leader, the Cistercian monk Bernard of Clairvaux (1091–1153), attempted a rescue but met with dismal failure. In October 1187, Saladin (r. 1138–1193), king of Egypt and Syria, reconquered Jerusalem, a victory so completely brilliant and unexpected that Pope Urban III was said to have dropped dead upon hearing it. Save for a brief interlude in the thir-

See the Map
The Major Crusades at MyHistoryLab.com

teenth century, the holiest of cities remained thereafter in Islamic hands until the twentieth century.

A Third Crusade in the twelfth century (1189–1192) attempted yet another rescue, led by the most powerful Western rulers: Hohenstaufen emperor Frederick Barbarossa, Richard the Lion-Hearted, king of England, and Philip Augustus, king of France. Instead, it became a tragicomic commentary on the passing of the original crusading spirit. Frederick Barbarossa accidentally drowned while fording the Saleph River, a small stream, near the end of his journey across Asia Minor. Richard the Lion-Hearted and Philip Augustus reached the outskirts of Jerusalem, only to shatter the Crusaders' unity and chances of victory by their intense personal rivalry. Philip Augustus returned to France and made war on Richard's continental territories. Richard, in turn, fell captive to the Emperor Henry VI while returning to England.

Document — Pope Urban II (r. 1088–1099) Preaches the First Crusade

When Pope Urban II summoned the First Crusade in a sermon at the Council of Clermont on November 26, 1095, he painted a most savage picture of the Muslims who controlled Jerusalem. Urban also promised the Crusaders, who responded by the tens of thousands, remission of their unrepented sins and assurance of heaven. Robert the Monk is one of four witnesses who has left us this summary of the sermon, which exists in five different accounts, a sign of its wide reporting and dissemination.

■ *Is the pope engaging in a propaganda and smear campaign? What images of the enemy does he create, and how accurate and fair are they? Did the Christian church have a greater claim to Jerusalem than the people then living there? Does a religious connection with the past entitle one group to confiscate the land of another?*

From the confines of Jerusalem and the city of Constantinople a horrible tale has gone forth and very frequently has been brought to our ears, namely, that a race from the kingdom of the Persians [that is, the Seljuk Turks], an accursed race, a race utterly alienated from God, a generation forsooth which has not directed its heart and has not entrusted its spirit to God, has invaded the lands of those Christians and has depopulated them by the sword, pillage and fire; it has led away a part of the captives into its own country, and a part it has destroyed by cruel tortures; it has either entirely destroyed the churches of God or appropriated them for the rites of its own religion. They destroy the altars, after having defiled them with their uncleanness. They circumcise the Christians, and the blood of the circumcision they either spread upon the altars or pour into the vases of the baptismal font. When they wish to torture people by a base death, they perforate their navels, and dragging forth the extremity of the intestines, bind it to a stake; then with flogging they lead the victim around until the viscera having gushed forth and the victim falls prostrate upon the ground. Others they bind to a post and pierce with arrows. Others they compel to extend their necks and then, attacking them with naked swords, attempt to cut through the neck with a single blow. What shall I say of the abominable rape of the women? The king-

dom of the Greeks is now dismembered by them and deprived of territory so vast in extent that it can not be traversed in a march of two months. On whom therefore is the labor of avenging these wrongs and of recovering this territory incumbent, if not upon you? . . .

Jerusalem is the navel of the world; the land is fruitful above others, like another paradise of delights. This the Redeemer of the human race has made illustrious by His advent, has beautified by residence, has consecrated by suffering, has redeemed by death, has glorified by burial. This royal city, therefore, situated at the centre of the world, is now held captive by His enemies, and is in subjection to those who do not know God, to the worship of the heathens. She seeks therefore and desires to be liberated, and does not cease to implore you to come to her aid. From you especially she asks succor, because, as we have already said, God has conferred upon you above all nations great glory in arms.

Accordingly undertake this journey for the remission of your sins, with the assurance of the imperishable glory of the kingdom of heaven.

Source: Translations and reprints from *Original Sources of European History*, Vol. 1 (Philadelphia: Department of History, University of Pennsylvania, 1910), pp. 5–7.

●◖●─Read the Document
The Magna Carta 1215
at **MyHistoryLab.com**

The English paid a handsome ransom for their adventurous king's release. Popular resentment of taxes levied for that ransom became part of the background of the revolt against the English monarchy that led to royal recognition of English freedoms in the Magna Carta of 1215.

The long-term results of the first three Crusades had little to do with their original purpose. Politically and religiously they were a failure. The Holy Land reverted as firmly as ever

to Muslim hands. But the Crusades had been a safety valve for violence-prone Europeans. More importantly, they stimulated Western trade with the East, as Venetian, Pisan, and Genoan merchants followed the Crusaders across Byzantium to lucrative new markets. The need to resupply the Christian settlements in the Near East also created new trade routes and reopened old ones long

((◖●─Hear the Audio
at **MyHistoryLab.com**

closed by Islamic warships in the Mediterranean.

A Closer Look

European Embrace of a Black Saint

Saint Maurice, patron saint of Magdeburg, Germany, was a third-century Egyptian Christian, who commanded the Egyptian legion of the Roman army in Gaul. In 286 C.E. he and his soldiers were executed for impiety after refusing to worship the Roman gods. Maurice's cult began in 515, and he became a favorite saint of Charlemagne and other pious, warring German kings.

Portrayed as a white man for centuries, Saint Maurice first appeared as a black man in the mid-thirteenth century. In the era of the Crusades, rulers had their eyes on new possessions in the Orient, and an Eastern-looking patron saint (Maurice) seemed the perfect talisman as Western merchants and armies ventured forth to trade and conquer. At this time, artists also began to paint as a black man one of the three Magi who visited baby Jesus on his birthday. The name Maurice was close to the German word for black dye ("Mauro") and later Moors ("Mohren"). Progressively, the third-century saint was transformed into a black African. By the fifteenth and sixteenth centuries, his head adorned the coats-of-arms of leading Nuremberg families who traded in the Near East, among them the Tuchers, Nuremberg's great cloth merchants, and Albrecht Dürer, Germany's most famous Renaissance artist.

Questions

1. Did Charlemagne and other German kings embrace Maurice as their favorite saint for mercenary, religious, or military motives?

2. Was racism behind the portrayal of Maurice as a white man for eleven centuries, before painters presented him as the black saint he had always been?

3. Why would some of Nuremberg's wealthy, leading families adorn their coats-of-arms with the head of an African saint?

myhistorylab   To examine this image in an interactive fashion, please go to **www.myhistorylab.com**

Chronology

The Crusades

1095	Pope Urban II launches the First Crusade
1099	The Crusaders take Jerusalem
1147–1149	The Second Crusade
1187	The Muslims retake Jerusalem under Saladin
1189–1192	Third Crusade
1202–1204	Fourth Crusade

The Fourth Crusade It is a commentary on both the degeneration of the original crusading ideal and the Crusaders' true historical importance that a Fourth Crusade transformed itself into a piratical commercial venture controlled by the Venetians. Launched in 1202, 30,000 Crusaders arrived in Venice to set sail for Egypt. When they could not pay the price of transport, the Venetians negotiated an alternative venture: the conquest of Zara, a rival Christian port city on the Adriatic. As a shocked world watched, the Crusaders obliged the Venetians. Zara, however, proved to be only their first digression; in 1204, they besieged Constantinople itself.

This stunning event brought Venice new lands and maritime rights that assured its domination of the eastern Mediterranean. Constantinople was now the center for Western trade throughout the Near East. Although its capture embarrassed reigning Pope Innocent III, the papacy was soon sharing the spoils, gleeful at the prospect of extending Roman Christianity East. A confidant of the pope became patriarch of Constantinople and launched a mission to win the Greeks and the Slavs to the Roman Church. Western control of Constantinople continued until 1261, when Eastern emperor Michael Paleologus, helped by the Genoese, who envied their great rival's windfall in the East, finally recaptured the city. This fifty-year-plus occupation of Constantinople did nothing to heal the political and religious divisions between East and West.

Towns and Townspeople

In the eleventh and twelfth centuries, most towns were small and held only about 5 percent of western Europe's population, but they contained the most creative segments of medieval society.

The Chartering of Towns Towns were originally dominated by feudal lords, both lay and clerical, who granted charters to those who would agree to live and work within them. The charters guaranteed the towns' safety and gave their inhabitants an independence unknown to peasants who worked the land. The purpose was originally to concentrate skilled laborers who could manufacture the finished goods desired by lords and bishops.

Foundry in Florence. Skilled workers were an integral component of the commerce of medieval towns. This scene shows the manufacture of cannons in a foundry in Florence.

✳ Map Exploration

To explore this map further, go to **http://www.myhistorylab.com**

Map 15–2. Medieval Trade Routes and Regional Products. Trade in Europe varied in intensity and geographical extent in different periods during the Middle Ages. The map shows some of the channels that came to be used in interregional commerce. Labels tell part of what was carried in that commerce.

As towns grew and beckoned, many serfs took their skills to the new urban centers. There they found the freedom and profits that could lift an industrious craftsperson into higher social ranks. As this migration of serfs to the towns accelerated, the lords in the countryside offered serfs more favorable terms of tenure to keep them on the land. The growth of towns thus improved the lot of serfs generally.

◆•◆•┌Read the Document
Medieval Town Customs Town Chester England
at **MyHistoryLab.com**

The Rise of Merchants Rural society not only gave the towns their craftspeople and day laborers, but the first merchants themselves may also have been enterprising serfs. Certainly, some of the long-distance traders were people who had nothing to lose and everything to gain from the enormous risks of foreign trade. They traveled together in armed caravans and convoys, buying goods and products as cheaply as possible at the source and selling them for all they could get in Western ports (see Map 15–2).

At first the merchants were disliked because they were outside the traditional social groups of nobility, clergy, and peasantry. Over time, however, the powerful grew to respect the merchants, and the weak always tried to imitate them, because the merchants left a trail of wealth behind them wherever they went.

As the traders established themselves in towns, they grew in wealth and numbers, formed their own protective associations, and soon found themselves able to challenge traditional seigneurial authority. Merchants especially wanted to end the arbitrary tolls and tariffs regional magnates imposed over the surrounding countryside. Such regulations hampered the flow of commerce on which both merchant and craftsman in the growing urban export industries depended.

Townspeople needed simple and uniform laws and a government sympathetic to their new forms of business activity, not the fortress mentality of the lords of the countryside. The result was often a struggle with the old nobility within and outside the towns. This conflict led towns in the High and Late Middle Ages to form their own independent communes and to ally themselves with kings against the nobility in the countryside, a development that would eventually rearrange the centers of power in medieval Europe and dissolve classic feudal government.

Because the merchants were the engine of the urban economy, small shopkeepers and artisans identified far more with them than with aloof lords and bishops, who had been medieval society's traditional masters. The lesser nobility (small knights) outside the towns also recognized the new mercantile economy as the wave of the future. During the eleventh and twelfth centuries, the burgher upper classes increased their economic strength and successfully challenged the old noble urban lords for control of the towns.

New Models of Government With urban autonomy came new models of self-government. Around 1100 the old urban nobility and the new burgher upper class merged into an urban patriciate. It was a marriage between those wealthy by birth (inherited property) and those whose fortunes came from long-distance trade. From this new ruling class was born the aristocratic town council, which henceforth governed towns.

Enriching and complicating the situation, small artisans and craftspeople also slowly developed their own protective associations or **guilds** and began to gain a voice in government. The towns' opportunities for the "little person" had created the slogan "Town air brings freedom." Within town walls people thought of themselves as citizens with basic rights, not subjects at the mercy of their masters' whim.

Towns and Kings By providing kings with the resources they needed to curb factious noblemen, towns became a major force in the transition from feudal societies to na-

tional governments. Towns were a ready source of educated bureaucrats and lawyers who knew Roman law, the tool for running the state. Money was also to be found in the towns in great quantity, enabling kings to hire their own armies and free themselves from dependence on the nobility. In turn, towns won royal political recognition and had their constitutions guaranteed. In France, towns became integrated early into royal government. In Germany, they fell under ever-tighter control by the princes. In Italy, uniquely, towns became genuine city-states during the Renaissance.

Jews in Christian Society Towns also attracted Jews who plied trades in small businesses. Many became wealthy as moneylenders to kings, popes, and businesspeople. Jewish intellectual and religious culture both dazzled and threatened Christians. These various factors encouraged suspicion and distrust among Christians and led to an unprecedented surge in anti-Jewish sentiment in the late twelfth and early thirteenth centuries.

Schools and Universities In the twelfth century, Byzantine and Spanish Islamic scholars made it possible for the philosophical works of Aristotle, the writings of Euclid and Ptolemy, the texts of Greek physicians and Arab mathematicians, and the corpus of Roman law to circulate among Western scholars. Islamic scholars wrote thought-provoking commentaries on Greek texts that were subsequently translated into Latin and made available to Western scholars and students. The resulting intellectual ferment gave rise to Western universities as we know them today. The first important one was established in 1158 in Bologna, which became the model for the universities of Spain, Italy, and southern France, and gained renown for the revival of Roman law. The University of Paris became the model for northern European universities and the study of theology. (See Document, "Student Life at the University of Paris" on page 436.)

In the High Middle Ages the learning process was basic. People assumed that truth was already known and only needed to be properly organized, elucidated, and defended. Students wrote commentaries on authoritative texts, especially those of Aristotle and the Church Fathers. Teachers did not encourage students to strive independently for undiscovered truth beyond the received knowledge of the experts. Rather, students learned to organize and harmonize the accepted truths of tradition, which were drilled into them.

This method of study was known as **Scholasticism**. Students summarized and compared the traditional authorities in their field, elaborated their arguments pro and con, and drew the logical conclusions. With the arrival of Aristotle's works in the West, logic and dialectic became the new tools for disciplining thought and knowledge. Dialectic was

The University of Bologna in central Italy was distinguished as the center for the revival of Roman law. This carving on the tomb of a Bolognese professor of law shows students attending one of his lectures.

the art of discovering a truth by pondering the arguments against it. Together with aspiring philosophers, theologians, and lawyers, even medical students learned their vocation by debating the authoritative texts in their field, not by clinical medical practice.

Abelard   No one promoted the new Aristotelian learning more boldly and controversially than Peter Abelard (1079–1142), the leading philosopher and theologian of his time and the first European scholar to gain a large student audience. He ended up, however, not as an academic superstar, but as an obscure abbot of a monastery in Brittany. That was because his bold subjection of church teaching to Aristotelian logic and critical reasoning made him many powerful enemies at a time when there was no tenure to protect genius and free speech in schools and universities. Accused of multiple transgressions of church doctrine, he wrote an autobiography recounting the "calamities" that befell him over a lifetime. His critics especially condemned his subjective interpretations. He likened the trinitarian bonds among God the Father, the Son, and the Holy Spirit to those created among people by sworn documents and covenants. Rather than a God-begotten cosmic ransom of hu-

mankind from the Devil, Christ's crucifixion was said to redeem Christians by virtue of its impact on their hearts and minds when they heard and pondered the story. Abelard's ethical teaching stressed intent: The consent of the doer made an act good or evil, not the deed itself. Inner feelings were also said to be more important for receiving divine forgiveness than the sacrament of penance performed by the priest.

Between his native genius and youthful disrespect for seniority and tradition, Abelard gained powerful enemies in high places. He gave those enemies the opportunity to strike him down when in Paris, where he was Master of Students at Notre Dame, he seduced the bright, seventeen-year-old niece of a powerful canon (her name was Heloise), who hired Abelard to be her tutor in his home. The passionate affair ended in public scandal, with Heloise pregnant. Unable to marry her officially (university teachers had to be single and celibate), they wed secretly. Intent on punishing Abelard and ending his career, the enraged uncle not only exposed their affair and secret marriage but also hired men to castrate Abelard.

Thereafter both entered cloisters in nearby Paris: Heloise at Argenteuil, Abelard at St. Denis. She continued to love Abelard and relive their passion in her mind, while Abelard be-

Document — Student Life at the University of Paris

As the following account by Jacques de Vitry makes clear, not all students at the University of Paris in the thirteenth century were there to gain knowledge. Students fought constantly and subjected each other to ethnic insults and slurs.

■ *Why were students from different lands so prejudiced against one another? Was the rivalry among faculty members as intense as that among students? What are the student criticisms of the faculty? Do they sound credible?*

Almost all the students at Paris, foreigners and natives, did absolutely nothing except learn or hear something new. Some studied merely to acquire knowledge, which is curiosity; others to acquire fame, which is vanity; others still for the sake of gain, which is cupidity and the vice of simony. Very few studied for their own edification, or that of others. They wrangled and disputed not merely about the various sects or about some discussions; but the differences between the countries also caused dissensions, hatreds and virulent animosities among them, and they impudently uttered all kinds of affronts and insults against one another.

They affirmed that the English were drunkards and had tails; the sons of France proud, effeminate and carefully adorned like women. They said that the Germans were furious and obscene at their feasts; the Normans, vain and boastful; the Poitevins, traitors and always adventurers. The Burgundians they considered vulgar and stupid. The Bretons were reputed to be fickle and changeable, and were often reproached for the death of Arthur. The Lombards were called avaricious, vicious and cowardly; the Romans, seditious, turbulent and slanderous; the Sicilians, tyrannical and cruel; the inhabitants of Brabant, men of blood, incendiaries, brigands, and ravishers; the Flemish, fickle, prodigal, gluttonous, yielding as butter, and slothful. After such insults from words they often came to blows.

I will not speak of those logicians [professors of logic and dialectic] before whose eyes flitted constantly "the lice of Egypt," that is to say, all the sophistical subtleties, so that no one could comprehend their eloquent discourses in which, as say Isaiah, "there is no wisdom." As to the doctors of theology, "seated in Moses' set," they were swollen with learning, but their charity was not edifying. Teaching and not practicing, they have "become as sounding brass or a tinkling cymbal," or like a canal of stone, always dry, which ought to carry water to "the bed of spices." They not only hated one another, but by their flatteries they enticed away the students of others; each one seeking his own glory, but caring not a whit about the welfare of souls.

Source: Translations and reprints from the *Original Sources of European History*, Vol. 2 (Philadelphia: Department of History, University of Pennsylvania, 1902), pp. 19–20.

came a self-condemning monk's monk, who assured Heloise in his letters that his "love" for her had only been wretched desire. The famous philosopher ended his life as a platitudinous monk. In 1121, a church synod ordered his writings burned. Another synod in 1140 condemned nineteen propositions from his works as heresy. Retracting his teaching, Abelard lived out the remaining two years of his life in the monastery of St. Denis. Heloise lived another twenty years and gained renown for her positive efforts to reform the rules for the cloistered life of women, under which she had suffered so much. Their story is a revelation of contemporary academic and religious life, the relationship of men and women, and the power of a reform-minded and controlling church.

●◆━┃Read the Document
Abelard Defends Himself
at **MyHistoryLab.com**

Society

The Order of Life

In the art and literature of the Middle Ages, three basic social groups were represented: those who fought as mounted knights (the landed nobility), those who prayed (the clergy), and those who labored in fields and shops (the peasantry and village artisans). After the revival of towns in the eleventh century, a fourth social group emerged: the long-distance traders and merchants.

Nobles By the Late Middle Ages, a distinguishable higher and lower nobility had evolved, living in both

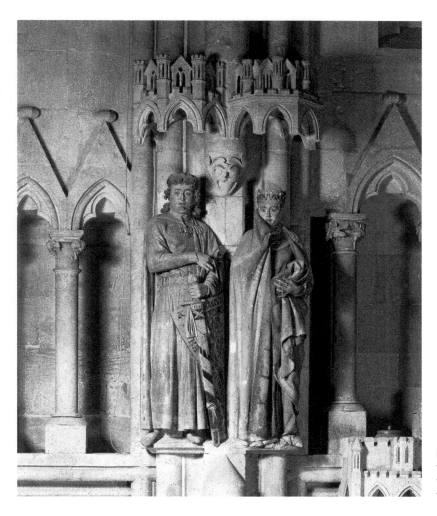

Ekkehard and Uta. ca. 1240–1250. This famous noble pair founded Naumburg Cathedral in Germany in the middle of the thirteenth century and are exemplary studies of medieval nobility.

town and country. The higher were the great landowners and territorial magnates, long the dominant powers in their regions; the lower were petty landlords, the descendants of minor knights, newly rich merchants, or wealthy farmers.

Arms were the nobleman's profession, waging war his sole occupation. The nobility accordingly celebrated physical strength, courage, and the constant activity of warfare. Warring brought new riches and a chance to gain honor and glory, whereas peace meant boredom and economic stagnation. In the eighth century the adoption of stirrups by mounted knights gave armies the edge.

No medieval social group was absolutely uniform. Noblemen formed a broad spectrum—from minor vassals without subordinate vassals to mighty barons, the principal vassals of a king or prince, who had many vassals of their own. Dignity and status within the nobility were directly related to the exercise of authority over others; a chief with many vassals far excelled the small country nobleman who was lord over none but himself.

By the Late Middle Ages, several factors forced the landed nobility into a steep economic and political decline from which it never recovered. Climatic changes and agricultural failures created large famines, while the great plague brought about unprecedented population losses. Changing military tactics occasioned by the use of infantry and heavy artillery during the Hundred Years' War made the noble cavalry nearly obsolete. And the alliance of wealthy towns with the king weakened the nobility within their own domains. After the fourteenth century, land and wealth counted for far more than lineage as qualification for entrance into the highest social class.

Clergy Unlike the nobility and the peasantry, the clergy was an open estate: One was a cleric by religious training and ordination, not because of birth or military prowess.

Dominicans (left) and Franciscans (right). Unlike the other religious orders, the Dominicans and Franciscans did not live in cloisters but wandered about preaching and combating heresy. They depended for support on their own labor and the kindness of the laity. *Cliche Bibliothèque Nationale de France, Paris.*

There were two basic types of clerical vocation: regular and secular. The **regular clergy** comprised the orders of monks who lived according to a special ascetic rule (*regula*) in cloisters separated from the world. In the thirteenth century, two new orders—the Franciscans and the Dominicans—gained the sanction of the church. Their members went out into the world to preach the church's mission and to combat heresy.

The **secular clergy**, those who lived and worked directly among the laity in the world (*saeculum*), formed a vast hierarchy. At the top were the wealthy cardinals, archbishops, and bishops who were drawn almost exclusively from the nobility. Below them were the urban priests, the cathedral canons, and the court clerks. Finally, there was the great mass of poor parish priests, who were neither financially nor intellectually much above the common people they served.

During most of the Middle Ages, the clergy were the first estate, and theology was the queen of the sciences. How did the clergy attain such prominence? A lot of it was self-proclaimed. However, there were also popular respect and reverence for the clergy's role as mediator between God and humanity. The priest brought the Son of God down to earth when he celebrated the sacrament of the Eucharist; his absolution released penitents from punishment for sin. It was declared improper for mere laypeople to sit in judgment on such a priest.

Peasants The largest and lowest social group in medieval society was one on whose labor the welfare of all others depended: the agrarian peasantry. Many peasants lived and worked on the manors of the nobility, the vital cells of rural social life. The lord of the manor required a certain amount of produce (grain, eggs, and the like) and services from the peasant families and held both judicial and police powers. He owned and operated the machines that processed crops into food and drink. The lord also had the right to subject his tenants to exactions known as *banalities*. He could, for example, force them to breed their cows with his bull and to pay for the privilege; to grind their bread grains in his mill; to bake their bread in his oven; to make their wine in his wine press; to buy their beer from his brewery; and even to surrender to him the choice parts of all animals slaughtered on his lands. The lord also collected as an inheritance tax a serf's best animal. Without the lord's permission, a serf could neither travel nor marry outside the manor in which he served.

However, the serfs' status was not chattel slavery. It was to a lord's advantage to keep his serfs healthy and happy; his welfare, like theirs, depended on a successful harvest. Serfs had their own dwellings and modest strips of land, and they lived off the produce of their own labor and organization. They could also market for their own profit any surpluses that remained after the harvest. And serfs could pass their property (their dwellings and field strips) on to their children, along with their worldly goods.

Two basic changes occurred in the evolution of the manor from the early to the later Middle Ages. The first was the increasing importance of the single-family holding. As family farms replaced manorial units, land and property remained in the possession of a single family from generation to generation. Second was the conversion of the serf's dues into money payments, a change made possible by the revival of trade and the rise of the towns. This development, completed by the thirteenth century, permitted serfs to hold their land as rent-paying tenants and to overcome their servile status.

By the mid-fourteenth century, a declining nobility in England and France, faced with the ravages of the great plague and the Hundred Years' War, tried to turn back the

Medieval Marketplace. A fifteenth-century rendering of an eleventh- or twelfth-century marketplace. Medieval women were active in all trades, but especially in the food and clothing industries. *© Scala/Art Resource, New York.*

historical clock by increasing taxes on the peasantry and restricting their migration to the cities. The response was armed revolt. The revolts of the agrarian peasantry, like those of the urban proletariat, were brutally crushed. They stand out at the end of the Middle Ages as violent testimony to the breakup of medieval society. As growing national sentiment would break its political unity, and heretical movements end its nominal religious unity, the peasantry's revolts revealed the absence of medieval social unity.

Medieval Women

The image and the reality of medieval women are two very different things. The image was strongly influenced by the views of male Christian clergy, whose ideal was the celibate life of chastity, poverty, and obedience. Drawing on both the Bible and classical medical, philosophical, and legal writings predating Christianity, Christian theologians depicted women as physically, mentally, and morally weaker than men. On the basis of such assumptions,

Christian clergy considered marriage a debased state by comparison with the religious life, and in their writings praised virgins and celibate widows over wives. In marriage, a woman's role was to be obedient to her husband, who, as the stronger partner, had a duty to protect and discipline her.

This image suggests that medieval women had two basic options in life: to become either a subjugated housewife or a confined nun. In reality, the vast majority of medieval women were neither.

Image and Status Both within and outside the church, this image of women is contradicted. Together with the cult of the Virgin Mary, the chivalric romances and courtly love literature of the twelfth and thirteenth centuries put women on pedestals and treated them as superior to men in purity. If the church harbored misogynist sentiments, it also condemned them, as in the case of the thirteenth-century *Romance of the Rose* and other popular bawdy literature.

The learned churchman Peter Lombard (1100–1169) asked why God created Eve from Adam's rib rather than taking her from his head or one of his feet. His answer: God took Eve from Adam's side because woman was created neither to rule over man nor to be enslaved by him but rather to stand squarely at his side, as a companion and partner in mutual aid and trust. By such insistence on the spiritual equality of men and women and their shared responsibility to one another, the church also helped elevate the dignity of women.

Germanic law treated women better than Roman law had done, recognizing basic rights that forbade their treatment as chattel. Unlike Roman women, who as teens married much older men, German women married husbands of similar age. Another practice unknown to the Romans was the groom's conveyance of a portion, or dowry (*dos*), to his bride, which became her own in the event of his death. All major Germanic law codes recognized the economic freedom of women: their right to inherit, administer, dispose of, and confer property and wealth on their children. They could also press charges in court against men for bodily injury and rape, the latter receiving punishments ranging from fines, flogging, and banishment to blinding, castration, and death.

Life Choices The nunnery was an option for single women from the higher social classes. Entrance required a dowry and could be almost as expensive as a wedding, though usually cheaper. Within the nunnery, a woman could rise to leadership as an abbess or a mother superior, exercising a degree of authority denied her in much of secular life. However, the nunneries of the established religious orders remained under male supervision, so that even abbesses had to answer to higher male authority.

In the ninth century, under the influence of Christianity, the Carolingians made monogamy official policy. Heretofore they had practiced polygamy and concubinage and permitted divorce. The result was both a boon and a burden to women. On one hand, wives gained a greater dignity and legal security. On the other hand, a wife's labor as household manager and bearer of children greatly increased. And the Carolingian wife was now also the sole object of her husband's wrath and pleasure. Such demands clearly took their toll. The mortality rates of Frankish women increased, and their life span decreased after the ninth century.

Under such conditions, the cloister became an appealing refuge for women. However, the number of women in cloisters was never very large. In late medieval England no more than 3,500 women entered the cloister.

Working Women The vast majority of medieval women were neither housewives nor nuns, but working women. The evidence suggests they were respected and loved by their husbands, perhaps because they worked shoulder by shoulder with them in running the household and often home-based businesses as well. Between the ages of 10 and 15, girls were apprenticed in a trade and learned to be skilled workers much like boys. If they married, they often continued their trade, operating their bake or dress shops next to their husbands' business, or becoming assistants and partners in the shops of their husbands. Women appeared in virtually every "blue-collar" trade, from butcher to goldsmith, but worked mostly in the food and clothing industries. Women belonged to guilds, just like men, and they became craftmasters. By the fifteenth century, townswomen increasingly had the opportunity to go to school and gain vernacular literacy.

Although women did not have as wide a range of vocations as men, their vocational destinies were just as fixed. Unlike men, however, women were excluded from the learned professions of scholarship, medicine, and law by reason of gender alone. Their freedom of movement within a profession was often more regulated than a man's, and their wages for the same work were not as great. Still, women remained as prominent and as creative a part of workaday medieval society as men.

◆●◆ Read the Document
The Battle of Hastings 1066
at **MyHistoryLab.com**

Growth of National Monarchies

England and France: Hastings (1066) to Bouvines (1214)

William the Conqueror The most important change in English political life was occasioned in 1066 by the death of the childless Anglo-Saxon ruler Edward the Confessor (r. 1042–1066), so named because of his reputation of piety. Edward's mother was a Norman princess, which gave Duke William of Normandy (d. 1087) a hereditary claim to the English throne. The Anglo-Saxon assembly, however, chose instead Harold Godwinsson (ca. 1022–1066), who had earlier solemnly promised the throne to William. That reneging brought the swift conquest of England by the powerful Normans. William's forces defeated Harold's army at Hastings on October 14, 1066, and William was crowned king of England in Westminster Abbey within weeks of the invasion.

Thereafter William established a strong monarchy but retained the Anglo-Saxon tax system, the practice of court writs (legal warnings) as a flexible form of central control over localities, and the Anglo-Saxon quasi-democratic tradi-

Battle of Hastings. William the Conqueror on horseback urging his troops into combat with the English at the battle of Hastings (October 14, 1066). *Detail from the Bayeux Tapestry, scene 51, c. 1073–1083. Musee de la Tapisserie, Bayeaux, France. Photo copyright Bridgeman-Giraudon/Art Resource, New York.*

tion of frequent *parleying*—that is, the holding of conferences between the king and lesser powers who had vested interests in royal decisions. The result was a balancing of monarchical and parliamentary elements that remains true of English government today.

Popular Rebellion and the Magna Carta William's grandson, Henry II (r. 1154–1189), brought to the throne greatly expanded French holdings through inheritance from his father (Maine, Touraine, and Anjou) and his marriage to Eleanor of Aquitaine (1122–1204), a union that created the so-called Angevin or English-French empire. As Henry II acquired new lands abroad, he became more autocratic at home. The result was strong political resistance from both the nobility and the clergy.

Under Henry's successors, the brothers Richard the Lion-Hearted (r. 1189–1199) and John (r. 1199–1216), burdensome taxation in support of foreign Crusades and a failing war with France turned resistance into outright rebellion. The danger of despotism became acute under the rule of King John, prompting the English barons to take matters into their own hands. With the full support of the clergy and the townspeople, they forced the king's grudging recognition of the **Magna Carta** ("Great Charter") in 1215, a document that reaffirmed traditional rights and personal liberties still enshrined in English law.

This famous cornerstone of modern English law put limits on royal power and secured the rights of the privileged to be represented at the highest levels of government in important matters like taxation. The Great Charter enabled the English to avoid both a dissolution of the monarchy by the nobility and the abridgment of the rights of the nobility by the monarchy.

Philip II Augustus Powerful feudal princes dominated France from the beginning of the Capetian dynasty (987) until the reign of Philip II Augustus (1180–1223). During this period the Capetian kings wisely concentrated their limited resources on securing the territory surrounding Paris known as the Île-de-France. By the time of Philip II, Paris had become the center of French government and culture, and the Capetian Dynasty a secure hereditary monarchy. Thereafter, the kings of France were able to impose their will on the French nobles.

The Norman Conquest of England enabled the Capetian kings to establish a truly national monarchy. The Duke of Normandy, who after 1066 was master of England, was also a vassal of the French king in Paris. Capetian kings understandably watched with alarm as the power of their Norman vassal grew.

Philip Augustus faced both an internal and an international struggle, and he succeeded at both. His armies occupied all the English territories on the French coast except for Aquitaine. At Bouvines on July 27, 1214, the French won handily over the English and their German allies. The victory unified France around the monarchy and thereby laid the foundation for French ascendancy in the Late Middle Ages.

◉ See the Map
England and France ca 1180 at **MyHistoryLab.com**

France in the Thirteenth Century: Reign of Louis IX

Louis IX (r. 1226–1270), the grandson of Philip Augustus, embodied the medieval view of the perfect ruler. He inherited a unified and secure kingdom.

Louis's greatest achievements lay at home. Under his reign the efficient French bureaucracy became an instrument of order and fair play in local government. He sent forth royal commissioners to monitor the royal officials responsible for local governmental administration and ensure justice. These royal ambassadors were received as genuine tribunes of the people. Louis further abolished private wars and serfdom within his own royal domain, gave his subjects the right of appeal from local to higher courts, and made the tax system more equitable. The French people came to associate their king with justice, and national feeling, the glue of nationhood, grew strong during his reign.

During Louis's reign, French society and culture became an example to all of Europe, a pattern that would continue into the modern period. Northern France became the showcase of monastic reform, chivalry, and Gothic art and architecture. Louis's reign also coincided with the golden age of Scholasticism, which saw the convergence of Europe's greatest thinkers on Paris, among them Saint Thomas Aquinas.

The Hohenstaufen Empire (1152–1272)

While stable governments developed in both England and France during the Middle Ages, the Holy Roman Empire fragmented in disunity and blood feuding (see Map 15–3).

Frederick I Barbarossa Frederick I Barbarossa (1152–1190), the first of the Hohenstaufens, reestablished imperial authority but also initiated a new phase in the contest between popes and emperors. Never have rulers and popes despised and persecuted one another more than they did during the Hohenstaufen Dynasty. Frederick attempted to hold the empire together by

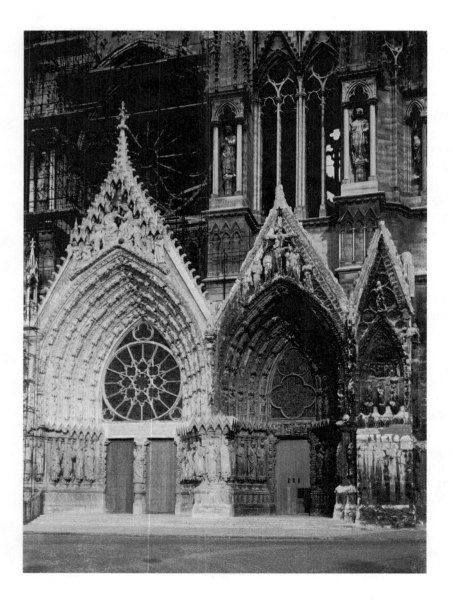

Gothic Cathedral. The portal of Reims Cathedral, where the kings of France were crowned. The cathedral was built in the Gothic style—emblematic of the High Middle Ages—that originated in France in the mid-twelfth century. The earlier Romanesque (Roman-like) style from which it evolved is characterized by fortresslike buildings with thick stone walls, rounded arches and vaults, and few windows. The Gothic style, in contrast, is characterized by soaring structures, their interiors flooded with colored light from vast expanses of stained-glass.

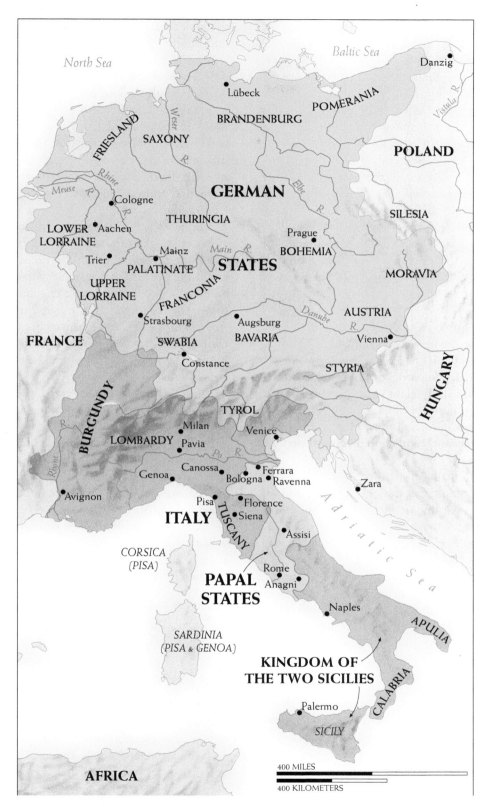

Map 15–3. **Germany and Italy in the Middle Ages.** Medieval Germany and Italy were divided lands. The Holy Roman Empire (Germany) embraced hundreds of independent territories that the emperor ruled only in name. The papacy controlled Rome and tried to enforce its will in central Italy. Under the Hohenstaufens (mid-twelfth to mid-thirteenth century), internal German divisions and papal conflict reached new heights; German rulers sought to extend their power to southern Italy and Sicily.

stressing feudal bonds, but his reign ended with stalemate in Germany and defeat in Italy. In 1186 his son—the future Henry VI (r. 1190–1197)—married Constance, heiress to the kingdom of Sicily. That alliance became a fatal distraction for the Hohenstaufens. This union of the empire with Sicily left Rome encircled, thereby ensuring the undying hostility of a papacy already thoroughly distrustful of the emperor.

When Henry VI died in September 1197, chaos followed. Germany was thrown into anarchy and civil war. Meanwhile, Henry VI's 4-year-old son, Frederick, who had a direct hereditary claim to the imperial crown, had for his own safety been made—fatefully, it would prove—a ward of Pope Innocent III (r. 1198–1215), who proclaimed and practiced as none before him the doctrine of the plenitude of papal power. Innocent had both the will and the means to challenge the Hohenstaufens.

Frederick II Hohenstaufen support had meanwhile remained alive in Germany, where in December 1212 young Frederick, with papal support, became Emperor Frederick II. But Frederick soon disappointed papal hopes. He was Sicilian and only nine of his thirty-eight years as emperor were spent in Germany. To secure the imperial title for himself and his sons, he gave the German princes what they wanted. The German princes became undisputed lords over their territories—in effect, petty kings.

Frederick had an equally disastrous relationship with the papacy, which excommunicated him four times and led the German princes against him, launching the church into European politics on a massive scale. This transformation of the papacy into a formidable political and military power soon made the church highly vulnerable to criticism from religious reformers and royal apologists.

When Frederick died in 1250, the German monarchy died with him. The princes established an electoral college in 1257 to pick the emperor, and the "king of the Romans" became their puppet. Between 1250 and 1272 the Hohenstaufen Dynasty slowly faded into oblivion.

See the Map
The Hundred Years War
at **MyHistoryLab.com**

....

Political and Social Breakdown

Hundred Years' War

The Causes of the War The Hundred Years' War, which began in May 1337 and lasted until October 1453, started when the English king Edward III (r. 1327–1377), the grandson of Philip the Fair of France (r. 1285–1314), claimed the French throne. But the war was more than a dynastic quarrel. England and France were territorial and economic rivals with a long history of prejudice and animosity between them. These factors made the Hundred Years' War a struggle for national identity.

Although France had three times the population of England, was far wealthier, and fought on its own soil, most of the major battles were stunning English victories. The primary reason for these French failures was internal disunity caused by endemic social conflicts. Unlike England, France was still struggling to make the transition from a fragmented feudal society to a centralized modern state.

France's defeats also resulted from incompetent leadership and English military superiority. The English infantry was more disciplined than the French, and English archers could fire six arrows a minute with enough force to pierce an inch of wood or the armor of a knight at 200 yards. Eventually, thanks in part to the inspiring leadership of Joan of Arc (1412–1431), and a sense of national identity and self-confidence, the French were able to expel the English from France. By 1453, all that remained to the English was their coastal enclave of Calais.

Charles forgot his liberator as quickly as he had embraced her. When the Burgundians captured Joan in May 1430, he could have secured her release but did not. The Burgundians and the English wanted her publicly discredited, believing this would demoralize French resistance. She was turned over to the Inquisition in English-held Rouen, where, after ten weeks of interrogation, she was executed on May 30, 1431.

The Hundred Years' War had lasting political and social consequences. It devastated France, but it also awakened French nationalism and hastened the country's transition from a feudal monarchy to a centralized state. In both France

See the Map
100 Years War
at **MyHistoryLab.com**

and England the burden of the war fell most heavily on the peasantry, who were forced to support it with taxes and services.

The Black Death

Preconditions and Causes In the fourteenth century, nine-tenths of the population worked the land. The three-field system of crop production increased the amount of arable land and with it the food supply. But as that supply grew, so did the population. It is estimated that Europe's population doubled between the years 1000 and 1300 and began thereafter to outstrip food production. There were now more people than there was food to feed them or jobs to employ them, and the average

See the Map
Black Death and
Peasant Revolts
at **MyHistoryLab.com**

European faced the probability of extreme hunger at least once during his or her expected thirty-five-year life span.

Black Death. Men and women carrying plague victims in coffins to the burial ground in Tournai, Belgium, 1349.

Between 1315 and 1317, cold weather and crop failures produced the greatest famine of the Middle Ages. Densely populated urban areas such as the industrial towns of the Netherlands experienced great suffering. Decades of over-population, economic depression, famine, and bad health progressively weakened Europe's population and made it highly vulnerable to a virulent bubonic plague that struck with full force in 1348.

●●•[Read the Document
Black Death 1349 Henry Knighton
at **MyHistoryLab.com**

The **Black Death**, so called by contemporaries because of the way it discolored the body, was most likely introduced by rats from Black Sea areas, the epidemic following the trade routes from Asia into Europe. Appearing in Sicily in late 1347, it entered Europe through the port cities of Venice, Genoa, and Pisa in 1348, and from there it swept rapidly through Spain and southern France and into northern Europe. Areas that lay outside the major trade routes, such as Bohemia, appear to have remained virtually unaffected. Bubonic plague made numerous reappearances in succeeding decades. It is estimated that western Europe had lost as much as two-fifths of its population by the early fifteenth century. (See Map 15–4 on page 446.)

Popular Remedies   Transmitted by rat- or human-borne fleas, the plague often reached a victim's lungs during the course of the disease. From the lungs, it was spread from person to person by the victim's sneezing and wheezing. Contemporary physicians had little understanding of these processes, so the most rudimentary prophylaxis was lacking. Throughout much of western Europe, the plague brought with it an obsession with death and dying, engendering a deep pessimism that endured for decades.

Popular wisdom held that a corruption in the atmosphere caused the disease. Some blamed poisonous fumes released by earthquakes. Many wore aromatic amulets as a remedy. According to the contemporary observations of Boccaccio, who recorded the reactions in the *Decameron* (1353), some sought a remedy in moderation and a temperate life, others gave themselves over entirely to their passions (sexual promiscuity ran high within the stricken areas), and still others, "the most sound, perhaps, in judgment," chose flight and seclusion as the best medicine.

One extreme reaction was the procession of flagellants, religious fanatics who beat themselves in ritual penance, believing such action would bring divine intervention. The terror created by the flagellants, whose dirty

Map 15–4. Spread of the Black Death. Apparently introduced by seaborne rats from areas around the Black Sea where plague-infested rodents have long been known, the Black Death had great human, social, and economic consequences. According to one of the lower estimates, it killed 25 million in Europe. The map charts the spread of the plague in the mid-fourteenth century. Generally following trade routes, it reached Scandinavia by 1350, and some believe it then went on to Iceland and even Greenland. Areas off the main trade routes were largely spared.

bodies may have transported the disease, became so socially disruptive and threatening that the church finally outlawed such processions.

In some places, Jews were cast as scapegoats. Centuries of Christian propaganda had bred hatred toward Jews, as had their role as society's moneylenders. Pogroms occurred in several cities, sometimes incited by the flagellants.

Social and Economic Consequences Whole villages vanished in the wake of the plague. Among the social and economic consequences of such high depopulation were a shrunken labor supply and a decline in the value of the estates of the nobility. As the number of farm laborers decreased, wages increased and those of skilled artisans soared. Many serfs chose to commute their labor services by money payments and pursue more interesting and rewarding jobs in skilled craft industries in the cities. Agricultural prices fell because of lowered demand, and the price of luxury and manufactured goods—the work of skilled artisans—rose. The noble landholders suffered the greatest decline in power. They were forced to pay more for finished products and for farm labor, while receiving a smaller return on their agricultural produce. Everywhere rents declined after the plague.

Watch the Video
The Plague
at **MyHistoryLab.com**

Peasants Revolt To recoup their losses, some landowners converted arable land to sheep pasture, substituting more profitable wool production for labor-intensive grain crops. Others abandoned the farms, leasing them to the highest bidder. Landowners also sought to reverse their misfortune by new repressive legislation that forced peasants to stay on their farms while freezing their wages at low levels. In 1351, the English Parliament passed a Statute of Laborers, which limited wages to pre-plague levels and restricted the ability of peasants to leave the land of their masters. Opposition to such legislation was also a prominent factor in the English peasants' revolt in 1381. In France the direct tax on the peasantry, the **taille**, was increased, and opposition to it helped ignite the French peasant uprising known as the Jacquerie. The consequences of both revolts were modest compared to the German Peasants' Revolt in 1525 (see Chapter 16).

Read the Document
Peasant Revolt in England
at **MyHistoryLab.com**

Cities Rebound Although the plague hit urban populations hard, the cities and their skilled industries in time prospered from its effects. Cities had always protected their interests, passing legislation as they grew to regulate competition from rural areas and to control immigration. After the plague, the reach of such laws extended beyond the cities to include the surrounding lands of nobles and landlords, many of whom now peacefully integrated into urban life.

The omnipresence of death also whetted the appetite for goods that only skilled industries could produce. Expensive cloths and jewelry, furs from the north, and silks from the south were in great demand in the decades after the plague. Initially, this new demand could not be met. The basic unit of urban industry, the master and his apprentices (usually one or two), purposely kept its numbers low, jealously guarding its privileges. The first wave of plague turned this already restricted supply of skilled artisans into a shortage almost overnight. As a result, the prices of manufactured and luxury items rose to new heights, which in turn encouraged workers to migrate from the countryside to the city and learn the skills of artisans. Townspeople profited coming and going. As wealth poured into the cities and per capita income rose, agricultural products from the countryside, now less in demand, declined.

There was also gain and loss for the church. It suffered as a landholder and was politically weakened, yet at the same time it received new revenues from the vastly increased demand for religious services for the dead and the dying, along with new gifts and bequests.

New Conflicts and Opportunities

By increasing the importance of skilled artisans, the plague contributed to new social conflicts within the cities. The economic and political power of local artisans and trade guilds grew steadily in the Late Middle Ages, along with the demand for their goods and services. The merchant and patrician classes found it increasingly difficult to maintain their traditional dominance and grudgingly gave guild masters a voice in city government. As the guilds won political power, they encouraged restrictive legislation to protect local industries. The restrictions, in turn, caused conflict between master artisans, who wanted to keep their numbers low and expand their industries at a snail's pace, and the many journeymen, who were eager to rise to the rank of master. To the long-existing conflict between the guilds and the ruling urban patriciate was now added a conflict within the guilds themselves.

Also after 1350, the two traditional "containers" of monarchy—the landed nobility and the church—were put on the defensive as a consequence of the plague. Kings now exploited growing national sentiment in an effort to centralize their governments and economies. At the same time, the battles of the Hundred Years' War demonstrated the military superiority of paid professional armies over the traditional noble cavalry, thus bringing into question the latter's future role. The plague also killed many members of the clergy—perhaps one-third of the German clergy fell victim as they dutifully ministered to the sick and dying. This reduction in clerical ranks occurred in the same century that saw the pope move from Rome to Avignon (1309–1377) and the Great Schism (1378–1417) divide the church into warring factions.

Ecclesiastical Breakdown and Revival: The Late Medieval Church

Boniface VIII and Philip the Fair

By the fourteenth century popes faced rulers far more powerful than the papacy. When Pope Boniface VIII (r. 1294–1303) issued a bull, *Clericis Laicos*, that forbade lay taxation of the clergy without prior papal approval, King Philip the Fair of France (r. 1285–1314) unleashed

◆◆◆[Read the Document

Unam Sanctam 1302 Pope
Boniface VIII
at **MyHistoryLab.com**

a ruthless antipapal campaign. Boniface made a last-ditch stand against state control of national churches on November 18, 1302, when he issued the bull *Unam Sanctam*, which declared that temporal authority was "subject" to the spiritual power of the church.

The French responded with force. Philip sent troops who beat the pope badly and might even have executed him had not an aroused populace liberated the pope and returned him safely to Rome.

There was no papal retaliation. No pope ever again so seriously threatened kings and emperors. Future relations between church and state would henceforth tilt toward state control of religion within particular monarchies.

The Great Schism (1378–1417) and the Conciliar Movement to 1449

After Boniface VIII's death, his successor, Clement V (r. 1305–1314), moved the papal court to Avignon on the southeastern border with France, where it remained until Pope Gregory XI (r. 1370–1378) reestablished the papacy in Rome in January 1377. His successor, Pope Urban VI (r. 1378– 1389), proclaimed his intention to reform the papal government in the **Curia**. This announcement alarmed the cardinals, most of whom were French. Not wanting to surrender the benefits of a papacy under French influence, the French king, Charles V (r. 1364–1380), supported a schism in the church, known thereafter as the **Great Schism**. On September 20, 1378, thirteen cardinals, all but one of whom were French, elected a cousin of the French king as Pope Clement VII (r. 1378–1397). Clement returned to Avignon. Thereafter allegiance to the two papal courts divided along po-

Papal Authority. Pope Boniface VIII (r. 1294–1303), who opposed the taxation of the clergy by the kings of France and England, issued one of the strongest declarations of papal authority, the bull *Unam Sanctam*. This statue is in the Museo Civico, Bologna, Italy. *Scala/Art Resource, New York.*

litical lines: Acknowledging Urban VI were England and its allies—the **Holy Roman Empire** (based on the old Roman Empire, mostly Germany and Northern Italy), Hungary, Bohemia, and Poland. Supporting Clement VII were France and its orbit—Naples, Scotland, Castile, and Aragon. The church, however, only recognized the Roman line of popes as official.

In 1409 a council at Pisa deposed both the Roman and the Avignon popes and elected its own new pope. But neither Rome nor Avignon accepted its action, so after 1409 there were three contending popes. This intolerable situation ended when the emperor Sigismund (r. 1410–1437) prevailed on the Pisan pope to summon a legal council of the church in Constance in 1414, a council also recognized by the reigning Roman pope Gregory XII (r. 1406–1415). After the three contending popes had either resigned or been deposed, the council elected a new pope, Martin V (r. 1417–1431), in November 1417, reuniting the church.

Under Pope Eugenius IV (r. 1431–1447), the papacy regained much of its prestige and authority, and in 1460 the papal bull *Execrabilis* condemned all appeals to councils as "completely null and void." But the conciliar movement had planted deep within the conscience of all Western peoples the conviction that the leader of an institution must be responsive to its members and not act against their best interests.

The Renaissance in Italy (1375–1527)

The **Renaissance** is the term used to describe fourteenth-and fifteenth-century efforts to revive ancient learning. Most scholars agree that it was a transition from the medieval to the modern world. Medieval Europe, especially before the twelfth century, had been a fragmented feudal society with an agricultural economy, its thought and culture dominated by the church. Renaissance Europe, especially after the fourteenth century, was characterized by growing national consciousness and political centralization, an urban economy based on organized commerce and capitalism, and ever-greater lay and secular control of thought and culture.

The distinctive features and achievements of the Renaissance are most strikingly revealed in Italy from roughly 1375 to 1527, the year of the infamous sack of Rome by imperial soldiers. What was achieved in Italy during these centuries also deeply influenced northern Europe.

The Italian City-State: Social Conflict and Despotism

Renaissance society took distinctive shape within the cities of late medieval Italy. Italy was the natural gateway between East and West. Venice, Genoa, and Pisa traded uninterruptedly with the Near East throughout the Middle Ages and maintained vibrant urban societies. During the thirteenth and fourteenth centuries, the trade-rich Italian cities became powerful city-states, dominating the political and economic life of the surrounding countryside. By the fifteenth century, the great Italian cities had become the bankers for much of Europe. There were five such major, competitive states in Italy: the duchy of Milan, the republics of Florence and Venice, the Papal States, and the kingdom of Naples. (See Map 15–5).

Social strife and competition for political power were so intense within the cities that for survival's sake, most had evolved into despotisms by the fifteenth century. Venice, ruled by a successful merchant oligarchy, was the notable exception. Elsewhere, the new social classes and divisions within society produced by rapid urban growth fueled chronic, near-anarchic conflict.

In Florence, these social divisions produced conflict at every level of society. True stability was not established until the ascent to power in 1434 of Cosimo de' Medici (1389–1464). The wealthiest Florentine and a most astute statesman, Cosimo controlled the city internally from behind the scenes, skillfully manipulating the constitution and influencing elections. His grandson Lorenzo the Magnificent (1449–1492, r. 1478–1492) ruled Florence in an almost totalitarian fashion.

Despotism was less subtle elsewhere in Italy. To prevent internal social conflict and foreign intrigue from paralyzing their cities, the dominant groups in many cities cooperated in the hiring of a strongman, known as a *podesta*, to maintain law and order. Because these despots could not depend on the divided populace, they operated through mercenary armies.

Political turbulence and warfare also gave birth to diplomacy, through which the various city-states stayed abreast of foreign military developments and, if shrewd enough, gained power and advantage without actually going to war. Most city-states established resident embassies during the fifteenth century, their ambassadors serving as the watchful eyes and ears at rival courts. Renaissance culture was promoted as vigorously by despots as by republicans and by popes as enthusiastically as by humanists.

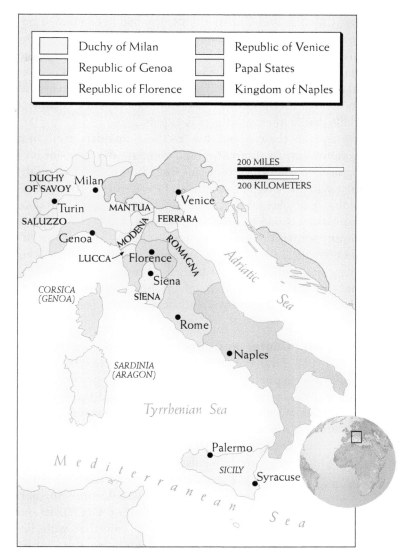

Map 15–5. Renaissance Italy. The city-states of Renaissance Italy were self-contained principalities whose internal strife was monitored by their despots and whose external conflicts were successfully controlled by treaties.

Humanism

Humanism was the scholarly study of the Latin and Greek classics and the ancient Church Fathers, both for their own sake and to promote a rebirth of ancient norms and values. Humanists advocated the ***studia humanitatis***, a liberal arts program that embraced grammar, rhetoric, poetry, history, politics, and moral philosophy.

The first humanists were orators and poets. They wrote original literature in both the classical and vernacular languages, inspired by the newly discovered works of the ancients, and they taught rhetoric within the universities. They were sought as secretaries, speech writers, and diplomats in princely and papal courts.

Classical and Christian antiquity had been studied before the Italian Renaissance—during the Carolingian renaissance of the ninth century, for example. However, the Italian Renaissance of the Late Middle Ages was more secular and lay dominated, had broader interests, recovered more manuscripts, and possessed far superior technical skills than earlier rebirths of antiquity.

Unlike their Scholastic rivals, humanists were not content only to summarize and compare the views of recognized authorities on a question but instead went directly to the original source and drew their own conclusions. Avidly searching out manuscript collections, Italian humanists made the full sources of Greek and Latin antiquity available to scholars during the fourteenth and fifteenth centuries. Mastery of Latin and Greek was their surgeon's tool. There is a kernel of truth—but only a kernel—in the arrogant boast of the humanists that the period between themselves and classical civilization was a "dark middle age."

Petrarch, Dante, and Boccaccio Francesco Petrarch (1304–1374) was the father of humanism. He left the legal profession to pursue his love of letters and poetry. Petrarch celebrated ancient Rome in his writings and tirelessly collected ancient manuscripts; among his finds were letters by Cicero. His critical textual studies, elitism, and contempt for the allegedly useless learning of the Scholastics were shared by many later humanists.

•◦•━Read the Document
Letters to Cicero 14th century
Petrarch at **MyHistoryLab.com**

•◦•━Read the Document
Dante's Divine Comedy 1321
Dante at **MyHistoryLab.com**

Petrarch was far more secular in orientation than Dante Alighieri (1265–1321), whose *Vita Nuova* and *Divine Comedy*—together with Petrarch's sonnets—form the cornerstones of Italian vernacular literature.

Also pioneering humanist studies was Petrarch's student and friend Giovanni Boccaccio (1313–1375), author of the *Decameron*, 100 bawdy tales told by three men and seven women in a country retreat from the plague that ravaged Florence in 1348. An avid collector of manuscripts, Boccaccio also assembled an encyclopedia of Greek and Roman mythology.

Educational Reforms and Goals The classical ideal of a useful education that produces well-rounded, effective people inspired far-reaching reforms in traditional education. The most influential Italian Renaissance tract on education, Pietro Paolo Vergerio's (1349–1420) *On the Morals That Befit a Free Man*, was written directly from classical models. Vittorino da Feltre (d. 1446) directed his students to a highly disciplined reading of ancient authors, together with vigorous physical exercise and games with intellectual pursuits.

Jan van Eyck, "Adam and Eve" (1432). In the wings of the Dutch painter Jan van Eyck's earliest work, the Ghent Altarpiece, Adam and Eve appear after their fall. Unlike the Italian Renaissance masters, the Netherlandish master portrays them as true-to-life humans, not heroic, idealized figures. Above their heads their son Cain kills his brother Abel, serving as a commentary on "humankind after the Fall."

Educated and cultured noblewomen also had a prominent place at Renaissance courts, among whom was Christine de Pisan (1365–1434). She was an expert in classical, French, and Italian languages and literature and became a well-known woman of letters in the courts of Europe. Her most famous work, *The City of Ladies*, describes the accomplishments of the great women of history.

Renaissance Art in and Beyond Italy

Throughout Renaissance Europe, the values and interests of the laity were less subordinated to those of the clergy than in previous centuries. In education, culture, and religion, a more this-worldly spirit was evident. The secular world and secular learning along with many purely human pursuits were again appreciated as ends in themselves.

This perspective on life is especially prominent in the painting and sculpture of the High Renaissance, the late fifteenth and early sixteenth centuries, when Renaissance art reached its maturity. In imitation of Greek and Roman art, painters and sculptors created well-proportioned and even heroic figures, as they strove to present the perfect human form. Whereas Byzantine and Gothic art had been religious and edgy in their representation of the human body, Renaissance art, especially in the fifteenth century, reproduced nature and human nature realistically, in both its physical beauty and grotesqueness.

Italian Renaissance artists led the way. They took advantage of new technical skills and materials developed during the fifteenth century: oil paints, the technique of shading to enhance realism (**chiaroscuro**), and sizing figures to convey to the viewer a feeling of continuity with a painting (linear perspective). Compared with their flat, two-dimensional Byzantine and Gothic counterparts, the new artists could fill a canvas or wood panel with energy and life in three dimensions.

The Italian artists Leonardo da Vinci (1452–1519) and Michelangelo Buonarroti (1475–1564) personified the Renaissance ideal of the universal person, one who is a master of many skills and trades. A military engineer and an advocate of scientific experimentation, Leonardo dissected corpses to learn anatomy and was a self-taught botanist. He foresaw such modern machines as airplanes and submarines. The variety of his interests tended to shorten his attention span, so that he constantly moved

View the Image
Da Vinci Mona Lisa
at **MyHistoryLab.com**

"Michelangelo's Creation of Adam"   The High Italian Renaissance obsession with the muscular, robust, heroic body finds expression in Michelangelo's rendering of the "The Creation of Adam" in the Sistine Chapel.

Document

Pico della Mirandola States the Renaissance Image of Man

One of the most eloquent Renaissance descriptions of the abilities of humankind comes from the Italian humanist Pico della Mirandola (1463–1494). In his famed *Oration on the Dignity of Man* (ca. 1486), Pico described humans as free to become whatever they choose.

■ *In what does the dignity of humankind consist? Does Pico reject the biblical description of Adam and Eve's fall? Does he exaggerate a person's ability to choose freely to be whatever he or she wishes? What inspired such seeming hubris during the Renaissance?*

The best of artisans [God] ordained that that creature (man) to whom He [God] had been able to give nothing proper to himself should have joint possession of whatever had been peculiar to each of the different kinds of being. He therefore took man as a creature of indeterminate nature and, assigning him a place in the middle of the world, addressed him thus: "Neither a fixed abode nor a form that is thine alone or any function peculiar to thyself have we given thee, Adam, to the end that according to thy longing and according to thy judgment thou mayest have and possess what abode, what form, and what functions thou thyself shalt desire. The nature of all other beings is limited and constrained within the bounds of laws prescribed by Us. Thou, constrained by no limits, in accordance with thine own free will, in whose hand We have placed thee, shall ordain for thyself the limits of thy nature. We have set thee at the world's center that thou mayest from thence more easily observe whatever is in the world. We have made thee neither of heaven nor of earth, neither mortal nor immortal, so that with freedom of choice and with honor, as though the maker and molder of thyself, thou mayest fashion thyself in whatever shape thou shalt prefer. Thou shalt have the power to degenerate into the lower forms of life, which are brutish. Thou shalt have the power, out of thy soul's judgment, to be reborn into the higher forms, which are divine." O supreme generosity of God the Father, O highest and most marvelous felicity of man! To him it is granted to have whatever he chooses, to be whatever he wills.

Source: The Renaissance Philosophy of man selections in translation by G. Pico della Mirandola. Copyright 1961 by University of Chicago Press -Books. Reproduced with permission of University of Chicago Press -Books in the formats Textbook and Other Book via Copyright Clearance Center.

from one activity to another. As a painter, his great skill lay in conveying inner moods through complex facial features, such as that seen in the most famous of his paintings, the Mona Lisa.

■ View the Image
Michelangelo's David
at **MyHistoryLab.com**

The melancholy genius Michelangelo also excelled in a variety of arts and crafts. His 18-foot godlike sculpture *David* is a perfect example of the Renaissance artist's devotion to harmony, symmetry, and proportion, which can also be seen in his extreme glorification of the human form.

Four different popes commissioned his works, the best known of which are the frescoes for the Sistine Chapel, painted for Pope Julius II (r. 1503–1513). His later works mark, artistically and philosophically, the passing of High Renaissance painting and the advent of a modernizing, experimental style known as **mannerism**, which reached its peak in the late sixteenth and early seventeenth centuries. It derived its name from the fact that it permitted the artist to express his own individual perceptions and feelings to paint, compose, or write in a "mannered" or "affected" way. Tintoretto (d. 1594) and the

■ Watch the Video
The Art of El Greco
at **MyHistoryLab.com**

Spaniard El Greco (d. 1614) would become its supreme representatives.

Italy's Political Decline: The French Invasions (1494–1527)

Autonomous city-states of Italy had always preserved their peace and safety from foreign invasion by cooperation with each other. However, in 1494 Naples, supported by Florence and the Borgia pope Alexander VI (1492–1503), prepared to attack Milan. At this point, the Milanese despot Ludovico il Moro (r. 1476–1499) invited the French to revive their dynastic claim to Naples. But France also had dynastic claims to Milan, and the French appetite for new territory became insatiable once French armies had crossed the Alps and reestablished themselves in Italy.

The French king Charles VIII (r. 1483–1498) responded rapidly to Ludovico's call. Within five months he had crossed the Alps (August 1495) and raced as conqueror through Florence and the Papal States into Naples.

Charles's lightning march through Italy alarmed Ferdinand of Aragon (r. 1479–1516), who was also king of Sicily, and helped to create a counteralliance: the League of Venice, which was able to force Charles to retreat.

The French returned to Italy under Charles's successor, Louis XII (r. 1498–1515), this time assisted by the Borgia pope Alexander VI (1492–1503). Alexander, probably the most corrupt pope in history, sought to secure a political base in Romagna, officially part of the Papal States, for his son Cesare.

Seeing that a French alliance could allow him to reestablish control over the region, Alexander agreed to abandon the League of Venice, which made the league too weak to resist a French reconquest of Milan. Louis successfully invaded Milan in August 1499. In 1500 he and Ferdinand of Aragon divided Naples between themselves, while the pope and Cesare Borgia conquered Romagna without opposition.

In 1503 Cardinal Giuliano della Rovere became Pope Julius II (1503–1513). He suppressed the Borgias and placed their newly conquered lands in Romagna under papal jurisdiction. After fully securing the Papal States with French aid, Julius changed sides and sought to rid Italy of his former ally, the French invaders. Julius, Ferdinand of Aragon, and Venice formed a Holy League in October 1511, and soon Emperor Maximilian I (r. 1493–1519) and the Swiss joined them. By 1512 the French were in full retreat.

The French invaded Italy again under Louis's successor, Francis I (r. 1515–1547). French armies massacred Swiss soldiers of the Holy League at Marignano in September 1515. That victory won from the Medici pope Leo X (r. 1513–1521) an agreement known as the Concordat of Bologna (August 1516), which gave the French king control over the French clergy and the right to collect taxes from them, in exchange for French recognition of the pope's superiority over church councils. This helped keep France Catholic after the outbreak of the Protestant Reformation. But the new French entry into Italy also led to the first of four major wars with Spain in the first half of the sixteenth century: the Habsburg-Valois wars, none of which France won.

See the Map
Empire and the Papacy in Italy at **MyHistoryLab.com**

Niccolò Machiavelli

The foreign invasions made a shambles of Italy. One who watched as French, Spanish, and German armies wreaked havoc on his country was Niccolò Machiavelli (1469–1527). The more he saw, the more convinced he became that Italian political unity and independence were ends that justified any means. Machiavelli admired the heroic acts of ancient Roman rulers, what Renaissance people called their *Virtù*. Romanticizing the old Roman citizenry, he lamented the absence of heroism among his compatriots. Such a perspective caused his interpretation of both ancient and contemporary history to be exaggerated.

The juxtaposition of what Machiavelli believed the ancient Romans had been with the failure of contemporary Romans to realize such high ideals made him the famous cynic we know in the popular epithet *Machiavellian*. Only an unscrupulous strongman, he concluded, using duplicity and terror, could impose order on so divided and selfish a people. Machiavelli seems to have been in earnest when he advised rulers to discover the advantages of fraud and brutality. He apparently hoped to see a strong ruler

Read the Document
The Prince 1519 Machiavelli
at **MyHistoryLab.com**

Niccolò Machiavelli. Santi di Tito's portrait of Machiavelli, perhaps the most famous Italian political theorist, who advised Renaissance princes to practice artful deception and inspire fear in their subjects if they wished to succeed. *Scala/Art Resource, New York.*

emerge from the Medici family. The Medicis, however, were not destined to be Italy's deliverers. The second Medici pope, Clement VII (r. 1523–1534), watched helplessly as Rome was sacked by the army of Emperor Charles V (r. 1519–1556) in 1527, the year of Machiavelli's death.

Revival of Monarchy: Nation Building in the Fifteenth Century

With the emergence of sovereign rulers after 1450, unified national monarchies progressively replaced fragmented and divisive feudal governance, but the dynastic and chivalric ideals of feudalism did not disappear. Minor territorial princes survived, and representative assemblies even grew in influence in some regions. But by the late fifteenth and early sixteenth centuries, the old problem of the one and the many was being decided clearly in favor of monarchy.

In the feudal monarchy of the High Middle Ages, the basic powers of government were divided between the king and his semiautonomous vassals. The nobility and the towns acted with varying degrees of unity and success through such evolving representative bodies as the English Parliament, the French Estates General, and the Spanish Cortes to thwart the centralization of royal power. However, as a result of the Hundred Years' War and the schism in the church, the landed nobility and the clergy were in decline in the Late Middle Ages. The increasingly important towns now began to ally with the king. Loyal, businesswise townspeople, not the nobility and the clergy, staffed the royal offices, becoming the king's lawyers, bookkeepers, military tacticians, and diplomats. This new alliance between king and town would slowly break the bonds of feudal society and make possible the rise of the modern sovereign state.

In a sovereign state, the powers of taxation, war making, and law enforcement are no longer the local right of semiautonomous vassals but are concentrated in the monarch and exercised by his chosen agents. Taxes, wars, and laws become national rather than merely regional matters. Only because monarchs were able to act independently of the nobility and the representative assemblies could they overcome the decentralization that had been the basic obstacle to nation building.

Monarchies also began to create standing national armies in the fifteenth century. As the noble cavalry receded and the infantry and the artillery became the backbone of armies, mercenary soldiers were recruited from Switzerland and Germany to form the mainstay of the "king's army."

•••-[Read the Document
Vladimir of Kiev's Acceptance of Christianity
at **MyHistoryLab.com**

Chronology

Major Political Events of the Italian Renaissance (1375–1527)

1378–1382	Ciompi revolt in Florence
1434	Medici rule in Florence established by Cosimo de' Medici
1454–1455	Treaty of Lodi allies Milan, Naples, and Florence (in effect until 1494)
1494	Charles VIII of France invades Italy
1495	League of Venice unites Venice, Milan, the Papal States, the Holy Roman Empire, and Spain against France
1499	Louis XII invades Milan (the second French invasion of Italy)
1500	The Borgias conquer Romagna
1512–1513	The Holy League (Pope Julius II, Ferdinand of Aragon, Emperor Maximilian I, and Venice) defeats the French
1513	Machiavelli writes *The Prince*
1515	Francis I leads the third French invasion of Italy
1516	Concordat of Bologna between France and the papacy
1527	Sack of Rome by imperial soldiers

The growing cost of warfare increased the need to develop new national sources of royal income. The expansion of royal revenues was especially hampered by the stubborn belief among the highest classes that they were immune from government taxation. The nobility guarded their properties and traditional rights and despised taxation as an insult and a humiliation. Royal revenues accordingly grew at the expense of those least able to resist and least able to pay. Monarchs had several options. As feudal lords they could collect rents from their royal domain. They might also levy national taxes on basic food and clothing, such as the *gabelle* or salt tax in France and the *alcabala* or 10 percent sales tax on commercial transactions in Spain. Kings could also levy direct taxes on the peasantry and on commercial transactions in towns under royal protection. This they did through agreeable representative assemblies of the privileged classes in which the peasantry did not sit. The French *taille* was such a tax. Sale of public offices and the issuance of high-interest government bonds appeared in the fifteenth century as innovative fund-raising devices. But kings did not levy taxes on the powerful nobility. They turned for loans to rich nobles, as they did to the great bankers of Italy and Germany, bargaining with the privileged classes, who often remained as much the kings' creditors and competitors as their subjects.

Medieval Russia

In the late tenth century Prince Vladimir of Kiev (r. 972–1015), then Russia's dominant city, received delegations of Muslims, Roman Catholics, Jews, and Greek Orthodox Christians, each group hoping to win the Russians to its religion. Prince Vladimir chose Greek Orthodoxy, which became the religion of Russia, adding a new cultural bond to the long-standing commercial ties the Russians had with the Byzantine Empire.

Vladimir's successor, Yaroslav the Wise (r. 1016–1054), developed Kiev into a magnificent political and cultural center, but after his death, rivalry among princes challenged Kiev's dominance, and it became just one of several national centers.

Mongol Rule (1243–1480) and Russian Liberation
Mongol (or Tatar) armies (see Chapters 8 and 12) invaded Russia in 1223, and Kiev fell in 1240. Russian cities became tribute-paying principalities of the segment of the Mongol Empire called the **Golden Horde**, which had its capital at Sarai, on the lower Volga. Mongol rule further divided Russia from the West but left Russian political institutions and religion largely intact. Thanks to their far-flung trade, the Mongolians brought most Russians greater peace and prosperity than they had enjoyed before.

The princes of Moscow cooperated with the Mongols and grew wealthy. They then gradually expanded the principality through land purchases, colonization, and conquest. In 1380 Grand Duke Dimitri of Moscow (1350–1389) defeated Tatar forces at Kulikov Meadow in a victory that marked the beginning of the decline of Mongolian hegemony. Another century would pass before Ivan III, called Ivan the Great (d. 1505), would bring all of northern Russia under Moscow's control and end Mongol rule in 1480 (see Map 15–6 on page 456). By the last quarter of the fifteenth century, Moscow had replaced Kiev as the political and religious center of Russia. In Russian eyes it was destined to become the "third Rome" after the fall of Constantinople to the Turks in 1453.

France

There were two cornerstones of French nation building in the fifteenth century. The first was the collapse of the English holdings in France following the Hundred Years' War. The second was the defeat of Charles the Bold (r. 1467–1477) and the duchy of Burgundy. Perhaps Europe's strongest political power in the mid-fifteenth century, Burgundy aspired to lead a dominant middle kingdom between France and the Holy Roman Empire. It might have succeeded had not the Continental powers joined together in opposition. When Charles the Bold was killed at Nancy in 1477, the dream of Burgundian empire died with him.

The dissolution of Burgundy ended its constant intrigue against the French king and left Louis XI (r. 1461–1483) free to secure the monarchy. The newly acquired Burgundian lands and his own Angevin inheritance permitted the king to double the size of his kingdom. Louis harnessed the nobility and expanded trade and industry.

A strong nation is a two-edged sword. It was because Louis's successors inherited such a secure and efficient government that France was able to pursue Italian conquests in the 1490s and to fight a long series of losing wars with the Habsburgs in the first half of the sixteenth century. By the mid-sixteenth century France was again a defeated nation and almost as divided internally as it had been during the Hundred Years' War.

Spain

Spain, too, became a strong country in the late fifteenth century. Both Castile and Aragon had been poorly ruled, divided kingdoms in the mid-fifteenth century. The marriage of Isabella of Castile (r. 1474–1504) and Ferdinand of Aragon (r. 1479–1516) changed that situation. The two future sovereigns married in 1469, despite strong protests from neighboring Portugal and France, both of which foresaw the formidable European power such a union would create. Castile was by far the richer and more populous of the two, having an estimated 5 million inhabitants to Aragon's population of under 1 million. Castile was also distinguished by its lucrative sheep-farming industry, which was run by a government-backed organization called the *Mesta*, another example of developing centralized economic planning. Although the two kingdoms were dynastically united by the marriage of Ferdinand and Isabella in 1469, each retained its own government agencies—separate laws, armies, coinage, and taxation—and cultural traditions.

Ferdinand and Isabella could do together what neither was able to accomplish alone, namely, subdue their realms, secure their borders, and venture abroad militarily. Townspeople allied themselves with the crown and

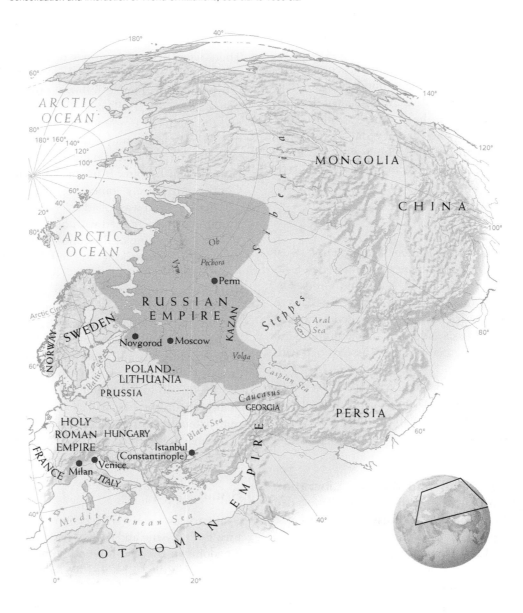

Map 15–6. Russia, ca. 1500.

progressively replaced the nobility within the royal administration. The crown also extended its authority over the wealthy chivalric orders, a further circumscription of the power of the nobility.

Spain had long been remarkable as a place where three religions—Islam, Judaism, and Christianity—coexisted with a certain degree of toleration. This toleration ended dramatically under Ferdinand and Isabella, who made Spain the prime example of state-controlled religion. Ferdinand and Isabella exercised almost total control over the Spanish church as they placed religion in the service of

national unity. They appointed the higher clergy and the officers of the Inquisition. The Inquisition, run by Tomás de Torquemada (d. 1498), Isabella's confessor, was a key national agency established in 1479 to monitor the activity of converted Jews (*conversos*) and Muslims (*Moriscos*) in Spain. In 1492 the Jews were exiled and their properties were confiscated. In 1502 nonconverting Moors in Granada were driven into exile. Spanish spiritual life remained largely uniform and regimented, a major reason for Spain's remaining a loyal Catholic country throughout the

See the Map
Spain 1491
at **MyHistoryLab.com**

sixteenth century and providing a base of operation for the European Counter-Reformation.

Ferdinand and Isabella had wide horizons. They contracted anti-French marriage alliances that came to determine much of European history in the sixteenth century. In 1496 their eldest daughter, Joanna, later known as "the Mad" (1479–1555), married Archduke Philip (1478–1506), the son of Emperor Maximilian I (r. 1493–1519). Their son, Charles I, the first ruler over a united Spain, came by his inheritance and election as Emperor Charles V in 1519 to rule over a European kingdom almost equal in size to that of Charlemagne. A second daughter, Catherine of Aragon (1485–1536), married King Henry VIII of England. It was the failure of Catherine's marriage that would become the key factor in the emergence of the Anglican Church and the English Reformation.

The new Spanish power was also evident in Ferdinand and Isabella's promotion of overseas exploration. Their patronage of the Genoese adventurer Christopher Columbus (1451–1506), who discovered the islands of the Caribbean while sailing west in search of a shorter route to the spice markets of the Far East, led to the creation of the Spanish Empire in Mexico and Peru, whose gold and silver mines helped to make Spain Europe's dominant power in the sixteenth century.

England

The last half of the fifteenth century was a period of especially difficult political trial for the English. Following the Hundred Years' War, a defeated England was subjected to internal warfare between two rival branches of the royal family, the House of York and the House of Lancaster. This conflict, known to us today as the Wars of the Roses (as York's symbol, according to legend, was a white rose, and Lancaster's a red rose), kept England in turmoil from 1455 to 1485.

The Lancastrian monarchy of Henry VI (r. 1422–1461) was consistently challenged by the Duke of York and his supporters in the prosperous southern towns. In 1461 Edward IV (r. 1461–1483), son of the Duke of York, seized power and, assisted by loyal and able ministers, effectively bent Parliament to his will. His brother and successor was Richard III (r. 1483–1485), whose reign saw the growth of support for the exiled Lancastrian Henry Tudor. Henry returned to England to defeat Richard on Bosworth Field in August 1485.

Henry Tudor ruled as Henry VII (r. 1485–1509), the first of the new Tudor Dynasty that would endure until 1603. To bring the rival royal families together and to make the hereditary claim of his offspring to the throne uncontestable, Henry married Edward IV's daughter,

Elizabeth of York. He succeeded in disciplining the English nobility through a special and much-feared instrument of the royal will known as the Court of Star Chamber. Henry shrewdly construed legal precedents to the advantage of the Crown, using English law to further his own ends. He confiscated so much noble land and so many fortunes that he governed without dependence on Parliament for royal funds, always a cornerstone of a strong monarchy. Henry thus began to shape a monarchy that would become one of early modern Europe's most exemplary governments during the reign of his granddaughter, Elizabeth I (r. 1558–1603).

Summary

Medieval Society In theory, medieval society was divided into three main groups: clergy (those who prayed), nobility (those who fought as mounted warriors), and laborers (peasants and artisans). The rise of merchants, self-governing towns, and universities helped break down this division. By supporting rulers against the nobility, towns gave kings the resources—money and university-trained bureaucrats and lawyers—to build national governments. Much of medieval history involved the struggle by rulers to assert their authority over powerful local lords and the church.

Church and State The medieval papacy sought to extend its power over both church and state. In the tenth century, the Cluny reform movement increased popular respect for the church and strengthened the papacy. In the Investiture Controversy, the papacy secured the independence of the clergy by enlisting the support of the German princes against the Holy Roman Emperors, thus weakening imperial power in Germany. The First Crusade further strengthened papal prestige. But by the end of the thirteenth century, kings had become more powerful than popes, and the French king, Philip the Fair, was able to defy the papacy. In the fourteenth century, the Great Schism further weakened papal prestige. Although it was able to fend off a movement to make church councils superior to popes, the papacy never recovered its authority over national rulers.

The Renaissance The Renaissance, which began in the Italian city-states in the late fourteenth century, marks the transition from the medieval to the modern world. Humanism, the scholarly study of the Greek and Latin classics and the ancient Church fathers, promoted a rebirth of ancient norms and values and the classical ideal of an educated, well-rounded person. The growth of secular values led to a great burst of artistic activity by artists such as da Vinci, Raphael, and Michelangelo. The political weakness of the Italian states invited foreign intervention by France, Spain, and the Habsburgs. The sack of Rome by imperial forces in 1527 marks the end of the Renaissance.

Nation Building By the fifteenth century, England, France, and Spain had developed into strong national monarchies with centralized bureaucracies and professional armies. Although medieval institutions, such as the English Parliament, in theory limited royal power, in practice monarchs in these countries held unchallenged authority. The Great Schism, the Hundred Years' War, and the Black Death had weakened the church and the nobility, while townspeople supported the kings. A similar process was beginning in Russia where the rulers of Moscow were extending their authority after throwing off Mongol rule. In the Empire, however, regional lords had defeated the emperors' attempts to build a strong central state.

Key Terms

Black Death (p. 445)	**Magna Carta** (p. 441)
chiaroscuro (p. 451)	**mannerism** (p. 452)
Crusades (p. 426)	**regular clergy** (p. 438)
Curia (p. 448)	**Renaissance** (p. 448)
Golden Horde (p. 455)	**Scholasticism** (p. 434)
Great Schism (p. 448)	**secular clergy** (p. 438)
guilds (p. 434)	***studia humanitatis*** (p. 449)
Holy Roman Empire (p. 448)	***taille*** (p. 447)
Humanism (p. 449)	**vernacular** (p. 425)

Review Questions

1. How do you account for the success of the Cluny reform movement? Can major features of the modern Catholic Church be found in the Cluny reforms?

2. Was the Investiture Controversy a political or a religious conflict? Summarize the respective arguments of Gregory VII and Henry IV. Is the conflict a precedent for the modern doctrine of the separation of church and state?

3. Why did Germany remain divided while France and England began to coalesce into reasonably strong states during the High Middle Ages?

4. How did the responsibilities of the nobility differ from those of the clergy and the peasantry during the High Middle Ages? How did each social class contribute to the stability of society?

Note: *To learn more about the topics in this chapter, please turn to the Suggested Readings at the end of the book. For additional sources related to this chapter please see MyHistoryLab.com.*

PEARSON
myhistorylab Connections

Reinforce what you learned in this chapter by studying the many documents,
images, maps, review tools, and videos available at **www.myhistorylab.com**.

Read and Review

✓●—[Study and Review   Chapter 15

●●—[Read the Document   *Expulsion Jews from France 12th
Century, p. 427*
Arab-Syrian Gentleman Discusses Franks, p. 428
The Magna Carta 1215, p. 430
*Issue of the Day: The Crusades - Political, Economical or
Religious?, p. 432*
Medieval Town Customs Town Chester England, p. 433
Abelard Defends Himself, p. 436
The Battle of Hastings1066, p. 440
Black Death 1349 Henry Knighton, p. 445
Peasant Revolt in England, p. 447
Unam Sanctam 1302 Pope Boniface VIII, p. 448
Letters to Cicero 14th century Petrarch, p. 450
Dante's Divine Comedy 1321 Dante, p. 450
The Prince 1519 Machiavelli, p. 453
Vladimir of Kiev's Acceptance of Christianity, p. 454

●—[See the Map   *The Crusades, p. 428*
The Major Crusades, p. 429
England and France ca 1180, p. 441
The Hundred Years War, p. 444
100 Years War, p. 444
Black Death and Peasant Revolts, p. 444
Empire and the Papacy in Italy, p. 453
Spain 1491, p. 456

●—[View the Image   *Da Vinci Mona Lisa, p. 451*
Michelangelo's David, p. 452

●—[Watch the Video   *The Art of El Greco, p. 452*

Research and Explore

●—[Watch the Video   *The Plague*

●—[See the Map   *Medieval Manor*

((●—[Hear the Audio

Hear the audio file for Chapter 15 at
www.myhistorylab.com.

16 | Europe, 1500–1650: Expansion, Reformation, and Religious Wars

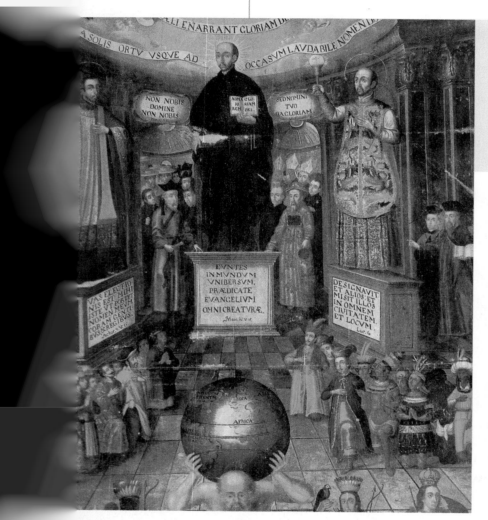

Allegory of the Jesuits and their missions in the four continents from the church of San Pedro, Lima, Peru. Anonymous painter (eighteenth century). St. Ignatius is flanked on his left by Francis Xavier, sporting a chasuble with Asian motifs. In the background, Jesuits living all over the world and occupying a variety of hierarchies within the church, including those wearing Chinese costumes and prelate robes, preside over the conversion of the faithful in India, China, Africa, and the Americas. Like Atlas, the Jesuits carry the globe on their shoulders.

- The Discovery of a New World
- The Reformation
- The Reformation's Achievements
- The Wars of Religion
- Superstition and Enlightenment: The Battle Within

IN THE SECOND DECADE OF THE SIXTEENTH CENTURY, a powerful religious movement began in Saxony in Germany and spread rapidly throughout northern Europe, deeply affecting society and politics as well as the spiritual lives of men and women. Attacking what they believed to be superstitions and corrupt practices that robbed people of both their money and their peace of mind, Protestant reformers led a revolt against the medieval church. In a short period of time, hundreds of thousands of people from all social classes set aside the beliefs of centuries and adopted a more simplified religious practice.

Protestants, more impressed by the human potential for evil than by the inclination to do good, encouraged parents, teachers, and magistrates to be firm disciplinarians. On the other hand, Protestants also embraced many Renaissance values, especially humanist educational reforms and the study of ancient languages. Here they found tools to master Scripture and challenge the papacy.

Protestantism was not the only reform movement to grow out of the grievances and reforms of the Late Middle Ages. Within the church itself a reform was emerging that would give birth to new religious orders, rebut Protestantism, and win back a great many of its converts.

As different groups identified their political and social goals with either Protestantism or Catholicism, 100 years of bloody opposition between Protestants and Catholics darkened the second half of the sixteenth century and the first half of the seventeenth. The political conflict that had previously been confined to central Europe and a struggle for Lutheran rights and freedoms then shifted to western Europe—to France, the Netherlands, England, and Scotland—and became a struggle for Calvinist recognition. In France, Calvinists fought Catholic rulers for the right to form their own communities, practice their chosen religion openly, and exclude from their lands those they deemed heretical. During the Thirty Years' War (1618–1648), international armies of varying religious persuasions clashed in central and northern Europe. By 1649 English Puritans had overthrown the Stuart monarchy and the Anglican Church.

For Europe the late fifteenth and the sixteenth centuries were years of unprecedented territorial expansion. Permanent colonies were established in the Americas, and the exploitation of the New World's human and mineral resources had begun. Imported American gold and silver spurred scientific invention and a new weapons industry. The new bullion helped create an international traffic in African slaves as rival tribes sold their captives to the Portuguese. Slaves came in ever-increasing numbers to work the mines and the plantations of the New World as replacements for faltering American natives. ■

The Discovery of a New World

The discovery of the Americas dramatically expanded the horizons of Europeans, both geographically and intellectually. Knowledge of the New World's inhabitants and exploitation of its mineral and human wealth set new cultural and economic forces in motion throughout western Europe. Beginning with the successful

((•• Hear the Audio
at **MyHistoryLab.com**

voyages of the Portuguese and Spanish in the fifteenth century, commercial supremacy progressively shifted from the Mediterranean and Baltic seas to the Atlantic seaboard, setting the stage for global expansion (see Map 16–1 on page 464).

The Portuguese Chart the Course

Seventy-seven years before Columbus, Prince Henry "the Navigator" (1394–1406), ruler of a strong and united Portugal, captured the West African Muslim city of Ceuta at the mouth of the Mediterranean Sea. There began the Portuguese exploration of the African coast, first in search of Guinea gold and slaves, and by century's end a sea route to Asia's spice markets (see Chapter 14). Topping the list of spices were pepper and cloves as they both preserved and enhanced the dull diet of most Europeans. Initially the catch of raiders, African slaves were taken by Portuguese traders in direct exchanges with tribal chiefs, who swapped their captured enemies for horses, corn, and finished goods (cloth and brassware). Over the second half of the fifteenth century, Portuguese ships delivered 150,000 slaves to Europe.

Before there was a sea route to the Orient, spices were obtained through the Venetians, who bought or bartered them from Eastern Muslim merchants. The Portuguese beat this Venetian-Mameluk (Turkish) monopoly by going

Christopher Columbus in old age (d. 1506) by Sebastiano del Piombo.

European Expansion

Europe

The Europeans turned to the Atlantic as a result of its weakness in the East where the Muslims dominated. However, a recovering Europe was now able to compete for access to valuable goods in eastern markets by navigating the high seas. In the late fifteenth and the sixteenth centuries, Europeans sailed far from their own shores to Africa, Southern and Eastern Asia, and the New World of the Americas. From Japan to Peru, they directly confronted civilizations other than their own and that of Islam, with which they already had contact in the form of trade and, more often, by force of arms. A major motivation for the voyages, which began with a reconnaissance of the West African coast, was to circumvent the Muslim monopoly on the movement of spices from the Indian Ocean into Europe, a grip that had only strengthened with the rise of the Ottomans. A wealthier, more self-confident Europe, now recovered from the great plague-induced population decline of the fourteenth century—its taste for Asian spices long since whetted during the Crusades—was ready to take those spices at their sources.

For much the same reasons (trade and self-aggrandizement), voyages of exploration also set forth from Ming China—especially between 1405 and 1433—reaching India, the Arabian Gulf, and East Africa. Had those voyages been followed up, they might have prevented Europeans from establishing a presence in the Indian Ocean. But the Chinese now faced both serious pressures on their northern and western borders and the problem of administrating a vast, multicultural empire stretching into Central Asia, where non-Chinese rivals had to be kept under control. Moreover, the dominant directly to the source by sea. Overland routes to India and China had become too difficult and unprofitable by the fifteenth century. The route by sea posed different obstacles and risks: fear of the unknown, making the first voyages of exploration slow and tentative. Venturing down the African coast, Portuguese square riggers were turned out into the deep ocean by cape after cape, and the farther out they sailed to round them, the greater the sailors' fear that they would not return home.

In addition to spice markets, the voyages sought allies against western Europe's archenemies, the Muslims. In 1455, a very self-interested pope gave the Portuguese explorers virtual carte blanche from the coast of Guinea to the Indies, granting them all the spoils of war: land, goods, and slaves. The church expected mass conversions in the wake of conquest, a Christian coup as well as mercantile advantage.

Bartholomew Dias pioneered the eastern Portuguese Empire after safely rounding the Cape of Good Hope at the tip of Africa in 1487. A decade later, in 1498, Vasco da Gama stood on the shores of India. When he returned to Portugal, he carried a cargo worth sixty times the cost of the voyage. Later, the Portuguese established successful colonies in Goa and Calcutta, whence they successfully challenged the Arabs and the Venetians for control of the European spice trade.

The Portuguese concentrated their explorations on the Indian Ocean. In their wake, the Spanish turned out into the Atlantic Ocean in search of a shorter route to the East Indies by sailing due West. But rather than beating the Portuguese to Asia, Columbus instead discovered the Americas.

The Spanish Voyages of Christopher Columbus

Thirty-three days after departing the Canary Islands, on October 12, 1492, Columbus landed in San Salvador (Watlings Island) in the eastern Bahamas. Thinking he was in the East Indies, he mistook his first landfall as an outer island of Japan. The error was understandable given the information he relied on: Marco Polo's thirteenth-century account of his years in China and Nuremberg mapmaker Martin Behaim's spherical map of the presumed world. That map showed nothing but ocean between the west coast of Europe and the east coast of Asia, with Cipangu, or Japan, in between (see Map 16–2 on page 465).

Naked and extremely friendly natives met Columbus and his crew on the beaches of the New World. They were Taino Indians, who spoke a variant of a language known as Arawak. Believing the island on which he

Neo-Confucian philosophy espoused by the scholar-bureaucrats in the imperial court disdained merchants and commerce, extolling instead a peasant agrarian economy.

These factors led the Chinese to turn inward and abandon overseas trade and exploration precisely at the moment when Europeans were exploring the coast of Africa on their way to the Indian Ocean. It was a fateful choice because it meant that the Asian power best able to resist the establishment of European commercial and colonial empires in the Indian Ocean had abdicated that role, leaving a vacuum of power for Europeans to fill. Still, Chinese merchants continued to ply ocean trade routes and settle as far from home as the Philippines and, in later centuries, the west coasts of North and South America. Wherever there was commerce in Chinese goods, there were Chinese merchants, albeit now operating without support from their government.

Although parallels may be drawn between the court culture of the Forbidden Palace in Beijing and that of King Louis XIV in seventeenth-century France, the Chinese government, with its philosophy of Confucianism, remained more unified and patriarchal than its counterparts in the West. At first the Chinese tolerated other religions, warmly embracing Jesuit missionaries, doing so in part because political power in China was not bound to a particular religion. The Japanese, too, were admirers of the Jesuits, who arrived in Japan with the Portuguese in 1543. The admiration was mutual, leading to 300,000 Christian converts by 1600. Tolerance of Christianity did not last as long in Japan as in China. Hideyoshi, in his drive for internal unity, banned Christianity in the late sixteenth century. Nonetheless, China and Japan, as well as many Islamic societies, including the Ottomans and the Mughals, demonstrated more tolerance for foreign religions, such as Christianity, than did the West for Islam or for Asian religious traditions.

Focus Questions

- Why did Europeans launch voyages of exploration in the fifteenth and sixteenth centuries? What role did the Crusades and the rise of the Ottoman Empire play in this enterprise?
- Why did the Chinese voyages of exploration under the Ming come to a halt? What were the consequences for world history?
- What was the biological impact of the European discovery of America?

landed to be the East Indies, Columbus called the natives Indians. The natives' generosity amazed Columbus, as they freely gave his men all the corn and yams they desired, along with sexual favors. "They never say no," Columbus marveled, as he observed how easily they could be enslaved by the Spanish.

On the heels of Columbus, Amerigo Vespucci (1451–1512), after whom America is named, and Ferdinand Magellan (1480–1521) carefully explored the coastline of South America. Their travels proved that the new lands discovered by Columbus were not the outermost territory of the Far East, but an entirely unknown continent that opened on the still greater Pacific Ocean.

Impact on Europe and America

Columbus's first voyage marked the beginning of more than three centuries of Spanish conquest, exploitation, and administration of a vast American Empire. What began as voyages of discovery became expeditions of conquest similar to the warfare Christian Aragón and Castile waged against Islamic Moors.

The voyages to the New World had important consequences for both Europe and America. They created Europe's largest trading bloc and spurred other European countries to undertake colonial ventures. The wealth extracted from its American possessions financed Spain's commanding role in the sixteenth century, while fueling a European-wide economic expansion.

European expansion also had a profound biological impact. Europeans introduced numerous species of fruits, vegetables, and animals from Europe into the Americas, and vice versa. European expansion also led to a spread of European diseases. Vast numbers of indigenous American peoples died from measles and smallpox, which broke out in massive epidemics among populations with no natural or acquired immunity. (See the discussion of the "Columbian Exchange" in Chapter 17.)

The voyages also began a long period of conquest during which native populations were also devastated by warfare and slave labor. In both South and North America, Spanish rule left a lasting footprint of Roman Catholicism, economic dependency, and hierarchical social structure.

The Reformation

The **Reformation** was a sixteenth-century religious movement that sought to reform the church. It led to the establishment of Protestantism and the religious division of Western Christendom.

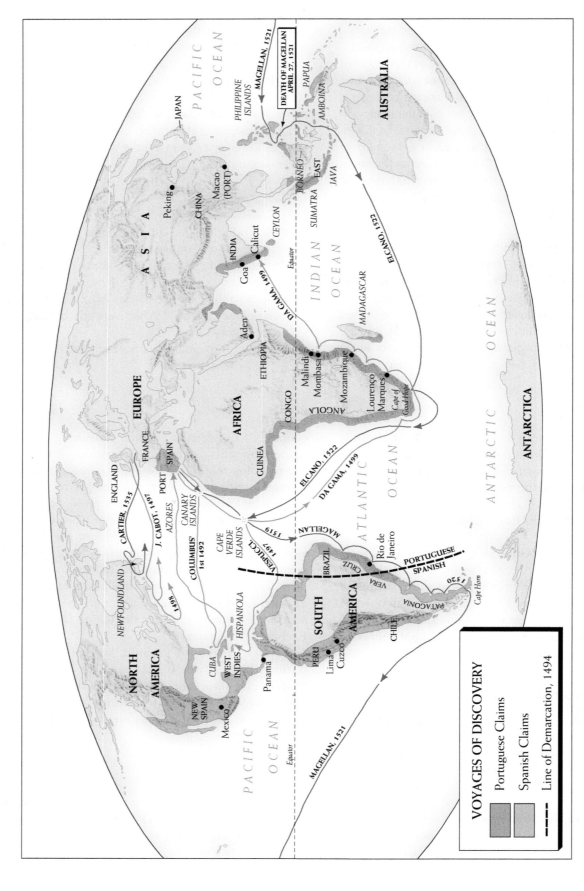

Map 16–1. European Voyages of Discovery and the Colonial Claims of Spain and Portugal in the Fifteenth and Sixteenth Centuries. The map dramatizes Europe's global expansion in the fifteenth and sixteenth centuries.

VOYAGES OF DISCOVERY

Portuguese Claims
Spanish Claims
Line of Demarcation, 1494

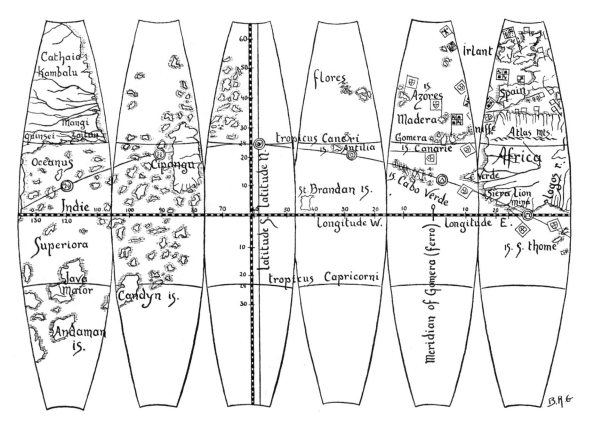

Map 16–2 Martin Behaim's "Globe Apple." What Columbus knew of the world in 1492 was contained in this map by Nuremberg geographer Martin Behaim (1440–1507), creator of the first spherical globe of the earth. The ocean section of Behaim's globe is reproduced here. Departing the Canary Islands (in the second section from the right), Columbus expected his first major landfall to be Japan, or what he calls Cipangu (in the second section from the left). When he landed at San Salvador, he thought he was on an outer island of Japan; after reaching Cuba, he believed it to be Japan. Only slowly did it dawn on him that these new lands had never before been seen by Europeans. *From Admiral of the Ocean Sea by Samuel Eliot Morison. Copyright © 1942, renewed 1970 by Samuel Eliot Morison. By permission of Little, Brown, and Company.*

Religion and Society

The Reformation first broke out in the free imperial cities of Germany and Switzerland. There were sixty-five such cities, and each was a small kingdom unto itself. Most had Protestant movements. Some turned Protestant and remained so, while others developed mixed confessions that allowed Catholics and Protestants to coexist.

Certain groups favored the Reformation more than others. In many places, trade guilds were in the forefront of the Reformation. Evidence suggests that people who felt bullied by either local or distant authority—a guild by an autocratic local government, a city by a prince or king—saw in the Protestant movement an ally.

Social and political experience thus coalesced with the larger religious issues in both town and countryside. When Martin Luther wrote, preached, and sang about a priesthood of all believers and ridiculed papal laws as arbitrary human inventions, they touched political as well as religious nerves in German and Swiss cities.

Popular Movements and Criticism of the Church

The Protestant Reformation could not have occurred without the monumental crises of the late medieval church and the Renaissance papacy. Laity and clerics alike began to seek a more heartfelt, idealistic religious piety. The Late Middle Ages saw independent lay and clerical efforts to reform local religious practice.

A variety of factors contributed to lay criticism of the church. The laity in the cities were becoming increasingly knowledgeable about the world and those who controlled their lives. They traveled widely—as soldiers, pilgrims, explorers, and traders. New postal systems and the printing

The Gutenberg Bible. Print and Protestantism would drive the history of the sixteenth century. Well established by the mid-fifteenth century, the printing press made possible the diffusion of both secular and religious learning. In addition to humanistic scholarship, print also served the educational and propaganda campaigns of princes and religious reformers, increasing literacy in both Latin and vernacular languages. Among the printed works preparing the way, none was more stimulating than Gutenberg's Latin Bible. In the mid-1520s Martin Luther made separate German translations of the New and the Old Testaments, which henceforth would become the battering rams of the Protestant Reformation.

press increased the information at their disposal. The new age of books and libraries raised literacy and heightened lay curiosity, confidence, and criticism.

Secular Control over Religious Life

On the eve of the Reformation, Rome's international network of church offices began to fall apart in many areas, hurried along by a growing sense of regional identity—incipient nationalism—and local secular administrative competence. Rare was the late medieval German town that did not have complaints about the maladministration, concubinage, or fiscalism of its clergy, especially the higher clergy (bishops, abbots, and prelates).

City governments also sought to restrict the growth of ecclesiastical properties and clerical privileges and to improve local religious life by bringing the clergy under the local tax code and by endowing new clerical positions for well-trained and conscientious preachers.

The Northern Renaissance

The scholarly works of northern humanists created a climate favorable to religious and educational reforms. These scholars tended to come from more diverse social backgrounds and to be more devoted to religious reforms and new lay freedoms than were their Italian counterparts.

The growth of schools and lay education combined with the invention of cheap paper to create a mass audience for printed books. In response, Johann Gutenberg (d. 1468) invented printing with movable type in the German city of Mainz around 1450. Thereafter, books were rapidly and handsomely produced on topics both profound and practical. By 1500, printing presses operated in at least 60 German cities and in more than 200 throughout Europe. A new medium now existed for politicians, humanists, and reformers alike.

● View the Image
Early Print Shop
at **MyHistoryLab.com**

The Electoral Princes of Saxony, by Lucas Cranach the Elder (ca. 1532). The three princes Luther served were Frederick the Wise, John the Constant, and John Frederick the Magnanimous.

The most famous of the northern humanists was Desiderius Erasmus (1466–1536), the "prince of the humanists." Idealistic and pacifistic, Erasmus gained fame as both an educational and a religious reformer. He aspired to unite the classical ideals of humanity and civic virtue with the Christian ideals of love and piety. He believed that disciplined study of the classics and the Bible, if begun early enough, was the best way to reform both individuals and society. He summarized his own beliefs with the phrase *philosophia Christi*, a simple, ethical piety in imitation of Christ. He set this ideal against what he believed to be the dogmatic, ceremonial, and factious religious practice of the Late Middle Ages. To promote his own religious beliefs, Erasmus edited the works of the Church Fathers and made a Greek edition of the New Testament (1516), which became the basis for a new, more accurate Latin translation (1519). Martin Luther later used both of these works as the basis for his famous German translation.

Whereas in Germany, England, and France, humanism helped the Protestants, in Spain it entered the service of the Catholic Church. Here the key figure was Francisco Jiménez de Cisneros (1437–1517), a confessor to Queen Isabella, and after 1508 Grand Inquisitor—a position from which he was able to enforce the strictest religious orthodoxy. Jiménez was a conduit for humanist scholarship and learning. He founded the University of Alcalá near Madrid in 1509, printed a Greek edition of the New Testament, and translated many religious tracts that aided clerical reform and control of lay religious life. His greatest achievement, taking fifteen years to complete, was the Complutensian Polyglot Bible, a six-volume work that placed the Hebrew, Greek, and Latin versions of the Bible in parallel columns.

Martin Luther and German Reformation to 1525

Unlike France and England, late medieval Germany lacked the political unity to enforce "national" religious reforms during the Late Middle Ages. There were neither lasting Statutes of Provisors and Praemunire, as in England, nor a Pragmatic Sanction of Bourges, as in France, both limiting papal jurisdiction and taxation on a national scale. What happened on a unified national level in England and France occurred only locally and piecemeal within German territories and towns. As popular resentment of clerical immunities and ecclesiastical abuses spread among German cities and towns, opposition to Rome formed. By 1517 it was pervasive enough to provide a solid foundation for Martin Luther's reform.

●—View the Image
Martin Luther
at **MyHistoryLab.com**

Luther (1483–1546), the son of a successful Thüringian miner, was educated in Mansfeld, Magdeburg (where the Brothers of the Common Life were his teachers), and Eisenach. Between 1501 and 1505 he attended the University of Erfurt, where the nominalist teachings of William of Ockham and Gabriel Biel (d. 1495) prevailed. After receiving his master of arts degree in 1505, Luther registered with the law faculty, following his parents' wishes, but he never began the study of law. To the disappointment of his family, he instead entered the Order of the Hermits of Saint Augustine in Erfurt on July 17, 1505.

Ordained in 1507, Luther pursued a traditional course of study. By 1511, he moved to the Augustinian monastery in Wittenberg, where he earned his doctorate in theology in 1512. Thereafter, he became a leader within the monastery, the new university, and the spiritual life of the city.

Justification by Faith Alone Reformation theology grew out of a problem that was then common to many clergy and laity: the failure of traditional medieval religion to provide either full personal or intellectual satisfaction. Luther was especially plagued by the disproportion between his own sense of sinfulness and the perfect righteousness that God required for salvation. Traditional church teaching and the sacrament of penance proved no consolation. Luther wrote that he came to despise the phrase "righteousness of God," for it seemed to demand of him a perfection he knew neither he nor any other human being could ever achieve. His insight into the meaning of "justification by faith alone" was a gradual process that extended between 1513 and 1518. The righteousness that God demands, he concluded, did not result from many religious works and ceremonies, but was given in full measure to those who believed and trusted in Jesus Christ.

The Attack on Indulgences An **indulgence** was a remission of the penalty imposed by priests on penitents as a "work of satisfaction" for mortal sins. According to medieval theology, after the priest absolved a penitent's guilt, the penitent still remained under an eternal penalty, a punishment God justly imposed for sin. Once absolved, however, that eternal penalty was reduced to a manageable "work of satisfaction" that the penitent might perform here and now (for example, through prayers, fasting, almsgiving, retreats, and pilgrimages). Penitents who defaulted on such prescribed works of satisfaction later suffered for them in purgatory.

At this point, indulgences, which had earlier been given to Crusaders who did not complete their penances because they had fallen in battle, became an aid to laity, made genuinely anxious by their belief in a future suffering in purgatory for neglected penances or unrepented sins. In 1343, Pope Clement VI (r. 1342–1352) had proclaimed the existence of a "treasury of merit," an infinite reservoir of good works in the church's possession that could be dispensed at the pope's discretion. On the basis of this treasury, the church sold "letters of indulgence," which covered the works of satisfaction owed by penitents. In 1476, Pope Sixtus IV (r. 1471–1484) extended indulgences also to sinners in purgatory.

Originally, indulgences had been given for a true self-sacrifice, such as for going on a Crusade to the Holy Land. By Luther's time, they were regularly dispensed for small cash payments. They were presented to the laity as remitting not only their future punishments, but also those of their dead relatives presumed to be stranded in purgatory.

●◦●▬[Read the Document
Erasmus Julius Excluded Heaven
at **MyHistoryLab.com** In 1517, Pope Leo X (r. 1513–1521) revived a plenary Jubilee Indulgence that had first been issued by Pope Julius II (r. 1503–1513), whose proceeds were to be used to rebuild St. Peter's Basilica in Rome. Such an indulgence promised forgiveness of all outstanding unrepented sins upon completion of certain acts. Such indulgences were preached on the borders of Saxony in the territories of the future Archbishop Albrecht of Mainz, who was much in need of revenues because of the large debts he had incurred in order to hold three ecclesiastical appointments simultaneously. The selling of the indulgence was a joint venture by Albrecht, the Augsburg banking house of Fugger, and Pope Leo X, with half the proceeds going to the pope and half to Albrecht and his creditors. The famous indulgence preacher John Tetzel (d. 1519) was enlisted to preach the indulgence in Albrecht's territories because he was a seasoned professional who knew how to stir ordinary people to action. As he exhorted on one occasion:

> *Don't you hear the voices of your dead parents and other relatives crying out, "Have mercy on us, for we suffer great punishment and pain. From this you could release us with a few alms. . . . We have created you, fed you, cared for you, and left you our temporal goods. Why do you treat us so cruelly and leave us to suffer in the flames, when it takes only a little to save us?"*[1]

When Luther, according to tradition, posted his ninety-five theses against indulgences on the door of Castle Church in Wittenberg, on October 31, 1517, he protested the impression that indulgences actually remitted sins and released the dead from punishment in purgatory. Luther believed such claims turned salvation into something that could be bought and sold.

Election of Charles V Luther's **ninety-five theses** made him famous overnight. They were embraced by humanists and other proponents of reform, but they prompted official proceedings against him. In October, he was called before the general of the Dominican order in Augsburg. As sanctions were being prepared against Luther, Emperor Maxim-

---

[1] *Die Reformation in Augenzeugen Berichten*, ed. by Helmar Junghans (Dusseldorf: Karl Rauch Verlag, 1967), p. 44.

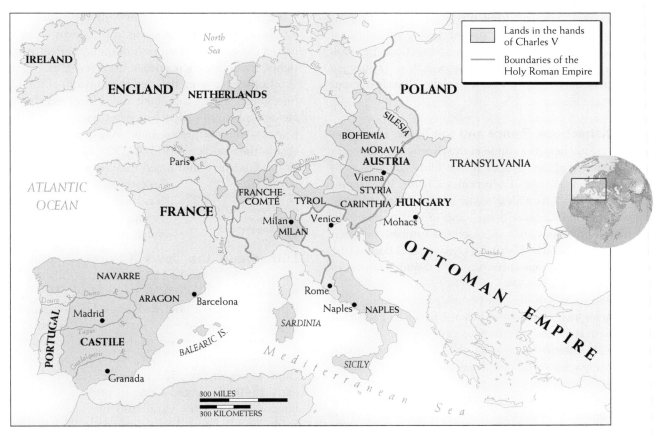

Map 16–3. The Empire of Charles V. Dynastic marriages and good fortune concentrated into Charles's hands rule over the lands shown here, plus Spain's overseas possessions. Crowns and titles rained down on him; election in 1519 as emperor gave him new burdens and responsibilities.

ilian I died (January 12, 1519), and this event, fortunately for the Reformation, turned attention away from heresy in Saxony to the contest for a new emperor.

The pope backed the French king, Francis I. However, the Hapsburg Charles I of Spain, a youth of 19, easily succeeded his grandfather as Emperor Charles V. (See Map 16–3.)

Read the Document

Martin Luther's Ninety-Five Theses 1517 at **MyHistoryLab.com**

Luther's Excommunication and the Diet of Worms

In the same month in which Charles was elected emperor, Luther entered a debate in Leipzig (June 27, 1519) with the Ingolstadt professor John Eck. Luther challenged the infallibility of the pope and the inerrancy of church councils, appealing for the first time to the sole authority of Scripture alone. He then burned all his bridges to the old church by defending the teaching of John Huss, a heretic condemned and executed by Rome.

In 1520, Luther described the pillars of his reform in three pamphlets. (1) The *Address to the Christian Nobility of the German Nation* urged the German princes to force re-forms on the Roman church, especially to curtail its political and economic power in Germany. Here, Luther also famously declared "all Christians to be of the same estate," by which he meant one Christian people under God's law and grace"—a strictly spiritual equality that the leaders of later peasant revolts willfully interpreted as social and political equality. (2) The *Babylonian Captivity of the Church* reduced the seven sacraments of the church to two, baptism and the Eucharist, and exalted the authority of Scripture, church councils, and secular princes over that of the pope. (3) The *Freedom of a Christian* summarized the new theology for the laity, describing a "happy union" between the soul and Christ by faith alone, in which everything the soul had (sin, death, and damnation) became Christ's and everything Christ had (purity, life, and heaven) became the believer's.

In April 1521, Luther defended his religious teaching before the imperial **Diet of Worms**, over which newly elected Emperor Charles V presided. Ordered to recant, Luther declared that he could not act against Scripture, reason, and his own conscience. On May 26, 1521, he was declared an "outlaw" to secular as well as religious authority and placed under the imperial ban. For his own protection, he took refuge in Wartburg Castle in Thuringia where he spent almost a year translating the New Testament into German.

Imperial Distractions: France and the Turks The Reformation was greatly helped in these early years by the emperor's war with France and the advance of the Ottoman Turks into eastern Germany. Against both adversaries Charles V, who also remained a Spanish king with dynastic responsibilities outside the empire, needed German troops, and to that end he promoted friendly relations with the German princes. Between 1521 and 1559, Spain (the Habsburg Dynasty) and France (the Valois Dynasty) fought four major wars over disputed territories in Italy and along their borders.

Thus preoccupied, the emperor agreed through his representatives at the German Diet of Speyer in 1526 that each German territory was free to enforce the Edict of Worms (1521) against Luther "so as to be able to answer in good conscience to God and the emperor." That concession, in effect, gave the German princes territorial sovereignty in religious matters and the Reformation time to put down deep roots.

How the Reformation Spread In the late 1520s and on into the 1530s, the Reformation passed from the hands of the theologians and pamphleteers into those of the magistrates and princes. In many cities, the magistrates followed the lead of Protestant preachers in mandating the religious reform. In numerous instances, magistrates had themselves worked for decades to bring about basic church reforms. Reform now ceased to be slogans and became laws all townspeople had to obey. The religious reform thus became a territorial political movement led by the German princes. Soon they, too, were pushing Protestant faith and politics onto their neighbors. By the 1530s, Protestant cities and lands formed powerful defensive alliances as they prepared for war with the Catholic emperor.

The Peasants' Revolt In its first decade, the Protestant movement suffered more from internal division than from imperial interference. By 1525, Luther was as much an object of protest within Germany as was the pope. Like the German humanists, the German peasantry had believed Luther to be an ally. Since the late fifteenth century, the peasantry had been organized against the territorial princes who were overriding traditional peasant laws and customs and were attempting to subject them to new regulations and

taxes. Peasant leaders saw in Luther's gospel of Christian freedom a point of view close to their own. They openly solicited the reformer's support of their political and economic rights, including their release from serfdom.

Luther, however, believed the freedom of the Christian to be an inner release from guilt and anxiety, not the right to create an egalitarian society by violent revolution, as the German peasants misinterpreted him. When the peasants revolted against their landlords in 1524–1525, Luther condemned them as "un-Christian" and urged the princes to crush their revolt.

An estimated 70,000 to 100,000 peasants died by the time the revolt was put down. Had Luther joined them, he would have been among them.

Luther and the Jews Also controversial is Luther's stand on the Jews. In 1523, he had published a pamphlet entitled "Jesus Christ Was Born a Jew." Therein, he urged Christians to be kinder and gentler to German Jews in the hope that "some" or even "many" might assimilate to Christian society and convert to the new reformed Christianity. The Jews, however, did not come his way, and Luther soon came to regret his 1523 pamphlet. In the late 1530s and early 1540s, he urged German princes forcibly to remove nonconverting Jews to a land of their own, as France, Spain, and Bohemia had already done. Although far short of making Judaism a capital crime, as imperial law had done with Anabaptism in 1529, Luther's proposals ran along a similar line: assimilation or exile.

Execution of a Peasant Leader. The punishment of a peasant leader in a village near Heilbronn. After the defeat of rebellious peasants in and around the city of Heilbronn, Jacob Rorbach, a well-to-do peasant leader from a nearby village, was tied to a stake and slowly roasted to death. © *Badische Landesbibliothek.*

Document

German Peasants Protest Rising Feudal Exactions

In the late fifteenth and early sixteenth centuries, German feudal lords, both secular and ecclesiastical, tried to increase the earnings from their lands by raising demands on their peasant tenants. As the lords restricted the traditional freedoms and property rights of peasants, massive revolts occurred in southern Germany in 1525. The following, representative statement of peasant grievances, summarized in twelve articles, came from the town of Memmingen.

■ *Are the peasants more interested in material than in spiritual freedom? Which of their demands are the most revolutionary, and which are the least problematic for their lords to grant? Why do some centuries exhibit greater social and political equality than others?*

1. It is our humble petition and desire that in the future each community should choose and appoint a pastor, and that we should have the right to depose him should he conduct himself improperly. . . .

2. We are ready and willing to pay the fair tithe of grain. . . . The small tithes [of cattle], whether [to] ecclesiastical or lay lords, we will not pay at all, for the Lord God created cattle for the free use of man. . . .

3. We . . . take it for granted that you will release us from serfdom as true Christians, unless it should be shown us from the Gospel that we are serfs.

4. It has been the custom heretofore that no poor man should be allowed to catch venison or wildfowl or fish in flowing water, which seems to us quite unseemly and unbrotherly as well as selfish and not agreeable to the Word of God. . . .

5. We are aggrieved in the matter of woodcutting, for the noblemen have appropriated all the woods to themselves. . . .

6. In regard to the excessive services demanded of us which are increased from day to day, we ask that this matter be properly looked into so that we shall not continue to be oppressed in this way. . . .

7. We will not hereafter allow ourselves to be further oppressed by our lords, but will let them demand only what is just and proper according to the word of the agreement between the lord and the peasant. The lord should no longer try to force more services or other dues from the peasant without payment. . . .

8. We are greatly burdened because our holdings cannot support the rent exacted from them. . . . We ask that the lords may appoint persons of honor to inspect these holdings and fix a rent in accordance with justice. . . .

9. We are burdened with a great evil in the constant making of new laws. . . . In our opinion we should be judged according to the old written law. . . .

10. We are aggrieved by the appropriation . . . of meadows and fields which at one time belonged to a community as a whole. These we will take again into our own hands. . . .

11. We will entirely abolish the due called Todfall [that is, *heriot* or *death tax*, by which the lord received the best horse, cow, or garment of a family upon the death of a serf] and will no longer endure it, nor allow widows and orphans to be thus shamefully robbed against God's will, and in violation of justice and right. . . .

12. It is our conclusion and final resolution, that if any one or more of the articles here set forth should not be in agreement with the Word of God, as we think they are, such article we will willingly retract.

Source: Translations and Reprints from the Original Sources of European History, Vol. 2 (Philadelphia: Department of History, University of Pennsylvania, 1897).

Zwingli and the Swiss Reformation

Although Luther's was the first, Switzerland and France had their own independent reform movements almost simultaneously with Germany's. Switzerland was a loose confederacy of thirteen autonomous cantons or states. Some became Protestant, some remained Catholic, and a few managed to effect a compromise. The two preconditions of the Swiss Reformation were the growth of national sentiment and a desire for church reform.

The Reformation in Zurich Ulrich Zwingli (1484–1531), the leader of the Swiss Reformation, was the people's priest in Zurich. His reform guideline was simple and effective: Whatever lacked literal support in Scripture was to be neither believed nor practiced by Christians. After a public disputation in January 1523, based on that Scripture test, Zurich became a Protestant city and the center of the Swiss Reformation. Its harsh discipline in pursuit of its religious ideals made it one of the first examples of a "puritanical" Protestant city.

See the Map
The Swiss Confederation
at **MyHistoryLab.com**

The Marburg Colloquy Landgrave Philip of Hesse (1504–1567) sought to unite Swiss and German Protestants in a mutual defense pact, a potentially significant political alliance. His efforts were spoiled, however, by theological disagreements between Luther and Zwingli over the nature of Christ's presence in the Eucharist. Zwingli interpreted Christ's words, "This is my body," to be symbolic, not literal. Christ, he argued, was only spiritually, not bodily, present in the bread and wine of the Eucharist. Luther, to the contrary, insisted that Christ's human nature shared the properties of his divine nature; hence, where Christ was spiritually present, he was also truly present as well, this because of his special nature as man and God. This was not the Eucharistic miracle of **transubstantiation**, as Rome taught it, but **consubstantiation**: Christ's body and blood being one with, but not of, the bread and wine of the Eucharist, thus fulfilling Christ's biblical promise that he would be truly present to faith whenever the Eucharistic meal was served.

In early October Philip of Hesse brought the two Protestant leaders together in his castle in Marburg hoping to work out their differences, only to see Luther leave thinking Zwingli was a dangerous fanatic. The disagreement splintered the Protestant movement and weakened it theologically, politically, and militarily.

Anabaptists and Radical Protestants

The moderate pace and small ethical results of the Lutheran and Zwinglian reformations discontented many who had desired a more rapid and thorough implementation of primitive Christianity. The most important of these groups were the Anabaptists, the sixteenth-century ancestors of the modern-day Mennonites and Amish. They distinguished themselves by replacing infant baptism with adult baptism in imitation of Jesus (*Anabaptism* derives from the Greek word meaning "to rebaptize").

Anabaptists also physically separated from established society to form their own communities in imitation of the first Christians. Because of the sacred unity of religious and civic life, the political authorities viewed the Anabaptists' renunciation of so many centuries of respected church practice as a clear and present threat to basic social bonds and the Christian gospel.

In 1529 rebaptism became a capital offense throughout the Holy Roman Empire. Between 1525 and 1618, 1,000 to 5,000 Anabaptists are estimated to have been executed for rebaptizing themselves as adults.

View the Image
Anabaptist Torture in Muenster
at **MyHistoryLab.com**

John Calvin and the Genevan Reformation

Calvinism was the religious ideology that inspired and accompanied massive political resistance in France, the Netherlands, and Scotland. Believing in both divine predestination and the individual's responsibility to create a godly society, Calvinists became zealous reformers. In a famous and controversial study, *The Protestant Ethic and the Spirit of Capitalism* (1904), the German sociologist Max Weber argued that this

Christ Blessing the Children, by Lucas Cranach the Elder (1538). This novel painting was a Lutheran protest against the Anabaptists, who refused to recognize the efficacy of infant baptism. Appealing to the example of Jesus, who had been baptized as an adult, Anabaptists (the name means "rebaptism") disavowed their infant baptism and sought another when they were old enough to grasp what it meant. Here, Jesus joins a throng of new mothers to caress, kiss, and commend their babies to God. After 1529, Anabaptism became a capital offense in the Holy Roman Empire.

combination of religious confidence and self-disciplined activism produced an ethic congenial to emergent capitalism, bringing Calvinism and later Puritanism into close association with the development of modern capitalist societies, a religion determined to restructure societies as well as to save souls.

Political Revolt and Religious Reform in Geneva

Whereas in Saxony religious reform paved the way for a political revolution against the emperor, in Geneva a political revolution against a local prince-bishop laid the foundation for religious change. In late 1533 the Protestant city of Bern sent Protestant reformers to Geneva, and by the summer of 1535, they had triumphed. On May 21, 1536, the city was exhorted "to live according to the Gospel and the Word of God . . . without . . . any more masses, statues, idols, or other papal abuses."

John Calvin (1509–1564), a reform-minded humanist and lawyer, arrived in Geneva in July 1536, after these events. He was persuaded to stay on and assist the Reformation. Before a year had passed, he had drawn up articles for the governance of the new church, as well as a catechism to guide and discipline the people. These strong measures made many suspect that the reformers were out to create a "new papacy," and later, in February 1538, they were exiled from the city.

Read the Document
Calvin Ecclesiastical Ordinances at **MyHistoryLab.com**

Calvin went to Strasbourg, a model Protestant city, to pastor the French exiles. During his Strasbourg stay, he wrote biblical commentaries and published a second edition of his *Institutes of the Christian Religion*, considered the definitive theological statement of the Protestant belief.

Calvin's Geneva

In 1540 Geneva elected officials favorable to Calvin, and he was invited to return. Within months of his arrival, new ecclesiastical ordinances allowed the magistrates and the clergy to cooperate in matters of discipline.

Calvin and his followers were motivated above all by a desire to make society godly. The "elect," Calvin taught, should live a manifestly God-pleasing life, if they were truly God's elect. The consistory, a judicial body composed of clergy and laity, became his instrument of power. It enforced the strictest moral discipline and meted out harsh punishments for moral and religious transgressions.

After 1555 the city's magistrates were all devout Calvinists, and Geneva became the home to thousands of exiled Protestants who had been driven out of France, England, and Scotland. Refugees—more than 5,000 strong—now made up over one-third of the population of Geneva, greatly strengthening the reformers' position in the city.

Two "liberal thinkers" who challenged Calvin's theology of predestination and the bondage of the will were Michael Servetus (1511–1553), a physician and Unitarian, and Jacobus

A Portrait of the Young John Calvin. *Bibliothèque Publique et Universitaire, Geneva.*

Read the Document
Calvin on Predestination 16th century at **MyHistoryLab.com**

Arminius (1560–1609), a Dutch theologian. Servetus, who had long ridiculed Calvin by mail, visited Geneva in person, there to be apprehended and executed with Calvin's blessing for alleged blasphemy against the Holy Trinity.

Political Consolidation of the Lutheran Reformation

In the 1530s German Lutherans formed regional consistories, which oversaw and administered the new Protestant churches. These consistories replaced the old Catholic episcopates. Under the leadership of Philip Melanchthon (1497–1560), educational reforms established compulsory primary education, schools for girls, a humanist revision of the school curriculum, and catechetical instruction of the laity in the new religion.

The Reformation also dug in elsewhere. Introduced into Denmark by Christian II (r. 1513–1523), Lutheranism became the state religion under Christian III (r. 1536–1559). In Sweden, Gustavus Vasa (r. 1523–1560) confiscated church property and subjected the clergy to royal authority (1527). In politically splintered Poland, Lutherans, Calvinists, and others found room to practice their beliefs. The absence of a central political authority made Poland a model of religious pluralism and toleration in the second half of the sixteenth century.

Chronology

Progress of Protestant Reformation on the Continent

1517	Luther posts ninety-five theses against indulgences
1519	Charles I of Spain elected Holy Roman emperor (as Charles V)
1519	Luther challenges infallibility of pope and inerrancy of church councils at Leipzig Debate
1521	Papal bull excommunicates Luther for heresy
1521	Diet of Worms condemns Luther
1521–1522	Luther translates the New Testament into German
1524–1525	Peasants' Revolt in Germany
1529	Marburg Colloquy between Luther and Zwingli
1530	Diet of Augsburg fails to settle religious differences
1531	Formation of Protestant Schmalkaldic League
1536	Calvin arrives in Geneva
1540	Jesuits, founded by Ignatius of Loyola, recognized as order by pope
1545–1563	Council of Trent institutes reforms and responds to the Reformation
1546	Luther dies
1547	Armies of Charles V crush Schmalkaldic League
1555	Peace of Augsburg recognizes rights of Lutherans to worship as they please

Reaction against Protestants: The "Interim"
Emperor Charles V made abortive efforts in 1540–1541 to enforce a compromise between Protestants and Catholics. As these efforts failed, he crushed the Protestant Schmalkaldic League in 1547. The Schmalkaldic League was formed in 1531 as a defensive league consisting of Lutheran Saxony and Hesse against the Imperial army, which beseiged and occupied Wittenberg in 1547, the year after Martin Luther's death. The emperor then established puppet rulers in Saxony and Hesse and issued as imperial law the Augsburg Interim, an order demanding Protestants everywhere to readopt Catholic beliefs and practices. Fortunately for Protestants, the Reformation was too entrenched by 1547 to be ended even by brute force. Confronted by fierce Protestant resistance and weary from three decades of war, the emperor relented.

The Peace of Augsburg in September 1555 made the division of Christendom permanent. It enforced in law what had already been established in practice: *cuius regio, eius religio*, "his kingdom, his religion," meaning that the ruler of a land would henceforth determine its religion. Under this edict, Lutherans were permitted to retain all church lands forcibly seized before 1552.

The Peace of Augsburg did not recognize Calvinism as a legal form of Christian belief and practice. This made the Calvinists all the more determined not only to secure the right to worship publicly as they pleased, but also to shape society according to their own religious convictions. They now took the lead in organizing national revolutions throughout northern Europe.

The English Reformation to 1553

Late medieval England had a well-earned reputation for defending the rights of the Crown against the pope. It was, however, the unhappy marriage of King Henry VIII (r. 1509–1547) that ensured the success of the English protest against the church.

The King's Affair Henry married Catherine of Aragón (d. 1536), a daughter of Ferdinand and Isabella of Spain and the aunt of Emperor Charles V, in 1509. By 1527 the union had produced only a single surviving child, a daughter, Mary. People at this time believed it unnatural for women to rule over men, and Henry was justifiably concerned about the political consequences of leaving behind only a female heir. At best, a woman ruler meant a contested reign, at worst, turmoil and revolution. Henry came to believe that his union with Catherine, who had numerous miscarriages and stillbirths, had been cursed by God because Catherine had briefly been the wife of his late brother, Arthur.

By 1527 Henry was thoroughly enamored of Anne Boleyn (ca. 1504–1536), one of Catherine's ladies in waiting, and determined to put Catherine aside and marry Anne. This he could not do, however, in Catholic England without a papal annulment of his marriage to Catherine. Therein lay a grave problem for the English king. Not only had eighteen years of marriage passed with little offspring, but also in 1527 the reigning pope, Clement VII (r. 1523–1534), was a prisoner of Emperor Charles V, Catherine's nephew. The pope could hardly annul a marriage that had been created by a papal dispensation in the first place, nor did he want to see his aunt dismissed by the English king.

These difficulties did not, however, discourage the king from pursuing a divorce against all odds. After Cardinal Wolsey (1475–1530), Lord Chancellor of England since 1515, failed to secure the papal annulment, Henry turned to his heavy-handed ministers, Thomas Cranmer (1489–1556) and Thomas Cromwell (1485–1540), to find a way out. Both harbored Lutheran sympathies, and neither was squeamish. Finding the way to a papal annulment closed, Henry's new advisers proposed a simple, failsafe solution: Why not have the king simply declare his supremacy over English spiritual affairs, as he did over English temporal affairs? Then the king could settle his own affair.

Reformation Parliament In 1529 Parliament convened for what would be a seven-year session that earned it the title of "Reformation Parliament." It passed a flood of legislation that harassed and finally placed royal reins on the clergy. In January 1531 the clergy publicly recognized Henry as head of the church in England "as far as the law of Christ allows." In 1533 Parliament passed the Submission of the Clergy, effectively placing canon law under royal control and thereby the clergy under royal jurisdiction.

In January 1533 Henry wed the pregnant Anne Boleyn, with Thomas Cranmer officiating. In 1534 Parliament ended all payments by the English clergy and laity to Rome and gave Henry sole jurisdiction over high ecclesiastical appointments. The Act of Succession in the same year made Anne Boleyn's children legitimate heirs to the throne, and the Act of Supremacy declared Henry "the only supreme head on earth of the church of England."

Read the Document
The Act of Supremacy (England), 1534
at **MyHistoryLab.com**

The Protestant Reformation under Edward VI

Despite his political break with Rome, Henry remained decidedly conservative in his religious beliefs, and Catholic doctrine remained prominent in a country seething with Protestant sentiment. Henry forbade the English clergy to marry and threatened to execute clergy caught twice in concubinage. The Six Articles of 1539 reaffirmed transubstantiation, denied the Eucharistic cup to the laity, declared celibate vows inviolable, provided for private Masses, and ordered the continuation of auricular confession.

Edward VI (r. 1547–1553), Henry's son by his third wife, Jane Seymour, became king at age 10. Under his regents, England enacted much of the Protestant Reformation. Henry's Six Articles and laws against heresy were repealed, and clerical marriage and Communion with the cup were sanctioned. An Act of Uniformity imposed Thomas Cranmer's Book of Common Prayer on all English churches, which were stripped of their images and altars. Cranmer's forty-two-article confession of faith set forth a moderate Protestant doctrine.

View the Image
Thomas Cranmer's Execution
at **MyHistoryLab.com**

These changes were short-lived because in 1553 Catherine of Aragón's daughter, Mary Tudor (d. 1558), succeeded to the throne and restored Catholic doctrine and practice with a single-mindedness that rivaled that of her father. It was not until the reign of Anne Boleyn's daughter, Elizabeth I (r. 1558–1603), that a lasting religious settlement was worked out in England.

Catholic Reform and Counter-Reformation

The Protestant Reformation did not take the medieval church completely by surprise. There were many internal criticisms and efforts at reform before there was a **Counter-Reformation** in reaction to Protestant successes.

Sources of Catholic Reform Before the Reformation began, ambitious proposals had been made for church reform. But sixteenth-century popes, mindful of how the Councils of Constance and Basel had stripped the pope of his traditional powers, quickly squelched such efforts to bring about basic changes in the laws and institutions of the church. Despite such papal foot-dragging, the church was not without its reformers. Many new religious orders sprang up in the sixteenth century to lead a broad revival of piety within the church.

Ignatius of Loyola and the Society of Jesus Of the various reform groups, none was more instrumental in the success of the Counter-Reformation than the Society of Jesus, the new order of Jesuits. Organized by Ignatius of Loyola in the 1530s, it was officially recognized by the church in 1540. Within a century the society had more than 15,000 members scattered throughout the world, with thriving missions in India, Japan, and the Americas.

Watch the Video
at **MyHistoryLab.com**

Ignatius of Loyola (1491–1556) was a heroic figure. A dashing courtier and caballero in his youth, he began his spiritual pilgrimage in 1521 after having been seriously wounded in the legs during a battle with the French. During a lengthy and painful convalescence, he read Christian classics. So impressed was he with the heroic self-sacrifice of the church's saints and their methods of overcoming mental anguish and pain that he underwent a profound religious conversion. Henceforth, he too would serve the church as a soldier of Christ.

View the Image
Ignatius of Loyola
at **MyHistoryLab.com**

After recuperating, Ignatius applied the lessons he had learned during his convalescence to a program of religious and moral self-discipline that came to be embodied in the *Spiritual Exercises*. This psychologically perceptive devotional guide contained mental and emotional exercises designed to teach one absolute spiritual self-

The Miracle of St. Ignatius of Loyola, by Peter Paul Rubens. Here, the founder of the Society of Jesus, surrounded by angels and members of the new Jesuit Order, preaches to an aroused assembly.

mastery. A person could shape his or her own behavior, even create a new religious self, through disciplined study and regular practice.

Whereas in Jesuit eyes Protestants had distinguished themselves by disobedience to church authority and by religious innovation, the exercises of Ignatius were intended to teach good Catholics to submit without question to higher church authority and spiritual direction. Perfect discipline and self-control were the essential conditions of such obedience. To these were added the enthusiasm of traditional spirituality and mysticism and uncompromising loyalty to the church's cause above all else. (See Document, "Ignatius of Loyola's 'Rules for Thinking with the Church.'") This potent combination helped counter the Reformation and win many Protestants back to the Catholic fold, especially in Austria and Germany.

The Council of Trent (1545–1563) The broad success of the Reformation and the insistence of Emperor Charles V forced Pope Paul III (r. 1534–1549) to call a general council of the church to reassert church doctrine. The pope also appointed a reform commission, whose report, presented in February 1537, bluntly criticized the fiscality and simony[2] of the papal Curia (court) as the primary source of the church's loss of esteem. The report was so critical that Pope Paul attempted unsuccessfully to suppress its publication; Protestants reprinted and circulated it widely.

The long-delayed council met in 1545 in the imperial city of Trent in northern Italy. There were three sessions,

---

[2] The sin of selling sacred or spiritual things, in this instance church offices.

spread over eighteen years, with long interruptions due to war, plague, and politics. Unlike the general councils of the fifteenth century, Trent was strictly under the pope's control, with high Italian prelates prominent in the proceedings.

The council's most important reforms concerned internal church discipline. The selling of church offices and other religious goods was forbidden. Trent strengthened the authority of local bishops so they could effectively discipline popular religious practice. Bishops who resided in Rome were forced to move to their appointed seats of authority. They had to preach regularly and conduct annual visitations. Parish priests were required to be neatly dressed, better educated, strictly celibate, and active among their parishioners. To train better priests, Trent also called for the establishment of a seminary in every diocese.

The Council did not make a single doctrinal concession to the Protestants, however. In the face of Protestant criticism, the Council of Trent reaffirmed the traditional scholastic education of the clergy; the role of good works in salvation; the authority of tradition; the seven sacraments; transubstantiation (see page XXX), the withholding of the Eucharistic cup from the laity; clerical celibacy; the reality of purgatory; the veneration of saints, relics, and sacred images; and the granting of letters of indulgence.

Rulers initially resisted Trent's reform decrees, fearing a revival of papal political power within their lands. But in time the new legislation took hold, and parish life revived under the guidance of a devout and better-trained clergy.

●●●─| Read the Document
Council of Trent 1545–1563
at **MyHistoryLab.com**

The Reformation's Achievements

Though politically conservative, the Reformation brought about far-reaching changes in traditional religious practices and institutions in many lands. By the end of the sixteenth century, what had disappeared or was radically altered was often dramatic.

Document
Ignatius of Loyola's "Rules for Thinking with the Church"

As leaders of the Counter-Reformation, the Jesuits attempted to live by and instill in others the strictest obedience to church authority. The following are some of the eighteen rules Ignatius included in his *Spiritual Exercises* to give Catholics positive direction. These rules also indicate the Catholic reformers' refusal to compromise with Protestants.

■ *Would Protestants find any of Ignatius's "rules" acceptable? Might any of them be controversial among Catholic laity as well as among Protestant laity?*

In order to have the proper attitude of mind in the Church Militant we should observe the following rules:

1. Putting aside all private judgment, we should keep our minds prepared and ready to obey promptly and in all things the true spouse of Christ our Lord, our Holy Mother, the hierarchical Church.
2. To praise sacramental confession and the reception of the Most Holy Sacrament once a year, and much better once a month, and better still every week. . . .
3. To praise the frequent hearing of Mass. . . .
4. To praise highly the religious life, virginity, and continence; and also matrimony, but not as highly. . . .
5. To praise the vows of religion, obedience, poverty, chastity, and other works of perfection and supererogation. . . .
6. To praise the relics of the saints . . . [and] the stations, pilgrimages, indulgences, jubilees, Crusade indulgences, and the lighting of candles in the churches.
7. To praise the precepts concerning fasts and abstinences . . . and acts of penance. . . .
8. To praise the adornments and buildings of churches as well as sacred images. . . .
9. To praise all the precepts of the church. . . .
10. To approve and praise the directions and recommendations of our superiors as well as their personal behaviour. . . .
11. To praise both the positive and scholastic theology. . . .
12. We must be on our guard against making comparisons between the living and those who have already gone to their reward, for it is no small error to say, for example: "This man knows more than St. Augustine"; "He is another Saint Francis, or even greater." . . .
13. If we wish to be sure that we are right in all things, we should always be ready to accept this principle: I will believe that the white that I see is black, if the hierarchical Church so defines it. For I believe that between . . . Christ our Lord and . . . His Church, there is but one spirit, which governs and directs us for the salvation of our souls.

Source: From The Spiritual Exercises of St. Ignatius, trans. by Anthony Mottola, pp. 139–141. Copyright © 1964 by Doubleday, a division of Bantam, Doubleday, Dell Publishing Group, Inc. Used by permission of Doubleday, a division of Random House, Inc.

Religion in Fifteenth-Century Life

In the fifteenth century, on the streets of the great cities of central Europe that later turned Protestant (for example, Zurich, Strasbourg, Nuremberg, and Geneva), the clergy and the religious were everywhere. They made up 6 to 8 percent of the total urban population, and they exercised considerable political as well as spiritual power. They legislated and taxed; they tried cases in special church courts; and they enforced their laws with threats of excommunication.

The church calendar regulated daily life. About one-third of the year was given over to some kind of religious observance or celebration. There were frequent periods of fasting. On almost a hundred days out of the year a pious Christian could not, without special dispensation, eat eggs, butter, fat, or meat.

Monasteries and especially nunneries were prominent and influential institutions. The children of society's most powerful citizens resided there. Local aristocrats were closely identified with particular churches and chapels, whose walls recorded their lineage and proclaimed their generosity. On the streets, friars from near and far begged alms from passersby. In the churches the Mass and liturgy were read entirely in Latin. Images of saints were regularly displayed, and on certain holidays their relics were paraded about and venerated.

There was a booming business at local religious shrines. Pilgrims gathered there by the hundreds, even thousands—many sick and dying, there in search of a cure or a miracle, but many were there for diversion and entertainment. Several times during the year special preachers arrived in the city to sell letters of indulgence.

Many clergy walked the streets with concubines and children, although they were sworn to celibacy and forbidden marriage. The church tolerated such relationships upon payment of penitential fines.

People everywhere could be heard complaining about the clergy's exemption from taxation and, in many instances, also from the civil criminal code. People also grumbled about having to support church offices whose occupants actually lived and worked elsewhere. Townspeople also expressed concern that the church had too much influence over education and culture.

Religion in Sixteenth-Century Life

In these same cities after the Reformation had firmly established itself, few changes in politics and society were evident. The same aristocratic families governed as before, and the rich generally got richer and the poor poorer. But overall numbers of clergy fell by two-thirds, and religious holidays shrank by one-third. Monasteries and nunneries were nearly empty. Many were transformed into hospices for the sick and poor or into educational institutions, their endowments also turned over to these new purposes. A few cloisters remained for very devout old monks and nuns, who could not be pensioned off or who lacked families and friends to care for them. But these remaining cloisters died out with their inhabitants.

In the churches, which had also been reduced in number by at least a third, worship was conducted almost completely in the vernacular. In some, particularly those in Zwinglian cities, the walls were stripped bare and whitewashed to make sure the congregation meditated only on God's Word. The laity observed no obligatory fasts. Indulgence preachers no longer appeared. Local shrines were closed down, and anyone found openly venerating saints, relics, and images was subject to fine and punishment.

Copies of Luther's translation of the New Testament, or more often excerpts from it, could be found in private homes, and meditation on them was encouraged by the new clergy. The clergy could marry, and most did. They paid taxes and were punished for their crimes in civil courts. Domestic moral life was regulated by committees composed of roughly equal numbers of laity and clergy, over whose decisions secular magistrates had the last word.

Not all Protestant clergy remained enthusiastic about this new lay authority in religion. And the laity themselves were also ambivalent about certain aspects of the Reformation. Over half of the original converts returned to the Catholic fold before the end of the sixteenth century. Whereas half of Europe could be counted in the Protestant camp in the mid-sixteenth century, only a fifth would be there by the mid-seventeenth century.[3]

See the Map
Europe After the Reformation
at **MyHistoryLab.com**

Family Life in Early Modern Europe

Changes in the timing and duration of marriage, family size, and infant and child care suggest that family life was under a variety of social and economic pressures in the sixteenth and seventeenth centuries. The Reformation was only one factor in these changes and not the major one.

Later Marriages Between 1500 and 1800, men and women in western Europe and England married at later ages than they had in previous centuries: men in their mid- to late 20s, and women in their early to mid-20s. The canonical, or church-sanctioned, age for marriage remained 14 for men and 12 for women. The church also recognized as valid free, private exchanges of vows between a man and a woman otherwise qualified. After the Reformation, which condemned such clandestine unions, both Protestants and Catholics required parental consent and public vows in church before a marriage could be deemed fully licit.

Arranged Marriages Marriage tended to be "arranged" in the sense that the parents met and discussed the terms of the marriage before the prospective bride and bridegroom became directly party to the preparations. But the wealth and social standing of the bride and the bridegroom were not the only things considered when youth married. By the fifteenth century, it was usual for the future bride and bridegroom to have known each other and to have had some prior relationship. Also, parents respected their emotional feeling for one another. Parents did not force total strangers to live together, and children had a legal right to protest and resist a coerced marriage, which was by definition invalid. The best marriage was one desired by the bride and groom and their families.

---

3 Geoffrey Parker, *Europe in Crisis, 1598–1648* (Ithaca, NY: Cornell University Press, 1979), p. 50.

A Closer Look

A Contemporary Commentary on the Sexes

G.1431; R6. MGVK f1   Taming of the Lion   [334 x 477]   1524   Berlin

TAMING THE LION

A   No man is ever so high or good
That he cannot be managed by a woman
Who does his will
In friendly love and service.

B   Although he is tyrannical wild,
He is soon calmed by a woman.
She boldly strokes his open mouth,
His anger fades, he does not bite.

C   The lion, most lordly of beasts,
Famous for his strength and nobility,
Favors us women with heartfelt gifts
And good humor accompanies his kindness.

D   How wonderfully you reflect
Your taming at woman's hand,
Bearing patiently what another
Does to you against your will.

E   O powerful king and greatest lord
Your equal is neither near nor far.

Excelling all, both large and small,
Upon your head should lie a crown.

F   Lord lion, although you are feared by all,
A woman knows how to saddle you,
Bending you to her will by love.
True love finds a home with a good man.

G   How well you have been groomed!
Now how lively and cheerful!
One so spirited
May have the company of women.

H   Lord lion, you may have your every wish.
Cover your trail with your tail
And you will not be tracked down.
Those who love in secret know this well.

Lion I let the women amuse themselves by serving me.
What harm can they possibly do me?
If I want, I can suddenly turn fierce again.
He is a fool who lets himself be taught by women.

Questions

1. In the scene above, who are the takers and who are the givers? Who controls the relationship between the sexes? Is the lion a truly forbidding patriarch or is the matriarch the one on top?

2. How does this artistic portrayal of womankind compare with the lives of historical women featured in the chapter?

3. Compare the scene with: "Christ Blessing the Children" (World Civilization, 8/ed. ch. 17, p. 503); Columbus and his crew with the women of the East Indies (World Civilization, 8/ed. ch. 17, p. 495); and Hans Baldung Grien's portrayal of witches (World Civilization, 8/ed. ch. 17, p.519).

4. What general conclusions can be drawn about the relationship of the sexes?

Portrait of His Wife and Two Elder Children, by Hans Holbein the Younger (1528). German-English painter Hans Holbein's painting of his wife and two of his children.

Family Size The west European family was conjugal, or nuclear, consisting of a father and a mother and two to four children who survived into adulthood. This nuclear family lived within a larger household, including in-laws, servants, laborers, and boarders. The average husband and wife had six to seven children, a new birth about every two years. Of these, an estimated one-third died by age 5, and one-half by their teens. Rare was the family, at any social level, that did not experience infant mortality and child death.

Wet Nursing The church allied with the physicians of early modern Europe on another intimate family matter. Both condemned women who hired wet nurses to suckle their newborn children. The practice was especially popular among upper-class women. It appears to have increased the risk of infant mortality by exposing infants to a strange and shared milk supply from women who were often not as healthy as the infants' own mothers and lived under less sanitary conditions. But nursing was distasteful to some upper-class women, whose husbands agreed. Among women, vanity and convenience appear to have been motives for hiring a wet nurse, while for husbands, a great deal more was at stake. Because the church forbade sexual intercourse to lactating women, a nursing wife often became a reluctant lover. In addition, nursing had a contraceptive effect (about 75 percent effective). Some women prolonged nursing their children to delay a new pregnancy, and some husbands cooperated in this form of family planning. For other husbands, however, especially noblemen and royalty who desired an abundance of male heirs, nursing seemed to rob them of offspring and jeopardize their patrimony—hence their support of hired wet nurses.

Loving Families? The traditional western European family had features that seem cold and distant. Children between the ages of 8 and 13 were sent from their homes into apprenticeships, school, or employment in the homes of relatives, friends, and occasionally strangers. The emotional ties between spouses also seem to have been as tenuous as those between parents and children. Widowers and widows often remarried within a few months of a spouse's death, and marriages between partners of widely disparate ages also suggest limited affection.

In response to such modern-day criticism, it must be remembered that a well-apprenticed child was a self-supporting child, and hence one with a future. Given the primitive living conditions, contemporaries appreciated the utilitarian and humane side of marriage, and understood when widowers and widows quickly remarried. Marriages with extreme age disparity were no more the norm in early modern Europe than was the practice of wet nursing, and each received just as much criticism and ridicule.

●●●┤Read the Document
Office and Dutie Husband Juan
Luis Vives at **MyHistoryLab.com**

The Wars of Religion

After the Council of Trent adjourned in 1563, Catholics began a Jesuit-led counteroffensive against Protestants. At the time of John Calvin's death in 1564, Geneva had become both a refuge for Europe's persecuted Protestants and an international school for Protestant resistance, producing leaders fully equal to the new Catholic challenge.

Genevan Calvinism and the reformed Catholicism of the Council of Trent were two equally dogmatic, aggressive, and irreconcilable church systems. Calvinists may have looked like "new papists" to critics when they dominated cities like Geneva, but when as minorities they found their civil and religious rights denied in the empire and elsewhere, they became true firebrands and revolutionaries.

Calvinism adopted a presbyterian organization that magnified regional and local religious authority. Boards of presbyters, or elders, representing the many individual Calvinist congregations, directly shaped the policy of the church at large. By contrast, the Counter-Reformation sponsored a centralized episcopal church system, hierarchically arranged from pope to parish priest and stressing absolute obedience to the person at the top. The high clergy—the pope and his bishops—not the synods of local churches, ruled supreme. Calvinism attracted proponents of political decentralization who opposed totalitarian rulers, whereas Catholicism remained congenial to proponents of absolute monarchy determined to maintain "one king, one church, one law."

The wars of religion were both internal national conflicts and truly international wars. Catholic and Protestant subjects struggled to control France, the Netherlands, and England. The Catholic governments of France and Spain conspired and finally sent armies against Protestant regimes in England and the Netherlands. The outbreak of the Thirty Years' War in 1618 made the international dimensions of the religious conflict especially clear; before it ended in 1648, the war drew every major European nation directly or indirectly into its deadly net.

French Wars of Religion (1562–1598)

When Henry II (r. 1547–1559) died accidentally during a tournament in 1559, his sickly 15-year-old son, Francis II (d. 1560), came to the throne under the regency of the queen mother, Catherine de Médicis (1519–1589). With the monarchy so weakened, three powerful families began to compete to control France. They were the Bourbons, whose power lay in the south and west; the Montmorency-Châtillons, who controlled the center of France; and the Guises, who were dominant in eastern France. The Guises were by far the strongest, and the name of *Guise* was interchangeable with militant, ultra-Catholicism. The Bourbon and Montmorency-Châtillon families, in contrast, developed strong Huguenot sympathies, largely for political reasons. (French Protestants were called **Huguenots** after Besançon Hughes, the leader of Geneva's political revolt against the Savoyards in the late 1520s.) The Bourbon Louis I, prince of Condé (d. 1569), and the Montmorency-Châtillon admiral Gaspard de Coligny

(1519–1572) became the political leaders of the French Protestant resistance.

Over two-fifths of the French aristocracy became Huguenots. Many apparently hoped to establish within France a principle of territorial sovereignty akin to that secured within the Holy Roman Empire by the Peace of Augsburg (1555). Calvinism thus indirectly served the forces of political decentralization.

Catherine de Médicis and the Guises Following Francis II's death in 1560, Catherine de Médicis continued as regent for her second son, Charles IX (r. 1560–1574). Fearing the Guises, Catherine sought allies among the Protestants. Early in 1562 she granted Protestants freedom to worship publicly outside towns—although only privately within them—and to hold synods, or church assemblies. In March of the same year this royal toleration ended when the Duke of Guise surprised a Protestant congregation worshiping illegally at Vassy in Champagne and proceeded to massacre several score—an event that marked the beginning of the French wars of religion.

On August 22, 1572, four days after the Huguenot Henry of Navarre married Charles IX's sister, the Huguenot leader Coligny was wounded by an assassin's bullet. Catherine had apparently been a part of this Guise plot to eliminate Coligny. After its failure, she feared both the king's reaction to her complicity and the Huguenot response under a recovered Coligny. Catherine convinced Charles that a Huguenot coup was afoot, inspired by Coligny, and that only the swift execution of Protestant leaders could save the Crown from a Protestant attack on Paris. On the eve of Saint Bartholomew's Day, August 24, 1572, Coligny and 3,000 fellow Huguenots were butchered in Paris. Within three days an estimated 20,000 Huguenots were executed in coordinated attacks throughout France.

●◆─ [Read the Document
Account Massacre St Bartholomew 1572 at **MyHistoryLab.com**

This event changed the nature of the struggle between Protestants and Catholics both within and beyond the borders of France. It was thereafter no longer an internal contest between Guise and Bourbon factions for French political influence, nor was it simply a Huguenot campaign to win basic religious freedoms. Henceforth, in Protestant eyes, it became an international struggle to the death against an adversary whose cruelty justified any means of resistance.

The Rise to Power of Henry of Navarre Henry III (r. 1574–1589), the last Valois king, found the monarchy wedged between a radical Catholic League and vengeful Huguenots. He sought to steer a middle course, and in this effort he received support from a growing body of neutral

The St. Bartholemew's Day Massacre. In this notorious event, here depicted by the contemporary Protestant painter François Dubois, 3,000 Protestants were slaughtered in Paris and an estimated 20,000 others died throughout France. The massacre transformed the religious struggle in France from a contest for political power into an all-out war between Protestants and Catholics.

Catholics and Huguenots who put the political survival of France above its religious unity. Such *politiques*, as they were called, were prepared to compromise religious creeds to save the nation.

In the mid-1580s the Catholic League became dominant in Paris, and Henry III had to flee Paris. Forced by his weakened position into guerrilla tactics, the king had both the Duke and the Cardinal of Guise assassinated. The Catholic League reacted with a fury that matched the earlier Huguenot response to the Massacre of Saint Bartholomew's Day. The king now struck an alliance with his Protestant cousin and heir, Henry of Navarre, in April 1589.

As the two Henrys prepared to attack Paris, however, a fanatical Dominican friar murdered Henry III. Thereupon the Bourbon Huguenot Henry of Navarre became Henry IV of France (r. 1589–1610).

A *politique*, weary of religious strife, Henry put political peace above religious unity. He believed that a royal policy of tolerant Catholicism would be the best way to achieve such peace. On July 25, 1593, he publicly abjured the Protestant faith and embraced the traditional and majority religion of his country. "Paris is worth a Mass," he is reported to have said.

The Edict of Nantes Five years later, on April 13, 1598, Henry IV's famous Edict of Nantes proclaimed a formal religious settlement. The Edict recognized minority religious rights within what was to remain an officially Catholic country. This religious truce granted the Huguenots, who now numbered well over a million, freedom of public worship, the right of assembly, admission to public offices and universities, and permission to maintain fortified towns. Concession of the right to fortify towns revealed the continuing distrust between French Protestants and Catholics. The edict only transformed a long hot war between irreconcilable enemies into a long cold war.

•◦•—Read the Document

The Edict of Nantes 1598
at **MyHistoryLab.com**

A Catholic fanatic assassinated Henry IV in May 1610. Although Henry is best remembered for the Edict of Nantes, the political and economic policies he put in place were equally important. They laid the foundations for the transformation of France into the absolutist state it would become in the seventeenth century. Ironically, in pursuit of the political and religious unity that had escaped Henry IV, his grandson Louis XIV (r. 1643–1715), calling for "one king, one church, one law," would later revoke the Edict of Nantes in 1685 (see Chapter 19).

Document — Theodore Beza Defends the Right to Resist Tyranny

"Although having long urged their flocks not to take up arms in defense of religion, after the St. Bartholomew's Day Massacre of French Protestants, Protestant pamphleteers defended the right of the persecuted to resist tyrants with armed force. In 1574 Calvin's successor in Geneva, Theodore Beza reminded kings of their obligation to protect their subjects and lower magistrates to remove higher ones, if the latter failed to keep their oaths of office. Finally "the People, who are prior to all magistrates" may also deprive tyrants of their power."

■ *What makes Beza's political theories radical?*

■ *Are there similarities between Beza's argument and the American Declaration of Independence? If so, how?*

It is apparent that there is mutual obligation between the king and the officers of a kingdom; that the government of the kingdom is not in the hands of the king in its entirety, but only the sovereign degree; that each of the officers has a share in accord with his degree; and that there are definite conditions on either side. If these conditions are not observed by the inferior officers, it is the part of the sovereign to dismiss and punish them. . . . If the king, hereditary or elective, clearly goes back on the conditions without which he would not have been recognized and acknowledged, can there be any doubt that the lesser magistrates of the kingdom, of the cities, and of the provinces, the administration of which they have received from the sovereignty itself, are free of their oath, at least to the extent that they are entitled to resist flagrant oppression of the realm which they swore to defend and protect according to their office and their particular jurisdiction? . . .

We must now speak of the third class of subjects, which though admittedly subject to the sovereign in a certain respect, is, in another respect, and in cases of necessity the protector of the rights of the sovereignty itself, and is established to hold the sovereignty to his duty, and even, if need be, constrain and punish him. . . . The people is prior to all the magistrates, and does not exist for them, but they for it. . . . Whenever law and equity prevailed, nations neither created nor accepted kings except upon definite conditions. From this it follows that when kings flagrantly violate these terms, those who have the power to give them their authority have no less power to deprive them of it.

Source: Constitutionalism and Resistance in the Sixteenth Century: Three Treatises by Hotman, Beza, and Mornay, trans. and ed. by Julian H. Franklin (New York: Pegasus, 1969). pp. 111–114.

Imperial Spain and the Reign of Philip II (1556–1598)

Until the English defeated his mighty Armada in 1588, no one person stood larger in the second half of the sixteenth century than Philip II of Spain. During the first half of his reign, he focused attention on the Mediterranean and Turkish expansion. On October 7, 1571, a Holy League of Spain, Venice, and the pope defeated the Turks at Lepanto in the largest naval battle of the sixteenth century. Before the engagement ended, 30,000 Turks had died, and over one-third of the Turkish fleet was sunk or captured.

Revolt in the Netherlands The spectacular Spanish military success in southern Europe would not be repeated in northern Europe when Philip attempted to impose his will within the Netherlands and on England and France. The resistance of the Netherlands especially proved the undoing of Spanish dreams of world empire.

The Netherlands were the richest land in Europe, its merchant towns Europe's most independent; many of these towns, like magnificent Antwerp, were Calvinist strongholds. A stubborn opposition to the Spanish overlords formed under William of Nassau, the Prince of Orange (r. 1533–1584). Like other successful rulers in this period, William of Orange was a *politique* who placed the Netherlands' political autonomy and well-being above religious creeds. He personally passed through successive Catholic, Lutheran, and Calvinist stages.

The year 1564 saw the first fusion of political and religious opposition to Spanish rule, the result of Philip II's unwise insistence that the decrees of the Council of Trent be enforced throughout the Netherlands. A national covenant was soon drawn up ("the Compromise"), in which a solemn pledge was made to resist the decrees of Trent and the Inquisition.

Philip dispatched the Duke of Alba (1508–1582) to suppress the revolt. His army marched northward from Milan in 1567 in a show of combined Spanish and papal might. A special tribunal, known to the Spanish as the Council of Troubles and among the Netherlanders as the Council of Blood, reigned over the land.

William of Orange had been an exile in Germany during these turbulent years. He now emerged as the leader of a broad movement for the Netherlands' independence from Spain. After a decade of persecution and warfare, the ten largely Catholic southern provinces (roughly modern Belgium) came together in 1576 with the seven largely Protestant northern provinces (roughly the modern Netherlands) in unified opposition to Spain. This union, known as the Pacification of Ghent, declared internal regional sovereignty in matters of religion.

See the Map
The Netherlands During the Dutch Revolt, ca. 1580
at **MyHistoryLab.com**

The Milch Cow. This sixteenth-century satirical painting depicts the Netherlands as a land all the great powers of Europe wish to exploit. Elizabeth of England is feeding her (England had long-standing commerical ties with Flanders); Philip II of Spain is attempting to ride her (Spain was trying to reassert its control over the entire region); William of Orange is trying to milk her (he was the leader of the anti-Spanish rebellion); and the king of France holds her by the tail (France hoped to profit from the rebellion at Spain's expense). *The "Milch Cow." Rijksmuseum, Amsterdam.*

In January 1579 the southern provinces formed the Union of Arras and made peace with Spain, while the northern provinces formed the Union of Utrecht and continued the struggle. They drove out all Spanish soldiers by 1593, but did not formally conclude peace with Spain until 1609. Not until the Peace of Westphalia (1648) did Spain fully recognize them.

England and Spain (1558–1603)

Elizabeth I Elizabeth I (r. 1558–1603), the daughter of Henry VIII and Anne Boleyn, was perhaps the most astute politician of the sixteenth century in both domestic and foreign policy. She repealed the anti-Protestant legislation of her predecessor Mary Tudor and guided a religious settlement through Parliament that prevented England from being torn asunder by religious differences in the sixteenth century, as the Continent was.

Catholic extremists hoped to replace Elizabeth with the Catholic Mary Stuart, Queen of Scots. But Elizabeth acted swiftly against Catholic assassination plots and rarely let emotion override her political instincts.

Elizabeth dealt cautiously with the Puritans—Protestants who sought to "purify" the national church of every vestige of "popery" and to make its Protestant doctrine more precise. The Puritans had two special grievances: (1) the retention of Catholic ceremony and vestments within the Church of England, and (2) the continuation of the episcopal system of church governance.

Sixteenth-century Puritans were not separatists, however. They worked through Parliament to create an alternative national church of semiautonomous congregations governed by representative presbyteries (hence, Presbyterians), following the model of Calvin and Geneva. The more extreme Puritans wanted every congregation to be autonomous, a law unto itself, with no higher control. They came to be known as Congregationalists. Elizabeth refused to tolerate this group, whose views she considered subversive.

Deterioration of Relations with Spain A series of events led inexorably to war between England and Spain, despite the sincere desires of both Philip II and Elizabeth to avoid it. Following Spain's victory at Lepanto in 1571, England signed a mutual defense pact with France. Also in the 1570s, Elizabeth's famous seamen, John Hawkins (1532–1595) and Sir Francis Drake (?1545–1596), began to prey regularly on Spanish shipping in the Americas. Drake's circumnavigation of the globe between 1577 and 1580 was one in a series of dramatic demonstrations of English ascendancy on the high seas. In 1585 Elizabeth signed a treaty

Elizabeth I (1558–1603) Standing on a Map of England in 1592.
An astute, if sometimes erratic, politician in foreign and domestic policy, Elizabeth was one of the most successful rulers of the sixteenth century.
National Portrait Gallery, London/SuperStock.

that committed English soldiers to the Netherlands. These events made a tinderbox of English-Spanish relations. The spark that finally touched it off was Elizabeth's reluctant execution of Mary, Queen of Scots (1542–1587) on February 18, 1587, for complicity in a plot to assassinate Elizabeth. Philip II ordered his Armada to make ready.

On May 30, 1588, a mighty fleet of 130 ships bearing 25,000 sailors and soldiers under the command of the Duke of Medina-Sidonia set sail for England. But the day belonged completely to the English. The barges that were to transport Spanish soldiers from the galleons onto English shores were prevented from leaving Calais and Dunkirk. The swifter English and Netherlands ships, assisted by an "English wind," dispersed the waiting Spanish fleet, over a third of which never returned to Spain. The Armada's defeat gave heart to Protestant resistance everywhere. Spain never fully recovered from it. By the time of Philip's death on September 13, 1598, his forces had been rebuffed by the French and the Dutch. His seventeenth-century successors were all inferior leaders who never knew responsibilities equal to Philip's; nor did Spain ever again know such imperial grandeur. The French soon dominated the Continent, while the Dutch and the English whittled away Spain's overseas empire.

Elizabeth died on March 23, 1603, leaving behind her a strong nation poised to expand into a global empire.

The Thirty Years' War (1618–1648)

The Thirty Years' War was the last and most destructive of the wars of religion. What made it so devastating was the now entrenched hatred of the opposing confessions, each determined to sacrifice all to regain the religious status quo ante.

Fragmented Germany   During the second half of the sixteenth century, Germany was an almost ungovernable land of 360 autonomous political entities. It was not a unified nation like Spain, England, or even strife-torn France (see Map 16–4 on page 486). The Peace of Augsburg (1555) had given each land a significant degree of sovereignty within its own borders, raising great power pretensions.

Religious Division   The Holy Roman Empire was about equally divided between Catholics and Protestants, the latter having perhaps a slight numerical edge by 1600 (see Map 16–5 on page 487). The terms of the Peace of Augsburg (1555) had attempted to freeze in place the territorial holdings of the Lutherans and the Catholics. However, in the intervening years, the Lutherans gained political control in many former Catholic areas, as did the Catholics in a few previously Lutheran areas. There was also religious strife between liberal and conservative Protestants, and majority Lutherans and growing numbers of Calvinists.

As elsewhere in Europe, Calvinism was the political and religious leaven within the Holy Roman Empire. Unrecognized as a legal religion by the Peace of Augsburg, Calvinism established a foothold within the empire when Elector Frederick III (r. 1559–1576), a devout convert to Calvinism, made it the official religion within the Palatinate. By 1609 Palatine Calvinists headed a Protestant defensive alliance supported by Spain's sixteenth-century enemies: England, France, and the Netherlands.

If the Calvinists were active within the Holy Roman Empire, so also were their Catholic counterparts, the Jesuits. Staunchly Catholic Bavaria, supported by Spain, became militarily and ideologically for the Counter-Reformation what the Palatinate was for Protestantism. From Bavaria, the Jesuits launched successful missions throughout the empire. In 1609 Maximilian, Duke of Bavaria (1573–1651), organized a Catholic League to counter a new Protestant alliance that had been formed by the Calvinist Elector Palatine, Frederick IV (r. 1583–1610). When the League fielded a great army under the command of the Count of Tilly (1559–1632), the stage was set, internally and internationally, for the Thirty Years' War, the worst European catastrophe since the Black Death of the fourteenth century.

Map 16–4. The Holy Roman Empire ca. 1618. On the eve of the Thirty Years' War the empire was politically and religiously fragmented, as this somewhat simplified map reveals. Lutherans dominated the north and Catholics the south, while Calvinists controlled the United Provinces and the Palatinate and also had an important presence in Switzerland and Brandenburg.

The Treaty of Westphalia In 1648 all hostilities within the Holy Roman Empire were brought to an end by the Treaty of Westphalia. It reasserted the major feature of the religious settlement of the Peace of Augsburg (1555), as rulers were again permitted to determine the religion of their lands. The treaty also gave the Calvinists their long-sought legal recognition while still denying it to sectarians.

By confirming the territorial sovereignty of Germany's many political entities, the Treaty of Westphalia perpetu-ated German division and political weakness. However, two German states attained international significance during the seventeenth century: Austria and Branden-burg-Prussia. The petty regionalism within the empire also reflected on a small scale the drift of larger European politics. During the seventeenth century distinctive na-tion-states reached maturity and estab-lished the pecking list of competitive na-tion-states in the modern world.

See the **Map** Europe After the Peace of Westphalia, 1648 at **MyHistoryLab.com**

✳ Map Exploration

To explore this map further, go to **http://www.myhistorylab.com**

Map 16–5. **Religious Division ca. 1600.** By 1600 few could expect Christians to return to a uniform religious allegiance. In Spain and southern Italy Catholicism remained relatively unchallenged, but note the existence elsewhere of large religious minorities, both Catholic and Protestant.

Superstition and Enlightenment: The Battle Within

Religious reform and warfare permanently changed religious institutions in major European lands. They also moved intellectuals to rethink human nature and society. One side of that reconsideration was dark and cynical, perhaps because the peak years of religious warfare had also been those of the great European witch hunts. Another side, however, was brilliantly skeptical and constructive, reflecting the growing scientific movement of the years between 1500 and 1700.

Witch Hunts and Panic

Why did great witch panics occur in the second half of the sixteenth and early seventeenth centuries? The misfortune created by religious division and warfare was a major factor. Some argue that the Reformation spurred the panics by ridiculing the traditional church defenses against the devil and demons, compelling people to protect themselves by searching out and executing witches. Political consolidation by secular governments and the papacy probably played a greater role, with both aggressively conforming their realms and eliminating competition for the loyalty of their subjects.

Two Witches by Hans Baldung Grien (1523) German artist Hans Baldung Grien presents the powers and temptations of two enchanted, monumental witches as they sow the wind.

Village Origins The roots of witch beliefs are found in both popular and elite culture. In village societies, feared and respected "cunning folk" helped people cope with natural disasters and disabilities by magical means. For local people, these were important services that kept village life moving forward in times of calamity.

For good or ill, the possession of magical powers made one an important person within village society. Claims to such powers were often made by those who were most in need of security and influence, particularly women, and especially old, impoverished single or widowed women.

Read the Document
Malleus Maleficarum 1486
at **MyHistoryLab.com**

Influence of the Clergy Popular belief in magic was the essential foundation of the witch hunts. Had ordinary people not believed that "gifted persons" could help or harm by magical means, and had they not been willing to make accusations against them, the hunts would never have occurred. The contribution of learned, Christian society was equally great. The Christian clergy also was perceived to practice 'magic,' that of the holy sacraments, transforming bread and wine into the body and blood of Christ, and eternal punishments for sins into temporal ones. And they also exorcised demons.

Attacking accused witches became a way for the church to extend its spiritual hegemony, especially in new areas being conformed by church and state to higher Christian society. As spiritual authorities revered and feared by villagers or townspeople, local cunning folk posed an obstacle to that mission. To accuse, try, and execute witches was a declaration of moral and political authority over a village or territory.

Why Women? Roughly 80 percent of the victims of witch hunts were women, most of them single and between 45 and 60 years of age. This suggests that misogyny fueled the witch hunts. Inspired by male hatred and sexual fear of women, and occurring at a time when women were breaking out from under male control, witch hunts seem a conspiracy of males against females.

Older single women claiming supernatural powers may, however, have been vulnerable for basic social reasons. As a dependent social group ever in need of public assistance, they were natural targets for the peculiar "social engineering" of the witch hunts. Because of their economic straits, more women than men laid claim to the supernatural powers that made them influential in village society. Such women found themselves on the front lines in disproportionate numbers when the church declared war on the practitioners of black magic. Also, many of these women were midwives, a vocation associated with the deaths of mothers and infants in childbirth, making them targets of resentment.

End of the Witch Hunts When and why did the witch hunts end? The emergence of a scientific worldview in the seventeenth century made it harder to believe that words and thoughts could impact physical things. A witch's curse was now merely words. Given the advances in medicine, the rise of insurance companies, and the availability of lawyers, people gained protection for themselves when physical affliction and natural calamity struck. Witch hunts also tended to get terribly out of hand.

Watch the Video
at **MyHistoryLab.com**

Not only were they dysfunctional, but they threatened total anarchy as well.

Writers and Philosophers

By the end of the sixteenth century, many could not embrace either old Catholic or new Protestant absolutes. Intellectually and politically, the seventeenth century became a period of transition, one that had been well prepared for by the humanists and scientists of the Renaissance. In the budding early modern world, the brightest and the best powerfully exposed medieval authorities and intellectual traditions (see Chapter 21). The writers and philosophers of the late sixteenth and seventeenth centuries were aware that they lived in a period of transition. Some embraced the emerging new science wholeheartedly (Hobbes and Locke), others tried to straddle the two ages (Cervantes and Shakespeare), and still others ignored or opposed the new developments that seemed mortally to threaten traditional values (Pascal).

William Shakespeare There is much less factual knowledge about William Shakespeare (1564–1616), the greatest playwright in the English language, than one would expect of such an important figure. He apparently worked as a schoolteacher for a time and in this capacity acquired his broad knowledge of Renaissance learning and literature. His work shows none of the Puritan distress over worldliness. He took the new commercialism and the bawdy pleasures of the Elizabethan Age in stride and with amusement. In politics and religion, he was a man of his time and not inclined to offend his queen.

That Shakespeare was interested in politics is apparent from his history plays and the references to contemporary political events that fill all his plays. He seems to have viewed government simply, however, through the character of the individual ruler, whether Richard III or Elizabeth Tudor, not in terms of ideal systems or social goals. By modern standards he was a political conservative, accepting the social rankings and the power structure of his day and demonstrating unquestioned patriotism.

Shakespeare knew the theater as one who participated in every phase of its life. A member and principal dramatist of a famous company of actors known as the King's Men, he was a playwright, actor, and part owner of a theater. His work brought together in an original synthesis the best past and current achievements in the dramatic arts. He particularly mastered the psychology of human motivation and passion and had a unique talent for psychological penetration.

Shakespeare wrote histories, comedies, and tragedies. The tragedies are considered his unique achievement; he wrote four of them within a three-year period: *Hamlet* (1603), *Othello* (1604), *King Lear* (1605), and *Macbeth* (1606). The most original of the tragedies, *Romeo and Juliet* (1597), transformed an old popular story into a moving drama of "star-cross'd lovers."

In his lifetime and ever since, Shakespeare has been immensely popular with both audiences and readers. As Ben Jonson (1572–1637), a contemporary classical dramatist who created his own school of poets, put it in a tribute affixed to the *First Folio* edition of Shakespeare's plays (1623): "He was not of an age, but for all time."

Blaise Pascal Blaise Pascal (1623–1662) was a French mathematician and a physical scientist widely acclaimed by his contemporaries. Torn between the continuing dogmatism and the new skepticism of the seventeenth century, he aspired to write a work that would refute two groups: the Jesuits, whose casuistry (i.e., confessional tactics designed to minimize and even excuse sinful acts) he considered a distortion of Christian teaching, and the skeptics, who either denied religion altogether (atheists) or accepted it only as it conformed to reason (deists). Pascal never realized such a definitive work, and his views on these matters exist only in piecemeal form. He wrote against the Jesuits in his *Provincial Letters* (1656–1657), and he left behind a provocative collection of reflections on humankind and religion that was published posthumously under the title *Pensées*.

Early on, Pascal was influenced by the Jansenists, seventeenth-century Catholic opponents of the Jesuits. Although the Jansenists were good Catholics, they shared with the Calvinists Saint Augustine's belief in the total sinfulness of human beings, their eternal predestination by God, and their complete dependence on faith and grace for knowledge of God and salvation.

Pascal believed that reason and science, though attesting to human dignity, remained of no avail in religion. Here only the reasons of the heart and a "leap of faith" could prevail. Pascal saw two essential truths in the Christian religion: A loving God, worthy of human attainment, exists; and human beings, because they are corrupted in nature, are utterly unworthy of God. Pascal believed that the atheists and deists of the age had spurned the lesson of reason. For him, rational analysis of the human condition attested to humankind's utter mortality and corruption, and it exposed the weakness of reason itself in resolving the problems of human nature and destiny. Reason should rather drive those who truly heed it to faith and dependence on divine grace.

Pascal made a famous wager with the skeptics. It is a better bet, he argued, to believe that God exists and to stake everything on his promised mercy than not to do so; if God does exist, everything will be gained by the believer, whereas the loss incurred by having believed in God should he prove not to exist is, by comparison, very slight.

Pascal was convinced that belief in God measurably improved earthly life psychologically and disciplined it morally, regardless of whether God proved in the end to exist. He thought that the surrender of traditional religious values posed great danger. Pascal urged his contemporaries to seek self-understanding by "learned ignorance" and to discover humankind's greatness by recognizing its misery. Thereby he hoped to counter what he believed to be the false optimism of the new rationalism and science.

Thomas Hobbes Thomas Hobbes (1588–1679) was the most original political philosopher of the seventeenth century. Although he never broke with the Church of England, he came to share basic Calvinist beliefs, especially the low view of human nature and the ideal of a commonwealth based on a covenant, both of which find eloquent expression in his political philosophy.

Hobbes was an urbane and much-traveled man and one of the most enthusiastic supporters of the new scientific movement. During the 1630s he visited Paris, where he came to know Descartes; after the outbreak of the Puritan Revolution (see Chapter 19) in 1640, he lived as an exile in Paris until 1651. Hobbes also spent time with Galileo (see Chapter 21) in Italy and took a special interest in the works of William Harvey. Harvey was a physiologist famed for the discovery of how blood circulated through the body; his scientific writings influenced Hobbes's own tracts on bodily motions.

Hobbes was driven to the vocation of political philosophy by the English Civil War (see Chapter 19). In 1651 his

Leviathan. Thomas Hobbes's political treatise, *Leviathan*, portrayed rulers as absolute lords over their lands, incorporating in their persons the individual wills of all their people.

▸ Read the Document
Leviathan
at **MyHistoryLab.com**

Leviathan appeared. Its subject was the political consequences of human passions, and its originality lay in (1) its designation of natural law, rather than common law (i.e., custom or precedent), as the basis of all positive law and (2) its defense of a representative theory of absolute authority against the theory of the divine right of kings. Hobbes maintained that statute law found its justification only as an expression of the law of nature and that rulers derived their authority from the consent of the people.

Hobbes viewed humankind and society in a thoroughly materialistic and mechanical way. He defined human beings as a collection of material particles in motion. He claimed that all their psychological processes begin with and are derived from bare sensation and that all their motivations are egotistical, intended to increase pleasure and minimize pain.

Despite this seemingly low estimate of human beings, Hobbes believed much could be accomplished by the reasoned use of science. All was contingent, however, on the correct use of that greatest of all human powers, one compounded of the powers of most people: the commonwealth, in which people are united by their consent in one all-powerful person.

The key to Hobbes's political philosophy is a brilliant myth of the original state of humankind. According to this myth, human beings in the natural state are generally inclined to a "perpetual and restless desire of power after power that ceases only in death."[4] As all people desire—and in the state of nature have a natural right to—everything, their equality breeds enmity, competition, and diffidence, and the desire for glory begets perpetual quarreling—"a war of every man against every man."[5]

Whereas earlier and later philosophers saw the original human state as a paradise from which humans had fallen, Hobbes viewed it as a corruption from which only society had delivered them. Contrary to the views of Aristotle and Christian thinkers like Thomas Aquinas, Hobbes saw human beings not as sociable, reasonable, political animals, but as self-centered beasts, laws unto themselves and utterly wild, until the state, the great Leviathan, imposed rule on them by brute force.

John Locke John Locke (1632–1704) proved to be the most influential political thinker of the seventeenth century.[6] His political philosophy came to be embodied in England's so-called Glorious Revolution of 1688–1689 (Chapter 19). Although he was not as original as Hobbes, his political writings were a major source of Enlightenment criticism of Hobbes's absolutism and gave inspiration to both the American and French Revolutions.

Locke's two most famous works are the *Essay Concerning Human Understanding* (1690) (discussed in Chapter 21) and *Two Treatises of Government* (1690). Locke wrote *Two Treatises of Government* as a refutation to the argument that rulers were absolute in their power. Rulers, Locke argued, remain bound to the law of nature, which is the voice of reason, teaching that "all mankind [are] equal and independ-

---

[4] *Leviathan*, Parts I and II, ed. by H. W. Schneider (Indianapolis, IN: Bobbs-Merrill, 1958), p. 86.

[5] Ibid., p. 106.

[6] Locke's scientific writings are discussed in Chapter 24.

Document | John Locke Explains the Sources of Human Knowledge

An Essay Concerning Human Understanding (1690) may be the most influential philosophical work written in the English language. Locke's fundamental idea, explicated in the following passage, is that human knowledge is grounded in the experiences of the senses and the mind's reflection on them. He rejected belief in innate ideas. His emphasis on experience led to the wider belief that human beings are creatures of their environment. After Locke, numerous writers argued that human beings could be improved if the environment in which they lived was reformed.

■ *How did Locke's views on sensation and experience influence the way people viewed the world?*

■ *Why is Locke's explanation for the sources of human knowledge so important?*

Let us then suppose the mind to be, as we say, white paper void of all characters, without any *ideas*. How comes it to be furnished? Whence comes it by that vast store which the busy and boundless fancy of man has painted on it with an almost endless variety? Whence has it all the materials of reason and knowledge? To this I answer, in one word, from *experience*; in that all our knowledge is funded, and from that it ultimately derives itself. Our observation, employed either about *external sensible objects, or about the internal operations of our minds perceived and reflected on by ourselves, is that which supplies our understanding with all the materials of thinking.* These two are the fountains of knowledge, from whence all the ideas we have, or can naturally have, do spring.

First, *our senses*, conversant about particular sensible objects, do *convey into the mind* several distinct *perceptions* of things, according to those various ways wherein those objects do affect them. And thus we come by those *ideas* we have of *yellow, white, heat, cold, soft, hard, bitter, sweet*, and all those which we call sensible qualities. . . . This great source of most of the *ideas* we

have, depending wholly upon our senses, and derived by them to the understanding. I call SENSATION.

Secondly, the other fountain from which experience furnisheth the understanding with *ideas* is the *perception of the operations of our own minds* within us, as it is employed about the ideas it has got. . . . And such are *perception, thinking, doubting, believing, reasoning, knowing, willing*, and all the different actings of our own minds. . . . I call this REFLECTION, the *ideas* it affords being such only as the mind gets by reflecting on its own operations within itself. . . . These two, I say, viz. external material things as the objects of SENSATION, and the operations of our own minds within as the objects of REFLECTION, are to me the only originals from whence all our *ideas* take their beginnings. . . .

The understanding seems to me not to have the least glimmering of any *ideas* which it doth not receive from one of these two.

Source: John Locke, *An Essay Concerning Human Understanding*, Vol. 1 (London: Everyman's Library, 1961), pp. 77–78.

---

ent, [and] no one ought to harm another in his life, health, liberty, or possessions,"[7] inasmuch as all human beings are the images and property of God. According to Locke, people enter social contracts, empowering legislatures and monarchs to "umpire" their disputes, precisely to preserve their natural rights, and not to give rulers an absolute power over them. (See Document, "John Locke Explains the Sources of Human Knowledge.")

"Whenever that end [the preservation of life, liberty, and property] is manifestly neglected or opposed, the [people's] trust must necessarily be forfeited and the power devolved into the hands of those that gave it, who may place it anew where they think best for their safety and security."[8] From Locke's point of view, absolute monarchy was "inconsistent" with civil society and could be "no form of civil government at all."[9]

---

[7] *The Second Treatise of Government*, ed. by T. P. Peardon (Indianapolis, IN: Bobbs-Merrill, 1952), chap. 2, sects. 4–6, pp. 4–6.

[8] Ibid., chap. 13, sect. 149, p. 84.

[9] Ibid.

Summary

Voyages of Discovery In the late fifteenth century, Europe began to expand around the globe. Driven by both mercenary and religious motives, the Portuguese pioneered a sea route around Africa to India and the Far East, and the Spanish discovered the Americas. Social, political, and biological consequences were immense for Europeans, Native Americans, Africans, and Asians. In time, a truly global world would emerge.

The Reformation The Reformation began in Germany with Martin Luther's attack on indulgences in 1517. Despite Emperor Charles V's opposition to the Reformation, Luther had the support of many German princes. The Reformation shattered the religious unity of Europe. In Switzerland, Zwingli and Calvin launched their own versions of Protestantism. In England, Henry VIII repudiated papal authority when the pope refused to grant him a divorce. The different Protestant sects were often as hostile to each other as they were to Catholicism. The Reformation also led to far-reaching changes in religious practices and social attitudes, including steps toward the advancement of women.

Key Terms

consubstantiation (p. 472)

Counter-Reformation (p. 475)

Diet of Worms (p. 469)

Huguenots (p. 482)

indulgence (p. 468)

ninety-five theses (p. 468)

Reformation (p. 463)

transubstantiation (p. 472)

Review Questions

1. What impact did European expansion have on the societies of both the Old and New Worlds?

2. What were the main problems of the church that contributed to the Protestant Reformation? Why was the church unable to suppress dissent as it had earlier?

3. How did the theologies of Luther, Zwingli, and Calvin differ? Were their differences only religious, or did they have political consequences for the Reformation as well?

4. Why did the Reformation begin in Germany and not in France, Italy, England, or Spain?

5. What was the Catholic Reformation? Did the Council of Trent alter the character of traditional Catholicism?

6. Why did Henry VIII break with the Catholic Church? Was the "new" religion he established really Protestant?

7. Were the wars of religion really over religion? Explain.

8. Henry of Navarre (later Henry IV of France), Elizabeth I, and William of Orange have been called *politiques*. What does that term mean, and how might it apply to each?

9. Why was England more successful than other lands in resolving its internal political and religious divisions peacefully during the sixteenth and seventeenth centuries?

10. "The Thirty Years' War is the outstanding example in European history of meaningless conflict." Evaluate this statement and provide specific reasons.

Note: *To learn more about the topics in this chapter, please turn to the Suggested Readings at the end of the book. For additional sources related to this chapter please see MyHistoryLab.com.*

PEARSON myhistorylab Connections

Reinforce what you learned in this chapter by studying the many documents, images, maps, review tools, and videos available at **www.myhistorylab.com**.

Read and Review

✓●─ **Study** and **Review**   Chapter 16

●●●─ Read the Document   *Duarte Barbosas to Africa India, p. 462*
Columbus journal and letter , p. 463
Erasmus Julius Excluded Heaven, p. 468
Martin Luther's Ninety-Five Theses 1517, p. 469
Against Murderous Thieving Hordes Peasants, p. 470
Calvin Ecclesiastical Ordinances, p. 473
Calvin on Predestination 16th century, p. 473
The Act of Supremacy (England), 1534, p. 475
Council of Trent 1545–1563, p. 476
Office and Dutie Husband Juan Luis Vives, p. 480
Account Massacre St Bartholomew 157, p. 481
The Edict of Nantes 1598, p. 482
Malleus Maleficarum 1486 , p. 488
Leviathan, p. 490

●─ See the Map   *Religious Divisions of Europe/Religious Divisions of Europe, p. 470*
The Swiss Confederation, p. 472
Europe After the Reformation, p. 478
The Netherlands During the Dutch Revolt, ca. 1580, p. 484
Europe After the Peace of Westphalia, 1648, p. 486

●─ View the Image   *Early Print Shop, p. 466*
Martin Luther, p. 467
Martin Luther Statue in Hesse Germany, p. 470
Anabaptist Torture in Muenster, p. 472
Thomas Cranmer's Execution, p. 475
Ignatius of Loyola, p. 475

Research and Explore

●─ Watch the Video   *Jesuits*

●─ Watch the Video   *Witch Hunts*

((●─ Hear the Audio

Hear the audio file for Chapter 16 at
www.myhistorylab.com.

Christianity is based on the teaching of Jesus of Nazareth, a Jew who lived in Palestine during the Roman occupation. His simple message of faith in God and self-sacrificial love of one's neighbor attracted many people. The Roman authorities, perceiving his large following as a threat, crucifed him. After Jesus' crucifixion, his followers proclaimed that he had been resurrected from the dead and that he would return in glory to defeat sin, death, and the devil, and take all true believers with him to heaven—a radical vision of judgment and immortality that has driven Christianity's appeal since its inception. In the teachings of the early church, Jesus became the Christ, the son of God, the long-awaited Messiah of Jewish prophecy. His followers called themselves Christians.

Christianity proclaimed the very incarnation of God in a man, the visible presence of eternity in time. According to early Christian teaching, the power of God's incarnation in Jesus lived on in the preaching and sacraments of the church under the guidance of the Holy Spirit. According to the Christian message, in Jesus, eternity has made itself accessible to every person here and now and forevermore.

The new religion attracted both the poor and powerless and the socially rising and well-to-do. For some, the gospel of Jesus promised a better material life. For others, it imparted a sense of spiritual self-worth regardless of one's place or prospects in society.

In the late second century the Romans began persecuting Christians as "heretics" (because of their rejection of the traditional Roman gods) and as social revolutionaries (for their loyalty to a lord higher than the emperor of Rome). At the same time dissenting Christians, particularly sects claiming direct spiritual knowledge of God apart from Scripture, internally divided the young church. To meet these challenges the church established effective weapons against state terrorism and Christian heresy: an ordained clergy, a hierarchical church organization, orthodox creeds, and a biblical canon (the New Testament). Christianity not only gained legal status within the Roman Empire, but also, by the fourth century, most favored religious status thanks to Emperor Constantine's embrace of it.

After the fall of the Western Roman Empire in the fifth century C.E., Christianity became one of history's great success stories. Aided by the enterprise of its popes and the example of its monks, the church cultivated an appealing lay piety centered on the Lord's Prayer, the Apostles' Creed, veneration of the Virgin, and the sacrament of the Eucharist. Clergy became both royal teachers and bureaucrats within the kingdom of the Franks. Despite a growing schism between the Eastern (Byzantine) and Western churches, and a final split in 1054, by 1000 the church held real economic and political power. In the

Pentecost. This exquisite enamel plaque, from the Mosan school that flourished in France in the eleventh and twelfth centuries, shows the descent of the Holy Spirit upon the apostles, fifty days after the resurrection of Jesus, on the ancient Jewish festival called the "feast of weeks," or Pentecost. *Mosan, The Pentecost, ca. 1150-1175. Champleve enamel on copper gilt; 4 1/16 x 4 1/6 in. (10.3 x 10.3 cm). The Metropolitan Museum of Art, The Cloisters Collection, 1965 (65.105). Photograph 1989 The Metropolitan Museum of Art.*

eleventh century reform-minded prelates put an end to presumptuous secular interference in its most intimate spiritual affairs by ending the lay investiture of clergy in their spiritual offices. For several centuries thereafter the church remained a formidable international force, able to challenge kings and emperors and inspire Crusades to the Holy Land.

By the fifteenth century the new states of Europe had stripped the church of much of its political power. It was thereafter progressively confined to spiritual and moral authority. Christianity's greatest struggles ever since have been not with kings and emperors over political power, but with materialistic philosophies and worldly ideologies, matters of spiritual and moral hegemony within an increasingly pluralistic and secular world. Since the sixteenth century a succession of humanists, skeptics, Deists, Rationalists, Marxists, Freudians, Darwinians, and atheists have attempted to explain away some of traditional Christianity's most basic teachings. In addition, the church has endured major internal upheavals. After the Protestant Reformation (1517–1555) made the Bible widely available to the laity, the possibilities for internal criticism of Christianity multiplied geometrically. Beginning with the split between Lutherans and Zwinglians in the 1520s, Protestant Christianity has fragmented into hundreds of sects, each claiming to have the true interpretation of Scripture. The Roman Catholic Church, by contrast, has maintained its unity and ministry throughout perilous times, although present-day discontent with papal authority threatens the modern Catholic church almost as seriously as the Protestant Reformation once did.

Christianity has remained remarkably resilient. It possesses a simple, almost magically appealing gospel of faith and love in and through Jesus. In a present-day world whose religious needs and passions still run deep, evangelical Christianity has experienced a remarkable revival. The Roman Catholic Church, still troubled by challenges to papal authority, has become more pluralistic than in earlier periods. The pope has become a world figure, traveling to all continents to represent the church and advance its position on issues of public and private morality. A major ecumenical movement emerging in the 1960s has promoted unprecedented cooperation among evangelical Christian denominations. Everywhere Christians of all stripes are politically active, spreading their divine, moral, and social messages. Meanwhile, old hot-button issues, such as the ordination of women, are being overtaken by new ones, particularly the marriage of gay men and women and the removal of clergy who do not maintain the moral discipline of their holy orders.

■ **Over the centuries what have been some of the chief factors attracting people to Christianity?**

■ **What forces have led to disunity among Christians in the past? What factors cause tensions among modern Christians?**

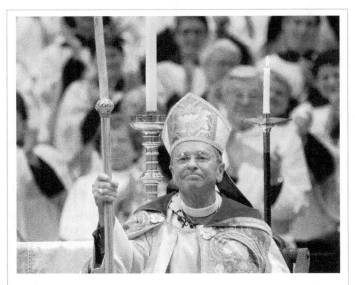

Gay bishop. V. Gene Robinson is applauded after his investiture as the Episcopal Church's bishop of New Hampshire in March 2004. Robinson is the Episcopal Church's first openly gay bishop. The issue of homosexuality has divided Christian churches across the world.

17 Conquest and Exploitation: The Development of the Transatlantic Economy

■ Periods of European Overseas Expansion

■ Mercantilist Theory of Economic Exploitation

■ Establishment of the Spanish Empire in America

■ Economies of Exploitation in the Spanish Empire

■ Colonial Brazil

■ French and British Colonies in North America

■ The Columbian Exchange: Disease, Animals, and Agriculture

■ Slavery in the Americas

■ Africa and the Transatlantic Slave Trade

TO BE SOLD on board the Ship *Bance-Yland*, on tuesday the 6th of *May* next, at *Afhley-Ferry*; a choice cargo of about 250 fine healthy NEGROES, juft arrived from the Windward & Rice Coaft. —The utmoft care has already been taken, and fhall be continued, to keep them free from the leaft danger of being infected with the SMALL-POX, no boat having been on board, and all other communication with people from *Charles-Town* prevented.

Auftin, Laurens, & Appleby.

N. B. Full one Half of the above Negroes have had the SMALL-POX in their own Country.

Slave Auction Notice. Africans who survived the voyage across the Atlantic were immediately sold into slavery in the Americas. This eighteenth-century advertisement relates to a group of slaves whose ship had stopped at Charleston, South Carolina, and then landed elsewhere in the region to auction its human cargo. Notice the concern to assure potential buyers that the slaves were healthy, as a smallpox epidemic was then raging on the mainland.

THE LATE-FIFTEENTH-CENTURY EUROPEAN encounter with the American continents changed the entire world. The more than two and a half centuries of European domination and government that followed the encounter made the Americas a region where European languages, legal and political institutions, trade patterns, and religion prevail. African populations, economies, and political structures were altered by the slave trade into the Americas. These developments gave Europe more influence over other world cultures and civilizations than it would otherwise have achieved.

Within decades of the European voyages of discovery, Native Americans, Europeans, and Africans began to interact in a manner unprecedented in human history. The Native Americans of North and South America encountered bands of European conquerors and European Roman Catholic missionaries. Technological and military superiority as well as political divisions among the Native Americans allowed the Europeans to realize their material and religious ambitions. By the middle of the sixteenth century Europeans had begun to import Africans into the American continents as chattel slaves, converting them to Christianity in the process. Consequently, by the close of the sixteenth century Europe, the Americas, and Africa had become linked in a vast transatlantic economy that extracted material and agricultural wealth from the American continents largely on the basis of the nonfree labor of impressed Native Americans and imported African slaves.

The next century would see English and French colonists settling in North America and the Caribbean, introducing different political values and, through the English, Protestantism. These North American colonists were also part of the transatlantic economy, and many would become economically involved directly or indirectly with African slavery. As they exploited the American wilderness, the colonists interacted with the Native Americans of North America, sometimes destroying indigenous cultures and eradicating whole indigenous peoples, sometimes converting Native Americans to Christianity; Native Americans, too, were drawn into the transatlantic economy.

Beginning in the sixteenth century, the importation of African slaves and the use of slave labor were fundamental to the plantation economy that eventually extended from Maryland to Brazil. Slavery also extended into the British colonies north of Maryland, though not in the context of plantations. The slave trade intimately connected the economy of certain sections of Africa to the transatlantic economy. The slave trade had a devastating effect on the African people and cultures involved in it, but it also enriched the Americas with African culture and religion. ■

((•—Hear the Audio at MyHistoryLab.com

Periods of European Overseas Expansion

Since the late fifteenth century, European contacts with the rest of the world have gone through four distinct stages. The first was that of the European discovery, exploration, initial conquest, and settlement of the Americas and commercial expansion elsewhere in the world. By the close of the seventeenth century Spain governed South America,

El Morro, Puerto Rico. This fortress was built by the Spanish in the sixteenth century to protect Spain's valuable trading rights against British, Dutch, and pirate ships.

The Atlantic World

The Atlantic World

The exchanges of people, goods, ideas, and plants, animals, and microcosms between the American, European, and African continents in the fifteenth and sixteenth centuries transformed world history. In the Americas, the native peoples—whose ancestors had migrated from Asia millennia before—had established a wide variety of civilizations. Some of their most remarkable architectural monuments and cities were constructed during the very centuries when European civilizations were reeling from the collapse of Roman power (see Chapter 13). While trade and culture had long linked parts of Africa and regions in Eurasia (see Chapter 14), the civilizations of the Americas and the civilizations of Eurasia and Africa had had no significant contact with each other prior to the era of European exploration.

Within half a century of the landing of Columbus, millions of America's native peoples in Florida, the Caribbean islands, Mesoamerica, and South America had encountered the impact of Europeans intent on conquest, exploitation, and religious conversion. The Europeans' rapid conquest was the result of several factors—their advanced weapons and navies; the new diseases they brought with them; and internal divisions among the Native Americans. Thereafter, Spain and Portugal dominated Central and South America (what we now, as a result of this history, term Latin America), and England, France, and Holland set

except for Portuguese-ruled Brazil. French and British colonies had been established in North America. France, Britain, the Netherlands, and Spain controlled various islands in the Caribbean. The French, British, and Dutch held outposts in Asia.

The second era was one of colonial trade rivalry among Spain, France, and Great Britain. The Anglo-French side of the contest has often been compared to a second Hundred Years' War. During this second period both the British colonies of the North American seaboard and the Spanish colonies of Mexico and Central and South America emancipated themselves from European control. This era may be said to have closed during the 1820s (see Chapter 22).

The third stage of European contact with the non-European world occurred in the nineteenth century when European governments carved formal empires in Africa and Asia. Those nineteenth-century empires also included new areas of European settlement such as Australia, New Zealand, and South Africa. The bases of these empires were trade, national honor, racial theories, religious expansion, and military superiority (see Chapter 24).

The last phase of European dominion occurred during the mid-twentieth century with the decolonization of peoples who had previously been under European colonial rule (see Chapters 31 and 32).

During the four and a half centuries before decolonization, Europeans exerted political dominance over much of the rest of the world that was out of all proportion to Europe's size or population. Europeans frequently treated other peoples as social, intellectual, and economic inferiors. They ravaged existing cultures because of greed, religious zeal, or political ambition. These actions have significantly affected the contemporary relationship between Europe and its former colonies. What allowed the Europeans to exert such influence and domination for so long over so much of the world was not any innate cultural superiority, but rather a technological supremacy related to naval power and gunpowder. Ships and guns allowed the Europeans to exercise their will almost wherever they chose.

Mercantilist Theory of Economic Exploitation

The early modern European empires of the sixteenth through the eighteenth centuries—empires based on commerce—existed primarily to enrich trade. Extensive trade rivalries sprang up around the world. The protection of these empires required naval power. Spain dominated the largest of these empires and constructed elaborate naval, commercial, and political structures to exploit and govern it. Finally, these out to settle North America. The Europeans imported their own food crops, such as wheat and apples, while also taking advantage of American plants, such as potatoes, corn, tomatoes, and tobacco.

Throughout the Americas and the Caribbean basin, Europeans established economies of exploitation. In Latin America, they developed various institutions to extract native labor. Plantation owners from the Mid-Atlantic English colonies through the Caribbean and into Brazil preferred slaves forcibly imported from Africa. African slaves were hardier than indigenous laborers, who lacked immunity to European diseases, and they could be better controlled than indentured servants from Europe. With the exception of tobacco, plantation crops derived largely from the Old World; some Africans were already familiar with the cultivation of, for example, rice. The emergent Atlantic World drew the economies and peoples of Europe, Africa, and the Americas into a vast worldwide web of production based on slave labor.

Slavery had its gravest impact on the lives of the millions of humans who over the centuries were torn from their birthplaces, their families, and their cultures. The slave trade corroded the political and social structures of African societies. African slaves suffered from high mortality and sharply reduced birthrates; they were subjected to harsh working conditions and brutally dehumanizing treatment.

Focus Questions

- How did the encounter of Europe and Africa with the Americas change the global ecological balance?
- Why was the Spanish Empire based on economies of exploitation? How was the labor of non-European peoples drawn into the economy of this empire?
- How and why did the plantation economy develop? Why did it rely on African slaves for its labor? What were the consequences of the slave trade for individuals and institutions in each of the three continents constituting the Atlantic world?
- Why do we think of the plantation economy as a global, rather than regional, system of production? Why was it the "engine" of Atlantic basin trade?

empires depended extensively on slave labor. Indeed, the Atlantic slave trade was a major way in which European merchants enriched themselves. That trade in turn forcibly brought together the lives and cultures of peoples in Africa and the New World.

To the extent that any formal economic theory lay behind the conduct of these empires, it was mercantilism, that practical creed of hard-headed businesspeople. The terms **mercantilism** and *mercantile system* (coined by later opponents) designate a system in which governments heavily regulate trade and commerce in hope of increasing individual national wealth. Economic writers of the time believed that a nation had to gain a favorable trade balance of gold and silver bullion. A nation was truly wealthy only if it amassed more bullion than its rivals.

From beginning to end, the economic well-being of the home country was the primary concern of mercantilist writers. Colonies existed to provide markets and natural resources for the industries of the home country. In turn, the home country furnished military security and political administration for the colonies. For decades both sides assumed that the colonies were the inferior partner in the relationship. The mercantilist statesmen and traders regarded the world as an arena of scarce resources and economic limitation. They assumed that one national economy could grow only at the expense of others. The home country and its colonies were to trade exclusively with each other. To that end, they tried to forge trade-tight systems of national commerce through navigation laws, tariffs, bounties to encourage production, and prohibitions against trading with the subjects of other monarchs. National monopoly was the ruling principle

Mercantilist ideas were always neater on paper than in practice. By the early eighteenth century, mercantilist assumptions were far removed from the economic realities of the colonies. The colonial and home markets simply did not mesh. Spain could not produce enough goods for South America. Economic production in the British North American colonies challenged English manufacturing and led to British attempts to limit certain colonial industries, such as iron and hat making.

Colonists of different countries wished to trade with each other. English colonists could buy sugar more cheaply from the French West Indies than from English suppliers. The traders and merchants of one nation always hoped to break the monopoly of another. For all these reasons, the eighteenth century became the "golden age of smugglers."[1] The governments could not control the activities of all their subjects. Clashes among colonists could and did lead to war between governments. Consequently, the problems associated with the European mercantile empires led to conflicts around the world.

---

[1] Walter Dorn, *Competition for Empire, 1740–1763* (New York: Harper, 1940), p. 266.

tempting at first to appease him with gifts of gold that only whetted Spanish appetites. Cortés succeeded in forging alliances with some subject peoples and, most importantly, with Tlaxcala, an independent state and traditional enemy of the Aztecs. His forces including several thousand of his native allies then marched on the Aztec capital of Tenochtitlán (modern Mexico City), where Moctezuma welcomed him. Cortés soon seized Moctezuma, making him a prisoner in his own capital. Moctezuma died in unexplained circumstances, and the Aztecs' wary acceptance of the Spaniards turned to open hostility.

Read the Document
2nd Letter Hernán Cortéz to King Charles V
at **MyHistoryLab.com**

The Spaniards and their allies were driven from Tenochtitlán and nearly wiped out, but they ultimately returned and laid siege to the city. The Aztecs, under their last ruler, Cuauhtemoc (ca. 1495–1525), resisted fiercely but were finally defeated in late 1521. Cortés razed Tenochtitlán, building his own capital over its ruins, and proclaimed the Aztec Empire to be New Spain. (See Document, "A Spaniard Describes the Glory of the Aztec Capital" on page 502.)

Read the Document
del Castillo History of Conquest
at **MyHistoryLab.com**

In 1532, largely inspired by Cortés's example in Mexico, Francisco Pizarro (ca. 1478–1541) landed on the western coast of South America to take on the Inca Empire, about which he knew almost nothing. His force included about 200 men armed with guns, swords, and horses, the military power of which the Incas did not understand. Pizarro lured the Inca ruler Atahualpa (ca. 1500–1533) into a conference and then seized him. The imprisoned Atahualpa tried to ransom himself with a hoard of gold, but instead of releasing him Pizarro treacherously had him garroted in 1533. The Spaniards fought their way to Cuzco, the Inca capital, and captured it, effectively ending the Inca Empire. The Spanish faced insurrections, however, and fought among themselves for decades. Effective royal control was not established until the late 1560s.

Establishment of the Spanish Empire in America

Conquest of the Aztecs and the Incas

Within twenty years of the arrival of Columbus (1451–1506), Spanish explorers in search of gold had claimed the major islands of the Caribbean and brutally suppressed the native peoples. These actions presaged what was to occur on the continent. The Caribbean islands became the staging areas for the further exploration and conquest of other parts of the Americas (see Map 17–1).

In 1519 Hernán Cortés (1485–1547) landed in Mexico with about 500 men and a few horses. He opened communication with nearby communities and then with Moctezuma II (1466–1520), the Aztec emperor. Moctezuma may initially have believed Cortés to be the god Quetzalcoatl, who, according to legend, had been driven away centuries earlier but had promised to return. Whatever the reason, Moctezuma hesitated to confront Cortés, at-

Map 17–1. European Explorations and Conquests, ca. 1550. By the middle of the sixteenth century, Spain controlled vast territories in the Americas.

The conquests of Mexico and Peru are among the most dramatic and brutal events in modern world history. Small military forces armed with advanced weapons and in alliance with indigenous enemies of the ruling Aztecs and Incas subdued, in a remarkably brief time, these two advanced, powerful peoples. The spread of European diseases, especially smallpox, among the Native Americans also aided the conquest. The native populations had long lived in isolation, and many of them succumbed to the new diseases. But beyond the drama and bloodshed, these conquests, as well as those of other Native American peoples, marked a fundamental turning point. Whole civilizations with long histories and a record of enormous social, architectural, and technological achievement were effectively destroyed. Native American cultures endured, accommodating to European dominance, but there was never any doubt about which culture had the upper hand.

The Roman Catholic Church in Spanish America

The Spanish conquest of the West Indies, Mexico, and the South American continent opened that vast region to the Roman Catholic faith. As it had in the Castilian reconquest of the Iberian Peninsula from the Moors, religion played a central role in the conquest of the New World. In this re-

spect the crusade against Islamic civilization in Spain and the crusade against the indigenous religions of the Americas were closely related. In both cases the Castilian monarchy received approval from church authorities for a policy of military conquest on the grounds of converting non-Christians to the Christian faith and eradicating their indigenous religious practices. The mission of conversion justified military conquest and the extension of political control and dominance. As a consequence of this policy, the Roman Catholic Church in the colonial New World was always a conservative force working to protect the political power and prestige of the conquerors and the interests of the Spanish authorities.

The relationship between political authority and the propagation of religious doctrine was even closer in the New World than on the Iberian Peninsula. Recognizing that it could not support a continentwide missionary effort from its own resources, the papacy turned over much of the control of the church in the New World directly to the Spanish monarchy. The zeal of both the Spanish monarchy and the papacy increased early in the sixteenth century as the papacy and the Habsburg monarchy fought the new enemy of Protestantism, which they were determined should have no foothold in America. As a consequence, the Roman Catholicism that spread throughout the Spanish domains of America took the form of the increasingly zealous faith associated with the Counter-Reformation.

Document

A Spaniard Describes the Glory of the Aztec Capital

On November 8, 1519, a group of approximately 500 Spaniards and several thousand of their native allies under the command of Hernán Cortés entered the Aztec capital of Tenochtitlán. One of them was Bernal Díaz del Castillo (b. 1492) who later wrote *The Conquest of New Spain*, a chronicle of his experience. This excerpt gives some sense of the magnificence of the Aztec capital.

■ *Which elements of Aztec life especially astonished Díaz? What can one conclude about the social and political life of the Aztec elite from the manner in which Moctezuma was attended? Which forms of wealth were most apparent?*

Early next day we left Iztapalapa [where Cortés's forces had been camped] with a large escort of these great Caciques [Aztec nobles], and followed the causeway, which is eight yards wide and goes so straight to the city of Mexico [Tenochtitlán] that I do not think it curves at all. Wide though it was, it was so crowded with people that there was hardly room for them all. Some were going to Mexico and others coming away, besides those who had come out to see us, and we could hardly get through the crowds that were there. For the towers and the cues [temples] were full, and they came in canoes from all parts of the lake. No wonder, since they had never seen horses or men like us before.

With such wonderful sights to gaze on we did not know what to say, or if this was real that we saw before our eyes. On the land side there were great cities, and on the lake many more. The lake was crowded with canoes. At intervals along the causeway there were many bridges, and before us was the great city of Mexico. . . .

We marched along our causeway to a point where another small causeway branches off to another city . . . and there, beside some towerlike buildings, which were their shrines, we were met by many more Caciques and dignitaries in very rich cloaks. The different chieftains wore different brilliant liveries, and the causeways were full of them. . . .

. . . When we came near to Mexico, at the place where there were some other small towers, the great Moctezuma descended from his litter, and these other great Caciques supported him beneath a marvelously rich canopy of green feathers, decorated with gold work, silver, pearls . . . which hung from a sort of border. It was a marvelous sight. The great Moctezuma was magnificently clad, in their fashion and wore sandals . . . the soles of which are of gold and the upper parts ornamented with precious stones. And the four lords who supported him were richly clad also in garments that seem to have been kept ready for them on the road so they could accompany their master . . . and many more lords . . . walked before the great Moctezuma, sweeping the ground on which he was to tread, and laying down cloaks so that his feet should not touch the earth. Not one of these chieftains dared to look him in the face. All kept their eyes lowered most reverently except those four lords, his nephews, who were supporting him.

. . . Who could now count the multitude of men, women, and boys in the streets, on the rooftops and in canoes on the waterways, who had come out to see us? . . .

They led us to our quarters, which were in some large houses capable of accommodating us all and had formerly belonged to the great Moctezuma's father. . . . Here Moctezuma now kept the great shrines of his gods, and a secret chamber containing gold bars and jewels. This was the treasure he had inherited from his father, which he never touched.

Source: From *The Conquest of Spain* translated by J.M. Cohen © 1963 Reprinted by permission of Penguin Group, UK

During the sixteenth century the Roman Catholic Church, represented more often than not by the mendicant orders such as the Franciscans and Dominicans, and later by the newly formed Jesuits, sought to convert the Native Americans. The conversion effort involved attempts to eradicate surviving indigenous religious practices. Thus religious conversion represented, among other things, an attempt to destroy significant parts of the Native American culture. But conversion did not bring acceptance of Native Americans by the Spanish; even until late in the eighteenth century, there were few Native American Christian priests.

Spanish Conquest of Mexico. A sixteenth-century drawing depicts a battle during the Spanish conquest of Mexico. The Aztecs are on the right. Note how the Spaniards bring up the rear, behind their native allies, the Tlaxcalteca.

of their own. Those who spoke for the church did not challenge Spanish domination or any but the most extreme modes of Spanish economic exploitation. The church at best only modestly moderated the forces exploiting human labor and material wealth. By the end of the colonial era in the late eighteenth century, the Roman Catholic Church had become one of the single most conservative forces in Latin America and would continue to be so for at least the next century and a half.

Real tension, however, existed between the early Spanish conquerors and the mendicant friars who sought to minister to the Native Americans. Without conquest the church could not convert the Native Americans, but the priests often deplored the harsh conditions imposed on the native peoples. By far the most effective and outspoken clerical critic of the Spanish conquerors was Bartolomé de Las Casas (1474–1566), a Dominican. He contended that conquest was not necessary for conversion. One result of his campaign was new royal regulations after 1550. Another result of Las Casas's criticism was the emergence of the **Black Legend**, according to which all Spanish treatment of the Native Americans was unprincipled and inhumane. Those who created this view of Spanish behavior drew heavily on Las Casas's writings. Although substantially true, the "Black Legend" nonetheless exaggerated the case against Spain. Certainly the rulers of the native empires—as the Aztec demands for sacrificial victims attest—had often themselves been exceedingly cruel to their subject peoples.

By the end of the sixteenth century the church in Spanish America had become largely an institution upholding the colonial status quo. Although individual priests did defend the communal rights of Native American tribes, the colonial church prospered as the Spanish elite prospered through its exploitation of the resources and peoples of the New World. The church became a great landowner through crown grants and through bequests from Catholics who died in the New World. The monasteries took on an economic as well as a spiritual life

Read the Document
The New Laws for the Indies for Good Treatment
at **MyHistoryLab.com**

Read the Document
Account of Devastation of Indies
at **MyHistoryLab.com**

Economies of Exploitation in the Spanish Empire

The colonial economy of Spanish America was an economy of exploitation in two senses. First, the organization of labor within the Spanish Empire in one situation after another involved structures of highly dependent servitude or slavery. Second, the resources of the continent were exploited in mercantilist fashion for the economic advantage of Spain.

Varieties of Economic Activity

The early **conquistadores** ("conquerors") had primarily been interested in gold, but by the middle of the sixteenth century silver mining provided the chief source of metallic wealth. The great silver mining centers were Potosí in present-day Bolivia and smaller sites in northern Mexico. The Spanish Crown was particularly interested in mining because it received one-fifth (the *quinto*) of all mining revenues. The Crown thus maintained a monopoly over the production and sale of mercury, which was required for separating silver from the other impurities in the ore. Silver mining was a flourishing source of wealth for the Spanish until the early seventeenth century, when the industry underwent a recession because of lack of new investment and the increasing costs involved in deeper mines. Nonetheless, silver predominated during the colonial era and experienced a major boom, especially in Mexico, during the eighteenth century. Its production for the benefit of Spaniards and the Spanish Crown epitomized

Document — A Contemporary Describes Forced Indian Labor at Potosí

The Potosí range in Bolivia was the site of the great silver mining industry in the Spanish Empire. The vast wealth of the region became legendary almost as soon as mining commenced there in the 1540s. Native Americans, most of whom were forced laborers working under the *mita* system of conscription, did virtually all of the work underground. This description, written by a Spanish friar in the early seventeenth century, portrays both the large size of the enterprise and the harsh conditions that the Native Americans endured. At any one time only one-third of the 13,300 conscripted Native Americans were employed. The labor force was changed every four months.

■ *How efficient does the description suggest the mines were? What would have been the likely effects of working so long underground surrounded by burning candles?*

According to His Majesty's warrant, the mine owners on this massive range have a right to the *mita* [conscripted labor] of 13,300 Indians in the working and exploitation of the mines, both those which have been discovered, those now discovered, and those which shall be discovered. It is the duty of the Corregidor [municipal governor] of Potosí to have them rounded up and to see that they come in from all the provinces between Cuzco over the whole of El Collao and as far as the frontiers of Tarija and Tomina. . . .

The *mita* Indians go up every Monday morning to the locality of Guayna Potosí which is at the foot of the range; the Corregidor arrives with all the provincial captains or chiefs who have charge of the Indians assigned them, and he there checks off and reports to each mine and smelter owner the number of Indians assigned him for his mine or smelter; that keeps him busy till 1 P.M., by which time the Indians are already turned over to these mine and smelter owners.

After each has eaten his ration, they climb up the hill, each to his mine, and go in, staying there from that hour until Saturday evening without coming out of the mine; their wives bring them food, but they stay constantly underground, excavating and carrying out the ore from which they get the silver. They all have tallow candles, lighted day and night; that is the light they work with, for as they are underground, they have need of it all the time. . . .

These Indians have different functions in the handling of the silver ore; some break it up with bar or pick, and dig down in, following the vein in the mine; others bring it up; others up above keep separating the good and the poor in piles; others are occupied in taking it down from the range to the mills on herds of llamas; every day they bring up more than 8,000 of these native beasts of burden for this task. These teamsters who carry the metal do not belong to the *mita*, but are mingados—hired.

Source: From Antonio Vázquez de Espinosa, *Compendium and Description of the Indies* (ca. 1620), trans. by Charles Upson Clark (Washington, DC: Smithsonian Institution Press, 1968), p. 62, quoted in Helen Delpar, ed., *The Borzoi Reader in Latin American History* (New York: Alfred A. Knopf, 1972), pp. 92–93.

the wholly extractive economy on which Latin American colonial life was based.

The activities associated with this extractive economy—mining the ore, smelting it, harvesting wood to feed the smelters' fires—required extensive labor. From the initial contact with America, there were too few Spanish colonists to provide the needed labor. Furthermore, the social status and expectations of those colonists who did come to the Americas made them unlikely to provide wage labor. Consequently, the Spaniards looked first to the Native American population and then to imported African slaves. Indigenous labor dominated on the continent and African labor in the Caribbean. (See Document, "A Contemporary Describes Forced Indian Labor at Potosí.")

Encomienda The Spanish devised a series of institutions to exploit Native American labor. The first was the **encomienda**, a formal grant by the Crown of the right to the labor of a specific number of Native Americans for a particular time. An *encomienda* usually involved a few hundred Native Americans but might grant the right to the labor of several thousand. The *encomienda* was first used on Hispaniola but spread to the continent as the conquest took place. *Encomienda* as an institution persisted in some parts of Latin America well into the eighteenth century but had generally declined by the middle of the sixteenth. Some Native Americans substituted payments in kind or cash for labor.

Repartimiento The passing of the *encomienda* led to another arrangement of labor servitude, the ***repartimiento***, which was largely copied from the draft labor practices of the Incas. *Repartimiento*, in an adaptation of the Incan *mita*, required adult male Native Americans to devote a set number of days of labor annually to Spanish economic enterprises. In the mines of Potosí, the *repartimiento* was known as the *mita*. The time limitation on *repartimiento* led some Spanish managers to use their workers in an extremely harsh manner, under the assumption that more fresh workers would soon be appearing on the scene. Native Americans sometimes did not survive their days of labor rotation.

The Hacienda Outside the mines, the major institution using dependent labor in the Spanish colonies was the ***hacienda***. This institution, which dominated rural and agricultural life in Spanish colonies on the continent, developed when the crown, partly to counter the extension of the *encomienda*, made available grants of land. These grants led to the establishment of large landed estates owned by ***peninsulares***, whites born in Spain, or Creoles, whites born in America. The Crown thus continued to use the resources of the New World for patronage without directly impinging on the Native Americans because the grazing that occurred on the *haciendas* required far less labor than did the mines. The establishment of *haciendas* represented the transfer of the principal of the large unit of privately owned land, which was characteristic of Europe and especially of Spain, to the New World. Such estates would become one of the most important features of Latin American life. Laborers on the *hacienda* usually stood in some relation of formal servitude to the owner.

The Silver Mines of Potosí. Worked by conscripted Indian laborers under extremely harsh conditions, these mines provided Spain with a vast treasure in silver.

Furthermore, they were usually required to buy goods for everyday living on credit from the owner. They were rarely able to repay the resulting debts and thus could not move to work for new landowners. This system was known as **debt peonage**. There were two major products of the *hacienda* economy: foodstuffs for mining areas and urban centers, and leather goods used in vast quantities on mining machinery. Both farming and ranching were thus subordinate to the mine economy.

Commercial Regulation and the Flota System

Because Queen Isabella of Castile (r. 1474–1504) had commissioned Columbus, the technical legal link between the New World and Spain was the Crown of Castile. Its powers both at home and in America were subject to few limitations. Government of America was assigned to the Council of the Indies, which, in conjunction with the monarch, nominated the viceroys of New Spain and Peru. These viceroys were the chief executives in the New World and carried out the laws promulgated by the Council of the Indies. Each of the viceroyalties included subordinate judicial councils known as *audiencias*. There were also a variety of local officers, the most important of which were the *corregidores*, who presided over municipal councils. These offices provided the monarchy with a vast array of opportunities for patronage, usually bestowed on persons born in Spain. Virtually all political power flowed from the top of this political structure downward; in effect, there was little or no local initiative or self-government (see Map 17–2 on page 506).

The colonial political structures existed largely to support Spain's commercial goals. Spanish control of its American empire involved a system of monopolistic trade regulation that was more rigid in appearance than in practice. The trade monopoly was often breached. The Casa de Contratación (House of Trade) in Seville regulated all trade with the New World. Cádiz was the only Spanish port to be used for the American trade. In America there were similarly specific ports for trade both with Spain and with non-Spanish merchants. The non-Spanish trade was highly restricted. The Casa de Contratación was the single most influential institution of the Spanish Empire, and its members worked closely with the Consulado (Merchant Guild) of Seville and other groups involved with American commerce in Cádiz. The entire organization was geared to benefit the Spanish monarchy and these privileged merchant groups.

A complicated system of trade and bullion fleets administered from Seville provided the key to maintaining the trade monopoly. Each year a fleet of commercial vessels (the *flota*) controlled by Seville merchants, escorted by warships, carried merchandise from Spain to a few specified ports in America. These included Portobello, Veracruz, and

Map Exploration

To explore this map further, go to **http://www.myhistorylab.com**

DISPUTED BY
ENGLAND,
RUSSIA,
AND SPAIN

NEW
FRANCE

VICEROYALTY
OF
NEW SPAIN

ENGLISH
COLONIES

ATLANTIC

Rio Grande

EFFECTIVE FRONTIER OF
SPANISH SETTLEMENT

OCEAN

Gulf of Mexico

Mexico
City
• Veracruz
• Acapulco

Santo Domingo

Caribbean Sea

Cartagena   Caracas
Portobelo

VICEROYALTY OF
NEW GRANADA
Separated From
Bogotá   Viceroyalty of
Peru,
1717,1739

GUIANA

• Quito

Amazon R.

VICEROYALTY
OF
PERU

VICEROYALTY
OF
BRAZIL
(Portugal)

Pernambuco

• Lima

Bahia

PACIFIC

• Portosi

OCEAN

VICEROYALTY
OF
LA PLATA
Separated From the
Viceroyalty of Peru,
1776

São Paulo
Rio de Janeiro

Santiago •

Buenos
Aires

AUDIENCIA
OF CHILE

Claimed but not
settled by Spain

→ Manila galleon

→ Treasure fleet to Spain

– – Treaty of Tordesillas
demarcation line

Map 17–2. The Americas, ca. 1750. Spain organized its vast holdings in the New World into viceroyalties, each of which had its own governor and other administrative officials. The English colonies clung to the North American seaboard. French possessions centered on the St. Lawrence River and the Great Lakes. Portuguese holdings in Brazil were mostly confined to the coast.

Sugar plantations of Brazil and the West Indies were a major source of the demand for slave labor. Slaves are here shown grinding sugarcane and refining sugar, which was then exported to the consumer markets in Europe.

Cartagena. There were no authorized ports on the Pacific coast. Areas far to the south, such as Buenos Aires, received goods only after the shipments had been unloaded at one of the authorized ports. After selling their wares, the ships were loaded with silver and gold bullion, usually wintered in heavily fortified Caribbean ports, and then sailed back to Spain. Each year a Spanish ship also crossed the Pacific from Manila, in the Spanish colony of the Philippines, to the Mexican port of Acapulco, bringing Chinese silk and porcelain. It returned to Manila laden with Mexican silver. So the Spanish Empire became part of a global exchange of trade. The flota system always worked imperfectly, but trade outside it was illegal. Regulations prohibited the Spanish colonists within the American Empire from trading directly with each other and from building their own shipping and commercial industry. Foreign merchants were also forbidden to breach the Spanish monopoly. (See Document: "Visitors Describe the Portobello Fair" on page 508.)

Colonial Brazil

Spain and Portugal originally had rival claims to the Americas. In 1494, by the Treaty of Tordesillas, the pope divided the seaborne empires of Spain and Portugal by drawing a line west of the Cape Verde Islands. In 1500 a Portuguese explorer landed on the coast of what is present-day Brazil, which extended east of the papal line of division, and thus Portugal gained a major hold on the South American continent.

See the Map
Spanish and Portuguese Exploration
at **MyHistoryLab.com**

Portugal had fewer human and material resources to devote to its New World empire than did Spain. The Crown granted captaincies to private persons that permitted them to attempt to exploit the region. The native people in the lands that Portugal governed lived for the most part in small, nomadic groups. In this respect they differed from the native peoples of Spanish America, with their centralized empires, cities, and organized political structures. As a result, labor practices in the two regions were also different. The Portuguese imported Africans as slaves rather than using the Native American population, as did the Spanish in most areas.

By the mid-sixteenth century, sugar production had gained preeminence in the Brazilian economy, although some minerals were discovered and some cattle was raised. Because sugarcane was grown on large estates (*fazendas*) with African slave labor, the dominance of sugar also meant the dominance of slavery.

Toward the close of the seventeenth century, sugar prices declined and the economy suffered. In the early eighteenth century, however, significant deposits of gold were discovered in southern Brazil. Immigrants from Portugal joined the ensuing gold rush, and economic activity moved suddenly toward the south. Instead of reducing Brazil's reliance on slave labor, the expansion of gold mining actually led to the increased importation of African slaves. Nowhere, except perhaps in the West Indies, was slavery as important as it was in Brazil, where it persisted until 1888.

Document   Visitors Describe the Portobello Fair

The Spanish tried to restrict all trade within their Latin American Empire to a few designated ports. Each year, a fair was held in some of these ports. The most famous such port was Portobello on the Isthmus of Panama. In the 1730s, two visitors described the event. This fair was the chief means of facilitating trade between the western coast of South America and Spain.

■ *What products were sold at the fair? How does this passage illustrate the inefficiency of monopoly trade in the Spanish Empire and the many chances for smuggling?*

The town of Portobello, so thinly inhabited, by reason of its noxious air, the scarcity of provisions, and the soil, becomes, at the time of the [Spanish] galleons one of the most populous places in all South America. . . .

The ships are no sooner moored in the harbour, than the first work is, to erect, in the square, a tent made of the ship's sails, for receiving its cargo; at which the proprietors of the goods are present, in order to find their bales, by the marks which distinguish them. These bales are drawn on sledges, to their respective places by the crew of every ship, and the money given them is proportionally divided.

Whilst the seamen and European traders are thus employed, the land is covered with droves of mules from Panama, each drove consisting of above a hundred, loaded with chests of gold and silver, on account of the merchants of Peru. Some unload them at the exchange, others in the middle of the square; yet, amidst the hurry and confusion of such crowds, no theft, loss, or disturbance is ever known. He who has seen this place during the *tiempo muerto*, or dead time, solitary, poor, and a perpetual silence reigning everywhere; the harbour quite empty, and every place wearing a melancholy aspect; must be filled with astonishment at the sudden change, to see the bustling multitudes, every house crowded, the square and streets encumbered with bales and chests of gold and silver of all kinds; the harbour full of ships and vessels, some bringing by the way of Rio de Chape the goods of Peru, such as *cacao, quinquina,* or Jesuit's bark, Vicuña wool, and bezoar stones; others coming from Carthagena, loaded with provisions; and thus a spot, at all times detested for its deleterious qualities, becomes the staple of the riches of the old and new world, and the scene of one of the most considerable branches of commerce in the whole earth.

The ships being unloaded, and the merchants of Peru, together with the president of Panama, arrived, the fair comes under deliberation. And for this purpose the deputies of the several parties repair on board the commodore of the galleons, where, in the presence of the commodore, and the president of Panama, . . . the prices of the several kinds of merchandizes are settled. . . . The purchases and sales, as likewise the exchanges of money, are transacted by brokers, both from Spain and Peru. After this, every one begins to dispose of his goods; the Spanish brokers embarking their chests of money, and those of Peru sending away the goods they have purchased, in vessels called *chatas* and *bongos,* up the river Chagres. And thus the fair of Portobello ends.

Source: From George Juan and Antonio de Ulloa, *A Voyage to South America,* Vol. 1 (London, 1772), pp. 103–110, as quoted in Benjamin Keen, ed., *Readings in Latin-American Civilization, 1492 to the Present* (New York: Houghton Mifflin, 1955), pp. 107–108.

The taxation and administration associated with gold mining brought new, unexpected wealth to the eighteenth-century Portuguese monarchy, allowing it to rule without recourse to the Cortés or traditional parliament for taxation. Through transatlantic trade, the new wealth generated from Brazilian gold also filtered into all the major trading nations, which could sell their goods to Portugal as well as profit from the slave trade.

As in the Spanish Empire, the Portuguese Crown attempted to establish a strong network of regulation around Brazilian trade. Brazil, however, required less direct control by the Portuguese than the Spanish Empire required from Spain. As a result, Brazil's colonial settlers may have felt less resentment toward the Portuguese government than the settlers of the Spanish Empire felt toward the Spanish administrators. In Brazil, where the basic unit of production was the plantation, there were fewer large cities than in Spanish America. The Crown's determination in Spanish America to have precious metals sent to Spain required a vast colonial administration. The sugar plantations of Brazil, in contrast, did not require such direct administration. Consequently, the Portuguese were willing to allow more local autonomy than was Spain. More local officials were allowed to serve in the government in Brazil than in Spanish America, where the administration was dominated by officials born in Spain. In Spanish America the use of Native American labor, which was important to the colonial economy, required government supervision. Brazil, less dependent on Native American labor, felt no such constraints. Indeed, the Portuguese government condoned policies whereby indigenous tribes were driven into the back country or exterminated. Throughout the eighteenth century the Portuguese government also favored the continued importation of slaves.

French and British Colonies in North America

Both England and France had important sugar islands in the Caribbean. England held Jamaica and Barbados, and France held Saint Domingue (Haiti), Guadeloupe, and Martinique. The plantations on these islands were worked by African slaves, and the trade and commerce of the northern British colonies were closely related to meeting the needs of these islands. The major presence of both nations, however, spread across different parts of the North American continent.

French explorers had pressed down the St. Lawrence River valley in Canada during the seventeenth century. French fur traders and Roman Catholic Jesuit missionaries had followed in their wake, with the French government supporting the missionary effort. By the end of the seventeenth century a significant but sparsely populated French presence existed in Canada (see Map 17–2). Trade rather than extensive settlements characterized the French effort. The largest settlement was Quebec, founded in 1608. Some French settlers married Native American women; the absence of a drive to permanently claim land reduced conflict between the French and the Native Americans. It was primarily through the fur trade that French Canada functioned as part of the early transatlantic economy.

◀•••[Read the Document
Albanel from Jesuit Relation
at **MyHistoryLab.com**

Beginning with the first successful settlement in Jamestown, Virginia, in 1607 and ending with

●◯[See the **Map**
European Empires ca 1600
at **MyHistoryLab.com**

the establishment of Georgia in 1733, the eastern seaboard of the United States became populated by a series of English colonies. Other nations, including the Dutch and Swedes, had founded settlements, but all of them were eventually taken over during the seventeenth century by the English.

A wide variety of reasons led to the founding of the English colonies. Settlement for enrichment from farming and trade accounted for some settlements, such as Virginia and New Amsterdam (and after 1664, New York). Other colonies, such as the Carolinas, were developed by royal favorites who were given vast land tracts. James Oglethorpe founded Georgia as a refuge for English debtors. But the pursuit of religious liberty constituted the major driving force of the Pilgrim and Puritan founders of Massachusetts, the Baptist Roger Williams in Rhode Island, the Quaker William Penn in Pennsylvania, and the Roman Catholic Lord Baltimore in Maryland.

With the exception of Maryland, these colonies were Protestant. The Church of England dominated the southern colonies. In New England, varieties of Protestantism associated with or derived from Calvinism were in the ascendancy. In their religious affiliations, the English-speaking colonies manifested two important traits derived from the English experience. First, much of their religious life was organized around self-governing congregations. Second, their religious outlook derived from those forms of Protestantism that were

Fur Trade. A Native American hands a pelt to a European buyer while two spectators—one European, one Indian—nonchalantly observe the transaction. By 1700 the fur trade had decimated the beaver population in southern Canada and New England. *1777 engraving. © The Granger Collection, New York.*

suspicious of central political authority and especially of potentially despotic monarchs. In this regard, their cultural and political outlook differed sharply from the cultural and political outlook associated with the Roman Catholicism of the Spanish Empire. In a sense, the values of the extreme Reformation and Counter-Reformation confronted each other on the two American continents.

The English colonists had complex interactions with the Native American populations. Unlike the Spanish to the south or the French to the north, they had only modest interest in missionary enterprise. As in South America, new diseases imported from Europe took a high death toll among the native population. Unlike Mexico and Peru, however, North America had no large Native American cities. The Native American populations were far more dispersed, and intertribal animosity was intense.

The English often encountered well-organized resistance, as from the Powhatan conspiracy in Virginia and the Pequots in New England. The results of Native American warfare with the English, however, could be no less devastating than those of the native peoples with the Spanish. Between 1634 and 1638 English settlers almost completely eradicated the Pequot tribe in what is present-day Connecticut. During one encounter at Mystic in 1637 the English set fire to an enclosed Pequot village and prevented its inhabitants from escaping with the result of a loss of life of over 400 native people. At the end of the conflict in 1638, most of the few remaining Pequots were sold into slavery on Bermuda or in the West Indies. Later in the century in King Philip's War (1675–1676) the Native Americans killed significant numbers of English settlers and for a time slowed the pace of English settlement. But in the end the English settlers clearly dominated.

By the early eighteenth century the most powerful of the Native American groups was the Iroquois Nation, organized in New York. The Iroquois battled successfully against other tribes and long negotiated successfully with both the Dutch and the English. The English often used one tribe against another, and the Native Americans also tried to use the English

Roanoke. The first successful English colonies in North America in the seventeenth century were preceded by two failed efforts on Roanoke Island in what is now North Carolina in the late sixteenth century. John White accompanied both attempts, the second as governor. White was a perceptive and sensitive observer whose watercolor paintings provide invaluable information about Native American life in the coastal Carolina region at the time of contact. This painting shows the Algonquin village of Secoton. The houses were bark covered. In the lower left is a mortuary temple. The dancers in the lower right are performing a fertility ceremony. The man sitting in the platform in the upper right is keeping birds away from the corn crop.

or the French in their own conflicts. The outcome of these later struggles between the English settlers and the Native Americans was rarely full victory for either side; rather, the result was mutual exhaustion, with the Native Americans temporarily retreating beyond the reach of English settlements and the English temporarily restraining their initial claims. From the late seventeenth century through the American Revolution, however, the Native Americans of North America were drawn into the Anglo-French wars that were fought in North America as well as Europe. Indeed, Native American alliances became important for the Anglo-French conflict on the Continent, which was intimately related to their rivalry over transatlantic trade (see Chapter 19).

((•─[Hear the Audio
at **MyHistoryLab.com**

The largest economic activity throughout the English-speaking colonies was agriculture. From New England through the Middle Atlantic states there were mostly small farms tilled by free white labor; from Virginia southward the plantation economy, dependent on slavery, predominated. During the early eighteenth century the chief products raised on these plantations were tobacco, indigo, rice, and sugar. Although slavery was a dominant institution in the South, all of the colonies included slaves. The principal port cities along the seaboard—Boston, Newport, New York, Philadelphia, Baltimore, and Charleston—resembled small provincial English cities. They were primarily trading centers through which goods moved back and forth between the colonies and England and the West Indies. The commercial economies of these cities were all related to the transatlantic slave trade.

Cities in the northern British colonies had significant slave populations. By 1741 New York City had a slave population second only to that in Charleston, South Carolina. In that year rumors of a slave conspiracy swept New York City. In the reaction to these rumors scores of slaves were arrested. By the end of the affair thirteen African Americans were burned at the stake and seventeen others were hanged. At the same time four white citizens were executed. This incident illustrates the significance of northern slave populations, the anxieties that their presence aroused, and the manner in which the enslavement of Africans penetrated the society and economy of the northern colonies.

Until the 1760s the political values of the American colonists largely resembled those of their English counterparts. The colonials were thoroughly familiar with events in England. They sent many of their children there to be educated. They were monarchists but, like their English counterparts, suspicious of monarchical power. Their politics involved vast amounts of patronage and individual favors. Their society was clearly hierarchical, with an elite that functioned like a colonial aristocracy and many ordinary people who were dependent on that aristocracy. Throughout the colonies

during the eighteenth century, the Anglican Church grew in influence and membership. The prosperity of the colonies might eventually have led them to separate from England, but in 1750 few people thought that would occur.

The Columbian Exchange: Disease, Animals, and Agriculture

The European encounter with the Americas produced remarkable ecological transformations that have shaped the world to the present moment (see Map 17–3 on page 512). Alfred Crosby, the leading historian of the process, has named this cross-continental flow the **Columbian Exchange**.

Diseases Enter the Americas

With the exception of a few ships that had gone astray or, in the case of the Vikings, that had gone in search of new lands, the American continents had been biologically separated from Europe, Africa, and Asia for tens of thousands of years. In the Americas no native animals could serve as major beasts of burden except for the llama, which could not transport more than about a hundred pounds. Nor did animals constitute a major source of protein for Native Americans, whose diets consisted largely of maize, beans, peppers, yams, and potatoes. At the same time, the American continents included areas of vast grassland without grazing animals that would have transformed those plants into animal protein. Moreover, it also appears that native peoples had lived on the long-isolated American continents without experiencing such major epidemics as would decimate their populations in the decades after the encounter.

By the second voyage of Columbus (1493), that picture began to change in remarkable ways. On his return voyage to Hispaniola and other islands of the Caribbean, Columbus brought a number of animals and plants that were previously unknown to the New World. The men on all his voyages and those on subsequent European voyages also carried diseases novel to the Americas.

The diseases thus transported by Europeans ultimately accounted for the conquest of the people of the Americas as much as the advanced European weaponry. Much controversy surrounds the question of the actual size of the populations of Native Americans in the Caribbean islands, Mexico, Peru, and the North Atlantic coast. All accounts present those populations as quite significant, with those of Mexico in particular numbering many millions. In the first two centuries after the encounter, wherever Eu-

•●•─[Read the Document
Smallpox epidemic in Mexico 1520 and Smallpox epidemic in New England at **MyHistoryLab.com**

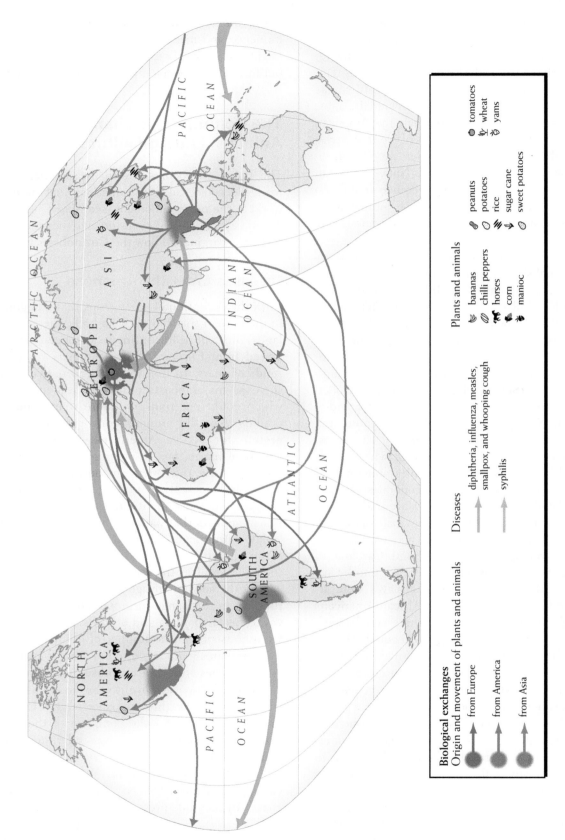

Map 17–3. Biological Exchanges. The worldwide movement of plants, animals, and diseases.

Biological exchanges
Origin and movement of plants and animals

- from Europe
- from America
- from Asia

Diseases

- diphtheria, influenza, measles, smallpox, and whooping cough
- syphilis

Plants and animals

- bananas
- chilli peppers
- horses
- corn
- manioc
- peanuts
- potatoes
- rice
- sugar cane
- sweet potatoes
- tomatoes
- wheat
- yams

Smallpox. Introduced by Europeans to the Americas, smallpox had a devastating effect on Native American populations. It swept through the Aztec capital of Tenochtitlán soon after the Spaniards arrived, contributing to the fall of the city. This illustration of the effect of the plague in the Aztec capital is from a post-conquest history known as the Florentine Codex, compiled for Spanish church authorities by Aztec survivors.

ropeans went either as settlers or as conquerors, extremely large numbers of Native Americans died from diseases they had never before encountered. The most deadly such disease was smallpox, which destroyed millions of people.

Beyond the devastation wrought by that disease, bubonic plague, typhoid, typhus, influenza, measles, chicken pox, whooping cough, malaria, and diphtheria produced deadly results in more localized epidemics. For example, an unknown disease, but quite possibly typhus, caused major losses among the Native Americans of New England between approximately 1616 and 1619.

On the reverse side of the equation it appears almost certain that syphilis, which became a rampant venereal disease in Europe at the close of the fifteenth century and eventually spread around the globe, originated in the New World. Until the discovery of penicillin in the 1940s, syphilis remained a major concern of public health throughout the world.

Animals and Agriculture

The introduction of European livestock to the Americas revolutionized the agriculture of two continents. The most important new animals were pigs, cattle, horses, goats, and sheep. Once transported to the New World, these animals multiplied at unprecedented rates. These animals were first introduced in the islands of the Caribbean, during the first forty years of Spanish settlement and exploitation. This event proved to be the foundation for the later Spanish conquest of both Mexico and Peru: It provided the Spanish with strong breeds of animals, especially horses, acclimated to the Americas when they set out to conquer the mainland of South America.

The horse became first the animal of the conquest and then the animal of colonial Latin American culture. Native Americans had no experience with such large animals who would obey the will of a human rider. The mounted Spanish

Overview The Columbian Exchange

To the Americas	
Diseases	smallpox, influenza, bubonic plague, typhoid, typhus, measles, chicken pox, malaria, and diphtheria
Animals	pigs, cattle, horses, goats, sheep, chickens
Plants	apples, peaches, pears, apricots, plums, oranges, mangos, lemons, olives, melons, almonds, grapes, bananas, cherries, sugarcane, rice, wheat, oats, barley, onions, radishes, okra, dandelions, cabbages, and other green vegetables
From the Americas	
Diseases	syphilis (?)
Animals	turkeys
Plants	maize, tomatoes, sweet peppers, chilis, potatoes, sweet potatoes, squash, pumpkins, manioc (tapioca), beans, cocoa, peanuts, pecans, pineapples, guavas, avocados, blueberries, and tobacco

Watch the Video at **MyHistoryLab.com**

horseman struck fear into Native Americans, and for good reason. After the conquest, however, the Americas from Mexico southward became the largest horse-breeding region of the world, with ranches raising thousands of animals. Horses became relatively cheap, and even Native Americans could acquire them. By the nineteenth century, the possession of horses would allow the Plains Indians of North America to resist the advance of their white conquerors.

Europeans also brought their own plants to the New World, including peaches, oranges, grapes, melons, bananas, rice, onions, radishes, and various green vegetables. Socially, for three centuries the most significant of these crops was sugarcane, whose cultivation created the major demand for slavery throughout the transatlantic plantation economy. Nutritionally, European wheat would, over the course of time, allow the Americas not only to feed themselves, but also to export large amounts of grain throughout the world.

No significant animals from the Americas, except the turkey, actually came to be raised in Europe. The Americas did, however, send to Europe a series of plants that eventually changed the European diet: maize, potatoes, sweet potatoes, peppers, beans, manioc (tapioca), peanuts, squash, pumpkins, pineapples, cocoa, and tomatoes. Africa was also the recipient of many of these same foodstuffs. All of these foods, to a greater or lesser degree, eventually entered the diet of Europeans and Africans and of European settlers and their descendants in the Americas. Maize and the potato had the most transforming impact. Each of these two crops became a major staple in European farming, as well as in the European diet. Both crops grow rapidly, supplying food quickly and steadily if not attacked by disease. Tobacco, we should note, originated in the Americas, too.

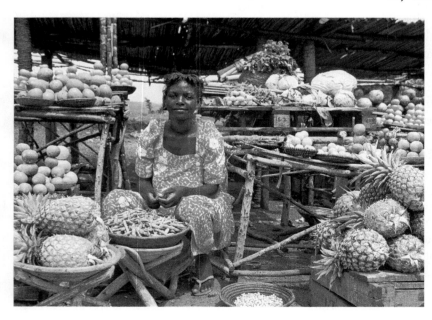

Global Foods. A woman in the African country of Uganda offers beans and pineapples for sale, both of which originated in the Americas.

✳ Map Exploration

To explore this map further, go to **http://www.myhistorylab.com**

Map 17–4. The Slave Trade, 1400–1860. Slavery is an ancient institution, and complex slave-trading routes were in existence in Africa, the Middle East, and Asia for centuries, but it was the need to supply labor for the plantations of the Americas that led to the greatest movement of peoples across the face of the earth.

Slavery in the Americas

Slavery was the final mode of forced or subservient labor in the New World. Unlike the labor exploitation of Native Americans discussed earlier in this chapter, enslavement of Africans and their descendants extended throughout not only the Spanish Empire but also Portuguese Brazil and the English-speaking colonies of North America. The heartland of transatlantic slavery lay in the Caribbean islands.

The Background of Slavery

Virtually every premodern state around the globe depended on slavery to some extent (see Map 17–4). The Mediterranean and African worlds were no exception, in both the pre-Islamic and the Islamic periods. Slave institutions in sub-Saharan Africa were ancient and included traffic with the Mediterranean world. The Islamic states of southwestern Asia and North Africa continued and even increased this traffic, importing slaves from both the

Sudan and Horn of Africa as well as the East African coast, although they took fewer slaves from Africa than from eastern Europe and Central Asia. Central Asia, for example, was the source of most of the (largely Turkish) slave-soldier dynasties that came to rule many Islamic states from India to North Africa. (Hence it is not surprising that the word *slave* is derived ultimately from *Slav*.) Both Mediterranean Christian and Islamic peoples were using slaves—mostly Greeks, Bulgarians, Turkish prisoners of war, and Black Sea Tartars, but also Africans—well before the voyages of discovery opened sub-Saharan sources of slaves for the new European colonies overseas.

Read the Document
Slavery in Africa late 1700s Mungo Park at **MyHistoryLab.com**

Not all forms of slavery were as dehumanizing as the **chattel slavery** that came to predominate (with the sanction of Christian authorities) during the colonization of the Americas. All slavery, however, involved the forceful exploitation and degradation of some human beings for the profit of others, the denial of basic freedoms, and sometimes the sundering, often violently, of even the closest family ties. Although there were some variations in the legal and social structures of slavery in the Atlantic world, slaves brought from Africa and their descendants were invariably chattel slaves: They were outright possessions of their masters, indistinguishable from any material possession; they were not recognized as persons under the law, so they had no legal rights; they could not claim any control over their bodies, their time, their labor, or even their own children.

Establishment of Slavery

As the number of Native Americans in South America declined due to disease and exploitation, the Spanish and the Portuguese turned to the labor of imported African slaves.

By the late sixteenth century, in the islands of the West Indies and the major cities of South America, the population of black slaves equaled or surpassed the white European population.

On much of the South American continent dominated by Spain, the number of slaves declined during the late seventeenth century, and the institution became less fundamental there than elsewhere. Slavery continued to prosper, however, in Brazil and especially in the Caribbean. Starting with the importation of slaves to Jamestown in 1619, slavery spread into the British North American colonies and later became a fundamental institution there.

One of the forces that led to the spread of slavery in Brazil and the West Indies was the cultivation of sugar. Sugarcane required a large investment in land and equipment, and only slave labor could provide enough workers for the extremely profitable sugar plantations. As the production of sugar expanded, so did the demand for slaves, and more slaves were imported.

By the close of the seventeenth century the Caribbean islands were the world center for sugar production. As the European appetite for sugar continued to grow, the slave population continued to expand. By 1725, slaves may have constituted almost 90 percent of the population of Jamaica. The situation was similar throughout the West Indies. There and elsewhere, in Brazil and the southern British colonies, prosperity and slavery went hand in hand. The wealthiest and most prized of the colonies were those that raised consumer staples, such as sugar, rice, tobacco, or cotton, by slave labor.

Sugar plantation. African slaves on the Caribbean island of Antigua bring sugar cane to a windmill where it will be crushed into juice. A white overseer closely watches the proceedings.

African American Culture. This eighteenth-century painting depicts a celebration in the slave quarters on a South Carolina plantation. One planter's description of a slave dance seems to fit this scene: the men leading the women in "a slow shuffling gait, edging along by some unseen exertion of the feet, from one side to the other—sometimes curtseying down and remaining in that posture while the edging motion from one side to the other continued." The women, he wrote, "always carried a handkerchief held at arm's length, which was waved in a graceful motion to and fro as she moved." *Abby Aldrich Rockefeller Folk Art Museum, Colonial Williamsburg Foundation, VA.*

The Plantation Economy and Transatlantic Trade

The **plantation economy** was composed of plantations that stretched from Maryland through the West Indies and into Brazil. They formed a vast corridor of slave societies in which social and economic subordination was based on both involuntary servitude and race. This kind of society, in its total dependence on slave labor and racial differences, was novel in world history; it had not existed before the European discovery and exploitation of the Americas. The social and economic influence of plantation slavery touched not only the plantation societies themselves, but also West Africa, western Europe, and New England. It persisted from the sixteenth century through the second half of the nineteenth century, ending with the British effort to outlaw the slave trade during the first half of the nineteenth century, the Latin American Wars of Independence, the Emancipation Proclamation of 1862 in the United States, and the Brazilian emancipation of 1888. Every society in which it existed still contends with its long-term effects.

The slave trade was part of the larger system of transatlantic trade that linked Europe, Africa, and the European colonies in South America, the Caribbean, and North America. In this system the Americas supplied labor-intensive raw materials such as tobacco, sugar, coffee, precious metals, cotton, and indigo. Europe supplied manufactured goods, including textiles, liquor, guns, metal wares, and beads, not to mention various forms of cash, including even gold. And Africa supplied gold, ivory, wood, palm oil, gum, and other products, as well as the slaves who provided the labor to create the American products. By the eighteenth century slaves were the predominant African export.

See the Map
Atlantic Slave Trade
at **MyHistoryLab.com**

Slavery on the Plantations

The plantations in the Americas at which the African slaves eventually arrived were always in a fairly isolated rural setting. Their products, however, were agricultural goods produced for an external overseas market that was part of a larger integrated transatlantic economy. The plantation might raise food for its owners and their slaves, but the main production—whether sugar, tobacco, or later, cotton and coffee—was intended for export. In turn, plantation owners imported from other parts of the world virtually all the finished or manufactured goods they used or consumed.

The life conditions of plantation slaves differed from colony to colony. Most owners possessed relatively few slaves, and vast slaveholdings were the exception. Black slaves living in Portuguese areas had the fewest legal protections. In the Spanish colonies the church attempted to provide some small protection for black slaves but devoted much more effort toward protecting the Native Americans. Slave codes were developed in the British and the French colonies during the seventeenth century, but they provided only the most limited protection. Virtually all slave owners feared a slave revolt; slave-related legislation and other regulations were intended to prevent such an event. Slave laws favored the master rather than the slave. Masters were permitted to punish slaves by whipping and other harsh corporal punishment. Furthermore, slaves were often forbidden to gather in large groups lest they plan a revolt. In most slave-owning societies, the marriages of slaves were not recognized by law. The child of an enslaved woman was born a slave, the property of the mother's owner. Slave families could be separated at whim by the owner or the owner's heirs.

Read the Document
Overseer in Cotton Plantation
at **MyHistoryLab.com**

The daily life of most slaves during these centuries was one of hard agricultural labor, poor diet and clothing, and inadequate housing. The death rate among slaves was high. Their welfare and their lives were sacrificed to the ongoing expansion of the plantations that made their owners wealthy and that produced goods demanded by consumers in Europe. Scholars have argued that slaves in one area or another had a better existence than others, but it is generally accepted that slaves in all plantation societies suffered under difficult conditions. The specifics of those conditions may have varied, but they were not significantly better in one place than another.

The African slaves who were transported to the Americas were, like the Native Americans, converted to Christianity: in the Spanish domains to Roman Catholicism, and in the English colonies to various forms of Protestantism. In both cases, they were forbidden to practice their traditional faiths. Slave owners often did not know whether particular activities were religious, but they erred on the side of caution: Activities that were not directly related to economic production, or that suggested links to African culture, were suppressed. Although some African practices survived in muted forms, and slaves did manage to mix Christianity with African religion, the conversion of Africans to Christianity nonetheless represented another example of the crushing of a set of non-European cultural values in the context of the New World economies and social structures.

The European settlers in the Americas and the slave traders were also prejudiced against black Africans. Many Europeans thought Africans were savage or less than civilized. Others looked down on them simply because they were slaves. These attitudes had been shared by both Christians and Muslims in the Mediterranean world, where slavery had long existed. Furthermore, many European languages and European cultures attached negative connotations to the idea and image of blackness. In virtually all plantation societies, race was an important element in keeping black slaves subservient. Although racial thinking in regard to slavery became more important in the nineteenth century, the fact that slaves were differentiated from the rest of the population by race as well as by their status as chattel property was fundamental to the system.

Africa and the Transatlantic Slave Trade

It was the establishment of plantations demanding the use of slave labor that drew Africa and its peoples into the heart of the transatlantic economy. As Native American peoples were decimated by conquest and European dis-

Chronology

Conquest of the Americas and the Transatlantic Slave Trade

1494	Treaty of Tordesillas divides the seaborne empires of Spain and Portugal
1500	The Portuguese arrive in Brazil
1519–1521	Hernan Cortés conquers the Aztec Empire
1531–1533	Francisco Pizarro conquers the Inca Empire
1607	Jamestown, Virginia, first permanent English settlement in North America
1608	The French found Quebec
1619	First African slaves brought to British North America
1700s	Over 6 million slaves imported from Africa to the Americas
1794	Slavery abolished throughout the French Empire
1807	The importation of slaves abolished in British domains
1808	The importation of slaves abolished in the United States
1817–1820	Spain abolishes the slave trade
1833	Slavery abolished throughout the British Empire
1865	Thirteenth Amendment to the Constitution abolished slavery in the United States
1850	Importation of slaves abolished in Brazil
1874–1928	Indigenous African slavery abolished
1888	Slavery abolished in Brazil

eases or proved unsatisfactory as plantation laborers, colonial entrepreneurs began to look elsewhere for people to work their plantations. First the Portuguese, and then the Spanish, Dutch, French, and English (others would follow, including Americans) turned to West, central, and, to a lesser degree, southeastern Africa for an ample supply of slaves. Thus the transatlantic slave trade was not overtly the result of racist principles, but of the economic needs of the colonial powers and their willingness to exploit weaker peoples to satisfy those needs. However, this willingness was based on the tacit racist assumption that non-European, nonwhite tribal peoples were subhuman and could be enslaved for European purposes.

Slaves in the streets of Zanzibar, nineteenth century. Slaving was part of East African trade for centuries. *Corbis-Bettmann.*

The Portuguese, who were the principal carriers throughout most of the early history of the trade, had a virtual monopoly of slavery until the Dutch broke it in the 1640s and briefly became the chief carriers. The French and the English came into the trade only in the late seventeenth century, yet during the eighteenth century, which saw the greatest number of slaves shipped, they carried almost half the total traffic. Americans, too, were latecomers but avid slavers who managed to make considerable profits before and even after Britain and the United States outlawed the transatlantic slave trade in 1807 and 1808, respectively.

If gold and the search for a sea route to Asia brought the first European ships to Africa, slaves were the main commodity for which they returned for a long time. Slaving was an important part of the massive new overseas trade that financed much European and American economic development that so dramatically changed the West during the nineteenth century. The success and considerable profits of this trade, bought at the price of immense human suffering, helped propel Europe and some of its colonial offshoots in the Americas into world dominance.

Slavery and Slaving in Africa

The trade that long before the fifteenth century supplied African slaves to the Islamic lands of the Mediterranean and to southwestern and southern Asia has conventionally been termed the "Oriental" slave trade. The savannahs of the Sudan and the Horn of Africa were the two prime sources of slaves for this trade. The Afro-European trade, conventionally called the **"Occidental" slave trade**, can be traced at least to the thirteenth century, when Euro-

peans established sugarcane plantations on Cyprus soon after Muslim forces had driven them out of the Holy Land. In Cypress, as later in Brazil and the Caribbean islands, slaves proved an especially profitable workforce for the labor-intensive process of sugar production. This industry subsequently spread westward to Crete and Sicily and, in the fifteenth century, to the Portuguese Atlantic islands of Madeira and São Tomé.

The Portuguese in particular developed the plantation system of slave labor as they began their expansion into the Atlantic and beyond. Although the savannah and Horn regions were the earliest sources for this trade, voyages beginning in the fifteenth century by first the Portuguese and then other Europeans opened the western coasts of Africa as far south as Angola, making them the prime slaving areas. A third but less important source region for both Occidental and Oriental trades was the eastern coast of Africa below the Horn.

Prior to the full development of the transatlantic slave trade by about 1650, slavery and slave trading had been no more significant in Africa than anywhere else in the world.[2] Indigenous African slavery resembled that of other premodern societies. It was apparently most common, if still limited, in the areas of the savannah and Horn, presumably because these areas were involved in external slave trading. In the western and central Sudan, slavery came largely to be regulated by Islamic norms, but in the Horn, specifically in Ethiopia, slavery was practiced in both Christian and Muslim communities. Estimates suggest that about 10,000 slaves per year, most of them female, were taken from sub-Saharan Africa through the Oriental slave trade.

By about 1650 the newer Occidental slave trade of the Europeans had become as large as the Oriental trade and for the ensuing two centuries far surpassed it. It affected adversely all of Africa, disrupting especially western and central African societies. As a result of the demand for young male slaves on the plantations of the Americas, West Africa experienced a sharp drain on its productive male population. Between 1640 and 1690, although the price of a slave at the coast remained constant, the number of slaves sold to European carriers doubled, indicating the increasing participation of Africans in the expanding trade. With the growing demand for slaves came an increase in internal warfare in western and central Africa. Moreover, as the external trade destroyed the regional male–female population balance, an internal market for female slaves in particular arose.

---

[2] The summary follows closely that of P. Manning, *Slavery and African Life: Occidental, Oriental, and African Slave Trades* (Cambridge: Cambridge University Press, 1990), pp. 127–140.

These developments accelerated during the eighteenth century—at the height of the Occidental trade. It was also during this period that African states and slave traders were most heavily involved as regulators and suppliers of the trade. Slave prices at times increased accordingly. Owing to population depletion and regional migrations, however, the actual number of slaves sold declined in some areas. The population declined sharply in the coastal and inland areas hardest hit by the ravages of the trade in the later eighteenth century and continued to decline in places even until 1850.

As European nations, followed by nations in the Americas, slowly began to outlaw first the slave trade and then slavery itself in the nineteenth century, occidental demand slowed and prices for slaves sank. The result was that the Oriental and internal trades increased. Slave exports from East Africa and the Sudan and Horn increased significantly after about 1780, and indigenous African slavery, predominantly of women, also expanded. Indeed, by about 1850 the internal African trade surpassed the combined Oriental and (now outlawed and decreasing) Occidental trade.

View the Image
West African Slave Market
at **MyHistoryLab.com**

This traffic was dominated by the same figures—merchants, warlords, and rulers—who had previously profited from external trade.

Indigenous African slavery began a real decline only at the end of the nineteenth century, in part because of the dominance of European colonial regimes and in part because of internal changes. The formal end of African indigenous slavery occurred over a long period, beginning in 1874 in the Gold Coast and ending only in 1928 in Sierra Leone. Late in the twentieth century, however, in various locations around the world—mostly places with endemic, severe poverty and weak civil authority, including the Sudan—patterns emerged of involuntary servitude and human trafficking that constitute modern-day slavery.

The African Side of the Transatlantic Trade

Africans were actively involved in the transatlantic slave trade. Except for the Portuguese in central Africa, European slave traders generally obtained their human cargoes from private or government-sponsored African middlemen

King Affonso I of the Kongo holds an audience with European ambassadors who kneel before him.

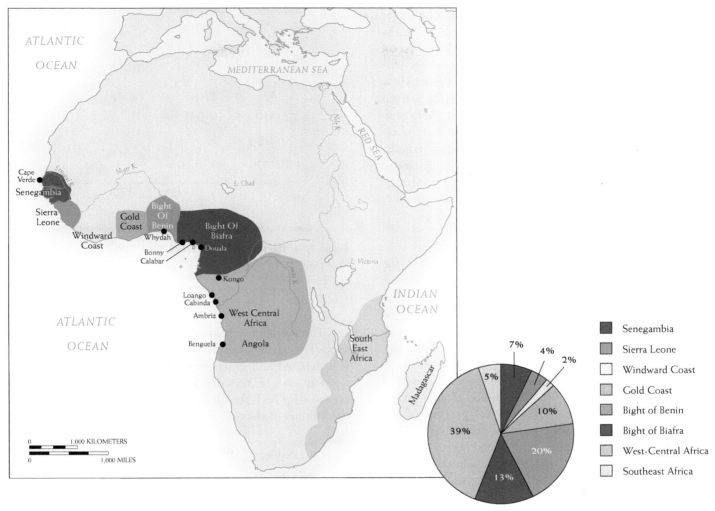

Map 17–5. Origins of African Slaves Sent to the Americas. Captive Africans came from eight regions. West Central Africa sent more captives to the Americas than any other region.

at coastal forts or simply at anchorages along the coast. A system of forts built by Europeans mostly between 1640 and 1750, for example, dominated the Gold Coast. This situation was the result of both the desire and ability of Africans to control inland trade and the vulnerability of Europeans to tropical disease (a new European arrival stood a less than 50 percent chance of surviving a year on the tropical African coast). Thus it was largely African middlemen who undertook the actual capture or procurement of slaves and the difficult, dangerous task of marching them to the coast. These middlemen were generally either wealthy merchants who could mount slaving expeditions inland or the agents of African chieftaincies or kingdoms who sought to profit from the trade.

The media of exchange were varied. At first they usually involved mixed barter for goods that ranged from gold dust or firearms to beads and alcohol. As time went on, they came increasingly to involve some form of monetary payment. This exchange drained productive resources (human beings) in return for nonproductive wealth.

The chief western and central African slaving regions provided different numbers of slaves at different times, and the total number of exported slaves varied sharply between periods (see Map 17–5). When one area was unable to produce sufficient numbers to meet demand (whether as a result of depopulation of choice areas, local warfare, or changing state policies), the European traders shifted their buying to other points. Thus, between 1526 and 1550 the major sources of the slaves for the transatlantic trade were the Kongo-Angola region (34 percent), the Guinea coast of Cape Verde (25.6 percent), and Senegambia (23.5 percent).[3] By contrast, between 1761 and 1810 the French drew some 52 percent of their slaves from Angola and 24 percent from the Bight of Benin, but only 4.8 percent from Senegambia, whereas the British relied most heavily on the Bight of Biafra and central Africa.[4] Traders naturally went where population density and the presence of active African merchant or state suppliers promised the best numbers and prices, although prices do not seem to have varied radically in a given period.

The Extent of the Slave Trade

Historians now estimate that from the sixteenth through the nineteenth centuries there were over 35,000 transatlantic slave ship voyages forcibly transporting more than 11 million Africans to America; many other Africans were lost in passage or through other brutality associated with the trade. The slave trade varied sharply in extent from period to period (see Figure 17–1). Only about 3 percent of the total Occidental trade occurred before 1600, and only about 14 percent between 1600 and 1700. The period of greatest activity, 1701–1810, accounted for over 60 percent of the total, and even the final half-century of slaving until 1870 accounted for over 20 percent of the total. Despite Great Britain's abolishing the slave trade in its colonies in 1807 and the United States in 1808, the Portuguese still transported more than a million slaves to Brazil between 1811 and 1870. Other nations also continued to trade in slaves in the nineteenth century. In fact, more slaves landed in the Americas in these final years of the trade than during the entire seventeenth century.[5] We would do well to remember how long it actually took the "modern" Western nations to abolish the trade in African slaves.

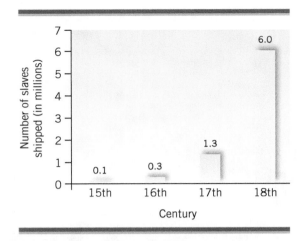

Figure 17–1 The Atlantic Slave Trade, 1400–1800. From Jorge Caizares-Esguerra; Eric Seeman, *The Atlantic in Global History; 1500–2000,* © 2007. Electronically reproduced by permission of Pearson Education, Inc., Upper Saddle River, New Jersey.

The overall number of African slaves exported during the Occidental trade—effectively, between 1451 and 1870—is still debated and must be seen in the larger context of all types of slaving in Africa in the same period. A major unknown—for both the Occidental and the Oriental trades—is the number of slaves who died under the brutal conditions to which they were subjected when captured and transported overland and by sea. The **Middle Passage**, the portion of the slave's journey that saw Africans packed onto dangerous and unhealthy boats for the voyage across the Atlantic Ocean, claimed untold numbers. The most reliable estimates pertain only to those slaves who actually landed abroad, and these estimates are more reliable for the Occidental trade than for the older, smaller, and more dispersed Oriental trade. As already noted, those who actually reached an American or Old World destination in the Occidental trade totaled more than 10 million.

View the Image
Diagram Slave Ship Filled for Middle Passage at **MyHistoryLab.com**

Another 5 million or more were lost to the Oriental trade. Finally, the Occidental trade spurred an apparently huge increase in internal slavery, and according to the estimate of one expert, an additional 15 million people were enslaved within African societies themselves.[6]

Consequences of the Slave Trade for Africa

The statistics in the previous section hint at the massive impact slave trading had on African life and history. Still, the question of specific effects remains difficult and dis-

---

[3] Scholars have spent decades attempting to assemble trustworthy statistics on the slave trade; the recent database by David Eltis et al., [Pls. give first name for Eltis.] *The Trans-Atlantic Slave Trade: A Database on CD-ROM* (Cambridge: Cambridge University Press, 2000), has marshaled a great deal of information in one spot, but new data continue to emerge. See Philip Curtin, *The Atlantic Slave Trade: A Census* (Madison: University of Wisconsin Press, 1969), p. 101.

[4] Curtin, *The Atlantic Slave Trade*, pp. 101, 129; James A. Rawley, *The Trans-Atlantic Slave Trade: A History* (New York: W. W. Norton, 1981), p. 129. Note that precise statistics are subject to revision in light of more recent scholarship; see, for example, Eltis et al., *The Trans-Atlantic Slave Trade: A Database on CD-ROM.*

[5] Rawley, *The Transatlantic Slave Trade*, p. 429; Curtin, *Atlantic Slave Trade*, p. 268.

[6] Manning, *Slavery and African Life*, pp. 37, 170–171.

puted. Modern scholarship has tended to emphasize the importance for African history of the coming of the maritime European powers in general and the transatlantic slave trade in particular. Regarding the slave trade, it is safe to say that the impact was considerable, however much that general conclusion must be qualified in the light of particular cases. (See Document, "A Slave Trader Describes the Atlantic Passage" on page 524) Consider some examples.

We do not know for certain if the transatlantic trade brought net population loss or gain to specific areas of West Africa. The wide and rapid spread of maize and cassava cultivation in forest regions after these plants had been imported from the Americas may have fueled African population increases that offset regional human loss through slaving. We know, however, that slaving took away many of the strongest young men in many areas and, in the Oriental trade zones, most of the young women.

Similarly, we do not know if more slaves were captured as by-products of local wars or from targeted slave raiding, but we do know they were captured and removed from their societies.

Nor do we know if slaving always inhibited development of trade or perhaps sometimes stimulated it because commerce in a range of African products—from ivory to wood and hides—often accompanied that in slaves. Still, we do know that in general, the exchange of productive human beings for money or goods that were generally not used to build a productive economy was a great loss for African society as a whole.

Finally, because we do not yet have accurate estimates of the total population of Africa at different times over the four centuries of the transatlantic slave trade, we cannot determine with certainty its demographic impact.

Job ben Solomon. Captured by Mandingo enemies and sold to a Maryland tobacco planter, Job ben Solomon accomplished the nearly impossible feat of returning to Africa as a freeman. By demonstrating his talents as a Muslim scholar, including his ability to write the entire Qur'an from memory, he astonished his owners and eventually convinced them to let him go home. *"The Fortunate Slave," An Illustration of African Slavery in the early eighteenth century by Douglas Grant (1968). From "Some Memoirs of the Life of Job," by Thomas Bluett 1734. Photo by Robert D. Rubic/Precision Chromes, Inc., Rare Books Division, the New York Public Library, Lenox and Tilden Foundations/Art Resource, New York.*

We can, however, make some educated guesses. If, for example, tropical Africa had possibly 50 million inhabitants in 1600, it would then have had 30 percent of the combined population of the Americas, the Middle East, Europe, and North Africa. If in 1900, after the depredations of the slave trade, it had 70 million inhabitants, its population would have dropped to only slightly more than 10 percent of the combined population of the same world regions. Accordingly, current best estimates indicate that overall African population growth suffered significantly as a result of the devastating numbers of people lost to enslavement or to the increased warfare and decreased birthrate tied to the slave trade. Figures like these also give some idea of slavery's probable impact on Africa's ability to engage with developments that, elsewhere in the world, led to the emergence of the modern industrializing world.[7]

---

[7] On all of the preceding points regarding the probable impact of the trade, see Manning, *Slavery and African Life*, pp. 126–148, 168–176. Also consult Eltis et al., *The Trans-Atlantic Slave Trade: A Database on CD-ROM* (an expanded and enhanced version was published in 2008).

Document   A Slave Trader Describes the Atlantic Passage

During 1693 and 1694, Captain Thomas Phillips carried slaves from Africa to Barbados on the ship Hannibal. The financial backer of the voyage was the Royal African Company of London, which held an English crown monopoly on slave trading. Phillips sailed to the west coast of Africa, where he purchased the Africans who were sold into slavery by an African king. Then he set sail westward.

■ *Who are the various people described in this document who in one way or another were involved in or profited from the slave trade? What dangers did the Africans face on the voyage? What contemporary attitudes could have led this captain to treat and think of his human cargo simply as goods to be transported? What are the grounds of his self-pity for the difficulties he met?*

Having bought my complement of 700 slaves, 480 men and 220 women, and finish'd all my business at Whidaw [on the Gold Coast of Africa], I took my leave of the old king and his *cappasheirs* [attendants], and parted, with many affectionate expressions on both sides, being forced to promise him that I would return again the next year, with several things he desired me to bring from England. . . . I set sail the 27th of July in the morning, accompany'd with the East-India Merchant, who had bought 650 slaves, for the Island of St. Thomas . . . from which we took our departure on August 25th and set sail for Barbadoes.

We spent in our passage from St. Thomas to Barbadoes two months eleven days, from the 25th of August to the 4th of November following: in which time there happened such sickness and mortality among my poor men and Negroes. Of the first we buried 14, and of the last 320, which was a great detriment to our voyage, the Royal African Company losing ten pounds by every slave that died, and the owners of the ship ten pounds ten shillings, being the freight agreed on to be paid by the charter-party for every Negro delivered alive ashore to the African Company's agents at Barbadoes. . . . The loss in all amounted to near 6500 pounds sterling.

The distemper which my men as well as the blacks mostly died of was the white flux, which was so violent and inveterate that no medicine would in the least check it, so that when any of our men were seized with it, we esteemed him a dead man, as he generally proved. . . .

The Negroes are so incident to [subject to] the small-pox that few ships that carry them escape without it, and sometimes it makes vast havoc and destruction among them. But tho' we had 100 at a time sick of it, and that it went thro' the ship, yet we lost not above a dozen by it. All the assistance we gave the diseased was only as much water as they desir'd to drink, and some palm-oil to anoint their sores, and they would generally recover without any other helps but what kind nature gave them. . . .

But what the smallpox spar'd, the flux swept off, to our great regret, after all our pains and care to give them their messes in due order and season, keeping their lodgings as clean and sweet as possible, and enduring so much misery and stench so long among a parcel of creatures nastier than swine, and after all our expectations to be defeated by their mortality. . . .

No gold-finders can endure so much noisome slavery as they do who carry Negroes; for those have some respite and satisfaction, but we endure twice the misery; and yet by their mortality our voyages are ruin'd, and we pine and fret ourselves to death, and take so much pains to so little purpose.

Source: From Thomas Phillips, "Journal," *A Collection of Voyages and Travels,* Vol. 6, ed. by Awnsham and John Churchill (London, 1746), as quoted in Thomas Howard, ed., *Black Voyage: Eyewitness Accounts of the Atlantic Slave Trade* (Boston: Little, Brown, and Company, 1971), pp. 85–87.

A Closer Look

The Slave Ship *Brookes*

This print, published in 1788 in England by the Plymouth Chapter of the Society for Effecting the Abolition of the Slave Trade, became the single most important and widely circulated abolitionist image of the horrific conditions of the Middle Passage. It records the main decks of the 320-ton slave ship *Brookes*, which measured 25 feet wide and 100 feet long.

The average space for each African destined for slavery in the Americas was 78 inches by 16 inches. The Africans were normally shackled to ensure discipline and to prevent their injuring the crew. Iron shackles also prevented Africans from committing suicide on the voyage.

Through the most inhumane use of space efficiency, 609 slaves could be crammed onboard for the nightmarish passage to America. A Parliamentary inquiry in 1788 found that the ship had been designed to carry no more than approximately 450 persons.

(See Document: *"A Slave Trader Describes the Atlantic Passage."*)

Questions

1. What response is this image, showing the crowded conditions on the slave ship *Brookes,* expected to arouse in the viewer? How do you think the response of viewers in the early twenty-first century might differ from those in the late-eighteenth and early-nineteenth centuries?

2. In recent years some commentators have criticized this image as indicating passivity on the part of the enslaved Africans and activity only on the part of the abolitionists. Why might this interpretation be directed toward the image?

3. Do you think that British viewers of this image of the *Brookes* would necessarily have associated their own nation with the slave trade? Why or why not?

myhistorylab   To examine this image in an interactive fashion, please go to **www.myhistorylab.com**

It is important to remember that even in West and central Africa, which bore the brunt of the transatlantic trade, its impact and the response to it were so varied in different places and times that even accurate overall statistics could be misleading for particular cases. In a few cases, kingdoms such as Dahomey (the present Republic of Benin) seem to have sought and derived immense economic profit for a time by making slaving a state monopoly. Other kingdoms, such as Benin, sought to stay almost completely out of slaving and derived no gain from it. In many instances, including the rise of Asante power or the fall of the Yoruba Oyo Empire, it now appears that increased slaving was in part a result as well as a cause of regional instability and change. Increased warfare meant increased numbers of prisoners to be enslaved and a surplus to be sold off; however, whether slaving gave good cause for war is still a major question in each regional context.

Similarly, if one can establish, as seems evident, a major increase in indigenous slavery as a result of the external trade to Occident and Orient during the centuries in question, we have to assume major social consequences for African society as a whole, but the specific consequences would differ according to the specifics of regional situations. For example, in West Africa relatively more men were taken as slaves than women, whereas in the Sahelian Sudanic regions relatively more women than men were taken. In the west the loss of so many men increased the pressures for polygamy and possibly the regional use of women slaves as well, whereas in the Sahelian Sudanic regions the loss of women may have stimulated polyandry and reduced the birthrate significantly.

Even though slavery existed previously in Africa, the scale of the transatlantic trade was unprecedented and hence had an unprecedented impact on indigenous social, political, and economic realities. In general, the slave trade measurably changed patterns of life and balances of power in the main affected areas, whether by stimulating trade or warfare (or at least raiding for new supplies), by disrupting previous market and political structures, by substantially increasing slavery inside Africa, or by disturbing the male–female ratio (and hence the workforce balance and birthrate patterns) and consequently the basic social institution of monogamous marriage.

If the overseas slave trade did not substantially and irrevocably change every region it touched, at the least it siphoned indigenous energy into ultimately counterproductive or destructive directions. This, in turn, meant the inhibition of true economic development, especially in central and coastal West Africa. The transatlantic slave trade must by any standard be described as one of the most tragic aspects of European involvement in Africa.

Summary

European Conquest of the New World. The contact between the native peoples of the American continents and the European explorers of the fifteenth and sixteenth centuries transformed world history. In the Americas, the native peoples had established a wide variety of civilizations. Some of their most remarkable architectural monuments and cities were constructed during the centuries when European civilizations were feeble in comparison. Until the European explorations, the civilizations of the Americas, Eurasia, and Africa had had no significant contact with each other.

Within half a century of the landing of Columbus, millions of America's native peoples had encountered Europeans intent on conquest, exploitation, and religious conversion. Because of their advanced weapons, navies, and the new diseases they brought with them, as well as internal divisions among the Native Americans, the Europeans achieved a rapid conquest.

The Transatlantic Economy. In both North and South America, economies of exploitation were established. In Latin America, various institutions were developed to extract native labor. From the Mid-Atlantic English colonies through the Caribbean and into Brazil, slave-labor plantation systems were established. The slaves were forcibly imported from Africa and sold in the Americas to plantation owners. The economies and peoples of Europe, Africa, and the Americas were thus drawn into a vast worldwide web of production based on slave labor.

Watch the Video
at **MyHistoryLab.com**

Slavery. The impact of slavery in the Americas was not limited to the life of the black slaves. Whites in the New World numbered about 12 million in 1820, compared to some 6 million blacks. However, only about 2 million whites had migrated there, compared to some 10 million or more Africans forcibly imported as slaves. Such numbers reveal the effects of brutal slave conditions and the high mortality and low birthrates of slave populations.

None of these statistics, however, enables us to assess the role that slavery has played in the Americas or, in particular, the United States. The United States actually received only a bit more than a quarter as many slaves as did Brazil alone or the British and French Caribbean regions together, yet the forced migration of Africans as slaves into the United States had profound consequences. Consider just the American Civil War and the endurance of racism and inequality, or, more positively, the African contribution to American industrial development, language, music, literature, and artistic culture.

On the African continent, the impact of the slave trade was immense, though difficult to document specifically for many areas. The social, economic, and personal effects were enormous in any case, given the extent and duration of the trade. Certainly the loss of population and productive resources helped set the stage for European colonization. The Atlantic slave trade's impact continues to be felt at both ends of the original "trade."

Key Terms

Black Legend (p. 503)

chattel slavery (p. 516)

Columbian Exchange (p. 510)

conquistadores (p. 503)

debt peonage (p. 505)

encomienda (p. 504)

hacienda (p. 505)

mercantilism (p. 499)

Middle Passage (p. 522)

"Occidental" slave trade (p. 519)

peninsulares (p. 505)

plantation economy (p. 517)

repartimiento (p. 505)

Review Questions

1. How were small groups of Spaniards able to conquer the Aztec and Inca empires?

2. What was the basis of the mercantilist theory of economics? What was the relationship between the colonial economies and those of the homelands?

3. Describe the economies of Spanish America and Brazil. What were the similarities and differences between them and the British and French colonies in the Caribbean and North America? What role did the various colonies play in the transatlantic economy?

4. Explain the chief factors involved in the Columbian Exchange. Which animals from Europe flourished in the Americas? Why? Which American plants produced broad impact in Europe and elsewhere in the world?

5. Why did forced labor and slavery develop in tropical colonies? How was slavery in the Americas different from slavery in earlier societies?

6. What historical patterns emerged in the slave trade(s) within and out of Africa? Consider the gender and age distribution of slaves, their places of origin, and their destinations.

7. Compare and contrast the Oriental and Occidental slave trades. What was the effect of the transatlantic slave trade on West African societies? On East Africa? What role did Africans themselves play in the slave trade?

Note: *To learn more about the topics in this chapter, please turn to the Suggested Readings at the end of the book. For additional sources related to this chapter please see MyHistoryLab.com.*

myhistorylab Connections

Reinforce what you learned in this chapter by studying the many documents, images, maps, review tools, and videos available at **www.myhistorylab.com**.

Read and Review

✔●┤Study and Review   Chapter 17

●┤Read the Document   *2nd Letter Hernán Cortéz to King Charles V, p. 500*
del Castillo History of Conquest, p. 500
The New Laws for the Indies for Good Treatment, p. 503
Account of Devastation of Indies, p. 503
Albanel from Jesuit Relation, p. 509
Smallpox epidemic in Mexico 1520 and Smallpox epidemic in New England, p. 511
Slavery in Africa late 1700s Mungo Park, p. 516
Overseer in Cotton Plantation , p. 517

●┤See the Map   *Spanish and Portuguese Exploration, p. 507*
European Empires ca 1600, p. 509
Atlantic Slave Trade, p. 517

●┤View the Image   *West African Slave Market, p. 520*
Diagram Slave Ship Filled for Middle Passage, p. 522

Research and Explore

●┤Watch the Video   *Columbian Exchange*

●┤Watch the Video   *Triangle Trade Routes*

((●┤**Hear** the **Audio**

Hear the audio file for Chapter 17 at
www.myhistorylab.com.

18 | East Asia in the Late Traditional Era

Late Imperial China

■ Ming (1368–1644) and Qing (1644–1911) Dynasties

Japan

■ Warring States Era (1467–1600)

■ Tokugawa Era (1600–1868)

Korea and Vietnam

■ Korea

■ Vietnam

Seventeenth-century screen painting of a Shintō river festival in Tsushima (a town near Nagoya city) held annually in July to ward off epidemics in the heat of the summer. Among the throng of spectators at the river's edge are shopkeepers, other townspeople, Buddhist priests, and palanquin bearers (at the left). Of the five boats on the river (which are not shown), each with 550 lanterns, only one mast with five red lanterns can be seen at the center of the panel. *Tosa (attributed to): people along the river. Detail from screen representing the River Festival. 17th century. Painting on paper. Photo: Arnaudet. Musée des Arts Asiatiques-Guimet, Paris, France. Reunion des Musées Nationaux/Art Resource, New York.*

W HEN WE COMPARE EAST ASIAN countries, we find shared cultural traits. This affinity is immediately apparent if we look at Chinese, Japanese, Korean, and Vietnamese paintings side by side. Less visible, but no less basic, was a range of social values shared at least by their elites. To the extent that it was based on Confucianism, the similarity may have been greatest in the mid–nineteenth century, when China, Japan, Korea, and Vietnam had become more Confucian than ever before.

But when we look at their histories and institutions, the similarities are fewer. China and Japan were furthest apart; each had gone its own way. Korea and Vietnam, even while forging an identity in reaction to their borrowings from China, were more directly influenced by China in their culture and institutions.

East Asia in the Late Traditional Era

East Asia

Why did the West, and not East Asia or anywhere else, open the door to modernity? Why did an industrial revolution not develop within the sophisticated commercial economies of Japan and China? The answer, obviously, must be found within Western history. Still, a few comparisons with the West may illuminate aspects of premodern East Asia.

1. The sociologist Max Weber saw Western capitalism as inspired by the Protestant ethic—which he found lacking in India, China, and Catholic Europe. But is the East Asian family-centered ethic of frugality, savings, and hard work not a "Protestant ethic" of sorts? And if a deeper Calvinist anxiety about salvation is required, as Weber theorized, then why has East Asia achieved such explosive growth since World War II?

2. Was the scientific revolution of the seventeenth century critical to the industrial revolution? Some historians say that industry was well under way before science began to make a substantial contribution from the late nineteenth century.

3. The self-educated technicians of England who invented the water loom and steam engine reaped enormous honors and rewards. In China and Japan no patents protected inventors, and no economists wrote of inventors as the benefactors of society. Wealth and honors were reserved for officials and gentry, who were literary and political in orientation and despised those who worked with their hands. (Of course, in earlier dynasties, the Chinese had been brilliantly inventive without patent protection.)

4. Bureaucracy is sometimes viewed as a key component of modernity. Bureaucracy does for administration what the assembly line does for production: It breaks complex

---

For China, the Ming (1368–1644) and Qing dynasties (1644–1911) were just two more centralized bureaucratic regimes of a kind that had been in place for centuries. In the Tang (618–907) the Chinese had forged a pattern of government so efficient and closely geared to the deeper familial and educational constitution of the society that, thereafter, they rebuilt it after each dynastic breakdown. This pattern continued during the Ming and the Qing, giving their histories a recognizable cyclical cast, even though they are also replete with historical trends that cut across dynastic lines.

Japanese political history, in contrast, is not cyclical. Each period of Japanese history reflects a new and different configuration. The centralized governments of the Nara and early Heian gave way to a manorial social order within which a powerful, local warrior class emerged. From this "feudal" class arose first the Kamakura *bakufu*, and then the Ashikaga. These in turn were followed by an era of Warring States and then a lengthy period of centralized "feudalism." Superficially at least, Japan's history was more like that of Europe than that of China. Neither Europe nor Japan ever found a pattern of rule that worked so well, was so sat-

isfactory to the rulers, and was so deeply embedded in the institutions of the society that it was re-created over and over again. In fact, from a Japanese or European point of view, that is not how history works.

This chapter underlines the dynamism of both China and Japan during these late centuries. "Late traditional society" does not mean "late static society." In both countries the society became more integrated and the apparatus of government more sophisticated than ever before. These advances shaped Chinese and Japanese responses to the West during the nineteenth century. Even Korea and Vietnam did not lack dynamism, though they also had problems aplenty. But we must especially note that it was during these centuries that the West was transformed. In fact, Greece and Rome apart, most of what seems important in Western history—the Renaissance, the Reformation, the Scientific Revolution, the formation of nation-states, the industrial revolution, the Enlightenment, and the democratic revolution—happened while the Ming and the Qing dynasties were reigning in China. As we view East Asia from the perspective of Europe, it appears to have been caught in a tar pit of slow motion. But in fact the West had simply accelerated. ■

tasks into simple ones, to achieve huge gains in efficiency. In the West bureaucracies appeared only in recent centuries. They strengthened monarchies and nation-states against landed aristocrats; they represented the triumph of ability over hereditary privilege. Chinese bureaucrats shared many of the same virtues. They were an elite of talent educated in the Confucian classics, as British officials were educated in those of Greece and Rome. But they were somehow different. They had wielded power for at least a millennium and were a segment of the landed gentry class in a country from which hereditary aristocrats had long since disappeared. Despite their talent, in the nineteenth century they would constitute a major obstacle to modernity. Were samurai bureaucrats of the Tokugawa era closer to their Western counterparts?

Putting aside comparisons with Europe, we also note the difference between Chinese and Japanese attitudes toward outside civilizations. When the Jesuits tried to introduce science, the Chinese response was occasional curiosity and general indifference. A few Jesuits were appointed as interpreters or court astronomers, or were used to cast cannons for China's armies. The Chinese lack of interest in foreign cultures can be explained by the coherence of China's core institutions: the emperor, bureaucracy, examination system, Confucian schools, and gentry. These were so deeply rooted and highly appreciated as to constitute a closed system. In contrast, despite a national policy of seclusion, the Japanese reached out for Dutch medicine and science—as they had earlier reached out for Chinese Neo-Confucianism. In the middle of the nineteenth century, this openness helps explain their rapid advance.

That Vietnam and Korea did not achieve industrial revolutions requires less explanation. They were smaller and less commercially developed than China or Japan. Vietnam was preoccupied with wars and its expansion to the south. In Korea—sometimes called the "hermit kingdom"—the elites were open only to Chinese culture and engaged in endless factional struggles.

Late Imperial China

Ming (1368–1644) and Qing (1644–1911) Dynasties

The Ming and the Qing were China's last dynasties. The first was Chinese; the second was a dynasty of conquest in which the ruling house and an important segment of the military were foreign (Manchus). They were nevertheless remarkably similar in their institutions and pattern of rule—so much so that historians sometimes speak of "Ming-Qing despotism" as if it were a single system. The two dynasties are also coupled as a result of certain demographic and economic trends that began during the Ming and continued through the Qing.

Land and People

China's population doubled from about 60 or 90 million in 1368 at the start of the Ming Dynasty to about 125 million in 1644 at its end. The population then tripled during the early and middle Qing Dynasty, reaching about 410 million people several decades into the mid-nineteenth century. This population density stimulated the growth of commerce and gave new prominence to the scholar-gentry class.

An increase in the food supply paralleled population growth. During the Ming, the spread of Song agricultural technology and new strains of rice accounted for 40 percent of the higher yields, and newly cultivated lands accounted for the rest. During the Qing, half the increased food supply was due to new lands and the other half to better seeds, fertilizers, and irrigation. New crops introduced from America during the late Ming, such as maize, sweet potatoes, and peanuts (which could be planted on dry sandy uplands and did not compete with rice), also bolstered the food supply. By the nineteenth century maize was grown in all parts of China.

In north China the population had declined from 32 million to 11 million during the Mongol conquests. The Ming government repopulated its open lands, resettling villages, building water control systems, and reopening the Grand Canal in 1415. The movement of people to the north continued until the nineteenth century. In the north, most farmers owned the land they worked and at times used hired labor. The land consisted mainly of irrigated dry fields, and the chief crops were millet, sorghum, and wheat.

South and southwest China also saw an influx of migrants from the densely populated lower Yangtse region, many settling in hilly or mountainous border areas that were agriculturally marginal. The White Lotus Rebellion of 1796–1804 occurred in such a recently settled area far from

Fishermen on Autumn River, a Ming Dynasty scroll painting by Dai Qin (1390–1460). Tai Chin, "Fisherman on an Autumn River" (1390–1460). A painting in ink and color on paper by the Ming artist Dai Quin. *Courtesy of Freer Gallery of Art, Smithsonian Institution, Washington, DC.*

centers of governmental authority. The Miao Wars of the late eighteenth century also were precipitated by the movement of Chinese settlers into southwestern uplands previously left to the slash-and-burn agriculture of the Miao tribes. Other

See the Map
Ming and Qing China
at **MyHistoryLab.com**

Chinese crossed over to Taiwan or emigrated overseas. During the Qing Dynasty, large Chinese mercantile communities became established in Southeast Asia.

The Yangzi basin, meanwhile, became even more densely populated. The lower Yangzi region and the delta, well supplied with waterways, had long been the rice basket of China, but from the late Ming agricultural cash crops, such as silk and cotton, predominated. Cotton was so widely grown in the delta that food had to be brought in from other areas by the early nineteenth century. In the lower Yangzi absentee landlords owned almost half of the land. A typical landlord's holdings were subdivided among tenants, who paid fixed rents in kind. South China also had extensive absentee landlordism, but far more land was owned collectively by clans, which managed the land and distributed rents among their members.

There are many unanswered questions regarding the population growth during these six centuries (1368–1911). Was there a decline in the death rate, and, if so, why? Or was it simply that new lands and technology enabled more mouths to be fed? Did the population oblige by promptly increasing? Certainly the Ming–Qing era was the longest continuous period of good government in Chinese history. The good years of Ming rule were longer than such periods in earlier dynasties, and the transition to Qing rule was quicker and less destructive. How much did these long periods of good government contribute to the population growth? Epidemic disease was not absent. In the great

plagues from 1586 to 1589 and from 1639 to 1644, as many as 20 to 30 percent of the people died in the most populous regions of China, and in specific counties and villages the figure was often higher. Another epidemic occurred in 1756, and a cholera epidemic from 1820 to 1822. The growth of China's population more than overcame such losses. Because of the growth in agriculture and population, most accounts view the eighteenth century as the most prosperous in Chinese history. But by the early nineteenth century the Chinese standard of living may have begun to decline. An ever-increasing population was no blessing.

China's Third Commercial Revolution

Commerce in China flourished between 300 B.C.E. and 220 C.E. (the late Zhou through the Han dynasties), only to decline in the centuries of disunity that followed. In Chapter 7 we read Sima Qian's description of wealthy Han merchants. Between 850 and 1250 (late Tang through Song) commerce again surged, only to contract during Mongol rule. At the end of the Mongol Dynasty, warlords confiscated merchant wealth. Early Ming emperors, isolationist and agrarian in orientation, restricted the use of foreign goods, required licenses for junks (coastal sailing ships), and attempted to encase foreign trade within the constraints of the tribute system. The early Ming also operated government monopolies that stifled enterprise and depressed the southeastern coastal region by their restrictions on maritime trade and shipping. But in the mid-sixteenth century commerce started to grow again, buoyed by the surge of population and agriculture and aided by a relaxation of government controls. If the growth during the Han and Song dynasties may be called, respectively, China's first and second com-

A porcelain enameled plate, from the Ming Dynasty, late sixteenth century.

Plate, Ming Dynasty, late 16th–early 17th century, "Kraakporselein," probably from the Ching-te Chen kilns. Porcelain, painted in underglaze blue. Diameter 14 1/4 in. The Metropolitan Museum of Art, Rogers Fund, 1916 (16.13). Photograph (c)1980 The Metropolitan Museum of Art. Art Resource, New York.

mercial revolutions, then the expansion between 1500 and 1800 was the third. This revolution was partly the extension to other parts of China of changes begun earlier in the Yangzi area, but it had new features as well. By the early nineteenth century China was the most highly commercialized nonindustrial society in the world.

One stimulus to commerce was imported silver, which played the role in the Ming-Qing economy that copper cash had played in the Song Dynasty. The Chinese balance of trade was favorable. Beginning in the mid-sixteenth century silver from mines in western Japan entered China, and from the 1570s, Spanish galleons sailing from Acapulco to China via Manila brought in Mexican and Peruvian silver. In exchange, Chinese silks and porcelains were sold in the shops of Mexico City. The late Ming court also opened silver mines in Guizhou and Yunnan provinces. In the eighteenth century copper mines were opened in south China. Also, private Shaanxi banks opened branches throughout China to facilitate the transfer of funds from one area to another and extend credit for trade. Eventually they opened offices in Singapore, Japan, and Russia as well.

As in Europe, so in China, the influx of silver and the overall increase in liquidity led to inflation and commercial growth. The price of land rose steadily. During the sixteenth century the thirty or forty early Ming taxes on land that were payable in grain, labor service, and cash were consolidated into one tax payable in silver, the so-called Single Whip Reform. To obtain the silver, farmers sold their grain in the market, and some switched from grain to cash crops. Moreover, by the early nineteenth century there were six times as many farm families as in the mid-fourteenth century.

Urban growth between 1500 and 1800, responding to flourishing local markets, was mainly at the level of intermediate market towns. These towns grew more rapidly than the population as a whole and provided the link between the local markets and the larger provincial capitals and cities such as Beijing, Hangzhou, or Guangzhou. The commercial integration of local, intermediate, and large cities was not entirely new, having occurred during the Song Dynasty in the lower Yangtse region, but now it spread over all of China. Interregional trade also gained. Where Song trade between regions was mainly in luxury goods such as silk, lacquerware, porcelains, medicines, and paintings, early Qing traders also dealt in staples, such as grain, timber, salt, iron, and cotton. This is not to suggest that China developed a national economy. Seven or eight regional economies, each the size of a large European nation, were still the focus for most economic activity. However, a new level of trade developed among them, especially where water transport made such trade economical. A final feature of eighteenth-century Chinese economic life was the so-called putting out system in textiles, under which merchant capitalists organized and financed each stage of production from fiber to dyed cloth.

Women and the Commercial Revolution The Confucian family ideal changed little during the Ming and Qing dynasties. A woman was expected first to obey her parents, then her husband, and finally her son—when he became the new family head. Physically, women became more restricted. Footbinding, which had begun among the elite during the Song Dynasty, spread through the upper classes during the Ming and to some commoners during the mid- to late Qing (see Figure 18–1). Most girls were subjected to this cruel and deformative procedure. Even in villages, women with big— that is to say, normal—feet were sometimes considered unmarriageable. One exception to the rule was the Hakka people of south China. Hakka women with unbound feet worked in the fields alongside their male kinsmen. Another exception was the Manchus. One Manchu (Qing) emperor even issued an edict banning footbinding, but the Chinese ignored it.

As population grew and the size of the average landholding shrank, more women worked at home, spinning, weaving, and making other products for the burgeoning commercial markets. As their contribution to the household income grew, their voice in household decisions often became larger than Confucian doctrines would suggest. But at the same time, women's property rights—to inheritance and control of dowries—became more limited than in previous dynasties. Furthermore, the same commercial revolution increased the number of rich townsmen who could afford concubines and patronize tea houses, restaurants, and brothels. (See Document, "The Thin Horse Market.")

Political System

One might expect these massive demographic and economic changes to have produced, if not a bourgeois revolution, at least some profound change in the political superstructure of China. They did not. Government during the Ming and Qing was much like that of the Song or Yuan, only improved and made stronger. Historians sometimes describe it as the "perfected" late imperial system. This system, they argue, was able to contain and use the new economic energies that destroyed the weaker late feudal polities of Europe. The sources of strength of the perfected Ming–Qing system were the spread of education, Confucianism ideology, stronger

emperors, better government finances, more competent officials, and a larger gentry class with an expanded role in local society.

Role of Confucianism Confucian teachings were more widespread in late imperial China than ever before. There were more schools in villages and towns. Academies preparing candidates for the civil service examinations multiplied. Publishing flourished, bookstores abounded, and literacy outpaced population growth. The Confucian view of society was patriarchal. The family, headed by the father, was the basic unit. The emperor, the son of heaven and the ruler-father of the empire, stood at its apex. In between were the district magistrates, the "father-mother officials." The idea of the state as the family writ large was not just a matter of metaphor but carried with it duties and obligations that were binding at every level.

The sociopolitical worldview of Confucianism was also buttressed by Neo-Confucian metaphysics, which gave a unitary character to Ming and Qing culture. This is not, of course, to deny the existence of different schools of Confucian thought. The vitality of late Ming thinkers was especially notable. Still, in comparison to Europe, where religious philosophies were less involved with the state and where a revolution in science was reshaping both religious and political doctrines, the greater unity and integration of the Chinese worldview cannot be denied.

Figure 18–1. A Bound Foot. This diagram shows the twisted and cramped bone structure of a bound ("lily") foot, as compared with that of a normal foot. Bound tightly with cloth from the age of 5, a little girl's foot grew painfully into this deformed but erotically admired shape. *From FAIRBANK. East Asia, 2/E © 1989 Wadsworth, a part of Cengage Learning, Inc. Reproduced by permission.*

Document | The Thin Horse Market

In China, ancestors without descendants to perform the rites ran the danger of becoming hungry ghosts or wandering spirits. Consequently, having a son who would continue the family line was an act of filial piety. If a wife failed to produce an heir, an official, a merchant, or wealthy landowner might take a concubine and try again. Or he might do so simply because he was able to, because it gave him pleasure, and because it was socially acceptable. For a poor peasant household, after a bad harvest and faced with high taxes, the sale of a comely daughter often seemed preferable to the sale of ancestral land.

■ *Concubines usually had no choice in the matter, but neither did many brides in pre-modern China. Was a woman better off as the wife of a poor peasant, experiencing hardship, hunger, and want, or as the concubine in a wealthy household with servants, good food, and the likelihood that her children would receive an education? What does the following passage tell us about attitudes toward women in premodern China?*

Upwards of a hundred people in Yangzhou earn a living in the "thin horse" business.* If someone shows an interest in taking a concubine, a team of a broker, a drudge, and a scout stick to him like flies. Early in the morning, the teams gather to wait outside the doors of potential customers, who usually give their business to the first team to arrive. Any teams coming late have to wait for the next opportunity. The winning team then leads their customer to the broker's house. The customer is then served tea and seated to wait for the women. The broker leads out each of them, who do what the matchmaker tells them to do. After each of her short commands, the woman bows to the customer, walks forward, turns toward the light so the customer can see her face clearly, draws back her sleeves to show him her hands, glances shyly at him to show her eyes, says her age so he can hear her voice, and finally lifts her skirt to reveal whether her feet are bound. An experienced customer could figure out the size of her feet by listening to the noise she made as she entered the room. If her skirt made noise when she walked in, she had to have a pair of big feet under her skirt. As one woman finishes, another comes out, each house having at least five or six. If the customer finds a woman to his liking, he puts a gold hairpin in her hair at the temple, a procedure called "inserting the ornament." If no one satisfies him, he gives a few hundred cash to the broker or the servants.

If the first broker gets tired, others will willingly take his place. Even if a customer has the stamina to keep looking for four or five days, he cannot finish visiting all the houses. Nevertheless, after seeing fifty to sixty white-faced, red-dressed women, they all begin to look alike and

he cannot decide which are pretty or ugly. It is like the difficulty of recognizing a character after writing it hundreds or thousands of times. Therefore, the customer usually chooses someone once his mind and eyes can no longer discriminate. The owner of the woman brings out a piece of red paper on which are listed the "betrothal presents," including gold jewelry and cloth. Once he agrees to the deal, he is sent home. Before he even arrives back at his lodgings, a band and a load of food and wine are already waiting there. Before long, presents he was to send are prepared and sent back with the band. Then a sedan chair and all the trimmings—colorful lanterns, happy candles, attendants, sacrificial foods—wait outside for the customer's arrangement. The cooks and the entertainer for the wedding celebration also arrive together with foods, wine, candy, tables, chairs, and tableware. Without the customer's order, the colorful sedan chair for the girl and the small sedan chair for her companion are dispatched to get the girl. The new concubine performs the bowing ceremony with music and singing and considerable clamor. The next morning before noon the laborers ask for rewards from the man, then leave to prepare another wedding for another customer in the same manner.

*A horse market is for the sale of horses. A "thin horse" market is the market for concubines. The name implies a measure of criticism.

Emperor In Ming–Qing times the emperor was stronger than ever. The Secretariat of high officials that had coordinated government affairs during the Song and the Yuan was abolished by the first Ming emperor, who personally made all important and many unimportant decisions. His successors, often aided by Grand Secretaries, continued this pattern of direct, personal rule. During the late fourteenth and fifteenth centuries the emperor was the bottleneck official, without whose active participation the business of government would bog down.

Then, during the sixteenth and early seventeenth centuries, a series of emperors appeared who were not interested in government. One spent his days on wine, women, and sports; another on Daoist rites; and still another emperor, who never learned to write, passed his days making furniture. During this era Grand Secretaries or eunuchs exercised the emperor's authority. But the Qing reestablished the pattern of personal government by emperors.

◆●▸ Read the Document
Mitamura at **MyHistoryLab.com**

Emperors wielded despotic powers at their courts. They had personal secret police and prisons where those who gave even minor offense might be tortured. Even high officials might suffer the humiliating, and sometimes fatal, punishment of having their bared buttocks beaten with bamboo rods at court—a practice inherited from the Mongols. The dedication and loyalty even of officials who were mistreated attest to the depth of their Confucian ethical formation. One censor who had served three emperors ran afoul of a powerful eunuch. The eunuch obtained an imperial order and had the official tortured to death in 1625. In his deathbed notes to his sons, the official blamed the villain for his agonies but wrote that he welcomed death because his body belonged to his "ruler-father." An earlier mid-sixteenth century incident involved Hai Rui, the most famous censor of the Ming period:

> Hai presented himself at the palace gate to submit a memorial denouncing some of the emperor's notorious idiosyncrasies. The emperor flew into a rage and ordered that Hai not be permitted to escape. "Never fear, sire," the eunuch go-between told the emperor. "He has said goodbye to his family, has brought his coffin with him, and waits at the gate!" Shih-tsung [the emperor] was so taken aback by this news that he forgave Hai for his impertinence.[1]

During the Qing the life-and-death authority of emperors did not diminish, but officials were generally better treated. As foreign rulers, the Manchu emperors took care not to alienate Chinese officials.

---

[1]C. O. Hucker, *China's Imperial Past* (Stanford, CA: Stanford University Press, 1975), p. 206.

The Forbidden Palace in Beijing, rebuilt when the third Ming emperor moved the capital from Nanjing to Beijing, was an icon of the emperor's majesty. Unlike the Kremlin, which consists of an assortment of buildings inside a wall, the entire palace complex in Beijing focused on the single figure of the ruler. Designed geometrically, its massive outer and inner walls, vast courtyards, and halls progress stage by stage to the raised area of the audience hall. During the Tang, emperors sat together with their grand councilors while discussing matters of government. In the Song, officials stood in the emperor's presence. By the Ming, the emperor sat on an elevated dais above the officials, who knelt before him. Behind the audience hall were the emperor's private chambers and his harem. In 1425 the palace had 6,300 cooks serving 10,000 persons daily. These numbers later increased. By the seventeenth century there were 9,000 palace ladies and perhaps 70,000 eunuchs. The glory of the emperor extended to his family, whose members were awarded vast estates in north China.

Bureaucracy A second component of the Ming–Qing system was the government itself. The formal organization of offices was little different from that in the Tang or the Song. At the top were the military, the censorate, and the administrative branch, and beneath the administration were the six ministries and the web of provincial, prefectural, and district offices. But government was better financed at this time than during earlier dynasties. China's productivity became steadily greater, whereas the apparatus of government grew only slowly. Government finances had their ups and downs, but as late as the 1580s huge surpluses were still being accumulated at both the central and the provincial levels. These surpluses probably braked the process of dynastic decline. Only during the last fifty years of the Ming did soaring military expenses bankrupt government finances.

In the second half of the seventeenth century the Manchus reestablished a strong central government and restored the flow of taxes to levels close to those of the Ming. In fact, revenues were so ample that early in the eighteenth century the emperors were able to freeze taxes on agriculture at the 1711 level and fix quotas for each province.

This contributed to the general prosperity of the eighteenth century but led to problems during the nineteenth century. Because agricultural productivity continued to rise, even though local officials collected some of the surplus, fixed quotas meant a declining share of the product. Both cultivators and gentry probably benefited from the new wealth, with the latter obtaining the larger share.

If the Ming–Qing system can be spoken of as perfected, the good government it brought to China was largely a product of the ethical commitment and the ex-

Document

The Seven Transformations of an Examination Candidate

The Chinese civil service examination was a grueling ordeal. Like a chess tournament, it required physical strength. Chinese critics said, "To pass the provincial examination a man needed the spiritual strength of a dragon-horse, the physique of a donkey, the insensitivity of a wood louse, and the endurance of a camel." The following selection is by a seventeenth-century writer who never succeeded in passing.

■ *Is the style of this passage overdone, or is it effective? What is distinctively Chinese about it?*

When he first enters the examination compound and walks along, panting under his heavy load of luggage, he is just like a beggar. Next, while undergoing the personal body search and being scolded by the clerks and shouted at by the soldiers, he is just like a prisoner. When he finally enters his cell and, along with the other candidates, stretches his neck to peer out, he is just like the larva of a bee. When the examination is finished at last and he leaves, his mind in a haze and his legs tottering, he is just like a sick bird that has been released from a cage. While he is wondering when the results will be announced and waiting to learn whether he passed or failed, so nervous that he is startled even by the rustling of the trees and the grass and is unable to sit or stand still, his restlessness is like that of a monkey on a leash. When at last the results are announced and he has definitely failed, he loses his vitality like one dead, rolls over on his side, and lies there without moving, like a poisoned fly. Then, when he pulls himself together and stands up, he is provoked by every sight and sound, gradually flings away everything within his reach, and complains of the illiteracy of the examiners. When he calms down at last, he finds everything in the room broken. At this time he is like a pigeon smashing its own precious eggs. These are the seven transformations of a candidate.

Source: From I. Miyazaki, *China's Examination Hell,* trans. by C. Schirokauer. Copyright © 1976 Weatherhill, pp. 57–58.

---

ceptional ability of its officials. No officials in the world today approach in power or prestige those of the Ming and the Qing. When the Portuguese arrived early in the sixteenth century, they called these officials "mandarins." (This term began as a Sanskrit word for "counselor" that became Hindi, entered Malay, and was then picked up by the Portuguese and adopted by other Europeans.) As in the Song, the rewards of an official career were so great that the competition to enter it was intense. As population and the number of schools grew, entrance became increasingly competitive. (See Document, "The Seven Transformations of an Examination Candidate.")

After being screened at the district office, a candidate took the county examination. If he passed, he became a member of the gentry. He gained the cap and sash of the scholar and exemption from state labor service. Even this examination required years of arduous study. About half a million passed each year. The second hurdle was the provincial examination held every third year. Only one in a hundred or more was successful. The final hurdle was the metropolitan examination, also held triennially. During the Ming, fewer than ninety passed each year. As in earlier dynasties, regional quotas were set to prevent the Yangzi region from dominating the officialdom.

Gentry A final component in the Ming–Qing system—if not new, at least vastly more significant than in earlier dynasties—was the **gentry** class. It was an intermediate layer between the elite bureaucracy above and the village below. The lowest level of bureaucratic government was the office of the district magistrate. Although the population increased sixfold during the Ming and the Qing, the number of district magistrates increased only from 1,171 to 1,470. Thus the average district, which had had a population of 50,000 in the early Ming and 100,000 in the late Ming, had two or three times that number by the early nineteenth century. The district magistrate came to his district as an outsider. The "law of avoidance," designed to prevent conflicts of interest, prevented him from serving in his home province. His office compound had a large staff of secretaries, advisers, specialists, clerks, and runners; but even then, he could not govern such a large population directly. To govern effectively, the magistrate had to obtain the cooperation of the local literati or gentry.

Examination Stalls. The dilapidated remains of the examination stalls at Nanjing. Doors to individual cubicles can be seen to the right and left of the three-story gate. Thousands of such cubicles made up the old examination stalls. Those who passed the exams governed China.

By *gentry* we do not mean a rural elite, like English squires. The Chinese gentry was largely urban, living in market towns or district seats. Socially and educationally, its members were of the same class as the magistrate—a world apart from clerks, runners, or village headmen. They usually owned land, which enabled them to avoid manual labor and to send their children to private academies. As absentee landlords whose lands were worked by sharecroppers, they were often exploitative; rebels at the end of the Ming attacked landlords as they did government offices. But the gentry were also local leaders. They represented community interests, which they interpreted conservatively, vis-à-vis the bureaucracy. They also performed quasi-official functions on behalf of their communities: maintaining schools and Confucian temples; repairing roads, bridges, canals, and dikes; and writing local histories.

The gentry class was the matrix from which officials arose; it was the local upholder of Confucian values. During the mid-nineteenth century, at a time of crisis, it would become the sustainer of the dynasty.

Pattern of Manchu Rule The collapse of the Ming Dynasty in 1644 and the establishment of Manchu rule was less of a break than might be imagined. First, the transition was short. Second, the Manchus, unlike the Mongols, were already partially Sinicized at the time of the conquest. They had been vassals of the Chinese state during the Ming, organized by tribal units into commanderies. Even before entering China, they had had the experience of ruling over Chinese who had settled in Manchuria to the north of the Great Wall.

In the late sixteenth century an able leader unified the Manchurian tribes and proclaimed a new dynasty. While still based in Mukden (more recently, Shenyang), the dynasty established a Confucian government with six ministries, a censorate, and other Chinese institutions. When the Ming collapsed and rebel forces took over China, the Manchus presented themselves as the conservative upholders of the Confucian order. The Chinese gentry preferred the Manchus to Chinese rebel leaders, whom they regarded as bandits. After the Manchu conquest, a few scholars and officials became famous as Ming loyalists. Most, however, served the new dynasty. The Qing as a Chinese dynasty dates from 1644, when the capital was moved from Shenyang (Mukden) to Beijing. All of south China was taken by 1659, with the aid of Ming generals who switched their allegiance to the new regime.

As a tiny fraction of China's population, the Manchus adopted institutions to maintain themselves as an ethnically separate elite group. One such institution was their military organization. The basic unit was the banner—the unit took the name of its flag. There were eight Manchu banners, eight Mongol, and eight Chinese. There were more companies (of 300 men each) in the Manchu banners than in either of the other two; together with their steppe allies, the Mongols, the Manchu troops outnumbered Chinese troops by more than two to one. Furthermore, the Chinese banners were mainly Manchurian Chinese, who had been part of the regime from its inception. Manchu garrison forces were segregated and were not under the jurisdiction of Chinese officials. They were given stipends and lands to cultivate. They were forbidden to marry Chinese, their children had to study Manchu, and they were not permitted to practice footbinding. In 1668 northern and central Manchuria were cordoned off by a willow palisade as a Manchu strategic tribal territory and closed to Chinese immigrants.

In addition to the Manchu banners, there were also Chinese constabulary forces known as "armies of the green standard." At first the distinction between the banners and the Chinese military was critical. Later, as the dynasty became Sinicized and accepted, the ethnic basis of its military strength became less important.

The second institutional feature of Manchu government was what has been termed "dyarchy": the appointment of two persons, one Chinese and one Manchu, to each key post in the central government. Early in the dynasty the Chinese appointments were often bannermen or bondservants who were personally loyal to the Manchus. At the provincial level Manchu governor-generals oversaw Chinese governors. Most officials and virtually all district magistrates beneath the governors were Chinese.

Emperor Qianlong. The great Manchu emperor Qianlong (r. 1736–1795). *Unidentified Artist, 16th century. Qing Dynasty (1644–1911. Hanging scroll; ink and color on silk; Overall: 63 1/2 x 30 1/2in. (161.3 x 77.5cm). The Metropolitan Museum of Art, Rogers Fund, 1942. (42.141.8). Photograph © 1980 The Metropolitan Museum of Art. Art Resource, New York.*

Chronology

Late Imperial China

Ming Dynasty 1368–1644

1368–1398	Reign of first Ming emperor; Chinese armies invade Manchuria, Mongolia, and eastern Central Asia
1402–1424	Reign of third Ming emperor; Chinese armies invade Vietnam and Mongolia
1405–1433	Voyages of Zheng He to India and Africa
1415	Grand Canal reopened
1472–1529	Wang Yangming, philosopher
1592–1598	Chinese army battles Japanese army in Korea

Qing (Manchu) Dynasty 1644–1911

1668	Manchuria closed to Chinese immigrants (by Willow Palisade)
1661–1722	Reign of Kangxi
1681	Suppression of revolts by Chinese generals
1683	Taiwan captured
1689	China and Russia sign Treaty of Nerchinsk
1736–1795	Reign of Qianlong
1793	Macartney mission

A particular strength of the Manchu Dynasty was the long reigns of two extremely able emperors, Kangxi (1661–1722) and Qianlong (1736–1795). Kangxi was born in 1654, ten years after the start of the dynasty. He ascended the throne at the age of 7, began to rule at 13, and held sway until his death in 1722. He was a man of great vigor. He rose at dawn to read memorials (official documents) before beginning his daily routine of audiences with officials. He sired thirty-six sons and twenty daughters by thirty consorts. He presided over palace examinations. Well versed in the Confucian classics, he won the support of scholars by his patronage of the *Ming History*, a new dictionary, and a 5,000-volume encyclopedia.

Kangxi also displayed an interest in European science: He studied with Jesuit court astronomers whom the Qing had inherited from the Ming. He opened four ports to foreign trade and carried out public works, improving the dikes on the Huai and Yellow rivers and dredging the Grand Canal. During his reign he made six tours of

China's southern provinces. Kangxi, in short, was a model emperor. But he was also responsible for the various policies that sought to preserve a separate Manchu identity. Like Kublai Khan (r. 1271–1294) before him, he built a summer palace on the plains of Manchuria, where he hunted, hawked, and rode horseback with the freedom of a steppe lord.

Qianlong began his reign in 1736, fourteen years after the death of his grandfather Kangxi, and ruled until 1795. During his reign the Qing Dynasty attained its highest level of prosperity and power. Like Kangxi, he was vigorous, wise, conscientious, careful, and hard-working. He visited south China on inspection tours. He patronized scholars on a grand scale: His *Four Treasures* of the classics, treating history, letters, and philosophy, put 15,000 copyists to work for almost fifteen years. (But he also carried out a literary inquisition against works critical of Manchu rule.)

Only in his last years did Qianlong lose his grip and permit a court favorite to practice corruption on an almost unprecedented scale. In 1796 the White Lotus Rebellion broke out. Qianlong's successor put down the rebellion and permitted the corrupt court favorite to take his own life. The ample financial reserves that had existed throughout the eighteenth century were never reestablished. China nevertheless entered the nineteenth century with its government intact and with a peaceful and stable society. There were few visible signs of what was soon to come.

Ming–Qing Foreign Relations

Ming Some scholars have contended that post-Song China was not an aggressive or imperialist state. They cite its inability to resist foreign conquest; the civility, self-restraint, and gentlemanliness of its officials; and the Song adage that good men should not be used to make soldiers, just as good iron is not used to make nails. The early Ming convincingly disproves this contention. The first Ming emperor (r. 1368–1398) oversaw the vigorous expansion of China's borders. At his death, China controlled the northern steppe from Hami at the gateway of Central Asia to the Sungari River in Manchuria and had regained control of the southern tier of Chinese provinces as well. The Mongols were expelled from Yunnan in 1382 (see Map 18–1).

During the reign of the third Ming emperor (1402–1424), China became even more aggressive. The emperor sent troops into northern Vietnam, which became a Chinese province for two decades. He also personally led five expeditions into the Gobi Desert in pursuit of Mongol troops.

Whenever possible, the third emperor and his successors "managed" China's frontiers with the tribute system. In this system the ambassadors of vassal kings acted out their political subordination to the universal ruler of the celestial kingdom. An ambassador approached the emperor respectfully, performed the kowtow (kneeling three times and each

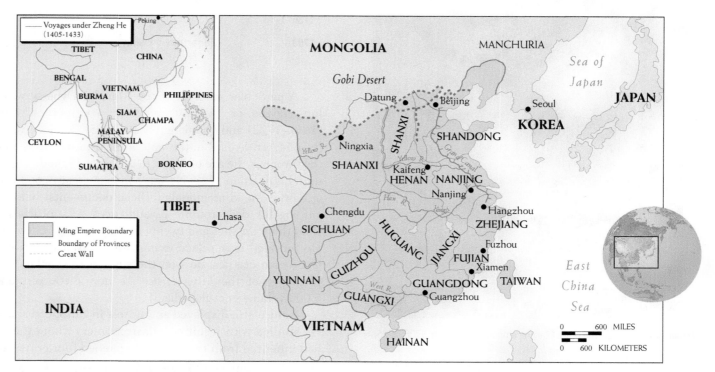

Map 18–1. The Ming Empire and the Voyages of Zheng He. The inset map shows the voyages of Zheng He to Southeast Asia and India. Some ships of his fleet even reached East Africa. (Zheng himself did not.)

Giraffe with Attendant. Some emperors had private zoos and gladly received exotic animals as gifts from tribute states. A painting by Shen Du (1357–1438), *"The Tribute: Giraffe with Attendant." Philadelphia Museum of Art: Gift of John T. Dorrance, 1977.*

time bowing his head to the floor three times), and presented his gifts. In return, the vassal kings were sent seals confirming their status, given permission to use the Chinese calendar and year-period names, and appointed to the Ming nobility.

The system conferred notable benefits on those willing to participate. While in Beijing, the ambassadors were housed and fed in a style appropriate to their status. The gifts they received were often more valuable than those they brought. In addition, they were permitted to trade private goods in the markets of the city. So attractive were these perquisites that some Central Asian merchants invented imaginary kingdoms of which they appointed themselves the emissaries. Eventually China had to set limits on the size, frequency, and cargoes of these missions. The most far-ranging ventures of the third Ming emperor were the maritime expeditions that sailed to Southeast Asia, India, the Arabian Gulf, and East Africa between 1405 and 1433. They were commanded by the eunuch Zheng He, a Muslim from Yunnan (see Map 18–1). The first of these armadas had sixty-two major ships and hundreds of smaller vessels and carried 28,000 sailors, soldiers, and merchants. Navigating by compass, the expeditions followed the sea routes

of the Arab traders. Trade was not the primary purpose of the expeditions, although some eunuchs used the opportunity to make fortunes, and records show that giraffes, zebras, and other exotic items were presented at the Chinese court. Probably the expeditions were intended to make China's glory known to distant kingdoms and to enroll them in the tribute system. Zheng He's soldiers installed a new king in Java. They captured and brought back to China hostile kings from Borneo and Ceylon, and they signed up nineteen other states as Chinese tributaries.

Read the Document
A Ming Naval Expedition 15th century at **MyHistoryLab.com**

The expeditions ended as abruptly as they had begun. They were costly and offered little return at a time when the dynasty was fighting in Mongolia and building the new capital at Beijing. What was remarkable about these expeditions was not that they came half a century earlier than the Portuguese voyages of discovery, but that China had the necessary maritime technology and yet decided not to use it. China lacked the combination of restlessness, greed, religious faith, and curiosity that would motivate the Portuguese.

The chief threat to the Ming Dynasty was the Mongols. In disarray after the collapse of their rule in China, the Mongols had broken up into eastern, western, and southern tribes. The Chinese, "using the barbarian to control the barbarian," made allies of the southern tribes (those settled just north of the Great Wall) against the more fearsome grassland Mongols. This policy worked most of the time, but twice the Mongols formed confederations—pale imitations of the war machine of Genghis—strong enough to defeat Chinese armies: In the 1430s they captured the emperor, and in 1550 they overran Beijing. The Mongol forces involved in the latter attack were defeated by a Chinese army in the 1560s and signed a peace treaty in 1571.

A second foreign threat to the Ming Dynasty was the Japanese and the Chinese pirates associated with them. Warrior-lords of decentralized Japan had begun raids on Korea and the northeastern Chinese coast during the thirteenth and early fourteenth centuries; they extended their activities down the coast to southeastern China and beyond during the fifteenth and sixteenth centuries. Hitherto, the coast had been China's most secure frontier. China built defenses and used a scorched-earth policy to make raiding less profitable but mostly had to put up with the depredations. The most serious threat from Japan was its invasions of Korea in 1592 and 1597–1598. Korea resisted with some initial success. China sent troops only after Japanese armies had occupied the entire Korean peninsula. Eventually the Japanese armies withdrew, but the strain on Ming finances had severely weakened the dynasty.

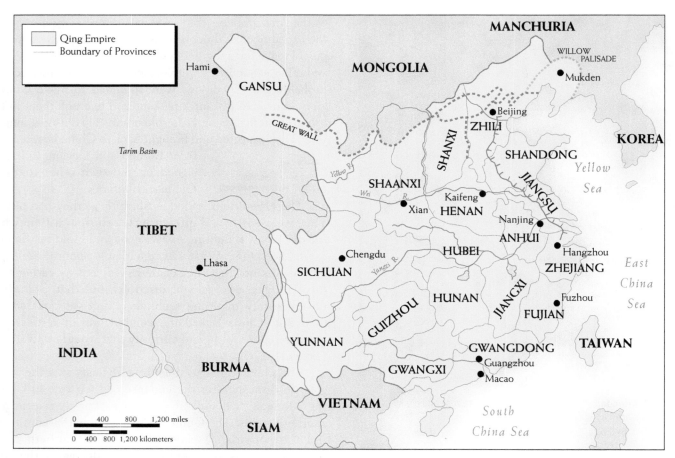

Map 18–2. The Qing Empire at Its Peak. The Willow Palisade was the line of demarcation between the Manchurian homeland of the Qing rulers and China. Chinese were excluded from Manchuria.

Qing The final foreign threat to the Ming was the Manchus, who, as we have seen, were the mouse that swallowed the elephant. After coming to power in 1644, the Manchu court spent decades consolidating its rule within China. The last Ming prince was pursued into Burma and killed in 1662. But then the three Chinese generals who had helped the Manchus conquer the south revolted. The Qing was also opposed by the Sino-Japanese pirate state of Koxinga on Taiwan. The emperor Kangxi suppressed the revolts by 1681; most Chinese troops in the Manchu armies remained loyal. In 1683 he took Taiwan, which became a part of China for the first time (see Map 18–2).

As always, the principal foreign threats to China, even to the Manchu Dynasty, which had itself come from the north, came from the north and northwest. Russia had begun expanding east across Siberia and south against the remnants of the Golden Horde during the reign of Ivan the Terrible (1533–1584). By the 1660s Russian traders, trappers, and adventurers had reached northern Manchuria, where they built forts and traded with the eastern Mongols. One is reminded of the French penetration of Canada dur-

ing the same decades. To prevent a rapprochement between the Russians and Mongols, Kangxi set up military colonies in Manchuria during the 1680s and drove the Russians from the lower Amur River. This victory during the early years of the reign of Peter the Great (1682–1725) led to the 1689 Treaty of Nerchinsk. Negotiated with the assistance of Jesuit translators, this treaty excluded Russia from northern Manchuria while permitting its caravans to visit Beijing.

In the west the situation was more complex, with a three-corner relationship among Russia, the western Mongols, and Tibet. Kangxi, and then Qianlong, campaigned against the Mongols, invaded Tibet, and in 1727 signed a new treaty with Russia. During the campaigns the Chinese temporarily came to control millions of square miles of new territories. These areas became protectorates under a "barbarian management office," separate from the administration for China itself. It is a telling comment on the persistence of the Chinese concept of empire that ever since that time, even after China's borders contracted during the nineteenth century, the Chinese have insisted that the Manchu conquests of non-Chinese peoples define their legitimate borders. The roots of the present-day contention over borders between China and the countries of the former Soviet Union go back to these events during the eighteenth century, as does the Chinese claim to Tibet.

Contacts with the West   Europeans had made their way to China during the Tang and the Yuan dynasties. But only with Europe's oceanic expansion in the sixteenth century did they arrive in large numbers. Some came as missionaries, of whom the most calculating, disciplined, enterprising, and successful were the Jesuits. On first arriving in Ming China, they put on the robes of the Buddhist monk; on learning something of the country, they switched to the gowns of the Confucian scholar. They studied Chinese and the Confucian classics and engaged in conversations with scholars. They used their knowledge of astronomy, geography, engraving, and firearms to win entry to the court at Beijing and appointments in the bureau of astronomy.

When the Manchus came to power in 1644, the Jesuits kept their position. They appealed to the curiosity of the court with instruments such as telescopes, clocks, and clavichords. They tried to propagate Christianity. They attacked Daoism and Buddhism as superstitions but argued that Confucianism as a rational philosophy complemented Christianity, just as Aristotle's teaching complemented Christian theology in Europe. They handled the problem of the Confucian rites of ancestor worship by interpreting them as secular and nonantagonistic to Christianity. A few high court officials were converted. Kangxi was sympathetic to the scholarly personalities of the Jesuits and appreciated the cannon they cast but was unsympathetic to their religion: "I had asked [the Jesuit] Verbiest why God had not forgiven his son without making him die, but though he had tried to answer I had not understood him.[2]

Meanwhile, their Franciscan and Dominican rivals had reported to Rome that the Jesuits condoned the Confucian rites. The ensuing debate was long and complex, but in the end, papal bulls issued in 1715 and 1742 decided against the Jesuits and forbade Chinese Christians to participate in the family rites of ancestor worship. Thereupon the emperor banned Christianity in China, churches were seized, missionaries were forced to flee, and congregations declined.

Other Europeans came to China to trade. The Portuguese came first in the early sixteenth century but behaved badly and were expelled. They returned in midcentury and were permitted to trade on a tiny peninsula at Macao that was walled off from China. They were followed by Dutch from the East Indies (Indonesia), by the British East India Company in 1699, and by Americans in 1784.

Le Pere Adam Schaal.

Jesuit Missionary.   A late-seventeenth-century color engraving of the Jesuit missionary Johann Adam Schall depicts him in traditional Confucian dress holding a sextant and a compass. A globe is behind him on the left.

At first the Westerners mingled with ships from Southeast Asia in a fairly open multiport pattern of trade. Then, during the early eighteenth century, the more restrictive "Canton system" evolved. Westerners could trade only at Guangzhou—or "Canton" as it was known to Westerners. They were barred from entering the city proper but were assigned land outside its walls along the river. They could not bring their wives to China. They were subject to the harsh dispositions of Chinese law. They were under the control of official merchant guilds. Nevertheless, the trade was profitable to both sides.

The British East India Company developed a triangular commerce among China, India, and Britain that enabled the English to drink tea and wear silk. Private fortunes were built. For China this trade produced a huge influx of specie, and the Chinese officials in charge grew immensely wealthy. Chafing under the various restrictions, the British government in 1793 sent the Macartney mission to China to negotiate the opening of other ports, fixed tariffs, representation at Beijing, and so on. The emperor Qianlong graciously permitted Lord Macartney (1736–1806) to present his gifts—which the Chinese described as tribute, even though Macartney refused to perform the kowtow—but he turned down Macartney's requests. (See Document, "Qianlong's Edict to King George III of England.") Western trade remained encapsulated at Guangzhou, distant from Beijing and little noted elsewhere in China.

---

[2] J. Spence, *Emperor of China: Self-Portrait of K'ang-Hsi* (New York: Alfred A. Knopf, 1974), p. 84.

Document   Qianlong's Edict to King George III of England

The Chinese emperor rejected the requests of the 1793 Macartney mission for change in the restrictive Canton system. His edict reflects the Chinese sense of their superiority to other peoples and their belief that China was the "central kingdom" of the world.

■ *What philosophical principles underlie the emperor's sense of superiority?*

You, O King, are so inclined toward our civilization that you have sent a special envoy across the seas to bring to our Court your memorial of congratulations on the occasion of my birthday and to present your native products as an expression of your thoughtfulness. On perusing your memorial, so simply worded and sincerely conceived, I am impressed by your genuine respectfulness and friendliness and greatly pleased. . . .

The Celestial Court has pacified and possessed the territory within the four seas. Its sole aim is to do its utmost to achieve good government and to manage political affairs, attaching no value to strange jewels and precious objects. The various articles presented by you, O King, this time are accepted by my special order to the office in charge of such functions in consideration of the offerings having come from a long distance with sincere good wishes. As a matter of fact, the virtue and prestige of the Celestial Dynasty having spread far and wide, the kings of the myriad nations come by land and sea with all sorts of precious things. Consequently there is nothing we lack, as your principal envoy and others have themselves observed. We have never set much store on strange or ingenious objects, nor do we need any more of your country's manufactures.

Source: Reprinted by permission of the publisher from *China's Response to the West; A Documentary Survey, 1839–1923* by Ssu-yu Teng and John Fairbank, pp. 19, 24–27, 155–156, 240–241, Cambridge Mass: Harvard University Press, Copyright (c) 1954, 1979 by the President and Fellows of Harvard College, Copyright renewed 1982 by Ssu-yu Teng and John King Fairbank.

Ming–Qing Culture

One thing that can be said of Ming–Qing culture, like population or agricultural productivity, is that there was more of it. Whether considering gentry, scholar officials, or a professionalized class of literati, their numbers and works were far greater than in previous dynasties. Even local literary figures or philosophers were likely to publish their collected works or have them published by admiring disciples. Bookstores came of age in the Ming, selling the Confucian classics; commentaries on them; collections of Tang and Song poetry; and also colored prints, novels, erotica, and model answers for the civil service examinations.

Chinese culture had begun to turn inward during the Song in reaction to Buddhism. This tendency was accelerated by the Chinese antipathy to Mongol rule and continued into the Ming and Qing, when Chinese culture became virtually impervious to outside influences. Even works on mathematics and science translated into Chinese by the Jesuits left few traces in Chinese scholarly writings. Chinese cultural self-sufficiency, of course, reflected a tradition and a social order that had stood the test of time, but it also indicated a closed system of ideas with weaknesses that would become apparent in the nineteenth century. Orthodox thought during these five centuries was Zhu Xi Neo-Confucianism. From the mid- to the late Ming, some perturbations were caused by the Zen-like teachings of the philosopher Wang Yangming (1472–1529), whose activism caused him to be jailed, beaten, and exiled at one point in an otherwise illustrious official career.

Several other original thinkers' refusal to accept bureaucratic posts under the Qing won them plaudits during the anti-Manchu nationalism of the early twentieth century, but they had only a limited influence on their own times. The most interesting was Gu Yanwu, who wrote on both philology and statecraft. He used philology and historical phonetics to get at the original meanings of the classics and contrasted their practical ethics with the "empty words" of Wang Yangming. Gu's successors extended his philological studies, developing empirical methods for textual studies, but lost sight of their implications for politics. The Manchus clamped down on unorthodox thought, and the seventeenth-century burst of creativity guttered out into a narrow, bookish, conservative scholasticism. Not until the end of the nineteenth century did thinkers draw from these studies the

Ming Dynasty Ink Painting by Wu Wei (1479–1508). The seated human figure is a part of the tranquility of nature. Nature, densely concentrated at the left and lower portions of the painting, stretches off into space in the middle and upper-right portion. *Wu Wei, "Scholar Seated under a Tree", China. Ink & traces of colour on silk. 14.7 x 8.25. Chinese and Japanese Special Fund. Photograph © 2007 Courtesy Museum of Fine Arts, Boston.*

kind of radical inferences that philological studies of the Bible had produced in Europe.

Ming and Qing Chinese esteemed most highly, and not without reason, the traditional categories of high culture: painting, calligraphy, poetry, and philosophy. Porcelains of great beauty were also produced. In the early Ming the blue-on-white glazes predominated. During the later Ming and Qing, more decorative wares with enamel painted over the glaze became widespread. The pottery industry of Europe was begun during the sixteenth century to imitate these wares, and Chinese and Japanese influences have dominated Western ceramics down to the present. Chinese today, however, look back and see the novel as the characteristic cultural achievement of the Ming and Qing.

The novel in China grew out of plot-books used by earlier storytellers. Like the stories, Chinese novels consisted of episodes strung together, and chapters in early novels often ended with an admonition to the reader not to miss the next exciting development. Ming and Qing novels were usually written by scholars who had failed the examinations, which may account for their caustic comments on officials. As most novels were written in colloquial Chinese, which was not quite respectable in the society of scholars, their authors wrote under pseudonyms.

Two collections of lively short stories are available in English: *Stories from a Ming Collection* and *The Courtesan's Jewel Box.* Many other stories were pornographic. In fact, the Ming may have invented the humorous pornographic novel. One example available in English is *The Carnal Prayer Mat.* This genre was suppressed in China during the Qing and rediscovered in Japanese collections in the twentieth century.

Short descriptions of several major novels may convey something of their flavor:

1. *The Romance of the Three Kingdoms*, published in 1522, tells of the political and military struggles in China in the aftermath of the Han Dynasty. Like Shakespeare, the author, whose identity is uncertain, used a historical setting to create a dramatic world in which human character determines the outcome of events. More than twenty editions had appeared by the end of the Ming, and the novel was also extremely popular in Japan and Korea.

2. *All Men Are Brothers* (also translated as *The Water Margin*) tells of 108 bandit heroes who flee government repression during the late northern Song, establish a hideout on a mountain amid marshes, and like Robin Hood, avenge the wrongs perpetrated by corrupt officials. Separate episodes tell why each had to leave society and of their many daring and funny adventures. Of all Chinese novels, this was the most popular. It was officially banned as subversive during the Qing but was widely read nonetheless.

3. *The Golden Lotus* is a pornographic novel about the sexual adventures of an urban merchant. It gives vivid descriptions of individual women and satirical descriptions of venal officials and greedy monks. In the end the hero dies of his excesses, and his family—all six wives and their children—disintegrates. The early English translation of this novel had long passages in Latin to protect those whose minds were not disciplined by the study of that language. Despite its literary merits, the book, like all of its genre, was proscribed during the era of Mao Zedong. In the recent decade it has become available again.

Document — A Star in Heaven

Among the officials whose stories are told in *The Scholars* is Fan Chin, thin and sallow with a grizzled beard and threadbare linen gown, who finally passes the county examination at the age of 54. On his return home, he is given a feast and advice by his domineering father-in-law, Butcher Hu. But when Fan Chin asks Hu for money to travel to the provincial examination, he gets the following reaction.

■ *Why did a satire such as* The Scholars *not undermine the premises on which Qing society rested?*

Butcher Hu spat in his face and let loose a stream of abuse. "Don't forget who you are!" he bellowed. "Just passing one examination and you become like a toad thinking to dine on the flesh of a swan. I hear you passed the examination not because of your essay, but because the examiner took pity on your old age. Now, like a fool, you aspire to be an official. Don't you know that those who have passed the higher examination are all stars in heaven! Haven't you seen the Changs in the city? Those officials all have tons of money and generously proportioned faces and ears. Now look at you with your protruding mouth and monkey chin. Piss on the ground and take a good look at yourself in the puddle! A miserable creature like you can't even hope to swallow a swan's fart! Forget it!

[Fan Chin takes the examination anyway. When he returns home, he discovers that his family has been hungry for two days. Fan goes to the market to sell a chicken. In the meantime, heralds on horseback arrive to proclaim he has passed the provincial examination. Returning home, Fan sees the posted announcement and falls into a dead faint. When revived, he begins ranting incoherently. A herald suggests that Butcher Hu, whom Fan fears, bring him to his senses with a slap. Butcher Hu demurs.]

"He may be my son-in-law," he said, "but now he has become a member of the gentry, a star in heaven. How can I hit a star in heaven? I've heard from Buddhist priests that whoever strikes a star in heaven will be carried away by the King of Hell, struck one hundred times with an iron rod, consigned to the eighteenth hell, and never return to human form again. I wouldn't dare do it."

[Eventually Butcher Hu slaps him, and Fan recovers in time to receive a visit from a member of the local gentry, who is wearing "an official's gauze cap, sunflower-coloured gown, gilt belt and black shoes." "Sir," he says to Fan, "although we live in the same district, I regret that we have never become acquainted." After paying his respects, the visitor presents Fan with fifty taels of silver and a more appropriate house. Soon others give him land, goods, money, rice, and servants. The chapter ends with the maids cleaning up under the supervision of Fan Chin's wife after several days of feasting. Fan Chin's mother enters the courtyard.]

"You must be very careful," the old lady warned her daughter-in-law and the maids. "These things all belong to someone else, so don't break them."

The maids replied:" How can you say they belong to others, madam? They all belong to you."

"Oh no! How could our house have such things?" she said with a smile. "How can you talk of their belonging to others?" the maids replied in unison. "And not only these things, but all of us and the house, too, belong to you."

When the old lady heard this, she picked up the bowls and dishes of fine porcelain and the cups and chopsticks inlaid with silver and examined them one by one. She burbled: "These things are all mine." Laughing wildly, she fell over backward, choked on phlegm, and lost consciousness.

If you want to know what became of the old lady, please read the next chapter.

Translation by Shang Wei.

4. *The Dream of the Red Chamber* (also translated as *The Story of the Stone*) is generally considered China's greatest novel. It tells the story of a youth growing up in a wealthy but declining family during the early Qing. Critics praise its subtlety and psychological insight. Anthropologists mine the novel for information on the Chinese extended family and for its depiction of social relations. Like other Ming and Qing novels, it was recognized as a respectable work of art only during the twentieth century, after Western novels entered China.

5. *The Scholars* is a social satire of the early Qing that pokes fun at scholars and officials. (See Document, "A Star in Heaven.")

Japan

The two segments of "late traditional" Japan could not be more different. The Warring States era (1467–1600)—really the last phase of Japan's medieval history—saw the unleashing of internal wars and anarchy that scourged the old society from the bottom up. Within a century all vestiges of the old manorial or estate system had been scrapped, and virtually all of the Ashikaga lords had been overthrown. The Tokugawa era (1600–1868) that followed saw Japan reunited and stable, with a more competent government than ever. The culture was also brilliantly transformed, preparing it for the challenge it would face during the mid-nineteenth century.

Warring States Era (1467–1600)

War is the universal solvent of old institutions. Nowhere in history was this clearer than in Japan between 1467 and 1600. In 1467 a dispute arose over who would be the next Ashikaga shōgun. The dispute led to war between two territorial lords who supported the respective contenders. Other lords used the opportunity to gain territory at the expense of weaker neighbors, and wars raged throughout Japan for eleven years. Most of Kyoto was destroyed in the fighting, and the authority of the Ashikaga *bakufu* came to an end. This first war ended in 1477, but the fighting resumed and continued for more than a century.

War of All Against All

Even before 1467 the Ashikaga equilibrium had been precarious. Regional **daimyo** (dye-myoh) lords had relied on their relationship to the *bakufu* to hold their stronger vassals in check, while relying on these vassals to preserve their independence against strong neighbors. The collapse of *bakufu* authority after 1467 pulled the linchpin from the system. It left the regional lords standing alone, removing the last barrier to internecine wars.

The regional lords, however, were too weak to stand alone. A region was a hodgepodge of competing jurisdictions. Lands might be "public," or in estates, and some were starting to look like private fiefs. Revenues might be paid to nobles in Kyoto, to regional lords, or to local samurai strongmen. Most regions contained military bands that were not the vassals of the daimyo. Several daimyo had lands in the territories of other lords. Occasionally, vassals were militarily more powerful than their daimyo lords. Some local vassals commanded bands of village warriors. Once the regional daimyo were forced to stand alone, they became prey to the stronger among their vassals as well as to neighboring states.

By the end of the sixteenth century all Ashikaga daimyo had fallen, with one exception in remote southern Kyushu. In their place emerged hundreds of little "Warring States daimyo," each with his own warrior band. In one prefecture along the Inland Sea, the remains of 200 hillside castles of such daimyo have been identified. The constant wars among these men were not unlike those of the early feudal era in Europe.

A Japanese term for "survival of the fittest"—"the strong eat and the weak become the meat"—is often applied to this century of warfare. Of the daimyo bands, the most efficient in revamping their domain for military ends survived. The less ruthless, who clung to old ways, were defeated and absorbed. It was an age, as one Warring States general put it, "when only muscle counts." Another said, "The warrior doesn't care if he's called a dog or beast, the main thing is winning.[3]

Early in this period, when there were hundreds of small states, castles were built on a bluff above a river or on a mountainside with natural defenses against surprise attacks. Inuyama Castle, today a thirty-minute bus ride from Nagoya, is the most impressive surviving example.

As fighting continued, hundreds of local states gave way to tens of regional states. The castles of such regional states were often located on plains, and as castle towns grew up around them, merchants flocked to supply the needs of their growing soldiery. Eventually, alliances of these regional states fought it out, until in the late sixteenth century all of Japan was brought under the hegemony of a single lord. Oda Nobunaga (1534–1582) completed the initial unification of central Honshu and would have finished the job had a treacherous vassal not assassinated him in 1582. Toyotomi Hideyoshi (1536–1598), who had begun life as a lowly foot soldier, completed the unification in 1590. After his death his vassal generals once again went to war, and it was only with the victory of Tokugawa Ieyasu (1542–1616) at the battle of Sekigahara in 1600 that true unification was finally achieved. Ieyasu's unification of 1600 superficially resembled that of the Minamoto in 1185 but was in fact based on a sweeping transformation of Japan's society.

Foot Soldier Revolution

During the Warring States period, the foot soldier replaced the aristocratic mounted warrior as the backbone of the military in Japan. Soldiers were still called *samurai*. They were still the vassals of daimyo or, sometimes, the vassals of vassals of daimyo, but their numbers, social status, and techniques of warfare changed dramatically. As a result, Japanese society changed from what it had been only a century earlier.

---

[3]G. Elison and B. L. Smith, eds., *Warlords, Artists, and Commoners* (Honolulu: Hawaii University Press, 1981), p. 57.

Daimyo Castle. Construction of the "White Heron" castle in Himeji was begun during the Warring States era and was completed shortly after 1600. During the Tokugawa peace, it remained as a monument to the glory of the daimyo. Today it can be seen from the "bullet train" as it runs westward from Kobe.

The changes began on the land. Ashikaga daimyo had diverted more and more land revenues for their own use, but Warring States daimyo took them all. Public lands and estates, including those of the imperial house, were seized and converted into fiefs. Soldiers were paid stipends from the revenues of the daimyo's lands, and important vassals, usually the officers or commanders of the daimyo's army, were awarded fiefs of their own. The governance of fiefs was essentially private, in the hands of the fief holder.

Inheritance patterns changed to fit the new circumstances. Multigeniture—the division of a warrior's rights to revenues from land among his children—was not appropriate to a society with a hereditary military class. It had impoverished the Kamakura vassals. To protect the integrity of the warrior's household economy, multigeniture had begun to give way to single inheritance during the Ashikaga period. After 1467 single inheritance became universal. As the fief was often passed to the most able son, not necessarily the eldest, the pattern is usually called *unigeniture* rather than *primogeniture*.

With larger revenues, Warring States daimyo built bigger armies. They recruited mainly from the peasantry. Some of the new soldiers moved to the castle town of the daimyo. Others lived on the land or remained in their villages, farming in peace and fighting in war. The growth of the military class had begun earlier. Accounts of twelfth-century battles tell of fighting by tens of hundreds of warriors, sometimes more. Scroll paintings of the Heiji wars corroborate these figures. By the fourteenth century battles involved thousands or tens of thousands of troops. By the late sixteenth century hundreds of thousands were deployed in major campaigns. Screen paintings show massed troops in fixed emplacements with officers riding about on horseback. Of course, special cavalry strike forces were still used.

In the mid-fourteenth century a new weapon was developed: a thrusting spear with a thick shaft and a heavy chisel-like blade. Held in both hands, it could penetrate medieval armor as a sword could not. It could also be swung about like a quarterstaff. It was used by soldiers positioned at intervals of 3 feet, in a pincushion tactic to impale charging cavalry. The weapon spelled the end of the aristocratic warrior in Japan, just as the pikes used by Swiss soldiers ended knighthood in northern Europe during the fifteenth century. After 1467 this spear became the principal weapon of Warring States Japan. Not surprisingly, its spread coincided with the recruitment of peasant soldiers, for it required only short training. By the early sixteenth century it was every warrior's dream to be the "number one spearman" of his lord. Even generals trained in its use. One famous general wrote that "one hundred spearmen are more effective than ten thousand swords."

A second change in military technology was the introduction of the musket by the Portuguese in the mid-sixteenth century. Warring States generals quickly adopted it. Its superiority was proved in the battle of Nagashino in 1575, in which Oda Nobunaga and Tokugawa Ieyasu used spear and musket platoons against the cavalry of a famous military tactician. Massing 3,000 muskets behind a bamboo barrier-fence and firing in volleys, Nobunaga decimated the forces of his enemy. As individual combat gave way to mass armies, warfare became increasingly pitiless, cruel, and bloody.

How, then, should one characterize the society that emerged from the Warring States? Does the word *feudal* apply, with its suggestion of lords and vassals and manorial life on the fiefs of aristocratic warriors? In some respects, it does: By the late sixteenth century all warriors in Japan were part of a pyramid of vassals and lords headed by a single overlord; warriors of rank held fiefs and vassals of their own.

In other respects Japan resembled postfeudal Europe. First, most of the military class was made up of soldiers, not aristocrats. Even though they were called samurai and were vassals, they were something new. They were not given fiefs but were paid with stipends of so many bales of rice. Second, unlike, say, feudal England, where the military class was about one quarter of 1 percent of the population, in mid-sixteenth-century Japan it may have reached 7 or 8 percent. It was more the size of Europe's mercenary armies during the fifteenth or sixteenth century. Third, the recruitment of village warriors added significantly to the power of Warring States daimyo but gave rise to problems as well. Taxes became harder to collect. Local samurai were often involved in uprisings. When organized by Pure Land Buddhist congregations, these uprisings sometimes involved whole provinces. Again, the parallels with postfeudal Europe seem closer. Fourth, even in a feudal society, not everything is feudal. The commercial growth of the Kamakura and Ashikaga periods continued through the dark decades of the Warring States era.

Chronology

Warring States Japan and the Era of Unification (1467–1600)

1467–1568	Battles throughout Japan
1543	Portuguese arrive in Japan
1568	Oda Nobunaga takes Kyoto and partially unifies Japan
1575	Battle of Nagashino
1582	Nobunaga assassinated
1588	Hideyoshi starts sword hunt
1590	Hideyoshi completes unification
1592, 1597–1598	Hideyoshi sends armies to Korea
1597	Hideyoshi bans Christianity
1598	Hideyoshi dies, his generals battle for succession
1600	Battle of Sekigahara; Tokugawa Ieyasu reunifies Japan

Foreign Relations and Trade

Japanese pirate-traders plied the seas of East Asia during the fifteenth and sixteenth centuries. To halt their depredations, the Ming emperor invited the third Ashikaga shōgun to trade with China. An agreement was reached in 1404, and the shōgun was appointed the "King of Japan." During the next century and a half, periodic "tribute missions" were sent to China. The opening of official trade channels did not, however, end piracy. It stopped only after Japan was reunified at the close of the sixteenth century.

The content of the trade reflected the progress of Japanese crafts. Early Japanese exports to China were raw materials such as raw copper, sulfur, or silver, but by the sixteenth century manufactured goods were rising in importance and included swords, spears, wine bottles, folding fans, picture scrolls, screen paintings, ink slabs, and the like. In exchange, Japan received copper cash, porcelains, paintings, books, and medicines.

After establishing his hegemony over Japan, Hideyoshi permitted only ships with his vermilion seal to trade with China, a policy the Tokugawa continued. Between 1604 and

Arrival of the Portuguese in Japan. Detail of central section of the boat. Portuguese merchants arrived in Japan in 1543 from India and the East Indies. Their crews were multiethnic, and they brought Jesuit priests as well. *"Arrival of the Portuguese in Japan" Detail—central section of the boat, 1594–1618. Screen. Paint, gold, paper. Museo, Soares Dos Reis, Porto, Portugal. Bridgeman-Giraudon/Art Resource, New York.*

1635 over 350 ships went to China in this "vermilion-seal trade." Then, in 1635, the imposition of seclusion ended Japan's foreign trade: No Japanese could leave Japan; the construction of large ships was prohibited; trade with the continent was limited to a small community of Chinese merchants in Nagasaki and to quiet trading with China and Korea through the Ryukyu and Tsushima islands.

Overlapping Japan's maritime expansion in the seas of East Asia was the arrival of European ships. Portuguese pirate-traders made their way to Goa in India, to Malacca, and to Macao in China and arrived in Japan in 1543. Spanish galleons came in 1587 via Mexico and the Philippines. These eastern and western waves of Iberian expansion were followed by the Dutch and the English after the turn of the century.

The Portuguese, from a tiny country with a population of 1.5 million, were motivated by a desire for booty and profits and by religious zeal. Their ships were superior. Taking advantage of the Chinese ban on maritime commerce, they became important as shippers. They carried Southeast Asian goods and Japanese silver to China and Chinese silk to Japan and then used their profits to buy Southeast Asian spices for the European market. The Portuguese, initially at least, found it easier to trade with the daimyo of a disunited Japan than to deal with the authorities of a united China. A few Kyushu daimyo, thinking to attract Portuguese traders, even converted to Christianity.

Traders brought with them Jesuit missionaries. The Society of Jesus had been founded in 1540 to act as soldiers in the pope's campaign against the Reformation. Only nine years later Saint Francis Xavier (1506–1552) arrived in Japan. He soon wrote back that the Japanese were "the best [people] who have yet been discovered." Another Jesuit wrote that the Japanese "are all white, courteous, and highly civilized, so much so that they surpass all other known races of the world." The Japanese, for their part, also appeared to admire the Jesuits for their asceticism, devoutness, and learning.

As they had attempted to convert scholar-officials in China, so the Jesuits in Japan directed their efforts toward the samurai. Moving to Kyoto, they won the favor of Nobunaga, who was engaged in campaigns against warrior monks on Mount Hiei and against Pure Land strongholds in Osaka. Portuguese and Christian objects became fashionable. Painters produced "Southern Barbarian screens" that depicted the "black ships" of the Portuguese. Christian symbols were used on lacquer boxes and saddles. Nobunaga himself occasionally wore Portuguese clothes and a cross and said he might become a Christian if only the Jesuits would drop their insistence on monogamy. Christian converts increased from a few in the early years to 130,000 in 1579 and to about 300,000 in 1600. That is to say, in the late sixteenth century a higher percentage of Japanese were Christian than today.

It is difficult to explain why Christianity met with greater success in Japan than in other Asian lands. When introduced, it was seen as a new Buddhist sect. There seemed little difference to the Japanese between the cosmic Buddha of Shingon and the Christian God, between the paradise of Amida and the Christian heaven, or between prayers to Kannon—the female *bodhisattva* of mercy—and to the Virgin Mary. The Japanese also noted the theological similarity between the pietism of the Pure Land sect and that of Christianity. To Japanese ears, the passage in Romans 10:13, "whosoever shall call upon the name of the Lord shall be saved," was reminiscent of the Pure Land practice of invoking the name of Amida. The Jesuits, too, noted these parallels and felt that the devil had established these sects in Japan to test their faith. Xavier, who, despite his admirable personal characteristics, was narrow-minded, referred to the historical Buddha and Amida as "two demons." Although this intolerance gave rise to certain tensions and animosities, Christianity spread, and to no small measure as a result of the personal example of the Jesuits.

The fortunes of Christianity began to decline in 1597, when Hideyoshi banned Christianity and had six Spanish Franciscans and twenty Japanese converts crucified in Nagasaki. Hideyoshi was aware of Spanish colonialism in the Philippines, and it was rumored that a Spanish pilot had boasted that merchants and priests represented the first step toward the conquest of Japan. Sporadic persecutions continued until 1614, when Tokugawa Ieyasu began a serious movement to extirpate the foreign religion. Faced with torture, some Christians recanted. More than 3,000 others were martyred.

The last resistance was an uprising near Nagasaki in 1637 and 1638 in which 37,000 Christians died. After that, Christianity survived in Japan only as a hidden religion with secret rites and devotions to "Maria-Kannon," the mother of Jesus represented or disguised as the Buddhist goddess of mercy holding a child in her arms. A few of these "hidden Christians" reemerged in the later nineteenth century. Otherwise, apart from muskets and techniques of castle building, all that remained of the Portuguese influence were certain loan words that became a permanent part of the Japanese language: *pan* for bread, *birōdo* for velvet, *kasutera* for sponge cake, *karuta* for playing cards, and *tempura* for that familiar Japanese dish.

Tokugawa Era (1600–1868)

Political Engineering and Economic Growth during the Seventeenth Century

From 1467 to 1590 Japan's energies were absorbed in ever bigger wars. But after the unifications of 1590 and 1600 Japan's leaders sought to create a peaceful, stable, orderly society. Like a great tanker that requires many times its own length to come about, Japan made this transition slowly. Many of the values and habits of mind of the Warring States era continued into the seventeenth century. By the middle or late seventeenth century, however, its society and political system had been radically reengineered. Vigorous economic and demographic growth had also occurred. This combination of political and economic change made the seventeenth century a period of great dynamism.

Hideyoshi's Rule One pressing problem faced by Japan's unifiers was how to cope with an armed peasantry. In war, village warriors fought for their lord: The benefit they offered the lord was greater than their cost. In peace, only the cost remained: their resistance to taxation and the threat of local uprisings. Accordingly, in the summer of 1588 Hideyoshi ordered a "sword hunt" to disarm the peasants. Records of the collected weaponry exist for only one county of 3,400 households in Kaga, a domain on the Sea of Japan: 1,073 swords, 1,540 short swords, 700 daggers, 160 spears, 500 suits of armor, and other miscellaneous items. Once the hunt was completed, the 5 percent of the population who remained samurai used their monopoly on weapons to control the other 95 percent.

Hideyoshi next moved to freeze the social classes. Samurai were prohibited from quitting the service of their lord. Peasants were barred from abandoning their fields to become townspeople. The Tokugawa continued this policy after 1600 and by and large succeeded. Samurai, farmers, and townspeople tended to marry within their respective classes, and each class developed a unique cultural character. The authorities even attempted to dictate lifestyles, prescribing who could ride in palanquins, who could wear silk, and who was permitted to build fancy gates in front of their houses.

But to grasp the class structure of Tokugawa society, we must note the vast range of social gradations within each class. A farmer who was a landlord and a district official was a more important figure than most lower samurai and lived in a different social world from a landless "water-drinking" peasant too poor to buy tea. A townsman could be the head of a great wholesale house, or a humble street peddler or clog mender. A samurai could be an elder, a key decision maker of his domain, with an income of thousands of bushels of rice and several hundred vassals of his own, or an impecunious foot soldier who stood guard at the castle gate.

"Picture-treading" Plaque. Fumi-e, or "picture-treading" plaques are bronze images representing Christ or the Virgin, which were used by the Tokugawa with increasing intensity from 1614 onward to extirpate the foreign religion. In the *fumi-e* ceremony suspected converts were obliged to tread on the plaques to show that they rejected Christianity.

Having disarmed the peasantry, Hideyoshi ordered cadastral surveys on his own lands and on those of his vassals. The surveys defined each parcel of land by location, size, soil quality, product, and cultivator's name. For the first time, an attempt was made to standardize the rods used to measure land and the boxes used to measure quantities of rice. These standards marked the beginning of the detailed record keeping that characterized the Tokugawa era. Hideyoshi's survey laid the foundations for a systematic land tax. Based on these surveys, domains and fiefs were henceforth ranked in terms of their assessed yield.

●●○—Read the Document
Injunctions Tokugawa Shogunate
at **MyHistoryLab.com**

Establishment of Tokugawa Rule Bedazzled by his own power and military successes, and against all the evidence of Warring States political behavior, Hideyoshi assumed that his vassals would honor their sworn oaths of loyalty to his heir. He was especially trustful of his great ally Tokugawa Ieyasu, whose domains were larger than his own. His trust was misplaced. After his death in 1598, Hideyoshi's former vassals, paying little attention to his heir, broke apart into two opposing camps and fought a great battle in 1600 from which the alliance headed by Tokugawa Ieyasu emerged victorious. Ieyasu was wise, effective in maintaining alliances, and a master strategist, but above all patient. In comparing the three unifiers, the Japanese tell the story that when a cuckoo failed to sing, Nobunaga said, "I'll kill it if it doesn't sing"; Hideyoshi said, "I'll make it sing"; but Ieyasu sat down and said, "I'll wait until it sings."

Like the Minamoto of twelfth-century Kamakura, Ieyasu spurned the Kyoto court and established his headquarters in Edo (today's Tokyo), in the center of his military holdings in eastern Japan (see Map 18–3 on page 552). He took the title of shōgun in 1603 and called his government the *bakufu*. In Edo he built a great castle, surrounded by massive fortifications of stone and concentric moats. The inner portion of these moats and stone walls remains today as the Imperial Palace. Ieyasu then used his military power to reorganize Japan.

Map Exploration

To explore this map further, go to **http://www.myhistorylab.com**

Legend:

□ Major outside daimyo domains that played key roles in the 1853-68 restoration period

▨ Main areas of Shogunal Rule

— Tōkaidō (Trunk Road)

MANCHURIA

HOKKAIDO

HONSHU

Sea of Japan

Seoul

KOREA

Yellow Sea

Pusan

CHŌSHŪ

TSUSHIMA

HIZEN

KYUSHU

Nagasaki

East China Sea

SATSUMA

Edo

Nagoya

Hyōgo Kyōto
Osaka

Inland Sea

SHIKOKU

TOSA

PACIFIC OCEAN

TANEGASHIMA

0   100   200   300 MILES
0 100 200 300 KILOMETERS

Map 18–3. Tokugawa Japan and the Korean Peninsula. The area between Edo and Osaka in central Honshu was both the political base of the Tokugawa *bakufu* and its rice basket. The domains that would overthrow the Tokugawa *bakufu* in the late nineteenth century were mostly in outlying areas of southwestern Japan.

Ieyasu's first move was to confiscate the lands of his defeated enemies and to reward his vassals and allies. During the first quarter of the seventeenth century the *bakufu* confiscated the domains of 150 daimyo, some belonging to former enemies and some taken over for infractions of the Tokugawa legal code, and transferred 229 daimyo from one domain to another. The transfers completed the work of Hideyoshi's sword hunt by severing long-standing ties between daimyo and their disarmed former village retainers. When a daimyo was transferred to a new fief, he took his samurai retainers with him. During the second quarter of the seventeenth century transfers and confiscations ended, and the system settled down.

The reshuffling of domains had not been random. The configuration that emerged was, first, that of a huge central Tokugawa domain. It contained the following: most of the domains of "house daimyo"—those who had been Tokugawa vassals before 1600; the fiefs of the 5,000 Tokugawa bannermen (upper samurai); and the lands that furnished the stipends of the other 17,000 Tokugawa direct retainers (middle and lower samurai). Then, strategically placed around the Tokugawa heartland were the domains of the "related daimyo." These domains had been founded by the second and third sons of early shōgun and furnished a successor to the main Tokugawa line when a shōgun had

Edo Castle. Edo first became a castle town in the mid-fifteenth century. Tokugawa Ieyasu made the castle his residence and headquarters in 1590, and, after his great victory in 1600, rebuilt and extended it. This early Edo period screen painting shows (upper right) the keep or inner citadel, which was not rebuilt after a fire in 1657. Korean envoys (bottom center) enter the castle grounds. They have brought tiger skins and other gifts. Onlookers gawk at their unfamiliar garb. Warriors (top, far right) practice archery. The inner castle compounds shown in the painting were only the central part of an elaborate system of moats, stone-block ramparts, and gates. In 1868, after the Meiji Restoration, Edo was renamed Tokyo (Eastern Capital) and became the residence of the emperor.

no heir. Beyond the related daimyo was a second tier of "outside daimyo" who had fought as allies of Tokugawa Ieyasu in 1600 but became his vassals only after the battle was over.

Finally, at the antipodes of the system were those outside daimyo who had been permitted to survive despite having fought against the Tokugawa in 1600. Their domains were drastically reduced. They remained the "enemies" within the system, although they had submitted and become Tokugawa vassals after 1600. Thus, the entire layout of domains constituted a defensive system, with the staunchest Tokugawa supporters nearest to the center.

The Tokugawa also established other systemic controls. Legal codes regulated the imperial court, temples and shrines, and daimyo. Military houses were enjoined to use men of ability and to practice frugality. They were prohibited from engaging in drinking parties, wanton revelry, sexual indulgence, habitual gambling, or the ostentatious display of wealth. Only with *bakufu* consent could daimyo marry or repair their castles.

Read the Document
Shohatto at **MyHistoryLab.com**

A second control was a hostage system, firmly established by 1642, that required the wives and children of daimyo to reside permanently in Edo and the daimyo themselves to spend every second year in Edo. Like the policy of Louis XIV (r. 1643–1715) at Versailles, this requirement transformed feudal lords into courtiers. The palatial Edo compounds of the daimyo contained hundreds or thousands of retainers and servants and occupied much of the city.

A third key control, established during the 1630s, was the national policy of seclusion. Seclusion was no barrier to cultural imports from China and Korea.

Daimyo. A daimyo seated in a palanquin carried by commoner porters. The screen at the side is rolled up so that he can observe the sights of Edo. Surrounding the palanquin are several dozen of his samurai retainers. In the right foreground are Edo townsmen.

The Commercial District of Osaka, the "kitchen" of Tokugawa Japan. Warehouses bear the crests of their merchant houses. Ships (upper right) loaded with rice, cotton goods, sake, and other goods are about to depart for Edo (Tokyo). Their captains vied with one another to arrive first and get the best price.

But except for small Chinese and Dutch trading contingents at Nagasaki, no foreigners were permitted to enter Japan, and on pain of death, no Japanese were allowed to go abroad. Nor could oceangoing ships be built. This policy was strictly enforced until 1854. Like the case of a watch, seclusion enclosed the workings of the entire system. Cut off from substantial outside political contacts, for Japanese, Japan became the world.

An interesting parallel can be drawn between Europe and Tokugawa Japan. Between the fifteenth and eighteenth centuries France moved from a late feudal pattern toward ever greater centralization, whereas Germany moved toward a decentralized order of many independent states. In Japan these two tendencies were delicately balanced. On the one hand, representing the forces of centralization was the *bakufu*, which governed its own domain and also administered the controls over the whole system. Its offices were staffed by its vassals—its highest councils by house daimyo and high-ranking bannermen, and lesser posts by lower-ranking vassals of ability. The pool of rank was always larger than that of the available posts.

On the other hand, representing decentralization were the domains of the 260 or so daimyo. Except for the house daimyo, they were excluded from service in the *bakufu*. Their domain governments, like miniature *bakufu*, were staffed by their samurai vassals. Each domain had its own autonomous military, finances, judiciary, schools, paper money, and so on. This balance between centralization and decentralization has led Japanese scholars to label the Tokugawa polity the "*bakufu*-domain system."

The Seventeenth-Century Economy The political dynamism of the period from Hideyoshi through the first century of Tokugawa rule was matched by economic growth. By the late sixteenth century there existed a backlog of agricul-

tural techniques, the spread of which had been impeded by regionalism and wars: methods of water control and irrigation that made double-cropping easier, better tools, new seed strains, the use of bony fish or of night soil from cities as fertilizers, and so on. During the seventeenth century these techniques were widely applied. Resources no longer needed for war were allocated to land reclamation. The result was a doubling of agricultural production, as well as a doubling of population from 12 million in 1600 to 24 million in 1700. The production of agricultural by-products—cotton, silk, indigo, lumber, dyes, *sake*, and so on—also grew, especially in central Japan and along the shores of the Inland Sea.

Peace also sustained growth in commerce. The merchants in Warring States Japan, like geese that lay golden eggs, had always been at risk. They had to pay for security, and they operated within cramped regional economies. On coming to power, Nobunaga and Hideyoshi knew that political unification alone was not enough. They recognized that prosperity would make their rule easier, and, acknowledging the enterprise of merchants, they abolished the medieval guilds and freed Japan's central markets from monopolistic restrictions. The result was a burgeoning of trade and the formation of a national market network atop the domain economies. As this network expanded during the seventeenth century, economic functions became more differentiated and efficient. The economic chain that began with a local buyer might extend to a merchant house in a regional port, to coastal shippers, to warehousers in Osaka or Edo, and then to great wholesale houses.

Seclusion ended much foreign trade. One might expect the sharp decline in trade to have dampened Japan's domestic economy. Instead, commerce continued to grow for the remainder of the seventeenth century.

To explain this growth, we must look at the tax system and the pattern of consumption in the castle towns and Edo. Tokugawa tax policy was based on land, not commerce.

Taxes took about one-third of the peasant's production. It was a heavier tax rate than that in neighboring China and bespeaks the effective grasp that the military class had on Japanese society. Most taxes were paid in grain. Even as late as the mid-nineteenth century, only a third was collected in money payments. Thus, the 87 percent of the population who lived in the countryside paid almost one-third of the country's agricultural wealth to the 5 percent in the military class. The remaining 8 percent of townspeople also lived off the tax flow by providing goods and services for samurai. This distribution of benefits was mirrored in the three-area city planning common to all castle towns: a large parklike area with castle, trees, stone walls, and moats for the daimyo and his government; an extensive samurai quarter; and a meaner townspeople's quarter. Moreover, just as the castle towns were the consumption centers of the regional tax economies, so was Edo the national consumption center and a super-castle town. It had the same three-area layout, although on a far grander scale. When the daimyo of Kaga, from a great domain on the Japan Sea, was in attendance at Edo, he was served by 8,000 samurai. When he returned to his domain, 4,000 stayed on in Edo to manage the Kaga estates: 267 acres of houses and gardens, barracks, schools, warehouses, and so on. One of these estates, with its magnificent red gate still intact, is today the main campus of Tokyo University. Other daimyo had establishments proportional to their domains. By 1700 Edo had a population of about 1 million.

To support their Edo establishments, the daimyo sold tax rice in Osaka. The "kitchen of Japan," Osaka became the redistribution center from which competing fleets of coastal shippers brought to Edo food, clothing, lumber, oil, and other supplies. By 1700 Osaka's population was about 400,000. Kyoto, rebuilt after its destruction in the early Warring States period, was almost as big. It continued as a center of handicraft production. It also was the location of the "captive" imperial court, which, after suffering penury during the Warring States era, was given support lands equivalent in revenues to those of a small daimyo.

The system of alternate-year attendance at Edo contributed to the development of overland transportation. The most traveled grand trunk road was the Tōkaidō Road between Edo and Kyoto (see Map 18–3). The artist Hiroshige (1797–1858) made a series of woodblock prints that depicted the scenery at its fifty-three post stations. The post stations had official inns for traveling daimyo and requisitioned supplies and horses as a tax obligation from adjacent villages. These stations often grew into thriving local towns.

The growth of a national economy led to a richness and diversity in urban life. Townsmen governed their districts. Samurai city managers watched over the city as a whole. Public schools, police, and companies of firefighters provided public services—a proverb of the time was "Fires are the flowers of Edo." But there were also servants, cooks, messengers, restaurant owners, priests, doctors, teachers, sword sharpeners, book lenders, instructors in the martial arts, prostitutes, and bathhouse attendants. In the world of popular arts there were woodblock printers and artists, book publishers, puppeteers, acrobatic troupes, storytellers, and **Kabuki** and **Nō** actors. Merchant establishments included money changers, pawnbrokers, peddlers, small shops, single-price retail establishments like the House of Mitsui, and great wholesale merchants. Merchant households furnished the raw materials for the personae of Edo fiction: the skinflint merchant who pinches every penny, the profligate son who runs through an inheritance to an inevitable bankruptcy, an erring wife, or the clerk involved in a hopeless affair with a prostitute. (See Document, "The Virtuous Wife" on page 556)

Eighteenth and Early Nineteenth Centuries

By the late seventeenth century the political engineering of the Tokugawa state was complete. After that, few major new laws were enacted, and few important changes were made in governing institutions. In the economy, too, from the early eighteenth century, dynamic growth gave way to slower growth within a high-level equilibrium. In the words of some historians, the society had become "frozen," "unchanging," or "strangely preserved." Yet changes of a different kind were under way.

The Forty-Seven Rōnin   The eighteenth century began with high drama. In the spring of 1701 a daimyo on duty at Edo Castle drew his sword and slightly wounded a *bakufu* official who had insulted him. Even to unsheath a sword within the castle was punishable by death. On the same day the daimyo was ordered to commit *harakiri* (literally, to cut his stomach), and his domain was confiscated. Fearing an attempt at revenge, the *bakufu* police kept an eye on the daimyo's retainers —now *rōnin*, or "masterless samurai." The retainers dissembled, working at lowly jobs, staying at home with their families, or leading lives of drunkenness and debauchery.

Twenty-one months later, on a snowy night in January, forty-seven of the retainers gathered in Edo, attacked the residence of the *bakufu* official, took his head, and then surrendered to the authorities. Their act struck the imagination of the citizenry of Edo and was widely acclaimed. But the *bakufu* council, after deliberating for two months, ordered all forty-seven to commit *harakiri*. The incident embodied the perennial theme of duty versus human feelings. Writers of Kabuki drama and puppet theater quickly took up the incident, and to this day it has been reworked into novels,

Document — The Virtuous Wife

The three-generation stem family, composed of the older parents, their eldest son and his "bride," and their children, was the ideal during the Edo period. The principal family bond was between the parents and their elder son. The son's "bride," at least until she produced children of her own, was less than a full family member, as the adage "the womb is borrowed" suggests. Kaibara Ekken (1630–1714), an early Confucian moralist, propounded an ethic appropriate to such a family in his *Greater Learning for Women*. It reflects the "wisdom" of his age.

■ *Can people accept and practice any ethic that serves their society? Or are some ethics more "natural" than others? How did a girl raised in Tokugawa society feel? Could she embrace Ekken's teachings? Or does the following passage suggest, at least obliquely, that some human feelings are universal and difficult to deny?*

GIRL'S INSTRUCTION

Seeing that it is a girl's destiny, on reaching womanhood, to go to a new home, and live in submission to her father-in-law, it is even more incumbent upon her than it is on a boy to receive with all reverence her parents' instructions. Should her parents, through their tenderness, allow her to grow up self-willed, she will infallibly show herself capricious in her husband's house, and thus alienate his affection; while, if her father-in-law be a man of correct principles, the girl will find the yoke of these principles intolerable. She will hate and decry her father-in-law, and the end of these domestic dissensions will be her dismissal from her husband's house and the covering of herself with ignominy. Her parents, forgetting the faulty education they gave her, may, indeed, lay all the blame on the father-in-law. But they will be in error; for the whole disaster should rightly be attributed to the faulty education the girl received from her parents.

THE INFIRMITIES OF WOMAN

The five worst infirmities that afflict the female are indocility, discontent, slander, jealousy, and silliness. Without any doubt, these five infirmities are found in seven or eight out of every ten women, and it is from these that arises the inferiority of women to men. A woman should cure them by self-inspection and self-reproach.

THE WIFE'S MISCELLANEOUS DUTIES

A woman has no particular lord. She must look to her husband as her lord, and must serve him with all worship and reverence, not despising or thinking lightly of him. The great lifelong duty of a woman is obedience. In her dealings with her husband, both the expression of her countenance and style of her address should be courteous, humble, and conciliatory, never peevish and intractable, never rude and arrogant—that should be a woman's first and chiefest care. When the husband issues his instructions, the wife must never disobey them. In doubtful cases she should inquire of her husband, and obediently follow his commands. If ever her husband should inquire of her, she should answer to the point—to answer in a careless fashion would be a mark of rudeness. Should her husband be roused at any time to anger, she must obey him with fear and trembling, and not set herself up against him in anger and forwardness. A woman should look on her husband as if he were Heaven itself, and never weary of thinking how she may yield to her husband and thus escape celestial castigation.

Source: Kaibara Ekken, *Greater Learning for Women*, in K. Hoshino, *The Way of Contentment* (London: John Murray, 1913, reprinted 1979), pp. 33–34, 44–45.

movies, and television scripts. Just as in Western theater there have been different Hamlets, so have there been many characterizations of Ōishi Kuranosuke, the leader of the band of forty-seven.

Viewed historically, three points may be noted about the incident. First, in a similar situation the more practical samurai of the Warring States period would have forgotten their former lord and rushed to find a new one. Loyalty was highly valued because disloyalty was a live option. But this was no longer true in the Tokugawa era. With the authority of the daimyo backed by that of the shōgun, there was no room for disloyalty. So loyalty became deeply internalized and was viewed almost as a religious obligation. It was also easier for Tokugawa samurai to be loyal unto death because, for the most part, there was so little likelihood in an era of peace that such a loyalty would be called for. In any case, in 1701 it was this Tokugawa species of absolute loyalty that moved the forty-seven *rōnin*.

Second, the incident tells something of the state in Tokugawa Japan. The 1615 "Laws for the Military Houses" contains the passage: "Law is the basis of the social order. Reason may be violated in the name of law, but law may not be violated in the name of reason. Those who break laws deserve heavy punishments."[4] One Tokugawa law forbade private vendettas. So, despite the moral purity of their act—which all recognized, even those who condemned them to death—the forty-seven "virtuous warriors" had to die. The state was above ethics. Their death sentence was a bureaucratic necessity.

Third, the males did not have a monopoly on loyalty and idealism. In the drama, at least, samurai wives and daughters displayed the same heroic spirit of self-sacrifice.

Cycles of Reform   Most political history of late Tokugawa Japan is written in terms of alternating cycles of laxity and reform. Even during the mid-seventeenth century the expenses of the *bakufu* and daimyo states were often greater than their income. In part, the reason was structural: Taxes were based on agriculture in an economy that was becoming commercial. In part, it was simple mathematics: After the samurai were paid their stipends, not enough was left for the expenses of domain governments and the costs of the Edo establishments. In part, it was the toll of extraordinary costs, such as a *bakufu* levy, the wedding of a daimyo's daughter, or the rebuilding of a castle after a fire. And finally, in part, it was a growing taste for luxury among daimyo and retainers of rank.

Over the years a familiar pattern emerged. To make ends meet, domains would borrow from merchants. Then, as finances became even more straitened, a reformist clique of officials would appear, take power, retrench the domain's finances, eliminate extravagance, and return the domain to a more frugal and austere way of life. Debts would be repaid or repudiated. A side effect of reform was the depression of the local merchant economy. But no one likes to practice frugality forever. So, after some of the goals of the reform had been achieved, a new clique would take over the government and a new round of spending would begin. The *bakufu* carried out three great reforms on Tokugawa lands:

1716–1733	Tokugawa Yoshimune	17 years
1787–1793	Matsudaira Sadanobu	6 years
1841–1843	Mizuno Tadakuni	2 years

The first two reforms were long and successful; the third was not. Its failure set the stage for the *bakufu*'s ineffective response to the West in the mid-nineteenth century. Daimyo domains also carried out reforms. Some were successful, enabling them to respond more effectively to the political crisis of the mid-nineteenth century.

Bureaucratization   The balance between centralization and decentralization lasted until the end of the Tokugawa era. Not a single domain ever tried to overthrow the *bakufu* hegemony. Nor did the *bakufu* ever try to extend its control over the domains. But bureaucracy grew steadily both within the *bakufu* and within each domain. One development was the extension of public authority into areas that had been private. In 1600 most samurai fiefs were run by their samurai fief holders. They collected the taxes, often at a heavier rate than the domain set, and they appointed fief stewards to oversee the fiefs. By 1850, however, district officials administered all but the largest of samurai fiefs. They collected the standard domain taxes and forwarded their income to the samurai. In periods of retrenchment, samurai were often paid only half the amount due.

Along with the growth of bureaucracy was the proliferation of administrative codes and government by paperwork. Surviving domain archives house room after room of records of every imaginable kind, mostly from the late eighteenth and early nineteenth centuries: records of births, adoptions, name changes, samurai ranks, fief registers, stipend registers, land and tax registers, court proceedings, domain history, and so on. Administrative codes for the *bakufu* exchequer, for example, grew from a single page during the seventeenth century to forty pages in the late Tokugawa. They define, among other things, an elaborate structure of offices and suboffices, their jurisdictional boundaries, and detailed instructions about how many copies of each document should be made and to which offices they should be forwarded.

Of course, bureaucratization had limits. Only samurai could aspire to official posts. They came to the office wearing their two swords. Decision-making posts were limited to upper-ranking samurai. In periods of financial crises—endemic in the late Tokugawa—a demand arose for men of ability, and middle- or lower-middle-ranking samurai joined domain decision making by becoming staff assistants to bureaucrats of rank.

---

[4] R. Tsunoda, W. T. de Bary, and D. Keene, *Sources of the Japanese Tradition* (New York: Columbia University Press, 1958), p. 336.

A Closer Look

Bridal Procession

Yohime, the twenty-first daughter of the eleventh shogun, approaches the main Edo estate of the Kaga daimyo.

An array of samurai precedes the bride's palanquin. Among them are men bearing gifts for the daimyo, which are covered by a cloth with the Tokugawa crest.

A red gate built in 1827 in celebration of the wedding. Extending from the gate is the wall that circled the huge Edo estate of the Kaga daimyo. In modern times his estate became the main campus of Tokyo University. The gate still stands today and is routinely used by students.

Yohime rides in a palanquin decorated with the hollyhock crest of the Tokugawa House. She is on her way to marry the Kaga daimyo, lord of the largest domain in Japan. The eleventh shogun had twenty-eight sons and twenty-seven daughters by more than forty concubines.

Behind the palanquin are Yohime's ladies in waiting. They are of a number befitting her status.

Questions

1. What was the political meaning of such a marriage?

2. What does this print say of the steeply hierarchical nature of the Tokugawa warrior class?

myhistorylab To examine this image in an interactive fashion, please go to **www.myhistorylab.com**

The Later Tokugawa Economy By 1700 the economy approached the limit of expansion within the available technology. The population, an important index, reached 26 million early in the eighteenth century and was at the same figure in the mid-nineteenth century, a period during which the population of China more than doubled. Within this constant figure were various smaller movements. Population declined during epidemics in the 1750s and the 1760s and during famines in the 1780s. The northeast never fully recovered. Southwestern Japan along the Inland Sea gained in population. Central Japan stayed even; it was more urban, and like most premodern cities, Tokugawa cities had higher death rates than rural areas.

After 1700 taxes became stabilized, and few land surveys were conducted. Evidence suggests little increase in grain production and only slow growth in agricultural by-products. Some families, in an attempt to raise their standard of living, made conscious efforts to limit their size. Contraception and abortion were commonplace, and infanticide (euphemistically called *mabiki*, the term for thinning out rice shoots in a paddy) was practiced in hard times. But periodic disease, shortages of food, and late marriages among the poor were more important factors. A study of one rural village showed the daughters of poor farmers marrying at 22 and having an average of 4.6 children, whereas for the daughters of rich farmers the figures were 19 and 6.2, respectively. A study of another domain showed that the size of the average farm household declined from 7 to 4.25 members.

During the Tokugawa some farmers remained independent small cultivators, but others became landlords or tenants. By the mid-nineteenth century tenants worked about a quarter of all cultivated lands. Most landlords were small, lived in their villages, and often were village leaders. They were not at all like the Chinese gentry. The misery of the lower stratum of rural society contributed to an increase in peasant uprisings during the late eighteenth and early nineteenth centuries. Authorities had no difficulty in quelling them, although some involved thousands of protestors and were locally destructive. No uprising in Japan even remotely approached those of late Manchu China.

Commerce grew slowly during the late Tokugawa. In the early eighteenth century it was reencased within guilds. Merchants paid set fees, which were usually not especially high, in return for monopoly privileges in central marketplaces. Guilds were also reestablished in the domains, and some domains established domain-run monopolies on products such as wax, paper, indigo, or sugar. The problem facing domain leaders was how to tax profits without injuring the competitive standing of domain exports. Most late Tokugawa commercial growth was in countryside industries— *sake*, soy sauce, dyes, silks, or cotton—and was especially prominent in central and western Japan. Some industries were organized and financed by city merchants under the putting-out system. Others competed with city merchants, shipping directly to end markets to circumvent monopoly controls. The expansion of labor in such rural industries contributed to the population shrinkage in late Tokugawa cities.

The largest question about the Tokugawa economy concerns its relation to Japan's amazing industrialization, which began later in the nineteenth century. Some scholars have suggested that Japan had a "running start." Others have stressed Japanese backwardness in comparison with European late developers. The question is still unresolved.

Languages of East Asia

The two main language families in present-day East Asia are the Sinitic and the Ural-Altaic. They are as different from each other as they are from European tongues. The Sinitic languages are Chinese, Thai, Burmese, and Tibetan. Within Chinese are several mutually unintelligible dialects. Standard Chinese, based on the Beijing dialect, is further from Cantonese than Spanish is from French. Ural-Altaic languages are spoken to the east, north, and west of China. They include Japanese, Korean, Manchurian, Mongolian, the Turkic languages, and, in Europe, Finnish and Hungarian. The origins of Vietnamese are debated.

Tokugawa Culture

If *The Tale of Genji* represents the classical culture of the aristocratic Heian court, and if Nō drama or an ink painting by Sesshū represents the austere samurai culture of medieval Japan, then a satire by Saikaku (1642–1693), a drama by Chikamatsu (1653–1724), or a woodblock print of a beauty by Utamaro (1753–1806) may be taken to represent the new urban culture of the Tokugawa era. In such works, one discerns a new secular consciousness, an exquisite taste put to plebeian ends, occasional vulgarities, and a sense of humor only occasionally encountered in the earlier Japanese tradition.

But there was more to Tokugawa culture than the arts and literature of the townspeople. Two hundred and fifty years of peace and prosperity provided a base for an ever more complex culture and a broader popular participation in cultural life. In the villages Buddhism became more deeply rooted; new folk religions proliferated; by the early nineteenth century most well-to-do farmers could read and write. The aristocratic culture of the ranking samurai houses also remained vigorous. Nō plays continued to be staged. The medieval tradition of black ink paintings was continued by the Kanō school and other artists.

Mother Bathing Her Son. Woodblock print by Kitagawa Utamaro (1753–1806). Utamaro was so popular a master of his genre that publishers hired unknown artists to produce fakes in his name. This led him to sign some works "the genuine Utamaro." He boasted of his high fees, comparing himself to a great courtesan and his imitators to streetwalkers. Note the tub's skillful design, the mother's wooden clog and her simple yet elegant kimono. A second kimono hangs to dry at the upper-right corner. *The Nelson-Atkins Museum of Art, Kansas City, Missouri (Purchase: Nelson Trust). © The Nelson Gallery Foundation. All Reproduction Rights Reserved.*

The Ashikaga tradition of restraint, simplicity, and naturalness in architecture was extended. The imperial villa in Katsura outside of Kyoto has its roots in medieval architecture and to this day inspires Japanese architects. The gilded and colored screen paintings that had surged in popularity during Hideyoshi's rule developed further, culminating in the powerful works of Ogata Kōrin (1658–1716).

Zen Buddhism, having declined during the Warring States period, was revitalized by the monk Hakuin (1686–1769). One of the great cultural figures of the Tokugawa era, Hakuin was also a writer, a painter, a calligrapher, and a sculptor. His autobiographical writings have been translated as *The Embossed Tea Kettle*.

Some scholars have argued that Tokugawa urban culture had a double structure. On the one hand were the samurai, serious and high-minded, who produced a vast body of Chinese-style paintings, poetry, and philosophical treatises. On the other hand was the culture of the townspeople: lowbrow, irreverent, secular, satirical, and often scatological. The samurai esteemed Song-style paintings of mountains or waterfalls, often adorned with quotations from the Confucian classics or Tang poetry. The townspeople collected prints of local beauties, actors, courtesans, and scenes from everyday life. Samurai moralists saw money as the root of evil. Merchants saw it as their goal in life; in Osaka, they even held an "abacus festival," at which their adding machines were consecrated to the gods of wealth and commerce.

In poetry, too, a double structure appeared. Bashō (1644–1694) was born a samurai but gave up his status to live as a wandering poet. He is famous for his travel journal, *The Narrow Road of Oku*, and especially for his haiku, little word-picture poems:

> *Such stillness—*
> *The cries of the cicadas*
> *Sink into the rocks.*

> *A crow perches*
> *On a leafless branch*
> *An autumn evening.*

Or, on visiting a battlefield of the past, he wrote:

> *The summer grass*
> *All that is left*
> *Of a warrior's dream.*[5]

Contrast Bashō's sense of the transience of life with the worldly humor of the townsman:

> *From a mountain temple*
> *The snores of a monk and*
> *the voice of the cuckoo.*

> *Showing a love-letter*
> *to her mother*
> *From a man she doesn't love.*

> *Even the most virtuous woman*
> *will undo her sash*
> *For a flea.*[6]

This is not to say, of course, that townspeople did not write proper haiku as well.

---

[5] Basho haiku from *Anthology of Japanese Literature*, compiled and edited by Donald Keene, copyright © 1955 by Grove Press, Inc. Used by permission of Grove/Atlantic, Inc.

[6] R. H. Blyth, *Japanese Humor* (Tokyo: Japanese Travel Bureau, 1957), p. 141.

Literature and Drama Is cultural creativity more likely during periods of economic growth and political change or during periods of stability? The greatest works of literature and philosophy of Tokugawa Japan were produced between 1650 and 1725, just as the initial political transformation was being completed but the economy was still growing and the society was not yet set in its ways.

One of the major literary figures and certainly the most entertaining was Ihara Saikaku (1642–1693), who is generally credited with having re-created Japanese fiction. Saikaku was heir to an Osaka merchant house. He was raised to be its master, but after his wife died he let the head clerk manage the business and devoted himself to poetry, theater, and the pleasure quarters. At the age of 40 he wrote and illustrated *The Life of an Amorous Man*, the story of a modern and bawdy Prince Genji who cuts a swath through bathhouse girls, shrine maidens, courtesans, and boy actors. The overnight success of the work led to a sequel, *The Life of an Amorous Woman*, the tale of a woman undone by passion and of her downward spiral through the minutely graded circles of the Osaka demimonde. Saikaku also wrote more than twenty other works, including *The Japanese Family Storehouse*, which humorously chronicles the contradictions between the pursuit of wealth and the pursuit of pleasure.

A second major figure of Osaka culture at the turn of the century was the dramatist Chikamatsu Monzaemon (1653–1724). Born a samurai in Echizen province, Chikamatsu entered the service of a court aristocrat in Kyoto and then, in 1705, moved to Osaka to write for both the Kabuki and the puppet theater. Kabuki had begun early in the seventeenth century as suggestive skits and erotic dances performed by troupes of actresses. In 1629 the *bakufu* forbade women to perform on the stage. By the 1660s Kabuki had evolved into a more serious drama with male actors playing both male and female roles. Actors entered the stage on a raised runway or "flower path" through the audience. Famous actors took great liberties in interpreting plays, to roars of approval from the audience. There was a ready market for woodblock prints of actors in their most famous roles—like posters of rock musicians today, but done with incomparably greater artistry.

The three main types of Kabuki plays were dance pieces, which were influenced by the tradition of the Nō; domestic dramas; and historical pieces. Chikamatsu wrote all three. In contrast to Saikaku's protagonists, the men and women in Chikamatsu's dramas struggle to fulfill the duties and obligations of their stations in life. Only when their passions become uncontrollable, which is generally the case, do the plays end in tragedy. The emotional intensity of the ending is heightened by the restraint shown by the actors before they reach their breaking point. In some plays the hero and heroine leave duty behind and, hoping for felicity in the next world, set out on a flight to death. Indeed, this ending was banned by *bakufu* authorities when the excessive popularity of the drama led to its imitation in real life.

It is interesting to compare Kabuki and the Nō drama. Nō is like early Greek drama in that the chorus provides the narrative line. In Nō, the stylization of action is extreme. In Kabuki, as in Elizabethan drama, the actors declaim their lines in the dramatic realism demanded by the commoner theatergoers of seventeenth-century Japan. But to convey the illusion of realism required some deviation from it. As Chikamatsu himself noted about Kabuki: "Many things are said by the female characters which real women could not utter. . . . It is because they say what could not come from a real woman's lips that their true emotions are disclosed." For him, "Art is something that lies in the slender margin between the real and the unreal.[7] Yet, for all that Chikamatsu was concerned with the refinements of his craft and the balance between emotional expressiveness and unspoken restraints, he never talked of the mysterious "no mind" as the key to an actor's power. His dramas are a world removed from the religiosity of the medieval Nō.

In the early eighteenth century Kabuki was displaced in popularity by the puppet theater (Bunraku). Many of Chikamatsu's plays were written for this genre. The word *puppet* does not do justice to the half-life-sized human figures, which rival Nō masks in their artistry. Manipulated by a team of three, a puppet does not only kneel and bow or engage in swordplay but can also mimic brushing a tear from the eye with its kimono sleeve or threading a needle. In the late eighteenth century the puppet theater, in turn, declined, and as the center of culture shifted from Osaka to Edo, Kabuki again blossomed as Japan's premier form of drama.

Confucian Thought The most important change in Tokugawa intellectual life was that the ruling elite abandoned the religious teachings of Buddhism in favor of the more secular worldview of Confucius, opening many avenues for further changes. (See Document, "A Tokugawa Skeptic.") The reworking occurred slowly. During the seventeenth century samurai were enjoined never to forget the arts of war and to be ever ready to die for their lord. One samurai in his deathbed poem lamented dying on *tatami* — with his boots off, as it were. In this period, most samurai were illiterate and saw book learning as unmanly. Nakae Tōju (1608–1648), a samurai and a Confucian scholar, recounted that as a youth he swaggered around with his friends during the day and studied secretly at night so as not to be thought a sissy. Schools, too, were slow to develop. One Japanese scholar has noted that in 1687 only four domains had proper domain schools, and in 1715, only ten.

---

[7]Tsunoda, de Bary, and Keene, *Japanese Tradition*, p. 448.

Document A Tokugawa Skeptic

Confucian teachings, though hardly scientific, placed a premium on rational argument. Some scholars used this rationalism to attack Buddhism. Others directed their attack against superstitions and explanations of natural phenomena that they found wanting. The following passages by Miura Baien (1723–1789), the son of a Kyushu doctor, exemplify such a rationalism.

■ *Does modern science answer the kind of question that Baien is raising? Are some superstitions in modern societies still vulnerable to his critique?*

Why do a pair of dark things on the forehead see; why do a pair of holes in the head hear? Why don't eyes hear, why don't ears see? When most people come to these points they just leave them alone, but I simply can't leave them alone. . . . They refer the question to past authority, and when they find a book that deals with it, they accept whatever answer it gives. I can't convince myself entirely in that way. When they discuss the natural world, they do so in a wild, hit-or-miss manner; when they talk of life and death, they do so in an absurd or obscure manner. Though their evidence may be flimsy and their arguments preposterous, this does not disturb people at all.

[It is] a human peculiarity . . . to view everything as human. Take, for example, children's picture books, The Betrothal of Rats or Monsters and Goblins. Rats are never kept as rats in their true shape; instead all of them are turned into human forms. The bridegroom appears in the book in ceremonial robes with a pair of swords, while the bride is shown with a flowing gown on and snowy cap of cotton, and is carried in a palanquin with an escort of footmen and young guards. In the book of Monsters and Goblins, no cases are found of an umbrella turning into a tea-mortar, or of a broom changing into a bucket. But all monsters and goblins are given eyes and noses and hands and feet, so as to look like members of the human family. . . .

It is such an imagination as this that populates heaven with a supreme God, and earth with gods of wind and thunder. Monstrous in form, they all move by foot, and do their work by hand. Wind is put in bags, thunder is beaten out on drums. If they are real bags, how are they made? And there must be skin to make a drum. If such imaginings are carried further, the sun will be unable to go on revolving unless it gets feet, and nature will be helpless in her work unless she has hands.

Source: From *Sources of Japanese Tradition* by Tsunoda and de Bary. Copyright © 1960 Columbia University Press. Reprinted by permission of the publisher.

The great figures of Tokugawa Confucianism lived during the same years as Saikaku and Chikamatsu, in the late seventeenth and early eighteenth centuries. They are great because they succeeded in the difficult task of adapting Chinese Confucianism to fit Japanese society. One problem, for example, was that in Chinese Confucianism there was no place for a shōgun, whereas in the Japanese tradition of sunline emperors there was no room for the Mandate of Heaven. Most Tokugawa thinkers handled this discrepancy by saying that heaven gave the emperor his mandate and that the emperor then entrusted political authority to the shōgun. One philosopher suggested that the divine emperor acted for heaven and gave the mandate to the shōgun. Neither solution was very comfortable, for, in fact, the emperor was as much a puppet as those in the Osaka theater.

Another problem was the difference between China's centralized bureaucratic government and Japan's "feudal" system of lord–vassal relationships. Samurai loyalty was clearly not that of a scholar-official to the Chinese emperor. Some Japanese thinkers solved this problem rather ingeniously by saying that it was China that had deviated from the feudal society of the Zhou sages, whereas in Japan, Tokugawa Ieyasu had re-created just such a society.

A third problem concerned the "central flowery kingdom" and the barbarians around it. No philosopher could quite bring himself to say that Japan was the real middle kingdom and China the barbarian, but some argued that centrality was relative, and still others suggested that China under barbarian Manchu rule had lost its claim to universality. These are just a few of a large range of problems related to Japanese political organization, Shintō, and to Japanese family practices. By the early eighteenth century these problems had been addressed, and a revised Confucianism acceptable for use in Japan had come into being.

Another point to note is the continuing vitality of Japanese thought—Confucian and otherwise—into the mid-nineteenth century. This vitality is partly explained by the disputes among different schools of Confucianism and partly, perhaps, by Japan's lack of an examination system. The best energies of its samurai youth were not channeled into writing the conventional and sterile "eight-legged essay" that was required in the Chinese examination system. Official preferment—within the constraints of Japan's hereditary system—was often obtained by writing a proposal for domain reforms, although this could sometimes lead to punishments as well.

The vitality was also a result of the rapid expansion of schools from the early eighteenth century. By the early nineteenth century every domain had its own official school and a school on its Edo estate. Commoner schools (*terakoya*), in which reading, writing, and the rudiments of Confucianism were taught, grew apace. In the first half of the nineteenth century private academies also appeared throughout the country. By the late Tokugawa era about 40 to 50 percent of the male population and 15 to 20 percent of the female population was literate—a far higher rate than in most of the world, and on a par with European late developers.

Other Developments in Thought For Tokugawa scholars, the emotional problem of how to deal with China was vexing. Their response was usually ambivalent. They praised China as the teacher country and respected its creative tradition. They studied its history, philosophy, and literature, and began a tradition of scholarship on China that has remained powerful to this day. But they also sought to retain a separate Japanese identity. Most scholars dealt with this problem by adapting Confucianism to fit Japan. But two schools—never in the mainstream of Tokugawa thought, but growing in importance during the eighteenth and early nineteenth centuries—arrived at more radical positions. The schools of National Studies and Dutch Studies were diametrically opposed in most respects but alike in criticizing the Chinese influence on Japanese life and culture.

National Studies began as philological studies of ancient Japanese texts. One source of its inspiration was Shintō; another was the Neo-Confucian School of Ancient Learning. Just as the School of Ancient Learning had sought to discover the original, true meanings of the Chinese classics before they were contaminated by Song metaphysics, so the scholars in the National Studies tradition tried to find in the Japanese classics the original true character of Japan before it had been contaminated by Chinese ideas. On studying the *Record of Ancient Matters, The Collection of Myriad Leaves,* or *The Tale of Genji,* they found that the early Japanese spirit was free, spontaneous, clean, lofty, and honest, in contrast to the Chinese spirit, which they characterized as rigid, cramped, and artificial. Some writings of this school appear to borrow the anti-Confucian logic of Daoism.

Chronology

Tokugawa Era (1600–1868)

1600	Tokugawa Ieyasu reunifies Japan
1615	"Laws of Military Houses" issued
1639	Seclusion policy adopted
1642	Edo hostage system in place
1644–1694	Bashō, poet
1653–1724	Chikamatsu Monzaemon, dramatist
1701	The forty-seven *rōnin* avenge their lord
1853, 1854	Commodore Matthew Perry visits Japan

A second characteristic of National Studies was its reaffirmation of Japan's unique creation and, by extension, the uniqueness of its emperor. Motoori Norinaga (1730–1801) wrote of Shintō creationism as the "Right Way":

Heaven and Earth, all the gods and all phenomena, were brought into existence by the creative spirits of two deities. . . . This . . . is a miraculously divine act the reason for which is beyond the comprehension of the human intellect.

But in foreign countries where the Right Way has not been transmitted, this act of divine creativity is not known. Men there have tried to explain the principle of Heaven and earth and all phenomena by such theories as the yin and yang, the hexagrams of the Book of Changes, and the Five Elements. But all of these are fallacious theories stemming from the assumptions of the human intellect and they in no wise represent the true principle.

The "special dispensation of our Imperial Land" means that ours is the native land of the Heaven-Shining Goddess who casts her light over all countries in the four seas. Thus our country is the source and fountainhead of all other countries, and in all matters it excels all the others.[8]

National Studies became influential during the late Tokugawa era. It had a small but not unimportant influence on the Meiji Restoration. Its doctrines continued thereafter as one strain of modern Japanese ultranationalism. Its most enduring achievement was in Japanese linguistics. Even today, scholars admire Motoori's philology. Moreover, in an age when the prestige of things Chinese was overwhelming,

[8]Tsunoda, de Bary, and Keene, *Japanese Tradition,* pp. 521, 523.

Motoori helped redress the balance by appreciating and giving a name to the aesthetic sensibility found in the Japanese classics. The phrase he used was *mono no aware*, which means, literally, "the poignancy of things."

But National Studies had several weaknesses that prevented it from becoming the mainstream of Japanese thought. First, even the most refined sensibility is no substitute for philosophy. In its celebration of the primitive, National Studies ran headlong into the greater rationality of Confucian thought. Second, National Studies was chiefly literary, and apart from its enthusiasm for the divine emperor, it had little to offer politically in an age when political philosophy was central in both the domain and the *bakufu* schools.

Dutch Studies   A second development was Dutch Studies. After Christianity had been proscribed and the policy of seclusion adopted, all Western books were banned in Japan. Some knowledge of Dutch was maintained among the official interpreters who dealt with the Dutch at Nagasaki. The ban on Western books (except for those propagating Christianity) was ended in 1720 by the shōgun Tokugawa Yoshimune (r. 1716–1745), following the advice of a scholar whom he had appointed to reform the Japanese calendar.

During the remainder of the eighteenth century, a school of "Dutch medicine" became established in Japan. Japanese pioneers early recognized that Western anatomy texts were superior to Chinese. The first Japanese dissection of a corpse occurred in 1754. In 1774 a Dutch translation of a German anatomy text was translated into Japanese. By the midcentury there were schools of Dutch Studies in the main cities of Japan, and instruction was available in some domains as well. Fukuzawa Yukichi (1835–1901), who studied Dutch and Dutch science during the mid-1850s at a school begun in 1838 in Osaka, wrote in his *Autobiography* of the hostility of his fellow students toward Chinese learning:

> *Though we often had discussions on many subjects, we seldom touched upon political subjects as most of us were students of medicine. Of course, we were all for free intercourse with Western countries, but there were few among us who took a serious interest in that problem. The only subject that bore our constant attack was Chinese medicine. And by hating Chinese medicine so thoroughly, we came to dislike everything that had any connection with Chinese culture. Our general opinion was that we should rid our country of the influences of the Chinese altogether. Whenever we met a young student of Chinese literature, we simply felt sorry for him. Particularly were the students of Chinese medicine the butt of our ridicule.*[9]

While medicine was the primary occupation of those who studied Dutch, some knowledge of Western astronomy, geography, botany, physics, chemistry, and arts also entered Japan. Works on science occasionally influenced other thinkers as well. Yamagata Bantō (1748–1821) was a rich and scholarly Osaka merchant who devised a rationalistic philosophy based on a synthesis of Neo-Confucianism and Western science. After studying a work on astronomy, he wrote in 1820 that conditions on other planets "varied only according to their size and their proximity to the sun." Bantō also speculated that "grass and trees will appear, insects will develop; if there are insects, fish, shellfish, animals and birds will not be absent, and finally there will be people too." Bantō qualified his argument with the naturalistic supposition that Mercury and Venus would probably lack human life, "since these two planets are near to the sun and too hot." He contrasted his rational arguments regarding evolution with the "slap-dash" arguments of Buddhists and Shintoists.[10]

From the late eighteenth century the Japanese began to be aware of the West, and especially of Russia, as a threat to Japan. In 1791 a concerned scholar wrote *A Discussion of the Military Problems of a Maritime Nation*, advocating a strong navy and coastal defenses. During the early nineteenth century such concerns mounted. A sudden expansion in Dutch Studies occurred after Commodore Matthew Perry's visits to Japan in 1853 and 1854. During the 1860s Dutch Studies became Western Studies, as English, French, German, and Russian were added to the languages studied at the *bakufu* Institute for the Investigation of Barbarian Books. In sum, Dutch Studies was not a major influence on Tokugawa thought. It cannot begin to compare with Neo-Confucianism. But it laid a foundation on which the Japanese built quickly when the need arose.

Korea and Vietnam

Korea and Vietnam are an unlikely duo. Korea was a northern land with an Altaic language; Vietnam to the southeast of China had jungles and elephants and was hot. Yet both countries, like Japan, took in Tang civilization and adapted it to their own purposes. Chinese civilization in the sixth and seventh centuries was the only high civilization in the area. Chinese laws, philosophies, and political institutions may be thought of as a technology of a kind. That other countries would borrow them was little different from Third World countries today that borrow the science, technology, and political ideas of the recent West.

---

[9]E. Kiyooka, trans., *The Autobiography of Fukuzawa Yukichi* (New York: Columbia University Press, 1966), p. 91.

[10]M. Jansen, ed., *Changing Japanese Attitudes toward Modernization* (Princeton, NJ: Princeton University Press, 1965), p. 144.

But Koreans and Vietnamese also gained identities separate from China. In time, they took pride in their independence. Were Korea and Vietnam like Germany, which became civilized by borrowing the heartland Greco-Christian culture of the Mediterranean area but kept its Germanic tongue and other elements from its earlier culture?

Korea

Geography shaped Korean history. A range of mountains along its northern rim divides the Korean peninsula from Manchuria, making it a distinct geographical unit. Mountains continue south through the eastern third of Korea, while in the west and south are coastal plains and broad river valleys. The combination of mountains, rice paddies, and sea makes Korea a beautiful land. The traditional name for Korea may be translated as the "land of the morning calm." Two further geograph-ical factors affected Korean history. One was that the north-western corner of Korea was only 300 miles from the north-eastern corner of historical China: close enough for Korea to be vulnerable to invasions by its powerful neighbor but far enough away so that most of the time China found it easier to treat Korea as a tributary than to control it directly. The second factor was that the southern rim of Korea was just 100 miles distant from the Japanese southern island of Kyushu across the Tsushima Straits (see Map 18–4).

Early History

During its old and new stone ages, Tungusic tribes moving south from northeast Asia peopled Korea. They spoke an Altaic tongue—related to Japanese and to Manchurian, Mongolian, and Turkic. They lived by hunting, gathering, and fishing, and, like other early peoples of northeast Asia, made comb-patterned pottery and practiced an animistic

Map 18–4. Early Korean States.

religion. They worshiped the sun, moon, sea, and other forces of nature, and they communicated with the spirits of the dead through shamans. Important leaders were buried in megalithic tomb mounds. The early society was transformed by the introduction of bronze in 1300 B.C.E., agriculture in 1000 B.C.E., and iron in 400–300 B.C.E. Most of the population originally lived in small coastal or riverside villages, and only gradually spread inland. Koreans were still ruled by tribal chiefdoms in 108 B.C.E. when the Han emperor Wudi sent an army into north Korea to menace the flank of the Hunnish Xiongnu Empire that spread across the steppe to the north of China. Wudi built a Chinese city—near Pyongyang, the present-day capital of North Korea—which survived into the fourth century C.E., and established commanderies and prefectures to administer the land.

Between the fourth and seventh centuries C.E., as Chinese control collapsed, three archaic states emerged from earlier tribal confederations. Silla, one of the three, aided by armies from Tang China, conquered the other two in the seventh century. The Tang armies wanted to stay and rule Korea, but they withdrew after battles with Silla troops, and Silla was recognized by China in 675 as an autonomous tribute state. The period of Silla rule may be likened to eighth-century Nara Japan: The capital was laid out, like Chang'an, on a checkerboard pattern. Korea borrowed Chinese writing, established government offices on the Chinese model, sent annual embassies to the Tang court, and sent thousands of students to study at the Tang capital. It embraced Chinese Buddhism, arts, and philosophies. Yet within the Silla government, birth mattered more than scholarship and rule by aristocrats continued, while in village Korea, the worship of nature deities was only lightly touched by the Buddhism that spread among the ruling elites.

Silla underwent a normal end-of-dynasty decline, with coups, wars, and barbarian attacks across the frontier. Rebel kingdoms fought until 918, when a warlord general founded a new dynasty, the Koryo. The English word "Korea" is derived from this dynastic name. This was a creative period. Korean scholars advanced in their mastery of Chinese principles of government. New genres of poetry and literature appeared. Korean potters made celadon vases rivaling those of China. The craft of history advanced: The earliest surviving history of Korea was compiled in 1145. Printing using movable metallic type was invented during the thirteenth century. Most important of all was the growth of Buddhism. Temples, monasteries, and nunneries were built throughout the land, and Buddhist arts flourished. During the thirteenth century, Buddhist scholars produced in classical Chinese a printed edition of the *Tripitaka*, a huge compendium of sutras and other sacred writings.

The Koryo was more "Chinese" than the Silla: government offices resembled those in China, and Chinese-type laws were enacted. But even then, the aristocracy monopolized posts in the central government, and only a third of the 300 district magistates were sent out from the capital; the rest were appointed from local nobles or dignitaries. Apart from nobles, Koryo society was made up of commoners (the "good people") and slaves. Commoners were burdened by heavy taxes of rice, labor, and military service. Hereditary slaves were almost one-third of the population.

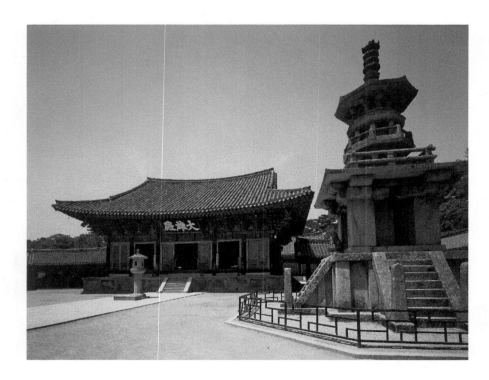

Pulguksa temple, built in 751 (and recently restored) near the ancient Silla capital of Kyongju. At right is a stupa containing a *sutra*, or relic of the Buddha.

Despite cultural advances, the Koryo state was weak. For one thing, the Koryo economy was undeveloped: Trade was by barter, money did not circulate, and Chinese missions commented on the extravagance of officials in the capital and the squalor of commoners and slaves in Korea's villages. For another, the dynasty was aristocratic from the start, and as centuries passed, private estates and armies arose, and civil officials were replaced by military figures. For still another, frequent Mongol incursions from across the northern border weakened state finances. The Koryo court survived as long as it did by becoming in succession the tributary of the Song, Liao, Jin, and Mongol dynasties.

Choson Dynasty

In 1392, a Koryo general, Yi Songgye, was sent to fight invading Ming (Chinese) armies. He decided that assuming power in Korea was the better part of valor; Forthwith, he made peace with the Chinese and founded the Choson Dynasty. The extraordinary longevity of the dynasty, from 1392 to 1910, was directly related to its status as a tributary of Ming and then Qing China (see Map 18–5). It served China's interest to prop up an obliging Korean state.

Ten to fifteen percent of Korea's population in the fifteenth century was composed of noble families (**yangban** [*yahng-bahn*]), who were the ruling class. Most had possessed *yangban* status during the previous dynasty; only families that had opposed the Yi's coming to power lost their position. About 30 percent of the population, or slightly more, were slaves. Early Choson Korea was the only "slave society" in the history of East Asia. Korean scholars argue that Korean slaves were not like slaves in other lands. There were no slave auctions, and, in line with Confucian teachings, wives and husbands were not separated. But slaves were nonetheless property. They were often attached to land, they could be given as gifts, and their children were slaves to be used as their owners willed. During the eighteenth and nineteenth centuries, the number declined sharply—possibly because it was easier to tax agricultural slaves than to own them. By the nineteenth century, only smaller numbers of household slaves remained. A majority of the Korean population were commoner farmers, who were heavily taxed and usually bore their lot stoically.

If the preceding Koryo period was Korea's age of Buddhist faith, the Choson was its Neo-Confucian age. Confucian teachings as interpreted by Zhu Xi became firmly established as the state orthodoxy. Civil and military examinations, for which only the *yangban* had the time and means to prepare, became the primary route to official promotion. Schools and academies increased in number. By the late fifteenth century, Korean philosophers were making original contributions to Zhu Xi philosophy, which later influenced thinkers in Japan.

Map 18–5. Korea during the Choson Era.

The shift from Buddhism to Neo-Confucianism as the ideology of the ruling elite may be seen as "East Asian" in that it paralleled changes that had occurred in China during the Song Dynasty and would occur in Japan during the Tokugawa era.

The history of Choson kings and their courts is filled with colorful drama, like European courts in the age of feudal monarchy. There were good ministers and bad, usurpations, assassinations, purges, and reforms. The *yangban* domination of the bureaucracy enabled them to resist any reform by the throne that would have injured their propertied interests. But they were united only in defense of their prerogatives, and more often were divided into factions that waged bitter struggles. The struggles can

A Badge of Rank. In Choson Korea—as in China—the rank of an official was indicated by the embroidered square affixed to his gown. Some squares showed ducks, pheasants, egrets, leopards, or tigers. Here we see a crane flying among the clouds and rainbows below.

be explained, in part, by the fact that those who passed the exams outnumbered the official posts available. Contention between bureaucratic cliques for control of the government in Seoul was almost constant, losers often being executed or imprisoned. As the struggles continued, the effectiveness of government declined, except for a brief recovery during the early eighteenth century. High officials in Seoul used their power to garner private agricultural estates and establish schools to prepare their kinsmen for examinations.

Wise rulers and periods of good government should also be noted. An early ruler, King Sejong (r. 1418-1450), reformed land taxes, made loans of grain to farmers during spring planting, and encouraged the spread of better agricultural technology. He also reformed the army and navy, attacked pirate strongholds on Tsushima Island, and expanded Korea's borders north of the Yalu River. In 1420, he established a Hall of Worthies—much like the Hanlin Academy of China—to encourage scholarship. Scholars at his court made sundials, water clocks, and astronomical instruments. But even Sejong suffered setbacks. The outstanding achievement of the Hall of Worthies was the creation of an alphabetic script known as *hangul*. But the script was never widely used and then only for informal purposes. Chinese remained the language of scholarship and official communications: It had prestige, authority,

and the support of the educated *yangban* class. Sejong also promoted the use of coins and paper money to stimulate commerce, but they never caught on. Artisans for the most part were attached to noble households and barter remained the rule. King Sejong was also unable to provide for an orderly succession: He had twenty sons and fourteen daughters, but after his death, his uncle usurped the Korean throne.

Invasions by foreign troops also threatened Korea at mid-dynasty. Having unified Japan, Hideyoshi decided to conquer China, and the path to China was through Korea. His samurai armies devastated Korea twice, once in 1592 and again in 1597. The invasions ended only with Hideyoshi's death in 1598. On both occasions the Ming court sent troops to aid its Korean tributary, but the Chinese armies, in turn, devastated the land almost as much as had the Japanese. A third disaster occurred in 1627 and 1637 when Manchu troops invaded pro-Ming Korea and laid waste to Seoul and to the northwest. The Korean court, just in time, switched its allegiance to the new Qing Dynasty and was able to continue its rule. The consequence of these four decades of invasions was a drop in taxable land to about a quarter of the level of the late-sixteenth-century. Behind this statistic lay a grim reality of famine, death and untold misery.

Chronology

Korean History

Prior to 108 B.C.E.	Tribal village society
108 B.C.E.–313 C.E.	Chinese commanderies
313–675	Three archaic states
675–918	Silla rule and Chinese influence
918–1392	Koryo Dynasty
1392–1910	Choson Dynasty
r.1418–1450	King Sejong: Reforms and Hangul
1592, 1597	Hideyoshi invasions
1627, 1637	Manchu invasions
1671	Famine
1811, 1862	Peasant rebellions

From the mid-seventeenth century on, Korea offers a mixed picture. Literacy rose, and a new popular fiction of fables, romances, and novels appeared. Women writers became important for the first time. Some *yangban* scholars reacted against what they perceived as the overly metaphysical nature of Neo-Confucianism. Calling for "practical learning" to renew Korean society, they outlined plans for administrative reforms and the encouragement of commerce. But their recommendations were not adopted, and Korean society continued its decline. More Koreans died in the famine of 1671 than during Hideyoshi's invasions. Excessive taxation, drought, floods, pestilence, and famine became commonplace. Robberies occurred in daytime Seoul, and bandits plagued the countryside. Disgruntled officials led peasants in month-long revolts in 1811 and 1862. Because of the concentration of officials, wealth, and military power at Seoul, and because of Qing support for the ruling house, neither revolt succeeded in toppling the dynasty, but the revolts left Korea with neither the will nor the means to meet the challenges it would soon face.

Vietnam

Vietnam in Southeast Asia

Four movements shaped the historical civilizations of Southeast Asia. Vietnam was touched by each and by a fifth as well. The first was the movement of peoples and languages from north to south. Ranges of mountains rising in Tibet and south China extend southward, dividing Southeast Asia into river valleys. The Mon and Burmese peoples had moved from the southeast slopes of the Tibetan plateau into the Upper Irrawaddy by 500 B.C.E. and continued south along the Irrawaddy and Salween rivers, founding the kingdom of Pagan in 847 C.E. Thai tribes moved south from China down the valley of the Chao Phraya River somewhat later, founding the kingdoms of Sukhothai (1238–1419) and Ayutthaya (1350–1767). Even today Thai-speaking peoples are still to be found in several southern China provinces. The origins of the Vietnamese are less clear, but they, too, first inhabited the north and moved into present-day central and southern Vietnam only in recent historical times.

A second movement was the Indianization of Southeast Asia. Between the first and fifteenth centuries Indian traders and missionaries crossed the Bay of Bengal and established outposts throughout Southeast Asia. As Hinduism and Buddhism spread through the region, Indian-type states with god-kings were established, and Indian scripts, legal codes, literature, drama, art, and music were adopted by the indigenous peoples. Today, Burma, Thailand, and Cambodia retain an Indian-type Buddhism; on the walls of Bangkok temples are painted scenes from the great Hindu epic, the *Mahabharata*. This early wave of Buddhism reached Vietnam, but was later supplanted by Chinese Buddhism. Vietnam, too, first received Buddhism as part of this early Indian wave, though it was later replaced by the Chinese form of that religion.

A third dynamic movement was that of Arab and Indian traders who sailed across the Indian Ocean to dominate trade with the Spice Islands (the Moluccas of present-day Indonesia) between the thirteenth and fifteenth centuries. Settling on the coasts and islands of Southeast Asia, they married into local ruling families and spread the teachings of Islam. Local rulers who converted became sultans. Today Malaysia and Indonesia are predominantly Muslim. The majestic Buddhist temple at Borobudur in central Java is a monument of an earlier age, submerged today in a sea of Islamic practice. Only the Hindu island of Bali to the east of Java retains the Indian religion that once covered the entire Indonesian archipelago. The Cham state (located in what today is central Vietnam) also became Muslim. Islam did not directly affect the Vietnamese, though Arab and Indian traders en route to China would visit Vietnamese coastal harbors or travel up the Red River to Hanoi.

A fourth movement, much later, was the Chinese **diaspora.** The emigration of Chinese throughout the world but especially to Southeast Asia began as a trickle and gathered momentum after 1842, after the Opium War. Most Chinese went, initially, as indentured labor to work on plantations. But in time many moved to cities and opened shops. The mercantile ethos of the Chinese was more advanced than that of peoples to the south. Today, the casual visitor to Bangkok sees shopkeepers reading Chinese newspapers in front of their shops. Their children became educated; some entered banking or law. In most of Southeast Asia the urban economies were largely developed and controlled by Chinese. This created resentments and, occasionally, anti-Chinese riots. To appease the powers that be, Chinese companies routinely appointed non-Chinese politicians or generals to their boards of directors. Assimilation occurred, but at a generational pace. The greatest concentrations of Chinese, apart from Singapore (three quarters of the population), were in Malaysia, Indonesia, and Thailand. But many of the "boat people" who fled Vietnam after the Vietnam War were Chinese Vietnamese.

A fifth movement or event, which affected only Vietnam and made it a part of East Asia, was conquest by China.

Vietnamese Origins

The story of Vietnam might first consider its present-day geography. Vietnam is like two baskets on a carrying pole. One basket is the Red River basin, centering on Hanoi in the north, the other the delta of the Mekong River centering on

Saigon (today Ho Chi Minh City) in the south. The carrying pole is the narrow mountainous strip of central Vietnam, with little river valleys opening to the South China Sea (see Map 18–6).

Vietnamese, until the late fifteenth century, inhabited only the northern part of present-day Vietnam, that is to say, the basin of the Red River, which flows from west to east and empties into the Gulf of Tongking. The Chams, a wholly different people, who are closer to Indonesians than to Vietnamese, occupied central Vietnam and part of the southeastern coast. Their kingdom was called Champa. They were a seafaring people who engaged in trade and piracy, and like the Indonesians they became Hindu-Buddhist and later Muslim. They waged intermittent wars against the Vietnamese to their north. A third people, the Khmers or Cambodians, inhabited the Mekong River Delta, the area that is today south Vietnam. The Khmers were a part of the Hindu-Buddhist Cambodian Empire that had its capital at Angkor in present-day Cambodia.

The early history of the Vietnamese in the Red River valley is known only through archaeology. Agriculture began early; slash-and-burn-techniques were practiced in the highlands and crude paddy fields in the lowlands. Bronze entered during the first millennium B.C.E., and iron during the first or second century B.C.E. Pots made on potting wheels and bronze arrowheads and fishhooks are found in excavations, but plows were still tipped with stone. The people lived in villages under tribal leaders and worshiped the spirits of nature; men tattooed their bodies.

Bronze drum engraved with intricate geometric designs from circa 800 B.C.E. Vietnam. An artifact of the early Bronze Age, it was made for ceremonial purposes. Whether early Vietnamese bronze technology was indigenous or whether it came from China is an open question.

A Millennium of Chinese Rule: 111 B.C.E.–939 C.E.

Vietnamese political history began in 208 B.C.E. when a renegade Han Dynasty general formed the state of Nan Yueh. Its capital was near the present-day Chinese city of Guangzhou (Canton). It ruled over peoples in both southeastern China and the Red River basin. The Chinese ideograph for Yueh is read *Viet* in Vietnamese. The name Vietnam, literally, "Viet to the south," is derived from the name of this early state. Nan Yueh lasted for a century until Han armies conquered it and brought it under Chinese control in 111 B.C.E. After that, the Red River basin was ruled by China for more than 1,000 years.

For the first seven centuries, Vietnam was governed by a Chinese military commandery, which consisted, initially, of a fort, Chinese troops, and a governor. It was like commanderies established in Korea and other border regions to rule over non-Chinese "barbarian" populations. The governor ruled indirectly through local Vietnamese chiefs or magnates. Refugees fleeing China after the fall of the Former Han Dynasty in 8 C.E. were appointed as officials in Vietnam.

In a famous incident of 39 C.E. the Vietnamese revolted against Chinese rule. The revolt was led by the Trung sisters—the husband of one sister had been executed by the Chinese. The sisters later were made into national heroes. As a fifteenth-century Vietnamese poet exclaimed:

All the male heroes bowed their heads in submission;
Only the two sisters proudly stood up to avenge the country.

But at the time there was little sense of "country," and the only consequence of the revolt was a further strengthening of Chinese controls.

Vietnamese society slowly evolved during the centuries of Chinese rule. Early Vietnam had a matrilineal tribal society, practiced slash-and-burn agriculture, and often moved their settlements when the lands became exhausted. New agricultural techniques and metal plows, introduced from China, led to permanent settlements and denser populations. Tribes gave way to villages, and descent became patrilineal—though women continued to enjoy a higher status than women in China. Buddhism entered, replacing or mingling with earlier animistic beliefs. Chinese officials sometimes married Vietnamese women, and a Sino-Vietnamese

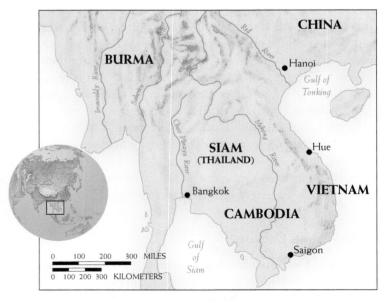

CHINA

BURMA

Hanoi

Gulf of Tonking

SIAM
(THAILAND)

Hue

Bangkok

VIETNAM

CAMBODIA

Saigon

Gulf of Siam

0   100   200   300   MILES

0   100 200 300   KILOMETERS

Map 18–6. Vietnam and Neighboring Southeast Asia

social elite arose in the capital. The influence of Chinese higher culture was initially confined to this elite.

During the Tang Dynasty (618–907), Vietnam was still considered a border region, but Chinese administration became stronger. Elements of Chinese law and, possibly, the Chinese land and tax system were introduced at this time. The Red River basin was also divided into provinces, which the Chinese referred to collectively as **Annam**, the "pacified south." When the French came to Vietnam in the nineteenth century, they picked up the term and called the north Vietnamese *Annamese*.

Since it was during the Tang that Japan and Korea also took in Chinese learning, one can ask whether Vietnam was a parallel case. In some ways it was. In all three societies Buddhism entered, flourished in the capitals, and gradually percolated into local areas, where it absorbed elements from earlier indigenous religions. In all three, other aspects of China's higher culture affected mainly the elites of the society, while an older way of life continued in villages with only small changes. But where Japanese and Korean rulers reached out for Chinese learning and technology and used it for their own ends, the Vietnamese had it thrust upon them. In the ninth century the Japanese devised a phonetic syllabary for the transcription of their language, and by the year 1000 they were writing works such as *The Tale of Genji*—reflecting a new culture in which native and Chinese elements were fused. In Vietnam, where both the rulers and the written language were Chinese, no such transformation occurred.

An Independent Vietnam

Ten major revolts occurred in what is now north Vietnam during the thousand years of Chinese rule—not an unusual number for a Chinese border region with a non-Chinese population. The last revolt, which took place in 939 when China was weak, led to the establishment of an independent Vietnamese government. Vietnam never again became a part of China.

The history of Vietnam's second millennium is conventionally broken into dynastic blocks named after the ruling families:

Ly	1009–1225
Tran	1225–1400
Le	1428–1787
Nguyen	1802–1880s

But Vietnamese "dynasties" were not strong, centralized, bureaucratic states like those of China. There were tensions between the center and peripheries. At the center were the social elites who ruled the population of the Red River Delta. At the periphery were magnates, powerful local figures, who controlled upland peoples and possessed armies of their own. Thanh Hoa, a province 100 miles south of Hanoi, was of particular importance, with magnates who often opposed the "dynasty." Often, several independent states coexisted during the time span of a single "dynasty."

Chinese invasions also affected Vietnamese history. Some Chinese dynasties, as they expanded, attempted to reconquer the "south" that had once been a part of China. Ming armies occupied Vietnam for twenty years beginning in 1407. But Vietnam was distant and hard to control. Rather than engaging in wars, Chinese rulers found it easier to enroll Vietnam as a tributary: Vietnamese dynasties sent ambassadors who professed the Vietnamese ruler's submission to the Chinese emperor. In official communications to China the Vietnamese rulers styled themselves as "kings," indicating a subordinate status.

Their submission, however, was purely formal. Within Vietnam, Vietnamese rulers styled themselves as "emperors" and claimed that their mandate to rule came directly from heaven. It was separate but equal to the mandate received by the Chinese emperor. They also denied the universality of the Chinese imperium by referring to China not as the Middle Kingdom but as the Northern Court—their own government being the Southern Court. In 1076, a Vietnamese general fighting Chinese troops wrote the following poem:

> *The Southern emperor rules the Southern land*
> *Our destiny is writ in Heaven's Book*
> *How dare you bandits trespass on our soil*
> *You shall meet your undoing at our hands.*

The poem proclaims the independence of Vietnam and a sense of a separate national identity. But the poem was written in Chinese, the only written language existing in Vietnam, and is couched in the vocabulary of Chinese political thought.

The March South

After twenty years of exploitative Ming rule, Le Loi, a landowner from Thanh Hoa, drove out the occupying Chinese armies in 1427. He used war-elephants in his attack against the Chinese forces. After his victory, he established the Le Dynasty (1428–1787).

Two momentous developments began in Vietnam during the fifteenth century and continued during the centuries that followed. One was a more extensive adoption of Chinese institutions. For Vietnam's rulers, Chinese institutions and culture were not so much "Chinese" as they were an advanced technology that could be used for their own purposes. The reforms of Le Thanh Tong (1442–1497), an immensely talented early ruler, were especially notable. He divided his

Document   On Husband-Sharing

The position of women in Vietnam may have been higher than in China, but Vietnamese officials still had concubines when they could afford them. The eighteenth-century poet Ho Xuang Huong gives her view on the subject.

■ *Should this poem be read as a criticism of the prevailing Confucian ethos?*

One rolls in warm blankets,
The other freezes:
Down with this husband-sharing!
You're lucky ever to have him,
He comes perhaps twice a month,
Or less.
Ah—to fight for—this!

Turned to a half-servant, an unpaid maid!
Had I known
I would have stayed single.

Source: From *A Thousand Years of Vietnamese Poetry*, by Nguyen Ngoc Bich. Copyright © 1975 by The Asia Society. Reprinted by permission.

realm into thirteen provinces and then into prefectures, counties, and departments. He weakened the nobility by holding civil service examinations for the selection of officials, and set up nine ranks of civil and military officials. He established schools, introduced Neo-Confucian learning, and promoted public works. He registered the population and reinstituted a Chinese-type land tax. In the decades after his death, some of these reforms broke down, but in time other reformers appeared and continued his work. Chinese institutions and culture proved far more powerful than Chinese armies.

The second development, also begun by Le Thanh Tong, was what Vietnamese historians call "the march to the south." The "march" took more than two centuries. In the first leg of the march, in 1471, Le armies moved south to conquer the Muslim state of Champa in what is today central Vietnam. (See Map 18–5.) To secure the Champa lands, Le established self-supporting colonies of Vietnamese soldier-peasants along the coast of the former kingdom. These gradually merged with the local population. To rule the Muslim Chams, in 1483 he promulgated a Confucian-tinged legal code that remained in effect for a century or more. It appealed to "universal" values that both Vietnamese and Chams could accept. Successors to the Le throne, however, were unable to maintain control over the central coast, and autonomous Vietnamese states arose. These impeded the passage of settlers from the densely populated Red River basin to the south during the sixteenth and early seventeenth centuries.

The second leg of the march south was the conquest of the Mekong Delta (the present-day south Vietnam). Within Vietnam there had emerged a balance between the Trinh

(the Le had become figureheads), who held power in Hanoi, and the Nguyen, who ruled the central coast from their capital at Hue. The Nguyen gradually extended their power to

Chronology

Vietnamese History

111 B.C.E. 939 C.E.	Vietnam as a part of China
First 7 Centuries	Rule by Chinese commanderies
7th and 8th Centuries	Sinification during Tang rule
939–1880s	An independent Vietnam
Ly Dynasty 1009–1225	
Tran Dynasty 1225–1400	
Occupation by Ming troops 1407–1426	
Le Dynasty 1428–1787	
1442–1487	Reforms by Le Thanh Tong
1471	Conquest of Champa
1698	Rule over Saigon
1757	Control of Mekong Delta
Nguyen Dynasty 1802–1880s	
1802	Nguyen unites Vietnam with Hue as its capital

Hue. A gate from the imperial citadel.

the sparsely settled Mekong Delta in the south: They seized control of Saigon in 1698, and by 1757 ruled the south as far west as the Gulf of Siam. Political control facilitated the flow of people from the north and the central coast to the south, though Vietnamese remained a minority in southern Vietnam throughout the eighteenth century.

The last phase of premodern Vietnamese history was the Nguyen conquest of the north in 1802. This led to the founding of the Nguyen Dynasty with its capital at Hue. Several French advisers and adventurers who had aided the first Nguyen emperor were rewarded with high posts in the new government. But from the time of the second emperor, the Nguyen Dynasty turned against the French and began a new wave of borrowing from China. It adopted the law codes of Qing China, recruited civil and military officials by examination, and established in Hue Chinese institutions such as the Six Boards, Hanlin Academy, and a Censorate. These moves were designed to placate Confucian scholars in the north, strengthen the authority of the court, and weaken the generals who had helped the dynasty's rise.

During the first half of the nineteenth century, Vietnam was governed better than in any previous era and better than any other Southeast Asian state. By any traditional standard, it was competent. But it had weaknesses as well. There were tensions between the north, which was overpopulated, well schooled, and furnished most of the official class, and the south, which was ethnically diverse, educationally backward, and poorly represented in government. Commerce and artisanal skills were less developed than in China and Japan, only small amounts of specie circulated, and periodic markets were more common than market towns. The government rested on a society composed largely of self-sufficient villages. In sum, Vietnam entered the second half of the nineteenth century less prepared than China or Japan for the challenges it would soon face.

Summary

China China's last two imperial dynasties were the Ming (1368–1644) and the Qing or Manchus (1644–1911). Although China could not match the dynamism of the West during these years, its society became more integrated and its government more sophisticated. The population reached 410 million, cities grew, and commerce expanded. Chinese government rested on a Confucian bureaucracy and gentry class. Under the Manchus, China expanded to the west, north and east, establishing claims to Tibet, Central Asia, Mongolia, and Taiwan. Trade with the West grew, especially with Britain, but Chinese officials controlled it until the Opium War of 1839–1842.

Japan After a century of civil war among warrior states (the Warring States era, 1467–1600), the Tokugawa shōgun (1600–1868) restored order. Their Edo government controlled the military houses and encouraged economic growth. Japan became closed to the outside world except for a small Dutch presence at Nagasaki. Japanese drama, literature, and art flourished, as did commercial life.

Korea and Vietnam The gap between "late traditional" history and "early modern" history is especially clear in Korea and Vietnam prior to the nineteenth century. Both countries were tributaries of China. The development of both combined Chinese elements with their respective internal dynamics. Vietnam was notable for its conquest and peopling of the Mekong Delta, Korea, for its Confucian culture, *yangban* aristocracy, and slavery.

Key Terms

Annam (p. 571)

daimyo (p. 547)

diaspora (p. 569)

gentry (p. 537)

Kabuki (p. 555)

Nō (p. 555)

National Studies (p. 563)

yangban (p. 567)

Review Questions

1. What factors led to economic and population growth in late traditional China? Was the pattern the same in Japan during those centuries?

2. How was Manchu rule like Mongol rule during the Yuan Dynasty? How was it like the rule by Chinese emperors during the Ming?

3. What were the social and administrative foundations of the absolute power of Ming–Qing emperors?

4. How did advances in military technology change warfare in sixteenth-century Japan? How was the strategic balance of power reflected in the government created by Tokugawa Ieyasu?

5. Did literacy ruin the samurai as warrior vassalle? How did literate samurai "fit" the changed society of the late eighteenth century?

6. Do critiques of imperialism presume the acceptance of some notion of human rights? Without such an acceptance are not Hideyoshi's invasion of Korea, the Chinese conquest of Tibet, and the Vietnamese "march to the South" simply the normal actions of strong states?

Note: To learn more about the topics in this chapter, please turn to the Suggested Readings at the end of the book. For additional sources related to this chapter please see MyHistoryLab.com.

PEARSON myhistorylab Connections

Reinforce what you learned in this chapter by studying the many documents, images, maps, review tools, and videos available at **www.myhistorylab.com**.

Read and Review

✓• Study and Review **Chapter 18**

•• Read the Document **Mitamura, p. 536**
A Ming Naval Expedition 15th century p. 541
Injunctions Tokugawa Shogunate p. 551
Shohatto p. 553

👁 See the Map **Ming and Qing China, p. 532**

Research and Explore

👁 See the Map *Trade Routes in Southeast Asia, 1300–1650*

👁 See the Map *Voyages of Zheng-He, p. 540*

(((•• Hear the **Audio**

Hear the audio file for Chapter 18 at
www.myhistorylab.com.

19 | State Building and Society in Early Modern Europe

■ European Political Consolidation

■ European Warfare: From Continental to World Conflict

■ The Old Regime

■ Family Structures and the Family Economy

■ The Revolution in Agriculture

■ The Eighteenth-Century Industrial Revolution: An Event in World History

■ European Cities

■ The Jewish Population: Age of the Ghetto

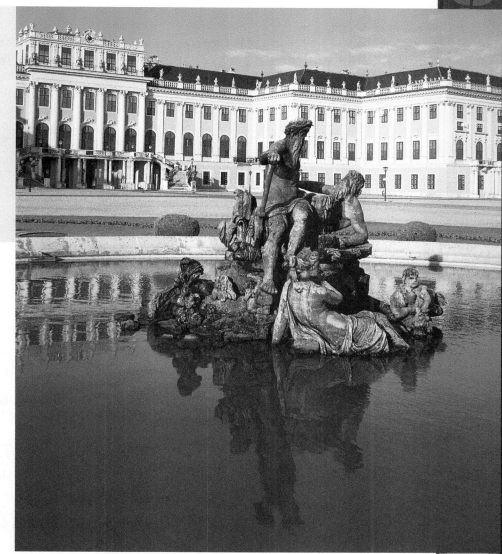

Schonbrunn Palace, Vienna. To symbolize his vast royal authority, Louis XIV of France constructed a vast new palace at Versailles outside Paris as the center of his government. Subsequently, other European monarchs built similar palaces. Between 1743 and 1763 the Austrian Empress Maria Theresa carried out the construction of the Schonbrunn Palace on the outskirts of Vienna to symbolize Habsburg authority.

FOR APPROXIMATELY THREE AND A HALF CENTURIES Commencing in the early seventeenth century northwestern Europe became the chief driving force in one world historical development after another. Such had not been the situation before that time and would not be the situation after World War II. Two broad factors accounted for this rise of European dominance.

First, by the mid-eighteenth century five major states had come to dominate European politics and would continue to do so until at least World War I. They were Great Britain, France, Austria, Prussia, and Russia. These states established their preeminence at the expense of Spain, Portugal, the United Provinces of the Netherlands, Poland, Sweden, and the Ottoman Empire. Equally essential to their rise was the weakness of the Holy

Early Modern Europe

Europe

During the seventeenth and eighteenth centuries political and economic developments in Europe set the continent on a path that by the nineteenth century resulted in a period of European world domination that ultimately proved temporary. The major states of northwestern Europe consolidated themselves politically and militarily in strong, often aggressive political units. The economy of this region of Europe would take the first steps toward industrialization and the capacity to produce vast quantities of both consumer and capital goods. The Netherlands, France, and Great Britain developed sophisticated financial structures that fueled overseas commercial empires, protected by strong navies.

These world-transforming developments occurred slowly. At the beginning of this era of political and economic consolidation, much of Europe resembled other major world civilizations. European states displayed certain problems that also characterized the governments of China and Japan during the same epochs. In particular, as in Japan, the problem of a balance between centralization and decentralization arose in virtually all the European states. In France, Russia, and Prussia, the forces of centralization proved quite strong. In Austria the forces of decentralization were powerful. England achieved a rather delicate balance. Furthermore, as in Tokugawa, Japan, European states of the eighteenth century generally saw an increase in legal codification and in the growth of bureaucracy. Only in Prussia did the military influence on society resemble that in Japan.

The role of the personality of the monarch in Europe bore some resemblance to that of certain Manchu emperors in China, such as Kangxi (1662–1722) and Qianlong (r. 1736–1795). Louis XIV and Peter the Great had no less influence on their nations than did these great Manchu emperors. All of them built up military strength and fostered innovation. However, although European rulers developed

Roman Empire after the Peace of Westphalia (1648). The five rising states engaged in warfare within each other and extended much of that conflict around the world, producing the most extensive European impact on the non-European world since the early sixteenth century when the Spanish had conquered the civilizations of Mexico and Peru.

The second factor in the dominance of Europe on the world scene was that during these centuries the peoples living primarily in northwestern Europe undertook a series of economic advances that laid the foundation for the social and economic transformation of the world. For the first time in their history Europeans commenced to achieve a more or less stable food supply. For reasons still much debated, the population of Europe began a major period of growth. New inventions in the manufacture of textiles transformed Europe's productive capacity, and the invention of the steam engine, powered by coal as a fuel, opened the way for moving manufacturing from the countryside to cities. Furthermore, the production of iron greatly expanded. These develop-ments, known collectively as the industrial revolution, gave Europe a productive and military capacity previously unknown in human history. ■

European Political Consolidation

Two Models of European Political Development

In the second half of the sixteenth century, changes in European military organization, weapons, and tactics sharply increased the cost of warfare. Because traditional sources of state income could not finance these growing military costs, monarchs sought new revenues. Monarchies that succeeded in building a secure financial base independent of the support of noble estates, diets, or assemblies achieved what later became known as absolute rule. The French monarchy was the most successful example of such centralized government. The English monarchy, by contrast, failed to make itself absolute, but rather by the end of the seventeenth century could govern only with and through Parliament. These differing paths of political development led to state bureaucracies, none of them put together so brilliant a group of trained civil servants as those who administered China. The roots of the Chinese civil service went back centuries, and Chinese civil servants, unlike those in Europe, tended to resist modernization of the Chinese government and economy for both practical and ideological reasons. Civil servants in Europe tended to foster rather than obstruct modernization, which posed no threat to their power or worldview.

The global commercial empires of the Netherlands, France, Spain, and England gave rise to fierce commercial rivalries. The drive for empire and commercial supremacy propelled these states into contact with Africa, Latin America, India, China, and Japan. Spain and Portugal had long exploited Latin America as their own monopoly, an arrangement that England challenged in the eighteenth century. China's lack of interest in dominating the Indian Ocean opened the way for European adventurers and traders in India. France and England fought for commercial supremacy in India, and by the 1760s England had, in effect, conquered the subcontinent. The slave trade between Africa and the New World flourished throughout the seventeenth and eighteenth centuries. European merchants and navies also sought to penetrate East Asia, although their success was limited until the advent of nineteenth-century "gunboat diplomacy."

As this term implies, European success in Africa, Asia, and the Indian Ocean was always closely linked to its sophisticated military technology, especially the construction of sturdy ships able to carry heavy cannons. As a result of these developments, European commerce dominated the world for the next two centuries. Moreover, beginning in the early eighteenth century with the slow but later steady growth of industrialism, the political power of the European states became linked to a qualitatively different economic base than any seen elsewhere in the world. That political and economic combination allowed Europe to dominate the world from the 1750s to World War II.

Focus Questions

- How did European states resemble those in other parts of the world in the mid-eighteenth century? How did they differ?
- What was the relationship between military technology, especially naval power, and the growth of European colonial empires?
- What factors led to the political and economic transformation of western Europe and its emergence as a region that would eventually (for a time) dominate much of the world?

the two distinct models of government—**absolutism** in France and **parliamentary monarchy** in England—that shaped subsequent political development in Europe.

Toward Parliamentary Government in England

When Elizabeth I died in 1603 without children, the English Crown passed to James VI of Scotland, the son of Mary, Queen of Scots, who became James I of England, the first of the Stuart Dynasty. In their pursuit of adequate income, Stuart monarchs of seventeenth-century England threatened the local political interests and economic well-being of the nobility and the landed and commercial elites represented in Parliament. These groups in turn over the course of the decades invoked traditional English liberties to effectively resist the monarchs. Furthermore, **Puritans** in the Church of England, whose Protestant religious views derived from John Calvin, wished to see a more radical reformation carried out in England. While attempting to rule as much as possible without Parliament, both James I (r. 1603–1625) and his son Charles I (r. 1625–1649) also resisted the Puritan demands and at the same time favored peaceful relations with the Roman Catholic powers Spain and France. Consequently,

the first two Stuarts confronted a combined political and religious opposition to their efforts to make the English monarchy the supreme power in the land. Many of the same political leaders who saw themselves defending traditional English liberties against the monarchy also saw themselves as having to protect the Protestant Reformation in England.

●●●○ Read the Document
The Divine Right of Kings 1598 James I
at **MyHistoryLab.com**

By 1642 the conflict between Charles I and Parliament over religion and arbitrary taxation erupted into civil war. In 1645 the parliamentary and Puritan forces triumphed. Disputes continued, and in 1649 a rump Parliament from whom any opposing members had been removed voted for the execution of Charles I. Thereafter, Parliament abolished the monarchy, the House of Lords, and the established Church of England. What replaced them was a Puritan republic led by Oliver Cromwell (1599–1658), the victorious general in the civil war. Cromwell himself soon encountered difficulties with Parliament and from 1653 onward governed as a military dictator.

●●●○ View the Image
Allegorical View Cromwell as Savior England
at **MyHistoryLab.com**

●●●○ Read the Document
Cromwell Abolishes the English Monarchy 1651
at **MyHistoryLab.com**

Charles I ruled for several years without calling Parliament, but once he began a war with Scotland, he needed revenues that only Parliament could supply. *Anthony van Dyck, "Portrait of Charles I. Hunting," c. 1635. Oil on Canvas. 8'11" × 6'11 1/2" (2.72 × 2.12 m). Musee du Louvre, Paris. RMN Reunion des Musees Nationaux/Art Resource, New York.*

After Cromwell died in 1658, disillusionment with Puritan strictness and political uncertainty led to the restoration of the Stuart monarchy under Charles II (r. 1660–1685). The restored monarch would have extended very considerable religious toleration, but the restored Parliament dominated by conservative members of the Church of England imposed a restrictive religious code on the land. Thereafter the Church of England found itself opposed by both Protestant Non-Conformists and Roman Catholics. Charles II in 1670 entered a secret treaty with Louis XIV of France to oppose the Dutch. As a result of that treaty, Charles again attempted to extend religious toleration. Parliament resisted by passing a Test Act that required all officials to take an oath, which no Roman Catholic could in good conscience take.

James, Duke of York, Charles's brother, was a Roman Catholic and became monarch in 1685. Immediately he extended toleration to both Roman Catholics and the Protestant Non-Conformists. In June 1688 James II (r. 1685–1688) imprisoned seven Anglican bishops who had refused to publicize his suspension of laws against Catholics. Under the guise of a policy of enlightened toleration, James was actually seeking to subject all English institutions to the power of the monarchy.

The English political classes had hoped that James would be succeeded by Mary (r. 1689–1694), his Protestant eldest daughter. She was the wife of William of Orange(1650–1702), stadtholder (the chief magistrate) of the Netherlands, great-grandson of William the Silent (1533–1584), and the leader of European opposition to Louis XIV. But on June 20, 1688, James II's Catholic second wife gave birth to a son. There was now a Catholic male heir to the throne. The Parliamentary opposition invited William to invade England to preserve its "traditional liberties," that is, the Protestant Church of England and parliamentary government.

The "Glorious Revolution"

William of Orange arrived with his army in November 1688 and was received without significant opposition by the English people. James fled to France, and Parliament in 1689 proclaimed William III and Mary II the new monarchs, thus completing the bloodless **Glorious Revolution**. William and Mary, in turn, recognized a Bill of Rights that limited the powers of the monarchy and guaranteed the civil liberties of the English privileged classes. Henceforth, England's monarchs would be subject to law and would rule by the consent of Parliament, which was to be called into session every three years. The Bill of Rights also prohibited Roman Catholics from occupying the English throne. The Toleration Act of 1689 permitted worship by all Protestants but outlawed Roman Catholics and those who denied the Christian doctrine of the Trinity. (See Document, "John Locke Denounces the Idea of Absolute Monarchy.")

Read the **Document**
The English Bill of Rights, 1689
at **MyHistoryLab.com**

The Revolution of 1688 has traditionally been seen as a relatively peaceful event. Recent scholarship, however, has disclosed considerable resistance in both Scotland and Ireland, which resulted in significant loss of life. Conversely, events in England itself now appear to have been driven not only by the long recognized actions of the political elite but also by a genuinely popular resistance to James II. Furthermore, the political results of the revolution went well beyond the assertion of parliamentary authority. In one area of government policy after another the reign of William and Mary marked important new departures for Britain, including policies favoring more modern economic activity resembling that of the Netherlands as well as a redirection of foreign policy toward direct opposition to France.

The measure closing this century of strife was the Act of Settlement in 1701. This bill provided for the English Crown to go to the Protestant House of Hanover in Germany if Anne (r. 1702–1714), the second daughter of James II and the heir to the childless William III, died without issue. Thus, at Anne's death in 1714, the Elector of Hanover became King George I of England (r. 1714–1727), the third foreigner to occupy the English throne in just over a century.

Document — John Locke Denounces the Idea of Absolute Monarchy

John Locke (1632–1704) was the most important English philosopher of the late seventeenth century. As will be seen in Chapter 21, he wrote on a wide variety of subjects, including both political philosophy and religious toleration. In 1690 he published his second Treatise of Civil Government. In this work he defended limitations on government and rooted political authority in the consent of the governed. He drafted the treatise in the late 1670s in response to Tory assertions of absolute monarchy set forth by supporters of Charles II. The treatise was published in the wake of the Revolution of 1688 and was read at the time as a justification of that event. Locke's thought would almost a century later influence the American Declaration of Independence.

In the passages below Locke explains that under absolute monarchy citizens must submit to an authority from which they can make no appeal. Consequently, there is a necessary conflict between citizens and the absolute monarchy. It was to escape such conflict and to secure property and liberty that human beings had left the state of nature to found civil society. This document should be read in conjunction with the document presented later in this chapter, "Bishop Bossuet Defends the Divine Right of Kings."

■ *What are the purposes of civil society according to Locke? Why is it so important that citizens have the right to a neutral authority for judicial decisions? Why does Locke find an absolute monarch in conflict with his subjects and they with him? How do Locke's views serve to provide a foundation for parliamentary government?*

Man being born . . . with a title to perfect freedom, and an uncontrolled enjoyment of all the rights and privileges of the law of nature, equally with any other man, or number of men in the world, hath by nature a power, not only to preserve his property, that is, his life, liberty and estate, against the injuries and attempts of other men; but to judge of, and punish the breaches of that law in others, as he is persuaded the offence deserve. . . . [T]here and there only is political society, where every one of the members hath quitted this natural power, resigned it up into the hands of the community in all cases that excludes him not from appealing for protection to the law established by it. And thus all private judgment of every particular member being excluded, the community comes to be umpire, by settled standing rules, indifferent, and the same to all parties; and by men having authority from the community, for the execution of those rules, decides all the differences that may happen between any members of that society concerning any matter of right . . .

Whenever therefore any number of men are so united into one society, as to quit every one his executive power of the law of nature, and to resign it to the public, there and there only is a political, or civil society. . . .

Hence it is evident, that absolute monarchy, which by some men is counted the only government in the world, is indeed inconsistent with civil society, and so can be no form of civil government at all; for the end of civil society, being to avoid, and remedy those inconveniencies of the state of nature, which necessarily follow from every man's being judge in his own case, by setting up a known authority, to which every one of that society may appeal upon any injury received, or controversy that may arise, and which every one of the society ought to obey; wherever any persons are, who have not such an authority to appeal to, for the decision of any difference between them, there those persons are still in the state of nature; and so is every absolute prince, in respect of those who are under his dominion.

For he being supposed to have all, both legislative and executive power in himself alone, there is no judge to be found, no appeal lies open to any one, who may fairly, and indifferently, and with authority decide, and from whose decision relief and redress may be expected of any injury or inconveniency, that may be suffered from the prince, or by his order: so that such a man, however intitled, czar, or grand seignior, or how you please, is as much in the state of nature, with all under his dominion, as he is with the rest of mankind: for where-ever any two men are, who have no standing rule, and common judge to appeal to on earth, for the determination of controversies of right betwixt them, there they are still in the state of nature, and under all the inconveniencies of it.

Source: John Locke, *Of Civil Government*, paragraphs 87, 89, 90, 91 in *Two Treatises of Government*, A New Edition (London: 1824), pp. 179–183.

Under the Hanoverians, Britain achieved political stability and economic prosperity during the first quarter of the eighteenth century. Robert Walpole (1676–1745) eventually became George I's chief minister. Walpole's ascendancy from 1721 to 1742 was based on royal support, his ability to handle the House of Commons, and his iron-fisted control of government patronage. He maintained peace abroad and promoted the status quo at home. Because the dominant economic groups were represented in Parliament, they were willing to pay the taxes to support a powerful military force, particularly a strong navy. As a result, Great Britain became not only a European power of the first order, but also eventually a world power.

The power of the British monarchs and their ministers had real limits. Parliament could not wholly ignore popular pressure. Even with the extensive use of patronage, many members of Parliament maintained independent views. Newspapers and public debate flourished. Free speech could be exercised, as could freedom of association. There was no large standing army. Walpole's enemies could and did openly oppose his policies in a fashion impossible on the Continent. Consequently, the English state embodied both very considerable military power and political liberty. British political life became the model for all progressive Europeans who questioned the absolutist political developments of the Continent. Furthermore, many of the political values that had emerged in the British Isles during the seventeenth century also took deep root among their North American colonies.

Rise of Absolute Monarchy in France: The World of Louis XIV

The French monarchy trod a very different political path. Louis XIV (r. 1643–1715) came to the throne at the age of 5. During his childhood Cardinal Mazarin (1602–1661), his chief minister, tried to impose direct royal administration on France. These efforts aroused a series of widespread rebellions among French nobles between 1649 and 1652 known as the Fronde (after the slingshot used by street boys).

Chronology

England

1603	James VI of Scotland becomes James I of England
1625	Charles I becomes king of England
1629	Charles I dissolves Parliament and embarks on eleven years of personal rule
1640	April–May, Short Parliament; November, Long Parliament convenes
1642	Outbreak of the Civil War
1649	Charles I executed
1649–1660	Various attempts at a Puritan Commonwealth
1660	Charles II restored to the English throne
1670	Secret Treaty of Dover between France and England
1672	Parliament passes the Test Act
1685	James II becomes king of England
1688	Glorious Revolution
1689	William III and Mary II come to the throne of England
1701	Act of Settlement provides for Hanoverian Succession
1702–1714	Queen Anne, the last of the Stuarts
1714	George I of Hanover becomes king of England
1721–1742	Ascendancy of Sir Robert Walpole

Louis XIV of France (r. 1643–1715) was the dominant European monarch in the second half of the seventeenth century. The powerful centralized monarchy he created established the prototype for the mode of government later termed absolutism.

Years of Personal Rule

On the death of Mazarin in 1661 Louis XIV assumed personal control of the government at the age of 23. Convinced by the Fronde that heavy-handed policies could endanger the monarchy, Louis concentrated unprecedented authority in the monarchy, but he took care not to intrude excessively on local social and political institutions. He appointed no chief minister. Rebellious nobles would now be challenging the king directly; they could not claim to be resisting only a bad minister.

More than any other monarch of the day, Louis XIV used the physical setting of his court to exert political control. The palace at Versailles, built between 1676 and 1708 on the outskirts of Paris, became Louis' permanent residence after 1682. It was a temple to royalty, architecturally designed and artistically decorated to proclaim the glory of the Sun King, as Louis was known. A spectacular estate with magnificent fountains and gardens, it housed thousands of the more important nobles, royal officials, and servants. Moments near the king were important to most court nobles because he had effectively excluded them from the real business of government. The king's rising and dressing were times of rare intimacy, when nobles could whisper their special requests in his ear. Fortunate nobles held his night candle as they accompanied him to his bed.

Document Bishop Bossuet Defends the Divine Right of Kings

The revolutions of the seventeenth century caused many to fear anarchy far more than tyranny; among them was the influential French bishop Jacques-Bénigne Bossuet (1627–1704), the leader of French Catholicism in the second half of the seventeenth century. Louis XIV made him court preacher and tutor to his son, for whom Bossuet wrote a celebrated *Discourse on Universal History*. In the following excerpt, Bossuet defends the divine right and absolute power of kings. He depicts kings as embracing in their person the whole body of the state and the will of the people they govern and, as such, as being immune from judgment by any mere mortal. Compare this document with "John Locke Denounces the Idea of Absolute Monarchy."

■ *Why might Bossuet have wished to make such extravagant claims for absolute royal power? How might these claims be transferred to any form of government? What are the religious bases for Bossuet's argument? How does this argument for absolute royal authority lead also to the need for a single uniform religion in France?*

The royal power is absolute. . . . The prince need render account of his acts to no one. "I counsel thee to keep the king's commandment, and that in regard of the oath of God. Be not hasty to go out of his sight; stand not on an evil thing for he doeth whatsoever pleaseth him. Where the word of a king is, there is power; and who may say unto him, What doest thou? Whoso keepeth the commandment shall feel no evil thing" [Eccles. 8:2–5]. Without this absolute authority the king could neither do good nor repress evil. It is necessary that his power be such that no one can hope to escape him, and finally, the only protection of individuals against the public authority should be their innocence. This confirms the teaching of St. Paul: "Wilt thou then not be afraid of the power? Do that which is good" [Rom. 13:3].

God is infinite, God is all. The prince, as prince, is not regarded as a private person: he is a public personage, all the state is in him; the will of all the people is included in his. As all perfection and all strength are united in God, so all the power of individuals is united in the person of the prince. What grandeur that a single man should embody so much! . . .

Behold an immense people united in a single person; behold this holy power, paternal and absolute; behold the secret cause which governs the whole body of the state, contained in a single head: you see the image of God in the king, and you have the idea of royal majesty. God is holiness itself, goodness itself, and power itself. In these things lies the majesty of God. In the image of these things lies the majesty of the prince.

Source: From *Politics Drawn from the Very Words of Holy Scripture*, as quoted in James Harvey Robinson, ed., *Readings in European History*, vol. 2 (Boston: Athenaeum, 1906), pp. 275–276.

A Closer Look

Versailles

Louis XIV constructed his great palace at Versailles, as painted here in 1668 by Pierre Patel the Elder (1605–1676), to demonstrate the new centralized power he sought to embody in the French monarchy.

The outer wings, extending from the front of the central structure, housed governmental offices.

The central building is the hunting lodge his father Louis XIII had built earlier in the century. Its interior and that of the wings added to it were decorated with themes from mythology presenting Louis XIV as the "Sun King," around whom all his kingdom revolved.

The gardens and ponds behind the main structure were the sites of elaborate entertainment, concerts, and fireworks.

Pierre Patel, "Perspective View of Versailles." Châteaux de Versailles et de Trianon, Versailles, France. Photo copyright Bridgeman-Giraudon/Art Resource, New York.

Questions

1. How might the size alone of Versailles, as experienced by visitors and by viewers of paintings and prints of the structure, have served to overawe Louis's subjects? What other buildings of the day might have approached Versailles in size? In particular, how might French nobility have reacted to the setting?

2. Do you think some people who saw Versailles or images of it might have wondered how this extraordinary royal community was financed and might have drawn critical conclusions about the structure of French taxes?

3. By the end of his life Louis rarely ventured outside Versailles, and neither did his eighteenth-century royal successors. How might the limitation of so much royal experience to the region of Versailles have distorted the monarchs' view of their kingdom.

4. How might the images of Louis in mythological scenes have created a sense that he and his power were vaster than those of ordinary mortals?

myhistorylab To examine this image in an interactive fashion, please go to **www.myhistorylab.com**

An important source for Louis' concept of royal authority was his devout tutor, the political theorist Bishop Jacques-Bénigne Bossuet (1627–1704). In direct contrast to the English Puritan challenges to royal authority, Bossuet defended what he called the **divine right of kings**. He cited examples of Old Testament rulers divinely appointed by and answerable only to God. Medieval popes had insisted that only God could judge a pope; so Bossuet argued that only God could judge the king. Although kings might be duty bound to reflect God's will in their rule, as God's regents on earth they could not be bound to the dictates of mere nobles and parliaments. Such assumptions lay behind Louis XIV's alleged declaration: "*L'état, c'est moi*" ("I am the state"). (See Document, "Bishop Bossuet Defends the Divine Right of Kings.")

Louis was determined to unify France religiously. In October 1685 he revoked the Edict of Nantes (1598), which had extended protections to the Huguenots. Protestant churches and schools were closed, Protestant ministers exiled, nonconverting laity forced to be galley slaves, and Protestant children ceremonially baptized by Catholic priests. The revocation prompted the emigration of more than a quarter of a million people, who formed new communities and joined the resistance to France in England, Germany, Holland, and the New World.

Chronology

France

1649–1652	The *Fronde*, a revolt of nobility and townspeople against the Crown
1661	Louis assumes personal rule
1667	Louis XIV invades Flanders
1672	France invades the United Provinces
1678–1679	Peace of Nijmegen
1682	Louis establishes his court at Versailles
1685	Edict of Nantes revoked
1689–1697	Nine Years' War between France and the League of Augsburg
1697	Peace of Ryswick
1702–1714	War of the Spanish Succession
1713	Treaty of Utrecht between England and France
1714	Treaty of Rastadt between the emperor and France

As will be seen later in the chapter, Louis used most of the wealth and authority he had amassed to lead France into a long series of wars that ultimately weakened the nation by the time of his death in 1715. Yet despite those failures, he had established a model of strong centralized monarchy that other monarchs in central and eastern Europe would copy.

Russia Enters the European Political Arena

The emergence of Russia as an active European power was a wholly new factor in European politics. Previously, Russia had been considered part of Europe only by courtesy, and before 1673 it did not send permanent ambassadors to western Europe. Geographically and politically, it lay on the periphery. Hemmed in by Sweden on the Baltic and by the Ottoman Empire on the Black Sea, Russia had no warm-water ports. Its chief outlet for trade to the west was Archangel on the White Sea, which was ice-free for only part of the year.

Birth of the Romanov Dynasty

View the Image
Ivan the Terrible
at **MyHistoryLab.com**

The second half of the sixteenth century had witnessed enormous political turmoil during the last half of the reign of Ivan IV (r. 1533–1584), later known as Ivan the Terrible.

His achievement might be compared with that of his near-contemporary Akbar the Great (r. 1556–1605), who consolidated the Mughal Empire (See Chapter 20.) A period known as the Time of Troubles followed Ivan's death. In

View the Image
Michael Romanov
at **MyHistoryLab.com**

1613, hoping to end the uncertainty, an assembly of nobles elected as tsar a 17-year-old boy named Michael Romanov (r. 1613–1645).

Thus began the dynasty that ruled Russia until 1917. Nonetheless, Russia remained weak and impoverished. The *boyars*, the old nobility, controlled the bureaucracy, while the *streltsy*, or guards of the Moscow garrison, persistently posed the danger of mutiny.

Peter the Great

In 1682, another boy—10 years old at the time—ascended the fragile Russian throne as co-ruler with his half brother. His name was Peter (r. 1682–1725), and Russia would never be the same after him. He and his sickly brother, who died in 1696, had come to power on the shoulders of the *streltsy*, who expected to be rewarded for their support. Like Louis XIV, the dangers and turmoil of his youth convinced Peter of two things: First, the power of the tsar must be made secure from the jealousy of the *boyars* and the greed of the *streltsy*; second, the military power of Russia must be increased.

Peter the Great (r. 1682–1725), seeking to make Russia a military power, reorganized the country's political and economic structures. His reign saw Russia enter fully into European power politics. Here he is depicted as a latter-day St. George, slaying a dragon. *The Apotheosis of Tsar Peter I the Great 1672–1725 by unknown artist 1710. Historical Museum Moscow Russia. E.T. Archive. Art Archive/Picture Desk Inc./Kobal Collection.*

Northwestern Europe, particularly the military resources of the maritime powers, fascinated Peter I, who eventually became known as Peter the Great. In 1697, he made a famous visit in transparent disguise to western Europe. There he spent his happiest moments inspecting shipyards, docks, and the manufacture of military hardware in England and the Netherlands. Peter returned to Moscow determined to copy the technology he had seen abroad, for he knew warfare would be necessary to make Russia a great power.

Taming the Streltsy and Boyars In 1698, before Peter's return from abroad, the *streltsy* had rebelled. On his return, Peter brutally suppressed the revolt with private tortures and public executions, in which his own ministers took part. Approximately a thousand of the rebels were put to death, and their corpses remained on public display to discourage future disloyalty.

Peter then built a new military establishment that would serve the tsar and not itself. He introduced effective and ruthless policies of conscription, drafting an unprecedented 130,000 soldiers during the first decade of the eighteenth century and almost 300,000 troops by the end of his reign. He adopted policies for the officer corps and general military discipline patterned on those of western European armies.

Peter also determined to make a sustained attack on the *boyars* and their attachment to traditional Russian culture. After his European journey, he personally shaved the long beards of the court *boyars* and sheared off the customary long hand-covering sleeves of their shirts and coats, which had made them the butt of jokes among other European courts. Peter became highly skilled at balancing one group against another, while never completely excluding any, as he set about to organize Russian government and military forces along the lines of the more powerful European states.

Developing a Navy In the mid-1690s, Peter oversaw the construction of ships to protect his interests in the Black Sea against the Ottoman Empire. In 1695, he began a war with the Ottomans. Part of the reason for Peter's trip to western Europe in 1697 had been to learn how to build still better warships, this time for combat on the Baltic. The construction of a Baltic fleet, largely constructed on the Finnish coast, was essential in the Great Northern War with Sweden (1700–1721), a struggle that over the years accounted for many of Peter's major steps toward Westernizing his realm.

View the Image
Battle of Poltava, 1709
at **MyHistoryLab.com**

When the Great Northern War came to a close in 1721, the Peace of Nystad confirmed the Russian conquest of Estonia, Livonia, and part of Finland. Henceforth, Russia possessed ice-free ports and a permanent influence on European affairs.

Founding St. Petersburg At one point, the domestic and foreign policies of Peter the Great intersected. This was at the site on the Gulf of Finland where he founded his new capital city of St. Petersburg in 1703. There he built government structures and compelled the *boyars* to construct town houses. He thus imitated those European monarchs who had copied Louis XIV by constructing smaller versions of Versailles. The founding of St. Petersburg went beyond establishing a central imperial court, however; it symbolized a new Western orientation of Russia and Peter's determination to hold his position on the Baltic coast.

Hear the Audio
at **MyHistoryLab.com**

The Case of Peter's Son Aleksei and Reforms of Peter the Great's Final Years Other reforms arose from Peter's family difficulties. Peter's son Aleksei had been born to his first wife, whom he had divorced in 1698.

Vue des bords de la Neva en descendant la riviere entre le Palais d'hyver de Sa Majesté Imperiale & les batimens de l'Academie des Sciences

Saint Petersburg. Peter the Great built Saint Petersburg on the Gulf of Finland to provide Russia with better contact with western Europe. He moved Russia's capital there from Moscow in 1703. This is an eighteenth-century view of the city.

Increasingly distrustful of his son, Peter became convinced by late 1717 that his court opponents looked to Aleksei as a focus for possible sedition while Russia remained at war with Sweden. Peter undertook an investigation during which he personally interrogated Aleksei, who was eventually condemned to death and died under mysterious circumstances on June 26, 1718.

Read the Document
Peter the Great with Alexis Russia
at **MyHistoryLab.com**

The interrogations surrounding Aleksei had revealed greater degrees of court opposition than Peter had suspected. Recognizing he could not eliminate his numerous opponents the way he had attacked the *streltsy* in 1698, Peter undertook radical administrative reforms designed to bring the nobility and the Russian Orthodox Church more closely under the authority of persons loyal to the tsar.

Administrative Colleges In December 1717 Peter reorganized his domestic administration to sustain his own personal authority and to fight rampant corruption. To achieve this goal, Peter looked to Swedish institutions called *colleges*—bureaus of several persons operating according to written instructions rather than departments headed by a single minister. These colleges, eight of which he imposed on Russian administration, were to look after matters such as the collection of taxes, foreign relations, war, and economic affairs. Each college was to receive advice from a foreigner. Peter used his appointive power to balance the influence in these colleges between nobles and persons he was certain would be personally loyal to himself.

Achieving Secular Control of the Church Peter also moved to suppress the independence of the Russian Orthodox Church, where some bishops and clergy had displayed sympathy for the tsar's son. In 1721, Peter simply abolished the position of *patriarch*, the bishop who had been head of the church. In its place he established a government department called the *Holy Synod*, which consisted of several bishops headed by a layman called the *procurator general*. This body would govern the church in accordance with the tsar's secular requirements.

Table of Ranks In 1722 Peter published a **Table of Ranks** intended to draw the nobility into state service. That table equated a person's social position and privileges with his rank in the bureaucracy or the military, rather than with his lineage among the traditional landed nobility, many of whom continued to resent the changes Peter had introduced into Russia. Peter thus made the social standing of individual *boyars* a function of their willingness to serve the central state.

For all the numerous decisive actions Peter had taken since 1717, he still had not settled on a successor. Consequently, when he died in 1725, there was no clear line of succession to the throne. For more than thirty years, soldiers and nobles again determined who ruled Russia.

See the Map
Expansion of Russia
Under Peter Great
at **MyHistoryLab.com**

Peter had laid the foundations of a modern Russia, but not the foundations of a stable state.

Chronology

Rise of Russian Power

1533–1584	Reign of Ivan the Terrible
1584–1613	Time of Troubles
1613	Michael Romanov becomes tsar
1682	Peter the Great becomes tsar as a boy
1689	Peter assumes personal rule
1697	European tour of Peter the Great
1698	Peter suppresses the *streltsy*
1700	The Great Northern War opens between Russia and Sweden; Russia defeated at Narva by Charles XII
1703	Saint Petersburg founded
1709	Russia defeats Sweden at Poltava
1718	Death of Aleksei, son of Peter the Great
1721	Peace of Nystad ends the Great Northern War
1721	Peter establishes control over the Russian church
1722	The Table of Ranks
1725	Peter dies, leaving an uncertain succession

The Habsburg Empire and the Pragmatic Sanction

After 1648 the Habsburg family retained a firm hold on the title of Holy Roman Emperor, but the power of the emperor depended less on force of arms than on the cooperation he could elicit from the various political bodies in the empire. These included large German units (such as Saxony, Hanover, Bavaria, and Brandenburg) and scores of small German cities, bishoprics, principalities, and territories of independent knights. While establishing their new dominance among the German states, the Habsburgs also began to consolidate their power and influence within their hereditary possessions outside the Holy Roman Empire, which included the Crown of Saint Wenceslas, encompassing the kingdom of Bohemia (in the modern Czech Republic) and the duchies of Moravia and Silesia; and the Crown of Saint Stephen, which ruled Hungary, Croatia, and Transylvania. In each of their many territories, the Habsburgs ruled by virtue of a different title and needed the cooperation of the local nobility, which was not always forthcoming. They repeatedly had to bargain with nobles in one part of Europe to maintain their position in another.

Despite these internal difficulties, Leopold I (r. 1658–1705) managed to resist the advances of the Turks into central Europe, which included a siege of Vienna in 1683, and to thwart the aggression of Louis XIV. He achieved Ottoman recognition of his sovereignty over Hungary in 1699 and extended his territorial holdings over much of the Balkan Peninsula and present-day western Romania (see Map 19–1).

Map 19–1. The Austrian Habsburg Empire, 1521–1772. The empire had three main units—Austria, Bohemia, and Hungary. Expansion was mainly eastward: eastern Hungary from the Ottomans (seventeenth century) and Galicia from Poland (1772). Meantime, Silesia was lost after 1740, but the Habsburgs remained Holy Roman Emperors.

In the early eighteenth century the Habsburg emperor Charles VI (r. 1711–1740) had no male heir, and there was only a weak precedent for a female ruler of the Habsburg domains. Charles feared that on his death the Austrian Habsburg lands might fall prey to the surrounding powers. Determined to prevent that disaster and to provide his domains with the semblance of legal unity, he devoted most of his reign to seeking the approval of his family, the estates of his realms, and the major foreign powers for a document called the **Pragmatic Sanction**.

This instrument provided the legal basis for a single line of inheritance within the Habsburg Dynasty through Charles VI's daughter Maria Theresa (1740–1780). After extracting various concessions from Charles, the nobles of the various Habsburg domains and the other European rulers agreed to the document. Consequently, when Charles VI died in October 1740, he believed that he had secured legal unity for the Habsburg Empire and a safe succession for his daughter. Despite the Pragmatic Sanction, however, his failure to provide his daughter with a strong army or a full treasury left her inheritance open to foreign

aggression. Less than two months after his death, the fragility of the foreign agreements became apparent. In December 1740 Frederick II of Prussia invaded the Habsburg province of Silesia. Maria Theresa had to fight for her inheritance.

The Rise of Prussia

The rise of Prussia occurred within the German power vacuum created by the Peace of Westphalia. It is the story of the extraordinary Hohenzollern family, which had ruled Brandenburg since 1417. Through inheritance the family had acquired a series of territories, most of which were not contiguous with Brandenburg. By the late seventeenth century, however, the scattered Hohenzollern holdings represented a block of territory within the Holy Roman Empire second in size only to that of the Habsburgs.

See the Map
Growth of Brandenburg-Prussia, 1618–1786
at **MyHistoryLab.com**

Beginning in the mid-seventeenth century, Hohenzollern rulers forged their geographically separated holdings into a powerful state by collecting taxes simply on their own

A Prussian Military Camp. This print shows a Prussian encampment in the Pomerania, on the south coast of the Baltic Sea. By 1800 this entire region had come under Prussian control.

authority and then building an army that allowed them to continue to enforce their will without the approval of the nobility.

There was, however, a political and social trade-off between the Hohenzollerns and their various nobles. In exchange for their obedience to the Hohenzollerns, the *Junkers*, or German noble landlords received the right to demand obedience from their serfs. Furthermore taxes fell most heavily on the backs of the peasants and the urban classes. As the years passed, *Junkers* increasingly dominated the army officer corps, and this dominance became even more pronounced during the eighteenth century. All officials and army officers took an oath of loyalty directly to the Hohenzollern rulers. The army and the Elector thus came to embody the otherwise absent unity of the state. The army made Prussia a valuable potential military ally. As a result of providing aid to the Habsburg emperor in 1701, the Hohenzollerns were permitted the title of "King" in Prussia, one of their parcels of territory that lay inside Poland and outside the authority of the Holy Roman Emperor.

Under Frederick William I (r. 1713–1740), the Prussian military grew from about 39,000 in 1713 to over 80,000 in 1740, making it the third- or fourth-largest army in Europe. Prussia's population, in contrast, ranked thirteenth in size. Separate laws applied to the army and to civilians. Laws, customs, and royal attention made the officer corps the highest social class of the state. Military service thus attracted the sons of *Junkers*.

Although Frederick William I built the best army in Europe, he avoided conflict. His army was a symbol of Prussian power and unity, not an instrument for foreign adventures or aggression. At his death in 1740 he passed on to his son Frederick II (Frederick the Great, r. 1740–1786) this superb

military machine, but not the wisdom to refrain from using it. Almost immediately on coming to the throne, Frederick II upset the Pragmatic Sanction and invaded Silesia (see Map 19–2). He thus crystallized the Austrian-Prussian rivalry for the control of Germany that would dominate central European affairs for over a century.

European Warfare: From Continental to World Conflict

Whereas religious zeal had largely fueled the European wars of the Reformation era, dynastic and commercial rivalry drove wars from the reign of Louis XIV through the conclusion of the Seven Years' War in 1763. Each round of warfare was geographically more widespread than the last, and eventually these wars became genuinely worldwide. Through these conflicts the European powers extended their military and political presence to match their expanding commercial presence in the Americas and in Asia.

The Wars of Louis XIV

By the late 1660s France had become superior to any other European nation in administrative bureaucracy, armed forces, and national unity. Louis XIV could afford to raise and maintain a large and powerful army and was in a position to dominate Europe.

Beginning in 1667, Louis XIV led France into four major wars of expansion, each with a widening scope. In 1667 and then again in 1672 Louis invaded Flanders. His second war against the Dutch, during which he was allied with England, led the Dutch to rally around the leadership of William Prince of Orange, the future William III of England. He forged an alliance with the Holy Roman Emperor, Spain, Lorraine, and Brandenburg against Louis, by then regarded as a menace to the whole of western Europe, Catholic and Protestant alike. Louis' second war ended inconclusively with the Peace of Nijmegen, signed with different parties in successive years (1678, 1679).

In 1681 Louis' forces occupied the free city of Strasbourg, prompting new defensive coalitions to form against him. One of these coalitions, the League of Augsburg, grew to include England, Spain, Sweden, the United Provinces, and the major German states including the Habsburg emperor. One of the chief reasons prompting William of Orange to consent to become monarch of England in 1688 was to draw that nation and its wealth into this coalition against France. Between 1689 and 1697 the League of Augsburg and France battled each other on European fronts in the Nine Years' War, while England and France struggled to control North America. The Peace of Ryswick, signed in September 1697, secured Holland's borders and thwarted Louis' expansion into Germany.

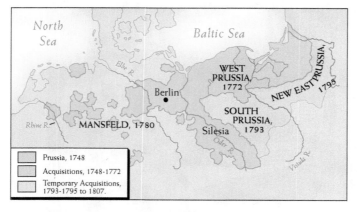

Map 19–2. Prussian Expansions 1748–1795. In the seventeenth century Brandenburg-Prussia expanded mainly by acquiring dynastic titles in geographically separated lands. In the eighteenth century it expanded through aggression to the east, seizing Silesia in 1740 and various parts of Poland in 1772, 1793, and 1795.

Map Exploration

To explore this map further, go to **http://www.myhistorylab.com**

Map 19–3. Europe in 1714. The War of the Spanish Succession ended a year before the death of Louis XIV. The Bourbons had secured the Spanish throne, but Spain had forfeited its possessions in Flanders and Italy.

Then on November 1, 1700, Charles II of Spain (r. 1665–1700) died without direct heirs. He left his entire inheritance to Louis' grandson Philip of Anjou, who became Philip V of Spain (r. 1700–1746). Spain and the trade with its American empire appeared to have fallen to France. In September 1701 England, Holland, and the Holy Roman Empire formed the Grand Alliance to preserve the balance of power by once and for all securing Flanders as a neutral barrier between Holland and France and by gaining for the emperor his fair share of the Spanish inheritance.

The War of the Spanish Succession (1701–1714) soon enveloped western Europe (see Map 19–3). France finally made peace with England at Utrecht in July 1713 and with Holland and the emperor at Rastadt in March 1714. Philip V remained king of Spain, but England got Gibraltar, at the southern tip of Spain, making it a Mediterranean power. Louis also formally recognized the right of the House of Hanover to accede to the English throne. At the conclusion of this long war, France was economically and politically

See the Map
Europe After the Treaty of Utrecht, 1714
at **MyHistoryLab.com**

A Dutch Merchant and His Wife in Batavia (Java). Attributed to Jacob Cuyp (1594–1651), this painting from 1650 shows the Dutch merchant Jacob Mathieusen and his wife in front of Batavia's harbor, on the island of Java in the East Indies. The merchant points to his ships while a slave shelters the couple from the tropical sun with a parasol.

exhausted. The European wars of the next generation occurred not only in Europe but also throughout the European overseas empires.

The Eighteenth-Century Colonial Arena

The Treaty of Utrecht established the boundaries of empire during the first half of the eighteenth century. Except for Brazil, which was governed by Portugal, Spain controlled all of mainland South America, as well as Florida, Mexico, and the entire western half of what is the present-day United States. Spain also ruled Cuba and half of Hispaniola. The British Empire consisted of the colonies along the North Atlantic seaboard, Nova Scotia, Newfoundland, Jamaica, and Barbados. Britain also possessed a few trading stations on the Indian subcontinent. The Dutch controlled Surinam, or Dutch Guiana, in South America; Cape Town at the southern tip of Africa; various trading stations in Ceylon and Bengal; and, most important, the trade with Java in what is today Indonesia.

The French had also established an empire in America and southern Asia. It covered the Saint Lawrence River valley; the Ohio and Mississippi river valleys; Saint Domingue (Haiti), Guadeloupe, and Martinique in the West Indies; and trading stations in India and West Africa. The economy of their West Indian islands resembled those of the Spanish and the British. Their holdings in Canada were sparsely populated, Quebec being the largest settlement, and the economy was based on agriculture and the fur trade. French and English settlers in North America clashed throughout the eighteenth century.

Each of the powers sought to make its imperial holdings into impenetrable trading areas. The Spanish government, however, lacked the capacity to maintain a commercial monopoly over its sprawling territory.

The Treaty of Utrecht gave the British a thirty-year *asiento*, or contract, to furnish slaves to the Spanish Empire and the right to send one ship each year to the trading fair at Portobello on the Spanish Main (present-day Panama). Nothing but friction arose from these rights. Much to the chagrin of the British, the Spanish government under the Bourbons took its own alleged trading monopoly seriously and maintained coastal patrols that searched English vessels for contraband.

War of Jenkins's Ear

In 1731, during one such search, there was a fight, and an English captain named Robert Jenkins had his ear cut off by the Spaniards. Thereafter, he preserved his ear in a jar of brandy. This incident was of little importance until 1738, when Jenkins appeared before the British Parliament, reportedly brandishing his ear as an example of Spanish atrocities to British merchants in the West Indies. British commercial interests put great pressure on Parliament to do something about Spanish interference in their trade. Robert Walpole could not resist these pressures, and in late 1739 Great Britain went to war with Spain. This might have been a relatively minor clash, but as a result of the Prussian invasion of Silesia, it became the opening encounter in a series of worldwide European wars.

The War of the Austrian Succession (1740–1748)

In December 1740, as noted earlier in the chapter, the new king of Prussia, Frederick II, ignored the Pragmatic Sanction and seized the Austrian province of Silesia. In response to the Prussian aggression, the young Maria Theresa of Austria recognized Hungary as the most important of her crowns and promised the Magyars considerable local autonomy. She thus preserved the Habsburg state, but at great cost to the power of the central monarchy.

The war over the Austrian Succession and the British-Spanish commercial conflict could have remained separate disputes. What united them was the role of France, whose aggressive court aristocrats drove the government to support the Prussian aggression against Austria, the traditional enemy of France.

This proved to be one of the most fateful decisions in world history. French aid to Prussia helped consolidate a new and powerful German state that could, and indeed later did, endanger France itself. The French move against Austria also brought Great Britain into the Continental war

Chronology

European Conflicts of the Mid-Eighteenth Century

1739	Outbreak of War of Jenkins's Ear between England and Spain
1740	War of the Austrian Succession commences
1748	Treaty of Aix-la-Chapelle
1756	Convention of Westminster between England and Prussia
1756	Seven Years' War opens
1759	British forces capture Quebec
1763	Treaty of Hubertusburg
1763	Treaty of Paris

against France and Prussia in an attempt to ensure that Belgium remained in the friendly hands of Austria. In 1744 the British-French conflict expanded beyond the Continent when France decided to support Spain against Britain in the New World. The war ended in military stalemate in 1748 with the Treaty of Aix-la-Chapelle. Prussia retained Silesia, but the treaty was a truce rather than a permanent peace.

View of the Taking of Quebeck by the English Forces Commanded by Genl. Wolfe Sep: 13. 1759.

The Taking of Quebec. The capture of Quebec in September 1759 by British forces, followed by the seizure of Montreal a year later, signaled the demise of French power in Canada.

The Seven Years' War (1756–1763)

Before the rivalries again erupted into war, a dramatic shift of alliances took place. In 1756 Prussia and Great Britain signed the Convention of Westminster, a defensive alliance aimed at preventing the entry of foreign troops into the Germanies. Frederick feared invasions by both Russia and France. The convention meant that Great Britain, the ally of Austria since the wars of Louis XIV, had now joined forces with Austria's major eighteenth-century enemy. Later in 1756 Austria achieved a defensive alliance with France. Thus the traditional European alliances of the previous century were reversed.

In August 1756, what would become the Seven Years' War opened when Frederick II invaded Saxony. Frederick considered this a preemptive strike against a conspiracy by Saxony, Austria, and France to destroy Prussian power. In the spring of 1757 France and Austria made a new alliance dedicated to the destruction of Prussia. They were eventually joined by Sweden, Russia, and the smaller German states. Two factors, in addition to Frederick's strong leadership (it was after this war that he came to be called Frederick the Great), saved Prussia—British financial aid and the death in 1762 of Empress Elizabeth of Russia (r. 1741–1762). Her successor Tsar Peter III (d. 1762), a fervent admirer of Frederick, immediately made peace with Prussia, thus allowing Frederick to hold off Austria and France. The Treaty of Hubertusburg of 1763 closed the Continental conflict with no significant changes in prewar borders.

More impressive to the rest of Europe than the survival of Prussia were the victories of Great Britain in every theater of conflict. The architect of victory was William Pitt the Elder (1708–1778). Although Pitt had previously criticized British involvement with the Continent, once he was named secretary of state in charge of the war in 1757 he reversed himself and pumped huge financial subsidies to Frederick the Great. But North America was Pitt's real concern. Put simply, he wanted all of North America east of the Mississippi for Great Britain, and that was exactly what he won as he directed unprecedented resources into the overseas colonial conflict. In what Americans know as the French and Indian War, the French government was unwilling and unable to direct similar resources against the English in America. In September 1759 the British took Quebec City. Montreal fell the next year. The French Empire in Canada was coming to an end.

Pitt's colonial vision, however, was global. The French West Indies fell to the British fleets. On the Indian subcontinent the British forces under Robert Clive (1725–1774) defeated the French in 1757 at the battle of Plassey. This victory opened the way for the eventual conquest of all India by the British East India Company. Never had any other European power experienced such a complete worldwide military victory nor one that affected so many non-Europeans.

The Treaty of Paris of 1763 was somewhat less triumphant. Pitt was no longer in office. George III (r. 1760–1820) had succeeded to the British throne and by 1762 had replaced Pitt with a new minister who was responsible for the peace settlement, in which Britain received all of Canada, the Ohio River valley, and the eastern half of the Mississippi River valley. France retained footholds in India at Pondicherry and Chandernagore and regained the West Indies sugar islands of Guadeloupe and Martinique.

The midcentury wars among European powers resulted in a new balance of power on the European continent and the high seas (see Map 19–4). Great Britain gained a world empire, and Prussia was recognized as a great continental power. With the surrender of Canada, France retreated from North America and thus opened the way for a continent largely dominated by the English language and Protestantism. By contrast, Latin America remained dominated by the Spanish and Portuguese languages and Roman Catholicism. For many years, West Africa would continue to furnish slaves to the economies of both Americas. On the subcontinent of India the foundations were laid for almost two centuries of British dominance.

The Old Regime

During the turmoil of the French Revolution and its aftermath, it became customary to refer to the patterns of social, political, and economic relationships that had existed in France before 1789 as the *ancien régime*, or the **Old Regime**. The term has come to be applied generally to the social life and institutions of all prerevolutionary Continental Europe. Politically, it meant the rule of theoretically absolute monarchies with growing bureaucracies and aristocratically led armies. Economically, the Old Regime was characterized by food shortages, the predominance of agriculture, slow transport, a low level of iron production, comparatively unsophisticated financial institutions, and, in some cases, competitive commercial overseas empires. Socially, men and women saw themselves less as individuals than as members of distinct corporate bodies that possessed certain privileges or rights as a group. Few persons outside the political, commercial, and intellectual elite actually wanted change or innovation. Except for the early industrial development in Britain, the economy was also predominantly traditional.

Hierarchy and Privilege

The medieval sense of hierarchy became more rigid during the eighteenth century. What enforced the hierarchy was the corporate nature of social relationships.

Eighteenth-century Europeans did not enjoy what Americans regard as individual rights. Instead, persons enjoyed such rights and privileges as were guaranteed to whatever communities or groups of which they were a part. The "community" might include the village, the municipality, the nobility, the church, the guild, a university, or the parish. In turn, each of these bodies enjoyed certain privileges—some great, some small. The privileges might involve exemption from taxation or degrading punishment, the right to practice a trade or craft, the right of one's children to pursue a particular occupation, or for the church, the right to collect the tithe.

Aristocracy

The eighteenth century was the great age of the aristocracy. The nobility constituted approximately 1 to 5 percent of the population of any given country. In every European state, it

An Aristocratic Couple. Portraits such as this one of the English landowner Robert Andrews and his wife, by Thomas Gainsborough (1728–1788), contain many clues to the aristocratic dominance of landed society: Andrews's gun and dog indicate his exclusive right to hunt game on his land. His wife's sitting against the expanse of his landed estate suggests the character of their legal relationship, whereby he could have controlled her property, which would have thus become an extension of his. The market price of the wheat raised on his estate (known in England as corn) would have been protected by various import laws enacted by the English Parliament whose membership was dominated by landowners such as Andrews himself. © *National Gallery, London/Art Resource.*

Map 19–4. The Colonial Arena. The acquisition of overseas colonies by European powers led to intense rivalries on a global scale. Territories frequently changed hands during the eighteenth century.

was the single wealthiest sector of the population; possessed the widest degree of social, political, and economic power; and dominated polite society. Land provided the aristocracy with its largest source of income, but the influence of aristocrats was felt in every area of life. Across the Continent, to be an aristocrat was a matter of birth and legal privilege, but in almost every other respect, aristocrats differed markedly from country to country. The smallest, wealthiest, best defined, and most socially responsible aristocracy resided in Great Britain. As one moved eastward across Europe the aristocracy became more numerous, not always wealthy, but possessing increasing degrees of arbitrary, repressive power over those below them in the social structure.

Throughout the century, in a Europeanwide **aristocratic resurgence**, the various nobilities sought to protect their social position and privileges against the expanding power of the monarchies and the growing wealth of commercial groups. First, all nobilities attempted to restrict entry into their ranks and institutions.

Second, they attempted to monopolize appointments to the officer corps of the armies, the bureaucracies, the government ministries, and the church. The nobles thus hoped to control the power of the monarchies.

Third, the nobles attempted to use institutions they already controlled against the monarchies. These institutions included the British Parliament, the French *parlements*, local aristocratic estates, and provincial diets.

Fourth, the aristocracies pressed the peasantry for higher rents or long-forgotten feudal dues. This was part of the nobility's effort to shore up its position by appealing to tradition and reasserting old privileges that had lapsed. To contemporaries, this aristocratic resurgence was one of the most fundamental political facts of the day and one to which monarchs had to pay attention.

◆●◆─┤**Read the Document**
Domat Social Order Monarchy
at **MyHistoryLab.com**

The Land and Its Tillers

Land was the economic basis of eighteenth-century life in Europe, as it was throughout the rest of the world. Well over three-fourths of all Europeans lived on the land, and most never traveled more than a few miles from their birthplaces. With the exception of the nobility and the wealthier

◆●◆─┤**Read the Document**
Voltaire Condition 18th century
France
at **MyHistoryLab.com**

landowners, the dwellers on the land were poor, and by any modern standard, their lives were hard.

Peasants and Serfs

Those people who worked the land were subject to immense influence and in some cases direct control by the landowners. This situation prevailed in different degrees for free peasants, such as English tenants and most French cultivators, and for the serfs of Germany, Austria, and Russia, who were legally bound to a particular plot of land and a particular lord. In all cases, the class that owned the land also controlled the local government and the courts.

Landlord power increased as one moved from west to east. Most French peasants owned some land, but a few were serfs. However, nearly all peasants were subject to certain feudal dues and to forced labor on the lord's estate for a certain number of days each year. Because French peasants rarely owned enough land to support their families, they were also subject to feudal dues attached to the plots of land they rented.

In Prussia and Austria, despite attempts by the monarchies late in the century to improve the lot of the serfs, the landlords continued to exercise almost complete control over them. Moreover, throughout Continental Europe the burden of state taxation fell on the tillers of the soil. Many peasants, serfs, and other agricultural laborers were forced to undertake supplemental work to pay the tax collector. Through various legal privileges and the ability to demand further concessions from the monarchs, the landlords escaped the payment of numerous taxes. They also presided over the manorial courts.

Road Work. Eighteenth-century France had some of the best roads in the world, but they were often built with forced labor. French peasants were required to work part of each year on such projects. This system, called the *corvée*, was not abolished until the French Revolution in 1789. *Joseph Vernet, "Construction of a Road." Louvre, Paris, France/Bridgeman-Giraudon/Art Resource, New York.*

The condition of the serfs was the worst in Russia. The Russian custom of reckoning one's wealth by the number of owned "souls" (that is, male serfs) rather than by the size of an estate reveals the contrast between Russia and Western Europe. Russian serfs were, in effect, regarded merely as economic commodities. Their services were attached to an individual lord rather than to a particular plot of land. Russian landlords could demand as many as six days a week of labor, and like Prussian and Austrian landlords, they could punish their serfs or even exile them to Siberia. Although serfs had little recourse against their lords, custom, tradition, and law did provide a few protections. For example, the marriages of serfs, unlike those of most slaves throughout the world, were legally recognized. The landlord could not disband the family of a serf. (See Document, "Russian Serfs Lament Their Condition" on page 596.)

The Russian monarchy itself contributed to the degradation of the serfs. Peter the Great gave whole villages to favored nobles. Catherine the Great (r. 1762–1796) confirmed the authority of the nobles over their serfs in exchange for the nobility's political cooperation. This situation led to considerable unrest. There were more than fifty peasant revolts between 1762 and 1769. They culminated between 1773 and 1774 in Pugachev's Rebellion, during which all of southern Russia was in ferment. Emelyan Pugachev (1726–1775) promised the serfs land and freedom. The rebellion was brutally suppressed, and any thought of liberalizing the condition of the serfs was set aside for a generation.

Pugachev's was the largest peasant uprising of the eighteenth century. Smaller peasant revolts or disturbances occurred in Bohemia in 1775, in Transylvania in 1784, in Moravia in 1786, and in Austria in 1789. Western Europe was more tranquil, but England experienced numerous enclosure riots. Rural rebellions were violent, but the peasants and serfs normally directed their wrath against property rather than persons. The rebels usually sought to reassert traditional or customary rights against practices they perceived as innovations. In this respect, the peasant revolts were conservative in nature.

Family Structures and the Family Economy

In preindustrial Europe, the household was the basic unit of production and consumption. That is to say, very few productive establishments employed more than a handful of people not belonging to the owner's family. The household mode of organization predominated on farms, in artisans' workshops, and in small merchants' shops. With that mode of economic organization, there developed what is known as the **family economy**.

The Family Economy

Throughout Europe people thought and worked in terms of sustaining the economic life of the family, and family members saw themselves as working together in an interdependent rather than an independent or individualistic manner.

Farm Family. Painted by the English artist Francis Wheatley (1747–1801) near the close of the eighteenth century, this scene is part of a series illustrating a day in the life of an idealized farm family. Note the artist's assumptions about the division of labor by gender. Men work in the fields, women work in the home or look after the needs of men and children. As other illustrations in this chapter show, many eighteenth-century women in fact worked outside the home, but considerable social pressure was developing at this time to restrict them to domestic roles. This painting and the others in the series are thus more prescriptive than descriptive, intended in part to persuade their viewers that women belonged in their separate family sphere. Many, perhaps most, families living in the countryside could not maintain the closeness that these paintings extol. To survive, many had to send members to work on other farms or even to other regions. *Francis Wheatley (RA) (1747–1801), "Evening," signed and dated 1799, oil on canvas, 17 1/2 × 21 1/2 in. (44.5 × 54.5 cm), Yale Center for British Art, Paul Mellon Collection, Bridgman Art Library (B1977.14.118).*

Document   Russian Serfs Lament Their Condition

As with other illiterate groups in European history, it is difficult to recapture the voices of Russian serfs. The following verses from "The Slaves' Lament," a popular ballad from the era of the Pugachev Rebellion (1773–1775), indicate that the serfs were aware of how the legislation of that era, which favored the landowning classes, affected their lives. The verses embody the resentment that Pugachev's Rebellion ignited. Note how the verses suggest that the tsar may be more favorable to serfs than their landowners are. Throughout this ballad, serfs present themselves as slaves.

■ *What specific complaints about landlords are expressed in these verses? What charges indicate that serfs may believe their situation has worsened? What hope do they seem to place in the tsar? What idealized picture of the world do the serfs believe they would themselves create?*

O woe to us slaves living for the masters!
We do not know how to serve their ferocity!
Service is like a sharp scythe;
And kindness is like the morning dew.
Brothers, how annoying it is to us
And how shameful and insulting
That another who is not worthy to be equal with us
Has so many of us in his power.
And if we steal from the lord one half kopeck,
The law commands us to be killed like a louse.
And if the master steals ten thousand,
Nobody will judge who should be hanged.
The injustice of the Russian sheriffs has increased:
Whoever brings a present is right beyond argument.
They have stopped putting their trust in the Creator for
*   authority,*
And have become accustomed to own us like cattle.
All nations rebuke us and wonder at our stupidity,
That such stupid people are born in Russia.
And indeed, stupidity was rooted in us long ago,
as each honour here has been given to vagrants.
The master can kill the servant like a gelding;
The denunciation by a slave cannot be believed.
Unjust judges have composed a decree
That we should be tyrannically whipped with a knout
*   for that.*
Better that we should agree to serve the tsar.

Better to live in dark woods
Than to be before the eyes of these tyrants;
They look on us cruelly with their eyes
And eat us as iron eats rye. No one wants to serve the tsar
But only to grind us down to the end.
And they try to collect unjust bribes,
And they are not frightened that people die cruelly.
Ah brothers, if we got our freedom,
We would not take the lands or the fields for ourselves.
We would go into service as soldiers, brothers,
And would be friendly among ourselves,
Would destroy all injustice
And remove the root of evil lords.
They [the landlords] sell all the good rye to the merchants,
And give us like pigs the bad.
The greedy lords eat meat at fast time,
And even when meat is allowed, the slaves
must cook meatless cabbage soup.
O brothers, it is our misfortune
always to have rye kasha.
The lords drink and make merry,
And do not allow the slaves even to burst out laughing.

Source: From Paul Dukes, trans. and ed., *Russia under Catherine the Great: Select Documents on Government and Society* (Oriental Research Partners, 1978), pp. 115–117. Reprinted by permission of Oriental Research Partners.

The goal of the family household was to produce or secure through wages enough food to support its members. In the countryside, that effort virtually always involved farming. In cities and towns, artisan production or working for another person was the usual pattern. Almost everyone lived within a household because ordinary people could rarely support themselves independently. Indeed, except for members of religious orders, people living outside a household were viewed with great suspicion as potentially criminal or disruptive or, at least, potentially dependent on the charity of others.

Marriage and the family within this economy meant that everyone in the household had to work. On a farm, much of the effort went directly into raising food or producing other agricultural goods that could be exchanged for food. In western Europe, however, few people had enough land to support their households from farming alone. For this reason, one or more family members might work elsewhere and send wages home. For example, the father or older children might be migrant workers, perhaps many miles from home. The burden of the farm work would then fall on the wife and the younger children. This was not uncommon. Within this family economy, all of the goods and income produced went to the benefit of the household rather than to the individual family member.

The family economy also dominated the life of skilled urban artisans. The father was usually the chief craftsman. He generally had one or more servants in his employ, but he would also expect his children to work in the enterprise. His eldest child was usually trained in the trade. His wife often sold the wares or had a small shop. The wife of a merchant also often ran the husband's business, especially when he traveled to purchase new goods. In any case, everyone in the family was involved. If business was poor, family members would look for employment elsewhere, not to support themselves but to help the family unit survive.

Women and the Family Economy

The family economy established many of the chief constraints on the lives and the personal experiences of women in preindustrial society. For women, marriage was an institution of economic necessity as well as one that fulfilled sexual and psychological needs. A woman outside a household was highly vulnerable. Unless she was an aristocrat or a member of a religious order, she could probably not support herself by her own efforts alone. Consequently, much of a woman's life was devoted first to aiding the maintenance of her parents' household and then to getting her own household to live in as an adult. In most cases, bearing and rearing children were subordinate to these goals.

As a child, certainly by the age of 7, a girl was expected to begin to contribute to the household work. On a farm, she might look after chickens or water animals or carry food to adult men and women working the land. In an urban artisan's household, she would do some form of light work, perhaps involving cleaning or carrying and later sewing or weaving. The girl would remain in her parents' home as long as she made a real contribution to the family enterprise or until her labor elsewhere was more valuable to the family. An artisan's daughter might not leave home until marriage because she could learn increasingly valuable skills from her parents.

The labor of the much larger number of girls growing up on farms quickly became of little value to the family. These girls would then leave home, usually by the age of 12 or 14. They might go to another farm but were more likely to migrate to a nearby town or city. They would rarely travel more than 30 miles from their parents' household and would then normally become servants in the household of an employer. (See Document, "Priscilla Wakefield Demands More Occupations Be Opened to Women" on page 598.)

Having migrated from home, the young woman made it her chief goal to accumulate a dowry. Her savings would allow her to make the necessary contribution to form a household with her husband. Marriage within the family economy was a joint economic undertaking, and the wife was expected to make an immediate contribution of capital for the establishment of the household. A young woman might well work for ten years or more to accumulate a dowry. This practice meant that marriage was usually postponed until a woman's mid- to late 20s.

A married woman's work was in many ways a function of her husband's occupation. If the peasant household possessed enough land to support itself, the wife spent much of her time literally carrying things for her husband—water, food, seed, harvested grain, and the like. But few peasants had such adequate landholdings. If the husband had to do work other than farming, such as fishing or migrant labor, the wife might do the plowing, planting, and harvesting. In the city, the wife of an artisan or merchant often acted as a business manager. She might manage the household finances and participate in the trade or business. When her husband died, she might take over the business, perhaps hiring an artisan.

Finally, if economic disaster struck the family, more often than not it was the wife who took the lead in sending off family members to find work elsewhere or even to beg in the streets. In all phases of life within the family economy, women led active, often decisive roles. Industriousness rather than idleness was their lot in life. Finding a functional place in the household was essential to their well-being, but once that place had been found, their function was essential to the ongoing well-being of the household.

Read the Document
Gluckel of Hamlen Memoirs
at **MyHistoryLab.com**

The Revolution in Agriculture

The main goal of traditional European peasant society was to ensure the stability of the local food supply. That supply was never certain and became more uncertain the farther east one traveled. A failed harvest meant not only hardship, but also death from either outright starvation or protracted debility. Food was often harder to find in the country than

Document

Priscilla Wakefield Demands More Occupations Be Opened to Women

At the end of the eighteenth century, several English women writers began to demand a wider life for women. Priscilla Wakefield was among such authors. She was concerned that women found themselves able to pursue only occupations that paid poorly or were excluded from work on the grounds of their alleged physical weakness. She also believed that women should receive equal wages for equal work. Many of the issues she raised have yet to be adequately addressed on behalf of women.

■ *From reading this passage, what do you understand to have been the arguments at the end of the eighteenth century to limit the kinds of employment that women might enter? Why did women receive lower wages for work similar to or the same as that done by men? What occupations traditionally filled by men does Wakefield believe women might also pursue?*

Another heavy discouragement to the industry of women, is the inequality of the reward of their labor, compared with that of men; an injustice which pervades every species of employment performed by both sexes.

In employments which depend on bodily strength, the distinction is just; for it cannot be pretended that the generality of women can earn as much as men, when the produce of their labor is the result of corporeal exertion; but it is a subject of great regret, that this inequality should prevail even where an equal share of skill and application is exerted. Male stay-makers, mantua-makers, and hairdressers, are better paid than female artists of the same professions; but surely it will never be urged as an apology for this disproportion, that women are not as capable of making stays, gowns, dressing hair, and similar arts, as men; if they are not superior to them, it can only be accounted for upon this principle, that the prices they receive for their labor are not sufficient to repay them for the expense of qualifying themselves for their business; and that they sink under the mortification of being regarded as artisans of inferior estimation. . . .

Besides these employments which are commonly performed by women, and those already shown to be suitable for such persons as are above the condition of hard labor, there are some professions and trades customarily in the hands of men, which might be conveniently exercised by either sex.—Watchmaking requiring more ingenuity than strength, seems peculiarly adapted to women; as do many parts of the business of stationer, particularly, ruling account books or making pens. The compounding of medicines in an apothecary's shop, requires no other talents than care and exactness; and if opening a vein occasionally be a indispensable requisite, a woman may acquire the capacity of doing it, for those of her own sex at least, without any reasonable objection. . . . Pastry and confectionery appear particularly consonant to the habits of women, though generally performed by men; perhaps the heat of the ovens, and the strength requisite to fill and empty them, may render male assistants necessary; but certain women are most eligible to mix up the ingredients, and prepare the various kinds of cakes for baking.—Light turnery and toy-making depend more upon dexterity and invention than force, and are therefore suitable work for women and children. . . .

Farming, as far as respects the theory, is commensurate with the powers of the female mind: nor is the practice of inspecting agricultural processes incompatible with the delicacy of their frames if their constitution be good.

Source: From Priscilla Wakefield, *Reflections on the Present Condition of the Female Sex* (1798), (London, 1817), pp. 125–127, as quoted in Bridget Hill, ed., *Eighteenth-Century Women: An Anthology.* Copyright © 1984 George Allen & Unwin, pp. 227–228.

in cities because city governments usually stored reserve supplies of grain.

During the century, historians now believe, bread prices slowly but steadily rose, spurred largely by population growth. This put pressure on all of the poor. The prices rose faster than urban wages but brought no appreciable advantage to the small peasant producer. On the other hand, the rise in grain prices benefited landowners and those wealthier peasants who had surplus grain to sell. The increasing price of grain allowed landlords to improve their income and lifestyle. They began a series of innovations in farm production that is known as the **agricultural revolution**.

French Peasants. During the seventeenth century the French Le Nain brothers painted scenes of French peasant life. Although the images softened many of the harsh realities of peasant existence, the clothing and the interiors were based on actual models and convey the character of the life of better-off French peasants whose lives would have continued very much the same into the eighteenth century.

New Crops and New Methods

This movement began during the sixteenth and seventeenth centuries in the Low Countries, where Dutch landlords and farmers devised better ways to build dykes and to drain land so that they could farm more extensive areas. They also experimented with new crops, such as clover and turnips, that would increase the supply of animal fodder and replenish the soil.

These methods were extensively adopted in England during the early eighteenth century. There, new methods of farming, new crops, and new modes of landholding eventually led to greater productivity. This advance in food production was necessary for an industrial society to develop. It ensured adequate food for the cities and freed surplus agricultural labor for industrial production.

Enclosure Replaces Open-Field Method Many of the agricultural innovations, which were adopted only slowly, were incompatible with the existing organization of land in Britain. Small cultivators who lived in village communities still farmed most of the soil. Each farmer tilled an assortment of unconnected strips. The two- or three-field systems of rotation left much land fallow and unproductive each year. Animals grazed on the common land in the summer and on the stubble of the harvest in the winter. Until at least the middle of the eighteenth century the decisions about which crops would be planted were made communally. The entire system discouraged improvement and favored the poorer farmers, who needed the common land and stubble fields for their animals. The village method made it almost impossible to increase pasture land and with it the size of herds and the production of manure for fertilizer. Traditional methods aimed to produce a steady, but not a growing, supply of food.

In 1700 approximately half the arable land in Britain was farmed by this open-field method. By the second half of the century the rising price of wheat encouraged landlords to consolidate or enclose their lands to increase production. The **enclosures** were intended to use land more rationally and to raise profits. The process involved the

The Lincolnshire Ox. (1790) by George Stubbs. The "Lincolnshire Ox" was a prize Hereford that grew to an enormous size by being fed solely on grass. The fascination with the Lincolnshire Ox, which was displayed for over a year in London, was characteristic of the general interest in agricultural improvements.

fencing of common lands, the reclamation of previously untilled waste, and the transformation of strips into block fields. These procedures disrupted the economic and social life of the countryside. Riots often ensued. Because many British farmers either owned their strips or rented them in a manner that amounted to ownership, the larger landlords usually had to resort to parliamentary acts to legalize the enclosure of the land, which they owned but rented to the farmers. Because the large landowners controlled Parliament, such measures passed easily. Between 1761 and 1792, almost 500,000 acres were enclosed through parliamentary acts, as compared with 75,000 acres between 1727 and 1760. In 1801 a general enclosure act streamlined the process.

See the Map
English Common Lands
Enclosed by Acts
at **MyHistoryLab.com**

The enclosures have remained controversial. By permitting the extension of both farming and innovation, they increased food production on larger agricultural units. However, they also disrupted the small traditional communities. They forced off the land some independent farmers, who had needed the common pasturage, and very poor cottagers, who had lived on the reclaimed waste land. However, the enclosures did not depopulate the countryside. In some counties where the enclosures took place, the population increased. New soil had come into production, and services subsidiary to farming also expanded.

Population Expansion

Agricultural improvement was both a cause and a result of an immense expansion in the population of Europe. The current population explosion seems to have had its origins in the eighteenth century. Exact figures are lacking, but the best estimates suggest that in 1700 Europe's population, excluding the European provinces of the Ottoman Empire, was between 100 million and 120 million people. By 1800 the figure had risen to over 180 million, and by 1850 to 260 million (see Figure 19–1). The population of England and Wales rose from 6 million in 1750 to over 10 million in 1800. France grew from 18 million in 1715 to approximately 26 million in 1789. Russia's population increased from 19 million in 1722 to 29 million in 1766. Such extraordinary sustained growth put new demands on all resources and considerable pressure on existing social organization.

Read the Document
Friend Men Treatise Population
at **MyHistoryLab.com**

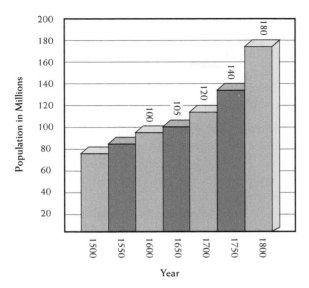

Figure 19–1. **Population of Europe, 1500–1800.**

The population expansion occurred across the Continent in both the country and the cities. Only a limited consensus exists about the causes of this growth. There was a clear decline in the death rate. There were fewer wars and somewhat fewer epidemics in the early eighteenth century. Hygiene and sanitation also improved. But changes in the food supply itself may have been the chief reason for sustained population growth. One contributing factor was improved and expanding grain production. Another, even more important factor, was the introduction in the eighteenth century of widespread cultivation of a New World tuber, the potato. Enough potatoes could be raised on a single acre to feed one peasant's family for an entire year. With this more certain food supply, more children could be reared, and more could survive.

The Eighteenth-Century Industrial Revolution: An Event in World History

In the second half of the eighteenth century the European economy began very slowly to industrialize. This development, more than any other single factor, distinguished Europe and eventually North America from the rest of the world for the next two centuries. While this economic development was occurring, people did not call it a *revolution*. That term came to be applied to the experience of British technological advances in productivity only after the French Revolution, when Continental writers contended that what had taken place in Britain was the economic equivalent of the political events in France. From this comparison arose the concept of an *industrial* revolu-

((•─[Hear the Audio
at MyHistoryLab.com

tion. The process, however, was revolutionary less in its pace, which was on the whole rather slow, than in its implications for the future of European society.

The European **industrial revolution** of the eighteenth century constituted the achievement of sustained economic growth despite subsequent downturns and depressions. At considerable social cost and dislocation, industrialism produced more goods and services than ever before in human history and eventually overcame the economy of scarcity. The new means of production demanded new kinds of skills, new discipline in work, and a large labor force. In the long run, industrialism clearly raised the standard of living; the poverty in which most Europeans had always lived was overcome.

Over time the wealth produced by industrialism upset the political and social structures of the Old Regime and led to political and social reforms. The economic elite of the emerging industrial society would eventually challenge the political dominance of the aristocracy. Industrialization also undermined traditional communities and, along with the growth of cities, displaced many people. These processes repeated themselves virtually everywhere that industrialization occurred during the next two centuries.

The consumer products of the industrializing businesses gave Europeans vast amounts of new goods to sell throughout the world and thus encouraged more international trade in which Western nations supplied the finished goods in exchange for raw materials. Furthermore, by the early nineteenth century iron and steel production and the new technologies of manufacture allowed European states and later the United States to build more powerful military forces, especially navies, than those of Africa, Latin America, or Asia. Both the economic and the military dominance of the West arose directly from the industrial achievement.

Much of the history of the non-Western world from the middle of the eighteenth century to the present can be understood in terms of how the nonindustrialized nations initially reacted to the penetration of their world by Europeans and Americans made wealthy and powerful through industrialized economies. Africa and Latin America became generally dependent economies. Japan, by the middle of the nineteenth century, decided it must imitate the European pattern and did so successfully. China did not make that decision and became indirectly ruled by Europeans. The Chinese revolutions of the twentieth century largely represented efforts to achieve real self-direction. Southeast Asia and the Middle East became drawn into the network of resource supply to the West; they could achieve movement toward economic independence only through imitation or, like Arab nations in the early 1970s, by refusing to supply oil to the West. The process of industrialization that commenced in small factories in eighteenth-century Europe has changed the world more than any other single development in the last two centuries.

Industrial Leadership of Great Britain

Great Britain was the home of the industrial revolution and, until the late nineteenth century, remained the industrial leader of Europe and the world (see Map 19–5). Several factors contributed to the early start of industrialization in Britain. Britain was the single largest free-trade area in Europe, with good roads and waterways without tolls or other internal trade barriers. There were rich deposits of coal and iron ore. The political structure was stable, and property was absolutely secure. The rule of law characterized Britain and produced a climate for secure investing and other economic enterprise. Property rights were powerfully secure. A sound system of banking and public credit created a good investment climate. Taxation in Britain was heavy, but it received legal approval from Parliament. Taxes were efficiently and fairly collected, largely from indirect taxes, with all regions and persons from all classes paying the same taxes. Besides satisfying domestic consumer demand, the British economy also benefited from the demand for goods from the North American colonies. Finally, British society was relatively mobile. Persons who had money or could earn it could rise socially.

New Methods of Textile Production Although eighteenth-century European society was devoted primarily to agriculture, small-scale household manufacturing permeated the countryside. The peasant family living in a one- or two-room cottage, not the factory, was the basic unit of production. The family economy, rather than the industrial factory economy, characterized the century. The same peasants who tilled the land in spring and summer often spun thread or wove textiles in winter.

Map 19–5. The Industrial Revolution in Britain. Richly endowed with coal and iron ore and possessing many natural ports and a network of navigable waterways, Britain exploited these advantages to become the world's first industrial nation.

Overview   Why the Industrial Revolution Began in Britain

Great Britain was the home of the industrial revolution, and until the middle of the nineteenth century, it maintained the industrial leadership of Europe. Several factors contributed to the early industrialization of Britain.

Natural Resources	Britain had extensive deposits of coal and iron ore.
Infrastructure	Britain had an extensive network of roads and canals that facilitated the shipment of raw materials and goods.
Society	1. The predominance of London: London was the largest city in Europe and the social, commercial, financial, and political center of Britain. It was thus both an enormous market for consumer goods itself and created a demand for these goods in the rest of Britain, which sought to emulate London fashions.
	2. The prevalence of newspapers: Newspapers thrived in Britain, and advertisements in them increased consumer demand for goods.
	3. Wealth in Britain brought status: British society was relatively mobile. Wealthy merchants and entrepreneurs could rise socially, enter the aristocracy, and enjoy political influence.
Government, Financial Institutions, and Empire	1. The rule of law: Britain had a stable government that guaranteed property rights.
	2. Britain was a free-trade area. No internal tolls inhibited the shipment of goods and raw materials within Britain.
	3. Britain had a sound system of banking and public credit that created a stable climate for investing in commerce and industry.
	4. Taxes were collected efficiently and fairly. No class was exempt from paying taxes.
	5. The colonial empire: British colonies were both a market for British goods and sources of raw materials for British manufacturers.

Under the **domestic or putting-out system**, agents of urban textile merchants took wool or other unfinished fiber to the homes of peasants, who spun it into thread. The agent then transported the thread to other peasants, who wove it into the finished product. The merchant sold the wares. In literally thousands of peasant cottages from Ireland to Austria stood either a spinning wheel or a hand loom. Sometimes the spinners or weavers owned their own equipment, but more often than not, by the middle of the century, the merchant capitalist owned the machinery as well as the raw material.

By midcentury production bottlenecks had developed within the domestic system. The demand for cotton textiles was growing more rapidly than production. This demand arose particularly in Great Britain, whose growing population wanted cotton textiles, as did its colonies in North America. The most famous inventions of the industrial revolution were devised in response to this consumer demand for cotton textiles.

Cotton textile weavers had the technical capacity to produce enough fabric to satisfy demand. However, the spinners could not produce as much thread as the weavers needed and could use. This imbalance had been created during the 1730s by John Kay's invention of the flying shuttle, which increased the productivity of the weavers. Thereafter, manufacturers and merchants offered prizes for the invention of a machine to eliminate this bottleneck. In about 1765 James Hargreaves (d. 1778) invented the **spinning jenny**. Initially, this machine allowed 16 spindles of thread to be spun, but by the close of the century it included as many as 120 spindles.

The spinning jenny broke the bottleneck between the productive capacity of the spinners and the weavers, but it was still a piece of machinery that was used in the cottage. The invention that took cotton textile manufacture from the home to the factory was Richard Arkwright's (1732–1792) **water frame**, patented in 1769. It was a water-powered device designed to permit the production of a purely cotton fabric rather than a cotton fabric containing linen fiber for durability. Eventually

Arkwright lost his patent rights, and other manufacturers were able to use his invention freely. As a result, numerous factories sprang up in the countryside near streams that provided the necessary water power. From the 1780s onward the cotton industry could meet an ever-expanding demand. Between 1780 and 1800 cotton output increased by 800 percent. By 1815 cotton composed 40 percent of the value of British domestic exports, and by 1830 just over 50 percent.

The Steam Engine The new technology in textile manufacture vastly increased cotton production and revolutionized a major consumer industry. But the invention that more than any other enabled industrialization to grow on itself and expand into one area of production after another was the steam engine. This machine provided for the first time in human history a steady and essentially unlimited source of inanimate power. Unlike engines powered by water or wind, the steam engine, driven by the burning of coal, was a portable source of industrial power that did not fail or falter as the seasons of the year changed. Unlike human or animal power, the steam engine depended on mineral energy that never tired. Finally, the steam engine could be applied to many industrial and, eventually, transportation uses.

The first practical engine using steam power was invented by Thomas Newcomen (1663–1729) in the early eighteenth century. It was large, inefficient in its use of energy, and practically untransportable. Nonetheless, English mine operators used it to pump water out of coal and tin mines. By the late eighteenth century almost a hundred Newcomen machines were operating in the mining districts of England.

During the 1760s James Watt (1736–1819) began to experiment with a model of a Newcomen machine at the University of Glasgow. He gradually understood that if the condenser were separated from the piston and the cylinder, much greater efficiency would result. In 1769 he patented his new invention, but his design required exceedingly precise metalwork. Watt soon found a partner in Matthew Boulton (1728–1809), a toy manufacturer in Birmingham, the city with the most skilled metalworkers in Britain. Watt and Boulton in turn consulted with John Wilkinson (1728–1808), a cannon manufacturer, to find ways to drill the precise metal cylinders required by Watt's design. In 1776 the Watt steam engine found its first commercial application pumping water from mines.

The use of the steam engine spread slowly because until 1800 Watt retained the exclusive patent rights and was reluctant to modify the engine. Boulton eventually persuaded him to adapt the engines for use in running cotton mills. By the early nineteenth century the steam engine had become the prime mover for all industry. With its eventual application to ships and then to wagons on iron rails, it also revolutionized transportation.

Blacksmith Shop. During the eighteenth century, most goods were produced in small workshops, such as this English blacksmith shop shown in a painting by Joseph Wright of Derby (1734–1797), or in the homes of artisans. Not until very late in the century, with the early stages of industrialization, did a few factories appear.

Iron Production The manufacture of high-quality iron has been basic to modern industrial development. It constitutes the chief element of all heavy industry and land or sea transport and is the material out of which most productive machinery itself has been manufactured. During the early eighteenth century British ironmakers produced less than 25,000 tons annually. Three factors held back the production of the metal. First, charcoal rather than coke was used to smelt the ore. Charcoal, which is derived from wood, was becoming scarce, and it did not burn at as high a temperature as coke, which is derived from coal. Second, until the perfection of the steam engine, insufficient blasts could be achieved in the furnaces. Finally, the demand for iron was limited. The elimination of the first two problems got rid of the third.

In the course of the century, British ironmakers began to use coke, and the steam engine provided new power for the blast furnaces. Coke was abundant because of Britain's large coal deposits. The steam engine both improved iron production and increased the demand for iron.

In 1784 Henry Cort (1740–1800) introduced a new method for melting and stirring the molten ore. Cort's process produced a purer iron. He also developed a rolling mill that

Chronology

Major Inventions in the Textile-Manufacturing Revolution

1733	John Kay's flying shuttle
1765	James Hargreaves's spinning jenny (patent 1770)
1769	James Watt's steam engine patent
1769	Richard Arkwright's water frame patent
1787	Edmund Cartwright's power loom

continually shaped the still-molten metal into bars, rails, or other forms. Previously, the metal had been pounded into these forms.

All of these innovations achieved a better, more versatile, and cheaper product. The demand for iron grew as its price went down. By the early nineteenth century annual British iron production amounted to over a million tons. The lower cost of iron in turn lowered the cost of steam engines and allowed them to be used more widely.

European Cities

Patterns of Preindustrial Urbanization

Remarkable changes occurred in the pattern of city growth between 1500 and 1800. In 1500 there were approximately 156 cities within Europe (excluding Hungary and Russia) with a population greater than 10,000. Only four of those cities—Paris, Milan, Venice, and Naples—had more than 100,000 inhabitants. By 1800 approximately 363 cities had 10,000 or more inhabitants, and 17 of those had populations larger than 100,000. The percentage of the European population living in urban areas had risen from just over 5 percent to just over 9 percent. The urban concentration had also shifted from southern Mediterranean Europe to the north.

Urban Classes

Social divisions were as marked in the cities of the eighteenth century as they were in the industrial centers of the nineteenth.

The Upper Classes At the top of the urban social structure stood a generally small group of nobles, large merchants, bankers, financiers, clergy, and government officials. These men (and they were always men) controlled the political and economic affairs of the town. Normally they constituted a self-appointed and self-electing oligarchy who governed the city through its corporation or city council. These rights of self-government had generally been granted by a royal charter that gave the city corporation its authority and the power to select its own members. In a few cities on the Continent artisan guilds controlled the corporations, but most councils were under the influence of the local nobility and the commercial elite.

The Middle Class The prosperous but not immensely wealthy merchants, tradesmen, bankers, and professional people were the most dynamic element of the urban population and constituted the group traditionally regarded as the middle class, or *bourgeoisie*. The middle class had less wealth than most nobles, but more than urban artisans. Middle-class people lived in the cities and towns, and their sources of income had little or nothing to do with the land. The middle class normally supported reform, change, and economic growth. Middle-class businessmen and professionals often found their pursuit of profit and prestige blocked by aristocratic privilege and social exclusiveness. The bourgeoisie (and some progressive aristocrats) also wanted more rational regulations for trade and commerce.

During the eighteenth century the middle class and the aristocracy frequently collided. The middle class often imitated the lifestyle of the nobles, and the nobles increasingly embraced the commercial spirit of the middle class. The bourgeoisie was not rising to challenge the nobility; both were seeking to enhance their existing power and prestige. However, tradition and political connection gave the advantage to the nobility. Consequently, as the century passed, the middle class increasingly resented the aristocracy. That resentment became more bitter as the bourgeoisie grew wealthier and more numerous, and the aristocratic control of political and ecclesiastical power tightened. The growing influence of the nobility seemed to mean that the middle class would continue to be excluded from the political decisions of the day.

On the other hand, the middle class tended to fear the lower urban classes as much as they resented the nobility. The lower orders constituted a potentially violent element in society; a potential threat to property; and, in their poverty, a drain on national resources. The lower orders, however, were much more varied than either the city aristocracy or the middle class cared to admit.

Artisans The segment of the urban population that suffered from both the grasping of the middle class and the local nobility was made up of shopkeepers, artisans, and wage earners. These people constituted the single largest group in any city. They included grocers, butchers, fishmongers, carpenters, cabinetmakers, smiths, printers, handloom weavers, and tailors, to give but a few examples. They

Dress Shop. Consumption of all forms of consumer goods increased greatly in the eighteenth century. This engraving illustrates a shop, probably in Paris. Here women, working apparently for a woman manager, are making dresses and hats to meet the demands of the fashion trade.

had their own culture, values, and institutions. Like the peasants of the countryside, they were in many respects conservative. Their economic position was highly vulnerable. If a poor harvest raised the price of food, their own businesses suffered.

The entire life of these artisans and shopkeepers centered on their work. They usually lived near or at their place of employment. Most of them worked in shops with fewer than a half-dozen other craftsmen. Their primary institution had historically been the guild, but by the eighteenth century most guilds had lost a considerable amount of their traditional influence.

Nevertheless, the guilds were not to be ignored. They played a conservative role. They did not seek economic growth or innovation. They attempted to preserve the jobs and the skills of their members. They still were able in many countries to determine who might and might not pursue a particular craft. They attempted to prevent too many people from learning a particular skill. The guilds also provided a framework for social and economic advancement. A young boy might become an apprentice to learn a craft or trade. After several years

he would be made a journeyman. Still later, if successful, he might become a master. The artisan could also receive certain social benefits from the guilds, including aid for his family during sickness or the promise of admission into the guild for his son. The guilds constituted the chief protection for artisans against the operation of the commercial market. They were particularly strong in central Europe.

The Jewish Population: Age of the Ghetto

Although the small Jewish communities of Amsterdam and other western European cities became famous for their intellectual life and financial institutions, most European Jews lived in eastern Europe. In the eighteenth century and thereafter, no fewer than 3 million Jews dwelled in Poland, Lithuania, and Ukraine. There were perhaps 150,000 in the Habsburg lands, primarily in Bohemia, around 1760. Fewer than 100,000 lived in Germany and approximately 40,000 in France. England and Holland had Jewish populations of fewer than 10,000. There were even smaller groups of Jews in Italy.

Document Belorussian Jews Petition Catherine the Great

In the 1780s, through military expansion, Empress Catherine the Great of Russia annexed Belorussia, bringing a new Jewish minority under her imperial government. In response to her decree governing many aspects of the region's law and economy, Belorussian Jews petitioned the empress to protect certain of their traditional rights regarding distillation and sale of spirits. They also petitioned for protection in court and for the right to retain their own traditional practices and courts for matters relating to their own community. The petition indicates how in Russia, as elsewhere in Europe, Jews were treated as a people apart. It also illustrates how Jews, like other minorities in Old Regime Europe, sought both to receive the protection of monarchies against arbitrary local officials and to maintain the integrity of long-standing social practices. The document also illustrates the Jews' dependence on the goodwill of the surrounding non-Jewish community.

■ *In the first part of the petition, how do the petitioners attempt to appeal to long-standing custom to defend their interests? How do both parts of the petition suggest that Jewish law and practice, distinct from the rest of the society, governed Jewish social life? In the context of this petition, which non-Jewish authorities may actually or potentially influence Jewish life?*

2. According to an ancient custom, when the squires built a new village, they summoned the Jews to reside there and gave them certain privileges for several years and then permanent liberty to distill spirits, brew beer and mead, and sell these drinks. On this basis, the Jews built houses and distillation plants at considerable expense. . . . A new decree of Her Imperial Majesty . . . reserved [this right] to the squires. . . . But a decree of the governor-general of Belorussia has now forbidden the squires to farm out distillation in their villages to Jews, even if the squires want to do this. As a result, the poor Jews who built houses in small villages and promoted both this trade and distillation have been deprived of these and left completely impoverished. But until all the Jewish people are totally ruined, the Jewish merchants suffer restraints equally with the poor rural Jews, since their law obliges them to assist all who share their religious faith. They therefore request an imperial decree authorizing the squire, if he wishes, to farm out distillation to Jews in rural areas.

3. Although, with Her Imperial Majesty's permission, Jews may be elected as officials . . . Jews are allotted fewer votes than other people and hence no Jew can ever attain office. Consequently, Jews have no one to defend them in courts and find themselves in a desperate situation—given their fear and ignorance of Russian—in case of misfortune, even if innocent. To consummate all the good already bestowed, Jews dare to petition that an equal number of electors be required from Jews as from others (or, at least, that in matters involving Jews and non-Jews, a representative from the Jewish community hold equal rights with non-Jews, be present to accompany Jews in court, and attend the interrogation of Jews). But cases involving only Jews (except for promissory notes and debts) should be handled solely in Jewish courts, because Jews assume obligations among themselves, make agreements and conclude all kinds of deals in the Jewish language and in accordance with Jewish rites and laws (which are not known to others). Moreover, those who transgress their laws and order should be judged in Jewish courts. Similarly, preserve intact all their customs and holidays in the spirit of their faith, as is mercifully assured in the imperial manifesto.

Source: From Supplication to Revolution: A Documentary Social History of Imperial Russia edited by Gregory L. Freeze. Copyright © 1988 by Oxford University Press, Inc. Used by permission of Oxford University Press, Inc.

In 1762 Catherine the Great of Russia specifically excluded Jews from a manifesto that welcomed foreigners to settle in Russia. (See Document, "Belorussian Jews Petition Catherine the Great.") However, she relaxed the exclusion a few years later. After the first partition of Poland in 1772, to be discussed in Chapter 22, Russia had a large Jewish population. The partition also resulted in larger Jewish communities in Prussia and Austria.

Jews dwelled in most nations without enjoying the rights and privileges of other subjects of the monarchs, unless such rights were specifically granted to them. They were regarded as aliens whose status might well be changed at the whim of local rulers or the monarchical government.

No matter where they lived, the Jews of Europe under the Old Regime resided apart from non-Jews. In cities they usually lived in distinct districts known as **ghettos**, and in the countryside, in primarily Jewish villages. Thus this period in Jewish history, which may be said to have begun with the expulsion of the Jews from Spain in 1492, is known as the age of the ghetto, or separate community. Jews were also treated as a distinct people religiously and legally. In Poland for much of the century they were virtually self-governing. Elsewhere they lived under the burden of discriminatory legislation. Except in England, Jews could not mix in the mainstream of the societies in which they lived.

During the seventeenth century a few Jews helped finance the wars of major rulers. These financiers often grew close to the rulers and came to be known as "court Jews." They tended to marry among themselves. Perhaps the most famous was Samuel Oppenheimer (1630–1703), who helped the Habsburgs finance their struggle against the Turks, including the defense of Vienna. Their position at court and their financial abilities may have brought them privilege and fame, but court Jews, including Oppenheimer, often failed to have their loans repaid.

Unlike the court Jews, however, most European Jews lived in poverty. They occupied the most undesirable sections of cities or poor rural villages. A few were moneylenders, but most worked at the lowest occupations. Their religious beliefs, rituals, and community set them apart. A wall of laws and social institutions—as well as the physical walls of the ghetto—kept them in positions of social inferiority.

Under the Old Regime, it is important to emphasize, this discrimination was based on religious separateness. Jews who converted to Christianity were welcomed, even if not always warmly, into the major political and social institutions of European society. But until the late eighteenth century those Jews who remained loyal to their faith were subject to various religious, civil, and social disabilities. They were not free to pursue the professions or often change residence, and they stood outside the political structures of the nations in which they lived. Jews could be expelled from the cities where they dwelled, and their property could be confiscated. They were regarded as socially and religiously inferior. They could be required to listen to sermons that insulted them and their religion. Their children could be taken away from them and given Christian instruction. And they knew their non-Jewish neighbors might suddenly turn violently against them. As will be seen in subsequent chapters, however, the end of the Old Regime brought major changes in the lives of Jews and in their relationship to the larger culture.

Ghetto in Cracow. During the Old Regime, European Jews were separated from non-Jews, typically in districts known as ghettos. Relegated to the least desirable section of a city or to rural villages, most lived in poverty. This watercolor painting depicts a street in Kazimlesz, the Jewish quarter of Cracow, Poland. *Judaica Collection. Max Berger, Vienna Austria/©Erich Lessing/Art Resource, New York.*

Summary

Models of European Political Development. In the seventeenth and eighteenth centuries, five great powers emerged in Europe: France, Britain, Austria, Prussia, and Russia. Through their military strength, economic development, and in some cases colonial empires, they would affect virtually every other world civilization.

Britain. In the seventeenth century, conflict between the Stuart kings and Parliament arising out of political, religious, and economic issues led to civil war, the execution of Charles I, a short-lived English republic under Oliver Cromwell, and in 1688–1689 the Glorious Revolution that finally limited royal authority and established the supremacy of Parliament. Although eighteenth-century England was not a democracy, its people had more rights and liberties than the subjects of the absolutist monarchs who ruled the other great European powers.

In a series of worldwide colonial struggles with France, Britain used its commercial resources and navy to profit from France's entanglements in Europe and emerge supreme in North America and India.

France. Under Louis XIV (r. 1643–1715), France became the model of an absolute monarchy. Louis used his splendid court at Versailles to overawe the French aristocracy and promote a glittering image of French culture that impressed all of Europe. However, he was not able completely to overcome opposition from the French elites who sought to reassert their influence under his successors. His revocation of the Edict of Nantes weakened France by driving thousands of French Protestants into exile.

Louis pursued an aggressive foreign policy that expanded France's borders but cost France dearly in wealth and resources and provoked strong opposition from the other European powers. In the War of the Spanish Succession, he succeeded in placing his grandson on the throne of Spain, but the war left France exhausted.

Russia. Russia became a great power under Peter the Great (r. 1682–1725). Peter curbed the power of the Russian church and aristocracy and opened Russia to Western technology and military and commercial influences. He built his new capital at Saint Petersburg. He also built an efficient army and navy and established a centralized bureaucracy to collect revenue.

Central Europe. The Habsburgs remained Holy Roman Emperors, but their power rested on their hereditary domains—Austria, Hungary, Bohemia, and northern Italy. Although the Habsburgs reconquered Hungary from the Ottomans, the rise of Prussia under the Hohenzollerns challenged Habsburg dominance in central Europe. The Hohenzollern rulers built Prussia from a collection of scattered German states into a great power by developing an efficient bureaucracy and a powerful army. Under Frederick II (r. 1740–1786), Prussia emerged from a series of wars with Austria, France, and Russia as one of the strongest European states and the rival to Habsburg power in central Europe.

The Old Regime. Eighteenth-century European society was traditional, hierarchical, corporate, and privileged—features that had characterized Europe and the world for centuries. All societies also confronted the scarce food supplies. For the eighteenth century, however, an improved food supply helped support a larger population. New agricultural techniques and the expanding population created pressures on social structures.

Commerce also grew during the eighteenth century. Agriculture became more commercialized, with more money payments; cities expanded.

Changes in European Society. European society stood on the brink of a new era in which the social, economic, and political relationships of centuries would be destroyed. The commercial spirit and the values of the marketplace clashed with the traditions of peasants and guilds. That commercial spirit brought social change; by the early nineteenth century it led to a conception of human beings as individuals rather than as members of communities.

The expansion of the European population further stimulated change and challenge to tradition, hierarchy, and corporateness. The traditional economic and social organization (the family economy) had presupposed a stable or declining population. A larger population created the need for new ways to solve old problems. The social hierarchy had to accommodate more people. Corporate groups, such as the guilds, had to confront an expanded labor force. New wealth meant that birth would cease to determine social relationships.

Furthermore, the eighteenth century witnessed the beginning of industrial production in response to the demands for consumer goods by the expanding population. New inventions greatly increasing productive capacity first appeared in the English textile industry. Thereafter industrial modes of production spread to the manufacture of iron. The steam engine provided a portable source of energy, allowing factories to be moved from the countryside into cities.

Industrialization also affected Europe's relations with much of the non-European world. For the first time in history, major changes in one region of Europe left virtually no corner of the globe untouched. By the close of the eighteenth century, a movement toward world interconnectedness and interdependence had begun.

Key Terms

absolutism (p. 577)

agricultural revolution (p. 598)

aristocratic resurgence (p. 594)

boyars (p. 583)

divine right of kings (p. 583)

domestic or putting-out system (p. 603)

enclosures (p. 599)

family economy (p. 595)

ghettos (p. 608)

Glorious Revolution (p. 578)

industrial revolution (p. 601)

Junkers (p. 588)

Old Regime (p. 592)

parliamentary monarchy (p. 577)

Pragmatic Sanction (p. 587)

Puritans (p. 577)

spinning jenny (p. 603)

streltsy (p. 583)

Table of Ranks (p. 585)

water frame (p. 603)

Review Questions

1. By the end of the seventeenth century, England and France had different systems of government with different religious policies. What were the main differences? Similarities? Why did each nation develop as it did?

2. How and why did Russia emerge as a great power? Discuss the character of Peter the Great. How were his domestic reforms related to his military ambitions? What were his methods of reform? To what extent did he succeed?

3. What were the main points of conflict between Britain and France in North America, the West Indies, and India? What were the results of these conflicts by 1763? Which countries emerged stronger from the Seven Years' War and why?

4. Why were so many people living in the European countryside dependent on the aristocracy?

5. How would you define the term *family economy*? In what ways were the lives of women constrained by the family economy in preindustrial Europe? What active roles were possible for women?

6. What caused the agricultural revolution? How did technological innovations help change European agriculture? To what extent did the English aristocracy contribute to the agricultural revolution? What were some of the reasons for peasant revolts in Europe in the eighteenth century?

7. What factors led to the industrial revolution of the eighteenth century? What were some of the technological innovations, and why were they important? Why did Great Britain take the lead in the industrial revolution? How did the consumer contribute to the industrial revolution?

8. Describe city life during the eighteenth century. Were all European cities of the same character? What changes had taken place in the distribution of population in cities and towns? Compare the lifestyle of the upper class with those of the middle and lower classes.

9. What was the status of European Jews in the Old Regime? How were they made to live as a people apart from the rest of the European population? What were the sources of prejudice against Jews in Europe?

Note: *To learn more about the topics in this chapter, please turn to the Suggested Readings at the end of the book. For additional sources related to this chapter please see MyHistoryLab.com.*

myhistorylab Connections

Reinforce what you learned in this chapter by studying the many documents, images, maps, review tools, and videos available at **www.myhistorylab.com**.

Read and Review

✓●─[Study and Review Chapter 19

●●●─[Read the Document *The Divine Right of Kings 1598 James I, p. 577*

Cromwell Abolishes the English Monarchy 1651, p. 577

The English Bill of Rights, 1689, p. 578

Peter Great with Alexis Russia, p. 585

Domat Social Order Monarchy, p. 594

Voltaire Condition 18th century France, p. 594

Gluckel of Hamlen Memoirs, p. 597

Friend Men Treatise Population, p. 600

◉─[See the Map *Growth of Brandenburg-Prussia, 1618–1786, p. 587*

Europe After the Treaty of Utrecht, 1714, p. 589

English Common Lands Enclosed by Acts, p. 600

◉─[View the Image *Allegorical View Cromwell as Savior England, p. 577*

Ivan the Terrible, p. 583

Michael Romanov, p. 583

Battle of Poltava, 1709, p. 584

Research and Explore

◉─[See the Map *Russia under Peter the Great*

◉─[See the Map *Rise of Prussia, 1440–1795*

─((●●─[Hear the Audio ─●─

Hear the audio file for Chapter 19 at
www.myhistorylab.com.

20 | The Last Great Islamic Empires, 1500–1800

- The Ottoman Empire and the Eastern Mediterranean World
- The Safavid Empire and the West Asian World
- The Mughals
- Central Asia: Islamization in the Post-Timur Era
- Power Shifts in the Southern Oceans

Akbar Inspecting the Construction of Fatehpur-Sikri, ca. 1590. Sometime around 1570, construction began on a new Mughal capital, Fatehpur-Sikri ("City of Victory"), a few miles southwest of Agra. Akbar (r. 1556–1605), the emperor who ordered the building of Fatehpur-Sikri, had a keen interest in architecture. Here he stands at the construction site, gesturing to a mason as the imperial entourage looks on. In every sense, he lived up to his epithet as the "architect of the spiritual and material world."

BETWEEN 1450 AND 1650 ISLAMIC CULTURE, SOCIETY, AND statecraft blossomed. The creation of three powerful empires and several strong regional states was the culmination of long processes in the Islamic eastern Mediterranean and West Asia. During this time the ideal of a universal Islamic caliphate yielded to the reality of multiple secular, albeit distinctively "Islamic," sultanates.

The simultaneous growth of the "gunpowder empires" of the Ottomans, Safavids, and Mughals marked the global apogee of Islamic civilizational and economic strength. By 1600 the Ottoman Turks controlled Asia Minor, the Fertile Crescent, the Balkans, Crimean Europe, the eastern Mediterranean, and Arabia; the Safavids ruled all of greater Iran; and descendants of Timur—the Timurid line known as the Mughals—governed Afghanistan and most of South Asia. Around these empires were arrayed Islamic khanates of Central Asia and Russia, sultanates of Southeast Asia, savannah empires of West Africa, the port cities of East Africa, the Sharifian state of Morocco, and regional empires of the Sudan in which Islam was significant (see Map 20–1).

In 1600 Islamic civilization seemed as strong as that of Europe, China, or Japan, yet military, economic, and political strength were partially deceptive. By around 1800, Ottoman, Safavid, and Mughal military power was waning in contrast to European military and trading expansion and empire building, even though Islamic social and cultural life still flour-

ished and the Ottomans, Safavids, and Mughals continued to be seen as powers into the early 1800s.

Hindus were the chief religious group the Muslims displaced in parts of Southeast Asia. Islam never ousted the Indian Buddhist cultures of Burma (Myanmar), Thailand, and Indochina (Vietnam), but it did take hold in most of Malaysia, Sumatra, Java, and the "Spice Islands" of the Moluccas. By 1500, Islam, long a fixture in North, West, and Central Africa, had also spread along the East African coast.

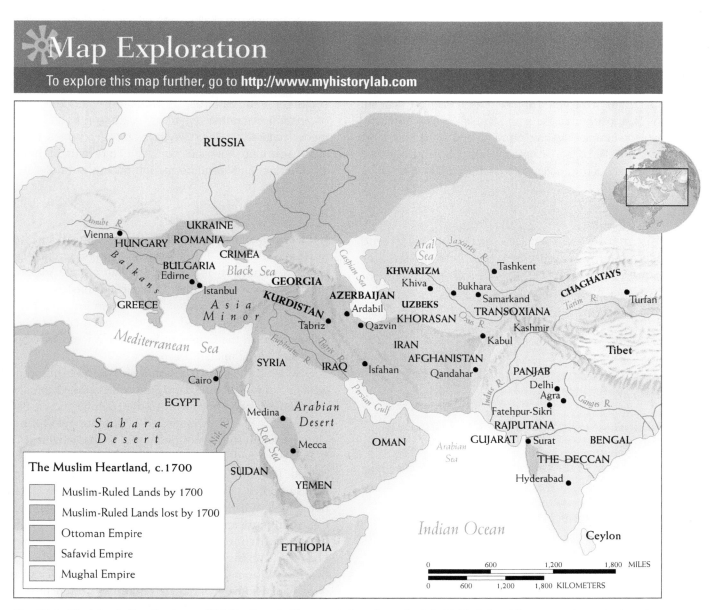

✳ Map Exploration

To explore this map further, go to **http://www.myhistorylab.com**

The Muslim Heartland, c.1700

- Muslim-Ruled Lands by 1700
- Muslim-Ruled Lands lost by 1700
- Ottoman Empire
- Safavid Empire
- Mughal Empire

Map 20–1. The Islamic Heartlands, ca. 1700. The three rival "gunpowder" empires—the Safavid, Mughal, and Ottoman empires—dominated the Islamic heartlands.

The Last Great Islamic Empires

Ottomans
Safavids
Mughals

The Islamic region's vitality between 1450 and 1800 was exemplified by the three great, prosperous imperial states of the Ottomans, Safavids, and Mughals. Each built extensive civilian and military bureaucracies, enjoyed inspired military and civilian leaders, revived Islamic social and cultural life, and improved on their predecessors.

While Islamic ideology, society, and culture were important to the success of the Ottomans, Safavids, and Mughals, military, social, and commercial innovations were key to each dynasty's rise to global importance. Their rulers built arguably the greatest cities in the world of their time in Istanbul, Isfahan, and Delhi. They patronized the arts, stimulating new traditions of Islamic literature, calligraphy, painting, and architecture. Yet all were essentially conservative societies. Economically they remained closely tied to agricultural production, long-distance trade, and taxation based on land. Perhaps because they were so successful, these societies did not undergo the kind of social or religiopolitical revolutions that rocked Europe after 1500. Thus, much like the societies of China and Japan in the same period, they did not experience the sort of generative changes in material and intellectual life that the comparatively underdeveloped western European societies, for all their diversity, saw in the sixteenth, seventeenth, and eighteenth centuries. There was no compelling challenge to traditional Islamic ideals of societal organization and human responsibility, even though many Islamic movements in the eighteenth century did call for communal and personal reform.

As one historian has put it, the striking growth of Islamic societies and cultures in this age was "not one of *origination*, but rather one of *culmination* in a culture long already mature." In their heydays, these empires produced much scientific work, but no scientific revolution; much art, architecture, and literature of high quality, but none that de-

In this chapter we turn first to the period's three major Islamic empires and then briefly to the smaller Islamic political-cultural centers of Central, South, and Southeast Asia, where European power was encroaching on what had been a virtual Muslim monopoly on maritime trade. ■

The Ottoman Empire and the Eastern Mediterranean World

Origins and Development of the Ottoman State before 1600

The Turkish dynasty of the Ottomans rose to prominence originally as one of the western Oghuz Turkish groups that moved from the Central Asian steppes to Anatolia as Muslim settlers and frontier warriors (ghazis).[1] The Ottomans reached Anatolia (Asia Minor) in the time of the Seljuks of Rum (1098–1308), the first western Turks to have founded a lasting state there (see Chapter 12). By about 1300, the newcomers ruled one of several small military states along the Byzantine-Seljuk frontier in western Anatolia. In the ensuing century, several vigorous leaders expanded their territory east into central Anatolia and (in 1356) west across the Dardanelles into the European Byzantine lands of Macedonia and modern Bulgaria. Exchanging grants of revenue-producing, conquered land (*timar*s) for military service, the Ottomans built both a formidable fighting force and a loyal military aristocracy.

By 1402 the center of Ottoman rule had shifted northwest to Edirne on the Balkan Peninsula itself. Ottoman control then extended northwest to the Danube and east across central Anatolia. Only encircled Constantinople formed an alien pocket in these dominions, and it finally fell in 1453 to Sultan Mehmed II, "the Conqueror" (r. 1451–1481). Renamed "Istanbul," it became the Ottoman capital. After centuries of power, Byzantium, the center of Eastern Christendom, had vanished, although the Ottomans allowed the Christian patriarch to continue to preside in Istanbul over the Eastern church. The conquest of Constantinople was both the culmination of previous war efforts and a springboard for Ottoman European ambitions. As their extraordinary, expansionist conquests continued, often justified in the name of Islam, they became in Christian European eyes the feared scourge of God.

---

[1]The Ottomans, sometimes called *Osmanlis*, are named after Osman (1259–1326), also rendered *Othman* or *Uthman*, a *ghazi* said to have founded the dynasty when he set up a border state in about 1288 on the Byzantine frontier in northwestern Anatolia.

●●▶[Read the Document
Mehmed II (15th century)
at **MyHistoryLab.com**

parted radically from previous traditions; political consolidation and also expansion, but no conquest of significant new markets or territories; prosperous long-distance trade, but no beginnings of a real commercial or industrial revolution. By the mid-nineteenth century, all three empires were at various stages of economic, political, social, and military disarray in comparison to Europe. By contrast, western Europe, having lagged behind the Islamic world in economic, social, and cultural development as well as political and military might since the Early Middle Ages, was by the nineteenth century in the midst of industrial, financial, social, and military revolutions and poised to challenge successfully the Islamic empires from the Mediterranean to South Asia.

Thus it is not entirely surprising that European global expansionism gradually dominated Africa, India, Indonesia, and the heartland culture of the Islamic world, rather than the reverse. Neither the great imperial Islamic states, the smaller Islamic sultanates and emirates, the diverse Hindu kingdoms, nor the varied African states (let alone the smaller societies of Africa, the Americas, and the South Pacific) fared well in their eventual clashes with European expansion during this age. The growing European domination of the seas, of the flow of gold and silver, and of global consumable products allowed Europeans to contain as well as to bypass the major Islamic lands in their quest for commercial empires. (Ironically, the Islamic states' hold on the Silk Road from the east may have been one factor in Europe's turn to the Atlantic.)

Industrial development and military technology joined economic wealth, social prosperity, and political stability by the early 1800s to give western Europe global military supremacy for the first time. Before 1800 the Europeans were able to bring only minor Islamic states under colonial administrations. However, the footholds they gained in Africa, India, and Southeast Asia laid the groundwork for rapid colonial expansion by the 1850s. The age of the last great Islamic empires was the beginning of the first great modern European empires. The colonialism of the nineteenth century accompanied the aggressive advance of European industrial, commercial, and military power that would hold sway into the mid-twentieth century.

Focus Questions

■ How did the trajectory of development between the Islamic empires and Europe differ in the period from 1500 to 1850?

■ Why, after centuries as the "underdog," was Europe by the early nineteenth century finally able to challenge the power of the Islamic empires?

■ Why was the Islamic world, more than China and Japan, increasingly subject to European intrusion during the early modern period?

Istanbul, from a 1537 Turkish map. Its strategic location on the Bosphorus Straits enabled it to dominate trade in the eastern Mediterranean.

By 1512 Ottoman rule was secure in virtually all of southeastern Europe and north of the Black Sea in most of the Ukraine. Under Selim I (r. 1512–1520) and Süleyman, "the Lawgiver" (known in the West as "the Magnificent," r. 1520–1566), Ottoman sovereignty only expanded. Selim subjugated the Egyptian Mamluks (1517) and annexed Syria-Palestine, most of North Africa, the Yemen, and Mecca and Medina. He also nullified the Shi'ite threat from Iran in the East (see below). Süleyman took control of Kurdistan, Georgia (in the Caucasus), Mesopotamia, and Iraq, and advanced Ottoman borders in eastern Europe. Having won much of Hungary and nearly taken Vienna by siege in 1526–1529, he was able by battle and treaty to bring virtually all of Hungary under direct rule in the 1540s.

See the Map
The Ottoman Empire to 1566
at **MyHistoryLab.com**

The Ottoman ruler could now claim to be the Abbasid heir and caliph for all Muslims. This was symbolized by the addition (by Selim I, after the Mamluk conquest in 1517) of the title "Protector of the Sacred Places [Mecca and Medina]" to that of emperor, **padishah**. At this point, Ottoman military might was unmatched globally, except possibly by China. Its vast territories—home to numerous linguistic and ethnic groups—made it truly an empire (see Map 20–2 on page 616).

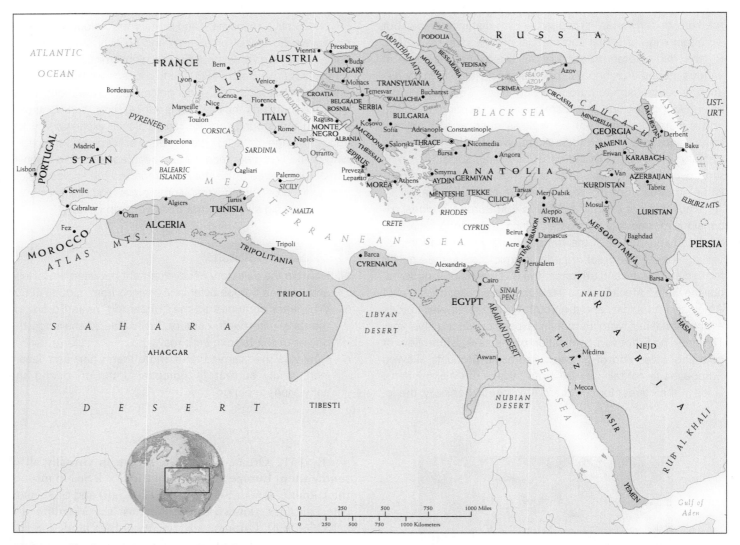

Map 20–2. The Ottoman Empire at Its Zenith. This large and multi-ethnic empire spanned three continents and lasted more than 400 years. Here at its largest extent around 1600.

The "Classical" Ottoman Order

Mehmed II was the true founder of the Ottoman Empire. He replaced tribal chieftains with loyal servants of the ruler, initiated a tradition of formal governmental legislation with his **Qanun-name** (*"Lawbook"*), and organized the *ulama* hierarchically under a single "Shaykh of Islam." In the next century Süleyman earned his title "Lawgiver" by his legislation touching all aspects of life and all social ranks, his reconciliation of customary law and **Shari'a** (religious law), and his regularization of both law and bureaucracy.

The entire Ottoman state was organized as one vast military institution. All members, whatever their function, held military ranks as the standing "army" of the state under the hereditary leadership of the sultan. This centralized state was supported by the productivity of its Muslim and non-Muslim subjects, such as Jewish and Armenian merchants. The ruling class was Muslim, shared the common Ottoman culture, and had to give utter allegiance to the sultan. The state organization included the palace, the administrative or ruling institution, the military institution, and the religious or learned institution. The palace included the sultan, his **harem**, his ministers, and the servants. The privy council, headed by the grand vizier, together with the chancery, the imperial treasury, and the remaining civil bureaucracy, formed the backbone of the ruling or administrative institution. Although men held the keys to power, women also had important roles, most often concealed to the public eye. Traditional Turkish customs assumed that power was vested collectively in the family. Women had some ceremonial functions, but also played

◄●Read the Document

Ogier Ghiselin de Busbecq, "Süleyman the Lawgiver" at **MyHistoryLab.com** vital roles in court politics, especially in selecting officers and negotiating economic policy.

Several measures helped ensure the ongoing strength of the sultan at the apex of the ruling institution. Young Ottoman princes received administrative and leadership training in the provinces, which kept them from being sheltered in the palace and gave them experience of life outside the capital. Stability of succession was traditionally guaranteed by the practice of fratricide in the ruling family, which, legalized formally in Mehmed II's *Qanun-name*, continued until the late sixteenth century. Thus, while theoretically left to God, succession to the sultanate went to the aspirant who could assert himself and seize power, after which he was expected to execute his brothers to eliminate future competing claims to the throne.

The Ottomans co-opted the legal-religious and educational-intellectual roles of the religious scholars, or *ulama*, for the service of the state, making them an arm of the government under a single religious authority, the **Grand Mufti** or "Shaykh of Islam." This highly organized branch of state was open only to Muslim men and included the entire system of courts and judges. It was based on a comprehensive network ranging from local mosque schools to the four elite madrasas built around the Süleymaniye Mosque in Istanbul during Süleyman's reign. Scholars' ranks within the graded *ulama* hierarchy reflected the level of schooling and teaching they had attained.

While the *ulama* were thus under state control, the state itself was formally committed to maintaining the divinely ordained *Shari'a*, and *ulama* enjoyed great esteem. This structure may explain why, whereas the *ulama* in both Safavid Iran and Mughal India often differed with their rulers, the Ottoman *ulama* usually functioned tamely as part of the state apparatus.

Although the religious establishment upheld the supremacy of the *Shari'a* and the sultan recognized its authority, the functional law of the land was the highly organized state administrative law—the practical code, or **Qanun**, established by the ruler. Still, the *Shari'a* as interpreted by the *ulama* theoretically governed the *Qanun*, and the sultan often formally applied traditional religious norms in his regulations. The conformity of these regulations to the *Shari'a* sometimes reflected the genuine piety of a particular administrator or ruler and sometimes was only a pious fiction, something also true for Safavid Iran and Mughal India.

The key ingredient to Ottoman power, however, was the military. The Ottoman rulers kept its loyalty by checking the power of the old landed aristocracy through careful registry and control of *timar* lands and by employing slave soldiers loyal only to the sultan. The army was based originally on the provincial cavalry whose officers were supported with

Süleyman the Lawgiver. Süleyman giving advice to the Crown Prince, Mehmed Khan. From a contemporaneous Ottoman miniature. *Suleyman I (Kanuni); Shehzade by Talikizade Suphi. Folio 79a of the Talikizade Shehnamesi, Library at the Topkapi Palace Museum, A3592, Photograph courtesy of Talat Halman.*

timar land revenues in lieu of cash wages. The state held all conquered agricultural land as direct property, granting peasants hereditary land use but not ownership. Careful records were kept of the revenue due on all lands, and as long as the state was strong, so was its control over productive land and the cavalry-gentry whom *timar* revenues supported. But even as early as 1400 Ottoman rulers tried to reduce the cavalry-gentry's preeminence by employing specialized infantry troops of well-trained, well-paid slave soldiers (equipped, unlike the cavalry, with firearms) who obeyed the sultan alone.

To sustain the quality of these slave troops, the Ottomans developed a unique institution: the provincial slave levy, or **devshirme**. This institution selected young Christian boys from the provincial (primarily the Balkan) peasantry to be raised as Muslims. They were trained to serve in both army and bureaucracy at all levels, from provincial officer to grand vizier. The most famous slave corps was the *yeni cheri*

Topkapi Palace, Istanbul. Inside the imperial harem, this elegant room was used to entertain the sultan, who watched the proceedings from his large throne.

(young troops), or **Janissaries**, the elite infantry troops of the empire. Muslim boys were not allowed into the slave corps, although some parents tried to buy them a place, since it offered the most promising careers in the empire. Until 1572 marriage was forbidden to slave soldiers, further ensuring loyalty and preventing hereditary claims on office.

After Süleyman: Challenges and Change

The reign of Süleyman marked the peak of Ottoman prestige and power. Further territorial gains were made in the seventeenth century, and the Ottoman state long remained a major force in European and Asian politics, but beginning with the reign of Süleyman's weak son, Selim II (1566–1574), the empire was plagued by military corruption, governmental decentralization, and maritime setbacks. Economically there were agricultural failures, commercial imbalances, and inflation. Yet culturally and intellectually, the seventeenth and eighteenth centuries were periods of impressive activity and accomplishments. Overall, in these

✓●─Study and Review
at **MyHistoryLab.com**

two centuries the state alternated between decline and vitality.

Political and Military Developments The post-Süleyman era began on a sour note with the loss of territory in the Caucasus and Mesopotamia to the Safavids of Iran (1603). By this time the Ottoman military apparatus was already weakened, partly from fighting two-front wars with the Safavids and the Habsburgs and partly by European advances in military and naval technology. The Janissaries became increasingly disruptive. By 1600 they had largely replaced the provincial cavalry as new warfare styles made cavalry obsolete. By 1600 Muslims were allowed into the Janissary corps, marriage was possible, and the *devshirme* was declining in use

(it ended just over a century later). During the seventeenth century, the Janissaries became increasingly corrupt as they tampered with politics, trying to influence decision-making and even dynastic succession. Finally, the increasing employment of mercenaries resulted—during peacetime—in the release of masses of unemployed armed men into the countryside, leading to the sacking of provincial towns, banditry, and revolts, all of which disrupted society.

Murad IV (r. 1623–1640) introduced reforms and ruled with an iron hand, but his death left again a weak central authority. The Köprülüs, father and son, two capable viziers (r.

◉─See the Map
The Decline of the Ottoman Empire
at **MyHistoryLab.com**

1656–1676), briefly renewed strong administrative control and military success, but thereafter the central institutions decayed.

Economic Developments Financing the Ottoman state became ever more difficult. The increase in the Janissary corps from 12,000 to 36,000 men during the sixteenth century drained state coffers. Inflation grew as the coinage was

Devshirme. An Ottoman portrayal of the *devshirme*. This miniature painting (c. 1558) depicts the recruiting of Christian youths for the sultan's elite Janissary corps. The boys, dressed in red, are at the bottom, while their parents, who look pleased, congregate on the right. *Arifi, "Suleymanname," Topkapi Palace Museum, II 1517, fol. 31b, photograph courtesy of Talat Halman.*

debased. In contrast to mercantilist and protectionist policies of European powers, the Ottomans discouraged exports and encouraged imports since too many exports would have raised domestic prices. This damaged the economy in the long run. The population doubled in the sixteenth century, and unemployment grew after 1600. Increased decentralization paved the way for the rise of provincial notables (**ayan**), who became virtually independent in the eighteenth century. Tax farming went hand-in-glove with the rise of large private estates. New taxes were imposed, old emergency levies regularized, and taxes demanded in cash rather than in kind—and increasingly on a communal rather than individual basis.

Culture and Society The seventeenth and eighteenth centuries were an era of genuine vitality in poetry, prose, music, painting, cartography, historiography, astronomy, and other fields. The Ottomans' patronage of the arts and sciences was one way to assert their claim to Islamic and universal authority. The seventeenth century saw especially lively intellectual exchange, both religious and secular. But it was also a time when the *ulama* became an aristocratic, increasingly corrupt elite. Major religious posts became hereditary sinecures for sons and other relatives of a handful of families who had produced prominent *ulama*, and the posts were often sold or leased. (See Document, "The Distinctiveness of Ottoman Identity and Culture" on page 620.)

In literature and the arts, the seventeenth and eighteenth centuries were highly productive. Of many individuals who were learned in many fields, Katib Chelebi (d. 1657) was the most illustrious; he wrote histories, social commentary, geographies, and encyclopedic works. Other important writers were the great historian of the Ottomans, Na'ima (d. 1716), the tireless traveler and travel writer Evliya Chelebi (d. ca. 1685), and probably the greatest Ottoman poet, Nedim (d. 1730). Ottoman art had been highly eclectic in the first century after Mehmed II, but in the later sixteenth century a more conservative turn produced distinctively Ottoman artistic and architectural forms. The greatest name here is that of the imperial master architect Sinan (d. 1578). The first half of the eighteenth century was the golden age of Ottoman poetry and art; it also saw the first Ottoman printing press and the beginning of strong European influence in the arts, architecture, and manners. In the popular sphere, the now classical form of Turkish theater (in which two men play male and female parts) began as early as the sixteenth century, perhaps under Jewish immigrant influence.

Socially, the period saw the consolidation of Ottoman society as a multiethnic, multireligious state. The empire encompassed a dizzying array of languages, religions, and ethnic identities. All subjects, Muslim and non-Muslim,

were organized into smaller communities called **millets** that were responsible for their community members from the cradle to the grave. The millets thus administered their educational, charitable, and judicial affairs and assisted the central government in collecting taxes. Typically the millets were headed by a religious leader and enjoyed some degree of internal autonomy. Thus, early on, the Ottoman Empire became a haven for numerous minority groups, especially Jews. Considerable immigration of Jews into Ottoman societies following their expulsion from Spain during the Spanish Inquisition (1492) had brought new craftsmen, physicians, bankers, scholars, and even entertainers. The large Christian population of the empire was generally well treated, but in the eighteenth and nineteenth centuries they began to suffer from increasing taxes and other discrimination. As a result Ottoman Christians looked as never before to Christian Europe and Russia for liberation.

Chronology

The Ottoman Empire

1301	Foundation of early Ottoman principality in Bursa by Osman
1356	Ottomans cross Dardanelles into Europe
1451–1481	Rule of Sultan Mehmed II, "the Conqueror"
1453	Fall of Constantinople to Mehmed the Conqueror
1512–1520	Rule of Selim I
1517	Ottoman conquest of Egypt, assumption of claim to Abbasid caliphal succession from Mamluks
1520–1566	Rule of Süleyman, "the Lawgiver"
1526–1529	First Ottoman siege of Vienna
1578	Death of Ottoman master architect, Sinan
1656–1676	Governance of Koprülüs as viziers
1683	Second Ottoman siege of Vienna
1699	Treaty of Karlowitz, loss of Hungarian and other European territory
1774	Loss of Crimea to Russia; tsar becomes formal protector of Ottoman Orthodox Christians
1918	End of empire at the end of World War I

Document

The Distinctiveness of Ottoman Identity and Culture

Presiding over a pluralistic culture, the Ottoman Turks, themselves a people from the periphery of the central Islamic lands, developed an "Ottoman" identity and culture that was especially evident in their ruling elite. The following selections from members of that elite describe some of the values and qualities they saw as important to Ottoman identity. In the first, Mustafa Ali (d. 1600), a major historian, intellectual, and state official, lists the special divine favors granted to the Ottoman rulers. In the second, another historian, Kinalizade Ali, uses an ancient political saying attributed to Aristotle and others to describe the prerequisites for an ordered polity under the Shari'a.

■ *Compare the two passages. What common themes emerge?*

1. THE GIFTS OF DIVINE FAVOR GIVEN THE OTTOMAN DYNASTY

The first gift: They reside all by themselves in a palace like unique jewels in the depth of the oyster-shell, and totally sever all relations with relatives and dependents. The slave girls and slave pages that have access to their honored private quarters (harem), who are evidently at least three to four thousand individuals, are all strangers and the person of the monarch is like a single gem in their midst....

The second gift: Their religious convictions being immaculate and their character like a shining mirror, it has never happened that a single member of that noble family ever swerved from the road of orthodoxy or that one valiant sultan befriended himself with an unseemly doctrine.

The third gift: The Lord, the Creator and Protector, has always hidden that great race under His protection and it has never been heard that the plague would have entered their flourishing palace or that an individual belonging to that blemishless progeny would have been struck by the horror of the pestilence and would have died of it.

The fourth gift: Whenever they conquered a province and, destroying and eradicating its castles and estates, were confronted with the necessity of appointing a magistrate and assigning a substantial force on their own authority they considered it a sign of weakness, like Alexander the Great, to appoint again one of the great of that province and to assign him certain revenues; may [that province] be as far away as can be, they would opt to send one of the attendants of their Gate of Happiness [there] as san-jaq begi, and to Yemen and Ethiopia and to very remote places like Algeria a begler-begi. No such absolute power was given to the earlier sovereigns.

The fifth gift: The various special troops in their victory-oriented army and the various tools of war and battle use that are given to them were not available to the brawny fists of anyone of the countless armies [of previous times]. To their attacks going downward and going upward are the same, to their victory-imprinted military music low and high notes are of the same level and equal. In their eyes, as it were, the conquest of a castle is like destroying a spider's web, and in their God-assisted hands to beat the enemies is clearly like pulling out a hair from the beard of a decrepit old man.

The sixth gift: The coherence of the figures in the registers of their revenues and the order of the recordings in the ledgers of their expenses are so strict that they and their salaried classes are free of worries. Consequently, their income exceeds their necessary expenses, their gain is larger than [the expenses for] the important affairs of state.

2. THE NEED OF AUTHORITY TO UPHOLD THE SHARI'A

> There can be no royal authority without the military
> There can be no military without wealth
> The subjects produce the wealth
> Justice preserves the subjects' loyalty to the sovereign
> Justice requires harmony in the world
> The world is a garden, its walls are the state
> The Holy Law [Shari'a] orders the state
> There is no support for the Holy Law except through royal authority.

Source: Selection 1 from Andreas Tietze, *Mustafa Ali's Counsel for Sultans of 1581*, Verlag Der Osterreichischen Akademie Der Wissenshaften, Vienna, 1979, pp. 38–39. Selection 2 from Cornell H. Fleischer, *Bureaucrat and Intellectual in the Ottoman Empire: The Historian Mustafa Ali (1541–1600)*, Princeton, NJ: Princeton University Press, 1986, p. 262.

Still, state policy encouraged just treatment of all subjects; for example, "rescripts of justice" (mostly against the malpractices of tax collectors) were often issued. Although royal decrees reserved special privileges for Muslims, they seldom affected mass behavior. In the eighteenth century, however, relations between Muslims and non-Muslims deteriorated, in part because of the remarkable rise in the socioeconomic status of non-Muslims—in particular the rich mercantile middle class. Non-Muslims virtually monopolized foreign trade, and in this period European countries gave many of them citizenship, which allowed them the trade privileges granted to foreign governments by the sultan.

One of the major social institutions of later Ottoman society, the coffeehouse, flourished from the mid-1500s on. Probably originally a Sufi institution that came with coffee from the Yemen to the Mediterranean, the coffeehouse rapidly became a major shared social space. Here men gathered to drink coffee, play games, watch puppet shows, read books, discuss public affairs, and even engage in political agitation. Despite coffee-drinking bans by the shaykh of Islam because of its stimulant qualities, neither the coffee habit nor coffeehouses, like the new, similarly imported habit of cigarette smoking, could be suppressed. Different types of coffeehouses developed, each identified by its focus: music, theater, recitation, poetry, or Janissary or other professional affiliation (e.g., firefighting). The coffeehouse stimulated the development of a common Ottoman urban culture among lower and middle classes.

●◆●⌐[Read the Document
Portrait of an Ottoman Gentleman
at **MyHistoryLab.com**

The Decline of Ottoman Military and Political Power

After their failure in 1683 to take Vienna, the Ottomans were driven out of Hungary and Belgrade and never again threatened Europe. In 1774 Russia took the Crimea and became the formal protector of Orthodox Christians in the Ottoman Empire (1774). Whereas in the seventeenth century the Empire was a relatively self-contained, self-sufficient empire, by the late 1700s it was increasingly dependent on international market systems, particularly those of western Europe. Previously its economic growth had been based on conquest and control of land as a source of wealth. But as its expansion was stopped, the sultanate was not fully prepared to adjust to changes in an increasingly European-dominated world economy geared toward capitalist accumulation and industrialization. Henceforth, the Ottomans were prey to the West, never regaining their earlier power and influence before their collapse in 1918.

Outflanked by Russia to the north and European sea power south and west, the Ottomans were blocked in the east by their Safavid foes in Iran. They could not sustain sufficiently the external trade needed to support their expensive wars, especially when, in the eighteenth century, Italian, French, British, and Dutch traders obtained special concessions for their trade in the Fertile Crescent, Persian Gulf, and Red Sea regions, which Ottoman merchants did not receive. Ultimately, Ottoman dependence on a decentralized agrarian-age, local-market economy proved insufficient to face the rising commercial and industrial powers of Europe.

A Turkish Coffeehouse. This early nineteenth-century rendering of a coffeehouse in Istanbul reflects the exoticism that Europeans cultivated in their portrayals of things Islamic.

The Safavid Empire and the West Asian World

Origins

As noted in Chapter 12, Iranian history changed after 1500 under the Safavid Dynasty. The Safavids had begun in the fourteenth century as hereditary Turkish spiritual leaders of a Sunni **sufi** order in Azerbaijan, in northwestern Iran. In the 1400s the Safavid order evolved a new, militant Shi'ite sufi ideology. By claiming descent from the imams of Twelver Shi'ism (see Chapter 12), Safavid spiritual masters (*shaykhs* or **pirs**) became the focus of Shi'ite religious allegiance. Many adherents were won to the *tariqa*, or sufi brotherhood, and eventually to Shi'ism from among the Turkoman tribesmen of eastern Anatolia, northern Syria, and northwestern Iran. These mounted warriors were called *Qizilbash* ("Red Heads") after their distinctive crimson uniform hats that signaled allegiance to the twelve Shi'ite imams and their own Safavid sufi master.

The growing strength of the Safavid brotherhood engendered conflicts with the dominant Sunni Turkoman groups around Tabriz. The Safavids emerged victorious in 1501 under the leadership of the young Safavid sufi-master designate Isma'il. Recognized as a divinely appointed representative of the "hidden" imam (see Chapter 10), Isma'il gained sovereignty over the southern Caucasus, Azerbaijan, the Tigris-Euphrates valley, and all of western Iran by 1506 (see Map 20–3). By 1512, unified under a common religious identity and in league with Babur, the Timurid ruler of Kabul, the Safavids took from the Uzbek Turks all of eastern Iran from the Oxus south to the Arabian Sea. Because of the loss of these territories, the largely pastoralist Uzbeks became implacable foes of the Safavids. Throughout the ensuing century the Safavids were often forced to fight a debilitating two-front war against Uzbeks in the east and Ottomans in the west.

See the Map
Atlas Map: Iran Under the Safavids, ca. 1252–1524, at **MyHistoryLab.com**

Strong central rule now united traditional Iranian lands for the first time since the heyday of the Abbasid Caliphate.

Map 20–3. The Safavid Empire. The Safavid Empire had a difficult time maintaining cohesive borders in the face of numerous invasions from both east and west.

In 1514 the better-armed Ottoman army of Selim I soundly defeated the Safavid forces at Chaldiran in Iranian Azerbaijan, initiating an extended series of Ottoman-Safavid border wars over the next two centuries. Chaldiran marked the beginning of Qizilbash disaffection with Shah Isma'il and fueled subsequent efforts to seize power from the Safavids. Furthermore, this defeat brought Ottoman control to the Fertile Crescent, forcing the Safavids to move their capital and their focus eastward to Qazwin and subsequently Isfahan.

Shah Abbas I

Isma'il's successor, Tahmasp I (r. 1524–1576), survived repeated attacks by both Ottomans and Uzbeks, in part through the strength of Shi'ite religious feeling and the allegiance of the Iranian bureaucracy. Twelve years later, however, the most able Safavid ruler, Shah Abbas I (r. 1588–1629) brought real leadership to Safavid Iran. He regained provincial land for the state and used the revenue to support new troops from his Caucasian territories as a counterweight to the unruly Qizilbash. They, like the Ottoman cavalry, were supported by land-revenue assignments. Abbas not only pushed the Ottomans out of Azerbaijan and Iraq but also repelled new Uzbek invasions in Khorasan and sought alliances with the Ottomans' European enemies. This latter tactic, used by several Safavid rulers, reflected one of various military and economic divisions in the often-assumed unity of the Islamic world. Empires, Islamic or not, were essentially divided from each other by self-interested desire for absolute control of their territories and their resources. Abbas also broke the century-long Portuguese monopoly on trade along Persian shores and opened trade relations with the English and Dutch East India commercial companies. His reign brought considerable prosperity to Iran, symbolized by the

Dancing Sufis, their arms raised in ecstasy, congregate at the tomb of the great Persian poet, Sa'di (d. 1292).

magnificent capital he built at Isfahan, which epitomized Safavid grandeur and vision—evidenced most vividly in its regal central square, the Maydan-i Shah.

Read the Document
Fathers Simon and Vincent Report on Shah Abbas I, the Safavid Ruler of Persia
at **MyHistoryLab.com**

It was a regime based on existing Persian bureaucratic institutions, which in turn stemmed from Seljuk institutions. Shah Isma'il ruthlessly enforced Shi'ite conformity, which slowly took root across the realm—perhaps bolstered by a rising Iranian self-consciousness and identity in the face of the Sunni Ottomans, Arabs, Uzbeks, and Mughals who surrounded Iran. In the latter part of his reign, Shah Isma'il began to develop a more centralized bureaucracy at the expense of his sufi enthusiasts. He was determined to rule no longer as leader of a Sufi brotherhood but rather to govern, both culturally and politically, through a reconstruction of the historic Iranian monarchy. Although Isma'il had loyal tribal and religious support internally, he had tenuous ties with his neighbors, especially the Ottoman sultans, who

Read the Document
Shah Isma'il Describes Himself to His Followers
at **MyHistoryLab.com**

vigorously fought the spread of his Sufi-inspired Shi'ite monarchy into eastern Anatolian lands widely populated by other sufi orders.

The enduring element of Safavid consolidation of power was the replacement in Iran of Sunni with Shi'ite Islam as the majority faith. Because Twelver Shi'ism was not widely grounded in Iranian religious tradition, while various sufi traditions were, the Safavids imported religious scholars (*ulama*), primarily from today's Lebanon and Syria, placing them in the service of the state to lend legitimacy

Maydan-i-Shah. The enormous rectangular-shaped plaza at the top of this aerial photo of central Isfahan connects with the equally impressive Masjd-i-Shah Mosque, constructed between 1611 and 1638.

to the government. They discouraged pilgrimage to Mecca and instead emphasized visits to Karbala and the shrine of Husayn, the Prophet Muhammad's grandson. Eventually, however, government–*ulama* relations became strained. By the 1600s, the *ulama* withdrew from political participation, refusing to confer direct legitimacy on the Shah.

Safavid Decline

After Shah Abbas, the empire rarely again enjoyed able leadership. This lack of competent leadership contributed finally to decline and collapse, the chief causes of which were (1) continued two-front pressure from Ottoman and Uzbek forces, (2) economic decline, (3) social unrest among the provincial elites, and (4) the increasing landholding power of the Shi'ite *ulama*. The conservative *ulama* introduced a form of Islamic legalism and emphasized their own authority as interpreters of the law over that of the monarch. They persecuted religious minorities and encouraged anti-Sunni hatred. Some of the Iranian *ulama* and merchant class sought closer ties with European commercial communities. Local administrators were content to maintain the traditional decentralized Safavid system in their own interests, which only increased dependency on the increasingly corrupt Safavid family.

In the end, an Afghan leader captured Isfahan and forced Husayn I (1694–1722) to abdicate. A few Safavid princes managed to retake control of western Iran, but the empire's greatness was gone. A revived, formally Safavid monarchy under the talented Qizilbash tribal leader Nadir Shah (r. 1736–1747) and several successors restored much of Iran's lost territories. However, Nadir Shah's military ventures, which included invading Northwest India and conquering Delhi, sapped the empire's finances. After Nadir's brutal, autocratic reign ended in 1747, Iran's provincial elites, *ulama*, and merchants struggled to regain some political and economic stability over the next sixty years. Only by the early nineteenth century was some success achieved under the Qajar kings (see Chapter 26).

Culture and Learning

In the long run, the most impressive achievement of Safavid times beyond the conversion of Iran to Shi'ite Islam, was the cultural and intellectual renaissance of the sixteenth and seventeenth centuries. The traditions of painting, with their origins in the powerful miniatures of the preceding century—notably those from Herat after 1450, exemplified by the work of the painter Bihzad (1440–1514) in late Timurid times—were cultivated and modified in Safavid times. Portraiture and scenes from everyday life became popular. Among the most developed crafts were those producing ceramic tiles, porcelains, shawls, and carpets. The magnificent city of Isfahan and especially the exquisite gardens and grand arches and domes constructed under Shah Abbas give

Safavid Art. *Woman with a Veil,* by Riza Abbasi, ca. 1595. In Safavid times, artists began to depict everyday life and people, such as this graceful, sinuous young woman.

breathtaking evidence of the developed sense of proportion, color, and design as well as the superb architectural technology and urban planning of Safavid times. So impressive was the scope of Isfahan that it was said to be "half the world," a lofty epithet suggesting it to be the quintessence of Iranian global preeminence. It marks a high point in the sophisticated use of space and lavish deployment of ceramic tiles to decorate the facades and domes of major buildings.

The lasting visible legacies of Safavid rule are its cultural artifacts, buildings, roads, town squares, homes, gardens, and bridges. These were financed and handsomely decorated out of Safavid fortunes from trade in silk, silver, and other long-distance commodities, as was Safavid patronage of literature, theology, philosophy, painting, crafts, and architecture. The Safavid age also saw a distinctively Shi'ite and sufi piety develop to give a firmly Shi'ite character to Iranian culture and traditions. It focused on commemorating the suffering of the imams, life as a struggle for social justice, and loyalty to the Shi'ite *ulama*, who alone provided guidance in the absence of the hidden imam (see Chapter 10).

In intellectual life, the *Ishraqi* or "Illuminationist" school of theological-philosophical thought joined with the mystical, sufi bent of Iranian Islamic thought and the long Islamic traditions of Aristotelianism and Platonism in the form of Shi'ite religious speculation about the nature of divine truth and its accessibility to human reason and imagination. Transcendence and a "realm of images" were key concepts for the illuminationists. They conceived of transcendence in terms of a divine light identified with the Light of Truth, expressed most fully in Muhammad and the Shi'ite imams. The realm of images was a sphere of being in which the attuned spirit could experience true visions. These ideas

Chronology

The Safavid Empire

1334	Death of Safi al-Din, founder of Safavid Sufi order
1501	Rise of Sufi Safavid shahs under Shah Isma'il I
1501–1510	Safavid conquest of greater Iran; Shi'ite state founded
1588–1629	Rule of Shah Abbas I
1722	Afghan invasion and abdication of Sultan Husayn
1722–1737	Rise of pretenders to the Safavid throne under Safavid banner of Tahmasp II and his son, Abbas III
1736–1747	Rule of Sunni Afshar leader, Nadir Shah; revival of Sunni monarchy in Iran
1739	Nadir Shah invades northern India, sacks Delhi

reconceived human experience of the Divine in a way that transcended logic, requiring individual experience. At stake were basic notions of the human psyche and the larger cosmos. The most prominent Iranian exponent of the *Ishraqi* school was Mulla Sadra (d. 1640).

The Mughals

Origins

In the early sixteenth century, invaders from northwest of the Oxus River, following an age-old pattern of Indian history, initiated a new era in the subcontinent. They ended the political fragmentation that by 1500 had reduced the Delhi sultanate to only one among many Indian states. These invaders were Chaghatay Turks descended from Timur (Tamerlane) and known to history as the **Mughals** (a Persianate form of *Mongol*). In 1525–1527 the founder of the Mughal Dynasty, Babur, marched on India, dethroned the last sultan of Delhi, and defeated a Rajput confederacy. Before his death in 1530, he ruled an empire stretching from the Oxus to Bihar, and the Himalayas to the Deccan (see Map 20–4). But the real founder of the Mughal Empire and the greatest Indian ruler since Ashoka (ca. 264-223 B.C.E.) was Akbar "the Great" (r. 1556–1605). Indeed, he was, if not greater, at least as great a ruler as his famous contemporaries, England's Elizabeth I (r. 1558–1603), the Holy Roman Emperor Charles V (r. 1519–1556), Süleyman the Magnificent (r. 1520–1566), and Shah Abbas I (r. 1587–1629).

Hear the Audio at MyHistoryLab.com

Akbar's Reign

Akbar began his reign with impressive military successes. He added North India and the northern Deccan to the Mughal dominions. Even more significant were his governmental reforms, cultural patronage, and religious toleration. He completely reorganized central and provincial government and rationalized the tax system. His marriages with Rajput princesses and his appointment of Hindus to positions of power eased Muslim-Hindu tensions. So did his cancellation of the poll tax on non-Muslims (1564) and his efforts to reduce the power of the more literalist, "hard-line" *ulama*. Under his leadership the Mughal Empire became a truly Indian empire.

Study and Review at MyHistoryLab.com

Akbar was a religious eclectic who showed not only tolerance of all faiths but also unusual interest in different religious traditions. He frequently brought together representatives of many faiths—Jain and Buddhist monks, Brahmans, *ulama*, Parsis (Zoroastrians), and Jesuits—to discuss religion. These de-

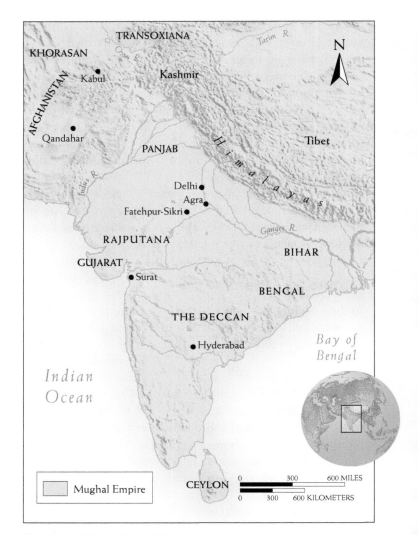

Map 20–4. India under the Mughals.

View the Image Akbar, Emperor of India at MyHistoryLab.com

bates took place in a special hall in Akbar's magnificent palace complex at Fatehpur-Sikri outside the Mughal capital, Agra.

The Last Great Mughals

Akbar's three immediate successors were Jahangir (r. 1605–1627), Shah Jahan (r. 1628–1658), and Awrangzeb (r. 1658–1707). They left behind significant achievements, but the problems of sustaining an Indian empire gradually undercut Mughal strength. The reigns of Jahangir and Shah Jahan were arguably the golden age of Mughal culture, notably in architecture and painting, when a distinctive Mughal style based on traditional Hindi and Persian styles solidified. But the costs of new building, military campaigns, and the erosion of Akbar's administrative and tax reforms brought economic decline. Jahangir set a fateful precedent in permitting English merchants to establish a trading post, or "factory," at Surat on the western coast in Gujarat. Shah Jahan brought the Deccan wholly under Mughal control but lost Qandahar to Safavid forces in 1648. His wars further strained the Mughal economy. No less a burden on the treasury were his elaborate building projects, the most magnificent of which was the white-stoned Taj

See the Map
Mughal Empire
at **MyHistoryLab.com**

Mahal (built in 1632–1653), the unparalleled tomb with its Persian-style dome that he built for his beloved consort, Mumtaz.

With Shah Jahan, internal disorder and instability hastened the decline of Mughal power. Religious toleration retreated; the narrow religious conservatism of his son, Awrangzeb, all but reversed Akbar's earlier policies. He persecuted non-Muslims, destroying Hindu temples, reimposing the poll tax (1679), and alienating the Rajput leaders, whose forebears Akbar had so carefully cultivated. His intransigent policies coincided with and likely contributed to the rise of the Sikh movement's militant reformism throughout the Punjab and Hindu Maratha nationalism in western India.

Sikhs and Marathas

In the late sixteenth and early seventeenth centuries the Sikhs, who trace their origins to the irenic teachings of Guru Nanak (d. 1538), became a distinctive religious movement. Neither Muslim nor Hindu, they had their own scripture, ritual, and

moralistic, reformist ideals. Awrangzeb earned their pitched opposition by persecution culminating in the martyrdom of their ninth leader, or *guru*, Teg Bahadur, in 1675. Thereafter, the tenth and last Sikh guru, Gobind Singh (d. 1708), developed the Sikhs into a formidable military force whose repeated uprisings plagued Awrangzeb and his successors.

The Hindu Marathas, led by the charismatic Shivaji (d. 1680), rose in religious and nationalistic fervor to found their own regional empire around 1646. At Shivaji's death, the Maratha state controlled the mountainous western coast, and its army was the most disciplined force in India. Despite Awrangzeb's subsequent defeat of the Marathas and his conquest of the entire south of India, the Marathas continued to fight. After his death they built a confederation of almost all the Deccan states under their leadership. After about 1740, while

See the Map
The Maratha Kingdoms
at **MyHistoryLab.com**

formally acknowledging Mughal sovereignty, the Marathas actually controlled far more of India than did the Mughals.

Political Decline

In addition to the Rajput, Sikh, and Maratha wars, other factors sealed the fate of the once-great Mughal Empire after Awrangzeb's death in 1707: the rise in the Deccan of the powerful Islamic state of Hyderabad in 1724; the Persian

Fatehpur-Sikri. The Diwan-i-Khas, the reception hall for for important guests in the vast imperial palace complex. *Nickolay Stanev/Shutterstock*

A Closer Look

The Mughal Emperor Jahangir Honoring a Muslim Saint over Kings and Emperors

Bichitr (d. late 1650s), the Mughal miniaturist master who painted from ca. 1620, depicts the Emperor Jahangir (r. 1605-27) seated on an hourglass throne with sands running through it, showing preference to the sufi saint and shaykh of the Chishti sufi order, Husayn, over three temporal rulers: the Ottoman emperor, the king of England, and a Hindu prince. One of the inscriptions reads, "although to all appearances kings stand before him, Jahangir looks inwardly towards the [sufi] dervishes."

Jahangir presents a book to Shaykh Husayn, descendant of the great saint Mu'inuddin Chishti, apparently ignoring the two great temporal rulers (an Ottoman prince and English King James I) ranked beneath Husayn on the left side of the painting (along with the lowest figure, representing the artist himself wearing a red turban). This presumably points to Jahangir's piety and preference of spirituality over temporal power(s).

The portrait of King James I of England was copied by Bichitr from an English portrait by John de Critz (d. 1642) given to Jahangir by Sir Thomas Roe, British ambassador to the Mughal court from 1615 to 1619. The realistic style of the original is faithfully reproduced here to scale.

The naked cupid figures are clearly copied also from a European painting, as are the two clothed cupids writing on the hourglass at the bottom of the throne.

Jahangir is seated on the hourglass throne and hence above time itself, just as his elevated seat puts him high above the earthly potentates depicted and even above Shaykh Husayn. The two clothed cupid figures are inscribing the throne with the wish that Jahangir might live a thousand years. The stool below the throne carries Bichitr's name, on which Jahangir would have to step to mount the throne.

Bichitr, Jahangir Preferring a Sufi Shakikh to Kings, ca. 1660–70, Album Page; Opaque watercolor, gold and ink on paper, 25.3 × 18.1 cm. Courtesy of the Freer Gallery of Art, Smithsonian Institution, Washington, DC.

Questions

1. What allegorical meaning might Jahangir's elevated seat above the hourglass, the royal rulers, and even the Muslim saint suggest here?

2. The radiant sun disk combined with the crescent moon is clearly symbolic or allegorical as well, and one of the inscriptions speaks of Jahangir as "light of the faith." What might Bichitr be saying with these about Jahangir's exalted status?

3. What do the disparate elements of the painting tell us about the relative international awareness of the Indian court in the early 1600s?

invasion of North India by Nadir Shah in 1739; invasions (1748–1761) by the Afghan tribal leader Ahmad Shah Durrani (r. 1747–1773), "founder of modern Afghanistan"; and British victories over Bengali forces at Plassey in Bengal (1757) and over the French on the southeastern coast (1740–1763). By 1819 the dominance of the British East India Company had eclipsed Mughal, as it did Maratha and almost all regional Indian power, even though the Mughal line did not officially end until 1858.

Religious Developments

The period from about 1500 to 1650 was of major importance for Indian religious life. Akbar's eclecticism mirrored the atmosphere of the sixteenth century in India. A number of religious figures preached a spiritually or mystically oriented piety that transcended the legalism of both the *ulama* and the Brahmans and rejected caste distinctions. In these ideas, we can see both Muslim Sufi and Hindu *bhakti* influences at work. We mentioned in Chapter 12 two forerunners of such reformers, Ramananda and Kabir. Guru Nanak, spiritual father of the Sikh movement, took up Kabir's ideas and preached faith and devotion to one loving, merciful God—a message repeated by his successors. (See Document, "Guru Arjun's Faith.") He opposed narrow allegiance to particular creeds and excessive pride in external religious observance. Nanak's hymns of praise contain both Hindu and Muslim ideas and imagery. Dadu (d. 1603) preached a similar message. He was born a Muslim but, like Kabir and Nanak, preached that one must transcend either Muslim or Hindu allegiance in love and service of God.

Read the Document
A Sikh Guru's Testimony of Faith
at **MyHistoryLab.com**

There was also an upsurge of *bhakti* devotionalism that amounted to a Hindu revival. It was epitomized by the Bengali Krishna devotee Chaitanya (d. ca. 1533), who stressed total devotion to Lord Krishna. The forebears of present-day Hare Krishna devotees, his followers spread widely his ecstatic public praise of God and his message that all are equal in God's sight. The other major Hindu devotional figure in this era was Tulasidas (d. 1623), whose Hindi retelling of the Sanskrit *Ramayana* epic remains among the most popular works of Indian literature. Tulasidas used the story of Rama's adventures to present *bhakti* ideas that remain as alive in current everyday Hindu life as do his verses.

Muslim eclectic tendencies came primarily from Sufis. By 1500 many Sufi retreat centers had been established in India. The Sufis' enthusiastic forms of worship and inclina-

Document   Guru Arjun's Faith

These lines are from the pen of the fifth Sikh guru, Arjun (d. 1606). Here he repeats the teaching of Kabir, the fifteenth-century Indian saint whose teachings are included with those of Guru Nanak and other poets in the Sikh holy scripture, the Adi Granth (later, after additions The Guru Granth Sahib). This teaching focuses on the error of clinging to a doctrinaire communalist faith, be it Hindu or Muslim.

■ *Why might syncretic teachings, such as those of the Sikhs, have been appealing in seventeenth-century India?*

I practice not fasting, nor observe the [month of] Ramadan:
I serve Him who will preserve me at the last hour.
The one Lord of the earth is my God,
Who judgeth both Hindus and Muslims.
I go not on a pilgrimage to Mecca, nor worship at Hindu places of Pilgrimage.
I serve the one God and no other.
I neither worship as the Hindus, nor pray as the Muslims.
I take the Formless God into my heart, and there make obeisance unto Him.

I am neither a Hindu nor a Muslim.
The soul and the body belong to God whether He be called Allah or Ram.
Kabir hath delivered this lecture.
When I meet a true guru or pir, I recognize my own Master.

Source: From Max Arthur Macauliffe, *The Sikh Religion*, 6 vols. (Oxford: Clarendon Press, 1909), p. 422.

Chronology

India: The Mughals and Contemporary Indian Powers

1525–1527	Rule of Babur, founder of Indian Timurid state
1538	Death of Guru Nanak, founder of Sikh tradition
1556–1605	Rule of Akbar "the Great"
1605–1627	Rule of Jahangir
1628–1658	Rule of Shah Jahan, builder of the Taj Mahal
1646	Founding of Maratha Empire
1658–1707	Rule of Awrangzeb
1680	Death of Maratha leader, Shivaji
1708	Death of tenth and last Sikh guru, Gobind Singh
1724	Rise of Hyderabad state
1739	Iranian invasion of North India under Nadir Shah
1757	British East India Company victory over Bengali and French forces at Plassey
1857–1858	Indian Uprising and the death of the last Mughal ruler, Bahadur Shah II

tion to play down the externals of religion proved particularly congenial to Indian sensibilities. Such Sufis were, however, often opposed by more puritanical *ulama*, many of whom held powerful positions as royal advisers and judges. To check *ulama* puritan bigotry, Akbar named himself the supreme spiritual authority in the empire, ordering that toleration be the law of the land.

Akbar's death was followed by the inevitable reaction. It was evident in the work of the Indian leader of the Central Asian Sufi order of the Naqshbandiya, Ahmad Sirhindi (d. 1624). He sought to purge Sufism of its extreme tendencies, including popular practices not sanctioned by the schools of law. He especially condemned practices reflecting Hindu influence and rejected toleration of Hindus themselves. Among Akbar's successors, Awrangzeb, as noted earlier, was known for strictures against non-Muslims. While his persecutions are often exaggerated, his narrowness of spirit did finally win out. The possibilities for Hindu-Muslim rapprochement in Akbar's time gradually waned, presaging the communal strife that has marred South Asian history in recent times.

Central Asia: Islamization in the Post-Timur Era

We can trace the solid footing of Islam in Central Asia to the post-Timur era of the fifteenth century. Even in the preceding century, as the peoples of western Central Asia had begun to shift from nomadic to settled existence, the familiar pattern of Islamic diffusion from trading and urban centers to the countryside had set in. Islamization by Sunni and Shi'ite Sufis, traders, and tribal rulers went on apace thereafter, even as far as western China and Mongolia. It was slowed only in the late 1500s by the conversion of the tribes of Mongolia proper to the Buddhism of the Tibetan lamas. Thus, after 1500 the Shi'ite Safavid Empire was bounded by Sunni Islamic states in India, Afghanistan, Anatolia, Mesopotamia, Transoxiana, and western Turkistan (Khwarizm, between the Aral and Caspian seas). In these last two areas, the most important states were ruled by Uzbek and Chaghatay Turks.

Uzbeks and Chaghatays

During the fifteenth century Timur's heirs had ruled Transoxiana and most of Iran (see Chapter 12). North of the Jaxartes River (Syr Darya) and the Aral Sea, a new steppe khanate had been formed by the unification in 1428 of Turkish and Mongol clans known as the Uzbeks. In time, an Uzbek leader descended from Genghis Khan, Muhammad Shaybani (d. 1510), invaded Transoxiana (1495–1500). There he founded a new Uzbek Islamic empire that replaced Timurid rule, which shifted south to Kabul and eventually India under the Mughals. Muhammad's line continued Uzbek rule in Transoxiana at Bukhara into the eighteenth century, while another Uzbek line ruled the independent khanate of Khiva in western Turkestan from 1512 to 1872.

Of the other Central Asian Islamic states after 1500, the most significant was ruled by Chaghatay Turks. The Chaghatays had been the successors of Genghis Khan in the whole region from the Aral Sea and the Oxus River to China (see Map 20–1). After 1350 Timur's invasion broke up their khanate. From about 1514 a revived Chaghatay state flourished in eastern Turkestan—the Tarim basin and the territory north of it, between Tashkent in the west and the Turfan oasis in the east. Although Chaghatay rule lasted until 1678 in part of the Tarim basin, their real power was lost after about 1555 to various Khoja princes—Sunni zealots claiming to be *Sharifs* (descendants of the Prophet).

Consequences of the Shi'ite Rift

On the face of it, the Ottoman, Mughal, Safavid, and Central Asian Islamic states had much in common: Muslim faith and culture, similar systems of taxation and law, the Persian lan-

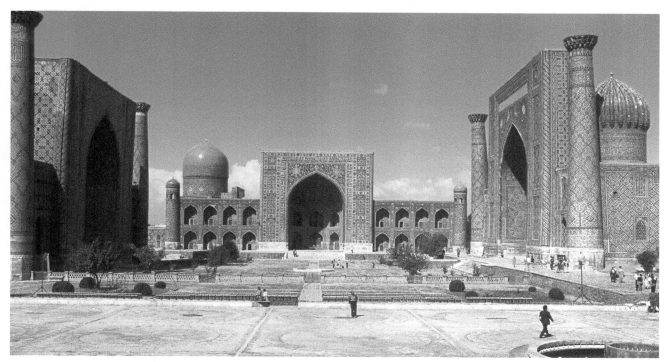

The Great Central Square of the Registan, in Samarkand, with the seventeenth-century Shir Dar Madrasa on the right and the fifteenth-century Ulugh Beg Madrasa on the left. Samarkand and other major Central Asian cities were centers of Islamic culture and learning as well as political power.

guage, and Turkish rulers. Yet the deep religious division between the Shi'ite Safavids and all their Sunni neighbors proved stronger than their common bonds. The result was a serious geographic division that isolated Central Asian Muslims.

Shi'ite-Sunni political competition was sharpened by Safavid militancy, to which the Sunni states responded in kind. Attempts to form alliances with non-Muslim states, previously unheard of in the Islamic world, became a commonplace of Shi'ite political strategy. The Sunnis also resorted to such tactics: The Ottomans, for example, made common cause with Protestants against their common Catholic Habsburg enemies. Although trade continued, the presence of a militant Shi'ite state astride the major overland trade routes of the larger Islamic world hurt the international flow of Islamic commerce.

The Safavid Shi'ite schism also changed the shared cultural traditions of the "Abode of Islam." This change was especially reflected in the fate of Persian literary culture. As a result of its ever stronger association with Shi'ism after the rise of the Safavids, Persian made little further progress as a potential common language alongside Arabic in Sunni lands. Outside Iran it was destined to remain a language of high culture, the court, and bureaucracy, where it (much like French in eighteenth- and nineteenth-century Europe) was the mark of the educated person: Being a master of Persian and Persian classic texts defined to a great extent what it meant to be an Ottoman or Mughal "gentleman." In

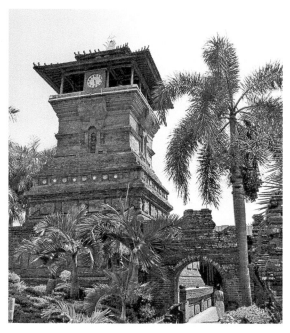

Kudus Mosque. On the island of Java (dates to the first half of the sixteenth century). The mosque combines Hindu, Buddhist, and Islamic architectural elements.

India, Urdu became the common, shared Muslim idiom (see Chapter 12), and in Ottoman and Central Asian lands, various Turkic tongues were spoken in everyday life. Educated Sunnis cultivated Persian letters inspired by the Persian classics but largely ignored Safavid Persian literature.

Central Asia was ultimately the Islamic region most decisively affected by the Shi'ite presence in Iran. Combined with the growing pressure of Christian Russian power, Iran's militant Shi'ism isolated Central Asia from the rest of the Muslim world. Political, economic, cultural, and religious interchange with other Islamic lands became increasingly difficult after 1500. However healthy Islam remained in this region, its contact with the original Islamic heartlands and India shrank. Contact came primarily through a few pilgrims, members of Sufi orders, *ulama*, and students. Central Asian Islam mostly developed in isolation on the periphery of the central Islamic lands.

Power Shifts in the Southern Oceans

Southern-Oceans Trade

Along the southern rim of Asia, from East Africa to Indonesia, the period from 1000 to 1500 witnessed a gradual spread of Islamic religion and culture to new regions and peoples. In ports of Java, Sumatra, the Malay Peninsula, South India, Gujarat, East Africa, Madagascar, and Zanzibar,

Map 20–5. **The Spread of Islam in Southeast Asia, 1300–1900.**

Afro-Indian merchant. This superb painting of an Indian of African origin shows the many connections linking the Indian Ocean world together. The man in this image is a merchant, probably a member of the Janjeera people, originally from Ethiopia. Janjeera merchants immigrated to India in the Middle Ages. Some remained there, and from the fifteenth century they and their descendants obtained positions of power and authority in local governments. The sumptuous dress and dignified bearing of this man suggest wealth and influence.

Islamic traders established thriving communities. Their enclaves often became centers of local life. Initially, the Muslims' economic stature especially attracted the socially mobile groups in these cosmopolitan ports; many also found Muslim ideas and practices compelling. Typically, these first conversions were followed by Islam's transmission to surrounding areas and finally to inland centers. In this, Sufi orders and their preachers and holy men played the main roles. However, conquest by Muslim coastal states accelerated the process in Indonesia and East Africa.

The international trade network Muslims inherited from the Indian Ocean to the South China sea was ancient. Before 1200, much of the trade in these waters had been dominated by Hindu or Buddhist kingdoms of the Malay Peninsula or Sumatra (see Chapter 12). Arab traders had also been active in the Indian Ocean. Hindu culture, along with an Indonesian language, had been carried as far west as Madagascar in the first millennium C.E. Hindus were the chief religious community the Muslims displaced. In the East, Islam never ousted the Indian Buddhist cultures of Burma (Myanmar), Thailand, and Indochina, although Muslim traders thrived in their port cities. Islam did, however, gradually win most of Malaysia, Sumatra, Java, and the "Spice Islands" of the Moluccas—the coastal areas first, then inland regions (see Map 20–5).

Control of the Southern Seas

The Portuguese reached the East African coast in 1498. In the ensuing three centuries, the history of the lands along the sea trade routes of Asia, from East Africa to Indonesia, was intertwined not only with Islamic religious, cultural, and commercial networks, but also with the rising power of Christian western Europe. The key attractions of these diverse lands were their commercial and strategic possibilities (see Map 20–6).

In the sixteenth century the Europeans began to displace by force the Muslims who, by 1500, dominated the maritime southern rim of Asia. European success was based on two key factors: the national support systems that backed their naval and commercial ventures, and their superior warships. This combination enabled the Portuguese to carve out a major power base in the early sixteenth century along the west coast of India at the expense of the Muslims who dominated Indian maritime trade. They did so through superior

naval power and by exploiting indigenous rivalries and terrorizing all who opposed them.

However, in the southern-seas trade centers, Islamization continued, even in the face of Christian proselytizing and growing European political and commercial presence. The Muslims, unlike most of the European Christians, never kept aloof from the native populations and were everywhere largely assimilated. They rarely abandoned their faith, which proved generally attractive to new peoples they encountered. The result was typically an Islamized, racially mixed population.

As a result, while European gunboat imperialism had considerable military and economic success, often at the

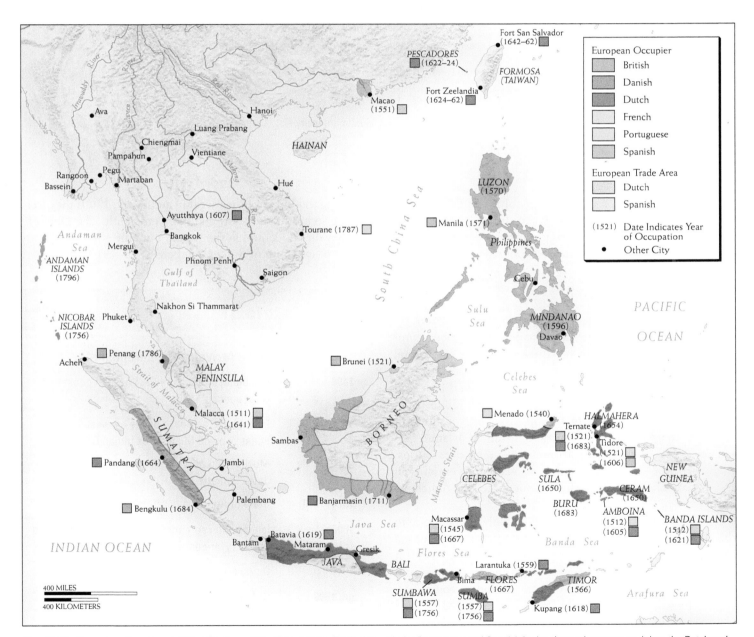

Map 20–6. European Commercial Penetration of Southeast Asia. Beginning with the Portuguese and Spanish in the sixteenth century, and then the Dutch and British in the seventeenth, European powers established commercial bases throughout Southeast Asia, often cooperating with local Islamic, Hindi, or Buddhist rulers.

Overview — The Religions of Southeast Asia

Predominately Buddhist	Burma (Myanmar)
	Thailand, with a significant Muslim minority
	Cambodia
	Laos
	Vietnam, with a large Roman Catholic minority
	Singapore, with Muslim, Christian, and Hindu minorities
Predominately Muslim	Indonesia, with a large Christian minority, and the Hindu island of Bali
	Malaysia, with Hindu, Buddhist, Chineese, and Christian minorities
	Brunei
Predominately Christian	The Philippines, with a sizable Muslim minority
	East Timor

expense of Islamic states, European culture and Christianity made little headway against Islam. From East Africa to the Pacific, only in the northern Philippines and East Timor did a substantial population become largely Christian.

The East Indies: Acheh

The Indonesian archipelago's history has always been heavily influenced by international demand for its spices, peppers, and other produce. By the fifteenth century its coastal Islamic states were centered on the trading ports of the Malay Peninsula, the north shores of Sumatra and Java, and the Moluccas, or "Spice Islands." The last great Hindu kingdom of inland Java was defeated by an Islamic coalition of states in the early 1500s. Several substantial Islamic sultanates arose in the sixteenth and seventeenth centuries, even as Europeans were carving out economic empires in the region. The most powerful Islamic state was Acheh, in northwestern Sumatra (ca. 1524–1910).

In its early years Acheh provided the only counterpoise to the Portuguese presence across the straits in Malacca (Malaysia). Although the Acheh sultans were unable to defeat the better-armed invaders, neither could the Portuguese subdue them. Despite Portuguese control of Indies commerce, Acheh throve and dominated the Sumatran pepper trade until nearly 1600. In the first half of the seventeenth century the sultanate controlled both coasts of Sumatra and parts of the Malay Peninsula. Meanwhile, the Dutch replaced the Portuguese in

milking the Indies of their wealth, and by the 1700s they were doing so just as ruthlessly and more efficiently. The Dutch finally won full control in the region, but only after nearly forty years of intermittent war with Acheh (1873–1910).

Chronology

The Southern Seas: Arrival of the Europeans

1498	Portuguese reach the East African coast and west coast of India
1500–1512	Portuguese establish bases on west Indian coast, replace Muslims as Indian Ocean power
early 1500s	Muslim sultanates replace Hindu states in Java, Sumatra
1524–1910	State of Acheh in northwestern Sumatra
1600s	Islamization spreads widely; connected spread of Malay language in the archipelago
1641	Dutch conquest of Malacca
ca. 1800	Dutch replace Muslim states as main archipelago power
1873–1910	War between Holland and Acheh

Summary

The Last Islamic Empires from the Mediterranean Sea to the Indian Ocean. The period from 1500 to 1800 marks the cultural and political bloom and gradual demise of the last Islamic empires. Islamic social, economic, political, and military vitality in the first half of this period was exemplified in the Ottoman, Safavid, and Mughal empires. All three built vast bureaucracies and arguably the greatest cities in the world at the time. They patronized the arts. Yet they were conservative societies. Economically they remained tied to agricultural production, local trade, and land taxation. They did not undergo the social or religiopolitical revolutions or changes in material and intellectual life that rocked western Europe after 1500. There was no compelling challenge to traditional Islamic ideals, even though numerous eighteenth-century Islamic reform movements did arise.

Decline. By the latter half of this period, these empires were in economic, political, and military decline, even if intellectual and artistic vigor held on.

Thus, it is not surprising that in these three centuries European expansionist intrusion into Africa, the Islamic heartlands, India, and Indonesia largely precipitated the decline of these global regions rather than the reverse. None of the Islamic states fared well in their clashes with Europeans in this age. Their growing domination of the world's seas and continents allowed the Europeans to contain or bypass the major Islamic lands in their quest for gold, silver, spices and plantation cash crops fueling their economic empires.

By the early 1800s industrial development joined economic wealth, social privilege, and political stability to give Europe global military supremacy for the first time. Before 1850, the Europeans were able to bring only minor Islamic states under colonial administration. However, the footholds they gained in Africa, India, and Southeast Asia laid the groundwork for rapid colonial expansion after 1850. The age of the last great Islamic empires was the beginning of the first great modern European empires.

Review Questions

1. Why did the Ottoman Empire expand so rapidly into Europe? Why did it lose some of its European territory?

2. Why were the Safavids successful in Iran? What roles did religion, geographic position, and access to the Indian Ocean have in this development? Who were the Safavids' major foes?

3. What were the most important elements uniting all Islamic states? Why was there still a lack of unity from 1500 to 1850? How and why were European powers able to promote division among Islamic states?

4. What were Akbar's main policies toward Hindus? His main governmental reforms? Why did he succeed and his followers fail in these policies?

5. How and why did the Sikhs develop into a formidable military power? Why did they become separatist in their orientation to the larger Indian world?

6. What were the key concepts in *Ishraqi* or "illuminationist" thinking? Define each.

7. Compare Sunni–Shi'ite differences and similarities (1500–1800) with those of the Protestant–Catholic split in the Christian world during that same period. For example, can we compare relations between England and Spain in the sixteenth century to those between the Ottomans and the Safavids? Explain.

8. Why were outside powers attracted to the southern seas lands? Why were the European powers able to gain control in most of them?

Note: *To learn more about the topics in this chapter, please turn to the Suggested Readings at the end of the book. For additional sources related to this chapter please see MyHistoryLab.com.*

Key Terms

ayan (p. 619)

devshirme (p. 617)

Grand Mufti (p. 617)

harem (p. 616)

Janissaries (p. 618)

millets (p. 619)

Mughals (p. 626)

padishah (p. 615)

pirs (p. 622)

Qanun (p. 617)

Qanun-name (p. 616)

Shari'a (p. 616)

sufi (SOO-fee) (p. 622)

myhistorylab Connections

Reinforce what you learned in this chapter by studying the many documents, images, maps, review tools, and videos available at **www.myhistorylab.com**.

Read and Review

✔●─[Study and Review **Chapter 20**

●●●─[Read the Document *Mehmed II (15th century), p. 614*
Ogier Ghiselin de Busbecq, "Süleyman the Lawgiver", p. 616
Women in Ottoman Society, p. 617
Portrait of an Ottoman Gentleman, p. 621
Shah Isma'il Describes Himself to His Followers, p. 623
Fathers Simon and Vincent Report on Shah Abbas I, the Safavid Ruler of Persia, p. 623
A Sikh Guru's Testimony of Faith, p. 629

👁─[See the Map *The Ottoman Empire to 1566, p. 615*
Atlas Map: Iran Under the Safavids, ca. 1252–1524, p. 622
Mughal Empire, p. 627
The Maratha Kingdoms, p. 627

●─[View the Image *Akbar, Emperor of India, p. 626*

Research and Explore

●─[Watch the Video *Why Does It Matter How We Use The Term "Empire"?*

👁─[See the Map *The Decline of the Ottoman Empire, p. 618*

((●●─[Hear the Audio

Hear the audio file for Chapter 20 at
www.myhistorylab.com.

21 | The Age of European Enlightenment

- The Scientific Revolution
- The Enlightenment
- The Enlightenment and Religion
- The Enlightenment and Society
- Enlightened Absolutism

NO SINGLE INTELLECTUAL FORCE DURING the past three centuries has so transformed every region of the world as has Western science and the technology that has flowed from its understanding of nature. The widespread application of scientific knowledge in everyday life as well as farming and manufacture could make itself felt first in Europe and then elsewhere only as the conviction became prevalent that change and reform were both possible and desirable. This attitude is now commonplace, but it came into its own in Europe only after 1700. The capacity and even eagerness to embrace change, especially change as justified on the grounds of science, represents one of the primary intellectual inheritances from that age. The movement of people and ideas that fostered such thinking is called the *Enlightenment*. Its leading voices combined confidence in the human mind inspired by the Scientific Revolution and faith in the power of rational criticism to challenge the intellectual authority of tradition and revealed religion. Its writers believed that human

Enlightenment Salon. The salon of Madame Marie-Thérse Geoffrin (1699–1777) was one of the most important gathering spots for Enlightenment writers during the middle of the eighteenth century. Well-connected women such as Madame Geoffrin were instrumental in helping the *philosophes* they patronized to bring their ideas to the attention of influential people in French society and politics. *Chäteaux de Malmaison et Bois-Preau, Rueil-Malmaison. Bridgeman-Giraudon/Art Resource, New York.*

The European Enlightenment

Europe

Of all the movements of modern European thought, the most influential are the Scientific Revolution and the Enlightenment. A direct line of intellectual descent exists from those movements to the science and social criticism of the present day. From the eighteenth century to the present, the writers of the Enlightenment provided a pattern for intellectuals who wished to make their societies more rational, scientific, economically productive, reform-minded, and religiously tolerant. The Enlightenment model of society in the West (and via the West in the rest of the world) became synonymous with "modern."

This particular view of modernization tended to make the European and later North American experience come to be regarded as the necessary pattern for all advanced societies.

This outlook originated with the majority of Enlightenment writers themselves. A minority of those writers of the eighteenth century, as do many present-day commentators, questioned whether even a rational, critical, and economically productive Europe should be the pattern for all human societies. Thus the Enlightenment also fostered its own internal self-criticism.

In terms of political thought, the heritage of the Enlightenment was complex with different strands of political thought often in tension or outright conflict with each other. Virtually all Enlightenment writers believed in some form of religious toleration or recognition of religious pluralism. Beyond that viewpoint there was much disagreement. Some Enlightenment thinkers drawing on the English political experience championed constitutionalism and modes of government in which the authority of the central government stand sharply circum-

beings could comprehend the operation of physical nature and mold it to the ends of material and moral improvement. The rationality of the physical universe became a standard against which the customs and traditions of society could be measured and criticized. Such criticism penetrated every corner of contemporary society. As a result, the spirit of innovation and improvement came to characterize modern Western society. This outlook would become perhaps the most important European cultural export to the rest of the world. ■

The Scientific Revolution

The sixteenth and seventeenth centuries witnessed a sweeping change in the scientific view of the universe. From being considered the center of the universe, the earth was now seen as only another planet orbiting about the sun. The sun itself became one of millions of stars. This transformation led to a vast rethinking of moral and religious matters as well as of scientific theory. Science and the scientific method became so impressive and so influential that they set a new standard for evaluating knowledge in the Western world.

The process that established the new view of the universe is normally termed the **Scientific Revolution**. The revolution-in-science metaphor must be used carefully, however. Not everything associated with the "new" science was necessarily new. Sixteenth- and seventeenth-century natural philosophers were often reexamining and rethinking theories and data from the ancient world and the Late Middle Ages. Moreover, the word *revolution* normally denotes rapid, collective political change involving large numbers of people. The Scientific Revolution was *not* rapid. It was a complex movement with many false starts and brilliant people suggesting wrong as well as useful ideas. Nor did it involve more than a few hundred people who labored in widely separated studies and crude laboratories located in Poland, Italy, Bohemia, France, and Great Britain. Furthermore, the achievements of the new science were not simply the function of isolated brilliant scientific minds. The leading figures of the Scientific Revolution often drew upon the aid of artisans and craftspeople to help them construct new instruments for experimentation and to carry out their experiments. Thus, the Scientific Revolution involved a reappropriation of older knowledge as well as new discoveries. In addition, because the practice of science involves social activity as well as knowledge, the revolution also saw the establishment of new social institutions to support the emerging scientific enterprise.

👁 See the Map
Science and the Enlightenment, ca.1450
at **MyHistoryLab.com**

scribed. Montesquieu, for example, influenced the Constitution of the United States and the numerous constitutions that document later influenced. Another strand of Enlightenment political thought, found in Voltaire, contributed to the growth of strong monarchical governments, associated with enlightened absolutism. Such writers believed that a monarch and a strong central bureaucracy could formulate and impose rational solutions to political and social problems and hence overcome competing social and political interests. Still another variety of Enlightenment political thought, arising from Rousseau, led to the socialist concern with inequality of wealth and a desire for radical democratic government. Because of the complexity of Enlightenment political thought, modern governments displaying liberalism, socialism, and bureaucratic centralism may find roots in eighteenth-century thinkers.

Present-day political movements that find themselves essentially at odds with the Enlightenment heritage are those attached to radical Islamic groups who define themselves in opposition to most Western values. Those values tend to be derived from the Enlightenment. Most particularly these groups oppose the religious pluralism, cultural relativism, and expansion of traditional social roles for women that have flowed over time from the expansion of Enlightenment values.

As we observed in Chapter 17, the seventeenth and eighteenth centuries, whose ideas fostered the Enlightenment, also saw the rise of European colonial empires and the establishment of plantation economies based on slavery. Europeans' treatment of non-Europeans, as well as their warfare against each other in this era, often belied the principles of the Enlightenment. Certain Enlightenment writers—a minority—sharply criticized those empires. In this respect, contemporary critics of Western influence throughout the world can find roots in this eighteenth-century critique of empire.

Focus Questions

- How did Enlightenment values as well as Enlightenment admiration of science become one of the chief defining qualities of societies regarded as advanced, progressive, and modern?
- How has the political thought of the Enlightenment influenced the development of modern political philosophies and modern governments?
- How could modes of thought developed to criticize various aspects of eighteenth-century European society be transferred to other traditions of world civilizations?

Nicolaus Copernicus Rejects an Earth-Centered Universe

Nicolaus Copernicus (1473–1543) was a Polish astronomer who enjoyed a high reputation during his lifetime. He had been educated first in Cracow and later in Italy, and he had not been known for strikingly original or unorthodox thought. In 1543, the year of his death, Copernicus published *On the Revolutions of the Heavenly Spheres*. Copernicus's book was "a revolution-making rather than a revolutionary text."[1]

What Copernicus did was to provide an intellectual springboard for a complete criticism of the then-dominant view of the position of the earth in the universe.

Read the Document

Nicolaus Copernicus: On the Revolution of the Heavenly Spheres (1500s) at **MyHistoryLab.com**

The Ptolemaic System At the time of Copernicus, the standard explanation of the place of the Earth in the heavens was the **Ptolemaic system**. It combined the mathematical astronomy of Ptolemy, contained in his work entitled the *Almagest* (150 C.E.), with the physical cosmology of Aristotle. Over the centuries, commentators on Ptolemy's work had developed several alternative Ptolemaic systems,

on the basis of which they made mathematical calculations relating to astronomy. Most of these writers assumed that the earth was the center of the universe, an outlook known as *geocentricism*. Drawing upon Aristotle, these commentators assumed that above the earth lay a series of concentric spheres, probably fluid in character, one of which contained the moon, another the sun, and still others the planets and the stars. At the outer regions of these spheres lay the realm of God and the angels. The earth had to be the center because of its heaviness. The stars and the other heavenly bodies had to be enclosed in the spheres so that they could move, since nothing could move unless something was actually moving it. The state of rest was presumed natural; motion required explanation. This was the astronomy found in such works as Dante's *Divine Comedy*.

Numerous problems were associated with the Ptolemaic model, and these had long been recognized. The most important was the observed motions of the planets. At certain times the planets actually appeared to be going backwards. The Ptolemaic model accounted for these motions primarily through *epicycles*. The planet moved uniformly about a small circle (an epicycle), while the center of the epicyle moved uniformly about a larger circle (called a deferent), with the earth at or near its center. The combination of these two motions, as viewed from the earth, was meant to replicate the changing planetary positions among the

---

[1]Thomas S. Kuhn, *The Copernican Revolution: Planetary Astronomy in the Development of Western Thought* (New York: Vintage, 1959), p. 135.

fixed stars—and did so to a high degree of accuracy. The circles employed in Ptolemaic systems were not meant to represent the actual paths of anything; that is, they were not orbits. Rather, they were the components of purely mathematical models meant to predict planetary positions. Other intellectual, but nonobservational, difficulties related to the immense speed at which the spheres had to move around the Earth. To say the least, the Ptolemaic systems were cluttered. They were effective, however, as long as one assumed Aristotelian physics.

Copernicus's Universe

Copernicus's *On the Revolutions of the Heavenly Spheres* adopted many elements of the Ptolemaic model but transferred them to a *heliocentric* (sun-centered) model, which assumed that the Earth moved about the sun in a circle. Copernicus's model, which retained epicyles, was actually no more accurate than Ptolemy's. However, Copernicus could claim certain advantages over the ancient model. In particular, the epicyles were smaller. The retrograde motion of the planets now stood explained as a result of an optical illusion arising from an observer viewing the planets from a moving earth. The order of the planets from the sun became more clearly intelligible when it was understood as being a result of their increasing periods of revolution based on the planets' increasing distance from the sun.

The repositioning of the earth had not been Copernicus's goal. Rather, Copernicus appears to have set out to achieve new intelligibility and mathematical elegance for astronomy. The means of doing so was to reject Aristotle's cosmology and to remove the earth from the center of the universe. His system was no more accurate than the existing ones for predicting the location of the planets, as he had used no new evidence. The major impact of his work was to provide another way of confronting some of the difficulties inherent in Ptolemaic astronomy. The Copernican system did not immediately replace the old astronomy, but it allowed other people who were also discontented with the Ptolemaic view to think in new directions. Indeed, for at least a century, the Copernican system was embraced by a distinct minority of natural philosophers and astronomers.

((•—[Hear the Audio at **MyHistoryLab.com**

The Ptolemaic System. The "Emperor's Astronomy" (dedicated to the Holy Roman Emperor Charles V) elegantly depicts the cosmos and heavens according to the 1,400-year-old Ptolemaic system, which maintained that the sun revolved around the earth. By means of hand-colored maps, Petrus Apianus (1495–1552) laid out the mechanics of a universe that was earth- and human-centered. Within three years of Apianus's book, this view was challenged by Copernicus's assertion that the earth revolved around the sun.

Tycho Brahe and Johannes Kepler

The next major step toward the conception of a sun-centered system was taken by the Danish astronomer Tycho Brahe (1546–1601). He spent most of his life opposing Copernicus and advocating a different kind of earth-centered system. He suggested that the moon and the sun revolved around the earth and that the other planets revolved around the sun. However, in attacking Copernicus, he gave Copernicus's ideas more publicity. More important, his major weapon against Copernican astronomy was a series of new astronomical observations made with the naked eye. Brahe constructed the most accurate tables of observations that had been drawn up for centuries.

When Brahe died, these tables came into the possession of Johannes Kepler (1571–1630), a German astronomer. Kepler was a convinced Copernican, but for philosophical, not scientific, reasons. Kepler was deeply influenced by Renaissance Neo-Platonists who, following upon Plato's (ca. 428–ca. 328 B.C.E.) association of knowledge with light, honored the sun. These Neo-Platonists were also determined to discover mathematical harmonies that would support a sun-centered universe. After much work, Kepler discovered that to keep the sun at the center of things, he must abandon the Copernican concept of circular orbits. The mathematical relationships that emerged from a consideration of Brahe's observations suggested that the orbits of the planets were elliptical. Kepler published his findings in 1609 in a book entitled *On the Motion of Mars*. He had solved the problems of planetary orbits by using Copernicus's sun-centered universe and Brahe's empirical data.

Kepler had, however, also defined a new problem. None of the available theories could explain why the planetary orbits were elliptical. That solution awaited the work of Sir Isaac Newton.

Tycho Brahe in the Uranienburg observatory on the Danish island of Hven (1587). Brahe made the most important observations of the stars since antiquity. Kepler used his data to solve the problem of planetary motion in a way that supported Copernicus's sun-centered view of the universe. Ironically, Brahe himself had opposed Copernicus's view.

Galileo Galilei

From Copernicus to Brahe to Kepler, there had been little new information about the heavens that might not have been known to Ptolemy. However, in 1609 an Italian scientist named Galileo Galilei (1564–1642) first turned a telescope on the heavens. He saw stars where none had been known to exist, mountains on the moon, spots moving across the sun, and moons orbiting Jupiter. The heavens were far more complex than anyone had formerly suspected. None of these discoveries proved that the earth orbited the sun, but they did suggest the complete inadequacy of the Ptolemaic system. It simply could not accommodate these new phenomena. Some of Galileo's colleagues at the University of Padua were so unnerved that they refused to look through the telescope, because it revealed the heavens to be different from the teachings of the church and from Ptolemaic theories. (See Document, "Galileo Discusses the Relationship of Science to the Bible.")

Galileo publicized his findings and arguments for the Copernican system in numerous works, the most famous of which was his *Dialogues on the Two Chief Systems of the World* (1632). This book brought down on him the condemnation of the Roman Catholic Church. He was compelled to recant his opinions. However, he is reputed to have muttered after the recantation, "*E pur si muove*" ("It [the earth] still moves").

Galileo's most important achievement was to articulate the concept of a universe totally subject to mathematical laws. More than any other writer of the century, he argued that nature in its most minute details displayed mathematical regularity. Copernicus had thought that the heavens conformed to mathematical regularity; Galileo saw this regularity throughout all physical nature. He believed that the smallest atom behaved with the same mathematical precision as the largest heavenly sphere.

Galileo stood as one of the foremost champions of the application of mathematics to scientific investigation and of the goal of reducing phenomena to mathematical formulas. However, earlier in the century the English philosopher Francis Bacon had advocated a method based solely on empiricism. As the century passed, both empirical induction and mathematical analysis proved fundamental to scientific investigation.

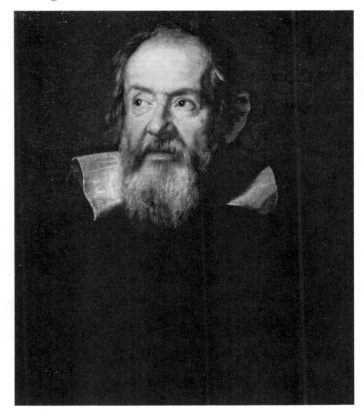

Portrait of Galileo Galilei (1636) by the Flemish Baroque painter Justus Sustermans.

Document

Galileo Discusses the Relationship of Science to the Bible

Both Protestant and Roman Catholic religious authorities were often critical of the discoveries and theories of sixteenth- and seventeenth-century science because of tensions with the literal reading of the Bible. For years before his condemnation by the Roman Catholic Church in 1633, Galileo had contended that scientific theory and religious piety were compatible. In his *Letter to the Grand Duchess Christiana* (of Tuscany), written in 1615, he argued that God had revealed truth in both the Bible and physical nature and that the truth of physical nature did not contradict the Bible if the Bible were properly understood. Galileo encountered difficulties regarding this letter because it represented a layman telling Roman Catholic Church authorities how to read the Bible.

■ *Why does Galileo see a difference between the text of scripture and the knowledge of nature achieved through the senses? To which does he seem to give priority? Why might church authorities have difficulty with his arguments? Why might some Roman Catholic authorities think he was behaving as a Protestant might?*

The reason produced for condemning the opinion that the Earth moves and the sun stands still is that in many places in the Bible one may read that the sun moves and the Earth stands still. . . .

With regard to this argument, I think in the first place that it is very pious to say and prudent to affirm that the holy Bible can never speak untruth—whenever its true meaning is understood. But I believe nobody will deny that it is often very abstruse, and may say things which are quite different from what its bare words signify. . . .

This being granted, I think that in discussions of physical problems we ought to begin not from the authority of scriptural passages, but from sense-experiences and necessary demonstrations; for the holy Bible and the phenomena of nature proceed alike from the divine Word, the former as the dictate of the Holy Ghost and the latter as the observant executrix of God's commands. It is necessary for the Bible, in order to be accommodated to the understanding of every man, to speak many things which appear to differ from the absolute truth so far as the bare meaning of the words is concerned. But Nature, on the other hand, is inexorable and immutable; she never transgresses the laws imposed upon her, or cares a whit whether her abstruse reasons and methods of operation are understandable to men. For that reason it appears that nothing physical which sense-experience sets before our eyes, or which necessary demonstrations

prove to us, ought to be called in question (much less condemned) upon the testimony of biblical passages which may have some different meaning beneath their words. For the Bible is not chained in every expression to conditions as strict as those which govern all physical effects; nor is God any less excellently revealed in Nature's actions than in the sacred statements of the Bible. . . .

From this I do not mean to infer that we need not have an extraordinary esteem for the passages of holy Scripture. On the contrary, having arrived at any certainties in physics, we ought to utilize these as the most appropriate aids in the true exposition of the Bible and in the investigation of those meanings which are necessarily contained therein for these must be concordant with demonstrated truths. I should judge the authority of the Bible was designed to persuade men of those articles and propositions which, surpassing all human reasoning, could not be made credible by science, or by any other means than through the very mouth of the Holy Spirit. . . .

But I do not feel obliged to believe that the same God who has endowed us with senses, reason, and intellect has intended to forgo their use and by some other means to give us knowledge which we can attain by them.

Source: From *Discoveries and Opinions of Galileo,* by Galileo Galilei. Copyright © 1957 by Stillman Drake. Used by permission of Doubleday, a division of Random House, Inc.

Francis Bacon: The Empirical Method

Bacon (1561–1626) was an Englishman of almost universal accomplishment. He was a lawyer, a high royal official, and the author of histories, moral essays, and philosophical discourses. Traditionally, he has been regarded as the father of **empiricism** and of experimentation in science. Much of this reputation was actually unearned. Bacon was not a natural philosopher, except in the most amateur fashion. His real accomplishment was setting an intellectual tone and helping to create a climate conducive to scientific work.

In books such as *The Advancement of Learning* (1605), the *Novum Organum* (1620), and the *New Atlantis* (1627), Bacon attacked the scholastic belief that most truth had already been discovered and only required

••▶ Read the Document
Francis Bacon, from Novum
Organum at **MyHistoryLab.com**

explanation, as well as the scholastic reverence for authority in intellectual life.

He believed that scholastic thinkers paid too much attention to tradition and to the knowledge of the ancients. Bacon believed that human knowledge should produce useful results—deeds rather than words. In particular, knowledge of nature should be brought to the aid of the human condition. These goals required the modification or abandonment of scholastic modes of learning and thinking. Bacon contended, "The [scholastic] logic now in use serves more to fix and give stability to the errors which have their foundation in commonly received notions than to help the search after truth."[2] Scholastic philosophers could not escape from their syllogisms to examine the foundations of their thought and intellectual presuppositions. Bacon urged that philosophers and investigators of nature examine the evidence of their senses before constructing logical speculations. In a famous passage, he divided all philosophers into "men of experiment and men of dogmas" and then observed:

> *The men of experiment are like the ant, they only collect and use; the reasoners resemble spiders, who make cobwebs out of their own substance. But the bee takes a middle course: it gathers its material from the flowers of the garden and of the field, but transforms and digests it by a power of its own. Not unlike this is the true business of philosophy.*[3]

By directing natural philosophy toward an examination of empirical evidence, Bacon hoped that it would achieve new knowledge and thus new capabilities for humankind.

Most of the people in Bacon's day, including the intellectuals, thought that the best era of human history lay in antiquity. Bacon dissented vigorously from that view. He wanted seventeenth-century Europeans to have confidence in themselves and their own abilities rather than in the people and methods of the past. Bacon was one of the first major European writers to champion the desirability of innovation and change. He looked to a future of material improvement achieved through the empirical examination of nature. His own theory of induction from empirical evidence was unsystematic, but his insistence on appealing to experience influenced others whose methods were more productive. He and others of his outlook received almost daily support from the reports not only of European explorers, but also of ordinary

seamen who now sailed all over the world and could describe wondrous cultures, as well as plants and animals, unknown to the European ancients.

Bacon believed that science had a practical purpose and its goal was human improvement. Bacon in this manner linked science and material progress in the public mind. This was a powerful idea and has continued to influence Western civilization to the present day. It has made science and those who can appeal to the authority of science major forces for change and technological innovation. Thus, though not making any major scientific contribution himself, Bacon directed investigators of nature to a new method and a new purpose. As a person actively associated with politics, Bacon also believed that the pursuit of new knowledge would increase the power of governments and monarchies. Again, his thought in this area opened the way for the eventual strong linkage between governments, the scientific enterprise, and sponsorship of technological advancement.

Isaac Newton Discovers the Laws of Gravitation

The question that continued to perplex seventeenth-century scientists who accepted the theories of Copernicus, Kepler, and Galileo was how the planets and other heavenly bodies

Newton's Telescope. Behind it is a copy of *Principia Mathematica,* his most famous work.

[2]Quoted in Franklin Baumer, *Main Currents of Western Thought,* 4th ed. (New Haven, CT: Yale University Press, 1978), p. 281.

[3]Quoted in Baumer, *Main Currents,* p. 288.

moved in an orderly fashion. Many unsatisfactory theories had been set forth to deal with the question. It was this issue of planetary motion that the Englishman Isaac Newton (1642–1727) addressed and, in so doing, established a basis for physics that endured for more than two centuries.

In 1687 Newton published *The Mathematical Principles of Natural Philosophy*, better known by its Latin title of *Principia Mathematica*. Much of the research and thinking for this great work had taken place more than fifteen years earlier. Galileo's mathematical bias permeated Newton's thought, as did his view that inertia applied to bodies both at rest and in motion. Newton reasoned that the planets and all other physical objects in the universe moved through mutual attraction, or gravity. Every object in the universe affected every other object through gravity. The attraction of gravity explained why the planets moved in an orderly, rather than a chaotic, manner. Newton had found that "the force of gravity towards the whole planet did arise from and was compounded of the forces of gravity towards all its parts, and towards every one part was in the inverse proportion of the squares of the distances from the part."[4] Newton proved this relationship mathematically; he made no attempt to explain the nature of gravity itself.

Newton was a great mathematical genius, but he also upheld the importance of empirical data and observation. Like Francis Bacon, he believed that one must observe phenomena before attempting to explain them. The final test of any theory or hypothesis for him was whether it described what was actually observed. Consequently, as Newton's own theory of universal gravitation became increasingly accepted, so, too, was Baconian empiricism.

●●►┐**Read the Document**
Isaac Newton, from Opticks
at **MyHistoryLab.com**

Women and Learning. René Descartes, the French philosopher, is on the right, tutoring Queen Christina (1626–1689) of Sweden, seated on the left.
Pierre-Louis the Younger Dumesnil (1698–1781), "Christina of Sweden (1626–89) and her Court: detail of the Queen and Rene Descartes (1596–1650) at the Table." Oil on canvas. Chateau de Versailles, France/Bridgeman Art Library.

Women in the World of the Scientific Revolution

The same factors that had long excluded women from participating in most European intellectual life continued to exclude them from working in the emerging natural philosophy. Traditionally, the institutions of European intellectual life had all but excluded women. Both monasteries and universities had been institutions associated with celibate male clerical culture. Except for a few exceptions in Italy, women had not been admitted to either medieval or early modern European universities; they would continue to be excluded from them until the end of the nineteenth century. Women could and did exercise much influence over princely courts where natural philosophers, such as Galileo, sought patronage, but they usually did not determine those patronage decisions or benefit

●●►┐**Read the Document**
Galileo Galilei, Letter to the Grand Duchess Christina (1630s)
at **MyHistoryLab.com**

from them. Queen Christina of Sweden was an exception by engaging René Descartes, the major French philosopher of science, to provide the regulations for a new science academy. When various scientific societies were founded, women were not admitted to membership.

Yet a few isolated women from two very different social settings did manage to engage in the new scientific activity—noblewomen and women from the artisan class. In both cases, they could do so only through their husbands or other men in their families.

The social standing of certain noblewomen allowed them to command the attention of ambitious natural philosophers who were part of their husband's social circle. Margaret Cavendish (1623–1673) actually made significant contributions to the scientific literature of the day. After she

---

[4]Quoted in A. Rupert Hall, *From Galileo to Newton, 1630–1720* (London: Fontana, 1970), p. 300.

had been privately tutored and become widely read, her marriage to the duke of Newcastle introduced her into a circle of natural philosophers. Her most important works were *Observations upon Experimental Philosophy* (1666) and *Grounds of Natural Philosophy* (1668). She was the only woman in the seventeenth century to be allowed to visit a meeting of the Royal Society of London.

Women associated with artisan crafts actually achieved greater freedom in pursuing the new sciences than did noblewomen. Traditionally, women had worked in artisan workshops, often with their husbands; and might take over the business when their spouse died. In Germany, much astronomy occurred in these settings, with women assisting their fathers or husbands. One such German female astronomer, Maria Cunitz, published a book on astronomy that many people thought her husband had written until he added a preface supporting her sole authorship. Elisabetha and Johannes Hevelius constituted a wife-and-husband astronomical team, as did Maria Winkelmann and her husband Gottfried Kirch. In each case, the wife served as the assistant to an artisan astronomer. Although Winkelmann discovered a comet in 1702, not until 1930 was the discovery ascribed to her rather than to her husband. Nonetheless, contemporary philosophers did recognize her abilities and understanding of astronomy. Winkelmann had worked jointly with her husband who was the official astronomer of the Berlin Academy of Sciences and was responsible for establishing an official calendar published by the Academy. When her husband died in 1710, Winkelmann applied for permission to continue the work, basing her application for the post on the guild's tradition of allowing women to continue their husband's work—in this case the completion of observations required for creating an accurate calendar. After much debate, the Academy formally rejected her application on the grounds of her gender, although its members knew of her ability and previous accomplishments. Years later, she returned to the Berlin Academy as an assistant to her son, who had been appointed astronomer. Again, the Academy insisted that she leave, forcing her to abandon astronomy. She died in 1720.

Such policies of exclusion, however, did not altogether prevent women from acquiring knowledge about the scientific endeav-ors of the age. Margaret Cavendish had composed a *Description of a New World, Called the Blazing World* (1666) to introduce women to the new science. Other examples of scientific writings for a female audience were Bernard de Fontenelle's *Conversations on the Plurality of Worlds* and Francesco Algarotti's *Newtonianism for Ladies* (1737). During the 1730s, Emilie du Châtelet aided Voltaire in his composition of an important French popularization of Newton's science. Her knowledge of mathematics was more extensive than his and crucial to his completing his book.

Still, with only a few exceptions, women were barred from science and medicine until the late nineteenth century, and not until the twentieth century did they enter these fields in any significant numbers. Not only did the institutions of science exclude them, but also the ideas associated with medical practice, philosophy, and biology suggested that women and their minds were essentially different from, and inferior to, those of men. By the early eighteenth century, despite isolated precedents of women pursuing natural knowledge, reading scientific literature, and engaging socially with natural philosophers, it had become a fundamental assumption of European intellectual life that the pursuit of natural knowledge was a male vocation.

John Locke

John Locke (1632–1704) attempted to achieve for philosophy a lawful picture of the human mind similar to that which Newton had presented of nature. Locke's three most famous works were *An Essay Concerning Human Understanding* (1690), *Two Treatises of Government*, and his *Letter Concerning Toleration* (1689). Each of them sounded philosophical themes that later writers of the Enlightenment found welcome. No other philosopher had so profound an impact on European and American thought during the eighteenth century.

In *An Essay Concerning Human Understanding*, Locke envisioned the human mind as being blank, or what he termed using Latin as a *tabula rasa*, at the

John Locke (1632–1704), defender of the rights of the people against rulers who think their power is absolute. *By courtesy of the National Portrait Gallery, London.*

Overview · Major Figures in the Scientific Revolution

Nicolaus Copernicus (1473–1543)	On the basis of mathematical analysis argued that the earth moved around the sun.
Tycho Brahe (1546–1601)	Compiled accurate tables of astronomical observations.
Johannes Kepler (1571–1601)	Used Brahe's data to argue that the orbits of the planets were elliptical.
Galileo Galilei (1564–1642)	First astronomer to use a telescope. Argued that mathematical laws governed the universe.
Francis Bacon (1561–1626)	Maintained that scientific thought must conform to empirical evidence. Championed innovation and change.
Isaac Newton (1642–1727)	Described the effect of gravity mathematically and established a theoretical basis for physics that endured until the late nineteenth century.
John Locke (1632–1704)	Argued that the human mind is a blank slate that may be molded by modifying the environment. Human beings could thus take charge of their own destiny without divine aid.

time of an individual's birth. In Locke's view, contrary to that of much medieval philosophy, there are no innate ideas (i.e., ideas people are born with); all knowledge is derived from actual sense experience. Each individual mind grows through experience as it confronts the world of sensation. Human ideas are either simple (that is, passive receptions from daily experience) or complex (that is, products of sustained mental exercise). What people know is not the external world in itself, but the results of the interaction of their minds with the outside world. Locke's thinking thus represented an early form of behaviorism. Human nature is changeable and can be molded by modifying the surrounding physical and social environment. Locke also, in effect, rejected the Christian view that human beings were creatures permanently flawed by original sin. Human beings, he proposed, do not need to wait for the grace of God or other divine aid to better their lives. They can take charge of their own destiny.

Read the Document

John Locke, Essay Concerning Human Understanding
at **MyHistoryLab.com**

Locke wrote *Two Treatises of Government* during the reign of Charles II (r. 1660–1685). Locke argued that rulers are not absolute in their power. They remain bound by the law of nature. That law is the voice of reason, teaching that human beings are equal and independent and that they should not harm one another or disturb one another's property because all persons are the images and property of God. According to Locke, people enter political contracts, empowering legislatures and monarchs to judge their disputes in order to preserve their natural rights (which include the possession of property) but not to give rulers an absolute power over them. Locke also contended that a monarch who violated the trust that had

been placed in him could be overthrown. This argument reappeared in the American Declaration of Independence in 1776. But in eighteenth-century Europe it was Locke's argument against absolutism and in favor of limited government that was most influential.

Locke's *Letter Concerning Toleration* contended that each person was responsible for his own religious salvation. Governments existed to protect property and the civil order. Matters only became confused when governments undertook to legislate on religion and require conformity to a single church. Yet Locke himself drew the line in England against toleration of Roman Catholics and Unitarians. During the eighteenth century, however, the logic of his argument was extended to advocate toleration for those faiths as well.

Hear the Audio
at **MyHistoryLab.com**

The Enlightenment

The eighteenth-century movement that came to be known as the **Enlightenment** included a number of writers living at different times in various countries. Its early exponents, known as the ***philosophes***, popularized the rationalism and scientific ideas of the seventeenth century. They worked to expose contemporary social and political abuses and argued that reform was necessary and possible.

Hear the Audio
at **MyHistoryLab.com**

Many of them also championed the advancement of economic growth and technological innovation. The advancement of their causes and ideas was anything but steady. They confronted vested interests, political oppres-

● See the Map
Science and the
Enlightenment, ca.1450
at **MyHistoryLab.com**

sion, and religious condemnation. Yet by midcentury they had brought enlightened ideas to the European public in a variety of formats.

Voltaire

One of the earliest and by far the most influential of the *philosophes* was François Marie Arouet, known to posterity as Voltaire (1694–1778). During the 1720s Voltaire had offended the French authorities by certain of his writings. He was arrested and briefly imprisoned. Later he went to England, visiting its best literary circles, observing its tolerant intellectual and religious climate, relishing the freedom he felt in its moderate political atmosphere, and admiring its science and economic prosperity. In 1733 he published *Letters on the English*, which appeared in French the next year. The book praised the virtues of the English and indirectly criticized the abuses of French society. In 1738 he published *Elements of the Philosophy of Newton*, which popularized the thought of the great scientist. Both works enhanced his reputation.

●●● Read the Document
Voltaire, Letters On England
at **MyHistoryLab.com**

Thereafter, Voltaire lived part of the time in France and part near Geneva, just across the French border, where the royal authorities could not bother him. His essays, history, plays, stories, and letters made him the literary dictator of Europe. He turned the bitter venom of his satire and sarcasm against one evil after another in French and European life. His most famous satire is *Candide* (1759), in which he attacked war, religious persecution, and what he regarded as unwarranted optimism about the human condition. Like most *philosophes*, Voltaire believed that human society could and should be improved. But he was never certain that reform, if achieved, would be permanent. It is important to recognize that the optimism often associated with the Enlightenment constituted a tempered hopefulness rather than a glib certainty. Pessimism was an undercurrent in most of the works of the period.

The *Encyclopedia*

The midcentury witnessed the publication of the *Encyclopedia*, one of the greatest monuments of the Enlightenment. Under the heroic leadership of Denis Diderot (1713–1784) and Jean le Rond d'Alem-

Voltaire. Philosopher, dramatist, poet, historian, and popularizer of scientific ideas, Voltaire (1694–1778) was the most famous and influential of the eighteenth-century philosophers. His sharp satire and criticism of religious institutions opened the way for a more general critique of the European political and social status quo.

bert (1717–1783), the first volume appeared in 1751. When completed in 1772, it numbered seventeen volumes of text and eleven of plates. The *Encyclopedia* was the product of the collective effort of more than one hundred authors, and its editors had solicited articles from all the major French *philosophes*. The project reached fruition only after numerous attempts to censor it and to halt its

Denis Diderot was the heroic editor of the *Encyclopedia*, which was published in seventeen volumes of text and eleven volumes of prints between 1751 and 1772. Through its pages many of the chief ideas of the Enlightenment reached a broad audience of readers. *Jean-Simon Berthelemy (1743–1811), "Denis Diderot" (1713–1784). Writer and Encyelopaedist. Oil on canvas, 55 x 46 cm. Inv.: P 2082. Photo: Bulloz. Musee de la Ville de Paris, Musee Carnavalet, Paris, France/Art Resource, New York.*

Document

The *Encyclopedia* Praises Mechanical Arts and Artisans

One of the most remarkable features of the *Encyclopedia* is the vast quantity of information it included about the mechanical arts of the day. Not only are there many articles on such work, but a large number of engravings portrayed eighteenth-century French artisans in their workplace. In the "Preliminary Discourse," which served as a general introduction to the *Encyclopedia*, D'Alembert explained the importance of the mechanical arts as well as the manner whereby the authors had explored these arts and the workshops where they were carried out.

■ *How does D'Alembert defend the importance of the mechanical arts? Why does he think they have not always received proper attention and appreciation? How did the authors of the Encyclopedia familiarize themselves with such work? What kind of conversation might have occurred between one of those authors and a skilled artisan operating his machinery?*

The mechanical arts, which are dependent upon manual operation and are subjugated (. . .) to a sort of routine, have been left to those among men whom prejudices have placed in the lowest class. . . . However, the advantage that the liberal arts have over the mechanical arts . . . is sufficiently counterbalanced by the quite superior usefulness which the latter for the most part have for us. It is this very usefulness which reduced them perforce to purely mechanical operations in order to make them accessible to a larger number of men. But while justly respecting great geniuses for their enlightenment, society ought not to degrade the hands by which it is saved. . . .

* * * * * * * * *

Too much has been written on the sciences; not enough has been written well on the mechanical arts. . . . Thus everything impelled us to go directly to the workers.

We approached the most capable of them. . . . We took the trouble of going into their shops, of questioning them, of writing at their dictation, of developing their thoughts and of drawing therefrom the terms peculiar to their professions, of setting up tables of these terms and of working out definitions for them, of conversing with those from whom we obtained memoranda, and (an almost indispensable precaution) of correcting through long and frequent conversations with others what some of them imperfectly, obscurely, and sometimes unreliably had explained. There are some artisans who are also men of letters, and we would be able to cite them here; but their numbers are very small. Most of those who engage in the mechanical art have embraced them only by necessity and work only by instinct. . . .

But there are some trades so unusual and some operations so subtle that unless one does the work oneself, unless one operates a machine with one's own hands, and sees the work being created under one's own eyes, it is difficult to speak of it with precision. Thus several times we had to get possession of the machines, to construct them, and to put a hand to the work. It was necessary to become apprentices, so to speak, and to manufacture some poor object ourselves in order to learn how to teach others the way good specimens are made.

Source: Schwab, Preliminary Discourse Encyclopedia of Diderot, 1st Edition, © 1963, pp 41–42, 122–123 Reprinted by permission of Pearson Education, Inc., Upper Saddle River, NJ.

publication. The *Encyclopedia* set forth the most advanced critical ideas in religion, government, and philosophy. This criticism often had to be hidden in obscure articles or under the cover of irony. The articles represented a collective plea for freedom of expression. However, the large volumes also provided important information on manufacturing, canal building, ship construction, improved agriculture, and other technological innovations of the day. The pages of the *Encyclopedia* constitute one of the first examples of linking together the ideals of scientific and technological progress. (See Document: "The *Encyclopedia* Praises Mechanical Arts and Artisans.")

Between 14,000 and 16,000 copies of various editions of the *Encyclopedia* were sold before 1789. The project had been designed to secularize learning and to undermine the intellectual assumptions remaining from the Middle Ages and the Reformation. The articles on politics, ethics, and society ignored concerns about divine law and concentrated

The Enlightenment and Religion

Throughout the century, in the eyes of many *philosophes*, the chief enemy of the improvement of humankind and the enjoyment of happiness was the church. The hatred of the *philosophes* for the church and Christianity was summed up in Voltaire's cry of "Crush the Infamous Thing." Almost all varieties of Christianity, but especially Roman Catholicism, invited the criticism of the *philosophes*. Intellectually, the churches perpetuated a religious rather than a scientific view of humankind and physical nature. The clergy taught that human beings were basically sinful and that they required divine grace to become worthy creatures. The doctrine of original sin in either its Catholic or its Protestant formulation suggested that meaningful improvement in human nature was impossible. Religious concerns turned human interest away from this world to the world to come. For the *philosophes*, the concept of predestination suggested that the fate of the human soul after death bore little or no relationship to virtuous living. Through their disagreements over obscure doctrines, the various churches favored the politics of intolerance and bigotry that in the past had caused human suffering, torture, and war.

Deism

The *philosophes* believed that religion should be reasonable and lead to moral behavior. The Newtonian worldview had convinced many writers that nature was rational. Therefore, the God who had created nature must also be rational, and the religion through which that God was worshiped should be rational. Moreover, Lockean philosophy, which limited human knowledge to empirical experience, cast doubt on whether divine revelation was possible. These considerations gave rise to a movement for enlightened religion known as **deism**.

The title of one of its earliest expositions, *Christianity Not Mysterious* (1696) by John Toland, indicates the general tenor of this religious outlook. Toland and later writers wished to consider religion a natural and rational, rather than a supernatural and mystical, phenomenon. In this respect the deists differed from Newton and Locke, who had regarded themselves as distinctly Christian. Newton had believed that God might interfere with the natural order, whereas the deists regarded God as resembling a divine watchmaker who had set the mechanism of nature to work and then let them operate without intervention.

There were two major points in the deists' creed. The first was a belief in the existence of God, which they thought could be empirically deduced from the contemplation of nature.

Illustration from the Encyclopedia. Denis Diderot in the *Encyclopedia* included illustrations of machinery and working people from across the globe. Diderot was also deeply hostile to slavery. This engraving illustrated a sugar mill and sugar boiling house run with slave labor in the New World. The sugar produced in such mills was used in the European coffeehouses where the ideas of the *philosophes* were often discussed.

●●●—[Read the Document

Diderot's Encyclopedia–Plate Illustrating Agricultural Techniques
at **MyHistoryLab.com**

on humanity and its immediate well-being. The encyclopedists looked to antiquity rather than to the Christian centuries for their intellectual and ethical models. The future welfare of humankind lay not in pleasing God or following divine commandments, but rather in harnessing the power of the earth and its resources and in living at peace with one's fellow human beings. The good life was to be achieved through the application of reason to human relationships.

With the publication of the *Encyclopedia*, enlightened thought became more fully diffused over the Continent. Enlightened ideas penetrated German and Russian intellectual and political circles (see Map 21–1 on page 650).

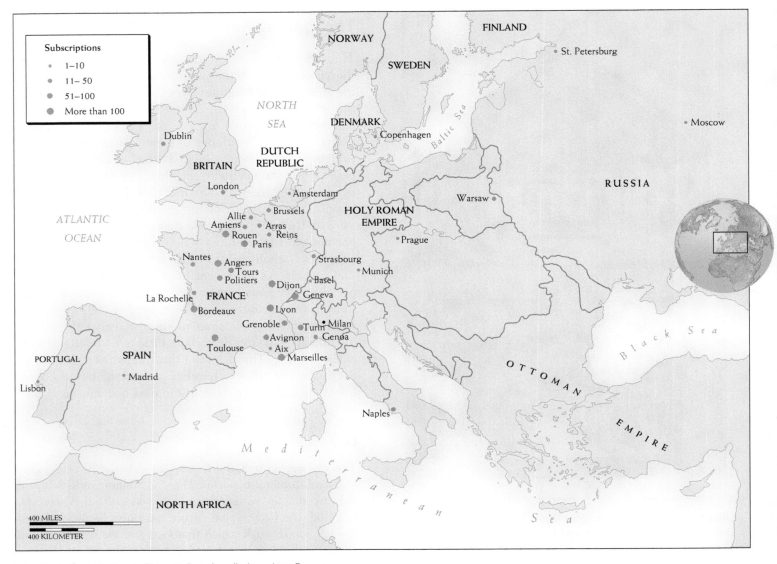

Map 21–1. Subscriptions to Diderot's *Encyclopedia* throughout Europe.

Because nature provided evidence of a rational God, that Deity must also favor rational morality. Consequently, the second point in the deists' creed was a belief in life after death, when rewards and punishments would be meted out according to the virtue of the life a person led on this earth.

Deism was empirical, tolerant, reasonable, and capable of encouraging virtuous living. It was the major positive religious component of the Enlightenment. Voltaire declared:

> *The great name of Deist, which is not sufficiently revered, is the only name one ought to take. The only gospel one ought to read is the great book of Nature, written by the hand of God and sealed with his seal. The only religion that ought to be professed is the religion of worshiping God and being a good man.*[5]

[5]Quoted in J. H. Randall, *The Making of the Modern Mind*, rev. ed. (New York: Houghton Mifflin, 1940), p. 292.

If such a faith became widely accepted, it would overcome the fanaticism and rivalry of the various Christian sects. Religious conflict and persecutions would end. There would also be little or no necessity for a priestly class to foment fanaticism, denominational hatred, and bigotry.

Toleration

A primary social condition for such a life was the establishment of religious toleration. Voltaire took the lead in championing this cause. In 1762 the political authorities in Toulouse ordered the execution of a Huguenot named Jean Calas (1698–1762). He stood accused of having murdered his son to prevent him from converting to Roman Catholicism. Calas had been viciously tortured and publicly strangled without ever having confessed his guilt. The confession would not have saved his life, but it

Chronology

Major Publication Dates of the Enlightenment

1687 Newton's *Principia Mathematica*

1690 Locke's *Essay Concerning Human Understanding*

1696 Toland's *Christianity Not Mysterious*

1733 Voltaire's *Letters on the English*

1738 Voltaire's *Elements of the Philosophy of Newton*

1748 Montesquieu's *Spirit of the Laws*

1750 Rousseau's *Discourse on the Moral Effects of the Arts and Sciences*

1751 First volume of the *Encyclopedia* edited by Diderot and d'Alembert

1755 Rousseau's *Discourse on the Origin of Inequality*

1762 Rousseau's *Social Contract*

1763 Voltaire's *Treatise on Tolerance*

1776 Smith's *Wealth of Nations*

1779 Lessing's *Nathan the Wise*

1792 Wollstonecraft's *A Vindication of the Rights of Woman*

would have given the Catholics good propaganda to use against Protestants.

Voltaire learned of the case only after Calas's death. He made the dead man's cause his own. In 1763 he published a *Treatise on Tolerance* and hounded the authorities for a new investigation. Finally, in 1765 the judicial decision against the unfortunate man was reversed. For Voltaire, the case illustrated the fruits of religious fanaticism and the need for rational reform of judicial processes. Somewhat later in the century the German playwright and critic Gotthold Lessing (1729–1781) wrote *Nathan the Wise* (1779) as a plea for toleration not only of different Christian sects, but also of religious faiths other than Christianity. All of these calls for toleration stated, in effect, that human life should not be subordinated to dogmatic religion. Secular values and considerations were more important than religious ones.

Read the Document
Voltaire, "On Universal Toleration
at **MyHistoryLab.com**

Islam in Enlightenment Thought

Islam, except in the Balkan Peninsula, had few adherents in eighteenth-century Europe. Although European merchants traded with the Ottoman Empire or with those parts of South Asia where Islam prevailed, most Europeans came to know what little they did know about the Islamic world and Islam as a religion through books—the religious commentaries of Christian missionaries, histories, and the reports of

travelers—that with rare exceptions were hostile to Islam and deeply misleading.

Islam continued to be seen as a rival to Christianity. European writers repeated what other Christian critics had said for centuries. They portrayed Islam as a false religion and Muhammad as an impostor and a false prophet because he had not performed miracles. Furthermore, they also attacked Islam as an exceptionally carnal or sexually promiscuous religion because of its teaching that heaven was a place of sensuous delights, its permission for a man to have more than one wife, Muhammad's own polygamy, and the presence of harems in the Islamic world.

Christian authors also ignored the Islamic understanding of the life and mission of Muhammad. They referred to Islam as Muhammadanism, thus implying that Muhammad was divine rather than a human being with whom God had chosen to communicate. For Muslims, the suggestion that Muhammad was divine is blasphemous.

Enlightenment *philosophes* spoke with two voices regarding Islam. Voltaire indicated his opinion along with that of many of his contemporaries in the title of his 1742 tragedy, *Fanaticism, or Mohammed the Prophet*. Although he sometimes spoke well of the Qur'an, Voltaire declared in a later historical work, "We must suppose that Muhammad, like all enthusiasts, violently impressed by his own ideas, retailed them in good faith, fortified them with fancies, deceived himself in deceiving others, and finally sustained with deceit a doctrine he believed to be good."[6] Thus for Voltaire, Muhammad and Islam in general represented simply one more examples of the religious fanaticism he had so often criticized among Christians.

Some Enlightenment writers, however, spoke well of the Islamic faith. The deist John Toland, who opposed prejudice against both Jews and Muslims, contended that Islam derived from early Christian writings and was thus a form of Christianity. These views so offended most of his contemporaries that Toland became known as a "Mohametan" Christian. Edward Gibbon (1737–1794), who blamed Christianity for contributing to the fall of the Roman Empire, wrote with respect of Muhammad's leadership and Islam's success in conquering so vast a territory in the first century of its existence. Other commentators approved of Islam's tolerance and the charitable work of Muslims.

Some *philosophes* criticized Islam on cultural and political grounds. In *The Persian Letters* (1721), supposedly written by two Muslim Persians visiting Europe, Charles Louis de Secondat, baron de Montesquieu (1689–1755), who became a major political philosopher, used Islamic culture as a foil to criticize his own European society. But by the time he wrote his more influential *Spirit of the Laws* (1748), discussed

[6]Quoted in Theodore Besterman, *Voltaire* (New York: Harcourt, Brace, & World, 1969), p. 409.

Map of Turkey and View of Constantinople (Istanbul). Few Europeans visited the Ottoman Empire. What little they knew about it came from reports of travelers and from illustrations such as this view of Istanbul, the empire's capital.

more fully later in this chapter, Montesquieu associated Islamic society with the passivity that he ascribed to people subject to political despotism. Like other Europeans, Montesquieu believed the excessive influence of Islamic religious leaders prevented the Ottoman Empire from adapting itself to new advances in technology.

One of the most positive commentators on eighteenth-century Islam was a woman. Between 1716 and 1718, Lady Mary Wortley Montagu (1689–1762) lived in Constantinople with her husband, the British ambassador to Turkey. She wrote a series of letters about her experiences there that were published the year after her death. In these *Turkish Embassy Letters*, she praised much about Ottoman society and urged the English to copy the Turkish practice of vaccination against smallpox. Unlike European males, Montagu had access to the private quarters of women in Istanbul. In contrast to the constraints under which English women found themselves, she thought upper-class Turkish women were remarkably free and well treated by their husbands despite having to wear clothing that completely covered them in public. In fact, Montagu thought the anonymity these coverings bestowed allowed Turkish women to move freely about Istanbul. She also considered the magnificent Ottoman architec-

Read the Document
Lady Mary Wortley Montagu, Letters: (a) on Constantinople; (b) on Smallpox; (c) on Vaccination in Turkey at **MyHistoryLab.com**

ture better than anything in western Europe. Montagu repeatedly criticized the misinformation that prevailed in Europe about the Ottoman Empire and declared that many of the hostile comments about Islam and Islamic morality were simply wrong.

Yet the European voices demanding fairness and expressing empathy for Islam were rare throughout the eighteenth century. As one historian has commented, "The basic Christian attitude was still what it had been for a millennium: a rejection of the claim of Muslims that Muhammed was a prophet and the Qur'an the word of God, mingled with a memory of periods of fear and conflict, and also, a few thinkers and scholars apart, with legends, usually hostile and often contemptuous."[7]

Nor were Muslims very curious about the Christian West. Only a handful of people from the Ottoman or Safavid empires visited western Europe in the eighteenth century,

[7]A. Hourani, *Islam in European Thought* (Cambridge: Cambridge University Press, 1991), p. 136.

Printing Shops. Shops such as this were the productive centers for the book trade and newspaper publishing, which spread the ideas of the Enlightenment.

and no Islamic writers showed much interest in contemporary European authors. The *ulama,* the Islamic religious establishment, reinforced these attitudes. They taught that God's revelations to Muhammad meant Islam had superseded Christianity as a religion and that therefore there was little to be learned from the Christian culture of Europe.

The Enlightenment and Society

Although the *philosophes* wrote much about religion, humanity was the center of their interest. As one writer in the *Encyclopedia* observed, "Man is the unique point to which we must refer everything, if we wish to interest and please amongst considerations the most arid and details the most dry."[8] The *philosophes* believed that the application of human reason to society would reveal laws in human relationships similar to those found in physical nature. Although the term did not appear until later, the idea of social science originated with the Enlightenment. The purpose of discovering social laws was to remove the inhumanity that existed through ignorance of them.

Montesquieu and *The Spirit of the Laws*

Charles Louis de Secondat, Baron de Montesquieu, was a French noble of the robe and a magistrate. His work *The Spirit of the Laws* (1748), perhaps the single most influential book of the century, exhibits the internal tensions of the Enlightenment. Montesquieu pursued an empirical method,

taking illustrative examples from the political experience of both ancient and modern nations. From them he concluded that no single set of political laws could apply to all peoples at all times and in all places. Rather, the good political life depended on the relationship of many political variables. Only a careful examination and evaluation of these elements could reveal what mode of government would prove most beneficial to a particular people. A century later such speculations would have been classified as sociology.

View the Image
The Spirit of the Laws, Montesquieu-Frontispiece at **MyHistoryLab.com**

As far as France was concerned, Montesquieu believed in a monarchy whose power was tempered and limited by various intermediary institutions, including the aristocracy, the towns, and the other corporate bodies that enjoyed particular liberties that the monarch must respect. These corporate bodies might be said to represent various segments of the general population and thus of public opinion. In France he regarded the *parlements,* judicial courts dominated by aristocrats like himself, as the major example of an intermediary association. Their role was to limit the power of the monarchy and thus to preserve the liberty of the subjects. In championing these aristocratic bodies and the general role of the aristocracy, Montesquieu was a political conservative. He adopted that stance, however, in the hope of achieving reform, for he considered the oppressive and inefficient absolutism of the monarchy responsible for the degradation of French life.

One of Montesquieu's most influential ideas was that of division of power. He took Great Britain for his model of a government with power wisely separated among different branches. There he believed he had found a system in which executive power resided in the king, legislative power in the Parliament, and judicial power in the courts. He thought any

[8]Quoted in F. L. Baumer, *Main Currents of Western Thought,* 4th ed. (New Haven, CT: Yale University Press, 1978), p. 374.

two branches could check and balance the power of the other. His perception of the eighteenth-century British constitution was incorrect because he failed to see how patronage and electoral corruption allowed a handful of aristocrats to dominate the government. Moreover, he was also unaware of the emerging cabinet system, which meant that the executive power was slowly becoming a creature of the Parliament. Nevertheless, the analysis illustrated Montesquieu's strong sense of the need to limit the exercise of power through a constitution and for legislatures, not monarchs, to make laws. Although Montesquieu set out to defend the political privileges of the French aristocracy, his ideas had a profound and enduring effect on the liberal democracies of the next two centuries.

●◆─┤Read the Document
Baron de Montesquieu, Excerpt from The Spirit of the Laws at **MyHistoryLab.com**

Adam Smith on Economic Growth and Social Progress

The most important economic work of the Enlightenment was Adam Smith's (1723–1790) *Inquiry into the Nature and Causes of the Wealth of Nations* (1776). Smith, who was for a time a professor at Glasgow, believed that economic liberty was the foundation of a natural economic system. As a result, he urged that the mercantile system of England—including the navigation acts, the bounties, most tariffs, special trading monopolies, and the domestic regulation of labor and manufacture—be abolished. These regulations were intended to preserve the wealth of the nation, to capture wealth from other nations, and to maximize the work available for the nation's laborers. Smith argued, however, that they hindered the expansion of wealth and production. The best way to encourage economic growth, he maintained, was to unleash individuals to pursue their own selfish economic interests. As self-interested individuals sought to enrich themselves by meeting the needs of others in the marketplace and in a society ruled by law, the economy would expand. Consumers would find their wants met as manufacturers and merchants competed for their business.

Smith is usually regarded as the founder of ***laissez-faire*** economic thought and policy, which favors a limited role for the government in economic life. *The Wealth of Nations* was, however, a complex book. Smith was no simple dogmatist. For example, he did not oppose all government activity touching the economy. The state, he argued, should provide schools, armies, navies, and roads. It should also undertake certain commercial ventures, such as the opening of dangerous new trade routes that were economically desirable, but too expensive or risky for private enterprise.

Within *The Wealth of Nations*, Smith, like other Scottish thinkers of the day, embraced an important theory of human social and economic development, known as the *four-stage theory*. According to this theory, human societies can be classified as hunting and gathering, pastoral or herding, agricultural, and commercial. The hunters and gatherers have little or no settled life. Pastoral societies are groups of nomads who tend their herds and develop some private property. Agricultural or farming societies are settled and have clear-cut property arrangements. Finally, in the commercial state there exist advanced cities, the manufacture of numerous items for wide consumption, extensive trade between cities and the countryside, and elaborate forms of property and financial arrangements. Smith and other Scottish writers described the passage of human society through these stages as a movement from barbarism to civilization.

The four-stage theory implicitly evaluated the later stages of economic development and the people dwelling in them as higher, more progressive, and more civilized than the earlier ones. A social theorist using this theory could thus very quickly look at a society and, on the basis of the state of its economic development and organizations, rank it in terms of the stage it had achieved. In point of fact, the commercial stage, the highest rank in the theory, described society as it appeared in northwestern Europe. Thus, Smith's theory allowed Europeans to look about the world and always find themselves dwelling at the highest level of human achievement. This outlook served as one of the major justifications in the minds of Europeans for their economic and imperial domination of the world during the next century. Europeans thus imbued with the spirit of the Enlightenment presented themselves as carrying out a civilizing mission to the rest of the world.

●◆─┤Read the Document
Adam Smith, Intro to the Wealth of Nations (1776) and Wealth of Nations, Adam Smith (1776) at **MyHistoryLab.com**

Rousseau

Jean-Jacques Rousseau (1712–1778) held a different view of political power. Rousseau was a strange, isolated genius who never felt comfortable with the other *philosophes*. Yet perhaps more than any other writer of the mid-eighteenth century, he transcended the thought and values of his own time. Rousseau had a deep antipathy toward the world and the society in which he lived. It seemed to him impossible for human beings living according to contemporary commercial values to achieve moral, virtuous, or sincere lives. In 1750, in his *Discourse on the Moral Effects of the Arts and Sciences,* he questioned the concepts of material and intellectual progress and the morality of a society in which commerce and industry were regarded as the most important human activities. He felt that the real purpose of society was to nurture better people. In 1755, in a *Discourse on the Origin of Inequality*, Rousseau blamed much of the evil in the world on maldistribution of property. Human

Rousseau. The writings of Jean-Jacques Rousseau (1712–1778) raised some of the most profound social and ethical questions of the Enlightenment. This portrait by Maurice Quentin was made ca. 1740.

beings dwelling in what his contemporaries regarded as normal social relations involving private property and various kinds of social inequality had in Rousseau's view departed from the natural goodness of humanity that had existed in a pre-social state of nature.

Rousseau carried these same concerns into his political thought. His most extensive discussion of politics appeared in *The Social Contract* (1762). This highly abstract book does not propose specific reforms but outlines the kind of political structure that Rousseau believed would overcome the evils of contemporary politics and society.

In the tradition of John Locke, most eighteenth-century political thinkers regarded society as a collection of independent individuals pursuing personal, selfish goals. These writers wished to liberate these individuals from the undue bonds of government. Rousseau picked up the stick from the other end. His book opens with the declaration, "All men are born free, but everywhere they are in chains."[9] The rest of the volume constitutes a defense of the chains of a properly organized society over its members. Rousseau suggested

[9]Jean-Jacques Rousseau, *The Social Contract and Discourses*, trans. by G. D. H. Cole (New York: Dutton, 1950), p. 3.

that society is more important than its individual members because they are what they are only as a result of their relationship to the larger community. Independent human beings living alone can achieve little. Through their relationship to the larger community, they become moral creatures capable of significant action. The question then becomes what kind of community allows people to behave morally. Rousseau sought to project the vision of a society in which each person could maintain personal freedom while also behaving as a loyal member of the larger community. He drew on the traditions of Plato and Calvin to define freedom as obedience to law. In his case, the law to be obeyed was that created by the general will. This concept normally indicated the will of the majority of voting citizens who acted with adequate information and under the influence of virtuous customs and morals. Such democratic participation in decision making would bind the individual citizen to the community. Rousseau believed that the general will must always be right and that to obey the general will was to be free. This argument led him to the notorious conclusion that some people must be forced to be free. His politics thus constituted a justification for radical direct democracy and for collective action against individual citizens.

Rousseau had, in effect, assaulted the eighteenth-century cult of the individual and the fruits of selfishness. He stood at odds with the commercial spirit that was transforming society. Adam Smith wanted people to be prosperous; Rousseau wanted them to be good even if it meant they might remain poor. He saw human beings not as independent individuals, but as creatures enmeshed in necessary social relationships. He believed that loyalty to the community should be encouraged. As one device to that end, he suggested a civic religion based on deism. Such a shared tolerant religious faith would unify society. Rousseau's chief intellectual inspiration arose from his study of Plato and the ancient Greek *polis*. Especially in Sparta, he thought he had discovered human beings dwelling in a moral society inspired by a common purpose. He hoped that modern human beings might also create such a moral commonwealth in which virtuous living would not become subordinate to commercial profit.

Enlightened Critics of European Empire

Most European thinkers associated with the Enlightenment favored the extension of European empires across the world. Like the Scottish writers who embraced the four-stage theory, they believed that the extension of the political structures and economies of northwestern Europe amounted to the spread of progress and civilization. The Scottish commentators and their followers were not without their criticisms of European civilization, but on the whole they believed it superior.

Document Denis Diderot Condemns European Empires

Denis Diderot was one of the most prolific writers of the Enlightenment. He is most famous as editor of the *Encyclopedia*. Some of his writings were published without being directly attributed to him. Among these were his contributions to Abbé G. T. Raynal's *History of the Two Indies*, published in various changing editions after 1772. Diderot's contributions appear to have been made in 1780. The entire *History* was critical of the European colonial empires that had arisen since the Spanish encounter with the New World. Diderot was particularly concerned to condemn the inhumane treatment of the native populations of the Americas, the greed displayed by all Europeans, and the establishment of various forms of forced labor.

■ *What is the basis for Diderot's view that Europeans have behaved tyrannically? How does he portray the behavior of Europeans once they have left their own native countries and find themselves in foreign areas? What are the specific social results he associates with European greed?*

Let the European nations make their own judgment and give themselves the name they deserve. . . . Their explorers arrive in a region of the New World unoccupied by anyone from the Old World, and immediately bury a small strip of metal on which they have engraved these words: *This country belongs to us.* And why does it belong to you? . . . You have no right to the natural products of the country where you land, and you claim a right over your fellow-men. Instead of recognizing this man as a brother you only see him as a slave, a beast of burden. Oh my fellow citizens! You think like that and you behave like that; and you have ideas of justice, a morality, a holy religion . . . in common with those whom you treat so tyrannically. This reproach should especially be addressed to the Spaniards.

Beyond the Equator a man is neither English, Dutch, French, Spanish, nor Portuguese. He retains only those principles and prejudices of his native country which justify or excuse his conduct. He crawls when he is weak; he is violent when strong; he is in a hurry to acquire, in a hurry to enjoy, and capable of every crime which will lead him most quickly to his goals. He is a domestic tiger returning to the forest; the thirst for blood takes hold of him once more. This is how all the Europeans, every one of them, indistinctly, have appeared in the countries of the New World. There they have assumed a common frenzy—the thirst for gold.

The Spaniard, the first to be thrown up by the waves onto the shores of the New World, thought he had no duty to people who did not share his color, customs, or religion. He saw in them only tools for his greed, and he clapped them in irons. These weak men, not used to work, soon died in the foul air of the mines, or in other occupations which were virtually as lethal. Then people called for slaves from Africa. Their number has gone up as more land has been cultivated. The Portuguese, Dutch, English, French, Danes, all the nations, free or subjected, have without remorse sought to increase their fortune in the sweat, blood and despair of these unfortunates. What a horrible system!

Source: Denis Diderot, *Political Writings*, John Hope Mason and Robert Wokler, eds. (Cambridge: Cambridge University Press, 1998), pp. 177, 178, 186.

There were, however, a few minority Enlightenment voices who criticized the European empires. The topic that most frequently allowed such criticism were discussions of the European conquest of the Americas, the treatment of Native Americans, and the enslavement of Africans on the two American continents. The most important of these critics were Denis Diderot and two German philosophers, Immanuel Kant (1724–1804) and Johann Gottfried Herder (1744–1803).

What sets of ideas allowed these figures from the Enlightenment to criticize empire? As Sankar Muthu has recently written, "The first and most basic idea is that human beings deserve some modicum of moral and political respect simply because of the fact that they are human."[10] In other words, the Enlightenment critics of empire argued for the existence of a form of shared humanity that the sixteenth-century European conquerors and their successors in the Americas and in other

[10]Sankar Muthu, *Enlightenment against Empire* (Princeton, NJ: Princeton University Press, 2003), p. 268. This section draws primarily from this excellent recent book.

areas of imperial conquest had ignored. Immanuel Kant, the German philosopher, wrote, "When America, the Negro countries, the Spice Islands, the Cape, and so forth were discovered, they were to them [the Europeans], countries belonging to no one, since they counted the inhabitants as *nothing*."[11] Kant, Denis Diderot, and the German philosopher of history Herder rejected this dismissive outlook and the harsh policies that had flowed from it. They believed no single definition of human nature could be made the standard throughout the world and then used to dehumanize people whose appearance or culture differed from that standard.

A second of these critical ideas was the conviction that the people whom Europeans had encountered in the Americas had actually possessed cultures that should have been respected and understood rather than being destroyed. Some Europeans in the early years of the encounter with America had actually argued that the native peoples were human, but that their way of life was so low, they could not be treated as being equally human with Europeans. In the late eighteenth century Herder directly rejected such a view, " 'European culture' is a mere abstraction, an empty concept. Where does or did it actually exist in its entirety? In which nation? In which period? . . . Only a misanthrope could regard European culture as the universal condition of our species. The culture of man is not the culture of the European; it manifests itself according to time and place in every people."[12] For Herder, human beings living in different societies possessed the capacity as human beings to develop in culturally different fashions. He thus strongly embraced an outlook later known as cultural relativism.

A third idea, closely related to the second, was that human beings may develop distinct cultures possessing intrinsic values that cannot be directly compared. The reason they may not be compared one to the detriment of another is that each culture possesses deep inner social and linguistic complexities that make any simple comparison impossible. Indeed, Diderot, Kant, and Herder argued that one fundamental aspect of humanity is the ability to develop a variety of distinctly different cultures.

These arguments critical of empire often involved criticism of New World slavery and were part of the antislavery movement to be discussed in a later chapter. Whereas the antislavery arguments took strong hold in both Europe and America from the late eighteenth century onward, the arguments critical of empire did not. They stand generally isolated from the rest of Enlightenment political thought and would not be strongly revived until new anticolonial voices were raised in Europe and the non-European world at the close of the nineteenth century.

---

[11]Quoted in ibid., p.267.
[12]F. M. Barnard, *Self-direction and Political Legitimacy: Rousseau and Herder* (Oxford: Clarendon Press, 1988), p. 227.

Women in the Thought and Practice of the Enlightenment

Women, especially in France, helped significantly to promote the careers of the *philosophes*. In Paris the salons of women such as Marie-Thérèse Geoffrin (1699–1777), Julie de Lespinasse (1733–1776), and Claudine de Tencin (1689–1749) gave the *philosophes* access to useful social and political contacts and a receptive environment for their ideas. These women were well connected to major political figures who could help protect the *philosophes* and secure them pensions. The marquise de Pompadour (1721–1764), the mistress of Louis XV, for example, played a key role in overcoming efforts to censor the *Encyclopedia*. She also helped block the circulation of works attacking the *philosophes*.

Nonetheless, the *philosophes* were on the whole not strong feminists. Although many criticized the education women received as overly religious and tended to reject ascetic views of sexual relations, the *philosophes* advocated no radical changes in the social condition of women.

Montesquieu, for example, maintained in general that the status of women in a society was the result of climate, the political regime, culture, and women's physiological nature. He believed women were not naturally inferior to men and should have a wider role in society. He was well aware of the personal, emotional, and sexual repression women endured in his day. Yet there were limits to his willingness to consider change in women's social role. He retained a traditional view of marriage and family and expected men to dominate those institutions. Furthermore, although he supported the right of women to divorce and opposed laws that directly oppressed them, he upheld the ideal of female chastity.

The views about women expressed in the *Encyclopedia* were less generous. The editors, Diderot and d'Alembert, recruited men almost exclusively as contributors and saw no need to include many articles by women. Most of the articles that dealt with women specifically or that discussed women in connection with other subjects often emphasized their physical weakness and inferiority, usually attributed to menstruation or childbearing. Contributors disagreed on the social equality of women. Some favored it, others opposed it, and still others were indifferent. The articles conveyed a general sense that women were reared to be frivolous and unconcerned with important issues. The encyclopedists discussed women primarily in a family context—as daughters, wives, and mothers—and considered motherhood their most important occupation. On sexual behavior, the encyclopedists upheld an unquestioned double standard.

In contrast to the articles, however, illustrations in the *Encyclopedia* showed women deeply involved in the economic activities of the day. The illustrations also showed the

Document — Rousseau Argues for Separate Spheres for Men and Women

Rousseau published *Émile*, a novel about education, in 1762. In it he made one of the strongest and most influential arguments of the eighteenth century for distinct social roles for men and women. Furthermore, he portrayed women as fundamentally subordinate to men. See page 660 for a contemporary rebuttal.

■ *How does Rousseau move from the physical differences between men and women to an argument for distinct social roles and social spheres? What would be the proper kinds of social activities for women in Rousseau's vision? What kind of education would he think appropriate for women?*

There is no parity between the two sexes in regard to the consequences of sex. The male is male only at certain moments. The female is female her whole life or at least during her whole youth. Everything constantly recalls her sex to her; and, to fulfill its functions well, she needs a constitution which corresponds to it. She needs care during her pregnancy; she needs rest at the time of childbirth; she needs a soft and sedentary life to suckle her children; she needs patience and gentleness, a zeal and an affection that nothing can rebuff in order to raise her children. She serves as the link between them and their father; she alone makes him love them and gives him the confidence to call them his own. How much tenderness and care is required to maintain the union of the whole family! And, finally, all this must come not from virtues but from tastes, or else the human species would soon be extinguished.

The strictness of the relative duties of the two sexes is not and cannot be the same. When woman complains on this score about unjust man-made inequality, she is wrong. This inequality is not a human institution—or, at least, it is the work not of prejudice but of reason. It is up to the sex that nature has charged with the bearing of children to be responsible for them to the other sex. Doubtless it is not permitted to any one to violate his faith, and every unfaithful husband who deprives his wife of the only reward of the austere duties of her sex is an unjust and barbarous man. But the unfaithful woman does more; she dissolves the family and breaks all the bonds of nature. . . .

Once it is demonstrated that man and woman are not and ought not be constituted in the same way in either character or temperament, it follows that they ought not to have the same education. In following nature's directions, man and woman ought to act in concert, but they ought not to do the same things. The goal of their labors is common, but their labors themselves are different, and consequently so are the tastes directing them. . . .

The good constitution of children initially depends on that of their mothers. The first education of men depends on the care of women. Men's morals, their passions, their tastes, their pleasures, their very happiness also depend on women. Thus the whole education of women ought to relate to men. To please men, to be useful to them, to make herself loved and honored by them, to raise them when young, to care for them when grown, to counsel them, to console them, to make their lives agreeable and sweet—these are the duties of women at all times, and they ought to be taught from childhood. So long as one does not return to this principle, one will deviate from the goal, and all the precepts taught to women will be of no use for their happiness or for ours.

Source: Excerpt from *Emile: On Education* by Jean-Jacques Rousseau, and Micheal Wu. Copyright © 1979 Jean Jacques Rousseau, Michael Wu. Reprinted by permission of Basic Books, a member of the Perseus Books Group.

activities of lower- and working-class women, about whom the articles have little to say.

Rousseau urged a traditional role for women. In his novel *Émile* (1762) he declared that women should be educated for a position subordinate to men, emphasizing especially women's function in bearing and rearing children. He portrayed them as weaker and inferior to men in virtually all respects except perhaps for their capacity for feeling and giving love. He excluded them from political life. Women were assigned the domestic sphere alone. Many of These attitudes were not new—some have roots as ancient as Roman law—but Rousseau's powerful presentation and the influence of his other writings gave them new life, including in the legislation of the French Revolution. (See Document, "Rousseau Argues for Separate Spheres for Men and Women.")

Document

Mary Wollstonecraft Criticizes Rousseau's View of Women

Mary Wollstonecraft published *A Vindication of the Rights of Woman* in 1792, thirty years after Rousseau's *Émile* had appeared. She criticized and rejected Rousseau's argument for distinct and separate spheres for men and women as defending the continued bondage of women to men and as hindering the wider education of the entire human race.

■ *What specific criticisms does Wollstonecraft direct against Rousseau's views? Why does Wollstonecraft put so much emphasis on a new kind of education for women?*

The most perfect education . . . is such an exercise of the understanding as is best calculated to strengthen the body and form the heart. Or, in other words, to enable the individual to attain such habits of virtue as will render it independent. In fact, it is a farce to call any being virtuous whose virtues do not result from the exercise of its own reason. This was Rousseau's opinion respecting men: I extend it to women. . . .

I may be accused of arrogance; still I must declare what I firmly believe, that all the writers who have written on the subject of female education and manners from Rousseau to Dr. Gregory [a Scottish physician], have contributed to render women more artificial, weak characters, than they would other wise have been; and, consequently, more useless members of society. . . .

. . . Strengthen the female mind by enlarging it, and there will be an end to blind obedience; but, as blind obedience is ever sought for by power, tyrants and sensualists are in the right when they endeavour to keep women in the dark, because the former only wants slaves, and the latter a play-thing. The sensualist, indeed, has been the most dangerous of tyrants, and women have been duped by their lovers, as princes by their ministers, whilst dreaming that they reigned over them.

. . . Rousseau declares that a woman should never, for a moment, feel herself independent, that she should be governed by fear to exercise her natural cunning, and made a coquettish slave in order to render her a more alluring object of desire, a sweeter companion to man, whenever he chooses to relax himself. He carries the arguments, which he pretends to draw from the indications of nature, still further, and insinuates that truth and fortitude, the corner stones of all human virtue, should be cultivated with certain restrictions, because, with respect to the female character, obedience is the grand lesson which ought to be impressed with unrelenting rigour.

What nonsense! When will a great man arise with sufficient strength of mind to put away the fumes which pride and sensuality have thus spread over the subject! If women are by nature inferior to men, their virtues must be the same in quality, if not in degree, or virtue is a relative idea; consequently, their conduct should be founded on the same principles, and have the same aim.

Connected with man as daughters, wives, and mothers, their moral character may be estimated by their manner of fulfilling those simple duties; but the end, the grand end of their exertions should be to unfold their own faculties and acquire the dignity of conscious virtue. . . .

But avoiding . . . any direct comparison of the two sexes collectively, or frankly acknowledging the inferiority of women, according to the present appearance of things, I shall only insist that men have increased that inferiority till women are almost sunk below the standard of rational creatures. Let their faculties have room to unfold, and their virtues to gain strength, and then determine where the whole sex must stand in the intellectual scale. . . .

. . . I . . . will venture to assert, that till women are more rationally educated, the progress of human virtue and improvement in knowledge must receive continual checks. . . .

The mother, who wishes to give true dignity of character to her daughter, must regardless of the sneers of ignorance, proceed on a plan diametrically opposite to that which Rousseau has recommended with all the deluding charms of eloquence and philosophical sophistry: for his eloquence renders absurdities plausible, and his dogmatic conclusions puzzle, without convincing, those who have not ability to refute them.

Source: Excerpts from *A Vindication of The Rights of Woman* by Mary Wollstoncraft, edited by Carol H. Posner. Copyright © 1988, 1975 by W.W. Norton & Company, Inc. Used by permission of W.W. Norton & Company, Inc.

Paradoxically, despite these views and his own ill treatment of the many women who bore his many children, Rousseau achieved a vast following among women in the eighteenth century. He is credited with persuading thousands of upper-class women to breast-feed their own children rather than putting them out to wet nurses. One explanation for this influence is that his writings, although they did not advocate liberating women or expanding their social or economic roles, did stress the importance of their emotions and subjective feelings. He portrayed the domestic life and the role of wife and mother as a noble and fulfilling vocation, giving middle- and upper-class women a sense that their daily occupations had purpose. He assigned them a degree of influence in the domestic sphere that they could not have competing with men outside it.

In 1792 in *A Vindication of the Rights of Woman*, Mary Wollstonecraft, (1759–1797) brought Rousseau before the judgment of the rational Enlightenment ideal of progressive knowledge. Wollstonecraft (who, like so many women of her day, died shortly after childbirth of puerperal fever) accused Rousseau and others after him who upheld traditional roles for women of attempting to narrow women's vision and limit their experience. She argued that to confine women to the separate domestic sphere because of their supposed physiological limitations was to make them the sensual slaves of men. Confined in this separate sphere, as the victims of male tyranny, they could never achieve their own moral or intellectual identity. Denying good education to women would impede the progress of all humanity. Wollstonecraft was demanding for women the kind of intellectual liberty that male writers of the Enlightenment had been championing for men for more than a century. (See Document, "Mary Wollstonecraft Criticizes Rousseau's View of Women.")

Enlightened Absolutism

During the last third of the century it seemed that several European rulers had embraced many of the reforms set forth by the *philosophes*. *Enlightened absolutism* is the term used to describe this phenomenon. The phrase indicates monarchical government dedicated to the rational strengthening of the central absolutist administration at the cost of lesser centers of political power. The monarchs most closely associated with it—Frederick II of Prussia, Joseph II of Austria, and Catherine II of Russia—often found that the political and social realities of their realms caused them to moderate both their enlightenment and their absolutism. Frederick II corresponded with the *philosophes*, invited Voltaire to his court, and even wrote history and political tracts. Catherine II, who was a master of what would later be called public relations, consciously sought to create the image of being enlightened. She read the works of the *philosophes*, became a friend of Diderot and Voltaire, and made frequent references to their ideas, all in the hope that her nation might seem more modern and Western. Joseph II continued numerous initiatives begun by his mother, Maria Theresa, and imposed a series of religious, legal, and social reforms that contemporaries believed he had derived from suggestions of the *philosophes*.

((• —[**Hear** the **Audio**
at **MyHistoryLab.com**

Despite such appearances, the relationship between these rulers and the writers of the Enlightenment was more complicated. The rulers did wish to see their subjects enjoy better health, more accessible education, a more rational political administration, and economic prosperity. In many of these policies, they were more advanced than the rulers of western Europe. However, the humanitarian and liberating zeal of the Enlightenment directed only part of their policies. Frederick II, Joseph II, and Catherine II were also determined to play major diplomatic and military roles in Europe. In no small measure they sought the rational economic and social integration of their realms, so they could achieve military strength. After the Seven Years' War all the states of Europe understood that they would require stronger armed forces, which meant they needed new revenues. The search for new revenues and for more political support for their rule led these monarchs to make "enlightened" reforms. Consequently, they and their advisers used rationality to pursue many goals admired by the *philosophes* but also to further what the *philosophes* considered irrational militarism.

Joseph II of Austria

No eighteenth-century ruler so embodied rational, impersonal force as the emperor Joseph II of Austria. He was the son of Maria Theresa (r. 1740–1780) and co-ruler with her from 1765 to 1780. During the next ten years he ruled alone. He lived very simply, sleeping on straw and eating little but beef. He lived in a town house in Vienna rather than the elaborate royal palace on the outskirts of the city. He prided himself on a narrow, passionless rationality, which he sought to impose by his own will on the various Habsburg domains. Despite his eccentricities and cold personality, Joseph II genuinely and sincerely wished to improve the lot of his peoples. His well-intentioned efforts led to a series of aristocratic and peasant rebellions from Hungary to the Austrian Netherlands.

Of all the rising states of the eighteenth century, Austria was the most diverse in its people and problems. The Habsburgs never succeeded in creating either a unified administrative structure or a strong aristocratic loyalty. The price of preserving the monarchy during the War of the Austrian Succession (1740–1748) had been guarantees of considerable aristocratic independence, especially in Hungary.

During and after the conflict, however, Maria Theresa had strengthened her powers in Austria and Bohemia. Through major administrative reorganization she imposed a much more efficient system of tax collection that extracted funds even from the clergy and the nobles, and she established several central councils to deal with governmental problems. She was particularly concerned about bringing all

A Closer Look

An Eighteenth-Century Artist Appeals to the Ancient World

JACQUES LOUIS DAVID completed *The Oath of the Horatii* in 1784. Like many of his other works, it used themes from the supposedly morally austere ancient Roman Republic to criticize the political life of his own day. David intended the painting to contrast ancient civic virtue with the luxurious aristocratic culture of contemporary France.

The Horatii take an oath their father administers to protect the Roman Republic against enemies even if it means sacrificing their own lives. One of these enemies is romantically involved with one of their sisters in the right of the painting. Patriotism must be upheld over other relationships.

The sharp division of the painting with a male world on the left and a female world on the right illustrates how eighteenth-century republican thinkers, such as Rousseau, excluded women from civic life and political participation.

The sisters and mother of the Horatii weep in a separate part of the scene. The emotion of the women and their uncertain political loyalty suggests that civic virtue pertains only to men.

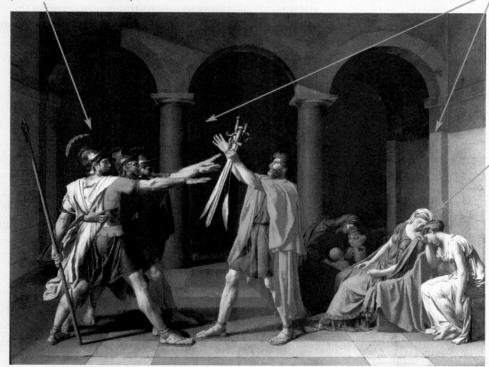

Jacques Louis David (1748–1825) "The Oath of the Horatii," c. 1784, oil on canvas, 330 x 425 cm Inv: 3692. Photo: G. Blot / C. Jean. © Reunion des Musees Nationaux/Art Resource, New York/Louvre, Paris, France.

Questions

1. The Enlightenment is usually associated with modern or progressive ideas. How and why did enlightened writers and readers still find the ancient world important to their reformist agendas?

2. How does the portrayal of women in this painting enter into the contemporary debate over the role of women in public life as seen in the Rousseau and Wollstonecraft documents in this chapter? How might Wollstonecraft have commented on this painting?

3. Do you think this painting and similar images of ancient virtue would have effectively undermined social respect and confidence in the eighteenth-century French aristocracy, or was the audience for such paintings too small?

educational institutions into the service of the Crown so that she could have enough educated officials, and she expanded primary education on the local level.

Maria Theresa was also concerned about the welfare of the peasants and serfs. The extension of the authority of the royal bureaucracy over that of the local nobilities helped the peasants, as did the empress's decrees limiting the services that landowners could demand from them. This concern arose from her desire to ensure a good military recruitment pool. In all these policies and in her general desire to stimulate prosperity and military strength by royal initiative, Maria Theresa anticipated the policies of her son.

Joseph II, however, was more determined, and his projected reforms were more wide ranging than his mother's. He was ambitious to expand at the expense of Poland, Bavaria, and the Ottoman Empire. But his greatest ambition was to change the authority of the Habsburg emperor over his various realms. He sought to overcome the pluralism of the Habsburg holdings by increasing the power of the central monarchy in areas of political and social life that Maria Theresa had wisely not disturbed. In particular, Joseph sought to lessen Hungarian autonomy. He refused to have himself crowned king of Hungary and even had the Crown of Saint Stephen sent to Vienna. He thus avoided having to guarantee existing or new Hungarian privileges in a coronation oath. He reorganized local government in Hungary to increase the authority of his own officials, and he required the use of the German language in all governmental matters. But the Magyar nobility resisted, and in 1790 Joseph had to rescind most of his centralizing measures.

Another target of Joseph's assertion of royal absolutism was religion. In October 1781 Joseph extended freedom of worship to Lutherans, Calvinists, and the Greek Orthodox. They were permitted to have their own churches, sponsor schools, enter skilled trades, and hold academic appointments and positions in the public service. From 1781 through 1789 Joseph relieved the Jews of certain taxes and signs of personal degradation and gave them the right of private worship. Despite these benefits, the Jews still did not enjoy general legal rights equal to those of other Habsburg subjects.

Above all, Joseph sought to bring the various institutions of the Roman Catholic Church directly under his control. He forbade direct communication between the bishops of his realms and the pope. He regarded most orders of monks and nuns as unproductive. Consequently, he dissolved over 600 monasteries and confiscated their lands, although he excepted certain orders that ran schools or hospitals. He also dissolved the traditional Roman Catholic seminaries, which he believed taught priests too great a loyalty to the papacy and too little concern for their future parishioners. In their place he sponsored eight general seminaries that emphasized parish duties. In effect, Joseph's policies made Roman

Catholic priests the employees of the state and ended the influence of the church as an independent institution in Habsburg lands. In many respects, the ecclesiastical policies of Joseph II, known as *Josephinism*, prefigured those of the French Revolution.

With regard to serfdom and the land, Joseph II again pursued policies initiated by Maria Theresa to more far-reaching ends. He abolished the legal status of serfdom defined in terms of servitude to another person. He gave peasants much more personal freedom. They could marry, engage in skilled work, or have their children trained in such skills without permission of the landlord. The procedures of the manorial courts were reformed, and avenues of appeal to royal officials were opened. Joseph also encouraged landlords to change land leases, so that it would be easier for peasants to inherit them or to transfer them to another peasant without bringing into doubt the landlord's title of ownership. Joseph believed that reducing traditional burdens would make the peasant tillers of the land more productive and industrious.

In 1789 Joseph proposed a new and daring system of land taxation. All proprietors were to be taxed, regardless of social status. No longer were the peasants alone to bear the burden of taxation. He commuted compulsory service into a monetary tax, split between the landlord and the state. The decree was drawn up, but resistance from the nobles delayed its implementation. Then in 1790 Joseph died, and the decree never went into effect. However, his measures had stirred up turmoil throughout the Habsburg realms. Peasants revolted over disagreements about the interpretation of their newly granted rights. The nobles of the various realms protested the taxation scheme.

On Joseph's death, the Crown went to his brother Leopold II (r. 1790–1792). Although sympathetic to Joseph's goals, Leopold had to repeal many of the most controversial decrees, such as that changing taxation.

Catherine the Great of Russia

After the death of Peter the Great in 1725, the court nobles and the army determined the Russian succession. As a result, the Crown fell into the hands of people with little talent until 1741, when Peter's daughter Elizabeth came to the throne. At her death in 1762 Elizabeth was succeeded by Peter III, one of her nephews. He was a weak and possibly insane ruler who had been married in 1745 to a young German princess, the future Catherine the Great (r. 1762–1796). Catherine had neither love nor loyalty for her demented husband. After a few months of rule Peter III was deposed and murdered with Catherine's approval, if not aid. On his deposition she was immediately proclaimed empress.

View the Image
Catherine the Great
at **MyHistoryLab.com**

Catherine the Great ascended to the Russian throne after the murder of her husband. She tried initially to enact major reforms, but she never intended to abandon absolutism. She assured the nobility of their rights and by the end of her reign had imposed press censorship.

Catherine's familiarity with the Enlightenment and the general culture of western Europe convinced her that Russia must make major reforms if it was to remain a great power. Consequently, in 1767 Catherine summoned a Legislative Commission to advise her on revising the law and government of Russia. There were over 500 delegates drawn from all sectors of Russian life. Before the commission convened, Catherine wrote a set of *Instructions*, containing ideas drawn from the political writings of the *philosophes*. The revision of Russian law, however, did not occur for more than half a century. In 1768 Catherine dismissed the commission before several of its key committees had reported. Yet the commission had gathered a vast amount of information about the conditions of local administration and economic life throughout Russia. The inconclusive debates and the absence of programs from the delegates themselves suggested that most Russians saw no alternative to an autocratic monarchy. Catherine herself had no intention of departing from absolutism.

●●○─Read the Document
Catherine the Great's Constitution
(1767) at **MyHistoryLab.com**

Catherine proceeded to carry out limited reforms on her own authority while supporting the rights and local power of the nobility. In 1775 she reorganized local government to solve problems brought to light by the Legislative Commission. She put most local offices into the hands of nobles rather than creating a royal bureaucracy. In 1785 Catherine

issued the Charter of the Nobility, which guaranteed many noble rights and privileges. She issued a similar charter to the towns of her realms. In part, the empress had to favor the nobles. There were too few educated subjects in her realm to establish an independent bureaucracy, and the treasury could not afford an army strictly loyal to the Crown. So Catherine wisely made a virtue of necessity. She strengthened the stability of her Crown by a convenient alliance with her nobles and urban leaders.

Catherine continued the Russian drive for warm-water ports (see Map 21–2 on page 664). This led to warfare with the Turks between 1768 and 1774, when the Treaty of Kuchuk-Kainardji gave Russia a direct outlet on the Black Sea, free navigation rights in its waters, and free access through the Bosphorus. Moreover, the Crimea became an independent state, which Catherine painlessly annexed in 1783.

Charter of Nobility. Granted by Empress Catherine II in 1785, this charter concluded the legal consolidation of Russian nobility as a class and provided for its political and corporate rights, privileges, and principles of self-organization. In this printing, the imperial title is hand written in gold and is surrounded by engraved coats of arms of the provinces of the Russian Empire.

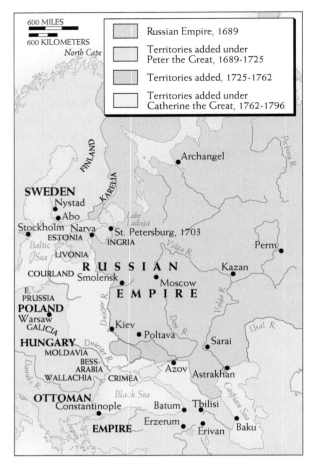

Map 21–2. Expansion of Russia, 1689–1796. The overriding territorial aim of the two most powerful Russian monarchs of the eighteenth century, Peter the Great (in the first quarter of the century) and Catherine the Great (in the last half of the century), was to secure navigable outlets to the sea in both the north and the south for Russia's vast empire; hence Peter's push to the Baltic Sea and Catherine's to the Black Sea. Russia also expanded into Central Asia and Siberia during this time period.

The Partition of Poland

These Russian military successes made the other states of eastern Europe uneasy. Their anxieties were allayed by the First Partition of Poland. The Russian victories along the Danube River in what is today Romania were most unwelcome to Austria, which had its own ambitions there. At the same time, the Ottoman Empire was pressing Prussia for aid against Russia. Frederick the Great made a proposal to Russia and Austria that would give each something it wanted, prevent conflict among them, and save appearances. After long, complicated, secret negotiations, the three powers agreed that Russia would abandon the Danubian provinces in return for a large chunk of Polish territory with almost 2 million inhabitants. As a reward for remaining neutral, Prussia annexed most of the Polish territory between East Prussia and Prussia proper, which allowed Frederick to

Chronology

Russia from Peter the Great through Catherine the Great

1725	Death of Peter the Great
1741–1762	Elizabeth
1762	Peter III
1762	Catherine II (the Great) becomes empress
1767	Legislative Commission summoned
1768	War with Turkey
1771–1774	Pugachev's Rebellion
1772	First Partition of Poland
1774	Treaty of Kuchuk-Kainardji ends war with Turkey
1775	Reorganization of local government
1783	Russia annexes the Crimea
1785	Catherine issues the Charter of the Nobility
1793	Second Partition of Poland
1795	Third Partition of Poland
1796	Death of Catherine the Great

unite two previously separate sections of his realm. Finally, Austria took Galicia, with its important salt mines, and other Polish territory with over 2.5 million inhabitants. The Polish state had lost approximately one-third of its territory.

There were two additional partitions of Poland by Russia and Prussia, and one more by Austria. They occurred in 1793 and 1795 and removed Poland from the map of Europe until 1919. The great powers contended that they were saving themselves, and by implication the rest of Europe, from Polish anarchy. The argument was plausible to some contemporaries because of the fears spurred by the French Revolution. However, the truth was that Poland's political weakness made the country and its resources a rich field for plunderous aggression.

Summary

The Scientific Revolution. The scientific ideas of the sixteenth and seventeenth centuries changed the way Western intellectuals thought about the world and humankind. Instead of a view of nature and humanity based on Scripture and Divine Revelation, Western thinkers came to rely on mathematical laws, empirical data, and experimentation. Copernicus, Kepler, and Galileo overturned the ancient idea, sanctioned by the Bible, that the earth was the center

◆◆┤Read the Document

Immanuel Kant defines the
Enlightenment, 1784
at **MyHistoryLab.com**

of the universe and that the sun and the planets revolved around it. Galileo maintained that the world was governed by mathematical laws. Francis Bacon urged the necessity for observation and experimentation. Newton showed the effects of gravity and established an enduring basis for physics. Locke argued that human beings are shaped by their sense experiences and are hence creatures of their environment subject to reform and possible progress.

The Enlightenment. The Enlightenment *philosophes* used reason as a basis for reform and to advocate progressive social, economic, and political movements. Voltaire attacked religious intolerance and advocated strong central government to impose rational solutions to social and political problems. Montesquieu and other *philosophes* argued for limited, constitutional government. Rousseau wished to reform society in the name of virtue rather than material happiness. He maintained that in the pursuit of virtue the needs of society were more important than those of the individual. The competing strands of the Enlightenment continue to pervade Western society.

Enlightened Absolutism. Enlightened absolutism was a form of monarchical government dedicated to the rational strengthening of the central government. Many of the reforms enlightened monarchs imposed were influenced by the ideas of the *philosophes*, but the chief goal of these rulers was to increase their own authority and military strength, as witnessed by the partitions of Poland among Russia, Prussia, and Austria at the end of the eighteenth century. The most important enlightened monarchs were Frederick II of Prussia, Joseph II of Austria, and Catherine the Great of Russia.

Review Questions

1. What was the Scientific Revolution? What were the major contributions of Copernicus, Brahe, Kepler, Galileo, Bacon, and Newton? Do you think they regarded themselves as revolutionaries?

2. Define the Enlightenment. Is it best seen as a single movement or as a series of related movements? What was the relationship of the Enlightenment to the New Science? How did the Enlightenment further the idea of progress and the superiority of European civilization?

3. Why did the *philosophes* believe they must comment so extensively on religion? Why did they criticize Christianity? Why did some of them champion deism? What were the differing views of the *philosophes* toward Islam?

4. Was there a single Enlightenment view of politics? Why could writers so dedicated to reform have so many different political paths to achieve reform? Why did some Enlightenment writers argue for the superiority of European culture? Why did others criticize European empires?

5. Define enlightened absolutism. What were the similarities in the policies of Frederick the Great, Joseph II, and Catherine the Great? To what extent do their policies actually seem to stem from the ideas of the Enlightenment *philosophes*?

Note: To learn more about the topics in this chapter, please turn to the Suggested Readings at the end of the book. For additional sources related to this chapter please see MyHistoryLab.com.

Key Terms

deism (p. 649)

empiricism (p. 642)

Enlightenment (p. 646)

laissez-faire (p. 654)

philosophes (p. 646)

Ptolemaic system (p. 639)

Scientific Revolution (p. 638)

myhistorylab Connections

Reinforce what you learned in this chapter by studying the many documents, images, maps, review tools, and videos available at **www.myhistorylab.com**.

Read and Review

✓●─[Study and Review] **Chapter 21**

●●●─[Read the Document] *Nicolaus Copernicus: On the Revolution of the Heavenly Spheres (1500s), p. 639*

Francis Bacon, from Novum Organum, p. 643

Isaac Newton, from Opticks, p. 644

Galileo Galilei, Letter to the Grand Duchess Christina (1630s), p. 644

John Locke, Essay Concerning Human Understanding, p. 646

Voltaire, Letters On England, p. 647

Diderot's Encyclopedia – Plate Illustrating Agricultural Techniques p. 649

Voltaire, "On Universal Toleration", p. 651

Lady Mary Wortley Montagu, Letters:
(a) on Constantinople;
(b) on Smallpox;
(c) on Vaccination in Turkey, p. 652

Baron de Montesquieu, Excerpt from The Spirit of the Laws, p. 654

Adam Smith, Intro to the Wealth of Nations (1776) and Wealth of Nations, Adam Smith (1776), p. 654

Catherine the Great's Constitution (1767), p. 663

Immanuel Kant Defines the Enlightenment, 1784, p. 665

◉●─[View the Image] *The Spirit of the Laws, Montesquieu-Frontispiece, p. 653*

Catherine the Great, p. 662

Research and Explore

◉─[See the Map] *Science and the Enlightenment, p.638 and p. 647*

─ ((●●─[Hear the Audio ─

Hear the audio file for Chapter 21 at
www.myhistorylab.com.

22 Revolutions in the Transatlantic World

- Revolution in the British Colonies in North America
- Revolution in France
- Wars of Independence in Latin America
- Toward the Abolition of Slavery in the Transatlantic Economy

BETWEEN 1776 AND 1824 A WORLD-TRANSFORMING series of revolutions occurred in France and the Americas. In half a century the peoples of the two American continents established their independence of European political control. In Europe the French monarchy collapsed from the forces of aristocratic resistance and popular revolution. All the revolutionary leaders sought to establish new governments based largely, though never entirely, on Enlightenment principles.

From start to finish these revolutions were connected. The financial pressures from the Seven Years' War (1756–1763) had led Britain, Spain, and France to undertake a search for revenue that politically destabilized the Americas and France itself. Once the American Revolution began, France aided the colonists, thus exacerbating its own financial problem. In turn the French Revolution and the ensuing Napoleonic Wars created situations in Spain and Portugal to which the colonial elites in Latin America responded by seeking independence. Thus the transatlantic revolutions, despite their

Guerrilla Warfare. Haitian slaves ambush French forces during their successful revolt led by Toussaint L'Ouverture and Jean-Jacques Dessalines in 1794. The Haitian revolution was the largest emancipation of slaves to occur in the eighteenth century.

The Transatlantic Revolutions

The Atlantic World

The revolutions and the crusade against slavery that occurred throughout the transatlantic world between 1776 and the 1830s transformed the political, social, and economic life of three continents. First in North America, then in France and other parts of Europe, and finally in South America bold political experiments challenged colonial government, monarchies, and aristocratic governments and laid the foundations for modern liberal democracy. These revolutions and the effort to abolish slavery owed much to the philosophical inspiration of the Enlightenment and bear witness to the immense influence of the Enlightenment in world history.

As a result of the events of this age of transatlantic revolution, the largest republic since ancient times was established in North America. In Europe the absolutist governments were overthrown across the continent by the impact of the French Revolution and the armies of Napoleon.

Slaves on Haiti overthrew the French colonial regime and established the first black republic. By the close of the first quarter of the nineteenth century, wars of independence across Latin America had closed the era of European empire with the establishment of republics everywhere except Brazil.

No less important, this era witnessed the beginning of an international effort to bring about the abolition of the slave economies that had long dominated the transatlantic economy.

The expanding forms of political liberty found their counterparts in an economic life freed from the constraints of the old colonial empires and eventually from the economies based on plantation slave labor. The new American republic constituted a vast free-trade zone with its commerce and ports open to the entire world.

For the first time since the encounter with Europe, all of Latin America could trade freely with its own peoples and those of the rest of the world.

individual characters and developments, were interconnected events in world history. Furthermore, the era witnessed the commencement of a vast international crusade, first to abolish the slave trade and then to abolish slavery in the transatlantic world. The same Enlightenment ideas that inspired many of the revolutionaries also inspired the opponents of slavery as did religious convictions. The political and economic dislocations of the revolutionary era helped the antislavery forces achieve their goals. The political, social, and economic life of the transatlantic world would never be the same again. ■

Revolution in the British Colonies in North America

Resistance to the Imperial Search for Revenue

After the Treaty of Paris in 1763 ended the Seven Years' War (see Chapter 19), the British government faced two imperial problems. The first was the sheer cost of empire, which the British felt they could no longer carry alone. The second was that the defeat of the French required the British to organize a vast expanse of new territory: all of North America east of the Mississippi, with its French settlers and, more important, its native Indian population (see Map 22–1 on page 670).

The British drive for revenue began in 1764 with the Sugar Act, which attempted to produce more revenue from imports into the colonies by the rigorous collection of what was actually a reduced tax on sugar. Smugglers were to be tried in admiralty courts without juries. The next year, Parliament passed the Stamp Act, which put a tax on legal documents and certain other items such as newspapers. The British considered these taxes legal and just because they had been approved by Parliament and because the revenue was to be spent in the colonies. The Americans responded that they alone through their assemblies had the right to tax themselves and that they were not represented in Parliament. Furthermore, the Americans feared that if colonial government were financed from Britain, they would cease to control it.

In October 1765 the Stamp Act Congress met in America and drew up a protest to the Crown. (See Document, "The Stamp Act Congress Addresses George III.") There was much disorder in the colonies, particularly in Massachusetts,

In Europe the reforms of the French Revolution and the new Napoleonic Code of law removed many regional economic barriers and led to more standard weights and measures.

National law formed the framework for economic activity. The movement to abolish slavery fostered a wage economy of free laborers. That kind of economy generated its own set of problems and social dislocation, including a sort of sharecropping serfdom for many former slaves, but it was nonetheless an economy of free human beings who were the chattel of no other human being.

Finally, the age of transatlantic revolutions saw the emergence of nationalism as a political force. All of the revolutions, because of their popular political base, had given power to the idea of nations defined by their own character and historical past rather than by dynastic rulers. Americans saw themselves as forming a new kind of nation. The French had demonstrated the power of a nation fully mobilized for military purposes. In turn France's aggression had aroused national sentiment, especially in Great Britain, Spain, and Germany. The new nations of Latin America also sought to define themselves by their heritage and historical experience rather than by their past in the Spanish and Portuguese empires.

These various revolutions, their political doctrines, and their social and economic departures provided examples to peoples elsewhere in the world. But even more important,

the transformations of the transatlantic revolutions and eventual abolition of slavery meant that new political classes and newly organized independent nations would become actors on the world scene. Europeans would have to deal with a score of new nations in the Americas. The rest of the world confronted new nations freed from the direction and authority of European powers. In turn, the political changes in Europe meant that those nations and their relationships with the rest of the world would be directed by a broader range of political groups and forces than in the past. Ironically, however, by the close of the nineteenth century several of the European nations as well as the United States that had become liberal democratic states would commence a new wave of colonialism throughout Africa and Asia and would impose new economic dominance on the republics of Latin America.

Focus Questions

- What is the relationship between the Enlightenment and the transatlantic revolutions? Between the Enlightenment and the crusade against slavery?
- How did the transatlantic revolutions fundamentally alter the relationship between Europe and the Americas?
- What is the relationship between the transatlantic revolutions and nationalism? Why did such a relationship exist?

led by groups known as the Sons of Liberty. The colonists agreed to boycott British goods. In 1766 Parliament repealed the Stamp Act but, through the Declaratory Act, claimed the power to legislate for the colonies.

American Political Ideas

The political ideas of the American colonists had largely arisen from the struggle of seventeenth-century English aristocrats and gentry against the absolutism of the Stuart monarchs. The American colonists believed that the English Revolution of 1688 had established many of their own fundamental political liberties. The colonists claimed that, through the measures imposed from 1763 to 1776, George III (r. 1760–1820) and the British Parliament were attacking those liberties and dissolving the bonds of moral and political allegiance that had formerly united the two peoples. Consequently, the colonists employed a theory that had originally been developed to justify an aristocratic rebellion in England to support their own popular revolution.

These Whig political ideas, largely derived from John Locke (1632–1704), were only a part of the English ideological heritage that affected the Americans. Throughout the eighteenth century they had become familiar with a series of

British political writers called the *Commonwealthmen*. These writers held republican political ideas that had their intellectual roots in the most radical thought of the Puritan revolution. They had relentlessly criticized the government patronage and parliamentary management of Robert Walpole (1676–1745) and his successors. They argued that such government was corrupt and that it undermined liberty. They regarded much parliamentary taxation as simply a means of financing political corruption. They also attacked standing armies as instruments of tyranny. In Great Britain this republican political tradition had only a marginal impact. In the colonies, however, these radical books and pamphlets were read widely and were often accepted at face value. The policy of Great Britain toward America after the Treaty of Paris made many colonists believe that the worst fears of the Commonwealthmen were coming true.

Crisis and Independence

In 1767 Charles Townshend (1725–1767) led Parliament to regulate and tax colonial imports. The colonists again resisted. The ministry sent over its own customs agents to administer the laws. To protect these new officers, the British sent troops to Boston in 1768. The obvious tensions resulted, and

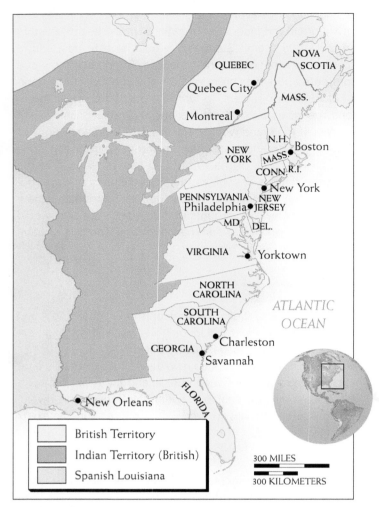

Map 22–1. North America in 1763. In the year of the victory over France, the English colonies lay along the Atlantic seaboard. The difficulties of organizing authority over the previous French territory in Canada and west of the Appalachian Mountains would contribute to the tensions that would precipitate the American Revolution.

Boston Massacre. This view of the Boston Massacre of March 5, 1770, by Paul Revere owes more to propaganda than to fact. There was no order to fire, and the innocent citizens portrayed here were really an angry, violent mob.

in March 1770 British troops killed five citizens in the Boston Massacre. In that same year Parliament repealed the Townshend duties except for the one on tea.

In May 1773 Parliament allowed the East India Company to import tea directly into the American colonies. Although the law lowered the price of tea, it retained the tax without the colonists' consent. In some cities the colonists refused to permit the tea to be unloaded; in Boston, a shipload of tea was thrown into the harbor, an event known since as the Boston Tea Party.

The British ministry of Lord North (1732–1792) was determined to assert the authority of Parliament over the resistant colonies. In 1774 Parliament passed a series of laws known in American history as the Intolerable Acts. These measures closed the port of Boston, reorganized the government of Massachusetts, allowed troops to be quartered in private homes, and removed the trials of royal customs offi-

cials to England. In the same year Parliament approved the Quebec Act, which extended the boundaries of Quebec to include the Ohio River valley. The Americans regarded the Quebec Act as an attempt to prevent the extension of their mode of self-government westward beyond the Appalachian Mountains.

During these years committees of correspondence, composed of citizens critical of Britain, had been established throughout the colonies. In September 1774 these committees organized the First Continental Congress in Philadelphia. This body hoped to persuade Parliament to restore self-government in the colonies and to abandon its attempt at direct supervision of colonial affairs. Conciliation, however, was not forthcoming. By April 1775 the battles of Lexington and Concord had been fought. In June the colonists were defeated at the battle of Bunker Hill.

The Second Continental Congress gathered in May 1775. It still sought conciliation with Britain but soon undertook the government of the colonies. By August 1775 George III had declared the colonies in rebellion. During the winter Thomas Paine's (1737–1809) pamphlet *Common Sense* galvanized public opinion in favor of separation from Great Britain. A colonial army and navy were organized. In April 1776 the Continental Congress opened American ports to the trade of all nations. Finally, on July 4, 1776, the Continental Congress adopted the Declaration of Independence. Thereafter, the War of the American Revolution continued until 1781, when the forces of George Washington (1732–1799) defeated those of Lord Cornwallis

Document The Stamp Act Congress Addresses George III

In 1765 the Stamp Act Congress met to protest the British imposition of taxes on the colonies. American leaders believed Great Britain had no right to impose such taxation. Their argument was that they were not and could not be represented in Parliament and that they were subject to the taxation only of their own assemblies. Later clauses implied that the taxation would prevent the colonists from purchasing manufactured goods from Britain and demanded the repeal of the act.

■ *Why does the Congress insist on the same rights for subjects born in the colonies as those born in England? On what grounds does the Congress declare that Parliament may not levy taxes in the colonies? Why is the Congress so concerned about what courts may try cases arising from the Stamp Act?*

The Members of this Congress, sincerely devoted, with the warmest sentiments of affection and duty to His Majesty's person and government . . . and with minds deeply impressed by a sense of the present and impending misfortunes of the British colonies on this continent; having considered as maturely as time will permit, the circumstances of the said colonies, esteem it our indispensable duty to make the following declarations of our humble opinion, respecting the most essential rights and liberties of the colonists, and of the grievances under which they labor, by reason of several late acts of Parliament.

1. That His Majesty's subjects in these colonies, owe the same allegiance to the crown of Great Britain, that is owing from his subjects born within the realm, and all due subordination to that august body the Parliament of Great Britain.
2. That His Majesty's liege subjects in these colonies are entitled to all the inherent rights and liberties of his natural born subjects, within the kingdom of Great Britain.
3. That it is inseparably essential to the freedom of a people, and the undoubted right of Englishmen, that no taxes be imposed on them but with their own consent, given personally, or by their representatives.
4. That the people of these colonies are not, and cannot, be represented in the House of Commons in Great Britain.

5. That the only representatives of the people of these colonies are persons chosen therein by themselves, and that no taxes ever have been, or can be constitutionally imposed on them, but by their respective legislatures.
6. That all supplies to the crown being free gifts of the people, it is unreasonable and inconsistent with the principles and spirit of the British constitution, for the people of Great Britain to grant to His Majesty the property of the colonists.
7. That trial by jury, is the inherent and invaluable right of every British subject in these colonies.
8. That the late act of Parliament entitled, *An act for granting and supplying certain stamp duties, and other duties, in the British colonies and plantations, in America, etc.* by imposing taxes on the inhabitants of these colonies, and the said act, and several other acts, by extending the jurisdiction of the courts of admiralty beyond its ancient limits, have a manifest tendency to subvert the rights and liberties of the colonists.

Source: From *Journal of the First Congress of the American Colonies . . .* 1765 (New York, 1845), pp. 27–29, as quoted in Oscar Handlin, ed., *Readings in American History.* Copyright © 1957 Alfred A. Knopf, pp. 116–117.

(1738–1805) at Yorktown. Early in 1778, however, the war had widened into a European conflict when Benjamin Franklin (1706–1790) persuaded the French government to support the rebellion. In 1779 the Spanish also came to the aid of the colonies. The 1783 Treaty of Paris concluded the conflict, and the thirteen American colonies had established their independence.

As the crisis with Britain unfolded during the 1760s and 1770s, the American colonists came to see themselves as first preserving traditional English liberties against a tyrannical Crown and corrupt Parliament and then as developing a new sense of liberty. By the mid-1770s the colonists had embraced republican political ideals. They would govern themselves through elected assemblies without any monarchical

Chronology

The American Revolution

1760	George III becomes king
1763	Treaty of Paris concludes the Seven Years' War
1764	Sugar Act
1765	Stamp Act
1766	Sugar Act repealed and Declaratory Act passed
1767	Townshend Acts
1770	Lord North becomes George III's chief minister
1770	Boston Massacre
1773	Boston Tea Party
1774	Intolerable Acts
1774	First Continental Congress
1775	Second Continental Congress
1776	Declaration of Independence
1778	France enters the war on the side of America
1781	British forces surrender at Yorktown
1783	Treaty of Paris concludes War of the American Revolution

authority. The Constitutional Convention met in 1787. After the constitution was adopted in 1788, Americans would insist on a bill of rights specifically protecting civil liberties. The Americans would reject the aristocratic social hierarchy that had existed in the colonies. They would embrace democratic ideals, even if the franchise remained limited. They would assert the equality of white male citizens not only before the law but also in ordinary social relations. They would reject social status based on birth and inheritance and assert the necessity of liberty for all citizens to improve their social standing and economic lot by engaging in free commercial activity. They did not free their slaves, nor did they address the rights of women or Native Americans, but the American Revolution produced a society freer than any the world had seen, one that would expand the circle of political and social liberty. The political and social values of the American Revolution would inspire the wars of independence in Latin America.

((•─[Hear the Audio
at MyHistoryLab.com

Revolution in France

The French monarchy emerged from the Seven Years' War both defeated and deeply in debt. The later French support for the American Revolution exacerbated the financial difficulties. Given France's economic vitality, the government debt was neither overly large nor disproportionate to the debts of other European powers. The problem was the government's inability to collect sufficient taxes to service and repay the debt.

Between 1786 and 1788 Louis XVI (r. 1774–1792) appointed several different ministers to deal with the financial crisis. All failed to persuade the aristocracy and the church to pay more taxes. As these negotiations dragged on, the *parlement* of Paris declared that only the Estates General could institute new taxes. The Estates General had not met since 1614. Consequently, in July 1788, Louis XVI agreed to convene the Estates General the next year.

Revolutions of 1789

The Estates General Becomes the National Assembly
The Estates General had three divisions: the First Estate of the clergy, the Second Estate of the nobility, and the **Third Estate**, representing everyone else in the kingdom. Before the Estates General met at Versailles in May 1789, there had been much public debate over its organization. The monarchy had agreed that the Third Estate should have twice as many members as either the nobility or the clergy. Then there arose the question of how voting should be organized. The nobility wanted all votes to be taken by Estate, which would have allowed the nobles and clergy to outvote the Third Estate. The Third Estate wanted each member to vote individually so that, with its larger membership, it would dominate.

From the beginning the Third Estate, composed largely of local officials, professional men, and lawyers, refused to sit as a separate order as the king desired. For several weeks there was a standoff. Then, on June 1 the Third Estate invited the clergy and the nobles to join it in organizing a new legislative body. A few of the lower clergy did so. On June 17 that body declared itself the National Assembly.

Three days later, finding themselves accidentally locked out of their usual meeting place, the National Assembly moved to a nearby tennis court, where its members took the famous Tennis Court Oath to continue to sit until they had given France a constitution.

●─[View the Image
Oath of the Tennis Court,
at **MyHistoryLab.com**

Louis XVI ordered the National Assembly to desist, but shortly afterward most of the clergy and many nobles joined the assembly. On June 27 the king capitulated and formally requested the First and Second Estates to meet with the National Assembly, where voting would occur by head rather than by order. Government by the privileged orders thus ended, and the National Assembly became the National Constituent Assembly.

Fall of the Bastille Two new factors soon intruded. First, Louis XVI attempted to regain the initiative by mustering troops near Versailles and Paris. This was the beginning of a steady, and consistently poorly executed, royal attempt to halt the revolution. Most of the National Constituent Assembly wished to create some form of constitutional monarchy, but from the start Louis's refusal to cooperate thwarted that effort.

The second new factor was the populace of Paris. The mustering of royal troops created anxiety in the city, where there had been several bread riots. By June the Parisians were organizing a citizen militia and collecting arms.

On July 14 around 800 people, mostly small shopkeepers, tradespeople, artisans, and wage earners, marched to the Bastille in search of weapons for the militia. This great fortress had once held political prisoners. Through miscalculations and ineptitude by the governor of the fortress, the troops in the Bastille fired into the crowd, killing ninety-eight people and wounding many others. The crowd then stormed the fortress, released its seven prisoners, none of whom was there for political reasons, and killed several soldiers and the governor. They found no weapons.

This was the first of many crucial *journées*, or days, when the populace of Paris would redirect the course of the revolution. The fall of the Bastille signaled that the political future of the nation would not be decided solely by the National Constituent Assembly. As the news spread, similar disturbances

Storming of the Bastille. On July 14, 1789, crowds stormed the Bastille, a prison in Paris. This event, whose only practical effect was to free a few prisoners, marked the first time the populace of Paris redirected the course of the revolution. *Anonymous, France, eighteenth century, "Seige of the Bastille, 14 July, 1789." Musée de la Ville de Paris, Musée Carnavalet, Paris, France. Bridgeman-Giraudon/Art Resource, N.Y.*

took place in the provincial cities. A few days later Louis XVI, again bowing to events, came to Paris and recognized both the new elected government of the city and its National Guard. The citizens of Paris were, for the time, being satisfied.

The Great Fear and Surrender of Feudal Privileges As popular urban disturbances erupted in various cities, a movement known as the Great Fear swept across much of the French countryside. Peasants were reclaiming rights and property that they had lost through the aristocratic resurgence of the last quarter century, as well as venting their anger against the injustices of rural life. The Great Fear, which was an intensification of peasant disturbances that had begun during the spring, witnessed the burning of châteaux, the destruction of records and documents, and the refusal by peasants to pay feudal dues.

On the night of August 4, 1789, aristocrats in the National Constituent Assembly attempted to halt the disorder in the countryside. By prearrangement, liberal nobles and churchmen rose in the assembly and surrendered hunting and fishing rights, judicial authority, tithes, and special exemptions. In a sense, these nobles gave up what they had already lost and what they could not have regained without civil war. Later, many would also be compensated for their losses. Nonetheless, after August 4 all French citizens were subject to the same and equal laws.

Declaration of the Rights of Man and Citizen On August 26, 1789, the assembly issued the Declaration of the Rights of Man and Citizen. This declaration drew together much of the political language of the Enlightenment and was also influenced by the Declaration of Rights adopted by Virginia in America in June 1776. The French declaration proclaimed that all men were "born and remain free and equal in rights." Their natural rights were "liberty, property, security, and resistance to oppression." Governments existed to protect those rights. All political sovereignty resided in the nation and its representatives. All citizens were to be equal before the law and were to be "equally admissible to all public dignities, offices and employments, according to their capacity, and with no other distinction than that of their virtues and talents." There were to be due process of law and presumption of innocence until proof of guilt. Freedom of religion was affirmed. Taxation was to be apportioned equally according to capacity to pay. Property constituted "an inviolable and sacred right."[1] Louis XVI stalled before ratifying both the declaration and the aristocratic renunciation of feudalism. His hesitations fanned suspicions that he might try to resort to force. Moreover, bread shortages continued. On October 5 several thousand Parisian women marched to

[1]Quoted in Georges Lefebvre, *The Coming of the French Revolution*, trans. by R. R. Palmer (Princeton, NJ: Princeton University Press, 1967), pp. 221–223.

A Closer Look

Challenging the French Political Order

This late eighteenth-century cartoon satirizes the French social and political structure as the events and tensions leading up to the outbreak of the French Revolution unfolded. This image embodies the highly radical critique of the French political structure that erupted from about 1787, when the nobility and church refused to aid the financial crisis of the monarchy.

Behind the king ride a Roman Catholic bishop and a noble magistrate. The bishop holds a document associating the clergy with religious persecution and protection of church property. The noble holds a statement championing the powers of the aristocratic *parlements*.

Louis XVI is portrayed as the chief rider of the poor citizen holding a whip and declaring that feudal dues and the rights of the landowners should prevail. This positioning of the king suggests that the cartoon was drawn after the calling of the Estates General when, until the representation of the Third Estate was doubled, Louis was seen as siding with the church and nobility against the people. Prior to then, he had been seen as a paternal protector of the French people.

At the bottom of the heap is a poor, blinded ordinary French citizen in the chains of taxation and feudal obligations. The image suggests that the chains of obligation and the orders of privilege maintaining the chains need to be removed.

Questions

1. This image points to the monarchy, the aristocracy, and established French Roman Catholic Church as political units in conflict with each other. How did they come into conflict? How did their conflicts allow the poor French citizens shown here at the bottom of the heap to come to the fore as agents of social and political change?

2. Does this cartoon illustrate all of the political and social tensions ready to erupt in France at the time of the Revolution? What others emerged? Why did all of these conflicts then lead to the intervention of foreign

powers against the revolution? Why are no foreign powers portrayed in this cartoon?

3. If leaders of the American Revolution had viewed this cartoon and then wanted to draw one of their own, how might theirs have appeared? How might one drawn by the leaders of the Haitian Revolution have drawn it? What common forces did all of the revolutions of the day seek to overturn—or were there common forces?

Women's March. The women of Paris marched to Versailles on October 7, 1789. The following day the royal family was forced to return to Paris with them. Henceforth, the French government would function under the constant threat of mob violence. *Anonymous, 18th century, "To Versailles, to Versailles." The Women of Paris going to Versailles, October 7, 1789. French, Musée de la Ville de Paris, Musée Carnavalet, Paris, France. Photograph copyright Bridgeman-Giraudon/Art Resource, New York.*

Read the Document
Declaration of the Rights of Man and the Citizen 1789 at **MyHistoryLab.com**

Versailles, demanding more bread. This was one of several occasions when women played a major role in the actions of the Parisian crowd. On this day they milled about the palace, and many stayed the night. Under this pressure the king agreed to sanction the decrees of the assembly. The Parisians believed that the king had to be kept under the watchful eye of the people. Consequently they demanded that Louis and his family return to Paris. The monarch had no real choice. On October 6, 1789, his carriage followed the crowd into the city, where he and his family settled in the palace of the Tuileries. The National Constituent Assembly soon followed. Thereafter, both Paris and France remained relatively stable and peaceful until the summer of 1792.

Reconstruction of France

Once established in Paris, the National Constituent Assembly set about reorganizing France. Throughout its proceedings the Assembly was determined to protect property and to limit the impact on national life of small-property owners as well as of the unpropertied elements of the nation. While championing civic equality before the law, the Assembly spurned social equality and extensive democracy. The Assembly thus charted a general course that, to a greater or lesser degree, nineteenth-century liberals across Europe and in other areas of the world would follow.

Political Reorganization The Constitution of 1791, the product of the National Constituent Assembly's deliberations, established a constitutional monarchy. There

was a unicameral Legislative Assembly vested with powers of war and peace. The monarch could delay but not halt legislation. The system of voting was complex and restricted. Only about 50,000 citizens of the French nation of 26 million could actually elect or serve in the Legislative Assembly.

The exclusion of women from both voting and holding office did not pass unnoticed. In 1791 Olympe de Gouges (d. 1793), a butcher's daughter who became a major radical in Paris, composed a *Declaration of the Rights of Woman*, which she ironically addressed to Queen Marie Antoinette (1755–1793). Much of the document reprinted the *Declaration of the Rights of Man and Citizen*, adding the word *woman* to the various original clauses. That strategy demanded that women be regarded as citizens and not merely as daughters, sisters, wives, and mothers of citizens. Olympe de Gouges further outlined rights that would permit women to own property and require men to recognize the paternity of their children. She called for equality of the sexes in marriage and improved education for women. Her demands illustrated how the public listing of rights in the *Declaration of the Rights of Man and Citizen* created universal civic expectations even among those it did not cover. (See Document: "Olympe de Gouges Issues a Declaration of the Rights of Woman." on page 676)

New Administrative Units The National Constituent Assembly abolished the ancient French provinces, such as Burgundy, and replaced them with eighty-three departments (*départements*) of generally equal size named after rivers, mountains, and other geographical features. The ancient judicial courts, including the seigneurial courts and the *parlements*, were suppressed and replaced by established uniform courts with elected judges and prosecutors. Legal procedures were simplified, and the most degrading punishments abolished.

Economic Policy In economic matters the National Constituent Assembly suppressed the guilds and liberated the grain trade. The assembly established the metric system to provide the nation with uniform weights and measures. These policies of economic freedom and uniformity disappointed both peasants and urban workers caught in the cycle of inflation. By the decrees of 1790 the Assembly placed the burden of proof on the peasants to rid themselves of the residual feudal dues for which compensation was to be paid. On June 14, 1791, the Assembly enacted the Chapelier Law forbidding worker associations, thereby crushing the attempts of urban workers to protect their wages. Peasants and workers were to be left to the mercy of the free marketplace.

The National Constituent Assembly decided to pay the troublesome royal debt by confiscating and then

Document
Olympe de Gouges Issues a Declaration of the Rights of Woman

On August 26, 1789, the National Assembly passed the Declaration of the Rights of Man and Citizen, the very broad principles of which could be extended beyond the domestic male French citizens to whom it applied. Within months various civically disadvantaged groups stepped forward to demand inclusion within the newly proclaimed realm of civic rights.

In September 1791 Olympe de Gouges published a Declaration of the Rights of Woman that paralleled in many respects the Declaration of the Rights of Man and Citizen proclaimed two years earlier. A self-educated woman and butcher's daughter, she had written widely on a number of reform topics. Radical as she was, she remained loyal to the monarchy and was eventually executed by the revolutionary government in 1793.

■ *What are the specific parallels that de Gouges drew between the rights of man and the rights of woman? How does her declaration suggest civic responsibilities for women as well as rights? How does her language suggest her familiarity with Enlightenment writers?*

Mothers, daughters, sisters [and] representatives of the nation demand to be constituted into a national assembly. . . . Consequently, the sex that is as superior in beauty as it is in courage during the sufferings of maternity recognizes and declares in the presence and Woman and of Female Citizens.

ARTICLE I

Woman is born free and lives equal to man in her rights. Social distinctions can be based only on the common utility.

ARTICLE IV

Liberty and justice consist of restoring all that belongs to others; thus, the only limits on the exercise of the natural rights of woman are perpetual male tyranny; these limits are to be reformed by the laws of nature and reason. . . .

ARTICLE VI

The law must be the expression of the general will; all female and male citizens must contribute either personally or through their representatives to its formation; it must be the same for all: male and female citizens, being equal in the eyes of the law, must be equally admitted to all honors, positions, and public employment according to their capacity and without other distinctions besides those of their virtues and talents. . . .

ARTICLE XVII

Property belongs to both sexes whether united or separate; for each it is an inviolable and sacred right no one can be deprived of it, since it is the true patrimony of nature, unless the legally determined public need obviously dictates it, and then only with a just and prior indemnity.

POSTSCRIPT

Woman, wake up; the tocsin of reason is being heard throughout the whole universe; discover your rights.

Source: From women in Revolutionary Paris, 1789–1795: Selected Documents Translated With Notes and Commentary. Translated with notes and commentary by Darlene Gay levy, Harriet Branson Applewhite, and Mary Durhan Johnson. Copyright © 1979 by the Board of Trustees of the University of Illinois. Used by permission of the editors and the University of Illinois Press.

selling the lands of the Roman Catholic Church in France. The Assembly then authorized the issuance of **assignats**, or government bonds, the value of which was guaranteed by the revenue to be generated from the sale of church property. When the *assignats* began to circulate as currency, the Assembly issued even larger quantities of them to liquidate the national debt. However, within a few months the value of *assignats* began to fall. Inflation increased and put new stress on the lives of the urban poor.

Civil Constitution of the Clergy In July 1790 the National Constituent Assembly issued the Civil Constitution of the Clergy, which transformed the Roman Catholic Church in France into a branch of the secular state. This measure reduced the number of bishoprics, made borders of dioceses conform to those of the new departments, and provided for the election of priests and bishops, who henceforth became salaried employees of the state. The Assembly consulted neither the pope nor the French clergy about these broad changes. The king approved the measure only with the greatest reluctance.

Document

A Free Person of Color from St. Domingue Demands Recognition of His Status

In the spring of 1791 Julian Raymond, a free person of color from the French Caribbean colony of St. Domingue (Haiti), petitioned the French National Assembly invoking the Declaration of Man and Citizen to recognize persons such as himself as free citizens. The National Assembly did so in May 1791, but later rescinded the decree. Only in March 1792 did the Assembly firmly recognize the civic equality of such persons. The background for the request and for the confusion of the French National Assembly over the matter was the eruption of the slave revolution in Haiti.

■ *How does Raymond portray himself as free but still clearly victimized the Assembly in St. Domingue composed only of white members? In a slave society such as that on St. Domingue, how might a person such as Raymond be legally free but still subject to various modes of discrimination? How can he invoke the principles of the Declaration of the Rights of Man and Citizen to apply pressure on the French National Assembly?*

Remaining to this day under the oppression of the white colonists, we dare hope that we do not ask the National Assembly in vain for the rights, which it has declared, belong to every man.

In our just protests, if the troubles, the calumnies that you have witnessed until today under the legislation of white colonists, and finally, if the truths which we had the honor of presenting yesterday to the bar of the Assembly do not overcome the unjust pretensions of the while colonial legislators who want to [proceed] without our participation, we beg the Assembly not to jeopardize the little remaining liberty we have, that of being able to abandon the ground soaked with the blood of our brothers and of permitting us to flee the sharp knife of the laws they will prepare against u.

If the Assembly has decided to pass a law which lets our fate depend on twenty-nine whites [in the colonial Assembly], our decided enemies, we demand to add an amendment to the decree which would be rendered in this situation, that free men of color can emigrate with their fortunes so that they can be neither disturbed nor hindered by the whites.

Mr. President, this is the last recourse which remains for us to escape the vengeance of the white colonists who menace us for not having given up our claims to the rights which the National Assembly has declared belong to every man.

Source: From: MASON. The French Revolution, 1/E. © 1999 Wadsworth, a part of Cengage Learning, Inc. Reproduced by permission. www.cengage.com/permissions.

The Civil Constitution of the Clergy was the major blunder of the National Constituent Assembly. The measure roused immense opposition within the French church, even from bishops who had long championed Gallican liberties over papal domination. Faced with this resistance, the Assembly unwisely ruled that all clergy must take an oath to support the Civil Constitution. Only seven bishops and about half the clergy did so. In reprisal, the assembly designated the clergy who had not taken the oath as "refractory" and removed them from their clerical functions. Refractory priests immediately attempted to celebrate Mass.

In February 1791 the pope condemned not only the Civil Constitution of the Clergy but also the *Declaration of the Rights of Man and Citizen*. That condemnation marked the opening of a Roman Catholic offensive against liberalism in Europe and revolution throughout the world that continued for over a century. Within France itself, the pope's action meant that religious devotion and revolutionary loyalty became incompatible for many people. French citizens quickly divided between those who supported the constitutional priests and those who resorted to the refractory clergy. Louis XVI and his family favored the refactory clergy.

Counterrevolutionary Activity In the summer of 1791 the queen and some nobles who had already left the country persuaded Louis XVI also to flee. The escape failed when Louis, along with his family, was recognized and stopped in the town of Varennes. On June 24 soldiers escorted the royal family back to Paris. Thereafter, the leaders of the National Constituent Assembly knew that the chief counterrevolutionary sat on the French throne.

Execution of Louis XVI. On January 21, 1793, the Convention executed Louis XVI. *Execution of Louis XVI. Aquatint. French, 18th century. Musée de la Ville de Paris, Musée Carnavalet, Paris, France. Giraudon/Art Resource, New York.*

Two months later, on August 27, 1791, Emperor Leopold II of Austria (r. 1790–1792), who was the brother of Marie Antoinette, and Frederick William II (r. 1786–1797), the king of Prussia, issued the Declaration of Pillnitz. The two monarchs promised to intervene in France to protect the royal family and to preserve the monarchy if the other major European powers agreed. The latter provision rendered the statement meaningless because Great Britain would not have given its consent. In France, however, the revolutionaries felt surrounded by aristocratic and monarchical foes.

Near its close in September 1791 the National Constituent Assembly forbade any of its own members to sit in the Legislative Assembly then being elected. This new body met on October 1 to confront immense problems.

A Second Revolution

Since the earliest days of the revolution, various clubs of politically like-minded persons had organized themselves in Paris. The best organized were the **Jacobins**, whose name derived from the fact that the group met in a former Dominican (Jacobin) monastery located in the Rue St. Jacques. The Paris club was linked to other local clubs in the provinces. In the Legislative Assembly a group of Jacobins known as the *Girondists* (because many of them came from the department of the Gironde) assumed leadership.[2] They led the Legislative Assembly on April 20, 1792, to declare war on Austria, by this time governed by Francis II (r. 1792–1835) and allied to Prussia.

---

[2] The Girondists are also frequently called the *Brissotins* after Jacques-Pierre Brissot (1754–1793), who was their chief representative in early 1792.

End of the Monarchy The war radicalized the revolution and led to what is usually called the second revolution, which overthrew the constitutional monarchy and established a republic. The war initially went poorly, and the revolution seemed in danger. Late in July, under radical working-class pressure, the government of Paris passed from the elected council to a committee, or commune, of representatives from the sections (municipal wards) of Paris. On August 10, 1792, a large crowd invaded the Tuileries and forced Louis XVI and Marie Antoinette to take refuge in the Legislative Assembly itself. During the disturbance several hundred of the royal Swiss guards and many Parisians died. Thereafter, the royal family was imprisoned in comfortable quarters, but the king was suspended from his political functions.

The Convention and the Role of Sans-Culottes

During the first week of September, in what are known as the September Massacres, the Paris Commune summarily killed about 1,200 people in the city jails. Many were aristocrats or priests, but most were simply common criminals. The crowd had assumed that the prisoners were all counter-revolutionaries. The Paris Commune then compelled the Legislative Assembly to call for the election, by universal manhood suffrage, of a new assembly to write a democratic constitution. That body, called the **Convention** after its American counterpart of 1787, met on September 21, 1792.

As its first act the Convention declared France a republic, that is, a nation governed by an elected assembly without a king. The second revolution had been the work of Jacobins more radical than the Girondists and of the people of Paris known as the **sans-culottes**. This term means "without breeches" and was derived from the long trousers that, as working people, they wore instead of aristocratic knee breeches. The *sans-culottes* were shopkeepers, artisans, wage earners, and a few factory workers. The politics of the Old Regime had ignored them, and the policies of the National Constituent Assembly had left them victims of unregulated economic liberty.

The *sans-culottes*, whose labor and military service were needed for the war effort, generally knew what they wanted. They sought immediate price controls for relief from food shortages and rising prices. They believed that all people had a right to subsistence and profoundly resented most forms of social inequality. They felt intense hostility toward the aristocracy and the original leaders of the revolution, whom they believed simply wanted to take over the social privileges of the aristocracy. They did not demand the abolition of property, but advocated a community of relatively small-property owners. They were antimonarchical, strongly republican, and suspicious even of representative government.

In contrast, the Jacobins were republicans who sought representative government. Their hatred of the aristocracy did not extend to a general suspicion of wealth. Basically, the Jacobins favored an unregulated economy. However, from Louis XVI's flight to Varennes onward, the more extreme Jacobins began to cooperate with leaders of the Parisian *sans-culottes* and the Paris Commune to overthrow the monarchy. Once the Convention began its deliberations, these advanced Jacobins, known as the Mountain because of their seats high in the assembly hall, worked with *sans-culottes* to carry the revolution forward and win the war.

In December 1792 Louis XVI was put on trial as mere "Citizen Capet" (Capet was the family name of the royal family's medieval forebears). The Girondists sought to spare his life, but the Mountain defeated the effort. By a narrow majority, Louis was convicted of conspiring against the liberty of the people and the security of the state. Condemned to death, he was beheaded on January 21, 1793.

The next month, the Convention declared war on Great Britain, Holland, and Spain. France was now at war with virtually all of Europe. Civil war soon followed. In March 1793 aristocratic officers and priests commenced a royalist revolt in the Vendée in western France and roused much local popular support. The Girondists had led the country into the war but had proved themselves incapable either of winning it or of suppressing the enemies of the revolution at home. The Mountain stood ready to take up the task.

See the Map
Revolutionary France
at **MyHistoryLab.com**

The Reign of Terror and Its Aftermath

The **Reign of Terror** is the name given to the months of quasi-judicial executions and murders stretching from the autumn of 1793 to the midsummer of 1794. The Terror can be understood only in the context of the internal and external wars, on the one hand, and the revolutionary expectations of the Convention and the *sans-culottes*, on the other.

Committee of Public Safety In April 1793 the Convention established a Committee of General Security and a Committee of Public Safety to perform the executive duties of the government. The Committee of Public Safety eventually enjoyed almost dictatorial power. The committee conceived of their task as saving the revolution from mortal enemies at home and abroad. They generally enjoyed a working political relationship with the *sans-culottes* of Paris, but it was an alliance of expediency for the committee.

The major problem was to secure domestic support for the war. In early June 1793 the Parisian *sans-culottes* invaded the Convention and secured the expulsion of the Girondist members. That gave the Mountain complete control. On June 22 the Convention approved a fully democratic constitution but suspended its operation until after the war emergency. August 23 saw a **levée en masse**, or general military requisition of population, which conscripted males into the army and directed economic production for military purposes. On September 29 a maximum on prices was established in accord with the *sans-culottes*'s demands. During these same months the armies of the revolution also crushed many of the counterrevolutionary disturbances in the provinces.

The Society of Revolutionary Republican Women
Revolutionary women established their own distinct institutions to fight the internal enemies of the revolution. In May 1793 Pauline Léon and Claire Lacombe founded the Society of Revolutionary Republican Women. Its members and other women filled the galleries of the Convention to hear the debates and cheer their favorite speakers. The Society became increasingly radical, however. Its members sought stricter controls on the price of food and other commodities, worked to ferret out food hoarders, and brawled with working market women thought to be insufficiently revolutionary. The women of the Society also demanded the right to wear the revolutionary cap or cockade usually worn only by male citizens. By October 1793 the Jacobins in the Convention had begun to fear the turmoil the Society was causing and banned all women's clubs and societies.

There were other examples of repression of women in 1793. Olympe de Gouges, author of the *Declaration of the Rights of Woman*, opposed the Terror and accused certain Jacobins of corruption. She was tried and guillotined in November 1793. In the same year women were formally excluded from the French army and from attending the galleries of the Convention.

Revolutionary Calendar. To symbolize the beginning of a new era in human history, French revolutionary legislators established a new calendar. This calendar for Year Two (1794) proclaims the indivisible unity of the revolution and the goals of Liberty, Equality, and Fraternity.

The Republic of Virtue The pressures of war made it relatively easy to dispense with legal due process. However, the people in the Convention and the Committee of Public Safety also believed they had made a new departure in world history. They had established a republic in which civic virtue rather than aristocratic and monarchical corruption might flourish.

Dechristianization The most dramatic departure of the republic of virtue was an attempt to dechristianize France. In October 1793 the Convention proclaimed a new calendar dating from the first day of the French Republic. There were twelve months of thirty days with names associated with the seasons and climate. Every tenth day, rather than every seventh, was a holiday. Many of the most important events of the next few years became known by their dates on the revolutionary calendar.[3]

In November 1793 the convention decreed the Cathedral of Notre Dame to be a Temple of Reason. The legislature then sent trusted members, known as deputies, on

---

[3]From summer to spring, the months on the revolutionary calendar were *Messidor, Thermidor, Fructidor, Vendémiaire, Brumaire, Frimaire, Nivose, Pluviose, Ventose, Germinal, Floréal,* and *Prairial.*

mission into the provinces to enforce dechristianization by closing churches, persecuting clergy and believers, and occasionally forcing priests to marry. This religious policy roused much opposition and deeply separated the French provinces from the revolutionary government in Paris.

Progress of the Terror During late 1793 and early 1794 Maximilien Robespierre (1758–1794) emerged as the chief figure on the Committee of Public Safety. The Jacobin Club provided his primary forum and base of power. A shrewd and sensitive politician, he had opposed the war in 1792, believing it to be a measure that might aid the monarchy. He largely depended on the support of the *sans-culottes* of Paris but continued to dress as he had before the revolution and opposed dechristianization as a political blunder. For him, the republic of virtue meant wholehearted support of republican government and the renunciation of selfish gains from political life. He once told the Convention:

If the mainspring of popular government in peacetime is virtue, amid revolution it is at the same time virtue and terror: virtue, without which terror is fatal; terror, without which virtue is impotent. Terror is nothing but prompt, severe, inflexible justice; it is therefore an emanation of virtue."[4]

The Reign of Terror manifested itself through a series of revolutionary tribunals established by the Convention during the summer of 1793. The tribunals were to try the enemies of the Republic, but the definition of enemy remained uncertain and shifted as the months passed. The first victims were Marie Antoinette, other members of the royal family, and aristocrats, who were executed in October 1793. They were followed by Girondist politicians who had been prominent in the Legislative Assembly.

By early 1794 the Terror had moved to the provinces, where the deputies on mission presided over the summary execution of thousands of people who had allegedly supported internal opposition to the revolution. In Paris during the late winter of 1794 Robespierre turned the Terror against republican political figures of the left and right. On March 24 he secured the execution of certain extreme *sans-culottes* leaders. Shortly thereafter he moved against more conservative republicans. Robespierre thus exterminated the leadership from both groups that might have threatened his own position. Finally, on June 10 he secured passage of a law that permitted the revolutionary tribunal tzo convict suspects without hearing substantial evidence.

In May 1794, at the height of his power, Robespierre, considering the worship of reason too abstract for most cit-

---

[4]Quoted in Richard T. Bienvenu, *The Ninth of Thermidor: The Fall of Robespierre* (New York: Oxford University Press, 1968), p. 38.

Document
The Paris Jacobin Club Alerts the Nations to Internal Enemies of the Revolution

By early 1793, the revolutionary groups in Paris stood sharply divided among themselves. The Girondists, who had led the nation into war, faced military reversals. General Dumouriez, a former revolutionary commander, had changed sides and was leading an army against France. At this point, on April 5, the radical Jacobin Club of Paris sent a circular to its provincial clubs, painting a dire picture of the fate of the revolution. While Dumouriez was marching against Paris, the Jacobins accused members of the government and its administrators of conspiring to betray the revolution. The circular suggested that some people were cooperating with England in the war against France. The Jacobins also portrayed as counterrevolutionaries all those political figures who had opposed the execution of Louis XVI. The distortion of the motives of political enemies, the appeal to a possible reversal of the revolution, and the accusations of internal conspiracy served to justify the demand for justice against enemies of the revolution.

■ *How did the Jacobins use the war to call for actions against their own domestic political enemies? What real and imagined forces did they see threatening the revolution?*

Friends, we are betrayed! To arms! To arms! The terrible hour is at hand when the defenders of the *Patrie* must vanquish or bury themselves under the bloody ruins of the Republic. Frenchmen, never was your liberty in such great peril! At last our enemies have put the finishing touch to their foul perfidy, and to complete it their accomplice Dumouriez is marching on Paris. . . .

But Brothers, not all your dangers are to be found there! . . . You must be convinced of a grievous truth! Your greatest enemies are in your midst, they direct your operations. O Vengeance!!! . . .

Yes, brothers and friends, yes, it is in the Senate that patricidal hands tear at your vitals! Yes, the counterrevolution is in the Government. . . , in the National Convention. It is there, at the center of your security and your hope, that criminal delegates hold the threads of the web that they have woven with the horde of despots who come to butcher us! . . . It is there that a sacriligious cabal is directed by the English court . . . and others. . . .

Let us rise! Yes, let us rise! Let us arrest all the enemies of our revolution, and all suspected persons. Let us exterminate, without pity, all conspirators, unless we wish to be exterminated ourselves. . . .

Let the departments, the districts, the municipalities, and all the popular societies unite and concur in protesting to the Convention, by dispatching thereto a veritable rain of petitions manifesting the formal wish for the immediate recall of all unfaithful members who have betrayed their duty by not wishing the death of the tyrant, and above all, against those who have led astray so many of their colleagues. Such delegates are traitors, royalists, or fatuous men. The Republic condemns the friends of kings! . . .

Let us all unite equally to demand that the thunder or indictments be loosed against generals who are traitors to the Republic, against prevaricating ministers, against postal administrators, and against all unfaithful agents of the government. Therein lies our most salutary means of defence; but let us repel the traitors and tyrants.

Source: From John Hall Stewart, *Documentary Survey of the French Revolution*, 1st Edition, © 1951. Reprinted by permission of Pearson Education, Inc., Upper Saddle River, NJ.

izens, abolished it and established the Cult of the Supreme Being. He did not long preside over this new religion. On June 26 he made an ill-tempered speech in the Convention, declaring the existence of a conspiracy among other leaders of the government against him and the revolution. Such accusations against unnamed persons had usually preceded his earlier attacks. On July 27 (the Ninth of Thermidor) members of the Convention, by prearrangement, shouted him down when he rose to speak. Robespierre was arrested that night and executed the next day.

The Reign of Terror soon ended, having claimed as many as 40,000 victims. Most were peasants and *sans-culottes* who had rebelled against the revolutionary government. By the late summer of 1794 those provincial uprisings had been crushed, and the war against foreign enemies was also going well. Those factors, combined with the feeling in Paris that the revolution had consumed enough of its own children, brought the Terror to an end. (See Document, "The Paris Jacobin Club Alerts the Nations to Internal Enemies of the Revolution.")

Chronology

The French Revolution

1789	May 5	Estates General opens at Versailles
	June 17	Third Estate declares itself the National Assembly
	June 20	National Assembly takes the Tennis Court Oath
	July 14	Fall of the Bastille
	August 4	Nobles surrender their feudal rights in a meeting of the National Constituent Assembly
	August 26	*Declaration of the Rights of Man and Citizen*
	October 5–6	Parisian women march to Versailles and force Louis XVI and his family to return to Paris
1790	July 12–14	Civil Constitution of the Clergy adopted and accepted by the king
1791	June 20–24	Louis XVI and his family attempt to flee France and are stopped at Varennes
1792	April 20	France declares war on Austria
	August 10	Tuileries palace stormed, and Louis XVI takes refuge in the Legislative Assembly
	September	September Massacres; monarchy abolished
1793	January 21	Louis XVI executed
	February 1	France declares war on Great Britain
	March	Counterrevolution breaks out in the Vendée
	April 6	Committee of Public Safety formed
	July	Robespierre enters Committee of Public Safety
	August 23	*Levée en masse* proclaimed
	October 16	Queen Marie Antoinette executed
	November 10	Cult of Reason proclaimed; revolutionary calendar beginning in September
1794	May 7	Cult of the Supreme Being proclaimed
	June 8	Robespierre leads the celebration of Festival of the Supreme Being
	July 28	Robespierre executed
1795	August 22	Constitution of the Year III adopted, establishing the Directory

The Thermidorian Reaction: End of the Terror and Establishment of the Directory The tempering of the revolution, called the **Thermidorian Reaction**, began in July 1794. It destroyed the machinery of terror and set up a new constitutional regime. The influence of generally wealthy middle-class and professional people replaced that of the *sans-culottes*. Many of the people responsible for the Terror were removed from public life. The Paris Jacobin Club was closed, and provincial Jacobin clubs were forbidden to correspond with each other.

The Thermidorian Reaction also involved still further political reconstruction. In place of the fully democratic constitution of 1793, which had never gone into effect, the Convention issued the Constitution of the Year III. It was a conservative document that provided for a bicameral legislative government heavily favoring property owners. The executive body, consisting of a five-person Directory, was elected by the upper legislative house, known as the Council of Elders.

◆●▶ Read the Document
Maximilien Robespierre "Speech to National Convention: The Terror Justified" at **MyHistoryLab.com**

By the Treaty of Basel of March 1795, the Convention concluded peace with Prussia and Spain. With the war effort succeeding, the Convention severed its ties with the *sans-culottes*. True to their belief in an unregulated economy, the Thermidorians repealed the ceiling on prices. When food riots resulted during the winter of 1794–1795, the Convention put them down to prove that the era of the *sans-culottes journées* had ended. On October 5, 1795 (13 Vendémiaire) the sections (municipal units, each with its own assembly) of Paris rebelled against the Convention. For the first time in the history of the revolution, artillery was turned against the people of Paris. A general named Napoleon Bonaparte (1769–1821) commanded the cannon and with what he termed a "whiff of grapeshot" dispersed the crowd. Other enemies of the Directory would be more difficult to disperse.

The Napoleonic Era

Napoleon Bonaparte was born in 1769 to a poor family of lesser nobles in Corsica. Because France had annexed Corsica in 1768, he went to French schools, pursued a military career, and in 1785 obtained a commission as a French artillery officer. He strongly favored the revolution and was a fiery Jacobin. In 1793 he played a leading role in recovering the port of Toulon from the British. As a reward the government appointed him a brigadier general. His defense of the new regime on 13 Vendémiaire won him another promotion and a command in Italy. By October 1797 he had crushed the Austrian army in Italy and concluded on his own initiative the Treaty of Campo Formio, which took Austria out of the war. Soon all of Italy and Switzerland lay under French domination.

In November 1797 the triumphant Bonaparte returned to Paris to be hailed as a hero and to confront France's only remaining enemy, Britain. Judging it impossible to cross the Channel and invade England at that time, he chose to capture Egypt from the Ottoman Empire. He thus hoped to drive the British fleet from the Mediterranean, cut off British communication with India, damage British trade, and threaten the British Empire. But the invasion of Egypt was a failure. Admiral Horatio Nelson (1758–1805) destroyed the French fleet at Aboukir on August 1, 1798. The French army could then neither accomplish anything of importance in the Near East nor get home. The French invasion of Egypt had alarmed Russia, which had its own ambitions in the Near East. The Russians, the Austrians, and the Ottomans joined Britain to form the Second Coalition. In 1799 the Russian and Austrian armies defeated the French

●◦●⌐Read the Document

Madame de Remusat on the Rise of Napoleon at **MyHistoryLab.com**

in Italy and Switzerland and threatened to invade France.

Napoleon. In December 1799 Napoleon seized power and established himself as First Consul. The title of "Consul" came from the ancient Roman Republic; by 1894 Napoleon would assume the title of "Emperor" as the French Republic gave way to the Napoleonic Empire. The simplicity of this modest military dress as First Consul also gave way to flowing imperial robes.

Having heard of these misfortunes, Napoleon abandoned his army in Egypt and returned to France in October 1799. On November 10, 1799 (19 Brumaire) his troops overthrew the Directory. Bonaparte issued the Constitution of the Year VII in December 1799, establishing himself as the First Consul. The constitution received overwhelming approval from the electorate in a largely rigged plebiscite. The establishment of the **Consulate**, in effect, closed the revolution in France.

The Consulate in France (1799–1804) Bonaparte quickly justified the public's confidence by achieving peace with France's enemies. Russia had already left the Second Coalition. A campaign in Italy brought another victory over Austria at Marengo in 1800. The Treaty of Lunéville early in 1801 took Austria out of the war and confirmed the earlier settlement of Campo Formio. Britain was now alone and, in 1802, concluded the Treaty of Amiens, which temporarily brought peace to Europe.

Bonaparte also restored peace and order at home. Although he used generosity, flattery, and bribery to win over some of his enemies, issued a general amnesty, and employed persons from all political factions, Bonaparte was ruthless and efficient in suppressing political opposition. He established a highly centralized administration in which all departments were managed by prefects directly responsible to the central government in Paris. He employed secret police. He stamped out, once and for all, the royalist rebellion in the west and moved against other royalist plots.

((•●⌐Hear the Audio

Napoleon 1 at **MyHistoryLab.com**

Napoleon also alleviated the hostility of French Catholics. In 1801 he concluded a concordat with Pope Pius VII (r. 1800–1823), to the shock and dismay of his anticlerical supporters. The concordat declared that "Roman Catholicism is the religion of the great majority of French citizens." This was merely a statement of fact and fell far short of what the pope had wanted—religious dominance for the Roman Catholic Church. Both refractory and constitutional clergy were forced to resign. Their replacements received their spiritual investiture from the pope, but the state named the bishops and paid their salaries and the salary of one priest in each parish. In return, the church gave up its claims to its confiscated property. The clergy had to swear an oath of loyalty to the state, and the Organic Articles of 1802, which were actually distinct from the concordat, established the supremacy of state over church. Similar laws were applied to the Protestant and Jewish religious communities, reducing still further the privileged position of the Catholic Church.

In 1802 another plebiscite appointed Napoleon consul for life, and he soon produced still another new constitution, which granted him what amounted to full power. He transformed the basic laws and institutions of France on the basis of both liberal principles derived from the Enlightenment and the early years of the revolution and conservative principles going back to the Old Regime, on the one hand, and the spirit that had triumphed at Thermidor, on the other. This was especially true of the Civil Code of 1804, usually called the Napoleonic Code. However, these laws stopped far short of the full equality advocated by liberal rationalists. Fathers were granted extensive control over their children and men over their wives. Labor unions were still forbidden, and the rights of workers were inferior to those of their employers.

In 1804 Bonaparte seized on a bomb attack on his life to make himself emperor. He argued that the establishment of a dynasty would make the new regime secure and make further attempts on his life useless. Still another new constitution, ratified by a plebiscite, was promulgated, designating Napoleon Emperor of the French instead of First Consul of the Republic. Napoleon summoned the pope to Notre Dame to take part in the coronation. But at the last minute the pope agreed that Napoleon should actually crown himself. The emperor had no intention of allowing anyone to think that his power and authority depended on the approval of the church. Henceforth he was called Napoleon I.

Napoleon's Empire (1804–1814) Between his coronation as emperor and his final defeat at Waterloo (1815), Napoleon conquered most of Europe in military campaigns that astonished the world. France's victories changed the map of Europe, ended the Old Regime and its feudal trappings in western Europe, and forced the eastern European states to reorganize themselves to resist Napoleon's armies.

Everywhere, Napoleon's advance unleashed the powerful force of nationalism.

The Treaty of Amiens with Britain (1802) could not last. Napoleon intervened militarily to extend French influence in Europe. The British issued an ultimatum. When Napoleon ignored it, Britain declared war, in May 1803. William Pitt the Younger (1759–1806) returned to office as prime minister in 1804 and began to construct the Third Coalition. By August 1805 he had persuaded Russia and Austria to move once again against French aggression. On October 21, 1805, Lord Nelson destroyed the combined French and Spanish fleets at the battle of Trafalgar just off the Spanish coast. Nelson was killed, but the British lost no ships. Trafalgar put an end to the French hope of invading Britain and guaranteed British control of the sea.

On land, however, the story was different. Between mid-October 1805 and July 1807 Napoleon had defeated the armies of Austria, Prussia, and Russia in stunning victories. The most famous of the victories was that of Austerlitz on December 2, 1805. Through these campaigns he forced Austria to withdraw from northern Italy, where Napoleon himself was recognized as king. He replaced the ancient Holy Roman Empire with the Confederation of the Rhine. On July 7, 1807, Napoleon and Emperor Alexander I (r. 1800–1825) of Russia concluded the Treaty of Tilsit, which confirmed France's gains in central and eastern Europe. Prussia and Russia became allies of Napoleon.

See the Map
Napoleon's Empire
in 1812
at **MyHistoryLab.com**

Napoleon knew that he could not be genuinely secure until he had defeated Britain. Unable to compete with the British navy, he adopted economic warfare to cut off all

William Pitt and Napoleon. In this early nineteenth-century cartoon, England, personified by a caricature of William Pitt, and France, personified by a caricature of Napoleon, are carving out their areas of interest around the globe.

British trade with the European continent. He thus hoped to cripple British commercial and financial power, cause domestic unrest and revolution, and drive the British from the war. On November 21, 1806, he had issued the Berlin Decrees forbidding his allies to import British goods. The Milan Decree of 1807 attempted to halt neutral nations, such as the United States, from trading with Britain. Nonetheless, the British economy survived because of its access to the growing markets of North and South America and the eastern Mediterranean. Known as the Continental System, Napoleon's policies harmed the European economies and roused resentment against France.

The Wars of Liberation   In 1807, as part of the strategy of crippling the British economy, a French army invaded the Iberian Peninsula to force Portugal to abandon its traditional alliance with Britain. The army stayed in Spain to protect lines of supply and communication. When a revolt broke out in Madrid in 1808, Napoleon deposed the Bourbons and placed his brother Joseph (1768–1844) on the Spanish throne. Attacks on the privileges of the church increased public outrage.

In Spain, Napoleon faced a kind of warfare that was not vulnerable to his usual tactics. Guerrilla bands cut communications, killed stragglers, destroyed isolated units, and then disappeared. The British landed an army under Sir Arthur Wellesley (1769–1852), later the Duke of Wellington, to support the Spanish insurgents. Thus began the long peninsular campaign that would drain French strength and play a critical role in Napoleon's eventual defeat.

Encouraged by the French troubles in Spain, the Austrians renewed the war in 1809. The French army nonetheless marched swiftly into Austria and won the battle of Wagram. The resulting peace deprived Austria of much territory and 3.5 million subjects. Another spoil of victory was the Archduchess Marie Louise (1791–1847), Francis I's 18-year-old daughter, whom Napoleon married for dynastic purposes after divorcing his wife Josephine de Beauharnais (1763–1814), who had borne him no children.

The Franco-Russian alliance concluded at Tilsit was faltering. The Continental System had harmed the Russian economy. Napoleon's organization of a Polish state, the Grand Duchy of Warsaw, on the Russian doorstep and its enlargement in 1809 after the battle of Wagram angered Alexander I. Napoleon's annexation of Holland in violation of the Treaty of Tilsit, his recognition of the French Marshal Bernadotte as the future king of Sweden (r. 1818–1844), and his marriage to an Austrian princess further disturbed the tsar. At the end of 1810 Russia withdrew from the Continental System and began to prepare for war (see Map 22–2 on page 686).

Determined to stifle the Russian military threat, Napoleon amassed an army of over 600,000 men, including over 400,000 non-French soldiers drawn from his empire and allies. He intended the usual short campaign crowned by a decisive battle, but the Russians retreated before his advance. His vast superiority in numbers—the Russians had only about 160,000 troops—made it foolish for them to risk a battle. Instead, they destroyed all food and supplies as they retreated. The so-called Grand Army of Napoleon could not live off the country, and Russia was too vast for supply lines. Terrible rains, fierce heat, shortages of food and water, and the courage of the Russian rear guard eroded the morale of Napoleon's army.

In September 1812 Russian public opinion forced the army to stand and fight. At Borodino, not far west of Moscow, the bloodiest battle of the Napoleonic era cost the French 30,000 casualties and the Russians almost twice as many. Yet the Russian army was not destroyed. Napoleon had won nothing substantial. By October, after occupying Moscow, the Grand Army was forced to retreat. By December Napoleon realized that the Russian fiasco would encourage plots against him at home. He returned to Paris, leaving the remnants of his army to struggle westward. Perhaps only as many as 100,000 lived to tell the tale of their terrible ordeal. Even

Francisco de Goya, *The Third of May, 1808*, 1814–1815. Napoleon sent troops into Spain in 1807 after the king of Spain had agreed to aid France against Portugal, which was assisting Britain. By early 1808 Spain had essentially become an occupied nation. On May 2 riots took place in Madrid between French troops and Spanish civilians. In response to the riots, the French marshall Joachim Murat ordered numerous executions, especially of artisans and clergy, during the night of May 2 and 3. *Francisco de Goya, "Los fusilamientos del 3 de Mayo, 1808," 1814. Oil on canvas, 8'60 × 11'40. © Museo Nacional Del Prado, Madrid.*

Map 22–2. Napoleonic Europe in late 1812. By mid-1812 the areas shown in peach were incorporated into France, and most of the rest of Europe was directly controlled by or allied with Napoleon. But Russia had withdrawn from the failing Continental System, and the decline of Napoleon was about to begin.

as the news of the disaster reached the West, the total defeat of Napoleon was far from certain. He was able to suppress his opponents in Paris and raise another 350,000 men.

In 1813 patriotic pressure and national ambition brought together the last and most powerful coalition against Napoleon. Financed by the British, the Russians drove westward to be joined by Prussia and then Austria. From the west Wellington marched his peninsular army into France. Napoleon waged a skillful campaign in central Europe and defeated the allies at Dresden. In October, however, he met decisive defeat at Leipzig from the combined armies of his enemies, in what the Germans called the Battle of the Nations. At the end of March 1814 the allied army marched into Paris. Napoleon abdicated and went into exile on the island of Elba off the coast of northern Italy.

The Congress of Vienna and the European Settlement

Once Napoleon was removed, the allies began to pursue their own separate ambitions. The key person in achieving eventual agreement among the allies was Robert Stewart, Viscount Castlereagh (1769–1822), the British foreign secretary. Even before the victorious armies had entered Paris, he achieved the Treaty of Chaumont on March 9, 1814, providing for the restoration of the Bourbons to the French throne and the contraction of France to its 1792 frontiers. Even more important, Britain, Austria, Russia, and Prussia formed a Quadruple Alliance for twenty years to preserve whatever settlement they later agreed on. Remaining problems—and there were many—and final details were left for a conference to be held at Vienna.

Chronology

Napoleonic Europe

1797	Napoleon concludes Treaty of Campo Formio
1798	Nelson defeats French navy at Aboukir
1799	Consulate established
1801	Concordat between France and papacy
1802	Treaty of Amiens
1803	War renewed between France and Britain
1804	Execution of Duke of Enghien; Napoleonic Civil Code issued; Napoleon crowned emperor
1805	Nelson defeats French fleet at Trafalgar (October 21); battle of Austerlitz (December 2)
1806	Continental System established by Berlin Decrees
1807	Treaty of Tilsit
1808	Beginning of Spanish resistance to Napoleonic domination
1809	Battle of Wagram; Napoleon marries Archduchess Marie Louise of Austria
1812	Invasion of Russia
1813	Leipzig (Battle of the Nations)
1814	Treaty of Chaumont (March) establishes Quadruple Alliance; Congress of Vienna convenes (September)
1815	Napoleon returns from Elba (March 1); Waterloo (June 18); Holy Alliance formed (September 26); Quadruple Alliance renewed (November 20)
1821	Napoleon dies on Saint Helena

Political Cartoon of the Congress of Vienna. In this cartoon depiction, Talleyrand simply watches which way the wind is blowing; Castlereagh hesitates, while the monarchs of Russia, Prussia, and Austria form the dance of the Holy Alliance. The King of Saxony holds onto his crown and the republic of Geneva pays homage to the Kingdom of Sardinia.

The Congress of Vienna assembled in September 1814 but did not conclude its work until November 1815. The four great powers conducted the important work of the conference. The victors agreed that no single state should be allowed to dominate Europe. They constructed a series of states to serve as barriers to any new French expansion (see Map 22–3 on page 688). Thus, they established the kingdom of the Netherlands, including Belgium in the north, and added Genoa to Piedmont in the south. Prussia, whose power was increased by acquisitions in eastern Europe, was given important new territories in the west to deter French aggression along the Rhine River.

Austria was given full control of northern Italy to prevent a repetition of Napoleon's conquests there. Most of Napoleon's arrangements in the rest of Germany were left untouched. The Holy Roman Empire was not revived. The Congress established the rule of legitimate monarchs and rejected any hint of the republican and democratic politics that had flowed from the French Revolution.

However, the settlement of eastern Europe sharply divided the victors. Alexander I wanted Russia to govern all of Poland. Prussia was willing if it received all of Saxony. Austria, however, refused to surrender its share of Poland or to see Prussian power grow and Russia penetrate deeper into central Europe. The Polish-Saxon question enabled France to rejoin the great powers. The French Foreign Minister Talleyrand (1754–1838) suggested that the weight of France, added to that of Britain and Austria, might bring Alexander to his senses. When news of a secret treaty among the three leaked out, the tsar agreed to become ruler of a smaller Poland, and Frederick William III of Prussia (r. 1797–1840) agreed to settle for part of Saxony. Thereafter, France was included as a fifth great power in all deliberations.

Napoleon's escape from Elba on March 1, 1815, further restored unity among the victors. He promised a liberal constitution and a peaceful foreign policy, but the allies declared him an outlaw (a new device under international law) and sent their armies to crush him. Wellington, with the crucial help of the Prussians, defeated Napoleon at Waterloo in Bel-

●●◖Read the Document
Napoleon's Exile to St. Helena
(1815) at **MyHistoryLab.com**

Map Exploration

To explore this map further, go to **http://www.myhistorylab.com**

Map 22–3 Europe 1815, after the Congress of Vienna. The Congress of Vienna achieved the post-Napoleonic territorial adjustments shown on the map. The most notable arrangements dealt with areas along France's borders (the Netherlands, Prussia, Switzerland, and Piedmont) and in Poland and northern Italy.

See the Map
Europe After the Congress of Vienna, 1815
at **MyHistoryLab.com**

gium on June 18, 1815. Napoleon again abdicated and was exiled to Saint Helena, a tiny Atlantic island off the coast of Africa, where he died in 1821.

The Hundred Days, as the period of Napoleon's return is called, made the peace settlement somewhat harsher for France, but the other main outlines of the Vienna Settlement remained in place. The Quadruple Alliance between England, Austria, Prussia, and Russia was renewed on November 20, 1815. Henceforth, it was as much a coalition for the maintenance of peace as for the pursuit of victory over France. A coalition with such a purpose had not previously existed in European international relations. Its existence and later operation represented an important new departure in European affairs. Unlike the situation in the eighteenth century, certain European powers were determined to prevent the outbreak of future war. The statesmen at Vienna, unlike their eighteenth-century counterparts, had seen the armies of the French Revolution change major frontiers of the European states and overturn the political and social order of much of the Continent. They had seen unprecedented military destruction. They were determined to prevent a recurrence of those upheavals. The shared purpose of the diplomats was to establish a framework for future stability, not to punish a defeated France. The great powers through the Vienna Settlement framed international relations in such a manner that the major powers would respect that settlement and not as in the eighteenth century use military force to change it.

The Congress of Vienna succeeded in preventing future French aggression and in arranging an acceptable settlement for Europe that produced a long-lasting peace. Its work has been criticized for failing to recognize and provide for the great forces that would stir the nineteenth century—nationalism and democracy—but such criticism is inappropriate. The settlement, like all such agreements, was aimed at solving past ills, and in that it succeeded. The Vienna Settlement remained essentially intact for almost half a century and spared Europe a general war until 1914.

Wars of Independence in Latin America

The wars of the French Revolution, particularly those of Napoleon, sparked movements for independence throughout Latin America. Between 1804 and 1824 France was driven from Haiti, Portugal lost control of Brazil, and Spain was forced to withdraw from all of its American empire except for Cuba and Puerto Rico. Three centuries of Iberian colonial government over the South American continent ended.

Eighteenth-Century Developments

Spain was one of the defeated powers in 1763. Charles III (r. 1759–1788) and the government circles in Spain were convinced that the American colonial system had to be changed. After 1765 the monarch abolished the monopolies of Seville and Cádiz and permitted other Spanish commercial centers to trade with America. He also opened more South American and Caribbean ports to trade and authorized commerce between American ports. In 1776 he organized a fourth viceroyalty in the region of the Río de la Plata, which included much of present-day Argentina, Uruguay, Paraguay, and Bolivia. Charles III also attempted to make tax collection more efficient and to eliminate bureaucratic corruption. To achieve those ends, he introduced into the empire *intendents*, who were royal bureaucrats loyal only to the Crown.

These reforms, which took place during the same years as the unsuccessful British effort to reorganize its authority in its North American colonies, largely succeeded in returning the empire to direct Spanish control. Many **peninsulares**, whites born in Spain, went to the New World to fill new posts at the expense of **creoles**, whites born in America. Expand-

View the Image
Slave Revolt in Saint Domingue, 1791
at **MyHistoryLab.com**

ing trade likewise brought more Spanish merchants to Latin America. The economy retained its export orientation, and economic life continued to be organized for the benefit of Spain. There matters stood until the early nineteenth century.

Revolution in Haiti

Between 1791 and 1804, the French colony of Haiti (St. Domingue) achieved independence. This event was of key importance for two reasons. First, it was sparked by policies of the French Revolution overflowing into its New World Empire. Second, the Haitian Revolution demonstrated that slaves of African origins could lead a revolt against white masters and mulatto freemen. The example of the Haitian Revolution for years thereafter terrified slaveholders throughout the Americas.

The relationship between slaves and masters on Haiti had been filled with violence throughout the eighteenth century. The French colonial masters had frequently used racial divisions between black slaves and mulatto freemen to their own political advantage. Once the French Revolution had broken out in France, the French National Assembly in 1791 decreed that free property-owning mulattos on Haiti should enjoy the same rights as white plantation owners. The Colonial Assembly in Haiti resisted the orders from France. (See Document: "A Free Person of Color from St. Domingue Demands Recognition of His Status" on page 677).

In 1791, a full-fledged slave rebellion shook Haiti. It arose as a result of a secret conspiracy among the slaves. François-Dominique Toussaint L'Ouverture (1743?–1803), himself a former slave, quickly emerged as its leader. The rebellion involved enormous violence and loss of life on both sides. Although the slave rebellion collapsed, mulattos and free black people on Haiti, who hoped to gain the rights the French National Assembly had promised, then took up arms against the white colonial masters. French officials sent by the revolutionary government in Paris soon backed them. Slaves now came to the aid of an invading French force, and in early 1793, the French abolished slavery in Haiti.

By this time both Spain and Great Britain were attempting to intervene in Haitian events to expand their own influence in the Caribbean. Both were opposed to the end of slavery, and both coveted Haiti's rich sugar-producing lands. Toussaint L'Ouverture and his force of ex-slaves again supported the French against the Spanish and the British. By 1800, his army had achieved dominance throughout the island of Hispaniola. He imposed an authoritarian constitution on Haiti and made himself governor-general for life, but he preserved formal ties with France.

The French government under Napoleon distrusted L'Ouverture and feared his example would undermine French authority elsewhere. In 1802, Napoleon sent an army to Haiti to capture L'Ouverture, who spent the remainder of his life

Toussaint L'Ouverture. L'Ouverture (1744–1803) began the revolt that led to Haitian independence in 1804.

imprisoned in France. Other Haitian military leaders of slave origin, the most important of whom was Jean-Jacques Dessalines (1758–1806), continued to resist. When Napoleon found himself again at war with Britain in 1803, he abandoned his American empire, selling Louisiana to the United States and withdrawing his forces from Haiti. Haiti declared independence in 1804.

Thus, the Haitian slave-led rebellion became the first successful assault on colonial government in Latin America. Haiti's experience also foreshadowed a less fortunate trend in decolonization: the break with the colonial power was not clean. In Haiti's case, France required exorbitant reparations payments before formally recognizing Haitian independence in 1825. The reparations were later reduced, but they crippled Haiti's economy for decades, and are credited as factors in laying the groundwork for the once-wealthy nation's current poverty.

First Movements towards Independence on the South American Continent

Generally speaking, on the South American continent it was the Creole elite—merchants, landowners, and professional people—who led the movements against Spain and Portugal. Few Indians, blacks, mestizos, mulattos, or slaves became involved in or benefited from the end of Iberian rule. Indeed, the Haitian slave revolt haunted the Creoles, as did an Indian revolt in the Andes in 1780 and 1781. The Creoles were determined that political independence from Spain and Portugal should not cause social disruption or the loss of their social and economic privileges. In this respect the Creole revolutionaries were not unlike American revolutionaries in the Southern colonies who wanted to reject British rule but keep their slaves, or French revolutionaries who wanted to depose the king but not extend liberty to the French working class.

Creole complaints resembled those of the American colonists against Great Britain. Latin American merchants wanted to trade more freely within the region and with North American and European markets. They wanted commercial regulations that would benefit them rather than Spain.

Creoles also feared that Spanish imperial regulations might affect landholdings, access to commissions in the army, local government policy, and the treatment of slaves and Indians in ways that would harm their interests. They also deeply resented Spanish policies favoring *peninsulares* for political patronage, including appointments in the colonial government, church, and army. They believed the *peninsulares* improperly secured all the best positions. Seen in this light, the royal patronage system represented another device with which Spain extracted wealth and income from America for its own people rather than its colonial subjects.

From the 1790s onward Spain suffered military reverses in the wars associated with the French Revolution and Napoleon, and the commercial situation turned sharply against the inhabitants of the Spanish Empire. The military pressures led the Spanish monarchy into a desperate search for new revenues, including increased taxation and the confiscation of property in the American Empire. The policies harmed the economic life of the Creole elite.

Creole leaders had read the Enlightenment *philosophes* and regarded their reforms as potentially beneficial to the region. They were also well aware of the events and the political philosophy of the American Revolution. But something more than reform programs and revolutionary example was required to transform Creole discontent into revolt against the Spanish government. That transforming event occurred in Europe when Napoleon toppled the Portuguese monarchy in 1807 and the Spanish government in 1808 and then placed his own brother on the thrones of both countries. The Portuguese royal family fled to Brazil and established its government there. But the Bourbon monarchy of Spain seemed wholly vanquished.

Eighteenth-Century Developments in the Spanish Empire

The French government under Napoleon distrusted L'Ouverture and feared his example would undermine French authority elsewhere. In 1802, Napoleon sent an army to Haiti to capture L'Ouverture, who spent the remainder of his life imprisoned in France. Other Haitian military leaders of slave origin, the most important of whom was Jean-Jacques Dessalines (1758– 1806), continued to resist. When Napoleon found himself again at war with Britain in 1803, he abandoned his American empire, selling Louisiana to the United States and withdrawing his forces from Haiti. Haiti declared independence in 1804.

Thus, the Haitian slave-led rebellion became the first successful assault on colonial government in Latin America. Haiti's experience also foreshadowed a less fortunate trend in decolonization: the break with the colonial power was not clean. In Haiti's case, France required exorbitant reparations payments before formally recognizing Haitian independence in 1825. The reparations were later reduced, but they crippled Haiti's economy for decades, and are credited as factors in laying the groundwork for the once-wealthy nation's current poverty.

San Martín in Río de la Plata

The first region to assert its independence was the Río de la Plata, or modern Argentina. As early as 1806 the citizens of Buenos Aires had fought off a British invasion and thus had learned that they could look to themselves rather than Spain for effective political and military action. In 1810 the junta in Buenos Aires not only thrust off Spanish authority but also sent liberation forces against Paraguay and Uruguay. The armies were defeated, but Spain nonetheless soon lost control in the two areas. Paraguay asserted its own independence. Uruguay was eventually absorbed by Brazil.

Undiscouraged by these early defeats, the Buenos Aires government remained determined to liberate Peru, the greatest stronghold of royalist power and loyalty on the continent. By 1814 José de San Martín (1778–1850), the leading general of the Río de la Plata forces, had organized and led a disciplined army in a daring march over the Andes Mountains. By early 1817 he had occupied Santiago in Chile and established the Chilean independence leader Bernardo O'Higgins (1778–1842) as supreme dictator. San Martín then constructed a naval force that in 1820 transported his army to Peru. The next year, he drove royalist forces from Lima and assumed the title of Protector of Peru (see Map 22–4).

Simón Bolívar's Liberation of Venezuela

While San Martín had been liberating the southern portion of the Continent, Simón Bolívar (1783–1830) had been pursuing a similar task in the north. In 1810, as a firm advocate of both independence and republicanism, Bolívar had helped organize a liberating junta in Caracas, Venezuela. Between 1811 and 1814 civil war broke out throughout Venezuela as both royalists, on the one hand, and slaves and *llaneros* (Venezuelan cowboys), on the other, challenged the authority of the republican government. (See Document, "Bolívar Denounces Spanish Rule in Latin America." on page 692) Bolívar had to go into exile. In

Map 22–4 The Independence Campaigns of San Martín and Bolívar.
José de San Martín and Simón Bolívar fought for independence in different parts of South America in the early 1800s. In 1822 they collaborated to liberate Quito, but they disagreed over post-independence political structures: San Martín was a monarchist, while Bolívar was a republican.

View the Image
The Great Liberator
Independence Leader,
Caudillo, and Future President
Simón Bolívar
at **MyHistoryLab.com**

Read the Document
Simon de Bolívar, "Address to
Second National Congress"
(Venezuela), 1819
at **MyHistoryLab.com**

1816, with help from Haiti, he launched a new invasion against Venezuela. He first captured Bogotá, capital of New Granada (including modern Colombia, Bolivia, and Ecuador), as a base for attacking Venezuela. By the summer of 1821 his forces had captured Caracas, and he had been named president.

A year later, in July 1822, the armies of Bolívar and San Martín joined to liberate Quito. At a famous meeting in Guayaquil the two leaders sharply disagreed about the future political structure of Latin America. San Martín believed that monarchies were required; Bolívar maintained his republicanism. Not long thereafter San Martín quietly retired from public life and went into exile in Europe. Meanwhile, Bolívar purposefully allowed the political situation in Peru to fall into confusion, and in 1823 he sent troops to establish his control. On

Document

Bolívar Denounces Spanish Rule in Latin America

In September 1815 Simón Bolívar published a long statement, often called *The Jamaica Letter*, in which he explained the political and economic difficulties under which the Creole elite of the Spanish Empire had lived. He defined Americans as referring to those persons in Latin America who were neither Indian nor European by birth. He also implicitly excluded black slaves. Consequently his attack on Spain was voiced on behalf of the white population of the South American continent who had been born there and who demanded rights of political participation and economic freedom.

■ *Why does Bolívar describe the Creole elite as having lived in a permanent political infancy? What are the economic disadvantages that he describes, and why had those become more burdensome in the half century before he wrote this letter? How had Spanish economic regulation prevented the Creole elite from achieving positions of responsibility in Latin America? How does this document compare with others concerned with movements of independence and nationalism?*

The role of the inhabitants of the American hemisphere has for centuries been purely passive. Politically they were non-existent. We are still in a position lower than slavery, and therefore it is more difficult for us to rise to the enjoyment of freedom. . . . We have been harassed by a conduct which has not only deprived us of our rights but has kept us in a sort of permanent infancy with regard to public affairs. If we could at least have managed our domestic affairs and our internal administration, we could have acquainted ourselves with the processes and mechanics of public affairs. . . .

Americans today, and perhaps to a greater extent than ever before, who live within the Spanish system occupy a position in society no better than that of serfs destined for labor, or at best they have no more status than that of mere consumers. Yet even this status is surrounded with galling restrictions, such as being forbidden to grow European crops, or to store products which are royal monopolies, or to establish factories of a type the [Spanish] Peninsula itself does not possess. To this add the exclusive trading privileges, even in articles of prime necessity, and the barriers between American provinces, designed to prevent all exchange of trade, traffic, and understanding. In short, do you wish to know what our future held?—simply the cultivation of the fields of indigo, grain, coffee, sugar cane, cacao, and cotton; cattle raising on the broad plains; hunting wild game in the jungles; digging in the earth to mine its gold—but even these limitations could never satisfy the greed of Spain.

So negative was our existence that I can find nothing comparable in any other civilized society, examine as I may the entire history of time and the politics of all nations. Is it not an outrage and a violation of human rights to expect a land so splendidly endowed, so vast, rich, and populous, to remain merely passive?

As I have just explained, we were cut off and, as it were, removed from the world in relation to the science of government and administration of the state. We were never viceroys or governors, save in the rarest of instances; seldom archbishops and bishops; diplomats never; as military men, only subordinates; as nobles, without royal privileges. In brief, we were neither magistrates nor financiers and seldom merchants.

Source: From Harold A. Bierck Jr., ed., *Selected Writings of Bolívar*, Vol. 1. Copyright © 1951 The Colonial Press, pp. 110–112.

December 9, 1824, at the battle of Ayacucho, the Spanish royalist forces suffered a major defeat at the hands of the liberating army. The battle marked the conclusion of Spain's effort to retain its American empire.

Independence in New Spain

The drive for independence in New Spain, which included present-day Mexico as well as Texas, California, and the rest of the southwestern United States, clearly illustrates the socially conservative outcome of the Latin American colonial revolutions. As elsewhere, a local governing junta was organized. But before it had undertaken any significant measures, a Creole priest, Miguel Hidalgo y Costilla (1753–1811), issued a call for rebellion to the Indians in his parish. They and other repressed groups of black and mestizo urban and rural workers responded. Father Hidalgo set forth a program of social change, including hints of land reform. Soon he stood at the head of a rather

Simón Bolívar. Bolívar was the liberator of much of Latin America. He inclined toward a policy of political liberalism.

◆◆┤Read the Document
Jose Morelos, Sentiments of the Nation (Mexico), 1813, at **MyHistoryLab.com**

unorganized group of 80,000 followers and marched on Mexico City. Both Hidalgo's forces and the royalist army that opposed them committed numerous atrocities. In July 1811 he was captured and executed. Leadership of his movement then fell to José María Morelos y Pavón (1765–1815), a mestizo priest. Far more radical than Hidalgo, he called for an end to forced labor and for substantial land reforms. He was executed in 1815, ending five years of popular uprising.

In 1820, however, the conservative political groups in Mexico, both Creole and Spanish, found their recently achieved security challenged from an unexpected source. A revolution in Spain had forced Ferdinand VII (r. 1813–1833) to accept a liberal constitution. Conservative Mexicans feared that the new liberal monarchy would attempt to impose liberal reforms on Mexico. Therefore, for the most conservative of reasons, they rallied to a former royalist general, Agustín de Iturbide (1783–1824), who in 1821 declared Mexico independent of Spain. Shortly thereafter, Iturbide was declared emperor. His own regime did not last long, but an independent Mexico, governed by persons determined to resist any significant social reform, had been created.

Great Britain was highly sympathetic to the independence movements in the different regions of Latin America.

By breaking the hold of the Spanish Empire the movement toward independence opened the markets of the continent to British trade and investment. Consequently in 1823 Great Britain supported the American Monroe Doctrine that prohibited further colonization and intervention by European powers in America. Britain soon recognized the Spanish colonies as independent states. Through the rest of the century, British commercial interests dominated Latin America.

Brazilian Independence

Brazilian independence, in contrast to that of Spanish Latin America, came simply and peacefully. As already noted, the Portuguese royal family, along with several thousand government officials and members of the court, took refuge in Brazil in 1807. Their arrival immediately transformed Rio de Janeiro into a court city. The prince regent Joao (r. 1816–1826) addressed many of the local complaints, equivalent to those of the Spanish Creoles. In 1815 he made Brazil a kingdom, which meant that it was no longer to be regarded merely as a colony of Portugal. This transformation was in many respects long overdue because Brazil was far larger and more prosperous than Portugal itself. Then in 1820 a revolution occurred in Portugal, and its leaders demanded Joao's return to Lisbon. They also demanded the return of Brazil to colonial status. Joao, who had become Joao VI in 1816, returned to Portugal but left his son Pedro (r. 1822–1831) as regent in Brazil, encouraging him to be sympathetic to the political aspirations of the Brazilians. In September 1822 Pedro embraced Brazilian independence against Portugal's recolonializing efforts. By the end of the year he had become emperor of an independent Brazil, which remained a monarchy until 1889. Thus in contrast to virtually all other nations of Latin America, Brazil achieved independence in a way that left no real dispute as to where the center of political authority lay.

Another factor aided the peaceful transition to independence in Brazil. The political and social elite there were determined to preserve slavery against the forces (see pages 694–695) that were challenging that institution. The wars of independence elsewhere had led to the abolition of slavery or moved the independent states closer to abolition. Any attempt to gain independence from Portugal through warfare might have caused social as well as political turmoil that would open the slavery question.

Toward the Abolition of Slavery in the Transatlantic Economy

In 1750 almost no one seriously questioned the institution of slavery; by 1888 slavery no longer existed in the transatlantic economy. This vast transformation of economic and social life occurred as the result of an international effort, first to abolish the slave trade and then to abolish the insti-

Chronology

The Wars of Latin American Independence

1759–1788		Charles III of Spain carries out imperial reforms
1776		Organization of Viceroyalty of Río de la Plata
1780–1781		Revolt of Indians in the Andes
1794		Toussaint L'Ouverture leads slave revolt in Haiti
1804		Independence of Haiti
1807		Portuguese royal family flees to Brazil
1808		Spanish monarchy falls to Napoleon
1808–1810		Creole Committees organized to govern much of Latin America
1810		Buenos Aires junta sends forces to liberate Paraguay and Uruguay
1811		Miguel Hidalgo y Costilla leads rebellion in New Spain and is executed
1811–1815		José María Morelos y Pavón leads rebellion in New Spain and is executed
1814		San Martín organizes army
1815		Brazil declared a kingdom
1816		Bolívar invades Venezuela
1817		San Martín occupies Santiago, Chile
1820		Revolution in Spain
1821	February 24	New Spain declares independence
	June 29	Bolívar captures Caracas, Venezuela
	July 28	San Martín liberates Peru
1822	July 26–27	San Martín and Bolívar quarrel at Guayaquil; San Martín goes into exile in Europe
	September 7	Dom Pedro declares Brazilian independence
1824		Battle of Ayacucho—final Spanish defeat

tution of slavery itself. At no previous time in world history had a society actually attempted to abolish slavery. Its eventual abolition in the transatlantic world stands as one of the most permanent achievements of the forces unleashed by the eighteenth-century Enlightenment and revolutions.

The eighteenth-century crusade against slavery in the plantation economy that stretched from Maryland south to Brazil (see Chapter 17) originated among writers of the Enlightenment and religious critics of slavery. Although some authors associated with the Enlightenment, including John Locke, were reluctant to question slavery or even defended it, the general Enlightenment rhetoric of equality stood in sharp contrast to the radical inequality of slavery. Montesquieu satirized slavery in *The Spirit of the Laws*. Adam Smith's emphasis in *The Wealth of Nations* on free labor and the efficiency of free markets undermined economic defenses of slavery. Much eighteenth-century literature idealized primitive peoples living in cultures very different from those of Europe and portrayed them as embodying a lost human virtue. This literature allowed some Europeans to look upon African slaves in the Americas as having been betrayed and robbed of an original innocence. In such a climate, slavery, once considered the natural and deserved result of some deficiency in slaves themselves, grew to be regarded as undeserved and unacceptable. Other Enlightenment ethical thinking led reformers to believe that by working against slavery, which for virtually the first time was defined as an unmitigated evil, they would realize their own highest moral character.

The initial religious protest against slavery originated among English Quakers, a radical Protestant religious group founded by George Fox in the seventeenth century. By the early eighteenth century it had solidified itself into a small, but relatively wealthy, sect in England. Members of Quaker congregations at that time actually owned slaves in the West Indies and participated in the transatlantic slave trade. During the Seven Years' War (1756–1763), however, many Quakers experienced economic hardship. Furthermore, the war created other difficulties for the English population as a whole. Certain Quakers decided that the presence of the evil of slavery in the world explained these troubles. They then sought to remove this evil from their own lives and from the lives of their congregations by taking action against the whole system of slavery that characterized the transatlantic economy.

Just as the slave system was a transatlantic affair, so was the crusade against it. There were Quaker communities in America, and soon Quakers in both Philadelphia and England wrote and organized against the institution. By the earliest stages of the American Revolution small groups of reformers, usually spearheaded by Quakers, had established an antislavery network. The turmoil of the American Revolution and the founding of the American republic gave these groups the occasion for some of their earliest successes. Emancipation gradually, but nonetheless steadily, spread among the northern states.

In 1787 the Continental Congress forbade slavery in the newly organized Northwest Territory north of the Ohio River.

Despite these American developments, Great Britain became and remained the center for the antislavery movement. In 1772 a decision by the chief justice affirmed that slaves brought into Great Britain could not forcibly be removed. During the early 1780s the antislavery reformers in Great Britain decided to work toward ending the slave trade rather than the institution of slavery itself. The horrors of the slave trade caught the public's attention in 1783 when the captain of the slave ship *Zong* threw more than 130 slaves overboard in order to collect insurance. Soon after, groups from the Church of England and the English Quakers formed the Society for the Abolition of the Slave Trade. The most famous of the new leaders was William Wilberforce, who, each year for the rest of his life, introduced a bill to end the slave trade.

For the reformers, attacking the trade rather than the institution appeared a less radical and more achievable reform. To many, the slave trade appeared a more obvious crime than the holding of slaves, which seemed a more passive act. Furthermore, attacking slavery itself involved serious issues of property rights, which might alienate potential supporters of the abolition of the slave trade. The antislavery groups also believed that if the trade were ended, planters would have to treat their remaining slaves more humanely.

While the British reformers worked for the abolition of the slave trade, slaves themselves in certain areas took matters into their own hands. Indeed, the largest emancipation of slaves to occur in the eighteenth century came on the island of Saint Domingue (Haiti), France's wealthiest colony, as a result of the slave revolt of 1794 led by Toussaint L'Ouverture and Jean-Jacques Dessalines (see Map 22–5). The revolt in Haiti and Haiti's eventual independence in 1804 stood as a warning to slave owners throughout the West Indies. Other slave revolts occurred, such as those in Virginia led by Gabriel Prosser in 1800 and by Nat Turner in 1831, in South Carolina led by Denmark Vesey in 1822, in British-controlled Demarra in 1823 and 1824, and in Jamaica in 1831. Each of these was brutally suppressed.

For complicated economic reasons some British West Indies planters began to consider abolition of the slave trade useful to their interests. Within the West Indies themselves the planters were experiencing soil exhaustion and competition from newly tilled islands opened for sugar cultivation. Some older plantations were being abandoned while others operated with low profitability. With the new islands there was a glut of sugar on the market, and as a consequence the price was falling. Under these conditions some British West Indies planters, for reasons that had nothing to do with religion or enlightened humanitarianism, began to favor curtailing the slave trade. Without new slaves, competing French planters would lack the labor they needed to exploit their islands.

Then, during the Napoleonic Wars, the British captured a number of the valuable French islands. In 1805 to protect the planters of the older British West Indies islands, the British Cabinet forbade the importation of slaves into the newly acquired French islands. By 1807 the abolition sentiment was strong enough for Parliament to pass Wilberforce's often proposed measure prohibiting slave trading from any British port.

Thereafter the suppression of this trade became one of the fundamental pillars of nineteenth-century British foreign policy. The British navy maintained a squadron of ships around the coast of West Africa to halt slave traders. Although the French and Americans also patrolled the West African coast, neither was deeply committed to ending the slave trade. Nonetheless, in 1824 the American Congress had made slave trading a capital offense.

Leaders of the Latin American wars of independence, disposed by Enlightenment ideas to disapprove of slavery, had sought the support of slaves by promises of emancipation. Once free of Spanish domination, the newly independent nations slowly freed their slave populations in order to maintain good relations with Great Britain from whom they needed economic support. Despite the gradual nature of this abolition, slavery would disappear from all nations of Latin America by the middle of the century with the important exception of Brazil.

Having slowly recognized that the abolition of the slave trade had not actually improved the lot of slaves, British reformers in 1823 adopted as a new goal the gradual emancipation of slaves and founded the Abolition Society. The savagery with which West Indian planters put down slave revolts

Map 22–5 The Haitian Revolution.

Spanish Slave Ship. After 1807 the British Royal Navy patrolled the West African coast attempting to intercept slave-trading ships. In 1846 the British ship HMS *Albatross* captured a Spanish slave ship, the *Albanoz,* and freed the slaves. A British officer depicted the appalling conditions in the slavehold in this watercolor.

in 1823 and 1824 and again in 1831 strengthened the resolve of the antislavery reformers. By 1830 the reformers abandoned the goal of gradual abolition and demanded immediate complete abolition of slavery. In 1833, following passage of the Reform Bill in Great Britain, they achieved that goal when Parliament abolished the right of British subjects to hold slaves. In the British West Indies, 750,000 slaves were freed within a few years.

The other old colonial powers in the New World tended to be much slower in their abolition of slavery. Portugal did little or nothing about slavery in Brazil, and when that nation became independent, its new government continued slavery. Portugal ended slavery elsewhere in its American possessions in 1836; the Swedes, in 1847; the Danes, in 1848; but the Dutch not until 1863. France had witnessed a significant antislavery movement throughout the first half of the century but did not abolish slavery in its West Indian possessions until the revolutions of 1848.

Despite all of these considerable achievements of the antislavery movement, during the first thirty years of the nineteenth century the institution of slavery actually revived and achieved new footholds in the transatlantic world. These areas included the lower south of the United States for the cultivation of cotton, Brazil for the cultivation of coffee, and Cuba for the cultivation of sugar. World demand for those products made the slave system economically viable in those regions. Slavery would end in the United States only after American abolitionists brought it to the center of American politics in the 1850s and the Civil War was fought during the next decade. In

Cuba it would persist until 1886, and full emancipation would occur in Brazil only in 1888 (see Chapters 24, 25, and 26).

The emancipation crusade, like slave trading itself, drew Europeans into African affairs. In 1787 the British established a colony for poor free blacks from Britain in Sierra Leone, which actually succeeded only after the British navy began to settle Africans rescued from captured slave-trading ships. The French established a smaller experiment at Libreville in Gabon. The most famous and lasting attempt to settle former black slaves in Africa was the establishment of Liberia through the efforts of the American Colonization Society after 1817. Liberia became an independent republic in 1847. All of these efforts to move former slaves back to Africa had only modest success, but they did affect the future of West Africa itself.

Other antislavery reformers were less interested in establishing outposts for settlement of former slaves than in transforming the African economy itself. These reformers attempted to spread both Christianity and free trade to Africa, hoping to exchange British manufactured goods, particularly textiles, for tropical goods produced by Africans. These commercial efforts of the antislavery movement marked the first serious intrusions of European powers well beyond the coast of West Africa into the heart of the continent.

After the American Civil War finally halted any large-scale demand for slaves from Africa, the antislavery reformers began to focus on ending the slave trade in East Africa and the Indian Ocean. This new drive against slavery and the slave trade in Africa itself became one of the rationales for European interference in Africa during the second half of the century and served as one of the foundations for establishing the late-century colonial empires.

Summary

The Transatlantic Revolutions. The revolutions and the crusade against slavery that occurred throughout the transatlantic world between 1776 and the 1830s transformed three continents. In North America, in France and other parts of Europe, and in South America, political experiments challenged government and the rule of monarchies and aristocracies. The foundations of modern liberal democracy were laid. The largest republic since ancient times had been established in North America. In Latin America, republicanism triumphed everywhere except Brazil. Never again could government be undertaken in these regions without some form of participation by the governed.

Economic and Social Liberalization. The expanding forms of political liberty found their counterparts in an economic life freed from the constraints of the old colonial empires and the slavery that marked their plantations. The new American republic constituted a vast free-trade zone. Its commerce was open to the world. And for the first time since the encounter with Europe, Latin America could trade freely among its own peoples and those of the rest of the world. In France and Europe, where the Napoleonic armies had carried the doctrines of the rights of man, economic life had been rationalized and freed from the domination of local authorities and local weights and measures. National law formed the framework for economic activity. The movement to abolish slavery fostered a wage economy of free laborers. That kind of economy would generate its own set of problems and social dislocation, but it was nonetheless an economy of free human beings.

Nationalism. Finally, the age of transatlantic revolutions saw the emergence of nationalism as a political force, a development that will be more fully discussed in Chapter 23. All of the revolutions, because of their popular political base, had given power to the idea of nations defined by their own character and historical past rather than by dynastic rulers. The Americans saw themselves as forming a new kind of nation. The French had demonstrated the power of a nation mobilized for military purposes. In turn, the aggression of France had aroused national sentiment, especially in Great Britain, Spain, and Germany. The new nations of Latin America also sought to define themselves by their heritage and historical experience rather than by their past in the Spanish and Portuguese empires.

These various revolutions, their political doctrines, and their social and economic departures provided examples to peoples elsewhere in the world. But even more important, the transatlantic revolutions and eventual abolition of slavery meant that new political classes and independent nations would become actors on the world scene. Europeans would have to deal with a score of new nations in the Americas. The rest of the world confronted new nations freed from the direction and authority of European powers. The political changes in Europe meant that those nations and their relationships with the rest of the world would be directed by a broader range of groups than in the past.

Key Terms

assignats (p. 676)

Consulate (p. 683)

Convention (p. 678)

creoles (p. 689)

Jacobins (p. 678)

levée en masse (p. 679)

peninsulares (p. 689)

Reign of Terror (p. 679)

sans-culottes (p. 678)

Thermidorean Reaction (p. 682)

Third Estate (p. 672)

Review Questions

1. Discuss the American Revolution in the context of transatlantic history. To what extent were the colonists influenced by their position in the transatlantic economy? To what extent were they influenced by European ideas and political developments? How did their demands for liberty compare and contrast with the ideas of liberty championed during the French Revolution?

2. How was the Estates General transformed into the National Assembly? How does the *Declaration of the Rights of Man and Citizen* reflect the social and political values of the eighteenth-century Enlightenment? What were the chief ways in which France and its government were reorganized in the early years of the revolution? Why has the Civil Constitution of the Clergy been called the greatest blunder of the National Assembly?

3. Why were some political factions dissatisfied with the constitutional settlement of 1791 in France? What was the revolution of 1792, and why did it occur? What were the causes of the Reign of Terror, and what political coalitions made it possible?

4. How did Napoleon rise to power? What were his major domestic achievements? Did his rule more nearly fulfill or betray the ideals of the French Revolution? Why did Napoleon decide to invade Russia? Why did he fail? What were the major outlines of the peace settlement achieved by the Congress of Vienna?

5. What political changes took place in Latin America in the twenty years between 1804 and 1824? What were the main reasons for Creole discontent with Spanish rule? Who were some of the primary leaders of Latin American independence, and why were they successful? How were the movements to Latin American independence influenced by the American and French Revolutions? What were the factors that made the Latin American wars of independence different from those two revolutions?

6. A motto of the French Revolution was "liberty, equality, and fraternity." How might one compare the American Revolution, the French Revolution, and the Latin American wars of independence in regard to the achievement of these goals? Which groups in each country or region benefited from the revolution, and which gained little or nothing from the changes?

7. What intellectual and religious factors contributed to the rise of the antislavery movement? To what extent did nonhumanitarian forces contribute to it? What opposition did it meet? Why did slavery receive a new lease on life during the same years that the antislavery movement emerged?

Note: To learn more about the topics in this chapter, please turn to the Suggested Readings at the end of the book. For additional sources related to this chapter please see MyHistoryLab.com.

PEARSON myhistorylab™ Connections

Reinforce what you learned in this chapter by studying the many documents, images, maps, review tools, and videos available at **www.myhistorylab.com**.

Read and Review

✔●—[Study and Review **Chapter 22**

●●●—[Read the Document *Declaration of the Rights of Man and the Citizen 1789, p. 675*
Maximilien Robespierre "Speech to National Convention: The Terror Justified", p. 682
Madame de Remusat on the Rise of Napoleon, p. 683
Napoleon's Exile to St. Helena (1815), p. 687
Simon de Bolívar, "Address to Second National Congress" (Venezuela), 1819, p. 691
Jose Morelos, Sentiments of the Nation (Mexico), 1813, p. 693

👁—[See the Map *Revolutionary France, p. 679*
Napoleon's Empire in 1812, p. 684

🔅—[View the Image *Oath of the Tennis Court, p. 672*
Slave Revolt in Saint Domingue, 1791, p. 689
The Great Liberator Independence Leader, Caudillo, and Future President Simón Bolívar, p. 691

((●—[Hear the Audio *Napoleon, 1, p. 683*

Research and Explore

📹—[Watch the Video *Revolution in the Atlantic World*

👁—[See the Map *Europe after the Congress of Vienna, 1815, p. 688*

((●—[Hear the Audio

Hear the audio file for Chapter 22 at
www.myhistorylab.com.

23

Political Consolidation in Nineteenth-Century Europe and North America

- The Emergence of Nationalism in Europe
- Early Nineteenth-Century Political Liberalism
- Efforts to Liberalize Early Nineteenth-Century European Political Structures
- Testing the New American Republic
- The Canadian Experience
- Midcentury Political Consolidation in Europe
- Unrest of Nationalities in Eastern Europe
- Racial Theory and Anti-Semitism

DURING THE NINETEENTH CENTURY TWO fundamental long-term developments occurred in the northern transatlantic world that would have a profound impact over the decades in every culture on the face of the earth. First, in both Europe and North America there took place a process of political consolidation that made the nation-states of that region the strongest of the period. Second, and directly contributing to that political strength, there emerged in Europe and North America powerful, new industrial economies with a new kind of society no longer based primarily on the land. As a direct result of this political consolidation and industrialization, the nations of the northern transatlantic became the world's major military powers. By the close of the nineteenth century, and well into the twentieth, this political and military power allowed the nations of

Garibaldi at Naples, by Antonio Licata. One of the extraordinary figures of the nineteenth century, Giuseppe Garibaldi (1807–1882) was the forceful and spiritual leader of the movement for Italian unification, which was achieved, after many conflicts, in 1861.

European and North American Political Consolidation

Europe, North America

During the first three quarters of the nineteenth century the nations of Europe and North America underwent major political consolidation. Great Britain emerged from the Napoleonic Wars as the strongest power on the globe and maintained that position for more than a century. France experienced decades of changing political regimes but remained a major political and military force. However, the third quarter of the century saw Germany and Italy transformed from relatively soft regions of small principalities into major unified nation-states. Similarly, the Austrian Empire reorganized itself. As will be seen in Chapter 24, Russia also undertook major political and social reforms to consolidate the strength of the tsarist government. On the other side of the Atlantic the United States became a major nation aspiring to stretch across the North American continent as did Canada. These developments laid the foundation for the major transatlantic state system of the late nineteenth and early twentieth centuries.

The movement toward strong, centralized national states in Europe and North America during the nineteenth century had counterparts elsewhere in the world. In Asia during this same period, Japan sought to imitate the military and economic power of the European states. Late nineteenth-century Latin America enjoyed one of its most successful and stable periods. The governments of that region established centralized regimes on the basis of relatively prosperous economies. In the United States the Civil War established the power of the central federal government over that of the individual states. The role of the war in forging a single American nation was similar to the role that military force played in the unifications of Italy and Germany and the suppression of the Paris Commune.

In the cases of Italy and Germany many people regarded the triumph of nationalism as a positive achievement. However, the last half of the century also saw various national and ethnic groups use the power of the national state to repress or dominate other minority groups. Examples include the Hungarian treatment of smaller subject nationalities and the British treatment of the Irish. To some extent, this phenomenon can be explained by the geographical borders of the new nations that were carved out of former European monarchies

Europe and the United States to exert unprecedented political, military, and economic influence around the globe.

The present chapter will examine the process of political consolidation in the northern transatlantic world, while Chapter 24 will explore the social changes that occurred there in the nineteenth century. Although we will consider the two processes separately, each contributed to the other. ■

The Emergence of Nationalism in Europe

Nationalism proved to be the single most powerful political ideology in Europe during the nineteenth and early twentieth centuries. As a political idea, **nationalism** is based on the relatively modern concept that a nation is composed of people who are joined together by the bonds of common language, customs, culture, and history, and who, because of those bonds, should share the same government. That is to say, political and ethnic boundaries should coincide. This idea came into its own in Europe during the late eighteenth and early nineteenth centuries. Early nineteenth-century nationalists directly opposed the principle upheld at the Congress of Vienna in 1814—that legitimate monarchies or family dynasties, rather than ethnicity, should provide the basis for political unity. Nationalists naturally protested multinational states such as the Austrian or Russian Empires, which embraced a wide variety of diverse ethnic groups that were often hostile to each other. Nationalists also objected to peoples of the same ethnic group, such as Germans and Italians, dwelling in political units smaller than those of the ethnic nation. Consequently, nationalists challenged both the domestic and the international order of the Vienna settlement.

and empires, such as the Austro-Hungarian Empire. In many cases, the new national boundaries ignored the reality that many, perhaps most, regions were home to more than one ethnic group, with religions, languages, and ethnicities different from those of their rulers and the governing class. In the premodern world, loyalty to a ruling dynasty, rather than shared history, language, or ethnicity, was the primary determinant of group identity or membership in a polity above the local level. People saw themselves first as members of a tribe, clan, village, or town, and second as the subjects of a ruler who might not even speak their language and whose authority often impinged very little on their daily lives. Thus ethnic or linguistic minorities posed less of an obstacle to monarchical rulers than to governments of nation-states, where national identity is often based on shared language and ethnicity. This problem has continued to bedevil national states in Europe and elsewhere in the world into the modern era and is an important cause for many recent conflicts in regions as diverse as eastern Europe, Asia, and Africa.

Elsewhere around the globe during the nineteenth century strong central governments often simply repressed minority populations, especially indigenous peoples, or allowed them fewer rights of civic participation and protection. In almost all cases the repression of minority groups generated social and political problems that haunted the twentieth century. Native Americans failed to gain rights in Latin America. In the United States the westward movement brought warfare against Native Americans, and legislation facilitated the segregation of American black citizens. In Canada, English speakers fared better than French speakers. In Australia, Aborigines were killed or forcibly relocated in many regions before and after that country's government gained sovereignty from England.

Finally, the emergence of strong European nation-states set the stage for the extension of their rivalries from Europe to other areas of the globe. The militarily and economically strong states of Europe soon turned to foreign adventures that subjugated vast areas of Africa and Asia. This imperialism led many colonized peoples to become aware that only strong nationalistic movements of their own could eventually end subjugation by the militarily stronger Europeans. Consequently, during the first quarter of the twentieth century, the nationalistic principle that less than fifty years earlier had dominated European politics began to influence the politics of the peoples on whom Europeans had imposed their government and administration. As these former colonies achieved independence and established their own nation-states, however, their governments experienced problems similar to those of the European nations in balancing the demands for unity of the majority with the rights of the diverse ethnic and religious minorities inhabiting their territory.

Focus Questions

- What role has military and economic power played in strengthening nation-states?
- Why do most nation-states have ethnic minorities? Why have these minorities tended to be oppressed?
- How did the rivalry among the European nation-states affect other regions of the world? What relationship did it have on the development of nationalism outside of Europe?

Creating Nations

Nationalists actually created nations in the nineteenth century. During the first half of the century various writers from various scholarly fields using the printed word spread a nationalistic concept of the nation. They were frequently historians who chronicled a people's past or writers and literary scholars who established a national literature by collecting and publishing earlier writings in the people's language. In effect, they gave a people a sense of their past and a literature of their own. In time schoolteachers, by imparting a nation's official language and history, spread nationalistic ideas. The language to be used in the schools and in government offices was always a point of contention for nationalists. In France and Italy official versions of the national language were imposed in the schools and replaced local dialects. In parts of Scandinavia and eastern Europe nationalists attempted to resurrect from earlier times what they regarded as purer versions of the national language. Often modern scholars or linguists virtually invented these resurrected languages. This process of establishing national languages led to far more linguistic uniformity within European nations than had existed before the nineteenth century. In most countries spoken and written proficiency in the official printed language became a path to social and political advancement and employment within government bureaucracies. The growth of a uniform language helped to persuade people who had not thought of themselves as constituting a nation that they were a nation. Yet even in 1850, perhaps less than half of the inhabitants of France, for example, spoke official French (see Map 23–1 on page 702).

Meaning of Nationhood

Nationalists used a variety of arguments and metaphors to express what they meant by nationhood. Some argued, for example, that gathering Italians into a unified Italy or

Map 23–1. Languages of Europe. Although this map provides a good overview of the main languages of nineteenth-century Europe, it does not show the vast number of dialects that were the primary tongue of most speakers. A speaker of the Piedmont dialect from northwestern Italy, for example, would not understand a speaker from Sicily.

Germans into a unified Germany, thus eliminating the petty dynastic states that governed those regions, would promote economic and administrative efficiency. Some nationalists claimed that nations, like biological species in the natural world, were distinct creations of God. Other nationalists claimed a place for their nations in the divine order of things. Throughout the nineteenth century, for example, Polish nationalists portrayed Poland as the suffering Christ among nations, thus implicitly suggesting that Poland, like Christ, would experience resurrection and a new life. (See Document, "Mazzini Defines Nationality.")

A significant difficulty associated with nationalism was, and is, determining which ethnic groups could be considered nations, with claims to territory and political autonomy. In theory, any of them could, but in reality nationhood came to be associated with groups that were large enough to support

a viable economy, that had a history of significant cultural association, that possessed a cultural elite that could nourish and spread the national language, and that could conquer other peoples to establish and protect their own independence. Throughout the century many smaller ethnic groups claimed to fulfill these criteria but could not effectively achieve either independence or recognition. They could and did, however, create domestic unrest within the political units they inhabited. Such was the situation in Europe. A similar situation, though in many ways quite different, prevailed for a time in the United States, where by the middle of the century leaders of many Southern states began to make statements that resembled those of nationalist leaders in Europe. One can view the defeat of the Confederate States of America, discussed later in this chapter, as an example of the military failure of a region to establish itself as a kind of nationality.

Document   Mazzini Defines Nationality

No political force in the nineteenth century was stronger than nationalism. It replaced dynastic political loyalty with loyalty based on ethnicity. In 1835 the Italian nationalist and patriot Giuseppe Mazzini (1805–1872) explained his understanding of the concept. Note how he combined a generally democratic view of politics with a religious concept of the divine destiny of nations.

■ *What specific qualities of a people does Mazzini associate with nationalism? How and why does Mazzini relate nationalism to divine purposes? How does this view of nationality relate to the goals of liberal freedom? How does it compare to other perspectives on nationalism and independence movements (for example, two documents presented later in this chapter—"Parnell Calls for Home Rule for Ireland" and "Herzl Calls for the Establishment of a Jewish State")?*

The essential characteristics of a nationality are common ideas, common principles, and a common purpose. A nation is an association of those who are brought together by language, by given geographical conditions or by the role assigned them by history, who acknowledge the same principles and who march together to the conquest of a single definite goal under the rule of a uniform body of law.

The life of a nation consists in harmonious activity (that is, the employment of all individual abilities and energies comprised within the association) towards this single goal. . . .

But nationality means even more than this. Nationality also consists in the share of mankind's labors which God assigns to a people. This mission is the task which a people must perform to the end that the Divine Idea shall be realized in this world; it is the work which gives a people its rights as a member of Mankind; it is the baptismal rite which endows a people with its own character and its rank in the brotherhood of nations. . . .

Nationality depends for its very existence upon its sacredness within and beyond its borders.

If nationality is to be inviolable for all, friends and foes alike, it must be regarded inside a country as holy, like a religion, and outside a country as a grave mission. It is necessary too that the ideas arising within a country grow steadily, as part of the general law of Humanity which is the source of all nationality. It is necessary that these ideas be shown to other lands in their beauty and purity, free from any alien mixture, from any slavish fears, from any skeptical hesitancy, strong and active; embracing in their evolution every aspect and manifestation of the life of the nation. These ideas, a necessary component in the order of universal destiny, must retain their originality even as they enter harmoniously into mankind's general progress.

The people must be the basis of nationality; its logically derived and vigorously applied principles its means; the strength of all its strength; the improvement of the life of all and the happiness of the greatest possible number its results; and the accomplishment of the task assigned to it by God its goal. This is what we mean by nationality.

Source: From *Absolutism to Revolution, 1648–1848*, 2nd ed., Herbert H. Rowen, ed. Copyright © 1969. Reprinted by permission of Prentice Hall, Upper Saddle River, NJ.

Regions of Nationalistic Pressure in Europe

During the nineteenth century nationalists challenged the political status quo in six major areas of Europe. England had brought Ireland under direct rule in 1800, allowing the Irish to elect members to the British Parliament in Westminster. Irish nationalists, however, wanted independence or at least self-government. The "Irish problem" would haunt British politics for the next two centuries. German nationalists sought political unity for all German-speaking peoples, challenging the multinational Austrian Empire and pitting Prussia and Austria against each other. Italian nationalists sought to unify the peninsula and drive out the Austrians. Polish nationalists struggled, primarily against Russia, to restore Poland as an independent nation. In eastern Europe a host of national groups, including Hungarians, Czechs, Slovenes, and others, sought either autonomy or formal recognition within the Austrian Empire. Finally, in the Balkans national groups, including Serbs, Greeks, Albanians,

A CONVENTION OF HEMMERS AND STITCHERS HELD AT LYNN, FEB. 28, FOR ADOPTING A LIST OF PRICES; MRS. E. HALL, PRESIDING.—(See page 284.)

Female Liberal Political Activism. The ideas of political liberalism spoke deeply to the situation of women throughout the transatlantic world. Women demanded entrance into the political forum as demonstrated by the first women's rights convention in Seneca Falls, New York in 1848, and this meeting of women strikers in Lynn, Massachusetts in 1860.

Romanians, and Bulgarians, sought independence from Ottoman and Russian control. Although there were never simultaneous disturbances in all six areas, any one of them could erupt into turmoil. During the century nationalists changed the political map and political culture of Europe in a way that the Confederate States of America failed to do in the mid-nineteenth-century United States.

Early Nineteenth-Century Political Liberalism

In the present-day United States, the word *liberal* carries meanings and connotations that have little or nothing to do with its significance for nineteenth-century Europeans. European conservatives of the last century saw liberals as more radical than they actually were; present-day Americans often think of nineteenth-century liberals as more conservative than they were.

Politics

European **liberalism** derived from the Enlightenment, the example of English liberties, and the so-called principles of 1789 as embodied in the French *Declaration of Rights of Man and Citizen*. Liberal political figures sought to establish a frame-

work of legal equality, religious toleration, and freedom of the press. They sought to limit the arbitrary power of the government against the persons and property of individual citizens. They generally believed that the legitimacy of government emanated from the freely given consent of the governed expressed through elected representative or parliamentary bodies. Most important, free government required that state or Crown ministers be responsible to the representatives of the nation rather than to the monarch.

These goals were limited. Such responsible government, however, existed in none of the major European countries in 1815. Even in Great Britain the ministers were at least as responsible to the monarch as to the House of Commons. The people who espoused these changes in government tended to be those who were excluded from the existing political processes, but whose wealth and education made them believe such exclusion was unjustified. Liberals were often academics, members of the learned professions, and people involved in the rapidly expanding commercial and manufacturing sectors. They believed in and were products of the career open to talent. The existing monarchical and aristocratic regimes often failed to recognize sufficiently their new status and to provide for their economic and professional interests.

Although European liberals wanted broader political participation, they were not democrats. Second only to their hostility to the privileged aristocracies was their general contempt for the lower, unpropertied classes. Liberals transformed the eighteenth-century concept of aristocratic liberty into a new concept of privilege based on wealth and property instead of birth. By midcentury this widely shared attitude meant that throughout Europe, liberals had separated themselves from both the rural and the urban working class. In the first half of the nineteenth century political liberals did not generally support the extension of political rights to women, but liberal political principles provided women with strong arguments to do so, as seen for example in the *Declaration of Female Independence* issued by the Seneca Falls Convention in the United States in 1848.

◆◆◇ Read the Document
The Seneca Falls Convention (1848)
at **myhistorylab.com**

Economics

The economic goals of the liberals also furthered their separation from the working class. European economic liberals opposed the old paternalistic legislation that established wages and labor practices by government regulation or by guild privileges. Labor was simply one more commodity to be bought and sold freely. Liberals sought what they regarded as structures of economic liberty in which people were free to use their talents and property to enrich themselves. The liberals contended that this would lead to more goods and services for everyone at lower prices, thus providing the basis for material progress.

The manufacturers of Great Britain, the landed and manufacturing middle class of France, and the commercial interests of Germany and Italy wanted to be able to manufacture and sell goods freely. They thus favored the removal of international tariffs as well as internal barriers to trade. To that end, liberals across the Continent and those who imitated them outside of Europe favored the rapid construction of railways from the 1830s onward.

The economic goals of European liberals found many followers outside Europe among groups that favored the expansion of free trade, new transport systems, and a free market in labor. In the United States people of this outlook often attacked slavery as an inefficient, paternalistic institution. In Latin America political liberals sought to remove paternalistic legislation that had protected Native Americans during the centuries of the Spanish Empire.

Relationship of Nationalism and Liberalism

Nationalism was not necessarily or logically linked to liberalism, and some conservative nationalists, for example, ignored the rights of national minorities. Liberalism and nationalism, however, were often complementary. Behind the concept of a people joined naturally together by the bonds of common language, customs, culture, and history lurked the idea of popular sovereignty. The idea of the career open to talent could be applied to suppressed national groups that were not permitted to realize their cultural or political potential. The efficient government and administration required by commerce and industry would mean replacing the small German and Italian states with larger political units. Moreover, nationalist groups in one country could gain the sympathy of liberals in other nations by espousing representative government and political liberty.

Liberalism and Nationalism in Modern World History

The wars of the French Revolution in Europe had demonstrated by the early nineteenth century that the ideals of political liberalism could easily spread across dynastic borders. In time those liberal ideals as well as those of nationalism would spread around the globe. It is for this reason that what began as a European development is so important not just for Europe but also for global history. The concept of

the rights of man and citizen could be used during the wars of independence in Latin America to challenge Spanish government. By the close of the nineteenth century those same ideals could be turned against the colonial government that Europeans imposed on Africa and Asia (see Chapter 26). Furthermore, the belief that people should have the right to govern themselves would inspire the settlers who spread across both the United States and Canada as well as those who came to live in Australia and New Zealand. Similarly, the belief that individual ethnic groups should constitute independent nations became a major political idea whereby peoples living under European colonial government during the late nineteenth century and even more importantly the twentieth century would challenge the right of Europeans and later Americans to govern them or to dominate their lives informally through economic power. Thus the political developments in Europe during the early nineteenth century would produce a profound impact around the globe during the next century.

Efforts to Liberalize Early Nineteenth-Century European Political Structures

European nations certainly did not move toward liberal political structures either rapidly or without considerable conflict. Indeed, after the Congress of Vienna most conservatives hoped that they had established walls against liberal advances. Three examples will indicate the different experiences that different European liberals confronted early in the nineteenth century.

Russia: The Decembrist Revolt of 1825 and the Autocracy of Nicholas I

In the process of driving Napoleon's army across Europe and then occupying defeated France, many officers in the Russian army were introduced to the ideas of the French Revolution and the Enlightenment. They realized how economically backward and politically stifled Russia was. Under these conditions, groups within the officer corps formed secret societies. These societies were small and divided in their goals; they agreed only that the government of Russia must change. Sometime during 1825 they seem to have decided to carry out a coup d'état in the next year.

Other events intervened, however. In late November 1825 Tsar Alexander I suddenly and unexpectedly died. His death created two crises. The first was a dynastic one: Alexander had no direct heir. His brother Constantine stood next in line to the throne. However, Constantine, who was the commander of Russian forces in Poland, had renounced any claim to be tsar. Through a series of secret instructions

Decembrist Revolt. When the Moscow regiment refused to swear allegiance to Nicholas, he ordered the cavalry and artillery to attack them. Although a total failure, the Decembrist Revolt came to symbolize the yearnings of all Russian liberals in the nineteenth century for a constitutional government. *The Insurrection of the Decembrists at Senate Square, St. Petersburg on 14th December, 1825 (w/c on paper) by Russian School (19th century). Private Collection/Bridgeman Art Library.*

made public only after his death, Alexander had named his younger brother, Nicholas (r. 1825–1855), as the new tsar. Once Alexander was dead, the legality of these instructions became uncertain. Constantine acknowledged Nicholas as tsar, and Nicholas acknowledged Constantine. This family muddle continued for about three weeks, during which Russia, to Europe's astonishment, actually had no ruler. Then, in early December, the army command reported to Nicholas the existence of a conspiracy among certain officers. Able to wait no longer, Nicholas had himself declared tsar.

The second crisis now unfolded—a plot by junior officers to rally the troops under their command to the cause of reform. On December 26, 1825, the army was to take the oath of allegiance to Nicholas, who was less popular than Constantine and was regarded as more conservative. Nearly all of the regiments took the oath. But the Moscow regiment, whose chief officers, surprisingly, were not secret society members, marched into the Senate Square in Saint Petersburg and refused to swear allegiance. Instead, they called for Constantine and a constitution. Attempts to settle the situ-

ation peacefully failed. Late in the afternoon Nicholas ordered cavalry and artillery to attack the insurgents. Five of the plotters were executed, and over 100 other officers were exiled to Siberia.

The immediate result of the revolt was the crushing of liberalism as even a moderate political influence in Russia. Nicholas I also manifested extreme conservatism in foreign affairs. Russia under Nicholas became the policeman of Europe, ever ready to provide troops to suppress liberal and nationalist movements. Except for a modest experiment early in the twentieth century tsarist Russia would never know genuinely liberal political structures.

Revolution in France (1830)

In 1824 Louis XVIII (r. 1814–1824), the Bourbon restored to the French throne by the Congress of Vienna, died. He was succeeded by his brother, Charles X (r. 1824–1830). The new king considered himself a monarch by divine right, and he also moved to restore lands that the French aristocrats

Liberty Leading the People by Eugene Delacroix is a famous evocation of the Revolution of 1830. *Giraudon/Art Resource, New York.*

Orléans, the head of the liberal branch of the royal family, the new monarch. Under what became known as the **July Monarchy**, Louis Philippe was called the king of the French rather than of France. The king had to cooperate with the Chamber of Deputies; he could not dispense with laws on his own authority. The revolutionary tricolor replaced the white flag of the Bourbons. The Charter, or constitution, was regarded as embodying the rights of the people rather than a concession granted by the monarch. Catholicism was recognized only as the religion of the majority of the people, not the official religion. Censorship was abolished. The franchise, though still restricted, was extended. Socially, however, the Revolution of 1830 proved quite conservative. The landed oligarchy retained its economic, political, and social influence. Money became the path to power and influence in the government. There was much corruption. Most important, the liberal monarchy displayed scant sympathy for the lower and working classes.

The Great Reform Bill in Britain (1832)

Passage of the **Great Reform Bill**, which became law in 1832, was the result of events different from those that occurred on the Continent. In Britain the forces of conservatism and reform compromised with each other. As a result, during the century Great Britain became for most people the exemplary liberal state not only of Europe but also of the world.

View the Image
Reform Bill of 1832–Cartoon
at **myhistorylab.com**

English determination to maintain the union with Ireland caused the first step in the reform process. England's relationship to Ireland was not unlike that of Russia's to Poland or Austria's to Hungary. The Act of Union in 1800 between England and Ireland suppressed the separate Irish Parliament. The Irish now sent representatives to the British Parliament at Westminster, but only Protestant Irishmen could be elected to represent overwhelmingly Catholic Ireland.

During the 1820s, under the leadership of Daniel O'Connell (1775–1847), Irish nationalists organized the Catholic Association to agitate for **Catholic emancipation**, as the movement for legal rights for Roman Catholics was known. In 1828 O'Connell was elected to Parliament but could not legally take his seat. The British ministry of the Duke of Wellington (1769–1852) realized that henceforth Ireland might elect a predominantly Catholic delegation to Parliament. If they were not seated, civil war might erupt. Consequently, in 1829 Wellington and Robert Peel (1788–1850) steered the Catholic Emancipation Act through Parliament. Roman Catholics could now become members of Parliament. This measure, together

had lost during the revolution. In addition, he pushed other conservative measures through the Chamber of Deputies. Opposition soon developed. After elections in 1827, Charles began to govern somewhat less conservatively, but French liberals wanted a genuinely constitutional regime. Matters came to a head in 1829 when Charles abandoned efforts to accommodate liberals and appointed an ultraroyalist ministry, but his efforts backfired.

In 1830 Charles X called for new elections, in which the liberals scored a stunning victory. Instead of attempting to accommodate the new Chamber of Deputies, the king and his ministers decided to undertake a royalist seizure of power. In June and July 1830 the ministry had sent a naval expedition against Algeria. On July 9 reports of its victory, and the consequent foundation of a French empire in North Africa, reached Paris. On July 25, 1830, under the euphoria of this foreign diversion, Charles X issued the Four Ordinances, which restricted freedom of the press, dissolved the recently elected Chamber of Deputies, and called for new elections under a franchise restricted to the wealthiest people in the country.

Liberal newspapers immediately called on the nation to reject the monarch's actions. The laboring populace of Paris, burdened since 1827 by an economic downturn, took to the streets and erected barricades. The king called out troops, and more than 1,800 people died during the ensuing battles in the city. On August 2 Charles X as result of the revolutionary disturbances abdicated and left France for exile in England. The liberals in the Chamber of Deputies named a new ministry composed of constitutional monarchists. They proclaimed Louis Philippe (r. 1830–1848), the Duke of

Daniel O'Connell, known as the "Liberator," was the preeminent leader of Catholic emancipation in the first half of the nineteenth century.

with the repeal in 1828 of restrictions against Protestant nonconformists, ended the monopoly held by members of the Church of England on British political life.

Catholic emancipation alienated many of Wellington's Tory supporters. In the election of 1830 many supporters of parliamentary reform were returned to Parliament. Even some Tories believed that parliamentary reform was necessary because they had concluded that Catholic emancipation could have been passed only by a corrupt House of Commons. The Wellington ministry soon fell. The Tories were badly divided, and King William IV (r. 1830–1837) turned to the Whigs under the leadership of Earl Grey (1764–1845) to form a government.

The Whig ministry soon presented the House of Commons with a major reform bill that had two broad goals. The first was to replace "rotten" boroughs, which had few voters, with representatives for the previously unrepresented manufacturing districts and cities. The second was to increase the number of voters in England and Wales. In 1831 the House of Commons narrowly defeated the bill. Grey called for a new election, in which a majority in favor of the bill was returned to the Commons. The House of Commons passed the reform

bill, but the House of Lords rejected it. Mass meetings were held throughout the country, and riots broke out in several cities. Finally, William IV agreed to create enough new peers to give a third reform bill a majority in the House of Lords. Under this pressure, the measure became law in 1832.

The Great Reform Act expanded the size of the English electorate, but it was not a democratic measure. The electorate was increased by over 200,000 persons, or by almost 50 percent. The basis of voting, however, remained a property qualification. Some working-class voters actually lost the vote when their old franchise rights were abolished. New urban boroughs gave the growing cities a voice in the House of Commons. Yet the passage of the Reform Act did not, as it was once thought, constitute the triumph of the middle-class interest in England. For every new urban electoral district, a new rural district was also drawn. It was expected that the aristocracy would dominate the rural elections.

Although passed with much turmoil and conflict, the Great Reform Act established the foundations for long-term political stability in Britain. During the 1840s a major working-class political movement known as **Chartism** would bring the demands of industrial workers into the political process. Despite the tensions created by Chartism, British political structures maintained themselves. Throughout the second half of the nineteenth century Great Britain continued to symbolize the confident liberal state. A large body of ideas emphasizing competition and individualism was accepted by the members of all classes. Even the leaders of trade unions during these years asked only to receive some of the fruits of prosperity and to prove their own social respectability. Parliament itself continued to provide an institution that permitted the absorption of new groups and interests into the existing political processes.

The most important example of the opening of parliamentary processes was the Second Reform Act passed by a Conservative government in 1867. It increased the number of voters from approximately 1,430,000 to 2,470,000. Britain had taken a major step toward democracy. Benjamin Disraeli (1804–1881), who led the Conservatives in the House of Commons, thought significant portions of the working class would eventually support Conservative candidates who were responsive to social issues. He also thought the growing suburban middle class would become more conservative.

Gladstone and Disraeli The election of 1868, however, which followed the Second Reform Act, dashed Disraeli's hopes. William Gladstone (1809–1898) became the new prime minister. His ministry of 1868–1874 witnessed the culmination of classical British liberalism. Gladstone introduced competitive examinations into the civil service, abolished the purchase of army officers' commissions, and introduced the secret ballot. He opened Oxford and Cambridge universities to students of all religious denominations and, by the Education Act of 1870, made the British government responsible for establishing and running elementary schools, which had been supported by the various churches.

The liberal policy of creating popular support for the nation by extending political liberty and reforming abuses had its conservative counterpart in concern about social reform. Disraeli succeeded Gladstone as prime minister in 1874. Whereas Gladstone looked to individualism, free trade, and competition to solve social problems, Disraeli believed the state should protect weaker citizens. In his view, paternalistic legislation would alleviate class antagonism. His most important measures were the Public Health Act of 1875, which consolidated and extended previous sanitary legislation, and the Artisans Dwelling Act of 1875, through which the government became actively involved in providing housing for the working class.

The Irish Question Ireland remained a major issue for the British government. From the late 1860s onward, Irish nationalists had sought to achieve **home rule** for Ireland, by which they meant more Irish control of local government. Their demands of the British government very much resembled the demands that first the Hungarians and then the Czechs made toward the Habsburg government, which will be considered later in this chapter. The Irish, like the Hungarians and Czechs in the Habsburg Empire, proved a profoundly disruptive force in British politics.

The leader of the Irish movement for home rule was Charles Stewart Parnell (1846–1891). By 1885 Parnell had organized eighty-five Irish members of the House of Commons into a tightly disciplined party that often voted as a bloc. In the election of 1885 the Irish Party emerged holding the balance of power between the English Liberals and Conservatives. The Irish could decide which party would take office. In December 1885 Gladstone announced support for home rule for Ireland, and Parnell gave his votes to the formation of a Liberal ministry. (See Document, "Parnell Calls for Home Rule for Ireland.") However, the issue split the Liberal Party. In 1886 a group known as the Liberal Unionists joined with the Conservatives to defeat Gladstone's Home Rule Bill. Gladstone called for a new election, which the Liberals lost. They remained permanently divided. The new Conservative ministry of Lord Salisbury (1830–1903) attempted to reconcile the Irish to the English government through public works and administrative reform. The policy had only marginal success.

In 1892 Gladstone returned to power and sponsored a second Home Rule Bill that passed the House of Commons but was defeated in the House of Lords. With the failure of this bill, further action on the Irish question was suspended until a Liberal ministry passed the third Home Rule Bill in the summer of 1914. However, implementation of home rule was suspended for the duration of World War I.

1848: Year of Revolutions in Europe

In 1848 a series of liberal and nationalistic revolutions and revolts spread across Europe (see Map 23–2 on page 711). No single factor caused this general revolutionary groundswell; rather, similar conditions existed in several countries. Severe food shortages had prevailed since 1846

A House of Commons Debate.
William Ewart Gladstone, standing on the right, is attacking Benjamin Disraeli, who sits with legs crossed and arms folded. Gladstone served in the British Parliament from the 1830s through the 1890s. Four times the Liberal Party prime minister, he was responsible for guiding major reforms through Parliament. Disraeli, regarded as the founder of modern British conservatism, served as prime minister from 1874 to 1880.

Document   Parnell Calls for Home Rule for Ireland

Since 1800, Ireland had been governed as part of Great Britain, sending representatives to the British Parliament in Westminster. Throughout the century, there had been tension and violent conflict between the Irish and their English governors. Agitation for home rule, whereby the Irish would directly control many of their own affairs, reached a peak in the 1880s. Charles Stewart Parnell was the chief leader for the cause of Irish nationalism during that decade. His program at the time was home rule for Ireland, by which he meant Irish administration of Irish domestic affairs while preserving an ill-defined union with England. In 1885, he made a speech outlining the resentments the Irish had felt toward the English since the Act of Union of 1800. He also drew direct parallels between the relationship of Ireland to England and that of Hungary to Austria. The efforts to achieve home rule failed during the nineteenth century.

■ *How does Parnell say the Act of Union affected Irish sentiment toward England? What parallel does he draw with Hungary and Austria? Why might Parnell be regarded as a moderate nationalist?*

It is not possible for human intelligence to forecast the future in the matter; but we can point to this—we can point to the fact that under 85 years of parliamentary connection with England, Ireland has become intensely disloyal and intensely disaffected; that notwithstanding the Whig policy of so-called conciliation, alternative conciliation and coercion . . . that disaffection has broadened, deepened, and intensified from day to day. Am I not, then, entitled to assume that one of the roots of this disaffection and feeling of disloyalty is the assumption by England of the management of our affairs. It is admitted that the present system can't go on, and what are you going to put in its place? My advice to English statesmen considering this question would be this—trust the Irish people altogether or trust them not at all . . . Whatever chance the English rulers may have of drawing to themselves the affection of the Irish people lies in destroying the abominable system of legislative union between the two countries by conceding fully and freely to Ireland their right to manage her own affairs. It is impossible for us to give guarantees, but we can point to the past; we can show that the record of English rule is a constant series of steps from bad to worse, that

the condition of English power is more insecure and more unstable at the present moment than it has ever been. We can point to the example of other countries; of Austria and of Hungary—to the fact that Hungary having been conceded self-government became one of the strongest factors in the Austrian empire. We can show the powers that have been freely conceded in the colonies [such as Canada and Australia have led to loyalty] . . .I am confident that the English statesman who is great enough . . .o carry out these teachings. . . to give Ireland full legislative liberty, full power to manage her own domestic concerns will be regarded in the future by his countrymen as one who has removed the greatest peril to the English empire—a peril, I firmly believe, which if not removed will find some day . . . an opportunity of revenging itself to the destruction of the British empire for the misfortunes, the oppressions, and the misgovernment of our country.

Source: From Charles Stewart Parnell, "Speech at Wicklow," October 5, 1885, as quoted in Raymond Phineas Stearns, *Pageant of Europe: Sources and Selections from the Renaissance to the Present Day* (New York: Harcourt, Brace and Company, 1948), pp. 634–635.

View the Image
Gladstone and Disraeli–Punch Cartoon
at **myhistorylab.com**
due to poor harvests. The commercial and industrial economy was in recession, with widespread unemployment. However, the dynamic for change in 1848 originated not with the working classes but with the political liberals, who were generally drawn from the middle classes. Throughout the Continent liberals were pushing for more representative governments, civil liberty, and unregulated economic life.

To put additional pressure on their governments, the liberals began to appeal for the support of the urban working classes, even though the goals of the two groups were different. The working classes sought improved employment and better working conditions rather than political reform for its own sake. The liberals refused to follow political revolution with social reform and thus isolated themselves from their temporary working-class allies. Once separated from potential mass support, the liberal revolutions became an easy prey to

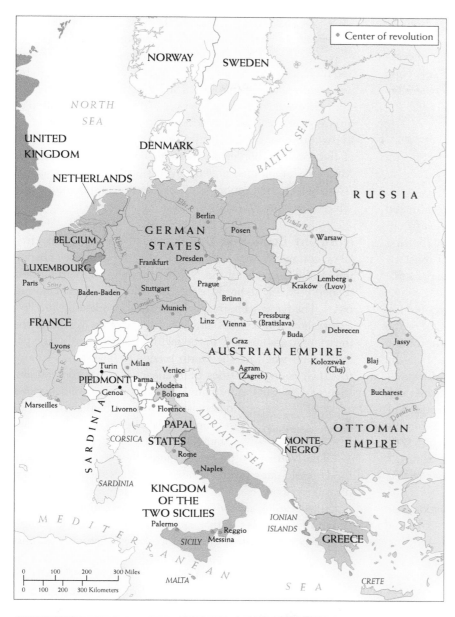

Map 23–2. Centers of Revolution in 1848–1849. The revolution that toppled the July Monarchy in Paris in 1848 soon spread to Austria and many of the German and Italian states. Yet by the end of 1849, most of these uprisings had been suppressed.

the armies of reactionary governments. As a result, the revolutions of 1848 failed to establish genuinely liberal or national states.

See the Map
European Centers of Rebellion and Revolution, 1820–1848
at **myhistorylab.com**

What are known in European history as the Revolutions of 1848 were confined to the Continent, where the results were important for the individual nation-states. In France the monarchy of Louis Philippe was overthrown and briefly replaced by a republic. In 1851 the republic was in turn overthrown in a military coup led by Louis Napoleon, a nephew of the first Napoleon. Thereafter Louis Napoleon created the Second Empire and took the title of Napoleon III. In Prussia and the Austrian Empire short-lived revolutions brought political liberals and nationalists to the fore, but in each case those revolutions were suppressed by the military. The same was true of efforts by Italian nationalists to thrust off Austrian rule of Italy.

From the standpoint of world history, however, the chief importance of the failed liberal and national Revolutions of 1848 was the emergence on the European continent of strongly conservative governments that would dominate the scene for the next quarter century. The turmoil of 1848 through 1850 ended the era of liberal revolution that had begun in 1789. Liberals and nationalists had discovered that rational argument and local insurrections would not help them to achieve their goals. The working class also adopted new tactics and organization. The era of the riot and urban insurrection was ending. In the future, workers would turn to trade unions and political parties to achieve their political and social goals. Finally, after the Revolutions of 1848, the political initiative in Europe passed for a time to the conservative political groups.

Read the Document
Metternich on the Revolutions of 1848
at **myhistorylab.com**

The defeat of liberal political forces in 1848 and the triumph of conservative powers also influenced the moderniza-

Revolutionary. In 1848, Ana Ipatescu helped to lead Transylvanian revolutionaries against Russian rule. (Transylvania is part of present-day Romania.) The revolutions of 1848 in eastern Europe were primarily the rising of nationalist groups. Although generally repressed in the revolutions of that year, subject nationalities would prove a source of political upheaval and unrest in the region throughout the rest of the century, ultimately providing the spark for the outbreak of World War I.

tion of Japan. Within a few years Japan would emerge from its long self-imposed isolation. After the Meiji Restoration the new leaders of Japan looked to European examples of successful modern nations. The nation they would most clearly copy was the conservative, militaristic Germany that emerged after the defeat of the liberals of 1848.

Testing the New American Republic

Toward Sectional Conflict

While the nations of western Europe very slowly embraced political liberalism, the United States of America was continuing its bold republican political experiment. By the first quarter of the century, however, serious sectional tensions had arisen, the most important of which related to the presence of black slavery in the Southern states.

The Constitutional Convention of 1788 had debated the sectional difference in a dispute over what proportion of the slave population, if any, would be counted in determining how many seats the Southern states were allotted in the House of Representatives. A compromise allowed the slaveholding states to count three-fifths of their slaves when calculating their population for representation in Congress. The Constitution also forbade any federal attempt to prevent the importation of slaves before 1808. Between 1788 and 1808 thousands of slaves were imported into the United States.

The westward movement, however, meant that slavery could not permanently be ignored. The Ordinance of 1787, passed by Congress under the Articles of Confederation, had prohibited slavery in the Northwest Territory, which embraced the future states of Ohio, Indiana, Illinois, Michigan, and Wis-

The Excelsior Iron Works, located in New York City. This print from the 1840s shows the works as a beehive of activity. Iron mills produced the material for railroads, ships, and machinery.

●●●–[Read the Document
"A Defense of the Slave Trade,"
July 1740 at **myhistorylab.com**

consin. Territory south of the Ohio River and beyond the Mississippi River was, however, open to slavery, and there it spread. By 1820 the number of slave and free states was evenly divided; this meant an equal number of senators from slave and free states. That year, Missouri was admitted as a slave state and Maine as a free one. It was also decided that in the future no slave states would be carved out of land north of the southern border of Missouri. For the time being, this Missouri Compromise ended congressional debate over slavery. Nonetheless, the economies of the North and the South were rapidly diverging.

Northern Economic Development Family farms, free labor, commerce, and early industrialization in textiles characterized the economy of the Northern states. Northern farmers tended primarily to produce foodstuffs for their local communities. The farms were relatively small and worked by families. Farm laborers were free. Similarly, free laborers worked in the towns, on the ships, and in the factories of the North. The political spokesmen for the North tended to favor tariffs to protect their young industries from cheaper foreign competition. In this favoring of tariffs, many Americans whose political views otherwise often resembled those of European liberals differed from their European counterparts.

((●–[Hear the Audio
Slavery 1 at **myhistorylab.com**

The North was the site of the earliest textile factories in the United States. Samuel Slater had established the first textile mill in Rhode Island in 1790. He had learned how to manufacture textiles in the new mills of industrializing Great Britain. His transfer of that technology to America illustrates how important British and European advances were transported to the United States. Much of the United States' early industrialization depended on such technological transfers. By the second decade of the nineteenth century the North had hundreds of cotton factories. These mills used cotton that was produced in the South, but most Southern cotton was sold overseas, mainly to the growing British textile industry.

During the second quarter of the century innovations in transportation led to the fuller integration of different parts of the Northern economy. Canals were built to link the major rivers with manufacturing and agricultural markets. The most famous was the Erie Canal, which connected the Hudson River to the Great Lakes. Other canals linked the Great Lakes to the Ohio River. Major efforts were undertaken to make the Ohio, Mississippi, and Missouri rivers

Map Exploration

To explore this map further, go to **http://www.myhistorylab.com**

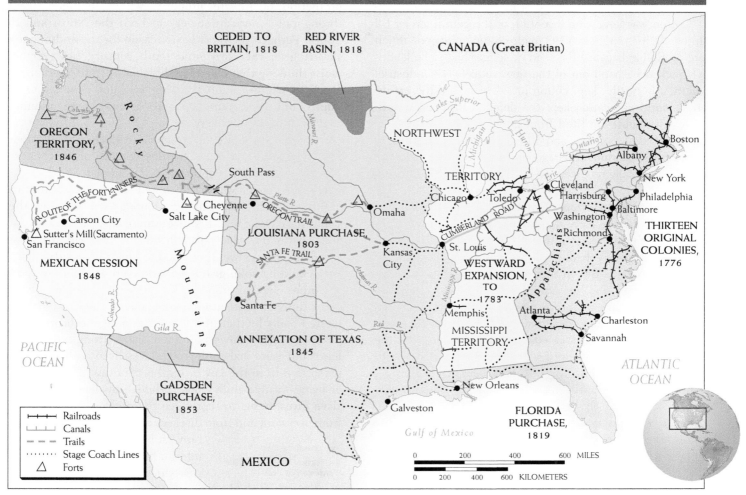

Map 23–3. The United States, 1776–1850. During the nineteenth century the United States expanded across the entire North American continent. The revolutionary settlement had provided most of the land east of the Mississippi. The single largest addition thereafter was the Louisiana Purchase of 1803. The annexation of Texas, and later the Mexican Cession following the Mexican War, added the major Southwestern territories. The borders of the Oregon Territory were settled through long, difficult negotiations with Great Britain.

navigable, which allowed steamboats to transport goods. But by the late 1840s, in America as in Europe, the major transportation innovation was the railroad. Most of the railways linked the Northeast and the West and fostered the commercial agriculture of the Midwest. Its products were sold in the Northeast and exported from Northern ports. Hence, the development of east–west railways undermined the older river-based trade routes along the Ohio and down the Mississippi. Few major lines ran north and south, so former ties between the sections based on the rivers weakened. The building of the early railways also aided the development of the Northern coal and iron industries. The further expansion of railways at midcentury caused new sectional tensions, as it became clear the railways could

open vast territories for settlement and could thus also open a national debate over the future of slavery. That prospect sharpened the sectional debate and led to civil war (see Map 23–3).

Rivers, canals, and railways allowed the upper Midwest to develop into a rich area for agriculture. In this sense much of the Northern economy was as rural and agricultural as the Southern. What most distinguished the two regions was free versus slave labor. The Southern economy depended on slavery and could expand only if slavery were allowed to expand as well.

The Southern Economy The overwhelmingly rural economy of the American South was dependent on cotton and slavery. In those respects, the Southern economy resembled the economies of many Latin American countries, which were based on exporting a single crop or natural resource and on slave labor. The South had to export goods, primarily raw cotton, either to the North or to Europe, primarily to Great Britain, to maintain its standard of living.

Cotton was king. The invention of the cotton gin by Eli Whitney (1765–1825) in 1793 made cotton cultivation much more profitable because the seed no longer had to be laboriously picked by hand out of the new cotton. The industrial revolution in textiles kept cotton prices high, and the expansion in world population kept the demand for cotton cloth steady. The South profited from growing the cotton, New England from shipping it, and other parts of the North from supplying the manufactured goods the South needed. The South had virtually no incentive to diversify its agriculture.

Slavery in the American South Slavery was abolished in the North by the early nineteenth century largely in response to the egalitarian values of the American Revolution. In any case, slavery had never been fundamental to the Northern economy. But in the South, the expansion of the cotton empire in the Mississippi Delta in the early nineteenth century gave slavery a new lease on life. Although most Southern families never owned slaves and relatively few slave owners had possessed more than a few slaves, the

Scars of Slavery. This Louisiana slave named Gordon was photographed in 1863 after he had escaped to Union lines during the Civil War. He bears the permanent scars of the violence that lay at the heart of the slave system. Few slaves were so brutally marked, but all lived with the threat of beatings if they failed to obey.

institution of slavery survived for many reasons. For one, it was economically viable, and no one could devise a political or social method acceptable to white Southerners to abolish it. No less important was the strong commitment to the protection of private property, which included slaves, throughout American society in both the North and the South. Perhaps the most basic reason for the endurance of slavery after the early nineteenth century, however, was racist thinking that considered blacks as fundamentally inferior to whites. Such thinking was not peculiar to the South, but it functioned there as one more argument against abolishing slavery.

What was the life of an American slave like? All American slaves were nonwhite, the descendants of Africans who had been forcibly captured and shipped in the most wretched of conditions to the United States (see Chapter 16). Despite much miscegenation among Africans and their white slave owners and Native Americans, the various slave codes defined as black virtually anyone who had African antecedents. Slaves were regarded as chattel property; that is, they could be sold, given away, or even gambled away like any other piece of property. They had no recourse to law or constitutional protections and could be, and often were, treated badly by their masters. Whipping and beating were permitted. State laws protected slaves from extreme violence but were laxly enforced; slaves lived with no serious protection from the law or legal authorities. Their standard of living was generally poor. Although owners wanted their slave investments to reproduce themselves, slaves suffered from overwork and from diseases associated with poor nutrition, substandard sanitation, and inferior housing thus harming their reproductive rate.

●●●┤Read the Document
The History of Mary Prince (1830s)
at **myhistorylab.com**

Slaves worked primarily in the fields, where they plowed, hoed, and harvested cotton, rice, sugar, tobacco, or corn. They were usually organized into work gangs supervised by white overseers. This work, like all farming, was seasonal, but during planting or harvest seasons, labor would extend from sunrise to sunset. Children would work in the fields as helpers. Older or more privileged slaves might work in the house, cleaning, cooking, or taking care of children.

Recent scholarship has emphasized how the slave communities helped preserve the family life and inner personalities of the slaves. Some elements of African culture persisted in the slave communities. African legends were passed on orally. Religion proved extraordinarily important. Not only did slaves adopt for their own cultural needs the Old Testament stories of the Jews' liberation from Egypt, but they also often combined elements of African religion with evangelical Protestantism. Yet despite these efforts to preserve a sense of community and even of family, the marriages and family lives of slaves had no legal recognition.

The integrity of the slave family could be violated at the master's whim or with changing economic circumstances. In addition, white masters and their sons often sexually exploited black slave women. Because slaves were property, they could be sold for profit or transported when the owner moved to a different region. Consequently, families could be, and were, separated by sale or perhaps after an owner's death. Many young children were reared and cared for by other slaves to whom they were not related. In a world of white dominance, the institutions, customs, and religions of the slave community were the only means black slaves had to protect the autonomy of their own personalities.

The Abolitionist Movement

During the 1830s a militant antislavery movement emerged in the North. Its leaders and followers refused to accept what they regarded as the moral compromise of living in a nation that tolerated slavery. Abolitionists such as William Lloyd Garrison, editor of the *Liberator*, condemned the Union and the Constitution as structures that perpetuated slavery. Former slaves who had escaped slavery, such as Frederick Douglass and Sojourner Truth, and freeborn black Americans, such as Daniel A. Payne, also joined the cause. (See Document, "Daniel A. Payne Denounces American Slavery.") The antislavery movement, which was initially only one of many American reform movements, gained new adherents during the 1840s as the question of extending slavery into the new territories came to the fore in 1847 toward the end of the Mexican War (1846–1848). That military victory added significant new territory in the Southwest and California, in addition to Texas, which had been annexed in 1845. Through negotiations with Britain the United States also acquired the vast Oregon Territory in the Northwest in 1846 (see Map 23–3).

See the Map
The Americas, 1800–1836
at **myhistorylab.com**

Victory in the Mexican War opened debate on the extension of slavery into the huge new territory it created. Southerners feared that the changing climate of national debate and the opening of territories where slavery might be prohibited would give the South a minority status and thus eventually overturn its political and social culture. Northerners came to believe that a slave-power conspiracy controlled the federal government. The Compromise of 1850 temporarily restored political calm and stability and reassured the South; but many Northerners came to believe that the compromise only demonstrated the strength of the slave-power conspiracy in Washington.

In 1854 the introduction of the Kansas-Nebraska Bill renewed the formal national political debate over slavery and galvanized the antislavery forces. The principle of the bill, introduced by Stephen A. Douglas (1813–1861), was that of popular sovereignty. The people of each new territory would decide whether slavery was to be permitted within its borders. Douglas was thus willing to repeal the Missouri Compromise, which had prohibited slavery in most of the Louisiana Territory. Popular sovereignty meant that every newly organized territory had to debate slavery. In 1854 the new Republican Party was organized largely in opposition to the Kansas-Nebraska Bill. Not everyone, however, was willing just to argue. For example, John Brown went to Kansas, where armed conflict had already broken out, and carried out virtual guerrilla warfare against slaveholding settlers. During 1854 "Bleeding Kansas" was in a state of civil war.

In 1857, in the Dred Scott decision, the Supreme Court effectively repealed the Missouri Compromise by declaring that Congress could not prohibit slavery in the territories. The decision further declared that slaves did not become free by living in free states and that slaves did not have rights that others were bound to respect. For radical antislavery Northerners, the decision raised the most serious questions about the morality of the Union itself, and it demonstrated again a Southern conspiracy to protect slavery. Thereafter, slavery dominated national political debate.

In 1859 John Brown seized the federal arsenal at Harpers Ferry, Virginia, as part of an effort to foment a possible slave rebellion. He was captured, tried, and hanged, further increasing sectional polarization. Radical Southerners feared more than ever a Northern conspiracy to attack the institution of slavery, while Northern radicals feared that the South would use the federal government to protect slavery. Thus the politics of both sections became radicalized.

The Republican Party had become the party that opposed slavery, although most Republicans did not favor outright abolition. In 1858 Abraham Lincoln (1809–1865) ran against Stephen Douglas for the U.S. Senate in Illinois. Lincoln lost but made a national reputation for himself in the debates leading up to the election. In 1860 Lincoln, the Republican candidate, was elected president. Neither he nor the Republican Party had campaigned for the abolition of slavery. Nonetheless, Southerners perceived his election as the victory of a party and a president dedicated to the eradication of slavery. In December 1860 Southern states began to secede and formed the Confederate States of America. Attempts at political compromise to maintain the Union failed, and when Confederate forces fired on Fort Sumter in Charleston harbor in April 1861, the most destructive war in U.S. history began.

The Civil War lasted almost exactly four years, and a different nation emerged from the violence. In 1863 Lincoln emancipated the slaves in the rebelling states. The Emancipation Proclamation transformed the Northern cause from that of suppressing a Southern rebellion into that of extending liberty. By the time the Confederacy was defeated in 1865, the South was occupied by Northern armies, its farms were often fallow, its transportation network was disrupted,

Document   Daniel A. Payne Denounces American Slavery

Daniel A. Payne was an African American who became an ordained Lutheran minister. He delivered this speech in June 1839, at his ordination. Though born in Charleston, South Carolina, he was the son of free African Americans. As a young man he had opened a school in that state to educate African American children. He had to abandon this effort after the legislature prohibited teaching free or enslaved African Americans to read and write. Later he became president of Wilberforce University in Xenia, Ohio, which was dedicated to the education of African Americans.

■ *On what grounds does Payne condemn slavery? What examples of moral brutalization does Payne associate with slavery? How does he bring in religious arguments against the evils of slavery?*

. . . I am opposed to slavery, not because it enslaves the black man, but because it enslaves *man*. And were all the slave-holders in this land men of color, and the slaves white men, I would be as thorough and uncompromising an abolitionist as I now am; for whatever and whenever I may see a being in the form of a man, enslaved by his fellow man, without respect to his complexion, I shall lift up my voice to plead his cause, against all the claims of his proud oppressor; and I shall do it not merely from the sympathy which man feels towards suffering man, but because God, *the living God*, whom I dare not disobey, has commanded me to open my mouth for the dumb, and to plead the cause of the oppressed.

Slavery brutalizes man. . . . This being God created but a little lower than the angels, and crowned him with glory and honor; but slavery hurls him down from his elevated position, to the level of brutes, strikes this crown of glory from his head and fastens upon his neck the galling yoke, and compels him to labor like an ox, through summer's sun and winter's snow, without remuneration. Does a man take the calf from the cow and sell it to the butcher? So slavery tears the child from the arms of the reluctant mother, and barters it to the soul trader for a young colt, or some other commodity! Does the bird catcher tear away the dove from his mate? So slavery separates the groaning husband from the embraces of his distracted and weeping wife! . . . The very moment that a man conceives the diabolic design of enslaving his brother's body, that very moment does he also conceive the still more heinous design of fettering his will, for well does he know that in order to make his dominion supreme over the body, he must fetter the living spring of all its motions. Hence, the first lesson the slave is taught is to yield his will unreservedly and exclusively to the dictates of his master. And if a slave desires to educate himself or his children, in obedience to the dictates of reason or the laws of God, he does not, he cannot do it without the consent of his master. . . .

In view of the moral agency of man, God hath most wisely and graciously given him a code of laws, and certain positive percepts, to control and regulate moral actions. This code of laws, and these positive percepts, with the divine influence which they are naturally calculated to exert on the mind of man, constitutes his moral government. . . .

Now, slavery nullifies these laws and percepts—weakens and destroys their influence over the human mind, and hinders men from yielding universal and entire obedience to them; therefore slavery subverts the moral government of God. This is the climax of the sin of slavery. . . .

. . . Slavery never legislates for the religious instruction of slaves, but, on the contrary, legislates to perpetuate their ignorance; and there are laws this very moment in the statute books of South Carolina and other states, prohibiting the religious instruction of slaves. . . .

In a word, slavery tramples the laws of the living God under its unhallowed feet—weakens and destroys the influence which those laws are calculated to exert over the mind of man, and constrains the oppressed to blaspheme the name of the Almighty.

Source: Speech originally printed in the *Lutheran Herald and Journal of the Fort Plain, N. Y., Franckean Synod*, Vol. 1, No. 15 (August 1, 1839) as reprinted in Philip S. Foner, ed., *The Voice of Black America: Major Speeches by Negroes in the United States, 1797–1971.* Copyright © 1972, New York: Simon & Schuster, pp. 67–71.

and many of its cities were in ruins. Southern political leaders had virtually no impact on the immediate postwar decisions. The Thirteenth, Fourteenth, and Fifteenth amendments to the Constitution largely recast the character of the Union. The Thirteenth abolished slavery, the Fourteenth granted citizenship to the former slaves, and the Fifteenth allowed them to vote. The Fourteenth Amendment also prohibited much political activity by people who had taken up arms

Harvest of death. Corpses of dead soldiers are strewn across the battlefield in Gettysburg, Pennsylvania. The battle, which lasted from July 1–3, 1863, resulted in 51,000 casualties.

against the Union. These amendments resolved the issues of slavery and the relative roles of the state and federal governments.

The Civil War and the Reconstruction era that followed it overturned the antebellum social and political structures of the South. The slaves were freed and for a time participated broadly and actively in the politics of the Southern states. For more than ten years federal troops occupied parts of the South. Many of the antebellum Southern leaders left political life. Economically, the South remained generally rural and still dependent on cotton. For the first time since the earliest colonial days, it became an area of free labor. Many of the freed slaves and poor whites who tilled the land remained hopelessly in debt to wealthier landowners. Attempts to bring manufacturing into the South met with limited success. Rampant racism also blocked free economic development. For the rest of the century the South remained in a semicolonial relationship to the North. More than ever, in order to pay for the goods and services it needed, the South had to export raw materials or partially finished goods to the North, according to the economic rules set by Northern manufacturers and financiers. Throughout the rural South, poverty was the norm.

Within the context of world history, the American Civil War is important for several reasons. With the exception of the Taiping Rebellion in China from 1851 to 1864, it was the greatest war with the most extensive casualties that occurred anywhere in the world between the defeat of Napoleon in 1815 and the onset of World War I in 1914. It resulted in the establishment of a continentwide free labor market, even though freed blacks lived in great poverty, and created an economic dependence not unlike that of the rural classes of Latin America. The free labor market, purged of slavery, helped open the entire North American continent to economic development. The war also allowed American political and economic interests to develop without the distraction of the debates over states' rights and the morality of slavery.

The Canadian Experience

Under the Treaty of Paris of 1763, all of Canada came under the control of Great Britain. Canada then, as now, included both an English-speaking and a French-speaking population. The latter was concentrated primarily in Quebec. The Quebec Act of 1774, which had so disturbed the English colonists along the Atlantic seaboard, made the Roman Catholic Church the established church in Quebec. During the American Revolution approximately 30,000 English loyalists fled the colonies and settled in Canada. They thus established a larger English presence and were strongly loyal to the British Crown.

The tension between the French and English populations led, in part, to the Constitutional Act of 1791, which divided the colony into Upper Canada (primarily English in ethnic composition) and Lower Canada (primarily French). Each section had its own legislature, and a governor-general presided over the two provinces on behalf of the British Crown. Newfoundland, Nova Scotia, New Brunswick, Cape Breton Island, and Prince Edward Island remained separate colonies.

In the early nineteenth century Canada's relations with the United States were often tense. There were local disputes over the fur trade and fear that the United States

Canadian rail passengers board a train of the Great Western Railway at Clifton Depot in southern Ontario, sometime in the late 1850s. As in the United States, the growth of railroads transformed Canada in the nineteenth century.

would dominate Canada. That apprehension, along with the Anglo-French ethnic divisions, came to constitute two of the major themes of Canadian history.

By the late 1830s the political situation in Canada was beginning to generate considerable internal pressure. Tension arose between long-established families with powerful economic interests in both Upper and Lower Canada and new settlers who hoped to achieve prosperity for themselves. There were quarrels over the influence of the British Crown in local affairs. In 1837 rebellions occurred in both Upper and Lower Canada. Although there were relatively few casualties, the British realized that some action had to be taken.

Road to Self-Government

The British government, operating in the more liberal political climate following the first Reform Act (1832), was determined to avoid another North American revolution. Consequently, it sent the Earl of Durham (1792–1840) to Canada with extensive powers to make reforms. In 1839 his *Report on the Affairs of British North America* advocated responsible government for Canada. Durham contended that both Canadian provinces should be united into one political unit. He thought that such political unification would eventually lead to a thoroughly English culture throughout Canada that would overwhelm the French influence in Quebec. He also believed that most Canadian affairs should be in the hands of a Canadian legislature and that only foreign policy and defense should remain under British control. In effect, Durham wanted Canadians generally to govern themselves, so that English culture would dominate. His policy was carried out in the Canada Act of 1840, which gave the nation a single legislature composed of two houses.

The Durham *Report* established the political pattern that the British government would, to a greater or lesser extent, follow with its other English-speaking colonies during the nineteenth century. Britain sought to foster responsible self-government in Australia, New Zealand, and South Africa. The Canadian experience thus had a considerable impact throughout the world. Until well into the twentieth century, however, the British government, like other Western imperial powers, also generally believed that nonwhite peoples, such as those of India, required direct British colonial administration.

Keeping a Distinctive Culture

Canadians did learn to exercise self-government, but distinct English and French cultures continued to exist. Within the legislature there were almost always trade-offs between the eastern and western sections of the nation. Furthermore, during the American Civil War, fears arose that the American republic might seek to invade or dominate Canada. One response to this fear was an attempt to unite the Maritime Provinces in 1862. Those discussions led to broader considerations of the desirability of a stronger federation among all the parts of Canada.

The result of those debates and discussions was the British North America Act of 1867, which created a Canadian federation. Canadians hoped to avoid what they regarded as flaws in the Constitution of the United States. The Canadian system of government was to be federal, but with much less emphasis on states' rights than in the United States. Canadians established a parliamentary mode of government but also chose to retain the presence of the British monarchy in the person of the governor-general as head of state. The person who was most responsible for establishing this new government and who led it for most of the period between 1867 and 1891 was John A. MacDonald (1815–1891).

Midcentury Political Consolidation in Europe

During the same period that the United States and Canada established themselves as strong unified political entities in North America, major political consolidation occurred in Europe that would have an enormous impact on the rest of the world. As has so often been true in modern European history, war made change possible. In this case a conflict disrupted the international balance that had prevailed since 1815 and quickly unleashed forces that upset the political situation in several of the involved states. The war itself was in some respects less important than the political consequences that flowed from it during the next decade.

The Crimean War

The Crimean War (1854–1856), named after the Black Sea peninsula on which it was largely fought, originated from a long-standing rivalry between Russia and the Ottoman Empire. Russia wanted to extend its influence over the Ottoman provinces of Moldavia and Walachia (now in Romania). In 1853 Russia went to war against the Ottomans on the pretext that the Ottomans had given Roman Catholic France, instead of Orthodox Russia, the right to protect Christians and Christian shrines in the Holy Land. The next year France and Great Britain supported the Ottoman Empire to protect their interests in the eastern Mediterranean, while Austria and Prussia remained neutral. The war quickly bogged down after the French and the British invaded the Crimea. In March 1856 a peace conference in Paris concluded a treaty highly unfavorable to Russia.

The Crimean War shattered the image of an invincible Russia that had prevailed since the close of the Napoleonic Wars. It also shattered the power of the Concert of Europe to settle international disputes on the Continent. The major European powers were no longer willing to cooperate to maintain the existing borders between themselves and their

A Closer Look

The Crimean War Recalled

Although the nineteenth century is often regarded as a relatively peaceful century because of its contrast with the twentieth, the third quarter of the century saw major armed conflicts in both Europe and North America. The wars of the third quarter of the nineteenth century brought European armies once again to the foreground in European culture and art. Beginning with the Crimean War (1853–1856) and ending with the wars of German unification (1870), the armed forces of the various nation states reforged European political life. In the United States, the Civil War resulted in unprecedented American casualties as the North firmly unified the nation under the federal government and ended slavery.

Over time these conflicts became the subject of historical paintings. Artists might record even the most difficult moments of warfare. Here, the English artist Elizabeth Thompson, Lady Butler, portrayed *Roll Call after an Engagement, Crimea*. A pioneering woman artist, she completed the work in 1874 two decades after the war, and Queen Victoria purchased it.

The abilities of the aristocratic officers leading the British army had been discredited, so Butler here portrays ordinary troops who had suffered grievously during the Crimean War.

A certain nostalgia for the comradeship of soldiers even under the most difficult circumstances penetrates this scene at a time when Britain had not engaged in a major war for many years.

Royal Collection Enterprises Ltd./Lady Elizabeth Thompson Butler (1846–1933), "The Roll Call: Calling the Roll after an Engagement, Crimea (unframed)." The Royal Collection (©2005, Her Majesty Queen Elizabeth II. Photo by SC.

The poor equipment of the troops during the war had been a public scandal, and the evident suffering of these troops recalls that.

Questions

1. Lady Butler had herself never witnessed war. How do you think she was able to portray this and other war scenes?

2. Do you view this painting as a realistic image of the experience of soldiers, or do you think it represents Lady Butler's interpretation?

3. How might one conclude that this painting represents warfare during an era of growing democratization?

4. Why do you think by the early twentieth century such paintings as *Roll Call after an Engagement, Crimea*, fell from favor?

myhistorylab   To examine this image in an interactive fashion, please go to **www.myhistorylab.com**

neighbors. For the next twenty-five years instability prevailed in European affairs, allowing a largely unchecked adventurism in foreign policy.

Italian Unification

Italian nationalists had long wanted to unite the small absolutist principalities of the peninsula into a single state but could not agree on how to do it. Romantic republicans such as Giuseppe Mazzini (1805–1872) and Giuseppe Garibaldi (1807–1882) sought to drive out the Austrians by popular military force and then to establish a republic. They not only failed but also frightened more moderate Italians. The person who eventually achieved unification was Count Camillo Cavour (1810–1861), the prime minister of Piedmont.

Piedmont (officially styled the Kingdom of Sardinia), in northwestern Italy, was the most independent state on the peninsula (see Map 23–4). It had unsuccessfully fought against Austria in 1848 and 1849. Following the second defeat, King Charles Albert (r. 1831–1849) abdicated in favor of his son, Victor Emmanuel II (r. 1849–1878). In 1852 the new monarch chose Cavour—a moderate liberal in economics and a strong monarchist who rejected republicanism—as his prime minister.

Cavour believed that if Italians proved themselves to be efficient and economically progressive, the great powers might decide that Italy could govern itself. He worked for free trade, railway construction, credit expansion, and agricultural improvement. Cavour also fostered the Nationalist Society, which established chapters in other Italian states to press for unification under the leadership of Piedmont. Furthermore, he believed that Italy could be unified only with the aid of France.

Cavour joined the French and British side in the Crimean War so that he would be able to raise the question of Italian unification at the peace conference. There he received no specific rewards but did gain the sympathy of Napoleon III (r. 1852–1870) of France. In 1858 Cavour and the French emperor met and plotted to start a war with Austria.

During the winter and spring of 1859 tension grew between Austria and Piedmont as Piedmont mobilized its army. In late April war erupted, and France came to Piedmont's aid. On June 4 the Austrians were defeated at Magenta, and on June 24, at Solferino in Lombardy. Fearing too extensive a Piedmontese victory, Napoleon III concluded a separate peace with Austria on July 11 at Villafranca. Piedmont received Lombardy, but the Veneto remained under Austrian control. Cavour felt betrayed by France, but nonetheless the war had driven Austria from most of northern Italy. Later that summer Parma, Modena, Tuscany, and the Romagna voted to unite with Piedmont.

At this point the forces of romantic republican nationalism compelled Cavour to pursue the complete unification of northern and southern Italy. This policy meant that Cavour

Chronology

German and Italian Unification

Year	Date	Event
1854		Crimean War opens
1855		Cavour leads Piedmont into war on side of France and England
1856	July 20	Treaty of Paris concludes Crimean War
1858		Secret conference between Louis Napoleon and Cavour
1859		War of Piedmont and France against Austria
1860		Garibaldi lands his forces in Sicily and conquers southern Italy
1861	March 17	Proclamation of the Kingdom of Italy
	June 6	Death of Cavour
1862		Bismarck becomes prime minister of Prussia
1864		Danish War
1866		Austro-Prussian War; Veneto ceded to Italy
1867		North German Confederation formed
1870	June 19- July 12	Crisis over Hohenzollern candidacy for the Spanish throne
	July 13	Bismarck publishes edited press dispatch
	July 19	France declares war on Prussia
	September 1	France defeated at Sedan and Napoleon III captured
	September 4	French Republic proclaimed
	October 2	Italian state annexes Rome
1871	January 18	Proclamation of the German Empire at Versailles
	March 28—May 28	Paris Commune
	May 10	Treaty of Frankfurt between France and Germany

Map 23–4. The Unification of Italy. Beginning with the association of Sardinia and Piedmont by the Congress of Vienna in 1815, unification was achieved through the expansion of Piedmont between 1859 and 1870. Both Cavour's statesmanship and the campaigns of ardent nationalists played large roles.

the strong monarchist had to work with Garibaldi the strong republican. In May 1860 Garibaldi landed in Sicily with more than 1,000 troops. He captured Palermo and prepared to attack the mainland. By September the city and kingdom of Naples, probably the most corrupt example of Italian absolutism, lay under his control. To forestall a republican victory in the cause of unification, Cavour rushed troops south to confront Garibaldi. On the way Cavour's troops conquered the Papal States except for the area around Rome, which remained under the direct control of the pope.

See the Map
The Unification of Italy, 1859–1870
at **myhistorylab.com**

Garibaldi's nationalism won out over his republicanism, and he unhappily accepted Piedmontese domination and a monarch as head of the unified Italian state. In late 1860 Naples and Sicily voted to join the northern union forged by Piedmont, and in March 1861 Victor Emmanuel II was proclaimed king of Italy. Three months later Cavour died. The new state was governed by the conservative constitution promulgated in 1848 by King Charles Albert. Italy gained the Veneto in 1866 as a result of the war between Austria and Prussia, and Rome in 1870 as a result of the Franco-Prussian War.

View the Image
Garibaldi Surrendering Power -
British Cartoon, 1860
at **myhistorylab.com**

German Unification

A united German nation was the single most important political development in Europe between 1848 and 1914. Germany was united by the conservative army and monarchy of Prussia and by Prussia's conservative prime minister, who sought to outflank the Prussian liberals.

William I (r. 1861–1888) regarded the Prussian army as his first concern. In 1860 his war minister and chief of staff proposed to enlarge the army and to increase the period of conscription from two to three years. The Prussian Parliament, created by the constitution of 1850, refused to approve the necessary taxes. A deadlock continued for two years between the monarch and the Parliament dominated by liberals.

Bismarck In September 1862 William I turned for help to the person who, more than any other single individual, shaped the next thirty years of European history: Otto von Bismarck (1815–1898). Bismarck came from Junker stock, and his outlook was deeply informed by the most traditional Prussian values, including admiration for the monarchy, the nobility, and the army. After being appointed prime minister and foreign minister in 1862, Bismarck immediately moved against the liberal Parliament. He contended that the Prussian constitution permitted the government to function on the basis of previously granted taxes. Therefore, taxes could be collected and spent, despite the parliamentary refusal to vote them. The army and most of the bureaucracy supported this interpretation of

the constitution. However, in 1863 new elections sustained the liberal majority in the Parliament. Bismarck had to find some way to attract popular support away from the liberals and toward the monarchy and the army. To that end, he set about uniting Germany through the conservative institutions of Prussia. The tactic amounted to diverting public attention from domestic matters to foreign affairs. It also meant that Prussia now assumed a position of leadership in the effort to unify Germany.

Bismarck pursued what was known as the *kleindeutsch*, or small German, solution to unification. Austria was to be excluded from German affairs when an opportunity presented itself. To achieve that end, Bismarck undertook two brief wars.

In 1864 he went to war with Denmark over the question of the duchies of Schleswig and Holstein, German-speaking areas that had long been administered by the Danish monarchy (see Map 23–5). The Austrians helped defeat Denmark and then with Prussia undertook the joint administration of the two duchies. Thereafter, Bismarck concluded various alliances with France and Italy to gain their support against Austria. War between Prussia and Austria broke out in the summer of 1866. This Seven Weeks' War led to the decisive defeat of Austria at Koniggratz. The Prussian victory and the consequent Treaty of Prague excluded the Habsburgs from German affairs. Prussia became the only major power among the German states.

Read the Document
A Letter from Bismarck (1866),
at **myhistorylab.com**

Creating Nations. The proclamation of the German Empire in the Hall of Mirrors at Versailles, January 18, 1871, after the defeat of France in the Franco-Prussian War. Kaiser Wilhelm I is standing at the top of the steps under the flags; Otto von Bismarck is in the center in a white uniform. The new nation possessed enormous economic resources and nationalistic ambitions.

Map 23–5. The Unification of Germany. Under Bismarck's leadership, and with the strong support of its royal house, Prussia used diplomatic and military means, on both the German and international stages, to forcibly unify the German states into a strong national entity.

In 1867 Hanover, Hesse, Nassau, and the city of Frankfurt, all of which had supported Austria during the war, were annexed by Prussia and their rulers deposed. Prussia and these newly incorporated territories, plus Schleswig and Holstein and the rest of the German states north of the Main River, constituted the North German Confederation. Prussia was its undisputed leader.

The Franco-Prussian War and the German Empire

Bismarck now awaited an opportunity to complete unification by bringing the states of southern Germany into the confederation. The occasion arose as a result of complex diplomacy surrounding the possibility of a cousin of William I of Prussia becoming king of Spain. France was, of course, opposed to the idea of a second state on its borders ruled by a Hohenzollern. Bismarck personally edited a press dispatch surrounding these negotiations to make it appear that William I had insulted the French ambassador, even though the king had not done so. Bismarck intended to goad France into war, and he succeeded. On July 19 France declared

war. Napoleon III hoped that victory would give his regime a new and stronger popular base. Once the war began, the states of southern Germany supported Prussia. On September 1, at Sedan, the Germans not only defeated the French army but also captured Napoleon III, who soon went into exile in England where he later died and is buried. By late September, Paris was besieged. It finally capitulated on January 28, 1871. Ten days earlier, in the Hall of Mirrors at the Palace of Versailles, the German Empire had been proclaimed. The rulers of the states of south Germany had requested William I to accept the imperial title. They, in turn, retained their thrones.

The unification of Germany established a strong, coherent state in the middle of Europe. It had been forged by the Prussian army and would be dominated by Prussian institutions. Its center of power rested on the monarchy and the military. It possessed enormous economic resources and nationalistic ambitions. For the next eighty years Europe would have to come to grips with this new political reality both on the Continent and abroad. The unification of Italy and Germany proved to many people that nationalistic goals could only be achieved by armed force. After its defeat at the hands

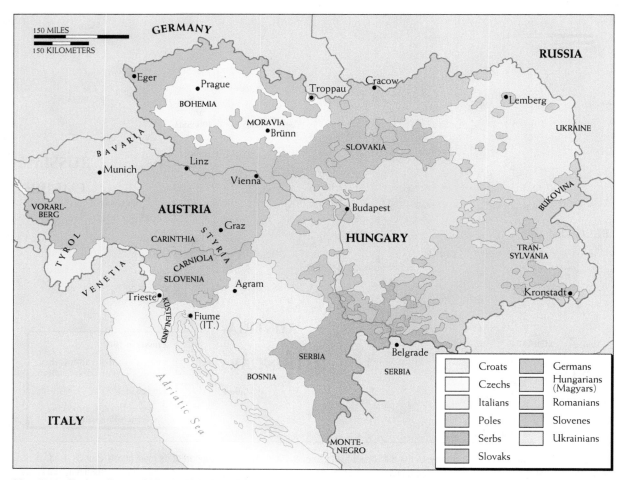

Map 23–6. Nationalities within the Habsburg Empire. The patchwork appearance reflects the unusual problem of the numerous ethnic groups that the Habsburgs could not, of course, meld into a modern national state. Only the Magyars were recognized in 1867, leaving nationalist Czechs, Slovaks, and the others chronically dissatisfied.

See the **Map**
The Unification of Germany, 1866–1871 at **myhistorylab.com**

of Prussia, France would within five years become a republic—the Third Republic—governed by a chamber of deputies, a senate, and a president.

Unrest of Nationalities in Eastern Europe

In the age of national states, liberal institutions, and industrialism, the Habsburg domains remained primarily dynastic, absolutist, and agrarian. Following the Revolutions of 1848 Emperor Francis Joseph (r. 1848–1916) and his ministers attempted to impose a centralized administration on the multinational empire. The system amounted to a military and bureaucratic government dominated by German-speaking Austrians. This situation was especially annoying to the Hungarians. The Austrian defeats in 1859 and 1866 and the consequent exclusion of Austria from Italy and from German affairs compelled Francis Joseph to come to terms with the Hungarian nobility. The subsequent **Ausgleich**, or

Compromise, of 1867 transformed the Habsburg Empire into a dual monarchy. Francis Joseph was crowned king of Hungary in Budapest. Except for the common monarch, foreign policy, and army, Austria and Hungary became almost separate states (see Map 23–6).

Many of the other national groups within the empire—including the Czechs, the Ruthenians, the Romanians, and the Serbo-Croatians—opposed the Compromise because it permitted the German-speaking Austrians and the Hungarian Magyars to dominate all other nationalities in their respective states. The Czechs of Bohemia were the most vocal group among the dissident nationalities. For over twenty years they were conciliated by generous Austrian patronage and posts in the bureaucracy. By the turn of the century, however, the Czechs had become more vocal. They and German-speaking groups in the Austrian Reichsrat, the Austrian Parliament, disrupted the proceedings of that body rather than permit a compromise on language issues. The emperor ruled thereafter by imperial decree with the support of the bureaucracy. Constitutionalism was dead in Austria. It flourished in Hungary only because the Magyars used it to dominate competing national groups.

Nationalist unrest within the Habsburg Empire not only caused internal political difficulties, but also constituted one of the major sources of political instability for all of central and eastern Europe. Virtually all the nationality problems had a foreign policy as well as a domestic political dimension. Both the Serbo-Croatians and the Poles believed they deserved a wholly independent state in union with their fellow nationals who lived outside the empire. Other national groups, such as Ukrainians, Romanians, and Bosnians, saw themselves as potentially linked to Russia, to Romania, to Serbia, or to a larger yet-to-be-established Slavic state. Many of these nationalities looked to Russia for protection. Out of these nationalistic tensions emerged much of the turmoil that would spark World War I. (See Document, "Lord Acton Condemns Nationalism" on page 726). The dominant German population of Austria proper was generally loyal to the emperor. However, a significant segment of the Austrian German population was strongly nationalistic and yearned to be part of the united German state being established by Bismarck. These nationalistic Germans in the Austrian Empire often hated the non-German national groups, particularly

⊙ See the Map
The Nationalities of Austria-Hungary, 1867 at **myhistorylab.com**

the Jews. Such attitudes would influence the youth and young adulthood of Adolf Hitler (1889–1945) and shape many of his political opinions.

Nationality problems touched each of the three great central and eastern European empires—the German, the Russian, and the Austrian. All had Polish populations. Each shared at least two other major national groups. Each nationality regarded its own aspirations and discontents as more important than the larger good or even survival of the empire they inhabited. The stirrings of nationalism affected the fate of all three empires from the 1860s through the outbreak of World War I. The government of each would be overturned during the war, and the Austrian Empire would disappear. These same unresolved problems of central and eastern European nationalism would then lead directly to World War II. During more recent years they have led to civil war in what was formerly Yugoslavia and to the breakup of what used to be called Czechoslovakia.

Racial Theory and Anti-Semitism

Articulated racial theory constituted a new component of late-century nationalistic unrest. Racial thinking, or **racism**, had long existed in Europe. Renaissance explorers had displayed considerable prejudice against nonwhites. Since at least the eighteenth century, biologists and anthropologists had classified human beings according to the color of their skin, their language, and their stage of civilization. Late eighteenth-century linguistic scholars had observed similarities between many of the European languages and Sanskrit. They then postulated the existence of an ancient race called the Aryans, who had spoken the original language from which the rest derived. During the Romantic period, writers had called the different cultures of Europe *races*. The debates over slavery in the European colonies and the United States had given further opportunity for the development of racial theory. However, in the late nineteenth century the concept of race emerged as a single dominant explanation of the history and the character of large groups of people.

Arthur de Gobineau (1816–1882), a reactionary French diplomat, enunciated the first important theory of race as the major determinant of human history. In his four-volume *Essay on the Inequality of the Human Races* (1853–1854), Gobineau portrayed the troubles of Western civilization as being the result of the long degeneration of the original white Aryan race. It had unwisely intermarried with the inferior yellow and black races, thus diluting the greatness and ability that originally existed in its blood. Gobineau saw no way to reverse this degeneration.

Gobineau's essay remained relatively obscure for years. Houston Stewart Chamberlain (1855–1927), an Englishman who settled in Germany, put racial theory on an alleged scientific basis in his widely read two-volume work entitled *Foundations of the Nineteenth Century* (1899). He championed the concept of biological determinism through race. Through the use of contemporary genetic theory, Chamberlain argued in opposition to Gobineau that the human race could be improved and even that a superior race could be developed. Chamberlain then added another element. He pointed to the Jews as the major enemy of European racial regeneration. Chamberlain's book and the lesser works on which it drew thus aided the spread of **anti-Semitism**. Other writings in Germany emphasized the supposed racial and cultural dangers posed by the Jews to traditional German national life.

During the late nineteenth century and the early twentieth, racial thinking became associated with the competitive ideas of Social Darwinism. Darwinian evolution (See Chapter 24) contended that species developed through a struggle for existence. Social thinkers transferred this concept of development through biological struggle to competition among nations, classes, and races. Consequently racial thinking embraced two interwoven images of biological determinism: race as a biological reality and competition as a reality of biological development. The result of this combination was a deadly vision of competition among races and nations for survival and domination. These ideas could and did support an image of Western superiority over non-Western peoples during the era of colonialism. Within Europe the same ideas could and did support policies of racial conflict and superiority that led to the Holocaust in the second quarter of the twentieth century.

Document   Lord Acton Condemns Nationalism

Lord Acton (1834–1902) was a major nineteenth-century English historian and commentator on contemporary religious and political events. In all his writings, he was deeply concerned with the character and preservation of liberty. His was one of the earliest voices to warn against the political dangers of nationalism.

■ *Why does Acton see the principle of nationality as dangerous to liberty? Why does he see nationalism as a threat to minority groups? Why does he see nationalism as a threat to democracy?*

The greatest adversary of the rights of nationality is the modern theory of nationality. By making the State and the nation commensurate with each other in theory, it reduces practically to a subject condition all other nationalities that may be within the boundary. It cannot admit them to an equality with the ruling nation which constitutes the State, because the State would then cease to be national, which would be a contradiction of the principle of its existence. According, therefore, to the degree of humanity and civilization in that dominant body which claims all the rights of the community, the inferior races are exterminated, or reduced to servitude, or outlawed, or put in a condition of dependence.

If we take the establishment of liberty for the realization of moral duties to be the end of civil society, we must conclude that those states are substantially the most perfect which, like the British and Austrian Empires, include various distinct nationalities without oppressing them. Those in which no mixture of races has occurred are imperfect; and those in which its effects have disappeared are decrepit. A State which is incompetent to satisfy different races condemns itself; a State which labors to neutralize, to absorb, or to expel them, destroys its own vitality; a State which does not include them is destitute of the chief basis of self-government. The theory of nationality, therefore, is a retrograde step in history. . . .

[N]ationality does not aim either at liberty or prosperity, both of which it sacrifices to the imperative necessity of making the nation the mold and measure of the State. Its course will be marked with material as well as moral ruin, in order that a new invention may prevail over the works of God and the interests of mankind. There is no principle of change, no phrase of political speculation conceivable, more comprehensive, more subversive, or more arbitrary than this. It is a confutation of democracy, because it sets limits to the exercise of the popular will, and substitutes for it a higher principle.

Source: From John Emerich Edward Dalbert-Acton, *First Baron Acton, Essays in the History of Liberty*, ed. by J. Rufus Fears (Indianapolis IN: Liberty Classics, 1985), pp. 431–433.

Anti-Semitism and the Birth of Zionism

Political and racial anti-Semitism, which cast such dark shadows across the twentieth century, emerged in part from this atmosphere of racial thought. Religious anti-Semitism dated from at least the Middle Ages. Since the French Revolution western European Jews had gradually gained entry into the civil life of Britain, France, Austria, and Germany (see Chapter 24). Popular anti-Semitism, which identified the Jewish community with money and banking interests, persisted. During the last third of the century, as finance capitalism changed the economic structure of Europe, people pressured by the changes became hostile toward the Jewish community. In Austria, Germany, and France various political leaders and parties used such anti-Semitism for their own considerable political advantage.

To this already ugly atmosphere, racial thought contributed the belief that no matter how much Jews assimilated themselves and their families into the culture and even the religion of their country, their Jewishness—and thus their alleged danger to the society—would remain. The problem of race was not in the character but in the blood of the Jew. An important Jewish response to this new, rabid outbreak of anti-Semitism was the launching in 1896 of the Zionist movement to found a separate Jewish state. Its founder was the Austro-Hungarian Theodor Herzl (1860–1904). The advance of political anti-Semitism, especially in Austria and France, as well as Herzl's personal experiences of discrimination, convinced him that liberal politics and the institutions of the liberal state could not protect the Jews in Europe or ensure that they would be treated justly. In 1896

Document | Herzl Calls for the Establishment of a Jewish State

In 1896 Theodor Herzl published his pamphlet *The Jewish State*. Herzl had become convinced that only the establishment of a separate state for Jews would halt the outbreaks of anti-Semitism that characterized late nineteenth-century European political and cultural life. Following the publication of this pamphlet, Herzl began to organize the Zionist movement among Jews in both eastern and western Europe.

■ *Why does Herzl define what he calls the Jewish Question as a national question? What objections does he anticipate to the founding of a Jewish state? Why does he believe that a Jewish state will prevent anti-Semitism?*

The idea which I develop in this pamphlet is an age-old one: the establishment of a Jewish State.

The world resounds with outcries against the Jews, and this is what awakens the dormant idea. . . .

I believe I understand anti-Semitism, a highly complex movement. I view it from the standpoint of a Jew, but without hatred or fear. I think I can discern in it the elements of vulgar sport, of common economic rivalry, of inherited prejudice, of religious intolerance—but also of a supposed need for self-defense. To my mind, the Jewish Question is neither a social nor a religious one, even though it may assume these and other guises. It is a national question, and to solve it we must first of all establish it as an international political problem which will have to be settled by the civilized nations of the world in council.

We are a people, one people.

Everywhere we have sincerely endeavored to merge with the national communities surrounding us and to preserve only the faith of our fathers. We are not permitted to do so. . . .

And will some people say that the venture is hopeless, because even if we obtain the land and the sovereignty only the poor people will go along? They are the very ones we need first! Only desperate men make good conquerors.

Will anybody say, Oh yes, if it were possible it would have been done by now?

It was not possible before. It is possible now. As recently as a hundred, even fifty years ago it would have been a dream. Today it is all real. The rich, who have an epicurean acquaintance with all technical advance, know very well what can be done with money. And this is how it will be: Precisely the poor and plain people, who have no idea of the power that man already exercises over the forces of Nature, will have the greatest faith in the new message. For they have never lost their hope of the Promised Land. . . .

Now, all this may seem to be a long-drawn-out affair. Even in the most favorable circumstances it might be many years before the founding of the State is under way. In the meantime, Jews will be ridiculed, offended, abused, whipped, plundered, and slain in a thousand different localities. But no; just as soon as we begin to implement the plan, anti-Semitism will immediately grind to a halt everywhere. . . .

Source: From Theodor Herzl, *The Jewish State*. © 1970 The Herzl Press, pp. 27, 33, 109, as quoted in William W. Hallo, David B. Ruderman, and Michael Stanislawski, eds., *Heritage: Civilization and the Jews Source Reader*. © 1984 Praeger, pp. 234–235.

Herzl published *The Jewish State*, in which he called for a separate state in which the Jews of the world might be assured of those rights and liberties that they should be enjoying in the liberal states of Europe. (See Document, "Herzl Calls for the Establishment of a Jewish State.") Furthermore, Herzl followed the tactics of late-century mass democratic politics by directing his appeal in particular to the economically poor Jews who lived in the ghettos of eastern Europe and the slums of western Europe. The original call to **Zionism** thus combined a rejection of the anti-Semitism of Europe with a desire to establish some of the ideals of both liberalism and socialism in a state outside Europe.

Racial thinking and revived anti-Semitism were part of a wider late-century aggressive nationalism. Previously, nationalism had been a literary and liberal movement. From the 1870s onward, however, nationalism became a movement with mass support, well-financed organizations, and political parties. Nationalists tended to redefine nationality in terms of race and blood. The new nationalism opposed the internationalism of both liberalism and socialism. The ideal of nationality was used to overcome the pluralism of class, religion, and geography. The nation and its duties replaced religion for many secularized people. It sometimes became a secular religion in the hands of state schoolteachers, who

DR. HERZL

Theodor Herzl. Herzl's visions of a Jewish state would eventually lead to the creation of Israel in 1948.

were replacing the clergy as the instructors of youth. This aggressive, racist nationalism would prove to be the most powerful ideology of the early twentieth century.

Summary

Nationalism. Nationalism is the modern concept that people who share the same customs, culture, language, and history should also share the same government. It became the most powerful European political ideology of the nineteenth and early twentieth centuries. Nationalists challenged both the domestic and the international order of the Vienna settlement in the decades after 1815.

Liberalism. Politically, nineteenth-century liberals sought to establish constitutional governments that recognized civil liberties and made the executive responsible to a legislature elected by men of wealth and property. Economically, liberals wanted a laissez-faire economy with minimal government involvement. People should be free to use their talents and property to enrich themselves without the state intervening to protect the working classes or the poor. Liberals often supported nationalists' efforts to create a single national state that could function as a more efficient economic

unit. Although efforts to liberalize tsarist Russia failed, liberalism largely triumphed in France after the Revolution of 1830 and in Britain after the passage of the Great Reform Bill. The British were, however, unable to resolve the problem of Irish nationalism in the nineteenth century.

Italian and German Unification. With French assistance, Piedmont and its premier Count Camillo Cavour managed to unite most of the Italian peninsula by 1860. The new Kingdom of Italy was formed from the northern Italian duchies, Austrian Lombardy, the Papal States, and the Kingdom of the Two Sicilies. Austrian Venetia was added in 1866, and Italy occupied Papal Rome in 1870.

Prussia achieved German unification under the leadership of Otto von Bismarck between 1864 and 1871. In three victorious wars against Denmark, Austria, and France, Bismarck forged the German states into a German Empire dominated by Prussia. Germany was henceforth the dominant power on the European continent.

North America. In the United States, westward expansion and war against Mexico brought vast new territories under the republic from the Mississippi River to the Pacific, but sectional conflict between North and South over economic issues and slavery led to the outbreak of the Civil War in 1861. Northern victory led to the abolition of slavery, the creation of a continentwide free labor market, and enormous economic development that would make the United States the world's leading industrial power in the twentieth century.

Canada in these years achieved self-government from Britain and created a united Canadian federation in 1867. However, Canada remained part of the British Empire and retained its connection with the British monarchy.

Eastern Europe. Nationalism created problems for the three eastern European empires—Germany, Russia, and Austria—but Habsburg Austria faced the greatest challenge from nationalism because it was a dynastic, not a national, state. Eleven different nationalities made up the Habsburg monarchy, each with its own national aspirations. In 1867 the Habsburgs worked out the *Ausgleich*, or Compromise, with the Magyars, by which Hungary became an autonomous kingdom under the Habsburg emperor. Thereafter the Habsburg monarchy became known as Austria-Hungary. However, Czechs, Croats, and other Slavs in the monarchy became increasingly dissatisfied.

Racism and Anti-Semitism. In the late nineteenth century, biological determinism, the concept that some peoples or races were inherently superior to others, took root in Western thought. In Germany, Austria, and France, some nationalists used the concept of race to blame the Jews for their countries' economic and political problems. Part of the Jewish response was the launching of the Zionist movement to found a separate Jewish state.

Key Terms

anti-Semitism (p. 725)

Ausgleich (p. 723)

Catholic emancipation (p. 708)

Chartism (p. 708)

Great Reform Bill (p. 708)

home rule (p. 709)

July Monarchy (p. 707)

kleindeutsch (p. 722)

liberalism (p. 704)

nationalism (p. 700)

racism (p. 725)

Zionism (p. 727)

Review Questions

1. Define nationalism. What were the goals of nationalists? What were the difficulties they confronted in realizing those goals? Why was nationalism a special threat to the Austrian Empire? What areas saw significant nationalist movements between 1815 and 1830? Which were successful and which unsuccessful?

2. What were the tenets of liberalism? Who were the liberals, and how did liberalism affect the political developments of the early nineteenth century? What relationship does liberalism have to nationalism?

3. Compare and contrast the movement toward political liberalism between 1815 and 1830 in Russia, France, and Great Britain.

4. What economic differences between the American North and South gave rise to sectional conflict? Why was slavery the core issue in that conflict? How did the westward movement contribute to making slavery so important an issue?

5. Why was it so difficult to unify Italy? What were the contributions of Mazzini, Cavour, and Garibaldi to Italian unification?

6. Who was Otto von Bismarck, and why did he try to unify Germany? What was Bismarck's method of unification, and why did he succeed? What effect did the unification of Germany have on the rest of Europe?

7. How did British politicians handle the Irish Question? What were the parallels between England's relationship with Ireland and the nationality problem of the Austrian Empire?

8. What were the origins of the modern idea of racial theory? Who were its major proponents? How did the rise of such a theory change European anti-Semitism?

Note: *To learn more about the topics in this chapter, please turn to the Suggested Readings at the end of the book. For additional sources related to this chapter please see MyHistoryLab.com.*

Reinforce what you learned in this chapter by studying the many documents, images, maps, review tools, and videos available at **www.myhistorylab.com**.

Read and Review

✓•⌐Study and Review **Chapter 23**

•⌐Read the Document *The Seneca Falls Convention (1848), p. 704*
Metternich on the Revolutions of 1848, p. 711
"A Defense of the Slave Trade," July 1740, p. 712
The History of Mary Prince (1830s), p. 714
A Letter from Bismarck (1866), p. 722

👁•⌐See the Map *The Americas, 1800–1836, p. 715*
The Nationalities of Austria-Hungary, 1867, p. 725

•⌐View the Image *Reform Bill of 1832–Cartoon, p. 707*
Gladstone and Disraeli–Punch Cartoon, p. 710
Garibaldi Surrendering Power - British Cartoon, 1860, p. 722

((•⌐Hear the Audio *Slavery, p. 712*

Research and Explore

👁•⌐See the Map *European Centers of Rebellion and Revolution, 1820–1848, p. 711*

👁•⌐See the Map *The Unification of Italy, 1859–1870, p. 722*

((•⌐Hear the Audio

Hear the audio file for Chapter 23 at
www.myhistorylab.com.

24 | Northern Transatlantic Economy and Society, 1815–1914

- European Factory Workers and Urban Artisans
- Nineteenth-Century European Women
- Jewish Emancipation
- European Labor, Socialism, and Politics to World War I
- North America and the New Industrial Economy
- The Emergence of Modern European Thought
- Islam and Late Nineteenth-Century European Thought

Russian society. A detail from the "Parade on Tsarina's Meadow" by G. G. Chernetson, 1831. Tsarina's Meadow was a vast space outside Saint Petersburg that often held military parades and reviews in nineteenth-century Russia. The different classes and ethnic groups of the Russian Empire can be seen mingling about.

DURING THE NINETEENTH CENTURY NORTHWESTERN Europe and the United States developed major industrial economies. These economies produced more goods and services than ever before in world history. This economic achievement undergirded the enormous international political power exerted by the industrial nations of the West from that time to the present.

The first half of the nineteenth century witnessed in Europe and to a lesser extent in the United States the emergence of a new kind of industrial labor force. These laborers worked in factories rather than in their homes or in small artisan workshops. More often than not the new industrial working class dwelled in cities. The presence and growth of this new labor force were the most important social developments of the century and

The Building of Northern Transatlantic Supremacy

North Atlantic

Between 1850 and 1914 Europe had more influence throughout the world than it had before or has had since. Although Europe and North America together were the most industrially advanced regions of the world, the preponderance of economic power lay with Europe. Its industrial base was more advanced than that of any other region, including the still-developing United States. European banks exercised vast influence across the globe. Europeans financed the building of railways in Africa, Asia, and the Americas. Financial power brought political influence. The armaments industry gave European armies and navies predominant power over the peoples of Africa and Asia, whereas the United States

began to exercise such power only as a result of the Spanish-American War. These economic developments established a pattern that still persists. First European, and later American, banks, companies, and corporations penetrated the economies and societies of Asia, Africa, and Latin America. These nonpolitical groups often expected their own governments to protect their interests. Thus, what started as commercial contact often evolved into the exercise of direct political influence even over nations that had never been European colonies.

During these years European culture was probably also enjoying its greatest influence. Capital cities in Latin America, especially Buenos Aires and Montevideo, adopted European-style architecture. Paris became synonymous with high fashion. Paris, London, and Vienna were world

would produce a vast influence on European and American political life. It was out of the social and political experience of this workforce that the political movement known as socialism arose.

In the second half of the nineteenth century European and American political, economic, and social life assumed many characteristics of our present-day world. In Europe nation-states with large electorates, political parties, centralized bureaucracies, and universal military service emerged. In the United States the politics associated with the Progressive movement brought the presidency to the center of American political life. On both sides of the North Atlantic, business adopted large-scale corporate structures, and the labor force organized itself into trade unions. The number of white-collar laborers grew as urban life became predominant throughout western Europe. But even as new vast cities arose in the United States, farming continued to spread across the central Midwest and upper Southwest. During this period, too, women began to assert new political awareness and to become politically active in both Europe and America.

During these same years Europe quietly became dependent on the resources and markets of the rest of the world. Farms in the United States, Canada, Latin America, Australia, and New Zealand supplied food to much of the world. Consequently climate changes in Kansas, Argentina, or New Zealand might now affect the European economy. However, before World War I Europe's industrial, military, and financial supremacy concealed this dependence. At the time Europeans assumed their supremacy to be natural, but the twentieth century would reveal it to have been temporary. Nevertheless, while it prevailed, Europeans dominated most of the other peoples of the earth and displayed extreme self-confidence. Toward the close of the nineteenth century the United States, having achieved the status of a major industrial power as well as an agricultural supplier, now entered the world stage as a military power, defeating Spain in the Spanish-American War in 1898. With that victory, the United States also acquired its first colonial territories.

During these same decades a number of major new sets of ideas arose. Theories of evolution in intellectual centers. The rest of the world regarded the advanced industrial and urban civilization of Europe as a model, in part because more non-Europeans were visiting and studying in Europe than ever before. During this period many American artists and writers flocked to Europe to absorb its culture. Another cultural feature of western Europe and the United States that affected the rest of the world during the era was the emerging role of women. In particular, the demand for the entrance of women into the political process and the professions became a hallmark of the twentieth century. On both sides of the Atlantic, women assumed leadership roles in social reform movements.

The nation that most clearly understood the nature of European power and sought to imitate it was Japan. After the Meiji restoration (1868), Japanese administrators came to Europe to study the new technology, political structures, and military organizations. The Japanese political and military reorganization that resulted proved sufficiently successful to allow them to defeat Russia in 1905, providing the first example of a non-European nation using Western weapons, organizations, and economic power to defeat a European nation. In the twentieth century other non-European nations found ways to import or manufacture technology that permitted them to challenge European and later American hegemony. Indeed, today the proliferation of weaponry usually developed in the United States or Europe has allowed regional powers to challenge Western dominance. This destabilizing arms trade began in the second half of the nineteenth century.

In contrast to Japan, China, India, the countries of the Middle East, and Africa were overwhelmed by Europe's economic and military power. In time, however, the peoples of those lands under European domination embraced the ideologies of revolutionary protest, most particularly those of nationalism and socialism. As people from the colonial world came to work or study in Europe, they encountered ideas and criticisms that were most effective against European and Western culture. They adapted those ideas to their own cultural contexts and then turned them against their colonial governors.

Focus Questions

- What was the relationship between nineteenth-century Europes economic power and its political hegemony around the globe?
- How did European colonies use ideologies fostered in Europe against their colonial rulers?

biology, relativity in physics, the irrational philosophy, and psychoanalysis in psychology came to the fore, shaping much of the intellectual outlook for the next century. ■

European Factory Workers and Urban Artisans

Although the seeds of industrial production had been sown in the eighteenth century, it was only in the nineteenth century that much of Europe headed toward a more fully industrial society. By 1830 only Great Britain had already attained that status, but new factories and railways were beginning to be constructed elsewhere in Europe. However, what characterized the second quarter of the century was less the triumph of industrialism than the final gasps of those economic groups that opposed it and were displaced by it. Intellectually, the period saw the formulation of the major creeds supporting and criticizing the new society.

((•●—[Hear the Audio
Industrial Revolution
at MyHistoryLab.com

The specter of poor harvests still haunted Europe. The worst such experience of the century was the Irish famine of 1845 to 1847. Perhaps as many as half a million Irish peasants, with no land or small simply starved when disease blighted the potato crop. Hundreds of thousands emigrated. By mid-century, the revolution in landholding had led to greater agricultural production. It also resulted in a vast uprooting of people from the countryside into cities and from Europe into the rest of the world. The countryside thus provided many of the workers for the new factories, as well as people with few economic skills who slowly immigrated to cities in hope of finding work.

In much of northern Europe both artisans and factory workers underwent a process of **proletarianization**. This term indicates the entry of workers into a wage economy and their gradual loss of significant ownership of the means of production, such as tools and equipment, and control over the conduct of their own trades. The process occurred rapidly wherever the factory system arose. The factory owner provided the financial capital to construct the factory, purchase the machinery, and secure the raw materials. The factory workers contributed their labor for a wage. Those workers also submitted to factory discipline, which meant that work conditions became largely determined by the demands for smooth operation of the machines. Closing of factory gates to late workers, fines for lateness, dismissal for drunkenness, and public scolding of faulty laborers constituted attempts to enforce regularity on humans that would match the regularity of cables, wheels,

Il Quarto Stato (The Fourth Estate), 1901. Giuseppe Pellizza da Volpedo (1868–1907) was a powerfully committed Italian socialist artist. The title of his painting is taken from the French socialist Jean Jaurès, who believed that workers would soon displace the traditional three estates of the clergy, aristocracy, and commoners. Pellizza and other artists embracing social realism moved painting away from nostalgic, sentimental depictions of peasants to images of industrial or farm laborers experiencing hunger, poverty, and awakening political consciousness. *Oil on canvas, 283 cm × 550 cm. Civica Galleria d'Arte Moderna-Milano. Photo by Marcello Saporetti.*

In the eighteenth century a European town or city workplace had usually consisted of a few artisans laboring for a master, first as apprentices and then as journeymen, according to established guild regulations and practices. The master owned the workshop and the larger equipment, and the apprentices and journeymen owned their tools. The journeyman could expect to become a master. This guild system had allowed considerable worker control over labor recruitment and training, production pace, product quality, and price.

In the nineteenth century the situation of the urban artisan changed. It became increasingly difficult for artisans to continue to exercise corporate or guild direction and control over their trades. The French Revolution had outlawed such organizations in France. Across Europe, political and economic liberals disapproved of labor and guild organizations and attempted to make them illegal.

Other destructive forces were also at work. The masters often found themselves under increased competitive pressure from larger, more heavily capitalized establishments or from the possibility of the introduction of machine production into a previously craft-dominated industry. In many workshops masters began to follow a practice, known in France as *confection*, whereby goods such as shoes, clothing, and furniture were produced in standard sizes and styles rather than by special orders for individual customers. This

and pistons. The factory workers had no direct say over the quality of the product or its price. It should be noted that for all their difficulties, factory conditions were often better than those of textile workers who resisted the factory mode of production. In particular, English hand-loom weavers, who continued to work in their homes, experienced decades of declining trade and growing poverty in their unsuccessful competition with power looms.

Urban artisans in the nineteenth century experienced proletarianization more slowly than factory workers, and machinery had little to do with the process. The emergence of factories in itself did not harm urban artisans. Many even prospered from the development. For example, the actual erection of factories and the expansion of cities benefited all craftsmen in the building trades, such as carpenters, roofers, joiners, and masons. The lower prices for machine-made textiles aided artisans involved in the making of clothing, such as tailors and hatters, by reducing the costs of their raw materials. Where the urban artisans encountered difficulty, and found their skills and livelihood threatened, was in the organization of production.

Overview

Major European Cities, 1850–1914

	1850	1880	1914
Berlin	419,000	1,122,000	2,071,000
Birmingham	233,000	437,000	840,000
Frankfurt	65,000	137,000	415,000
London	2,685,000	4,470,000	7,256,000
Madrid	281,000	398,000	600,000
Paris	1,053,000	2,269,000	2,888,000
Vienna	444,000	1,104,000	2,031,000

practice increased the division of labor in the workshop. Each artisan produced a smaller part of the uniform final product. Consequently, less skill was required of each artisan, and the particular skills possessed by a worker became less valuable. Masters also attempted to increase production and reduce their costs for piecework. Those attempts often led to work stoppages or strikes. Migrants from the countryside or small towns created, in some cases, a surplus of relatively unskilled workers who were willing to work for lower wages or under less favorable and protected conditions than traditional artisans. The dilution of skills and lower wages, caused not by machinery but by changes in the organization of artisan production, made it much more difficult for urban journeymen ever to hope to become masters with their own workshops where they would be in charge. Increasingly, these artisans became lifetime wage laborers whose skills were simply bought and sold in the marketplace.

✓ **Study** and **Review**
Industrial Side Effects
at **MyHistoryLab.com**

Nineteenth-Century European Women

Women in the Early Industrial Revolution

The industrial economy ultimately produced an immense impact on the home and the family life of women. First, it took virtually all productive work out of the home and allowed many families to live on the wages of the male spouse alone. That transformation prepared the way for a new concept of gender-determined roles in the home and in general domestic life. Women came to be associated with domestic duties such as housekeeping, food preparation, child rearing and nurturing, and household management. The man came to be associated almost exclusively with breadwinning. Children were reared to match these gender patterns. Previously, this domestic division of labor had prevailed only among the relatively small middle and gentry class. During the nineteenth century it came to characterize the working class as well. Second, industrialization created new modes of employment that allowed many young women to earn enough money to marry or, if necessary, to support themselves independently. Third, industrialism, though fostering more employment for women, lowered the skills required of them.

Because the early industrial revolution had begun in textile production, women and their labor were deeply involved from the start. While both spinning and weaving were still domestic industries, women usually worked in all stages of production. Hand spinning was virtually always a woman's task. When spinning was moved into factories and involved large machines, however, men displaced women. The higher wages commanded by male cotton-factory workers allowed many women to stop working or to work only to supplement their husbands'

wages. With the next generation of machines in the 1820s, unmarried women rapidly became employed in the factories. However, their jobs tended to require less skill than most work done by men and than women had previously exercised in the home production of textiles. There was thus a certain paradox in the impact of the factory on women. Many new jobs opened to them, but those jobs were less skilled than those that had been available to them before. Moreover, the women in the factories were almost always young and single or widows. At marriage or perhaps at the birth of the first child, a woman usually found that her husband earned enough money for her to leave the factory. Factory owners also disliked employing married women because of the likelihood of pregnancy, the influence of husbands, and the duties of child rearing.

◀▶ Read the Document
Industrial Society and Factory
Conditions (early 1800s)
at **MyHistoryLab.com**

In Britain and elsewhere by midcentury, industrial factory work accounted for less than half of all employment for women. The largest group of employed women in France

Women in Textile Factories. As textile production became increasingly automated in the nineteenth century, textile factories required fewer skilled workers and more unskilled attendants. To fill these unskilled positions, factory owners turned increasingly to unmarried women and widows, who worked for lower wages than men and were less likely to form labor organizations. The two women shown here, holding "shuttles" used in textile factories, worked in the Lowell Mills, in Massachusetts, around 1860.

continued to work on the land. In England they were do-mestic servants. Domestic industries, such as lace glove and garment making and other kinds of needlework, employed many women. Their conditions of labor were almost always harsh, whether they worked in their homes or sweated in workshops. Generally all work done by women commanded low wages and involved low skills. They had virtually no way to protect themselves from exploitation. The charwoman was a common sight across the Continent and symbolized the plight of working women.

Social Disabilities Confronted by All Women

During the early nineteenth century virtually all European women faced social and legal disabilities in property rights, family law, and education. By the close of the century each area had shown improvement. In this period European women, like European men, led lives that reflected their social rank. Yet within each rank, the experience of women was distinct from that of men. Women remained, generally speaking, economi-cally dependent and legally inferior, whatever their social class. Their position thus resembled that of women around the world: All women found their lives circumscribed by traditional social customs and expectations. (See Document, "English Women Industrial Workers Explain Their Economic Situation.")

Middle-Class Family. Family was central to the middle-class conception of a stable and respectable social life. This portrait of the Bellelli family is by Edgar Degas. Notice that the husband and father sits at his desk, suggesting his association with business and the world outside the home, whereas the wife and mother stands with their children, suggesting her domestic role.
Edgar Degas (1834–1917), The Bellelli Family, c. 1858–60. Musée d'Orsay, Paris, France. Photograph Copyright Bridgeman-Giraudon/Art Resource, New York.

Women and Property Until the last quarter of the nine-teenth century in most European countries no married women, whatever their social class, could own property in their own names. In effect, upon marriage women lost to their husbands' control any property they owned or that they might inherit or earn by their own labor. Their legal identities were subsumed into their husbands', and they had no independent standing before the law. The courts saw the theft of a woman's purse as a theft of her husband's property. Because European society was based on private property and wage earning, these disabilities put married women at a great dis-advantage, limiting their freedom to work, save, and relocate.

Reform of women's property rights came slowly. By 1882 Great Britain allowed married women to own property in their own right. In France, however, a married woman could not even open a savings account in her own name until 1895, and not until 1907 were married women granted possession of their own wages. In 1900 Germany allowed women to take jobs without their husbands' permission, but a German husband retained control of most of his wife's property except for her wages. Similar laws prevailed else-where in Europe.

Family Law European family law also worked to the dis-advantage of women. Legal codes required wives to obey their husbands. The Napoleonic Code and the remnants of Roman law made women legal mi-nors throughout Europe. Divorce was difficult for most of the century. In England until 1857 divorce required an act of Parliament. Most na-tions did not permit divorce by mutual consent. French law forbade divorce between 1816 and 1884. Thereafter the chief recognized legal cause for divorce was cruelty and injury, which had to be proven in court. In Great Britain adul-tery was the usual cause for divorce, but a woman had to prove her husband's adultery plus other offenses, whereas a man only had to prove his wife's adultery. In Germany only adultery or serious maltreatment was recognized as grounds for divorce. Across Europe extramarital sexual relations of husbands were more tolerated than those of wives. Everywhere, divorce required legal hearings and proof, making the process ex-pensive and all the more difficult for women who did not control their own property.

The authority of husbands also extended to children. A husband could take children away from their mother and give them to someone else to rear. Only the husband, in most countries, could permit his daughter to marry. In some countries he could virtually force his daughter to marry the man of his choice. In cases of divorce and separation, the

Document

English Women Industrial Workers Explain Their Economic Situation

In 1832, there was much discussion in the British press about factory legislation. Most of that discussion was concerned with the employment of children, but the *Examiner* newspaper made the suggestion that any factory laws should not only address the problem of child labor, but also, in time, eliminate women from employment in factories. That article provoked the following letter to the editor, composed by or on behalf of women factory workers, which stated the necessity of such employment for women and the unattractive alternatives.

■ *What reasons do these women give to prove the necessity of their holding manufacturing jobs? What changes in production methods have led women from the home to the factory? How does the situation of these women relate to the possibility of their marrying?*

Sir, Living as we do, in the densely populated manufacturing districts of Lancashire, and most of us belonging to that class of females who earn their bread either directly or indirectly by manufactories, we have looked with no little anxiety for your opinion on the Factory Bill. . . . You are for doing away with our services in manufactories altogether. So much the better, if you had pointed out any other more eligible and practical employment for the surplus female labour, that will want other channels for a subsistence. If our competition were withdrawn, and short hours substituted, we have no doubt but the effects would be as you have stated, "not to lower wages, as the male branch of the family would be enabled to earn as much as the whole had done," but for the thousands of females who are employed in manufactories, who have no legitimate claim on any male relative for employment or support, and who have, through a variety of circumstance, been early thrown on their own resources for a livelihood, what is to become of them?

In this neighbourhood, hand-loom has been almost totally superseded by power-loom weaving, and no inconsiderable number of females, who must depend on their own exertions, or their parishes for support, have been forced, of necessity into the manufactories, from their total inability to earn a livelihood at home.

It is a lamentable fact, that, in these parts of the country, there is scarcely any other mode of employment for female industry, if we except servitude and dressmaking. Of the former of these, there is no chance of employment for one-twentieth of the candidates that would rush into the field, to say nothing of lowering the wages of our sisters of the same craft; and of the latter, galling as some of the hardships of manufactories are (of which the indelicacy of mixing with the men is not the least), yet there are few women who have been so employed, that would change conditions with the ill-used genteel little slaves, who have to lose sleep and health, in catering to the whims and frivolities of the butter-flies of fashion.

We see no way of escape from starvation, but to accept the very tempting offers of the newspapers, held out as baits to us, fairly to ship ourselves off to Van Dieman's Land [Tasmania] on the very delicate errand of husband hunting, and having safely arrived at the "Land of Goshen," jump ashore, with a "Who wants me?" . . .

—*The Female Operatives of Todmorden*

Source: From *The Examiner*, February 26, 1832, as quoted in Ivy Pinchbeck, *Women Workers and the Industrial Revolution, 1750–1850* (New York: Augustus M. Kelley, 1969), pp. 199–200.

husband normally assumed authority over children no matter how he had treated them previously.

The sexual and reproductive rights of women, which have been so widely debated recently, could hardly be discussed in the nineteenth century. Both contraception and abortion were illegal. The law on rape normally worked against women. Wherever they turned—whether to physicians or lawyers—women confronted an official or legal world populated and controlled by men.

Educational Barriers Throughout the nineteenth century women had less access to education than men, and what was available to them was inferior. Not surprisingly, the percentage of illiterate women exceeded that of men. Most women were educated only enough for the domestic careers they were expected to follow.

University and professional education remained reserved for men until at least the third quarter of the century. The University of Zurich opened its doors to women in the

1860s. The University of London admitted women for degrees in 1878. Women were not awarded degrees at Oxford until 1920 or at Cambridge until 1921. They could not attend Sorbonne lectures until 1880. Just before the turn of the century universities and medical schools in the Austrian Empire allowed women to matriculate, but Prussian universities did not until after 1900. Russian women did not attend universities before 1914, but other institutions that awarded degrees were open to them. Italian universities were more open to both women students and women instructors than similar institutions elsewhere in Europe.

The absence of a system of private or public secondary education for women prevented most of them from gaining the qualifications they needed to enter a university whether or not the university prohibited them. Considerable evidence suggests that educated, professional men feared the competition of women. Women who attended universities and medical schools were sometimes labeled political radicals.

Chronology

Major Dates in Late Nineteenth-Century and Early Twentieth-Century European Women's History

1857	Revised English divorce law
1865	University of Zurich admits women for degrees
1869	John Stuart Mill's *The Subjection of Women*
1878	University of London admits women as candidates for degrees
1882	English Married Woman's Property Act
1894	Union of German Women's Organizations founded
1901	National Council of French Women founded
1903	British Women's Social and Political Union founded
1907	Norway permits women to vote on national issues
1910	British suffragettes adopt radical tactics
1918	Vote extended to some British women
1918	Weimar constitution allows German women to vote
1920–1921	Oxford and Cambridge Universities award degrees to women
1922	French Senate defeats bill extending vote to women
1928	Britain extends vote to women on same basis as men

By 1900 men in the educated elites also feared the challenge educated women posed to traditional gender roles in the home and workplace. Restricting their access to secondary and university education helped bar women from social and economic advancement. Women would benefit only marginally from the expansion of professional employment that occurred during the late nineteenth and early twentieth centuries. Although a few women did enter the professions, especially medicine, most nations prevented women from becoming lawyers until after World War I.

Schoolteaching at the elementary level, which was seen as a female job because of its association with the nurturing of children, became a professional haven for women. Trained at institutions that were equivalent to normal schools, women schoolteachers were regarded as educated, but not as university educated. Secondary education remained largely the province of men.

Read the Document
Ellen Key, from The Century of the Child at **MyHistoryLab.com**

The few women who pioneered in the professions and on government commissions and school boards or who dispersed birth control information faced grave social obstacles, personal humiliation, and often outright bigotry. These women and their male supporters were challenging that clear separation of life into male and female spheres that had emerged in middle-class European society during the nineteenth century. Women themselves often hesitated to support feminist causes or expanded opportunities for themselves because they had been so thoroughly acculturated into the recently stereotyped roles. Many women saw a real conflict between family responsibilities and feminism.

New Employment Patterns for Women

During the late nineteenth century two major developments affected the economic lives of women. The first was an expansion in the variety of jobs available outside the better paying learned professions. The second was a withdrawal of married women from the workforce. These two seemingly contradictory developments require explanation.

Availability of New Jobs The expansion of governmental bureaucracies, the emergence of corporations and other large-scale businesses, and the expansion of retail stores opened many new employment opportunities for women. The need for elementary schoolteachers, usually women, grew with compulsory education laws. Technological inventions and innovations, such as the typewriter and eventually the telephone exchange, also fostered female employment. Women by the thousands became secretaries and clerks for governments and private businesses. More thousands became shop assistants.

Although these jobs did open new and often better employment opportunities for women, they nonetheless required low-level skills and involved minimal training. They

Women Working at a Telephone Exchange. The invention of the telephone opened new employment opportunities for women.

were occupied primarily by unmarried women or widows. Few women had prominent positions.

Employers continued to pay women low wages because they assumed, often knowing better, that a woman did not need to support herself independently but could expect additional financial support from her father or husband. Consequently, a woman who did need to support herself independently could rarely find a job paying an adequate income or a position that paid as well as one held by a man who was supporting himself independently.

Withdrawal from the Labor Force Most of the women filling these new service positions were young and unmarried. After marriage, or certainly after the birth of her first child, a woman normally withdrew from the labor force. She either did not work or she worked at home. This pattern was not new, but it had become more common by the end of the nineteenth century. The industrial occupations that women had filled in the mid-nineteenth century, especially textile and garment making, were shrinking. Those industries thus offered fewer jobs for either married or unmarried women. Employers in offices and retail stores preferred young, unmarried women whose family responsibilities would not interfere with their work. The decline in the number of births also meant that fewer married women were needed to look after other women's children.

The real wages paid to male workers increased during this period, thus reducing families' need for a second income. Also, thanks to improving health conditions, men lived longer than

before, and so wives were less likely to be thrust into the workforce by an emergency. Smaller families also reduced the need for supplementary wages. Working children stayed at home longer and continued to contribute to the family's wage pool.

Finally, the cultural dominance of the middle class, with its generally idle wives, established a pattern of social expectations. The more prosperous a working-class family became, the less involved in employment its women were supposed to be. Indeed, the less income-producing work a wife did, the more prosperous and stable the family was considered.

Yet behind these generalities stands the enormous variety of social and economic experience late nineteenth-century women actually encountered. As might be expected, social class largely determined these individual experiences.

Late Nineteenth-Century Working-Class Women

Although less dominant than earlier in the century, the textile industry and garment making continued to employ many women. The German clothing-making trades illustrate the kind of vulnerable economic situation that women could encounter as a result of their limited skills and the organization of the trade. The manufacture of mass-made clothes in Germany was designed to require minimal capital investment by manufacturers and to protect them from significant risk. A major manufacturer would arrange to produce clothing through a putting-out system. He would purchase the material

Women Laundry Workers. Although new opportunities opened to them in the late nineteenth century, many working-class women, like these women ironing in a laundry, remained in traditional occupations. As the wine bottle suggests, alcoholism was a problem for women as well as men engaged in tedious work. The painting is by Edgar Degas (1834–1917). *Réunion des Musées Nationaux/Art Resource, New York.*

and then put it out for tailoring. The clothing was made not in a factory but usually in independently owned, small sweatshops or by workers in their homes.

In Berlin in 1896 there were more than 80,000 garment workers, mostly women. When business was good, employment for these women was high. If business became poor, however, less and less work was put out, idling many of them. In effect, the workers who actually sewed the clothing carried much of the risk of the enterprise. Some women did work in factories, but they too were subject to layoffs. Furthermore, women in the clothing trade were nearly always in positions less skilled than those of the male tailors or the male middlemen who owned the workshops.

The expectation of separate social and economic spheres for men and women and the definition of women's chief work as pertaining to the home contributed mightily to the exploitation of women workers outside the home. Because their wages were regarded merely as supplementing those of their husbands, they became particularly vulnerable to the economic exploitation that characterized the German putting-out system for clothing production. Women were nearly always treated as casual workers in Europe.

The Rise of Political Feminism

As can be seen from the previous discussion, liberal society and its values neither automatically nor inevitably improved the lot of women. In particular, it did not give them the vote or access to political activity. Male liberals feared that granting the vote to women would benefit political conservatives, because women were thought to be unduly controlled by the clergy. Consequently, anticlerical liberals often had difficulty working with feminists.

Obstacles to Achieving Equality Women were also often reluctant to support feminist causes. Political issues relating to gender were only one of several priorities for many women. Some were sensitive to their class and economic interests. Others subordinated feminist political issues to national unity and nationalistic patriotism. Still others would not support particular feminist organizations because of differences over tactics. The various social and tactical differences among women often led to sharp divisions within the feminists' own ranks. Except in England, it was often difficult for working-class and middle-class women to cooperate. Roman Catholic feminists were uncomfortable with radical secularist feminists.

Although liberal society and law presented women with many obstacles, they also provided feminists with many of their intellectual and political tools. As early as 1792 in Britain, Mary Wollstonecraft (1759–1797), in *The Vindication of the Rights of Women*, had applied the revolutionary doctrines of the rights of man to the predicament of the members of her own sex (see Chapter 21). John Stuart Mill (1806–1873), with his wife Harriet Taylor (1804–1858), had applied the logic of liberal freedom to the position of women in *The Subjection of Women* (1869). The arguments for utility and efficiency so dear to middle-class liberals could be used to expose the human and social waste implicit in the inferior role assigned to women.

Furthermore, the socialist criticism of capitalist society often, though by no means always, included a harsh indictment of the social and economic position to which women had been relegated. The earliest statements of feminism arose from critics of the existing order and were often associated with people who had unorthodox opinions about sexuality, family life, and property. This hardened resistance to the feminist message, especially on the Continent.

These difficulties prevented Continental feminists from raising the kind of massive public support or mounting the large demonstrations that feminists in Great Britain and the United States could. Everywhere in Europe, however, including Britain, the feminist cause was badly divided over both goals and tactics.

Votes for Women in Britain Europe's most advanced women's movement was in Great Britain. There Millicent Fawcett (1847–1929) led the moderate National Union of Women's Suffrage Societies. She believed Parliament would grant women the vote only when convinced that women would be respectable and responsible in their political activity. In 1908 this organization could rally almost half a million women in London. Fawcett was the wife of a former Liberal Party cabinet minister and economist. Her tactics were those of English liberals.

Emmeline Pankhurst (1858–1928) led a different and much more radical branch of British feminists. Pankhurst's husband had been active in both labor and Irish nationalist politics. Irish nationalists had developed numerous disruptive political tactics. Early labor politicians had also sometimes had confrontations with police over the right to hold meetings. In 1903 Pankhurst and her daughters founded the Women's Social and Political Union. For several years they and their followers, known derisively as **suffragettes**, lobbied publicly and privately for women's suffrage. By 1910, having failed to move the government, they turned to the violent tactics of arson, window breaking, and sabotage of postal boxes. They marched en masse on Parliament. The Liberal government of Herbert Asquith (1852–1928), prime minister from 1908 to 1916, imprisoned many of the demonstrators and force-fed those who went on hunger strikes in jail. The government refused to extend the franchise. Only in 1918, and then as a result of their contribution to the war effort, did some British women receive the vote.

Read the Document

John Stuart Mill on Enfranchisement of Women (1869) at **MyHistoryLab.com**

Political Feminism on the Continent The contrast of France and Germany shows how advanced the British women's movement was. In France, when Hubertine Auclert (1848–1914) began campaigning for the vote in the 1880s, she stood virtually alone. During the 1890s several women's organizations emerged. In 1901 the National Council of French Women (CNFF) was organized among upper-middle-class women, but it did not support the vote for women for several years. French Roman Catholic feminists, such as Marie Mauguet (1844–1928), supported the franchise. Almost all French feminists, however, rejected violence: They were also never able to organize mass rallies. The leaders of French feminism believed that the vote could be achieved through careful legalism. In 1919 the French Chamber of Deputies granted the vote to women, but in 1922 the French Senate defeated the bill. French women did not receive the right to vote until 1944 at the end of World War II.

In Germany feminist awareness and action were even more underdeveloped. German law actually forbade German women from political activity. Because no group in the German Empire enjoyed extensive political rights, women were not certain that they would benefit from demanding them. Any such demand would be regarded as subversive of both the state and society.

In 1894 the Union of German Women's Organizations (BDFK) was founded. By 1902 it was calling for the

Women's Suffrage. The creator of this poster cleverly reveals the hypocrisy and foolishness of denying the vote to women.

right to vote, but it was largely concerned with improving women's social conditions, their access to education, and their right to other protections. The group also worked to see women admitted to political or civic activity on the municipal level. Their work usually included education, child welfare, charity, and public health. The German Social Democratic Party supported women's suffrage, but that Socialist party was so disdained by the German authorities and German Roman Catholics that this support only made suffrage more suspect in their eyes. Women received the vote in Germany only in 1918 under the constitution of the Weimar Republic. Before World War I, only in Norway (1907) could women vote on national issues.

Jewish Emancipation

One of the most important social changes to occur throughout Europe during the nineteenth century was the emancipation of European Jews from the narrow life of the ghetto into a world of equal or nearly equal citizenship and social status. This transformation represented one of the major social impacts of political liberalism on European life.

Early Steps to Equal Citizenship

Jewish emancipation, slow and never fully completed, began in the late eighteenth century and continued throughout the nineteenth. It moved at different paces in different countries. In 1782 Joseph II (r. 1765–1790), the Habsburg emperor, issued a decree that placed the Jews of his empire under more or less the same laws as Christians. In France

the National Assembly recognized Jews as French citizens in 1789. During the Napoleonic Wars Jewish communities in Italy and Germany were allowed to mix on a generally equal footing with the Christian population.

These various steps toward political emancipation were frequently limited or partially repealed with changes in rulers or governments. Even in countries that granted them political rights, Jews could not own land and could be subject to discriminatory taxes. Nonetheless, by the first half of the nineteenth century Jews in western Europe and to a much lesser extent in central and eastern Europe had begun to acquire equal or nearly equal citizenship.

In Russia, however, the traditional modes of prejudice and discrimination continued unabated until World War I. Jews were treated as aliens under Russian rule. The government undermined Jewish community life, limited publication of Jewish books, restricted areas where Jews might live, required internal passports from Jews, and banned them from many forms of state service and from many institutions of higher education. The police and others were allowed to conduct **pogroms**—organized riots—against Jewish neighborhoods and villages.

Broadened Opportunities

After the revolutions of 1848, and especially in western Europe, the situation of European Jews improved for several decades. Throughout Germany, Italy, the Low Countries, and Scandinavia, Jews were allowed full rights of citizenship. After 1858 Jews in Great Britain could sit in Parliament. In Austria-Hungary full legal rights were extended to Jews in 1867. From approximately 1850 to 1880 there was relatively

Dedication of a New Synagogue. The social life of Europe became transformed in numerous ways during the nineteenth century. Beyond the expansion of cities and the rise of industrial society, there also occurred numerous changes in religious life. One of the most important of these changes was the gradual emancipation of European Jews from sharply restricted lives in urban ghettos to fuller political participation and social assimilation. This painting by G. E. Opitz portrays the dedication of a new synagogue in Alsace in 1820.

little organized or overt prejudice toward Jews. They entered the professions and other occupations once closed to them. They participated fully in the literary and cultural life of their nations. They were active in the arts and music. They became leaders in science and education. Jews intermarried freely with non-Jews as legal prohibitions against such marriages were repealed during the last quarter of the century.

Outside of Russia, Jewish political figures served in the highest offices of the state. Politically they tended to be aligned with liberal parties because such groups had championed equal rights. Later in the century, especially in eastern Europe, many Jews became associated with the Socialist parties.

The prejudice that had been associated with religious attitudes toward Jews seemed to have dissipated, although it still appeared in rural Russia and eastern Europe. From these regions hundreds of thousands of European Jews immigrated to the United States. Almost anywhere in Europe Jews might encounter prejudice on a personal level. But in western Europe, including England, France, Italy, Germany, and the Low Countries, the Jewish populations seem to have felt relatively secure from the old dangers of legalized persecution and discrimination.

That began to change during the last two decades of the nineteenth century. In the 1870s anti-Semitic sentiments attributing the economic stagnation of that decade to Jewish bankers and financial interests began to be voiced. In the 1880s organized anti-Semitism erupted in Germany as it did in France in the 1890s. As we saw in the previous chapter, those developments gave birth to Zionism, the movement to establish a Jewish state in Palestine. However, Zionism was initially a minority movement within the Jewish community. Most Jewish leaders believed the attacks on Jewish life to be temporary recurrences of older prejudice; they felt that their communities would remain safe under the legal protections that had been extended during the century. That analysis would be proved disastrously wrong during the 1930s and 1940s.

European Labor, Socialism, and Politics to World War I

The Working Classes in the Late Nineteenth Century

After 1848 European workers ceased taking to the streets to voice their grievances in the form of riots. They also stopped trying to revive the old paternalistic guilds. After midcentury the labor force accepted the fact of modern industrial production and its general downgrading of skills and attempted to receive more benefits from that system. Workers turned to new institutions and ideologies. Chief among them were trade unions, democratic political parties, and socialism.

Trade Union Membership Certificate. Trade unions continued to grow in late nineteenth-century Great Britain. The effort to curb the unions eventually led to the formation of the Labour Party. The British unions often had quite elaborate membership certificates, such as this one for the National Union of Gas Workers and General Labourers of Great Britain and Ireland.

Trade Unions Trade unionism came of age as legal protections were extended to unions throughout the second half of the century. Unions became fully legal in Great Britain in 1871 and were allowed to picket in 1875. In France the Third Republic fully legalized unions in 1884. After 1890 they could function in Germany with little disturbance. Initially, most trade unions were slow to enter the political process directly. As long as the traditional governing classes looked after labor interests, members of the working class rarely sought office themselves.

The midcentury organizational efforts of the unions aimed to improve the wages and working conditions of skilled workers. By the close of the century large industrial unions for unskilled workers were also being organized. They confronted extensive opposition from employers, and were often recognized only after long strikes. In the decade before 1914 strikes were common throughout Europe as the unions attempted to raise wages to keep up with inflation. However, despite the advances of unions and the growth of their membership in 1910 to approximately 3 million in

Britain, 2 million in Germany, and 977,000 in France, they never included a majority of the industrial labor force. The unions did represent a new collective fashion in which workers could associate to confront the economic difficulties of their lives and attain better security.

Democracy and Political Parties The democratic franchise gave workers direct political influence, which meant they could no longer be ignored. Except for Russia, all the major European states adopted broad-based, if not perfectly democratic, electoral systems. Democracy brought new modes of popular pressure to bear on all governments. It meant that discontented groups could now voice their grievances and advocate their programs within government rather than from outside it.

The advent of democracy witnessed the formation, for the first time in Europe, of organized mass political parties, such as had existed throughout the nineteenth century in the United States. In the liberal European states with narrow electoral bases, most voters had been men of property who understood what they had at stake in politics. Organization had been minimal. The expansion of the electorate brought into the political processes many people whose level of political consciousness and interest was low. This electorate had to be organized and taught the nature of power and influence in the liberal democratic state. The organized political party—with its workers, newspapers, offices, social life, and discipline—was the vehicle that mobilized the new voters. The largest single group in these mass electorates was the working class. The democratization of politics presented the Socialists with opportunities and required the traditional ruling class to vie with them for the support of the new voters.

Marxist Critique of the Industrial Order

During the 1840s Karl Marx (1818–1883) produced the most influential of all critiques of the newly emerged industrial order. His analysis became very important because later in the century it was adopted by the leading Socialist political party in Germany, which in turn influenced most other European Socialist parties, including a small group of exiled Russian Socialists led by V. I. Lenin. Marx was born in the Rhineland. His Jewish middle-class parents sent him to the University of Berlin, where he became deeply involved in radical politics. During 1842 and 1843 he edited the radical *Rhineland Gazette*. Soon the German authorities drove him into exile—first in Paris; then in Brussels; and finally, after 1849, in London.

In 1844 Marx met Friedrich Engels (1820–1895), another young middle-class German, whose father owned a textile factory in Manchester, England. The next year, Engels published *The Condition of the Working Class in England*,

Karl Marx. Marx's Socialist philosophy eventually triumphed over most alternative versions of socialism in Europe, but his monumental work has been subject to varying interpretations, criticisms, and revisions that continue to this day.

which presented a devastating picture of industrial life. The two men became fast friends. Late in 1847 they were asked to write a pamphlet for a newly organized and ultimately short-lived secret Communist league. *The Communist Manifesto*, published in German, appeared early in 1848. Marx, Engels, and the league had adopted the name *Communist* because the term was more self-consciously radical than *Socialist*. *Communism* implied the outright abolition of private property rather than some less extensive rearrangement of society. The *Manifesto* itself was a work of fewer than fifty pages. It would become the most influential political document of modern European history, but that development lay in the future. At the time it was simply one more political tract. Moreover, neither Marx nor his thought had any effect on the revolutionary events of 1848.

●•●—[**Read** the **Document**
The Communist Manifesto, Karl
Marx (1848) at **MyHistoryLab.com**

In *The Communist Manifesto* Marx and Engels contended that human history must be understood rationally and as a whole. According to their analysis, history is the record of humankind's coming to grips with physical nature to produce the goods necessary for survival. That basic productive process determines the structures, values, and ideas of a society. Historically, the organization of the means of production has always involved conflict between the classes that owned and controlled the means of production and those classes that worked for them. That necessary conflict has provided the engine for historical development; it is not an accidental by-product of mismanagement or bad intentions. Consequently, only a radical social transformation, not piecemeal reforms, can eliminate the social and economic evils inherent in the very structures of production. Such a revolution will occur as the inevitable outcome of the development of capitalism itself.

In Marx's and Engels's eyes, during the nineteenth century the class conflict that had characterized previous Western history had become a struggle between the bourgeoisie and the proletariat, or between the middle class and the workers. The character of capitalism ensured the sharpening of the struggle. Capitalist production and competition would steadily increase the size of the unpropertied proletariat. Large-scale mechanical production crushed both traditional and smaller industrial producers into the ranks of the proletariat. As the business structures grew larger and larger, smaller middle-class units would be squeezed out by the competitive pressures. Competition among the few remaining gigantic concerns would lead to more intense suffering by the proletariat. As the workers suffered increasingly from the competition among the ever-enlarging firms, they would foment revolution and finally overthrow the few remaining owners of the means of production. For a time the workers would organize the means of production through a dictatorship of the proletariat, which would eventually give way to a propertyless and classless communist society.

This proletarian revolution was inevitable, according to Marx and Engels. The structure of capitalism required competition and consolidation of enterprise. Although the class conflict involved in the contemporary process resembled that of the past, it differed in one major respect. The struggle between the capitalistic bourgeoisie and the industrial proletariat would culminate in a wholly new society that would be free of class conflict. The victorious proletariat, by its very nature, they contended, could not be a new oppressor class: "The proletarian movement is the self-conscious, independent movement of the immense majority, in the interest of the immense majority."[1] The result of the proletarian victory would be "an association, in which the free development of each is the condition for the free development of all."[2] The victory of the proletariat over the bourgeoisie represented the culmination of human history. For the first time, one group of people would not be oppressing another. Marx's analysis was conditioned by his own economic environment. The 1840s had seen much unemployment and deprivation. Capitalism, however, did not collapse as he predicted, nor did the middle class during the rest of the century or later become proletarianized. (See Document: "Karl Marx and Friedrich Engels Describe the Class Struggle.")

Instead, more and more people came to benefit from the industrial system. Nonetheless, within a generation Marxism had captured the imagination of many Socialists and large segments of the working class. Its doctrines were allegedly based on the empirical evidence of hard economic fact. This much proclaimed scientific aspect of **Marxism** helped the ideology, as science became more influential during the second half of the century. Marx had made the ultimate victory of socialism seem certain. His works also proclaimed that the path to socialism lay with revolution rather than reform. As Marxist thought permeated the international Socialist movement during the next seventy-five years, it would provide the ideological basis for some of the most momentous and ultimately repressive political movements in the history of virtually the entire modern world.

Germany: Social Democrats and Revisionism

The thought of Karl Marx ultimately came to exercise such vast influence because his ideas were adopted by the German Social Democratic Party (SPD). Founded in 1875, the SPD suffered twelve years of persecution by Otto von Bismarck (1815–1898), who believed socialism would undermine German politics and society. In 1878 there was an attempt to assassinate Emperor William I (r. 1861–1888). Bismarck unfairly blamed the Socialists and steered antisocialist laws through the Reichstag, the German Parliament. These measures suppressed the organization, meetings, newspapers, and other public activities of the SPD. Nonetheless, the SPD steadily polled more votes in elections to the Reichstag.

When repression failed, Bismarck enacted social welfare legislation to wean German workers from socialist loyalties. These measures provided health insurance, accident insurance, and old age and disability pensions. The German state itself thus organized a system of social security that did not change the system of property holding or politics.

In 1891, after forcing Bismarck's resignation, Emperor William II (r. 1888–1918) allowed the antisocialist legislation to expire. The SPD then had to decide how to operate as a legalized party. Their new direction was announced in the Erfurt Program of 1891. In good Marxist fashion, the program declared the imminent doom of capitalism and the necessity of socialist ownership of the means of production. However, these goals were to be achieved by legal political participation rather than by revolutionary activity. Since the revolution was inevitable, it was argued, the immediate task

---

[1] Robert C. Tucker, ed., *The Marx-Engels Reader* (New York: W. W. Norton, 1972), p. 353.

[2] Ibid.

Document

Karl Marx and Friedrich Engels Describe the Class Struggle

The Communist Manifesto (1848) is arguably the most influential political pamphlet of modern European history. In that relatively brief document, Karl Marx and Friedrich Engels portrayed human history as developing from ancient times to the present through a series of economic class struggles. In the contemporary world, they saw the complex struggles of the past reduced to a head-on economic, political, and social clash between the bourgeoisie, or capital-owning class, and the proletariat, or workers. Both groups had emerged in the course of history. The bourgeoisie had arisen from medieval townsmen asserting their liberty against feudal landowners and then against other groups of aristocrats. In turn, as the bourgeoisie came to dominate the economy and invest their capital in modern industry, they produced the contemporary wage-labor force. Over time this labor force came to see that its interests opposed that of its economic masters. The result was to be the final class conflict of history because, as Marx and Engels argued, the proletariat, unlike any previous group seeking to establish its liberty, was so large that its victory was also the victory of humanity itself.

■ *Whom do Marx and Engels portray as the previous enemies of the bourgeoisie? How did bourgeois economic development and dominance lead to a society based on the "cash nexus"? Why is the bourgeoisie responsible for the emergence of the proletariat? Why is the victory of the proletariat inevitable?*

The history of all hitherto existing society is the history of class struggles.. . .

Our epoch, the epoch of the bourgeoisie, possesses, however, this distinctive feature: it has simplified the class antagonisms. Society as a whole is more and more splitting up into two great hostile camps, into two great classes directly facing each other: Bourgeoisie and Proletariat. . . .

Each step in the development of the bourgeoisie was accompanied by a corresponding political advance of that class. . . .

The bourgeoisie, wherever it has gotten the upper hand, has put an end to all feudal, patriarchal, idyllic relations. It has pitilessly torn asunder the motley feudal ties that bound man to his "natural superiors," and has left remaining no other nexus between man and man than naked self-interest, than callous "cash payment". . . .

The proletariat goes through various stages of development. With its birth begins its struggle with the bourgeoisie. . . . . . .

But with the development of industry the proletariat not only increases in number; it becomes concentrated in greater masses, its strength grows, and it feels that strength more. The various interests and conditions of life within the ranks of the proletariat are more and more equalized, in proportion as machinery obliterates all distinctions of labour, and nearly everywhere reduces wages to the same low level. . . . . . .

The bourgeoisie finds itself involved in a constant battle. . . . . . .

Of all the classes that stand face to face with the bourgeoisie today, the proletariat alone is a really revolutionary class. . . . . . .

All previous historical movements were movements of minorities, or in the interest of minorities. The proletarian movement is the self-conscious, independent movement of the immense majority, in the interest of the immense majority. . . . . . .

The advance of industry, whose involuntary promoter is the bourgeoisie, replaces the isolation of the labourers, due to competition, by their revolutionary combination, due to association. The development of Modern Industry, therefore, cuts from under its feet the very foundation on which the bourgeoisie produces and appropriates products. What the bourgeoisie, therefore, produces, above all, is its own grave-diggers. Its fall and the victory of the proletariat are equally inevitable. . . . . . .

The proletarians have nothing to lose but their chains. They have a world to win.

Source: Excerpts from Karl Marx and Friedrich Engels in The Communist Manifesto in Lawrence H. Simon (ed) Selected Writings Copyright © 1994 Reprinted by permission of International Publishers Company, Inc., New York.

of Socialists was to improve workers' lives. In theory, the SPD was vehemently hostile to the German Empire, but in practice the party functioned within its institutions.

The SPD's situation, however, generated the most important internal socialist challenge to the orthodox Marxist analysis of capitalism and the socialist revolution. Eduard Bernstein (1850–1932) wrote what was regarded as his socialist heresy. Bernstein, who was familiar with the British **Fabians**, questioned whether Marx and his later orthodox followers had been correct in their pessimistic appraisal of capitalism and the necessity of revolution. In *Evolutionary Socialism* (1899), Bernstein pointed to the rising standard of living in Europe, the ongoing power of the middle class, and the opening of the franchise to the working class. He argued that a humane socialist society required not revolution, but more democracy and social reform. Bernstein's doctrines, known as **revisionism**, were widely debated among German Socialists and were finally condemned as theory, although the party actually pursued a peaceful, reformist program. His critics argued that evolution toward social democracy might be possible in liberal, parliamentary Britain but not in authoritarian, militaristic Germany with its basically powerless Reichstag. Therefore, the German SPD continued to advocate revolution.

The German debate over revisionism became important for the later history of Marxist socialism. The German SPD was, as noted, the most successful prewar Socialist Party. Its rejection of an ideology of reform socialism in favor of revolutionary socialism influenced all Socialists who looked to the German example. Most significant, Lenin adopted this position, as did the other leaders of the Russian Revolution. Thereafter, wherever Soviet Marxism was influential, the goal of its efforts would be revolution rather than reform.

Great Britain: The Labour Party and Fabianism

No form of socialism made significant progress in Great Britain, the most advanced industrial society of the day. The members of the growing trade unions normally supported Liberal Party candidates. The "new unionism" of the late 1880s and the 1890s organized the dock workers, the gas workers, and similar unskilled groups. Employer resistance to unions heightened class antagonism. In 1892 Keir Hardie (1856–1915) became the first independent worker elected to Parliament. In 1893 the Socialist Independent Labour Party was founded, but it remained ineffective.

In 1901, however, a decision by the House of Lords (Britain's supreme court) removed the legal protection previously accorded union funds. The Trades Union Congress responded by launching the Labour Party, which sent twenty-nine members to Parliament in the election of 1906. Their goals did not yet encompass socialism. The British

labor movement also became more militant. In scores of strikes, workers fought for wages to meet the rising cost of living. The government intervened to mediate these strikes, which in 1911 and 1912 involved the railways, the docks, and the mines.

British socialism itself remained primarily the preserve of intellectuals. The Socialists who exerted the most influence were from the Fabian Society, founded in 1884. The society took its name from Q. Fabius Maximus (d. 203 B.C.E.), the Roman general who defeated Hannibal by waiting before attacking. Its name thus indicated a gradualist approach to social reform. Its leading members were Sydney Webb (1859–1947) and Beatrice Webb (1858–1943), H. G. Wells (1866–1946), and George Bernard Shaw (1856–1950). Many of the Fabians were civil servants who believed that the problems of industry, the expansion of ownership, and the state direction of production could be solved and achieved gradually, peacefully, and democratically. They sought to educate the country to the rational wisdom of socialism. They were particularly interested in collective ownership on the municipal level, or so-called gas-and-water socialism.

Beatrice and Sidney Webb. These most influential British Fabian Socialists, shown in a photograph from the late 1920s, wrote many books on governmental and economic matters, served on special parliamentary commissions, and agitated for the enactment of socialist policies.

Russia: Industrial Development and the Birth of Bolshevism

Following its defeat in the Crimean War, the tsarist government in Russia had undertaken a series of major internal reforms. The most important of these was the emancipation of the serfs in 1861. That measure was extremely complicated and in effect required serfs to pay for their land. The poverty of the emancipated serfs became a political cause for groups of urban revolutionaries in Russia, the most important of which was named The People's Will, who succeeded in assassinating Tsar Alexander II (r. 1855–1881) in 1881. Thereafter, the government pursued a policy of general political repression.

At the same time in the late nineteenth century the tsarist government was determined to make Russia an industrial power. It favored the growth of heavy industries, such as railways, iron, and steel. A small, but significant, industrial proletariat arose. By 1900 Russia had approximately 3 million factory workers. Their working and living conditions were bad by any standard.

New political departures accompanied this economic development. In 1901 the Social Revolutionary Party was founded. It opposed industrialism and looked to the communal life of rural Russia as a model for the economic future. In 1903 the Constitutional Democratic Party, or Cadets, was formed. Liberal in outlook, the Cadets were drawn from people who participated in the *zemstvos* (local governments). They wanted a parliamentary regime with responsible ministries, civil liberties, and economic progress. The Cadets hoped to model themselves on the Liberal parties of western Europe.

Lenin's Early Thought and Career The situation for Russian Socialists differed radically from that in other major European countries. Russia had no representative political institutions and only a small working class. The compromises and accommodations achieved elsewhere were meaningless in Russia, where socialism in both theory and practice had to be revolutionary. The Russian Social Democratic Party had been established in 1898. It was Marxist, and its members greatly admired the German SPD, but tsarist repression meant that it had to function in exile.

The leading late nineteenth-century Russian Marxist was Georgii Plekhanov (1857–1918), based in Switzerland. His chief disciple was Vladimir Illich Ulyanov (1870–1924), who took the name of Lenin. The future leader of the communist revolution was the son of a high bureaucrat. His older brother had been executed in 1887 for participating in a plot against Alexander III (r. 1881–1894). In 1893 Lenin moved to Saint Petersburg, where he briefly practiced law. Soon he, too, was drawn to the revolutionary groups among the factory workers. In 1895 he was exiled to Siberia. After his release in 1900,

Hear the Audio
Socialism
at MyHistoryLab.com

Lenin spent most of the next seventeen years in Switzerland.

In Switzerland Lenin became deeply involved in the organizational and policy disputes of the exiled Russian Social Democrats. They all considered themselves Marxists but quarreled about the proper nature of a Marxist revolution in primarily rural Russia and the structure of their own party. The Social Democrats were modernizers who favored further industrial development. Most believed that Russia must develop a large proletariat before the revolution could come. This same majority hoped to mold a mass political party like the German SPD.

Lenin dissented from both positions. In *What Is to Be Done?* (1902), he condemned any accommodations. He also criticized a trade unionism that settled for short-term gains rather than true revolutionary change for the working class. Lenin further rejected the concept of a mass party composed of workers. Revolutionary consciousness would not arise spontaneously from the working class. It must be carried to them by a small, elite party. (See Document: "Lenin Argues for the Necessity of a Secret and Elite Party of Professional Revolutionaries.")

Establishment of the Bolsheviks In 1903, at the London Congress of the Russian Social Democratic Party, Lenin split

Chronology

Major Dates in the Development of Socialism

1864	International Working Men's Association (the First International) founded
1875	German Social Democratic Party founded
1876	First International dissolved
1878	German antisocialist laws passed
1884	British Fabian Society founded
1889	Second International founded
1891	German antisocialist laws permitted to expire
1891	German Social Democratic Party's Erfurt Program
1895	French *Confédération Générale du Travail* founded
1899	Eduard Bernstein's *Evolutionary Socialism*
1902	Formation of the British Labour party
1902	Lenin's *What Is to Be Done?*
1903	Bolshevik-Menshevik split

Document
Lenin Argues for the Necessity of a Secret and Elite Party of Professional Revolutionaries

Social democratic parties in western Europe had mass memberships and were generally democratic organizations. In this passage from *What Is to Be Done?* (1902), Lenin explains why the autocratic political conditions of Russia demanded a different kind of organization for the Russian Social Democratic Party. Lenin's ideas became the guiding principles of Bolshevik organization. Lenin departed from Marx's own thought by urging the necessity of fulminating revolution rather than waiting for it to occur as a necessary result of the collapse of capitalism.

■ *What does Lenin mean by "professional revolutionaries"? Why does Russia need such revolutionaries? How does Lenin reconcile his antidemocratic views to the goal of aiding the working class?*

I assert that it is far more difficult [for government police] to unearth a dozen wise men than a hundred fools. This position I will defend, no matter how much you instigate the masses against me for my "anti-democratic" views, etc. As I have stated repeatedly, by "wise men," in connection with organization, I mean professional revolutionaries, irrespective of whether they have developed from among students or working men. I assert: (1) that no revolutionary movement can endure without a stable organization of leaders maintaining continuity; (2) that the broader the popular mass drawn spontaneously into the struggle, which forms the basis of the movement and participates in it, the more urgent the need for such an organization, and the more solid this organization must be . . . . ; (3) that such an organization must consist chiefly of people professionally engaged in revolutionary activity; (4) that in an autocratic state [such as Russia],

the more we confine the membership of such an organization to people who are professionally engaged in revolutionary activity and who have been professionally trained in the art of combating the political police, the more difficult will it be to unearth the organization; and (5) the greater will be the number of people from the working class and from other social classes who will be able to join the movement and perform active work in it.

. . . .

The only serious organization principle for the active workers of our movement should be the strictest secrecy, the strictest selection of members, and the training of professional revolutionaries.

Source: Validmir Ilyich Lenin, *What Is To Be Done? Burning Questions of Our Movement*, Chapter 4 (first published 1902). Public domain, reprinted at http://www.marxists.org/archive/lenin/works/1901/witbd/index.htm

the party ranks. Although it lost most of the votes during the congress, Lenin's group mustered a slim majority near the close. Thereafter, his faction assumed the name **Bolsheviks**, meaning "majority," and the other, more moderate, democratic revolutionary faction became known as the **Mensheviks**, or "minority." There was, of course, a considerable public relations advantage to the name *Bolshevik*. (In 1912 the Bolsheviks organized separately from other Social Democrats.) In 1905 Lenin complemented his organizational theory with a program for revolution in Russia. His *Two Tactics of Social Democracy in the Bourgeois-Democratic Revolution* urged that the socialist revolution unite the proletariat and the peasants. He grasped better than any other revolutionary the profound discontent in the Russian countryside. He knew that an alliance of workers and peasants in rebellion probably could not be suppressed. Lenin's two principles of an elite party and a dual social revolution allowed the Bolsheviks, in late 1917, to

capture the leadership of the Russian Revolution and to transform the political face of the modern world.

The Revolution of 1905 and Its Aftermath The quarrels among the Russian Socialists had no immediate influence within Russia itself. In 1904 Russia went to war with Japan, but the result was defeat and political crisis. The Japanese captured Port Arthur, Russia's base on the eastern coast of China, early in 1905. A few days later, on January 22, a priest named Father Gapon (1870–1906) led thousands of workers to petition the tsar for improvements in industrial conditions. As the petitioners approached the Winter Palace in Saint Petersburg, troops opened fire. About 100 people were killed, and many more were wounded.

Revolutionary disturbances spread throughout Russia: Sailors mutinied, peasants revolted, and property was

See the Map
The Growth of Russia to 1914
at **MyHistoryLab.com**

A Closer Look

Bloody Sunday, Saint Petersburg 1905

On Bloody Sunday, January 22, 1905, troops of Tsar Nicholas II fired on a peaceful procession of workers at the Winter Palace who sought to present a petition for better working and living conditions. The scene in a Saint Petersburg square portrayed here, which can still be visited today, depicts one of the enduring images of events leading to the subsequent Russian Revolutions of 1905 and 1917. It figured in at least two movies: the 1925 antitsarist Soviet silent film called "The Ninth of January," and "Nicholas and Alexandra," the lavish 1971 movie that was sympathetic to the tsar and blamed Bloody Sunday on frightened and incompetent officials. While Nicholas had not ordered the troops to fire and was not even in Saint Petersburg on Bloody Sunday, the event all but destroyed any chance of reconciliation between the tsarist government and the Russian working class.

The workers are visibly defenseless in the face of the rifles being fired at them.

Although the square before the Winter Palace toward the right of the troops is large and might have allowed an escape route of sorts for the workers' procession, the troops forced the crowd into an area of narrow escape.

The view is the one that officials in the Winter Palace, which lay behind the row of troops with rifles, would have seen.

Questions

1. How did the invention of photography and the making of movies transform the recording and interpretation of the past?

2. Do you think the firing on the crowd in 1905 was as orderly affair as this picture from a later Bolshevik film made it appear?

3. How did the ongoing recollection and reenactment of this dramatic, violent moment in the Revolution of 1905 serve to continue to discredit the tsarist government and to champion the later Bolshevik Revolution?

attacked. An uncle of the tsar was assassinated. Liberal Constitutional Democratic leaders from the *zemstvos* demanded political reform. University students went on strike. In early October 1905 strikes broke out in Saint Petersburg,

Chronology

Major Dates in Turn-of-the-Century Russian History

1895		Lenin arrested and sent to Siberia
1897		Eleven-and-a-half-hour workday established
1898		Russian Social Democratic Party founded
1900		Lenin leaves Russia for western Europe
1901		Social Revolutionary Party founded
1903		Constitutional Democratic Party (Cadets) founded
1903		Bolshevik-Menshevik split
1904		Russo-Japanese War begins
1905	January	Japan defeats Russia
	January 22	Revolution breaks out in Saint Petersburg after Bloody Sunday massacre
	October 20	General strike
	October 26	*October Manifesto* establishes constitutional government
1906	May 10	Meeting of first *Duma*
	June	Stolypin appointed prime minister
	July 21	Dissolution of first *Duma*
	November	Land redemption payments canceled for peasants
1907	March 5–June 16	Second *Duma* seated and dismissed
1907		Franchise changed and a third *Duma* elected, which sits until 1912
1911		Stolypin assassinated by a social revolutionary
1912		Fourth *Duma* elected
1914		World War I breaks out

and worker groups, called *soviets*, virtually controlled the city. Tsar Nicholas II (r. 1894–1917) promised Russia constitutional government.

Early in 1906 the tsar announced the election of a parliament, the **Duma**, with two chambers. However, he reserved for himself ministerial appointments, financial policy, and military and foreign affairs. Nicholas named as his chief minister P. A. Stolypin (1862–1911). Neither the tsar nor his minister was sympathetic to the Duma. It would meet, disagreements would occur, and it would be dismissed. In 1906, however, the government canceled any redemptive payments the peasants still owed from the emancipation of the serfs in 1861. Thereafter Stolypin repressed rural discontent.

After Stolypin's assassination in 1911 by a social revolutionary, the tsarist government simply muddled along. But the imperial family became surrounded by scandal over the influence of Grigori Rasputin (1871?–1916), who seemed able to heal the tsar's hemophilic son, the heir to the throne. The undue influence of this strange and uncouth man, the continued social discontent, and the conservative resistance to liberal reforms rendered the position and policy of the tsar uncertain after 1911.

European Socialism in World History

The debates among late nineteenth- and early twentieth-century European Socialists were complicated and in some respects obscure. They proved significant, however, not only for European politics but also for political developments around the world, and that is the reason we have discussed them in some detail. The impact arose for two reasons. First, Europeans who immigrated to North and South America carried many of these socialist ideas and quarrels with them. They continued to debate the issues they had debated in Europe in their new homelands. Second, by the end of the nineteenth century numerous students from different parts of the European empires in Africa and Asia traveled to Europe for education. There they confronted these debates among European Socialists. Many of those students later returned home to become leaders of anticolonial political movements and carried with them again the ideas and quarrels about methods, theory, and tactics they had encountered among European Socialists.

North America and the New Industrial Economy

The full industrialization of the United States followed a pattern not unlike that of nineteenth-century Europe. The first industry to become thoroughly mechanized was textile manufacture, followed by growth in the iron and steel industries. There were certain significant differences, however.

Immigrant Labor. Chinese laborers, known as "coolies," performed most of the backbreaking work on the construction of the railroads in the American West. The workers depicted here are laying down track near Promontory, Utah.

The United States industrialized considerably later than Great Britain. Its major expansion in iron and steel took place after the Civil War and was thus approximately contemporary to the economic rise of the newly united Germany. In the United States there had always been enormous social respect for entrepreneurial enterprise. American manufacturers and commercial developers thus encountered little of the prejudice against trade and commerce that existed among the European aristocracy. Wealthy American businessmen had considerable political influence. The United States possessed an immense internal market that functioned without trade restraints for the shipment of unprocessed goods to factories or of finished products to their markets. Much of the capital for American industrial expansion came from British bankers who saw the United States as an area of secure investment. Finally, the United States had a relative shortage of labor and consequently relatively high wages, the factors that attracted so many immigrants to the industrial sector during the second half of the century.

In America as in Europe, however, the railways spurred the most intense industrial growth. The number of railway miles increased from approximately 50,000 in the mid-1860s to almost 200,000 by 1900. Much of the construction was made possible by vast European investments in the United States. The railways created enormous demand for iron, steel, coal, and lumber. They also stimulated settlement, vastly expanded markets, and helped to knit the country together.

European Immigration to the United States

The same conditions that made American life so difficult for black people and Native Americans (see Chapter 22) turned the United States into a land of vast opportunity for white European immigrants. These immigrants faced religious and ethnic discrimination as well as frequent poverty in the United States; however, for many of them and their children, the social and economic structures of the United States allowed for assimilation and remarkable upward social mobility. This was especially true of those immigrants, mostly from northern and western Europe, who arrived between approximately 1840 and 1890—the great period of German, English, Welsh, Scottish, and Irish immigration (see Map 24–1 on page 753). Among this group, the Irish undoubtedly encountered the most difficulties and resistance.

Toward the end of the century and well into the next—in what is sometimes known as the New Immigration—millions of people arrived from the Mediterranean, eastern Europe, and the Balkans. Most of these peoples left economically depressed areas and financed their immigration themselves. However, some American companies did send ships to Italy for immigrants to work in American factories and mines. These new immigrants, who generally came to work in the growing industrial cities, were perceived as fundamentally different from those who had come before them. They were seen and treated as of a lower class and inherently more difficult to assimilate than the earlier immigrants. Predominately Roman Catholic, Orthodox, and Jewish, they encountered much intolerance. The same kind of racial theory that spread through Europe during these years was present in the United States. These new immigrants were often regarded as being from less desirable racial stocks. As a result, turn-of-the-century immigrants often encountered serious prejudice and endured lives of enormous poverty. They also often settled into communities of people from their own ethnic background. What ultimately held them together were various private organizations,

✳ Map Exploration

To explore this map further, go to **http://www.myhistorylab.com**

- Emigration from Europe
- Emigration from Japan
- Emigration from China
- Emigration from India
- Migration from European Russia

PACIFIC OCEAN

NEW ZEALAND
AND
AUSTRALIA
2 million

CALIFORNIA

ALSAKA

JAPAN

UNITED
STATES
OF AMERICA
33.6 million
1821 to 1920

CANADA
2.3 million

ARCTIC
OCEAN

CHINA

SIAM

EAST INDIES

WEST INDIES

SWEDEN

RUSSIA
550,000
1860 to 1900

INDIA

IRELAND   U.K.
GERMANY
FRANCE
SPAIN   ITALY

• Odessa
2 million to USA
1890 to 1910

ARABIA

INDIAN
OCEAN

GUIANA

MOROCCO

ALGERIA
764,000

Slaves
to Arabia

SOUTH
AMERICA
3.6 million

BRAZIL   Slaves

CAPE
COLONY   NATAL
160,000
to 1888

ATLANTIC
OCEAN

Number of Immigrants		
From Asia		700,000
Main groups		
Chinese	370,000	
Japanese	275,000	
From Canada		2,200,000
From Europe		30,000,000
Main groups		
Germans	5,000,000	
Irish	4,500,000	
Italians	4,500,000	
Poles	2,600,000	
English	2,600,000	
Jews	2,000,000	
From Latin America		900,000

Map 24–1. Patterns of Global Migration, 1840–1900. Emigration was a global process by the late nineteenth century. But more immigrants went to the United States than to every other nation combined.

such as churches and synagogues, clubs, newspapers in their own languages, and social agencies they organized for themselves.

Although none of these immigrants faced the same legal discrimination as did American black people, the Jews encountered restricted covenants on real estate, obstacles to joining private clubs, and quotas for admission to many schools and universities. Asian immigrants to the West Coast of the United States faced even harsher prejudice.

Unions: Organization of Labor

The expansion of industrialism led to various attempts to organize labor unions. In America as in Europe, workers faced great resistance from employers and those who feared that labor unions might lead to socialism. Another difficulty arose from the social situation of the labor force itself. White laborers would not organize alongside black workers.

Different ethnic minorities would not cooperate. The ongoing flood of immigration ensured a supply of workers willing to work for low wages. The owners of businesses more often than not could divide and conquer the sprawling, ethnically mixed labor force.

The first effort at labor organization occurred in the 1870s with the National Labor Union and railroad unions. In 1881 the American Federation of Labor (AFL) was founded. In contrast to earlier organizations and the advanced European socialist movement, such as that in Germany, it did not seek to transform the life of workers in a radical fashion but rather focused on higher wages and better working conditions. The AFL concentrated on organizing skilled workers; it did not seek to organize whole industries. Among its most effective leaders was Samuel Gompers (1850–1924). Other unions, such as the United Mine Workers and the Railway Brotherhoods, organized workers by industry.

Ellis Island. In 1892 the federal government opened the immigration station on Ellis Island, located in New York City's harbor, where about 80 percent of the immigrants to the United States landed. As many as 5,000 passengers per day reported to federal immigration officers for questions about their background and for physical examinations, such as this eye exam. Only about 1 percent were quarantined or turned away for health problems.

The industrialization of the United States—again, like that of Europe—saw major periods of business crisis or downturn. Serious depressions occurred in both the 1870s and the 1890s. There was no government relief. What little relief there was came from local authorities and private charities. This pattern would continue until the Great Depression of the 1930s. The economic turmoil of the 1880s and 1890s spawned violent strikes. Perhaps the most famous of these incidents was the breaking of the Pullman strike in Chicago in 1894 by federal troops. The major goal of labor thereafter was to achieve the full legal right to organize. Although the Clayton Act of 1914 moved in that direction, the clear right to organize with the protection of the federal government was achieved only through the legislation of Franklin Roosevelt's (1882–1945) New Deal in the 1930s.

Socialism was a path not taken by American labor and one not allowed to be taken. The leaders of the conservative unions worked against the Socialists, and spokesmen for business did everything possible to block their influence. The federal and state governments actively sought to repress socialist activities wherever they appeared. After the Bolshevik Revolution of 1917, virtually all American Socialists were persecuted as Bolshevists during the 1920s and beyond. The United States thus became the land where many social issues tended to be addressed by trade unions rather than by Socialist parties. Furthermore, although many conservative American political and business leaders disliked them, unions were not legally attacked here as they were in Britain, which led to the founding of the British Labour Party after the turn of the century.

In many European countries, Socialist parties, or ministers like Bismarck who attempted to outflank the Socialists, had pressed their governments to pass legislation providing social security and other social services. As with so many other policies favorable to labor, no significant legislation of this kind was passed in the United States, at either the federal or state level, until the New Deal.

The Progressives

Much of the power in American politics in the decades after the Civil War, especially in cities, often lay in the hands of political bosses. This system depended on patronage at every level of government. In return for jobs, contracts, licenses, favors, and sometimes actual services, the boss expected and received political support. Government was a vehicle for distributing spoils. The point of boss politics was not merely venality; it was also a way, however crude and unattractive, of organizing the disorderly social and economic forces of the great cities. It was a way of managing cities that were growing as never before with highly diverse populations.

Toward the close of the century, reform-minded political figures began to emerge on the city and state levels. These reformers feared that people such as themselves from the white upper-middle classes might soon lose political and social influence. Deeply disturbed by the corruption of much of political life, these reformers found the urban environment with its slums an unacceptable picture of disorder. They wanted to see more efficient and less corrupt government. They also wanted the government to become a direct agent of change and reform. Pursuing these goals, they ushered in what has been called the *Progressive era*, which lasted from approximately 1890 through 1914. Although the Progressives were reformers, they were not always liberal by later standards. For example, Progressives in the South often disenfranchised blacks and poor whites by imposing literacy tests and similar devices.

The Progressives began their reform work on the local level, especially in the cities, before they launched into national politics. The disorder and extreme disparity of wealth and poverty in the cities disturbed them. Urban reformers believed that the politics of bosses and patronage robbed cities of the money needed to make them livable places. In place of patronage, they demanded social and municipal services to clean up the cities. They repeatedly attacked special interests who blocked reform. Progressive mayors called for lower utility rates and streetcar fares and also attacked police corruption.

Social Reform

Not only politicians joined the Progressive crusade. Churches began to address the question of social reform. It was in this era that the "Social Gospel" was first preached, with its message that Christianity involved civic action. Young men and women began to work in settlement houses in the slums. The most famous was Chicago's Hull House, led by Jane Addams (1860–1935). Other young persons from the middle class became active in housing and health reform, education, and charities. They conducted extensive surveys of the poorest parts of the great cities. These people believed that the urban environment could be cleaned up and social order made to prevail. Their vision of such social order was that of the white middle class.

Beginning in the mid-1890s, progressivism began to affect state governments. There the impulse toward reform involved various attempts to protect whole classes of persons who were perceived as unable to protect themselves against exploitation, especially children and women working under unwholesome conditions for low wages. Other aspects of progressivism at the state level involved the civil service requirements and the regulation of railways. Virtually all of these reformers partook of the cult of science that was so influential in the late nineteenth

Child Labor in the United States. A young girl works at a loom in a cotton mill in the Carolinas. At the dawn of the twentieth century, children worked in textile mills, particularly in the South, which was in the process of moving toward a less agriculturally based economy. It wasn't until the 1930s that state legislation effectively brought an end to child labor in textile mills.

century. They believed that the problems of society were susceptible to scientific, rational management. The general public interest should replace special interests.

One area of concern for the Progressive movement was child labor. In both the United States and Europe children had labored in both rural and industrial settings throughout the nineteenth century. Various reform efforts had attempted to limit the employment of children. Factory laws had been passed in England as early as the 1830s. In the United States at the close of the nineteenth century children worked in textile mills, especially in the South as that region attempted to move toward a less agriculturally based economy. Child labor was relatively cheap, and children often worked in mills along with their parents. In addition to working long hours around dangerous equipment in unhealthy conditions, these children rarely received significant education.

In the late nineteenth century labor organizations criticized the employment of children in the textile mills but to little effect. In 1994 the National Child Labor Committee was organized to work for reform. It published pamphlets and photographs of the harsh conditions endured by children. Federal legislation was passed during Woodrow Wil-

son's administration but was declared unconstitutional. During the 1920s the use of child labor in textile mills declined through changes in factory technology. In the next decade state legislation effectively brought an end to textile mill child labor. The federal Fair Labor Standards Act of 1938 established new standards for the employment of children. The problem of child labor especially in migrant agricultural work would continue and child labor exploitation remains an issue in many parts of the world today. American firms subcontracting to factors in South American and Asia have been accused of exploiting the labor of children in order to bring American consumers cheap clothing and related products.

●♦●⊢Read the Document
The Sadler Report: Child Labor in the United Kingdom, 1832
at **MyHistoryLab.com**

The Progressive Presidency

Roosevelt   Theodore Roosevelt became president in 1901 after the assassination of William McKinley (1843–1901). He had been police commissioner of New York City and later a reforming governor of New York State. Roosevelt, in effect, created the modern American presidency. By force

Document
Theodore Roosevelt States His Progressive Creed

In 1912 Theodore Roosevelt ran unsuccessfully for the presidency on the Progressive ticket challenging both traditional Republicans and Democrats. At the party convention he set forth his most important Progressive convictions. The issues Roosevelt raised in this speech still echo in American politics.

■ *Why does Roosevelt attack the old established parties? What political reforms does he advocate? What social reforms? Why have some people seen Roosevelt as one of the first presidents to be concerned with the environment?*

The Old parties are husks, with no real soul within either, divided on artificial lines, boss-ridden and privilege-controlled, each a jumble of incongruous elements, and neither daring to speak out wisely and fearlessly what should be said on the vital issues of the day. This new movement is a movement of truth, sincerity, and wisdom, a movement which proposes to put at the service of all our people the collective power of the people, through their governmental agencies. . . .

The first essential in the Progressive program is the right of the people to rule. . . . We should provide by a national law for presidential primaries. We should provide for the election of United States Senators by popular vote . . . there must be stringent and efficient corrupt-practices acts, applying to the primaries as well as the elections; and there should be publicity of campaign contributions during the campaign. . . .

We stand for a living wage. Wages are subnormal if they fail to provide a living for those who devote their time and energy to industrial occupations. The monetary equivalent of a living wage varies according to local conditions, but must include enough to secure the elements of a normal standard of living—a standard high enough to make morality possible, to provide for education and recreation, to care for immature members of the family, to maintain the family during periods of sickness, and to permit of reasonable saving for old age.

Hours are excessive if they fail to afford the worker sufficient time to recuperate and return to his work thoroughly refreshed. We hold that the night labor of women and children is abnormal and should be prohibited. We hold that the seven-day working week is abnormal, and we hold that one day of rest in seven should be provided by law. . . . Working women have the same need to combine for protection that working men have; the ballot is as necessary for one class as for the other . . . and therefore we favor woman suffrage.

I believe in a protective tariff, but I believe in it as a principle, approached from the standpoint of the interest of the whole people, and not as a bundle of preferences to be given to favored individuals. . . .

There can be no greater issue than that of conservation in this country. Just as we must conserve our men, women and children, so we must conserve the resources of the land on which they live. . . .

Our cause is based on the eternal principle of righteousness; and even though we who now lead may for the time fail, in the end the cause itself shall triumph. . . . I say in closing: We stand at Armageddon, and we battle for the Lord.

Source: From Theodore Roosevelt's "Confession of Faith before the Progressive National Convention," August 6, 1912, as quoted in Oscar Handlin, ed., *Readings in American History*. Copyright © 1957 Alfred A. Knopf, pp. 477–480.

of personality and intelligence, he began to make the presidency the most important and powerful branch of government. As president, he began to set the agenda for national affairs and to define the problems that the federal government was to address. He surrounded himself with strong advisers and Cabinet members. He used his own knowledge of party patronage to beat the bosses at their own game. (See Document, "Theodore Roosevelt States His Progressive Creed.")

In domestic policy, Roosevelt was determined to control the powerful business trusts. No centers of economic power, he believed, should, through their organization, be stronger than the federal government. He successfully moved against some of the most powerful financiers in the country, such as J. P. Morgan and John D. Rockefeller. Through legislation associated with the term "Square Deal," Roosevelt attempted to assert the public interest over that of the various powerful special interests. He was not opposed to big business in itself, but he wanted it to operate according to rules established by the government for the public good.

In 1902 Roosevelt brought the moral power of the presidency to the aid of mine workers who were on strike. He appointed a commission to arbitrate the dispute. This was a major intrusion of the federal government into the economic system. It reversed the policies that had prevailed a decade earlier, when the government had used federal troops to break strikes. Roosevelt sought to make the presidency and the federal government the guarantor of fairness in economic relations. Thus he fostered the passage of the Pure Food and Drug Act and the Meat Packing Act in 1906, which protected the public against adulterated foodstuffs. Here again, the regulatory principle came to the fore. His conservation policies ensured that millions of acres of national forests came under the care of the federal government.

Roosevelt was associated with a vigorous, imperialistic foreign policy that had roots in the 1890s. In 1898 McKinley had led the nation into the Spanish-American War, and the United States had emerged as an imperial power with control of Cuba, Puerto Rico, Guam, and the Philippines. Roosevelt believed that the United States should be a major world power, and he sent a war fleet around the world. In Latin America naval intervention assured the success of the Panamanian revolt of 1903 against Colombia. A treaty with the new Panamanian government allowed the United States to construct and control a canal across the Isthmus of Panama. The United States was thus following the model of the European great powers, which had been intervening in Africa and Asia. Like the other great powers, the imperialist policies of the United States were built on a conviction of racial superiority.

Roosevelt was succeeded in 1909 by William Howard Taft (1857–1930), his handpicked successor. Taft disappointed Roosevelt, and in 1912 the election was a three-way contest among Taft, Roosevelt (running as a third-party candidate), and Woodrow Wilson. The Democrat Wilson won and brought a different concept of progressivism to the White House.

Wilson Woodrow Wilson (1856–1924) was a former president of Princeton University and a reforming governor of New Jersey, where he had battled the bosses. While still an academic, he had criticized the weak presidency of the late nineteenth century. Wilson, like Roosevelt, accepted a modern industrialized nation. However, unlike Roosevelt, Wilson disliked big business almost in and of itself. He believed in economic competition in which the weak would receive protection from the government. Wilson termed his attitude and policy the New Freedom. Although he had pressed this idea during the campaign, in office he followed a policy of moderate regulation of business.

●●○─Read the Document
Speech Before Congress
at **MyHistoryLab.com**

Wilson also had a different view of the presidency. Rather than seeing in it the bully pulpit to lead public opinion that Roosevelt had, Wilson saw the office as responsible for leading Congress to legislative decisions. Wilson was the first American president since 1800 to deliver the State of the Union address to Congress in person. He presented Congress with a vast agenda of legislation and then worked carefully with the Democratic leadership to see that it was passed. Although Wilson appeared to be an advanced reformer, he retained many beliefs that disappointed his later admirers. For example, he reinstated racial segregation in the federal civil service and opposed female suffrage.

Wilson had long seen his real goals in terms of domestic reform. But war broke out in Europe in August 1914. Although Wilson was reelected in 1916 on the slogan "He Kept Us Out of War!" in April 1917 he nevertheless led the nation into the European conflict. The expertise that he and other Progressives had brought to the task of efficient domestic government was then turned to making the nation an effective military force. These two impulses—the first toward domestic reform, the second toward a strong international role—had long marked the Progressive movement and would shape American history in the years after the war.

The American Progressives resembled political leaders of their generation in Great Britain. The Conservative Benjamin Disraeli (1804–1881) and Liberals William Gladstone (1809–1898) and David Lloyd-George (1863–1945) had supported various measures of social reforms. Elsewhere in Europe political leaders in France and Germany had undertaken reforms in housing and urban life to forestall the advance of socialism and to address the problems of industrialization and urbanization. These leaders had favored unprecedented use of central government authority and the establishment of stronger governments.

The Emergence of Modern European Thought

The last quarter of the nineteenth century and the first decade of the twentieth century were the crucible of modern Western thought. Philosophers, scientists, psychologists, and artists began to portray physical reality, human nature, and society in ways different from those of the past. The vast change in thinking commenced in the realm of biology.

Darwin's Theory of Natural Selection

In 1859, Charles Darwin (1809–1882) published *On the Origin of Species*, which carried the mechanical interpretation of physical nature into the world of living things. (See Document, "Darwin Defends a Mechanistic View of

Document
Darwin Defends a Mechanistic View of Nature

In the closing paragraphs of *On the Origin of Species* (1859), Charles Darwin contrasted the view of nature he championed with that of his opponents. He argued that an interpretation of organic nature based on mechanistic laws was actually nobler than an interpretation based on divine creation. In the second edition, however, Darwin added the term *Creator* to these paragraphs.

■ *Why does Darwin believe a mechanistic creation suggests no less dignity than creation by God? How does the insertion of the term Creator change this passage? What is the grandeur that Darwin finds in his view of life?*

Authors of the highest eminence seem to be fully satisfied with the view that each species has been independently created. To my mind it accords better with what we know of the laws impressed on matter by the Creator, that the production and extinction of the past and present inhabitants of the world should have been due to secondary causes, like those determining the birth and death of the individual. When I view all beings not as special creations, but as the lineal descendants of some few beings which lived long before the first bed of the Cambrian [geological] system was deposited, they seem to me to become ennobled. . . .

It is interesting to contemplate a tangled bank, clothed with many plants of many kinds, with birds singing on the bushes, with various insects flitting about, and with worms crawling through the damp earth, and to reflect that these elaborately constructed forms, so different from each other, and dependent upon each other in so complex a manner, have all been produced by laws acting around us. These laws, taken in the largest sense, being Growth with Reproduction; Inheritance which is almost implied by reproduction; Variability from the indirect and direct action of the conditions of life, and from use and disuse: a Ratio of Increase so high as to lead to a Struggle for Life, and as a consequence to Natural Selection, entailing Divergence of Character and the Extinction of less-improved forms. Thus, from the war of nature, from famine and death, the most exalted object which we are capable of conceiving, namely the production of the higher animals, directly follows. There is grandeur in this view of life, with its several powers, having been originally breathed by the Creator into a few forms or into one; and that, whilst this planet has gone cycling on according to the fixed law of gravity, from so simple a beginning endless forms most beautiful and most wonderful have been, and are being evolved.

Source: Charles Darwin, *On the Origin of Species and the Descent of Man* (New York: Modern Library, n.d.), pp. 373–374.

Nature.") Both Darwin and his book have been much misunderstood. He did not originate the concept of evolution, which had been discussed widely before he wrote. What he and Alfred Russel Wallace (1823–1913) did, working independently, was to formulate the principle of natural selection, which explained how species had changed or evolved over time. Earlier writers had believed evolution might occur; Darwin and Wallace explained how it could occur.

The two scientists contended that more living organisms come into existence than can survive in their environment. Those organisms with a marginal advantage in the struggle for existence live long enough to propagate. This principle of survival of the fittest Darwin called **natural selection**. It was naturalistic and mechanistic, requiring no guiding mind behind the development in organic nature. What neither Darwin nor anyone else in his day could explain was the origin of those chance variations that provided some living things with the marginal chance for survival. Only after 1900, when the work on heredity of the Austrian monk Gregor Mendel (1822–1884) received public attention, did the mystery of those variations begin to be unraveled.

Darwin and Wallace's theory represented the triumph of naturalistic explanation, which removed the idea of preconceived divine purpose from organic nature. Eyes were not made for seeing according to the rational wisdom and purpose of God but had developed mechanistically over time. Thus the theory of evolution through natural selection not only contradicted the biblical narrative of the Creation, but it also undermined both the deistic argument for the existence of God from the design of the universe and the whole concept of fixity in nature or the universe at large. The world was a realm of flux. The idea that physical and organic nature might be constantly changing allowed people to believe that society, values, customs, and beliefs should also change.

●●●┤Read the Document
On Darwin's 1860s
at **MyHistoryLab.com**

Darwin's theories about the evolution of humankind from the higher primates aroused enormous controversy. This caricature shows him with a monkey's body holding a mirror to an apelike creature.

In 1871, in *The Descent of Man*, Darwin applied the principle of evolution by natural selection to human beings. Darwin was hardly the first person to treat human beings as animals, but he contended that humankind's moral nature and religious sentiments, as well as its physical frame, had developed naturalistically largely in response to the requirements of survival. Neither the origin nor the character of humankind, in Darwin's view, required the existence of a god for their explanation. Not since Copernicus had removed the earth from the center of the universe had the pride of Western human beings received so sharp a blow.

Darwin's theory of evolution by natural selection was controversial from the moment *On the Origin of Species* appeared. It encountered criticism from both the religious and the scientific communities. By the end of the century, scientists widely accepted the concept of evolution, but not yet Darwin's mechanism of natural selection. The acceptance of natural selection really dates from the 1920s and 1930s, when Darwin's theory was combined with modern genetics.

The Revolution in Physics

By the late 1870s, discontent arose over the belief of many physical scientists that their mechanistic models, solid atoms, and absolute time and space actually described the real universe.

In 1883, Ernst Mach (1838–1916) published *The Science of Mechanics*, in which he urged that scientists consider their concepts descriptive not of the physical world, but of the sensations experienced by the scientific observer. Scientists could describe only the sensations, not the physical world that underlay those sensations. In line with Mach, the French scientist Henri Poincaré (1854–1912) urged that the theories of scientists be regarded as hypothetical constructs of the human mind rather than as true descriptions of nature. In 1911, Hans Vaihinger (1852–1933) suggested that the concepts of science be considered "as if" descriptions of the physical world. By World War I, few scientists believed they could portray the "truth" about physical reality. Rather, they saw themselves as recording the observations of instruments and as offering useful hypothetical or symbolic models of nature.

X Rays and Radiation Discoveries in the laboratory paralleled the philosophical challenge to earlier physical science. In December 1895, Wilhelm Roentgen (1845–1923) published a paper on his discovery of X rays, a form of energy that penetrated various opaque materials. Major steps in the exploration of radioactivity followed within months of the publication of his paper.

In 1896, Henri Becquerel (1852–1908) discovered that uranium emitted a similar form of energy. The next year, J. J. Thomson (1856–1940), at Cambridge University, formulated the theory of the electron. The interior world of the atom had become a new area for human exploration. In 1902, Ernest Rutherford (1871–1937) explained the cause

Marie Curie (1869–1934) and Pierre Curie (1859–1906) were two of the most important figures in the advance of physics and chemistry. Marie was born in Poland but worked in France for most of her life. She is credited with the discovery of radium, for which she was awarded the Nobel Prize in Chemistry in 1911.

of radiation through the disintegration of the atoms of radioactive materials. Shortly thereafter, he speculated on the immense store of energy present in the atom.

Theories of Quantum Energy, Relativity, and Uncertainty The discovery of radioactivity and discontent with the existing mechanical models led to revolutionary theories in physics. In 1900, Max Planck (1858–1947) pioneered the articulation of the quantum theory of energy, according to which energy is a series of discrete quantities, or packets, rather than a continuous stream. In 1905, Albert Einstein (1879–1955) published his first epochmaking papers on **relativity**, in which he contended that time and space exist not separately, but rather as a combined continuum. Moreover, the measurement of time and space depends on the observer as well as on the entities being measured.

In 1927, Werner Heisenberg (1901–1976) set forth his uncertainty principle, according to which the behavior of subatomic particles is a matter of statistical probability rather than of exactly determinable cause and effect. Much that had seemed unquestionable about the physical universe had now become ambiguous.

Read the Document
Werner Heisenberg, "Uncertainty" (Germany) at **MyHistoryLab.com**

Friedrich Nietzsche and the Revolt against Reason

During the second half of the century, philosophers began to question the adequacy of rational thinking to address the human situation. No writer better exemplified this new attitude than the German philosopher Friedrich Nietzsche (1844–1900). His books remained unpopular until late in his life, when his brilliance had deteriorated into insanity. He was wholly at odds with the values of the age and attacked Christianity, democracy, nationalism, rationality, science, and progress. He sought less to change values than to probe their sources in the human character. He wanted not only to tear away the masks of respectable life, but also to explore how human beings made such masks.

His first important work was *The Birth of Tragedy* (1872), in which he urged that the nonrational aspects of human nature are as important and noble as the rational characteristics. He insisted on the positive function of instinct and ecstasy in human life. To limit human activity to strictly rational behavior was to impoverish human life. In this work, Nietzsche regarded Socrates as one of the major contributors to Western decadence because of the Greek philosopher's appeal for rationality. In Nietzsche's view, the strength for the heroic life and the highest artistic achievement arise from sources beyond rationality.

In later works, such as the prose poem *Thus Spake Zarathustra* (1883), Nietzsche criticized democracy and Christianity. Both, he said, would lead only to the mediocrity of

sheepish masses. He announced the death of God and proclaimed the coming of the *Overman* (Übermensch), who would embody heroism and greatness. The term was frequently interpreted as some mode of superman or superrace, but such was not Nietzsche's intention. He was critical of contemporary racism and anti-Semitism. He sought a return to the heroism that he associated with Greek life in the Homeric age. He thought the values of Christianity and of bourgeois morality prevented humankind from achieving life on a heroic level.

Two of Nietzsche's most profound works are *Beyond Good and Evil* (1886) and *The Genealogy of Morals* (1887). Both are difficult books. Nietzsche sought to discover not what is good and what is evil, but the social and psychological sources of the judgment of good and evil. He declared, "There are no moral phenomena at all, but only a moral interpretation of phenomena."[3] He dared to raise the question of whether morality itself was valuable: "We need a critique of moral values; the value of these values themselves must first be called in question."[4] In Nietzsche's view, morality was a human convention that had no independent existence. For Nietzsche, this discovery liberated human beings to create life-affirming values instead. Christianity, utilitarianism, and middle-class respectability could, in good conscience, be abandoned. Human beings could create a new moral order that would glorify pride, assertiveness, and strength rather than meekness, humility, and weakness.

Read the Document
Friedrich Nietzsche, Beyond Good and Evil at **MyHistoryLab.com**

The Birth of Psychoanalysis

A determination to probe beneath surface or public appearance united the major figures of late nineteenth-century science, art, and philosophy. They sought to discern the undercurrents, tensions, and complexities that lay beneath the calm surfaces of hard atoms, respectable families, rationality, and social relationships. No intellectual development more exemplified this trend than psychoanalysis through the work of Sigmund Freud (1856–1939).

Development of Freud's Early Theories Freud was born into an Austrian Jewish family that settled in Vienna. He planned to become a lawyer but soon moved to the study of physiology and medicine. In 1886, he opened his medical practice in Vienna, where he lived until driven out by the Nazis in 1938. Freud conducted all his research and writing from the base of his medical practice. His earliest medical interests had been psychic disorders, to which he sought to apply the critical method of science. In late 1885, he had studied in Paris with Jean-Martin Charcot (1825–1893), who

---

[3.]*The Basic Writings of Nietzsche*, ed. and trans. by Walter Kaufman (New York: Modern Library, 1968), p. 275.

[4] Ibid., p. 456.

Freud in the United States. In 1909 Freud and his then-devoted disciple Carl Jung visited Clark University in Worcester, Massachusetts, during Freud's only trip to the United States. Here Freud sits on the right holding a cane. Jung is sitting on the far left.

used hypnosis to treat cases of hysteria. In Vienna, he collaborated with another physician, Josef Breuer (1842–1925), and in 1895 they published *Studies in Hysteria*.

In the mid-1890s, Freud abandoned hypnosis and allowed his patients to talk freely and spontaneously about themselves. He found that they associated their particular neurotic symptoms with experiences related to earlier experiences, going back to childhood. He also noted that sexual matters were significant in his patients' problems. For a time, he thought that perhaps sexual incidents during childhood accounted for their illnesses.

◄●►[Read the Document
Richard Freiherr von Krafft-Ebing, Psychopathia Sexualia (Germany), 1886 at **MyHistoryLab.com**

By 1897, however, Freud had rejected this view. In its place he formulated a theory of infantile sexuality, according to which sexual drives and energy already exist in infants and do not simply emerge at puberty. For Freud, human beings are sexual creatures from birth through adulthood. He thus questioned in the most radical manner the concept of childhood innocence. He also portrayed the little acknowledged matter of sexuality as one of the bases of mental order and disorder.

Freud's Concern with Dreams During the same decade, Freud also examined the psychic phenomena of dreams. Romantic writers had taken dreams seriously, but few psychologists had examined them scientifically. Freud believed the seemingly irrational content of dreams must have a reasonable, scientific explanation. His research led him to reconsider the general nature of the human mind. He concluded that dreams allow unconscious wishes, desires, and drives that had been excluded from everyday conscious life to enjoy freer play in the mind. "The dream," he wrote, "is the [disguised] fulfillment of a [suppressed, repressed] wish."[5] During the waking hours, the mind represses or censors certain wishes, which are as important to the individual's psychological makeup as conscious thought is. In fact, Freud argued, unconscious drives and desires contribute to conscious behavior. Freud developed these concepts and related them to his idea of infantile sexuality in his most important book, *The Interpretation of Dreams*, published in 1900.

Freud's Later Thought In later books and essays, Freud developed a new model of the internal organization of the mind as an arena of struggle and conflict among three entities: the id, the superego, and the ego. The **id** consists of amoral, irrational, driving instincts for sexual gratification, aggression, and general physical and sensual pleasure. The **superego** embodies the external moral imperatives and expectations imposed on the personality by society and culture. The **ego** mediates between the impulses of the id and the asceticism of the superego and allows the personality to cope with the inner and outer demands of its existence. Consequently, everyday behavior displays the activity of the personality as its inner drives are partially repressed through the ego's coping with external moral expectations, as interpreted by the superego.

Despite his interest in the nonrational forces in human life and thought, Freud was a son of the Enlightenment. Like the *philosophes*, he was a realist who wanted human beings to live free of fear and illusions by rationally understanding themselves and their world. He saw the personalities of human beings as being determined by finite physical and mental forces in a finite world. He was hostile to religion and spoke of it as an illusion. Freud, like the writers of the eighteenth century, wished to see civilization and humane behavior prevail. More fully than those predecessors, however, he understood the immense sacrifice of instinctual drives required for rational civilized behavior. It has been a grave misreading of Freud to see him as urging humankind to thrust off all repression. He did indeed believe that excessive repression could lead to mental disorder, but he also believed civilization and the survival of humankind required some repression of sexuality and aggression. Freud thought the sacrifice and struggle were worthwhile, but he was pessimistic about the future of civilization in the West.

---

[5] *The Basic Writings of Sigmund Freud*, trans. by A. A. Brill (New York: The Modern Library, 1938), p. 235.

Islam and Late Nineteenth-Century European Thought

The few late nineteenth-century European thinkers who wrote about Islam interpreted it in terms of the growing contemporary scientific outlook, as a historical religious phenomenon without any reference to the supernatural. Islam, like the other great world religions, was seen as a product of a particular culture, and the same kind of analysis was applied to the Qur'an. In the works of scholars such as the influential French writer Ernest Renan (1823–1892), Islam was, like Judaism, a manifestation of the ancient Semitic mentality, which had given rise to a powerful monotheistic vision. Renan, and sociologists such as the German Max Weber, also dismissed Islam as a religion and culture incapable of developing science and closed to new ideas.

Al-Afghani. One of the most influential thinkers in the Muslim world in the nineteenth century, al-Afghani tried to reconcile modern science with Islam.

Renan's views were opposed in a French journal by Jamal al-din al-Afghani (1839–1897), an Egyptian intellectual, who argued that over time Islam, which had arisen 600 years after Christianity, would eventually produce cultures as modern as those in Europe. Al-Afghani was one of the rare Islamic writers who directly contested a European thinker (see Chapter 26).

The European racial and cultural outlooks that denigrated nonwhite peoples and their civilizations were also directed toward the Arab world. European authors who championed white racial superiority looked to India and the Aryan civilization that was supposed to have risen there and later influenced northern European life as the source of Europe's cultural superiority.

Christian missionaries reinforced these anti-Islamic attitudes. They blamed Islam for Arab economic backwardness, for mistreating women, and for condoning slavery. They also often came into conflict with Islamic religious authorities. Because the penalty for abjuring Islam is death, the missionaries made few converts among Muslims. So the missionaries turned their efforts to founding schools and hospitals, hoping these Christian foundations would eventually lead some Muslims to Christianity. Few Muslims converted, but these institutions did educate young Arabs in Western science and medicine, and many of their students became leaders in the Middle East. Eventually, as missionary families came to live for long periods of time among Arabs, they became more sympathetic to Arab political aspirations.

Within the Islamic world, and especially in the decaying Ottoman Empire, as political leaders continued to champion Western scientific education and technology, they confronted a variety of responses from religious thinkers. Some of these thinkers sought to combine modern thought with Islam. For example, the Salafi, or the salafiyya movement, believed there was no inherent contradiction between science and Islam. They believed Muhammad had wisely and properly addressed the issues of his day and that a reformed Islamic faith could do so again. The Arab world should cease direct imitation of the West and modernize itself on the basis of a pure, restored Islamic faith. The Salafi emphasized a rational reading of the Qur'an and saw Ottoman decline as the result of Muslim religious error. This outlook, which had originally sought to reconcile Islam with the modern world, eventually led many Muslims in the twentieth century to oppose Western influence.

Other Islamic religious leaders simply rejected the West and modern thought. They included the Mahdist movement in Sudan, the Sanussiya in Libya, and the Wahhabi movement in the Arabian Peninsula (see Chapter 26). Such religious-based opposition was strongest in those portions of the Middle East where the European presence was least direct, which is to say outside of Morocco, Algeria, Egypt, and Tunisia, which for all intents and purposes were under the control of Western powers by 1900, and Turkey, where Ottoman leaders had long been deeply involved with the West.

Summary

Workers. During the course of the nineteenth century, European workers underwent a process of proletarianization as industrialization spread across the Continent. To protect their interests, European workers joined trade unions and socialist parties, such as the Labour Party in Britain. The Marxist critique of modern capitalism strongly influenced European socialism when the German Social Democratic Party adopted the thought of Karl Marx. In Russia, Lenin founded the Bolsheviks as an elite Marxist party that advocated the overthrow of the tsarist regime through a revolution of workers and peasants.

Women. Nineteenth-century women were divided along class lines. Unlike working-class women, most women of the upper and middle classes adopted a cult of domesticity and did not work outside the home. Most jobs available to women were low paying and insecure. Women of all classes faced social, political, and legal disabilities that were only gradually improved in the late nineteenth and early twentieth centuries. Before World War I, only Norway allowed women to vote, and few women could earn university degrees or enter the professions.

Jewish Emancipation. With the exception of Russia, European countries had abolished their legal restrictions on Jews by the mid-nineteenth century. Jews became more fully integrated into European political and economic life. After 1880, however, anti-Semitism increased as Jews were blamed for economic and social problems.

The United States. By 1914, the United States had become the world's leading industrial power. However, despite the creation of a mass industrial workforce, socialism did not take root in the United States. Under presidents Theodore Roosevelt and Woodrow Wilson, the Progressive movement enacted a number of social and political reforms. The United States also embarked on a more aggressive foreign policy with the Spanish-American War, the acquisition of a colonial empire, interventions in Latin America, and, under Wilson, participation in World War I.

Modern European Thought. In 1850, learned Europeans regarded the physical world as rational, mechanical, and dependable. By the first decades of the twentieth century philosophers, scientists, psychologists, and artists began to portray physical reality, human nature, and society in ways that seem familiar to us today. Physicists probed the mysteries of the atom. The theories of evolutionary biology contended that human nature is part of the order of nature and does not stand apart from nature. Traditional morality and the primacy of reason were challenged by Nietzsche and Freud. Within the Islamic world, modern European thought produced a variety of often-conflicting responses.

Key Terms

Bolsheviks (p. 749)

Duma (p. 751)

ego (p. 762)

Fabians (p. 747)

id (p. 762)

Marxism (p. 745)

Mensheviks (p. 749)

natural selection (p. 759)

pogroms (p. 742)

proletarianization (p. 733)

relativity (p. 761)

revisionism (p. 747)

soviets (p. 751)

suffragettes (p. 741)

superego (p. 762)

Review Questions

1. What were the chief factors accounting for the proletarianization of the European labor force? How much of the change in the situation of workers was a result of technology and how much of the change in their organization?

2. How would you describe living conditions in European cities during the late nineteenth century? What factors contributed to those conditions? How did urban reform emerge?

3. How did the class position of a European woman determine much of her experience? How did industrialization change the social experience of working-class women? What social factors limited the opportunities of women regardless of their class? Why did women grow discontented with their lot? What factors led to change? To what extent had they improved their position by 1914? Was the emancipation of women inevitable? How did women approach their situation differently from country to country?

4. What were the major characteristics of Jewish emancipation in the nineteenth century? How did late-century economic developments contribute to increasing prejudice against Jews?

5. How did the ideas of Karl Marx come to dominate so much late nineteenth-century European socialism?

6. What was the status of the working-class groups in the United States and Europe in 1860? What improvements if any had been achieved by 1914?

7. What caused the emergence of trade unions and organized mass political parties in Europe?

8. How did the American Progressives, as reformers, differ from the various European Socialists? Why were the debates of "opportunism" and "revisionism" important to the socialist parties? Why were there so many disputes among Socialists?

9. Assess the value of industrialism for Russia. Were the tsars wise in attempting to modernize their country, or would they have been better off leaving it as it was? How did Lenin's view of socialism differ from that of Socialists in western Europe? Why did socialism not emerge as a major political force in the United States?

10. What were the major changes in science in the late nineteenth century? How did both Darwin and Einstein challenge assumptions of earlier science? How may both Nietzsche and Freud be seen to challenge confidence in human rationality?

11. What were the chief characteristics of Western attitudes toward Islam in the nineteenth century? How did Islamic thinkers respond to modern Western thought?

Note: To learn more about the topics in this chapter, please turn to the Suggested Readings at the end of the book. For additional sources related to this chapter please see MyHistoryLab.com.

myhistorylab Connections

Reinforce what you learned in this chapter by studying the many documents, images, maps, review tools, and videos available at **www.myhistorylab.com**.

Read and Review

✓•─Study and Review **Chapter 24**

•─Read the Document *Industrial Society and Factory Conditions (early 1800s), p. 735*
Ellen Key, from The Century of the Child, p. 738
John Stuart Mill on Enfranchisement of Women (1869), p. 741
The Communist Manifesto, Karl Marx (1848), p. 744
Socialism, p. 748
The Sadler Report: Child Labor in the United Kingdom, 1832, p. 756
Speech Before Congress, p. 759
On Darwin's 1860s, p. 760
Werner Heisenberg, "Uncertainty" (Germany), p. 761
Friedrich Nietzsche, Beyond Good and Evil, p. 761
Richard Freiherr von Krafft-Ebing, Psychopathia Sexualia (Germany), 1886, p. 762

((•─Hear the Audio *Industrial Revolution, p. 733*
Reform of Thought, p. 760

✓•─Study and Review *Industrial Side Effects, p. 735*

Research and Explore

●─See the Map *The Growth of Russia to 1914, p. 749*

((•─Hear the Audio

Hear the audio file for Chapter 24 at
www.myhistorylab.com.

25 Latin America from Independence to the 1940s

Mexico City. Juan O'Gorman (1905–1982) was best known as an architect whose most famous work is the library at the Universidad Nacional Autónoma de México. In 1932, he took the helm of Mexico City's department of building and construction. His interests in architecture, art (he became a renowned muralist), and the development of Mexico City are all on display in his 1949 painting, "La Ciudad de Mexico." The painting, complete with angels heralding "Viva Mexico," shows the city and the country as a work in progress.

- Independence without Revolution
- Economy of Dependence
- Search for Political Stability
- Three National Histories

BY THE MID-1820S, LATIN AMERICANS HAD DRIVEN out their colonial rulers and broken the colonial trade monopolies. Though rich in natural resources, the region did not achieve widespread prosperity and long-lasting political stability after independence. The wars of independence had not been popular grass-roots movements. They had originated with the creole elite, who were seeking to resist the imposition of European liberalism by Napoleon or, later, the Spanish liberals. In effect, the wars had been fought to break the colonial trade monopolies and to preserve the existing social structure. The military leaders of the wars held much of the political power in the new nations the wars had created.

The wars also destroyed much of the economic infrastructure of the region. Mines had been flooded, livestock depleted, and the workforce disrupted. Whereas previously colonial Latin America had been dependent on Spain for its exports and financial credits, it now became dependent on Great Britain and later on the United States.

Postindependence Latin America had much in common with other regions of the world—Africa and Asia, for example—during the nineteenth and early twentieth centuries. In all three regions, particular nations or areas would specialize in a particular niche in the increasingly integrated world economy. In Asia and Africa vast plantations produced products such as rubber; in Latin America plantations might produce sugar or coffee. In all three regions huge mining industries extracted resources such as copper, phosphates, gold, and diamonds. Virtually all such enterprises were dominated by Europeans or North Americans. Filling a particular niche by supplying a particular raw product might bring initial prosperity but provided too narrow an economic base for sustained economic well-being. In contrast, the economic advance of the United States and Europe was largely due to their ability to exploit niche economies around the globe. ■

Independence Without Revolution

Immediate Consequences of Latin American Independence

By the late 1820s the wars of independence left Latin America liberated from direct European control, but economically exhausted and politically unstable (see Map 25–1 on page 770.). Only Brazil tended to prosper immediately after independence. In contrast, the new republics of the former Spanish Empire felt themselves weak and vulnerable. Because the wars of independence had been largely civil wars, the new governments knew that many of their populations might welcome their collapse. Economic life on the continent contracted, and in 1830 overall production was lower than it had been in 1800. Difficult terrain over vast distances made interregional trade complicated, and few institutions fostered it. The old patterns of overseas trade had been disrupted. There was an absence of domestic funds for investment. Many wealthy *peninsulares* returned to Spain or departed for Spanish-governed Cuba. Consequently, Latin American governments and businesses looked to Britain for protection, markets, and capital investment.

((••┤**Hear** the **Audio**
Latin America
at **MyHistoryLab.com**

Independence itself also created several new sources of discontent. There was much disagreement about the character of the future government, even among those who had most wanted to oust the Spanish. Certain institutions, such as the Roman Catholic Church, that had enjoyed a privileged status in the colonial period sought to maintain those privileges under new and often unfriendly governments. Native American communities, which had also been somewhat protected by paternalistic colonial policies, found themselves subject to new exploitation once they were made equal citizens under the law. Major disagreements arose between the creole elites of different regions of the new nations. The agricultural hinterlands resented the predominance of the port cities, whose merchants set the terms of trade. Investors or merchants from one Latin American nation found themselves in conflict with those of others over transport tariffs on rivers or over mining regulations. Civilians often became rivals of the military for political authority.

Absence of Social Change

Yet no matter what the actual or potential conflict among various groups in the literate political and economic elites might be, they all opposed substantial social reform. The creole victors in the wars of independence granted equal rights to all persons, and except for Brazil, the independent states had abolished slavery by 1855. However, the right to vote depended on a property qualification, and peasants remained dependent on and often subservient to their landlords. The racial codes of the colonial empires disappeared, but not the racial prejudice. Although **mestizos**, **mulattos**, and even Indians who achieved economic success were assimilated into the higher ranks of the social structure, persons of white or nearly white complexion tended to constitute the elite of Latin America. The creole elite generally discriminated against the peoples of color in their midst. Most important, no major changes in landholding accompanied the wars of independence; the ruling classes of all the newly independent nations protected the interests of landholders.

Except for Mexico in 1910, no Latin American nation, from the wars of independence until the 1950s, experienced a fundamental revolution that overthrew the social and economic structures dating from the colonial period. The absence of such social revolution, which would necessarily have involved changes in landholding, is perhaps the single most important factor in Latin American history during the first century of independence. The rise and fall of political regimes represented quarrels among the elites and did not substantially change the structures or expectations of everyday life for most of the population. Throughout the social structure there was no mutually shared trust or allegiance to the political system.

Control of the Land

Most Latin Americans during the nineteenth century lived in the countryside. Agriculture continued to be dominated by large *haciendas*, or plantations. The landowners virtually ruled these estates as small domains. They were nearly a law unto themselves. The *latifundia* (the large rural estates)

Latin American History

Latin America

Since the early nineteenth century, Spanish- and Portuguese-speaking America stretching from the Rio Grande to Cape Horn has posed a paradox. Languages, religion, economic ties, and many political institutions render the area part of the Western world. Yet the economics, politics, and social life of Latin America have developed differently from other parts of the West. Exceedingly rich in natural resources, possessing gold, silver, nitrates, and oil, the region has been plagued with extreme poverty. As other Western nations have moved toward liberal democracy and social equality, the states of Latin America have had millions of citizens living in situations of marked inequality and social dependence. For almost two centuries, authoritarian regimes, uncertain democracy, and a general tendency toward instability have characterized Latin American political life.

Latin America shares many cultural features with Europe and North America. Its languages are primarily European, although much of its population speaks Native American languages. Its primary religion is Roman Catholicism. Its nations have often adopted the constitutional traditions of Europe and the United States. Many of its elite have studied abroad. Despite these important similarities, the economic and political development of Latin America has been different from that of much of Europe or the United States.

Three major explanations have been set forth to account for these difficulties that have led to so much tragedy and human suffering.

The first and most widely accepted view contends that after the wars of independence the new states of Latin America remained economically and culturally dependent on Europe and, later, the United States. In effect, proponents of this view—called **dependency theory**—argue that the colonial framework was never abolished. Under Spanish and Portuguese rule, Latin America's wealth was extracted and exported for the benefit of those powers. After independence, the creole elite turned toward foreign investors, first British and then American, to finance economic development and to provide the technology for mining, transport, and industry. As a result, Latin America again became dependent on wealthy foreign powers for investment and for markets. These foreign powers, interested in strong governments that

actually grew larger during the nineteenth century. Confiscated church lands and conquered Indian territories augmented existing estates or led to the establishment of new ones. These estates might include tens of thousands of acres and yet might be attended by a relatively sparse workforce. Work was labor intensive because little machinery was available; virtually no machinery was manufactured in Latin America. Herding and stockraising produced salted meat, leather, tallow, and wool for the export market. For some products—salted meats, for example—there was a limited manufacturing stage in Latin America. Other agricultural exports included cereal crops, tobacco, sugar, coffee, and cacao.

Landowners constituted a society unto themselves. Their families intermarried. They sometimes formed friendships or family alliances with members of the wealthy urban classes who were involved in export commerce or the law. Younger sons might enter the army or the church. The landowners served in the various postindependence national parliaments or congresses. Their wealth, literacy, and social connections made them the rulers of the countryside, and the army would protect them from any social uprising.

The landowners lived well and comfortably, though often on isolated estates. Most of the rural workforce was socially and economically dependent on them. In Brazil slavery persisted until 1888. In other rural areas many people lived as virtual slaves. **Debt peonage** was widespread and often tied a peasant to the land much as a European serf had been during the Middle Ages. A peon would become indebted to his landlord and could never repay the debt. Later in the nineteenth century the new lands that were opened were generally organized as large holdings with tenants rather than as small landholdings with independent farmers. This was markedly different from both the United States and Canada. Poor roads and limited railways made internal travel difficult and kept many people on the land. Little effort was made to provide even a primary education, leaving millions of Latin American peasants ignorant, lacking any significant technological skills, and incapable of improving their condition or of protesting or escaping their bondage to the land and its owners.

The second half of the nineteenth century witnessed a remarkable growth in Latin American urban life (see Figure 25–1). There took place some movement from the countryside to would protect their interests, threw their support behind dictators whose policies impoverished their people and suppressed democratic dissent.

A second explanation emphasizes the Iberian heritage. Its advocates contend that Latin America should be viewed as a region on the periphery of the Western world in the same manner that Spain, Portugal, and Italy lie on the Mediterranean periphery of Europe. All of these Latin nations, dominated by Roman Catholicism, have had similar unstable and often authoritarian governments. They have frequently tended toward some version of dictatorship, uneven development, anticlericalism, and social cleavage between urban and rural areas and between wealthy middle-class or landed elites and poor peasant populations. Viewed in this Iberian-Mediterranean context, Latin America seems less puzzling than when it is viewed in the context of northern Europe.

A third explanation emphasizes conscious political, economic, and cultural decisions the Latin American **creole** elite took after independence. This explanation contends that the elite, including the army officers who won the wars, sought to enrich themselves and to maintain their positions at the cost of all other segments of the population, who in many of these countries differed ethnically and racially from the elite. These officers, landowners, and urban middle-class leaders aligned their national economies with the industrializing regions of Europe and North America, with which they joined culturally as well, thus differentiating themselves from the lower classes and indigenous peoples and culture. They also

adopted European liberal political and economic ideologies to justify unlimited exploitation of economic resources on the basis of individualist enterprise. They then used the wealth generated by this exploitation to maintain their power. They embraced European concepts of progress to dismiss the legitimacy of the culture and communal values of the Indians or the peasants.

In addition to these views, it helps to consider Latin America within a global perspective. Beginning in the nineteenth century much of the region, like much of Asia and Africa, was drawn into an integrated worldwide economic system dominated by Europe and North America. Many nations in Latin America and elsewhere, having developed narrow economies based on the export of one or a few raw materials or semifinished products, became vulnerable to fluctuations in worldwide demand for these products and to political and economic interference from Europe and North America.

Focus Questions

■ What is dependency theory? How can it help to understand the history of Latin America since independence?

■ Is Latin America's Iberian heritage a likely explanation of why Latin America has developed along such different lines from those of North America?

■ What role did the creole elite play in the economic and political instability that has characterized Latin America in the modern era?

the city and an influx of European immigrants as well as some from Asia. The creole elite favored European immigration, which increased the size of the white population; Asian immigration was a source of inexpensive labor. Throughout this period there arose a political and social trade-off between the urban and rural elites. Each more or

	1870	1914
Rio de Janiero	275,000	1,000,000
Sao Paulo	31,000	450,000
Buenos Aires	178,000	1,200,000
Lima	90,000	200,000
Guayaquil, Ecuador	12,000	75,000
Mexico City	200,000	700,000

Figure 25–1 Population of Latin American Cities, 1870–1914
Source: United Nations.

less permitted the other to pursue its economic self-interest, to profit from the commodity export economy through commerce or production, and to repress any discontent. Nonetheless, the growth of the urban centers shifted political influence from the countryside to the cities and gave rise to an urban working class and all the social discontents associated with vast numbers of relatively poor people working in difficult situations. Urban growth in Latin America created social and political difficulties not unlike those that arose in Europe and the United States at about the same time.

Submissive Political Philosophies

The political philosophies embraced by the educated and propertied creole elites also discouraged any real challenge to the social order. The political ideas associated with European liberalism, which flourished in Latin America immediately after independence, supported republican government but also limited the franchise to property holders. Thus in Latin America, as in Europe, liberalism protected property and tended to ignore the social problems of the poor and

Map Exploration

To explore this map further, go to **http://www.myhistorylab.com**

Map 25–1. Latin America in 1830. By 1830 most of Latin America had been liberated from Europe. This map shows the initial borders of the states of the region with the dates of their independence. The United Provinces of La Plata formed the nucleus of what later become Argentina.

Peonage. This 1845 lithograph by Carlos Morel (1813–1894) shows a night watch by a group of peons or laborers in the Pampas, Argentina. The great landowners of Latin America ruled their huge estates as small domains. *Picture Desk, Inc./Kobal Collection.*

propertyless. In addition, the creole elite frequently exhibited racial prejudice toward the mulatto, mestizo, and Indian populations.

Economic liberalism and the need for British investment led to the championing of free trade. During the decades immediately after independence, Latin America actually exported less than it had under colonial rule. The region achieved a trade balance by exporting precious metals. Because these metals often came from stocks mined years earlier, this in effect amounted to a flight of capital. The general economic view was that Latin America would produce raw materials for export in exchange for manufactured goods imported from Europe, and especially from Britain.

For most of the nineteenth century the landed sector of the economy dominated because cheap imports from abroad and a shortage of local capital discouraged indigenous attempts at industrialism. Latin American liberals championed the extension of great landed estates and all the forms of social dependence associated with them. The produce of the new land could contribute raw materials or lightly processed goods for export to pay for the import of finished goods. Liberals thus favored confiscating land owned by the church and the Indian communities because these groups did not exploit their lands in a progressive manner, according to the liberals.

During the second half of the century, **positivism**—the political ideas stemming from the French positivist philosopher Auguste Comte (1798–1857)—swept across Latin America. Comte and his followers had advocated the cult of science and technological progress. This highly undemocratic outlook suggested that either technocrats or dictatorial governments could best achieve modernization. It was especially popular among military officers and influenced the ongoing Latin American struggle between civilian and military elites. The great slogan of Latin American positivism, emblazoned on the flag of the Brazilian republic, was "Order and Progress." Social or political groups that created disorder or challenged the existing social order were by definition unprogressive.

Toward the close of the century the military forces in various countries—following the model of European armies, especially Germany's—became more professionalized. Their new training often made the officer corps the most important educated elite in a country. Their education and attachment to the armies they served gave them considerable influence, generally of a conservative character.

Finally, the late nineteenth-century European theories of "scientific" racism were used to preserve the Latin American social status quo and the dominance of those of white or more nearly white complexions. Racial theory could attribute the economic backwardness of the region to its vast nonwhite or mixed-blood population. This explanation, of course, shifted responsibility for Latin America's economic difficulties away from the mostly white governing elites toward Indians, blacks, mestizos, and mulattos, who had long been exploited or repressed. (See Document, "A Peruvian Commentator Decries Racial Thinking" on page 772.)

This conservative intellectual heritage continued to affect twentieth-century political thought. First, it can be seen in the ongoing tendency of military groups in Latin America to view themselves as the guarantors of order. These groups were ready to intervene in political affairs and seize control from civilians to protect the status quo or to thwart social change. Second, it can be seen in the way the political elites of Latin America naturally and actively opposed communism after the Russian Revolution. Although many Latin American nations had small organized communist parties, governments used the fear of communism to resist virtually all political movements—communist or not—that advocated social reform or questioned property arrangements. From the 1920s onward, in Latin America as in Europe, the fear of communism brought support to conservative governments, whether civilian or military. Communism would become an

Document

A Peruvian Commentator Decries Racial Thinking

Manuel González Prada (1848–1918) was a Peruvian social and political critic. He had spent much time in France, where he became acquainted with Europe's advanced scientific thought and contemporary theories of race. (See Chapters 23 and 24.) He personally embraced much European idealism and strongly opposed social Darwinism and racism. In an essay published in 1904, entitled "Our Indians," Prada decried the treatment of the Native American Indians in Peru by the republican government and the racial ideas that supported such treatment. As noted in the first paragraph, he saw the case of Peruvian Indians as only one among many contemporary examples of peoples suffering serious discrimination and maltreatment on the basis of race. He contends that the republic of Peru, because of racial theory and the cultural assumptions of white superiority, put modern Peruvian Indians in a situation worse than their Inca forebears had experienced as a result of the Spanish Empire's various forced labor practices. The racial outlook that Prada condemns was widespread across Latin America and was one of several factors that held back Lain America's social and political progress.

■ *How does Prada present the situation of Peruvian Indians as one of numerous cases of the impact of racial thinking globally? How does he connect the degradation of Peruvian Indians with greed? Why does he see the treatment of Peruvian Indians as contradicting republican political ideals?*

How convenient an invention ethnology is in the hands of some men! If one grants the division of humanity into superior and inferior races and recognizes the superiority of the whites and their consequent right to govern the planet, nothing is more natural than the suppression of the Negro in Africa, the redskin in the United States, the Tagalog in the Philippines, or the Indian in Peru. . . .

[A]s a general rule, the dominant [group in Peru] approach the Indian only to deceive him, oppress him or corrupt him. And we should remember that not only the national half-caste acts with inhumanity and bad faith. When Europeans become wool traders, mine owners, or hacienda proprietors, they show themselves fine exactors, extortionists, rivaling the old *encomenderos* and the present day *hacendados*. The white skinned animal, wherever he is born, is afflicted with the disease of gold. In the final analysis he yields to the instinct of rapacity. . . . .

Does the Indian suffer less under the republic than under Spanish rule? While neither *corregimientos* nor *encomiendas* exist, forced labor and its recruitment remain. What we make him suffer is enough to call down upon us the execration of humanity. We hold him in ignorance and servitude, we debate him in the garrisons, we brutalize him with alcohol, we set him to destroying himself in civil war, and from time to time we organize hunting parties and massacres. . .

It is an unwritten axiom that the Indian has no rights, only obligations. In his case a personal complaint is considered insubordination, a collective claim a plot of rebellion. The Spanish royalists killed the Indian when he tried to escape the yoke of his conquerors; we republicans exterminate him when he protests against onerous taxes or tires of enduring in silence the inequities of some satrap.

Our form of government is in essence a great lie, because a state in which two or three million individuals live outside the law does not deserve to be called a democratic republic. . . .

The political and social organization of the ancient Inca empire astonishes revolutionary reformers today. . . . Morally speaking, the native of the republic is inferior to the native encountered by the conquerors; but moral depression because of political servitude is not the same as an absolute incapacity by organic constitution to achieve civilization.

Source: Manuel González Prada, from *Horas de lucha* (first published 1908) as quoted in Harold Eugene Davis, *Latin American Social Thought: The History of Its Development Since Independence, with Selected Readings* (Washington, DC: University Press of Washington D C, 1961), pp. 202, 203, 205.

even more powerful issue throughout the region after the successful Cuban Revolution of 1959 installed an actual Soviet-dominated communist state in Latin America.

Economy of Dependence

The wars of independence destroyed the Spanish and Portuguese colonial trade monopolies. Where previously only a few dozen ships called annually at any port, hundreds laden with goods from all over the world could now drop anchor. Consequently, Latin America had many new trading partners. Trade was free and the nations were politically independent, but the character of the demand for Latin American commodities by other nations continued to shape economic life in the most fundamental manner.

One of the chief reasons for this dependence on foreign trading partners was the absence of large internal markets. Had such markets existed during the colonial period itself, the newly independent nations might have been able to trade with each other rather than primarily with nations outside the region. Trade after independence flowed in the same direction that trade had flowed before independence because Europe remained the source of imports of finished goods. Furthermore, then as now, geographical barriers hindered internal trade. The jungles of the Amazon and the Andes Mountains prevented any easy east–west trade. No road systems allowed goods to travel between countries or even easily within them, and there was little domestic investment in transport. European and American investments in railways during the nineteenth century generally facilitated exports rather than internal trade.

New Exploitation of Resources

As previously noted, the wars of independence themselves sharply disrupted the Latin American economy. In both Mexico and Peru, mines were flooded; machinery fell in disrepair; labor became dispersed. Agricultural production was also disrupted. Between 1825 and 1850 the new nations attempted to set their economic houses in order, but with mixed results. Capital financing to restore the mining industry and establish new industries was totally inadequate. Virtually no domestic industries existed to manufacture heavy equipment or build ships. Both to restore old industries, such as mining, and to have access to modern transport, such as steamships and railroads, Latin Americans had to turn to Europe and North America. For many decades Britain exercised the predominant economic influence over Latin America. Britain had sought to break the old colonial monopoly. Once it was gone, the British rapidly established their own economic dominance. This desire to pour manu-

Brazilian Coffee being loaded onto a British ship. Most Latin American countries developed an export economy based on the exchange of agricultural products, raw materials, and semifinished goods for finished goods and services from abroad. Until recently, the coffee industry dominated both the political and economic life of Brazil.

factured goods into Latin America also led Britain and other nations to discourage the development of manufacturing industries there. Foreign investment did help revive the mining industry in Mexico, Peru, and Chile, but mining produces raw materials, not manufactured goods.

To pay for imports and foreign services, Latin American nations turned to the production of agricultural commodities for which there was great European demand. This shift meant that the rural areas of Latin America and the commercial centers serving agriculture became politically and economically more important than many of the old colonial urban centers. The production of wheat, beef, hides, hemp, coffee, cocoa, and other foodstuffs for the export market also raised the value of land and led governments to expand into previously unsettled territory and to confiscate the lands of the church. Because so much land was available, agricultural production was increased by extending areas of cultivation rather than by finding more efficient ways to farm areas already under cultivation. So much wealth could be accumulated through land speculation and land development that little incentive existed for alternative investments in manufacturing. It would also have been difficult, if not impossible, for new Latin American industries to compete with the cheap goods imported from more established industrial economies abroad.

After 1850 the Latin American republics became, relatively speaking, more prosperous. Chile exported copper and nitrates as well as wheat. Peru exported guano to be used as fertilizer. Coffee was becoming king in Venezuela, Brazil, Colombia, and Central America. Sugar continued to be produced in the West Indies as well as in Cuba, which remained under Spanish control. Argentina supplied hides and tallow. However, this limited prosperity and recovery were based on the export of agricultural commodities, extracted minerals, or nonreplenishable resources, such as guano, and the importation of finished goods from abroad.

Nevertheless, the period from approximately 1870 through 1930 came to be seen as a kind of golden age for the Latin American economy. There was more prosperity than ever before, especially in Chile, Argentina, Brazil, and Mexico. The economies of the Latin American nations grew because industrial production in Europe and the United States created a demand for three broad varieties of exports. First were foodstuffs raised in Latin America that were more or less like those that could be raised in Europe, chiefly wheat and beef products, for which Argentina became the great exporter. Second were distinctly tropical products, such as bananas, sugar, and coffee. Third were natural resources, including metals, of which copper was the most important; minerals, such as nitrates; and later, oil.

Both the trading patterns for these goods and the internal improvements in Latin American production deeply and inextricably linked the economy of the region to Europe and, after 1900, to the United States. The region could not control its own economic destiny. Europeans and North Americans provided capital and the technological and managerial skills to build bridges, roads, railroads, steam lines, and new mines. Most of the transport system was constructed to service the existing export economy rather than to foster the development of alternative forms of domestic economic development. Furthermore, whenever the economy of Europe or the United States floundered, Latin America was hurt. A decline in the prices of commodities and raw materials could, of course, force Latin America to reduce the amount of goods it imported, harming its European and North American trading partners. But the major economic difficulties almost always struck Latin America first and lasted there longest.

Banana Republic. For most of the twentieth century the United Fruit Company, an American conglomerate, exerted tremendous economic influence throughout Central America, with extensive coffee and banana plantations throughout the region. The company also wielded significant political power, especially in Guatemala, where workers in this photograph are harvesting bananas.

Increased Foreign Ownership and Influence

During the late nineteenth century the relative prosperity of the export sector increased the degree of economic dependence. The growing European demand generated by spreading industrialism gave Latin Americans a false sense of the long-term security of their export markets. The vast profits to be made through mining and agricultural exports discouraged investment in local industry, except as it served the export economy. Land still remained the most favored form of domestic investment. Foreigners saw no reason to capitalize local industry that might replace goods being imported. By late in the century the wealthy classes in Latin America had, in effect, lost control and even ownership of some of the most valuable sectors of their economy. For example, in 1901 British and other foreign investors owned approximately 80 percent of the Chilean nitrate industry. Foreigners also owned and operated most of the steamship lines and railroads.

The European and American economic penetration of Latin America was more subtle than that experienced by India or China, but it was no less real. Foreign ownership was not the only indication of economic dependence. Foreign powers used their political and military influence to protect their economic interests. Britain was the dominant power until the turn of the century. Its diplomats and military and naval officers were frequently involved directly or indirectly in the domestic political affairs of the Latin American nations. From the Spanish American War of 1898 onward, the United States began to exercise more direct influence in the region. In 1903, to facilitate its plans to build a canal across the Isthmus of Panama, the United States participated in the rebellion that allowed Panama to separate from Colombia. There were numerous other instances of U.S. military intervention in the Caribbean and in Central America. By the 1920s U.S. investments had become dominant as a result of two decades of "Dollar Diplomacy" exercised through economic influence and intervention. During that decade, largely as a result of economic dislocations arising from World War I, the United States generally replaced Great Britain as the dominant trading partner of Latin American nations. The role of the United States remains controversial, but from a structural standpoint it was just one more example of a dominant foreign power treating Latin America as a junior and dependent economic partner.

The United States' interventions were one cost to Latin America of being a dependent economy. More significant costs arose from fundamental shifts in world trade that were brought on by World War I and continued through the 1920s. First, the overall amount of trade carried on by European countries decreased, particularly during the war, when traditional trading partners divided into two warring camps. Second, during the 1920s world prices of agricultural commodities dropped steadily. Latin American nations had to produce more goods to pay for their imports, and no easy or rapid adjustment was possible. Third, various synthetic products manufactured in Europe or North America replaced the natural products long supplied by Latin American producers. Most important among these products were synthetic nitrates. Finally, petroleum began to replace other natural products as an absolute percentage of world trade. This shift meant that petroleum-exporting countries, such as Mexico, gained a greater share of export income.

Economic Crises and New Directions

The Great Depression turned the difficult economic conditions of the 1920s into a genuine crisis. Commodity prices virtually collapsed. The economic decline in Europe and the United States lessened the demand for Latin American products. The republics of Latin America could not repay their debts to foreign banks, and a number of them suspended interest payments. Those decisions in turn worsened the economic crisis in the more developed creditor nations. The depression led eventually to the beginning of a new economic era in Latin America. The new era, which really began after the conclusion of World War II, was marked by strong economic nationalism and a determination to create sectors of the various national economies that were not wholly dependent on events and wealth outside Latin America. These various drives toward economic independence have had mixed success, but they date only from the turmoil of the Depression.

Where did industrialism fit into this general picture of a dependent economy, or what is sometimes termed a **neocolonial economy**? The brief answer is, almost always, on the periphery of the export sector. Until the 1940s major industrialization did not occur in Latin America. There were, however, significant earlier developments. Before World War I light manufacturing was done in connection with preparing exports, such as beef processing in Argentina. Light-manufactured goods such as textiles were also produced. With the Depression, however, it became necessary to substitute domestically manufactured goods for those traditionally imported from abroad. Various nations pursued different policies of what was called **import substitution**, but all of these policies were undertaken because of the collapse of the export economy rather than because of any independent decision to industrialize. In that regard, the effort to industrialize was itself a result of being dependent.

By the mid-1940s there were three major varieties of manufacturing in Latin America. First, there were industries that, as in the past, transformed raw materials for export. They included sugar and other food processing, tin and copper mining, and petroleum refining. Second, there were industries addressing local demands, such as power plants, textiles, foundries, machine shops, and food companies. Third, there were industries depending generally on the transformation of imported materials. These industries were basically assembly plants whose owners could take advantage of inexpensive labor. None of this manufacturing was particularly sophisticated, and none of it involved heavy industry. Not until the 1950s would significant steel production, for example, occur in the region.

Search for Political Stability

The new states of independent Latin America, unlike the British colonies of North America, had little or no experience in self-government. The Spanish Empire had been ruled directly by the monarchy and by Spanish-born royal bureaucrats. Spain had persistently discriminated against the creole elite as well as against mulattos, mestizos, and Indians. This monarchical or paternalistic heritage survived in two forms. First, many traditionalists and conservatives favored the establishment of monarchies in Latin America, including José de San Martín (1778–1850). Monarchy was briefly established in Mexico. In Brazil, an emperor from the Portuguese royal family governed until 1889.

The second heritage of the colonial monarchy was the proclivity of the Latin American political elites to tolerate or actively to support strong executives. Few of the early republic constitutions endured or established a stable political life. They were frequently suspended or rewritten, so that a strong leader could consolidate his own power. Such figures, who appeared throughout Latin America during the nineteenth century, were called **caudillos**. They usually came from the army officer corps or enjoyed strong ties to the army. Whatever constitutional justification they provided for themselves, the real basis of their rule was force and repression. *Caudillos* might support conservative causes, such as protection of the church or strong central government, or they might pursue liberal policies, such as the confiscation of church land, the extension of landed estates, and the development of education.

These strongmen also encountered little opposition because of their repressive policies. Later in the century the new relative prosperity of expanding economies quieted potential discontent. The dictators became more skilled at both repression and patronage. The political and social elites also rallied to their support when, around the turn of the century, the young labor movement called strikes.

Even when *caudillos* were forced from office and parliamentary government was more or less restored, the regimes that replaced them were neither genuinely liberal nor democratic. Parliamentary governments usually ruled by courtesy of the military and in the economic interest of the existing elites. No matter who ruled, the life of the overwhelming mass of the population changed little. Except for the Mexican Revolution of 1910, Latin American politics was run by and for the elite.

Three National Histories

Three Latin American nations possess over 50 percent of the land, people, and wealth of the region. They are Argentina, Mexico, and Brazil. Their national histories illustrate the more general themes of Latin American history.

Argentina

Argentine history from independence to World War II can be divided into three general eras. From the rebellion against Spain in 1810 until midcentury, the question of which region of the nation would dominate political and economic life was foremost. From 1853 until 1916 Argentina experienced extraordinary economic expansion and large-scale immigration from Europe, which transformed its society and its position in the world. From 1916 to 1943 Argentines failed to establish a democratic state and struggled with the ramifications of an economy they did not really control.

Buenos Aires versus the Provinces In 1810 the junta in Buenos Aires had overturned Spanish government in the viceroyalty of Río de la Plata. However, the other regions of the viceroyalty refused to accept the leadership of the province and city of Buenos Aires. Paraguay, Uruguay, and Upper Peru (Bolivia) went their separate ways. Conflicts between Buenos Aires and the remaining provinces dominated the first seventy

years of Argentine history. It was the story of *porteños*, as the inhabitants of Buenos Aires were called, versus provincials. Eventually Buenos Aires established its primacy because of its capacity to dominate trade on the Río de la Plata and its control of the international customhouse, which assured revenue.

Between 1821 and 1827 Bernardino Rivadavia (1780–1845) worked to create a liberal political state but could not overcome the centrifugal forces of regionalism. His major accomplishment was a commercial treaty in 1823 that established Great Britain as a dominant trading partner. Thus began a deep intermeshing of trade and finance between the two nations that would continue for over a century. After Rivadavia's resignation in 1827 came the classical period of *caudillo* rule in Argentina. The strongman of the province of Buenos Aires was Juan Manuel de Rosas (1793–1877). In 1831 he negotiated the Pact of the Littoral, whereby Buenos Aires was put in charge of foreign relations, trade, and the customhouse, while the other provinces were left to run their own internal affairs. Within Buenos Aires, Rosas set up what amounted to dictatorial rule. He tolerated no dissent, no civil liberties, and no political power distinct from his own. One of his devices was the secret *Mazorca* (ear of corn) association, which terrorized his opponents. His major policies were expansion of trade and agriculture,

Juan Manuel de Rosas (1793–1877), a *caudillo* of Buenos Aires from 1827 to 1852. De Rosas was the archetypal *caudillo*, waging relentless war on the natives of Patagonia.

Read the **Document**
Domingo F. Sarmiento, "Civilization and Barbarism," 1845
at **MyHistoryLab.com**

suppression of the Indians, and nationalism. In Argentine history Rosas symbolized government by a single strong figure.

Expansion and Growth of the Republic Rosas's success in strengthening Buenos Aires bred resentment in other provinces. In 1852 Justo José de Urquiza (1800–1870), the *caudillo* of the state of Entre Rios, overthrew Rosas. The next year a federal constitution was promulgated for the Argentine Republic. Buenos Aires remained aloof until the republic conquered the province in 1859. Disputes continued and in 1880 the city of Buenos Aires was made a distinct federal province, separate from its rich hinterland. Provincials had hoped that this arrangement would lessen the influence of the city; however, the economic prosperity of the end of the century simply gave the capital new prominence.

The Argentine economy was overwhelmingly agricultural, the chief exports at midcentury being animal products. Internal transportation was poor, and the country was sparsely populated. Technological advances changed this situation during the last quarter of the century. In 1876 the first refrigerator ship, *La Frigiorique*, steamed into Buenos Aires. Henceforth, it would be possible to transport large quantities of Argentine beef to Europe. Furthermore, at about the same time it became clear that wheat farming could be extended throughout the pampas. In 1879 and 1880 a government army under General (and later President) Julio Roca (president 1880–1886, 1898–1904) carried out a major campaign against the Indian population known as the *Conquest of the Desert*. The British soon began to construct and manage railways to carry wheat from the interior to the coast, where it would be loaded on British and other foreign steamships. Government policy made the purchase of land by wealthy Argentines simple and cheap. The owners, in turn, rented the land to tenants. The predominance of both large landowners and foreign business interests thus continued throughout the most significant economic transformation in Argentine history.

The development of the **pampas** and the vastly increased production of beef and wheat made Argentina one of the wealthiest nations of Latin America and a major agricultural rival of the United States. The opening of land, even if only for tenant farming and not ownership, encouraged hundreds of thousands of Europeans, particularly from Spain and Italy, to immigrate to Argentina. The immigrants also provided workers for the food-processing, service, and transportation industries in Buenos Aires. By 1900 the new economic life and the thousands of new citizens had drastically changed Argentina. It became much more urbanized and industrialized. More people had reason to be politically discontent. Moreover, the children of the nineteenth-century immigrants often became the strongest Argentine nationalists during the twentieth century.

Chronology

Argentina

1810	Junta in Buenos Aires overthrows Spanish government
1827–1852	Era of Rosas's dictatorial government
1876	Ship refrigeration makes possible export of beef around the world
1879–1880	General Roca carries out *Conquest of the Desert* against the Indian population
1914–1918	Argentina remains neutral in World War I
1930s	Period of strong influence of nationalist military
1943–1956	Era of Juan and Eva Perón

The prosperity of economic expansion quieted most political opposition for some time. The conservative landed oligarchy continued to govern under presidents who sought to perpetuate a strong export economy. Like similar groups elsewhere, they ignored the social questions raised by urbanization and industrialization. However, they also ignored the political aspirations of the urban middle and professional classes, whose members wanted a greater share in political life and an end to political corruption. In

Immigrant Hotel, Buenos Aires, ca. 1900. More than 8 million people from Europe and Asia immigrated to South America and the Caribbean between 1860 and 1920. In this photograph, European immigrants dine in a communal hall at a hotel set aside specifically for them.

1890 these groups founded the Radical Party, which for many years achieved few successes. However, in 1912 the conservative government expanded the franchise and provided for the secret ballot.

Four years later, Hipólito Irigoyen (1850–1933), leader of the Radical Party, was elected president (first term 1916–1922). Without significant support in the legislature, his presidency brought fewer changes than might have been expected. He remained neutral in World War I, so Argentina could trade with both sides. Nonetheless, the war put great pressure on the economy, and much labor agitation resulted. Although previously sympathetic toward labor, Irigoyen as president used troops against strikers. The most violent labor clash occurred in January 1919, when troops quelled a general strike in Buenos Aires during what became known as the *Semana Trágica*, or Tragic Week. Thereafter, the Radical Party attempted to consolidate support among conservatives and pursued policies that benefited landowners and urban business interests. This was possible because of the close relationship between agricultural producers and processors and because both the landed and the middle classes wanted to resist concessions to the working classes.

The Military in Ascendance By the end of the 1920s the onetime reformist Radical Party had become corrupt and directionless. The worldwide commodity depression hurt exports. In 1930 the military staged a coup against the aged Irigoyen, who had returned to the presidency in 1928. The officers eventually returned power to conservative civilians,

Argentine president Juan Domingo Perón and his wife Eva address a throng of supporters from a balcony in Buenos Aires.

and Argentina remained heavily dependent on the British export market. U.S. interests also began to establish plants in Argentina, removing still more economic activity from Argentine control.

Throughout the 1930s a right-wing nationalistic movement, ***nacionalismo***, arose among writers, political journalists, and a few active politicians. This movement resembled the Fascist political movements then active in Europe. Its supporters were angered by British and American domination of the economy, equating their influence with imperialism. In politics the movement's supporters rejected liberalism and spread the fear of international communism. They also exhibited a strong anti-Semitic spirit and warmly supported the Roman Catholic Church. *Nacionalismo* was associated with a relatively progressive social policy rooted in the social values of the late nineteenth-century papacy of Leo XIII. It advocated social reforms that recognized the needs of workers and the poor but that also sought to promote social harmony rather than communist revolution or socialist reconstruction of the economy. The various writers who set forth these ideas also looked back to Rosas as a role model for Argentine politics. In effect these groups were anti-imperialistic, socially concerned, authoritarian, and sympathetic to the rule of a modern *caudillo*. The pressures that came to the fore as a result of World War II gave these attitudes and their supporters influence that they had not previously enjoyed.

World War II closed almost all of Europe to Argentine exports, creating a sudden economic crisis. The country's leadership seemed incapable of responding to the crisis, and in 1943 the military again seized control. Its leaders had lost patience with politicians more interested in patronage than in patriotism. Many of the officers were children of immigrants and were fiercely nationalistic. They regarded liberal politics as a system that permitted politicians to look after themselves. Some officers had become deeply impressed by the Fascist and Nazi movements and their rejection of European liberal politics. The officers also shared the Fascist and Nazi hostility to Britain. They contended that the government must address social questions, industrialize the country, and liberate it from foreign economic control. In all these respects, they echoed the *nacionalistas*.

Between 1943 and 1946 Juan Perón (1895–1974), one of the colonels involved in the 1943 coup, forged this social discontent and these authoritarian political attitudes into a remarkable political movement known as **Peronism**. It was authoritarian, initially militaristic, anticommunist, and socially progressive. Perón understood better than his fellow officers that political power could be exerted by appeals to the Argentine working class, particularly in Buenos Aires. He gained the support of the trade unions that were opposed to communism. In 1945 he had been arrested by other military leaders, but he was freed when it became clear that

Document

Eva Perón Explains the Sources of Her Popularity

The Peronist movement in Argentina drew broad support from workers and the poor. The movement involved a cult of personality around both Perón and his wife, Eva. In 1951 Eva Perón published a book entitled *My Mission in Life (La Razón de mi Vida)*. Here she explains how she sought to relate to her husband's political supporters.

■ *Why was Eva Perón's acceptance of the name "Evita" a political act? How did her use of this name separate her from the ruling elites of Argentina? What is the role she projects for herself in her relationship to various social groups in Argentina? Do you believe her discussion of herself to be sincere or politically opportunistic?*

When I chose to be "Evita," I chose the path of my people. . . .

Only the people call me "Evita." Only the *descamisados* [the "unshirted," as Perón's working-class followers were termed] learned to call me so. . . .

I appeared to them thus the day I went to meet the humble of my land, telling them that I preferred being "Evita" to being the wife of the president, if that "Evita" could help to mitigate some grief, or dry a tear.

If a man of the government, a leader, a politician, an ambassador, who normally calls me "Se–ora," should call me "Evita," it would sound as strange and out of place to me as if a street-urchin, a workingman, or a humble person of the people should call me "Señora." . . .

Now, if you ask me which I prefer, my reply would be immediately that I prefer the name by which I am known to the people.

When a street-urchin calls me "Evita," I feel as though I were the mother of all urchins, and of all the weak and the humble of my land.

When a working man calls me "Evita," I feel glad to be the companion of all the workingmen of my country and even of the whole world.

When a woman of my country calls me "Evita," I imagine myself her sister, and that of all the women of humanity.

And so, almost without noticing it, I have classified in these three examples the principal activities of "Evita" relating to the humble, the workers, and women.

The truth is that, without any artificial effort, at no personal cost, as though I had been born for all this, I feel myself responsible for the humble as though I were the mother of all of them; I fight shoulder to shoulder with the workers as though I were another of their companions from the workshop or factory; in front of the women who trust in me, I consider myself something like an elder sister, responsible to a certain degree for the destiny of all of them who have placed their hopes in me.

And certainly I do not deem this an honor but a responsibility. . . .

Yes. I confess that I have an ambition, one single, great personal ambition: I would like the name of "Evita" to figure somewhere in the history of my country.

Source: Sara Castro-Klarén Sylvia Malloy, and Beatriz Sarlo Excerpt from Women's Writings in Latin America: An Anthology Copyright © 1991 Sara Castro Klaren. Reprinted by permission of Westview Press, a member of the Perseus Book Group.

---

he alone could silence working-class discontent. In 1946 he made himself the voice of working-class democracy, even though after his election to the presidency he created an authoritarian regime that only marginally addressed industrial problems. He was greatly aided by his wife, the former actress Eva Duarte (1919–1952). She enjoyed charismatic support among trade-union members and the working class. (See Document, "Eva Perón Explains the Sources of Her Popularity.")

Perón became the most famous of the postwar Latin American dictators, but his power and appeal were rooted in the antiliberal attitudes that had been fostered by the corrup-

tion and aimlessness of Argentine politics during the Depression. He was the supreme twentieth-century embodiment of the *caudillo*. He was ousted in 1956, but long-term stability would elude Argentine politics after his departure.

Mexico

The heritage of Mexican independence was a combination of the thwarted social revolution led by Father Hidalgo and José María Morelos between 1811 and 1815 and the conservative political coup carried out in 1820 by the creole elite against a potentially liberal Spanish Crown. For the first century of independence conservative forces held sway, but in 1910 the Mexican people launched the most far-reaching revolution in Latin American history.

Turmoil Follows Independence The years from 1820 to 1876 were a time of political turmoil, economic floundering, and national humiliation. Newly independent Mexico attempted no liberal political experiments. Its first ruler was Agustín de Iturbide (1783–1824), who ruled until 1823 as an emperor. After this unsuccessful effort to adopt monarchical rule, Mexico was governed by a succession of presidents, most of whom were *caudillos* from the army or depended on the army for support. The strongest of these figures was Antonio López de Santa Anna (1795–1863), a general and a political opportunist always willing to modify his principles and policies to attain or retain power. Usually he supported conservative political and social interests. He ruled in a thoroughly dictatorial manner. More than once he was driven from office, but he inevitably returned until finally exiled in 1855.

The midcentury movement against Santa Anna's autocracy was called **La Reforma**. In theory, its supporters were liberal, but Mexican liberalism was associated primarily with anticlericalism, confiscation of church lands, and opposition to military influence on national life and politics. *La Reforma* aimed to produce political stability, civilian rule, and an economic policy that would attract foreign capital

The Execution of Maximilian of Mexico, June 19, 1867, by the French Impressionist painter Edouard Manet. Between 1867 and 1869 Manet completed a series of compositions depicting the execution of the Mexican emperor. This is the final and largest work. Edouard Manet (1832–1883), "The Execution of Emperor Maximilian of Mexico, June 19, 1867." *Oil on canvas. Location: Staedtische Kunsthalle, Mannheim, Germany. Art Resource, New York.*

and immigrants. Having deposed Santa Anna, the leaders of the reform movement passed legislation to break up large landed estates, particularly those owned by the church, and to promote the establishment of small farms. However, the actual content of the laws permitted existing large landowners to purchase additional land cheaply and thus made great estates even larger. The legislative attack on privileges of the church led to further civil war between 1857 and 1860. In January 1861 Benito Juárez (1806–1872) entered Mexico City as the temporary victor.

Political instability was matched by economic stagnation. After 1820 many Spanish officials and merchants fled Mexico, taking with them large quantities of gold and silver. The mines that had produced Mexico's colonial wealth were in poor condition, and the country lacked the investment capital or technological knowledge to repair them. The inefficiencies of the *hacienda* system left farming in a backward condition. Cheap imports of manufactured goods spelled the end of domestic industries. Transportation was primitive. The government's remedy for these weaknesses was massive foreign borrowing; as a result, interest payments became one of the largest portions of the national budget.

Foreign Intervention Political weakness and economic disarray invited foreign intervention. The territorial ambitions of the United States impinged on Mexico in two ways. In 1823 the Mexican government allowed Stephen F. Austin (1793–1836) to begin the colonization of Texas. During the next decade, the policies of Santa Anna stirred resentment among the Texas settlers, and in 1835 they rebelled. The next year Santa Anna destroyed the defenders of the Alamo but was decisively defeated at the battle of San Jacinto. Texas became an independent republic that was annexed by the United States in 1845. Border clashes between Mexican and U.S. forces enabled President James Polk to launch a war against Mexico in 1846 that saw the United States army occupy Mexico City. Through the treaty of Guadalupe Hidalgo (1848), the United States gained a vast portion of Mexican territory, including what is now New Mexico, Arizona, and California.

European intervention occurred as a direct result of Juárez's liberal victory in 1861. Mexican conservatives and clerics invited the Austrian Habsburg Archduke Maximilian (1832–1867) to become the emperor of Mexico. Napoleon III (r. 1852–1870) of France, who portrayed himself as a defender of the Roman Catholic Church, provided support for this Austrian imperial venture. In May 1862 French troops invaded Mexico, and two years later Maximilian became emperor. He disappointed his conservative supporters by accepting much of the former government's liberal policy toward the church but was unable to gain support from other segments of the population. By 1867 Juárez had organized strong resistance forces. He captured the unhappy emperor

A Closer Look

Benito Juárez

Benito Juárez (1806–1872) was one of the most remarkable figures to lead Mexico or any other Latin American nation during the nineteenth century. In 1861 he became the first and only Amerindian to hold the office of president in Mexico. Dedicated to bringing liberal reforms and economic advancement to Mexico, Juárez's political movement was known as *La Reforma* to indicate that it stood in favor of constitutional government in opposition to the autocracy of Santa Anna and conservative political groups in Mexico. He worked to defend and protect the rights of Native Americans in Mexico, and he opposed the political authority still often exercised by the Roman Catholic Church in Mexico. He also favored economic development in his nation. In all these respects he stood in agreement with most political liberals throughout the nineteenth-century transatlantic world. His most heroic moment came in his firm resistance during the 1860s to any kind of compromise with the effort of the Austrian Prince Maximilian to establish a conservative European empire over Mexico. The Mexican victory over Maximilian was the single most important example of an American nation rejecting and overcoming European efforts to impose direct political control over their nation.

    This portrait was painted in 1948 by the famous Mexican painter Diego Rivera (1886-1957). Rivera was himself a communist and a radical anticlerical. Note his emphasis in the portrait on Juárez as a civilian.

In the upper left is a portrayal of the execution of the Emperor Maximilian before a firing squad.

In the upper right Rivera pictures the construction of what appears to be a railroad bridge symbolizing Juárez's dedication to economic development, as do the tools for engineering drawings in the foreground.

Questions

1. How does Rivera's portrayal of Juárez present Juárez as a particular kind of Mexican patriot?

2. Looking at the portrait, could one discern that it had been painted after the violence of the Mexican Revolution and that it might be idealizing a Mexican leader of the third quarter of the nineteenth century?

3. Why might Rivera have wanted to trace the ideal of national and economic independence of Mexico to the middle of the previous century?

and executed him. The Mexicans had been victorious, but their vulnerability to foreign powers had again been exposed.

Díaz and Dictatorship   Once restored to office, the liberal leaders continued their measures against the church but failed to rally significant popular support. Consequently, in 1876 Porfirio Díaz (1830–1915), a liberal general, led a revolt on the grounds that he was restoring a true republic. Except for four years in the 1880s, when a surrogate held office, Díaz retained the presidency until 1911. He maintained what became one of the most successful dictatorships in Latin American history by giving almost every political sector something it wanted. He allowed landowners to purchase public land cheaply; he favored the army, whose support he required; and he made peace with the church by not enforcing anticlerical measures. Later, he freely used repression against opponents to diffuse their political activity and bribery to cement the loyalty of his supporters. Wealthy Mexicans grew even richer under Díaz, and Mexico became a respectable member of the international financial community. Unprecedented quantities of foreign capital flooded the nation. Foreign companies, especially from the United States, invested heavily in what, by 1900, appeared to be a thoroughly stable country.

Yet problems remained. The peasants wanted land and resented the ever-growing power of the landlords. Because food production actually declined during the Díaz regime, many Mexicans were malnourished. Labor unrest and strikes afflicted the textile and mining industries. Like other Latin American rulers and governments in Europe and the United States, Díaz used military force against workers.

Owing to inflation, real wages for the working class declined in the first decade of this century. The Panic of 1907 in the United States disrupted the Mexican economy. By 1910 the so-called *Pax Porfiriana* was unraveling.

Revolution   In 1908 the elderly Díaz announced that he would not seek reelection. Although he later changed his mind and was reelected in 1910, his first announcement spurred public discussion of Mexico's political and social future. In 1910 Francisco Madero (d. 1913), a wealthy landowner and moderate liberal opposed Diaz. Madero's campaign slogan was "Effective Suffrage—No Reelection," which ironically Díaz himself had coined two generations earlier. Díaz won, but Madero then led an insurrection that by May 1911 drove the dictator into European exile.

Shortly thereafter, Madero was elected president. He recognized the rights of trade unions to organize and to strike, but he was unwilling to undertake significant agrarian reform that might have changed the pattern of landholding. He ended by being distrusted both by conservatives, who wanted little or no change from the days of Díaz, and by reformist leaders, who thought the time had come for extensive social and political restructuring. Far more radical leaders emerged, calling for social change. Pancho Villa (1874–1923) in the north and Emiliano Zapata (1879–1919) in the south rallied mass followings of peasants who demanded fundamental structural changes in rural landholding. In late 1911 Zapata proclaimed his Plan of Ayala, which in effect set forth a program of large-scale peasant confiscation of land. Much of the struggle during

The Mexican Revolution. The forces of Emiliano Zapata march on Xochimilco in 1914. Women fought alongside men and played other prominent roles during the Mexican Revolution.

Document   Emiliano Zapata Issues the Plan of Ayala

By November 1911 the Díaz regime had fallen in Mexico, and Francisco Madero was attempting to establish a moderately liberal government. He was confronted by a major popular peasant revolution led in the valley of Morelos by Emiliano Zapata. On November 28 the rebel leader set forth his opposition to Madero and announced sweeping goals of land reform. Zapata never took dominant control of the Mexican Revolution, but the radical economic demands of his *Plan of Ayala* would influence the course of Mexican social development for the next thirty years.

■ *Why did Zapata place so much emphasis on collective ownership of natural resources? What is Zapata's vision of future economic life? Who would be the winners and losers from his proposed policies?*

. . . be it known: that the lands, woods, and water usurped by the *hacendados* [great landowners] . . . henceforth belong to the towns or citizens in possession of the deeds concerning these properties of which they were despoiled through the devious action of our oppressors. The possession of said properties shall be kept at all costs, arms in hand. The usurpers who think they have right to said goods may state their claims before special tribunals to be established upon the triumph of the Revolution.

. . . the immense majority of Mexico's villages and citizens own only the ground on which they stand. They suffer the horrors of poverty without being able to better their social status in any respect, or without being able to dedicate themselves to industry or agriculture due to the fact that the lands, woods, and water are monopolized by a few. For this reason, through prior compensation,

one-third of such monopolies will be expropriated from their powerful owners in order that the villages and citizens of Mexico may obtain *ejidos* [agricultural communities], colonies, town sites, and rural properties for sowing or tilling, and in order that the welfare and prosperity of the Mexican people will be promoted in every way.

The property of those *hacendados* . . . who directly or indirectly oppose the present plan shall be nationalized, and two-thirds of their remaining property shall be designated for war indemnities—pensions for the widows and orphans of the victims that succumb in the struggle for this plan.

Source: James W. Wilkie and Albert L. Michaels, eds. *Revolution In Mexico: Years of Upheaval 1910–1940.* Copyright © 1969 by Alfred A. Knopf, a division of Random House, Inc. Reprinted by permission.

the next ten years would be between supporters and opponents of such agrarian reform. (See Document, "Emiliano Zapata Issues the Plan of Ayala.")

Madero found himself squeezed between the conservative supporters of the deposed Díaz and the radical peasant revolutionaries. No one trusted Madero, and in early 1913 he was overthrown by General Victoriano Huerta (1854–1916), who had the help of the United States but was assassinated not long thereafter. Huerta, who was basically a dictator, failed to quash the peasant rebellion. His attacks against the forces of Zapata involved considerable loss of life. In the meantime, Venustiano Carranza (1859–1920), a wealthy landowner, joined Villa's cause. He soon put himself at the head of a large Constitutionalist Army—so called because it advocated the restoration of constitutional government in opposition to Huerta's political dictatorship—that initially received the support of both Zapata and Villa. Huerta's government collapsed on August 15, 1914, when

Constitutionalist forces entered Mexico City. Thereafter disputes erupted between Carranza and Villa and then between Carranza and Zapata. These conflicts arose both from simple political rivalry and from Carranza's refusal to embrace the kind of radical agrarian reform the two peasant leaders sought. Carranza eventually won out, thanks to his political skills and the effectiveness of his army.

Carranza's political skills also helped him build a broad base and edge out both Villa and Zapata as the chief leader of the revolution. One particularly skillful move followed an attempt by President Woodrow Wilson (1856–1924) of the United States to support Carranza by sending U.S. Marines to Veracruz in April 1914. Carranza shrewdly denounced the United States for this action, thus casting himself in the role of patriot and nationalist, and the Marines departed. In another skillful move, he addressed himself to the concerns of urban industrial workers as well as the land hunger of rural peasants, successfully separating the two groups. This division ultimately doomed the effort to implement an agrarian revolution. Carranza made many promises, especially about agrarian reform, that he had little or no intention of carrying out.

Beginning in early 1915 Carranza's military forces began an ultimately successful campaign against Villa and Zapata. The peasant leaders still commanded regional support but could not win control of the nation. During 1916 Carranza confronted U.S. military intervention along the border that continued until early 1917, when the United States became involved in World War I in Europe. By 1917, after years of deadly and destructive civil war, Carranza's forces were sufficiently confident to write a constitution. The Constitution of 1917 set forth a program for ongoing social revolution—never pursued with any vigor—and political reform. Perhaps its two most famous provisions were Articles 27 and 123. Article 27 provided for the government, on behalf of the nation, to become the owner of water and mineral rights and other subsoil property rights. This article abrogated all prerevolutionary contracts with foreign companies in regard to oil and minerals. Together with other provisions, it meant that peasant villages could reclaim land they had lost over the past half century. Article 123 guaranteed certain rights for the organization of labor. Many years would pass before all the provisions of the constitution could be enforced, but from 1917 onward it provided the ongoing goals of the revolution and the ideals toward which Mexican governments were expected to strive.

Carranza and his immediate subordinates were much more conservative than either Villa or Zapata. They recognized the agrarian problem but were cautious about changing existing property arrangements. Carranza and his chief supporters were associated with northwestern Mexico and admired the economic development they had seen in California. They were determined to modernize Mexican political life and attract capital investment; Mexican leaders would share these goals from that time onward. Thus despite all the radical rhetoric associated with the revolution and the vast upheaval among peasants that it involved, the Mexican Revolution saw the victory of a more or less middle-class political and economic elite who would attempt to govern the country through enlightened paternalism. Although turmoil would persist for many years, with Carranza's victory the general direction of Mexican political life had been established.

The decade after 1917 witnessed both confusion and consolidation. In 1919 Zapata was lured into an ambush and killed. Carranza was assassinated in 1920. Three years later Villa was also assassinated. In this turmoil, Carranza's generals provided stability. During the 1920s military leaders drawn from Carranza's revolutionary Constitutionalist Army served as presidents. They moved cautiously and hesitated to press land redistribution too quickly. They were opposed by the Roman Catholic Church, which at one point suspended all services for more than two years. In 1929

Plutarco Elías Calles (1877–1945) organized the **PRI**, the Institutional Revolutionary Party, which quickly became the most important political force in the nation. The Mexican political system became one dominated by a single party within which most political debate occurred, rather than a system dominated by a single strong leader. Despite external criticism and internal tensions, the PRI would oversee the longest period of political stability experienced by any Latin American nation in the twentieth century.

In 1934 Lázaro Cárdenas (1895–1970) was elected president. More than any of the other leaders to emerge after the revolution, he moved directly to fulfill the promises and programs of 1917. He turned tens of millions of acres of land over to peasant villages. In 1938, when Mexico was the third largest producer of petroleum, he expropriated the oil industry. His nationalization policy established PeMex, which remains the Mexican national oil company. Cárdenas left other mineral industries in private and generally foreign hands. His extensive reforms went through smoothly because he worked through bureaucratic and administrative means.

With the election of Manuel Ávila Camacho (1897–1955) in 1940, the era of revolutionary politics ended. Thereafter, the major issues in Mexico were those generally associated with postwar economic development. But unlike other Latin American nations, Mexico, because of its revolution, could confront those issues with a democratic perspective and a sense of collective social responsibility, no matter how imperfectly those goals might be realized.

Chronology

Mexico

1820–1823	Agustín de Iturbide rules unsuccessfully as emperor
1833–1855	Santa Anna dominates Mexican political scene
1846–1848	Mexico defeated by United States and loses considerable territory
1861	Victory of liberal forces under Juárez
1862–1867	French troops led by Archduke Maximilian of Austria unsuccessfully invade Mexico
1876–1911	Era of Porfirio Díaz
1911	Beginning of Mexican Revolution
1911	Zapata proclaims Plan of Ayala
1917	Forces of Carranza proclaim constitution
1929	Institutional Revolutionary Party organized

Brazil

Postcolonial Brazil, the largest Latin American country, differed in several important respects from other newly independent nations in the region. Its language and colonial heritage were Portuguese rather than Spanish. For the first sixty-seven years of its independence it had a relatively stable monarchical government. And most distinctively, it retained the institution of slavery until 1888.

Brazil had moved directly from being part of the Portuguese monarchy to becoming an independent empire in 1822. The first emperor, Pedro I (r. 1822–1831), while serving as regent for his father, the king of Portugal, had put himself at the head of the independence movement. Although he granted Brazil a constitution in 1823, Pedro's high-handed rule and his patronage of Portuguese courtiers rather than Brazilians led to his forced abdication in 1831. Brazilians then took hold of their own destinies.

After a decade of political uncertainty under a regency, Pedro II (r. 1831–1889), the 15-year-old son of Pedro I, assumed direct power in 1840 and governed Brazil until 1889. Pedro II made wise and shrewd use of patronage. He established a reputation as a constitutional monarch by asking leaders of both the conservative and the liberal political parties to form ministries. Consequently, Brazil enjoyed remarkable political stability. However, the government took few initiatives to develop the economy.

The Slavery Issue The great divisive issue in Brazil's social and political life was slavery. Sugar production remained the mainstay of the economy until the middle of the nineteenth century. Most sugar plantations were located in the coastal provinces of the northeast. Their owners were conservative and resistant to changes in production. Soil exhaustion and inefficient farming methods made profits

Antislavery Print. Slavery lasted longer in Brazil than in any other nation in North or South America. Antislavery groups circulated prints such as this one published in France to illustrate the brutality of slave life in Brazil.

impossible without the cheap labor of slaves. From about 1850 coffee cultivation began to spread in the southern provinces, marking a key shift in Brazilian agriculture. Coffee would soon become the nation's most important product. Coffee producers also used slave labor and wanted to retain slavery, but their profits were much larger than those of the sugar producers, so a transition to free labor would have been easier for them. Coffee planters also tended to see themselves as being on the side of economic progress. Hence, people investing in coffee were more open to emancipation than those who had invested in sugar.

As early as 1826 the Brazilian government had made a treaty with Great Britain, agreeing to suppress the slave trade. For many years Brazil refused to honor these treaty provisions but by 1850 had virtually ceased importing slaves, putting the sugar planters on the defensive and freeing the capital once spent on slaves for investments in coffee. The end of slave imports effectively doomed the institution of slavery because the birthrate among slaves was too low for the slave population to reproduce itself. It was nonetheless one thing to face this technical inevitability and another to abolish slavery.

Read the Document
Friederich Hassaurek, How to Conduct a Latin American Revolution, 1865
at **MyHistoryLab.com**

The Paraguayan War of 1865–1870 postponed consideration of the slave question. This conflict, which pitted Brazil, Argentina, and Uruguay against Paraguay, originated in border disputes and in larger commercial conflicts about ongoing Paraguayan access to the ports on the lower Plate River, in particular Montevideo. The conflict became a long, exceedingly destructive struggle because the dictator of Paraguay, Francisco Solano López (1827–1870), mobilized his entire country into a war of attrition and refused to surrender. His death in battle in 1870 finally ended the war, but only after more than half (and perhaps a larger portion) of the adult male population of Paraguay had been killed. The victorious powers installed a friendly government in Paraguay, which sold off state lands to foreign speculators.

The end of the war returned slavery to the forefront of Brazilian politics. Brazil and the Spanish colonies of Puerto Rico and Cuba were now the only slaveholding countries in the hemisphere. The emperor favored gradual emancipation. A law of 1871 set the stage for such emancipation by freeing slaves owned by the Crown and by decreeing legal freedom for future children of slaves. The law actually had little effect because it required the children of slaves to work on plantations until the age of 21. However, throughout the 1870s and 1880s the abolition movement gathered momentum in Brazil. Public figures from across the entire political spectrum called for an end to slavery. (See Document, "A Brazilian Liberal Denounces Slavery" on page 780.) Abolitionists helped slaves to escape. The army, many of whose officers held political views associated with positivism,

Document A Brazilian Liberal Denounces Slavery

Critics sharply attacked slavery in Brazil from the mid-nineteenth century onward. The first major attempt to emancipate slaves occurred in 1871. That law proposed gradual emancipation by liberating the children of slaves. The abolitionist movement continued to grow, resulting in the final emancipation of slaves in Brazil in 1888. In 1883 Joaquim Nabuco, a major leader of the abolitionist movement, published *O Abolicionismo*, which stands as one of the chief examples of Brazilian antislavery literature. Although not quoted in the following passage, Nabuco drew extensive parallels between the slavery of Brazil and the slavery that had existed in the United States before the Civil War. Here Nabuco seeks to demonstrate the manner in which the continuation of slavery prevents commercial economic development in Brazil and inhibits the country from embracing the progressive forces of the day. Note the manner in which Nabuco has absorbed the ideas of the eighteenth-century Enlightenment and nineteenth-century European liberalism.

■ *What values and outlooks does Nabuco associate with the expansion of commerce? Why does he see slavery as undermining those values? How and why does he see slavery inhibiting progressive social and intellectual forces? In this passage, what are some possible arguments against slavery that Nabuco does not raise?*

Slavery does not permit the existence of a true working class, nor is it compatible with the wage system and the personal dignity of the artisan. . . . [T]here can be no strong, respected, and intelligent working class where the employers of labor are accustomed to order slaves about. . . .

Slavery and industry are mutually exclusive terms, like slavery and colonization. The spirit of the former, spreading through a country, kills every one of the human faculties from which industry springs—initiative, inventiveness, individual energy, and every one of the elements that industry requires—the formation of capital, an abundance of labor, technical education of the workers, confidence in the future. . . .

. . .[C]ommerce, in the absence of industry and free labor, can function only as an agent of slavery, buying whatever it offers and selling whatever it needs. This is why in Brazil commerce does not develop or open new perspectives for the country. . . . Slavery distrusts commerce, as it distrusts any agency of progress, whether it is a business man's office, a railroad station, or a primary school; yet slavery needs commerce. . . . But so long as slavery endures, commerce must always be the servant of a class, and not an independent national agent. . . .

Of the classes whose growth slavery artificially stimulates, none is more numerous than that of government employees. . . . Officeholding is . . . the asylum of the descendants of formerly rich and noble families that have squandered the fortunes made from slavery. . . . But officeholding is also our political olive tree, that shelters all those young men of brains and ambition but no money who form the great majority of our talented people. . . .

Among the forces of progress and change around which slavery has created a vacuum as hostile to its interests, the press is notable—and not only the newspaper but the book, and everything that concerns education. . . . The slave hut and the school are poles that repel each other. . . .

Among the forces whose emergence slavery has impeded is public opinion, the consciousness of a common destiny. Under slavery there cannot exist that powerful force called public opinion, that simultaneously balances and offers a point of support to the individuals who represented the most advanced thought of the country. Just as slavery is incompatible with spontaneous immigration, so will it prevent the influx of new ideas. Itself incapable of invention, it will have nothing to do with progress.

Source: Excerpts from Benjamin Keen, Readings in Latin American Civilization 1492 to the Present Copyright © 1955 Reprinted by permission of The Estate of Benjamin Keen.

resented having to enforce laws protecting slavery. In 1888 Pedro II was in Europe for medical treatment, and his daughter was regent. She favored abolition rather than gradual emancipation. When Parliament in that year passed a law abolishing slavery without any compensation to the slave owners, she signed it, thus ending slavery in Brazil.

A Republic Replaces Monarchy The abolition of slavery brought to a head other issues that in 1889 caused the collapse of the monarchy. Planters who received no financial compensation for their slaves were resentful. Roman Catholic clerics were disaffected by disputes with the emperor over education. Pedro II was unwell; his daughter, the heir to the throne, was unpopular and distrusted. The officer corps of the army had been dissatisfied with what it regarded as insufficient political influence since its victory in the Paraguayan War. In November 1889 the army sent Pedro II into exile in France.

The Brazilian republic lasted from 1891 to 1930. Like the monarchy, it was dominated by a small group of wealthy persons, the most dominant of whom were the coffee planters. The political arrangement that allowed the republic to function smoothly was an agreement among the state governors. The president was to be chosen alternately from the states of São Paulo and Minas Gerais. In turn, the other eighteen governors had considerable local political latitude. Fixed elections and patronage kept the system in operation. Literacy replaced property as the qualification for voting, leaving few people qualified to vote. There was consequently little organized opposition and, for that matter, little political life at all within the republic.

From the 1890s onward the coffee industry dominated both the political and the economic life of the nation. Around 1900 Brazil was producing over three-fourths of the world's coffee. The crop's success led almost inevitably to overproduction. To meet this problem, the government devised policies for maintaining high prices that required large loans from foreign banks. High world coffee prices encouraged competition from other Latin American producers, which in turn required more price supports in Brazil. In addition to the international loans, maintaining the price of coffee required considerable payments to the government from all of the non-coffee-related sectors of the economy. These sectors in turn felt exploited by the coffee interests. As a result of these arrangements, throughout the life of the republic Brazil remained essentially a country producing a single product for export and few goods for internal consumption.

Economic Problems and Military Coups The end of slavery, the expansion of coffee production, and the beginning of a slow growth of urban industry attracted foreign immigrants to Brazil. They tended to settle in the cities and constituted the core of the early industrial labor force. In Brazil, as elsewhere, World War I caused major economic disruption. Urban labor discontent appeared. There was a general strike in São Paulo in 1917, with the inevitable military action against the strikers. The failure to address urban and industrial social problems and the political corruption of the republic led to attempted military coups in 1922 and 1924. Both revolts failed to bring down the republic, but they indicated profound discontent with a political structure designed primarily to protect the producers of a single agricultural commodity. The revolts also demonstrated that certain segments of the military were determined to change the political system. They wanted a modern nation that was not dependent on a single exportable product and a political system that depended on

Overview Latin American Products for Export 1820–1930

Argentina	animal products (meat, leather, wool), grain
Bolivia	tin, silver, wool
Brazil	coffee, sugar, rubber
Chile	copper
Colombia	coffee, cattle
Ecuador	bananas
Mexico	silver, cattle, oil
Peru	nitrates, silver
Uruguay	animal products (meat, leather)
Venezuela	coffee, cattle

more than corruption and recognized interests besides those of the coffee planters.

Coffee had ruled as the economic "king" of the Brazilian republic, and its collapse brought the republic down with it. In 1929 coffee prices hit record lows; currency exchange rates fell; and foreign loans were unavailable. Millions of bags of coffee lay in warehouses. Government reserves were depleted in an unsuccessful attempt to hold up the price of coffee and to pay for imports no longer being funded by coffee exports. The economic structure of the republic lay in shambles. In October 1930 a military coup installed Getulio Vargas (1883–1954) in the presidency. Vargas governed Brazil until 1945.

The Vargas years represent a major turning point in Brazilian history. Vargas was initially supported by the reform elements in the military, by professional middle-class groups, and by urban workers. In office, he moved first to the right and then to the left and then back again. He was an experimentalist and pragmatist who primarily wanted to hold on to power and to make Brazil a modern nation. Vargas was able to recognize the new social and economic groups shaping Brazilian political life. First with constitutionalism and then with dictatorship, he attempted to allow the government to act on behalf of those groups without allowing them to influence or direct the government in a genuinely democratic manner. However, despite the personal power that accrued to him, he did not form his own political party or movement as Perón would later do in Argentina or as the Mexican revolutionaries had done. Rather, Vargas attempted to function like a ringmaster directing the various forces in Brazilian life. His failure to establish a gen-

uinely stable institutional political framework for a Brazil that included many interest groups besides the coffee planters has influenced Brazil to the present day.

Vargas and his supporters sought to lessen Brazil's dependence on coffee by fostering industries that would produce domestically goods that had previously been imported from abroad. They thus attempted to create internal suppliers for goods needed in the internal Brazilian economy. The policy succeeded, and by the mid-1930s domestic manufacturing was increasing. These years mark the real beginning of Brazilian manufacturing. In the constitution of 1934 Vargas established a legal framework for labor relations. The structures were paternalistic but included an eight-hour day and a minimum wage. The constitution also asserted government responsibility to protect mineral and water rights.

In the Brazilian context these measures appeared reformist, if not necessarily liberal, and marked a departure from government policy dominated by the coffee oligarchy and politics by patronage. However, in the late 1930s Vargas confronted major political opposition from both the Brazilian Communist Party (founded in 1922) and a new right-wing movement called *Integralism*. In 1937, facing these political opponents, Vargas assumed personal dictatorial power. His regime thereafter was repressive. He claimed to have established an **Estado Novo** ("new state"). He wrapped himself in the flag of nationalism and order and presented himself as the protector of national stability against factions that would foster instability and of the national interest against international opponents.

Vargas and the Military.
Getulio Vargas became ruler of Brazil in 1930 through a military coup. Here he stands with his military supporters. One of the purposes of such pictures was to remind the public that any serious opposition might be put down by the military.

Like the European dictators of the same era, Vargas used censorship, secret police, and torture against his political opponents. He also used his newly assumed power to diversify and modernize the economy. In 1940 a five-year plan provided more state direction for the economy. His government favored the production of goods from heavy industry that would be used in Brazil itself. To maintain the support of workers and trade unions, the state also issued a progressive labor code. Siding with the Allies in World War II, Brazil built up large reserves of foreign currency through the export of foodstuffs. This economic activity and imposed political stability allowed the government to secure foreign loans for still further economic development. By the end of the war Brazil was becoming the major Latin American industrial power.

Participation in World War II on the side of the Allies had led many in Brazil to believe that they should not remain subject to a dictatorship. This attitude was widespread in the military, which had fought in Europe and established close contact with the United States. In 1945 Vargas promised that he would lead the nation toward democracy and hold presidential as well as congressional elections. His actions, however, suggested that he planned to manipulate the elections. In response, the military carried out a coup, and Vargas retired temporarily from political life.

The new regime, which was democratic, continued the general policy of economic development through foreign-financed industrialization. The state, however, assumed a much smaller role. When in 1950 Vargas was elected president, his return to office was anticlimactic. He was by then an elderly man, well past his prime. Yet in 1953 he established Petrobas, a state-owned petroleum exploration company. His presidency remained controversial. There was much criticism of him and of the corruption of his appointments. A member of his staff became involved in the assassination of a prominent civilian journalist. The military demanded that Vargas resign. Instead he took his own life in 1954, leaving a public testament in which he presented himself as the protector of the poor and of the broad national interest.

In the decade after Vargas's death, Brazil remained a democracy, though a highly unstable one. The government itself began to undertake vast projects such as the enormously costly construction of the new capital of Brasília, begun in 1957. Located far inland, Brasília required the creation of a vast road system. With Brasília under way, the government of Juscelino Kubitschek (1902–1976), who had supported the building of the new capital, fostered the establishment of a large automobile industry. The rapid growth of cities and the expansion of a working class radicalized political life. The political system could not readily accommodate itself to the concerns of workers and the urban poor. Widespread poverty and illiteracy continued to plague both the cities and the countryside. In a structural problem created by the constitu-

Chronology

Brazil

1822	Brazil becomes an independent empire
1840	Pedro II assumes personal rule
1840s and 1850s	Spread of coffee cultivation
1865–1870	Paraguayan War
1871	First law curbing slavery
1888	Slavery abolished
1889	Fall of the monarchy
1917	General strike in São Paulo
1929	Collapse of coffee prices
1930–1945	Vargas era
1957	Construction of Brasília begins
1964	Military takes control of the government

tion of 1946, the presidency was controlled by urban voters, whereas the congress was controlled by rural voters.

By the early 1960s, when President João Goulert (1918–1977) took office, Brazilian political life was in turmoil. Goulert's predecessors, including Vargas, had always attempted to balance interests or to move among various political forces without firmly favoring a single sector. After months of wavering, however, Goulert committed himself to a policy favored by the left. In 1964 he announced his support for land reform. Peasants had already tried to seize land, and landowners had fought them. Political conservatives and moderates expected some favors would be extended to urban radicals, which they might have tolerated, but vigorously resisted any hint of significant political or land reform in the countryside. Goulert also questioned the authority of the military hierarchy. Moreover, Brazil faced economic problems: Both industrial and farm production had fallen from the levels achieved in 1960, fostering discontent. In March 1964 the military, claiming to protect Brazil from communism, seized control of the government, ending its post–World War II experiment with democracy.

Summary

Economic Dependence. In the 1820s, Latin America threw off Spanish and Portuguese rule, but the traditional elites—landowners, military officers, the church—remained in control. A series of strongmen called *caudillos* dominated most Latin American republics. Nor did independence bring economic prosperity. Because Latin American economies remained dependent on producing agricultural commodities for

••◦─┤Read the Document
Francisco Bilbao, America in Danger,
1862 at **MyHistoryLab.com**

export, foreign nations, particularly Britain, dominated Latin American economic life. When commodity prices collapsed during the Great Depression, Latin American economies were devastated. The crisis did, however, lead to the beginnings of manufacturing in many Latin American countries in an effort to avoid dependence on imports.

Argentina. After independence, Buenos Aires came to dominate Argentina economically and politically. Agricultural exports, the growth of industry, and large-scale European immigration contributed to a strong export economy. However, urban social discontent and the growth of nationalism in the 1930s led to military intervention in politics and the corporatist dictatorship of Juan Perón from 1946 to 1956.

Mexico. In the first decades after independence Mexico was politically and economically unstable. Mexico lost half its territory to the United States and was invaded by France in the 1860s. The long-lasting dictatorship of Porfirio Díaz brought political stability but led to increasing discontent. The Mexican Revolution that began in 1911 produced cautious social and economic reform under the one-party rule of the PRI, the Institutional Revolutionary Party, which remained in power until the end of the century.

Brazil. Brazil was a stable constitutional monarchy after its independence until 1889. It also retained slavery until 1888. The establishment of a republic did not change Brazil's economic dependence on coffee exports, however, and the collapse of coffee prices in 1929 led to the dictatorship of Getulio Vargas. Though politically repressive, Vargas instituted social reforms and promoted industrial development, which continued to expand in the decade after his death in 1954.

Key Terms

caudillos (p. 776)

creole (p. 769)

debt peonage (p. 768)

dependency theory (p. 768)

Estado Novo (p. 788)

import substitution (p. 775)

La Reforma (p. 780)

mestizos (p. 767)

mulattos (p. 767)

nacionalismo (p. 778)

neo-colonial economy (p. 775)

pampas (p. 777)

Peronism (p. 778)

positivism (p. 771)

PRI (p. 784)

Review Questions

1. What was the condition of the Latin American economies after independence? What was their relation to Britain? Why were most Latin American states slow to develop an industrial base? What role did their economies play in the worldwide economy that developed in the nineteenth century?

2. Did the structure of Latin American societies change after independence? What role did the traditional elites play in the economic and political life of their nations? What was the condition of the mass of the population?

3. How did European and United States investment in Latin America affect the region economically? Politically?

4. Why did so many Latin American nations find it difficult to develop stable political regimes? What role did the military play?

5. What was the effect of increased European immigration on Argentina? How did the Argentine elite cope with growing urbanization and industrialization? Why was Juan Perón able to seize and hold power?

6. Did Mexico experience a real revolution in the early twentieth century? How does this experience distinguish Mexico from other Latin American countries? What caused the turmoil?

7. Why was the Brazilian experience of independence and early nationhood different from that of Spanish-speaking Latin America? What was the role of coffee in Brazil's economy? How did the Vargas regime change the Brazilian economy? Why did Brazilian democracy end in a military coup in 1964?

Note: *To learn more about the topics in this chapter, please turn to the Suggested Readings at the end of the book. For additional sources related to this chapter please see MyHistoryLab.com.*

myhistorylab Connections

Reinforce what you learned in this chapter by studying the many documents, images, maps, review tools, and videos available at **www.myhistorylab.com**.

Read and Review

✓● Study and Review Chapter 25

●●●●● Read the Document *Domingo F. Sarmiento, "Civilization and Barbarism," 1845, p. 777*

Friederich Hassaurek, "How to Conduct a Latin American Revolution", 1865, p. 785

Francisco Bilbao, "America in Danger", 1862, p. 790

((●●●─ Hear the Audio *Latin America, p. 767*

Research and Explore

◉● See the Map *The Americas, ca. 1900*

((●●●─ **Hear** the **Audio**

Hear the audio file for Chapter 25 at
www.myhistorylab.com.

26 | India, the Islamic Heartlands, and Africa, 1800–1945

- The Indian Experience
- British Dominance and Colonial Rule
- From British Crown Raj to Independence
- The Islamic Experience
- Islamic Responses to Declining Power and Independence
- Western Political and Economic Encroachment
- The Western Impact
- Islamic Responses to Foreign Encroachment
- The African Experience
- New States and Power Centers
- Islamic Reform Movements
- Increasing European Involvement: Exploration and Colonization
- Patterns in European Colonial Rule and African Resistance
- The Rise of African Nationalism

The Indian Mutiny of 1857. The mutinous Sepoy cavalry attacking British infantry at the battle of Cawnpore. Although the uprising was suppressed, it was not easily forgotten. In its aftermath the British reorganized the government of India.

THE EUROPEAN ENCROACHMENT ON the rest of the world from the late fifteenth century onward brought radical, often devastating changes. In the West itself, spiritual and material disruption accompanied the Renaissance, Reformation, Enlightenment, and Industrial and Scientific Revolutions. When Western expansion brought the ideas and innovations of these watershed European developments to Asia and Africa, the challenges and changes that ensued came much more rapidly than they had in the West. Furthermore, they were accompanied by the intrusion of European military and economic power. Consequently, they were received typically with virulent resistance or cautious adaptation.

To organize these complex processes under the rubric of "modernization" does not reflect the acute differences between the relatively lengthy and gradual processes of change in Western Europe and the more rapid and disruptive changes that European imperialism and colonialism brought to other global regions. Nor does it do justice to the degree to which the West appropriated the very concept of "modernity." Although every advanced society in any age has presumably viewed its culture as "modern," the dominance of the West in recent centuries has identified modernity with a novel set of ideas and institutions that evolved in Europe between the Renaissance and the early twentieth century, then were gradually exported to, or imposed upon, other societies around the world. The expression "the impact of modernity" refers too frequently to how "modern" Western civilization affected traditional cultures.

The consequences of the spread of Western culture have been so massive that non-Western peoples are often seen as merely its passive recipients. The European-American view of the world often assumes a simplistic dualism that enhances Western self-esteem by portraying the "modern" West and the "backward" "Orient" as opposites, as though all of the world outside Europe, North America, and their Westernized offshoots were some monolithic, archaic entity. Popular Western stereotypes of Arabs, Africans, Indians, Chinese, and others reinforce the Westerner's sense of being the true "modern" of recent history.

As parochial as such chauvinistic generalizations are, they may nonetheless have a grim historical core, as suggested by the crises that many non-Western cultures experienced underwent under the impact of the agents of Western "modernity." The impingement of the West has been significant in the recent history of African, Asian, and Indian civilizations. Not all non-Western societies have had equal success in retaining or reasserting their precolonial independence and identity, or in responding creatively to the challenges of Western-style modernity. The spectrum of postcolonial experience ranges from the largely positive Japanese response or the mixed Chinese experience to the painful, often destructive African experiences, with those of India, Latin America, and the Islamic heartlands somewhere in between.

Nevertheless, in all regions, Western modernity entered cultures that had their own flourishing social, religious, and political traditions. These traditions did not simply melt away upon the arrival of Westerners.

Rather, profound transformations occurred that sought to balance unforeseen challenges of modernity with familiar traditions. Those transformations continue to reverberate today. They occurred throughout Asia and Africa as these continents became the sites of a fierce European competion for raw materials and influence. The "great game" and the "scramble for colonies" would permanently alter the cultural, economical, and political landscapes of Asia, Africa, and Latin America, as well as Europe itself. ■

The Indian Experience

British Dominance and Colonial Rule

In the eighteenth century Britain became dominant in the southern seas, overtaking Portugal and Holland. In India the British defeated the French and regional Indian powers for domination of the subcontinent (see Chapter 20). By the early nineteenth century they had built the largest colonial empire in the Afro-Asian world. India, the greatest non-Westen traditional civilization to come under direct European colonial rule, was the "jewel in the crown" of that empire.

Building the Empire: The First Half of the Nineteenth Century

Penetrating the multiethnic, multilingual, and multiconfessional world of India was not a simple task for Britain, but required a multipronged approach. In order for British imperial plans to succeed, the British had to secure the economic and cultural bases for their control. This involved identifying how to extract as many natural resources as possible with minimal costs and also how to convince various Indian social and ethnic groups that cooperation with the British imperial enterprise was in their best interests.

As early as half a century before the British Crown assumed direct rule over India in 1858, the British wielded effective imperial control of India through the East India Company. As the Company's pressure on smaller states to pay "subsidies" for military "protection" brought ever more of them to collapse or rebellion, the British annexed more territory. Those areas not annexed were recognized as independent princely states. Ranging in size from less than one to more than 80,000 square miles (Hyderabad), these states remained independent only as long as they remained faithful allies to Britain and contributed money to their common "defense." Members of Indian elites often colluded with the British against local rulers. Mysore state, the Maratha confederation, and the Sikhs of the Panjab were overpowered

The Challenge of Modernity: India, Islam, and Africa

Africa

Middle
East

India

The period from 1800 to World War II was hard on the fortunes of South Asia, Africa, and the Islamic heartlands. For centuries there had been a rough, long-term balance in advances and setbacks in material and intellectual culture, commercial development, and political stability among the major cultural regions of the world. Suddenly, over a period of 150 years, Europe, long a relative backwater in world history, came to dominate the rest of the world.

The Middle East, Africa, Iran, Central Asia, India, and Southeast Asia, along with Central and Latin America—later the so-called Third World of "developing nations"—were most drastically affected by European imperialism and colonialism. Notwithstanding indigenous developments in these regions, this era's decisive development was new and unprecedented domination of the world's economy, intellectual life, and political and military history by a single segment of the global community. Certainly the histories of the less "developed" (in the sense of evolving toward European-style "modernity") nations of the world in this age had their own internal dynamics; in fact, many smaller African or Latin American societies were not even directly affected by Western dominance until recently. Still, the effects of Western military, economic, and cultural power were considerable. Though not synonymous with "progress" as Westerners and modernization theorists often think, these

between 1797 and 1853. The India that resulted was a mixture of small and large tributary states and provinces directly administered by the British (see Map 26–1 on page 796).

The economic impact of Company rule was extensive. To pay debts incurred by their military actions, Company administrators organized and exploited Indian land revenues. Squeezed by these demands, many peasants deserted their land; by the 1830s land revenues were in sharp decline. In addition, demand for Indian indigo, cotton, and opium in the China and British trade also diminished in the 1830s, and famines brought widespread suffering. The economic and social reforms (1828–1836) of Governor General Lord William Bentinck (1774–1839) could not turn things around substantially.

((•— Hear the Audio

India's Imperialism
at **myhistorylab.com**

Company rule, especially in the early 1800s, also affected the physical face of India. Company policies encouraged settled agriculture and small commodity production at the expense of the nomadic and pastoralist cultures that had flourished across North and central India. British "pacification" involved clearing land to deny natural cover to military enemies and often forced resettlement of peasants to pioneer farming in new regions. Early in the nineteenth century European entrepreneurs also undertook massive commercial logging. These activities caused extensive deforestation throughout the subcontinent. This ecological destruction was a major by-product of India's transformation into a more homogeneous peasant farming society, which provided a better base for colonial administration.[1]

•••—Read the Document

Dadabhai Naoroji, The Benefits of British Rule in India, 1871 at **myhistorylab.com**

The Indians were by no means passive in the face of this misuse of their lands and peoples. The first half of the nineteenth century saw almost constant revolt in one place or another. The revolts included peasant movements of noncooperation, Muslim farm workers' attacks on British and Hindu estate owners, grain riots, and tribal warfare. They culminated in a watershed event, the Indian Uprising of 1857 (the so-called Sepoy Mutiny or Rebellion). The commonly accepted image of this era as one of general tranquility preceding a "mutiny" against British custodianship was the product of British propaganda.

The immediate trigger of the Uprising of 1857 was the concern among Bengali troops that animal grease on newly issued rifles exposed them to ritual pollution. Behind this issue, however, lay a variety of grievances, including the recent addition of Sikhs, Gurkhas, and lower-caste soldiers to the army; the deteriorating economic conditions of many of the Hindu troops' higher-caste relatives back home; outrage at excessive tax rates, especially among troops from Meerut; and anger at the 1856 British annexation of the rich princely state of Awadh (home to many of the troops). One can also see in the revolt the desire to recover and rebuild a pre-British political order in North India. This was not an all-India affair: it centered on Delhi, where the last Mughal emperor joined the

---

[1]C. A. Bayly, *Indian Society and the Making of the British Empire* (Cambridge: Cambridge University Press, 1988), pp. 138–146.

effects have nevertheless been a hallmark of "modernity" in most of Asia, Africa, and Latin America. Whether by rejection, adaptation, or imitation, peoples worldwide have had to contend with the immense power of the West.

The vitality of many of the cultures and traditions that bore the brunt of the Western onslaught has been striking. Arab, Iranian, Indian, African, and other encounters with Western material and intellectual domination produced differing, often very creative responses. These have produced significant instances of political, economic, and intellectual independence only since 1945. However, they began much earlier. Thus modern Islamic reform began in the eighteenth century, although it has only recently become a major global factor. Indian national, as opposed to regional, consciousness developed from the late 1800s in response to British imperial domination, even though it did not bring union and independence until after World War II. Ironically, exposure of indigenous elites to European political and social philosophies gave future colonial-independence leaders intellectual resources for ideologies of self-rule framed in "modern" terms. Creative thinkers such as M.K. Gandhi (1869–1948) merged European thought with ideas from

● View the Image
Mahatma Gandhi
at **myhistorylab.com**

their own cultures to create new ideologies that could inspire Western sympathizers as well as their indigenous followers to oppose European oppression. African nationalist leaders such as Julius Nyerere (1922–1999) and Jomo Kenyatta (1889–1978) similarly found creative ways to combine European nationalist and indigenous cultural models.

Certainly one widespread result of the imperial–colonial experience has been to sharpen the cultural self-consciousness and self-confidence of those peoples most adversely affected by Western dominance. The experiences of Third World nations with outside domination may well prove not only to have been a source of misery and reversal, but also to have provided the necessary preparation for positive development and resurgence, despite the problems plaguing many of these nations.

Focus Questions

■ How did Western domination affect South Asia, the Islamic heartlands, and Africa in the nineteenth century?
■ How did these societies develop ideologies of resistance that helped them achieve independence?

● Read the Document
The Indian Revolt (1857)
at **myhistorylab.com**)

rebel cause, and it involved uprisings in other cities and towns from Chittagong in Bengal to Lahore and even Peshawar in the Panjab. There were also peasant uprisings in the countryside around Delhi and Lucknow.

Because their real power bases in Bengal and the Panjab were not destroyed, and their ability to communicate with and move new troops remained unimpaired, the British eventually won the day. With forces augmented by Panjabi Sikhs and Nepalese Gurkhas, they overcame the internally divided Indian opposition. By autumn 1857, the revolt was broken, often with great brutality, and it was finished before the end of the year. In the next year the East India Company was dissolved, and India came under direct rule of the British Crown.

The "Mutiny" of 1857 was not a nationalist revolution, but rather a series of spontaneous antiforeigner, anti-British uprisings. Still, it adumbrated the rise of an effective unified response and highlighted resentment of the burdens of foreign domination that were to grow increasingly oppressive for Indians of all regions and religions over the ensuing ninety years of Crown rule, known as the **Raj**.

British-Indian Relations

The overall impact of the British presence on the Indian masses, under Company and Crown rule, was brutal but impersonal, being largely economic. India was effectively integrated into Britain's economy, becoming a market for British goods and providing Britain with raw materials and

other products. Britain's involvement in India's internal affairs touched politics, education, the civil service, communications, and transportation, but the consequences of its domination and exploitation of India's labor and resources were even more far-reaching.

British cultural imperialism was never a major nor even an official policy of the East India Company. Like Warren Hastings (1732–1818), the Company's governor general from 1774 to 1785, many Britons expressed interest in and some openness to Indians and Indian culture. A few mixed and even intermarried with Indians. The Company itself required many of its India officers to learn Persian and Sanskrit. Nor did it try to propagate Christianity or impose Western culture; indeed, it opposed Christian missionary activity in India until the 1830s and 1840s (albeit partly because the caste system aided implementation of imperial policy). Nonetheless, the British-Indian relationship had a paternalistic, patronizing dimension, both before and after 1857. Even with Indians' improved access to English education and civil service posts of increasing responsibility from the late nineteenth century on, the fundamental imbalance between overlords and subjects remained and was frequently expressed in racial terms. The ethos of the British rulers included the understanding that their job was governing an inferior "race" that could not manage on their own. Even Indians whose university degrees or army training gave them impeccable British qualifications were

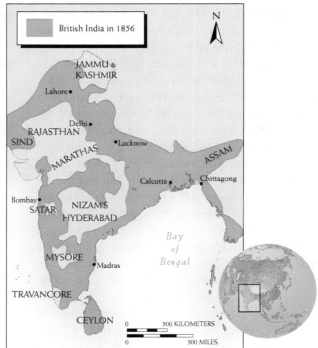

Map 26–1. **British India, 1820 and 1856.**

Portrait of Ram Mohan Roy, the most influential Indian thinker in the early nineteenth century.

never accepted as true equals. From army to civil service ranks, the command/administrative upper echelon was British; middle and lower echelons were Indian.

Despite this unequal relationship, British ideas and practice influenced a small but powerful Indian elite in business and political life as well as manners and customs. Christian conversion was rare, but Christian and secular values associated with the Enlightenment—the ideals of British liberalism, for example—did influence Hindu and Muslim educated classes.

In the nineteenth century, probably the most influential and controversial member of the Indian elite to engage the British on their own ground was Ram Mohan Roy (1772–1833). Roy, a Bengali Hindu, rose to the top of the native ranks of East India Company service and became a strong voice for reform, both of Hindu practice and of British colonial policies that deviated from European and Christian ideals. The spiritual father of the Brahmo Samaj (1828), a Hindu reform movement opposed to "barbarous" practices ranging from *sati* (immolation of widows on their husbands' funeral pyres) to "idol worship" and Brahmanic "ritualism," Roy was an avowed modernist seeking to meld the best of European-Christian morality and thought with the best of Hindu piety and thought. He was quick to oppose autocratic, unfair British legal and commercial practices and campaigned in India and England to reform Company policies. Influenced by Christian Scripture and great European thinkers, he drew upon both in his Hindu reform efforts. His wide-ranging writings and campaigns for

Read the Document

Lord William Bentinck, on the Suppression of Sati, 1829
at **myhistorylab.com**

education, political involvement, and social progress and against the "backward" practices and ideas of many of his Hindu compatriots alienated most contemporaneous leading Hindu thinkers and activists. Twentieth-century Indians have, however, often seen him as a visionary.

Cultural relations between Britain and India were not a one-way affair. During the Company era, and increasingly after 1858, Britons at home became aware of India and Indians. The image they received was filtered through the experience of other Britons who had been in the subcontinent and were not always sympathetic or objective interpreters. Even many Company officers who made India a career developed little interest in Indians beyond what they needed to know to extract economic gain from them. Others, however, studied Indian cultures and languages and became friends with some of the Indian elite. However, a stricter social segregation of white rulers from Indian subjects set in after direct Crown rule began in 1858.

Despite their keen interest in Indian culture, the British, much more than their Mughal predecessors, all too often treated Indians as backward heathens in need of "civilizing" influences from their own "enlightened" culture, law, political system, education, and religion. This dismissive attitude to Indian culture is vividly evident in the argument of the British historian and statesman Lord Macaulay (1800–1859) in favor of an English-language curriculum in Indian schools. (See Document, "Macaulay Writes on Indian Education.")

Document   Macaulay Writes on Indian Education

The decision in 1835 to encourage English-language study and British school curriculum in Indian schools was hotly disputed by both English and Indians. In the end it bred a new generation of elite Indians prepared to be advocates for their nation, as well as a bureaucratic class for the British Raj. It also worked to Hindu advantage because Muslims tended often to reject English schooling, thereby losing ground in the long run. This famous paper by Thomas Babington Macaulay expresses the thinking of the "Anglicists," who prevailed over the "Orientalists," and reveals British prejudices about the superiority of Western over Indian culture.

■ *When Macaulay writes, "English is better worth knowing than Sanscrit or Arabic," is he being objective or is he engaging in "cultural imperialism"? In your view, which are laudable, and which problematic, intentions of the writer?*

We now come to the gist of the matter. We have a fund to be employed as government shall direct for the intellectual improvement of the people of this country. The simple question is, what is the most useful way of employing it?

All parties seem to be agreed on one point, that the dialects commonly spoken among the natives of this part of India contain neither literary nor scientific information, and are, moreover, so poor and rude that, until they are enriched from some other quarter, it will not be easy to translate any valuable work into them. It seems to be admitted on all sides that the intellectual improvement of those classes of the people who have the means of pursuing higher studies can at present be affected only by means of some language not vernacular amongst them.

What then shall that language be? One-half of the committee maintain that it should be the English. The other half strongly recommend the Arabic and Sanscrit. The whole question seems to me to be, which language is the best worth knowing?

To sum up what I have said, I think it clear that we are free to employ our funds as we choose; that we ought to employ them in teaching what is best worth knowing; that English is

better worth knowing than Sanscrit or Arabic; that the natives are desirous to be taught English, and are not desirous to be taught Sanscrit or Arabic; that neither as the languages of law, nor as the languages of religion, have the Sanscrit and Arabic any peculiar claim to our engagement; that it is possible to make natives of this country thoroughly good English scholars; and that to this end our efforts ought to be directed. In one point I fully agree with the gentlemen to whose general views I am opposed. I feel with them, that it is impossible for us, with our limited means, to attempt to educate the body of the people. We must at present do our best to form a class who may be interpreters between us and the millions whom we govern; a class of persons, Indian in blood and color, but English in taste, in opinions, in morals, and in intellect. To that class we may leave it to refine the vernacular dialects of the country, to enrich those dialects with terms of science borrowed from the Western nomenclature, and to render them by degrees fit vehicles for conveying knowledge to the great mass of the population.

Source: From *Sources of Indian Tradition*, ed. by William Theodore de Bary. Copyright © 1958 by Columbia University Press. Reprinted with permission of the publisher.

Most Indians resented their subordinate status. Their late-nineteenth-century nationalist movement extended to the grass-roots level—among tribal groups, peasant farmers, and home or small-industry workers. Whatever their status, the distrust and animosity most Indians felt toward their foreign rulers continued to grow.[2]

From British Crown Raj to Independence

The Burden of Crown Rule

The Revolt of 1857 had numerous consequences beyond transferring administration of India from the Company to the Crown. In particular, the bloody conflict exacerbated mutual fear and hatred. Before the revolt, the British had maintained a largely native army under British command. After the revolt, they tried to maintain at least a 1:3 ratio of British to Indians. Because the army was financed by Indian, not British, revenues, this imposed huge economic burdens on India, diverting one-third of its total annual revenues to pay for its own military occupation.

British economic policies and accelerating population growth put great strains on India's poor. Cheap British machine-made goods were exchanged for Indian raw materials and home-industry products, which harmed or destroyed Indian craft industries and forced multitudes into poverty or onto the land. Industrialization, which might have provided work for India's unemployed masses, was avoided. During the American Civil War (1861–1865), which limited Britain's access to American cotton, there was a shift from food to cotton farming in India. This shift intensified the effects of a drought in the 1870s, leading to widespread famine. Many peasants were forced to immigrate to British South Africa to work as indentured servants.

●●●─┤Read the Document
Karl Marx, "The British Rule in India," 1853
at **myhistorylab.com**

The Revolt of 1857 also created a poisonous distrust of Indians within the British colonial administration. **Cantonments** segregating whites from "untrustworthy" natives became the rule in Indian towns and cities. Despite just intentions in royal statements and the opening of the civil service, at least nominally, to Indian candidates, the *Raj* discouraged equality between the Indians and British. One bright exception to this trend was the tenure (1880–1884) of the Marquess of Ripon (1827–1909) as viceroy of India.

British Officer Reclining. This photograph of a British officer reclining while being fanned and served by two Indian attendants provides a glimpse into the colonial lifestyle in British India. It also gives insight into race, class, and labor divides.

Ripon fought to erase legal discrimination by allowing Indian judges to try British as well as Indian citizens. His efforts earned him the hatred of most of his British compatriots in India, but he was an example to emerging Indian leaders of the best that British egalitarianism could produce. Although his British foes agitated to dilute his measures, in doing so they unwittingly gave Indians a model for their own political agitation.[3]

Indian Resistance

Indians soon took up political activism. In the late 1800s, they founded institutions that would help overcome traditional regionalism, build national feeling, and ultimately end colonial rule. In 1885 modernists formed the Indian National Congress to reform traditional Hindu and Muslim practices that did not match up to their liberal ideals and to change British Indian policies that were equally out of line with democratic ideals. Other Indians agitated for rejection of British rule altogether. The Muslim League developed as a counterbalance to the Hindu-dominated

[2]See, for example, Bayly, *Indian Society and the British Empire*, pp. 169–199; David Arnold, "Rebellious Hillmen: The Gudem-Rampa Risings, 1839–1924," in Ranajit Guha, ed., *Subaltern Studies* (Delhi: Oxford University Press, 1982), pp. 88–142; Ranajit Guha, *Elementary Aspects of Peasant Insurgency in Colonial India* (New Delhi, 1984); cf. Eric Stokes, *The Peasant and the Raj: Studies in Agrarian Society and Peasant Rebellion in Colonial India* (Cambridge: Cambridge University Press, 1978).

[3]Stanley Wolpert, *A New History of India*, 2nd ed. (New York: Oxford University Press, 1982), pp. 256–257.

Congress. The League eventually made common cause with Congress in seeking home rule but ultimately worked for, and gained, a separate Muslim state, Pakistan. Heavy-handed, erratic British policies in legal administration, political representation, and taxation strengthened growing desires for nationhood and independence.

Indian internal divisions were a major obstacle to achieving independence. These included the many language groups and princely states of the subcontinent, but these were not the only divisions, nor even the most critical. For much of British rule, every Indian politician was first a representative of his own region or state and second an Indian nationalist. Furthermore, the educated Indian elite had little in common with the masses of farmers and laborers beyond antagonism to foreign rule, which made unified resistance or political action difficult. Mistrust and conflict among Hindus, Muslims, Sikhs, and Jains also impeded concerted action.

Nevertheless, a nationalist movement with many sub-branches took root. There were three principal elements within the independence movement that led to the creation of India and Pakistan in 1947.

The first element consisted of the National Congress members who sought gradual reform and progress toward Indian self-governance, or *svarāj*. This did not preclude outright opposition to the British, but it did mean trying to deal with the colonial rulers to change the system from within wherever possible. Among the proponents of this approach were G. K. Gokhale (1866–1915), the champion of moderate, deliberate, peaceful work toward self-determination; the spiritual and political genius Mohandas K. Gandhi (1869–1948); and his follower Jawaharlal Nehru (1889–1964), later to become India's first prime minister. Gandhi was the major Indian leader after World War I who directed the all-India movement that finally drove the British out. An English-trained lawyer, he drew on not only his native Hindu (and Jain and Buddhist) heritage, but also the ideas of Christian and Western liberal thinkers like Henry David Thoreau (1817–1862) and Leo Tolstoy (1828–1910). In the end, Gandhi became a world figure as well as an Indian leader. (See Document, "Gandhi on Passive Resistance and *Svarāj*" on page 800.)

The second element consisted of militant Hindu nationalists, whose leader, the extremist B. G. Tilak (1856–1920), stressed use of Indian languages and revival of Hindu culture and learning. Tilak also subscribed to an anti-Muslim, Hindu communalist vision of Indian "self-governance." Where earlier in the nineteenth century foreign ideas had stimulated a Hindu renaissance and various reform movements, the Hindu extremists now looked to return to traditional Indian values and self-sufficiency. Al-though their movement dissipated in the common resistance effort after 1914, their religious and political ideas still influence Indian political life, as witnessed by today's resurgence of Hindu extremist groups and communal (especially Hindu-Muslim) strife.

Muslims were the third element, but there were divergent regional and sectarian Muslim constituencies. Generally, their leaders were hesitant to make common cause out of the fear that as a minority they stood to lose what power they had in a Hindu-majority, Indian nation. Muslims had been slower than Hindus to take up British ideas and education and thus lagged behind the Hindu intelligentsia in numbers and influence with the British or other Indians. Because Muslims were so prominent in the 1857 Revolt, the British were at first much less inclined to foster their advancement than that of Hindus. Nonetheless, the Muslims, distrusting the Hindu-dominated Indian National Congress, at first sought rapprochement with the British rather than risk submersion in Hindu-led opposition movements.

The man who did most to regain respect and a voice for Muslims in India under the Crown was Sayyid Ahmad Khan (1817–1898). A longtime supporter of modernist ideas and cooperation with the British, he could also be sharply critical of their mistakes in India. His opposition to Muslim participation in the National Congress foreshadowed later Hindu–Muslim tensions. He also founded the Muslim educational initiative that led to creation of the Muhammadan Anglo-Oriental College at Aligarh, which became the center

Chronology

India

1772–1833	Ram Mohan Roy, Hindu reformer
1774–1785	Administration of Warren Hastings
1817–1898	Sayyid Ahmad Khan, Muslim reformer
1835	Introduction of English education
1857–1858	Sepoy Revolt, or "Mutiny," followed by direct Crown rule as a British colony
1869–1948	Mohandas K. Gandhi
1873–1938	Muhammad Iqbal
1876–1949	Muhammad Ali Jinnah
1885	Indian National Congress formed
1889–1964	Jawaharlal Nehru
1947	Independence and partition

Document   Gandhi on Passive Resistance and *Svarāj*

Gandhi's powerful thinking and prose were already evident in his *Hind Svarāj*, or *Indian Home Rule*, of 1909. This was to remain his basic manifesto. The following excerpts reflect important points in his philosophy. *Svadeshî* refers to reliance only on what one produces at home (rather than on foreign goods).

■ *How does Gandhi relate passive resistance and svarāj to his theory of Indian self-rule? What are the advantages/disadvantages of his strategy for effecting political and social change? How does this document compare with others concerned with movements of independence and nationalism? See "The Stamp Act Congress Addresses George III" (Chapter 22) and "Mazzini Defines Nationality" (Chapter 23).*

Passive resistance is a method for securing rights by personal suffering; it is the reverse of armed resistance. When I refuse to do something repugnant to my conscience, I use soul-force. For instance, the government of the day has passed a law applicable to me. I do not like it. If by using violence I force the government to repeal the law, I am employing what may be termed body-force. If I do not obey the law and accept the penalty for its breach, I use soul-force. It involves sacrifice of self.

Everybody admits that sacrifice of self is infinitely superior to sacrifice of others. Moreover, if this kind of force is used in a cause that is unjust, only the person using it suffers. He does not make others suffer for his mistakes . . . .

. . . The real meaning of the statement that we are a law-abiding nation is that we are passive resisters. When we do not like certain laws, we do not break the heads of law-givers but we suffer and do not submit to the laws . . . .

If man will only realize that it is unmanly to obey laws that are unjust, no man's tyranny will enslave him. This is the key to self-rule or home-rule [*svarāj*] . . . .

Let each do his duty. If I do my duty, that is, serve myself, I shall be able to serve others. Before I leave you, I will take the liberty of repeating:

1. Real home-rule is self-rule or self-control.
2. The way to it is passive resistance: that is soul-force or love-force.
3. In order to exert this force, *Svadeshî* in every sense is necessary.
4. What we want to do should be done, not because we object to the English or because we want to retaliate, but because it is our duty to do so. Thus, supposing that the English remove the salt-tax, restore our money, give the highest posts to Indians, withdraw the English troops, we shall certainly not use their machine-made goods, nor use the English language, nor many of their industries. It is worth noting that these things are, in their nature, harmful; hence we do not want them. I bear no enmity towards the English but do towards their civilization. In my opinion, we have used the term *Svadeshî* without understanding its real significance. I have endeavored to explain it as I understand it, and my conscience testifies that my life henceforth is dedicated to its attainment.

Source: From *Sources of Indian Tradition*, ed. by William Theodore de Bary. Copyright © 1958 by Columbia University Press. Reprinted with permission of the publisher.

---

for modernist Muslim attempts to integrate Muslim faith with modern Western thought and learning. It remains a Muslim intellectual center in India today.

Hindu-Muslim Friction on the Road to Independence

In the twentieth century the rift between Indian Muslims and Hindus grew wider, despite periods of cooperation against the British. Muslim arguments for coexistence with Hindus floundered while fears of loss of communal identity and rights grew. In the end the great Indo-Muslim poet, thinker, and "spiritual father of Pakistan," Muhammad Iqbal (1873–1938), and the "founder of Pakistan," Muhammad Ali Jinnah (1876–1949), helped move Muslims to separatism.

The independence of India and Pakistan was achieved only with violence and suffering. Much blood was spilled in the long battle with the British and communal violence among Indians themselves—especially that between Hindus and Muslims during partition in 1947 and the subsequent (still

A Closer Look

Gandhi and His Spinning Wheel

Gandhi premised his civil disobedience and resistance movement against the British colonial hegemony over India on a return to basics of Indian life: attaining *swadeshi*, self-sufficiency (e.g., rejecting machine-made European clothing for home-industry spinning of simple Khadi cloth), moral independence and superiority (nonviolent civil disobedience in the face of British armed control), and *swaraj*, self-governance or home rule (replacing the British Raj). The spinning wheel (Hindi *Charkha*, etymologically related to Sanskrit *chakra*, "wheel") became the tangible symbol of these fundamentals in Gandhi's message and his practice, and was later taken onto the national flag of India. Note that it also carries associations of the *chakra* used in early Buddhist teaching and Ashokan symbolism, as noted in Chapter 4.

The simple wooden, 16-spoke spinning wheel, or *charkha*, became the major symbol of the independence movement that Gandhi led, referring both to making one's own clothing and to the nobility of physical work.

Note the simple loincloth, or *dhoti*, which Gandhi took up, along with a shoulder shawl, both made of simple khadi cotton, after he abandoned the European dress of his earlier life as a London-trained lawyer in South Africa.

Questions

1. Why do you think the emphasis, by the educated Gandhi and other members of the independence-movement elite, on the importance of simple work, such as spinning for one's own clothing, had such resonance for millions of Indians under British rule in the Subcontinent?

2. What elements might have made the identification of the *charkha* as spinning wheel with the Ashokan and Buddhist *chakra* so compelling as a conjoined symbol for India as a nation?

3. How might spinning one's own cloth relate to nonviolence (*ahimsa*) as well as to economic resistance to the British?

The Founding Father of Pakistan. Muhammad Ali Jinnah was president of India's Muslim League in the 1930s, when he advanced the "two nations" theory and made the first formal demand for a separate Muslim homeland. His ideas led to the establishment of Pakistan, of which he was founding president.

festering) dispute over Kashmir between India and Pakistan. Still, the victory of 1947 gave the peoples of the subcontinent, Indians and Pakistanis, at last a sense of agency and of political participation on their own terms, not those dictated by a foreign power. The British legacy was not all bad, for it also consisted of administrative and political unity and egalitarian and democratic ideals that Indian nationalists turned to their own uses for the two new nations.

●•●•[Read the Document
Gandhi Speaks against the Partition of India (pre-1947) at **myhistorylab.com**

The Islamic Experience

Islamic Responses to Declining Power and Independence

The eighteenth century saw the great Muslim empires weaken as the West became ascendant in international trade, military-political power, imperialist expansion, industrial specialization and productivity, and technological progress. Diverse Islamic peoples and states plunged from positions of global power into a struggle for survival. As with India, the decline of Islamic preeminence was due both to the rise of the modern West and to internal problems.

By the nineteenth century, Muslim empires—Mughal, Ottoman, Safavid/Qajar, Moroccan, and Central Asian—had declined politically, militarily, and economically in relation to western European empires (see Map 26–2 on page 803). They had become increasingly decentralized, less stable economically and politically, and dominated by entrenched hereditary elites. The circumnavigation of the globe made it no longer necessary to transit the Islamic heartlands to move between Europe and Asia. For millennia, these heartlands had benefited commercially from their geographic middle-man status. The shift in trade routes resulted in changes in Middle Eastern/Mediterranean economies that made them more peripheral to the world economy now centered on western Europe. Still, once various European nations had established footholds in South and Southeast Asia, they turned their attention after 1800 back to the Islamic heartlands. This Middle Eastern world (including Iran) became enmeshed in European imperial competition for industrial resources such as oil, and most of it came under Western political and economic domination. The interactions between Middle Eastern peoples and these new imperial powers were varied. There was some cooperation and accommodation, but for the most part the prevailing reality after 1800 was one of conflict.

Ultimately, the fundamental question engrossing Muslim reformers, politicians, and intellectuals was the basis of European ascendancy. Was European secular learning and technological superiority transferable to the Middle East or other regions? Could the once dominant Islamic world regain vitality by importing European values, education, and technology? Could Islamic values be adapted or reformed to foster the kind of societal progress Europe seemed to have managed without succumbing entirely to secularization?

During the eighteenth and nineteenth centuries a variety of reform movements sought to revive Islam as a comprehensive guide for living and to purify it of the more stultifying Islamic societal developments in preceding centuries. In major urban areas such as Cairo, Istanbul, and Damascus, influential reformers such as Muhammad Ali (see p. 806) and the sultan Mahmud II proposed adaptive reform that sought to reengineer the armies, institutions, and societies of the Middle East to conform to the political reality of European domination. In these same urban settings, a variety of intellectuals sought to redefine what it meant to be Muslim in a modern age by emphasizing the malleability of Islam in relation to contemporary society. The most famous of such reform efforts was the *Tanzimat* (see p. 806) in the Ottoman Empire. In the more rural areas, where neither urban Muslim ideas nor

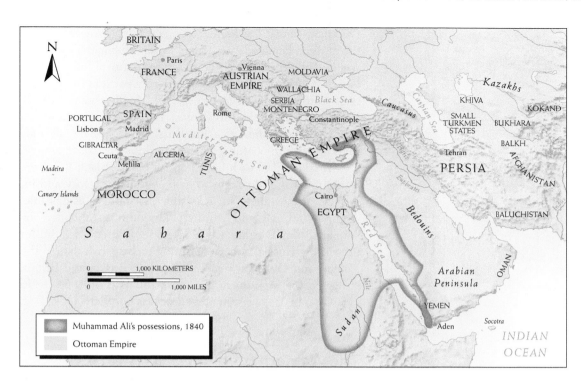

Map 26–2. West Asia, Central Asia, and the Mediterranean, ca. 1850. Compare this map with Map 20–2 on p. 616. Although the Ottoman Empire still technically ruled a large area, in actuality it had lost much control over regions on the periphery.

European power had penetrated to the same extent, other reformers stressed rejection of more flexible forms of Islam and of any Western or other values that might be held up as models.

The most famous movement that emphasized a strict construction of what "true" Islam entails was that of the **Wahhabis**, the followers of Ibn Abd al-Wahhab (1703–1792) in Arabia. It sought to combat the excesses of popular and Sufi piety, such as saint worship, visitations to saints' tombs, and faith in the intercession of Sufi masters and saints. It also sought to break the stranglehold of the *ulama*'s conformist positions on legal and religious issues, favoring instead exercise of independent judgment. The only authorities were to be the Qur'an and the traditions of the Prophet, not the scholastic norms of the traditional schools of legal and theological interpretation. Allied with a local Arab prince, Muhammad Ibn Sa'ud, the Wahhabi movement swept over the Arabian Peninsula. It was crushed in the early 1800s by Egyptian military forces representing the Ottoman regime. Still, the movement finally saw victory under a descendant of Ibn Sa'ud at the onset of the twentieth century and is the formal ideology of today's Saudi Arabia.

◆◆▸ Read the Document
Religious Minorities in the Middle East (late 19th-early 20th century) at **myhistorylab.com**

Other Muslim reform movements reflected similar revivalist, even militantly pietist responses to Islamic decadence and decline. Examples include that of Usman Dan Fodio in Africa in the late eighteenth century (see p. 812) and the Muslim Brotherhood in modern Egypt (see Chapter 33). Such groups called for a pristine Islam divested of the authoritarianism of the medieval legal schools, *ulama* theological conformity, and degenerate Sufi orders. Furthermore, such movements inspired an uncritical nostalgia for a time when Islamic societies were ascendant, even dominant. This vision still rallies movements from Africa to Indonesia. In Islamic societies everywhere it has provided one response to the challenge of Western-style "modernity" and one model for cultural and religious life.

Western Political and Economic Encroachment

From the late 1700s until World War II the political fortunes of Arab, Turkish, Persian, Indian, Southeast Asian, and African Islamic states were increasingly dictated externally by Western powers—including Britain, Russia, Germany, and France—and were at the mercy of the rivalries among them.

Western governments extracted from indigenous governments capitulations favorable to their own economic and political interests in exchange for promises of military protection or other considerations. These capitulations granted commercial concessions, protection, and "extraterritorial" legal status to European merchant enclaves. Such concessions (the earliest was from the sixteenth century) had originally been reciprocal and also served the commercial purposes of Muslim rulers and merchants. However, they eventually provided Western powers with pretexts for direct intervention in Ottoman, Iranian, Indian, and African affairs. The Ottoman

Frontispiece from the Arab Literary-Scientific Journal *al-Muqtataf*, founded by Yaqub Sarruf in the 1860s. A group of such periodicals provided a public arena for political debate despite Ottoman, Egyptian, and British censors. They were a way for the burgeoning educated middle class of the Arab world (especially in Egypt) to develop national identities and debate social, economic, and political issues and policies. The crossed pen and hammer suggest a call to action while the floral border is reminiscent of traditional Islamic manuscripts.

Empire, like the Mughal Empire, suffered from internal disunity; its provincial rulers, or *pashas*, were virtually independent. This, combined with increasing economic problems facing Asian and African agrarian societies, made it easy for Western powers—with their rapidly industrializing economies and increasingly effective militaries—to take control almost at will. Repeated Ottoman diplomatic and military defeats made that once great imperial power "the sick man of Europe" after 1800; a similar weakness allowed Westerners to control the fate of Indian and Iranian states as well.

The event that marked symbolically the onset of European domination of the Islamic heartlands was Egypt's invasion by Napoleon Bonaparte (1769–1821) in 1798 (see Chapter 22). The ease with which French forces were able to invade Egypt and topple the local government was suggestive of the weakened state of the Middle Eastern and wider Islamic world. It also demonstrated European technical advances in field artillery and infantry rifles. Eventually Britain, Russia, and the

Ottomans forced the French to evacuate Egypt in 1801, but the invasion heralded a new era of European imperialism in the region. The British had already wrested control of India and the Persian Gulf from the French; they now became the preeminent European power in the eastern Mediterranean as well. The French continued to contest British ascendancy in the larger Middle Eastern area, but Russia presented the most serious nineteenth-century challenge to Britain's colonial empire.

Russia had already won control of the Black Sea from the Ottomans and sought to gain as much territory and influence in Iran, the Caucasus, and Central Asia as possible. Afghanistan, an independent kingdom established by Ahmad Shah Durrani (r. 1737–1773), acted as a buffer preventing Russia from penetrating to British India. In the Iranian and Ottoman regions, however, Russia and Britain struggled for supremacy. The Crimean War of 1854–1856 (see Chapter 23) was one result of this conflict.

The Western Impact

Beyond the overt European political and commercial impact, Western political ideology, culture, and technology proved to be critical factors for change in Islamic societies. Outside of India, this was most strongly felt in Egypt, Lebanon, North Africa, and Anatolia (modern Turkey). Of all the Islamic states, including those in Africa and India, the ones least and last affected by Western "modernity" were Iran, Afghanistan, and the Central Asian khanates. The Iranian case deserves at least brief attention.

Iran The rulers of Iran from 1794 to 1925 were the Qajar shahs, a Turkoman Dynasty whose absolutist reign was not unlike that of the Safavids. Unlike the Safavids, however, the Qajars made no religious claims to descent from the Shi'ite *imams*. Under Qajar rule, in marked contrast to Safavid sovereignty, the Shi'ite *ulama* became less and less strongly connected with the state apparatus. This period saw the emergence of a Shi'i traditionalist doctrine that encouraged all Shi'ites, in the absence of a living *imam*, to choose a **mujtahid**—a qualified scholarly guide—from among the *ulama* and follow him in all matters requiring religious-legal interpretation. Consequently, the *ulama* gained strength as an independent power in the state. As guardians of law and faith, they became often the Qajars' chief critics (not least for their attempts to admit Western influences) and champions of popular grievances.

A prime demonstration of *ulama* power occurred when the Qajar Shah granted a fifty-year monopoly on tobacco sales to a British corporation in 1890. In 1891 the leading authority in the *ulama* spearheaded a tobacco boycott to protest the concession. This popular action, the first success-

Linking Asia and Europe. The opening of the Suez Canal in 1869 was a major engineering achievement. It also became a major international waterway, reducing the distance from London to Bombay by half.

ful mass protest in modern Iranian history, was supported by modernist-nationalist opponents of the Qajar regime who had strong connections to Iran's commercial, or **bazaari**, middle classes. In the face of such widespread opposition, the shah had to rescind the concession. On the one hand, this was a stunning victory for the power of public opinion and a symbolic blow against Western commercial interests in Iran. Yet ironically this action only made Iran more dependent on Western capital. The Iranian government was forced to pay an exorbitant compensation of around £500,000 sterling to the British corporation, which necessitated a foreign loan from a British bank. This was Iran's first foreign debt and made it more reliant on Western institutions thereafter.

Subject as it was to the machinations of outsiders such as Russia, Britain, and France, Iran inevitably felt the impact of Western ideas about education, science, law, and government. This occurred especially in the latter half of the century, when younger Iranian intellectuals began to warm to Western liberalism on economic, social, and political issues. As in other Islamic countries, the seeds of a new, secular nationalism were being sown where, previously, sectarian or communalist religious sentiments had held sway. It coincided and worked with a growing desire for a voice in government. An uneasy alliance of Iranian radical nationalists, liberal *bazaari*, and conservative *ulama* proved, on occasion, an effective counterforce to Qajar absolutism, beginning with the successful 1891–1892 Tobacco Boycott and ending with the revolutionary *mashruteh* or Iranian Constitutional Movement of 1906–1911, when the Qajar shahs were forced to cede their treaty-making powers and control of the country's finances to the *majlis* or National Consultative Assembly. Yet such alliances were not to endure for very long.

Islamic Responses to Foreign Encroachment

As the Iranian case shows, Western impingement on the Islamic world in the nineteenth and early twentieth centuries elicited varied responses. Every people or state had a different experience, according to its particular circumstances and history. Yet there were at least three typical styles of reaction: (1) emulation of Western ideas and institutions; (2) efforts to join Western innovations with traditional Islamic institutions; and (3) traditionalist rejection of things Western in favor of the status quo or a return to a purified Islamic *Umma*. Of course, none of these styles was confined to one class or group in Islamic societies, and none was uniform within a country or across political, ethnic, and cultural boundaries.

Read the Document
Ottoman
at **myhistorylab.com**

Emulation of the West

The career of the virtually independent Ottoman viceroy Muhammad Ali (ca. 1769–1849), pasha of Egypt from 1805 to 1849, exemplifies a strategy of emulation. Ali, who arrived in Alexandria as part of an Albanian regiment of Ottoman forces sent to fight the French in 1801, set out to rejuvenate Egypt's failing agriculture, introduce modern mechanized industry, modernize the army with European help, and introduce European education and culture in government schools. Although he ultimately failed to make Egypt as powerful as European states of his day, Muhammad Ali did set his country on the path to becoming a nation-state. His successors' financial and political successes, such as building the Suez Canal, also led to

Muhammad Ali (1769–1849), the famous viceroy of Egypt.

catastrophes such as indebtedness and the eventual occupation of Egypt by Britain, despite the heroic 1881–1882 uprising led by Urabi Pasha (1839–1911). From 1882 to 1956, Britain occupied the Suez Canal and parts of Egypt, and while some consider Muhammad Ali "the father of modern Egypt," others consider Urabi Pasha, an Egyptian-born military officer, "the father of Egyptian nationalist movements." But Muhammad Ali and Urabi Pasha were not the only Egyptian militant political figures who emerged. Sa'd Zaghlul Pasha (1857–1927), an Egyptian

statesman and patriot, led a *Wafd* or delegation to Paris in 1919 to protest the 1914 British protectorate imposed on Egypt and to demand immediate independence. Zaghlul Pasha and his compatriots did not reverse the British occupation, but the *Wafd* Party lasted well beyond the last occupying British troops.

Several Ottoman sultans and viziers tried to appropriate Western experience and success after Russia's devastating defeat of the Turks in 1774. Most notable were the reforms of Selim III (r. 1762–1808), Mahmud II (r. 1808–1839), and the so-called **Tanzimat**, or beneficial "legislation" (literally, "[re]ordering") era, from about 1839 to 1880. Selim made serious efforts at economic, administrative, and military reform. He brought European officers in to train a new military corps to supplant the conservative Janissaries. Mahmud's reforms were much like those of Muhammad Ali. Most important were his destruction of the Janissary corps, tax and bureaucratic reforms, and encouragement of Western military and educational methods among Ottoman elites. Like Selim and Muhammad Ali, he was less interested in promoting European enlightenment ideas about citizen rights and equity than in building a stronger, more modern centralized government, which often resulted in the consolidation of political power among a select few.

The Tanzimat reforms, introduced by several liberal Ottoman ministers of state, continued the efforts of Selim and Mahmud to bring the Ottoman state into line with ideals espoused by the European states. They were also intended to give European powers less cause to intervene in Ottoman affairs and to regenerate domestic confidence in the state.

Watch the Video
The Ottoman Tanzimat Period (1839-1876): The Middle East Confronts Modernity
at **myhistorylab.com**

Tanzimat. A sitting of the new (1909) Turkish Parliament following the abolition of the 1876 Constitution in 1878 by the Sultan Abdul Hamid II. Sessions were held in a lavish chamber with the delegates from the Balkans, Anatolia, and Fertile Crescent (Syria, Lebanon, Iraq, Jordan, and Palestine) seated facing a high podium at the front of the chamber.

The nineteenth-century Ottoman reforms failed to save the empire or truly to revive it as an economically sound, culturally vibrant, or militarily and politically powerful state. Nevertheless, they paved the way for the rise of Turkish nationalism, the 1908 "Young Turk" revolution, and ultimately the nationalist revolution of the 1920s that produced modern Turkey. (Ironically and tragically, this development simultaneously frustrated similar nationalist aspirations among old Ottoman minorities such as the Greeks, the Armenians, and the Kurds.)

The creation of the Turkish republic from the ashes of the Ottoman state after World War I is probably the most extreme effort to modernize and nationalize an Islamic state on a Western model. Others would argue that it is the most successful integration of Western models and Islamic institutions. This state was largely the child of Mustafa Kemal (1881–1938), known as "Atatürk" ("father of the Turks"), its founder and first president (1922–1938). Atatürk led Turkey through an intensive reform that sought to eliminate vestiges of the Ottoman past and orient Turkey more toward the West. He based his wide-ranging reforms on six principles fundamental to the doctrine known as "Kemalism": reformism, secularism, republicanism, nationalism, statism, and populism. Although Atatürk's major reforms ranged from introduction of a European-style code of civil law to abolition of the caliphate, Sufi orders, Arabic script, and the Arabic call to prayer, he attempted to inculcate pride in the ideal of a modern secular Turkish nation appealing to all segments of society. On the surface, Atatürk's reforms constituted a truly radical attempt to secularize an Islamic state and to separate religious from political and social institutions. At the same time, his reforms were largely a continuation of the transformation begun in the Ottoman era and had essentially the same goal as the Tanzimat movement, that is, making Turkey more responsive to the challenges of modernity. In the decades since, Turkey has maintained its independence, reaffirmed its commitment to democratic government, and emerged with a unique, but still distinctly Islamic, identity.

◆●─Read the Document
The Young Turk Revolution, 1908
at **myhistorylab.com**

Integration of Western and Islamic Ideas

The attempt to join modernization with traditional Islamic institutions and ideas is exemplified in the thought of Muslim intellectuals such as Jamal al-Din al-Afghani (1839–1897), Muhammad Abduh (1845–1905), and Muhammad Iqbal (1873–1938). These thinkers argued for progressive Islam rather than materialist Western secularism as the best answer for life in the modern world.

Afghani is best known for his emphasis on the unity of the Islamic world, or **pan-Islamism**, and on a populist, constitutionalist approach to political order. His ideas and his charismatic personality influenced political-activist movements in Egypt, Iran, Ottoman Turkey, and elsewhere.

Kemal Atatürk at the Wedding of His Adopted Daughter, Nebile, in 1929. Everything about this photo—the bride's dress, her father's white tie—suggests a European setting.

Afghani's Egyptian disciple, Muhammad Abduh, sought to modernize Muslim education. Abduh argued that a firm, revealed Qur'anic base could be combined harmoniously with modern science and its open questioning of reality. Through his efforts as Grand Mufti and head of state education, he introduced modernist reforms that affected even the curriculum of the most venerable traditionalist institution of higher learning in the Islamic world, the great al-Azhar in Cairo.

Muhammad Iqbal, the most celebrated Indian Muslim thinker of the twentieth century, argued for a modernist revival of Muslim faith through purifying and uplifting the individual self above enslavement to either reason or traditionalist conformity. Often credited with the original idea of a separate Muslim state in South Asia (today's Pakistan), Iqbal still felt that Islam was essentially nonexclusivist and supranationalist:

The truth is that Islam is not a church. It is a state conceived as a contractual organism . . . and animated by an ethical ideal which regards man not as an earth-rooted creature, defined by this or that portion of the earth, but as a spiritual being understood in terms of a social mechanism, and possessing rights and duties as a living factor in that mechanism . . . .[4]

---

[4]Quoted in K. Cragg and R. M. Speight, eds., *Islam from Within* (Belmont, CA: Wadsworth, 1980), p. 213.

Although Iqbal's poetry and essays excited Muslim fervor and dynamism, it is difficult to say how great his tangible impact on Islamic political and social life really was.

Women and Reform in the Middle East

Although the discussion of reform, religion, and modernity in the Middle East was dominated by men, there were also a number of Middle Eastern women who addressed the status of women in modern society. Most important were those who demanded political involvement for women in their country's affairs: notably, the Iranian women who confronted their fathers and brothers in the Iranian Parliament in December 1911 on the possibility that the men might capitulate to the Russian-British demands to remove the American reforming administrator, Morgan Schuster; the Egyptian women who, upon returning with their politician husbands in 1919 from Paris, where the Egyptian delegation (or *Wafd*) had been humiliated by the Versailles powers, threw off their veils and declared themselves the new Egyptian women; or the Palestinian women who convened a Women's Congress of Palestine in 1929 to address the political issues ensuing from the Wailing Wall riots of the same year. It is also noteworthy that there emerged in the late nineteenth and early twentieth centuries a number of journals and magazines devoted to women's concerns. These mainly focused on traditional issues such as cooking, parenting, and fashion, but there were other journals that sought to enlarge the domain of women and their role in the public sphere. Some articles stressed that women were essential to society and not to be excluded from commercial or political participation. Movements and demonstrations likewise supported such concerns. Thus Huda Sha'rawi (1879–1947) founded the Egyptian Feminist Union in 1923 to fight for women's suffrage, marriage-law reform, and equal access to education. In a well-publicized event, Sha'rawi and her colleague Saize Nabrawi made a dramatic gesture to highlight their feminist objectives. Standing in Cairo's bustling train station, they publicly removed their veils to emphasize that women should no longer be concealed from the rest of society. Sha'rawi's act, like that of the women who returned from Versailles in 1919, indicated that the veil was symbolic of women's inadequate public status in Egypt and other Middle Eastern countries. For those outside the Middle East today, veiling is often seen as the most important gender issue. Many Middle Eastern feminists stress, however, that women's inequality is rooted in wide-ranging cultural, political, and economical structures that need to be addressed much more than the veil issue.

Purification and Revival of Islam

A third kind of Muslim reaction to Western domination has emphasized Islamic values and ideals to the exclusion of "outside" forces. This approach has involved either the kind of purist, reformist revivalism already seen in Wahhabism or the kind of conservatism often associated with Sunni or Shi'ite "establishment" *ulama*, as in the case of Iran since 1979. Both conservative and revivalist Muslim thinkers share the conviction that the answers to the questions facing modern Muslims are to be found within, not outside, the Islamic tradition.

Traditionalist conservatism is much harder to pin down as the ethos of particular movements and organized groups than is reformist revivalism. Whereas Muslim revivalism (today commonly called "Islamism") usually focuses on the Qur'an and Prophetic example as sole authorities for Muslim life, Muslim conservatism typically champions those forms of Islamic life and thought embodied in traditional law, theology, and even Sufism. It is seen in the legalistic tendencies that have often resurfaced when Islamic norms have been threatened by the breakdown of traditional society and the rise of secularism. Although such conservatism has often been associated with reactionary forces in Islamic society, it has often also served to preserve basic Muslim values while allowing for gradual change that reformist revivalism cannot accept. Where conservatives have formed alliances with governments or simply been co-opted by them, the credibility of establishment *ulama* has often been destroyed. This is because the masses of Muslims have been increasingly attracted to Islamist agendas for rapid change.

Chronology

Islamic Heartlands, 1700–1938

1703–1792	Ibn Abd al-Wahhab
1737–1773	Rule of Ahmad Shah Durrani, founder of modern Afghanistan
1794–1925	Qajar shahs of Iran
1798	Napoleon Bonaparte invades Egypt
1805–1849	Muhammad Ali rules Egypt
ca. 1839–1880	Ottoman Tanzimat reforms
1839–1897	Jamal al-Din al-Afghani
1845–1905	Muhammad Abduh
1881-82	Urabi Pasha uprising
1882–1922	British occupation of Egypt
1891-92	Iranian Tobacco Boycott
1906-11	Iranian Constitutional Movement
1908	"Young Turk" revolution
1922–1938	Mustafa Kemal, "Atatürk," in power

Document   Tâhâ Hussein, "The Future of Culture in Egypt"

Tâhâ Hussein (1889–1973) was Egyptian minister of education from 1950 to 1952 and a leading Arab intellectual. Born in a poor village in upper Egypt, he became blind by the age of 3. He studied at Al-Azhar University and finished his doctorate at the Sorbonne in Paris. Hussein, like many contemporaneous intellectuals around the world, was very concerned with nationalism and how to reconcile modernity with traditional thought and practice. In his writings, he argued that Egypt was part of Mediterranean civilization and should follow European ideas in its quest to build a modern nation. In the following piece, "The Future of Culture in Egypt" (1938), Hussein argues for Westernization as a return to Egypt's real roots.

■ *What is Hussein trying to achieve by emphasizing Egypt's historic ties to Europe?*

The subject to be treated in this discourse is the future of culture in Egypt, now that our country has regained her freedom through the revival of the constitution and her honor through the realization of independence. We are living in an age characterized by the fact that freedom and independence do not constitute ends in themselves, but are merely means of attaining exalted, enduring, and generally practical goals . . .

I know of nothing that causes me more worry than this newly won independence and freedom of ours. I fear that they may beguile us into thinking that we have come to the end of the road when in fact we have just reached the beginning . . .

I do not want us to feel inferior to the Europeans because of our cultural shortcomings. This would cause us to despise ourselves and admit that they are not treating us unjustly when they are being arrogant. It is obnoxious for a man who is sensitive to dignity and honor to be compelled to acknowledge that he is not yet deserving of them. Let us keep this disgrace from ourselves and the nation. The way to do it is to take hold of our affairs with determination and vigor from today on, discard useless words for meaningful action, and establish our new life on a sound, constructive basis. . . .

At the outset we must answer this fundamental question: Is Egypt of the East or of the West? Naturally, I mean East or West in the cultural, not the geographical sense. It seems to me that there are two distinctly different and bitterly antagonistic cultures on the earth. Both have existed since time immemorial, the one in Europe, the other in the Far East. . . .

The Egyptian mind had no serious contact with the Far Eastern mind; nor did it live harmoniously with the Persian mind. The Egyptian mind has had regular, peaceful, and mutually beneficial relations only with the Near East and Greece. In short, it has been influenced from earliest times by the Mediterranean Sea and the various peoples living around it. . . .

In order to become equal partners in civilization with the Europeans, we must literally and forthrightly do everything that they do; we must share with them the present civilization, with its pleasant and unpleasant sides, and not content ourselves with words or mere gestures. Whoever advises any other course of action is either a deceiver or is himself deceived. Strangely enough we imitate the West in our everyday life, yet hypocritically deny the fact in our words. If we really detest European life, what is to hinder us from rejecting it completely? And if we genuinely respect the Europeans, as we certainly seem to do by our wholesale adoption of their practices, why do we not reconcile our words with our actions? Hypocrisy ill becomes those who are proud and anxious to overcome their defects.

Source: From *The Future of Culture in Egypt,* by Tâhâ Hussein, trans. by Sidney Glazer, Washington, DC: American Council of Learned Societies, 1954, pp. 1–5, 7–9, 15–17, 20, 25. No. 9 in ACLS Near Eastern Translation Project, copyright 1954. Reprinted in *The Islamic World,* eds. William H. McNeill and Marilyn Robinson Waldon, The University of Chicago Press, 1973.

Nationalism

Nationalism is a product of modern European history (see Chapter 23). Nationalist movements in the Islamic world, though internally driven, have often been influenced by Western models or arisen in reaction to Western imperialism and colonial occupation. During the late nineteenth century, many Asian and African intellectuals grappled with the question of identity and whether or not their ethnic or linguistic group constituted a distinct nation or part of a larger whole. (See Document, "Tâhâ Hussein, 'The Future of Culture in Egypt.'") The answer was not always self-evident and in fact proved quite complicated given the mosaic of ethnicities, religions, and language groups across Africa and Asia. Yet the often arbitrary, artificial divisions of the colonial world by European administrators eventually demanded African and Asian answers to these questions. In European capitals, especially after World War I, new "nations" were created and drawn on the maps of Africa and Asia. Thus nations such as Nigeria, Lebanon, Congo, or Iraq reflected imperialist priorities and interests rather than realities on the ground. With time, these borders have taken on an aura of legitimacy. However, building nations that were created artificially has proven to be a difficult and sometimes violent process. Nationalism has been an important aspect of the response to Western domination in the Islamic heartlands as in India. In Turkey in the 1920s it took a secularist form; in Libya, Iran, and elsewhere since the 1970s and 1980s it has taken an Islamic-revivalist form. As an Afro-Asian phenomenon, it will reappear in the next section ("The African Experience") and in Chapter 33.

The African Experience

The period between 1800 and 1945 saw striking change throughout Africa, especially in sub-Saharan Africa. North Africa and Egypt were more closely implicated in the politics of the Ottoman Empire and Europe throughout this period. Except for South Africa below the Transvaal, tropical and southern Africa did not come under colonial control until after 1880. Before then, internal developments—first, demographic and power shifts and then the rise of Islamic reform movements—overshadowed the increasing European presence in the continent.

New States and Power Centers

Southern Africa

In the south, below the Limpopo River, the first quarter of the nineteenth century saw devastating internal warfare, depopulation, and forced migrations of many Bantu peoples in what is known as the **mfecane**, or "crushing" era. Likely brought on by exploding population and fueled by increasing economic competition, the *mfecane* was marked by the rapid rise of sizable military states among the northern Nguni-speaking Bantu. Its result was warfare and chaos; widespread depopulation by death and emigration; and the creation of new, multitribal, multilingual Bantu states in the territory of modern Zimbabwe, Mozambique, Malawi, Zambia, and Tanzania.

The Nguni warrior-king Dingiswayo formed the first of the new military states between about 1800 and 1818. The most important state was formed by his successor, Shaka, leader of the Nguni-speaking Zulu nation and kingdom (ca. 1818–1828). Shaka's brutal military tactics led to Zulu conquest of a vast dominion in southeastern Africa and the virtual depop-

Moshoeshwe, king and founder of Lesotho. Not all of the Bantu peoples followed the militaristic example of Shaka. Moshoeshwe, prince of a sub-tribe of the Sotho Bantus, fought off Zulu attacks and led his people to a mountain stronghold in southern Africa, where, through diplomacy and determination, he founded a small nation that has endured to the present. The kingdom became the British protectorate of Basutoland in 1868. In 1966 it achieved independence as the kingdom of Lesotho under Moshoeshwe's great-grandson, King Moshoeshwe II.

Chronology

Southern Africa

ca. 1800–1818	Dingiswayo, Nguni Zulu king, forms new military state
ca. 1800–1825	The *mfecane* among the Bantu of southeastern Africa
1806	British take Cape Colony from the Dutch
ca. 1818–1828	Shaka's reign as head of the Nguni state; major warfare, destruction, and expansion
ca. 1825–1870	Sotho kingdom of King Moshoeshwe in Lesotho region
1835–1841	Great Trek of Boers into Natal and north onto the high veld beyond the Orange
1843	British annexation of Natal province
1852–1860	Creation of the Orange Free State and South African Republic

ulation of some 15,000 square miles. Refugees from Shaka's "total war" zone fled north into Sotho-speaking Bantu territory or south, putting increasing pressure on the southern Nguni peoples. Virtual chaos ensued, north and south of Zululand.

The net result, beyond widespread suffering and death, was the creation of diverse new states. Some groups tried to imitate the unique military state of Shaka; others fled to mountainous areas and built new, largely defensive states; others went west into the Kalahari. The most famous new state was Lesotho, the Sotho kingdom of King Moshoeshwe, which survived as long as he lived (from the 1820s until 1870). Moshoeshwe defended his people from the Zulu and held off Afrikaners, missionaries, and the British until his death.

The new state-building spawned by the *mfecane* was nullified by Boer expansion and British annexation of Natal province (1843). These developments stemmed from the **Great Trek** of Boer *voortrekers* between 1835 and 1841. This migration brought about 6,000 Afrikaners from the eastern Cape Colony northeastward into the more fertile regions of southern Africa, Natal, and especially the high veld above the Orange River. It resulted in the creation after 1850 of the Afrikaner republics of the Orange Free State between the Orange and Vaal rivers, and the South African Republic north of the Vaal.

East and Central Africa

Farther north in East and east central Africa, increasing external trade led to the formation of several strong regional states. In the Lakes region, peoples such as the Nyamwezi to the east of Lake Tanganyika and the Baganda west of Lake Victoria gained regional power from as early as the late 1700s through trade with the Arab-Swahili eastern coast and the eastern Congo states to the west. The chief traffic in this east–west commerce across central Africa involved slaves, ivory, copper, and, from the outside, Indian cloth, firearms, and other manufactured goods.

West Africa

In West Africa the slave trade was only slowly curtailed. However, European demand for other products—notably palm oil and gum arabic—gained importance by the 1820s. In the first half of the century *jihad* movements of the Fulbe (or Fulani) and others shattered the stability of the western savannah and forestlands from modern Senegal and Ghana through southern Nigeria. Protracted wars and dislocation gave rise to regional kingdoms, such as those of Asante and Dahomey (modern Benin), which flourished before succumbing to internal dissension and British and French colonial ambitions.

Islamic Reform Movements

The expansive vitality of Islam was one significant agent of change in sub-Saharan Africa before the European rush for colonies in the 1880s. It has remained a factor on the wider African scene ever since. In 1800 Islam was already an established tradition from West Africa across the Sudan to the Red Sea and along the East African coast, as well as over all of Arabic-speaking North Africa. It had long been widespread in the southern Sahara and northern Sahel and was common among merchant classes in parts of West Africa. Islam was the law of the land in the sultanate of Zanzibar and the waning Funj Sultanate on the Blue Nile in the

Elephant Tusks, Congo. Ivory was a prized possession used for decorative purposes and jewelry.

Document

Usman Dan Fodio on Evil and Good Government

Following in the tradition of the Wahhabis in Arabia and most previous Islamic reform movements, Dan Fodio stressed adherence to Muslim norms as expressed in the Shari'a, the Divine Law. In the two excerpts that follow, he enumerates some of the evils of the previous Hausa rulers and their "law" and then lists five principles of proper Islamic government.

■ *What does the first principle, that "authority shall not be given to one who seeks it," mean? What government abuses listed by Dan Fodio might be most appalling to the average Muslim? Why?*

One of the ways of their government [that is, of the Hausa or Habe kings] is succession to the emirate by hereditary right and by force to the exclusion of consultation. And one of the ways of their government is the building of their sovereignty upon three things: the people's persons, their honour, and their possessions; and whomsoever they wish to kill or exile or violate his honour or devour his wealth they do so in pursuit of their lusts, without any right in the Shari'a. One of the ways of their government is their imposing on the people monies not laid down by the Shari'a, being those which they call janghali and kurdin ghari and kurdin salla. One of the ways of their governments is their intentionally eating whatever food they wish, whether it is religiously permitted or forbidden, and wearing whatever clothes they wish, whether religiously permitted or forbidden, and drinking what beverages . . . they wish, whether religiously permitted or forbidden, and riding whatever riding beasts they wish, whether religiously permitted or forbidden, and taking what women they wish without marriage contract, and living in decorated palaces, whether religiously permitted or forbidden, and spreading soft (decorated) carpets as they wish, whether religiously permitted or forbidden . . . .

And I say—and help is with God—the foundations of government are five things: the first is that authority shall not be given to one who seeks it. The second is the necessity for consultation. The third is the abandoning of harshness. The fourth is justice. The fifth is good works. And as for its ministers, they are four. (The First) is a trustworthy wazir to wake the ruler if he sleeps, to make him see if he is blind, and to remind him if he forgets, and the greatest misfortune for the government and the subjects is that they should be denied honest wazirs. And among the conditions pertaining to the wazir is that he should be steadfast in compassion to the people, and merciful towards them. The second of the ministers of government is a judge whom the blame of a blamer cannot overtake concerning the affairs of God. The third is a chief of police who shall obtain justice for the weak from the strong. The fourth is a tax collector who shall discharge his duties and not oppress the subjects . . . .

Source: From translation of Usman Dan Fodio *Kitab al-Farq* by M. Hiskett. *Bulletin of the School of Oriental and African Studies*, London, 1960, Part 3., p. 559 Reprinted by permission of Oxford University Press, Oxford UK in the formats Text and Other Book via Copyright Clearance Center.

eastern Sudan. Even so, the rural populace was still often pagan or semi-pagan, and even ruling and urban elites of the towns were frequently only nominally Muslim.

The nineteenth century is notable for the number and strength of a series of militant Islamic revivalist and reform movements of *jihad*. Aimed at a more fully Muslim society and wider allegiance to Muslim values, these movements both fixed and spread Islam as a lasting part of the African scene. West African *jihad* movements originated in the seventeenth century with the activities of militant, reformist Sufi brotherhoods that came originally from the north, especially through Mauritania. These movements eventually spread to other regions, especially in the eighteenth century, and flourished among widely dispersed groups of people.

The most important of these *jihad* movements was led by a Fulbe Muslim scholar from Hausa territory in the central Sahel. Usman Dan Fodio (1754–1817) was influenced by the reformist ideas spreading throughout the eighteenth-century Islamic world, from India to Saudi Arabia and Africa. Shortly after 1804, he gathered an immense army of fervent supporters and conquered most of the Hausa lands of modern Nigeria, bringing an explicitly Islamic order to the region. Dan Fodio left behind an impressive sultanate centered on his new capital of Sokoto and governed by his son, Muhammad Bello, until 1837. In his wake the Fulbe became the ruling class in Hausa regions. Islam spread into the countryside, where it still predominates. (See Document, "Usman Dan Fodio on Evil and Good Government.")

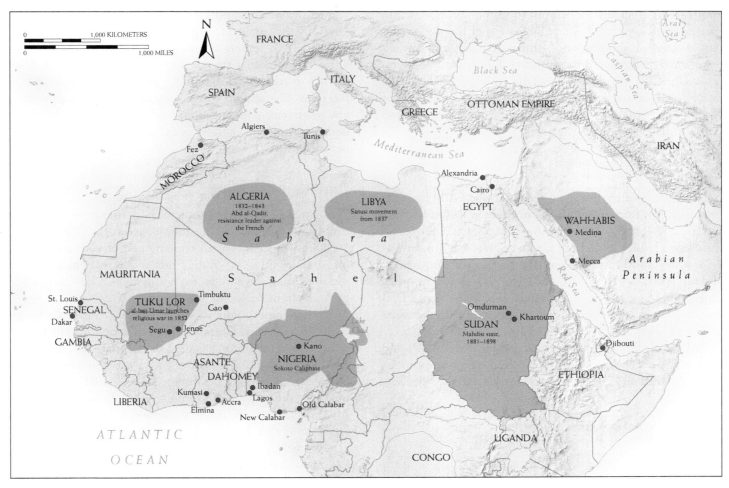

Map 26–3. Islamic Reform Movements in Africa and Arabia in the Nineteenth Century.

Other nineteenth-century reform movements had similar success in gaining at least ephemeral political power and spreading a reformist Islamic message among the masses. Most notable alongside several West African *jihad* movements were the Sanusi movement of Libya and the eastern Sahara (after about 1840) and the Mahdist uprising of the eastern Sudan (1880s and 1890s). The Libyan movement provided the focus for resistance to the Italian invasion of 1911. The Sudanese Muhammad Ahmad (1848–1885) condemned the widespread corruption of basic Islamic ideals and declared himself the awaited deliverer, or **Mahdi**, in 1881. He led the northern Sudan in rebellion against Ottoman-Egyptian control, defeating even the British forces from Egypt under Gordon at Khartoum. His successor governed the Sudan until the British finally destroyed the young Islamic state in 1899 (see Map 26–3).

Chronology

Islamic Reform Movements

1810	Dan Fodio founds Islamic sultanate in Hausa territory of northern and central Nigeria
after 1840	Sanusi movement in Libya and eastern Sahara
1881	Muhammad Ahmad declares himself the Mahdi (Sudan)

Increasing European Involvement: Exploration and Colonization

During the nineteenth century, Europe's growing involvement ended in its domination of African politics and economy. Before the mid-1800s, Europeans rarely ventured beyond the African coasts, although the transatlantic slave trade affected areas far inland. This changed drastically as, first, trading companies and explorers, then missionaries and, finally, colonial troops and governments moved into Africa. Ironically, the gradual elimination of the slave trade (largely through the efforts of British abolitionists) was accompanied by increased European exploration and more intense Christian missionary activity in Africa, which ushered in imperial and colonial ventures, the consequences of which were possibly more devastating for Africa's future than the slave trade had been.

Explorers

Nineteenth-century European explorers—mostly English, French, and German—gradually uncovered for Westerners the great "secrets" of Africa: the sources and courses of the Niger, Nile, Zambezi, and Congo rivers; natural wonders, such as Mount Kilimanjaro and Lake Tanganyika; and fabled places like Timbuktu. The history of European exploration is one of fortune hunting, self-promotion, violence, and mistakes as well as patience, perseverance, bravery, and dedication.

Many of the explorers were accomplished authors and lecturers; tales of their adventures stimulated European interest in Africa and opened the way for traders, missionaries,

Henry Morton Stanley and His Servant Kalula. Stanley was a journalist-turned-explorer who "found" abolitionist-turned-explorer David Livingstone near Lake Tanganyika in 1871. Stanley claimed to have greeted him with, "Dr. Livingstone, I presume."

and finally soldiers and governors from the Christian West. One of the greatest explorers was David Livingstone (1813–1873); among other things, he renamed Mosioa-Tunya ("smoke that thunders"), on the modern Zimbabwe-Zambia border, "Victoria Falls," after Britain's monarch at the time. Livingstone was a Scottish Presbyterian missionary, physician, and abolitionist who was in love with and dedicated to Africa and its peoples as few other Europeans before or after him.

Christian Missions

The latter nineteenth century saw a mounting influx of Protestant and Catholic missionaries (by 1900, some 10,000). They vied—with one another, or with Muslims—for African souls. Part of their motivation was eradication of the remaining slave trade, especially that in East Africa run by Arabs from Zanzibar.

Missionaries came to know African peoples far better than did explorers. Certainly, their accounts of Africa contained chauvinistic, misleading descriptions of "degraded" African culture and religion, but they also brought real knowledge of Africa to Europe. Their translation work and mission schools also brought alphabetic literacy to Africans. Although their settlements, often in remote areas, provided European governments with convenient pretexts for intervention in African tribal and state affairs, the missionaries were often idealists rather than opportunists and often found themselves at odds with colonial officers. Half of those who went into tropical regions died of diseases such as malaria, yellow fever, and sleeping sickness. If they were often paternalistic and instruments of their home countries' imperialism, they also fought to bring Africans medicine and education. Through their religious ideals, they provided Africans—intentionally or inadvertently—with weapons of principle to turn against their European exploiters. African Christian churches, for example, later played a leading role in resistance to apartheid in South Africa, despite white Christian racism there and elsewhere in Africa (see Chapter 33). Thus missionaries' roles in European domination of Africa cannot be monolithically or simply characterized.

The Colonial "Scramble for Africa"

Before 1850 the only significant European-African armed conflicts over African territory took place in South Africa and Algeria. In South Africa, as noted above, Boers came into conflict with Bantu tribes after leaving the British Cape Colony on their Great Trek to find new lands. The French invaded Algeria in 1830, settled Europeans on choice farmlands, and battled native resistance fighters. Over most

A Missionary Visit to a Zulu Kraal. The nineteenth-century European and American enthusiasm for working toward "the evangelization of the world in our time" found one of its major outlets in missionary efforts in Africa.

of Africa, the European presence was felt with real force only from the 1880s. By World War I virtually the whole continent (Ethiopia and Liberia were the only exceptions) was divided into a patchwork of territories under European colonial administrations (see Map 26–4 on page 816).

This foreign takeover of Africa was supported by the Europeans' mounting popular and commercial interests, which were fueled by publicity given African exploration and missionizing. European desire for Africa's industrial markets and natural resources, together with intra-European competition for power and prestige, pushed one European state after another to claim whatever segments of Africa they could (see Chapter 28).

The superior economic, technological, and military power the West commanded made this takeover possible. Technical expertise especially gave Europeans access to the African interior in the late 1800s. Except for the Nile and the Niger, all the great African rivers have impassable waterfalls a short way inland from the sea, where the coastal plains rise sharply to the largely highland interior. European-built steamboats above the falls and railroads around them (or where no navigable rivers ran) permitted new levels of commercial and colonial exploitation.

Great Britain and France were the vanguard of European nations seeking African additions to their colonies or markets. The British had the largest involvement, ranging south to north from the Cape Colony (taken from the Dutch in 1795) to Egypt (their effective **protectorate** from 1882), and west to east from trade in West Africa, colonies (such as Sierra Leone and Gambia, set up in 1807), protectorate rule (as in Niger districts after 1885), to their East African sphere of influence in the 1870s (and Zanzibar protectorate in 1890). The

British long resisted African colonial involvement and then chose "indirect" as preferable to "direct" colonial administration. Their rule was only slightly more enlightened than that of the French, who had earlier assembled a colonial empire under direct control. The French had long had government-supported trading outposts in Senegal and elsewhere in West Africa. After a bitter struggle (1830–1847) they conquered Algeria, creating the first major European

Men Sorting Diamonds, Kimberley, South Africa. Diamond mining in South Africa took off in the late 1860s. By 1880 Kimberley, the biggest mine in the region, had 30,000 people, second only to Cape Town. Whites such as these diamond sorters, monopolized the well-paid skilled jobs.

Map Exploration

To explore this map further, go to **http://www.myhistorylab.com**

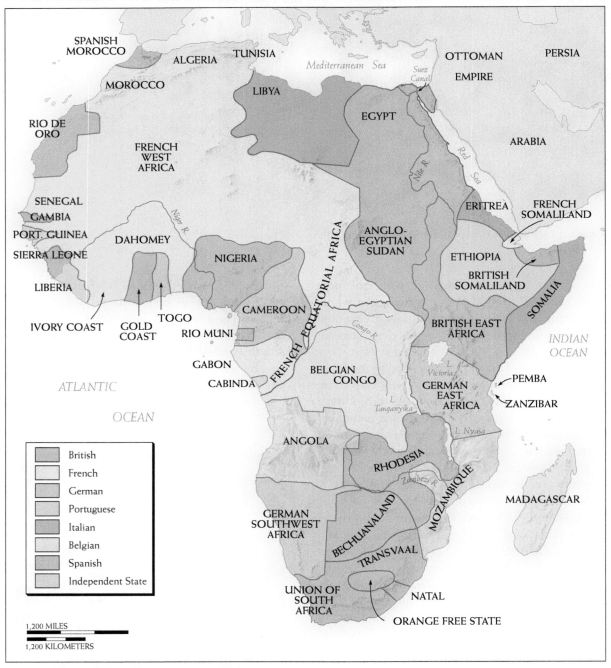

Map 26–4. Partition of Africa, 1880–1914. By 1914 the only countries in Africa that remained independent were Liberia and Ethiopia. The occupying powers included most large European states.

colony in Africa. Tunisia and the Ivory Coast became French protectorates (1880s), Dahomey was bloodily annexed (1894), and French Equatorial Africa was proclaimed in 1910.

Beginning in the mid-1880s the major European powers sought mutual agreement to their claims on segments of Africa. Belgium's Leopold II (r. 1865–1909) and Germany's Otto von Bismarck (1815–1898) laid claim to parts of

Mutesa of Buganda and His Court. Noted for his cunning and diplomatic skill and for his autocratic and often cruel conduct, Mutesa was one of the few African rulers able to maintain a powerful, successful army and court, which enabled him to deal effectively with Egyptian and British efforts to encroach on his sphere of influence.

the worst legacies of the European presence was the white racist state of South Africa, which ended only in 1994. No Western nation can have a clear conscience about its involvement in Africa.

African states were not, however, simply passive objects of European manipulation and conquest. Many astute native rulers sought, by diplomacy, trade, and warfare, to use the European presence to their advantage. The Bagandan king Mutesa in the 1870s (in today's Uganda), is an example of an African ruler who benefited, at least temporarily, from European interest in his territory. Direct armed resistance was always (even for Ethiopia) doomed because of European technological superiority. Nevertheless, such resistance was widespread and continued frequently into the twentieth century. Finally, colonial rule involved ongoing conflict and negotiation between European desires, backed by technological superiority, and the enduring power "on the ground" of African individuals and institutions.

British taxpayers were reluctant to fund colonial ventures. British colonial officials made a virtue of necessity: Only able to afford to pay a very small contingent of British administrators, they put British men in charge of existing African political structures, and they ruled through indigenous leaders. Often, early in colonial rule, they would make a show of removing a few high-profile, independent-minded indigenous leaders (thus they deposed and exiled Mutesa's successor in Uganda). The remaining "native chiefs" (in colonial parlance) and their British supervisors would then perform a delicate balancing act—the chiefs and the colonists depending on each other for power and legitimacy, but neither commanding perfect loyalty from their subjects.

Frederick Lugard, whose British parents were missionaries in India, had been an explorer, entrepreneur, and military leader in various parts of Africa before being appointed high commissioner of Northern Nigeria in 1900. During his tenure, he formalized this British style of colonial administration and named it, appropriately, **indirect rule**.

Other European powers typically ruled their colonies directly: willing to bankroll the placement of more Europeans in the colonies, they hired local Africans to work for them within European-style political structures. The French were the most explicit about their intentions, claiming that their goal was for Africans to "evolve"—through education, imitation, assimilation (and, perhaps, over generations)—into French citizens. In practice, however, French colonial officials were loath to share the prestige of citizenship.

Africa. France and England consolidated their African interests. Italy took African colonial territory in Eritrea, Somaliland, and Libya, although Ethiopia used its newly modernized army to defeat an Italian invasion in 1896 (postponing to 1935 Italy's conquest of Ethiopia). This **scramble for Africa** was largely completed by the outbreak of World War I. After the war Germany lost its African possessions to other colonial powers. Europe's African colonies did not gain independence until the changes in the global balance of power and attitudes toward colonialism that followed World War II (see Chapter 33).

Patterns in European Colonial Rule and African Resistance

European colonial rule in Africa is one of the uglier chapters of modern history. If German, French, Belgian, Portuguese, and Boer rule were notoriously brutal and produced worse atrocities, Britain was not exempt from oppressive misrule and exploitation. The paternalistic attitudes of late-nineteenth-century Europe and America amounted to sheer racism when applied in Africa. The regions with large-scale white settlements produced the worst exploitation at the expense of vastly larger native populations. Everywhere, white minorities exercised disproportionate power over the lives of black or brown majorities. Among

Mau Mau freedom fighters in a Kenyan hideout, around 1950.

Another important variation in the African colonial experience was between settler and non-settler colonies. Colonies with relatively high settler populations tended to be places where the environment could support plantation-style, export-oriented agriculture, and where diseases to which Europeans were most susceptible were less prevalent. Settler colonies included Kenya, Mozambique, Rhodesia (now Zimbabwe), South Africa, and Algeria.[5]

Africans resisted European domination in all its guises throughout the continent. Sometimes this resistance involved defensive battle against overt European aggression, as in the 1879 "Zulu war" when British forces attacked and, after bloody, costly battles, finally defeated the Zulus at Ulundi, destroying their independent state. Often the most efficient resistance was simply disengagement, shirking payment of colonial taxes or participation in forced labor. (See Document, "Oginga Odinga on European Influences." on page 819) Marches, riots, and rebellions, however, were more frequent and forceful than colonial administrators admitted, and accounts of such events were sometimes suppressed. Resistance tended to be more overt and sustained in settler colonies, where Africans and Europeans were in greatest direct contact. In places where Europeans had seized large fertile land tracts—the Kenyan highlands, for example—resistance could become violent and chronic, as in the **Mau Mau** uprising that began as a protest against

land alienation among Kenya's Kikuyu people. During the 1950s, tens of thousands of Kenyans were killed, and many more suspected insurgents and sympathizers incarcerated in detention camps, while the Mau Mau revolt became a nationalist insurgency.[6]

The Rise of African Nationalism

The key factor in European colonialism's demise was the rise of nationalism across Africa, especially after World War I. However little the colonial partition of Africa reflected native linguistic, racial, or cultural divisions, it still influenced both nationalist movements and the eventual shape of African states. The "national" consciousness of diverse peoples in a given colonial unit was fueled by shared opposition to foreign rule. It was also fed by the use of a common European tongue and through the assimilation of European thought by a growing educated native elite. These elites were typically

Champion of Negritude, Leopold Senghor.

[5]See E. Gilbert and J. T. Reynolds, *Africa in World History* (Upper Saddle River, NJ: Pearson Prentice Hall, 2004), Chapter 15, for more detailed coverage.

[6]The history of Mau Mau is still contested. British administrators deliberately destroyed much documentary evidence. For recent attempts to reconstruct events and their meanings, see D. Anderson, *Histories of the Hanged: The Dirty War in Kenya and the End of Empire* (New York: W.W. Norton, 2005), and C. Elkins, *Imperial Reckoning: The Untold Story of Britain's Gulag in Kenya* (New York: Henry Holt & Co., 2004).

Document   Oginga Odinga on European Influences

Oginga Odinga (ca. 1911–1994) was an early Kenyan nationalist leader. Born into a leading family of the Luo tribe, he grew up in western Kenya, near Lake Victoria. After Kenyan independence in 1963, he opposed many of President Jomo Kenyatta's policies. He published his autobiography, *Not Yet Uhuru*, in 1967; "Uhuru" in Swahili means "freedom" or "independence." Here Odinga argues that Kenya's postcolonial leaders worked at creating a new African elite (themselves) rather than serving the masses of Africans who worked for independence.

These are Odinga's recollections of his first experiences with Europeans.

■ *What made the strongest impression on Odinga? What overall attitude does he evidence toward Europeans? What can you infer here about Luo culture?*

We connected Whites and Government with five main things. There were the inoculations against the plague from which the children ran in fear. There were the tax collections. There was the order to the villagers to work on the roads. There were clothes, *kanzu*, the long robes copied from Arab garb at the coast, given free to the chiefs and elders to wear to encourage others in the tribe to clothe themselves in modern dress. There were the schools, which came later, and to which, in the beginning, only orphans, foster children, poor nieces and nephews and never the favourite sons were sent, for the villagers distrusted the pressure on them to send their children out of the home and away from herding the animals; and the more alert objected to the way the Christian missions taught 'This custom (yours) is bad, and this (ours) is good', for they could see that the children at the missions would grow up to despise Luo ways.

Source: Not Yet Uhuru: The Autobiography of Oginga Odinga. (New York: Hill and Wang, 1967), pp.2–3.

educated in mission schools and sometimes foreign universities. In the early twentieth century their ranks gradually increased. From them came the leaders of Africa's nationalist movements between the world wars and of Africa's (more than forty) new, self-governing nations created after World War II (see Chapter 33).

Mass political parties emerged in the postwar period, including the Convention People's Party in the Gold Coast (Ghana) under Kwame Nkrumah (1909–1972) and the African Democratic Assembly with members from numerous French (especially West) African colonies under the leadership of Félix Houphouët-Boigny (1905–1993), who became the first president of the Ivory Coast.

It is important to note, however, a countervailing trend: the emergence of movements seeking to transcend both colonial boundaries and ethnic or "tribal" divisions and foster an inclusive African identity. One example is **Negritude**, a literary and intellectual movement to celebrate all aspects of African civilization, exemplified in the writings of Leopold Senghor (1906–2001), who later became the first president of Senegal.

The most severe indigenous critiques of the Western treatment of Africa often drew on Western religious and political ideals. Twentieth-century African leaders learned well from the West and used their learning to help end Western domination. African independence movements were based on modern nationalist models from Europe and America rather than ancient ones derived from native tradition. The national independence movements typically ejected the colonial intruders and tried not to return to an earlier status quo. Their aim was to take over and to run the Western institutions introduced by colonialism. This legacy from the West is still visible today.

Summary

Western Encroachment. The century and a half that began in 1800 was a bleak one for Africa, the Indian subcontinent, and the Islamic heartlands. For centuries there had been a rough balance in material and intellectual culture, commerce, and political stability among the major regions of the world. Suddenly, over 150 years, the European sector of the global community came to dominate the rest of the world.

The Middle East, Africa, Iran, Central Asia, India, and Indonesia–Malaysia, along with Latin America—the so-called Third World of "developing nations"—were drastically affected by European imperialism and colonialism. Regardless of indigenous developments in these regions, the decisive reality in this era was unprecedented domination by a single segment of the global community. Western dominance, sometimes positive, often sordid and ugly, was by no means synonymous with "progress," as Westerners have typically liked to think. Nevertheless, it has been a hallmark of "modernity" in most of Asia, Africa, and Latin America.

Indigenous Reactions. The vitality of many of the cultures and traditions that bore the brunt of the Western onslaught has been striking. Arab, Iranian, Indian, African, and other encounters with Western material and intellectual domination produced varied responses and initiatives. These have played out in political, economic, and intellectual independence only since 1945; however, most encounters began much earlier, some well before 1800. Thus modern Islamic reform and resurgence began in the eighteenth century, although it has become a major global factor only in recent decades. Indian national consciousness developed from the eighteenth century onward in response to British domination, even though national union and independence came only after World War II.

Key Terms

bazaari (p. 805)

cantonments (p. 798)

Great Trek (p. 811)

indirect rule (p. 817)

Mahdi (p. 813)

Mau Mau (p. 818)

mfecane (p. 810)

mujtahid (p. 804)

Negritude (p. 819)

pan-Islamism (p. 807)

protectorate (p. 815)

Raj (p. 795)

scramble for Africa (p. 817)

Tanzimat (p. 806)

Wahhabis (p. 803)

Review Questions

1. What does the "impact of modernity" mean to traditional Afro-Asian-Indian cultures? What patterns of reaction can you discern? Why was the West able to impose itself on these cultures?

2. Why was India called the "jewel in the crown" of the British Empire? How did the British gain control of India? What policies did they follow in government and economics?

3. What kinds of political activism against British rule can you cite from Indian history after 1800? What kinds of success or failure did they have?

4. How was the Islamic world internally divided after 1800? How did those divisions influence the coming of European powers?

5. How did nationalism affect European control in South Asia, Africa, and the Middle East? How and when did its various manifestations arise? Did any successful "national states" emerge in these regions before 1945?

6. Discuss the new African states and power centers of sub-Saharan Africa before 1870. Why did no modern nation-state develop in the area? How did Islam affect the development of new entities? What role did trade play?

7. What were Europeans' three main interests in Africa? Why were Africans unable to stop the "scramble for Africa"?

8. What factors influenced Africans' experience of colonial rule in different regions?

9. What was the role of African nationalism in resisting foreign control?

Note: *To learn more about the topics in this chapter, please turn to the Suggested Readings at the end of the book. For additional sources related to this chapter please see MyHistoryLab.com.*

PEARSON myhistorylab Connections

Reinforce what you learned in this chapter by studying the many documents, images, maps, review tools, and videos available at **www.myhistorylab.com**.

Read and Review

✓●—Study and Review Chapter 26

●●●—Read the Document *Dadabhai Naoroji, The Benefits of British Rule in India, 1871, p. 794*
The Indian Revolt (1857), p. 795
Lord William Bentinck, on the Suppression of Sati, 1829, p. 796
Karl Marx, "The British Rule in India," 1853, p. 798
Amrita Lal Roy, English Rule in India, 1886, p. 799
Gandhi Speaks against the Partition of India (pre-1947), p. 802
Religious Minorities in the Middle East (late 19th-early 20th century), p. 803
Ottoman, p. 805
The Young Turk Revolution, 1908, p. 807

●●—View the Image *Mahatma Gandhi, p. 795*

((●●—Hear the Audio *India's Imperialism, p. 794*

●●—Watch the Video *Gandhi in India, p. 799*
The Ottoman Tanzimat Period (1839-1876): The Middle East Confronts Modernity, p. 806

Research and Explore

●●—Watch the Video *Imperialism and Colonialism: Empires in Africa*

●●—Watch the Video *The Three M's*

((●●—Hear the Audio

Hear the audio file for Chapter 26 at
www.myhistorylab.com.

The Islamic tradition is the youngest major world religious tradition. Since its inception during the lifetime of the Prophet Muhammad (d. 632 B.C.E.) it has grown, like the Christian and Buddhist traditions, into a worldwide community not limited by national boundaries or defined in racial or ethnic terms. It began among the Arabs but spread widely. Islam's historical heartlands are those Arabic-, Turkic-, and Persian-speaking lands of the Near East between Egypt and Afghanistan. However, today more than half of its faithful live in Asia east of Karachi, Pakistan; indeed, more Muslims live in sub-Saharan Africa than in all of the Arab lands. There are also growing Muslim minorities in the United States and Europe.

The central vision of Islam is a just and peaceful society in which people can freely worship God. It focuses on a human community of worshipers who recognize the absolute sovereignty and oneness of God and strive to do His will. Muslims believe His will is found first in God's revealed word, the Qur'an; then as elaborated and specified in the actions and words of his final prophet, Muhammad; and finally as interpreted and extended in the scriptural exegesis and legal traditions of the Muslim community over the past thirteen and a half centuries.

The Muslim vision thus centers on one God who has guided humankind throughout history by means of prophets or apostles and repeated revelations. God is the Creator of all, and in the end all will return to God. God's majesty would seem to make him a distant, threatening

deity of absolute justice; this aspect of the Divine exists in Muslim perceptions of the wide chasm between the human and the Divine. Still, there is an immanent as well as a transcendent side to the Divine in Muslim view. Muslims have given us some of the greatest images of God's nearness to his faithful worshiper, images that have a special place in the thought of Muslim mystics, who are known as *Sufis* (taken originally from *suf*, "wool," because of early Muslim ascetics' use of simple wool dress).

Muslims understand God's word in the Qur'an and the elaboration of that word by tradition to be a complete prescription for human life. Thus Islamic law is not law in the Western sense of civil, criminal, or international law. Rather, it (like Torah for Jews) is a comprehensive set of standards for the moral, ritual, social, political, economic, aesthetic, and even hygienic and dietary dimensions of life. By being faithful to God's law the Muslim hopes to gain salvation on the Last Day, when human history will end and all God's creatures who have ever lived will be resurrected and called to account for their thoughts and actions during life on earth. Some will be saved; others will be eternally damned.

Thus *Islam*, which means "submission [to God]," is taken as a name for the religiously defined system of life that Muslims have sought to institute wherever they have lived. Muslims have striven to organize their societies and polities around the ideals represented in the traditional picture of the Prophet's community in Medina and Mecca (622–632). This approach necessitates compromise in which power is given to temporal rulers and accepted by Muslim religious leaders as long as those rulers protect God's Law, the *Shari'a*. The ideal of a single international Muslim community, or *Umma*, has never fully been realized politically, but it remains an ideal.

Many reform movements over the centuries have called for greater adherence to rigorist interpretations of Islamic law and greater dominance of piety and religious values in sociopolitical as well as individual life. The most famous of these movements, that of the Wahhabis in eighteenth-century Arabia, remains influential in much of the Muslim world, including Saudi Arabia. The Wahhabis' puritanical zeal in fighting what they consider "innovations" in many regional Islamic contexts, such as Shi'ism, Sufi traditions, and all more liberal forms of Islamic practice, continues to the present day. Wahhabism has had considerable success in the past half century and was apparently the spawning ground of the extremist views of Osama bin Laden's al-Qa'ida terrorist organization. Largely Arab in its ethnic makeup, this group has turned from fighting Muslim states it regards as un-Islamic

Muhammad and Ali. This sixteenth-century Persian miniature shows the Prophet Muhammad and his kinsman Ali purifying the Ka'ba in Mecca of pagan idols. The Ka'ba is the geographical point toward which all Muslims face when performing ritual prayer. *Art Resource/Bildarchiv Preussischer Kulturbesitz.*

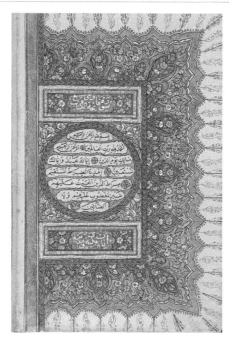

The Qur'an's First Chapter. This nineteenth-century hand-copied Koran in Arabic is open to the *Fatiha*, the opening chapter of Islam's holy book. In seven very short verses, the Fatiha sums up man's relation to God in prayer. Muslims repeat the invocation of verse one, "In the name of God, the Merciful Compassionate One," before eating, drinking, or performing any other significant act.

Muslim School Children in Malaysia, 1997. Though most non-Muslims associate Islam with the Middle East, Islam has deep roots in Southeast Asia. About 212 million Muslims live in Indonesia, making it the most populous Muslim country in the world.

to opposing what it considers the oppressive intrusion by the United States' benighted foreign policy in the Arab Islamic world. While mainstream Muslims everywhere reject bin Laden's extremism, Wahhabi zealotry has adherents on the fringes of Islamic communities around the world. In this respect, Islam is not unlike Christianity, Judaism, Hinduism, or other major religions, each of which has over its history spawned literalists, zealots, and extremists, who have urged violence in the name of their version of their parent faith.

The major sectarian, or minority, groups among Muslims are those of the Shi'ites, who have held out for an ideal of a temporal ruler who is also spiritual heir of Muhammad and God's designated deputy on earth. Most Shi'ites, notably those of Iran, hold that after eleven designated blood descendants of the prophets had each failed to be recognized by the majority of Muslims as the rightful leader, or *Imam*, the twelfth disappeared in the late ninth century and remains to this day physically absent from the world, although he is not dead. He will come again at the end of time to vindicate his faithful followers.

Muslim piety takes many forms. Common religious duties are central for Muslims everywhere: faith in God and trust in his Prophet; regular performance of ritual worship (*Salat*); fasting (*sawm*) dawn to sunset every day in Ramadan (ninth month of the lunar year); giving of one's wealth to the needy (*zakat*); and at least once in a lifetime, if able, making the pilgrimage to Mecca and its environs (*Hajj*). Other more regional or popular, but widespread practices are also important. Celebration of the Prophet's birthday indicates Muhammad's exalted popular status, even though any divine status for him is strongly rejected theologically. Recitation of the Qur'an permeates all Muslim practice, from daily worship to celebrations of all kinds. Visitation of saints' tombs is a prominent form of popular devotion. Muslims around the world also practice Sufi chanting or even ecstatic dancing.

Muslims vary enormously in their physical environment, language, ethnic background, and cultural heritage. What binds them now as in the past are not political allegiances but religious affinities and a shared heritage of religious faith and culture. How these allegiances and sensibilities will fare in the face of global challenges will be an important factor in shaping the world of the twenty-first century.

■ **How has the ideal of a single, international Muslim community influenced Islamic history? World history?**

■ **What impact have reform movements had on Islam since its inception? What impact do they have today?**

27 | Modern East Asia

Woodblock, Munakata Shikō, 1945. In modern Japan, woodblock prints are divided between modernists who, initially at least, took their inspiration from the West, and those who went through a "Western phase" and then built on the native folk art tradition. Among the latter, the greatest was Munakata Shikō (1903–1975). Munakata was born in Aomori Prefecture, a sparsely populated area in northernmost Honshu known for its long bitter winters, rocky soil, and strong folk religion tradition. At age 24 Munakata went to Tokyo, where for two years he experimented with oils, but then he switched to print-making. In 1937, at age 34, he took up the Buddhist subjects for which he is best known. His most famous prints are sensuous Buddhist deities and Bodhisattvas such as the one depicted here.

■ Modern Japan (1853–1945)

■ Overthrow of the Tokugawa Bakufu (1853–1868)

■ Building the Meiji State (1868–1890)

■ Growth of a Modern Economy

■ The Politics of Imperial Japan (1890–1945)

■ Japanese Militarism and German Nazism

■ Modern China (1839–1949)

■ Close of Manchu Rule

■ From Dynasty to Warlordism (1895–1926)

■ Cultural and Ideological Ferment: The May Fourth Movement

■ Nationalist China

FROM THE MID–NINETEENTH CENTURY, THE West was the expanding, aggressive, imperialistic force in world history. Its industrial goods and gunboats reached every part of the globe. It believed in free trade and had the military might to impose it on others. It was the trigger for change throughout the world. But the response to the Western impact depended on the internal array of forces in each country. In fact, the "response to the West" was only one small, though vital, part of the history of each country. Japan and China were both relatively successful in their responses, for neither became a colony.

The two countries were also similar in that their governing elites were educated in Confucianism. Unlike the otherworldly religions of Buddhism, Islam, or Christianity, Confucianism was just secular enough to crumble in the face of the more powerful secularism of nineteenth-century science and the doctrines associated with it. In both Japan and China, though much more rapidly in Japan, the leading intellectuals abandoned Confucianism in favor of Western secular doctrines. To be sure, many Confucian values, deeply embedded in the societies, survived the philosophies of which they had once been a part. In fact, one of the "breakdown products" of the Confucian sociopolitical identity was a strong new nationalism in both China and Japan.

But there the similarities end. In most other respects, modern Japan and China could hardly be more different. Perhaps the difference was only to be expected, given the pattern of recurrent dynasties in China's premodern history and of feudal evolution in Japan's.

View the Image
Japanese Woodcut on Perry's Arrival
at **myhistorylab.com**

The coming of Commodore Matthew Perry (1794–1858) in 1853–1854 precipitated a rapid political change in Japan.

Within fifteen years the old Tokugawa regime had collapsed, and the Japanese were building a modern state. Economic growth followed. By 1900 Japan had defeated China and within five years would defeat tsarist Russia in war. Sustained economic growth continued during the early twentieth century. After the Great Depression, Japan, like Italy and Germany, became an aggressive and militarized state and was eventually defeated in World War II. But after the war Japan reemerged more stable, more productive, and with a stronger parliamentary government than before.

The Chinese polity, in contrast, easily weathered the Opium War (1839–1842), an event of considerably greater magnitude than Perry's visit to Japan. The hold of tradition in China was remarkable, as was the effectiveness of traditional remedies in dealing with political ills. Only in its relations with the Western powers did traditional patterns not work. In one sense the strength of tradition was China's weakness, for it took seventy years after the Opium War to overthrow the dynasty. Only then were Chinese able to begin the modernization that Japanese had started in 1868, and even then they were unsuccessful.

Along with warlordism and the other problems that had accompanied the dissolution of past dynasties, new ills arose from the rending of the very fabric of the dynastic pattern. To these problems was added the unprecedented experience of being confronted by nations more powerful than itself. That China in some sense "failed" during this modern century is not a Western view imposed on China; it is the view the Chinese themselves hold. ■

Modern Japan (1853–1945)

Overthrow of the Tokugawa Bakufu (1853–1868)

From the seventeenth century into the nineteenth, the natural isolation of the islands of Japan was augmented by its policy of seclusion, making Japan into a little world of its own. The 260-odd domains were the states of this world, the *bakufu* in Edo was its hegemon, and the imperial court in Kyoto provided a sacerdotal or religious sanction for the *bakufu*-domain system. Then, in 1853 and 1854,

Read the Document
President Millard Fillmore, Letter to the Emperor of Japan, 1852
at **myhistorylab.com**

the American ships of Commodore Perry came and forced Japan to sign a Treaty of Friendship, opening it to foreign intercourse.

Fourteen years later the entire *bakufu*-domain system collapsed, and a new group of unusually talented leaders seized power. Seclusion, like the case of a watch, had been necessary to preserve the Tokugawa political mechanism. With the case removed, the jolt of the foreign intrusion caused the inner workings to fly apart.

But little changed during the first four years after Perry. The *bakufu* attended to its affairs and the domains to theirs. The daimyo continued to spend every other year living in Edo. Political action consisted mainly of daimyo cliques trying to influence *bakufu* policy. The break came in 1858

Read the Document
The Views of Ii Naosuke, 1853
at **myhistorylab.com**

when the *bakufu*, ignoring the imperial court's disapproval, was persuaded to sign a commercial treaty with the United States.

In reaction, some daimyo, who wanted a voice in national policy making, criticized the treaty as contravening the hallowed policy of seclusion. Younger samurai, frustrated by their exclusion from office, started a movement to "honor the emperor." The *bakufu*, in turn, purged its critics: Dissident daimyo were forced into retirement, while samurai critics were executed or imprisoned. The purge was effective until 1860, when the head of the *bakufu* council was himself

Global Perspective

Modern East Asia

East Asia

From the late nineteenth century most countries wanted to become modern. They coveted the wealth and power of the West. But what does it mean to be modern?

Three stages may be noted in Japan's development as the world's first and most advanced non-Western modernizer: preconditions, Westernization, and assimilation.

Even before contact with the modern West, Japan had some of the preconditions needed for industrialization: a fairly literate people, an ethic of duty and hard work, a market economy, secular thought, some bureaucracy, and a protonationalism. In sum, it had in place an adequate base for an "external modernization."

Building on these preconditions, Japan Westernized after 1868, adopting a range of new institutions: post offices, banks, customhouses, hospitals, police forces, joint stock companies, universities with faculties of science and engineering, and so on. Japanese thinkers brought in modern ideas and values: Spencer and Guizot, Turgenev and Tolstoy, Adam Smith and Marx. Japanese writers began experimenting with new forms.

Little by little Japan *assimilated* what it had borrowed. The zaibatsu combines were modern, with the most recent technologies, yet their business organizations were unlike those of the West. The spare beauty of traditional architecture was transferred to the glass, steel, concrete, and stone of the modern. A new literature, completely Japanese yet also completely modern, appeared.

Japan may serve as a useful model in that its modernization—as analyzed in terms of the above three stages—has gone further than that in any other non-Western country. We note the absence in India or the Islamic world of comparable preconditions. After the end of colonialism, countries in these areas had to create the necessary preconditions even

---

assassinated by extremist samurai. His successors lacked the nerve to continue his tough policies, opening the way for a new kind of politics between 1861 and 1868.

In 1861 two domains, Chōshū and Satsuma, emerged to mediate, to heal the breach that had opened between the *bakufu* and the court. Chōshū was the first to come forth: Its officials traveled between Kyoto and Edo, proposing a policy that favored the *bakufu* but made concessions to the court. Next Satsuma sallied forth with a policy that made further concessions and ousted Chōshū as "the friend of the court." In response, the moderate reformist government of Chōshū adopted the pro-emperor policy of its extremist faction and, in turn, ousted Satsuma. Beaten in the diplomatic game, Satsuma seized the court in 1863 in a military coup, and the Chōshū radicals returned disgruntled to their domain.

Four points may be noted about the 1861–1863 diplomatic phase of domain action: (1) Even after 250 years of *bakufu* rule, several domains were still viable, autonomous units that could act when the opportunity arose; (2) the two domains that acted first and most of those that followed were large domains with many samurai—Chōshū had 10,000 samurai families and substantial financial resources; (3) both Satsuma and Chōshū had fought against the Tokugawa in 1600 and remembered an earlier independence; (4)

by the 1861–1863 period, domain politics was no longer in the hands of daimyo and their high-ranking advisers. In both Satsuma and Chōshū the new politics had opened decision making to middle-ranking samurai officials in a way that would have been impossible before 1853.

The 1863 Satsuma coup at the Kyoto court initiated a military phase of politics in which battles determined every turning point. Events were complicated, for besides the court and the *bakufu*, there were more than 260 domains—somewhat like a circus with too many rings and sideshows. But most domains were too small to carry weight in national politics. Little "hereditary daimyo," for example, were influential only as *bakufu* officials. Of the larger domains, some were insolvent and others too closely associated with the *bakufu* to act independently. As long as Satsuma and Chōshū remained enemies, politics stalemated and the *bakufu* continued as hegemon. But when the two domains became allies in 1866, the *bakufu* was overthrown in less than two years.

A movement for a "union of court and camp" contributed to the *bakufu*'s downfall; daimyo, who earlier had criticized the *bakufu*, campaigned for a new counciliar rule in which they would participate together with the emperor. The movement came to nothing, but it led daimyo to withdraw support that might otherwise have gone to the *bakufu*.

as they borrowed the new technologies. The difficulty explains their limited success. In Africa the dearth of preconditions was even more pronounced.

China, like Japan but unlike countries of South Asia, the Middle East, or Africa, had many of the necessary preconditions—they might be called East Asian preconditions—in place. But when it came to Westernization, the government by Confucian literati that had long been China's outstanding asset became its greatest liability. It took decades to topple the dynasty and to advance beyond Confucian ideas.

Then, in the maelstrom of the May Fourth Movement, intellectual change occurred at a furious pace, but new doctrines alone could not provide a stable polity. Nationalism emerged as the common denominator of Chinese thought. The Nationalists (Guomindang) drew on it at the Huangpu Academy, during the march north, and in the Nanjing government. But other groups could also appeal to it. The Chinese communists won out by 1949.

It is beguiling to view the CCP cadres as a new class of literati operating the machinery of a monolithic, centralized state, with the teachings of Marx and Lenin replacing those of Confucius, and local party organization replacing the Confucian gentry. But this interpretation is too simple. Communism stressed science, materialism, and class conflict. It broke with the Chinese past.

Communism itself was also modified in China. Marx had predicted that socialist revolutions would break out in advanced economies where the contradictions of capitalism were sharpest. Lenin had shifted the emphasis from spontaneous revolutions by workers to the small but disciplined revolutionary party, the vanguard of the proletariat. He thereby changed communism into what it has been ever since: a movement capable of seizing power only in backward nations. At the level of doctrine, Mao Zedong modified Lenin's ideas only slightly—by theorizing that "progressive" peasants were a part of the proletariat. But he went beyond this theory in practice, virtually ignoring city workers while relying on China's villages for recruits for his armies, who were then indoctrinated using Leninist techniques.

Yet, the organizational techniques that were so effective in creating a party and army would prove less so for economic development. It would soon became clear that mass mobilization was no substitute for individual incentives.

Focus Questions

- Why are the preconditions necessary for modernization along Western lines? Why are they so important?
- Compare and contrast the process of modernization in Japan and China in the twentieth century. Which country was more successful? Why?

A second feature of this period was a strong antiforeignism. Samurai extremists assassinated foreigners as well as *bakufu* officials; one of their slogans was "expel the barbarians." Early on, Chōshū and Satsuma fired on foreign ships. But when Western gunboats bombarded those domains in retaliation, they dropped their xenophobic slogan and set about buying rifles and gunboats.

Another aspect of the military phase of politics from 1863 to 1868 was the formation of new rifle units, commanded mostly by lower samurai. These units transformed political power in Japan. For example, Chōshū troops armed with Spencers and Minies—mostly surplus left over from the U.S. Civil War—defeated a traditionally armed but numerically superior *bakufu* army in mid-1866 with a numbing force.

A final development was a cultural shift in the way Japanese saw themselves. The Tokugawa elites had seen themselves as civilized Confucians. They viewed the rest of the world, China and Korea excepted, as barbarian. But in the face of Western technology, this view became untenable. In 1868 Fukuzawa Yukichi (1835–1901), a student of Western studies and a *bakufu* translator, introduced a Western theory of history: The West, with its technology, science, and humane laws, was "civilized and enlightened," China, Japan, and countries like Turkey were "half civilized," and

other areas were barbarian. This theory stood the Confucian view on its head. Fukuzawa argued, furthermore, that technology was not detachable but grew out of the Western legal, political, economic, and educational systems. James Watt (1736–1819), he suggested, had been moved to invent the steam engine because patents protected inventions and gave inventors profits and honors. Fukuzawa also maintained that Western systems required political freedom and a citizenry with a spirit of independence. Fukuzawa's writings became immensely influential after the Restoration, eventually sparking the Civilization and Enlightenment Movement of the 1870s. (See Document, "A Japanese View of the Inventiveness of the West" on page 829)

....

Building the Meiji State (1868–1890)

Most attempts by non-Western nations to build modern states occurred during the twentieth century; the idea of a "developing nation" did not exist in the mid-nineteenth century. Yet Japan after the 1868 **Meiji Restoration** was just such a nation. (The years from 1868 to 1912 are referred to as the "Meiji period," after the era name of the new emperor.) It was committed to progress, by which it meant

A Closer Look

East Meets the West

Commodore Perry presents a letter from President Fillmore to Japanese representatives.

Perry came in 1853 with only four ships.

Commodore Matthew C. Perry (commodore is a rank equivalent to admiral) had fought against Barbary Pirates, taken Key West, and been active in the Spanish-American War. He entered Edo Bay in 1853 and threatened to shell Japanese installations on the shore if he were not given a treaty. He got the Treaty of Friendship in 1854 and retired from the navy in 1855.

Two-sworded *bakufu* officials face Perry. Perry did not know the difference between emperor and shogun and thought he was meeting officials of the emperor.

Americans and Japanese could not communicate. As an interpreter Perry used a Hong Kong Chinese, who spoke English and could write in Chinese, which the Japanese representatives could read. The interpreter wears his hair in a queue, the token of Chinese submission to their Manchu rulers.

Questions

1. What did Perry have in mind during this meeting? What did the *bakufu* representatives want?

2. How did so innocuous a meeting lead fifteen years later to the overthrow of Tokugawa rule?

myhist**o**rylab   To examine this image in an interactive fashion, please go to **www.myhistorylab.com**

Document

A Japanese View of the Inventiveness of the West

Serious Japanese thinkers reacted to their country's weakness with proposals to adopt Western science and industry. But the Civilization and Enlightenment Movement of the 1870s had its lighter side as well. In 1871 the novelist Kanagaki Robun wrote a satire about a man with an umbrella, a watch, and eau de cologne on his hair, eating with a friend in a new beef restaurant. Before the Restoration, Buddhism had banned beef eating as a defilement. The comic hero, however, wonders, "Why we in Japan haven't eaten such a clean thing before." He then goes on to rhapsodize about Western inventions. See also Document, "Liang Qichao Urges the Chinese to Reform" on page 853.

■ *What does a beef restaurant have to do with the marvels of Western technology?*

In the West they're free of superstitions. There it's the custom to do everything scientifically, and that's why they've invented amazing things like the steamship and the steam engine. Did you know that they engrave the plates for printing newspapers with telegraphic needles? And that they bring down wind from the sky with balloons? Aren't they wonderful inventions! Of course, there are good reasons behind these inventions. If you look at a map of the world you'll see some countries marked "tropical," which means that's where the sun shines closest. The people in those countries are all burnt black by the sun. The king of that part of the world tried all kinds of schemes before he hit on what is called a balloon. That's a big round bag they fill with air high up in the sky. They bring the bag down and open it, causing the cooling air inside the bag to spread out all over the country. That's a great invention. On the other hand, in

Russia, which is a cold country where the snow falls even in summer and the ice is so thick that people can't move, they invented the steam engine. You've got to admire them for it. I understand that they modeled the steam engine after the flaming chariot of hell, but anyway, what they do is to load a crowd of people on a wagon and light a fire in a pipe underneath. They keep feeding the fire inside the pipe with coal, so that the people riding on top can travel a great distance completely oblivious to the cold. Those people in the West can think up inventions like that, one after the other. . . . You say you must be going? Well, good-bye. Waitress! Another small bottle of *sake*. And some pickled onions to go with it!

Source: Excerpt from "The Beefeater" from *Modern Japanese Literature*, compiled and edited by Donald Keene, copyright © 1956 by Grove Press, Inc. Reprinted by permission of Grove/Atlantic, Inc.

achieving wealth and power of the kind Western industrial nations possessed. In retrospect, we are aware that Japan had important assets that contributed to the attainment of these goals. But it also had liabilities, and they loomed large in the eyes of the Meiji leaders. There was no blueprint for progress. The government faced tough decisions as it advanced by trial and error. It also demanded that the Japanese people make sacrifices for the sake of the future.

The announcement of the restoration of rule by an emperor was made on January 3, 1868. In the battles that followed, Chōshū and Satsuma troops defeated those of the *bakufu*. In May, Edo surrendered to the imperial forces. Within months Edo Castle became the imperial palace and Edo was renamed Tokyo, the "eastern capital." A year later the last *bakufu* holdouts surrendered in Hokkaido. At the start the Meiji government was made up of only a small group of samurai leaders from Chōshū, Satsuma, and a few

other domains. These men controlled the youthful emperor through a handful of Kyoto nobles. They controlled their own domains through domain officials and the samurai commanders of the domain armies. They have been described, only half humorously, as twelve bureaucrats in search of a bureaucracy. But such a description belittles the vision with which they defined the goals of the new government.

Centralization of Power

The immediate goal of these sumarai leaders was to centralize political power. What this entailed, concretely, was using the leverage of the Chōshū and Satsuma domain armies to abolish the domains. This was a ticklish operation in that many in these armies were loyal to their old domain and not to the young samurai leaders who had abandoned their domains to form the new central government. Nevertheless, by

Document On Wives and Concubines

During the 1870s and 1880s leading Japanese thinkers introduced a wide range of Western ideas into their country. Among them were freedom and equality as rights inherent in human nature. Debating the questions of equality in marriage and the rights of wives, intellectuals voiced a radical criticism of concubinage and prostitution. As a consequence of these debates, laws were passed during the 1880s and 1890s that strengthened the legal status of wives. Mori Arinori (1847–1889), who had studied in the United States and England, wrote the following passage in 1874. He later became a diplomat and, between 1885 and 1889, the minister of education.

■ *Think of comparable instances in American or European history where new ideas led to dramatic social change. How long did the changes last, and how deeply rooted did they become?*

The relation between man and wife is the fundamental of human morals. The moral path will be achieved by establishing this fundamental, and the country will only be firmly based if the moral path is realized. When people marry, rights and obligations emerge between them so that neither can take advantage of the other.

There have hitherto been a variety of marriage practices [in our country]. . . . Sometimes there may be one or even several concubines in addition to the wife, and sometimes a concubine may become the wife. Sometimes the wife and the concubines live in the same establishment. Sometimes they are separated, and the concubine is the favored one while the wife is neglected. . . .

Taking a concubine is by arbitrary decision of the man and with acquiescence of the concubine's family. The arrangement, known as *ukedashi*, is made by paying money to the family of the concubine. This means, in other words, that concubines are bought with money. Since concubines are generally geisha and prostitutes pa-

tronized by rich men and nobles, many descendants in the rich and noble houses are the children of bought women. Even though the wife is superior to the concubine in households where they live together, there is commonly jealousy and hatred between them because the husband generally favors the concubine. Therefore, there are numerous instances when, the wife and the concubines being scattered in separate establishments, the husband repairs to the abode of the one with whom he is infatuated and willfully resorts to scandalous conduct. . . .

Thus, I have here explained that our country has not yet established the fundamental of human morality, and I hope later to discuss how this situation injures our customs and obstructs enlightenment.

Source: Reprinted by permission of the publisher from *Meiroku Zasshi: Journal of The Japanese Enlightenment* by William R. Braisted, pp 104–105, Cambridge, Mass: Harvard University Press, Copyright © 1976 by the University of Tokyo Press.

1871 the young leaders had replaced the domains with prefectures controlled by the Tokyo government. To ensure a complete break with the past, each new prefectural governor was chosen from samurai of other regions. The first governor of the Chōshū area, for example, was a samurai of a former Tokugawa domain.

Having centralized political authority, in 1871 about half of the most important Meiji leaders went abroad for a year and a half—ostensibly to revise the "unequal treaties" of 1854 and 1858, but in fact to study the West. (See Document, "On Wives and Concubines.") They traveled in the United States and Europe visiting parliaments, schools, and factories.

●●—Read the Document
Japanese Impressions of American Culture (1860) at **myhistorylab.com**

On returning to Japan in 1872 they discovered that the stay-at-home officials were planning war with Korea. They quickly quashed the plan, insisting that the highest priority be given to domestic development.

The second task of the Meiji leaders was to stabilize government revenues, which fluctuated with the price of rice since the land tax was collected mostly in grain. The government converted the grain tax to a money tax, shifting the burden of fluctuations onto the shoulders of the nation's farmers. But a third of the revenues still went to pay for samurai stipends, so in 1873 the government raised a conscript army and subsequently abolished the samurai class. The samurai were paid off in government bonds; but as the bonds fell during the inflation of the 1870s, most former samurai became impoverished. What had begun as a reform of government finance ended as a social revolution.

Some samurai rebelled. Those in the domains that had carried out the Restoration were particularly indignant at their treatment. The last and greatest uprising, in 1877, was by Satsuma samurai led by Saigō Takamori (1827–1877), who had broken with the government over the issue of whether to invade Korea. When the uprising was suppressed in 1877, the Meiji government became militarily secure.

Political Parties

Other samurai opposed the government by forming political parties and campaigning for popular rights, elections, and a constitution. They drew heavily on liberal Western models that had become widely known through the Civilization and Enlightenment Movement. National assemblies, they argued, were the means by which advanced societies tapped the energies of their peoples; parties in a national assembly would unite the emperor and the people, thereby curbing the arbitrary actions of the Satsuma-Chōshū clique. Samurai were the mainstay of the early party movement, despite its doctrines proclaiming all classes to be equal.

Japan's first foreign mission, headed by Prince Iwakura, Ambassador Extraordinary and Plenipotentiary, leaving Yokohama for the United States and Europe on December 23, 1871.

Then, with the government's formation of prefectural assemblies in 1878, what had been in fact unofficial pressure groups became true political parties. Many farmers joined, wanting their taxes cut; the poor joined too, hoping to improve their condition. The parties were given another boost after a political crisis in 1881, when the government promised a constitution and a national assembly within ten years. During the 1880s the parties had ups and downs. When poorer peasants rebelled, the parties temporarily dissolved to dissociate themselves from the uprisings. But as the date for national elections approached, the parties regrouped and regained strength, and the ties between party notables and local men of influence grew closer.

The Constitution

The government viewed the party movement with distaste but was unsure how to counter it. The promise of a constitution had been one tactic. Itō Hirobumi (1841–1909), originally from Chōshū, went abroad to shop for a constitution that would serve the needs of the Meiji government. He found principles to his liking in Germany and brought home a German jurist to help adapt the conservative Prussian constitution of 1850 to Japanese uses. As promulgated in 1889, the Meiji Constitution was notable for the extensive powers granted to the emperor and for the severely limited powers it granted to the lower house in the **Diet** (the English term for Japan's bicameral national assembly).

The emperor was sovereign. According to the constitution, he was "sacred and inviolable." In Itō's commentaries the sacredness was defined in Shinto terms. As in Prussia, the emperor was given direct command of the armed forces. Yamagata Aritomo (1838–1922) had set up a German-type general staff system in 1878. The emperor had the right to name the prime minister and to appoint the cabinet. He could dissolve the lower house of the Diet and issue imperial ordinances when the Diet was not in session. The Imperial Household Ministry, which was outside the cabinet, administered the great wealth given to the imperial family during the 1880s—so that the emperor would never have to ask the Diet for funds. In every case, it was intended and understood that the Meiji leaders would act for the emperor in all

Read the Document
Emperor Meiji, The Constitution of the Empire of Japan at **myhistorylab.com**

of these matters. Finally, the constitution itself was presented as a gift from the emperor to his subjects.

The lower house of the Diet, in contrast, was given the authority only to approve budgets and pass laws. Both of these powers were hedged. The constitution stipulated that the previous year's budget would remain in effect if a new budget was not approved. The appointive House of Peers, the upper house of the Diet, had to approve any bill to become law. Furthermore, to ensure that the parties

The Promulgation of the Meiji Constitution in 1889. The emperor, standing under the canopy, was declared "sacred and inviolable." Seated on the throne, at the left, is the empress. *Shosai Ginko (Japanese, act. 1874–1897), View of the Issuance of the State Constitution in the State Chamber of the New Imperial Palace, March 2, 1889 (Meiji 22), Ink and color on paper, 14 1/8 x 28 3/8 in. The Metropolitan Museum of Art, Gift of Lincoln Kirstein, 1959 (JP3233-3235) Photograph © The Metropolitan Museum of Art. Art Resource, New York.*

themselves would represent the stable and responsible elements of Japanese society, the vote was given only to adult males paying 15 yen or more in taxes. In 1890 this was about 5 percent of the adult male population. In short, Itō had never intended to create a parliamentary system with full deliberative powers. What he devised was a constitutional system that included a parliament as one of its parts.

The government also created institutions designed to limit the future influence of the political parties. In 1884 it created a new nobility, honorable and conservative, with which to stock the future House of Peers. The nobility was composed of ex-nobles and the Meiji leaders themselves. Itō, born a lowly foot soldier in Chōshū, began in the new nobility as a count and ended as a prince. In 1885 he established a cabinet system and became the first prime minister, followed by Kuroda Kiyotaka (1840–1900) of Satsuma and then by Yamagata Aritomo of Chōshū. In 1887 Itō established a privy council, with himself as its head, to approve the constitution he had written. In 1888 new laws and civil service examinations were instituted to insulate the imperial bureaucracy from the tawdry concerns of political parties.

By this time the bureaucracy, which had begun as a loose collection of men of ability and of their

•◦◦—**Read the Document**
Japan: The Imperial Rescript on Education, 1890 at **myhistorylab.com**

protégés, had become highly systematized. Detailed administrative laws defined their functions and governed their behavior. They were well paid. In 1890 there were 24,000 officials; by 1908 there were 72,000.

Growth of a Modern Economy

The late Tokugawa economy was backward and not markedly different from the economies of other East Asian countries. Almost 80 percent of the population lived in the countryside at close to a subsistence level. Sophisticated but labor-intensive paddy-field techniques were used in farming. Taxes were high, as much as 35 percent of the product, and two-thirds of the land tax was paid in kind. That is to say, money had only partially penetrated the rural economy. Japan had not developed factory production with machinery, steam power, or large accumulations of capital.

Early Meiji reforms unshackled the late Tokugawa economy. Occupations were freed, which meant that farmers could trade and samurai could farm. Barriers on roads were abolished, as were the monopolistic guilds that had restricted access to central markets. The abolition of domains threw open regional economies that had been partially self-enclosed. Most large merchant houses were too closely tied to daimyo finances and went bankrupt, but there rose a groundswell of new commercial ventures and of traditional agriculturally based industries.

Silk was the wonder crop. The government introduced mechanical reeling, enabling Japan to win markets previously held by the hand-reeled silk of China. About two-thirds of Japanese silk production was exported, and not until the 1930s did cotton textiles become more important. Silk production rose from 2.3 million pounds in the post-Restoration era to 93 million in 1929.

A parallel unshackling occurred on the land. The land tax reform of the 1870s lowered taxes only slightly, but created a powerful incentive for growth by giving farmers a clear title to their land and by fixing the tax in money. The freedom to buy and sell land led to a rise in tenancy from an estimated 25 percent in 1868 to about 44 percent at the turn of the century. Progressive landlords bought fertilizer and farm equipment. Rice production rose from 149 million bushels a year during 1880–1884 to 316 million during 1935–1937. More food, combined with a drop in the death rate—the result of better hygiene—led to population growth: from about 30 million in 1868 to 45 million in 1900 to 73 million in 1940. Because the farm population remained constant, the extra hands were available for factory and other urban jobs.

First Phase: Model Industries

Modern industries developed in four phases. The first, which lasted until 1881, was the era of model industries. With military strength a goal, the Meiji government expanded the arsenals and the shipyards that it had inherited from the Tokugawa. It also built telegraph lines, made a start on railroads, developed coal and copper mines, and established factories for textiles, cement, glass, tools, and other products. Every new industry begun during the 1870s was the work of the government; many were initiated by the Ministry of Industry, set up in 1870 under Itō. The quantitative output of these early industries was insignificant, however. Essentially they were pilot-plant operations that doubled as "schools" for technologists and labor.

Just as important to economic development was a variety of other new institutions such as banks, post offices, ports, roads, commercial laws, a system of primary and secondary schools, and a government university. They were patterned after European and American examples, although the pattern was often altered to fit Japan's needs. For example, Tokyo Imperial University had a faculty of agriculture earlier than any university in Europe.

Silk-Weaving Mill in Japan, late nineteenth century. Note the division of labor: The women do the manual labor, while the man, dressed in formal attire, supervises.

Second Phase: 1880s–1890s

Substantial growth in the modern sector took place during the 1880s and 1890s. It was marked by the appearance of what would later become the great industrial combines known as *zaibatsu*. Accumulating capital was the greatest problem. Iwasaki Yatarō (1834–1885) used political connections. After the Restoration, he gained control of the ships that he had managed as a samurai official for the Tosa domain. He next acquired government ships that had been used to transport troops in 1874 and during the 1877 Satsuma Rebellion. From these beginnings he built a shipping line to compete with foreign companies, started a bank, and invested in the enterprises that later became the Mitsubishi combine.

Shibusawa Eiichi (1840–1931) was another maverick entrepreneur. Born in a peasant family that made indigo dye, he became a merchant, joined the pro-emperor movement, then switched sides and became a retainer of the last shogun. He spent two years in France and after 1868 entered the Finance Ministry. In 1873 he made the "heavenly descent" from government to private business. Founding the First Bank, he showed a talent for beginning new industries with other people's money. His initial success was the Osaka Cotton Spinning Mill, established as Japan's first joint stock company in 1882. The investors profited hugely, and money poured in to found new mills; by 1896 the production of yarn had reached 17 million pounds, and by 1913 it was more than ten times that amount. After the turn of the century cotton cloth replaced yarn as the focus of growth: Production rose more than 100-fold, from 22 million square yards in 1900 to 2,710 million in 1936.

Japan's First Railroad, planning began in 1869, one year after the Meiji Restoration, and the first line from the Shiodome station in Tokyo to the port of Yokohama was opened in 1872. In this woodblock print, onlookers (in the foreground) gape outside the fence while passengers in Western dress await the arrival of the train.

Another area of growth was railroads. Before railroads, coastal shipping carried the bulk of Japan's commerce. It cost as much during the early Meiji period to transport goods 50 miles overland as it did to ship them to Europe. Railroads gave Japan an internal circulatory system, opening up hitherto isolated regions. In 1872 Japan had 18 miles of track; in 1894, 2,100 miles; and in 1934, 14,500 miles.

Cotton textiles and railroads were followed during the 1890s by cement, bricks, matches, glass, beer, chemicals, and other private industries. One can only admire the foresight and vigor of the bold entrepreneurs who pioneered in these industries. At the same time, the role of government in creating a favorable climate for growth should not be forgotten: The society and the polity were stable, the yen was sound, capital was safe, and taxes on industry were low. In every respect, the conditions enjoyed by Japan's budding entrepreneurs differed from those of China.

Third Phase: 1905–1929

The economy continued to grow after the Russo-Japanese War in 1905 and spurted ahead during World War I. Light industries and textiles were central, but iron and steel, shipping, coal mining, electrical power, and chemicals also grew. An economic slump followed the war, and the economy grew slowly during the 1920s. One factor was renewed competition from a Europe at peace; another was the great earthquake that destroyed Tokyo in 1923. Tokyo was rebuilt with loans, but they led to inflation. Agricultural productivity also leveled off during the 1920s: It became cheaper to import foodstuffs from the newly acquired colonies of

Taiwan and Korea than to invest in new agricultural technology at home.

By the 1920s Japanese society, especially in the cities, was becoming modern. The Japanese ate better, were healthier, and lived longer. Personal savings rose with the standard of living. Urban workers opened postal saving accounts, drank beer, went to movies, and read newspapers. In 1890, 31 percent of girls and 64 percent of boys went to primary schools; by 1905 the figures were 90 and 96 percent, respectively; and by 1925 primary school education was universal. Japan had done what no other non-Western nation had even attempted: It had achieved universal literacy. During the 1920s, the 1930s, and the war years, increasing numbers of primary school graduates went on to middle and higher schools, or entered the new technical colleges. Nevertheless, an enormous cultural and social gap remained between the majority who had only a primary school education and the 3 percent who attended university. The gap would prove to be a basic weakness in the political democracy of the 1920s.

Despite overall improvements in the condition of the Japanese, the human costs of growth were high. (See Document, "Natsume Sōseki on the Costs of Rapid Modernization." on page 834) Because textiles played a large role in the early phase of growth, well into the twentieth century women accounted for more than half of the industrial labor force. They went to the mills after leaving primary school and returned to their villages before marrying. "Neither silk-reeling maids nor slops are kept for long," went the words of one song. Their working hours were long, their dormitories crowded, and their movements

Document
Natsume Sōseki on the Costs of Rapid Modernization

Natsume Sōseki (1867–1916) was one of the earliest of a series of great novelists to create a new literature in Japan after the turn of the twentieth century. Sōseki could often be humorous. One of his early works, *I Am a Cat*, looks at a Tokyo household from a feline perspective. He advocated ethical individualism as superior to state morality. He also wrote of human isolation in a changing society and of the dark side of human nature.

■ *What were the costs of Japan's rapid modernization? Was the uneasiness experienced by only a few advanced thinkers, or did it cut across the society? Was it different from alienation in the modern West?*

THE ENLIGHTENMENT OF PRESENT-DAY JAPAN

Let us set aside our half-baked understanding of new Western theories. If we truly do research and advance from A theory to B theory and on to C—without pursuing what is fashionable and without displaying what is new out of sheer vanity, let us say that by an orderly natural and internal process we reach in forty or fifty years after the Meiji Restoration the level of sophisticated civilization that it took Westerners one hundred years to attain. Westerners are mentally and physically more robust than Japanese and, even discounting hardships they experienced as pioneers, it took them one hundred years. If we can actually achieve this progress in less than half the time it took them, we can be proud of acquiring an amazing knowledge, but we will suffer a nervous prostration from which we will be unable to recover. Gasping for breath, we will fall groaning by the wayside.

PASSERS-BY

This is what your brother said. He suffers because nothing he does appears to him as either an end or a means. He is perpetually uneasy and cannot relax. He cannot sleep and so gets out of bed. But when he is awake, he cannot stay still, so he begins to walk. As he walks, he finds that he has to begin running. Once he has begun running, he cannot stop. To have to keep on running is bad enough, but he feels compelled to increase his speed with every step he takes. When he imagines what the end of all this will be, he is so frightened that he breaks out in a cold sweat. And the fear becomes unbearable.

I was surprised when I heard your brother's explanation. I myself have never experienced uneasiness of this kind. And so, though I could comprehend what he was saying, I could feel no sympathy for him. I was like a man who tries to imagine what it is like to have a splitting headache though he has never had one. I tried to think for a while. And my wandering mind hit upon this thing called "man's fate"; it was a rather vague concept in my mind, but I was happy to have found something consoling to say to your brother.

"This uneasiness of yours is no more than the uneasiness that all men experience. All you have to do is to realize that there is no need for you alone to worry so much about it. What I mean to say is that it is our fate to wander blindly through life."

Not only were my words vague in meaning but they lacked sincerity. Your brother gave me one shrewd, contemptuous glance; that was all my remarks deserved. He then said: "You know, our uneasiness comes from this thing called scientific progress. Science does not know where to stop and does not permit us to stop either. From walking to rickshaws, from rickshaws to horsedrawn cabs, from cabs to trains, from trains to automobiles, from automobiles to airships, from airships to airplanes—when will we ever be allowed to stop and rest? Where will it finally take us? It is really frightening."

"Yes, it is frightening," I said.

Your brother smiled. "You say so, but you don't really mean it. You aren't really frightened. This fear that you say you feel, it is only of the theoretical kind. My fear is different from yours. I feel in my heart. It is an alive, pulsating kind of fear."

Source: First selection from Natsume Sōseki, "The Enlightenment of Present-Day Japan," in *Sōseki zenshū,* Vol. 14, p. 279. Translation by T. Craig. Second selection from E. McClellan, *Two Japanese Novelists: Sōseki and Tōson* (Chicago: University of Chicago Press, 1974), pp. 49–50.

restricted. "Like the money in my employment contract, I remain sealed away," was another verse. Some contracted tuberculosis, the plague of late nineteenth- and early twentieth-century Japan, and were sent back to their villages to die. The following verse bluntly captures the public attitude towards women factory workers:

> If a woman working in an office is a willow,
> A poetess is a violet,
> And a female teacher is an orchid,
> Then a factory woman is a vegetable gourd.[1]

Fourth Phase: Depression and Recovery

The 1927 Japanese bank crisis and the 1929 worldwide Great Depression plunged Japan into unemployment and suffering. The distress was particularly acute in the rice-dependent northeast. The political consequences of these years were far-reaching. Yet most of Japan recovered by 1933 and even the northeast by 1935, more rapidly than other industrial nations.

An export boom and military procurements at home fueled the recovery. During the 1930s the production of pig iron, raw steel, and chemicals doubled. Japan constructed complete electric-power stations and became self-sufficient in machine tools and scientific instruments. Shipbuilding forged ahead; by 1937 Japan had a merchant fleet of 4.5 million tons, the third largest and certainly the newest in the world. The quality of Japan's manufacturers rose. The outcry in the West against Japanese exports at this time was not because of volume—a modest 3.6 percent of world exports in 1936—but because Japanese products for the first time were competitive in terms of quality.

··

The Politics of Imperial Japan (1890–1945)

Parliaments began in the West and have functioned better there than in the rest of the world. For Japan to establish a constitution during the nineteenth century was a bold experiment. Even so cautious a constitution as that of Meiji in that age had no precedent outside the West; most Western observers were skeptical of its chances for success. How are we now, in retrospect, to view the Japanese political experience after 1890?

---

[1]E. Patricia Tsurumi, "Whose History Is It Anyway? And Other Questions Historians Should Be Asking," in *Japan Review* (1995) 6:17–38, p. 21. By permission of the International Research Center for Japanese Studies.

Some say the Japanese were not ready for constitutional government and that the militarism of the 1930s was inevitable. In terms of an ideal democracy, Japanese society certainly had many weaknesses: a small middle class, weak trade unions, an independent military under the emperor, a strong emperor-centered nationalism, and so on. These weaknesses, others note, did not prevent the Diet from growing in importance, nor did they block the transfer of power from the bureaucratic Meiji leaders to political party leaders. The transfer clearly fell short of full parliamentary government. But had the Great Depression and other events not occurred, the advance toward parliamentary government might well have continued.

From Confrontation to the Founding of the Seiyūkai (1890–1900)

Two kinds of political history can be written about Japan under the Meiji Constitution. One would describe what the government did. It would include the drawing up of budgets, the building of modern military forces, the prosecution of wars, the formation of a banking system, the establishment of new universities, the reform of the tax system, and so on—all of those activities that characterize a modernizing state. The other kind of history would deal with politics, the struggles between different groups and bodies for power.

In 1890 the Meiji leaders—sometimes called *oligarchs*, the few who rule—were concerned with nation building, not politics. They saw the cabinet as "transcendental," as serving the emperor and nation above the ruck of partisan interests. They viewed the political parties as noisy, ineffective, and irresponsible. They saw the lower house of the Diet as a safety valve, a place to let off steam without interfering in the government's serious work of building a new Japan. But the oligarchs had miscalculated: The authority of the lower house to reject a budget made that body more powerful than they had intended. This drew the oligarchs, willy-nilly, into the political struggles they had hoped to avoid.

The first act of the parties in the new 1890 Diet was to slash the government's budget. Prime Minister Yamagata was furious but had to make concessions to get part of the cut restored. This pattern of applying pressure to the annual budget continued for almost a decade. Rising expenditures meant that the previous year's budget was never enough. The government tried to intimidate and bribe the parties, but failed. It even formed its own party and tried to win elections by enlisting the police and local officials for campaign support. The opposing political parties nevertheless maintained their control of the lower house. They were well organized in the prefectures, and enjoyed the support of rural voters who opposed the heavy land tax.

Russo-Japanese War. Japanese soldiers with flag and bayonets charge across a smoky field to engage Russian troops in the 1904–1905 Russo-Japanese War. Victory over Russia gave Japan Korea and a new international standing. The popularity of postcards, such as this one, reflected the new nationalism of Japan.

Unable either to coerce or defeat the opposing parties and determined that his Meiji Constitution not fail, in 1900 Itō Hirobumi formed a new party. The party was called the Rikken Seiyūkai, or Friends of Constitutional Government. The Seiyūkai was composed of ex-bureaucrats associated with Itō and politicians from the Liberal Party that a Tosa samurai, Itagaki Taisuke (1837–1919), had formed in 1881. For most of the next twenty years it was the most important party in Japan, providing parliamentary support for successive governments through its control of the lower house. This arrangement was satisfactory to both sides: Itō and subsequent prime ministers got the Diet support necessary for the government to function smoothly. The party politicians got cabinet posts and pork barrel legislation with which to reward their supporters. Itō had made the constitution work, but at the cost of relinquishing transcendental cabinets.

The Golden Years of Meiji

The years before and after the turn of the century represented the culmination of what the government had striven for since 1868. Economic development was under way. The unequal treaties were revised in two steps: Japan got rid of extraterritoriality in 1899 (by a treaty signed in 1894) and regained control of its own tariffs in 1911. However, it was events abroad that won Japan recognition as a world power.

The first event was a war with China in 1894–1895 over conflicting interests in Korea. From its victory Japan secured Taiwan, the Pescadores Islands, the Kwantung Peninsula in southern Manchuria, an indemnity, and a treaty giving it the same privileges in China as those enjoyed by the Western powers (see Map 27–1 on page 838). Russia, however, had its own expansionist plans and, obtaining French and German support, forced Japan to give up the Kwantung Peninsula, which included Port Arthur. Three years later, Russia took Kwantung for itself.

The second event was Japan's participation in 1900 in the international force that relieved the Boxers' siege of the foreign legations in Beijing. The Japanese troops were notable for their numbers and discipline.

The third event was the Anglo-Japanese Alliance of 1902. For Britain this alliance ensured Japanese support for its East Asian interests and warded off the likelihood of a Russo-Japanese agreement over spheres of influence in northeast Asia. For Japan the alliance meant it could fight Russia without fear that a third party would intervene.

The fourth event was the war with Russia that began in 1904, when Japanese torpedo boats launched a surprise attack on the Russian fleet at Port Arthur. On land, Japanese armies drove the Russians from their railway zones in Manchuria and seized Mukden in March 1905. The Russians sent their Baltic fleet to join the battle, but it was annihilated by Admiral Tōgō (1847–1934) at Tsushima Straits. After months of war, both countries were exhausted and Russia was plagued by revolution. President Theodore Roosevelt (1858–1919) proposed a peace conference at Portsmouth, New Hampshire. The resulting treaty gave Japan the Russian lease on the southern portion of the Liaotung Peninsula (which it called the Kwantung Peninsula), the Russian railway in south Manchuria, the southern half of Sakhalin, and a recognition of Japan's "paramount interest" in Korea, which it annexed in 1910.

Map 27–1. **Formation of the Japanese Empire.** The Japanese Empire grew in three stages: the Sino-Japanese War of 1894–1895, the Russo-Japanese War of 1904–1905, and Japanese conquests in Manchuria and northern China after 1931.

It is ironic that Japan, a country still not free of the system of unequal treaties, should itself have joined the imperialist scramble for colonies. Neither Japanese tradition, which had rarely looked to foreign expansion, nor Japan's economy, which was just building its modern industries and had no capital for export, explains the desire for colonies. The explanation is simpler: Japan wanted equality with the great Western powers, and military power and colonies were the best credentials. Political party leaders, most liberal thinkers, and conservative leaders alike shared the enthusiasm for empire.

See the Map
Japanese Colonial Expansion to 1914 at **myhistorylab.com**

Rise of the Parties to Power

The founding of the Seiyūkai by Itō in 1900 ended a decade of confrontation between the Diet and government. The aging oligarch Itō soon found intolerable the day-to-day experience of dealing with party politicians, who, unlike the bureaucrats, neither obeyed him nor paid him the respect that he thought his due. He relinquished the presidency of the party to the noble Saionji Kinmochi (1849–1940) in 1903. Saionji also found it too much to bear and passed the post to Hara Takashi (1856–1921) in 1914. With Hara, the office found the man.

Hara was an outsider. Born a generation after the founding fathers of the Meiji state in a politically unimportant northeastern domain, he began his political career as a newspaper reporter. He then entered the Foreign Office, eventually became ambassador to Korea, and then, an editor, bank official, company president, and Diet member. He helped Itō to found the Seiyūkai. The most able politician in Japan, Hara was painstaking, patient, paternalistic, and perspicacious. His goals for Japan centered on the expansion of national wealth and power and were no different from those of Itō or Yamagata. But he felt that these goals should be achieved by party government, not oligarchic rule, and so he worked unceasingly to expand the power of his party. The years between 1905 and 1921 were marked by the struggle between these two alternative conceptions of government.

The struggle can be represented as a rising curve of party strength and a descending curve of oligarchic influence. The rising curve had two vectors: a buildup of the Seiyūkai Party machine that enabled it to win elections and maintain itself as the majority (or plurality) party in the Diet, and the strengthening of the Diet vis-à-vis other elites within the government. To build up the party, Hara obtained campaign funds from industrialists and other moneyed interests, and promoted pork barrel legislation in the Diet: Local constituencies that supported Seiyūkai candidates got new schools, bridges, dams, roads, or even railroad lines. Seiyūkai politicians established ties with local notables, who brokered the votes of their communities. When serving as home minister, Hara was even willing to call on the police and local officials to aid Seiyūkai election campaigns.

In co-opting other governmental elites, the Seiyūkai had mixed success. The party steadily increased its representation in the cabinet. It gained some patronage appointments in the central bureaucracy and in the newly formed colonial bureaucracy, although most bureaucrats remained professionals and resisted the intrusion of outside political appointees. Some career bureaucrats, however, developed working relations with the party and became partly politicized. In the House of Peers, and in the privy council, which ratified treaties, the Seiyūkai fared less well. By and large, these bodies remained independent. The Seiyūkai had no success in penetrating the military services. At most, it exercised some restraints on military budgets in time of peace.

The descending curve of weakening oligarchic control reflected the aging of the "men of Meiji." In 1900 Itō was the last oligarch to become prime minister. From 1901 to 1912 Katsura Tarō (1847–1913), a Chōshū general and Yamagata's protégé, and Saionji, Itō's protégé, took turns in the post. Both had Seiyūkai support. Toward the end of the period, Katsura resented the fact that he had to consult Yamagata for every important decision. Changes within the elites also weakened the oligarchs. A younger generation of officers in the military services chafed at the continuing domination by Satsuma and Chōshū higher officers. In the civil bureaucracy younger officials who had graduated from the law faculty of Tokyo Imperial University were achieving positions of responsibility. Proud of their ability, they saw the bureaucracy as an independent service and resisted oligarchic control almost as much as they resisted that of the parties.

The oligarchs did, however, maintain their power to act for the emperor in appointing prime ministers. With the deaths of Itō in 1909 and Yamagata in 1922, Saionji and, later, ex-prime ministers took over this critical function.

As the rising and descending curves approached each other, the political parties advanced. Several turning points were critical. One came in 1912: When the army's demands for a larger budget were refused, it withdrew its minister, causing Saionji's cabinet to collapse. Katsura formed a new cabinet and tried to govern using imperial decrees in place of Diet support. This infuriated the parties, and even the usually compliant Seiyūkai withdrew its support. Massive popular demonstrations broke out, a movement was organized for the "Protection of the Constitution," and party orators shouted "Destroy the Satsuma-Chōshū cliques" and "Off with Katsura's head." Katsura tried to counter the popular forces aligned against him by forming a second political party, to rival the Seiyūkai. The party became politically important during the 1920s, but Katsura was forced to resign in 1913. The lower house had brought down an oligarchic prime minister.

The curves finally crossed in 1918 when Hara became prime minister. It was the first time a politician who was not a Meiji founding father or a protégé of one had obtained the post. He enacted reforms but did nothing to remedy the parliamentary shortcomings of the Meiji Constitution.

A parallel development was the liberalism that blossomed during World War I and culminated in the period of party governments from 1924 to 1932. Japan had joined the Allies in World War I and was influenced by democratic ideas from England and America. Scholars discussed revising the Meiji Constitution. Labor unions appeared, first liberal and often Christian, and later Marxist. A social movement was launched to improve conditions in Japan's industrial slums and to pass social and labor legislation. The Kenseikai, which had been out of power since 1916, grew steadily more liberal and adopted universal manhood suffrage as its particular goal. When Hara cut the tax qualification for voting from 10 to 3 yen—a substantial extension of the franchise—the Kenseikai criticized the change as insufficient and the Seiyūkai as the perpetrator of class despotism.

During a brief interlude of nonparty cabinets between 1922 and 1924, the Kenseikai launched the Second Movement for the Protection of the Constitution; liberal factions of the Seiyūkai joined in the movement. In 1924, the two parties formed a coalition government, and for the next eight years the presidents of one or the other of the two parties served as prime ministers.

The cabinets (1924–1926) of Katō Kōmei are considered the peak of parliamentary power in prewar Japan. Born in 1860, Katō graduated from Tokyo Imperial University at the age of 21 and entered the Mitsubishi firm. He married the boss's daughter, spent time in England, and joined the Foreign Ministry, becoming foreign minister at 40. For a country that esteemed age, his rise was meteoric. He subsequently became a Diet member, newspaper president, ambassador to England, and, from 1914, president of the

Kenseikai. Outspoken, cold, and haughty, Katō was widely respected, if not liked. He was an Anglophile who understood and advocated a British model of government. His ministry passed universal manhood suffrage, increased academic appointments to the House of Peers, and cut the military budget from 42 percent in 1922 to 29 percent in 1925. He also enacted social and labor legislation. In effect, he legalized the moderate socialist movement and outlawed revolutionary socialism. Katō's cabinet brought Japan close to a true parliamentary government.

Militarism and War (1927–1945)

The future of Japan's parliamentary government seemed assured during the mid-1920s. The economy was growing; society was stable; party leaders were experienced. Japan's international position was secure. By a decade later, however, party leaders had lost the gains of thirty-five years. By 1945 Japan had been defeated in a devastating war and was occupied by foreign troops for the first time in its history. How did this come about?

Put simply, a small shift in the balance of power among the governmental elites established by the Meiji Constitution produced a major change in Japan's foreign policy. The parties had been the obstreperous elite between 1890 and 1926 and had advanced their influence by forcing the other elites to compromise. From the late 1920s the military became the obstreperous elite and did the same. Beginning in 1932 military men replaced party presidents as prime ministers. In 1937 Japan went to war with China; and by the end of 1941 Japan was allied with Germany and Italy, had clashed with the Soviet Union, and had gone to war with the United States.

From their inception, the military services in Japan had been constructed on different principles from Japan's civilian society. Soldiers were not samurai. The rifle companies of Satsuma and Chōshū had broken decisively with that tradition, and universal conscription had put the new military on a changed footing. But the armed services had their own schools, which inculcated the values of discipline, bravery, loyalty, and obedience. Soldiers saw themselves as the true heirs of those who had founded the modern Japanese state and as the true guardians of Japanese tradition. They contrasted their loyalty to the emperor and their concern for all Japanese with the pandering to special interests by the political parties.

The military resented its diminished national stature during the 1920s, when military budgets were cut and the prestige of a military career had declined to the point where officers wore civilian clothes when off base. In particular, the fleet wing of the navy resented the decision by moderate admirals to accept a formula at the London Naval

Yearning for Military Heroes. Japanese patriotic society members dressed as samurai around 1925.

Conference of the Great Powers in 1930 that would limit Japan's naval strength. Furthermore, even during the liberal 1920s, the general staffs remained directly responsible to the emperor. With the passing of the Meiji oligarchs, this meant they were responsible only to themselves.

A Crisis in Manchuria The multilateral treaties (the 1921–1922 Washington Conference and the 1930 London Conference) that replaced the earlier system of bilateral treaties (such as the Anglo-Japanese Alliance) recognized the existing colonies but opposed new colonial ventures. The Western powers strongly supported the "open door" in China, which in their minds included Manchuria. Japan's position in Manchuria was ambiguous. Because Japan maintained its interests through a tame Chinese warlord, Manchuria was not, strictly speaking, a colony. But because Japan had gained its special position in Manchuria at the cost of 100,000 lives in the 1905 Russo-Japanese War, it saw its claim to Manchuria as similar to that of Western nations to their colonies.

From the late 1920s the Nationalists' unification of China threatened Japan's special position. Japanese army figures murdered the Manchurian warlord when he showed signs of independence. Faced with a crisis, the party government in Tokyo equivocated, hoping to preserve a status quo that was crumbling before its eyes. The army saw Manchuria as a buffer between the Soviet Union and the Japanese colony of Korea and was unwilling to make concessions. In 1931 the army provoked a crisis, took over Manchuria, and made it an independent state in 1932. When the League of Nations condemned Japan for violating the open door, Japan withdrew from the League in 1933.

The Great Depression Just as the crisis in Manchuria called into question Japan's place in the international political order, the Great Depression cast doubts on the international economic order and the *zaibatsu*. The *zaibatsu* ("moneyed cliques") were seen as rich capitalists in a country full of suffering and want, as the backers of the "established parties," and as internationalists at a time of rising nationalism.

Rural Japan was especially hard hit by the Depression. The real income of farmers fell by a third between 1926 and 1931 and recovered only slowly. Our images of the Depression in Japan, which may not be representative, come primarily from the northeast, where a crop failure in 1931 led to famine; children turned to begging for food from passing trains, and tenant farmers were forced to eat the inner bark of pine trees or to dig up the roots of wild plants. Urban workers suffered, too. The value of Japanese exports dropped 50 percent between 1929 and 1931. Workers' real income dropped from an index of 100 in 1929 to 69 in 1931. Unemployment rose to 3 million, and many factory workers returned to their villages, adding to the burden on the farm economy. Only the salaried middle class benefited from falling prices.

The government acted effectively to counter the Depression. Going off the gold standard led to an export boom. Japan recovered from the Depression more quickly than other nations. By 1936 its heavy industries were growing apace, and real wages were up. But the recovery came too late to help the political parties; by 1936 political trends that had begun during the worst years of the Depression had become irreversible.

The Depression galvanized the political left and right. The moderate left was composed mainly of socialists, who won eight Diet seats in 1928, eighteen in 1936, and thirty-seven in 1937. Supported by unionists and white-collar workers, they reemerged even stronger after World War II. The radical left consisted of many little Marxist parties and of the Japanese Communist Party, which had been founded in 1922. Though small and subject to governmental repression, they were important in intellectual and literary circles during the 1920s and 1930s.

The Radical Right and the Military The political right in pre-World War II Japan is difficult to define. Most Japanese, except for a few Marxist or Christian intellectuals, were imbued with an emperor-centered nationalism. During the 1930s, however, new right-wing organizations appeared and challenged the status quo. Civilian ultranationalists used Shinto myths and Confucian values to attack Western liberalism. Some bureaucrats looked to Nazi Germany and argued for the exclusion of party politicians from government. "Bureaucrats can run it better, and better serve the people's interest," they proclaimed. Military officers envisioned a "defense state" guided by themselves. They argued for military expansion and an autarchic empire insulated from the uncertainties of the world economy. Young officers of the revolutionary right advocated "direct action" against the elites of the parliamentary coalition and called for a second restoration of imperial power.

The last group precipitated political change. On May 15, 1932, junior army and navy officers attacked the Seiyūkai offices, the Bank of Japan, and the Tokyo police headquarters, and murdered Prime Minister Inukai. This attack occurred at the peak of right-wing agitation and the pit of the Depression. In these circumstances Saionji decided that it would be unwise to appoint another party president as the new prime minister; he chose instead a moderate admiral. For the next four years cabinets were led by moderate military men, but with continuing party participation. These cabinets were no more than a holding pattern; they satisfied neither the parties nor the radical young officers.

During 1936 and 1937 Japanese politics were buffeted by crosscurrents but continued to drift to the right. In the election of February 1936 the Minseitō, the successor to the Kenseikai, overturned the Seiyūkai-dominated Diet. It used as its slogan, "What shall it be, parliamentary government or Fascism?" A week later young officers responded with an attempted coup in Tokyo. Leading 1,400 soldiers, they attacked government offices, killed cabinet ministers, although missing the prime minister, and occupied the Diet, the Army ministry, and other government buildings. They called for a cabinet made up of military men, but Saionji and others close to the emperor stood firm. The navy also opposed the rebellion, and within three days it was suppressed. It was the last "direct action" by the radical right in prewar Japan. The ringleaders were swiftly tried and executed, and generals sympathetic to them were retired. The officers who purged the army radicals were tough-minded technocrats, who throughout the budget cuts of the 1920s had advocated the further modernization of Japan's weaponry. They included General Tōjō Hideki (1884–1948), who would lead Japan into World War II.

Suppression of the radical young officers did not end military meddling in politics. On the contrary, the services interfered more than ever in the formation of cabinets, blocking the appointment of party politicians or liberal bureaucrats. As a result, from 1936 on moderate prime ministers gave way to more outspokenly militaristic figures.

Opposition to militarism remained substantial nonetheless. In the 1937 election the prime minister, a former general whose political slogan was "Respect the gods and honor the emperor," tried to win control of the Diet by throwing government support to the Shōwakai, a small Nazi-like party. It performed miserably at the polls, gaining only 40 Diet seats, while the two major centrist parties, which had joined

Four years before Pearl Harbor, the Japanese invaded and occupied most of eastern China. Early in 1937, Japanese troops captured Nanjing, entering the city through its triple-arched gate. Chinese resistance led to a breakdown of military discipline and the "rape of Nanjing," an event still alive in Chinese memory decades later.

in opposition to the government, won 354. The Japanese people proved more level-headed than their leaders. But the centrists' victory was empty: Although a peacetime government could not rule without the Diet, the Diet could not oppose a government in wartime, and by summer, Japan was at war in China.

The Road to Pearl Harbor There were three critical junctures between the outbreak of war with China and World War II in the Pacific. The first was the decision in January 1938 to strike a knockout blow at the Nationalist government in Nanjing. The war had begun the previous year with a skirmish near Beijing and quickly spread. The Japanese army's leaders disagreed on whether to continue. Some held that the only threat to Japanese interests in Korea and Manchuria was the Soviet Union, and a long war in China would be foolish. But as Japanese armies advanced, the general staff argued that the only way to end the war was to convince the Chinese Nationalists that fighting was hopeless. The general staff got its way, and the army quickly occupied most of the cities and railroads of eastern China. When Nationalist leader Jiang Jieshi (Chiang Kai-shek 1887–1975) refused to surrender, a stalemate ensued that lasted until 1945. China was never an important theater in the Pacific War.

The second critical decision was the signing of the **Tripartite Pact** with Germany and Italy in September 1940. Japan had long admired Germany. In 1936 it joined Germany in the Anti-Comintern Pact against international communism. It wanted an alliance with Germany against the Soviet Union. Germany insisted, however, that any alliance would also have to be directed against the United States and Britain. The Japanese would not agree; the Japanese navy, especially, saw the American Pacific fleet as its only potential enemy and was unwilling to risk being dragged into a German war. After Japanese troops were defeated by Russian troops in an undeclared miniwar from May to September 1939 on the Mongolian border, sentiment rose in favor of an alliance with Germany, but then Germany "betrayed" Japan by signing a nonaggression pact with the Soviet Union. Japan then decided to improve its relations with the United States, but America insisted that Japan get out of China. By the late spring of 1940 German victories in Europe—the fall of Britain appeared imminent—again led military leaders in Japan to favor an alliance with Germany.

Japan signed the Tripartite Pact with three objectives in mind: to isolate the United States, to take over European colonies in Southeast Asia, and to improve its relations with the Soviet Union through the good offices of Germany. Japan achieved the last objective on its own when it signed a neutrality pact with the Soviet Union in April 1941. Two months later, Germany attacked the Soviet Union without consulting Japan. It compounded this second "betrayal" by asking Japan to attack the Soviet Union in the east. Japan waited and watched. When the German advance was stopped short of Moscow, Japan decided to honor the neutrality pact and turn south. This decision marked, in effect, the end of Japan's participation in the Axis. Thereafter, it fought its own war in Asia. Yet instead of deflecting American criticism as intended, the Tripartite Pact, by linking Japan to Germany, led to a hardening of America's position on China.

The third and fatal decision was to go to war with the United States. In June 1940, following Germany's defeat of France, Japanese troops had moved into northern French Indochina. The United States retaliated by limiting strategic exports to Japan. When Japanese troops took southern Indochina in July 1941, the United States embargoed all exports to Japan; they cut Japanese oil imports by 90 percent, producing the "crisis of the dwindling stockpile." The navy's general staff warned that oil reserves would last only two years; after that the navy would lose its capability to fight. Its general staff pressed for the capture of the oil-rich Dutch East Indies. But it was too dangerous to move against Dutch and British colonies in Southeast Asia with the United States on its flank in the Philippines. The navy, therefore, planned a preemptive strike against the United States, and on December 7, 1941, it bombed Pearl Harbor. The Japanese decision for war wagered Japan's land-based air power, shorter supply lines, and what it saw as greater will power against American productivity. At the Imperial Conference where the all-or-nothing decision was taken, the navy's chief of staff compared the war with the United States to a dangerous operation that might save the life of a critically ill patient.

Tōjō Hideki (1884–1948), prime minister at the time of the attack on Pearl Harbor in 1941 and one of the chief figures in the rise of Japanese militarism.

Japanese Militarism and German Nazism

Some features of Japanese militarism afford an interesting comparison with Nazi Germany. Both countries were late developers with elitist, academic bureaucracies and strong military traditions. Both had patriarchal family systems. The parliamentary systems of both were less well rooted than those of England, France, or the United States. Stricken by the Great Depression, both sought a solution in territorial expansion, justifying it in terms of being have-not nations. Both persecuted Socialists and then liberals. Both were modern enough in their military services, schools, governments, and communications to implement authoritarian regimes, but their values were not sufficiently modern or democratic to resist antiparliamentary forces.

The differences between the two countries are also striking. Despite the gap between its small educated elite and the rest of the population with only a middle-school education, and despite the cultural split between the more traditional rural areas and the Westernized cities, Japan was more homogeneous than Germany. It had no Catholic–Protestant split. It had no *Junker* class, nor was

its socialist movement a serious contender for political power. The political process during the 1930s was also different. In Germany parliament ruled; to come to power, the Nazis had to win an election. In this objective they were helped by the combination of the Great Depression and a runaway inflation that destroyed the German middle class and the centrist parties along with it. In Japan's constitutional system, the Diet was weaker. Control of the government was wrested from the Seiyūkai and Minseitō even while they continued to win elections. They remained strong at the polls because Japan did not suffer from inflation and the Depression did not decimate its middle class.

The process by which the two countries went to war was also different. In Germany the Nazis rose as a mass party, created a totalitarian state, and then made war. The authority of the Nazi Party lasted until Hitler died in a Berlin bunker. In Japan there was neither a mass party nor a single group of leaders in continuous control of the government. The spiritual mobilization of the population, the implementation of controls over industry, and the formation of a nationalism so intense that university students could be mobilized as suicide (*kamikaze*) pilots all followed the outbreak of hostilities. In Japan it was not the totalitarian state that made war as much as it was war that made the state totalitarian.

The Allies depicted General Tōjō, the prime minister at the outbreak of war, as the Japanese Hitler. Yet when American planes began to bomb Japan in 1944, he was removed

Chronology

Modern Japan

Overthrow of Tokugawa Bakufu

1853–1854	Perry obtains Treaty of Friendship
1858	*Bakufu* signs commercial treaty
1861–1863	Chōshū and Satsuma emerge
1866	Chōshū defeats *bakufu* army
1868	Meiji Restoration

Nation Building

1868–1871	Shaping a new state
1871–1873	Iwakura mission
1873–1878	Social revolution from above
1877	Satsuma Rebellion
1881	Promise of constitution
1889	Meiji Constitution promulgated
1890	First Diet session

Imperial Japan

1894–1895	Sino-Japanese War
1900	Seiyūkai formed
1904–1905	Russo-Japanese War
1910	Korea annexed

Era of Party Government

1918	Hara becomes prime minister
1924	Katō becomes prime minister
1925	Universal manhood suffrage passed

Militarism

1931	Japan takes Manchuria
1937	War with China
1941	Japan attacks Pearl Harbor
1945	Japan surrenders

from office by the elder statesmen close to the emperor and succeeded by increasingly moderate prime ministers. The military, to be sure, continued to prosecute the war. Even after the devastation of the atomic bombs, the Imperial Conference on August 14, 1945, was divided three to three over the Allied ultimatum demanding unconditional surrender. The emperor broke the deadlock, saying that the unendurable must be endured. It was the only important decision that he had ever been allowed to make.

Modern China (1839–1949)

China's modern century was not the century in which it became modern as much as it was the century in which it encountered the modern West. Its first phase, from the Opium War to the fall of the Qing Dynasty, was remarkably little affected by Western impact. Indeed, it was only during the decade before 1912 that the Confucian tradition began to be discarded in favor of new ideas from the West. The second phase of China's modern history, from 1912 to the establishment of a communist state in 1949, was a time of turmoil and suffering. The fighting incidental to the collapse of the dynasty gave way to decades of warlord rule; to partial military unification and continual military campaigns; to war with Japan; and then, while most countries were returning to peace, to four bitter years of civil war.

Close of Manchu Rule

The Opium War

The eighteenth-century three-country trade—British goods to India, Indian cotton to China, and Chinese tea to Britain—was in China's favor. Silver flowing into China spurred the monetization of Chinese markets. Then the British replaced cotton with Indian opium. By the 1820s the balance of trade was reversed, and silver began to flow out of China.

●❖–[Read the Document
William Hunter, "Description of European Factories in Guangzhou," 1824 at **myhistorylab.com**

A crisis arose in the 1830s when the British East India Company lost its monopoly on British trade with China. The opium trade became wide open. To check it, the Chinese government banned opium in 1836, closed the dens where it was smoked, and executed Chinese dealers. In 1839 the government sent Imperial Commissioner Lin Zexu (1785–1850) to Guangzhou (Canton) to superintend the ban. He continued the crackdown and destroyed over 20,000 chests—a six-month supply—of opium belonging to foreign merchants. This led to a confrontation between the Chinese and British. (See Document, "Commissioner Lin Urges Morality on Queen Victoria.")

Document

Commissioner Lin Urges Morality on Queen Victoria

In 1839 the British in China argued for free trade and protection for the legal rights of their citizens. The Chinese position was that behind such lofty arguments, the British were pushing opium.

■ *What does this document suggest about the Qing Dynasty's view of China's place in the world in 1839? Does the dynasty still view China as a universal empire? Do Lin's arguments leave the British queen any ground to stand on?*

A communication: magnificently our great Emperor soothes and pacifies China and the foreign countries, regarding all with the same kindness. If there is profit, then he shares it with the peoples of the world; if there is harm, then he removes it on behalf of the world. This is because he takes the mind of heaven and earth as his mind.

The kings of your honorable country by a tradition handed down from generation to generation have always been noted for their politeness and submissiveness. We have read your successive tributary memorials saying, "In general our countrymen who go to trade in China have always received His Majesty the Emperor's gracious treatment and equal justice," and so on. Privately we are delighted with the way in which the honorable rulers of your country deeply understand the grand principles and are grateful for the Celestial grace. For this reason the Celestial Court in soothing those from afar has redoubled its polite and kind treatment. The profit from trade has been enjoyed by them continuously for two hundred years. This is the source from which your country has become known for its wealth. But after a long period of commercial intercourse, there appear among the crowd of barbarians both good persons and bad, unevenly. Consequently there are those who smuggle opium to seduce the Chinese people and so cause the spread of the poison to all provinces. Such persons who only care to profit themselves, and disregard their harm to others, are not tolerated by the laws of heaven and are unanimously hated by human beings. His Majesty the Emperor, upon hearing of this, is in a towering rage. . . .

We find that your country is sixty or seventy thousand *li* [three *li* make one mile, ordinarily] from China. Yet there are barbarian ships that strive to come here for trade for the purpose of making a great profit. The wealth of China is used to profit the barbarians. That is to say, the great profit made by barbarians is all taken from the rightful share of China. By what right do they then in return use the poisonous drug to injure the Chinese people? Even though the barbarians may not necessarily intend to do us harm, yet in coveting profit to an extreme, they have no regard for injuring others. Let us ask, where is your conscience? I have heard that the smoking of opium is very strictly forbidden by your country; that is because the harm caused by opium is clearly understood. Since it is not permitted to do harm to your own country, then even less should you let it be passed on to the harm of other countries—how much less to China!

Suppose there were people from another country who carried opium for sale to England and seduced your people into buying and smoking it; certainly your honorable ruler would deeply hate it and be bitterly aroused. We have heard heretofore that your honorable ruler is kind and benevolent. Naturally you would not wish to give unto others what you yourself do not want.

Now we have set up regulations governing the Chinese people. He who sells opium shall receive the death penalty and he who smokes it also the death penalty. Now consider this: if the barbarians do not bring opium, then how can the Chinese people resell it, and how can they smoke it? The fact is that the wicked barbarians beguile the Chinese people into a death trap. How then can we grant life only to those barbarians? He who takes the life of even one person still has to atone for it with his own life; yet is the harm done by opium limited to the taking of one life only? Therefore in the new regulations, in regard to those barbarians who bring opium to China, the penalty is fixed at decapitation or strangulation. This is what is called getting rid of a harmful thing on behalf of mankind.

[However] all those who within the period of the coming one year (from England) or six months (from India) bring opium to China by mistake, but who voluntarily confess and completely surrender their opium, shall be exempt from their punishment. This may be called the height of kindness and the perfection of justice.

Source: Reprinted by permission of the publisher from *China's Response to the West; a document survey 1839–1923,* by Ssu-yu Teng and John Fairbank, pp. 19, 24–27, 155–156, 240–241, Cambridge, Mass: Harvard University Press, Copyright © 1954, 1979 by the President and Fellows of Harvard College, Copyright renwed 1982 by Ssu-yu Teng and John King Fairbank.

The Opium War, 1840. Armed Chinese junks were no match for British warships. The war ended in 1842 with the Treaty of Nanjing.

War broke out in November 1839 when Chinese war junks clashed with a British merchantman. The following June 16 British warships arrived at Guangzhou, and for the next two years the British bombarded forts, fought battles, seized cities, and attempted negotiations. The Chinese troops, with their antiquated weapons and old-style cannon, were ineffective. The war ended in August 1842 with the Treaty of Nanjing, the first of the "unequal treaties."

The treaty ended the "Canton system," which had restricted Western trade, and also provided Britain with a superb deep-water port at Hong Kong, a huge indemnity, and the opening of five ports: Guangzhou, Shanghai, Xiamen (Amoy), Ningbo, and Fuzhou. British merchants and their families could reside in the ports and freely engage in trade; Britain could appoint a consul for each city; and British residents gained extraterritoriality, under which they were subject to British and not Chinese law. The treaty also contained a "most-favored-nation" clause, a provision that any further rights gained by any other nation would automatically accrue to Britain as well.

•••⟨Read the Document
The Treaty of Nanjing, 1842
at **myhistorylab.com**

The treaty with Britain was followed in 1844 by similar treaties with the United States and France. The American treaty permitted churches in treaty ports, and the French treaty permitted the propagation of Catholicism.

After the treaties were signed, Chinese imports of opium rose from 30,000 chests to 87,000 in 1879, declined to 50,000 chests in 1906, and ended during World War I. But trade grew slowly. Western merchants blamed the lack of growth on hidden restraints. They also complained that, despite the treaties, Guangzhou remained closed to trade. Chinese authorities, for their part, were incensed by the export of coolies to work under harsh conditions in Cuba and Peru. A second war broke out in 1856, which continued sporadically until British and French troops captured Beijing in 1860. A new set of treaties provided for indemnities, opening eleven new ports, stationing foreign diplomats in Beijing, propagating Christianity anywhere in China, and legalizing the opium trade.

While the British fought China for trading rights, the Russians encroached on China's northern frontier. During the 1850s Russia established settlements along the Amur River. In 1858 China ceded the north bank of the Amur to Russia and in 1860 gave Russia the Maritime Province between the Ussuri River and the Pacific.

Rebellions against the Manchu

Far more immediate a threat to Manchu rule than foreign gunboats were the Taiping, Nian, and Muslim Rebellions that convulsed China between 1850 and 1873 (see Map 27–2). The torment and suffering they caused were unparalleled. Estimates of those killed during the twenty years of the **Taiping Rebellion** range from 20 to 30 million. Adding in losses due to other rebellions, droughts, and floods, China's population dropped by 60 million and did not recover to pre-rebellion levels until almost the end of the dynasty in 1912.

((•⟨Hear the Audio
China
at **myhistorylab.com**

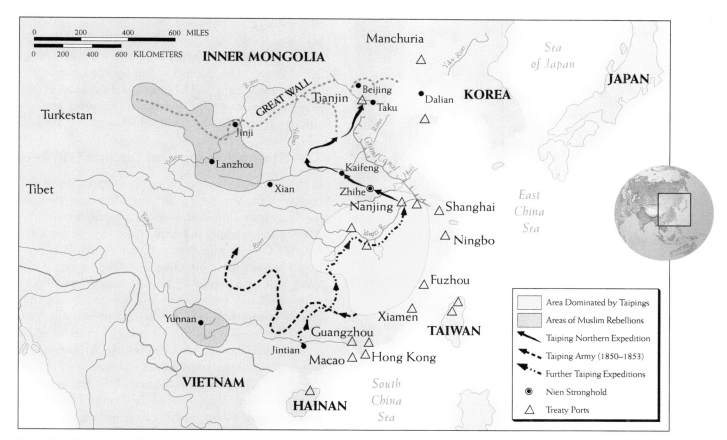

Map 27–2. The Taiping, Nian, and Muslim Rebellions. Between 1850 and 1873 China was wracked by rebellions that almost ended the Manchu Dynasty. The dynasty was saved by Chinese "gentry armies."

The Taipings were begun by Hong Xiuquan (1814–1864), a schoolteacher from a poor family in a minority Hakka group in the southern province of Guangdong. Hong had four times failed to pass the civil service examinations. He became ill and saw visions. Influenced by Protestant tracts, Hong announced that he was the younger brother of Jesus and that God had told him to rid China of evil demons—including Manchus, Confucians, Daoists, and Buddhists. He formed an Association of God Worshipers. His followers cut off their queues as a sign of resistance to the Manchus, who called them "long-haired rebels." The Taipings attacked local Confucian temples, arousing the opposition of the gentry. They were soon joined by peasants, miners, and workers. Hong proclaimed the Heavenly Kingdom of Great Peace in 1851 and two years later captured Nanjing and made it his capital. The fighting spread until the Taipings controlled most of the Yangzi basin; their armies of almost 1 million eventually entered sixteen of the eighteen Chinese provinces.

The Taiping ideology joined Old Testament Christianity with an ancient text often used by reformers, the *Zhou Rites*. The puritanical ethics of the Taipings came from the Old Testament, and the idea of sharing property equally came

from the *Zhou Rites*. The Taipings prohibited opium, tobacco, alcohol, gambling, adultery, prostitution, and footbinding. They upheld filial piety. They maintained that women were men's equals and appointed women to administrative and military posts. In short, like earlier rebels, the Taipings combined moral reform, religious fervor, and a vision of a transformed egalitarian society.

The movement had several weaknesses. Most Taiping leaders were too poorly educated to govern effectively, and the Taipings could not draw on Confucian gentry. When the Taiping area was divided into kingdoms, dissension broke out. The Taipings failed to cultivate the secret societies, which were also anti-Manchu. They also failed to cultivate Westerners, who had been neutral before the 1860 treaty settlements and aided the dynasty thereafter. Moreover, many Taiping ideals remained unfulfilled: land was not redistributed, and, although Taiping teachings emphasized frugality and the sanctity of monogamous marriage, Hong lived in luxury with many concubines.

Other rebellions were of lesser note but longer duration. The Nian were located north of the Taipings along the Huai River. They began as bandits who lived in walled villages, were

Between 1850 and 1864, China was wracked by a great civil war between the Taiping rebels and the gentry-led militia of the Qing government. The victory of the government delayed the collapse of the Qing Dynasty until 1912. The scene above shows troops arrayed in battle formation.

organized in secret societies, and lived by raiding the surrounding countryside. Eventually they built an army, collected taxes, and ruled 100,000 square miles. The Qing feared the Nian would join forces with the Taipings. An even longer revolt was that of Muslims against Chinese in the southwest and northwest. One rebel set up an Islamic kingdom with himself as sultan. Like the Taiping Rebellion, these rebellions took advantage of the weakened state of the dynasty and occurred in areas with few officials and no Qing armies.

Against the rebellions, the Manchu Banners and the Chinese Army of the Green Standard proved helpless: The one was useful only for defense, the other only against civilians. The first effective step was taken in 1852, when the court sent Zeng Guofan (1811–1872) to Hunan province in south-central China to organize a local army. Zeng was a product of the Confucian examination system and had served in Beijing. He saw the Manchu government, of which he was an elite member, as the upholder of morality and the social order, and Chinese rebels as destroyers of that order. Arriving in Hunan, he recruited local gentry as officers. They were of the class that, since the late Ming, had been growing in importance and performing many local government functions, in some cases organizing local militia. They were Confucian, and as landlords they had much to lose from rebel rule. They recruited soldiers from their local areas. Zeng's "Hunan Braves" stopped the Taipings' advance.

Until 1860, Manchu conservatives dominated the Qing court. They limited Zeng's role and were slow to uphold the treaties. In 1860, the conservatives lost their footing when the British and the French occupied Beijing. A new reform government began internal changes, adopted a policy of cooperation with the Western powers, and put Zeng in charge of suppressing the rebellions. Zeng appointed able officials to raise other regional armies. Li Hongzhang (1823–1901), with his Anhui army, was especially effective. Foreigners and Shanghai merchants gave their support. Revenues from the customs service and foreign ships and weapons strengthened Zeng's armies. The Taipings collapsed when Nanjing was captured in 1864. Zeng and Li suppressed the Nian by 1868, and Muslim rebellions were put down five years later. Scholar-officials, relying on local gentry, had saved the dynasty.

Self-Strengthening and Decline (1874–1895)

If we compare the period after the suppression of the rebellions with the late Song or the late Ming, the late Qing looks good. Despite administrative decentralization, China's resiliency and capacity to rebuild were impressive. On its borders the Qing regained some territories while losing others. But if we ask how effective was China's response to the West, or if we compare China to Japan, then China looks almost moribund. Historians often call these years the period of **self-strengthening**, after a catchphrase in vogue at the time. This term is not inappropriate, as the list of new initiatives taken during the period is long. Yet, because the firepower of Western naval forces doubled each decade, the forces that China faced at the end of the century were vastly more formidable than those of the Opium War. Despite self-strengthening, China was relatively weaker at the end of the period than at the start.

In 1895 Li Hongzhang met with Itō Hirobumi (1838–1909) to negotiate a peace treaty after China's defeat in the Sino-Japanese War. Itō asked with uncharacteristic bluntness: "Ten years ago when I was at Tianjin, I talked about reform with the Grand Secretary [Li]. Why is it that up to now not a single thing has been changed or reformed?" Li replied: "Affairs in my country have been so confined by tradition that I could not accomplish what I desired. . . . Now in the twinkling of an eye ten years have gone by, and everything is still the same. I am even more regretful. I am ashamed of having excessive wishes and lacking the power to fulfill them." Itō responded blandly: "The providence of heaven has no affection, except for the virtuous."[2] Considering that Li was the single most powerful figure in China during these decades, Itō's puzzlement was not surprising.

The Court at Beijing The situation at the court helps explain China's inability to act effectively. Prince Gong (1833–1898) and the empress dowager (1835–1908) were co-regents for the young emperor. For a Manchu noble, Prince Gong was a man of ideas. After signing the treaties of 1860, he established in 1861 a new office directly under the

---

[2] S. Y. Teng and J. K. Fairbank, *China's Response to the West* (Cambridge, MA: Harvard University Press, 1954), p. 126.

Grand Council to handle the court's foreign relations. He also established a school to train the Chinese in foreign languages. Over time, however, his position at the court grew weaker. Outmaneuvered by the empress dowager, he was ousted in 1884.

The empress dowager was the daughter of a Manchu official. She became an imperial concubine and produced the only male child of the former emperor. She was educated, clever, petty, strong-willed, and narrow-minded. She did not oppose change, except by circumstance, nor did she favor it. She had no conception of how to reform China. Her single goal was to gather political power into her own hands. She acquired this power by forging a combine of conservative bureaucrats, military commanders, and eunuchs, and by maintaining a balance between the court and the regional strength of the powerful governors' general. The result was a court barely able to survive, too weak to govern effectively, and not inclined to do more than approve of provincial initiatives.

Regional Governments The most vital figures during these decades were a handful of governors general whose names are legendary: Zeng Guofan, Li Hongzhang, Zuo Zongtang (1812–1885), and Zhang Zhidong (1837–1909). Each had a staff of 200 or 300 and an army, and governed two or three provinces. They were loyal to the dynasty that they had restored in the face of almost certain collapse, and in return for their allegiance they were allowed great autonomy.

The Empress Dowager Cixi (1835–1908) sits upon a throne. The empress dowager manipulated the levers of power at the Manchu court in Beijing.

Their first task was reconstruction. The rebellions in central China had destroyed the mulberry trees on which silkworms fed and, in the northwest, irrigation systems. Millions were hungry or homeless. The governors' response to these ills was massive and effective. Just as they had mobilized gentry to suppress the rebellions, now they obtained gentry cooperation in rebuilding. They set up refugee centers and soup kitchens, reduced taxes in the devastated Yangzi valley, reclaimed lands gone to waste, began water-control projects, and built granaries. By the early 1890s, China's late dynastic society was restored.

The governors' second task was self-strengthening—the adoption of Western arms and technology. Keenly aware of China's weakness, they built arsenals and shipyards during the 1860s and 1870s, and commercial ventures during the 1870s and 1880s. The China Merchants Steam Navigation Company was established in 1872, the Kaiping Coal Mine in 1876, and then a telegraph company, short stretches of railways, and cotton mills. The formula applied was "official supervision and merchant operation." Governors like Zeng made major decisions, but day-to-day operations were left to the merchants. This division of labor led to problems.

Li Hongzhang awarded the Steam Navigation Company a monopoly on shipments of tax rice and official cargos, and won tariff concessions for the company as well. For a time these advantages enabled it to compete successfully with foreign lines. But Li also used company ships to transport his troops; he rewarded political supporters with company funds; and he interfered in company operations by hiring and firing managers. Consequently, both investors and managers took profits quickly and did not reinvest. British lines soon dominated shipping in China's domestic waters.

Treaty Ports Conditions in the **treaty ports**, of which there were fourteen by the 1860s, were unlike the rest of China. The ports were little islands of privilege where foreigners lived in mansions staffed with servants, raced horses at the track, participated in amateur theatricals, drank (in Shanghai, at the longest bar in the world), and went to church on Sunday. But the ports were also islands of security, under the rule of foreign consuls, where capital was safe from confiscation, trade was free, and "squeeze" (extortion by officials) was the exception and not the rule. Foreign companies naturally located in the ports. British interests in 1865, for example, funded the Hong Kong and Shanghai Bank to finance international trade and make loans to Chinese firms and banks. Chinese merchants were attracted by the security of the ports and located their businesses on rented lands in the foreign concessions. Joint ventures were also begun by Chinese and foreign merchants. Well into the twentieth century foreign concessions remained the vital sector of China's modern economy.

The Bund. After the Opium War, Shanghai became a treaty port in 1842, and foreign settlements arose along the Huangpu River, north of the old walled city. British and other companies built offices along the river's muddy waterfront, which they called the "Bund"—an Anglo-Indian term derived from "band," the Urdu word for embankment. Before World War II, oceangoing ships docked along the Bund in the heart of commercial Shanghai. Today, this stretch of the river is fronted by the Zhongshan (Sun Yat-sen) Road. On one side are banks, insurance companies, and hotels; on the other is a park. Ships no longer dock.

The effects of the treaty ports on China were largely negative. The low tariffs mandated by the treaties gave Chinese industries little protection. Native cotton spinning was almost destroyed by imports of yarn. Chinese tea lost ground to Indian tea and Chinese silk to Japanese silk, as these countries developed products of standard quality and China did not. China had few products to export: pig bristles, soybeans, and vegetable oils. The level of foreign trade stayed low, and China's interior markets were affected only slightly.

By the 1870s, the foreign powers reached an accommodation with China. The Qing court would uphold the treaties; the foreign powers would prop up the dynasty. By 1900, the court's revenues from customs fees were larger than those from any other source, including the land tax.

The Maritime Customs Service, an efficient treaty-port institution, collected the fees. Sir Robert Hart (1835–1911), who headed the institution, saw himself as an official of the Chinese government. In 1895 the Maritime Customs Service had 700 Western and 3,500 Chinese employees.

View the Image
American Cartoon on Western Powers Carving up China at **myhistorylab.com**

The Borderlands: The Northwest, Vietnam, and Korea

China's other foreign relations were with fringe lands inhabited by non-Chinese but claimed by China as tributaries. Though distant from the pressing concerns of Chinese government, tributaries were nonetheless mirrors in which China saw reflected its own self-image as a universal empire. During the late nineteenth century this image was strengthened in the northwest but was dealt a fatal blow in Vietnam and Korea.

The French in Vietnam. Arrival in Saigon of Paul Beau (1857–1927), governor-general of Indochina 1902–1907, from "Le Petit Journal," November 1902.

The Northwest In the northwest, China confronted tsarist Russia. Both countries had been expanding onto the steppe since the seventeenth century. Both had firearms. Caught in a pincers between them, the once proud, powerful, and independent nomadic tribes were rendered impotent. Conservatives at the Manchu court ordered Zuo Zongtang to suppress a Muslim leader of an independent state in Chinese Turkestan (the Tarim basin, a part of the old Silk Road). Zuo led his army across 3,000 miles of deserts and by 1878 had conquered the area, which was subsequently renamed Xinjiang, or the "New Territories." A treaty signed with Russia in 1881 restored most of the Ili region in western Mongolia to Chinese control. These victories strengthened court conservatives who wished to take a stronger stance toward the West.

Vietnam To the south was Vietnam, which saw itself as an independent state, though it used Chinese writing, Chinese laws, and Chinese-type government institutions. China saw Vietnam as a tributary that could be aided or punished as necessary.

During the 1840s the second emperor of the Nguyen Dynasty reduced French influences and suppressed Christianity. Thousands were killed, including French and Vietnamese priests. The French, in response, seized Saigon and its provinces in 1859, established a protectorate over Cambodia in 1864, and took three more provinces in 1867 and Hanoi in 1882. China, flush with confidence after its victories in Central Asia, sent troops to aid its tributary in 1883. The result was a two-year war in which French warships ranged the coast of China, attacking shore batteries and sinking ships. In 1885 China was forced to sign a treaty abandoning claims to Vietnam. By 1893, France joined Vietnam, Cambodia, and Laos to form the Federation of Indochina, which remained a French colony until 1940.

Korea Unlike Vietnam, Korea actually saw itself as a Chinese tributary. The Korean ruler styled himself as a king and not an emperor. Korea was the only rim area of China that accepted the Chinese view of the tribute system.

During its last decades the Choson Dynasty was weak. It hung on to power, in part, by enforcing a policy of seclusion almost as total as that of Tokugawa Japan, which won it the name of the Hermit Kingdom. Its only foreign ties were tribute missions to China and occasional diplomatic or trade missions to Japan. In 1876 Japan "opened" Korea to international relations, using much the same tactics that Perry had used twenty-two years earlier against Japan. Japan then contended with China for influence in Korea's internal politics. Conservatives and moderate reformers in Korea looked to China for support. Radical reformers, weaker and fewer in number, looked to Japan, arguing that only sweeping changes like those in Japan would enable Korea to survive. The radicals, however, were soon suppressed.

In 1893 a popular religious sect rebelled against the weak and corrupt Seoul government. The government requested Chinese support and China sent troops, but Japan sent more. In 1894 war broke out between China and Japan. China and the Western powers expected an easy Chinese victory, but they had not understood the changes occurring within Japan. Japan won handily. Neither Chinese warships nor Chinese armies were a match for the discipline and superior tactics of the Japanese military. After this war, Taiwan became Japan's first colony. Defeat by Japan convinced many throughout China that basic changes were inevitable.

Students at Nanjing University. University students at Nanjing University study in the Severence Hall Reading Room in the early 1900s.

From Dynasty to Warlordism (1895–1926)

Confucian officials ruled China. Their intellectual formation was highly resistant to change. For most, the foreign crises of the nineteenth century were "coastal phenomena" that, like bee stings, were painful for a time but then forgotten. Few officials realized the magnitude of the foreign threat.

China's defeat by Japan, another Asian nation and one for which China had little regard, came as a shock. China responded with a new wave of reform proposals. The most influential thinker was Kang Youwei (1858–1927), who described China as "enfeebled" and "soundly asleep atop a pile of kindling." For this state of affairs, Kang blamed the "conservatives." They did not understand, Kang argued, that Confucius himself had been a reformer and not simply a transmitter of past wisdom. Confucius had invented the idea of a past golden age to persuade the rulers of his own age to adopt his ideas. All of history, Kang continued, was evolutionary, an advance from absolute monarchy to constitutional monarchy to democracy. Actually, Kang was not well versed in Western ideas; he equated the mystical Confucian virtue of humanity (*ren*) with electricity and ether. Nonetheless, his reinterpretation of the essentials of Confucianism removed a major barrier to the entry of Western ideas into China.

In 1898 the emperor himself became sympathetic to Kang's ideas and, on June 11, launched "one hundred days of reform." He took as his models Peter the Great (r. 1682–1725) and the Japanese Meiji emperor (r. 1867–1912). Edicts were issued for sweeping reforms of China's schools, railroads, police, laws, military services, bureaucracy, post offices, and examination system. But conservative resistance was nationwide, and the orders were implemented in only one province. At the court, the empress dowager regained control, and the reforms soon ended. Kang and most of his associates fled to Japan; one reformer who remained behind was executed.

The response of the Western powers to China's 1895 defeat has been described as "carving up the melon." Each nation defined a sphere of interest—usually a leasehold with railway rights and special commercial privileges. Russia took Port Arthur; Germany, Shandong; Britain, the New Territories at Hong Kong. New ports and cities were opened to foreign trade. The United States, busy acquiring the Philippines and Guam, was in a weaker position in China, so it enunciated an "open-door" policy: equal commercial opportunities for all nations and the preservation of China's territorial integrity.

There was in China at this time a religious society called the **Boxers**. The Chinese name translates more literally as "Righteous and Harmonious Fists." The Boxers had rituals, spells, and amulets that they believed made them impervious to bullets. They rebelled first in Shandung in 1898, and, gaining court support, entered Beijing in 1900. The court declared war on the treaty powers, and there followed a two-month siege of the foreign legation quarter. Pent-up resentments against decades of foreign encroachments fueled support for the rebellion. Eventually an international force captured Beijing, won a huge indemnity, and obtained the right to maintain permanent military forces in the capital. In the aftermath of the Boxer Rebellion, the Russians occupied Manchuria.

The defeat of the Boxers convinced even conservative Chinese leaders of the futility of old ways. A more powerful reform movement began, with the empress dowager herself in its vanguard. But as the movement gained momentum, the dynasty could not stay far enough in front and eventually was overrun.

Educational reforms began in 1901. Women, for the first time, were admitted to newly formed schools. In place of Confucianism, the instructors taught science, mathematics, geography, and an anti-imperialist version of Chinese history that fanned the flames of nationalism. Western doctrines, such as classical economics, liberalism, socialism, anarchism, and social Darwinism, were also introduced. Most of this knowledge entered via translations from Japanese, and in the process the modern vocabulary coined by Japanese scholars was implanted in China. By 1906 there were 8,000 Chinese students in Japan, which had become a hotbed of Chinese reformist and revolutionary societies.

Yuan Shikai (1859–1916) began military reforms; his New Army drew on Japanese and Western models. Young men from gentry families, spurred by patriotism, broke with the traditional Chinese animus against military careers and joined the New Army as officers. Their loyalty was to their commanders and nation, not to the dynasty.

Political reforms began with a modification of the examination system to accommodate Western learning. Then in 1905 the examination system was abolished altogether. Henceforth, officials would be directly recruited from graduates of the schools and from those who had studied abroad. Provincial assemblies were formed in 1909, and a consultative assembly with some elected members was established in Beijing in 1910. These representative bodies were intended to rally the new gentry nationalism in support of the court, but they became forums for the expression of interests at odds with those of the dynasty.

In sum, during the first decade of the twentieth century the three vital components of the imperial system—Confucian education, the bureaucracy, and the gentry—were changed in ways that a few decades earlier would have been unimaginable.

These changes sparked the 1911–1912 revolution, which began with an uprising against a government plan to nationalize railways. The players were:

1. Gentry who stood to lose their investments in the railways.

Document

Liang Qichao Urges the Chinese to Reform (1896)

Next to Kang Youwei, Liang Qichao (1873–1929) was the most influential thinker of late Qing China.

■ *What kind of reform program is Liang advocating? Compare his response to the challenge of the West with that by a Japanese commentator in "A Japanese View of the Inventiveness of the West," on page 829.*

On the *Harm of not Reforming.* Now here is a big mansion which has lasted a thousand years. The tiles and bricks are decayed and the beams and rafters are broken. It is still a magnificently big thing, but when wind and rain suddenly come up, its fall is foredoomed. Yet the people in the house are still happily playing or soundly sleeping and as indifferent as if they have seen or heard nothing. Even some who have noted the danger know only how to weep bitterly, folding their arms and waiting for death without thinking of any remedy. Sometimes there are people a little better off who try to repair the cracks, seal up the leaks, and patch up the ant holes in order to be able to go on living there in peace, even temporarily, in the hope that something better may turn up. These three types of people use their minds differently, but when a hurricane comes they will die together. . . . A nation is also like this. . . .

India is one of the oldest countries on the great earth. She followed tradition without change; she has been rendered a colony of England. Turkey's territory occupied three continents and had an established state for a thousand years; yet, because of observing the old ways without change, she has been dominated by six large countries, which have divided her territory. . . . The Moslems in central Asia have usually been well known for their bravery and skill in warfare, and yet they observe the old ways without changing. The Russians are swallowing them like a whale and nibbling them as silkworms eat mulberry leaves, almost in their entirety.

The age of China as a country is equal to that of India and the fertility of her land is superior to that of Turkey, but her conformity to the defective ways which have accumulated and her incapacity to stand up and reform make her also like a brother of these two countries. . . . Whenever there is a flood or drought, communications are severed, there is no way to transport famine relief, the dead are abandoned to fill the ditches or are disregarded, and nine out of ten houses are emptied. . . . The members of secret societies are scattered over the whole country, waiting for the chance to move. Industry is not developed, commerce is not discussed, the native goods daily become less salable. . . . "Leakage" [i.e., squeeze] becomes more serious day by day and our financial sources are almost dried up. Schools are not well-run and students, apart from the "eight-legged" essays, do not know how to do a thing. The good ones are working on small researches, flowery writing, and miscellaneous trifles. Tell them about the vast oceans, they open their eyes wide and disbelieve it.

Source: Reprinted by permission of the publisher from *China's Response to the West; a Document Survey 1839–1923,* by Ssu-yu Teng and John Fairbank, pp. 19, 24–27, 155–156, 240–241, Cambridge, Mass: Harvard University Press, Copyright © 1954, 1979 by the President and Fellows of Harvard College, Copyright renwed 1982 by Ssu-yu Teng and John King Fairbank.

2. Qing military commanders, who broke with Beijing, declaring their provinces independent.
3. Sun Zhongshan (or Sun Yat-sen) (1866–1925), a republican revolutionary. Born a peasant, he had learned English and become a Christian in Hawaii, studied medicine in Guangzhou and Hong Kong, organized the Revolutionary Alliance in Tokyo in 1905, and was also associated with the 1912 Nationalist Party.
4. Yuan Shikai, who was made a commander to preserve the

Read the Document
Long Yu, The Abdication Decree, 1912
at **myhistorylab.com**

dynasty. Instead, he arranged for the last child emperor to abdicate and for Sun to step aside, and he declared himself president of the new Republic of China.

The Nationalist Party won the election called in 1913. Yuan thereupon had its leader assassinated, crushed military governors who supported them, and forced Sun Zhongshan and other revolutionaries to flee again to Japan. Yuan was uncontested as the ruler of China, but mistaking the temper of the times, he proclaimed a new dynasty with himself as emperor. The idea of yet another dynasty met implacable opposition from all quarters, forcing Yuan to abandon the attempt. He died three months later. After Yuan, China fell into the hands of warlord armies. The years until the late 1920s were a time of agony, frustration, and travail for the Chinese people, but they were also a time of intense intellectual ferment.

Cultural and Ideological Ferment: The May Fourth Movement

In the century after the Opium War, China's leading thinkers responded to the West in terms of four successive modes of thought:

1. From the 1840s into the 1860s, the key event in China was the Taiping Rebellion. The success of gentry Confucianism in putting down the rebellion and reestablishing the social order underlined the effectiveness, vitality, and validity of traditional doctrines.

2. From the 1860s to the 1890s, the dominant intellectual modality was "ti-yong reformism." The essence (ti) was to remain Chinese, but useful contrivances (yong) could be borrowed from the West. This formula enabled a restabilized China to borrow and reform in small ways, such as building arsenals and railroads, while remaining Chinese at the core. It was the ideology of the "self-strengthening" movement.

3. During the last decade of the Manchu Dynasty, the ti–yong distinction came to be seen as inadequate. The ti itself was reinterpreted. The dominant view was that of Kang Youwei, who argued that Confucius had been a reformer and that Confucianism, properly understood, was a philosophy of change. This kind of thought underlay the reforms of 1900 through 1911.

4. A period of freedom and vigorous experimentation with new doctrines began in 1914 and extended into the 1920s. It is called the May Fourth Movement after an incident in Beijing in 1919 in which thousands of students protested the Versailles settlement that awarded former German possessions in Shandung to Japan. The new nationalism changed the complexion of Chinese thought. Instead of appealing to tradition, leading thinkers began to judge ideas in terms of their value in solving China's problems. It was not accidental that this era of intellectual excitement corresponded almost exactly with the period of warlord rule—which afforded a breathing space between the ideological constraints of the old dynasty and those of the Nationalist and Communist eras that would follow.

During the May Fourth era the center of advanced thought was Beijing. Cai Yuanpei (1868–1940), who had been minister of education under the republic, became the chancellor of Beijing University, and Chen Duxiu (1879–1942) became his dean of letters. Both men had a Confucian education and had passed the traditional examinations. Cai joined the party of Sun Zhongshan and studied in Germany. After the fall of Yuan Shikai, he made Beijing University into a haven for scholars who had returned from study in Japan or the West.

Chen Duxiu, a Francophile, had studied in Japan. In 1915 he launched *New Youth*, a magazine that played a role in the intellectual revolution of early twentieth-century China comparable to the *cahiers* in the French Revolution or the pamphlets of Thomas Paine in the American Revolution. In his magazine Chen blamed Confucius for Chinese ills. He called for a generation of progressive, cosmopolitan, and scientific youth who would uphold the values of liberty, equality, and fraternity.

The greatest modern Chinese writer was Lu Xun (1881–1936). Like most other leading intellectuals of the period, he was born into a scholar-official family. He went to Japan for eight years to study medicine but switched in midcourse to literature. His first work, *A Madman's Diary*, appeared in *New Youth* in 1918. Its protagonist is a pathetic figure whose madness takes the form of a belief that people eat people. Lu Xun's message was that only a madman's vision could truly comprehend an abnormal and inhumane society.

As the May Fourth Movement developed, ideas propounded in Beijing quickly spread to the rest of China, especially to its urban centers. Protest demonstrations against imperialist privilege broke out in Shanghai, Wuhan, and Guangzhou. Nationalism and anti-imperialist sentiment were stronger than liberalism, although few thinkers did not speak out for democracy.

At the onset of China's intellectual revolution, Marxism had small appeal; Marx's critique of capitalist society did not fit Chinese conditions. More persuasive was the anarchism of Peter Kropotkin (1842–1921), who taught that mutual aid was as much a part of evolution as the struggle for survival. But after the Russian Revolution of 1917, Marxism-Leninism entered China. The Leninist definition of imperialism as the crisis stage of capitalism had an immediate appeal; it blamed the West for China's ills and offered "feudal" China the possibility of leapfrogging over capitalism to socialism. As early as 1919 an entire issue of *New Youth* was devoted to Marxism. Marxist study groups formed in Beijing and other cities. In 1919 a student from Hunan, Mao Zedong, who had worked in the Beijing University library, returned to Changsha to form a study group. Chen Duxiu was converted to Marxism in 1920. Instructed in organizational techniques by a Comintern agent, Chen and others formed the Chinese Communist Party in Shang-

Document
Chen Duxiu's "Call to Youth" in 1915

Struggle, natural selection, and organic process are the images used by Chen Duxiu—so different from those of Confucianism!

■ *How does Chen's "Call to Youth" relate to the political conditions in China in 1915?*

The Chinese compliment others by saying, "He acts like an old man although still young." Englishmen and Americans encourage one another by saying, "Keep young while growing old." Such is one respect in which the different ways of thought of the East and West are manifested. Youth is like early spring, like the rising sun, like trees and grass in bud, like a newly sharpened blade. It is the most valuable period of life. The function of youth in society is the same as that of a fresh and vital cell in a human body. In the processes of metabolism, the old and the rotten are incessantly eliminated to be replaced by the fresh and living. . . . According to this standard, then, is the society of our nation flourishing, or is it about to perish? I cannot bear to answer. As for those old and rotten elements, I shall leave them to the process of natural selection. . . . I only, with tears, place my plea before the young and vital youth, in the hope that they will achieve self-awareness, and begin to struggle.

What is the struggle? It is to exert one's intellect, discard resolutely the old and the rotten, regard them as enemies and as the flood or savage beasts, keep away from their neighborhood and refuse to be contaminated by their poisonous germs. Alas! Do these words really fit the youth of our country? I have seen that, out of every ten youths who are young in age, five are old in physique; and out of every ten who are young in both age and physique, nine are old in mentality. Those with shining hair, smooth countenance, a straight back and a wide chest are indeed magnificent youths! Yet if you ask what thoughts and aims are entertained in their heads, then they all turn out to be the same as the old and rotten, like moles from the same hill. . . . It is the old and rotten air that fills society everywhere. One cannot even find a bit of fresh and vital air to comfort those of us who are suffocating in despair.

Source: Reprinted by permission of the publisher from *China's Response to the West; a Document Survey* 1839–1923, by Ssu-yu Teng and John Fairbank, pp. 19, 24–27, 155–156, 240–241, Cambridge, Mass: Harvard University Press, Copyright © 1954, 1979 by the President and Fellows of Harvard College, Copyright renwed 1982 by Ssu-yu Teng and John King Fairbank.

hai in 1921; Zhou Enlai (1898–1976) formed a similar group in Paris during the same year. The numbers involved were small but grew steadily.

Nationalist China

Guomindang Unification of China and the Nanjing Decade (1927–1937)

Sun Zhongshan (Sun Yat-sen) fled to Japan during the 1913–1916 rule by Yuan Shikai. He returned to Guangzhou in 1916, but despite his immense attractiveness as a leader he was a poor organizer, and his **Guomindang (GMD)**— Nationalist Party—made little headway. For a time in 1922 he was driven out of Guangzhou by a local warlord. From 1923 Sun received Soviet advice and support. With the help of Comintern agents such as Michael Borodin, he reorganized his party on the Leninist model, with an executive committee on top of a national party congress and, below this, provincial and county organizations and local party cells.

Since 1905 Sun had enunciated his "three principles of the people:" nationality, livelihood, and rights. After 1912 Sun's earlier nationalism, directed against Manchu rule, was redirected against Western imperialism. The "people's livelihood" meant equalizing landholdings and nationalizing major industries. "People's rights" meant democracy, although Sun argued that full democracy must be preceded by tutelage under a single-party dictatorship. Sun sent his loyal lieutenant Jiang Jieshi (Chiang Kai-shek) (1887–1975) to the Soviet Union for study. Jiang returned after four months with a cadre of Russian advisers and in 1924 established a military academy at Huangpu to the south of Guangzhou. The Huangpu cadets were to form a "party army." Sun died in 1925. By 1926 the Academy had graduated several thousand officers, and the GMD army numbered almost 100,000. The GMD had become the major political force in China, with 200,000 members, its leadership divided between a left and a right wing.

Changes that were occurring within Chinese society spurred party growth. Industries arose in the cities. Labor

Jiang Jieshi (or Chiang Kai-shek, 1887–1975), as a young revolutionary officer, stands behind Sun Zhongshan (or Sun Yat-sen, 1866–1925), father of China's 1911–1912 Republican Revolution, taken around 1925.

unions were organized in tobacco and textile factories. New ventures were begun outside the treaty ports, and even medium-sized towns had chambers of commerce. Entrepreneurs, merchants, officials, teachers, journalists, and the employees of foreign firms formed a new and politically conscious middle class.

The quicksilver element in cities was the several million students at government, Catholic, and Protestant schools. In May 1925 students demonstrated against the treatment of workers in foreign-owned factories at Shanghai. Police in the international settlement fired on the demonstrators, killing thirteen and wounding fifty. The incident further inflamed national and anti-imperialist feelings. Strikes and boycotts of foreign goods were called throughout China; those called in Hong Kong lasted fifteen months.

Under these conditions the Chinese Communist Party (CCP) also grew, and by 1926 it had 20,000 members. The party was influential in student organizations, labor unions, and even within the GMD. By an earlier agreement Sun had permitted CCP members to join the GMD as individuals but had enjoined them from organizing CCP cells within the party. Moscow approved of this policy; it felt that the CCP was too small to accomplish anything on its own and that by working within the GMD, its members could join in the "bourgeois, national, democratic struggle" against "imperialism and feudal warlordism." Zhou Enlai, for example, became deputy head of the political education department of the Huangpu Academy.

By 1926 the GMD had established a base in the area around Guangzhou. Jiang Jieshi felt ready to march north against the warlord domains, but, worried about the growing communist strength, he ousted the Soviet advisers and CCP members from the GMD offices in Guangzhou. The march north began in July. By the spring of 1927 Jiang's army reached the Yangzi, defeating and often absorbing warlord armies as it advanced.

After entering Shanghai in April 1927, Jiang carried out a further purge of CCP members in the GMD, of its party organization, and of the labor unions that it controlled. Hundreds were killed. The CCP responded by trying to gain control of the GMD left wing, which had established a separatist government at Wuhan, and by armed uprisings. Both attempts failed. The surviving CCP members fled to the mountainous border region of Hunan and Jiangxi to the southwest and established the "Jiangxi Soviet." The left wing of the GMD, disenchanted with the communists, rejoined the right wing at Nanjing, China's new capital. Jiang's army continued north, took Beijing, and gained the nominal submission of most northern Chinese warlords in 1928. By this time most foreign powers had recognized the Nanjing regime as the government of China.

Jiang Jieshi was the key figure in the Nanjing government. By training and temperament he believed in military force. He was unimaginative, strict, was feared more than loved, and, amid considerable corruption, was incorruptible. Jiang venerated Sun Zhongshan and his "three people's principles." The grandeur of Sun's tomb in Nanjing surpassed that of the Ming emperors. But where Sun, as a revolutionary, had looked back to the zeal of the Taiping rebels, Jiang, trying to consolidate his rule over provincial warlords, looked back to Zeng Guofan, who had put down the rebels and restabilized China. Like Zeng, Jiang was conservative and, though a Methodist, often appealed to Confucian values. The New Life Movement begun by Jiang in 1934 was an attempt to revitalize these values.

Jiang's power rested on the army, the party, and the Nanjing government. The army was dominated by the Huangpu clique, which was personally loyal to Jiang, and by officers trained in Japan. After 1927, German military advisers replaced Soviet advisers; they reorganized Jiang's army along German lines with a general staff system. The larger part of GMD revenues supported the military, which was expanded into a modernized force of 300,000. Huangpu graduates also controlled the secret military police and used it against communists and any others who opposed the government. Jiang became president of the party in 1938.

The densely populated central and lower Yangzi provinces were the base of GMD strength. The party was unable to control outlying areas, though some gains were made during the Nanjing decade. In 1931 Jiang attacked the Jiangxi Soviet. In 1934 the communists were forced to abandon their mountain base and flee to the southwest and then to Shaanxi province in northwestern China. Of the 90,000 troops that set out on this epic **Long March** of

6,000 miles, only 20,000 survived It was during this march that Mao Zedong wrested control of the CCP from the Moscow-trained, urban-oriented leaders and established his unorthodox view that a revolutionary Leninist party could base itself on the peasantry.

The Japanese had held special rights in Manchuria since the Russo-Japanese War of 1905. When Jiang's march north and the rise of Chinese nationalism threatened their position, field-grade officers of Japan's army in Manchuria engineered a military coup in 1931, and in 1932 established a puppet state and proclaimed Manchurian independence. In the years that followed, Japanese army units moved south to the Great Wall.

Map 27–3. The Northern Expeditions of the Guomindang. These expeditions, from 1926 to 1928, unified most of China under the Nationalist (Guomindang) government of Jiang Jieshi, inaugurating the Nanjing decade. Warlord armies continued to hold power on the periphery.

Chinese national sentiment demanded that Jiang resist, but Jiang, well aware of the disparity between his army and that of Japan, felt that the internal unification of China should take precedence over war against a foreign power. On a visit to Xian in 1936 Jiang was captured by a northern warlord and held until he agreed to join with the CCP in a united front against Japan. In the following year, however, a full-scale war with Japan broke out, and China's situation again changed.

War and Revolution (1937–1949)

In 1937 the GMD controlled most of China and was recognized as its government, whereas the CCP survivors of the Long March had just begun to rebuild their strength in arid Shaanxi, a remote area beyond the reach of Jiang's army. But by 1949 CCP forces had conquered China, including border areas never under GMD rule, and Jiang and the GMD had fled to Taiwan. What had happened?

The war with Japan was critical. It began in July 1937 with an unplanned clash at Beijing and then quickly spread. Battlefield victories soon convinced the Japanese military leaders to abandon negotiations in favor of a knockout blow. Beijing and Tianjin fell within a month, Shanghai in August, and Nanjing in December. The following year the Japanese took Guangzhou and Wuhan and set up puppet regimes in Beijing and Nanjing. In 1940, frustrated by trying to work with Jiang, the leader of the left wing of the GMD and many of his associates joined the Japanese puppet government. Japan proclaimed a "New Order in East Asia," which was to

Map 27–4. The Long March, 1934–1935. Arrows trace the Chinese communists' "Long March," from Jiangxi Soviet to Yan'an in northwestern China.

replace the system of unequal treaties. Japan expected Jiang to recognize his situation as hopeless and submit. Instead, in 1938 Jiang relocated his capital to Chongqing, far to the west behind the gorges of the Yangzi. He was joined by thousands of Chinese—students and professors, factory managers, and workers.

Jiang's stubborn resistance won admiration from all sides. But the Japanese occupied just those eastern cities, railways, and densely populated Yangzi valley territories that had constituted the GMD base. The withdrawal to Chongqing cut the GMD off from most of the Chinese population; programs for modernization ended; and the GMD's former tax revenues were lost. Inflation increased geometrically, reducing the real income of officials, teachers, and soldiers alike. By the end of World War II salaries were paid in large packages of almost worthless money, which was immediately spent for food or goods possessing real value. Inflation led to demoralization and exacerbated the already widespread corruption.

The United States sent advisers and military equipment to strengthen Jiang's forces after the start of the Pacific War. The advisers, however, were frustrated by Jiang, who wanted to husband his forces for the anticipated postwar confrontation with the communists. Within the GMD army a gap divided officers and men. Conditions in the camps were primitive, food was poor, and medical supplies were inadequate. The young saw conscription almost as a death sentence. Jiang's unwillingness to commit his troops against the Japanese also meant that the surge of anti-Japanese patriotism was not converted to popular support for the GMD.

For the communists, the Japanese occupation was an opportunity. Headquartered at Yan'an, they consolidated their base in Shaanxi province. They began campaigns to promote literacy and production drives to promote self-sufficiency. Soldiers grew food so as not to burden the peasants. The CCP abandoned its earlier policy of expropriating lands in favor of reductions in rents and interest. (This change led to the widespread American view that the CCP were not communists but agrarian reformers, despite their protests to the contrary.) The party took only those provincial and county posts needed to ensure their control and shared the rest with the GMD and other parties. It expanded village councils to include tenants and other previously excluded strata. But while compromising with other political and social groups, it strengthened the party internally.

CCP membership expanded from 40,000 in 1937 to 1.2 million in 1945. Schools were established to train party cadres. Even as the party expanded, it maintained orthodoxy by a rectification campaign begun in 1942. Those tainted by liberalism, individualism, or other impure tendencies were criticized, and made to confess their failings and repent at public meetings. Mao's thought was supreme. To the Chinese at large Mao represented himself as the successor to Sun; but within the CCP he presented himself as a theoretician in the line of Marx (1818–1883), Engels (1820–1895), Lenin (1870–1924), and Stalin (1879–1953).

Where the GMD ruled through officials and often in cooperation with local landlords, the communists learned to operate at the grass-roots level. They infiltrated Japanese-controlled areas and penetrated GMD organizations and military units. CCP armies were built up from 90,000 in

Mao Zedong (1893–1976) at his cave headquarters in Shaanxi province during World War II. He wears a padded winter jacket and writes with a Chinese brush. On his desk are the *Collected Works* of Lu Hsun.

1937 to 900,000 in 1945. These armies were supplemented by a rural people's militia and by guerrilla forces in nineteen mountainous "base areas." By most accounts the Yan'an leadership and its party, army, and mass organizations possessed a cohesion, determination, and high morale that were conspicuously lacking in Chongqing.

But the strength of the Chinese communists as of 1945 should not be overstated. Most Chinese villagers were influenced by neither the CCP nor the GMD, and although intellectuals in free China had become disaffected with the GMD, most did not positively support the CCP. When the war in the Pacific ended in 1945, China's future was unclear. The Soviet Union allowed CCP cadres to enter Manchuria, which it had seized during the last few days of the war, and blocked the entry of GMD troops until the following year. But even the Soviet Union recognized the GMD as the government of China and expected it to win the postwar struggle. The Allies directed Japanese armies to surrender to the GMD forces in 1945. The United States flew Jiang's troops from Chongqing to key eastern cities. His armies were three times larger than the communists' and far better equipped.

A civil war broke out early in 1946. Both sides recognized that the earlier united front had been a sham. Efforts by U.S. General George Marshall (1880–1959) to mediate were futile. Until the summer of 1947 GMD armies were victorious—even capturing Yan'an. But the tide turned in July as CCP armies went on the offensive in north China. They captured American military equipment left by the GMD forces, and by October 1948 the GMD forces had been driven from Manchuria. In January 1949 Beijing and Tianjin fell. By late spring CCP armies had crossed the Yangzi, taking Nanjing and Shanghai. A few months later all of China was in CCP hands. Many Chinese fled with Jiang to Taiwan or escaped to Hong Kong: they included not only GMD officials and generals, but entrepreneurs and academics as well. Not a few made their way to the United States.

In China apprehension was mixed with anticipation. The disciplined, well-behaved soldiers of the "Peoples' Liberation Army" were certainly a contrast to those of the GMD. As villages were liberated, lands were taken from landlords and given to the landless. In the cities crowds welcomed the CCP troops as liberators. The feeling was widespread that the future of China was once again in the hands of the Chinese.

Chronology

Modern China

Close of Manchu Rule

1839–1842	Opium War
1850–1873	Taiping and other rebellions
1870s–1880s	Self-strengthening movement
1894–1895	Sino-Japanese War
1898	One hundred days of reform
1898–1900	Boxer Rebellion
1911–1912	Republican revolution overthrows Qing Dynasty

Warlordism

1912–1916	Yuan Shikai president of Republic of China
1916–1928	Warlord era
1919	May Fourth incident

Nationalist China

1924	Founding of Huangpu Military Academy
1926–1928	Jiang's march north and Nationalist reunification of China
1928–1937	Nanjing decade
1934–1935	Chinese Communists' Long March to Yan'an
1937–1945	War with Japan
1945–1949	Civil war and the establishment of the People's Republic of China

Summary

Japan. The old Tokugawa regime collapsed quickly, just 15 years after the arrival of Perry in 1853. Samurai rebellions attempted to preserve vested interest in the decade after 1868, but they lost every battle. The new Meiji government began sweeping Westernizing reforms in every field. Japan received international recognition for its military victories in 1895 and 1905. Modern economic growth went hand in hand with universal education. In 1890, a parliament (the Diet) was formed, which made steady gains through the 1920s. But the Great Depression and a crisis in Manchuria led to the rise of militarism in the 1930s and eventually to war with the United States in 1941.

China. In the nineteenth century the Qing Dynasty was in decline. The Taiping and other rebellions threatened its existence. "Gentry armies" that combined modern weapons and traditional values put down the rebellions. Not until 1912, seventy years after the Opium War, did the Qing collapse. After that, China was ruled for a decade and a half by warlords, a pattern not unlike that seen in the aftermaths of previous dynasties. But China's defeat by Japan in 1895, the flood of Western ideas that entered during the decades after 1900, and a rising nationalism prevented the rise of a new dynasty. Instead, the Nationalist Party (Guomindang) of Sun Zhongshan and Jiang Jieshi was formed. It built an army, marched north, and unified China. Its new capital was Nanjing. Chinese communists, who had organized in the early 1920s, were forced to flee to the arid northwest. But the Japanese invasion in the late 1930s destroyed the Nationalists' base in eastern China. Consequently, the communists resurged and won the 1945-1949 civil war.

Key Terms

Boxers (p. 852)

Diet (p. 831)

Guomindang (GMD) (p. 855)

Long March (p. 857)

Meiji Restoration (p. 827)

Self-strengthening (p. 848)

Taiping Rebellion (p. 846)

treaty ports (p. 850)

Tripartite Pact (p. 842)

zaibatsu (p. 833)

Review Questions

1. After the Meiji Restoration, what steps did Japan's leaders take to achieve their goal of "wealth and power"?

2. What were the strengths and weaknesses of Japan's prewar parliamentary institutions? What led to the sudden rise of militarism during the 1930s?

3. Which had the greater impact on China, the Opium War or the Taiping Rebellion?

4. How did the Qing (Manchu) Dynasty recover from the Taiping Rebellion? Why was the recovery inadequate to prevent the overthrow of the dynasty in 1912?

5. Did the May Fourth Movement prepare the way for the Nationalist revolution? The communist revolution? Or was it incidental to both?

Note: To learn more about the topics in this chapter, please turn to the Suggested Readings at the end of the book. For additional sources related to this chapter please see MyHistoryLab.com.

PEARSON

myhistorylab Connections

Reinforce what you learned in this chapter by studying the many documents, images, maps, review tools, and videos available at **www.myhistorylab.com**.

Read and Review

✓●─[Study and Review **Chapter 27**

●●●─[Read the Document *President Millard Fillmore, Letter to the Emperor of Japan, 1852, p. 825*
The Views of Ii Naosuke, 1853 , p. 825
Japanese Impressions of American Culture (1860), p. 830
Emperor Meiji, The Constitution of the Empire of Japan, p. 831
Japan: The Imperial Rescript on Education, 1890, p. 832
William Hunter, "Description of European Factories in Guangzhou," 1824, p. 844
The Treaty of Nanjing, 1842, p. 846

●●─[View the Image *Japanese Woodcut on Perry's Arrival, p. 825*
American Cartoon on Western Powers Carving up China, p. 850

((●●─[Hear the Audio *China, p. 846*

Research and Explore

◉─[See the Map *Japanese Colonial Expansion to 1914, p. 838*

((●●─[**Hear** the **Audio**

Hear the audio file for Chapter 27 at
www.myhistorylab.com.

28 | Imperialism and World War I

- Expansion of European Power and the "New Imperialism"
- Emergence of the German Empire
- World War I
- The Russian Revolution
- End of World War I

During the second half of the nineteenth century, and especially after 1870, Europe exercised unprecedented influence and control over the rest of the world. North and South America, as well as Australia and New Zealand, almost became part of the European world as great streams of European immigrants populated them. Until the nineteenth century, Asia (with the significant exception of India) and most of Africa had gone their own ways, having little contact with Europe. But in the latter part of that century, almost all of Africa was divided among a number of European nations (see Chapter 26). Europe also imposed its economic and political power across Asia (see Map 28–1, on page 866 and Chapter 27). By the next century, European dominance had brought every part of the globe into a single world economy. Events in any corner of the world had significant effects thousands of miles away.

These developments helped foster competition and hostility among the great

The British Dominions Beyond the Seas:
Natives of the Greatest Empire the World
has ever Known.
SPECIALLY PAINTED FOR "THE ILLUSTRATED LONDON NEWS."

The global British Empire dominated the nineteenth-century European imperial experience. The empire was popularized in newspapers, books, and novels, as well as in thousands of illustrations and photographs. This illustration seeks to portray the worldwide reach of the British Empire and the varied peoples whom it governed abroad and, at the same time, as seen in the caption, to build domestic pride in the imperial achievement. Similar illustrations could be found portraying the empires of France, German, the Netherlands, Belgium, and Russia. "Citizens of the British Empire, the Greatest Empire the world has ever known..."

Imperialism and the Great War

Europe

European imperialism in the last part of the nineteenth century brought Western countries into contact with almost all the inhabited areas of the world and intensified their activity in places where they had already been interested. By the time of the outbreak of World War I, European nations had divided Africa among themselves for exploitation. The vast subcontinent of India had long been a British colony, producing primary products such as raw cotton that fed British industry. Much of China had fallen under European control and, Indochina was under French rule. The islands of the Pacific had been divided among Western powers. Much of the Middle East was under the nominal control of the Ottoman Empire, which was in its death throes and

under European influence. The Monroe Doctrine made Latin America a protectorate of the United States. Japan, pushed out of its isolation, had itself become an imperial power at the expense of China and Korea. What all of the Western imperial powers, as well as Japan, had in common was a need to extract raw materials from their colonies to feed their industries. Their colonies in turn were to serve as markets for Western manufactured goods, even at the expense of indigenous manufactures, as in the case of India's ancient cloth weaving industry. This, as well as the prestige that colonies afforded, helps explain why nations were so determined to obtain and retain colonies.

The emergence of a new, powerful German state at the center of Europe upset the old balance of power and threatened the peace established in 1815. Germany's Chancellor

powers of Europe and to bring on a terrible war that undermined Europe's strength and its influence in the world. The frenzy for imperial expansion that had seized Europeans in the late nineteenth century had done much to destroy Europe's peace and prosperity and its dominant place in the world. ■

Expansion of European Power and the "New Imperialism"

The explosive developments in nineteenth-century science, technology, industry, agriculture, transportation, communication, and military weapons provided the chief sources of European power. They made it possible for a few Europeans (or Americans) to impose their will, by force or the threat of force, on other peoples many times their number. Institutional as well as material advantages allowed Westerners to have their way. The growth of national states that commanded the loyalty, service, and resources of their inhabitants to a degree previously unknown was a Western phenomenon. It permitted the European nations to deploy their resources more effectively than ever before.

The Europeans also possessed another, less tangible, weapon: They considered their civilization and way of life to

be superior to all others. This gave them a self-confidence that was often unpleasantly arrogant and fostered their expansionist mood.

The first half of the century was generally hostile to colonial expansion. The loss of the American colonies had sobered even the British. The French acquired Algeria and part of Indochina, and the British added territory to their holdings in Canada, India, Australia, and New Zealand. The dominant doctrine of free trade, however, opposed political interference in other lands as economically unprofitable.

Britain ruled the waves and had great commercial advantages as a result of being the first country to experience the Industrial Revolution. Therefore, the British were usually content to trade and invest overseas without annexations. Yet they were prepared to interfere forcefully if a less industrialized country interfered with their trade. Still, at midcentury, in Britain as elsewhere, most people opposed further political or military involvement overseas.

In the last third of the century, however, the European states swiftly spread their control over perhaps 10 million square miles and 150 million people—about one-fifth of the world's land area and one-tenth of its population. During this period, European expansion went forward with great speed, and participation in it came to be regarded as necessary for a great power. The movement has been called the **New Imperialism**.

Watch the Video
The Origins of Modern Imperialism and Colonialism at **myhistorylab.com**

Bismarck created a new system of alliances that preserved the peace for as long as he remained in power, but the new German emperor, William II, abandoned this policy of restraint and sought greater power and influence for his country. The result was a new system of alliances that divided Europe into two armed camps and greatly increased the chances of a general war. What began as yet another Balkan War involving the European powers became a world war. As the terrible war of 1914–1918 dragged on, the real motives that had driven the European powers to fight gave way to public affirmations of the principles of nationalism and self-determination. Peoples under colonial rule took seriously the public statements, and sometimes the private promises, made to secure their cooperation in supplying the war effort and sought to win their independence and nationhood. For the most part they were disappointed by the peace settlement. The establishment of the League of Nations and the system of mandates in place of open colonial rule did not change much. The British Empire inherited vast territories from the defeated German and the defunct Ottoman Empires and was larger than ever. The French retained and expanded their holdings in Africa, the Pacific, and the Middle East. The Americans added to the islands they controlled in the Pacific. Japanese imperial ambitions were rewarded at China's expense.

A glance at the new map of the world might suggest that the old imperial nations, especially Britain and France, were more powerful than ever. However, that impression would be superficial and misleading. The great Western European powers paid an enormous price in lives and money for their victory in the war. Colonial peoples pressed for the rights that Western nations proclaimed as universal but denied to their colonies; influential minorities in the countries that ruled them sympathized with colonial aspirations for independence. Tension between colonies and their ruling nations was one cause of the instability in the world created by the Paris treaties of 1919.

Focus Questions

- Why were Western powers eager to obtain colonies?
- Why is World War I a turning point in history?
- How did World War I alter the relationship between imperial powers and colonized peoples?

The New Imperialism

The word *imperialism* is now used so loosely that it has almost lost real meaning. It may be useful to offer a definition that might be widely accepted: "the policy of extending a nation's authority by territorial acquisition or by establishing economic and political hegemony over other nations."[1] That definition seems to apply equally well to ancient Egypt and Mesopotamia and to the European performance in the late nineteenth century, but in Europe it new elements. Previous imperialisms had taken the form either of seizing land and settling it with the conqueror's people or of establishing trading centers to exploit the resources of the dominated area. The New Imperialism did not completely abandon these devices, but it introduced new ones.

The usual pattern of the New Imperialism was for a European nation to invest capital in a "less industrialized" country to develop its mines and agriculture, to build railroads, bridges, harbors, and telegraph systems, and to employ many natives in the process. This transformed the local economy and culture. To safeguard its investments, the dominant European state would make favorable arrangements with the local government, either by loaning it money or by intimidating it.

If these arrangements proved inadequate, the dominant power would establish more direct political control. Sometimes this meant full annexation and direct rule as a colony, or it could be a protectorate status, whereby the local ruler became a figurehead controlled by the dominant European state and maintained by its military power. In other instances, the European state established "spheres of influence" in which it received special commercial and legal privileges without direct political involvement.

Motives for the New Imperialism

A predominant interpretation of the motives for the New Imperialism has been economic, in the form given by the English radical economist J. A. Hobson (1858–1928) and later adapted by Lenin. As Lenin put it, "Imperialism is the monopoly stage of capitalism,"[2] the last stage of a dying system. Competition inevitably eliminates inefficient capitalists and therefore leads to monopoly. Powerful industrial and financial capitalists soon run out of profitable areas of investment in their own countries and persuade their governments to gain colonies in "less developed" countries. Here they can find higher profits from their investments, new markets for their products, and safe sources of raw materials.

---

[1] *American Heritage Dictionary of the English Language* (New York: Houghton Mifflin, 1969), p. 660.

[2] V. I. Lenin, *Imperialism, the Highest Stage of Capitalism* (New York: International Publishers, 1939), p. 88.

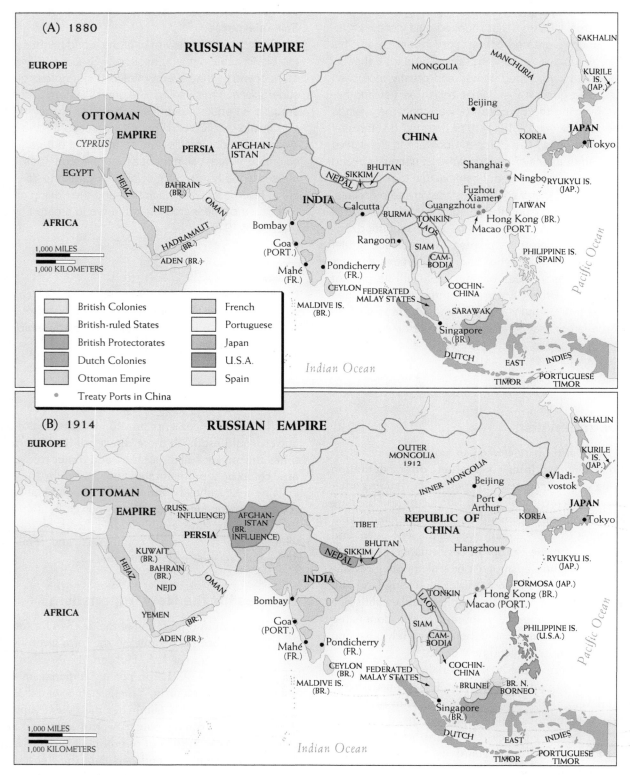

Map 28–1. Asia, 1880–1914. As in Africa (see Map 27–4 on page 859), the late nineteenth century saw imperialism spread widely and rapidly in Asia. Two new powers, Japan and the United States, joined the British, French, and Dutch in extending control both to islands and to the mainland and in exploiting an enfeebled China.

Knitting the World. The New Imperialism was not restricted to Europe. An advertisement for the Singer Sewing Machine Company, based in New York, shows a seamstress sewing together the two halves of the western Hemisphere. By the late nineteenth century, U.S. firms like Singer created a global demand for their goods. Singer sewing machines came with instruction booklets printed in fifty-four languages. Of the fifteen factories making the machines, only seven were in the United States.

Facts do not support this viewpoint, however. The European powers did invest considerable capital abroad, but not in a way that fit Hobson and Lenin's model. Britain, for example, made heavier investments abroad before 1875 than during the next two decades. Moreover, only a small percentage of British and European investments overseas, went to their new colonies. Most capital went into other European countries or to older, well-established areas like the United States, Canada, Australia, and New Zealand. Even when countries did invest in new areas, they often did not invest in their own colonies.

The facts are equally discouraging for those who emphasize the need for markets and raw materials. Colonies were not usually important markets for the great imperial nations, and all these states were forced to rely on areas that they did not control as sources of vital raw materials. It is not even clear that control of the new colonies was particularly profitable, though Britain, to be sure, benefited greatly from its rule of India. It is also true that some European business people and politicians hoped colonial expansion would cure the depression of 1873 to 1896.

Nevertheless, as one of the leading students of the subject, D.K. Fieldhouse has said, "No one can determine whether the accounts of empire ultimately closed with a favorable cash balance."[3] That is true of the European imperial nations collectively, and it is certain that for some of them, like Italy and Germany, empire was a losing proposition. Some individuals (like King Leopold II of the Belgians, in

[3]*The Colonial Empires* (New York: Delacorte, 1966), p. 393.

the Congo) and companies, of course, made great profits from particular colonial ventures, but such people were able to influence national policy only occasionally. Economic motives certainly played a part, but a full understanding of the New Imperialism requires a search for other motives.

At the time, advocates of imperialism gave various justifications for it. Some argued that the advanced European nations had a duty to bring the benefits of their higher culture and superior civilization to more so-called backward peoples. Religious groups demanded that Western governments support Christian missionaries politically and even militarily. Some politicians and diplomats supported imperialism as a tool of social policy. In Germany, for instance, some people suggested that imperial expansion would deflect public interest away from domestic politics and social reform. Yet Germany acquired few colonies, and such considerations played little, if any, role in its colonial policy. In Britain, Joseph Chamberlain (1836–1914), the colonial secretary from 1895 to 1903, argued for the empire as a source of profit and economic security that would finance a great program of domestic reform and welfare, but these arguments were made well after Britain had acquired most of its empire. Another apparently plausible justification for imperialism was that colonies would attract a European country's surplus population. In fact, most European emigrants went to areas their countries did not control, chiefly the Americas and Australia.

The "Scramble for Africa"

All these motives were on display in the late nineteenth century, when European imperial powers expanded their economic and political control of Africa. During this so-called scramble for Africa, which occurred between the late 1870s and about 1900, the European powers sought to maximize their control of African territory and raw materials. Motivated by intense economic and political competition, they rationalized their expansionary policies on both religious and cultural grounds. The imperial powers eventually divided almost all the continent among themselves.

For centuries, European slave-trading bases had dotted the African coastline, but few Europeans had penetrated the interior. This changed in the late 1870s. (See Chapter 26). The Congress of Vienna had prohibited the Atlantic slave trade in 1815, a ban that Western, primarily British, naval patrols enforced along the African coast. Those patrols and the abolition of slavery in the Americas during the nineteenth century meant that Africa was no longer a source for slave labor except in Central and East Africa, where Arab slave traders continued to export slaves to the Muslim world until at least the 1890s. Instead, Africa became an important supplier of raw materials, such as ivory, rubber, minerals, and notably, diamonds and gold to the

See the Map
Africa Before the Scramble at **myhistorylab.com**

Document   Social Darwinism and Imperialism

One of the intellectual foundations of the New Imperialism was the doctrine of "social Darwinism," a pseudoscientific application of Darwin's ideas about biology to nations and races. The impact of social Darwinism was substantial. In the selection that follows, an Englishman, Karl Pearson (1857–1936), attempts to connect concepts from evolutionary theory—the struggle for survival and the survival of the fittest— to the development of human societies.

■ *How does the author connect Darwin's ideas to the concept of human progress? Is it reasonable to equate biological species with human societies, races, or nations? How do the author's ideas justify imperial expansion? What arguments can you make against the author's assertions?*

History shows me one way, and one way only, in which a state of civilisation has been produced, namely, the struggle of race with race, and the survival of the physically and mentally fitter race. This dependence of progress on the survival of the fitter race, terribly black as it may seem to some of you, gives the struggle for existence its redeeming features; it is the fiery crucible out of which comes the finer metal. You may hope for a time when the sword shall be turned into the ploughshare, when American and German and English traders shall no longer compete in the markets of the world for raw materials, for their food supply, when the white man and the dark shall share the soil between them, and each till it as he lists. But, believe me, when that day comes mankind will no longer progress,- there will be nothing to check the fertility of inferior stock; the relentless law of heredity will not be controlled and guided by natural selection. Man will stagnate.... The path of progress is strewn with the wreck of nations; traces are everywhere to be seen of the hecatombs of inferior races, and of victims who found not the narrow way to the greater perfection. Yet these dead peoples are, in very truth, the stepping stones on which mankind has arisen to the higher intellectual and deeper emotional life of today.

Source: From Karl Pearson, *National Life from the Standpoint of Science*, 2d ed. (Cambridge, U.K.: Cambridge University Press, 1907), pp. 21, 26-27, 64.

West. The British, French, Belgians, Germans, Italians, and Portuguese sought to maximize their access to these resources. The competition was so fierce and the scramble for African territories so frantic and volatile that the imperial powers were constantly negotiating with each other about how to parcel Africa among them without the contest leading to war. To set the rules, the German chancellor Otto von Bismarck called a conference in Berlin in 1884–1885 that mapped out a European-controlled Africa. African colonies had become both trophies for European powers and possible bargaining chips in their economic and political competition with each other (See Map 28–2 on page 869).

North Africa In North Africa, the experience of European imperialism was slightly different from that in sub-Saharan Africa. Because much of North Africa was still technically part of the Ottoman Empire, the European powers secured their interests primarily in two ways: through economic penetration (investments and loans) and diplomatic pressure. Force, however, was always an option.

British Fort at Alexandria, Egypt. The opening of the Suez Canal in 1869 sharply reduced the time needed for travel from Europe to the Far East, and, for Great Britain, from England to its colony in India. Britain acquired a financial interest in the canal, giving it a strategic interest in Egypt. In 1882 Britain made Egypt a protectorate in order to secure the canal.

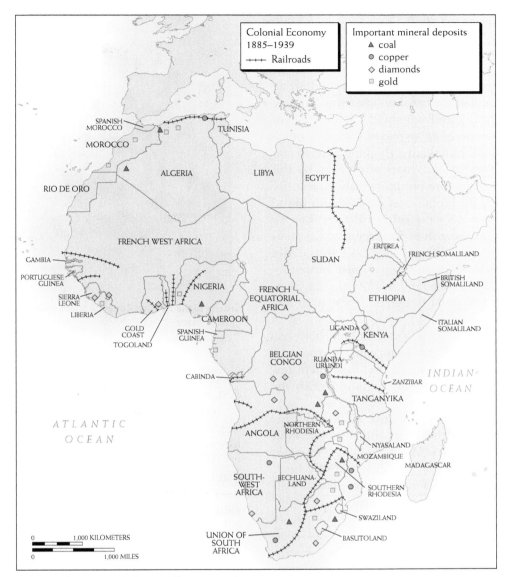

Colonial Economy 1885–1939
+++ Railroads

Important mineral deposits
▲ coal
◉ copper
◇ diamonds
▢ gold

Map 28–2. **The Colonial Economy of Africa, 1885–1939.** The economies of European colonies in Africa were based largely on the exploitation of natural resources. Note how all of the railroads terminated at a port to link the colonies to the world market.

By 1914, European powers controlled all of North Africa. France had begun the conquest of Algeria in 1830 (see Chapter 19). The French also took control of Tunisia in the early 1880s and of Morocco between 1901 and 1912. Italy seized Libya from Turkey in 1911–1912. Egypt, the richest North African country, fell under the control of Britain.

Egypt Egypt was an unusual case. For most of the nineteenth century, it had been a semi-independent province of the Ottoman Empire under the hereditary rule of a Muslim dynasty. The Khedives, as these rulers were titled, had tried to modernize the country by building new harbors, roads, and a European-style army. To pay for these projects, the Egyptian

government borrowed money from European creditors. To earn the money to repay these loans, it forced farmers to plant cash crops, particularly cotton that could be sold on the international market. This proved to be a mixed blessing. When cotton prices were high, for example, during the American Civil War (1861–1865), which cut off supplies of cotton from the Southern states, the Egyptian economy boomed, and government revenues soared. When cotton prices fell, as they did after the Civil War, so did Egyptian revenue. Ultimately, the Egyptian government became utterly dependent on European creditors. The construction of the Suez Canal was the final blow to Egypt's finances.

●●●─ **Read the Document**
A British View of Egyptian Agriculture, 1840
at **myhistorylab.com**

The Suez Canal was opened in 1869. Built by French engineers with European capital, it was one of the most remarkable engineering feats of the day. The canal connected the Mediterranean to the Red Sea, which meant that ships from Europe no longer had to sail around Africa to reach Asia. In particular, the canal reduced the shipping distance from India to Britain from about 12,000 miles to 7,000 miles. The canal therefore increased the speed of international contacts and, by reducing shipping costs, made many goods on the world market more affordable. Yet the tangible benefits to Egypt were not immediately clear. By 1876, the Khedive was bankrupt; most of his shares in the company that ran the canal were sold to Britain. Egypt's European creditors took more than 50 percent of Egyptian revenue each year to repay their loans and forced the Egyptian government to increase taxes to raise more revenue. This provoked a rebellion, and in 1881 the Egyptian army took over the government to defend Egypt from foreign exploitation.

An uncooperative Egyptian government was, however, not in the best interests of the European superpowers. Britain sent a fleet and army to Egypt that easily defeated the Egyptians and established seventy years of British supremacy in the country.

Egypt never became an official part of the British Empire. The Khedives, who became kings after Egypt severed its ties with Turkey during World War I, continued to reign, but the British exercised control through a relatively small number of British administrators and soldiers. The British used their experience from India to run Egypt.

Their primary goal was stability: Egypt had to repay its debts, and Britain was to retain control of the Suez Canal, which the British regarded as their "lifeline" to their empire in India and the Far East. They built a naval base at Alexandria and installed a large garrison in Cairo. They established municipal governments that were responsible for taxation and public services and further expanded cotton cultivation. They also prevented the Egyptians from establishing a textile industry that would compete with Britain's own textile mills.

Economically, this meant that while the Egyptian economy grew and tax revenues increased, per capita income actually declined among Egyptians, most of whom were peasant farmers who owned little or no land. Politically, it led to the growth of Egyptian nationalism and to increasing demands that the British leave Egypt.

The Belgian Congo Perhaps the most remarkable story in the European scramble for Africa was the acquisition of the Belgian Congo. In the 1880s, the lands drained by the vast Congo River and its tributaries became the personal property of King Leopold II of Belgium (r. 1865–1909). As

Cruelty in the Belgian Congo. A naked slave, tied to the ground, is whipped by an overseer.

a young monarch, he had become determined that Belgium, despite its small territory, must acquire colonies. No doubt he was inspired by the great commercial wealth that the neighboring Netherlands had accumulated from its long history of colonial trade.

The Belgian government, however, had no interest at that time in acquiring colonies. So despite being a constitutional monarch, Leopold used his own wealth and political guile to realize his colonial ambitions. He did so under the guise of humanitarian concern for Africans. In 1876, he gathered explorers, geographers, and antislavery reformers in Brussels and formed the International African Association. He then recruited the English-born journalist and explorer Henry Morton Stanley (1841–1904) to undertake a major expedition into the Congo. Stanley had previously made a great reputation by crossing Africa from east to west. Between 1879 and 1884, Stanley explored the Congo and on Leopold's behalf made "treaties" with local rulers who had no idea what they were signing. Leopold then won diplomatic recognition for those treaties and for his own allegedly humanitarian efforts in the region first from the United States and then in 1885 from a conference of European powers held in Berlin. The larger, stronger European states were willing to let Leopold govern the Congo to keep one another out. Leopold, thus, personally became the ruler of an African domain that was over seventy times the size of Belgium itself. Only after the Belgian government gave him an interest-free loan that he needed to pay for his activities in the Congo did he agree to bequeath the Congo to Belgium upon his death.

Although Leopold continued to cultivate the image of a humanitarian ruler by holding antislavery conferences in Belgium and manipulating public relations, his goal in the Congo was economic exploitation of the most brutal kind. Leopold's administration used slave labor, intimidation, torture, mutilation, and mass murder to extract rubber and ivory from what became known as the Congo Free State. Eventually, beginning with the African-American reporter George Washington Williams (1849–1891) and culminating with an international outcry led by the English journalist E. D. Morel (1873–1924) and the diplomat Roger Casement (1864–1916), Leopold's crimes were exposed, and he formally turned the Congo over to Belgium in 1908.

Read the Document
Edward D. Morel, The Black Man's Burden
at **myhistorylab.com**

The cruelties in the Congo, which became the basis for Joseph Conrad's classic novel *Heart of Darkness* (1902) and were recorded for posterity in photographs, eyewitness accounts, newspaper articles, and by an official Belgian commission. The most responsible historical estimates suggest that the exploitation carried out by Leopold's administration halved the population of the Congo in about thirty years. Millions of Africans died of murder, exploitation, starvation, and disease.

Southern Africa South Africa's fertile pastures and farm land and its vast deposits of coal, iron ore, gold, diamonds, and copper made it appealing to a host of people. The Afrikaners or Boers, descendants of seventeenth- and eighteenth-century Dutch settlers, had long inhabited the area around the Cape of Good Hope, and the British started to settle there after Britain took over from the Dutch during the Napoleonic Wars.

As the British expanded in southern Africa, although they met with considerable native resistance from the Zulu, Shona, and Ndebele peoples, they eventually established colonies in what is now South Africa, Botswana, Zambia, and Zimbabwe. In 1910, after a series of bloody wars with the white Afrikaners, who consistently resented and opposed British rule, the British formed a pact with them that guaranteed the rule of the European minority over the majority black and nonwhite population. Africans and people of mixed race whom the British referred to as "colored" were forbidden to own land, denied the right to vote, and excluded from positions of power. To preserve their political power and economic privileges, the white elite of South Africa eventually enforced a policy of racial apartheid—"separateness"—that turned the country into a totally segregated land. The result was decades of oppression, racial tensions, and economic exploitation.

Asia In Asia, the emergence of Japan as a great power frightened the other powers that were interested in China (see Chapter 27). The Russians were building a railroad across Siberia to Vladivostok and feared any threat to Manchuria. Together with France and Germany, they applied diplomatic pressure that forced Japan out of the Liaotung Peninsula in northern China and its harbor, Port Arthur. All pressed feverishly for concessions in China. Fearing that China, its markets, and its investment opportunities would soon be closed to U.S. citizens, the United States proposed the Open Door Policy in 1899. This policy opposed foreign annexations in China and allowed entrepreneurs of all nations to trade there on equal terms. British support helped win acceptance of the policy by all the powers except Russia.

The United States had only recently emerged as a force in international affairs. After freeing itself of British rule and consolidating its independence during the Napoleonic Wars, the Americans had busied themselves with westward expansion on the North American continent until the end of the nineteenth century. The Monroe Doctrine of 1823 had, in effect, made the entire Western Hemisphere an American protectorate. Cuba's attempt to

Chronology

Expansion of European Power and the New Imperialism	
1869	Suez Canal completed
1875	Britain gains control of the Suez Canal
1879–1884	Leopold II establishes his personal rule in the Congo
1880s	Britain establishes protectorate over Egypt
1882	France controls Algeria and Tunisia
1884–1885	Germany establishes protectorate over Southwest Africa (Namibia), Togoland, the Cameroons, and East Africa (Tanzania)
1898	Spanish-American War: United States acquires Puerto Rico, Philippines, and Guam, annexes Hawaiian Islands, and establishes protectorate over Cuba
1899	United States proposes Open Door Policy in Far East
1899–1902	Boer War in South Africa
1908	Belgium takes over the Congo from Leopold II

Map 28–3. The American Domain, ca. 1900. The United States claimed islands in the South Pacific and intervened repeatedly in Latin America to secure its economic interests.

gain independence from Spain was the spark for the new U.S. involvement in international affairs. Sympathy for the Cuban cause, U.S. investments on the island, the desire for Cuban sugar, and concern over the island's strategic importance in the Caribbean all helped persuade the United States to fight Spain.

Victory in the Spanish-American War of 1898 brought the United States an informal protectorate over Cuba and the annexation of Puerto Rico and drove Spain completely out of the Western Hemisphere. The United States forced Spain to sell the Philippine Islands and Guam, and Germany bought the other Spanish islands in the Pacific. The United States and Germany also divided Samoa between them. France and Britain took the remaining Pacific islands. The United States had dominated Hawaii for some time and annexed it in 1898, five years after an American-backed coup had overthrown the native Hawaiian monarchy. This burst of activity after the Spanish-American War made the United States an imperial and Pacific power (see Map 28–3).

Thus, by the turn of the century, most of the world had come under the control of the industrialized West. The one remaining area of great vulnerability was the Ottoman Empire. Its fate, however, was closely tied up with European developments and must be treated in that context.

Emergence of the German Empire

Formation of the Triple Alliance (1873–1890)

Prussia's victories over Austria and France and its creation of a large, powerful German Empire in 1871 revolutionized European diplomacy. The sudden appearance of a vast new state that brought together most of the German people to form a nation of great and growing population, wealth, industrial capacity, and military power posed new problems.

By 1870 the balance of power that had been created at the Congress of Vienna 1815 had altered radically. Britain retained its position and so did Russia, even though it was somewhat weakened by the Crimean War. Austria, however, had lost ground, and its position was further threatened by the forces of nationalism within the Austro-Hungarian Empire. French power and prestige were badly damaged by the Franco-Prussian War and the German annexation of Alsace-Lorraine. The French were both afraid of their powerful new neighbor and resentful of their defeat and their loss of territory and of their traditional position as the dominant Western European power.

Bismarck's Leadership (1873–1890)

Bismarck (1815–1898) continued to guide German policy until 1890. After 1871 he insisted that Germany was a satisfied power and wanted no further territorial gains, and he meant it. He wanted to avoid a new war that might undo his achievement. He tried to assuage French resentment by cultivating friendly relations and by supporting French colonial aspirations. He also prepared for the worst. If France could not be conciliated, it must be isolated. Bismarck sought to prevent an alliance between France and any other European power—especially Austria or Russia—that would threaten Germany with a war on two fronts.

Bismarck and the Kaiser. Bismarck and the young Kaiser William II meet in 1888. The two disagreed over many issues, and in 1890 William dismissed the aged chancellor.

War in the Balkans Bismarck's first move was to establish the Three Emperors' League in 1873, which brought together the three great conservative empires of Germany, Austria, and Russia. The league collapsed when Russia went to war with Turkey in 1877 as a result of uprisings in the Ottoman Balkan provinces. The tottering Ottoman Empire was preserved chiefly by the competing aims of those powers who awaited its demise. Ottoman weakness encouraged Serbia and Montenegro to come to the aid of their fellow Slavs in Bosnia and Herzegovina. Soon the rebellion spread to Bulgaria.

Then Russia entered the fray and created a major international crisis. The Russians hoped to expand at Ottoman expense and to achieve their most cherished goal: control of Constantinople and the Dardanelles. Russian intervention also reflected the influence of the **Pan-Slavic movement**, which sought to bring all the Slavic peoples, even those under Austrian or Ottoman rule, under the protection of Holy Mother Russia.

Before long the Ottoman Empire was forced to ask for peace. The Treaty of San Stefano of March 1878 was a Russian triumph, but a short-lived one. The Slavic states in the Balkans were freed of Ottoman rule, and Russia itself obtained territory and a heavy monetary indemnity. But the terms of the Russian victory alarmed the other great powers. Austria feared that the new Slav states in the Balkans and the powerful increase in Russian influence there would threaten its own Balkan provinces. The British were alarmed by the damage the Russian settlement would do to the European balance of power and especially by possible Russian control of the Dardanelles. Disraeli (1804–1881) was determined to resist, and British public opinion supported him. A popular song gave the language a new word for superpatriotism:

> *We don't want to fight.*
> *But by jingo if we do,*
> *We've got the men,*
> *We've got the ships,*
> *We've got the money too!*
> *The Russians will not have Constantinople!*

Congress of Berlin Even before San Stefano, Disraeli had sent a fleet to Constantinople. After the magnitude of Russia's appetite was known, Britain and Austria forced Russia to agree to an international conference at which the other great powers would review the provisions of San Stefano. The resulting Congress of Berlin met in June and July of 1878 under the presidency of Bismarck.

The decisions of the Congress were a blow to Russian ambitions. Bulgaria lost two-thirds of its territory and was deprived of access to the Aegean Sea. Austria-Hungary was given Bosnia and Herzegovina to "occupy and administer," although those provinces remained formally under Ottoman rule. Britain received Cyprus, and France gained permission to occupy Tunisia. These privileges were compensation for the gains that Russia was permitted to keep. Germany asked for nothing, but the Russians were bitterly disappointed. The Three Emperors' League was dead.

The major trouble spot now was in the south Slavic states of Serbia and Montenegro. They deeply resented the

Austrian occupation of Bosnia and Herzegovina, as did many of the natives of those provinces.

The south Slavic question, no less than the estrangement between Russia and Germany, was a threat to the peace of Europe.

German Alliances with Russia and Austria Bismarck could ignore the Balkans, but not the breach in his eastern alliance system. With Russia alienated, he concluded a secret treaty with Austria in 1879. The resulting Dual Alliance provided that if either Germany or Austria was attacked by Russia, the ally would help the attacked party. And if either was attacked by someone else, each promised at least to maintain neutrality. The treaty was renewed every five years until 1918. As the central point in German policy, it was criticized at the time; some have judged it mistaken in retrospect. It appeared to tie the German fortunes to those of the troubled Austro-Hungarian Empire and thus to borrow trouble. It also isolated the Russians and pushed them to alliances in the West.

Bismarck was aware of these dangers but discounted them. He never allowed the alliance to drag Germany into Austria's Balkan quarrels. He made it clear to the Austrians that the alliance was purely defensive and that Germany would never attack Russia.

Bismarck expected the news of the Austro-German negotiations to frighten Russia into seeking closer relations with Germany, and he was right. Russian diplomats soon approached him, and by 1881 he had renewed the Three Emperors' League on a firmer basis. Although it did not resolve all conflicts, it helped preserve peace.

The Triple Alliance In 1882 Italy, ambitious for colonial expansion and annoyed by the French preemption of Tunisia, asked to join the Dual Alliance. At this point Bismarck's policy was a complete success. He was allied with three of the great powers and friendly with Great Britain, which held aloof from all alliances. France was isolated and no threat. Although the Three Emperors' League was allowed to lapse, the Triple Alliance (Germany, Austria, and Italy) was renewed for another five years in 1887. To restore

German relations with Russia, Bismarck negotiated the Reinsurance Treaty that same year, in which both powers promised to remain neutral if either was attacked. All seemed smooth, but a change in the German monarchy soon overturned Bismarck's system. (See Document, "Bismarck Explains His Foreign Policy." on page 875).

In 1888 William II (r. 1888–1918) came to the German throne. Like many Germans of his generation, he was filled with a sense of Germany's destiny as the leading power of Europe. To achieve a "place in the sun," he and his contemporaries wanted a navy and colonies like Britain's. These aims, of course, ran counter to Bismarck's limited continental policy. In 1890 William used a disagreement over domestic policy to dismiss Bismarck.

During Bismarck's time, Germany was a force for European peace and was increasingly understood to be so. This position would not have been possible without its great military power. But it also required the leadership of a statesman who could exercise restraint and make a realistic estimate of what his country needed and what was possible.

Forging the Triple Entente (1890–1907)

Franco-Russian Alliance Almost immediately after Bismarck's retirement, his system of alliances collapsed. His successor, General Leo von Caprivi (1831–1899), refused the Russian request to renew the Reinsurance Treaty, which he considered incompatible with the Austrian alliance. Political isolation and the need for foreign capital unexpectedly drove the Russians towards France. The French, who were even more isolated, were glad to pour capital into Russia if it would help produce an alliance and security against Germany. In 1894 the Franco-Russian alliance was signed.

Britain and Germany Britain now became the key to the international situation. Colonial rivalries pitted the British against the Russians in Central Asia and against the French in Africa. Traditionally, Britain had also opposed Russian control of Constantinople and the Dardanelles and French control of the Low Countries. There was no reason to think that Britain would soon become friendly with its traditional rivals or abandon its usual friendliness towards the Germans. Yet within a decade of William II's accession, Germany had become the enemy in the minds of the British. The problem lay in the foreign and naval policies of the German emperor and his ministers.

At first Germany tried to win the British over to the Triple Alliance, but when Britain clung to "splendid isolation," German policy changed. The idea was to demonstrate Germany's worthiness as an ally by withdrawing support and even making trouble for Britain.

Document   Bismarck Explains His Foreign Policy

Otto von Bismarck, chancellor of the new German Empire, guided German foreign policy in the years from its establishment of the empire in 1871 until his dismissal from office in 1890. In that period and for another quarter century, Europe was free of war among the great powers. The system of alliances Bismarck took the lead in creating is often given credit for preserving that peace. The following passage from his memoirs, written in his retirement, sets forth in retrospect his intentions in creating this system.

■ *What alliances made up Bismarck's systems? How were they meant to preserve the peace? What is Bismarck's stated purpose for avoiding a war in Europe? Were there other reason too?*

The Triple Alliance which I originally sought to conclude after the peace of Frankfurt, and about which I had already sounded Vienna and St. Petersburg, from Meaux, in September 1870, was an alliance of the three emperors with the further idea of bringing into it monarchical Italy. It was designed for the struggle which, as I feared, was before us, between the two European tendencies which Napoleon called Republican and Cossack, and which I, according to our present ideas, should designate on the one side as the system of order on a monarchical basis, and on the other as the social republic to the level of which the antimonarchical development is wont to sink, either slowly or by leaps and bounds, until the conditions thus created become intolerable, and the disappointed populace are ready for a violent return to monarchical institutions in a Caesarean form, I consider that the task of escaping from this *circulus vitiosus*, or, if possible, of sparing the present generation and their children an entrance into it, ought to be more closely incumbent on the strong existing monarchies, those monarchies which still have a vigorous life, than any rivalry over the fragments of nations which people the Balkan peninsula. If the monarchical governments have no understanding of the necessity for holding together in the interests of political and social order, but make themselves subservient to the chauvinistic impulses of their subjects, I fear that the international revolutionary and social struggles which will have to be fought out will be all the more dangerous, and take such a form that the victory on the part of monarchical order will be more difficult. Since 1871 I have sought for the most certain assurance against those struggles in the alliance of the three emperors, and also in the effort to impart to the monarchical principle in Italy a firm support in that alliance.

Source: Otto von Bismarck, *Reflections and Reminiscences*, ed. by Theodore S. Hamerow (New York: Harper Torchbooks, 1968), pp. 236–237.

The Germans began to exert pressure against Britain in Africa by barring British attempts to build a railroad from Capetown to Cairo. They also openly sympathized with the Boers of South Africa in their resistance to British expansion. In 1896 William insulted the British by sending a congratulatory telegram to Paul Kruger (1825–1904), president of the Transvaal, for repulsing a British raid "without having to appeal to friendly powers for assistance."

In 1898 William's dream of a German navy began to achieve reality with the passage of a naval law providing for nineteen battleships. In 1900 a second law doubled that figure. The architect of the new navy was Admiral Alfred von Tirpitz (1849–1930), who openly proclaimed that Germany's naval policy was aimed at Britain. His "risk" theory argued that Germany could build a fleet strong enough, not to defeat the British, but to inflict enough damage to make the British navy inferior to those of other powers like France or the United States. The threat posed by the German navy did more to antagonize British opinion than anything else. As the German navy grew and German policies seemed to become more threatening, the British were alarmed enough to abandon their traditional attitudes and policies (see Figure 28–1 on page 876).

Entente Cordiale The first breach in Britain's isolation came in 1902 when an alliance was concluded with Japan to help defend British interests in the Far East against Russia. Next, Britain concluded a series of agreements

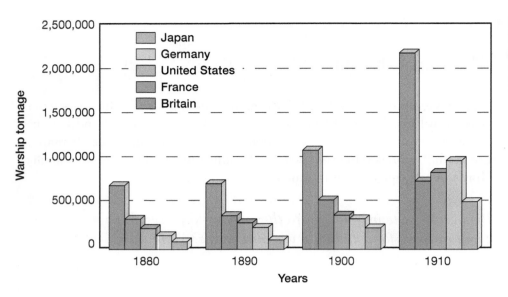

Figure 28–1 Warship Tonnage of the World's Navies, 1880–1910. Naval strength was the primary index of power before World War I.
Source: Paul Kennedy, Rise and Fall of the Great Powers (New York: Random House, 1987), p. 203.

with the French in 1904, collectively called the Entente Cordiale. It was not a formal treaty and had no military provisions, but it settled all outstanding colonial differences between the two nations. The Entente Cordiale was a big step towards aligning the British with Germany's great potential enemy.

First Moroccan Crisis At this point Germany decided to test the new understanding between Britain and France and to press for colonial gains. In March 1905 William II landed at Tangier, challenged the French predominance there in a speech in favor of Moroccan independence, and by implication asserted Germany's right to participate in Morocco's destiny. Germany's chancellor, Prince Bernhard von Bülow (1849–1929), intended to show France how weak it was and how little it could expect from Britain; he also hoped to gain significant colonial concessions.

The Germans might well have achieved their aims, but they demanded an international conference to exhibit their power more dramatically. The conference met in 1906 at Algeciras in Spain. Austria sided with its German ally, but Spain, Italy, and the United States voted with Britain and France. The Germans had overplayed their hand, and the French were confirmed in their position in Morocco. Moreover, German bullying had, driven Britain and France closer together. In the face of a possible German attack on France, Sir Edward Grey (1862–1933), the British foreign secretary, without making a firm commitment, authorized conversations between the British and French general staffs. As the years passed, their agreements became morally binding. By 1914 French and British military and naval plans were so mutually dependent that the two countries were effectively, if not formally, allies.

British Agreement with Russia Britain's new relationship with France was surprising. But hardly anyone believed that the British whale and the Russian bear would ever be allies. The Russo-Japanese War of 1904–1905 made such a development seem even less likely because Britain was allied with Russia's enemy. But Britain had behaved with restraint, and the Russians were chastened by their humiliating defeat. The defeat had also led to the Russian Revolution of 1905, which left Russia weak and reduced British apprehensions. The British were also concerned that Russia might again drift into the German orbit.

With French support, the British made overtures to the Russians and in 1907 concluded an agreement with them that settled Russo-British quarrels in Central Asia and Persia and opened the door for wider cooperation. The Triple Entente, an informal but powerful association of Britain, France, and Russia, was now ranged against the Triple Alliance. Because Italy was unreliable, Germany and Austria-Hungary stood surrounded by two great land powers and Great Britain.

William II and his ministers had turned Bismarck's nightmare of the prospect of a two-front war with France and Russia into a reality and had made it more horrible by adding Britain to the hostile coalition. Bismarck's alliance system had been intended to maintain peace, but the new one increased the risk of war and made the Balkans, where Austrian and Russian ambitions clashed, a likely spot for it. Bismarck's diplomacy had left France isolated and impotent; the new arrangement found France associated with the two greatest powers in Europe, apart from Germany. The Germans could rely only on Austria, where troubles made it more likely to need aid than to provide it.

World War I

The Road to War (1908–1914)

The situation in the Balkans was exceedingly complicated. The weak Ottoman Empire controlled the central strip running west from Constantinople to the Adriatic. North and south of it were the independent states of Romania, Montenegro, Serbia, and Greece; Bulgaria, though technically still part of the empire, was legally autonomous and practically independent. The Austro-Hungarian Empire included Croatia and Slovenia and since 1878 had "occupied and administered" Bosnia and Herzegovina.

Except for the Greeks and the Romanians, most of the inhabitants of the Balkans spoke variants of the same Slavic language and felt a cultural and historical kinship with one another and with Russia. For centuries they had been ruled by Austrians, Hungarians, or Turks, and the growing nationalism that characterized late-nineteenth-century Europe made many of them eager for liberty or at least autonomy. The more radical among them longed for a union of the south Slavic, or Yugoslav, peoples in a single nation. They looked to independent Serbia as the center of the new nation and hoped to detach all the Slavic provinces (especially Bosnia, which bordered on Serbia) from Austria. Serbia was to unite the Slavs at the expense of Austria, as Piedmont had united the Italians, and Prussia the Germans.

In 1908 a group of modernizing reformers called the Young Turks overthrew the Ottoman government. This threatened to revive the empire and to interfere with the plans of the European jackals to pounce on the Ottoman corpse. These events precipitated the first of a series of Balkan crises that would eventually lead to world war.

The Bosnian Crisis In 1908 the Austrian and Russian governments decided to act before Turkey became strong enough to resist. They agreed to call an international conference in which each of them would support the other's demands. Russia would agree to the Austrian annexation of Bosnia and Herzegovina, and Austria would support Russia's request to open the Dardanelles to Russian warships.

Austria, however, declared the annexation unilaterally before any conference was called. The British, ever concerned about their own position in the Mediterranean, rejected the Russian demand. The Russians, feeling betrayed by the British, were humiliated and furious. Their "little brothers," the Serbs, were enraged by the loss of Bosnia, which they had hoped one day to include in an independent south Slavic nation led by themselves. The Russians were too weak to do anything but accept the new situation. The Germans had not been warned in advance of Austria's plans and were unhappy

See the **Map**
Diplomatic Crises, 1905–1914
at **myhistorylab.com**

because the action threatened their relations with Russia. But Germany felt so dependent on the Dual Alliance that it assured Austria of its support. Austria had been given a free hand, and to an extent German policy was being made in Vienna. It was a dangerous precedent. At the same time, the failure of Britain and France to support Russia strained the Triple Entente and made it harder for them to oppose Russian interests again if they wanted to retain Russian friendship.

Second Moroccan Crisis The second Moroccan crisis, in 1911, emphasized the French and British need for mutual support. When France sent in an army to put down a rebellion, Germany took the opportunity to "protect German interests" in Morocco as a means of extorting colonial concessions in the French Congo. To add force to their demands, the Germans sent the gunboat *Panther* to the port of Agadir, allegedly to protect German citizens there. Once again, as in 1905, the Germans went too far. The *Panther*'s visit to Agadir alarmed Britain. For some time Anglo-German relations had been deteriorating for some time, chiefly because of the naval race, but negotiations failed to persuade William II and Tirpitz to slow down naval construction.

In this atmosphere, the British heard of the *Panther*'s arrival in Morocco. They mistakenly believed that the Germans meant to turn Agadir into a naval base on the Atlantic. The crisis passed when France yielded some insignificant bits of the Congo and Germany withdrew from Morocco. The main result was to increase British fear of, and hostility to, Germany and to draw Britain closer to France. Specific plans were now formulated for a British expeditionary force to help defend France against German attack. The British and French navies agreed to cooperate. If France were attacked by Germany, Britain had to help defend the French, for its own security was inextricably tied up with that of France.

The Balkan Wars After the second Moroccan crisis, Italy feared that the recognition of the French protectorate in Morocco would encourage France to move into Libya. Consequently, in 1911 Italy attacked the Ottoman Empire to anticipate the French, defeated the faltering Turks, and obtained Libya and the Dodecanese Islands in the Aegean. The Italian victory encouraged the Balkan states to try their luck. In 1912 Bulgaria, Greece, Montenegro, and Serbia attacked the Ottoman Empire and won easily (see Map 28–4 on page 878). After this First Balkan War the victors fell out among themselves. The Serbs and the Bulgarians quarreled about the division of Macedonia, and in 1913 a Second Balkan War erupted. This time the Ottoman Empire and Romania joined Greece and Serbia against Bulgaria, which lost much of what it had gained since 1878.

Map 28–4. **The Balkans, 1912–1913.** Two maps show the Balkans before (a) and after (b) the two Balkan Wars; note the Ottoman retreat. In (c) we see the geographical relationship of the Central Powers and their Bulgarian and Turkish allies.

The alarmed Austrians were determined to limit Serbian gains and especially to prevent the Serbs from obtaining a port on the Adriatic. An international conference sponsored by Britain in early 1913 resolved the matter in Austria's favor and called for an independent kingdom of Albania. But Austria felt humiliated by the public airing of Serbian demands. At first the Serbs defied the powers and stayed in Albania. Under Austrian pressure they withdrew, but in September 1913, after the Second Balkan War, the Serbs reoccupied sections of Albania. In mid-October Austria unilaterally issued an ultimatum to Serbia, which again withdrew from Albania. During this crisis many Austrians had wanted an all-out attack on Serbia to remove its threat once and for all. In Russia, Pan-Slavic sentiment pressed Czar Nicholas II (r. 1894–1917) to take a firm stand, but Russia nonetheless once again let Austria have its way.

The lessons learned from this crisis profoundly influenced behavior in the final crisis of 1914. The Russians had, as in 1908, been embarrassed by their passivity, and their allies were now more reluctant to restrain them. The Austrians were embarrassed by the results of accepting an international conference and were determined not to do it again. They had seen that a threat of direct force might obtain better results; they and their German allies did not miss the lesson.

Sarajevo and the Outbreak of War (June–August 1914)

The Assassination On June 28, 1914, a young Bosnian nationalist shot and killed the Austrian Archduke Francis Ferdinand (1863–1914), heir to the throne, and his wife as

they drove through the Bosnian capital of Sarajevo. The assassin was a member of a conspiracy hatched by a political terrorist society called Union or Death, better known as the Black Hand. The chief of intelligence of the Serbian army's general staff had helped plan the crime. Even though his

role was not actually known at the time, it was generally believed that Serbian officials were involved. The glee of the Serbian press supported that belief.

●●●━[Read the Document
Borijove Jevtic: The Murder of Archduke Franz Ferdinand at Sarajevo (28 June 1914) at **myhistorylab.com**

Germany and Austria's Response The assassination was condemned throughout Europe. To those Austrians who had long favored an attack on Serbia as a solution to the empire's Slavic problem, the opportunity seemed irresistible. But it was never easy for the Austria-Hungary to make a decision. Conrad von Hotzendorf (1852–1925), chief of the Austrian general staff, urged an attack as he had often done before. Count Stefan Tisza (1861–1918), speaking for Hungary, resisted. Count Leopold Berchtold (1863–1942), the Austro-Hungarian foreign minister, knew that German support would be required if Russia should decide to protect Serbia. He also knew that nothing could be done without Tisza's approval and that only German support could persuade the

((●━[Hear the Audio
World War 1 at **myhistorylab.com**

Hungarians to accept a war. The question of peace or war, therefore, had to be answered in Berlin.

William II and Chancellor Theobald von Bethmann-Hollweg (1856–1921), who succeeded Bernhard von Bùlow in 1909, readily promised German support for an attack on Serbia. It has often been said that they gave the Austrians a

Assassination of the Archduke. Above: The Austrian Archduke Franz Ferdinand and his wife in Sarajevo on June 28, 1914. Later in the day the royal couple were assassinated by young revolutionaries trained and supplied in Serbia, igniting the crisis that led to World War I. Below: Moments after the assassination the Austrian police captured one of the assassins.

"blank check," but their message was firmer than that. They urged the Austrians to move swiftly, while the other powers were still angry at Serbia. They also indicated that a failure to act would be taken as evidence of Austria-Hungary's weakness and uselessness as an ally. Therefore, the Austrians never wavered in their determination to attack Serbia. They hoped, with Germany's protection, to fight a limited war that would not bring on a general European conflict. However, they were prepared to risk even a widespread war. The Germans also knew that they risked a general war, but they hoped to "localize" the fight between Austria and Serbia.

These calculations proved to be incorrect. Bethmann-Hollweg hoped that the Austrians would strike swiftly and present the powers with a *fait accompli* while the outrage of

the assassination was still fresh. He also hoped that German support would deter Russian involvement. Failing that, he was prepared for a continental war that would bring rapid victory over France and allow a full-scale attack on the Russians, who were always slow to bring their strength into action. This policy depended on British neutrality, and the German chancellor convinced himself that the British could be persuaded to stand aloof.

However, the Austrians were slow to act. They did not even deliver their deliberately unacceptable ultimatum to Serbia until July 24, when the general hostility toward Serbia had begun to subside. Serbia further embarrassed the Austrians by returning so soft and conciliatory an answer that even the mercurial German emperor thought it

Chronology

Coming of World War I

1871	End of the Franco-Prussian War; creation of the German Empire; German annexation of Alsace-Lorraine
1873	Three Emperors' League (Germany, Russia, and Austria-Hungary)
1875	Russo-Turkish War
1878	Congress of Berlin
1879	Dual Alliance between Germany and Austria
1881	Three Emperors' League is renewed
1882	Italy joins Germany and Austria in Triple Alliance
1888	William II becomes German emperor
1890	Bismarck dismissed
1894	Franco-Russian alliance
1898	Germany begins to build battleship navy
1902	British alliance with Japan
1904	Entente Cordiale between Britain and France
1904–1905	Russo-Japanese War
1905	First Moroccan crisis
1907	British agreement with Russia
1908–1909	Bosnian crisis
1911	Second Moroccan crisis; Italy attacks Turkey
1912–1913	First and Second Balkan Wars
1914	Outbreak of World War I

removed all reason for war. But the Austrians were determined not to turn back. On July 28 they declared war on Serbia, even though they could not field an army until mid-August.

The Triple Entente's Response The Russians, previously so often forced to back off, responded angrily to the Austrian demands on Serbia. The most conservative elements of the Russian government feared that war would bring on revolution as it had in 1905. But nationalists, Pan-Slavs, and most of the politically conscious classes in general demanded action. The government ordered partial **mobilization**, against Austria only. This policy was militarily impossible, but its purpose was diplomatic: to pressure Austria to hold back its attack on Serbia.

Mobilization of any kind, however, was dangerous because it was generally understood to be equivalent to an act of war. It was especially alarming to General Helmuth von Moltke (1848–1916), head of the German general staff. The possibility that the Russians might start mobilization before the Germans could move would upset the delicate timing of Germany's only battle plan—the **Schlieffen Plan**, which required an attack on France first—and would endanger Germany. From this point on, Moltke pressed for German mobilization and war. The pressure of military necessity mounted until it became irresistible (see Map 28–5).

Map 28–5. The Schlieffen Plan of 1905. Germany's grand strategy for quickly winning the war against France in 1914 is shown by the wheeling arrows on the map. The crushing blows at France were, in the original plan, to be followed by the release of troops for use against Russia on Germany's Eastern Front. But the plan was not adequately implemented, and the war on the Western Front became a long contest instead.

The western European powers were not eager for war. France's president and prime minister were on their way back from a visit to Russia when the crisis flared up again on July 24. The Austrians had, in fact, timed their ultimatum precisely, so that these two men would be at sea at the crucial moment. Had they been in Paris they might have attempted to restrain the Russians. But the French ambassador to Russia gave the Russians the same assurances that Germany had given its ally. The British worked hard to avoid trouble by traditional means: a conference of the powers. Austria, still smarting from its humiliation after the London Conference of 1913, would not hear of it. The Germans privately supported the Austrians but were publicly conciliatory in the hope of keeping the British neutral.

Soon, however, Bethmann-Hollweg realized what he should have known from the first: If Germany attacked France, Britain must fight. Until July 30 his public appeals to Austria for restraint were a sham. Thereafter, he sincerely tried to persuade the Austrians to negotiate and to avoid a general war, but it was too late. While Bethmann-Hollweg was urging restraint on the Austrians, Moltke was pressing them to act. The Austrians wondered who was in charge in Berlin, but they could not retreat without losing their own self-respect and that of the Germans.

On July 30 Austria ordered mobilization against Russia. Bethmann-Hollweg resisted the enormous pressure to mobilize, not because he had any further hope of avoiding war but because he wanted Russia to mobilize against Germany first and appear to be the aggressor. Only thus could he win the support of the German nation for war, especially the pacifistic Social Democrats. His luck was good this time. The news of Russian general mobilization came only minutes before Germany would have mobilized in any case. The Schlieffen Plan went into effect. The Germans invaded Luxembourg on August 1 and Belgium on August 3. The invasion of Belgium violated the treaty of 1839, in which the British had guaranteed Belgian neutrality. This factor undermined the considerable sentiment in Britain for neutrality and united the nation against Germany. Germany then invaded France, and on August 4 Britain declared war on Germany.

The Great War had begun. As Sir Edward Grey put it, the lights were going out all over Europe. They would come on again, but Europe would never be the same.

Strategies and Stalemate (1914–1917)

The outbreak of war produced jubilation throughout Europe. No general war had been fought since Napoleon, and the horrors of modern warfare were not yet understood. The dominant memory was of Bismarck's swift and decisive campaigns, in which costs and casualties were light and the rewards great.

Trench Warfare. French infantry soldiers approach German soldiers during a battle near Champagne, France in 1917. This scene of trench warfare characterizes the twentieth century's first great international conflict.

Both sides expected to take the offensive, force a battle on favorable ground, and win a quick victory. The Triple Entente powers—or the Allies, as they came to be called—had superior numbers and financial resources as well as command of the sea. Germany and Austria, the Central Powers, had the advantages of internal lines of communication and of having launched their attack first.

After 1905 Germany's only war plan was the one developed by Count Alfred von Schlieffen (1833–1913), chief of the German general staff from 1891 to 1906 (see Map 28–5 on page 880). It aimed to outflank the French defenses by sweeping through Belgium to the Channel, then wheeling to the south and east to envelop the French and crush them against the German fortresses in Lorraine. In the east the Germans planned to stand on the defensive against Russia until France had been beaten, a task they thought would take only six weeks.

The apparent risk, besides the violation of Belgian neutrality and the consequent alienation of Britain, lay in weakening the German defenses against a direct attack across the frontier. Yet Schlieffen is said to have uttered the dying words, "It must come to a fight. Only make the right wing strong." The execution of his plan, however, was left to Helmuth von Moltke, the nephew of Bismarck's most effective general. Moltke was a gloomy and nervous man who lacked the talent of his illustrious uncle and the theoretical daring of Schlieffen. He added divisions to the left wing and even weakened the Russian front for the same purpose. The consequence of this hesitant strategy was the failure of the Schlieffen Plan by a narrow margin.

The War in the West The French had also put faith in the offensive, but with less reason than the Germans. They badly underestimated the numbers and the effectiveness of the German reserves and set too much store on the importance of the courage and spirit of their troops, which proved insufficient against modern weapons, especially the machine gun. The French offensive on Germany's western frontier failed totally. In a sense this defeat was better than a partial success because it released troops for use against the main German army. As a result, the French and the British were able to stop the Germans at the battle of the Marne in September 1914.

Thereafter, the war in the west became one of position instead of movement. Both sides dug in behind a wall of trenches protected by barbed wire that stretched from the North Sea to Switzerland. Strategically placed machine-gun nests made assaults difficult and dangerous. Nonetheless, both sides, attempted massive attacks initiated by artillery bombardments of unprecedented and horrible force and duration. Still, the defense was always able to prevent a breakthrough.

See the Map
The Actual German Advance, 1914
at **myhistorylab.com**

A German U-Boat. By this date German submarine warfare had been severely curtailed.

A Closer Look

The Development of the Armored Tank

Warfare frequently proves a source of technological innovation. Such was true of World War I, which witnessed the development of numerous new weapons. Among the most important of these was the tank — an armored vehicle using a caterpillar track rather than wheels for transport. The caterpillar track had been invented in Great Britain but was then purchased by the American Holt tractor company, which devised a caterpillar tractor in the first decade of the century to cultivate areas with either wet or loose earth where a wheeled vehicle would sink into the ground. During World War I the British modified the caterpillar tractor by introducing a heavily armored closed compartment for a crew armed with machine guns. These early slow-moving tanks could drive over trenches, small hills, and rough terrain and through mud and thus bring mobility to the combat zones where trench warfare had made any kind of effective assault on troops difficult. The tank was used primarily by France, and the United States in relatively small numbers in World War I, but rapidly moving tanks became the major weapons of later twentieth-century warfare.

In the first illustration notice how the design of the driver's area of the tractor was intended to allow the driver a wide area of vision and also was fully exposed.

Notice also how the caterpillar track on the tractor would allow it to move over difficult or wet ground without sinking.

In this illustration of a British World War I tank captured by the Germans, notice how the armament of the tank was intended to protect the crew from small arms fire while the opening on the top permitted the mounting of a machine gun.

Observe how the interior of the tank allowed for a small crew working in an extremely hot environment with little chance of escape if the tank was hit by artillery fire or became bogged down on difficult ground.

Questions

1. What technological developments prior to World War I made tank warfare possible? What military developments made it desirable?

2. What advantages does tank warfare offer?

3. How do tanks interact with other military units to achieve success?

4. What devices and tactics have modern armies developed to combat the tank?

myhistorylab To examine this image in an interactive fashion, please go to **www.myhistorylab.com**

Map 28–6. World War I in Europe. Despite the importance of military action in the Far East, in the Middle East, and at sea, the main theaters of activity in World War I were in the European areas shown here.

The War in the East In the east the war began auspiciously for the Allies. The Russians advanced into Austrian territory and inflicted heavy casualties, but Russian incompetence and German energy soon reversed the situation (see Map 28–6). A junior German officer, Erich Ludendorff (1865–1937), under the command of the elderly General Paul von Hindenburg (1847–1934), destroyed or captured an entire Russian army at the battle of Tannenberg; he also defeated the Russians at the Masurian Lakes. In 1915 the Central Powers pressed their advantage in the east and drove into the Baltic States and western Russia, inflicting over 2 million casualties in a single year. Russian confidence was badly shaken, but the Russian army stayed in the field.

As the battle lines hardened, both sides sought new allies. Turkey (because of its hostility to Russia) and Bulgaria (the enemy of Serbia) joined the Central Powers. Italy seemed an especially valuable prize, and both sides

bid for its support with promises of a division of the spoils of victory. Because what the Italians wanted most was held by Austria, the Allies could make the more attractive promises. The Italians sought the acquisition of *Italia Irredenta* ("unredeemed Italy"); they wanted to annex lands inhabited by Italians but still under Austrian rule, such as Trieste and the Trentino, as well as such multilingual regions as Istria and South Tirol and to such disparate places as Fiume, Corsica and Malta, among others. In a secret treaty of 1915 the Allies agreed to deliver to Italy most of **Italia Irredenta** (i.e., the Trentino, the South Tyrol, Trieste, and some of the Dalmatian Islands) after victory. By the spring of 1915 Italy was engaging Austrian armies. Although the Italian campaign distracted the Central Powers, it never produced significant results. Romania joined the Allies in 1916 but was quickly defeated and driven from the war.

In the Far East, Japan honored its alliance with Britain and entered the war. The Japanese quickly overran the German colonies in China and the Pacific and used the opportunity to improve their own position against China.

In 1915 the Allies undertook to break the deadlock in the fighting by going around it. The idea came chiefly from Winston Churchill (1874–1965), First Lord of the British Admiralty. He proposed an attack at Gallipoli on the Dardanelles and the swift capture of Constantinople. This policy would knock Turkey from the war, bring help to the Balkan front, and ease communication with Russia. Success depended on timing, speed, and daring leadership, but all of these qualities were lacking. The execution of the attack was inept and overly cautious. Troops were landed and, as resistance continued, the Allied commitment increased. Before the campaign was abandoned the Allies lost almost 150,000 men and diverted three times that number from more useful fighting.

Return to the West   Both sides turned back to the west in 1916 (see Map 28–5 on page 880). General Erich von Falkenhayn (1861–1922), who had succeeded Moltke in September 1914, sought success by an attack on the French stronghold of Verdun. The commander of Verdun, Henri Pétain (1856–1951), became a hero. "They shall not pass" became a slogan of national defiance. The Allies tried to end the impasse by launching a major offensive along the River Somme in July. Once again, the superiority of the defense was demonstrated. The only result was enormous casualties on both sides. On all fronts the losses were great and the results meager. The war on land dragged on with no end in sight.

Read the Document
British Soldiers on the Battle of the Somme at **myhistorylab.com**

The War at Sea   As the war continued, control of the sea became more important. The British ignored the distinction between war supplies (which were contraband according to international law) and food or other peaceful cargo, which was not subject to seizure. They imposed a strict blockade meant to starve out the enemy, regardless of international law. The Germans responded with submarine warfare meant to destroy British shipping and to starve the British. They declared the waters around the British Isles a war zone, where even neutral ships would not be safe. Both policies were unwelcome to neutrals, especially to the United States, which conducted extensive trade in the Atlantic, but the sinking of neutral ships by German submarines was both more dramatic and more offensive than Britain's blockade.

In 1915 the British liner *Lusitania* was torpedoed by a German submarine. Among the 1,200 drowned were 118 Americans. President Woodrow Wilson (1856–1924)

warned Germany that a repetition would not be accepted, and the Germans desisted rather than further anger the United States. This development gave the Allies a considerable advantage. The German fleet that had cost so much money and had caused so much trouble played no significant part in the war. The only battle it fought was at Jutland in the spring of 1916. The battle resulted in a standoff and confirmed British domination of the surface of the sea.

America Enters the War   In December 1916 President Wilson attempted to bring about a negotiated peace, but neither side was willing to give up its hopes for total victory. The war seemed likely to continue until one or both sides reached exhaustion. Two events early in 1917 changed the situation radically. On February 1 the Germans announced the resumption of unrestricted submarine warfare, which led the United States to break off diplomatic relations. On April 6 the United States declared war on Germany.

One of the deterrents to an earlier American intervention had been the presence of autocratic tsarist Russia among the Allies. Wilson could conceive of the war only as an idealistic crusade "to make the world safe for democracy." That problem was resolved in March of 1917 by a revolution in Russia that overthrew the tsarist government.

The Russian Revolution

The March Revolution in Russia was neither planned nor led by any political faction. It was the result of the collapse of the monarchy's ability to govern. Military and domestic failures produced massive casualties, widespread hunger, strikes by workers, and disorganization in the army. The peasant unrest that had plagued the countryside before 1914 did not subside during the conflict. All political factions were discontented.

See the Map
Russian Armies In the Eastern Front at **myhistorylab.com**

In early March 1917 strikes and worker demonstrations erupted in Petrograd, as Saint Petersburg had been renamed. The ill-disciplined troops in the city refused to fire on the demonstrators, and the tsar abdicated on March 15. The government of Russia fell into the hands of members of the Duma, who formed a provisional government composed chiefly of Constitutional Democrats with Western sympathies. The various Socialists, including both Social Revolutionaries and Social Democrats of the Menshevik wing, also began to organize the workers into councils called **soviets**. Initially, they allowed the provisional government to function without actually supporting it. But they became estranged as the Constitutional Democratic Party failed to control the army or to purge "reactionaries" from the government.

In this climate the provisional government decided to remain loyal to the existing Russian alliances and to continue the war against Germany. Its fate was sealed when a new offensive in the summer of 1917 collapsed. Disillusionment with the war, shortages of food and other necessities at home, and the growing demand by the peasants for land reform undermined the government, even after its leadership had been taken over by the moderate Socialist Alexander Kerensky (1881–1970).

Ever since April the Bolsheviks had been working against the provisional government. The Germans, in their most successful attempt at subversion, had rushed the brilliant Bolshevik leader V. I. Lenin (1870–1924) in a sealed train from his exile in Switzerland across Germany to Petrograd in the hope that he would cause trouble for the revolutionary government. The Bolsheviks demanded that all political power go to the soviets, which they controlled. The failure of the summer offensive encouraged them to attempt a coup, but it failed. Lenin fled to Finland, and his chief collaborator, Leon Trotsky (1877–1940), was imprisoned.

An abortive right-wing countercoup gave the Bolsheviks another chance. Trotsky, released from prison, led the powerful Petrograd Soviet. Lenin returned in October, insisted to his doubting colleagues that the time was ripe to take power, and by the extraordinary force of his personality persuaded them to act. Trotsky organized the coup that took place on November 6 and that concluded with an armed assault on the provisional government. The Bolsheviks, almost as much to their own astonishment as to that of the rest of the world, had come to rule Russia.

●●◀─[Read the Document
Bolshevik Seizure of Power, 1917
at **myhistorylab.com**

The victors moved to fulfill their promises and to assure their own security. The provisional government had decreed an election for late November to select a Constituent Assembly. The Social Revolutionaries won a large majority over the Bolsheviks. When the assembly gathered in January, it met for only a day before the Red Army, controlled by the Bolsheviks, dispersed it. All other political parties also ceased to function in any meaningful fashion. In November and January the Bolshevik government promulgated decrees that nationalized the land and turned it over to its peasant proprietors. Factory workers were put in charge of their plants. Banks were taken from their owners and seized for the state, and the debt of the tsarist government was repudiated. Property of the church reverted to the state.

The Bolshevik government also took Russia out of the war, which they believed benefited only capitalism. They signed an armistice with Germany in December 1917. On March 3, 1918, they accepted the Treaty of Brest-Litovsk, by which Russia yielded Finland, Poland, the Baltic states, and the Ukraine. Georgian territory in the Transcaucasus region was ceded to Turkey. The Bolsheviks also agreed to pay a heavy war indemnity. These terms were a terribly high price to pay for peace, but Lenin had no choice.

((●◀─[Hear the Audio
World War 3
at **myhistorylab.com** The Bolsheviks needed time to impose their rule on a devastated and chaotic Russia.

Until 1921 the New Bolshevik government confronted massive domestic resistance. A civil war erupted between the "Red" Russians supporting the revolution and the **"White" Russians**, who opposed the Bolshevik triumph. In the summer of 1918 the tsar and his family were murdered.

Overview

Casualties of the Major Belligerents in World War I

Country	Killed	Wounded
Austria-Hungary	1.1 million	3.62 million
Belgium	38,000	44,000
Britain	723,000	1.16 million
Bulgaria	88,000	152,000
France	1.4 million	2 million
Germany	2 million	4.2 million
Italy	578,000	947,000
Ottoman Empire	804,000	400,000
Romania	250,000	120,000
Russia	1.8 million	1.45 million
Serbia	278,000	138,000
United States	114,000	205,000
Total:	**9,173,000**	**14,436,000**

Loyal army officers continued to fight the revolution and received aid from the Allies. However, led by Trotsky, the Red Army eventually overcame the domestic opposition. By 1921 Lenin and his supporters were in firm control.

End of World War I

Military Resolution

The Treaty of Brest-Litovsk brought Germany to the peak of its success. The Germans controlled eastern Europe and its resources, especially food. By 1918 they were free to concentrate their forces on the Western Front. This turn of events would probably have been decisive had it not been balanced by American intervention. Still, American troops would not arrive in significant numbers for about a year, and both sides tried to win the war in 1917. An Allied attempt to break through in the west failed disastrously, bringing heavy losses to the British and the French and causing a mutiny in the French army. The Austrians, supported by the Germans, defeated the Italians at Caporetto and threatened to overrun Italy, before they were checked with the aid of Allied troops. The deadlock continued, but time was running out for the Central Powers.

In 1918 the Germans, persuaded chiefly by Ludendorff—second in command to Hindenburg, but the real leader of the army—decided to gamble everything on one last offensive. The German army pushed forward and even reached the Marne again but got no farther. They had no more reserves, and the entire nation was exhausted. The Allies, on the other hand, were bolstered by the arrival of American troops in ever-increasing numbers. They launched a counteroffensive that proved irresistible. As the Austrian fronts in the Balkans and Italy collapsed, the German high command knew that the end was imminent.

Ludendorff was determined that peace should be made before the German army could be thoroughly defeated in the field and that the responsibility should fall on civilians. For some time he had been the effective ruler of Germany under the aegis of the emperor. He now allowed a new government to be established on democratic principles and to seek peace immediately. The new government, under Prince Max of Baden (1867–1928), asked for peace on the basis of the **Fourteen Points** that President Wilson had declared as the American war aims. These were idealistic principles, including self-determination for nationalities, open diplomacy, freedom of the seas, disarmament, and establishment of a League of Nations to keep the peace. Wilson insisted that he would deal only with a democratic German government

Read the Document

Woodrow Wilson, The Fourteen Points (1918) at **myhistorylab.com**

because he wanted to be sure he was dealing with the German people and not merely their rulers.

The disintegration of the German army forced William II to abdicate on November 9, 1918. The majority branch of the Social Democratic Party proclaimed a republic to prevent the establishment of a soviet government under the control of their radical Leninist wing, which had earlier broken away as the Independent Socialist Party. Two days later this Republican-, Socialist-led government signed the armistice that ended the war by accepting German defeat. The German people were, in general, unaware that their army had been defeated in the field and was crumbling. No foreign soldier stood on German soil. Many Germans expected a negotiated and mild settlement. The real peace embittered the German people, many of whom came to believe that Germany had not been defeated but had been tricked by the enemy and betrayed—even stabbed in the back—by Republicans and Socialists at home.

The victors rejoiced, but they also had much to mourn. The casualties on all sides came to over 9 million dead and over 14 million wounded. The economic and financial

John Singer Sargent, *Gassed*, 1918–1919. Many new weapons were used extensively for the first time in the Great War of 1914–1918, including machine guns, barbed wire, tanks, airplanes, and several kinds of poison gas. The Germans were the first to employ gas as a weapon, firing a nonlethal kind of tear gas at the Russians on the Eastern Front in January 1915. By April, they had learned how to use the poison gas chlorine against the Allies on the Western Front. *Gassed*, by the American painter John Singer Sargent, can be compared to ancient Greek friezes depicting mythical battles. There is, however, an important difference in treatment: While Greek sculptures always portray an element of heroism along with death and suffering, Sargent's painting reveals only the horror of battle. *John Singer Sargent (1856-1925), "Gassed, an Oil Study". 1918-19 Oil on Canvas. Private Collection. Photo © Christies Images. The Bridgeman Art Library International*

resources of the European states were badly strained. The victorious Allies, formerly creditors to the world, became debtors to the new American colossus, itself barely touched by the calamities of war.

The old international order, moreover, was dead. Russia was ruled by a Bolshevik dictatorship that preached world revolution and the overthrow of capitalism everywhere. Germany was in chaos. Austria-Hungary had disintegrated into a swarm of small states competing for the remains of the ancient empire. These kinds of change stirred the colonial territories ruled by the European powers; overseas empires would never again be as secure as they had seemed before the war. Europe was no longer the center of the world, free to interfere when it wished or to ignore the outer regions if it chose. Its easy confidence in material and moral progress was shattered by the brutal reality of four years of horrible war. The memory of that war lived on to shake the nerve of the victorious Western powers as they confronted the new conditions of the postwar world.

Settlement at Paris

The Peacemakers The representatives of the victorious states gathered at Versailles and other Parisian suburbs in the first half of 1919. Wilson speaking for the United States, David Lloyd George (1863–1945) for Britain, Georges Clemenceau (1841–1929) for France, and Vittorio Emanuele Orlando (1860–1952) for Italy made up the Big Four. Japan, now recognized for the first time as a great power, also had an important part in the discussions.

Versailles. The German delegation signs the peace treaty ending World War I in the Hall of Mirrors of the Palace of Versailles on June 28, 1919. This painting by Sir William Orpen, completed in 1921, now hangs in the Imperial War Museum in London. U.S. President Woodrow Wilson is seated in the center, holding a clutch of papers.

Wilson's idealism came into conflict with the more practical war aims of the victorious powers and with many of the secret treaties that had been made before and during the war. The British and French people had been told that Germany would be made to pay for the war. Russia had been promised control of Constantinople in return for recognition of the French claim to Alsace-Lorraine and British control of Egypt. Romania had been promised Transylvania at the expense of Hungary. Some of the agreements contradicted others; Italy and Serbia had competing claims to the islands and shore of the Adriatic. During the war the British had encouraged Arab hopes of an independent Arab state carved out of the Ottoman Empire; those plans conflicted with the Balfour Declaration (1917), in which the British seemed to accept Zionism and to promise the Jews a national home in Palestine. Both of these plans conflicted with an Anglo-French agreement to divide the Near East between themselves.

●●●─Read the Document
The Balfour Declaration, 1917
at **myhistorylab.com**

The continuing national goals of the victors presented further obstacles to an idealistic "peace without victors." France was keenly conscious of its numerical inferiority to Germany and of the low birthrate that would keep it inferior. Naturally, France was eager to achieve a settlement that would permanently weaken Germany and preserve French political and military superiority. Italy sought the acquisition of *Italia Irredenta* ("unredeemed Italy"); Britain looked to its imperial interests; Japan pursued its own advantage in Asia; and the United States insisted on freedom of the seas, which favored American commerce, and on its right to maintain the Monroe Doctrine.

Finally, the peacemakers of 1919 faced a world still in turmoil. The greatest immediate threat appeared to be the spread of bolshevism. While Lenin and his colleagues were distracted by civil war, the Allies landed small armies in Russia to help overthrow the Bolshevik regime. Communist governments were established in Bavaria and Hungary. Berlin also experienced a dangerous communist uprising led by the "Spartacus group" (communist extremists). The Allies were sufficiently worried by these developments to allow and to support suppression of these communist movements by right-wing military forces. They even permitted an army of German volunteers to operate against the Bolsheviks in the Baltic states.

The fear of the spread of communism played a part in the thinking of the diplomats at Versailles, but it was far from dominant. The Germans kept playing on such fears as a way of getting better terms, but the Allies, especially the French, would not hear of it. Fear of Germany remained the chief concern for France; attention to interests that were more traditional and more immediate governed the policies of the other Allies.

The Peace The Paris settlement consisted of five separate treaties between the victors and the defeated powers. Formal sessions began on January 18, 1919, and the last treaty was signed on August 10, 1920. The notion of "a peace without victors" became a mockery when the Soviet Union (as Russia was now called) and Germany were excluded from the peace conference. The Germans were simply presented with a treaty and compelled to accept it, which fully justified their complaint that the treaty had not been negotiated but dictated. The principle of national self-determination was violated many times, as it was unavoidable. Nevertheless, the diplomats of the small nations were angered by their exclusion from decision making. The undeserved adulation accorded Wilson on his arrival gradually turned into equally undeserved scorn. He had not abandoned his ideals lightly but had merely given way to the irresistible force of reality.

Peacemakers. The Allies promoted Arab efforts to secure independence from Turkey in an effort to remove Turkey from the war. Delegates to the peace conference of 1919 in Paris included British Colonel T. E. Lawrence, who helped lead the rebellion against Turkey, and representatives from the Middle East. Prince Feisal, the third son of King Hussein, stands in the foreground of this picture; Lawrence is in the middle row, second from the right; and Brigadier General Nuri Pasha Said of Baghdad is second from the left.

The League of Nations Wilson put great faith in a new instrument for peace and justice, the **League of Nations**. Its covenant was an essential part of the peace treaty. The league was not intended as an international government, but as a body of sovereign states that agreed to pursue common policies and to consult in the common interest, especially when war threatened. In that case the members promised to submit the matter to arbitration, to an international court, or to the League Council. Refusal to abide by this agreement would justify league intervention in the form of economic and even military sanctions.

●▶ Read the Document
The Covenant of the League of Nations at **myhistorylab.com**

But the league was unlikely to be effective because it had no armed forces at its disposal. Action required the unanimous consent of its council, consisting of Britain, France, Italy, the United States, Japan, and four other states that had temporary seats. The Covenant of the League bound its members to "respect and preserve" the territorial integrity of all its members, which was generally seen as a device to ensure the security of the victorious powers. The exclusion of Germany and the Soviet Union from the League Assembly further undermined the league's claim to even-handedness.

Colonies Another provision of the covenant dealt with colonial areas. They were to be placed under the "tutelage" of one of the great powers under league supervision and encouraged to advance towards independence. Because there were no teeth in this provision, little advance was made. Provisions for disarmament were equally ineffective. Members of the league remained fully sovereign and continued to pursue their own national interests.

Germany In the West, the main territorial issue was the fate of Germany (see Map 28–7 on page 890). Although a united Germany was less than fifty years old, no one seems to have thought of undoing Bismarck's work and dividing it into its component parts. The French would have liked to have set up the Rhineland as a separate buffer state, but Lloyd George and Wilson would not permit that. Still, they could not ignore France's need for protection against a resurgent Germany. France received Alsace-Lorraine and the right to work the coal mines of the Saar for fifteen years. Germany west of the Rhine, and 50 kilometers east of it, was to be a demilitarized zone; Allied troops could stay on the west bank for fifteen years. In addition to this physical barrier to a new German attack, the treaty provided that Britain and the United States would guarantee to aid France if it were attacked by Germany. Such an attack was made more unlikely by the permanent disarmament of Germany. Its army was limited to 100,000 men on long-term service; its fleet was all but eliminated;

and it was forbidden to have war planes, submarines, tanks, heavy artillery, or poison gas. As long as these provisions were observed, France would be safe.

The East The settlement in the East ratified the collapse of the great defeated empires that had ruled it for centuries. Germany's frontier lost much of Silesia and part of Prussia. East Prussia was cut off from the rest of Germany by a corridor carved out to give the revived state of Poland access to the sea. The Austro-Hungarian Empire disappeared. Most of its German-speaking people were gathered in the small Republic of Austria, cut off from the Germans of Bohemia and forbidden to unite with Germany. The Magyars occupied the much-reduced kingdom of Hungary.

The Czechs of Bohemia and Moravia joined with the Slovaks and Ruthenians to the east to form Czechoslovakia, and this new state also included several million unhappy Germans. The southern Slavs were united in the kingdom of Serbs, Croats, and Slovenes, or Yugoslavia. Italy gained the Trentino and Trieste. Romania gained Transylvania from Hungary and Bessarabia from Russia. Bulgaria lost territory to Greece and Yugoslavia. Finland, Estonia, Latvia, and Lithuania became independent states, and much of Poland was carved out of formerly Russian soil. Similarly, in the Caucasus, the new nations of Georgia, Armenia, and Azerbaijan took advantage of the turmoil following the Russian Revolution to enjoy a period of independence from 1918 to 1921. Ukraine and Russia also achieved autonomy during this brief period.

The old Ottoman Empire also disappeared. The new Republic of Turkey was limited to little more than Constantinople and Asia Minor. Palestine and Iraq came under British control and Syria and Lebanon under French control as mandates of the League of Nations. Germany's former colonies in Africa were divided among Britain, France, Belgium, and South Africa. The German Pacific possessions went to Australia, New Zealand, and Japan.

◉▶ See the Map
Southeastern Europe, 1914
at **myhistorylab.com**

In theory, the mandate system was meant to have the "advanced nations" govern the former colonies in the interests of the native peoples until they became ready to govern themselves. They were thus divided into three categories—A, B, and C—in descending order of their readiness for independence. In practice, most mandated territories were treated as colonies by the powers under whose "tutelage" they came. Not even one Class A mandate had achieved full independence twenty years after the signing of the treaty. Colonialism was to remain a problem even after World War II.

◉▶ Watch the Video
The Continuing Legacy of World War I in the Middle East at **myhistorylab.com**

Map 28–7. **World War I Peace Settlement in Europe and the Middle East.** The map of central and Eastern Europe, as well as that of the Middle East, underwent drastic revision after World War I. The enormous territorial losses suffered by Germany, Austria-Hungary, the Ottoman Empire, Bulgaria, and Russia were the other side of the coin represented by gains for France, Italy, Greece, and Romania and by the appearance, or reappearance, of at least eight new independent states from Finland in the north to Yugoslavia in the south. The mandate system for former Ottoman territories outside Turkey proper laid the foundations for several new, mostly Arab, states in the Middle East.

Reparations Perhaps the most debated part of the peace settlement dealt with **reparations** for the damage done by Germany during the war. Before the armistice the Germans promised to pay compensation "for all damages done to the civilian population of the Allies and their property." The Americans judged that the amount would be between $15 billion and $25 billion and that Germany would be able to pay that amount. However, France and Britain, worried about repaying their war debts to the United States, were eager to have Germany pay the full cost of the war, including pensions to survivors and dependents. There was general agreement that Germany could not afford to pay such a sum, whatever it might be, and no sum was fixed at the conference. In the meantime Germany was to pay $5 billion annually until 1921. At that time a final figure would be set, which Germany would have to pay within thirty years. The French did not regret the outcome. Either Germany would pay and be bled into impotence, or Germany would refuse to pay and justify French intervention.

To justify these huge reparations, the Allies inserted the notorious Clause 231, the **war guilt clause**, into the treaty:

The Allied and Associated Governments affirm, and Germany accepts, the responsibility of Germany and her allies for causing all the loss and damage to which the Allied and Associated Governments and their nationals have been subjected as a consequence of the war imposed upon them by aggression of Germany and her allies.

The Germans, of course, bitterly resented the charge. They had lost territories containing millions of Germans and great quantities of badly needed natural resources; they were presented with an astronomical and apparently unlimited reparations bill. To add insult to injury, they had to admit to a war guilt that they did not feel. Finally, they had to accept the entire treaty as it was written by the victors, without any opportunity for negotiation. Germany's Chancellor Philipp Scheidemann (1865–1939) spoke of the treaty as the imprisonment of the German people and asked, "What hand would not wither that binds itself and us in these fetters?" But there was no choice. The Social Democrats and the Catholic Center Party formed a new government, and their representatives signed the treaty. These parties formed the backbone of the Weimar government that ruled Germany until 1933; they never overcame the stigma of accepting the Treaty of Versailles.

Evaluation of the Peace

Few peace settlements have been more attacked than the one negotiated in Paris in 1919. It was natural that the defeated powers should have objected to it, but the peace was soon bitterly criticized in the victorious countries as well. Many of the French thought that it failed to provide adequate security for France because it tied that security to promises of aid from the unreliable Anglo-Saxon countries. In England and the United States, liberals complained that the treaty violated the idealistic and liberal aims and principles that the Western leaders had professed. It was not a peace without victors. It did not end imperialism but attempted to promote the national interests of the winning nations. It violated the principles of national self-determination by leaving significant pockets of minorities outside the borders of their national homelands.

The most influential critic of the peace was John Maynard Keynes (1883–1946), a brilliant British economist who took part in the peace conference. When he saw the direction it was taking, he resigned in disgust and wrote a book called *The Economic Consequences of the Peace* (1920). It was a scathing attack, especially on reparations and the other economic clauses of the treaty. It was also a skillful assault on the negotiators, particularly on Wilson, who was depicted as a fool and a hypocrite. Keynes argued that the Treaty of Versailles was both immoral and unworkable. He called it a Carthaginian peace, referring to the utter destruction of Carthage by Rome after the Third Punic War (149–146 B.G.E.). He argued that such a peace would bring economic ruin and war to Europe unless it were repudiated. Keynes had a great effect on the British, who were already suspicious of France and glad of an excuse to withdraw from continental affairs. The decent and respectable position came to be one that aimed at revision of the treaty in favor of Germany.

Even more important was the book's influence in the United States. It fed the traditional tendency towards isolationism and gave powerful weapons to Wilson's enemies. Wilson's own political mistakes helped prevent American ratification of the treaty. Consequently, America was out of the League of Nations and not bound to defend France. Britain, therefore, was also free from its obligation to France. France was left to protect itself without adequate means to do so for long.

Many of the attacks on the Treaty of Versailles are unjustified. It was not a Carthaginian peace. Germany was neither dismembered nor ruined. Reparations could be and were scaled down, and until the great world depression of the 1930s the Germans recovered a high level of prosperity. Complaints against the peace should also be measured against the peace the victorious Germans had imposed on Russia at Brest-Litovsk and their plans for a European settlement in case of victory. Both were far more severe than anything enacted at Versailles. The attempt at achieving self-determination for nationalities was less than perfect, but it was the best solution Europe had ever accomplished in that direction.

The peace, nevertheless, was unsatisfactory in important ways. The elimination of the Austro-Hungarian Empire, however inevitable that might seem, created serious problems. Economically it was disastrous, for it separated raw materials from manufacturing areas and producers from their markets by new boundaries and tariff walls. In hard times, this separation created friction and hostility that aggravated other quarrels also created by the peace treaties. Poland and especially Czechoslovakia contained unhappy German minorities. Czechoslovakia itself was a collection of nationalities that did not find it easy to live together as a nation. Disputes over territories in eastern Europe promoted further tension. The peace was inadequate on another level as well. It rested on a defeat that Germany did not admit. The Germans believed they had been cheated rather than defeated. The high moral principles proclaimed by the Allies also undercut the validity of the peace, for it plainly fell far short of those principles.

Finally, the great weakness of the peace was its failure to accept reality. Germany and Russia were inevitably to play an important part in European affairs, yet they were excluded from the settlement and from the League of Nations. Given the many discontented parties, the peace was not self-enforcing, yet no satisfactory machinery for enforcing it was established. The league was never a serious force for this purpose. It was left to France, with no guarantee of support from Britain and no hope of help from the United States, to defend the new arrangements. Finland, the Baltic States, Poland, Romania, Czechoslovakia, and Yugoslavia were created or strengthened as a barrier to the westward expansion of Russian communism and as a safeguard to deter German revival. Most of these states, however, would have to rely on France in case of danger. France was simply not strong enough for the task if Germany were to rearm.

The tragedy of the Treaty of Versailles was that it was neither conciliatory enough to remove the desire for change, even at the cost of war, nor harsh enough to make another war impossible. A lasting peace required enforcing German disarmament while the more obnoxious clauses of the peace treaty were revised. Such a policy demanded continued attention to the problem, unity among the victors, and far-sighted leadership; none of these was present in adequate supply during the next two decades.

Summary

The New Imperialism. European imperialism in the last part of the nineteenth century brought the Western countries into contact with most of the world. By 1914, European nations had divided Africa among themselves and controlled large parts of Asia and the islands of the Pacific. Much of the Middle East was under the nominal control of the Ottoman Empire, which was in its death throes and under European influence. The Monroe Doctrine made Latin America a protectorate of the United States. Japan had become an imperial power at the expense of China and Korea.

World War I. The emergence of a new, powerful German state at the center of Europe upset the old balance of power. Bismarck, however, preserved the peace for as long as he remained in power. The new German emperor, William II, abandoned the policy of restraint and sought more power and influence for his country. The result was a system of alliances that divided Europe into two armed camps. What began as yet another Balkan War involving the European powers became a world war that influenced the rest of the world. As the devastating war of 1914–1918 dragged on, the real motives that had driven the European powers to fight gave way to public affirmations of the principles of nationalism and self-determination.

The Peace Settlement. The peoples under colonial rule took these statements seriously and sought to win their own independence and nationhood. For the most part they were disappointed by the peace settlement. The British and French Empires were larger than ever. The Americans added to the islands they controlled in the Pacific. Japanese imperial ambitions were rewarded at the expense of China.

However, the old imperial nations, especially Britain and France, had paid an enormous price in lives, money, and will for their victory in the war. Colonial peoples pressed for the rights that were proclaimed as universal by the West but denied to their colonies; influential minorities in the countries that ruled them sympathized with colonial aspirations for independence. Tension between colonies and their ruling nations was a cause of instability in the world created by the Paris treaties of 1919.

Key Terms

Fourteen Points (p. 886)

Italia Irredenta (p. 883)

League of Nations (p. 889)

mobilization (p. 890)

New Imperialism (p. 864)

Pan-Slavic movement (p. 873)

reparations (p. 891)

Schlieffen Plan (p. 880)

soviets (p. 884)

war guilt clause (p. 891)

"White" Russians (p. 885)

Review Questions

1. What role did Bismarck envisage for the new Germany after 1871? How successful was he in carrying out his vision? Was he wise to tie Germany to Austria-Hungary?

2. Why and in what stages did Britain abandon "splendid isolation" at the turn of the century? Were the policies it pursued instead wise ones, or should Britain have followed a different course?

3. How did developments in the Balkans lead to the outbreak of World War I? What was the role of Serbia? Of Austria? Of Russia? What was the aim of German policy in July 1914? Did Germany want a general war?

4. Why did Germany lose World War I? Could Germany have won, or was victory never a possibility? Assess the settlement of Versailles. What were its benefits to Europe, and what were its drawbacks? Was the settlement too harsh or too conciliatory? Could it have secured lasting peace in Europe? How might it have been improved?

5. Why was Lenin successful in establishing Bolshevik rule in Russia? What role did Trotsky play? Was it wise policy for Lenin to take Russia out of the war?

Note: *To learn more about the topics in this chapter, please turn to the Suggested Readings at the end of the book. For additional sources related to this chapter please see MyHistoryLab.com.*

PEARSON
myhistorylab Connections

Reinforce what you learned in this chapter by studying the many documents, images, maps, review tools, and videos available at **www.myhistorylab.com**.

Read and Review

✔●─ **Study** and **Review** Chapter 28

●❖─ Read the **Document** *A British View of Egyptian Agriculture, 1840, p. 869*
Edward D. Morel, The Black Man's Burden , p. 871
Serbian Society of National Defense, Program for Nationalism, p. 874
Borijove Jevtic: The Murder of Archduke Franz Ferdinand at Sarajevo (28 June 1914). p. 878
British Soldiers on the Battle of the Somme, p. 884
Bolshevik Seizure of Power, 1917, p. 885
Woodrow Wilson, The Fourteen Points (1918) , p. 886
The Balfour Declaration, 1917, p. 888
The Covenant of the League of Nations, p. 889

👁─ See the **Map** *Africa Before the Scramble, p. 867*
Congress of Berlin, p. 874
Diplomatic Crises, 1905–1914, p. 877
The Actual German Advance, 1914, p. 881
Russian Armies In the Eastern Front, p. 884
Southeastern Europe, 1914, p. 889

((●─ Hear the **Audio** *World War 1, p. 878*
World War 3, p. 885

●─ Watch the **Video** *The Origins of Modern Imperialism and Colonialism, p. 864*
The Continuing Legacy of World War I in the Middle East, p. 889

Research and Explore

●─ Watch the **Video** *New Imperialism*

●─ Watch the **Video** *World War I*

─ ((●─ **Hear** the **Audio** ─

Hear the audio file for Chapter 28 at
www.myhistorylab.com.

29 | Depression, European Dictators, and the American New Deal

- After Versailles: Demands for Revision and Enforcement
- Toward the Great Depression in Europe
- The Soviet Experiment
- The Fascist Experiment in Italy
- German Democracy and Dictatorship
- The Great Depression and the New Deal in the United States

IN THE TWO DECADES THAT FOLLOWED THE CONCLUSION OF the Paris Settlement, the Western world saw a number of experiments in politics and economic life. Two broad factors accounted for these experiments. First, the war, the Russian Revolution, and the peace treaty had transformed the political face of Europe. New political regimes had emerged in the wake of the collapse of the monarchies of Germany, Austria-Hungary, and Russia. These new governments immediately faced the problems of postwar reconstruction, economic dislocation, and nationalistic resentments. Most of these nations also included large groups who questioned the legitimacy of their governments.

Second, beginning in the early 1920s, economic dislocations that led to the economic downturn that became known as the Great Depression began to spread across the world. It occurred through the combination of financial turmoil in the more advanced industrial nations and a collapse of commodity prices in the commodity-exporting countries. Faced with

Weimar Germany. In this painting, which reflects the mood of social and political disillusionment that prevailed in much of Europe in the 1920s, George Grosz satirized conservative and right-wing groups in Weimar Germany, including the army, the courts, the newspapers, and the Nazi Party.

The Interwar Period in Europe and the United States

The West

The two decades between the great wars marked a period of immense political and economic transition around the globe. Many regions endured political turmoil and economic instability, followed by the establishment of militaristic authoritarian regimes. In Italy, it was the Fascists; in Germany, the Nazis; in the Soviet Union, Stalin's regime. Spain too came under the rule of a military dictator who rose to power with the assistance of the Nazis. Many Europeans, battered by the global economic crisis of the 1930s and, in the case of Germany, the harsh terms of the Treaty of Versailles, believed that only strong leaders could lead their countries to prosperity again in the global competition for resources and territory. In East Asia, Japan came into the grip of a right-wing militaristic government. China saw more than twenty years of civil war and revolution that would culminate with the communists' rise to power under Mao Tse-tung. Most of Latin America came under the sway of dictators or governments heavily influenced by the military.

With the exception of Russia (and later China), all of these governments were right wing in orientation. In fact, the Russian Revolution was a pivotal factor in the rise of right-wing and Fascist dictators, who often justified their power on the basis of their firm opposition to the "Red Menace" and the growing popularity enjoyed by socialism and communism in many European countries during the economic crisis of the 1930s.

To many observers in the late 1930s, the day of liberal parliamentary democracy appeared to be ending. The disruptions arising from World War I and the social and economic turmoil of the Depression seemed to pose problems that liberal governments could not address. Only the radical medicine of socialism, communism, or right-wing dictatorships seemed capable of resolving the crisis. The deep political divisions

political instability and economic crisis, governments contrived various political and economic responses. In Europe these efforts often produced authoritarian regimes. In the United States the response to the Depression led to a much-increased role for the federal government in the life of the nation. ■

or to enforce the Paris treaties contributed to domestic political turmoil across the Continent.

Toward the Great Depression in Europe

Three factors combined to bring about the intense severity and the extended length of the **Great Depression** with its accompanying extensive unemployment and loss of social security for millions of people around the globe. First, a financial crisis stemmed directly from the war and the peace settlement. To this was added a crisis in the production and distribution of goods in the world market. These two problems became intertwined in 1929, and as far as Europe was concerned they reached the breaking point in 1931. Finally, both of these difficulties became worse than they might have been because no major western European country or the United States provided strong, responsible economic leadership.

After Versailles: Demands for Revision and Enforcement

The Paris settlement fostered both resentment and discontent. Those resentments counted among the chief political factors in Europe for the next two decades. Germany had been humiliated. The arrangements for reparations led to endless haggling over payments. Various national groups in the successor states of the Austro-Hungarian Empire felt that injustice had been done in their particular cases of self-determination. There were demands for further border adjustments. On the other side, the victorious powers, especially France, often believed that the provisions of the treaty were being inadequately enforced. Consequently, throughout the 1920s and into the 1930s demands either to revise

Financial Tailspin The quest for payment of German reparations caused one of the major diplomatic crises of the 1920s; the crisis itself resulted in further economic upheaval. In early 1923 the Allies—France in particular—declared between the right and left in their populations brought some nations, such as France in the mid-1930s, to the brink of civil war. Spain became engulfed in the civil war that brought General Francisco Franco (1892–1975) to power in 1939.

The interwar period also departed from the nineteenth-century ideal of *laissez-faire* economics, in which central governments assumed little responsibility for guiding the economies of their countries. The German inflation of the early 1920s, the worldwide financial collapse of the late 1920s, the vast unemployment of the early 1930s, together with the agricultural crisis of both decades, roused demands for government action as millions of people experienced very real, and often sudden, economic hardship and suffering. One reason for these demands was simply that more governments throughout the world were responsible to mass democratic electorates. Governments that failed to adequately address the problems were put out of office. This happened to the Republicans in the United States, the Socialist and Liberal parties in Germany, the left-wing parties in Japan, and various political parties in Latin America that failed to deal with the Depression. Paradoxically, many democratic electorates actually turned themselves over to politically authoritarian regimes as they searched for social and economic stability.

Extreme forms of nationalism in both Europe and Japan also spawned authoritarianism. The authoritarian governments of Germany, Italy, and Japan all had agendas of nationalistic aggression. They shared the nineteenth-century conviction that territorial expansion was essential to national prestige and economic security. As a result, they were prepared to move wherever they saw fellow nationals living outside their borders (a legacy of the creation of nation-states in the eighteenth and nineteenth centuries) or where they could establish dominance over other peoples and thus become imperial powers. Japan moved against Manchuria and later other parts of Asia. Italy invaded Ethiopia. Germany sought union with German-speaking peoples in Austria and Czechoslovakia and then sought to expand throughout eastern Europe. In turn, those actions challenged the dominance of Great Britain and the vital security interests of the United States. By the end of the 1930s the authoritarian regimes and the liberal democracies stood on the brink of a major confrontation.

Focus Questions

- Why did many people in the 1930s lose faith in liberal democracy and *laissez-faire* economics?
- What led many countries to adopt authoritarian regimes during this period? Why did authoritarian governments seem to pose a solution to economic hardship and social instabililty?
- What was the relationship between extreme nationalism and the outbreak of World War II?

Germany to be in technical default of its reparations payments. On January 11, to ensure receipt of the hard-won reparations, French troops occupied the Ruhr mining and manufacturing district. The **Weimar Republic** ordered passive resistance that amounted to a general strike in the largest industrial region of the nation. Confronted with this tactic, the French government sent French civilians to run the German mines and railroads. France got its way. The Germans paid, but its victory cost France dearly. The English, alienated by the French heavy-handedness, took no part in the occupation. Britain became more suspicious of France and more sympathetic to Germany. The cost of the Ruhr occupation, moreover, vastly increased French as well as German inflation and damaged the French economy.

The political and economic turmoil of the Ruhr invasion led to international attempts to ease the German payment of reparations. The most famous of these efforts were the Dawes Plan of 1924 and the Young Plan of 1929, both devised by Americans. At the same time, large amounts of American investment capital were pouring into Europe. However, by 1928 this lending decreased as American money became diverted into the booming New York stock market. The crash of Wall Street in October 1929—the result of virtually unregulated financial speculation—saw the loss of large

((•—Hear the Audio
Depression
at **MyHistoryLab.com**

amounts of money. Credit sharply contracted in the United States as numerous banks failed. Thereafter, little American capital was available for investment in Europe.

As credit for Europe began to run out, a major financial crisis struck the Continent. In May 1931 the Kreditanstalt— a primary lending institution and major bank for much of central and eastern Europe—collapsed. As a result, the German banking system came under severe pressure and was saved only through government guarantees. As the German difficulties increased, in June 1931 U.S. president Herbert Hoover (1874–1964) announced a one-year moratorium on all payments of international debts. The Hoover moratorium was a prelude to the end of reparations. The Lausanne Conference of the summer of 1932, in effect, brought the era of reparations to a close. The next year the debts owed to the United States were settled either through small token payments or simply through default.

Problems in Agricultural Commodities

The 1920s witnessed a contraction in the market demand for European goods relative to the Continent's productive capacity. This problem originated both within and outside

Jarrow Crusade. In what was known as the Jarrow Crusade during the autumn of 1936, a group of approximately 200 protesters marched from the town of Jarrow in northeastern England to London to demonstrate their need for employment and the plight of their town where the previous year the shipyard had been closed.

Europe. In both instances the difficulty arose from agriculture. Better methods of farming, improved strains of wheat, expanded tillage, and more extensive transport facilities all over the globe vastly increased the quantity of grain. World wheat prices fell to record lows. Although this helped consumers, it decreased the income of European farmers. At the same time, higher industrial wages raised the cost of the industrial goods that farmers or peasants used. Consequently, they also had great difficulty paying off their mortgages and normal annual operation debts. These problems were especially acute in central and eastern Europe and abetted farmers' disillusionment with liberal politics. German farmers, for example, would become prime supporters of the National Socialist Workers Party (Nazis).

Outside Europe similar problems affected other producers of agricultural commodities. The prices they received for their products plummeted. Government-held reserves reached record levels. This glut of major world commodities involved the supplies of wheat, sugar, coffee, rubber, wool, and lard. The people who produced these goods in underdeveloped nations could no longer make enough money to buy finished goods from industrial Europe. As world credit collapsed, the economic position of these commodity producers worsened. Commodity production had simply outstripped world demand.

The results of the collapse in the agricultural sector of the world economy and the financial turmoil were stagnation and depression for European industry. Coal, iron, and textiles had depended largely on international markets. Unemployment spread from these industries to those producing finished consumer goods. Persistent unemployment in Great Britain and, to a lesser extent, in Germany during the 1920s had created "soft" domestic markets. The policies of reduced spending with which the governments confronted the Depression further weakened domestic demand. By the early 1930s the Depression was feeding on itself.

Depression and Government Policy The governments of the late 1920s and the early 1930s were not particularly well suited in either structure or ideology to confront the unemployment and social insecurity caused by the Depression. The electorates demanded action. The government response depended largely on the severity of the Depression in a particular country and on the self-confidence of the nation's political system.

Great Britain and France undertook moderate political experiments. In 1924 the Labour Party in Great Britain established itself as a viable governing party by forming a short-lived government. It again formed a ministry in 1929. Under the pressure of the Depression and at the urging of King George V (r. 1910–1936), the Labour prime minister Ramsay MacDonald (1866–1937) organized a National Government, which was a coalition of the Labour, Conservative, and Liberal parties. It remained in power until 1935, when a Conservative ministry led by Stanley Baldwin (1867–1947) replaced it.

The most important French political experiment was the **Popular Front** Ministry, which came to office in 1936. It was composed of Socialists, radicals, and communists—the first time that Socialists and communists had cooperated in a ministry. The Popular Front addressed major labor problems in the French economy. By 1938 various changes in the cabinet in effect brought the Popular Front to an end.

The political changes in Britain and France were only of domestic significance. But the political experiments of the 1920s and 1930s that reshaped world history and civilization involved the establishment of a Soviet government in Russia, a Fascist regime in Italy, and a Nazi dictatorship in Germany.

The Soviet Experiment

The consolidation of the Bolshevik Revolution in Russia established the most extensive and durable of all twentieth-century authoritarian governments. The Communist Party of the Soviet Union retained power from 1917 until the end of 1991, and its presence influenced the political history of Europe and much of the rest of the world, as did no other single factor. Unlike the Italian Fascists or the German National Socialists, the Bolsheviks seized power violently through revolution. For several years they confronted armed

Lenin. Anxiety over the spread of the Bolshevik Revolution was a fundamental factor of European politics during the 1920s and 1930s. Images like this Soviet portrait of Lenin as a heroic revolutionary conjured fears among people in the rest of Europe of a political force determined to overturn their social, political, and economic institutions. *Gemalde von A. M. Gerassimow, "Lenin as Agitator"/Art Resource/Bildarchiv Preussischer Kulturbesitz.*

opposition, and their leaders long felt insecure about their hold on the country. The Communist Party was neither a mass party nor a nationalistic one. Its early membership rarely exceeded more than 1 percent of the Russian population. The Bolsheviks confronted a much less industrialized economy than that in Italy or Germany. They believed in and practiced the collectivization of economic life attacked by the right-wing dictatorships. The Marxist-Leninist ideology was broader than the nationalism of the Fascists and the racism of the Nazis. Communism was an exportable commodity. The communists regarded their government and their revolution not as part of a national history but as epoch-making events in the history of the world and the development of humanity. Fear of communism and determination to stop its spread became one of the leading political forces in western Europe and the United States for most of the rest of the century.

War Communism

Within the Soviet Union the Red Army under the organizational genius of Leon Trotsky (1879–1940) had suppressed internal and foreign military opposition to the new government. Within months of the revolution, a new secret police, known as *Cheka*, appeared. Throughout the civil war Lenin (1870–1924) had declared that the Bolshevik Party, as the vanguard of the revolution, was imposing the dictatorship of the proletariat. Political and economic administration became highly centralized. All major decisions flowed from the top in a nondemocratic manner. Under the economic policy of **War Communism**, the revolutionary government confiscated and then operated the banks, the transport facilities, and heavy industry. The state also forcibly requisitioned grain and shipped it from the countryside to feed the army and the workers in the cities. The fact of the civil war permitted suppression of possible resistance to this economic policy.

War Communism helped the Red Army defeat its opponents. The revolution had survived and triumphed. The policy, however, generated domestic opposition to the Bolsheviks, who in 1920 numbered only about 600,000 members. The alliance of workers and peasants forged by the slogan of "Peace, Bread, and Land" had begun to dissolve. Many Russians were no longer willing to make the sacrifices demanded by the central party bureaucrats. In 1920 and 1921 serious strikes occurred. Peasants were discontented and resisted the requisition of grain. In March 1921 the navy mutinied at Kronstadt. The Red Army crushed the rebellion with grave loss of life. Each of these incidents suggested that the proletariat itself was opposing the dictatorship of the proletariat. Also, by late 1920 it had become clear that further revolution would not sweep across the rest of Europe. For the time being the Soviet Union would constitute a vast island of revolutionary socialism in the larger sea of worldwide capitalism.

The New Economic Policy

Under these difficult conditions Lenin made a crucial strategic retreat. In March 1921, following the Kronstadt mutiny, he outlined the **New Economic Policy**, normally referred to as NEP. Apart from what he termed "the commanding heights" of banking, heavy industry, transportation, and international commerce, considerable private economic enterprise was allowed. In particular, peasants could farm for a profit. They would pay taxes like other citizens, but they could sell their surplus grain on the open market. The NEP was consistent with Lenin's earlier conviction that the Russian peasantry held the key to the success of the revolution. After 1921 the countryside did become more stable, and a secure food supply seemed assured for the cities. Similar free enterprise flourished within light industry and domestic retail trade. By 1927 industrial production had reached its 1913 level. The revolution seemed to have transformed Russia into a land of small family farms and privately owned shops and businesses.

Stalin versus Trotsky

The NEP had caused sharp disputes within the Politburo, the highest governing committee of the Communist Party. To some members the partial return to capitalism seemed nothing less than a betrayal of sound Marxist principles. These frictions increased as Lenin's firm hand disappeared. In 1922 he suffered a stroke and never again dominated party affairs; in 1924 he died. In the ensuing power vacuum, an intense struggle for leadership of the party commenced, after which two factions emerged. One was led by Trotsky; the other by Josef Stalin (1879–1953), who had become general secretary of the party in 1922. Shortly before his death Lenin had criticized both men. He was especially harsh toward Stalin. However, the general secretary's base of power lay with the party membership and with the daily management of party affairs. Consequently, Stalin was able to withstand Lenin's posthumous strictures.

((•─ Hear the Audio Communism at MyHistoryLab.com

Each faction wanted to control the party, but the struggle was fought over the question of Russia's path toward industrialization and the future of the communist revolutionary movement. Trotsky, speaking for what became

✓•─ Study and Review Lenin, 1920, vs. Stalin, 1931 at MyHistoryLab.com

known as the left wing, urged rapid industrialization and looked to voluntary collectivization of farming by poor peasants as a means of increasing agricultural production. Trotsky further argued that the revolution in Russia could succeed only if new revolutions took place elsewhere. A right-wing faction opposed Trotsky. Although its chief ideological voice was that of Nikolai Bukharin (1888–1938), the editor of *Pravda*, the official party paper, Stalin was its true political manipulator. In the mid-1920s this group pressed for the continuation of Lenin's NEP and a policy of relatively slow industrialization.

Stalin was the ultimate victor in these intraparty rivalries. Unlike the other early Bolshevik leaders, he had not spent a long exile in western Europe, and he was much less an intellectual and internationalist than they had been. He was also much more brutal. His handling of various recalcitrant national groups within Russia after the revolution had shocked even Lenin. Stalin's power lay in his command of bureaucratic and administrative methods. He was neither a brilliant writer nor an effective public speaker; however, he mastered the crucial, if dull, details of party structure, including admission and promotion. That mastery meant that he could draw on the support of the lower levels of the party apparatus when he clashed with other leaders.

In the mid-1920s Stalin supported Bukharin's position on economic development. In 1924 he also enunciated, in opposition to Trotsky, the doctrine of "socialism in one country." He urged that socialism could be achieved in Russia alone; Russian success did not depend on the fate of the revolution elsewhere. Stalin thus nationalized the previously international scope of the Marxist revolution. By 1927 Trotsky had been removed from all his offices, ousted from the party, and exiled to Siberia. In 1929 he was expelled from Russia and eventually moved to Mexico, where he was murdered in 1940 by one of Stalin's agents. With the removal of Trotsky, Stalin was firmly in control of the Soviet state.

Decision for Rapid Industrialization

While the capitalist economies of western Europe floundered during the Depression, the Soviet Union registered tremendous industrial advances. Through 1928 Lenin's NEP, as championed by Bukharin with Stalin's support, had steered Soviet economic development. Private ownership and enterprise were permitted to flourish in the countryside to ensure enough food for the workers in the cities. A few farmers, the *kulaks*, had be-

Kulaks. During Stalin's drive to collectivize agriculture, wealthy peasants known as *kulaks* become the object of his wrath. Here a group of mostly peasant women demonstrate against the *kulaks*.

come prosperous. They probably numbered less than 5 percent of the rural population. During 1928 and 1929 they and other farmers withheld grain from the market because prices were too low. Food shortages occurred in the cities and caused potential unrest. The goals of the NEP were no longer being fulfilled.

Sometime during these troubled months, Stalin came to a momentous decision: Russia must industrialize rapidly to match the economic and military power of the West. Agriculture must be collectivized to produce sufficient grain for food and export and to free peasant labor for the factories. This program, which basically embraced Trotsky's earlier economic position, unleashed a second Russian revolution. The costs and character of Stalin's "socialism in one country" now became clear.

Read the Document
Stalin Demands Rapid Industrialization of the USSR (1931) at **MyHistoryLab.com**

Agricultural Policy In 1929 Stalin ordered party agents into the countryside to confiscate any hoarded wheat. The *kulaks* bore the blame for the grain shortages. As part of the general plan to erase the private ownership of land and to collectivize farming, the government undertook a program to eliminate the *kulaks* as a class. A *kulak*, however, soon came to mean any peasant who opposed Stalin's policy. In the countryside, peasants and farmers at all levels of wealth resisted stubbornly. They were determined to keep their land. They wreaked their own vengeance on the policy of **collectivization** by slaughtering more than 100 million horses and cattle between 1929 and 1933. The situation in the countryside amounted to open warfare. The peasant resistance caused Stalin to call a brief halt to the process in March 1930. He justified the slowdown on the grounds of "dizziness from success." (See Document: "Stalin Calls for the Liquidation of the *Kulaks* as a Class." on page 902)

Soon thereafter, the drive to collectivize the farms was renewed with vehemence, and the costs remained high. As many as 10 million peasants were killed, and millions of others were sent forcibly to collective farms or labor camps. Initially, because of the turmoil on the land, agricultural production fell. There was famine in 1932 and 1933. Milk and meat remained in short supply because of the livestock slaughter. Yet Stalin persevered. The *kulaks* were uprooted from their farms and sent to Siberia or other regions far from their homes. Peasants who remained had their lands incorporated into large collective farms. The state provided the machinery for these units through machine-tractor stations. The state thus retained control over major farm machines, a monopoly that was a powerful weapon.

Read the Document
Irina Ivanovna Kniazeva, "A Life in a Peasant Village" (USSR) 1917–1930s at **MyHistoryLab.com**

Stalin also used the drive to collectivization as a device to eradicate possible centers of anti-Russian

Propaganda. Stalin used intimidation and propaganda to support his drive to collectivize Soviet agriculture. The poster shows an idealized Soviet collective farm on which tractors owned by the state have replaced peasant labor. In reality, collectivization provoked fierce resistance and caused famines in which millions of peasants died. *1932 (colour litho) by Klutchis (fl. 1932). Deutsches Plakat Museum, Essen, Germany/Archives Charmet/The Bridgeman Art Library.*

nationalism within the Soviet Union. His chief area of concern was Ukraine. There during 1932 and 1933 his government demanded exceptionally high quotas of grain to be shipped to other regions of the Soviet Union. The result was a forced famine that cost the lives of millions of people in the Ukraine. This experience of vast loss of life, including starvation and executions, illustrates Stalin's willingness to direct the destructive power of the Soviet government against a particular ethnic group that he feared might become a center of nationalist political resistance to Soviet authority. Only the opening of the Soviet archives following the collapse of the Soviet Union revealed the horrendous extent of this deadly ethic policy.

Collectivization dramatically changed Russian farming. In 1928 approximately 98 percent of Russian farmland consisted of small peasant holdings. Ten years later, despite all the opposition, over 90 percent of the land had been collectivized, and the quantity of farm produce directly handled

Document

Stalin Calls for the Liquidation of the *Kulaks* as a Class

The core of Stalin's agricultural policy undertaken in the late 1920s and early 1930s was the replacement of private farms with large collective farms run by the state. The greatest obstacle to this policy was the *kulaks*, prosperous, productive peasants. In this speech of 1929, Stalin first explains why collective farms must replace small peasant farming to achieve an adequate food supply for the cities and the industrial workers. He then calls for the liquidation of the *kulaks* as a class. As might be expected, the *kulaks* resisted collectivization by destroying crops and farm animals. In turn, Communist Party agents killed millions of peasants to achieve collectivization.

■ *What were the goals of the collectivization of farms in the Soviet Union? How did the kulaks stand in the way of collectivization? How does Stalin dehumanize the kulaks by discussing them entirely as a class and as part of the capitalistic system?*

Can we advance our socialized industry at an accelerated rate as long as we have an agricultural base, such as is provided by small-peasant farming, which is incapable of expanded reproduction, and which, in addition, is the predominant force in our national economy? No, we cannot....

What, then, is the solution? The solution lies in enlarging the agricultural units, in making agriculture capable of accumulation, of expanded reproduction, and in thus transforming the agricultural bases of our national economy.

[T]he socialist way [to enlarge farming units], which is to introduce collective farms and state farms in agriculture, the way which leads to the amalgamation of the small-peasant farms into large collective farms, employing machinery and scientific methods of farming, and capable of developing further, for such agricultural enterprises can achieve expanded reproduction....

The characteristic feature in the work of our Party during the past year is that we, as a Party, as the Soviet power,

(a) have developed an offensive along the whole front against the capitalist elements in the countryside;
(b) that this offensive, as you know, has brought about and is bringing about very palpable, positive results.

What does this mean? It means that we have passed from the policy of restricting the exploiting proclivities of the *kulaks* to the policy of eliminating the *kulaks* as a class....

Until recently the Party adhered to the policy of restricting the exploiting proclivities of the *kulaks*....

Could we have undertaken such an offensive against the *kulaks* five years or three years ago? Could we then have counted on success in such an offensive? No, we

could not. That would have been the most dangerous adventurism. It would have been playing a very dangerous game at offensive. We would certainly have failed, and our failure would have strengthened the position of the *kulaks*. Why? Because we still lacked a wide network of state and collective farms in the rural districts which could be used as strongholds in a determined offensive against the *kulaks*. Because at that time we were not yet able to substitute for the capitalist production of the *kulaks* the socialist production of the collective farms and state farms....

Now we are able to carry on a determined offensive against the *kulaks*, to break their resistance, to eliminate them as a class and substitute for their output the output of the collective farms and state farms. Now, the *kulaks* are being expropriated by the masses of poor and middle peasants themselves, by the masses who are putting solid collectivization into practice. Now, the expropriation of the *kulaks* in the regions of solid collectivization is no longer just an administrative measure. Now, the expropriation of the *kulaks* is an integral part of the formation and development of the collective farms. Consequently it is now ridiculous and foolish to discourse on the expropriation of the *kulaks*. You do not lament the loss of the hair of one who has been beheaded.

Source: From Stalin, "Problems of Agrarian Policy in the USSR," Speech at a conference of Marxist students of the Agrarian question, December 27, 1929, in *Problems of Leninism*, pp. 391–393, 408–409, 411–412, as quoted in Robert V. Daniels, *A Documentary History of Communism*, rev. ed. (Hanover, NH: University Press of New England, 1984), pp. 224–227. Reprinted by permission.

by the government had risen by 40 percent. The government now had primary direction over the food supply. The farmers and peasants could no longer determine whether there would be stability or unrest in the cities. Stalin and the Communist Party had won the battle of the wheat fields, but they had not solved the problem of producing enough grain. That difficulty has plagued the former Soviet Union to the present day.

Five-Year Plans The Soviet revolution in agriculture had been undertaken for the sake of rapid industrialization. The increased grain supply was to feed the labor force and provide exports to finance the imports required for industrial development. The Soviet Union's industrial achievement between 1928 and World War II was one of the most striking accomplishments of the twentieth century. Russia made a more rapid advance toward economic growth than any other nation in the Western world has ever achieved during any similar period of time. By even the conservative estimates of Western observers, Soviet industrial production rose approximately 400 percent between 1928 and 1940. The production of iron, steel, coal, electrical power, tractors, combines, railway cars, and other heavy machinery was emphasized. Few consumer goods were produced. The labor

for this development was supplied internally. Capital was raised from the export of grain, even at the cost of internal shortage. The technology was generally borrowed from already industrialized nations.

The organizational vehicle for industrialization was a series of Five-Year Plans first begun in 1928. The State Planning Commission, or Gosplan, oversaw the program. It set goals of production and organized the economy to meet them. Coordinating all facets of production was immensely difficult and complicated. Deliveries of materials from mines or factories had to be assured before the next unit could carry out its part of the plan. There was many a slip between the cup and the lip. The troubles in the countryside were harmful. A vast program of propaganda was undertaken to sell the Five-Year Plans to the Russian people and to elicit cooperation. The industrial labor force, however, soon became subject to regimentation similar to that being imposed on the peasants. By the close of the 1930s the accomplishment of the three Five-Year Plans was truly impressive and probably allowed the Soviet Union to survive the German invasion. Industries that

Read the Document
John Scott, excerpt from Behind the Urals: An American Worker in Russia's City of Steel at **MyHistoryLab.com**

had never existed in Russia now challenged and in some cases, such as tractor production, surpassed those of their counterparts in the rest of the world. Large, new industrial cities had been built and populated by hundreds of thousands of people.

Party Congress, 1936. By the mid-1930s Stalin's purges had eliminated many leaders and other members from the Soviet Communist Party. This photograph of a meeting of a party congress in 1936 shows a number of the surviving leaders with Stalin, who sits fourth from the right in the front row. To his left is Vyacheslav Molotov, long-time foreign minister. The first person on the left in the front row is Nikita Khrushchev, who headed the Soviet Union in the late 1950s and early 1960s.

The Purges

Stalin's decisions to industrialize rapidly and to move against the peasants aroused internal political opposition because they were departures from Lenin's policies. In 1929 Stalin forced Bukharin, the fervent supporter of the NEP and his own former ally, off the Politburo. Little detailed information is known about further opposition, but it does seem to have existed among lower level party followers of Bukharin and other previous opponents of rapid industrialization. Sometime in 1933 Stalin began to fear that he would lose control over the party apparatus and that effective rivals might emerge. These fears resulted in the **Great Purges**, among the most mysterious and horrendous political events of the twentieth century. The purges were not understood at the time and are still not fully comprehended today.

On December 1, 1934, Sergei Kirov (1888–1934), the popular party chief of Leningrad (formerly Saint Petersburg and Petrograd) and a member of the Politburo, was assassinated. In the wake of the shooting thousands of people were arrested, and still more were expelled from the party and sent to labor camps. At the time it was believed that Kirov had been murdered by opponents of the regime. Direct or indirect complicity in the crime became the normal accusation against those whom Stalin attacked. It now seems practically certain that Stalin himself authorized Kirov's assassination to forestall any threat from the Leningrad leader.

The purges after Kirov's death were just the beginning of a larger process. Between 1936 and 1938 spectacular show trials were held in Moscow. Previous high Soviet leaders, including former members of the Politburo, publicly confessed political crimes. They were convicted and executed. It is still not certain why they made their palpably false confessions. Still other leaders and lower level party members were tried in private and shot. Thousands of people received no trial at all. The purges touched persons in all areas of party life. It is inexplicable why some were executed, others sent to labor camps, and still others left unmolested. After the civilian party members had been purged, the prosecutors turned against the army. Important officers, including heroes of the civil war, were killed. Within the party itself, hundreds of thousands of members were expelled, and applicants for membership were removed from the rolls. The exact numbers of executions, imprisonments, and expulsions are unknown but certainly ran into the millions.

The trials and purges astonished observers from outside the Soviet Union. Nothing quite like this phenomenon had ever been seen. Political murders and executions were not new, but the absurd confessions were novel. The scale of the political turmoil was also unprecedented. The Russians themselves did not believe or comprehend what was happening. There existed no national emergency or crisis; there were only accusations of sympathy for Trotsky or of complicity in Kirov's murder or of other nameless crimes. If a rational explanation is to be sought, it probably must be found in Stalin's concern for his own power. In effect, the purges created a new party structure that was absolutely loyal to him. New, younger party members replaced those executed or expelled. The newcomers knew little of old Russia or of the ideals of the original Bolsheviks. They had not been loyal to Lenin, Trotsky, or any Soviet leader except Stalin himself.

Despite the flagrant violence and widespread repression of the Soviet experiment, it found many sympathizers throughout the world. Some people did not know of its repression; others ignored those events. The Soviet Union almost immediately after the Bolshevik seizure of power had fostered the organization of Communist parties subservient to Moscow's influence throughout the world. Others who were not formally members of these parties often sympathized with what they believed or hoped were the goals of the Soviet Union. During at least the first fifty years of its existence the Soviet Union managed to capture the imagination of some intellectuals in the West and in other parts of the globe who hoped for a utopian egalitarian transformation of society. During much of the 1930s, to these and other people, the Soviet Union also appeared as an enemy to the Fascist experiments in Italy and Germany. To many people living in the European colonial empires, the Marxist ideology championed by the Soviet Union appeared to offer a vehicle for freeing themselves from the colonial situation. The Soviet Union welcomed and trained many such anticolonial leaders and offered other support to their causes. In the wake of the collapse of the Soviet Union at the close of the century and what is now known about its repression, it is difficult to understand the power its presence exercised over many people's political imaginations around the world, but that attraction was one of the most fundamental factors in world politics from the 1920s through at least the early 1970s.

The Fascist Experiment in Italy

The first authoritarian political experiment in western Europe that arose in part from fears of the spread of bolshevism occurred in Italy. The general term *fascist*, which has been used to describe the various right-wing dictatorships that arose between the wars, was derived from the Italian Fascist movement of Benito Mussolini (1883–1945).

•◦─┤Read the Document
Filippo Tommaso Marinetti, "Futuristic Manifesto" at **MyHistoryLab.com**

While scholars still dispute the exact meaning of **fascism** as a political term, the governments regarded as fascist were antidemocratic, anti-Marxist, anti-parliamentary, and frequently anti-Semitic. They hoped to hold back the spread of bolshevism, which seemed a real threat at the time. They sought a world that would be safe for the middle class, small businesses, owners of moderate amounts of property, and small farmers. The Fascist regimes rejected the political inheritance of the French Revolution and of nineteenth-century liberalism. Their adherents believed that normal parliamentary politics and parties sacrificed national honor and greatness to petty party disputes. They wanted to overcome the class conflict of Marxism and the party conflict of liberalism by consolidating the various groups and classes within the nation for great national purposes. As Mussolini declared in 1931, "The fascist conception of the state is all-embracing, and outside of the state no human or spiritual values can exist, let alone be desirable."[1] Fascist governments were usually single-party dictatorships characterized by terrorism and police surveillance.

((•●─┤Hear the Audio
Fascism at **MyHistoryLab.com**

These dictatorships were rooted in the base of mass political parties.

---

[1]Quoted in Denis Mack Smith, *Italy: A Modern History* (Ann Arbor: University of Michigan Press, 1959), p. 412.

Benito Mussolini became famous for bombastic public speeches delivered in settings surrounded by his fascist followers and military supporters.

Rise of Mussolini

The Italian *Fasci di Combattimento* ("Band of Combat") was founded in 1919 in Milan. Most of its members were war veterans who felt that the sacrifices of World War I had been in vain. They resented Italy's failure to gain the city of Fiume, toward the northern end of the Adriatic Sea, at the Paris conference. They feared socialism, inflation, and labor unrest.

Their leader or **Duce**, Benito Mussolini, was the son of a blacksmith. After having been a schoolteacher and a day laborer, he became active in Italian Socialist politics and by 1912 had become editor of the socialist newspaper *Avanti*. In 1914 Mussolini broke with the Socialists and supported Italian entry into the war on the side of the Allies. His interventionist position lost him the editorship of *Avanti*. He then established his own paper, *Il Popolo d'Italia*. Later he served in the army and was wounded. In 1919 Mussolini was just another Italian politician. His *Fasci* organization was one of many small political groups in a country characterized by such entities.

Postwar Italian politics was a muddle. During the war the Italian Parliament had virtually ceased to function. Ministers had ruled by decree. However, many Italians were dissatisfied with the parliamentary system as it then existed. They felt that Italy had emerged from the war as less than a victorious nation, had not been treated as a great power at the peace conference, and had not received the territories it deserved. The main spokesman for this discontent was the extreme nationalist writer Gabriele D'Annunzio (1863–1938). In 1919 he captured Fiume with a force of patriotic Italians. The Italian army, enforcing the terms of the Versailles Treaty, eventually drove him out. D'Annunzio had provided the example of the political use of a nongovernmental military force. Removing him from Fiume made the parliamentary ministry seem unpatriotic.

Between 1919 and 1921 Italy was also wracked by social turmoil. Numerous industrial strikes occurred, and workers occupied factories. Peasants seized uncultivated land from large estates. Parliamentary and constitutional government seemed incapable of dealing with this unrest. The Socialist Party had captured a plurality of seats in the Chamber of Deputies in 1919. A new Catholic Popular Party had also done well. Both appealed to the working and agrarian classes. However, neither party would cooperate with the other, and parliamentary deadlock resulted.

Under these conditions, many Italians honestly—and still others conveniently—believed that a communist revolution might break out.

Initially, Mussolini was uncertain which way the political winds were blowing. He first supported the factory occupations and land seizures. Never one to be concerned with consistency, however, he soon reversed himself. He had discovered that many upper-class and middle-class Italians who were pressured by inflation and who feared property loss had no sympathy for the workers or the peasants. They wanted order rather than some vague social justice that might harm their own interests. Consequently, Mussolini and his Fascists took direct action in the face of the government inaction. They formed local squads that terrorized Socialist supporters. They attacked strikers and farm workers and protected strikebreakers. Conservative land and factory owners were grateful to the terrorists. The officers and institutions of the law simply ignored these crimes. By early 1922 the Fascists controlled the local government in many parts of northern Italy.

In 1921 Mussolini and thirty-four of his followers had been elected to the Chamber of Deputies. Their importance grew as the local Fascists gained more direct power. The Fascist movement now had hundreds of thousands of supporters. In October 1922 the Fascists, dressed in their characteristic black shirts, began a march on Rome. Intimidated, King Victor Emmanuel III (r. 1900–1946) refused to authorize using the army against the marchers. No other single decision so ensured a Fascist seizure of power. The cabinet resigned in protest. On October 29 the monarch telegraphed Mussolini in Milan and asked

◄●—[Read the Document

Benito Mussolini, "The Political and Social Doctrine of Fascism" at **MyHistoryLab.com**

Document

Mussolini Heaps Contempt on Political Liberalism

The political tactics of the Italian Fascists wholly disrregarded the liberal belief in the rule of law and the consent of the governed. In 1923 Mussolini explained why the Fascists so hated and repudiated these liberal principles. Note his emphasis on the idea of the twentieth century as a new historical epoch requiring a new kind of politics and his undisguised praise of force in politics.

■ *Who would be some nineteenth-century liberal political leaders included in Mussolini's attack? Why might Mussolini's audience have been receptive to these views? What events or developments within liberal states allowed Mussolini to portray liberalism as so corrupt and powerless?*

Liberalism is not the last word, nor does it represent the definitive formula on the subject of the art of government.... Liberalism is the product and the technique of the nineteenth century.... It does not follow that the Liberal scheme of government, good for the nineteenth century, for a century, that is, dominated by two such phenomena as the growth of capitalism and the strengthening of the sentiment of nationalism, should be adapted to the twentieth century, which announces itself already with characteristics sufficiently different from those that marked the preceding century....

I challenge Liberal gentlemen to tell if ever in history there has been a government that was based solely on popular consent and that renounced all use of force whatsoever. A government so constructed there has never been and never will be. Consent is an ever-changing thing like the shifting sand on the sea coast, it can never be permanent: It can never be complete.... If it be accepted as an axiom that any system of government whatever creates malcontents, how are you going to prevent this discontent from overflowing and constituting a menace to the stability of the State? You will prevent it by force. By the assembling of the greatest force possible. By the inexorable use of this force whenever it is necessary. Take away from any government whatsoever force—and by force is meant physical, armed force—and leave it only its immortal principles, and that government will be at the mercy of the first organized group that decides to overthrow it. Fascism now throws these lifeless theories out to rot.... The truth evident now to all who are not warped by [liberal] dogmatism is that men have tired of liberty. They have made an orgy of it. Liberty is today no longer the chaste and austere virgin for whom the generations of the first half of the last century fought and died. For the gallant, restless and bitter youth who face the dawn of a new history there are other words that exercise a far greater fascination, and those words are: order, hierarchy, discipline....

Know then, once and for all, that Fascism knows no idols and worships no fetishes. It has already stepped over, and if it be necessary it will turn tranquilly and step again over, the more or less putrescent corpse of the Goddess of Liberty.

Source: From Benito Mussolini, "Force and Consent" (1923), as trans. in Jonathan F. Scott and Alexander Baltzly, eds., *Readings in European History Since 1814* (New York: F. S. Crofts, 1931), pp. 680–682.

him to become prime minister. The next day Mussolini arrived in Rome by sleeping car and, as head of the government, greeted his followers when they entered the city. (See Document: "Mussolini Heaps Contempt on Political Liberalism.")

Technically, Mussolini had come into office by legal means. The monarch did have the power to appoint the prime minister. Mussolini, however, had no majority in the Chamber of Deputies. Behind the legal façade of his assumption of power lay the months of terrorist disruption and intimidation and the threat of the Fascists' October march itself.

The Fascists in Power

Mussolini had not really expected to be appointed prime minister. He moved cautiously to consolidate his power. He succeeded because of the impotence of his rivals, his own effective use of his office, his power over the masses, and his sheer ruthlessness. On November 23, 1922, the king and Parliament granted Mussolini dictatorial authority for one year to bring order to the lower levels of the government. Wherever possible, Mussolini appointed Fascists to office. Late in 1924, at Mussolini's behest, Parliament changed the election law. Previously parties had been represented in the Chamber of Deputies in proportion to the popular vote cast for them. According to the new election law, the party that gained the largest popular vote (with a minimum of at least 25 percent) received two-thirds of the seats in the chamber. Coalition government, with all its compromises and hesitations, would no longer be necessary. In the election of 1924 the Fascists won a great victory and complete control of the Chamber of Deputies. They used that majority to end legitimate parliamentary life. A series of laws passed in 1925 and 1926 permitted Mussolini, in effect, to rule by decree. In 1926 all other political parties were dissolved, and Italy was transformed into a single-party, dictatorial state.

The Italian dictator made one important domestic departure that brought him significant political dividends. Through the Lateran Accord of February 1929 the Roman Catholic Church and the Italian state made peace with each other. Ever since the armies of Italian unification had seized papal lands in the 1860s the church had been hostile to the state. The popes had remained virtual prisoners in the Vatican after 1870. The agreement of 1929 recognized the pope as the temporal ruler of Vatican City. The Italian government agreed to pay an indemnity to the papacy for confiscated land. The state also recognized Catholicism as the religion of the nation, exempted church property from taxes, and allowed church law to govern marriage. The Lateran Accord brought further respectability to Mussolini's authoritarian regime.

German Democracy and Dictatorship

The Weimar Republic

The German Weimar Republic was born from the defeat of the imperial army, the revolution of 1918 against the Hohenzollerns, and the hopes of German Liberals and Social Democrats. Its name derived from the city in which its constitution was written and promulgated in August 1919. While the constitution was being debated, the republic, headed by the Social Democrats, accepted the humiliating terms of the Versailles Treaty. Although its officials had signed only under the threat of an Allied invasion, the republic was nevertheless permanently associated with the national disgrace and the economic burdens of the treaty. Throughout the 1920s the government of the republic was required to fulfill the economic and military provisions imposed by the Paris settlement. It became all too easy for nationalists and military figures whose policies had brought on the tragedy and defeat of the war to blame the young republic and the Socialists for the results of the conflict. In Germany, more than in other countries, the desire to revise the treaty was closely related to a desire to change the mode of domestic government.

((•—[Hear the **Audio**
Nazis 1
at **MyHistoryLab.com**

The Weimar Constitution was a highly enlightened document. It guaranteed civil liberties and provided for direct election, by universal suffrage, of the **Reichstag** and the president. It also, however, contained certain crucial structural flaws that eventually allowed it to be overthrown. Seats in the Reichstag were allotted according to a complicated system of proportional representation. This made it relatively easy for small political parties to gain seats and resulted in shifting party combinations that led to considerable instability. Ministers were technically responsible to the Reichstag, but the president appointed and removed the chancellor, the head of the cabinet. Perhaps most important, Article 48 allowed the president, in an emergency, to rule by decree. The constitution thus permitted the possibility of presidential dictatorship.

The new government suffered major and minor humiliations as well as considerable economic instability. In March 1920 the right-wing Kapp armed insurrection erupted in Berlin. Led by a conservative civil servant and supported by army officers, the attempted coup failed, but only after government officials had fled the city and workers had carried out a general strike. In the same month, strikes took place in the Ruhr mining district. The government sent in troops. Such extremism from both the left and the right would haunt the republic for all its days. In May 1921 the Allies presented a reparations bill for 132 billion gold marks. The German Republican government accepted this preposterous demand only after new Allied threats of occupation. Throughout the early 1920s there were numerous assassinations or attempted assassinations of important Republican leaders. Violence was the hallmark of the first five years of the republic.

Invasion of the Ruhr and Inflation Inflation brought on the major crisis of this period. The financing of the war and continued postwar deficit spending generated an immense rise in prices. Consequently, the value of German currency fell. By early 1921 the German mark traded against the American dollar at a ratio of 64 to 1, compared with a ratio of 4.2 to 1 in 1914. The German financial community contended that the value of the currency could not be stabilized until the reparations issue had been solved. In the meantime, the printing presses kept pouring forth paper money, which was used to redeem government bonds as they fell due.

The French invasion of the Ruhr in January 1923, launched to secure the payment of reparations, and the German response of passive economic resistance produced cataclysmic inflation. The Weimar government paid subsidies to the Ruhr labor force, who had laid down their tools. Unemployment soon spread from the Ruhr to other parts of the country, creating a new drain on the treasury and also reducing tax revenues. By this point the printing presses had

Inflation in Germany. During the German inflation of 1923 currency literally was not worth the paper on which it was printed and people used it as fuel for kitchen stoves.

difficulty providing enough paper currency to keep up with the daily rise in prices. Money was literally not worth the paper it was printed on. Stores were unwilling to exchange goods for the worthless currency, and farmers withheld produce from the market.

The moral and social values of thrift and prudence were thoroughly undermined. Middle-class savings, pensions, and insurance policies were wiped out, as were investments in government bonds. Simultaneously, debts and mortgages could not be paid off. Speculators in land, real estate, and industry made great fortunes. Union contracts generally allowed workers to keep up with rising prices. Thus inflation was not a disaster for everyone. To the middle class and the lower middle class, however, the inflation was yet one more trauma coming hard on the heels of the military defeat and the peace treaty. Only when the social and economic upheaval of these months is grasped can one understand the later German desire for order and security at almost any cost.

Hitler's Early Career Late in 1923 Adolf Hitler (1889–1945) made his first significant appearance on the German political scene. The son of a minor Austrian customs official, he had gone to Vienna, where he painted postcards for income and later found work as a day laborer. In Vienna he encountered Mayor Karl Lueger's (1844–1910) Christian Socialist Party, which prospered on an ideology of anti-Semitism and from the social anxieties of the lower middle class. Hitler absorbed the rabid German nationalism

and extreme anti-Semitism that flourished in Vienna. He came to hate Marxism, which he associated with Jews. During World War I Hitler fought in the German army, was wounded, rose to the rank of corporal, and won the Iron Cross for bravery.

After the conflict, Hitler settled in Munich. There he became associated with a small nationalistic, anti-Semitic political party that in 1920 adopted the name of National Socialist German Workers Party, better known simply as the **Nazis**. In the same year the group began to parade under a red banner with a black swastika. It issued a platform, or program, of Twenty-Five Points. Among other things, this platform called for the repudiation of the Versailles Treaty, the unification of Austria and Germany, the exclusion of Jews from German citizenship, agrarian reform, the prohibition of land speculation, the confiscation of war profits, state administration of the giant cartels, and the replacement of department stores with small retail shops. Originally the Nazis had called for a broad program of nationalization of industry in an attempt to compete directly with the Marxist political parties for the worker's vote. As the tactic failed, the Nazis redefined the meaning of the word *socialist* in the party name, so that it suggested a nationalistic outlook. In 1922, Hitler said

> *Whoever is prepared to make the national cause his own to such an extent that he knows no higher ideal than the welfare of his nation; whoever has understood our great national anthem, Deutschland, Deutschland, über Alles ["Germany, Germany, over All"], to mean that nothing in the wide world surpasses in his eyes this Germany, people and land, land and people—that man is a Socialist.[2]*

This definition, of course, had nothing to do with traditional German socialism. The "socialism" that Hitler and the Nazis had in mind was not state ownership of the means of production but the subordination of all economic enterprise to the welfare of the nation. It often implied protection for small economic enterprises. Increasingly, the Nazis discovered that their party appealed to virtually any economic group that was at risk and under pressure. They often tailored their messages to the particular local problems these groups confronted in different parts of Germany. The Nazis also found considerable support among war veterans, who faced economic and social displacement in Weimar society. The ongoing Nazi demand for revision of the Versailles Treaty appealed to a broad spectrum of economic groups as well as the disaffected war veterans. (See Document, "Hitler Denounces the Versailles Treaty" on page 909)

---

[2]Alan Bullock, *Hitler: A Study in Tyranny*, rev. ed. (New York: Harper & Row, 1964), p. 76.

Document   Hitler Denounces the Versailles Treaty

Demands for revision of the Versailles Treaty of 1919 were voiced in many European nations during the 1920s, but such demands were especially fundamental to German politics and constituted a fundamental platform of the National Socialist Movement. Hitler and his followers made denunciation of the treaty their single most uncompromising declaration. In this speech of April 17, 1923, Hitler explained how the treaty had undermined the German nation.

■ *How might the French invasion of the Ruhr and the resulting inflation have made this speech particularly effective? To what extent was Hitler's condemnation of the control the Versailles Treaty imposed on Germany correct? How does Hitler contrast his young Nazi movement with the young Weimar Republic? Why does the one appear a strong and the other a weak supporter of German national goals?*

With the armistice begins the humiliation of Germany. If the Republic on the day of its foundation had appealed to the country: "Germans, stand together! Up and resist the foe! The Fatherland, the Republic expects of you that you fight to your last breath," then millions who are now the enemies of the Republic would be fanatical Republicans. Today they are the foes of the Republic not because it is a Republic but because this Republic was founded at the moment when Germany was humiliated, because it so discredited the new flag that men's eyes must turn regretfully towards the old flag.

It was no Treaty of Peace which was signed, but a betrayal of Peace.

The Treaty was signed which demanded from Germany that she should perform what was for ever impossible of performance. But that was not the worst; after all that was only a question of material values. This was not the end: Commissions of Control were formed! For the first time in the history of the modern world there were planted on a State agents of foreign Powers to act as Hangmen and German soldiers were set to serve the foreigner. And if one of these Commissions was "insulted," a company of the German army had to defile before the French flag. We no longer feel the humiliation of such an act; but the outside world says, "What a people of ours!"

So long as this Treaty stands there can be no resurrection of the German people: no social reform of any kind is possible! The Treaty was made in order to bring 20 million Germans to their deaths and to ruin the German nation. But those who made the Treaty cannot set it aside. At its foundation our Movement formulated three demands;

1. Setting aside of the Peace Treaty.
2. Unification of all Germans.
3. Land and soil to feed our nation.

Our Movement could formulate these demands, since it was not our Movement which caused the War, it has not made the Republic, it did not sign the Peace Treaty.

There is thus one thing which is the first task of this Movement: it desires to make the German once more National, that his Fatherland shall stand for him above everything else. It desires to teach our people to understand afresh the truth of the old saying: He who would not be a hammer must be an anvil. An anvil are we today, and that anvil will be beaten until out of the anvil we fashion once more a hammer, a German sword!

Source: From speech delivered in Munich, April 17, 1923, by Adolph Hitler, from *The Speeches of Adolf Hitler, April 1922–August 1939,* trans. by Norman H. Baynes, 1969, pp. 56–57.

Soon after the promulgation of the Twenty-Five Points, the storm troopers, or **SA** (*Sturm Abteilung*), were organized under the leadership of Captain Ernst Roehm (1887–1934). It was a paramilitary organization that initially provided its members with food and uniforms and, later in the decade, with wages. In the mid-1920s the SA adopted its famous brown-shirted uniform. The storm troopers were the chief Nazi instrument for terror and intimidation before the party gained control of the government. They were a law unto themselves. The organization constituted a means of preserving military discipline and values outside the small army permitted by the Paris settlement. The existence of such a private party army was a sign of the potential for violence in the Weimar Republic and the widespread contempt for the law and the institutions of the republic.

The social and economic turmoil following the French occupation of the Ruhr and the German inflation gave the fledgling party an opportunity for direct action against the Weimar Republic, which seemed incapable of providing military or economic security. By this time, because of his immense oratorical skills and organizational abilities, Hitler personally dominated the Nazi Party. On November 9, 1923, Hitler and a band of followers, accompanied by General Erich Ludendorff (1865–1937), attempted an unsuccessful putsch (i.e., attempt to overthrow the government) at a beer hall in Munich. When the local authorities crushed the rising, sixteen Nazis were killed. Hitler and Ludendorff were arrested and tried for treason. The general was acquitted. Hitler used the trial to make himself into a national figure. In his defense, he condemned the republic, the Versailles Treaty, the Jews, and the weakened condition of his adopted country. He was convicted and sentenced to five years in prison. He actually spent only a few months in jail before being paroled. During this time, he dictated **Mein Kampf** ("My Struggle"). Another result of the brief imprisonment was his decision to seize political power by legal methods.

●●—[Read the Document
Adolph Hitler, excerpt from Mein Kampf at **MyHistoryLab.com**

The Stresemann Years The officials of the republic were attempting to repair the damage from the inflation. Gustav Stresemann (1878–1929) was responsible primarily for reconstruction of the republic and for its achievement of a sense of self-confidence. Stresemann abandoned the policy of passive resistance in the Ruhr. The country simply could not afford it. Then, with the aid of banker Hjalmar Schacht (1877–1970), he introduced a new German currency. The rate of exchange was 1 trillion of the old German marks for one new Rentenmark. Stresemann also moved against challenges from both the left and the right. He supported the crushing of both Hitler's abortive putsch and smaller communist disturbances. In late November 1923, after four months as chancellor, he resigned to become foreign minister, a post he held until his death in 1929. In that office he continued to influence the affairs of the republic.

In 1924 the Weimar Republic and the Allies renegotiated the reparation payments. The Dawes Plan lowered the annual payments and allowed them to fluctuate according to the fortunes of the German economy. The last French troops left the Ruhr in 1925. The same year, Field Marshal Paul von Hindenburg (1847–1934), a military hero and a conservative monarchist, was elected president of the republic. He governed in strict accordance with the constitution, but his election suggested that German politics had become more conservative. Conservative Germans seemed reconciled to the republic. This conservatism was in line with the prosperity of the latter 1920s. Foreign capital flowed into Germany, and employment, which had been poor throughout most of the postwar years, improved smartly. Giant industrial combines spread. The prosperity helped to establish broader acceptance and appreciation of the republic.

In foreign affairs, Stresemann pursued a conciliatory course. He fulfilled the provisions of the Versailles Treaty even as he attempted to revise it by diplomacy. He was willing to accept the settlement in the West but was a determined, if sometimes secret, revisionist in the East. He aimed to recover German-speaking territories lost to Poland and Czechoslovakia and possibly to unite with Austria, chiefly by diplomatic means. The first step, however, was to achieve respectability and economic recovery. That goal required a policy of accommodation and "fulfillment," for the moment at least.

Locarno These developments gave rise to the Locarno Agreements of October 1925. The spirit of conciliation led foreign ministers Austen Chamberlain (1863–1937) for Britain and Aristide Briand (1862–1932) for France to accept Stresemann's proposal for a fresh start. France and Germany both accepted the western frontier established at Versailles as legitimate. Britain and Italy agreed to intervene against the aggressor if either side violated the frontier or if Germany sent troops into the demilitarized Rhineland. Significantly, no such agreement was made about Germany's eastern frontier, but the Germans made treaties of arbitration with Poland and Czechoslovakia, and France strengthened its ties with those countries. France supported German membership in the League of Nations and agreed to withdraw its occupation troops from the Rhineland in 1930, five years earlier than specified at Versailles.

Germany was pleased to have achieved respectability and a guarantee against another Ruhr occupation, as well as the possibility of revision in the east. Britain enjoyed playing a more even-handed role. Italy was glad to be recognized as a great power. The French were happy, too, because the Germans voluntarily accepted the permanence of their western frontier, which was also guaranteed by Britain and Italy, and France maintained its allies in the east.

The Locarno Agreements brought new hope to Europe. Germany's entry into the League of Nations was greeted with enthusiasm. Chamberlain, Briand, and Stresemann all received the Nobel Peace Prize in 1925 and 1926. The spirit of Locarno was carried even further when the leading European states, Japan, and the United States signed the Kellogg-Briand Pact in 1928, renouncing "war as an instrument of national policy." The joy and optimism were not justified. France had merely recognized its inability to coerce Germany without help. Britain had shown its unwillingness to uphold the settlement in the east. Austen Chamberlain

Chronology

Major Political Events of the 1920s and 1930s

1919 August	Constitution of the Weimar Republic promulgated
1920	Kapp Putsch in Berlin
1921 March	Kronstadt mutiny leads Lenin to initiate his New Economic Policy
1922 October	Fascist march on Rome leads to Mussolini's assumption of power
1923 January	France invades the Ruhr
November	Hitler's Beer Hall Putsch
1924	Death of Lenin
1925	Locarno Agreements
1928	Kellogg-Briand Pact; first Five-Year Plan launched in USSR
1929 January	Trotsky expelled from USSR
February	Lateran Accord between the Vatican and the Italian state
October	New York stock market crash
November	Bukharin expelled from his offices in the Soviet Union; Stalin's central position thus affirmed
1930 March	Bruning government begins in Germany
	Stalin calls for moderation in his policy of agricultural collectivization because of "dizziness from success"
September	Nazis capture 107 seats in German Reichstag
1931 August	National Government formed in Britain
1932 March 13	Hindenburg defeats Hitler for German presidency
May 31	Franz von Papen forms German Cabinet
July 31	German Reichstag election
November 6	German Reichstag election
December 2	Kurt von Schleicher forms German Cabinet
1933 January 30	Hitler made German chancellor
February 27	Reichstag fire
March 5	Reichstag election
March 23	Enabling Act consolidates Nazi power
1934 June 30	Bloody purge of the Nazi Party
August 2	Death of Hindenburg
December 1	Assassination of Kirov leads to the beginning of Stalin's purges
1936 May	Popular Front government in France
July–August	Most famous of public purge trials in Russia

declared that no British government ever would "risk the bones of a British grenadier" for the Polish corridor. Germany was not reconciled to the eastern settlement. It maintained clandestine military connections with the Soviet Union and planned to continue to press for revision.

In both France and Germany, moreover, the conciliatory politicians represented only a part of the nation. In Germany especially, most people continued to reject Versailles and regarded Locarno as only an extension of it. When the Dawes Plan ran out in 1929, it was replaced by the Young Plan, which lowered the reparation payments, put a term on how long they must be made, and removed Germany entirely from outside supervision and control. The intensity of the outcry in Germany against the continuation of any reparations showed how far the Germans were from accepting their situation. Despite these problems, war was by no means inevitable. Europe, aided by American loans, was returning to prosperity. German leaders like Stresemann would certainly have continued to press for change, but there is little reason to think that they would have resorted to force, much less to a general war. Continued prosperity and diplomatic success might have won the loyalty of the German people for the Weimar Republic and moderate revisionism, but the Great Depression of the 1930s brought new forces to power.

Depression and Political Deadlock

The outflow of foreign, and especially American, capital from Germany that began in 1928 undermined the economic prosperity of the Weimar Republic. The resulting economic crisis brought parliamentary government to a halt. In 1928 a coalition of center parties and the Social Democrats governed. All went reasonably well until the Depression struck. Then the coalition partners differed sharply on economic policy. The Social Democrats refused to reduce social and unemployment insurance. The more conservative parties, remembering the inflation of 1923, insisted on a balanced budget. The coalition dissolved in March 1930. To resolve the parliamentary deadlock in the Reichstag, President von Hindenburg appointed Heinrich Brüning (1885–1970) as chancellor. Lacking a majority in the Reichstag, the new chancellor governed through emergency presidential decrees, as authorized by Article 48 of the constitution. The party divisions in the Reichstag prevented the overriding of the decrees. The Weimar Republic was transformed into a presidential dictatorship.

German unemployment rose from 2,258,000 in March 1930 to over 6,000,000 in March 1932. There had been persistent unemployment during the 1920s, but nothing of such magnitude or duration. The economic downturn and the parliamentary deadlock worked to the advantage of the more extreme political parties. In the election of 1928 the Nazis had won only 12 seats in the Reichstag, and the communists had won 54 seats. Two years later, after the election of 1930, the Nazis held 107 seats and the communists 77.

The power of the Nazis in the streets was also on the rise. The unemployment fed thousands of men into the storm troopers, which had 100,000 members in 1930 and almost 1 million in 1933. The SA freely and viciously attacked communists and Social Democrats. For the Nazis, politics meant the capture of power through terror and intimidation as well as through elections. Decency and civility in political life vanished. Nazi rallies resembled secular religious revivals. The Nazis paraded through the streets and the countryside. They gained powerful supporters and sympathizers in the business, military, and newspaper communities. Some intellectuals were also sympathetic. The Nazis transformed this discipline and enthusiasm born of economic despair and nationalistic frustration into impressive electoral results.

Hitler Comes to Power

For two years Brüning continued to govern through the confidence of Hindenburg. The economy did not improve, and the political situation deteriorated. In 1932 the 83-year-old president stood for reelection. Hitler ran against him and forced a runoff. The Nazi leader garnered 30.1 percent of the vote in the first election and 36.8 percent in the second. Although Hindenburg was returned to office, the vote convinced him that Brüning had lost the confidence of conservative German voters. In May 1932 he dismissed Brüning and appointed Franz von Papen (1878–1969) in his place. The new chancellor was one of a small group of extremely conservative advisers on whom the aged Hindenburg had become increasingly dependent. Others included the president's son and several military figures. With the continued paralysis in the Reichstag, their influence over the president amounted to control of the government. Consequently, the crucial decisions of the next several months were made by only a handful of people.

Papen and the circle around the president wanted to draw the Nazis into cooperation with them without giving Hitler effective power. The government needed the popular support on the right that only the Nazis seemed able to generate. The Hindenburg circle decided to convince Hitler that the Nazis could not come to power on their own. Papen removed the ban on Nazi meetings that Brüning had imposed and then called a Reichstag election for July 1932. The Nazis won 230 seats and polled 37.2 percent of the vote. Hitler would only enter the Cabinet if he were made chancellor. Hindenburg refused. Another election was called in November, partly to wear down the Nazis' financial resources. The Nazis gained only 196 seats, and their percentage of the popular vote dipped to 33.1 percent. The advisers around Hindenburg still refused to appoint Hitler to office.

In early December 1932 Papen resigned, and General Kurt von Schleicher (1882–1934) became chancellor. People were now afraid of civil war between the extreme left and the far right. Schleicher decided to try and fashion a broad-based coalition of conservative groups and trade unionists. The prospect of such a coalition, including groups from the political left, frightened the Hindenburg circle even more than the prospect of Hitler. They did not trust Schleicher's motives, which have never been clear. Consequently, they persuaded Hindenburg to appoint Hitler chancellor. To control him and to see that he did little mischief, Papen was named vice chancellor, and other traditional conservatives were appointed to the Cabinet. On January 30, 1933, Adolf Hitler became the chancellor of Germany.

((•— Hear the Audio
Nazis 2
at **MyHistoryLab.com**

Hitler had come into office by legal means. All the proper forms and procedures had been observed. This was important, for it permitted the civil service, the courts, and

Hitler. Hitler's mastery of the techniques of mass politics and propaganda—including huge staged rallies like this one in 1938—was an important factor in his rise to power.

the other agencies of the government to support him in good conscience. He had forged a rigidly disciplined party structure and had mastered the techniques of mass politics and propaganda. He understood how to touch the raw social and political nerves of the electorate. His support appears to have come from across the social spectrum. Pockets of resistance appeared among Roman Catholic voters in the country and small towns. Otherwise, support for Hitler was particularly strong among farmers, war veterans, and the young, who had especially suffered from the insecurity of the 1920s and the Depression of the early 1930s. Hitler promised them security against communists and Socialists, effective government in place of the petty politics of the other parties, and an uncompromising nationalist vision of a strong, restored Germany.

Much blame was once assigned to German big business for the rise of Hitler. However, there is little evidence that business contributions made any crucial difference to the Nazis' success or failure. Hitler's supporters were frequently suspicious of business and giant capitalism. They wanted a simpler world, one in which small property would be safe from both socialism and large-scale capitalist consolidation. These people looked to Hitler and the Nazis rather than to the Social Democrats because the Social Democrats, though concerned with social issues, never appeared sufficiently nationalistic. The Nazis won out over other conservative nationalistic parties because, unlike those conservatives, the Nazis did address the problem of social insecurities.

Hitler's Consolidation of Power

Once in office, Hitler moved with almost lightning speed to consolidate his control. This process had three facets: the capture of full legal authority, the crushing of alternative political groups, and the purging of rivals within the Nazi Party itself. On February 27, 1933, a mentally ill Dutch communist set fire to the Reichstag building in Berlin. The Nazis quickly turned the incident to their own advantage by claiming that the fire proved the existence of an immediate communist threat against the government. To the public, it seemed plausible that the communists might attempt some action against the state now that the Nazis were in power. Under Article 48, Hitler issued the Emergency Decree suspending civil liberties and proceeded to arrest communists or alleged communists. This decree was not revoked as long as Hitler ruled Germany.

In early March another Reichstag election took place. The Nazis still received only 43.9 percent of the vote. However, the arrest of the newly elected communist deputies and the political fear aroused by the fire meant that Hitler could control the Reichstag. On March 23, 1933, the

Reichstag passed an Enabling Act that permitted Hitler to rule by decree. Thereafter, there were no legal limits on his exercise of power. The Weimar Constitution was never formally repealed or amended. It had simply been supplanted by the February Emergency Decree and the March Enabling Act.

Perhaps better than anyone else, Hitler understood that he and his party had not inevitably come to power. His potential opponents had stood divided between 1929 and 1933. He intended to prevent them from regrouping. In a series of complex moves, Hitler outlawed or undermined various German institutions that might have served as rallying points for opposition. In early May 1933 the offices, banks, and newspapers of the free-trade unions were seized, and their leaders arrested. The Nazi Party itself, rather than any government agency, undertook this action. In late June and early July, the other German political parties were outlawed. By July 14, 1933, the National Socialists were the only legal party in Germany. During the same months the Nazis had taken control of the governments of the individual federal states in Germany. By the close of 1933 all major institutions of potential opposition had been eliminated.

The final element in Hitler's personal consolidation of power involved the Nazi Party itself. By late 1933 the SA, or storm troopers, consisted of approximately 1 million active members and a larger number of reserves. The commander of this party army was Ernst Roehm, a possible rival to Hitler himself. The German army officer corps, on whom Hitler depended to rebuild the national army, was jealous of the SA leadership. Consequently, to protect his own position and to shore up support with the regular army, on June 30, 1934, Hitler ordered the murder of key SA officers, including Roehm. Others killed between June 30 and July 2 included the former chancellor Kurt von Schleicher and his wife. The exact number of purged victims is unknown, but it has been estimated to have exceeded 100. The German army, which was the only institution in the nation that might have prevented the murders, did nothing. A month later, on August 2, 1934, President Hindenburg died. Thereafter, the offices of chancellor and president were combined. Hitler was now the **Führer**, or sole ruler of Germany and of the Nazi Party.

The Police State

As Hitler consolidated his power, he oversaw the organization of a police state. The chief vehicle of police surveillance was the **SS** (*Schutzstaffel*), or security units, commanded by Heinrich Himmler (1900–1945). This group had originated in the mid-1920s as a bodyguard for Hitler and had become a more elite paramilitary organization than the larger SA. In 1933 the SS had approximately 52,000 members. It was the instrument that carried out the blood purges of the party in 1934. By 1936 Himmler had become head of all police matters in Germany.

Anti-Jewish Policies. Soon after seizing power, the Nazi government began harassing German Jewish businesses. Non-Jewish German citizens were urged not to buy merchandise from shops owned by Jews.

The police character of the Nazi regime was all-pervasive, but the people who most consistently experienced its terror were the German Jews. Anti-Semitism had been a key plank of the Nazi program—anti-Semitism based on biological racial theories stemming from late nineteenth-century thought rather than from religious discrimination. Before World War II the Nazi attack on the Jews went through three stages of increasing intensity. In 1933, shortly after assuming power, the Nazis excluded Jews from the civil service. For a time they also attempted to enforce boycotts of Jewish shops and businesses. The boycotts won relatively little public support. In 1935 the Nuremberg Laws robbed German Jews of their citizenship. All persons with at least one Jewish grandparent were defined as Jews. The professions and the major occupations were closed to Jews. Marriage and sexual intercourse between Jews and non-Jews were prohibited. Legal exclusion and humiliation of the Jews became the order of the day. (See Document, "The Nazis Pass Their Racial Legislation." on page 915)

Document

The Nazis Pass Their Racial Legislation

Anti-Semitism was a fundamental tenet of the Nazi Party and became a major policy of the Nazi government. This comprehensive legislation of September 15, 1935, carried anti-Semitism into all areas of public life and into some of the most personal areas of private life as well. It was characteristically entitled the Law for the Protection of German Blood and Honor. Hardly any aspect of Nazi thought and action shocked the non-German world as much as this policy toward the Jews.

■ *How would this legislation have affected the normal daily interaction between Jews and non-Jews in Germany? Why are there specific prohibitions against mixed marriages and sexual relations between Jews and non-Jews? How does this legislation separate German Jews from the symbols of German national life?*

Imbued with the knowledge that the purity of German blood is the necessary prerequisite for the existence of the German nation, and inspired by an inflexible will to maintain the existence of the German nation for all future times, the Reichstag has unanimously adopted the following law, which is now enacted:

Article I: (1) Any marriages between Jews and citizens of German or kindred blood are herewith forbidden. Marriages entered into despite this law are invalid, even if they are arranged abroad as a means of circumventing this law.

(2) Annulment proceedings for marriages may be initiated only by the Public Prosecutor.

Article II: Extramarital relations between Jews and citizens of German or kindred blood are herewith forbidden.

Article III: Jews are forbidden to employ as servants to their households female subjects of German or kindred blood who are under the age of forty-five years.

Article IV: (1) Jews are prohibited from displaying the Reich and national flag and from showing the national colors.

(2) However, they may display the Jewish colors. The exercise of this right is under state protection.

Article V: (1) Anyone who acts contrary to the prohibition noted in Article I renders himself liable to penal servitude.

(2) The man who acts contrary to the prohibition of Article II will be punished by sentence to either a jail or penitentiary.

(3) Anyone who acts contrary to the provisions of Articles III or IV will be punished with a jail sentence up to a year and with a fine, or with one of these penalties.

Article VI: The Reich Minister of Interior, in conjunction with the Deputy to the Führer and the Reich Minister of Justice, will issue the required legal and administrative decrees for the implementation and amplification of this law.

Article VII: This law shall go into effect on the day following its promulgation, with the exception of Article III, which shall go into effect on January 1, 1936.

Source: Snyder, Louis, L. *Documents of German History.* Copyright © 1957 Rutgers, the State University. Reprinted by permission of Rutgers University Press.

The persecution of the Jews increased again in 1938. Business careers were forbidden. In November 1938, under orders from the Nazi Party, thousands of Jewish stores and synagogues were burned or otherwise destroyed. The Jewish community itself had to pay for the damage that occurred on this **Kristallnacht** because the government confiscated the insurance money. In all manner of other ways, large and petty, the German Jews were harassed. Through this persecution the Nazis were able to inculcate the rest of the population with the concept of a master race of pure German "Aryans" and also displayed their own contempt for civil liberties.

It was not until 1942, however, after the war had broken out, that Hitler decided to destroy all the Jews in Europe in what became known as the Final Solution. It is thought that over 6 million Jews, mostly from eastern European nations, died as a result of that staggering decision, unprecedented in its scope and implementation.

Women in Nazi Germany

The Nazis believed in separate social spheres for men and women. Men belonged in the world of action, women in the home, and the two spheres should not mix. Women who

Overview

Characteristics Shared by Fascist, Nazi, and Soviet Communist Regimes of the 1920s and 1930s

1. Well-organized, highly disciplined political parties
2. Intense nationalism (often denied while realized in practice in the Soviet Union)
3. Programs that promised to cure social, political, and economic malaise
4. A monopoly over mass communications and propaganda
5. Highly effective instruments of terror and police power
6. Real or imagined national, class, or racial enemies who could be demonized to whip up mass support
7. Command over modern technology and its capacity for immense destruction

sought to liberate themselves and to adopt roles traditionally followed by men in public life were considered to be exhibiting symptoms of cultural decline. Respect for women, the Nazis believed, should arise from their function as wives and mothers.

These attitudes stood in direct conflict with many of the social changes that German women, like women elsewhere in Europe, had experienced during the first three decades of the twentieth century. German women had become much more active and assertive. More of them worked in factories or were independently employed, and they had begun to enter the professions. Under the Weimar constitution, they voted. Throughout the Weimar period there was also a lively discussion of women's emancipation. For the Nazis these developments were signs of cultural weakness. They generally urged a much more traditional role for women in their new society. Nazi writers portrayed women as wives and mothers first and foremost.

The Nazis' point of view was supported by women of a generally conservative outlook and women who were following traditional roles as housewives, confirming the choices these women had made about how to lead their lives. In a period of high unemployment, the Nazi attitude also appealed to many men because it discouraged women from competing with them in the workplace. Such competition had begun during World War I, and many Nazis considered it symptomatic of the social confusion that had followed the German defeat.

The Nazi discussion of the role of women was also deeply rooted in Nazi racism. Nazi writers argued that the superiority of the pure German race depended on the purity of the blood of each and every individual. It was the special task of German mothers to preserve racial purity. Hitler particularly championed this view of women. They were to breed strong sons and daughters for the German nation. Nazi journalists often compared the role of women in childbirth to that of men in battle. Each served the state in particular social and gender roles. In both cases, the good of the nation was superior to that of the individual.

Most Nazis who discussed the role of women relegated them to the home. They also generally attacked feminist outlooks. Women were encouraged to bear many children because the Nazis believed the declining German birthrate was the result of emancipated women who had spurned their natural and proper roles as mothers. The Nazis established special medals for women who bore large families. They also sponsored schools that taught women how to care for and rear children (see photograph on page 917).

The Nazis also saw women as educators of the young and thus the special protectors of German cultural values. Through cooking, dress, music, and stories, mothers were to instill a love for the nation. As consumers for the home, women were to aid German-owned shops, to buy German-produced goods, and to avoid Jewish merchants.

The Nazis realized that in the midst of the Depression many women would need to work, but the party urged them to pursue employment that the Nazis considered natural to their character. These tasks included agriculture, teaching, nursing, social work, and domestic service. Nonetheless, despite some variation in the early and mid-1930s, the percentage of women employed in Germany changed little from the Weimar to the Hitler years: It was 37 percent in 1928 and the same again in 1939. Thereafter, because of the war effort, many more women were recruited into the German workforce.

The Great Depression and the New Deal in the United States

The United States emerged from World War I as a major world power. However, it retreated from that role when the Senate refused to ratify the Versailles Treaty and subsequently failed to join the League of Nations. In 1920 Warren Harding (1865–1923) became president and urged a return to what he termed "normalcy," which meant minimal

A Closer Look

The Nazi Party Rally

The Nazi rallies served as a centerpiece for the party's effort to generate mass support and to embody its broad appeal. These rallies were also often associated with raising money to support the party. The Nazis also intended their rallies to generate fervent nationalistic group solidarity demonstrating that whatever other divisions might exist in the nation, loyalty to the Nazi Party and to the nation would be more important than any other group loyalty.

The Nazi Party had used what later became the ever-present swastika (or hooked cross) symbol since 1920. Hitler himself claimed to have chosen the symbol, which he and other Nazis associated with an allegedly racially pure Aryan past. In fact, many cultures had used the swastika as a symbol, which dated to ancient times in Asia. Rediscovery of the symbol during nineteenth-century archaeological excavations led to its revived use by various groups prior to the Nazis, often, though not excusively, in relation to ideas of racial purity. By the 1920s it had become almost exclusively associated with the Nazis in the public mind and has remained so to the present. The Nazis adopted the swastika as the German national flag in 1935.

It should be noted that young women were enthusiastic supporters among the crowd at this 1938 Nazi rally, extending the Nazi salute. The image in the photo illustrates the gender divisions Nazi ideology fostered. Men were portrayed as defenders of the homeland, whereas women were to pursue traditional domestic roles and to bear children for the nation.

Questions

1. How might the holding of rallies serve to give the sense that loyalty to the Nazi Party and the nation overrode all other social and political loyalties?

2. How could the experience of attending Nazi rallies or viewing them through movies or news reels convey to the German and non-German public throughout Europe a sense of inevitable Nazi success and widespread support?

3. What events or experiences at Nazi rallies might not have been captured in photographs? How could photographs be used to shape the news in the 1930s and later?

myhistorylab   To examine this image in an interactive fashion, please go to **www.myhistorylab.com**

involvement abroad and conservative economic policies at home. Business interests clearly remained in the ascendant, with the federal government taking a relatively inactive role in national economic life. Indeed, government inactivity was the virtual creed of Harding's successor, President Calvin Coolidge (1872–1933).

The first seven or eight years of the decade witnessed remarkable American prosperity. New electrical appliances such as the radio, phonograph, washing machine, and vacuum cleaner appeared on the market. Large-scale advertising campaigns attempted to persuade consumers to purchase such items. Real wages rose for many groups of workers. Industry grew at a robust rate. Automobile manufacturers assumed a major role in national economic life. Henry Ford's (1863–1947) Model T exemplified the determination of the automobile industry to produce for a mass market. Increasing numbers of factories became mechanized. Engineers and efficiency experts were the heroes of the business world. For most of the 1920s the New York stock market boomed. All of this remarkable activity stood in marked contrast to the various economic dislocations occurring in Europe.

The material prosperity appeared, however, in a sharply divided society. Segregation remained a basic fact of life for black Americans throughout the South and to a lesser degree in other areas of the country. The Ku Klux Klan, which sought to terrorize blacks, Roman Catholics, and Jews, en-

joyed a resurgence. Lynchings of African Americans, both men and women, continued, especially in the South. The Prohibition Amendment of 1919 (repealed in 1933) forbade the manufacture and transport of alcoholic beverages. In the wake of this divisive national policy, major criminal operations arose to supply liquor and to disrupt the stability of civic life. Many immigrants came from Mexico and Puerto Rico. They settled in cities where their labor was desired, but where they were often not welcomed or assimilated. Finally, the wealth of the nation was overwhelmingly concentrated in relatively few hands.

Economic Collapse

In March 1929 Herbert Hoover became president, the third Republican in as many elections. On October 29, 1929, the New York stock market crashed. The other financial markets also went into a tailspin. During the next year the stock market continued to fall. The banks that had loaned people money with which to speculate in the market suffered great losses.

The financial collapse of 1929 triggered the Great Depression in America, although there were other underlying domestic causes. During the 1920s manufacturing firms had not made sufficient capital investment. The disproportionate amount of profits going to about 5 percent of the U.S. population had by the end of the decade begun to

Women members of the Ku Klux Klan in New Castle, Indiana, August 1, 1923. The revived Klan was a powerful presence in scores of American communities during the early 1920s, especially among native-born white Protestants, who feared cultural and political change. In addition to preaching "100 percent Americanism," local Klan chapters also served a social function for members and their families.

Unemployed Workers. The Great Depression brought unprecedented unemployment to the United States. In 1930 unemployed workers were photographed standing outside the Municipal Lodging House in New York City.

undermine the purchasing power of other consumers. Furthermore, agriculture had been in trouble for years. Finally, the economic difficulties in Europe and Latin America, which predated those in the United States, meant foreigners were less able to purchase goods produced in the United States.

The most pervasive problem of the Great Depression was the spread of unemployment. Joblessness hit poor unskilled workers most rapidly but then worked its way up the job ladder to touch factory and white-collar workers. As unemployment spread, small retail businesses suffered. In the major American manufacturing cities, hundreds of thousands of workers could not find jobs. The price of corn fell so low in some areas that it was not profitable to harvest the crop. By the early 1930s banks across the country began to fail, and people lost their savings.

●●●─Read the Document
The Great Depression:
An Oral Account (1932)
at **MyHistoryLab.com**

The federal government was not really equipped to address the emergency. There was no tradition of federal action to alleviate economic distress. President Hoover organized economic conferences in Washington and encouraged the Federal Reserve to make borrowing easier. He supported the ill-advised Hawley-Smoot Tariff Act of 1930, with which Congress had hoped to protect American industry by erecting a high tariff barrier. But fundamentally Hoover believed relief was a matter for local government and voluntary organizations. In many areas the local relief agencies had actually run out of money by 1931. By 1932 U. S. unemployment had risen to over 23 percent and thousands of banks had failed. The gross national product had fallen by over 15 percent since 1929, with international trade declining by approximately two-thirds during the same period.

New Role for Government

The election of 1932 was one of the most crucial in American history. Franklin Delano Roosevelt (1882–1945), in accepting the Democratic nomination, pledged his party to a "new deal for the American people." He overwhelmingly defeated Hoover and quickly set about redirecting federal policy to fight the Depression.

Roosevelt had been born into a moderately wealthy New York family. A distant cousin of Theodore Roosevelt (1858–1919), he had been educated at Harvard College and Columbia Law School. After serving in World War I as assistant secretary of the navy, in 1920 he ran as the Democratic vice presidential candidate. The next year, however, he was struck with polio and his legs became paralyzed. With extraordinary determination he went on to be elected governor of New York in 1928. As the newly elected president he attempted to convey to the nation the same kind of optimistic spirit that had informed his own personal struggle of the 1920s.

Roosevelt's first goal was to give the nation a sense that the federal government was acting to meet the economic challenge. The first 100 days of his administration became legendary. Coming into office at the height of the crisis in the banking system, he immediately closed all the banks and permitted only sound institutions to reopen. Congress convened in a special session and rapidly passed a new banking act. Shortly thereafter, Congress enacted the Agricultural Adjustment Act and the Farm Credit Act to aid the farm sector of the economy. To provide jobs, Roosevelt's administration sponsored the Civilian Conservation Corps. The Federal Emergency Relief Act provided funding for state and local relief agencies. To restore confidence, Roosevelt began making speeches, known as his "fireside chats," to the American people.

Roosevelt's most ambitious program was the National Industrial Recovery Act (NIRA), which established the National Recovery Administration (NRA). This agency attempted to foster codes written by various industries to regulate wages and prices. It was hoped that competition might be thus regulated to protect jobs and assure production.

The NIRA and other New Deal legislation, such as the Wagner Act of 1935, which established the National Labor Relations Board and the Fair Labor Standards Act of 1938, provided a larger role in the American economy for organized labor. It became easier for unions to organize. Union membership

The Works Progress Administration was one of the chief New Deal agencies designed to create public works projects that would generate employment, such as this group of men repairing a street.

grew rapidly and steadily. American unionism took on a new character during these years. Previously, most unions had organized by craft and had been affiliated with the American Federation of Labor. The major union gains of the 1930s, however, occurred through the organization of whole industries composed of workers in various crafts in a single union. The most important of these organizations were the United Mine Workers and United Automobile Workers. These new unions organized themselves into the Congress of Industrial Organizations. The CIO and the AFL were rivals until they merged in the 1950s. These new strong industrial labor organizations introduced a powerful new force to the American economic scene.

In 1935 the U.S. Supreme Court declared the NRA unconstitutional. Thereafter, Roosevelt de-emphasized centralized economic planning. There were no fewer federal agencies—indeed, their number increased—but they operated in general independence from each other.

Through New Deal legislation, the federal government was far more active in the economy than it had been in the past. The government itself attempted to provide relief for the unemployed in the industrial sector. The major institution of the relief effort was the **Works Progress Administration**. Created in 1935, the WPA began a massive program of large public works.

The programs of the New Deal years also involved the federal government directly in economic development rather than turning such development over to private enterprise. Through the Tennessee Valley Authority (TVA), the government became directly involved in the economy of the four states of the Tennessee River Valley. The TVA built dams and then produced and sold hydroelectricity. Never had the government undertaken such an extensive economic role. Another major new function for the government was providing security for the elderly, through the establishment of the Social Security Administration in 1935.

Hence, in one area of American life after another, it was decided that individual voluntary effort could not provide sufficient personal economic security and that the government must act to do so. These actions established a mixed economy in the United States—that is, one in which the federal government would play an ongoing active role alongside the private sector.

The New Deal changed much of American life. Yet despite its programs and new initiatives, it did not solve the unemployment problem. Indeed, in the late 1930s the economy began to falter again. It was the entry of the nation into World War II that brought the U.S. economy to full employment.

There were limitations to the liberalism of the New Deal, the most significant of which related to race. Southern Democratic senators provided Roosevelt with the necessary votes to pass his economic legislation. These same senators, who often chaired important Senate committees, opposed the passage of federal legislation to prohibit lynchings of which the overwhelming majority of victims since the 1870s had been African Americans. Roosevelt needed those southern senatorial votes and did not support anti-lynching legislation.

Despite such shortcomings, the New Deal did preserve American democracy and capitalism. The experience of the United States under the New Deal stood in marked contrast to the economic and political experiments taking place in Europe. Many businesspeople found Roosevelt far too liberal and his policies too activist. Nonetheless, the New Deal fundamentally preserved capitalism in a democratic setting, where, in contrast to Europe, there was a broad spectrum of political debate—much of it highly critical of the administration. The United States had demonstrated that a nation with a vast industrial economy could confront its gravest economic crisis and still preserve democracy.

Summary

Postwar Problems. The Versailles settlement bred political discontent and resentment throughout Europe among both victors and the defeated. In the 1920s there were endless wrangles over reparations between Germany and the Allied powers. After World War I, Europe never recovered its prewar prosperity or stability. The onset of the Great Depression in 1929 caused severe problems in both Europe and the United States and led to the Nazi seizure of power in Germany and FDR's New Deal in the United States.

The Soviet Union. The Bolsheviks had expected communist revolutions to break out across Europe. When that did not happen, they were forced to consolidate their regime within Russia. Lenin's New Economic Policy gave the state control over heavy industry, transportation, and international commerce but allowed for small-scale private enterprise and peasant farms. Stalin abandoned this policy to push for rapid industrialization. He abolished private enterprise, collectivized agriculture, and eliminated his opponents in a series of purges in which millions were imprisoned or killed. Despite the violence and oppression, Marxist parties around the world were subservient to the Soviet Union as the world's only communist state and the enemy of fascism.

Fascist Italy. Benito Mussolini came to power in Italy in 1922. Many Italians were dissatisfied with the terms of the Versailles Treaty and frightened by the social unrest that followed World War I. Mussolini promised order and a strong state. Although he achieved power by legal means, he soon transformed Italy into a single-party dictatorship. In 1929 he came to terms with the Catholic Church by negotiating the Lateran Accord, which recognized the pope as the independent ruler of Vatican City.

Nazi Germany. The postwar Weimar Republic in Germany was buffeted by social, political, and financial instability. Many Germans refused to accept Germany's defeat in World War I or the terms of the Versailles Treaty. Rampant inflation destroyed the savings of the middle class. The Great Depression brought financial collapse and massive unemployment. Many Germans looked to Adolf Hitler and the Nazi Party for solutions. Once Hitler came to power in 1933, he quickly established a one-party dictatorship based on police terror, propaganda, racial anti-Semitism, and the cult of Hitler as supreme leader. The Jews, in particular, were persecuted. Hitler also formed an alliance with the German army and began a program of rapid rearmament.

The United States. The United States emerged from World War I as a world power but retreated into isolation during the 1920s. The prosperity of the 1920s ended in the Great Depression. Franklin Delano Roosevelt's New Deal greatly expanded the power of the federal government in social and economic affairs and preserved capitalism in a democratic setting.

Review Questions

1. Explain the causes of the Great Depression. Why was it more severe, and why did it last longer, than previous economic downturns? Could it have been avoided?

2. How did Stalin achieve supreme power in the Soviet Union? Why did he decide that Russia had to industrialize rapidly? Why did this decision require the collectivization of agriculture? Was the policy a success? How did it affect the Russian people? What were the causes of the great purges?

3. Why was Italy dissatisfied and unstable after World War I? How did Mussolini achieve power? What were the characteristics of the fascist state?

4. Why did the Weimar Republic collapse in Germany? Discuss Hitler's rise to power. Which groups in Germany supported Hitler, and why were they pro-Nazi? How did he consolidate his power?

5. Compare the authoritarian regimes in the Soviet Union, Italy, and Germany. What characteristics did they have in common? What role did terror play in each?

6. Why did the United States economy collapse in 1929? What policies did Roosevelt use to combat the Depression? How did his policies affect the role of the federal government in national life?

Note: To learn more about the topics in this chapter, please turn to the Suggested Readings at the end of the book. For additional sources related to this chapter please see MyHistoryLab.com.

Key Terms

collectivization (p. 901)

Duce (p. 905)

fascism (p. 904)

Führer (p. 914)

Great Depression (p. 896)

Great Purges (p. 903)

Kristallnacht (p. 915)

Mein Kampf (p. 910)

Nazis (p. 908)

New Economic Policy (NEP) (p. 899)

Popular Front (p. 898)

Reichstag (p. 907)

SA (p. 909)

SS (p. 914)

War Communism (p. 899)

Weimar Republic (p. 897)

Works Progress Administration (p. 920)

PEARSON
myhistorylab Connections

Reinforce what you learned in this chapter by studying the many documents, images, maps, review tools, and videos available at **www.myhistorylab.com**.

Read and Review

✓●—[Study and Review   Chapter 29

•••—[Read the Document   *Stalin Demands Rapid Industrialization of the USSR (1931), p. 901*
Irina Ivanovna Kniazeva, A Life in a Peasant Village (USSR) 1917–1930s, p. 901
John Scott, excerpt from Behind the Urals: An American Worker in Russia's City of Steel, p. 903
Filippo Tommaso Marinetti, "Futuristic Manifesto", p. 904
Benito Mussolini, "The Political and Social Doctrine of Fascism", p. 905
Adolph Hitler, excerpt from Mein Kampf, p. 910
The Great Depression: An Oral Account (1932), p. 919

((●—[Hear the Audio   *Depression, p. 897*
Communism, p. 900
Fascism, p. 904
Nazis 1, p. 907
Nazis 2, p. 912

✓●—[Study and Review   *Lenin, 1920, vs. Stalin, 1931, p. 900*

Research and Explore

●—[View the Image   *Bread Line During the "Great Depression"*

●—[View the Image   *Works Project Administration (WPA)*

((●—[Hear the Audio

Hear the audio file for Chapter 29 at
www.myhistorylab.com.

30 | World War II

- Again the Road to War (1933–1939)
- World War II (1939–1945)
- The Domestic Fronts
- Preparations for Peace

The more idealistic survivors of the first World War, especially in the United States and Great Britain, thought of it as "the war to end all wars" and "a war to make the world safe for democracy." Only thus could they justify the awful slaughter, expense, and upheaval. How appalled they would have been had they known that only twenty years after the peace treaties a second great war would break out that would be more truly global than the first. In this war the democracies would be fighting for their lives against militaristic, nationalistic, authoritarian, and totalitarian states in Europe and Asia. Great Britain and the United States would be allied with the communist Soviet Union. The defeat of the militarists and dictators would not bring the longed-for peace, but rather a Cold War in which the European states became second-class powers, subordinate to the two new great powers, partially or fully non-European: the Soviet Union and the United States. ■

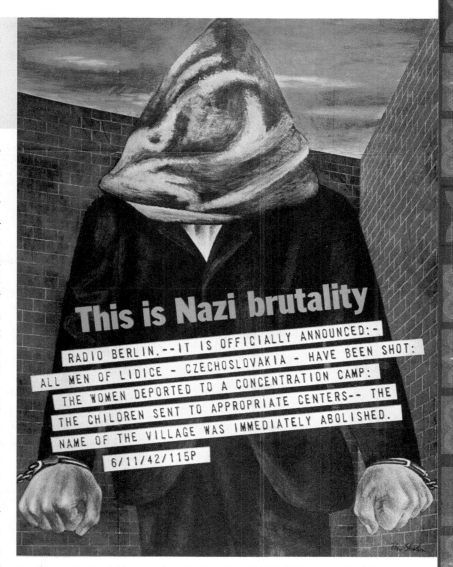

Nazi Terror. In this vivid poster, the artist Ben Shahn (1898–1969) memorialized the destruction of Lidice. The Czechoslovakian town was obliterated by the Nazis on June 11, 1942, in vengeance for the Czechs' resistance against their Nazi rulers.

World War II

World War II

The second great war of the twentieth century (1939–1945) grew out of the unsatisfactory resolution of the first. In retrospect, the two wars appear to some people to be one continuous conflict—a kind of twentieth-century Thirty Years' War—with the two main periods of fighting separated by an uneasy truce. To others, that point of view distorts the situation by implying that the second war was the inevitable result of the first and its inadequate peace treaties.

The latter opinion seems to be the sounder one. Whatever the flaws of the treaties of Paris, the world suffered an even more terrible war than the first as a result of failures of judgment and will on the part of the victorious democratic powers. The United States, which had become the wealthiest and potentially the strongest nation in the world, disarmed almost entirely and withdrew into a shortsighted and foolish isolation; it could play no important part in restraining the angry and ambitious dictators who brought on the war. Britain and France refused to face the reality of the threat the Axis powers posed until the most deadly war in history was required to put it down. If the victorious democracies had remained strong, responsible, and realistic, they could have remedied whatever injustices or mistakes arose from the treaties without endangering the peace.

Equally important, however, was the unwillingness of the victorious powers to adjust the peace treaties from World War I, or to compel compliance even in the face of Germany's obvious unwillingness or inability to pay the war

Again the Road to War (1933–1939)

World War I and the Versailles Treaty had only a marginal relationship to the world Depression of the 1930s. But in Germany, where the government's resistance to the reparations settlement had contributed to the vast inflation of 1923, economic and social discontent focused on the Versailles settlement as the cause of all ills. Throughout the late 1920s Adolf Hitler and the Nazi Party had never ceased denouncing Versailles as the source of all Germany's trouble; the economic woes of the early 1930s seemed to bear them out.

Nationalism and attention to the social question, along with party discipline, had been the sources of Nazi success. They continued to influence Hitler's foreign policy after he became chancellor in early 1933. Moreover, the Nazi destruction of the Weimar Republic and of political opposition meant that German foreign policy lay in Hitler's own hands. Consequently, it is important to know his goals and the plans he had for achieving them.

Hitler's Goals

From first to last, Hitler's racial theories and goals held the central place in his thought. He meant to go far beyond Germany's 1914 boundaries, which were the limit of the vision of his predecessors. He intended to bring the entire German people (*Volk*), understood as a racial group, together into a

See the Map
Expansion of Germany
in 1930s
at **MyHistoryLab.com**

single nation. The new Germany would include all the Germanic parts of the old Habsburg Empire, including Austria. This virile and growing nation would need more space to live (*Lebensraum*), which would be taken from the Slavs, a lesser race, fit only for servitude. The new Germany would be purified by the removal of the Jews, the most inferior race in Nazi theory. The plan always required the conquest of Poland and the Ukraine as the primary areas for the settlement of Germans and for the provision of badly needed food. (See Document, "Hitler States His Plans for Russia.")

However, neither *Mein Kampf* nor later statements of policy were blueprints for action. Hitler was a brilliant improviser who exploited opportunities as they arose. But he never lost sight of his goal, which would almost certainly require a major war.

Read the Document
Adolf Hitler, "The Obersalzberg
Speech" at **MyHistoryLab.com**

Destruction of Versailles

When Hitler came to power, Germany was too weak to permit the direct approach to his goals. The first problem was to shake off the fetters of Versailles and to make Germany a formidable military power. In October of 1933 Germany withdrew from an international disarmament conference and also from the League of Nations. These acts alarmed the French but were merely symbolic. In January of 1934 reparations the victors demanded. Here too, the United States' isolationism played a pivotal role, as the government insisted that its allies in World War I, France and Britain, whose economies were also struggling after the war, repay their debts to the United States. France and Britain, in turn, sought to fund their war debts using reparations extracted primarily from Germany. The inability of the democratic German government of the Weimar Republic to negotiate a better deal from the victors of World War I added to the perception of ordinary Germans that it was weak and inept, thus contributing to its downfall.

The second war itself was plainly a global war. In the second decade after World War I aggression on three continents foreshadowed the disaster to come. The Japanese occupation of Manchuria in 1931, though not technically a part of that war, was a significant precursor. Italy attacked Ethiopia in 1935. Italy, Germany, and the Soviet Union intervened in the Spanish Civil War (1936–1939). Japan attacked China in 1937. European colonies or former colonies, such as Australia and other South Pacific islands, the Philippines, and regions of the Middle East and North Africa became theaters of war or, like India, were drawn into the conflict by helping to supply the combatants. Men and women from all the inhabited continents thus took part. The use of atomic weapons brought the frightful struggle to a close, but the so-called conventional weapons did almost all the damage while state-sponsored genocide, such as Hitler's Holocaust, killed millions of civilians. The world reached a level of destructiveness that threatened the very survival of civilization, even without the use of atomic or nuclear devices.

The aftermath of World War II, and the victors' analysis of the causes of the conflict, led to the creation of the United Nations, an international organization designed to forestall future conflict through improved international diplomacy.

Focus Questions

- What was the relationship between World War I and World War II? Why was the isolationism of the United States after World War I such an important factor in the advent of World War II?
- Why was World War II truly a global war?
- What lessons did the world learn from the experiences of World War I and World War II?

Germany made a nonaggression pact with Poland that was of greater concern, for it put into question France's chief means of containing the Germans. At last, in March 1935 Hitler formally renounced the disarmament provisions of the Versailles Treaty with the formation of a German air force, and soon he reinstated conscription, which aimed at an army of half a million men.

His path was made easier because the League of Nations was ineffective at keeping the peace. In September 1931 Japan occupied Manchuria, provoking an appeal to the League of Nations by China. The league responded by sending out a commission under the Earl of Lytton (1876–1951). The Lytton Report condemned the Japanese for resorting to force, but the powers were unwilling to impose sanctions. Japan withdrew from the league and kept control of Manchuria.

The league formally condemned Hitler's decision to rearm Germany, but it took no steps to prevent it. France and Britain felt unable to object because they had not carried out their own promises to disarm. Instead, they met with Mussolini (1883–1945) in June 1935 to form the so-called Stresa Front and agreed to maintain the status quo in Europe by force if necessary. But Britain was desperate to maintain superiority at sea. Contrary to the Stresa accords and at the expense of French security needs, Britain soon made a separate naval agreement with Hitler, allowing him to rebuild the German fleet to 35 percent of the British navy.

Italy Attacks Ethiopia

The Italian attack on Ethiopia underscored the impotence of the League of Nations and the timidity of the Allies. Using a border incident as an excuse, Mussolini attacked Ethiopia in October 1935. His real intent was to avenge a humiliating defeat that the Italians had suffered in 1896, to begin the restoration of Roman imperial glory, and perhaps to divert Italians from the corruption of the Fascist regime and Italy's economic troubles.

The League of Nations condemned Italian aggression and voted economic sanctions. It imposed an arms embargo that limited loans and credits to and imports from Italy. But Britain and France, afraid of alienating Mussolini, refused to place an embargo on oil, the one economic sanction that could have prevented Italian victory. Even more important, the British did not prevent the movement of Italian troops and munitions through the Suez Canal. This wavering policy proved disastrous. The League of Nations and collective security were totally discredited, and Mussolini turned to Germany. By November 1, 1936, he could speak publicly of a Rome–Berlin "Axis."

Remilitarization of the Rhineland

The Ethiopian affair also influenced Hitler's evaluation of the strength and determination of the Western powers. On March 7, 1936, he took his greatest risk yet, sending a small armed force into the demilitarized Rhineland. This

Document Hitler States His Plans for Russia

As was revealed in detail only after World War II, Hitler had definite, if vainglorious, views on Russians and positive plans for Germany's exploitation of Russia in the event of Germany's victory.

■ *What were Hitler's plans for Russia under German rule? How did they fit his racial theories? How would he justify his plans for Russia and the Russians?*

The German colonists ought to live on handsome, spacious farms. The German services will be lodged in marvelous buildings, the governors in palaces. Beneath the shelter of the administrative services, we shall gradually organize all that is indispensable to the maintenance of a certain standard of living. Around the city, to a depth of thirty to forty kilometers, we shall have a belt of handsome villages connected by the best roads. What exists beyond that will be another world, in which we mean to let the Russians live as they like. It is merely necessary that we should rule them. In the event of a revolution, we shall only have to drop a few bombs on their cities, and the affair will be liquidated. Once a year we shall lead a troop of Kirghizes through the capital of the Reich, in order to strike their imaginations with the size of our monuments.

What India was for England, the territories of Russia will be for us.

When one contemplates this primitive world, one is convinced that nothing will drag it out of its indolence unless one compels the people to work. The Slavs are a mass of born slaves, who feel the need of a master. . . . It's better not to teach them to read. They won't love us for tormenting them with schools. Even to give them a locomotive to drive would be a mistake. . .

The Germans—this is essential—will have to constitute amongst themselves a closed society, like a fortress. The least of our stable-lads must be superior to any native.

For German youth, this will be a magnificent field of experiment. We'll attract to the Ukraine Danes, Dutch, Norwegians, Swedes. The army will find areas for maneuvers there, and our aviation will have the space it needs.

Source: Hitler's Secret Conversations, 1941–1944, trans. by Norman Cameron and R. H. Stevens (New York: Farrar, Straus & Young, 1953), pp. 20, 28–29.

---

was a breach not only of the Versailles Treaty but also of the Locarno Agreements of 1925, agreements that Germany had voluntarily made. It also removed one of the most important elements of French security. France and Britain had every right to resist. The French especially had a claim to retain the only element of security left after the Allies had failed to guarantee France's defense. Yet Britain and France made only a feeble protest with the League of Nations. British opinion would not support France. The French themselves were paralyzed by internal division and by military planning that was exclusively defensive. Both countries were further weakened by a growing pacifism.

A Germany that was rapidly rearming and had a defensible western frontier presented a completely new problem to the Western powers. Their response was the policy of **appeasement**. It was based on the assumption that Germany had real grievances, that Hitler's goals were limited and ultimately acceptable, and that the correct policy was to negotiate and make concessions before a crisis could

lead to war. Behind this approach was the general horror of another war. Memories of the last war were still fresh, and the prospect of aerial bombardment was terrifying. A firmer policy, moreover, would have required rapid rearmament. But British leaders especially were reluctant to pursue this path because of the expense and widespread belief that the arms race had been a major cause of the last war. As Germany armed, the French huddled behind their defensive wall, the Maginot Line, named for the Defense Minister André Maginot. It was a powerful series of concrete fortifications and diverse other defensive devices along the German border with France between 1930 and the beginning of the war in 1939.

The Spanish Civil War

The new European alignment that found the Western democracies on one side and the Fascist states on the other was made clearer by the Spanish Civil War, which broke out in July 1936. In 1931 the Spaniards had established a

Map 30–1. The Spanish Civil War, 1936–1939. The purple area on the map shows the large portion of Spain quickly overrun by Franco's insurgent armies during the first year of the war. In the following two years progress came more slowly for the Fascists as the war became a kind of international rehearsal for the coming World War II. Madrid's fall to Franco in the spring of 1939 had been preceded by that of Barcelona a few weeks earlier.

democratic republic. Elections in February 1936 brought to power a government ranging from Republicans of the left to communists and anarchists. The defeated groups, especially the Falangists, the Spanish version of Fascists, would not accept defeat at the polls. In July, General Francisco Franco (1892–1975) led an army from Spanish Morocco against the republic (see Map 30–1).

Thus began a civil war that lasted almost three years, killed hundreds of thousands, and provided a training ground for World War II. Germany and Italy aided Franco with troops and supplies, and the Soviet Union sent equipment and

●●●—Read the Document

Constancia de la Mora from "In Place of Splendor" at **MyHistoryLab.com**

advisers to the Republicans. Liberals and leftists from Europe and America volunteered to fight in the Republican ranks against fascism.

The civil war, fought on blatantly ideological lines, profoundly affected world politics. It brought Germany and Italy closer together, leading to the Rome–Berlin **Axis** Pact. The Axis powers were joined in the same year by Japan in the Anti-Comintern Pact, ostensibly against communism but really a new and powerful diplomatic alliance. In western Europe, the appeasement mentality reigned. Although international law

Pablo Picasso, *Guernica,* **1937.** The Spanish Civil War divided Europe, with Fascist Italy and Nazi Germany assisting Franco, and Soviet Russia aiding the republic. Before its end in 1939, the war in Spain took some 500,000 lives. On April 26, 1937, planes from the German Condor Legion bombed the Basque town of Guernica, killing some 1,000 men, women, and children and destroying about 70 percent of the buildings. It was the most effective aerial bombardment of a city up to that time, and its purpose was simply to create terror. *Pablo Picasso, "Guernica" 1937, Oil on canvas. 11'5 1/2 x 25'5 3/4. Museo Nacional Centro de Arte Reina Sofía/©2007 Estate of Pablo Picasso/Artists Rights Society (ARS), New York.*

permitted the sale of weapons and munitions to the legitimate Republican government, France and Britain forbade the export of war materials to either side. The United States passed new neutrality legislation to the same end. By early 1939 the Franco's forces had won effective control of Spain.

Austria and Czechoslovakia

In 1934 Mussolini, not yet allied with Hitler, had frustrated a Nazi coup in Austria by threatening military intervention. In 1938 the new diplomatic situation encouraged Hitler to try again. He seems to have hoped to achieve his goal by propaganda, bullying, and threats, but the Austrian Premier, Kurt von Schuschnigg (1897–1977), refused to collapse. On March 9 the premier announced a plebiscite for March 13, in which the Austrian people could decide whether to unite with Germany for themselves. Hitler dared not let the plebiscite take place and invaded Austria on March 12. Mussolini made no objection, and Hitler marched into Vienna to the cheers of his Austrian sympathizers.

The **Anschluss**, or union of Germany and Austria, had great strategic significance, especially for Czechoslovakia, one of the bulwarks of French security. The Czechs were now surrounded by Germany on three sides.

The very existence of Czechoslovakia was an affront to Hitler. It was democratic and pro-Western; it had been created as a check on Germany and was allied to both France and the Soviet Union. It also contained about 3.5 million ethnic Germans who lived in the Sudetenland near the German border. These Germans had been the dominant class in

the old Austro-Hungarian Empire, and they resented their new minority position. Supported by Hitler, they agitated for privileges and autonomy within the Czech state. The Czechs made many concessions; Hitler's intention, however, was not to improve the lot of the Sudeten Germans but to destroy Czechoslovakia.

The French, as usual, deferred to British leadership. The British prime minister was Neville Chamberlain (1869–1940), a man thoroughly committed to the policy of appeasement. He was determined not to allow Britain to go to war again. He pressed the Czechs to make further concessions to Germany, but no concession was enough.

On September 12, 1938, Hitler made a provocative speech that led to rioting in the Sudetenland and the declaration of martial law by the Czech government. On September 15 Chamberlain accepted the separation of the Sudetenland from Czechoslovakia. Moreover, he and the French premier, Edouard Daladier (1884–1970), threatened to desert the Czechs if they did not agree. A week later Chamberlain flew again to Germany only to find that Hitler had raised his demands: He wanted cession of the Sudetenland in three days and its immediate occupation by the German army.

Munich

France and Britain prepared for war. At the last moment Mussolini proposed a conference of Germany, Italy, France, and Britain, which met on September 29 at Munich. Hitler received almost everything he had demanded. The Sudetenland, the key to Czech security, became part of Germany,

Document

Winston Churchill Warns of the Effects of the Munich Agreement

Churchill delivered a speech on the Munich Agreement before the House of Commons on October 5, 1938. Following are excerpts from it.

■ *What was decided at Munich? Why were the representatives of Czechoslovakia not at the meeting? Why did Chamberlain think the meeting was successful? Munich was the high point of the policy called appeasement. How would its advocates defend this policy? Churchill was a leading opponent of appeasement. What are his objections to it?*

The Chancellor of the Exchequer [Sir John Simon] said it was the first time Herr Hitler had been made to retract—I think that was the word—in any degree. We really must not waste time after all this long Debate upon the difference between the positions reached at Berchtesgaden, at Godesberg and at Munich. They can be very simply epitomized, if the House will permit me to vary the metaphor. One pound was demanded at the pistol's point. When it was given, £2 were demanded at the pistol's point. Finally, the dictator consented to take £17s. 6d. and the rest in promises of good will for the future. . . .

I do not grudge our loyal, brave people, who were ready to do their duty no matter what the cost, who never flinched under the strain of last week—I do not grudge them the natural, spontaneous outbursts of joy and relief when they learned that the hard ordeal would no longer be required of them at the moment; but they should know the truth. They should know that there has been gross neglect and deficiency in our defenses; they should know that we have sustained a defeat without a war, the consequences of which will travel far with us along our road; they should know that we have passed an awful milestone in our history, when the whole equilibrium of Europe has been deranged, and that the terrible words have for the time being been pronounced against the Western democracies: "Thou art weighed in the balance and found wanting." And do not suppose that this is the end. This is only the beginning of the reckoning. This is only the first sip, the first foretaste of a bitter cup which will be proffered to us year by year unless, by a supreme recovery of moral health and martial vigor, we arise again and take our stand for freedom as in the olden time.

Source: Reproduced with permission of Curtis Brown Ltd, London on behalf of The Estate of Winston Churchill. Copyright © Winston Churchill.

thus depriving the Czechs of any chance of self-defense (see Map 30–2 on page 930). In return, the rest of Czechoslovakia was spared. Hitler promised, "I have no more territorial demands to make in Europe." Chamberlain told a cheering crowd that he had brought "peace with honour. I believe it is peace for our time." (See Document, "Winston Churchill Warns of the Effects of the Munich Agreement.")

Even in the short run, the appeasement of Hitler at Munich was a failure. Soon Poland and Hungary also tore bits of territory from Czechoslovakia, and the Slovaks demanded autonomy. Finally, on March 15, 1939, Hitler broke his promise and occupied Prague, putting an end to Czech independence and to illusions that his only goal was to restore Germans to the Reich. Munich remains an example of short-sighted policy that helped bring on a war in disadvantageous circumstances as a result of the very fear of war and the failure to prepare for it.

It was apparent that Poland was the next target of German expansion. In the spring of 1939 the Germans put pressure on Poland to restore the formerly German

Agreement at Munich. On September 29–30, 1938, Hitler met with the leaders of Britain and France at Munich to decide the fate of Czechoslovakia. The Allied leaders abandoned the small democratic nation in a vain attempt to appease Hitler and avoid war. Hitler sits in the center of the picture. To his right is British Prime Minister Neville Chamberlain.

Map Exploration

To explore this map further, go to **http://www.myhistorylab.com**

Map 30–2. Partitions of Czechoslovakia and Poland, 1938–1939. The immediate background of World War II is found in the complex international drama unfolding on Germany's eastern frontier in 1938 and 1939. Germany's expansion inevitably meant the victimization of Austria, Czechoslovakia, and Poland. With the failure of the Western powers' appeasement policy and the signing of a German-Soviet pact, the stage for the war was set.

city of Danzig and to allow a railroad and a highway through the Polish Corridor to connect East Prussia with the rest of Germany. When the Poles would not yield, the pressure mounted. On March 31 Chamberlain announced a Franco-British guarantee of Polish independence. Hitler did not take the guarantee seriously. He had come to hold the Western leaders in contempt. He knew that both countries were unprepared for war and that many of their populations were opposed to war for Poland.

Belief in the Polish guarantee was further undermined by France and Britain's inability to get effective help to the Poles. The French, still dominated by the defensive mentality of the Maginot Line, had no intention of attacking Germany's western front. The only way to defend Poland was to bring Russia into the alliance against Hitler, but a Russian alliance posed many problems. Each side was profoundly suspicious of the other. The French and British were hostile to Russia's communist ideology, and since Stalin's purge of the officer

((• Hear the Audio
World War II 1 at
MyHistoryLab.com

corps of the Red Army, they questioned the military value of an alliance with Russia. Besides, the Russians could not help Poland without the right to cross Romania and enter Poland. Both nations, suspicious of Russian intentions—and with good reason—refused to grant these rights. As a result, Western negotiations with Russia were slow and cautious.

The Nazi-Soviet Pact

The Russians also had good reason to hesitate. They resented being left out of the Munich Agreement. They were annoyed by the low priority that the West seemed to give to negotiations with Russia, compared with the urgency with which they dealt with Hitler. They feared, rightly, that the Western powers meant them to bear the burden of the war against Germany. As a result, they opened negotiations with Hitler, and on August 23, 1939, the world was shocked to learn of a

Nazi-Soviet nonaggression pact. Its secret provisions, which were easily guessed and soon carried out, divided Poland between the two powers and allowed Russia to annex the Baltic States and to take Bessarabia from Romania. The most bitter ideological enemies had become allies; communist parties in the West changed their line overnight from the ardent advocacy of resistance to Hitler to a policy of peace and quiet.

The Nazi-Soviet pact sealed Poland's fate, and the Franco-British commitment guaranteed a general war. On September 1, 1939, the Germans invaded Poland. Two days later Britain and France declared war on Germany. World War II had begun.

World War II (1939–1945)

World War II was truly global. Fighting took place in Europe and Asia, the Atlantic and the Pacific oceans, the Northern and Southern hemispheres. The demand for the fullest exploitation of material and human resources for increased production, the use of blockades, and the intensive bombing of civilian targets made the war of 1939 even more "total"—that is, comprehensive and intense—than that of 1914.

German Conquest of Europe

The speed of the German victory over Poland astonished everyone, not least the Russians, who hastened to collect their share of the booty before Hitler could deprive them of it. On September 17 they invaded Poland from the east, dividing the country with the Germans. They then absorbed Estonia, Latvia, and Lithuania into the Soviet Union. In November 1940 the Russians invaded Finland, but the Finns fought back fiercely. Although they were finally compelled to yield territory and bases to Russia, they retained their independence. Russian difficulties in Finland may well have encouraged Hitler to invade the Soviet Union in June 1941, just twenty-two months after the 1939 treaty.

Meanwhile, the Western Front was quiet. The French remained behind the Maginot Line while Hitler and Stalin swallowed Poland and the Baltic States. Britain hastily rearmed and imposed the traditional naval blockade. Cynics in the West called it the phony war, or *Sitzkrieg*, but Hitler shattered the stillness in the spring of 1940. In April, without warning and with swift success, the Germans invaded Denmark and Norway. Hitler now had both air and naval bases closer to Britain. A month later a combined land and air attack struck Belgium, the Netherlands, and Luxembourg. German air power and armored divisions were irresistible. The Dutch surrendered in a few days, and the Belgians, though aided by the French and the British, surrendered less than two weeks later. The British and French armies in Belgium were forced

to flee to the English Channel to seek escape from the beaches of Dunkirk. By the heroic effort of hundreds of Britons manning small boats, over 200,000 British and 100,000 French soldiers were saved, but casualties were high and much valuable equipment was abandoned.

The Maginot Line ran from Switzerland to the Belgian frontier. Until 1936 the French had expected the Belgians to continue the fortifications along their German border. After Hitler remilitarized the Rhineland without opposition, the Belgians lost faith in their French alliance and returned to neutrality, leaving the Maginot Line exposed on its left flank. Hitler's swift advance through Belgium therefore circumvented France's main line of defense. The French army, poorly and hesitantly led by generals who lacked a proper understanding of how to use tanks and planes, collapsed. Mussolini, eager to claim the spoils of victory when it was clearly safe to do so, attacked France on June 10, though without success. Less than a week later the new French government,

Chronology

Events Leading to World War II

1919 June	Versailles Treaty
1923 January	France occupies the Ruhr
1925 October	Locarno Agreements
1931 Spring	Onset of Great Depression in Europe
1933 January	Hitler comes to power
October	Germany withdraws from League of Nations
1935 March	Hitler renounces disarmament, starts an air force, and begins conscription
October	Mussolini attacks Ethiopia
1936 March	Germany reoccupies and remilitarizes the Rhineland
July	Outbreak of Spanish Civil War
October	Formation of the Rome–Berlin Axis
1938 March	Anschluss with Austria
September	Munich Conference and partition of Czechoslovakia
1939 March	Hitler occupies Prague; France and Great Britain guarantee Polish independence
August	Nazi-Soviet pact
September 1	Germany invades Poland
September 3	Britain and France declare war on Germany

Churchill and Roosevelt. The close cooperation between Prime Minister Winston Churchill of Britain and President Franklin Roosevelt of the United States helped to assure the effective alliance of their two countries in World War II.

under the ancient hero of Verdun, Henri Philippe Pétain (1856–1951), asked for an armistice. In two months Hitler had accomplished what Germany had failed to achieve in four years of bitter fighting in the previous war.

The terms of the armistice, signed on June 22, 1940, allowed the Germans to occupy more than half of France, including the Atlantic and English Channel coasts. To prevent the French from fleeing to North Africa to continue the fight, and even more to prevent them from turning their fleet over to Britain, Hitler left southern France unoccupied. Pétain set up a dictatorial regime at the resort city of Vichy and collaborated with the Germans to preserve as much autonomy as possible. Most of the French were too stunned to resist. Many thought that Hitler's victory was certain and saw no alternative to collaboration. A few, most notably General Charles de Gaulle (1890–1969), fled to Britain, where they organized the French National Committee of Liberation, or "Free French." The Vichy government controlled most of French North Africa and the navy. But the Free French began operating in central Africa and from London radioed messages of hope and defiance to France. As expectations of a quick German victory faded, a French Resistance movement arose.

Battle of Britain

Hitler expected the British to come to terms. He was prepared to allow Britain to retain its empire in return for giving Germany a free hand in Europe. If there was any chance that the British would consider such terms, that chance disappeared when Winston Churchill (1874–1965) replaced Chamberlain as prime minister in May 1940.

One of Churchill's greatest achievements was establishing a close relationship with the American president Franklin D. Roosevelt (1882–1945), who found ways to help the British despite strong political opposition from isolationists. In 1940 and 1941, before the United States was at war, America sent military supplies, traded destroyers for leases on British naval bases, and even convoyed ships across the Atlantic to help the British survive.

As Britain remained defiant, Hitler was forced to contemplate an invasion, which required control of the air. The first strikes by the German air force (**Luftwaffe**), directed against the airfields and fighter planes in southeastern England, began in August 1940. Had these attacks continued, Germany might soon have gained control of the air and, with it, the chance of a successful invasion. In early September, however, seeking revenge for British bombing raids on German cities, the *Luftwaffe* made London its major target. For two months, London was bombed every night. Much of the city was destroyed, and about 15,000 people were killed, but the theories of victory through air power alone proved vain. Casualties were much less than expected, and the bombings made the British people more resolute.

Moreover, the Royal Air Force (RAF), aided by the newly developed radar and an excellent system of communications, inflicted heavy losses on the *Luftwaffe*. Hitler lost the Battle of Britain in the air and was forced to abandon his plans for invasion.

Battle of Britain. A rubble-strewn street in London after the city had experienced a night of German bombing. Despite many casualties and widespread devastation, the German bombing of London did not break British morale or prevent the city from functioning.

German Attack on Russia

Operation Barbarossa, the code name for the invasion of Russia, was aimed at knocking Russia out of the war before winter could set in. Success depended in part on an early start, but here Hitler's Italian alliance proved costly. Mussolini was jealous of Hitler's success and annoyed at German condescension.

Consequently, Mussolini launched an attack against the British in Egypt and drove them back some 60 miles. Encouraged by this success, he also invaded Greece. But in North Africa the British counterattacked and drove into Libya, and the Greeks also repulsed the Italians. In March 1941 the British sent help to the Greeks, and Hitler was forced to divert his attention to the Balkans and to Africa. General Erwin Rommel (1891–1944), who would later earn the title "The Desert Fox," went to Africa and soon drove the British back into Egypt. In the Balkans the German army swiftly occupied Yugoslavia and crushed Greek resistance, but the price was a delay of six weeks for Barbarossa (see Map 30–3). This delay proved to be fatal the following winter in the Russian campaign.

Operation Barbarossa was launched against Russia on June 22, 1941, and it almost succeeded. Stalin panicked: He had not fortified his frontier or ordered his troops to withdraw when attacked. Two thousand planes

Map 30–3. Axis Europe 1941. On the eve of the German invasion of the Soviet Union, the Germany–Italy Axis bestrode most of western Europe by annexation, occupation, or alliance—from Norway and Finland in the north to Greece in the south and from Poland to France. Britain, the Soviets, a number of insurgent groups, and finally, the United States had before them the long struggle of conquering this Axis "fortress Europe."

were destroyed on the ground. By November Hitler had gone farther into Russia than Napoleon had: The German army stood at the gates of Leningrad, on the outskirts of Moscow, and on the Don River. Of the 4.5 million troops with which the Russians had begun the fighting, they had lost 2.5 million; of their 15,000 tanks, only 700 were left. A German victory seemed imminent.

But the Germans were unable to deliver the final blow. In August they delayed their advance so that they could decide on a course of action. One plan was to take Moscow before winter. Such a plan might have brought victory, for Moscow was Russia's transportation hub. Hitler, however, diverted significant forces to the south. By the time he was ready to return to the offensive near Moscow, it was too late. Winter struck the German army, which was not equipped to face it. Given precious time, Stalin was able to restore order and fortify the city. Even more important, troops had arrived from Siberia, where they had been placed to check a possible Japanese attack. In November and December the Russians counterattacked. The war had turned into one of attrition, and the Germans began to have visions of Napoleon's retreat.

Hitler's Europe

The demands and distractions of war and Hitler's ultimate defeat of course prevented him from fully carrying out his plans.

Roundup of Hungarian Jewish Women. World War II resulted in the near-total destruction of the Jews of Europe, victims of the Holocaust spawned by Hitler's racial theories of the superiority and inferiority of particular ethnic groups. Hitler placed special emphasis on the need to exterminate the Jews, to whom he attributed particular wickedness. This picture shows Hungarian Jewish women, after "disinfection" and head shaving, marching to the concentration or death camp at Auschwitz-Birkenau. *Photo by Bernhard Walter; source: National Archives and Records Administration*

Therefore, it is hard to be sure precisely what his intentions were, but the measures he took before his death give evidence of a regime probably unmatched in history for carefully planned terror and inhumanity. To give *Lebensraum* to the Germans at the expense of people he deemed inferior, Hitler established colonies of Germans in Poland, driving the local people from their land and using them as cheap labor. He had worse plans for Russia. The Russians would be driven to Central Asia and Siberia, where they would be kept in check by frontier colonies of German war veterans. Germans would settle the more desirable lands of European Russia.

Hitler's long-range plans included Germanization as well as colonization. In lands inhabited by people racially akin to the Germans, like Scandinavia, the Netherlands, and Switzerland, the natives would be absorbed into the German nation. Such peoples would be reeducated and purged of dissenting elements, but there would be little or no colonization. He even had plans, only slightly realized, of adopting selected people from those he considered the lesser races into those he considered the master race.

Hitler regarded the conquered lands merely as a source of plunder. From eastern Europe he removed everything useful, including entire industries. In Russia and Poland the Germans simply confiscated the land. In the west the conquered

⊙ **See the Map**
The Nazi Empire in 1942
at **MyHistoryLab.com**

countries were forced to support the occupying army at a rate several times the real cost. The Germans used the profits to strip the conquered peoples of most necessities. The Nazis were frank about their policies. One of Hitler's high officials said, "Whether nations live in prosperity or starve to death interests me only insofar as we need them as slaves for our culture."[1]

Racism and the Holocaust

The most horrible aspect of the Nazi rule in Europe arose from the inhumanity and brutality inherent in Hitler's racial doctrines. He considered the Slavs subhuman creatures like beasts who need not be treated as people. In Poland the upper and professional classes were either jailed, deported, or killed. Schools and churches were closed; marriage was controlled to keep down the Polish birthrate; and harsh living conditions were imposed. In Russia things were even worse. Hitler spoke of his Russian campaign as a war of extermination. Heinrich Himmler (1900–1945), head of Hitler's elite SS guard, formed extermination squads to eliminate 30 mil-

[1] Quoted by Gordon Wright, *The Ordeal of Total War, 1939–1945* (New York: Harper & Row, 1968), p. 117.

▪●▪ Read the Document

Wannsee Protocol
at **MyHistoryLab.com**

lion Slavs to make room for the Germans. Some 6 million Russian prisoners of war and deported civilian workers may have died under Nazi rule.

Hitler had special plans for the Jews. He meant to make all Europe *Judenrein* ("free of Jews"). For a time he thought of sending them to Madagascar but later decided on the "Final Solution of the Jewish problem": extermination. The Nazis built extermination camps in Germany and Poland and used the latest technology to kill millions of men, women, and children just because they were Jews. (See Document, "Mass Murder at Belsen.") Before the war was over, 6 million Jews had died in what has come to be called the **Holocaust**. Only about a million remained alive, mostly in pitiable condition (see Map 30–4).

◉ View the Image

Emaciated Woman at
Bergen-Belsen
at **MyHistoryLab.com**

The Road to Pearl Harbor

The war took on truly global proportions in December 1941. The Japanese were already at war with China, and between the outbreak of that war in 1937 and the opening of the World War II campaign in the Pacific, there were three critical junctures. The first was the decision in January 1938 to destroy the Chinese Nationalist Party government in Nanjing. The Japanese army quickly occupied most of the cities and railroads of eastern China, killing over 300,000 people and brutally raping 7,000 women (known today as the Rape of Nanjing), but Jiang Jieshi (Chiang Kai-shek) refused to give in. The result was a stalemate that lasted until 1945. China was never a major theater of the war in the Pacific.

The second critical decision was the Tripartite Pact with Germany and Italy in September 1940. Japan had long admired Germany. In 1936 it had joined Germany in the Anti-Comintern Pact directed against international communism. It also wanted an alliance with Germany against the Soviet Union. Germany insisted, however, that any alliance also be directed against the United States and Britain, to which the Japanese would not agree. The Japanese navy, in particular, was not interested in being dragged into a German war. After an undeclared miniwar with Russia from May to December 1939 on the Mongolian border, sentiment rose for an alliance with Germany, but then Germany "betrayed" Japan by signing a nonaggression pact with the Soviet Union. For a time Japan decided to improve its relations with the United States, but America insisted that Japan get out of China. By the late spring of 1940 German victories in Europe—the fall of Britain appeared imminent—again led the Japanese military to favor an alliance with Germany.

When Japan signed the Tripartite Pact it had three objectives: to isolate the United States, to take over the Southeast Asian colonies of Britain, France, and the Netherlands, and to improve its relations with the Soviet Union through the good offices of Germany.

The last objective was reached when Japan signed a neutrality pact with the Soviet Union in April 1941. Two months later Germany attacked the Soviet Union, without consulting Japan. Germany compounded this second "betrayal" by asking Japan to attack the Soviet Union in the east. Japan waited

Map 30–4. The Holocaust. The Nazi policy of ethnic cleansing—targeting Jews, Gypsies, political dissidents, and "social deviants"—began with imprisoning them in concentration camps, but by 1943 the *Endlösung*, or Final Solution, called for the systematic extermination of "undesirables."

Document | Mass Murder at Belsen

Hitler's calculated plan to wipe out Europe's Jews, was not widely known during the war. Kurt Gerstein, a colonel in the SS, was part of the apparatus of extermination. However, unlike most people involved, he tried to tell the world what was taking place. The following is an account of what he saw at the death camp at Belsen, Germany, in 1942.

■ *What were the reasons for Hitler's policy of exterminating millions of people? Why did many Germans take part in the process? Why did Colonel Gerstein not resist?*

A train arrived from Lemberg [Lvov]. There were forty-five cars containing 6,700 people, 1,450 of whom were already dead. Through the gratings on the windows, children could be seen peering out, terribly pale and frightened, their eyes filled with mortal dread. . . . The train entered the station, and two hundred Ukrainians wrenched open the doors and drove the people out of the carriages with their leather whips. Instructions came through a large loudspeaker telling them to remove all their clothing, artificial limbs, glasses, etc. They were to hand over all objects of value at the counter. . . . Shoes were to be carefully tied together, for otherwise no one would ever again have been able to find shoes belonging to each other in a pile that was a good eighty feet high. Then the women and girls were sent to the barber who, with two or three strokes of his scissors, cut off all their hair and dropped it into potato sacks. . . .

Then the column moved off. Headed by an extremely pretty young girl, they walked along the avenue, all naked, men, women, and children, with artificial limbs removed. I myself was stationed up on the ramp between the [gas] chambers with Captain Wirth.

Mothers with babies at their breasts came up, hesitated, and entered the chambers of death. At the corner stood a burly SS man with a priestlike voice. "Nothing at all is going to happen to you!" he told the poor wretches. "All you have to do when you get into the chambers is to breathe in deeply. That stretches the lungs. Inhaling is necessary to prevent disease and epidemics." When asked what would be done with them, he replied: "Well, of course, the men will have to work building houses and roads, but the women won't need to work. They can do housework or help in the kitchen, but only if they want to." For some of these poor creatures, this was a small ray of hope that was enough to make them walk the few steps to the chambers without resistance. Most of them knew what was going on. The smell told them what their fate was to be. They went up the small flight of steps and saw everything. Mothers with their babies clasped to their breasts, small children, adults, men, women, all naked; they hesitated, but they entered the chambers of death, thrust forward by the others behind them or by the leather whips of the SS [Storm Troopers]. Most went in without a word. . . . Many were saying prayers. I prayed with them. I pressed myself into a corner and cried aloud to my God and theirs. How gladly I should have gone into the chambers with them; how gladly I should have died with them. Then they would have found an SS officer in uniform in their gas chambers; they would have believed it was an accident and the story would have been buried and forgotten. But I could not do that yet. First, I had to make known what I had seen here. The chambers were filling up. The people were treading on each other's feet. There were 700–800 of them in an area of 270 square feet, in 1,590 cubic feet of space. The SS crushed them together as tightly as they possibly could. The doors closed. Meanwhile, the rest waited out in the open, all naked. "It's done exactly the same way in winter," I was told. "But they may catch their death!" I said "That's what they're here for," an SS man said. . . . The diesel exhaust gases were intended to kill those unfortunates. But the engine was not working. . . . The people in the gas chambers waited, in vain. I heard them weeping, sobbing. . . . After 2 hours and 49 minutes, measured by my stopwatch, the diesel started. Up to that moment, men and women had been shut up alive in those four chambers, four times 750 people in four times 1,590 cubic feet of space. Another twenty-five minutes dragged by. Many of those inside were already dead. They could be seen through the small window when the electric light went on for a moment and lit up the inside of the chamber. After twenty-eight minutes, few were left alive. At the end of thirty-two minutes, all were dead.

Source: Pius XII and the Third Reich: A Documentation, by Saul Friendlander. Copyright © 1966 by Alfred A. Knopf, Inc. Copyright © 1964 by Editions du Seuil. Originally published in French under the title. *Pie XII et le III Reich, Documents.* Reprinted by permission of Georges borchardt, Inc. for the author.

and watched. When the German advance faltered, Japan decided to honor the neutrality pact and turn south. This, in effect, was the end of Japan's participation in the Axis. Thereafter, it fought its own war in Asia. Yet instead of deflecting American criticism as intended, the pact, by linking Japan to Germany, hardened America's position on China.

The third and fateful decision was to go to war with the United States. In June 1941, following Germany's defeat of France, Japanese troops had occupied northern French Indochina. The United States retaliated by limiting strategic exports to Japan. In July 1941 Japanese troops took southern Indochina, and the United States embargoed all exports to Japan, cutting Japanese oil imports by 90 percent. The navy pressed for the capture of the oil-rich Dutch East Indies, but it would be too dangerous to move against Dutch and British colonies in Southeast Asia with the United States on its flank in the Philippines. The navy, therefore, planned a preemptive strike against the United States. The Japanese decision for war wagered Japan's land-based air power, shorter supply lines, and what it saw as greater will power against American productivity. At the Imperial Conference where the all-or-nothing decision was taken, the navy's chief of staff compared the war with the United States to a dangerous operation that might save a critically ill patient.

America's Entry into the War

On Sunday morning, December 7, 1941, even while Japanese representatives were discussing a settlement in Washington, Japan launched an air attack on Pearl Harbor, Hawaii, the chief American naval base in the Pacific. The next day, the United States and Britain declared war on Japan. Three days later, Germany and Italy declared war on the United States.

The Tide Turns

The potential power of the United States was enormous, but America was ill prepared for war. Although conscription had been introduced in 1940, the army was tiny, inexperienced, and poorly supplied. Nor was American industry ready for war. The Japanese swiftly captured Guam, Wake Island, and the Philippines (see Map 30–5 on page 938). They also attacked Hong Kong, Malaya, Burma, and Indonesia. By the summer of 1942, the Japanese Empire stretched from the western Aleutian Islands south almost to Australia, and from Burma east to the Gilbert Islands in the mid-Pacific.

●●● Read the Document
Japanese Total War Research Institute; Plan for the Greater East Asia Co-Prosperity Sphere, 1942 at **MyHistoryLab.com**

In the same year, the Germans almost reached the Caspian Sea in their drive for Russia's oil fields. In Africa, Rommel drove the British

Pearl Harbor. The successful Japanese attack on the American base at Pearl Harbor in Hawaii on December 7, 1941, together with simultaneous attacks on other Pacific bases, brought the United States into war against the Axis powers. For Japan, it was the opening phase of a campaign to capture European and American colonies in Southeast Asia. This picture shows the battleships USS *West Virginia* and USS *Tennessee* in flames as a small boat rescues a man from the water.

back toward the Suez Canal and was finally stopped at El Alamein, only 70 miles from Alexandria. Relations between the democracies and their Soviet ally were not close; German submarines were threatening British supplies; the Allies were being thrown back on every front, and the future looked bleak.

The tide turned at the battle of Midway in June 1942. A month earlier, both sides had suffered massive losses in the battle of the Coral Sea, but greater U.S. ship production made such trade-offs unprofitable for Japan. At Midway, American planes destroyed four Japanese aircraft carriers. Soon American Marines landed on Guadalcanal in the Solomon Islands and began to reverse the momentum of the war. The War in

the Pacific was far from over, but Japan was checked sufficiently to allow the Allies to concentrate their efforts first in the West.

Watch the Video
FDR on Winning the War at **MyHistoryLab.com**

Allied Landings in Africa, Sicily, and Italy   In November 1942, an Allied force landed in French North Africa. Even before that landing, the British Field Marshal Bernard Montgomery (1887–1976), after stopping Rommel at El Alamein, had begun a drive to the west (see Map 30–6 on page 939). The American general Dwight D. Eisenhower (1890–1969) had pushed eastward through Morocco and Algeria. The German army was trapped in

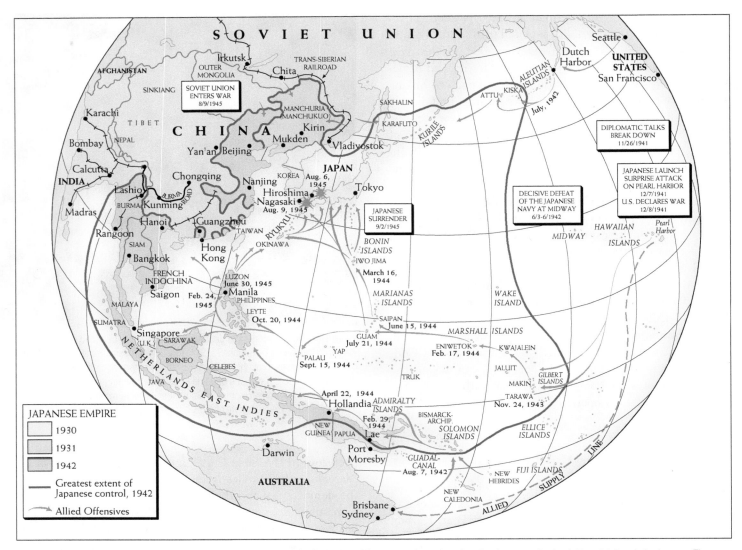

Map 30–5. The War in the Pacific. As in Europe, the Allies initially had trouble recapturing areas that the Japanese had quickly seized early in the war. The map shows the initial expansion of the Japanese and the long struggle of the Allies to push them back to their homeland and defeat them.

Tunisia and crushed. The Mediterranean was now under Allied control, and southern Europe was exposed. In July and August 1943 the Allies took Sicily. Mussolini was driven from power, the Allies landed in Italy, and Marshal Pietro Badoglio (1871–1956), the leader of the new Italian government, declared war on Germany. Churchill had spoken of Italy as the "soft underbelly" of the Axis, but German resistance was tough and determined. Still, the need to defend Italy strained the Germans' energy and resources and left them vulnerable on other fronts.

Battle of Stalingrad The Russian campaign became especially demanding. In the summer of 1942 the Germans resumed the offensive on all fronts but did not get far, except in the south. Their goal there was the oil fields near the Caspian Sea, and they got as far as Stalingrad on the Volga, a key point for protecting the flank of their southern army.

Hitler was determined to take the city and Stalin was determined to hold it. The battle of Stalingrad raged for months with unexampled ferocity. The Russians lost more men at Stalingrad than the Americans lost in combat during the entire war, but their heroic defenses prevailed. Because Hitler again overruled his generals and would not allow a retreat, an entire German army, some 740,000 men, was lost.

Stalingrad marked the turning point of the Russian campaign. Thereafter, as the German military and material resources dwindled, the Russians advanced westward inexorably.

Strategic Bombing In 1943 the Allies also gained ground in production and logistics. The industrial might of the United States began to come into full force. New technology and tactics made great strides in eliminating the submarine menace. In the same year the American and

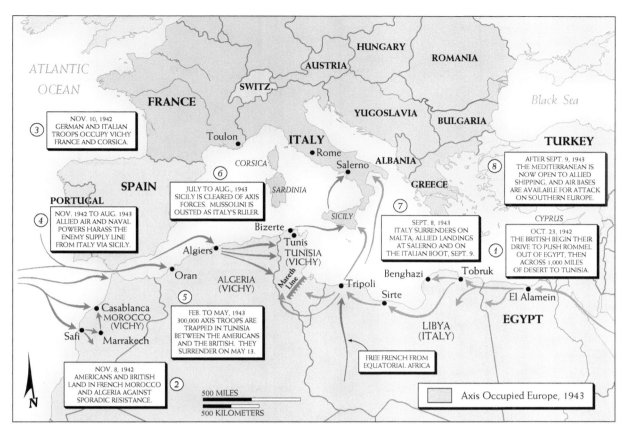

Map 30–6. North African Campaigns, 1942–1945. Control of North Africa was important to the Allies if they were to have access to Europe from the south. The map diagrams this theater of the war from Morocco to Egypt and the Suez Canal.

Stalingrad. Russian soldiers, in their heroic defense of Stalingrad, dug trenches from building to building in the city. The German defeat at Stalingrad in February 1943 marked the turning point of the Russian campaign. Thereafter the Russians advanced inexorably westward.

View the Image
Operation Overlord, Normandy, 1944
at **MyHistoryLab.com**

British air forces began a series of massive bombardments of Germany by night and day. This bombing did not have much effect on the war until 1944. Then the Americans introduced long-range fighters that could protect the bombers and allow accurate missions by day. By 1945 the Allies could bomb at will.

Defeat of Nazi Germany

On June 6, 1944 (D-Day), in one of greatest amphibious assaults ever attempted, Allied troops landed in force on the coast of Normandy (see Map 30–7 on page 940). By the beginning of September France had been liberated.

All went smoothly until December, when the Germans launched a counterattack called the Battle of the Bulge through the Forest of Ardennes. However, it was their last gasp. The Allies recovered the momentum and pushed eastward. They crossed the Rhine in March 1945, and German resistance crumbled. This time there could be no doubt that the Germans had lost the war on the battlefield.

In the east, the Russians were within reach of Berlin by March 1945. Because the Allies insisted on unconditional surrender, the Germans fought on until May. Hitler committed suicide in an underground hideaway in Berlin on May 1, 1945.

Map 30–7. Defeat of the Axis in Europe, 1942–1945. Here we see some major steps in the progress toward Allied victory against Axis Europe. From the south through Italy, the west through France, and the east through Russia, the Allies gradually conquered the continent to bring the war in Europe to a close.

D-Day. American soldiers land at Omaha Beach in Normandy on D-Day, June 6, 1944.

See the Map
World War II in Europe, 1939–1945 at
MyHistoryLab.com

The Russians occupied Berlin by agreement with their Western allies. The Third Reich had lasted a dozen years instead of the millennium predicted by Hitler.

Fall of the Japanese Empire

The war in Europe ended on May 8, 1945, and by then victory over Japan was in sight (see also Chapter 27). The original Japanese attack on the United States had been a calculated risk against the odds. The longer the war lasted, the greater the impact of American superiority in industrial production and human resources. Beginning in 1943 American forces began a campaign of "island hopping," selecting major bases and places strategically located along the enemy supply line. Starting from the Solomons, they moved northeast toward the Japanese homeland. Ameri-

Read the Document
The Franck Report at
MyHistoryLab.com

Read the **Document**
An Eyewitness to Hiroshima (1945) at **MyHistoryLab.com**

can bombers launched a terrible wave of bombings that destroyed Japanese industry and disabled the Japanese navy. But still the Japanese government, dominated by a military clique, refused to surrender.

View the **Image**
Nagasaki Atomic Bomb Attack–August 1945 at **MyHistoryLab.com**

Confronted with Japan's determination, the Americans made plans for a frontal assault on the Japanese homeland, which, they calculated, would cost unacceptable American casualties and even greater losses for the Japanese. At this point, science and technology presented the Americans with another choice. Since early in the war a secret program had been in progress. Its staff was working to use atomic energy for military purposes.

See the **Map**
World War II in the Pacific, 1939–1945 at **MyHistoryLab.com**

On August 6, 1945, an American plane dropped an atomic bomb on the city of Hiroshima. More than 70,000 of Hiroshima's 200,000 residents were killed. Two days later the Soviet Union declared war on Japan and invaded Manchuria. The next day a second atomic bomb fell, this time on Nagasaki. Even then the Japanese were prepared to face an invasion rather than give up. It was only the unprecedented intervention of Emperor Hirohito (r. 1926– 1989) that forced the government to surrender on August 14. And even then, the Cabinet made the condition that Japan could keep its emperor. President Harry Truman (1884–1972), who had come to office on April 12, 1945, on the sudden death of Franklin D. Roosevelt, accepted the condition. Peace was formally signed on September 2, 1945.

The Cost of War

World War II was the most terrible war in history. Military deaths are estimated at 15 million, and at least as many civilians were killed. If deaths linked indirectly to the war

Hiroshima. This photo, taken a few days after an atomic bomb was dropped, poignantly captures the total devastation wreaked on the city.

are included, as many as 40 million may have died. Most of Europe and significant parts of Asia were devastated. Yet the end of so devastating a war provided little opportunity for relaxation. The dawn of the Atomic Age that brought a dramatic end to the war made people conscious that another major war might destroy humanity. Everything depended on the conclusion of a stable peace, but even as the fighting ended, the victors began to quarrel.

The Domestic Fronts

World War II represented an effort of total war by all the belligerents. Never before in world history had so many men and women and so many resources been devoted to military effort. One result was the carnage that occurred on the battlefields and at sea. Another was an unprecedented organization of civilians on the various home fronts. Each domestic effort and experience was different, but almost no one escaped the impact of the conflict. Shortages, propaganda campaigns, and new political developments were ubiquitous. In this section we look at the home fronts of the principal European belligerents.

Germany: From Apparent Victory to Defeat

Hitler had expected to defeat all his enemies by rapid strokes, or ***blitzkrieg***. Such campaigns would scarcely have affected Germany's society and economy. During the first two years of the war, in fact, Hitler demanded few important sacrifices from the German people. Spending on domestic projects continued, and food was plentiful; the economy was not on a full wartime footing. The failure to knock out the Soviet Union changed everything. Because enough food could no longer be imported from the east, Germany had to mobilize for total war, and the government demanded major sacrifices.

A great expansion of the army and military production began in 1942. As minister for armaments and munitions, Albert Speer (1905–1981) guided the economy, and Germany met its military needs instead of making consumer goods. Major German business enterprises aided the growth of wartime production. Between 1942 and late 1944 the output of military products tripled, but as the war went on the army absorbed more men from industry, hurting the production of even military goods.

Beginning in 1942 everyday products became scarce. Prices and wages were controlled, but the German worker's standard of living fell. Burdensome food rationing began in April 1942, and shortages were severe until the Nazi government seized food from occupied Europe. To preserve their own home front, the Nazis passed on the suffering to their defeated neighbors.

By 1943 there were also serious labor shortages. The Nazis required German teenagers and retired workers to work in the factories, and increasing numbers of women joined

Youth Rally. Members of the Nazi German Women's Youth Movement perform calisthenics.

them. To achieve total mobilization the Germans closed retail businesses, raised the maximum age of women eligible for compulsory service, shifted non-German domestic workers to wartime industry, moved artists and entertainers into military service, closed theaters, and reduced such basic public services as mail and railways. Finally, the Nazis forced thousands of people from conquered lands to labor in Germany.

Hitler assigned women a special place in the war effort. The celebration of motherhood continued, with an emphasis on women who were the mothers of important military figures. Films portrayed ordinary women who became especially brave and patriotic during the war and remained faithful to their husbands who were at the front. Women were thereby depicted as mothers and wives who would send their sons and husbands off to war. The government portrayed other wartime activities of women as the natural fulfillment of their maternal roles. As air raid wardens they protected their families; as factory workers in munitions plants they aided their sons on the front lines. Women working on farms were providing for their soldier sons and husbands; as housewives they were helping to win the war by conserving food and managing their households frugally. Finally, by their faithful chastity, German women were protecting racial purity. They were not to marry or to engage in sexual relations with men who were not Germans. German women were thus supposed to demonstrate the kind of service and courage required by the war.

●●—[Read the Document
Gertrud Scholtz-Klink, "Speech to the Nazi Women's Organization" (Germany), 1935
at **MyHistoryLab.com**

The war years also saw an intensification of political propaganda on the domestic front beyond what occurred in other countries. Hitler and other Nazis genuinely believed

that weak domestic support had led to Germany's defeat in World War I, and they were determined that this would not happen again. Nazi propaganda blamed the outbreak of the war on the British and its prolongation on the policies of Germany's opponents. It also stressed the might of Germany and the inferiority of its foes.

Propaganda Minister Josef Goebbels (1897–1945) used radio and films to boost the Nazi cause. Movies of the collapse of Poland, Belgium, Holland, and France demonstrated German military might. Throughout the conquered territories the Nazis used the same mass media to frighten inhabitants about the possible consequences of an Allied victory. Later in the war the ministry broadcast exaggerated claims of Nazi victories. As the German armies were checked on the battlefield, especially in Russia, propaganda became a substitute for victory. To stiffen German resolve, the propaganda also aimed to frighten the German population about the consequences of defeat.

After May 1943, when the Allies began their major bombing offensive over Germany, the German people had much to fear. One German city after another endured heavy bombing, fires, and destruction. But the bombing did not undermine German morale—on the contrary, it may have confirmed the general fear of defeat at the hands of such savage opponents and increased German resistance.

World War II brought increased power to the Nazi Party in Germany. Every area of the economy and society came under the direct influence or control of the party. The Nazis were determined that they, rather than the traditionally honored German officer corps, would profit from the new authority flowing

Bombing of Cologne. The Allied campaign of aerial bombardment did terrible damage to German cities. This photograph shows the devastation it delivered to the city of Cologne on the Rhine.

to the central government because of the war effort. Throughout the war years there was virtually no serious opposition to Hitler or his ministers. In 1944 a small group of army officers made an attempt to assassinate Hitler; the effort failed, and there was no significant popular support for this act.

The war brought great changes to Germany, but what transformed the country afterward was the experience of defeat accompanied by vast physical destruction, invasion, and occupation. Hitler and the Nazis had brought the nation to such a complete and disastrous end that only a new kind of state with new political structures could emerge.

France: Defeat, Collaboration, and Resistance

In France the Vichy government cooperated closely with the Germans for a variety of reasons. Some of the collaborators believed that the Germans were sure to win, and so they wanted to be on the victorious side. A few actually sympathized with the Nazis' ideas and plans. Many conservatives regarded the French defeat as a judgment on what they saw as the corrupt, secularized, liberal Third Republic. But most of the French were not active collaborators and remained helpless and demoralized by defeat and German power.

Many conservatives and extreme rightists saw the Vichy government as a device to reshape the French national character and halt the decadence they associated with political and religious liberalism. The Roman Catholic clergy, who had lost power and influence under the Third Republic, gained status under Vichy. The church supported Pétain; his government supported religious education. Vichy adopted the church's views of the importance of family and spiritual values. Divorce was forbidden during the first three years of marriage and was made difficult thereafter; large families were rewarded.

The Vichy regime embraced an intense, chauvinistic nationalism. It encouraged the long-standing prejudice against foreigners working in France and it persecuted those who were not regarded as genuinely and thoroughly French. The chief victims were French Jews. Anti-Semitism was not new in France. Even before Germany undertook Hitler's "Final Solution" in 1942, the French had begun to remove Jews from government, education, and publishing. In 1941 the Germans began to intern Jews living in occupied France; soon they carried out killings and imposed large fines collectively on the Jews of the occupied zone. In the spring of 1942 the Germans began deporting Jews, ultimately over 60,000, to the extermination camps of eastern Europe. Although the Vichy government had no part in these decisions, it made no protest, and its own anti-Semitic policies facilitated the process.

A few Frenchmen had fled France to join de Gaulle's Free French forces soon after the defeat of 1940. Serious internal resistance to the German occupiers and to the Vichy government, however, did not develop only late in 1942. The Germans attempted to force young people in occupied France to work in German factories; some of them fled and joined the Resistance, but the total number of resisters was small. Many were deterred by fear. Some abhorred the violence that resistance inevitably entailed. As long as it appeared that the Germans would win the war, moreover, resistance seemed imprudent and futile. In all, less than 5 percent of the adult French population appear to have been involved in the Resistance.

By early 1944 the tide of battle had shifted. An Allied victory appeared inevitable, and the Vichy government was clearly doomed. Only then did an active Resistance assert itself. General de Gaulle urged the French people to resist their conquerors and their lackeys in the Vichy government. Within France, Resistance groups joined forces to plan for a better day. From Algiers on August 9, 1944, the Committee of National Liberation declared the authority of Vichy illegitimate. Soon French soldiers joined in the liberation of Paris and established a government for Free France. On October 21, 1945, France voted to adopt a new constitution as the basis of the Fourth Republic. The French people had experienced defeat, disgrace, deprivation, and suffering. Hostility and bitter quarrels over who had done what during the occupation and the Vichy period would divide them for decades.

Great Britain: Organization for Victory

On May 22, 1940, the British Parliament gave the government emergency powers. The government could now institute compulsory military service, food rationing, and various controls over the economy.

Churchill and the British war cabinet moved as quickly as possible to mobilize the nation. By the end of 1941 British production had already surpassed Germany's. To meet the heavy demands on the labor force, factory hours were extended, and women were brought into the workforce in great numbers. Unemployment disappeared, and the working classes had more money to spend than they had enjoyed for many years. To avoid inflation caused by increased demand for an inadequate supply of consumer goods, savings were encouraged, and taxes were raised to absorb the excess purchasing power.

The bombing "blitz" conducted by the German *Luftwaffe* against British targets in the winter and spring of 1940 to 1941 was the most immediate and dramatic experience of the war for the British people. The German air raids killed thousands and destroyed the homes of many more. Many families removed their children to the countryside. Gas masks were issued to thousands of city dwellers, who were frequently compelled to take shelter from the bombs in the London subways.

After the spring of 1941 Hitler needed most of his air force for the Russian front, but the bombing of Britain continued, killing more than 30,000 people. Terrible as it was, this toll was much smaller than the number of Germans killed by Allied bombing later in the war. In England as in Germany, however, the bombings, even such a terrible fire-bombing as the one at Dresden in February, 1945, did not break the people's spirit but seem to have made them more determined to resist.

During the worst months of the "blitz," Winston Churchill's remarkable speeches cheered and encouraged the British people. He united them with a sense of common suffering and purpose. They were called upon to make many sacrifices: Transportation facilities were strained simply from carrying enough coal for domestic heating and for running factories. Food and clothing for civilians were in short supply, and the government adopted strict rationing to achieve a fair distribution. Every scrap of land was farmed, increasing the productive portion by almost 4 million acres. Gasoline was in short supply, so private vehicles almost disappeared.

The British established their own propaganda machine to influence the Continent. The British Broadcasting Company (BBC) sent programs to every country in Europe in the local language to encourage resistance against the Nazis. At home the government used the radio to unify the nation. Soldiers at the front heard the same programs as their families at home.

For most of the British·population, strangely enough, the standard of living improved over the course of the war. The general health of the nation also improved for reasons that are still not clear. These gains should not be exaggerated, but many connected them with the government's active involvement in the economy and the lives of the citizens. This wartime experience may have contributed to the Labour Party's triumph in 1945, when the British voters repudiated Winston Churchill, the leader who had brought them through to victory in the war,

◀●▶ Read the Document
Winston Churchill, "Their Finest Hour" (Great Britain), 1940
at **MyHistoryLab.com**

many feared that a return to Conservative rule would bring a return to the economic misery of the 1930s.

The United States: American Women and African Americans in the War Effort

In the United States, the withdrawal of millions of men from the workforce and their induction into the armed forces created a demand for new workers, especially in the burgeoning defense industries. In part, the demand was filled by millions of women leaving the home to enter the labor force, some of them taking jobs in defense plants doing work usually done only by men. Economic pressures caused by the Great Depression of the 1930s had already brought many more women into the workforce than had been common before. Most came from poor families and worked in white-collar

jobs to support themselves or to help their families eke out a living. Even so, the heavy burden of housework and the widespread hostility to the idea of women working outside the home kept the vast majority of women at home.

America's entry into the war changed things quickly. The need for vast amounts of equipment to wage the war called for and attracted new groups to seek work in the many enlarged and newly created factories. African Americans from the South came to Northern and Western cities to seek well-paying jobs, and women, too, came forward in greater numbers than ever before. Prejudices of various kinds had kept them from many opportunities, but the needs of war overcame such prejudice. In October 1942, President Roosevelt made the new situation clear: "In some communities employers dislike to hire women. In others they are reluctant to hire Negroes. We can no longer afford to indulge such prejudice."

Many women already working moved over to jobs in the defense industries; others entered the workforce for the first time, lured less by wages than by patriotism. Their brothers and boyfriends were risking their lives for their country and its ideals of freedom and democracy. They were eager to do their part to support them, to be, in the words of a current song, the woman "behind the man behind the gun." Another popular song, "Rosie the Riveter," told of a young woman working in an aircraft factory to provide protection for her boyfriend in the Marines. Rosie came to be one of the best known symbols of the war effort when she appeared on the cover of the *Saturday Evening Post*. With her rivet gun on her lap she stamped on a copy of Hitler's *Mein Kampf*, the hated symbol of the enemy's evil.

The Soviet Union: "The Great Patriotic War"

No nation suffered greater loss of life or more extensive physical destruction during World War II than the Soviet Union. Perhaps as many as 16 million people were killed, and vast numbers of Soviet troops were taken prisoner. Hundreds of cities and towns and well over half the industrial and transportation facilities of the country were devastated. The Germans sent thousands of Soviet prisoners to work in factories in Germany as forced labor. The Germans also confiscated grain supplies and drew mineral resources and oil from the Soviet Union to serve their own war effort.

Stalin (1879–1953) conducted the war as virtual chief of the armed forces, and the State Committee for Defense provided strong central coordination. In the decade before the war, Stalin had already made the Soviet Union a highly centralized nation; he had attempted to manage the entire economy centrally through the Five-Year Plans, the collectivization of agriculture, and the purges. The country was thus on what amounted to a wartime footing long before the conflict erupted. When the war began, millions of citizens entered

A Closer Look

Rosie the Riveter

The entry of the United States into the Second World War called for rapid and vast increases in American industrial production to meet the needs of the United States and its allies. At the same time the removal of millions of American men from the workforce by the requirements of military service created unprecedented demands for workers to fill the gaps. To encourage women into war work, the United States government conducted a campaign of publicity to celebrate a new role for women as patriotic citizens fully capable of supporting the war effort by taking jobs even in heavy industry. The best known symbol created was "Rosie the Riveter," feminine but strong and able, the ideal woman worker: loyal, efficient, and patriotic. A hit song, "Rosie the Riveter", first used the name in 1942 and made it very popular. Soon, the government commissioned posters that featured Rosie over the caption "We Can Do It." Rosie became the most famous representation of a new and important role for women in winning the war.

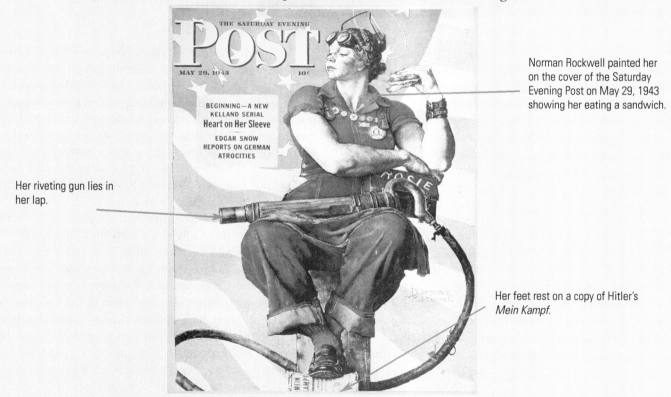

Norman Rockwell painted her on the cover of the Saturday Evening Post on May 29, 1943 showing her eating a sandwich.

Her riveting gun lies in her lap.

Her feet rest on a copy of Hitler's *Mein Kampf.*

Printed by permission of the Norman Rockwell Family Agency. Copyright © 1943 the Norman Rockwell Family Entities. © 1943 SEPS: Licensed by Curtis Publishing, Indianapolis, IN. All rights reserved. www.curtispublishing.com

Questions

1. Why was it necessary to lure great numbers of women into industrial jobs?
2. What is the significance of Rosie's footrest?
3. Based on what you have read about the years prior to U. S. involvement in World War 11, how much of a departure is this image from the "traditional" role of women at the time? Was this the precursor to a new direction for women in U.S. society or did things return to the way they had been once the war ended?

Home front. Russian women apply grease to howitzer shells at a munitions plant during World War II.

the army, but the army did not grow in influence at the expense of the state and the Communist Party—that is, Stalin.

Soviet propaganda differed from the propaganda of other nations. Because the Soviet government distrusted the loyalty of its citizens, it confiscated radios to prevent the people from listening to German propaganda. In large cities the government erected large loudspeakers to broadcast to the people in place of radios. Soviet propaganda emphasized Russian patriotism, not Marxist class conflict. The struggle was called "The Great Patriotic War." As in other countries, writers and playwrights helped sustain public support for the war. Sometimes they drew on communist themes, but they also portrayed the common Soviet citizen as contributing to a great patriotic struggle.

Great Russian novels of the past reappeared; more than half a million copies of Tolstoy's *War and Peace* were published during the siege of Leningrad. Other authors wrote straightforward propaganda fostering hatred of the Germans. Serge Eisenstein (1898–1948), the great filmmaker, produced a vast epic entitled *Ivan the Terrible*, which glorified one of the most brutal tsars of Russia's past. Musicians, such as Dimitri Shostakovich (1906–1975), wrote scores that sought to contribute to the struggle and evoke heroic emotions. The most important of these works was Shostakovich's Seventh Symphony, also known as the "Leningrad Symphony."

Stalin even made peace with the Russian Orthodox Church. He pursued friendly relations with church leaders and allowed them to enter the Kremlin. Stalin hoped that this new policy would give him more support at home and permit the Soviet Union to be viewed more favorably in those parts of eastern Europe where the Orthodox Church predominated.

Within occupied portions of the western Soviet Union, an active resistance movement arose against the Germans. The swiftness of the German invasion had stranded thousands of Soviet troops, some of whom escaped and carried on irregular resistance warfare behind enemy lines. Stalin supported partisan forces in lands held by the enemy for two reasons: He wanted to cause as much difficulty as possible for the Germans; and the Soviet-sponsored resistance reminded the peasants in the conquered regions that the Soviet government, with its policies of collectivization, had not disappeared. Stalin feared that the peasants' hatred of the communist government might lead them to collaborate with the invaders. When the Soviet army moved westward toward the end of the war, it incorporated the partisans into the regular army.

As the Soviet armies reclaimed the occupied areas and then moved across eastern and central Europe, the Soviet Union established itself as a world power second only to the United States. Stalin had been a reluctant belligerent, but he emerged a major victor. In that respect, the war and the extraordinary patriotic effort and sacrifice it generated consolidated the power of Stalin and the party more effectively than had the political and social policies of the previous decade.

Preparations for Peace

The split between the Soviet Union and its wartime allies that followed the war and began to emerge as it ended should cause no surprise. As the self-proclaimed center of world communism, the Soviet Union was openly dedicated to the overthrow of the capitalist nations, although this message was muted when the occasion demanded. On the other side, the Western allies were no less open about their hostility to communism and its chief purveyor, the Soviet Union.

Although cooperation against a common enemy and strenuous propaganda efforts in the West helped improve Western feeling toward the Soviet ally, Stalin remained suspicious and critical of the Western war effort. Likewise, Churchill never ceased planning to contain the Soviet advance into Europe. For some time Roosevelt seems to have hoped that the Allies could continue to work together after the war, but even he was losing faith by 1945. Differences in historical development and ideology, as well as traditional conflicts over political power and influence, soon dashed hopes of a mutually satisfactory peace settlement and continued cooperation to uphold it.

The Atlantic Charter

In August 1941, even before America entered the war, Roosevelt and Churchill had met off Newfoundland and agreed to the Atlantic Charter. A broad set of principles in the spirit of Wilson's Fourteen Points, it provided a theoretical basis for the peace they sought. When Russia and the United States joined Britain in the war, the three powers entered a purely military alliance in January 1942, leaving all political questions aside. The first political conference was the meeting of foreign ministers in Moscow in October 1943. The ministers reaffirmed earlier agreements to fight on until the enemy surrendered unconditionally and to continue cooperating after the war in a United Nations organization.

●•●─[Read the Document
Roosevelt and Churchill:
The Atlantic Charter, 1941
at **MyHistoryLab.com**

Tehran

The first meeting of the three leaders took place at Tehran, the capital of Iran, in 1943. Western promises to open a second front in France the next summer (1944) and Stalin's agreement to join in the war against Japan (when Germany was defeated) created an atmosphere of goodwill in which to discuss a postwar settlement. Stalin wanted to retain what he had gained in his pact with Hitler and to dismember Germany. Roosevelt and Churchill made no firm commitments.

The most important decision was for the Western Allies to attack Germany from Europe's west coast instead of from southern Europe by way of the Mediterranean. This decision meant, in retrospect, that Soviet forces would occupy eastern Europe and control its destiny. At Tehran in 1943 the Western Allies did not foresee this outcome clearly, for the Russians were still fighting deep within their own frontiers, and military considerations were paramount everywhere. Among other important concessions Roosevelt and Churchill made to Stalin was to move Poland's western border to the Oder and Neisse rivers.

By 1944 the situation was different. In August, Soviet armies were in sight of Warsaw, which had risen in expectation of liberation. But the Russians turned south into the Balkans, allowing the Polish rebels to be annihilated. The

Russians gained control of Romania and Hungary, gaining advances of which centuries of expansionist tsars had only dreamed. Alarmed by these developments, Churchill went to Moscow and met with Stalin in October. They agreed to share power in the Balkans on the basis of Soviet predominance in Romania and Bulgaria, Western predominance in Greece, and equality of influence in Yugoslavia and Hungary. These agreements were not enforceable without American approval, and the Americans were known to be hostile to such un-Wilsonian devices as "spheres of influence."

The three powers easily agreed on Germany's disarmament and denazification and on its division into four zones of occupation by France and the Big Three (the USSR, Britain, and the United States). Churchill, however, began to balk at Stalin's plan to dismember Germany and objected to his demand for reparations in the amount of $20 billion as well as for forced labor from all the zones, with Russia to get half of everything. These matters were left to fester and cause dissension in the future.

The settlement of eastern Europe remained a problem. Everyone agreed that the Soviet Union deserved neighboring governments that were friendly, but the West insisted that they also be independent, autonomous, and democratic. The Western leaders, and especially Churchill, were not eager to see eastern Europe fall under Russian domination. They, especially Roosevelt, were also truly committed to democracy and self-determination.

However, Stalin knew that independent, freely elected governments in Poland and Romania would not be safely friendly to Russia. He had already established a subservient government in Poland at Lublin in competition with the Polish government in exile in London. Under pressure from the Western leaders, however, Stalin agreed to reorganize the government and to include some Poles friendly to the West. He also signed a Declaration on Liberated Europe, promising self-determination and free democratic elections. Stalin was never free of the fear that the Allies might still make an arrangement with Germany and betray him. Yet he appeared eager to avoid conflict before the war with Germany was over, and he probably thought it worth endorsing some meaningless principles as the price of continued harmony. In any case, he wasted little time violating these agreements.

Yalta

The next meeting of the Big Three was at Yalta in the Crimea in February 1945. The Western armies had not yet crossed the Rhine, and the Soviet army was within 100 miles of Berlin. The war with Japan continued, and no atomic explosion had yet taken place. Roosevelt, faced with an invasion of Japan and prospective heavy losses, was eager to bring the Russians into the Pacific war as soon as possible.

Big Three at Potsdam. This photograph shows the "Big Three" at Potsdam. By the summer of 1945 only Stalin remained of the original leaders of the major Allies. Roosevelt and Churchill had been replaced by Harry Truman and Clement Attlee, respectively.

As a true Wilsonian, Roosevelt also suspected Churchill's determination to maintain the British Empire and Britain's colonial advantages. The Americans thought that Churchill's plan to set up British spheres of influence in Europe would encourage the Russians to do the same and lead to friction and war. To encourage Russian participation in the war against Japan, Roosevelt and Churchill made extensive concessions to Russia in Asia. Again in the tradition of Wilson, Roosevelt stressed a United Nations organization: "Through the United Nations, he hoped to achieve a self-enforcing peace settlement that would not require American troops, as well as an open world without spheres of influence in which American enterprise could work freely."[2] Soviet agreement on these points seemed well worth concessions elsewhere.

The Big Three at Yalta, at **MyHistoryLab.com**

Potsdam

The Big Three met for the last time in the Berlin suburb of Potsdam in July 1945. Much had changed since the last conference. Germany was defeated, and news of the successful experimental explosion of an atomic weapon reached the American president during the meetings. The cast of characters was also different: President Truman had replaced Roosevelt; and Clement Attlee (1883–1967), leader of the Labour Party, had replaced Churchill during the conference. Previous agreements were reaffirmed, but progress on undecided questions was slow.

Russia's western frontier was moved far into what had been Poland and included part of German East Prussia (see

<hr>

[2] Robert O. Paxton, *Europe in the Twentieth Century* (New York: Harcourt Brace Jovanovich, 1975), p. 487.

Map 30–8. Territorial Changes in Europe after World War II. The map shows the shifts in territory that followed the defeat of the Axis. No peace treaty formally ended the war with Germany.

Map 30–8). In compensation, Poland was allowed "temporary administration" over the rest of East Prussia and Germany east of the Oder-Neisse River line, a condition that became permanent. In effect, Poland was moved about 100 miles west, at Germany's expense, to accommodate the Soviet Union. The Allies agreed that Germany would be divided into occupation zones until the final peace treaty was signed; the country would remain divided until the end of the Cold War more than forty years later.

A Council of Foreign Ministers was established to draft peace treaties for Germany's allies. Growing disagreements made the job difficult, and it was not until February 1947 that Italy, Romania, Hungary, Bulgaria, and Finland signed treaties. The Russians signed their own agreements with the Japanese in 1956. These disagreements were foreshadowed at Potsdam.

Summary

The Coming of War. The second great war of the twentieth century (1939–1945) grew out of the unsatisfactory resolution of the first. In retrospect, the two wars appear to some people to be one continuous conflict, with the two main periods of fighting separated by an uneasy truce. To others, that point of view distorts the situation by implying that the second war was the inevitable result of the first and its inadequate peace treaties.

The latter opinion seems more sound. Whatever the flaws of the treaties of Paris, the world suffered an even more terrible war than the first as a result of failures of judgment and will on the part of the victorious democratic powers. The United States, which had become the wealthiest and potentially the strongest nation in the world, disarmed almost entirely and withdrew into foolish isolation; it could play no important part in restraining the ambitious dictators who would bring on the war. Britain and France refused to face the threat posed by the Axis powers until the deadliest war in history was required to put it down. If the victorious democracies had remained strong, responsible, and realistic, they could have remedied whatever injustices or mistakes arose from the treaties without endangering the peace.

World War II. The second war itself was plainly a world war. The Japanese occupation of Manchuria in 1931 was a precursor. Other precursors were Italy's attack on Ethiopia in 1935, the intervention of Italy, Germany, and the Soviet Union in the Spanish Civil War (1936–1939); and Japan's attack on China in 1937. These developments revealed that aggressive forces were on the march around the globe and that the defenders of the world order lacked the will to stop them. The formation of the Axis among Germany, Italy, and Japan guaranteed that the war would be fought around the world. Fighting and suffering took place in Asia, Africa, the islands of the Pacific, and Europe. The use of atomic weapons brought the struggle to a close, but conventional weapons did almost all the damage. The survival of civilization was threatened even without the use of nuclear devices.

This war was ended not with unsatisfactory peace treaties but with no treaty at all in the European area where it had begun. The world quickly split into two unfriendly camps: the Western led by the United States and the Eastern led by the Soviet Union. This division hastened the liberation of former colonial territories.

Key Terms

Anschluss (p. 928)

appeasement (p. 926)

Axis (p. 927)

blitzkrieg (p. 941)

Holocaust (p. 935)

Lebensraum (p. 924)

Luftwaffe (p. 932)

Review Questions

1. What were Hitler's foreign policy aims? Was he bent on conquest in the East and dominance in the West, or did he simply want to return Germany to its 1914 boundaries?

2. Why did Britain and France adopt a policy of appeasement in the 1930s? What were its main features? Did the appeasers buy the West valuable time to prepare for war by their actions at Munich in 1938?

3. How was Hitler able to defeat France so easily in 1940? Why was the air war against Britain a failure? Why did Hitler invade Russia? Why did the invasion ultimately fail? Could it have succeeded?

4. Why did Japan attack the United States at Pearl Harbor? What was the significance of American intervention in the war? Why did the United States drop atomic bombs on Japan? Did President Truman make the right decision when he ordered the bombs used?

5. What impact did World War II have on the civilian population of Europe? How did experiences on the domestic front of Great Britain differ from those of Germany and France? What impact did "The Great Patriotic War" have on the people of the Soviet Union? Did participation in World War II solidify Stalin's hold on power?

6. What was Hitler's "Final Solution" to the Jewish problem? Why did Hitler want to eliminate Slavs as well? Some historians have looked at the twentieth century and have seen a period of great destruction as well as of great progress. Was the twentieth century truly a "century of Holocaust"? Discuss the ramifications of these questions.

Note: *To learn more about the topics in this chapter, please turn to the Suggested Readings at the end of the book. For additional sources related to this chapter please see MyHistoryLab.com.*

myhistorylab Connections

Reinforce what you learned in this chapter by studying the many documents,
images, maps, review tools, and videos available at **www.myhistorylab.com**.

Read and Review

✔●—⌐Study and Review **Chapter 30**

●●●—⌐Read the Document *Adolf Hitler, "The Obersalzberg
Speech", p. 924*
Constancia de la Mora from "In Place of Splendor", p. 927
Wannsee Protocol, p. 935
*Japanese Total War Research Institute; Plan for the Greater
East Asia Co-Prosperity Sphere, 1942, p. 937*
The Franck Report , p. 940
An Eyewitness to Hiroshima (1945), p. 941
*Gertrud Scholtz-Klink, "Speech to the Nazi Women's
Organization" (Germany), 1935, p. 942*
*Winston Churchill, "Their Finest Hour" (Great Britain),
1940, p. 944*
Roosevelt and Churchill: The Atlantic Charter, 1941, p. 947

●—⌐See the Map *The Nazi Empire in 1942, p. 934*
World War II in Europe, 1939–1945, p. 940
World War II in the Pacific, 1939-1945, p. 941

●—⌐View the Image *Emaciated Woman at Bergen-Belsen,
p. 935*
Operation Overlord, Normandy, 1944, p. 939
Nagasaki Atomic Bomb Attack–August 1945, p. 941
The Big Three at Yalta, p. 948

((●—⌐Hear the Audio *World War II 1, p. 930*

●—⌐Watch the Video *FDR on Winning the War, p. 937*

Research and Explore

●—⌐See the Map *The Expansion of Germany in the 1930s,
p. 924*

●—⌐Watch the Video *The Big Three at Yalta, p. 948*

((●—⌐**Hear** the **Audio**

Hear the audio file for Chapter 30 at
www.myhistorylab.com.

31 The West Since World War II

- The Cold War Era
- Towards Western European Unification
- European Society in the Second Half of the Twentieth Century and Beyond
- American Domestic Scene since World War II
- The Soviet Union to 1989
- 1989: Year of Revolutions in Eastern Europe
- The Collapse of the Soviet Union
- The Collapse of Yugoslavia and Civil War
- Challenges to the Atlantic Alliance

IN THE MORE THAN HALF A CENTURY SINCE THE CONCLUSION of World War II, Europe's influence on the world scene has been transformed. The destruction and financial strains of the war left Europe exhausted and incapable of exercising the kind of power it had formerly exerted. Almost immediately after the war, the Cold War developed between the United States and the Soviet Union. Europe along with other parts of the world became a divided and contested territory, with America dominant in Western Europe and the Soviets dominant in Eastern Europe. The European powers themselves could not determine the outcome of that struggle for world dominance between the superpowers. Furthermore, less than five years after the war Europeans began to lose control of their overseas empires.

Within both the world context and the more narrow Western context, the greatest

The "beautiful game," by way of Europe. In the twentieth century the sport of soccer became the most popular game in the world. The World Cup, which takes place every four years, is a truly global event. The 2006 Cup attracted over 28 billion television viewers—the most watched event in history. Here Florent Malouda from France is taken down by two Italian players in the final in Berlin on July 10, 2006. Like several other players from the French squad, Malouda was an emigré. Indeed, the captain of the French team, Zinedine Zidane, who was ejected in a controversial call late in the game, has been quoted as saying, "First I am an Algerian from Marseille, and then a Frenchman." Italy went on to the win the match 5–3 in penalty kicks.

The West Since 1945

The West

Immediately after 1945 the nations of the West entered the Cold War. That ideological, economic, and military rivalry between the United States and the Soviet Union dominated political struggles throughout the world for more than half a century. It divided Europe between the North Atlantic Treaty Organization and Warsaw Pact military forces and forced nations outside of Europe, in Asia, Africa, and Latin America, to side with one or the other of the superpowers. Hence the Cold War too became a world war that had an important impact on non-Western nations. At times these other nations became theaters of conflict in which indigenous civil wars melded into the struggle between the United States and the Soviet Union, as in the case of Cuba, Angola, Korea, and Vietnam. A neutral stance in this conflict became extremely difficult for any nation to sustain.

In the later 1980s, however, the Cold War unexpectedly ended as the Soviet Union and the nations of Eastern Europe, their economies exhausted from failed experiments in central planning and repression, experienced enormous internal political changes and began the difficult transition to democracy and capitalism. These changes have clearly opened a new epoch of Western history. The United States has emerged from the Cold War as the single remaining superpower. Western Europe has achieved a new level of economic and political unity under the auspices of the European Union, although its peoples and governments are hesitant to press the process too far too rapidly. The economic success of the European Union has inspired other regional global treaties to promote free markets, including NAFTA (North American Free Trade Association), as well as the global WTO (World Trade Organization). Europe has also been more ambitious than the United States in promoting

change that took place after 1945 was the emergence of the United States as a fully active great power. The American retreat from leadership that occurred in 1919 was not repeated. The United States' decision to take an activist role in world affairs touched virtually every aspect of the postwar world. As a result of this acceptance of a leadership role, American domestic politics and its foreign policy became intertwined as in no previous period of American history.

Europe did not stagnate in this situation. Rather, its society continued to develop in new directions. Yet for forty-five years after World War II, Europe remained divided between a Western region generally characterized by democracies and an Eastern region characterized by Communist Party authoritarian states dominated by the Soviet Union. From the late 1970s onward there were political stirrings and economic stagnation in Eastern Europe and the Soviet Union. These stirrings culminated in 1989 with revolutions throughout Eastern Europe and in 1991 with the collapse of communist government in the Soviet Union itself. Since those events Europeans have been seeking to forge a new political direction. The movement toward unification, most

particularly of the currency, continues in western Europe. But the several nations that emerged from the former Soviet Union continue to experience political confusion and economic stagnation. The attacks of September 11, 2001, on the United States and the international events flowing therefrom have challenged the post–World War II Western alliance. The world financial crisis originating in 2008 have brought serious challenges to European economic life. ∎

The Cold War Era

Areas of Early Cold War Conflict

The tense relationship between the United States and the Soviet Union that dominated world history during the second half of the twentieth century originated in the closing months of World War II. In part, the new coldness between the Allies arose from the mutual feeling that each had violated previous agreements. The Russians were plainly asserting permanent control of Poland and Romania under puppet communist governments. The United States, on the

((•─[Hear the Audio
Cold War 1
at **MyHistoryLab.com**

other hand, was taking a harder line on the extent of German reparations to the Soviet Union.

international organizations such as the World Court designed to discipline countries that oppress their neighbors or threaten world peace. Eastern Europe and the former Soviet Union are experiencing economic turmoil and political uncertainty. Although some eastern European countries such as Poland, the Czech Republic, and Hungary are better prepared than others to join the European Union, the shared aspiration of all eastern European nations to become EU members bodes well for the future of this region. Except for Latvia, Estonia, and Lithuania, newly independent former regions of the Soviet Union such as Ukraine, Georgia, and Belarus have an even more difficult path ahead of them in developing their economies and societies. Together with the Islamic countries, such as Uzbekistan, Turkmenistan, and Kazakhstan, these countries face added difficulties from the legacy of repressive authoritarian government and centrally planned economies. The security of Europe's eastern borders will depend on the success of these eastern European nations and former Soviet republics in making the transition to democracy.

Another important factor in the history of both the United States and Europe since World War II has been the rising immigration from the rest of the world. Germany has seen the influx of significant numbers of Islamic *gastarbeiters* (guest workers) from Turkey, while France, Italy, and Spain receive numerous Islamic immigrants from North Africa and the Middle East, many from their former colonies. The United States, with its long history as an immigrant nation, has been more comfortable dealing with the influx of non-European immigrants, but struggles persist over language, cultural identity, and assimilation. Europe, less accustomed to non-European immigration, has found it even more difficult to accommodate immigrants whose religions, languages, and appearance differ from those of Europeans and who may not seek to assimilate to the cultures of the nations where they have come to reside.

Focus Questions

■ What was the Cold War, and why can we rightly call it a world war?

■ How has the relationship between the United States and Europe changed since World War II? How might it develop in the future?

■ What immediate and long-term factors accounted for the collapse of the Soviet Union?

■ How has immigration changed the face of Europe since 1945? What is the religious dimension of that immigration?

H-bomb Shelter. In 1950 Albert Einstein wrote that "Radioactive poisoning of the atmosphere and hence annihilation of any life on earth has been brought within the range of technical possibilities. . . . In the end, there beckons more and more clearly general annihilation." The U.S. government, however, fostered belief in manageable atomic warfare in spite of the evidence from Japan, and backyard bomb shelters were a 1950s fad. This one could house a small family for up to five days. Standard features included canned food and water, sterno stove, battery-powered radio, chemical toilet, flashlight, blankets, and first-aid kit. During peacetime, the shelter could be used as a spare bedroom, for storage space, or even to cultivate mushrooms.

Read the Document
Josef Stalin, excerpts from the "Soviet Victory" Speech, 1946 at **MyHistoryLab.com**

Read the Document
Iron Curtain Speech, Winston Churchill at **MyHistoryLab.com**

The new mood of hostility among the former allies appeared quickly. In February 1946 both Stalin and his foreign minister, Vyacheslav Molotov (1890–1986), gave public speeches in which they spoke of the Western democracies as enemies. A month later Churchill (1874–1965) delivered a speech in Fulton, Missouri, in which he spoke of an Iron Curtain that had descended on Europe, dividing a free and democratic West from an East under totalitarian rule. He warned against communist subversion and urged Western unity and strength to counter the new menace. In this atmosphere, difficulties grew.

The attempt to deal cooperatively with the problem of atomic energy was an early victim of the **Cold War**. The Americans put forward a plan to place the manufacture and control of atomic weapons under international control, but the Russians balked at proposed requirements for on-site inspection and for limits on veto power in the United Nations. The plan fell through. The United States continued to develop its own atomic weapons in secrecy, and the Russians did the same. By 1949, with the help of information obtained by Soviet spies in Britain and the United States, the Soviet Union had exploded its own atomic bomb, and the race for nuclear weapons was on.

The resistance of Westerners to what they increasingly perceived as Soviet intransigence and communist plans for subversion and expansion took clearer form in 1947. Since 1944 civil war had been raging in Greece between the royalist government restored by Britain and insurgents supported by the communist countries, chiefly Yugoslavia. In 1947 Britain informed the United States that it was financially no longer able to support the Greeks. On March 12 President Truman (1884–1972) asked Congress for legislation that would provide funds to support Greece and also Turkey, which was under Soviet pressure to yield control of the Dardanelles, and Congress complied. In what became known as the Truman Doctrine, the American president advocated a policy of supporting "free people who are resisting attempted subjugation by armed minorities or by outside pressures," by implication anywhere in the world.

◆◆◆ Read the Document
The Truman Doctrine (1947)
Harry S. Truman at
MyHistoryLab.com

American aid to Greece and Turkey took the form of military equipment and advisers. For Western Europe, where the menacing growth of communist parties was fueled by postwar poverty and hunger, the Americans devised the European Recovery Program. Named the **Marshall Plan** after George C. Marshall (1880–1959), the secretary of state who introduced it, this program provided broad economic aid to European states on condition only that they work together for their mutual benefit. The Soviet Union and its satellites were invited to participate. Finland and Czechoslovakia were willing, and Poland and Hungary showed interest. The Soviets, however, forbade them to take part.

◆◆◆ Read the Document
George C. Marshall,
The Marshall Plan, 1947
at **MyHistoryLab.com**

The Marshall Plan helped restore prosperity to Western Europe and set the stage for Europe's unprecedented postwar economic growth. It also led to the waning of communist strength in the West and to the establishment there of solid democratic regimes.

From the Western viewpoint, these moves marked the beginning of a policy of containment, a new and successful response to the Soviet and communist challenge. Stalin considered it a renewal of the old Western attempt to isolate and encircle the USSR. His answer was to replace all multiparty governments behind the Iron Curtain with thoroughly communist regimes completely under his control. He also called a meeting of all communist parties around the world at Warsaw in the autumn of 1947. There they organized the Communist Information Bureau (Cominform), a revival of the old Comintern, dedicated to spreading revolutionary communism throughout the world.

In February 1948 a more dramatic and brutal display of Stalin's new policy took place in Prague. The Communists expelled the democratic members of what had been a coalition government and murdered Jan Masaryk (1886–1948), the

Berlin Airlift. The Allied airlift in action during the Berlin Blockade. Every day for almost a year Western planes supplied the city until Stalin lifted the blockade in May 1949.

foreign minister and son of the founder of Czechoslovakia, Thomas Masaryk (1850–1937). President Eduard Benes (1884–1948) was forced to resign, and Czechoslovakia was brought fully under Soviet rule.

These Soviet actions, especially those in Czechoslovakia, increased American determination to go ahead with its own arrangements in Germany. The Russians swiftly dismantled German industry in the eastern zone, but the Americans chose to try to make Germany self-sufficient, which meant restoring rather than destroying its industrial capacity. To the Soviets the restoration of a powerful industrial Germany, even in the western zones only, was frightening and unacceptable.

Disagreement over Germany produced the most heated postwar debate. When the Western powers agreed to proceed with a separate constitution for the western sectors of Germany in February 1948, the Soviets walked out of the joint Allied Control Commission. In the summer of that year the Western powers issued a new currency in their zone. Berlin, though well within the Soviet zone, was governed by all four powers. The Soviets chose to seal off the city by closing all railroads and highways to West Germany. Their purpose was to drive the Western powers out of Berlin.

The Western allies responded to the Berlin Blockade with an airlift of supplies to the city that lasted almost a year. In May 1949 the Russians were forced to back down and to open access to Berlin. The incident greatly increased tensions and suspicions between the opponents. It hastened the separation of Germany into two states, a situation that would prevail for forty years. West Germany formally became the German Federal Republic in September 1949, and the eastern region became the German Democratic Republic a month later.

NATO and the Warsaw Pact

Meanwhile, the nations of Western Europe had been coming closer together. The Marshall Plan encouraged international cooperation. In March 1948 Belgium, the Netherlands, Luxembourg, France, and Britain signed the Treaty of Brussels, providing for cooperation in economic and military matters. In April 1949 these nations joined Italy, Denmark, Norway, Portugal, and Iceland to sign a treaty with Canada and the United States that formed the North Atlantic Treaty Organization (NATO). NATO committed its members to mutual assistance in case any of them was attacked. For the first time in history the United States committed itself to defend allies outside the Western Hemisphere. NATO formed

the West into a bloc. A few years later West Germany, Greece, and Turkey joined the alliance (see Map 31–1). The formation of NATO represented the culminating moment in the formulation of the United States' policy of containment, which had originated with the Truman Doctrine and Marshal Plan. This policy, formally ratified by U.S. decision makers in 1950, assumed that the Soviet Union by its fundamental political character sought to be an expansionist power the extension of which must be resisted or contained. (See Document, "The United States National Security Council Proposes to Contain the Soviet Union.")

Soviet relations with the states of Eastern Europe were governed by a series of bilateral treaties providing for close ties and mutual assistance in case of attack. In 1949 the Council of Mutual Assistance (COMECON) was formed to integrate the economies of these states. Unlike the NATO states, the Eastern alliance system was under direct Soviet domination through local communist parties controlled from Moscow and overawed by the presence of the Red Army. The Warsaw Pact of May 1955, which included Albania, Bulgaria, Czechoslovakia, East Germany, Hungary, Poland, Romania, and the Soviet

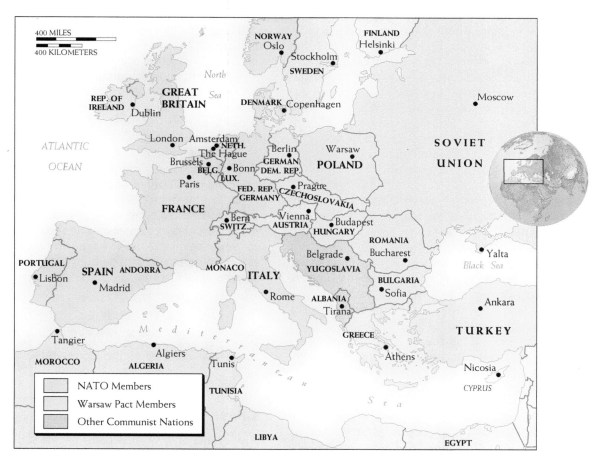

Map 31–1. Major Cold War European Alliance Systems. The North Atlantic Treaty Organization, which includes both Canada and the United States, stretches as far east as Turkey. By contrast, the Warsaw Pact nations were the contiguous communist states of Eastern Europe, with the Soviet Union, of course, as the dominant member.

Document

The United States National Security Council Proposes to Contain the Soviet Union

In response to the subjugation of Eastern Europe by Communist parties dominated by the Soviet Union and the occupation of these nations by Soviet troops, the United States government in 1950 adopted a policy of "containment" of the Soviet Union. This policy had been debated for many months and had for all practical purposes been in effect since the declaration of the Truman Doctrine in 1947. It was formally set forth after a period of implementation in what became known as the National Security Council Paper 68, arguably the most important statement of American foreign policy of the mid-twentieth century. The paper presented the Soviet Union as a nation determined to pursue an expansionist foreign policy and ideological struggle and as a long-term solution to that challenge proposed a policy of containing the influence of the Soviet Union diplomatically and militarily.

■ *How did the National Security Council characterize Soviet policy? How did the Council actively encourage U.S. engagement with the rest of the world? What were the goals of containment? Why did the Council urge that the Soviet Union always be given opportunity to save face and to back down with dignity?*

The fundamental design of those who control the Soviet Union and the international communist movement is to retain and solidify their absolute power, first in the Soviet Union and second in the areas now under their control. . . .

The design, therefore, calls for the complete subversion or forcible destruction of the machinery of government and structure of society in the countries of the non-Soviet world and their replacement by an apparatus and structure subservient to and controlled from the Kremlin. . . .

Our overall policy at the present time may be described as one designed to foster a world environment in which the American system can survive and flourish. It therefore rejects the concept of isolation and affirms the necessity of our positive participation in the world community.

This broad intention embraces two subsidiary policies. One is a policy which we would probably pursue even if there were no Soviet threat. It is a policy of attempting to develop a healthy international community. The other is the policy of "containing" the Soviet system. . . .

As for the policy of "containment," it is one which seeks by all means short of war to (1) block further expansion of Soviet power, (2) expose the falsities of Soviet pretensions, (3) induce a retraction of the Kremlin's control

and influence, and (4) in general, so foster the seeds of destruction within the Soviet system that the Kremlin is brought at least to the point of modifying its behavior to conform to generally accepted international standards. . . .

One of the most important ingredients of power is military strength. . . . Without superior aggregate military strength . . . a policy of "containment"—which is in effect a policy of calculated and gradual coercion—is no more than a policy of bluff.

At the same time, it is essential to the successful conduct of a policy of "containment" that we always leave open the possibility of negotiation with the USSR . . .

In "containment" it is desirable to exert pressure in a fashion which will avoid so far as possible directly challenging Soviet prestige, to keep open the possibility for the USSR to retreat before pressure with a minimum loss of face and to secure political advantage from the failure of the Kremlin to yield or take advantage of the openings we leave it.

Source: National Security Council, Paper Number 68, *Foreign Relations of the United States* (Washington, DC: U.S. Government Printing Office, 1977), Sections: III, IV, VI. as cited on http://www.seattleu.edu/artsci/history/us1945/docs/nsc68-1.htm.

((•—[Hear the Audio
Cold War 1, Slide 2
at **MyHistoryLab.com**

Union, merely gave formal recognition to a system that already existed. Europe stood divided into two unfriendly blocs.

In 1953 Stalin died, and later that year an armistice was concluded in Korea (see Chapter 32). Both events produced hope that international tensions might lessen, but the rivalry of power and polemics soon resumed.

Crises of 1956

The events of 1956 had considerable significance both for the Cold War and for what they implied about the realities of European power in the postwar era.

Suez In July 1956 President Gamal Abdel Nasser (1918–1970) of Egypt nationalized the Suez Canal. Great

Britain and France feared that this action would close the canal to their supplies of oil in the Persian Gulf. In October 1956 war broke out between Egypt and Israel. The British and French seized the opportunity to intervene; however, the United States refused to support their action. The Soviet Union protested vehemently. The Anglo-French forces had to be withdrawn, and control of the canal remained with Egypt.

The Suez intervention proved that without the support of the United States the nations of Western Europe could no longer undertake meaningful military operations to impose their will on the rest of the world. It also appeared that the United States and the Soviet Union had restrained their allies from undertaking actions that might have resulted in a wider conflict. The fact that neither of the superpowers wanted war constrained both Egypt and the Anglo-French forces.

Poland The autumn of 1956 also saw important developments in Eastern Europe that demonstrated similar limitations on independent action among the Soviet bloc nations. When the prime minister of Poland died, the Polish Communist Party leaders refused to choose, as his successor, the person selected by Moscow. Considerable tension developed. The Soviet leaders even visited Warsaw to make their opinions known. In the end, Wladyslaw Gomulka (1905–1982) emerged as the new communist leader of Poland. He was the choice of the Poles, and he proved acceptable to the Soviets because he promised continued economic and military cooperation and most particularly continued Polish membership in the Warsaw Pact. Within those limits he halted the collectivization of Polish agriculture and improved the relationship between the communist government and the Polish Roman Catholic Church.

Uprising in Hungary Hungary provided the second East European trouble spot for the Soviet Union. In late October demonstrations of sympathy for the Poles occurred in Budapest. When the communist government moved to stop the demonstrations, street fighting erupted. A new ministry headed by former premier Imre Nagy (1896–1958) was installed by the Hungarian Communist Party. Nagy was a communist who sought a more independent position for Hungary. He went much further in his demands than Gomulka and directly appealed for political support from noncommunist groups in Hungary. Nagy called for the removal of Soviet troops and the ultimate neutralization of Hungary. He even called for Hungarian withdrawal from the Warsaw Pact. These demands were wholly unacceptable to the Soviet Union. In early November Soviet troops invaded Hungary; deposed Nagy, who was later executed; and imposed Janos Kadar (1912–1989) as premier.

The Cold War Intensified

The events of 1956 ended the era of fully autonomous action by the European nation-states. In different ways and to differing degrees, the two superpowers had demonstrated the new political realities. After 1956 the Soviet Union began to talk about "peaceful coexistence" with the United States. In 1958 negotiations began between the two countries for limitations on the testing of nuclear weapons. However, in the same year the Soviet Union also announced that the status of West Berlin had to be changed and the Allied occupation forces withdrawn. The demand was refused. In 1959 tensions relaxed sufficiently for several Western leaders to visit Moscow and for Soviet Premier Nikita Khrushchev (1894–1971) to tour the United States. A summit meeting

Chronology

Major Dates in the Era of the Cold War

	Berlin Blockade
1949	Formation of the North Atlantic Treaty Organization (NATO)
1950	Outbreak of the Korean War
1953	Death of Stalin
1956 July	Egypt seizes the Suez Canal
October	Anglo-French attack on the Suez Canal; Hungarian Revolution
1957	Treaty of Rome establishes the European Economic Community (EEC)
1960	Paris Summit Conference collapses
1961	Berlin Wall erected
1962	Cuban Missile Crisis
1963	Russian-American Test Ban Treaty
1968	Russian invasion of Czechoslovakia
1975	Helsinki Accords
1979	Russian invasion of Afghanistan
1981	Military crackdown on Solidarity Movement in Poland
1985	Reagan–Gorbachev summit
1987	Major American-Soviet Arms Limitation Treaty
1989	Berlin Wall comes down
1991	Soviet Union dissolves

MISSILE EQUIPMENT
MARIEL PORT FACILITY
4 NOVEMBER 1962

Cuban Missile Crisis of 1962. The American ambassador to the United Nations displayed photographs to persuade the world of the threat to the United States less than 100 miles from its own shores.

was scheduled for May 1960 in Paris, and American President Dwight D. Eisenhower (1890–1969) was to go to Moscow. Just before the gathering, however, the Soviet Union shot down an American U-2 aircraft that was flying reconnaissance over Soviet territory. Khrushchev demanded an apology from President Eisenhower, who accepted responsibility but refused to apologize. Khrushchev then refused to take part in the summit conference, and Eisenhower's trip to the Soviet Union was canceled.

Read the Document
The Kitchen Debate
at **MyHistoryLab.com**

The Soviet actions aimed at destroying the possibility of the summit conference on the eve of its opening were not simply the result of the American spy flights. The Soviets had long been aware of the American flights but chose to protest at this time for two reasons. Khrushchev had hoped that the leaders of Britain, France, and the United States would be sufficiently divided over the future of Germany so that a united Allied front would be impossible. But the divisions did not come about as he had hoped, and, consequently, the conference would have been of little use to him. Second, by 1960 the communist world itself had become split between the Soviets and the Chinese. The Chinese accused the Russians of lacking revolutionary zeal. Khrushchev's action was, in part, a response to those charges and proof of the hard-line attitude of the Soviet Union toward the capitalist world.

The abortive Paris conference opened the most difficult period of the Cold War. In 1961 the new U.S. president, John F. Kennedy (1917–1963), and Premier Khrushchev met in Vienna. The conference was inconclusive, but Kennedy left wondering if the two nations could avoid war. Throughout 1961 thousands of refugees from East Germany had fled to West Berlin. In August 1961 the East Germans erected a

Watch the Video
Escaping the Berlin Wall
at **MyHistoryLab.com**

concrete wall along the border between East and West Berlin to halt this outflow. Henceforth, until November 1989, it was possible to cross only at designated checkpoints and with proper papers.

A year later the Cuban Missile Crisis brought the most dangerous days of the Cold War. The Soviet Union placed missiles in Cuba, a nation friendly to Soviet aims lying less than 100 miles from the United States. The United States blockaded Cuba, halted the shipment of new missiles, and

Watch the Video
Cold War Connections:
Russia, America, Berlin, and
Cuba at **MyHistoryLab.com**

demanded the removal of existing installations. After a tense week the Soviets backed down and the crisis ended.

Détente and Afterward

In 1963 the two powers concluded the Nuclear Test Ban Treaty. This agreement marked the start of a lessening in the sharp tensions between the United States and the Soviet Union that had commenced just after the end of World War II. In 1968 the Soviet Union invaded Czechoslovakia to block its growing independence and to overthrow the government of its relatively liberal leader, Alexander Dubcek (1921–1974). Although deplored by the United States, this action led to no renewal of tensions. During the presidency of Richard Nixon (1913–1994) the United States embarked on a policy of détente, or reduction of tension, with the Soviet Union. This policy involved trade agreements and mutual reduction of strategic armaments. The Soviet invasion of Afghanistan in 1979, though not directly affecting Europe, hardened relations between Washington and Moscow, and

Soviet Invasion of Czechoslovakia. In the summer of 1968 Soviet tanks rolled into Czechoslovakia, ending that country's experiment in liberalized communism, known as the Prague Spring. This picture shows defiant, flag-waving Czechs, some standing atop an overturned truck and others surrounding a Soviet tank, in the immediate aftermath of the invasion.

President Ronald Reagan and Premier Mikhail Gorbachev confer at a summit meeting in December 1989.

the U.S. Senate refused to ratify the Strategic Arms Limitation Treaty of 1979.

The administration of President Ronald Reagan (1911–2004) initially slowed arms limitation negotiations and successfully deployed a major new missile system in Europe. The United States also launched a new arms proposal, known as the Strategic Arms Defense Initiative, to create a system that would use highly developed technology in space to defend against nuclear attack. The proposal was controversial at home but played a major role in arms negotiations between the United States and the Soviet Union. One of the purposes of the Reagan arms buildup was simply to outspend the Soviet Union and force it to exhaust its own financial resources and continue to starve consumer industries.

President Reagan and Soviet leader Mikhail S. Gorbachev (b. 1931) held a friendly summit meeting in 1985, the first East–West summit in six years. Other meetings followed. Arms negotiations continued until, in December 1987, the United States and the Soviet Union agreed to dismantle over 2,000 medium- and shorter-range missiles. The treaty provided for mutual inspection. This action represented the most significant agreement since World War II between the two superpowers.

Thereafter, the political upheavals in Eastern Europe and the Soviet Union overwhelmed the issues of the Cold War. The Soviet Union abandoned its support for communist governments in Eastern Europe. By the close of 1991 the Soviet Union itself had collapsed and been replaced by the Commonwealth of Independent States. The era of the Cold War had concluded in a manner that virtually no one had predicted.

Towards Western European Unification

Since 1945, the nations of western Europe have taken unprecedented steps toward economic cooperation. The process of economic integration has not been steady, nor is it completed. The collapse of the Soviet Union and the emergence of new free governments in eastern Europe have further complicated an already difficult process.

The Marshall Plan and NATO gave the involved countries new experience in working with each other and demonstrated the productivity, efficiency, and simple possibility of cooperative action. In 1950 France, West Germany, Italy, and the "Benelux" countries (Belgium, the Netherlands, and Luxembourg) organized the European Coal and Steel Community. Its success reduced the suspicions of government and business groups about the concept of coordination and economic integration.

It took more, however, to draw European leaders toward further unity. The unsuccessful Suez intervention and the resulting diplomatic isolation of France and Britain persuaded many Europeans that only through unified action could they significantly influence the two superpowers or control their own destinies. Consequently, in 1957, through the Treaty of Rome, the six members of the Coal and Steel Community agreed to form a new organization: the **European Economic Community**. The members of the Common Market, as the EEC soon came to be called, sought to achieve the eventual elimination of tariffs, a free flow of capital and labor, and similar wage and social benefits in all the participating countries. The chief institutions of the EEC were a Council of Foreign Ministers and a High Commission composed of technocrats. The Council of Foreign Ministers came to be the dominant body.

Read the Document
A Common Market and European Integration (1960)
at **MyHistoryLab.com**

The Common Market was a stunning success. By 1968 all tariffs among the six members had been abolished well ahead of the planned schedule. Trade and labor migration among the members grew steadily. Moreover, nonmember states began to copy the Community and seek membership. In 1959 Britain, Denmark, Norway, Sweden, Switzerland, Austria, and Portugal formed the European Free Trade Area. However, by 1961 Great Britain had decided to seek Common Market membership. Twice—in 1963 and 1967—France vetoed British membership on the grounds that Britain was too closely tied to the United States and its policies to support the EEC wholeheartedly.

Nevertheless, the Common Market survived and continued to prosper. In 1973 Great Britain, Ireland, and Denmark became members. Throughout the late 1970s, however, and into the 1980s momentum slowed. Norway

The Euro. Some thousand people stand around a huge euro symbol in a park in Frankfurt's banking district in Germany, January, 1, 1997.

and Sweden, with relatively strong economies, declined to join. Although in 1982 Spain, Portugal, and Greece applied for membership and were eventually admitted, there continued to be sharp disagreements and a sense of stagnation within the Community.

Finally, in early l988 the leaders of the Community targeted the year 1992 for achieving a virtual free-trade zone throughout the Community, entailing the elimination of remaining trade barriers and other restrictive trade policies. In 1991 the leaders of the Community signed the Treaty of Maastricht, which made a series of specific institutional proposals that would lead to a unified currency and a strong central bank. This treaty was submitted to referendums in a number of European states where it encountered resistance. When the treaty finally went into effect in November 1993, the European Community was renamed the **European Union** (**EU**), the name it continues to carry.

Read the Document
Treaty on European Union at
MyHistoryLab.com

The most striking recent element of the expanding momentum of economic cooperation is the adoption of a common currency, the **euro**. Austria, Belgium, Cyprus, Finland, France, Germany, Greece, Ireland, Italy, Luxembourg, the Netherlands, Portugal, Malta, Slovakia, Slovenia, and Spain now constitute the the Eurozone region using this new currency, which first appeared in January 2002. Such a widespread common currency is unprecedented in European history.

In 2004 the European Union embraced the largest expansion in its history. Ten new members entered the Union: Cyprus, the Czech Republic, Estonia, Hungary, Latvia, Lithuania, Malta, Poland, Slovakia, and Slovenia (see Map 31–2). The Union now included an additional

75 million people speaking nine languages. This expansion presents enormous challenges because the economies in these nations, most of which are from the former Eastern Soviet bloc, are much less economically developed. They came to the Union in hopes that membership would foster prosperity; Their needs have placed new political strains on the existing structures. These new members of the EU will be permitted to adopt the euro only when their economies have become sufficiently strong.

In 2007 the heads of state of the European Union signed the Lisbon Treaty. The purpose of this agreement was to create new institutions within the Union that would allow it to function more nearly as a unitary body on the world scene. The treaty established a presidency and also created vehicles for unified policy on matters such as climate change. It strengthened the enforcement of rights for citizens of the Union. The treaty stirred considerable debate in the various countries of the Union, but in late 2009 it had received all the ratifications necessary for it to go into effect.

View the Image
European Union Flag
at **MyHistoryLab.com**

The most public challenge that now faces and divides the nations of the European Union is the possible future admission of Turkey. Some European political leaders strongly favor this step provided Turkey achieves the economic and democratic structures requisite for European Union membership. Other leaders oppose its future admission because, they contend, Turkey has historically not been part of Europe. Opponents to admission are also apprehensive about the influence of Islamist political activity in Turkey. The debate over the possible membership of Turkey serves as a proxy for debate over the future cultural and religious character of the Union itself.

In the early years of the Union, religion was not a major topic of discussion, but the possible admission of Turkey with its overwhelmingly Islamic population has brought the issue to the fore. Similarly, France's determination to assert the secular character of its state by attempting to forbid Muslim women students from wearing headscarves has raised much controversy. The Italian government has moved to remove crucifixes from classrooms in public schools. All of these factors and others have begun to stir more public discussion about the character of religious freedom and the relationship of church and state in the European Union. The Roman Catholic Church has vigorously asserted the role of Christianity in the formation of European identity and has urged the recognition of religious freedom as a human right. (See

See the Map
Contemporary Europe at
MyHistoryLab.com

Document, "Pope Benedict XVI Calls for the Recognition of Religious Freedom as a Human Right.")

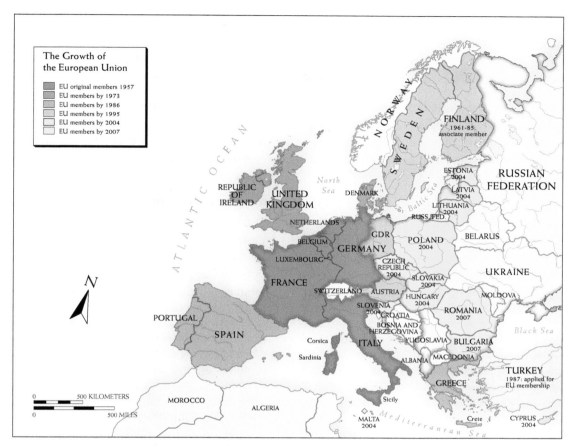

Map 31–2. **The Growth of the European Union.** This map traces the growth of membership in the European Union from its founding in 1957 through the introduction of its newest members in 2004. Note that even though Turkey has applied for membership it has not yet been admitted.

European Society in the Second Half of the Twentieth Century and Beyond

Toward a Welfare State Society

The Great Depression, the rise of authoritarian states in the wake of economic dislocation and mass unemployment, and World War II, which involved more people in a war effort than ever before, changed how many Europeans thought about social welfare. Governments began to spend more on social welfare than they did on the military. This reallocation of funds was a reaction to the state violence of the first half of the century and was possible because the NATO defense umbrella, which the United States primarily staffed and funded, protected Western Europe.

Creation of European Welfare States The modern European welfare state was broadly similar across the Continent. Before World War II, except in Scandinavia, the two basic models for social legislation were the German and the British. Bismarck had introduced social insurance in Germany during

the 1880s to undermine the German Social Democratic Party. In effect, the imperial German government provided workers with social insurance and thus some sense of social security while denying them significant political participation. In early-twentieth-century Britain, where all classes had access to the political system, social insurance was targeted toward the poor. In both the German and British systems, workers were insured only against the risks from disease, injury on the job, and old age. Unemployment was assumed to be only a short-term problem and often one that workers brought on themselves. People higher in the social structure could look out for themselves and did not need government help.

After World War II, the concept emerged that social insurance against predictable risks was a social right and should be available to all citizens. In Britain, William B. Beveridge (1879–1963) famously set forth this concept in 1942. Paradoxically, making coverage universal, as Beveridge recommended, appealed to conservatives as well as socialists. If medical care, old-age pensions, and other benefits were available to all, they would not become a device to redistribute income from one part of the population to another.

Document

Pope Benedict XVI Calls for the Recognition of Religious Freedom as a Human Right

On April 18, 2008, Pope Benedict XVI Addressed the United Nations General Assembly in New York City. In the course of a wide-ranging speech, the Pope paid special attention to religious freedom as a fundamental human right. He particularly defended religious freedom when its exercise stands in tension or conflict with the values of a surrounding secular society or other surrounding majority values.

■ *How did Pope Benedict XVI define religious freedom as a human right? How did he portray the relationship of the exercise of religious freedom to secular values and secular social institutions? How did he relate religious freedom to human betterment?*

Human rights. . . must include the right to religious freedom, understood as the expression of a dimension that is at once individual and communitarian — a vision that brings out the unity of the person while clearly distinguishing between the dimension of the citizen and that of the believer. The activity of the United Nations in recent years has ensured that public debate gives space to viewpoints inspired by a religious vision in all its dimensions, including ritual, worship, education, dissemination of information and the freedom to profess and choose religion. It is inconceivable, then, that believers should have to suppress a part of themselves — their faith — in order to be active citizens. It should never be necessary to deny God in order to enjoy one's rights.

The rights associated with religion are all the more in need of protection if they are considered to clash with a prevailing secular ideology or with majority religious positions of an exclusive nature. The full guarantee of religious liberty cannot be limited to the free exercise of worship, but has to give due consideration to the public dimension of religion, and hence to the possibility of believers playing their part in building the social order. . . .

Refusal to recognize the contribution to society that is rooted in the religious dimension and in the quest for the Absolute — by its nature, expressing communion between persons — would effectively privilege an individualistic approach, and would fragment the unity of the person. . . .

The United Nations remains a privileged setting in which the [Roman Catholic] Church is committed to contributing her experience "of humanity", developed over the centuries among peoples of every race and culture, and placing it at the disposal of all members of the international community. This experience and activity, directed towards attaining freedom for every believer, seeks also to increase the protection given to the rights of the person.

Those rights are grounded and shaped by the transcendent nature of the person, which permits men and women to pursue their journey of faith and their search for God in this world. Recognition of this dimension must be strengthened if we are to sustain humanity's hope for a better world and if we are to create the conditions for peace, development, cooperation, and guarantee of rights for future generations.

Source: Pope Benedict XVI's Address to the United Nations General Assembly, April I8, 2008 as reproduced on the Vatican City Website: http://www.vatican.va/holy_father/benedict_xvi/speeches/2008/april/documents/hf_ben-xvi_spe_20080418_un-visit_en.html

---

The first major European nation to begin to create a welfare state was Britain, in 1945–1951 under the Labour Party ministry of Clement Attlee (1883–1967). The most important element of this early legislation was the creation of the National Health Service. France and Germany did not adopt similar health care legislation until the 1970s because their governments initially refused to make coverage universal.

The spread of welfare legislation (including unemployment insurance) within Western Europe was related to both the Cold War and domestic political and economic policy. The communist states of Eastern Europe were promising their people social security as well as full employment. The capitalist states came to believe they had to provide similar security for their people, but, in fact, the social security of the communist states was often more rhetoric than reality.

Resistance to the Expansion of the Welfare State

Western European attitudes toward the welfare state have reflected three periods that have marked economic life since the end of the war. The first period was one of reconstruction from 1945 through the early 1950s. It was followed by the second period, twenty-five years of generally steady and

The March of Pain. Under the banner "The March of Pain," a crowd of angry protesters from the southern Italian city of Bari, members of an association for the handicapped, lobby for more government assistance. The demands of special interest groups on the welfare state increased dramatically in the 1960s and 1970s.

expanding economic growth. The third period brought first an era of inflation in the late 1970s and then one of relatively low growth and high unemployment from the 1990s to the present. During each of the first two periods, a general conviction existed, based on Keynesian economics, that the foundation of economic policy was government involvement in a mixed economy. From the late 1970s, more people came to believe the market should be allowed to regulate itself and that government should be less involved in, though not completely withdraw from, the economy.

The most influential political figure in reasserting the importance of markets and resisting the power of labor unions was Margaret Thatcher (b. 1925) of the British Conservative Party who served as prime minister from 1979 to 1990. She cut taxes and sought to curb inflation. She and her party were determined to roll back many of the socialist policies that Britain had enacted since the war. Her administration privatized many industries that Labour Party governments had nationalized. She also curbed the power of the trade unions in a series of bitter and often violent confrontations. Her goal was to make the British economy more efficient and competitive. Although her administration roused enormous controversy, she was able to push these policies through Parliament. Furthermore, over time the British Labour Party itself largely came to accept what was at the time known as the Thatcher Revolution.

While Thatcher redirected the British economy, the government-furnished welfare services now found across continental Europe began to encounter new challenges. The funding on which they are based assumed a growing population and low unemployment. As the proportion of the population consuming the services of the welfare state—the sick, the injured, the unemployed, and the elderly—increases relative to the number of able-bodied workers who pay for them, the costs of those services have risen. The leveling off of population growth in Europe has imperiled the benefits of the welfare state, which Europeans have come to take for granted. The low fertility rates across the Continent mean the next working generation will have fewer people to support the retired elderly population.

The general growth of confidence in the ability of market forces rather than government intervention to sustain social cohesion has also spread in the past twenty-five years and has raised questions about the existing welfare structures. Governments across the Continent, including those normally associated with left-of-center politics, such as the British Labour Party and the German Social Democratic Party, have limited further growth of the welfare state and have reduced benefits. In that respect, Europeans in the next few decades may look at the second half of the twentieth century as the Golden Age of welfare states and may find their own societies dealing with social welfare differently. (See Document, "Tony Blair Seeks to Redefine the British Welfare State." on page 964)

The Movement of Peoples

Many people migrated from, to, and within Europe during the half century following World War II.

External Migration   In the decade and a half after 1945 approximately half a million Europeans each year settled elsewhere in the world. This was the largest outward migration since the 1920s, when the rate was approximately 700,000 persons annually. While the earlier migrants had mostly been from rural areas, the later migrants often included educated city dwellers.

Decolonization in the postwar period contributed to an inward flow of European colonials from overseas (see Chapter 33). The most dramatic example of this phenomenon was the more than 1 million French colonials who moved to France after the end of the Algerian War. British citizens returned from various parts of the British Empire; Dutch people came back to the Netherlands from Indonesia, and Portuguese returned from Africa.

Decolonization also provoked a migration of non-European inhabitants of the former colonies to Europe. Great Britain, for example, received thousands of immigrants from India and Pakistan, as well as from its former African and Caribbean colonies. France received many immigrants from its former colonies in Indochina and the Arab world. This influx caused social tension and conflict. In Great Britain, for example, during the 1980s angry clashes took place between the police and non-European immigrants. France has had similar difficulties, which have contributed to the emergence there of the National Front, an extreme right-wing

Document | Tony Blair Seeks to Redefine the British Welfare State

Tony Blair (b. 1953) served as Labour Party prime minister of the United Kingdom from 1997 to 2007. During his time in office he championed what he termed New Labour and sought to redefine the British welfare state while still preserving many of its most basic outlines. In June 2002 he outlined his new understanding of the character of the welfare state and its role in promoting individual responsibility. In many respects his view of welfare and government social responsibility had been influenced by Margaret Thatcher's attack on earlier understandings of welfare and government social responsibility.

■ *How is it clear in this speech that Blair is trying to lead a traditional party of the left toward a new understanding of government social responsibility? What does Blair portray as duties of government? How does he seek to mesh government help for individuals while still assigning responsibility to the individuals receiving that help?*

In welfare, for too long, the right had let social division and chronic unemployment grow; the left argued for rights but were weak on responsibilities. We believe passionately in giving people the chance to get off benefit and into work. . . .

It's right for them, for the country, for society. But with the chance, comes a responsibility on the individual—to take the chance, to make something of their lives and use their ability and potential to the full. . . .

We must give the unemployed youth the skills to find a job; give the single mother the childcare she needs to go out and work; give the middle-aged man on a disability benefit the support and confidence to go back into the office.

And we must not only lift people out of poverty. We must transform their horizons, aspirations and hopes as well—through helping people get the skills they need for better jobs, and through giving them chance to save and build up a nest egg.

Only in this way will we drive up social mobility, the great force for equality in dynamic market economies.

To do all that, ours has to be an enabling welfare state—one which helps people to help themselves. . . .

Government has a responsibility to provide real opportunities for individuals to gain skills and to get into work that pays. But individuals also have a responsibility to grasp those opportunities.

We are now seeing the beginnings of a sea-change in how people view our welfare state. There is growing public support for a welfare state that tackles poverty at its source; that gets people into work; that offers people hope—in exchange for a commitment to help themselves. . . .

This is a welfare state which reflects all our responsibilities: the responsibility we have to engage actively with the jobless to provide them with opportunities; their responsibility to engage actively with us and take those opportunities. . . .

All of our reforms have the same underlying principles—opportunity, fairness and mutual responsibility. We want to give people the chance to fulfill their potential. We want to raise people's expectations and their self-belief, by giving them the tools to help themselves.

Source: Tony Blair, June 10, 2002 as made available at http://www.guardian.co.uk/society/2002/jun/10/socialexclusion.politics1.

group led by Jean-Marie Le Pen (b. 1928). This group has drawn strength from the racial and ethnic tensions that have developed as a tight job market provokes resentment among some working-class voters toward North African immigrants.

As a result of this external migration into Europe, large Islamic populations now exist in several European nations and have become political factors in France and Germany.

Internal Migration World War II and its aftermath created a vast refugee problem. Millions of people were displaced from their homes. Many cities in Germany and in central

and Eastern Europe had been bombed or overrun by invading armies. Hundreds of thousands of foreign workers had been moved into Germany to contribute to the war effort. There were thousands of prisoners of war. Some of these people were returned to their homeland willingly; others, unwillingly. Changes in borders after the war also caused many people to move or be moved. For example, Poland, Czechoslovakia, and Hungary sent millions of ethnic Germans to Germany. Hundreds of thousands of Poles left from territory taken over by the Soviet Union. An estimated 3 million East Germans migrated to West Germany (see Map 31–3.)

Map 31–3. Displaced Peoples in East and Central Europe, 1945–1950. World War II left millions of Europeans displaced. In an attempt to reestablish ethnic and linguistic uniformity within political boundaries, more than 31 million people were resettled between 1945 and 1952.

Once the Cold War set in, Soviet domination made it impossible for Eastern Europeans to migrate to other parts of Europe, whether for political or economic reasons. As a result, until the collapse of the Soviet Empire, most internal migration in Europe after the immediate postwar years occurred outside the communist bloc.

The major motivation for internal migration from the late 1950s onward was economic opportunity. The prosperous nations of northern and Western Europe had jobs that paid good wages and provided excellent benefits, often financed in part by the governments. Thus, there was a flow of workers from the poorer countries of Turkey, Greece, Yugoslavia, Italy, Spain, and Portugal into the wealthier countries of France, West Germany, Switzerland, and the Benelux nations. The establishment of the European Economic Community in 1957 facilitated this movement.

In the late 1980s politics again became a major factor in European migration. The pressure of thousands of refugees seeking to escape from Eastern Europe to the West contributed to the collapse of the communist governments of Eastern Europe in 1988 and 1989. Since 1989 people from all over Eastern Europe have migrated to the West. The civil war in the former Yugoslavia has also created many refugees. Europe has been in recession, however, and the new migrants are generating tension, resentment, and strife. Several nations have taken legal and administrative steps to restrict migration. The financial collapse that began in 2008 has led many people who had moved from eastern to western Europe in pursuit of employment to move back to their original countries of residence.

The New Muslim Population

Well into the twentieth century the European relationship with most of the Muslim world was either at arm's length or colonialist. Muslims from the Ottoman Empire, the greatest Muslim state, rarely traveled in Europe, and few Europeans traveled in the empire. Europeans encountered Muslims mainly as subjects, in colonies, such as Algeria, Egypt, the Indian subcontinent, sub-Saharan Africa, and the East Indies. In all of these regions from at least the midcentury onward, Christian missionaries often clashed with Muslim religious teachers.

At the same time most Europeans, with the exception of a few minority communities in the Balkans and the former Soviet Empire, regarded themselves and their national cultures as either Christian or secular. Indeed, until recently most Europeans paid little attention to Islam.

That indifference began to change in the 1960s and had dissolved by the end of the twentieth century as a sizable Muslim population settled in Europe. This highly diverse immigrant community had become an issue in Europe even before the events of September 11, 2001, discussed later in this chapter.

The immigration of Muslims into Europe and particularly Western Europe arose from two chief sources: European economic growth and decolonization. As the economies of Western Europe began to recover in the quarter century

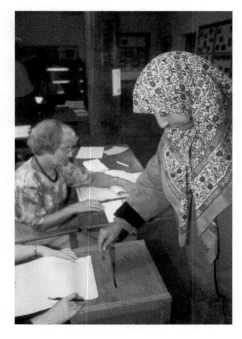

A Muslim woman wearing a traditional headscarf in Hamburg, Germany votes in the Bundestag elections. The presence of foreign-born Muslims whose labor is necessary for the prosperity of the European economy is an important issue in contemporary Europe. Many of these Muslims live in self-contained communities.

after World War II, a labor shortage developed. To fill this demand, Western Europe imported laborers, many of whom came from Muslim nations. For example, Turkish "guest workers" were invited to move to West Germany—on a temporary basis, it was presumed—in the 1960s, and Britain welcomed Pakistanis. The aftermath of decolonization and the quest for a better life led Muslims from East Africa and the Indian subcontinent to settle in Great Britain. The Algerian war brought many Muslims from North Africa into France. Today there are approximately 1.3 million Muslims in Great Britain, 3.2 million in Germany, and 4.2 million in France. Smaller but still significant numbers have settled in Italy, Spain, Sweden, Denmark, and the Netherlands, nations that had previously had generally homogeneous populations.

These Muslim immigrant communities share certain social and religious characteristics. Originally, many Muslims came to Europe expecting they would eventually return to their homes, an expectation their host countries shared. Neither the immigrants nor the host nations gave much thought to assimilation. Moreover, except for Great Britain, where all immigrants from the Commonwealth may vote immediately upon settling there, European governments made it difficult for Muslim, or any other, immigrants to take part in civic life. Unlike the United States, few European countries had any experience in dealing with large-scale immigration. The various Muslim communities have therefore generally remained unassimilated and self-contained. This apartness has provided internal community support for Muslim immigrants but prevented them from fully engaging with the societies in which they live. Many of their children have not learned European languages well, and Muslim women tend to remain strictly confined to their homes.

But the world around these communities has changed. Many of the largely unskilled jobs that the immigrants originally filled have disappeared. Most of the Muslim immigrants to Europe, unlike many who have settled in the United States and Canada, were neither highly skilled nor professionally educated. As a result, they and their adult children who may have grown up in Europe find it difficult to get jobs in the modern service economy. Furthermore, as European economic growth has slowed, European Muslims have become the target of politicians who seek to blame the immigrants for a host of problems, from crime to unemployment.

The radicalization of parts of the Islamic world has also touched the Muslim communities in Europe. Although Turkish Muslims living in Germany come from a nation that has been secularized since the 1920s and thus tend to be less religiously observant than Pakistani Muslims dwelling in Great Britain, Muslims from both countries have been involved in radical Islamic groups, and some belonged to organizations involved in the September 11, 2001, attack on the United States. By contrast, the French government has attempted to engage the Muslim community through the French Council for the Muslim religion founded in 2003 and to exert highly controversial secular control by legislating in 2010 against the wearing of the burqa in public by Muslim women.

Nonetheless, European Muslims are not a homogeneous group. They come from different countries, have different class backgrounds, and espouse different Islamic traditions. Many European Muslims and Muslim clerics disagree strongly with each other. Some emphasize a more traditional message; others preach a more radical one that is highly critical of the West. At the same time, these Muslim communities, so often now marked by deep poverty and unemployment, have become a major concern for European social workers who disagree among themselves about how their governments should respond to them.

New Patterns in the Work and Expectations of Women

In the decades since World War II the work patterns and social expectations of women have changed markedly. In all social ranks women have begun to assume larger economic and political roles. Women have entered the learned professions and are filling more major managerial positions than ever before in European history. (See Document, "Simone de Beauvoir Urges Economic Freedom for Women.")

Feminism Certain more or less traditional patterns continue to describe the position of women in both family and economic life. Despite enormous gains during the second half of the twentieth century, and despite the collapse of those authoritarian governments whose social policies inhibited the advancement of women into the mainstream of society, gender inequality remained a major characteristic of the social life of Europe at the opening of the twenty-first century.

Since World War II, European feminism, though less highly organized than American feminism, has set forth a new agenda. The most widely read postwar work on women's issues was undoubtedly Simone de Beauvoir's (1908–1986) *The Second Sex*, published in 1949. In that work, de Beauvoir explored the difference that being a woman rather than a man had made in her life. She was part of the French intellectual establishment and thus wrote from a privileged position. Over the years, however, she and other European feminists argued that at all levels, European women experienced distinct social and economic disadvantages. In the courts, for example, divorce and family laws favored men. European feminists also called attention to the social problems that women faced, including spousal abuse.

Simone de Beauvoir, here with her companion, the philosopher Jean-Paul Sartre, was the major feminist writer in postwar Europe.

More Married Women in the Workforce The number of married women in the workforce has risen sharply. Both middle-class and working-class married women have sought jobs outside the home. Because of the rather low birthrate in the 1930s, there were few young single women to be employed just after the war. Married women entered the job market to replace them. Some factories changed their work shifts to accommodate the needs of married women. Consumer conveniences and improvements in health care also made it easier for married women to enter the workforce by reducing the demands of child care on their time.

In the twentieth century children were no longer expected to make substantial contributions to family income. They spent much of their time in compulsory schools. When families needed more income than one worker can provide, both parents worked. Even without financial necessity, both parents were now likely to work when both were motivated to pursue careers.

Within Europe the age at which women have decided to bear children has risen. Women have tended to bear children in their early 20s in eastern Europe and in their late 20s in western Europe. In urban areas, childbearing occurs later and the birthrate is lower than elsewhere. Many women have begun to limit sharply the number of children they bear or to forgo childbearing and child rearing altogether. Both men and women continue to expect to marry, but the new careers open to women and the desire of couples to maintain as high a standard of living as possible have contributed to a declining birthrate.

Document | Simone de Beauvoir Urges Economic Freedom for Women

Simone de Beauvoir was the single most important feminist voice of mid-twentieth-century Europe. In *The Second Sex*, published in France in 1949, she explored the experience of women coming of age in a world of ideas, institutions, and social expectations shaped historically by men. Much of the book discusses the psychological strategies that modern European women had developed to deal with their status as "the second sex." Toward the end of her book, de Beauvoir argues strongly that economic freedom and advancement for women are fundamental to their personal fulfillment.

■ *Why does de Beauvoir argue that the achievement of civic rights must be accompanied by economic freedom for women? Why does the example of the small number of professional women illustrate issues for European women in general? How does she indicate that even professional women must overcome a culture in which the experience of women is fundamentally different from that of men? Do de Beauvoir's comments seem relevant for women at the opening of the twenty-first century? What similarities do you see with the views of Priscilla Wakefield (Chapter 19) and Mary Wollstonecraft (Chapter 21)?*

French law no longer includes obedience among a wife's duties, and every woman citizen has become a voter; these civic liberties remain abstract if there is no corresponding economic autonomy . . . It is through work that woman has been able, to a large extent, to close the gap separating her from the male; work alone can guarantee her concrete freedom. The system based on her dependence collapses as soon as she ceases to be a parasite; there is no longer need for a masculine mediator between her and the universe. . . . [W]hen she is productive and active, she regains her transcendence; she affirms herself concretely as subject in her projects; she senses her responsibility relative to the goals she pursues and to the money and rights she appropriates.

. . . [T]here are quite a lot of privileged women today who have gained economic and social autonomy in their professions. They are the ones who are at issue when the question of women's possibilities and their future is raised. While they are still only a minority, . . . they are the subject of continuing debate between feminists and antifeminists. The latter maintain that today's emancipated women do not

accomplish anything important, and that besides they have trouble finding their inner balance. The former exaggerate the emancipated women's achievements and are blind to their frustrations. In fact, there is no reason to assume that they are on the wrong track; and yet it is obvious that they are not comfortably settled in their new condition: they have come only halfway as yet. Even the woman who has emancipated herself economically from man is still not in a moral, social, or psychological situation identical to his. Her commitment to and focus on her profession depend on the context of her life as a whole. And, when she starts her adult life, she does not have the same past as a boy; society does not see her with the same eyes; she has a different perspective on the universe. Being a woman poses unique problems to an autonomous human being today.

American Domestic Scene Since World War II

Three major themes have characterized the postwar American experience—an opposition to the spread of communism, an expansion of civil rights to blacks and other minorities at home, and a determination to achieve ongoing economic growth. Virtually all of the major postwar political debates and social divisions have arisen from these issues.

Truman and Eisenhower Administrations

The foreign policy of President Harry Truman was directed against communist expansion in Europe and East Asia. He enunciated the Truman Doctrine in regard to Greece and Turkey and initiated the Marshall Plan for European reconstruction. As will be discussed more fully in Chapter 32 he led the United States to support the UN intervention against aggression in Korea. Domestically, the Truman administration pursued what may be regarded as a continuation of the New Deal. However, Truman encountered considerable opposition from conservative Republicans. The major achievement of those Republicans was the passage in 1947 of the Taft-Hartley Act, which limited labor union activity. Truman won the 1948 election against great odds. Through policies he termed the Fair Deal, he sought to extend economic security.

Those efforts, however, were frustrated as fear of a domestic communist menace swept much of the country. Senator Joseph McCarthy (1909–1957) of Wisconsin led the campaign against the perceived communist danger within the ranks of American citizens and government agencies. The patriotism and loyalty of scores of prominent Americans were challenged. That development, a frustration with the war in Korea, and perhaps the natural weariness of the electorate after twenty years of Democratic Party government led to the election of war hero Dwight Eisenhower in 1952.

In retrospect, the Eisenhower years now seem a period of calm after the war years of the 1940s and before the turmoil of the 1960s. Eisenhower, personally popular, ended the Korean War. The country was generally prosperous. Home building increased dramatically, and the vast interstate highway system was initiated. The president was less activist than either Roosevelt or Truman had been.

Beneath the apparent quiet of the Eisenhower years, however, stirred several forces that would lead to the disruptions of the 1960s. One of them flowed from the injustices of segregation and racial inequality. Another flowed from the long-term implications of some of the major foreign policy commitments the Eisenhower administration made in its effort to oppose the advance of communism. One of those commitments led to American involvement in Vietnam; indeed, that involvement began under Eisenhower.

Civil Rights

In 1954 the United States Supreme Court, in the decision of *Brown v. Board of Education of Topeka*, declared unconstitutional the segregation of the black and white races. Shortly thereafter the Court ordered the desegregation of schools. For the next ten years the struggle over school integration and civil rights for black Americans stirred the nation. Southern states attempted to resist school desegregation. In 1957 Eisenhower sent troops into Little Rock, Arkansas, to integrate the schools, but resistance continued in other Southern states.

While the battle raged over the schools, American blacks began to protest segregation in other areas. In 1955 the Reverend Martin Luther King Jr. (1929–1968) organized a boycott in Montgomery, Alabama, against segregated buses. The Montgomery bus boycott marked the beginning of the use of civil disobedience to fight racial discrimination in the United States. Drawing on the ideas of Henry David Thoreau

(1817–1862) and the experience of Mohandas Gandhi (1869–1948) in India, the leaders of the civil rights movement went to jail rather than obey laws they considered unjust. The civil rights struggle continued well into the 1960s. One of its most dramatic moments was the 1963 march on Washington by tens of thousands of supporters of civil rights legislation. The greatest achievements of the movement were the Civil Rights Act of 1964, which desegregated public accommodations, and the Voting Rights Act of 1965, which cleared the way for black Americans to vote. This legislation as well as ongoing protests against housing and job discrimination brought black citizens nearer to the mainstream of American life than they had ever been.

●◆●—[Read the Document
Martin Luther King, Jr., Letter
from Birmingham City Jail, 1963
at **MyHistoryLab.com**

However, much yet remained undone. In 1967 major race riots occurred in several American cities, resulting in significant loss of life. Those riots, followed by the assassination of Martin Luther King Jr. in 1968, weakened the civil rights movement. Although African Americans had more access to education and public office, especially in urban areas, they continued to lag behind other Americans economically and in their prospects for good health.

Martin Luther King Jr., pictured here with his wife Coretta, was the most prominent civil rights leader in the United States. Here he leads a protest march in 1965.

New Social Programs

The advance of the civil rights movement in the late 1950s and early 1960s represented the cutting edge of a new advance of political liberalism, which proved to be relatively short-lived. In 1960 John F. Kennedy narrowly won the presidential election. He saw himself as attempting to set the country moving again after the years of Eisenhower torpor. Kennedy defined his aims as seeking to move toward a New Frontier. One goal was to put a man on the moon. He also attempted unsuccessfully to expand medical care under the social security program. In the civil rights movement, however, he basically reacted rather than led.

Nevertheless, the reaction to Kennedy's assassination in 1963 provided the occasion for his successor, Lyndon Johnson (1908–1973), to press for activist legislation. Johnson set forth a bold domestic program known as the War on Poverty, which established major federal programs to create jobs and provide job training. Furthermore, new entitlements were added to the social security program, including Medicare, which provides medical services for the elderly and disabled. Johnson's drive for what he termed the Great Society brought to a close the era of major federal initiatives that had begun under Franklin Roosevelt. By the late 1960s the electorate had begun to become much more conservative.

The Vietnam War and Domestic Turmoil

Johnson's activist domestic vision quickly was overshadowed by the U.S. involvement in Vietnam (to be considered more fully in Chapter 32). By 1965 Johnson had decided to send tens of thousands of Americans to Vietnam. This policy led to the longest of American wars to that point in U.S. history. At home, the war and particularly the draft provoked vast public protests. Most young American men who were drafted went into the armed forces, but significant numbers, especially college and university students, resisted. Large-scale protests involving civil disobedience, often patterned after those of the civil rights movement, erupted on campuses throughout the country. In some cases units of the National Guard were sent to restore calm. At Kent State University in Ohio in 1970 the National Guard killed four protestors. In all these respects, the Vietnam War divided the nation as had no conflict since the Civil War.

The national unrest led Lyndon Johnson to decide not to seek reelection in 1968. Richard Nixon led the Republicans to victory. His election marked the beginning of an era of American politics dominated by conservative policies. Nixon campaigned on a platform of law and order. Perhaps the most important act of his administration was his reestablishment of diplomatic relations with the People's Republic of China. Initially, Nixon's policies toward Viet-

Kent State Protest. The clash between protesting students and the Ohio National Guard at Kent State University was the most violent moment in the protests against the U.S. involvement in Vietnam.

nam were no more successful than those of Johnson. Half of the casualties in the war occurred under his administration. Nonetheless, he concluded the war in 1972. That same year he was reelected, but soon thereafter the Watergate scandal began to erode his administration.

See the Map
The Vietnam War
at **MyHistoryLab.com**

The Watergate Scandal

On the surface, the Watergate scandal involved only the burglary of the Democratic Party national headquarters by White House operatives in 1972. The deeper issues related to questions of the extent of presidential authority and the right of the government to intrude into the personal lives of citizens. In 1973 Congress established a committee to investigate the scandal. Testimony before that committee revealed that President Nixon had recorded conversations in the White House. The Special Prosecutor, who had been appointed to investigate the charges, finally gained access to the tapes in the summer of 1974 through a Supreme Court decision. In the meantime the Judiciary Committee of the House of Representatives voted three articles of impeachment against Nixon. Shortly thereafter, some of the newly released tapes revealed that Nixon had ordered federal agencies to try to cover up White House participation in the burglary. After this revelation, Nixon became the only American president to resign (in August 1974).

The Watergate scandal further shook public confidence in the government. It also served as a distraction from the major problems facing the country, especially inflation, which had resulted from fighting the war in Vietnam while expanding federal domestic expenditures. The subsequent administrations of Gerald Ford (1974–1977, b. 1913) and Jimmy Carter (1977–1981, b. 1924) battled inflation and high interest rates without significant success. Furthermore, the Carter administration became bogged down in the Iran hostage crisis of 1980 after the Iranians took more than forty Americans hostage in 1979 and held them for over a year.

The Triumph of Political Conservatism

In 1980 Ronald Reagan was elected president by a large majority and reelected four years later. Reagan was the first fully ideological conservative to be elected in the postwar era. Reagan sought to reduce the role of the federal government in American life. The chief vehicle to this end was a major tax cut and reform of the taxation system. Thereafter the American economy experienced its longest peacetime expansion.

The straightforward conservatism of the Reagan administration proved offensive to many Americans who had traditionally supported a liberal political and social agenda. His policies were regarded as hostile to blacks and women. High officials were involved in scandals, particularly the sale of arms to Iran in exchange for the promised release of American hostages in Lebanon. Despite these difficulties, Reagan

•••—Read the Document

Republican Party Nomination Acceptance at **MyHistoryLab.com**

left office as probably the most popular and successful of the post–World War II American presidents.

In 1988 Vice President (under Reagan) George Herbert Walker Bush (b. 1924) was elected to succeed Reagan. He was immediately confronted by the major changes that Gorbachev was carrying out in the Soviet Union and the extraordinary transformations occurring in eastern Europe that are discussed later in this chapter. Bush kept the NATO alliance strong and close to the United States at a time when observers had begun to question its utility. In 1989 he sent troops into Panama to oust its dictator, Manuel Noriega (b. 1940). In the summer of 1990, in response to the invasion of Kuwait by Iraq, he initiated the largest mobilization of American troops since the Vietnam War. Using the United Nations, he forged a broad worldwide coalition against Iraq's aggression. In early 1991 the coalition launched Operation Desert Storm and forced Iraq out of Kuwait.

The victory in the Persian Gulf War was the high point of the Bush presidency. Thereafter, he stumbled in the face of the serious economic problems confronting the nation. In 1992 the Democratic nominee, Governor William Clinton (b. 1946) of Arkansas, won the election.

The Clinton presidency encountered difficulties almost from the beginning. During his first two years in office Clinton tried to bring about a dramatic change in health care finance and delivery. This effort ultimately failed and left the Clinton presidency with a reputation for being poorly managed. In 1994, in one of the most far-reaching changes in recent American politics, the Republican Party won majorities in both houses of Congress. The new Republican-controlled Congress undertook major changes in the funding of welfare, taxation, and government regulation. This Congress continued the conservative redirection of federal policy that had begun with the election of Ronald Reagan.

The presidential election of 1996 saw the reelection of President Clinton and of a Republican-dominated Congress and Senate. Scandals plagued both parties. The House of Representatives censured and fined Newt Gingrich, the Speaker of the House. A personal sexual scandal and allegations of perjury plagued President Clinton during 1998, although the Republicans lost seats in the House of Representatives in that year's election. In the wake of the election loss, Gingrich resigned from the House, and President Clinton was impeached. He was acquitted in early 1999 by the Senate. In terms of policy, Clinton was seen as moving the Democractic Party into a more conservative stance.

The presidential election of 2000 between Texas governor George W. Bush (the son of the former president) and Vice President Al Gore was the closest in modern American history. Gore won a majority of the popular vote but failed to win a majority in the electoral college. The pivotal electoral votes depended on which candidate carried Florida, where the final vote count was disputed for more than a month after the November election. After complicated legal disputes over how, or indeed whether, to recount the Florida vote, the U.S. Supreme Court voted 5 to 4 to halt the recount, which resulted in Bush being declared the winner in Florida and thus in the presidential election as well.

On September 11, 2001, a surprise terrorist attack on New York City and Washington, D.C., transformed the political life of the United States. As the nation rallied to respond, a period of remarkable bipartisan cooperation followed. In October 2001, the United States began a war against terrorism with air attacks against terrorist positions in Afghanistan. U.S. forces also attacked the forces of the extremist Islamic Taliban regime in Afghanistan, which had tolerated the presence of Islamic terrorists within the part of Afghanistan that was under its control. In 2003 as a second step in the response to the terrorist threat the United States

•••—Read the Document

Addresses by George W. Bush. 2001 at **MyHistoryLab.com**

invaded Iraq, an event fully discussed in the last section of this chapter and in Chapter 33.

In 2004 President Bush successfully overcame the challenge of Democratic candidate John Kerry to achieve reelection with a majority of both the popular and electoral college vote. In the subsequent congressional elections of 2006 the Democratic Party regained control of both houses of Congress in an election fought out largely over the American intervention in Iraq. In 2008 in the wake of criticism of the Bush foreign policy and the growing worldwide financial meltdown Senator Barack Obama of Illinois was elected as the first African American president of the United States. The Democratic Party expanded its control of both houses of Congress. The new administration faced the most challenging economic crisis since the Great Depression. Its initial moves involved extensive government spending in support of the financial system and the creation of new jobs.

The Soviet Union to 1989

The Soviet Union emerged from World War II as a major world power, but Stalin did little or nothing to modify the repressive regime he had fostered. Stalin's personal authority over the party and the nation remained unchallenged. In foreign policy he solidified Soviet control over Eastern Europe for the purposes of both communist expansion and Soviet national security. The Soviet army assured subservience to the goals of the Soviet Union. Such continued to be the situation until Stalin died on March 6, 1953.

The Khrushchev Years

No single leader immediately replaced Stalin, but by 1956 Nikita Khrushchev became premier, remaining in that position until 1964. He never enjoyed the extraordinary powers of Stalin.

The Kitchen Debate. One of the most famous incidents of the Cold War was a spontaneous debate between Nikita Khrushchev and Vice President Richard Nixon at a trade fair in Moscow. Because it took place at a display of kitchen appliances, it was sometimes called the Kitchen Debate.

•♦•[Read the Document
Nikita Khrushchev, Speech to the Twenty-Second Congress of the Communist Party, 1962 at **MyHistoryLab.com**

In 1956, at the Twentieth Congress of the Communist Party, Khrushchev made a secret speech (later published outside the Soviet Union) in which he denounced Stalin and his crimes against Socialist justice during the purges of the 1930. The speech caused shock and consternation in party circles and opened the way for limited, but genuine, internal criticism of the Soviet government. By 1958 all of Stalin's former supporters were gone, but none had been executed.

Under Khrushchev, intellectuals were somewhat freer to express their opinions. This so-called thaw in the cultural life of the country was closely related to the premier's interest in the opinions of experts on problems of industry and agriculture. He often went outside the usual bureaucratic channels in search of information and new ideas. Novels such as Aleksandr Solzhenitsyn's (b. 1918) *One Day in the Life of Ivan Denisovich* (1963) could be published. However, Boris Pasternak (1890–1960), the author of *Dr. Zhivago*, was not permitted to accept the Nobel Prize for literature in 1958. The intellectual liberalization of Soviet life during this period looked favorable largely in comparison with what had preceded it and continued to seem so later when freedom of expression declined again in the two decades after Khrushchev's fall.

In economic policy Khrushchev made moderate efforts to decentralize economic planning and execution. During the late 1950s he often boasted that Soviet production of consumer goods would overtake that of the West. Steel, oil, and electric power production continued to grow, but the consumer sector including housing improved only marginally. The ever-growing defense budget and the space program that successfully launched the first human-engineered earth satellite, *Sputnik*, in 1957 made major demands on the nation's productive resources.

Khrushchev strongly redirected Stalin's agricultural policy. He recognized that despite the collectivization of the 1930s the Soviet Union could not feed its own people. Khrushchev removed many of the most restrictive regulations on private cultivation. The machine-tractor stations were abandoned. Existing collective farms were further amalgamated. The government undertook an extensive "virgin lands" program to extend wheat cultivation by hundreds of thousands of acres. This policy initially increased grain production to new records. The applied farming techniques, however, proved inappropriate for the soil, and the new lands soon underwent severe erosion. The agricultural problem continued to grow over the decades. By the 1970s the Soviet Union imported vast quantities of grain from the United States and other countries. U.S. grain imports constituted a major facet of the policy of détente.

By 1964 high Communist Party leaders and many people lower in the party had concluded that Khrushchev had tried to do too much too soon and had done it too poorly. His foreign policy, culminating in the backdown over the Cuban Missile Crisis, appeared a failure. On October 16, 1964, after defeat in the Central Committee of the Communist Party, Khrushchev resigned. Leonid Brezhnev (1906–1982) eventually emerged as his successor.

Brezhnev

Domestically the Soviet government became markedly more repressive after 1964. Intellectuals enjoyed less and less freedom and had little direct access to the government leadership. In 1974 the government expelled Solzhenitsyn. Jewish citizens of the Soviet Union were harassed. Bureaucratic obstacles impeded emigration to Israel.

The internal repression gave rise to a dissident movement. Certain Soviet citizens dared to criticize the regime in public and to carry out small demonstrations against it. They accused the Soviet government of violating the human rights provisions of the 1975 Helsinki Accords. The dissidents included prominent citizens, such as the Nobel Prize–winning physicist Andrei Sakharov (1921–1989). The Soviet government responded with further repression.

In foreign policy the Brezhnev years witnessed attempts both to reach accommodation with the United States and to continue to expand Soviet influence and maintain Soviet leadership of the communist movement. Nonetheless, growing Soviet spending on defense, and particularly on naval expansion, put ongoing pressures on the consumer side of the economy.

In December 1979 the Soviet Union invaded Afghanistan. A Soviet presence had already existed in that country, but for reasons that still remain unclear, the Soviet government felt required to send in troops to ensure its influence in Central Asia. The Afghanistan invasion, in addition to exacerbating tensions with the United States, tied the hands of the Soviet government in its own sphere of influence in Eastern Europe. There seems little doubt that the Soviet hesitation to react more strongly to events in Poland during the 1980s, which are discussed in the next section, stemmed in part from having committed military resources to Afghanistan as well as from the broad condemnation the invasion provoked from some Western European Communist parties and from the governments of nations not aligned with the West. The Soviet government also clearly lost internal support as its army became bogged down and suffered steady losses.

Communism and Solidarity in Poland

In early July 1980 the Polish government raised meat prices. The result was hundreds of protest strikes across the country. On August 14 workers occupied the Lenin shipyard at Gdansk. The strike soon spread to other shipyards, transport facilities, and factories connected with the shipbuilding industry. The most important leader to emerge from among the strikers was Lech Walesa (b. 1944). The strike leaders refused to negotiate with the government through any of the government-controlled unions. The Gdansk strike ended on August 31 after the government promised the workers the right to organize an independent union. Less than a week later the Polish communist head of state was replaced; later that year the Polish courts recognized Solidarity as an independent union, and the state-controlled radio—for the first time in thirty years—broadcast a Roman Catholic Mass.

In the summer of 1981, for the first time in any European communist state, secret elections for the Polish party congress permitted real choices among the candidates. Poland remained a nation governed by a single party, but real debate was temporarily permitted within the party congress. This extraordinary Polish experiment came to a rapid close

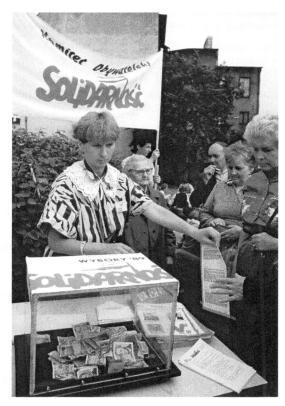

The Polish Trade Union "Solidarity" in 1989 successfully forced the Polish communist government to hold free elections. In June of that year Solidarity, whose members here are collecting funds for their campaign, won overwhelmingly.

in late 1981. General Wojciech Jaruzelski (b. 1923) became head of the party, and the army moved into the center of Polish events. In December 1981 martial law was declared. The government arrested several Solidarity leaders. Martial law would continue until the late 1980s.

Gorbachev Attempts to Redirect the Soviet Union

Both of Brezhnev's immediate successors, Yuri Andropov (1914–1984) and Constantin Chernenko (1911–1985), died after holding office for just short periods. In 1985 Mikhail S. Gorbachev (b. 1931) came to power. In what proved to be the last great attempt to reform the Soviet system and eliminate its repressive Stalinist heritage, Gorbachev immediately set about making the most remarkable changes that the Soviet Union had witnessed since the 1920s. His reforms unleashed forces that within seven years would force him to retire and end both communist rule and the Soviet Union as it had existed since the Bolshevik Revolution of 1917.

Initially, Gorbachev and his supporters challenged the way the party and bureaucracy had traditionally managed the Soviet government and economy. Under the policy of ***perestroika***, or restructuring, they proposed major economic and political reforms. The centralized economic ministries were reduced in size. A larger role was allowed for private enterprise on the local level. By early 1990, in a clear abandonment of traditional Marxist ideology, Gorbachev had begun to advocate private ownership of property. He and his advisers considered policies to liberalize the economy and move it rapidly toward a free market. Despite these organizational changes the Soviet economy, instead of growing, stagnated and even declined. Shortages of food, consumer goods, and housing became chronic. In a pattern that has continued to characterize Russian political life, old-fashioned communists blamed these results on the abandonment of centralized planning.

Read the Document
Mikhail Gorbachev on the Need for Economic Reform (1987) at **MyHistoryLab.com**

Democratic critics blamed overly slow reform and urged a more rapid move to a free market economy.

Gorbachev also allowed, within the Soviet context, an extraordinarily broad public discussion and criticism of Soviet history and Soviet Communist Party policy. This development was termed ***glasnost***, or openness. Certain communist , such as Bukharin (1888–1938), who had been executed by Stalin, once again received official public recognition for their positive contributions to Soviet history. Within factories, workers were permitted to criticize party officials and the economic plans of the party and the government. Censorship was relaxed and free expression encouraged. Dissidents were released from prison. In the summer of 1988 Gorbachev presided over a party congress that witnessed full debates. In 1988 a new constitution permitted openly contested elections. After real political campaigning, a novel experience for the Soviet Union, the Congress of People's Deputies was elected in 1989 and then formally elected Gorbachev as president.

1989: Year of Revolutions in Eastern Europe

In 1989 Soviet domination and communist rule in Eastern Europe came to an abrupt end. None of these revolutions could have taken place without the Soviet Union's refusal to intervene militarily as it had done in 1956 and 1968. For the first time since the end of World War II the peoples of Eastern Europe could shape their own political destiny without the almost certain military intervention of the Soviet Union. Once they realized the Soviets would stand back, thousands of ordinary citizens denounced Communist Party domination and asserted their desire for democracy.

The generally peaceful character of most of these revolutions was not inevitable. It may, in part, have resulted from the shock with which much of the world responded to the violent repression of prodemocracy protesters in Beijing's Tiananmen Square by the People's Republic of China in the late spring of 1989. The Communist Party officials of Eastern Europe and

View the Image
Statue of Lenin Toppled during Soviet Collapse at **MyHistoryLab.com**

the Soviet Union clearly decided at some point in 1989 that they could not offend world opinion with a similar attack on democratic demonstrators.

Statue of Lenin. The collapse of Communist Party governments in Eastern Europe and the Soviet Union was the most important political event of the closing years of the twentieth century. It was accompanied by the destruction of the public symbols of those governments. Throughout the region gigantic statues of Communist Party leaders were torn down. Here, Hungarians explore a toppled statue of Lenin.

Solidarity Reemerges in Poland

During the mid-1980s, Poland's government relaxed martial law. By 1984 several leaders of Solidarity had been released from prison and began again to work for free-trade unions and democratic government. An active underground press and several new dissenting political organizations emerged. Poland's economy continued to deteriorate, demonstrating the inability of communist governments to deliver economic growth and prosperity.

During 1987 the government released the last of its Solidarity prisoners in a sweeping amnesty. In 1988 new strikes occurred that even the leaders of Solidarity had not anticipated. This time the communist government failed to reimpose control. Solidarity was legalized.

Jaruzelski, with the tacit consent of the Soviet Union, repealed martial law and promised free elections to a parliament with increased powers. When elections were held in 1989, the communists lost overwhelmingly to Solidarity candidates. Late in the summer Jaruzelski, unable to find a communist who could forge a majority coalition in parliament, turned to Solidarity. On August 24, 1989, after negotiating with Lech Walesa, Jaruzelski named Tadeusz Mazowiecki (b. 1927) the first noncommunist prime minister of Poland since 1945. The appointment was made with Gorbachev's express approval.

Hungary Moves toward Independence

Hungary had for some time shown the greatest national economic independence of the Soviet Union in Eastern Europe. The Hungarian government had emphasized the production of food and consumer goods. It had also permitted a small stock exchange. In early 1989, as events unfolded in Poland, the Hungarian communist government began to take other independent actions. In January its Parliament permitted independent political parties. Soon thereafter the government permitted free travel between Hungary and Austria, opening the first breach in the Iron Curtain. Thousands of East Germans then moved into Austria through Hungary. From Austria they went to West Germany.

In May 1989 Premier Janos Kadar (1912–1989), who had been installed after the Soviet intervention in 1956, was voted from office by the Parliament. Thousands of people gave an honorary burial to the body of Imre Nagy, who had been executed in 1958. The Hungarian Communist Party changed its name to the Socialist Party and permitted the emergence of other opposition political parties. In October, Hungary promised free elections. By 1990 a coalition of democratic parties controlled the Parliament and governed the country.

The Breach of the Berlin Wall and German Reunification

In the autumn of 1989 popular demonstrations erupted in many East German cities with people demanding democracy and an end to Communist Party rule. Gorbachev told the leaders of the East German Communist Party that the Soviet Union would no longer support them. With startling swiftness, the communist leaders of the East German government resigned, making way for a younger generation of Communist Party leaders. These new leaders, who remained in office for just weeks, promised political and economic reform. They convinced few East Germans, however, and the emigration to the West continued. In November 1989, in one of the most emotional moments in European history since 1945, the government of East Germany ordered the opening of the Berlin Wall. Tens of thousands of East Berliners crossed into West Berlin to celebrate, to visit families, and to shop with money provided by the West German government. Shortly thereafter, free travel began between East and West Germany. By early 1990 the communist government of East Germany, after failing to reorganize itself, had been swept away in free elections.

The revolution in East Germany had broad ramifications for international relations. The citizens of the two Germanies were determined to reunify. With the collapse of Communist Party government in East Germany, there was no longer a viable distinction between them. Late in 1989 the ministers of the European Economic Community accepted in principle the unification of Germany. By February 1990 reunification had become a foregone conclusion, accepted by the United States, the Soviet Union, Great Britain, and France.

The Velvet Revolution in Czechoslovakia

Late in 1989, in "the velvet revolution," communist rule in Czechoslovakia quickly unraveled. In November, under popular pressure from street demonstrations and well-organized political opposition, the Communist Party began to retreat from office. The patterns were similar to those occurring elsewhere. The old leadership resigned, and younger communists replaced them, but the changes they offered were inadequate.

The popular new Czech leader who led the forces against the party was Václav Havel (b. 1936), a playwright and philosopher of international standing whom the government had frequently imprisoned. Havel and the group he represented, which called itself the Civic Forum, negotiated changes with the government. These included an end to the political dominance of the Communist Party (which had been written into the constitution), inclusion of

A Closer Look

Collapse of the Berlin Wall

No single structure so illustrated the divisions of the Cold War as the Berlin Wall, which was erected in 1961. The most symbolic moment in the collapse of communism across Eastern Europe came in November 1989 when that wall was breached.

The sight of hundreds of Germans standing on top of the wall would have been unthinkable just days before. Armed East German and Soviet guards had for over a quarter-century prevented Germans from crossing the wall except at a few heavily guarded checkpoints.

English graffiti had been placed on the wall to ensure that an international television audience, which was largely English-speaking, would understand the aspirations of those people who wanted the wall to come down.

The overwhelmingly youthful crowd indicates the repudiation of the Cold War divisions by the new generation of Germans and Europeans.

Questions

1. How did the vast numbers of photographs of this event, as well as amateur movies and videos, illustrate that the government could no longer control the manner in which information was dispersed?

2. In June 1989, the Chinese government had violently suppressed a vast rally in Tiananmen Square in Beijing. How does this picture from Berlin about six months later illustrate the decision of the Soviet and East German governments to behave differently in the face of popular opposition?

3. What does this picture both reveal and fail to reveal about the motives of the East Germans who crossed the Berlin Wall in November 1989?

myhistorylab To examine this image in an interactive fashion, please go to **www.myhistorylab.com**

noncommunists in the government, elimination of traditional Marxist education, removal of travel restrictions, and relaxation of censorship.

Early in December the tottering communist government admitted that the invasion of 1968 had been a mistake. The Soviet Union and other Warsaw Pact states did likewise. Shortly thereafter Civic Forum succeeded in forcing the resignation of Gustav Husak (b. 1913), who had been president of Czechoslovakia since 1968, and in guaranteeing a free election for his successor. In late December 1989 Havel was elected president.

Violent Revolution in Romania

The most violent upheaval of 1989 occurred in Romania, where President Nicolae Ceausescu (1918–1989) had governed without opposition for almost a quarter century. Romania was a one-party state with total centralized economic planning. Ceausescu, who had been at odds with the Soviet government for some time, maintained his Stalinist regime in the face of Gorbachev's reforms. He was supported by an army and a security force loyal to him. He had also placed his closest relatives in major political positions where they personally profited through corrupt practices.

On December 15 troubles erupted in the city of Timisoara in western Romania. The security forces sought to arrest a clergyman who had tried to protect the rights of ethnic Hungarians within Romania's borders. Over the next two days the Romanian security forces fired on demonstrators in Timisoara. Casualties ran into at least the hundreds. A few days later demonstrators in Bucharest publicly shouted against Ceausescu at a major rally, and by December 22 the city was in full revolt. Fighting, with many casualties, broke out between the army, which supported the revolution, and the security forces loyal to Ceausescu. The revolutionaries gained control of the television station and broadcast reports of the spreading revolution. Ceausescu and his wife attempted to flee the country but were captured, tried, and executed by firing squad on December 25. His death ended the shooting between the army and security forces. The provisional government in Bucharest announced that the first free elections since the end of World War II would take place in the spring of 1990.

The Collapse of the Soviet Union

Gorbachev clearly believed, as shown by his behavior toward Eastern Europe in 1989, that the Soviet Union could no longer afford to support communist governments in that region or intervene to uphold their authority. He was beginning to advance a similar view of the nature of the authority of the Communist Party within the Soviet Union.

Renunciation of Communist Political Monopoly

In early 1990 Gorbachev formally proposed to the Central Committee of the Soviet Communist Party that the party abandon its monopoly of power. After intense debate the Committee adopted his proposal, abandoning the Leninist position that only a single elite party could act as the vanguard of the revolution and forge a new Soviet society.

Gorbachev confronted challenges from three major political forces by 1990. One consisted of those groups—considered conservative in the Soviet context—whose members wanted to maintain the influence of the Communist Party and the Soviet army. They were deeply disturbed by the country's economic stagnation and political and social disorder. They still appeared to control significant groups in the economy and society. During late 1990 and early 1991 Gorbachev, who himself seems to have been disturbed by the nation's turmoil, began to appoint members of these factions to key positions in the government. In other words, Gorbachev seemed to be making a strategic retreat. He apparently believed that only these more conservative forces would give him the support he needed.

Gorbachev made this calculation because he was now facing opposition from members of a second group, those who wanted much more extensive and rapid change. Their leading spokesman was Boris Yeltsin (1931–2007). Yeltsin and those supporting him wanted to move quickly to a market economy and a more democratic government. Like Gorbachev, Yeltsin had risen through the Communist Party and had become disillusioned with its policies. Throughout the late 1980s he had been critical of Gorbachev. In 1990 he was elected president of the Russian Republic, the largest and most important of the Soviet Union's constituent republics. In the new political climate, that position gave him a firm political base from which to challenge Gorbachev's authority and increase his own.

The third force was regional unrest. Some of the republics of the Soviet Union had experienced considerable discontent in the past, but it had been repressed by the military or the Communist Party. Initially, the greatest unrest came from the three Baltic republics of Estonia, Latvia, and Lithuania.

During 1989 and 1990 the parliaments of the Baltic republics tried to increase their independence, and Lithuania actually declared independence. Discontent also arose in the Soviet Islamic republics in Central Asia. Riots broke out in Azerbaijan and Tajikistan. Throughout

1990 and 1991 Gorbachev sought to negotiate new constitutional arrangements between the republics and the central government. His failure to do so may have been the most important reason for the rapid collapse of the Soviet Union.

The August 1991 Coup

The turning point in all of these events came in August 1991 when the conservative forces that Gorbachev had brought into the government attempted a coup. Armed forces occupied Moscow, and Gorbachev himself was placed under house arrest while on vacation in the Crimea. The forces of political and economic reaction—led by people who, at the time, were associated with Gorbachev—had at last attempted to seize control. Boris Yeltsin denounced the coup and asked the world to help maintain the Soviet Union's movement toward democracy.

Within two days the coup collapsed. Gorbachev returned to Moscow, but in humiliation, having been victimized by the groups to whom he had turned for support. One of the largest public demonstrations in Russian history, perhaps the largest, celebrated the failure of the coup in Moscow. From that point on, Yeltsin steadily became the dominant political figure in the nation. In the months immediately after the coup the Communist Party, compromised by its participation in the coup, totally collapsed. The constitutional arrangements between the central government and the individual republics were revised. On December 25, 1991, the Soviet Union ceased to exist, Gorbachev left office, and the Commonwealth of Independent States came into being (see Map 31–4).

Map 31–4 The Commonwealth of Independent States. In December 1991 the Soviet Union broke up into its fifteen constituent republics. Eleven of these were loosely joined in the Commonwealth of Independent States. Also shown is the autonomous region of Chechnya, which has waged two bloody wars with Russia in the last decade.

The Yeltsin Years

As president of Russia, Boris Yeltsin was the head of the largest and most powerful of the new states. His popularity was high both in Russia and in the Commonwealth in 1992, but by 1993 he faced serious economic and political problems. Opposition to Yeltsin personally and to his economic and political reforms grew in the Russian Parliament. Its members were mostly former communists who wanted to slow or halt the movement toward reform. The impasse between the president and the Parliament crippled the government. In September 1993 Yeltsin suspended Parliament, which responded by deposing him. Parliament's leaders tried to provoke popular uprisings against Yeltsin in Moscow. The military, however, backed Yeltsin and eventually surrounded the Parliament building with troops and tanks. On October 4, 1993, after pro-Parliament rioters rampaged through Moscow, Yeltsin ordered the tanks to attack the Parliament building, crushing the revolt.

These actions temporarily consolidated Yeltsin's position and authority. The major Western powers, deeply concerned by the turmoil in Russia, supported him. The crushing of Parliament left Yeltsin far more dependent than before on the military, and the country's continuing economic problems bred unrest. In the December elections, for example, radical nationalists openly intolerant of non-Russian ethnic groups and advocating rebuilding Russia's empire made an uncomfortably strong showing, nearly capturing more seats in the new Parliament than supporters of Yeltsin. In 1994 the central government found itself at war in the province of Chechnya, a conflict from which the central government eventually emerged as the loser. This conflict demonstrated the government's very limited capacity to exercise its authority when faced with significant resistance. Further turmoil marked internal Russian political developments in the wake of the collapse of the Soviet Union. Nonetheless, Yeltsin achieved reelection to the presidency in 1996.

Thereafter Russian politics remained highly confused. President Yeltsin, who suffered from poor health, faced steady opposition in the Russian Parliament. The economic life of the nation remained stagnant at best. In 1998 Russia defaulted on its debt payments. Political assassinations occurred. The economic downturn contributed to further political unrest. In the face of these problems, Yeltsin resigned the presidency just as the new century opened. His resignation made the premier, Vladimir Putin, acting president. Putin was elected president in his own right in March 2001. Putin renewed the war against the rebels in Chechnya, which not only resulted in heavy casualties and enormous destruction there, but also strengthened Putin's political support in Russia itself.

The Chechen War spawned one of the major acts of recent terrorism. In September 2004, a group of Chechens captured an elementary school in Beslan, a community in the Russian republic of North Ossetia (in the north Caucasus), on the opening day of the term. Approximately 1,200 students, teachers, and parents were held hostage for several days. When government troops stormed the school, approximately 330 of the hostages were killed. By the middle of the decade, however, Russian forces had clearly established the upper hand over the Chechen rebels and the drive toward independence was firmly checked at a very high cost in lives on both sides.

In the wake of the Chechen War and as part of his determination that the central government would dominate Russia's economy and political life, Putin sought to diminish local autonomy and centralize power in his own hands. The central government also moved against leading oligarchs and other businessmen with some being imprisoned. Putin used the attacks on these enormously wealthy and economically powerful figures to generate support from the broad Russian public who regard the oligarchs as thieves and one of the causes of the economic hardship of the l990s. Putin also imprisoned political critics and opponents as well as moving against independent newspapers and television stations.

During Putin's presidency the Russian economy genuinely began to improve. Foreign debts were paid. The Russian rubble came to be regarded as a serious currency. Many more consumer goods were available. Much of this relative prosperity was the result of the oil resources available to the Russian Federation and the rising price of oil on the world market. Under Putin a clear trade-off occurred between political freedom and economic and political stability. In 2008 Putin left the elected presidency at the end of his second four-year term, turning the office over to his own handpicked successor Dmitri Medvedev (b. l965). At the same time, however, Putin assumed the office of prime minister and clearly remained the chief political figure in the country.

Putin, both as president and now prime minister, has been determined to use the nation's economic recovery and new wealth to allow Russia to reassert its position as a major power on both the regional and world scene. After the terrorist attacks on the United States in September 2001, Putin supported the American assault on Afghanistan, largely because the Russian government was afraid that Islamic extremism would spread beyond Chechnya to other regions in Russia and to the largely Muslim nations that bordered Russia in Central Asia and the Caucasus. This period of cooperation proved short-lived. Putin became one of the leading voices against the

Document
Vladimir Putin Outlines a Vision of the Russian Future

Vladimir Putin served as president of the Russian Federation from 1998 to 2008 when he moved to the office of prime minister. In one of his last presidential speeches he outlined his view of a democratic Russian future as well as his concerns about the relationship of the Russian Federation to NATO. His speech embraced a strong rhetoric of democracy, but at the same time placed very considerable limits on the kind of activity and criticism that democratic parties might exercise. Note that he made no provision about who might decide if they were behaving in a fashion dangerous to the national interest. In his own time in office he imprisoned numerous political opponents. Also note his concerns about the Russian Federation's future place and how he made a strong commitment to expansion of its military defense capacities.

■ *How does Putin seem to embrace democratic reform? What are the limits that he places on democratic activity? How might those limits lead to government interference with the activity of political parties? What are Putin's concerns regarding NATO and the place of the Russian Federation in world affairs.*

The desire of millions of our citizens for individual freedom and social justice is what defines the future of Russia's political system. The democratic state should become an effective instrument for civil society's self-organization. . . .

Russia's future political system will be centered on several large political parties that will have to work hard to maintain or affirm their leading positions, be open to change and broaden their dialogue with the voters.

Political parties must not forget their immense responsibility for Russia's future, for the nation's unity and for our country's stable development.

No matter how fierce the political battles and no matter how irreconcilable the differences between parties might be, they are never worth so much as to bring the country to the brink of chaos.

Irresponsible demagogy and attempts to divide society and use foreign help or intervention in domestic political struggles are not only immoral but are illegal. They belittle our people's dignity and undermine our democratic state. . . .

No matter what their differences, all of the different public forces in the country should act in accordance with one simple but essential principle: do nothing that would damage the interests of Russia and its citizens and act only for Russia's good, act in its national interests and in the interest of the prosperity and security of all its people. . . .

It is now clear that the world has entered a new spiral in the arms race. This does not depend on us and it is not we who began it. . . .

NATO itself is expanding and is bringing its military infrastructure ever closer to our borders. We have closed our bases in Cuba and Vietnam, but what have we got in return? New American bases in Romania and Bulgaria, and a new missile defense system with plans to install components of this system in Poland and the Czech Republic soon it seems. . . .

We are effectively being forced into a situation where we have to take measures in response, where we have no choice but to make the necessary decisions. . . .

Russia has a response to these new challenges and it always will. Russia will begin production of new types of weapons over these coming years, the quality of which is just as good and in some cases even surpasses those of other countries.

Source: Validmir Putin, Speech at Expanded Meeting of the State Council on Russia's Development Strategy through to 2020, February 8, 2008, President of Russia, Official Web Portal, http://www.kremlin.ru/eng/text/speeches/2008/02/08/1137_type829 12type82913_159643.shtml

American-led invasion of Iraq and has continued to criticize American policy in the region. Putin has also been sharply critical of the ongoing expansion of NATO, which has embraced nations directly bordering the Russian Federation. His government continued to attempt to exert influence in various of the new nations, such as the former Soviet republics of Ukraine and Georgia, that came into existence with the collapse of the former Soviet Union. (See Document, "Vladimir Putin Outlines a Vision of the Russian Future.")

This determination to assert Russian domination over recently independent nations that were once part of the former Soviet Union dramatically displayed itself in August 2008. That month troops of the Russian Federation invaded the republic of Georgia. What had provoked this attack was Georgia's having shortly before sent troops into South Ossetia. Russian troops first drove the Georgians out of South Ossetia and then continued into Georgia itself. South Ossetia, itself a part of the former Soviet Union, had been divided into regions dominated by Russia and Georgia. Georgia sought to assert further influence, only to be immediately and overwhelmingly blocked by Russian forces. Russia eventually withdrew after a cease-fire but had succeeded in demonstrating its power in the region and in creating potential instability in postwar Georgia.

The Russian invasion of Georgia marked a new departure in post-Soviet Russian foreign policy and a resurgence of Russian international influence following the collapse of the Soviet Union nearly twenty years earlier. During that period both the European Union and NATO had moved to expand their memberships by expanding into eastern Europe and into regions previously dominated by or part of the former Soviet Union. The Russian Federation found itself compelled to watch over these expansions without being able to stop them or otherwise significantly influence them. Discussions had taken place about the possibility of bringing both Ukraine and Georgia into NATO. The United States had indicated support for such inclusion. Putin and other leaders of the Russian Federation had witnessed the manner in which various regions of the former Yugoslavia, most recently Kosovo in February 2008, had broken away from Serbia and established their own independence. The Russian Federation feared that the example of Kosovo and the international recognition its independence had achieved might serve as a pattern for potential breakaway regions in the Russian Federation. It also feared encirclement by NATO member nations where the United States might locate military bases. The action taken against Georgia served to demonstrate the Russian Federation's ability to take military action on its borders and to give warning to other nations in the region of its capacity to intervene. At the same time the absence of any effective resistance to Russian actions in Georgia from either the United States or the European Union nations raised doubts about the capacity of either to influence events in the region of the Black Sea. Therefore, though the Russian incursion into Georgia was relatively brief, it demonstrated that the classic issues of European great power politics remain alive in the new Europe. The action also demonstrated Russian willingness to take advantage of American involve-

Russian Invasion of Georgia. The aftermath of an attack by a Russian warplane on an apartment block in Gori, Georgia during the conflict in South Ossetia in August 2008. Here a Georgian man cradles the body of a relative killed during the bombing, which killed at least five people.

ment in Iraq and Afghanistan to reassert its potential authority in those regions it has dominated since the wars of Catherine the Great in the eighteenth century.

In late 2008 another question suddenly confronted Russia. As one element in the worldwide financial crisis, commodity prices dropped sharply. These reductions included a reduction in the price of oil on the world market. It remains to be seen whether Russia will be able to maintain its economic growth and political resurgence in the face of dropping income from the sale of oil, which financed its new international influence during the past decade.

See the Map Successor Republics of the Soviet Union at **MyHistoryLab.com**

The Collapse of Yugoslavia and Civil War

Yugoslavia was created after World War I. Its borders included six major national groups—Serbs, Croats, Slovenes, Montenegrins, Macedonians, and Bosnians (Muslims)—among whom there have been ethnic disputes for centuries (see Map 31–5 on page 982). The Croats and Slovenes are Roman Catholic and use the Latin alphabet. The Serbs, Montenegrins, and Macedonians are Eastern Orthodox and use the Cyrillic alphabet. The Bosnians are Islamic. Most members of each group reside in a region with which they are associated historically—Serbia, Croatia, Slovenia, Montenegro, Macedonia, and Bosnia-Herzegovina—and these regions formerly

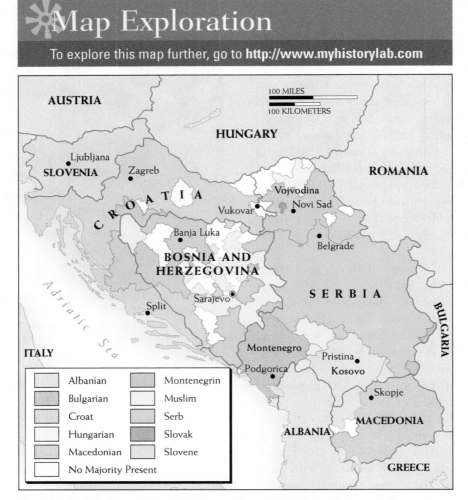

Map Exploration

To explore this map further, go to **http://www.myhistorylab.com**

Map 31–5. Ethnic Composition in the Former Yugoslavia. The rapid changes in Eastern Europe during the close of the 1980s intensified long-standing ethnic tensions in the former Yugoslavia. This map shows where Yugoslavia's ethnic population lived in 1991, before internal conflicts escalated.

constituted individual republics within Yugoslavia. Many Serbs, however, lived outside Serbia proper.

Yugoslavia's first communist leader, Marshal Tito (1892–1980), had acted independently of Stalin in the late 1940s and pursued his own foreign policy. He succeeded in muting ethnic differences by encouraging a cult of personality around him and by engaging in complex political power sharing. After his death serious economic difficulties undermined the authority of the central government, and Yugoslavia gradually dissolved into civil war.

In the late 1980s the old ethnic differences came to the fore again in Yugoslav politics. Nationalist leaders—most notably Slobodan Milošević (b. 1941) in Serbia and Franjo Tudjman (b. 1922) in Croatia—gained increasing authority. The Serbs contended that Serbia did not exercise sufficient influence in Yugoslavia and that Serbs living in Yugoslavia,

but outside Serbia, encountered systematic discrimination, especially from Croats. Ethnic tension and violence soon resulted. During the summer of 1990, in the wake of the changes in the former Soviet bloc nations, Slovenia and Croatia declared independence from the central Yugoslav government and were soon recognized by several European nations, including, most importantly, Germany. Recognition from the full European Community soon followed.

From this point on, violence escalated steadily. Serbia—concerned about Serbs living in Croatia and about the loss of lands and resources there—was determined to maintain a unitary Yugoslav state that it would dominate. Croatia was equally determined to secure independence. Croatian Serbs demanded safeguards against discrimination and violence, providing the Serbian army with a

Destruction of Sarajevo. An elderly parishioner walks through the ruins of St. Mary's Roman Catholic Church in Sarajevo. The church was destroyed by Serb shelling in May 1992.

pretext to move against Croatia. By June 1991 full-fledged war had erupted between the two republics. Serbia accused Croatia of reviving fascism, while Croatia accused Serbia of maintaining a Stalinist regime. At its core, however, the conflict was ethnic; as such, it highlighted the potential for violent ethnic conflict within the former Soviet Union.

The conflict took a new turn in 1992 as Croatian and Serbian forces determined to divide Bosnia-Herzegovina. The Muslims in Bosnia—who had lived alongside Serbs and Croats for generations—soon became crushed between the opposing forces. The Serbs in particular, pursuing a policy called ethnic cleansing, a euphemism redolent of some of the worst horrors of World War II, killed or forcibly moved many Bosnian Muslims.

More than any other single event, the unremitting bombardment of Sarajevo, the capital of Bosnia-Herzegovina, brought the violence of the Yugoslav civil war to the attention of the world. The United Nations attempted unsuccessfully to mediate the conflict and imposed sanctions, which had little influence. Early in 1994, however, a shell exploded in the marketplace in Sarajevo, killing dozens of

●●●Read the Document
Zlata Filipovi, from Zlata's Diary: A Child's Life in Sarajevo
at **MyHistoryLab.com**

people. Thereafter, NATO forced the Serbs to withdraw their artillery from around Sarajevo.

The events of the civil war came to a head in 1995 when NATO forces carried out strategic air strikes. Later that year under the leadership of the United States, the leaders of the warring forces completed a peace agreement in Dayton, Ohio. The agreement was of great complexity but recognized an independent Bosnia. The terms of the agreement

have been enforced by the presence of NATO troops, including many from the United States.

In the late 1990s Serbian aggression against ethnic Albanians in the province of Kosovo again provoked a NATO response. For months the world watched as the Serbian military drove Albanians from Kosovo where the Albanians constituted the majority of the population. Casualties, atrocities, and deaths were daily occurrences. These tactics resembled those that had been used earlier in the decade in Bosnia. In early 1999 NATO intervened and launched an air attack against the Serbian forces that was the largest military action in Europe since the close of World War II. Belgrade was repeatedly bombed. As a result, the Serbian army withdrew from Kosovo, and NATO ground forces entered the province to protect the ethnic Albanians. In 2000 a revolution overthrew the regime of Slobodan Milošević, and the new Yugoslav government handed him over in June 2001 to the Inter-

●●See the Map
The Former Yugoslavia after 1991
at **MyHistoryLab.com**

national War Crimes Tribunal at the Hague for trial as a war criminal. (Milošević died in prison in 2006 of natural causes.)

Challenges to the Atlantic Alliance

Challenges on the International Security Front

NATO has continued to exist following the collapse of the Soviet Union and has moved to expand its membership to include Poland, the Czech Republic, and Hungary. Yet the exact present purpose of NATO remains ill defined. Although initially taking a reluctant role in settling the civil war in the former Yugoslavia, NATO eventually attempted to assume the role of internal peacekeeper in the new Europe. The role was not welcomed by all NATO members or the broad European publics.

The sense of drift in NATO's purpose and continental Europe's inward-looking tendency manifested themselves in new and unexpected ways after al-Qa'ida's attacks on the United States on September 11, 2001. Initially Europeans deeply sympathized with the Americans' tragedy and loss of life. After all, many Europeans as well as many other non-Americans also died in the collapse of the Twin Towers. NATO aircraft patrolled the skies of the United States. Not long thereafter, however, a significant split developed as the United States government of President George W. Bush responded to the terrorist assault.

The September 11 attacks on the United States transformed and redirected American foreign policy into what the administration of President George W. Bush termed "a war on terrorism." In late 2001, the United States attacked

Chronology

The Breakup of Yugoslavia

1991 June	Slovenia declares independence
	Croatia declares independence
1992 January	Macedonia declares independence
April	Serbia and Montenegro proclaim a new Federal Republic of Yugoslavia
April	War erupts in Bosnia and Herzegovina after Muslims and Croats vote for independence
1995 November	Peace agreement reached in Dayton, Ohio
1998 March	War breaks out in Kosovo, a province of Serbia
1999 March	NATO bombing of Serbia begins
2000	Milošević regime overthrown

the Taliban government of Afghanistan, rapidly overthrowing it. The defeat of the Taliban destroyed al-Qa'ida's Afghan bases, but not its leadership, which appears to have survived, although it was dispersed and remains in hiding.

Following the Afghan campaign, the Bush administration set forth a policy of preemptive strikes and intervention against potential enemies of the United States. The administration argued that the danger of weapons of mass destruction—then believed to have been developed by governments such as that of Iraq—falling into the hands of international terrorist organizations posed so severe a danger to the security of the United States that the nation could not wait to respond to an attack but must stand prepared to take preemptive action. This argument, which aroused controversy both at home and abroad, marked a major departure from the United States' previous foreign policy.

The sharpest and thus far most lasting division arose in the months immediately before and after the American invasion of Iraq in 2003. The American invasion (which will be discussed more fully in Chapter 33), received the support of numerous European governments including most notably the United Kingdom, Italy, Poland, Bulgaria, and Spain. Other traditional European allies of the United States, however, most particularly France and Germany, sharply criticized American decision making and actions. Popular political opinion across Europe dissented vocally from American policy.

◆◆◆ Read the Document
Statement from Chancellor Schröder on the Iraq Crisis (2003) at **MyHistoryLab.com**

Once the invasion had been carried out and the occupation began, terrorists struck in Europe itself. On March 11, 2004, at least 190 people were killed in commuter train bombings in Madrid, Spain. The Madrid bombings were the largest act of terrorism against civilians in Europe since World War II. The al-Qa'ida–sponsored attack demonstrated that such terrorist attacks can directly influence European political processes. The terrorist attack occurred just before the Spanish election, in which the Spanish government, which had supported the American invasion of Iraq, was voted from office. The new Spanish government announced that it would withdraw Spanish troops from the conflict. On July 7, 2005, terrorist bombings struck the London bus and subway system with a considerable loss of life. Once more, as in Spain, terrorism struck a major European city. The British government, unlike the Spanish, continued to retain its armed forces in Iraq.

In the years following the American invasion of Iraq profound divisions have arisen between the United States and many of its historic postwar allies. Many Europeans see themselves, their values, and their emerging political community as different from those of the Americans. The long-term relationship will no doubt be worked through on many issues beyond the immediate one of Iraq. More than likely, external events and the wider conflict between the West and radical political Islam will be the determining factors characterizing the Atlantic alliance, as was the division between a democractic West and a communist Eastern block in the past.

Strains over Environmental Policy

Beginning in the 1960s and growing in intensity over the past two decades significant concern has arisen in all the major industrialized countries over the impact of economic development on the environment. This concern has involved issues of pollution of water from industrial and urban waste and pollution of the atmosphere from emissions of hydrocarbons set loose in the air by industrial plants and the ever-growing number of automobiles and other vehicles using internal combustion engines as well as coal-burning utility plants and other industrial sites. One result of this new interest in the environment has been the rise of politically active environmental movements around the world. Some of these movements have worked within the existing political system; others have taken more radical courses of action, including ecological terrorism, sabotage, and confrontation with police at major meetings of world leaders, particularly at the G-8 Summit meetings.

Environmental issues have proved divisive within the industrial democracies. Environmental activist groups and environmental political parties have urged action in various

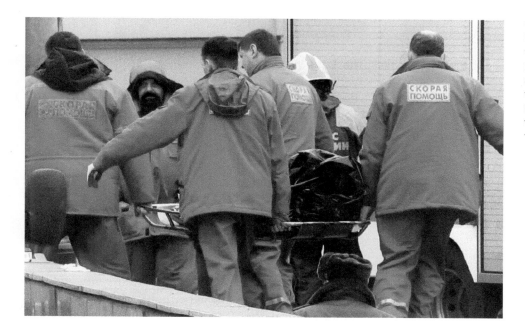

Suicide Bombing in Moscow Metro.
Russian emergency workers carry the body of a victim of a terrorist attack from the Lubyanka metro station in Moscow on March 29, 2010, after two female suicide bombers blew themselves up on packed metro trains in central Moscow's morning rush hour, killing at least forty people.

•◦•─Read the Document
European Criticism of American Environmental Policies, 2007 at **MyHistoryLab.com**

areas of concern. Other political groups have sought either slower action or little action on the grounds that addressing the threats to the environment may halt economic growth.

During the past decade the political tensions arising from environmentalism have begun to impinge upon international relations. The chief issue in debate has been the emission of what are termed greenhouse gases, which the scientific community has concluded is raising the temperature of the planet in such a way as to have a major negative impact around the globe.

In 1997 various members of the United Nations signed the Kyoto Protocol on Climate Change. This treaty set specific mandatory goals for the reduction of the emission of greenhouse gases in the most developed industrial countries against 1990 benchmarks. Those gases include carbon dioxide, methane, hydrofluorocarbons, and sulphur hexafluoride among others. The Kyoto Protocol received the support of numerous major nations, including Japan, Russia, and the European Union and became binding on its signatories in 2005. Whether the various targets that have been set by the treaty and by subsequent statements of various governments

•◦•─Read the Document
The Kyoto Protocol to the United Nations Framework Convention on Climate Change, Article Two at **MyHistoryLab.com**

will be able to do so or not remains to be seen. Some developing nations have actually been permitted to increase their emissions.

The United States has not ratified the protocol; indeed, in 2001 it withdrew entirely from the protocol. The Bush administration indicated that it feared implementation of the treaty would harm economic growth in the United States. The administration also criticized those parts of the

Watch the Video
The Role of the Environment in History at **MyHistoryLab.com**

treaty that permit developing nations such as China and India, which contribute major pollution, not to reduce their emissions. The administration contended that this portion of the treaty works to the disadvantage of the United States in world trade.

The U.S. stance on the treaty put it at odds with traditional European allies as well as Japan. Moreover, as the United States pursued its intervention in Iraq, numerous European governments saw American government as pressing unilateral policies on a number of fronts. Even supporters of the United States in Iraq, such as Great Britain, were critical of the environmental policies of the Bush administration.

In the spring of 2007 the United States sought to modify its position and to gain some measure of agreement on the environment with other nations. The United States has offered to enter into negotiations with all nations that are major contributors to greenhouse emissions including India and China. Moreover, in a reversal of policy, the United States offered to enter into negotiations for setting specific targets for elimination of emissions. At the same time the conservative government of Germany wanted the nations of the G-8 to promise to reduce their 1990 levels of greenhouse emissions by 50 percent by 2050. Other nations have proposed similar ambitious goals for the reduction of these gases. The Obama administration's exact position on international environmental issues remains to be determined, but it will probably pursue a less unilateral policy than the Bush administration.

Numerous factors account for the recent shifts in U.S. environmental policy statements. The American National Academy of Sciences has determined that the rate of

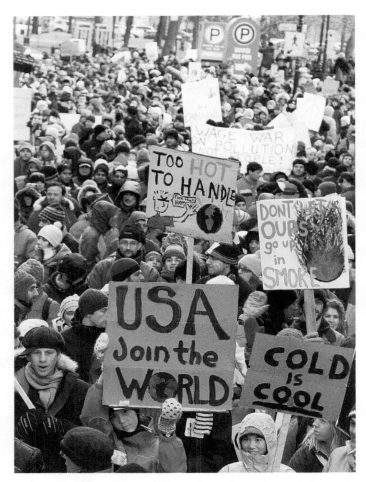

Protesters at the UN Climate Change Conference, Montreal. Thousands of people march through the streets of Montreal on December 3, 2005, as part of a worldwide day of protest against global warming. The demonstration coincided with a United Nations Climate Change Conference.

worldwide greenhouse emissions is growing faster than anyone has predicted. Many industrial and commercial companies have found it to their advantage to embrace the environmental cause. Several companies and industries have come to believe they can actually prosper by addressing climatic issues. Across the globe advocates for more rapid dealing with the growing environmental challenge appear to have been making great strides in persuading public opinion of the validity and urgency of their case, a development reflected by changes in the stance of various governments—even if they have not embraced the Kyoto Protocol.

Two developments clearly lie ahead in the immediate future. First, environmental pollution will continue to grow. Second, a period of protracted negotiations will ensue. Those negotiations will contribute to the ongoing tension between the United States and its traditional Atlantic partners.

Summary

The Cold War. U.S.-Soviet cooperation did not survive World War II. After 1945 Europe was divided into a Soviet-dominated zone in the East (the Warsaw Pact) and a U.S. led zone in the West (NATO). U.S.-Soviet rivalry played itself out around the world from the 1950s to the 1980s, although gradually a spirit of détente arose between the two powers, especially under President Ronald Reagan and Soviet leader Mikhail Gorbachev. The Cold War ended with the collapse of communist rule in Eastern Europe in 1989 and the disappearance of the Soviet Union in 1991.

Postwar European Society. Since World War II, European society has been marked by a rise in prosperity and consumerism, more rights and opportunities for women, moves toward political and economic unification symbolized by the adoption of a common currency, the euro, in 2002, and the publication of a draft constitution for a united Europe in 2003.

The United States. The major themes in postwar American history were opposition to communism at home and abroad, the expansion of civil rights to African Americans, and economic prosperity. Politically, the relatively liberal years from the late 1950s through the 1970s were succeeded by a growing conservatism especially under the presidencies of Ronald Reagan, George Bush, and George W. Bush. Even the Democratic President Bill Clinton was more a centrist than a liberal. After the terrorist attacks of September 11, 2001, the United States embarked on a war on terrorism that led to wars in Afghanistan and Iraq.

Eastern Europe. The failure of the communist regimes in Eastern Europe and the Soviet Union to produce economic prosperity or political liberalization led to their growing unpopularity. Soviet economic difficulties led Mikhail Gorbachev to institute liberal reforms that led to the collapse of the communist rule first in Eastern Europe, then in the Soviet Union itself. The disappearance of the Soviet Union led to independence for much of the former Soviet Empire. Russia itself has experienced social, economic, and political turmoil under presidents Boris Yeltsin and Vladimir Putin.

In the former Yugoslavia, the end of communist rule led to dismemberment and civil war. In the 1990s the NATO powers, led by the United States, intervened to halt the fighting and end a pattern of ethnic atrocities.

Key Terms

Cold War (p. 953)

euro (p. 960)

European Economic Community (p. 959)

European Union (EU) (p. 960)

glasnost (p. 974)

Marshall Plan (p. 954)

perestroika (p. 974)

Review Questions

1. What were the causes of the Cold War? How did the United States and the Soviet Union each react to what it perceived to be the other's hostility? What was the effect of the Cold War on Europe?

2. How did the outcome of World War II affect Europe's position in the world? What were the factors behind the movement toward European unification? How successful has this movement been?

3. What were the chief characteristics of Western European society in the decades since 1945? What was the experience of Eastern Europe during the same period, and why was it different?

4. What were the most important developments in the domestic history of the United States between 1945 and 1968? How did the Vietnam War affect American society? When did the shift to political conservatism occur in the United States? What did it mean for the role of the federal government?

5. Describe the Soviet economy between 1945 and 1990. Did it meet the needs of the Soviet people? What were the causes for the collapse of the Soviet Union? What role did Gorbachev play in that process?

6. Describe the collapse of communist rule in Eastern Europe. Why was it a relatively bloodless revolution? What problems have followed the collapse of communist rule?

7. Was the old Yugoslavia a national state? Why did it break apart and slide into civil war? How did the West respond to this crisis?

8. How did the American response to the attacks of September 11, 2001, cause significant rifts in the NATO alliance? Why do some European nations feel able to dissent from the U.S. position in the Middle East when they rarely did so during the Cold War?

9. What major factors in regard to environmental policy have divided the United States and European nations?

Note: *To learn more about the topics in this chapter, please turn to the Suggested Readings at the end of the book. For additional sources related to this chapter please see MyHistoryLab.com.*

myhistorylab Connections

Reinforce what you learned in this chapter by studying the many documents, images, maps, review tools, and videos available at **www.myhistorylab.com**.

Read and Review

✓●─Study and Review Chapter 31

●●●─Read the Document *Josef Stalin, excerpts from the "Soviet Victory" Speech, p. 953*
Iron Curtain Speech, Winston Churchill, p. 953
The Truman Doctrine (1947), Harry S. Truman, p. 954
George C. Marshall, The Marshall Plan, 1947, p. 954
Gamal Abdel Nasser, Speech on the Suez Canal (Egypt), 1956, p. 957
The Kitchen Debate, 958
A Common Market and European Integration (1960), p. 959
Treaty on European Union, p. 960
Martin Luther King, Jr., Letter from Birmingham City Jail, 1963, p. 969
Republican Party Nomination Acceptance, p. 971
Addresses by George W. Bush. 2001, p. 971
Nikita Khrushchev, Speech to the Twenty-Second Congress of the Communist Party, 1962, p. 972
Mikhail Gorbachev on the Need for Economic Reform (1987), p. 974
Zlata Filipovi, from Zlata's Diary: A Child's Life in Sarajevo, p. 983
Statement from Chancellor Schröder on the Iraq Crisis (2003), p. 984
European Criticism of American Environmental Policies, 2007, p. 985
The Kyoto Protocol to the United Nations Framework Convention on Climate Change, Article Two, p. 985

●─See the Map *Contemporary Europe, p. 960*
The Vietnam War, p. 970
Successor Republics of the Soviet Union, p. 981
The Former Yugoslavia after 1991, p. 983

●─View the Image *European Union Flag, p. 960*
Statue of Lenin Toppled during Soviet Collapse, p. 974

((●─Hear the Audio *Cold War 1, p. 952*
Cold War 1, Slide 2 , p. 956

●─Watch the Video *Escaping the Berlin Wall, p. 958*
Cold War Connections: Russia, America, Berlin, and Cuba, p. 958
The Role of the Environment in History, p. 985

Research and Explore

●─Watch the Video *Is the USA an Imperial Power? Is this an Imperial Age?*

●─Watch the Video *BP Environmental Disaster*

((●─**Hear** the **Audio**

Hear the audio file for Chapter 31 at
www.myhistorylab.com.

32

East Asia: The Recent Decades

- Japan
- China
- Taiwan
- Korea
- Vietnam

EAST ASIA'S HISTORY SINCE World War II divides into two phases. In the first, from 1945 to 1980, Japan, and then South Korea and Taiwan (along with Singapore and Hong Kong), demonstrated amazing economic growth. The values of the East Asian heritage, it appeared, almost automatically led to economic growth, if given half a chance. But in stark contrast, those East Asian nations that became communist—China, Vietnam, and North Korea—did poorly. Vietnam was wracked by wars. North Korea was impossibly totalitarian. The government of China proved incapable of tapping the talents and energies of its people—despite having gained undisputed authority over a territory comparable to the Qing Empire.

After 1980, the situation changed (see Map 32–1 on page 992). Those nations that had prospered during the first phase continued to do so. Japan was free and democratic, and despite new problems, enjoyed a European level of well-being. Hand in hand with economic benefits were social stability and a rich cultural life. South Korea and Taiwan

The Price of Growth. A coal-powered plant in Hebei province, northern China, February 2006. According to the Worldwatch Institute, sixteen of the world's twenty most polluted cities are in China. On average, China builds one coal-fired plant a week.

Modern East Asia

East Asia

Before World War II, only Europe, the United States, and Japan had successfully combined the ingredients needed for modern economic growth. It was as though these countries had a magic potion that the rest of the world lacked. Industrialization in East Asia during the second half of the twentieth century made clear that there was no magic potion: The West and Japan just got there first. The industrialization of East Asia raises issues that powerfully affect relations among nations.

One question is whether high-wage nations will be able to compete with those low-wage nations that have found the formula for growth. Until recently, advanced nations were satisfied with their share of world trade. They sold the products of their heavy industries and advanced technologies and bought raw materials and labor-intensive products. They assumed that their technological edge was permanent—that they would always be sufficiently ahead of the less-developed nations to maintain high wages for their workers. This assumption is now challenged. Since the 1960s, Taiwan, South Korea, Hong Kong, and Singapore have achieved modern growth in high technological fields well before their wages reached Western levels. This has made them formidable competitors in precisely those areas the West saw as its own. Since the late 1980s, China has done the same. The United States kept its market open and regained a measure of competitiveness during the 1990s, but at the cost of holding down wages, corporate restructuring, relocating jobs abroad, and huge trade deficits. Can it continue to pay this price? Will the new competition, combined with runaway immigration, create a permanent two-tier system of wages? China, the most recent East Asian industrializer, will transformed themselves into democracies and continued to prosper economically. But the most striking change was in China, which in 1978 launched a semicapitalist market economy. Long suppressed entrepreneurial abilities surfaced, production grew, and exports boomed. Within a few decades, China became an important player in global markets. Chinese society, too, was slowly transformed. Vietnam adopted a weaker version of the Chinese policy, encouraging private enterprise and opening its markets to foreign capital. Only North Korea resisted the changes sweeping the rest of the communist world. The rigidities of its singular brand of communism inflicted hunger and misery on its people and led its government to pursue desperate policies. ■

Japan

For Japan, already bogged down in its occupation of China, the decision in 1941 to go to war with the United States was a desperate gamble. By all objective measures—steel production, oil, machine tools, heavy chemicals, shipping—Japan was far weaker. The Japanese military, however, misread statements of isolationist sentiment in the United States during 1940 and 1941 and concluded that Americans had no stomach for a drawn-out war in the western Pacific. In terms of strategy, they bet Japan's shorter lines of supply against American productivity.

By early 1945 at war's end, the Japanese were poor, hungry, and ill-clothed. Cities were burned out, and factories were scarred by bombings; shipping was destroyed, railways were dilapidated, and trucks and cars were scarce. Yet, despite their wretchedness, the Japanese people steeled themselves for a final battle in defense of their homeland. Then, in early August, atomic bombs were dropped on Hiroshima and Nagasaki, and the Soviet Union declared war on Japan and invaded Manchuria. Even then, opinion at the hastily convened imperial conference was split: three favored surrender and three favored continuing the war. The emperor broke the deadlock, and Japan accepted the Allied terms of unconditional surrender. In the August 15 broadcast to the Japanese people, the emperor said that the "unendurable must be endured."

◉ See the Map
Japan in 1945
at **MyHistoryLab.com**

After years of wartime propaganda, the Japanese reacted with shock to the fact of surrender, deep sadness at having lost the war, relief that the bombing was over, and apprehension about what would come next. They expected a harsh and vindictive occupation; when they found it constructive, they turned to positive cooperation. Their receptivity to new democratic ideas and their repudiation of militarism led one Japanese writer to label the era "the second opening of Japan."

have fairly cheap labor for decades. As it advances, the impact on high-wage nations will be massive.

A second issue is natural resources. An oil crisis occurred in the early 1970s when demand outran supply. There were shortages at the pumps, a steep rise in the price of oil, and a transfer of wealth from industrial to oil-rich nations. Market forces, however, uncovered new sources of supply and the crisis faded. Yet oil reserves continue to dwindle. At some point demand, including new demand from China, India, and Brazil, will outstrip supply. Will struggles over scarce resources shape future international relations?

A third issue is population. Japan's population quadrupled in the course of industrialization and then leveled off. Its pattern resembled that of western Europe. China, in contrast, had a huge population when it began industrialization. Since it could ill afford a further quadrupling, it adopted tough policies to limit births. Its population may peak at 1.6 billion in 2030. Whether other less-developed nations in the world follow the Japanese or Chinese pattern will depend on their particular circumstances, but for many, the Chinese model may be unavoidable. More people are no blessing.

A fourth issue is politics. The recent history of Taiwan and South Korea suggests that East Asian dictatorships may evolve toward democracy as standards of living rise. Will this happen in China? China is prospering; its people are caught up in consumerism; but the Chinese Communist Party shows no signs of relaxing its monopoly on government. Also, postwar Taiwan and South Korea were less thoroughly authoritarian to begin with and were strongly influenced by the United States. It is too early to make predictions.

A final issue is pollution, the dark companion of industrial and demographic growth. When the world was underdeveloped, industrial wastes vanished harmlessly into the vast reaches of surrounding lands and seas. But as the world industrializes, pollution threatens. It is particularly severe in China. And even apart from disasters such as Minamata and Chernobyl, automobile fumes, industrial effluents, chimney gases, pesticides, garbage, and sewage cause lakes to die, forests to wither, and levels of toxins to rise.

Focus Questions

■ What is the impact of East Asian economic growth on the world's natural resources? On international relations?

■ Does recent history suggest that the Chinese government will become more democratic as its citizens become more prosperous?

The Occupation

General Douglas MacArthur was the Supreme Commander for the Allied Powers in Japan. His headquarters in Tokyo was staffed almost entirely by Americans, and the Occupation forces themselves were American, apart from British troops on Shikoku. The first phase of the Occupation focused on demilitarization and democratization. Civilians and soldiers abroad were returned to Japan, and the military was demobilized. Ultranationalist organizations were dissolved, and the Home Ministry was abolished. The police were decentralized, and political prisoners were freed. Following the model of the Nuremberg trials in Germany, wartime leaders were brought to trial for crimes against humanity. In addition, 210,000 officers, businessmen, teachers, and officials—the leaders of wartime Japan—were removed from office. The thoroughness of these reforms reflected the Occupation belief that Japanese society was tainted by feudal and militaristic values and that Japan's leaders had been joined in a huge conspiracy to wage war.

As a part of democratization, Shinto was disestablished as the state religion, labor unions were encouraged, and the holding companies of zaibatsu combines were dissolved. The old educational system, which had forced students at an early age to choose either an elite or a mass track, was changed to a single-track system that kept open

Emperor Hirohito and General MacArthur. The two men met at the U.S. Embassy in Tokyo in 1945. MacArthur felt the emperor contributed to the stability of Japan and made the work of the Occupation easier. The emperor was glad to be of use and relieved that he was not hanged as a war criminal.

Map 32–1. Contemporary East Asia.

longer the option of continuing in school. The most radical undertaking was a land reform that expropriated landlord holdings and sold them to landless tenants at a fractional cost. The effect, ironically, was to create a countryside of politically conservative small farmers. Needless to say, some reforms accelerated changes already under way in Japan, and all of the reforms depended on the cooperation—at times enthusiastic and at times reluctant—of Japanese officials.

Of the Occupation reforms, none was more important than the new constitution, written by the Government

Section of MacArthur's headquarters in 1947 and passed into law by the Japanese Diet. It fundamentally changed Japan's polity in five respects:

1. A British-style Parliament was established in which the cabinet became a committee of the majority party or coalition in the Diet. This broke with the Meiji Constitution, which had permitted the emperor (those who acted in his name) to appoint prime ministers without regard for the Diet. The new constitution added an American-style judiciary and elective prefectural governors.

2.   Women were given the vote.

3.   The rights to life, liberty, the pursuit of happiness, a free press, and free assembly were guaranteed. These were joined by newer rights, such as academic freedom, collective bargaining, sexual equality in marriage, and minimal standards of wholesome and cultural living.

4.   **Article 9 of the No-War Constitution** stipulated: "The Japanese people forever renounce war as a sovereign right of the nation" and will never maintain "land, sea, and air forces" or "other war potential." This article, though never strictly observed, made Japan into something unique in the world: a major power without commensurate military strength.

5.   The constitution defined the emperor as "the symbol of the state, deriving his position from the will of the people with whom resides sovereign power."

The Japanese people accepted the new constitution and embraced democracy with uncritical enthusiasm. The no-war clause was viewed by most as the guarantee of a peaceful future. Although it did not preclude the formation of a Self-Defense Force, it acted as a brake on military expenditures, which half a century later were only about 1 percent of Japan's gross domestic product. The Japanese had been readied for the changed status of the emperor by his speech on January 1, 1946, in which he renounced all claims to divinity. The Occupation saw to it that the emperor traveled about Japan in a manner appropriate to his new status as a symbol of the state. No one who saw this mild, rumpled-looking, and inarticulate man mistook him for a Shinto god. During the 1960s and 1970s, most, though not all, Japanese came to feel a considerable affection for Emperor Hirohito, who, they felt, had shared in their wartime and postwar hardships. They were saddened by his death in 1989 (See Document, "Two Views of the 'Symbol Emperor.'")

By late 1947, most of the Occupation reforms had been carried out. To create a climate in which the new democracy could take root and flourish, the Occupation in its second phase turned to economic recovery. It dropped plans to deconcentrate big business further, encouraged the Japanese government to curb inflation, and cracked down on communist unions that used strikes for political ends. The United States also gave Japan $2 billion in economic aid.

●●─[Read the Document
The Constitution of Japan (1947)
at **MyHistoryLab.com**

The outbreak of the Korean War in 1950 marked the start of the third and final phase of the Occupation. Caught up in the peninsular war, the American military no longer had time for Japan. Consequently, Japanese officials began to look to the cabinet and the Diet for policy decisions, not to the occupying forces. By the time Japan regained its sovereignty in April 1952, the effect of the changeover was hardly noticeable in the daily life of the Japanese people. On the same day as the peace treaty, Japan signed a security treaty with the United States, which provided for American bases and committed the United States to Japan's defense. Although attacked by the political left, the security treaty became the cornerstone of Japan's minimalist defense policy.

Parliamentary Politics

In 1945, Japan had a parliamentary potential that harked back to the rise of party power in the Diet between 1890 and 1932. It also had an authoritarian potential compounded of those factors that had led to the rise of militarism. Had the country been occupied by the Soviet Union, the efficiency of its bureaucracy, its wartime economic planning organs, its educated and disciplined work force, and its receptivity to change after defeat would doubtless have made Japan a model communist state. Occupied by the United States, the parliamentary potential emerged.

Japan's postwar politics can be divided into three periods. The first, from 1945 to 1955, was the continuation of prewar party politics as modified to fit the new political environment. Two conservative parties and a socialist party emerged. The conservative Liberals and the Democrats were the successors to the mainstream prewar parties. They resumed their struggle for power in the early postwar elections. The Japanese Socialist Party, which won 26 percent of the vote in 1947, was the heir of the moderate prewar Socialist Party, which had received 9 percent of the vote in 1937.

Opening the Olympics. In the 1964 Tokyo Olympics Japan stepped back onto the international stage after the disasters of the war years. Holding the Olympic torch is Sakai Yoshinori, who was born in Hiroshima on August 6, 1945, the day the atomic bomb was dropped.

Document   Two Views of the "Symbol Emperor"

The murkiest aspect of Japan's prewar emperor-centered ideology was the juxtaposition of the emperor as a modern monarch and the emperor as a living deity, ultimately descended from the sun goddess. In the first selection, former Prime Minister Yoshida Shigeru, a product of Meiji Japan, basically accepts the prewar ideology but argues that because in fact the emperor exercised little power before World War II, nothing was changed by the postwar constitution. In the second selection, Nobel Prize winner Ōe Kenzaburō, a humanistic and slightly leftist novelist, recognizes that the emperor has been stripped of his former authority but worries about a revival of his Shinto identity.

■ *What does Yoshida mean by "as naturally," and why does Ōe call the prewar emperor an "absolute ruler"?*

1. In regard to the question of the Imperial structure of government, as it existed in Japan, I pointed out that the Meiji Constitution had originated in the promises made to the Japanese people by the Emperor Meiji at the beginning of his reign, and there was little need to dwell on the fact that democracy, if we were to use the word, had always formed part of the traditions of our country, and was not—as some mistakenly imagined—something that was about to be introduced with the revision of the Constitution. As for the Imperial House, the idea and reality of the Throne had come into being among the Japanese people as naturally as the idea of the country itself; no question of antagonism between Throne and people could possibly arise; and nothing contained in the new Constitution could change that fact. The word "symbol" had been employed in the definition of the Emperor because we Japanese had always regarded the Emperor as the symbol of the country itself—a statement which any Japanese considering the issue dispassionately would be ready to recognize as an irrefutable fact.

2. Japan's emperor system, which had apparently lost its social and political influence after the defeat in the Pacific War, is beginning to flex its muscles again, and in some respects it has already recouped much of its lost power—with two differences: first, the Japanese today will not accept the prewar ideology-cum-theology that held the emperor to be both absolute ruler and living deity. Nevertheless, imperial rites performed quite recently were done in such a manner as to impress upon us that the emperor's lineage can be traced to a deity; I am referring here to the rituals associated with the present emperor's enthronement and the so-called Great Thanksgiving Service that followed it. These ceremonies provoked little objection from either the government or the people, indeed most Japanese seemed to take it all very much for granted.

For most of this first decade, the Liberals held power under Prime Minister Yoshida Shigeru (1878–1967). Before the war, Yoshida had been an ardent imperialist but had favored close ties with Britain and the United States and opposed the rise of militarism. After the war, as president of the Liberal Party, he cooperated closely with MacArthur and worked to rebuild Japan's economy. Pro-business and anticommunist, he was so autocratic in his dealings with bureaucrats and lesser politicians that he was nicknamed "one-man Yoshida."

The second period from 1955 to 1993 has been called the one-and-a-half party system. The "one" party was the Liberal Democratic Party (**LDP**), formed by a merger of the two conservative parties in 1955. It held power throughout this period. The "half party," so called because it was permanently out of power, was the Japanese Socialist Party. It had split in 1951 and reunited in 1955.

What did one-party rule for thirty-eight years mean? One-party rule is not usually associated with democratic government. In the years following 1955, the strength of the conservatives was simply the continuation of prewar constituencies, that is to say, the network of ties between local men of influence, prefectural assemblymen, and Diet politicians, and their ties to business and the bureaucracy. From

Chronology

Japan Since 1945

1948–1954	Yoshida ministries
1950–1953	Korean War
1952	Peace and security treaties
1955	Liberal and Democratic parties merge to form the LDP
1955–1973	Double-digit economic growth
1972	Japan recognizes the People's Republic of China
1973–1989	Economic growth continues at slower pace
1990	Bubble bursts and recession begins
1993	Socialists lose half of their Diet seats
1994–1996	Non-LDP coalitions govern; LDP-led coalitions reestablished
2001–2006	Koizumi Junichirō of the LDP as prime minister
2003	Japan sends troops to Iraq
2009	Hatoyama Ichirō becomes prime minister
2009	Hatoyama Yukio becomes prime minister
2010	Kan Naoto becomes prime minister

the 1960s onward, the LDP became identified as the party that was rebuilding Japan and maintaining Japan's security through close ties with the United States. It was recognized as more able than other parties. Despite the cozy relationships that developed between the LDP and business, periodic scandals, and a general distrust of politicians, the Japanese people voted to keep it in power. Rule by a single party for such a long period provided for an unusual continuity in government policies. Within the larger pattern of the LDP hegemony, several trends were notable:

1. From 1955 to 1960, Japanese politics was marked by ideological strife. The LDP was led by wartime figures who were purged after the war but had resumed their political careers. These leaders highhandedly modified several Occupation reforms, recentralized the police, strengthened central government controls over education, and discussed a revision of the constitution. Marxist Socialists, some of whom had been jailed during the war, led the opposition. The Socialists branded LDP rule the "tyranny of the majority," since legislation was often passed by "snap votes," and warned of the revival of authoritarianism. Diet sessions were marked by confrontation, rancor, and occasional violence. But after 1960, confrontation politics declined. Adopting a "low posture," the new LDP prime minister dropped controversial political issues and drew up a plan to double the national income in ten years. These moves inaugurated a more peaceful era. As prosperity grew during the 1970s and 1980s, ideological confrontation declined further. In many areas a consensus emerged as LDP consulted opposition politicians before presenting bills to the Diet.

2. A second trend was a steady decline in the LDP popular vote, from 63 percent in 1955 to 55 percent in 1963 to 43 percent in 1976. The decline mirrored Japan's economic growth: Farmers, small shopkeepers, and others, who traditionally voted for the LDP, became a smaller part of the population, while unionized laborers and white-collar workers, who tended to vote for the Socialists, increased. By the late 1970s, the conservatives faced the possibility that they would have to form a coalition to stay in power. But in the 1979 election the steady twenty-year decline in the LDP popular vote came to an end. For the next fourteen years the party enjoyed a stable majority in the powerful Lower House of the Diet—though not always in the Upper House—and maintained its rule.

3. Although it received less than half of the popular vote, the LDP maintained its Diet majority because its opposition fragmented: In 1960, non-Marxist members broke from the Socialist Party to form a competing Democratic Socialist Party. In 1964, the Value Creating Society (*Sōka Gakkai*), a Nichiren Buddhist sect that grew to include almost one-tenth of the Japanese population, formed the Clean Government Party (*Kōmeitō*). The Japanese Communist Party, which became less militant after the end of the Korean War, also gained ground, and during the 1970s received almost 10 percent of the popular vote. Competition at the polls between candidates of these smaller opposition parties benefited the larger LDP.

A third era of politics began in 1993, when the left collapsed. The Japanese Socialist Party had been the principal opposition party for almost fifty years. But the end of the Cold War, the worldwide rejection of Marxism, the decline of labor unions, and the widespread Japanese view that Socialist politicians had little to contribute to their recession-ridden country signaled the demise of socialism in Japan. In the 1993 election, the Socialists dropped from 136 to 70 seats in the Lower House of the Diet. In 1994, hungry for a taste of power after decades in the wilderness, the Socialists set aside their principles and joined the LDP in a coalition government. In the 1996 general election, voters showed their disapproval by stripping the Socialists of all but 26 seats; in the

2000 election the total dropped further to 19 seats. The Communist Party also slumped. In the 2003 election, Socialists and communists together garnered less than 5 percent of the seats in the 480-member Lower House.

The collapse of the left inaugurated an era of multiparty conservative politics. The players were the LDP, still the largest party, a shifting number of smaller conservative parties, and the Clean Government Party. Japanese electoral politics during the 1990s was punctuated by scandals and factional strife, but the overriding issue was the economy. In 1993 the LDP lost 52 of its 275 seats, a punishment for failing to end the recession. In its place, a non-LDP Conservative coalition held power between 1994 and 1996. Political scientists hailed this as the beginning of the two-party conservative government. The possibility was not absent. But as the economic crisis continued, voters again turned to the LDP in the hope that its more seasoned politicians would be better able to cope with the lagging economy. To some extent it did, and the LDP stayed in power until 2009. Most LDP prime ministers were easily forgettable. The quirky but charismatic Koizumi Junichirō held office from 2001 to 2006. But all LDP prime ministers offered Japan more of the same: dependency on the bureaucracy, pork barrel projects for LDP voters, and public works to keep employment up.

But more of the same was not enough. The electorate had tired of programs that led Japan deeper into debt. Also, the number of voters who saw themselves as "independents" increased. In the election of 2009, the LDP dropped from 293 seats in the Lower House to 119. The winner with 305 of the 480 Diet seats was the Democratic Party of Japan, a new party cobbled together 11 years earlier from a variety of small opposition parties. The first DPJ prime minister in September 2009 was Hatoyama Yukis. He was succeeded in June 2010 by Kan Naoto. They extended welfare, strenghthned cabinet power, curbed the bureaucracy, and tried to better relations with China while continuing to rely on the United States for Japan's security.

Economic Growth

The extraordinary story of the postwar East Asian economy started with Japan. Japanese productivity in 1945 was about the same as it had been in 1918. By 1955 it had recovered to prewar levels. Growth was expected to moderate. Instead, it forged ahead and continued at a double-digit pace for almost two decades. Shipbuilding, machine tools, steel, heavy chemicals, automobiles, consumer electronics, and optics led the way. Before the war, "made in Japan" often meant cheap, ten-cent-store goods. By the late 1970s, Sony, Toyota, Honda, Panasonic, Toshiba, Seiko, and Canon were known throughout the world for the quality of their products.

◉ View the Image
Japanese Technician
Testing Equipment
at MyHistoryLab.com

Nissan Motors. An almost completely automated assembly line at the company's Zama factory. The high cost of labor in Japan makes such robot-intensive production economical.

Several factors explain this growth. An infrastructure of banking, marketing, and manufacturing skills had carried over from prewar Japan. The international situation was favorable: Oil was cheap, access to raw materials and export markets was easy, and under American sponsorship Japan gained early entry into the World Bank, the International Monetary Fund, and other international organizations. A rate of savings close to 20 percent promoted reinvestment. Savings were necessary to supplement inadequate pensions.

A revolution in education helped. In prewar years education ended for most with middle school; only 3 percent attended university. By the early 1980s, almost all middle school graduates went on to high school, and a rising percentage of high school graduates went on to higher education. By the early 1980s, Japan was graduating more engineers than the United States, and virtually all were employed in productive, nonmilitary industries. (In contrast, the total number of lawyers practicing in Japan just about equaled a single year's graduating class from American law schools.) This upgrading of human capital and channeling of its best minds into productive careers enabled Japan to tap the huge backlog of technology that had developed in the United States during and after the war years. It proved cheaper to license or buy technology than to invent it. After "improvement engineering," Japan sold its products to the world.

High-quality, cheap labor was abundant. The population in 1950 was 83 million; by 2010 it approached 128 million. It is expected to stabilize and then decline in the twenty-first century. At the war's end, 47 percent of Japan's labor force was in agriculture; by 2010 only a tiny fraction worked the land. Until the mid-1960s more labor was available than jobs, which kept wages low. Labor organization proved no bar to economic growth. Industrial workers in Japan during the immediate postwar decades were more highly unionized than in the United States, but the basic component of Japanese labor organization was the company union rather than a trade union. Company-based unions regularly engaged in spring offensives and marched with red flags on May Day, but they took great pains not to impair their companies' productivity. Since the 1980s the strength of unions has slowly declined.

The government aided manufacturers with tariff protection, foreign exchange, and special depreciation allowances. Industries in advanced technologies got cheap loans, subsidies, and the products of government research laboratories. Small budgets for defense spending and welfare kept corporate taxes low. The Finance Ministry and the Ministry of Trade and Industry encouraged the Bank of Japan to back private banks in refinancing Japan's industries. Critics who spoke of "Japan Inc.," as if Japan were a single gigantic corporation, overstated the case: Competition between companies within Japan was often fierce; but government was more supportive of business than it was regulative.

By 1973 the Japanese economy was "mature." Double-digit growth gave way to 4 percent growth. Labor became expensive, research budgets grew as the backlog of cheap technology declined, welfare costs rose, and tough but costly antipollution policies were implemented. Behind the statistic of slower growth was a change in composition: Smokestack industries declined while service industries, pharmaceuticals, specialty chemicals, scientific equipment, computers, and robots grew. Japan's trade, hitherto balanced, began to generate huge surpluses. The world appetite for Japanese products was the main cause of these surpluses. But protectionist policies also contributed, which led to friction with the United States and Europe.

Convinced that their boom would never end, Japanese bid up the price of corporate shares and land to unrealistic levels—several times those of Europe and America. In 1991 the "bubble" burst: The price of land and stocks plummeted. Japanese who had bought shares of stock or real estate at exaggerated prices were hard hit; banks that had made housing or margin loans incurred huge losses. As banks and individuals retrenched, the economy slowed. Incremental growth

characterized the next two decades. Thousands of small companies went bankrupt; large companies restructured and cut research budgets; some workers were laid off or retired early; fewer new graduates were hired and unemployment rose.

Mixed trends appeared during the first decade of the twenty-first century. (1) As in the United States and Europe, some industrial production moved abroad in search of cheap, skilled labor. Sony television sets were no longer manufactured in Japan. (2) Chinese demand for Japanese high-tech products rose, helping Japan to recover from the world recessions in 2000 and 2007; Japanese economists began to speak of the "complementarity" of Japanese and Chinese markets. (3) The government had no program in place to address its national debt—relative to GDP, the largest of all industrial nations. Most working Japanese, still protected by the cocoon of lifetime employment, were unwilling to accept higher taxes. (Large personal savings and foreign currency reserves partially offset the national debt.)

But Japanese strengths remained formidable: Industry was restructured during the 1990s, with greater rewards for those who displayed talent. Japanese automobiles were coveted throughout the world, and the Japanese export surplus grew. Even Japan's management skills seemed exportable: Nissan's Tennessee plant took 17.37 hours to assemble an automobile, while at General Motors the average was 26.75. Equally notable was Japan's determination to maintain its lead in flat screens, fermentation chemistry, robotics, and materials research and to become a world force in biotechnology, medical instruments, and airplanes. Today, new science and engineering buildings on the Tokyo University campus dwarf the dreary prewar brick buildings of the faculties of law, letters, economics, and education.

At the dawn of the third millennium Japan's economy loomed large. It was second only to that of the United States, and almost as large as the economies of Germany and France combined. (See the comparative data in Figure 32–1.) Japan was at a European level of affluence, achieved by the peaceful development of human resources in a free society.

A Comparison of Japan with Germany and France Combined, 2009 Estimates		
	GDP (in trillions)	Population (in millions)	Per Capita GDP
Germany	$3.34	82	$40,731
France	$2.65	65	$40,769
Total	$5.99	147	$40,748 (average)
Japan	$5.09	127	$39,921

Figure 32–1. The above GDP figures represent purchasing power. Japanese economy is almost the equal of the two leading European Nations.

Society and Culture

The triple engines of change—Occupation reforms, economic growth, and rapid expansion of higher education—transformed Japanese society. In 1945, almost half of the population lived in villages organically rooted in the past; sixty years later most Japanese lived in cities, more than a quarter in the Tokyo–Osaka industrial corridor. As in the United States and Europe, a tiny percentage of the population produced the food for the rest. Families changed, too. In 1945 the three-generation extended family of grandparents, parents, and children was held up as the ideal, and most marriages were arranged. Fifty years later the nuclear family of parents and children was the norm, and most marriages were "love matches." In the 1950s and 1960s, companies and government offices built huge apartment blocks for their employees on the edges of cities. The apartments were small, but wives welcomed life without mothers-in-law. In the 1960s and 1970s, larger apartments, called "mansions" in Japanese, were built in cities and purchased by middle- and higher-income families; only the rich could afford city houses. As incomes rose, people bought rice cookers, washing machines, dryers, televisions, computers, and other electronic equipment. Consumerism was constrained only by the small size of living units.

The status of women rose. Occupation reforms had given women the vote, legal equality, and an equal share of the family inheritance. Women's colleges gained the right to award degrees, and women were admitted to hitherto all-male bastions, including the former imperial universities. Rising incomes and smaller families enabled parents to give daughters as well as sons a higher education. Co-ed excursions to ocean beaches or ski slopes became commonplace. Most women worked for a few years after completing their education and married later: The average age of marriage rose from 24 in 1970 to 28 in 2002. Wives usually stayed at home while their children were small, but many returned to work when their children entered middle school. In 1980, almost twice as many wives stayed at home than worked, while in 2002 more wives worked than stayed at home. A working wife had a greater say in household matters. With the shift toward nuclear families, wives became household authority figures, at least during the long hours that their husbands commuted and worked. Greater economic leeway also made divorce an option: The number of divorces tripled to European levels between 1970 and 2010.

In the new Japan, getting ahead depended more than ever on education. Middle school was compulsory, and by 2007 over half of high school graduates—about the same percentage as in the United States—went on to some form of higher education. The pressure to enter good schools started in kindergarten. Mothers routinely compared children's test scores and sent their children to after-school tutoring classes. Examinations determined admissions at every level, even for the cram schools that prepped failed candidates to retake university entrance examinations. Magazine articles regularly lamented the excesses of Japan's "examination society." They claimed that Japan's lockstep education was appropriate to the needs of assembly-line production but not to the needs of the "information age." But few changes were made. A few students rebelled against the rigid system, but most realized that the pressure to excel was for their own good and limited their rebellion to reading violent and sadistic *manga*.

The enormous prewar gap between a tiny educated elite and those with only a middle school education disappeared. More than 90 percent of Japanese saw themselves as middle class—though the percentage below the poverty line was about the same as in the United States. This consciousness was the social base for the new democracy. More education also explains Japan's tremendous consumption of newspapers, magazines, and books. Bookstores stock every variety of books imaginable: serious fiction, mysteries, histories, poetry, science fiction, romances, cookbooks, and translations, as well as books on investing, self-improvement, and home repairs.

In prewar Japan, the claims of the individual vis-à-vis the family, community, and state were weak. Postwar prosperity brought greater personal autonomy. Public opinion polls of workers reveal a desire for more meaningful jobs and a larger sphere of independence. Small pleasures have not replaced duties but are an expected part of everyday life. The young, taking affluence for granted, meet with

Middle School Students in a Japanese Literature Class. Girls and boys wear school uniforms and study together. Desks are pushed together to accommodate large classes. The teacher is dressed like a businessman.

Comic Book. Raised from childhood in the arts of *ninja*, the young heroine Azumi slays evil men. The popularity of this *Bigu Komikku* (Big Comic) led to a movie (*anime*, or animated) version. Was this the Japanese model for the American movie "Kill Bill?" Japan has specialized comics for every demographic group—children, teenage boys, teenage girls, and adults.

friends at coffeehouses or McDonald's, watch American movies and Japanese *anime*, and frequently travel abroad.

Attitudes toward minorities, who made up only about 2 percent of the population, improved during the postwar era. The Ainu of Hokkaido, though disesteemed and neglected, had mostly been absorbed into the majority population during the prewar century. In the postwar, the 20,000 or 30,000 who maintained or regained their ethnic identity formed political organizations, enlisted the support of leftist parties, and obtained welfare legislation. A larger minority group was the "outcasts," descended from Tokugawa butchers, leather workers, and undertakers. Their communities were especially numerous in western Japan. Though physically indistinguishable from other Japanese, their members were shunned as marriage partners and frequently barred from good jobs. Assimilation has been underway since the Meiji era, postwar political and legal action improved their condition, but social prejudices persist. A third minority in Japan is the Korean. In the early postwar decades they suffered social and occupational prejudices. Today over half a million still have Korean citizenship, since citizenship is determined by blood, not birthplace. (Since 1985, it has been possible but not easy for them to obtain Japanese citizenship.) But assimilation is underway. Except for the aged, most Koreans in Japan speak Japanese and have attended Japanese schools. In the 1980s, half of marriages in the

group were to Japanese; by the 1990s, the figure was 80 percent and since then has risen further.

As the new millennium began, a serious social problem facing Japan was the aging of its population. In 1980, there were five workers for every retired person; in 2010 there were fewer than two. Corporate pensions were underfunded, private savings were inadequate, and government and public pensions (the Japanese equivalent of Social Security) added to government deficits. A recurring question is how the old will be supported and how they will vote. This problem, of course, is not unique to Japan. All developed nations have experienced a shift from high to lower fertility and mortality, but the imbalance was particularly skewed by wartime population losses and postwar baby booms in Japan, Italy, and Germany.

Urban Japan is crowded and would be more livable with fewer people. With a birthrate lower than the death rate, a slow decline has already begun. Some Japanese welcome this opportunity to reduce population. Until Japan returns to a more normal population distribution, the problem of too few workers, they argue, can be solved by raising the retirement age, starting pensions later, and tapping the reservoir of nonworking, middle-aged women. Others, however, advocate incentives to encourage marriage and larger families. The average Japanese family today has 1.23 children, one of the lowest figures in the world. During the past two decades, people of Japanese descent from Brazil and Peru and illegal immigrants from other parts of Asia have taken the lowly jobs that Japanese shun. In the recession of 2008–2009, some illegal immigrants were deported, and some Brazilian Japanese were given one-way tickets home. The barriers to immigration are still high.

The rapid transformation of Japanese society might be expected to produce deep cultural strains and social dislocations. At the margin, these occurred. The growth among the urban poor of "new religions" such as the Value Creating Society was interpreted by some as an attempt to re-create a sense of community within an impersonal urban society. One aberrant apocalyptic cult released nerve gas in a Tokyo subway in 1995, leaving the Japanese shocked that something so "un-Japanese" could happen. White-collar workers, or "salary men," spent hours commuting to work in crowded buses and trains. In Japan's corporate world *karōshi*, or death from overwork, became a recognized phenomenon.

Yet the ability of the society—family, school, office, and workshop—to absorb strains and lend support to the individual was impressive. Lifetime employment gave both workers and salaried employees a sense of security. Even during the long recession of the 1990s, layoffs were exceptional. Japanese wives, if public opinion polls are to be

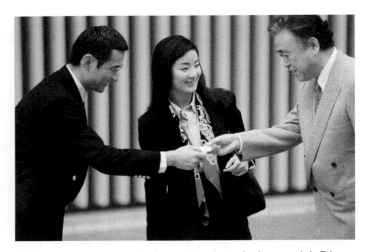

Body Language. Japanese businessmen exchange business cards in Tokyo. A businesswoman stands to one side and observes. An almost diplomatic formality governs such occasions.

believed, felt better off than their American counterparts. In Japan unwed mothers account for about 1 percent of births; in the United States the figure is about 40 percent, in Sweden, over 50 percent. Infant mortality in Japan is the lowest in the world and longevity the highest. Japan has less crime; big cities are safe at night; drugs are not a problem; since guns are tightly controlled, murders are far fewer. In 2008, 62 of every 100,000 Japanese were in prison; in the United States, the figure is 754. Despite crowded housing and omnipresent social pressures, by most comparative measures Japanese society was stable and orderly.

Japanese culture also remained vital. The traditional arts were maintained—poetry, painting, pottery, textiles, tea ceremony, flower arrangement, the Kabuki, and Nō drama. The best artists were designated as Living National Treasures and held in respect. In architecture, literature, painting, and dance, the prewar tradition of vigorous experiments with new or hybrid forms continued. The awareness of nature, so evident in films like Kurosawa Akira's *Rashomon* or *The Seven Samurai*, carried over to television dramas. Films by Itami Jūzō (*Tanpopo*), Suo Masayuki (*Shall We Dance*), and more recent directors combined humor with social satire. Symphony orchestras in Japan's major cities played Mozart and Stravinsky as well as native compositions with haunting passages played on the Japanese flute and zither. Clothing designers competed in Tokyo, New York, and Paris. College students formed rock bands, listened to jazz, watched *anime*, and read Japanese *manga* and science fiction along with writings by serious novelists. Postwar Japan amply supports an argument for parallelism between economic and cultural dynamics.

Japan and the World

At the start of the new millennium, Japan had three sets of critical international relationships: with the world, East Asia, and the United States. Toward the wider world, Japan was a trading partner and, as it described itself, a "UN nation." It gave more foreign aid to developing countries than did other nations. It was a member of major international economic organizations. Its economy depended on free trade, and it worked assiduously to ensure its continuance.

A second set was East Asian. For reasons of history and proximity, Japan was extraordinarily alert (and at moments insensitive) to developments in Korea, Taiwan, China, and the Russian Far East. Newspapers covered these nations in detail. Japan's relations with China, South Korea, and Taiwan have improved during recent decades, though wartime grievances linger. Toward China, Japanese felt a growing ambivalence. They appreciated Chinese imports of Japanese high-tech goods, which were vital to the Japanese economy, but they worried that China's growing military strength was altering the political balance in East Asia, if not posing a future threat. They envisioned a peaceful balance of powers in East Asia, not a Chinese hegemony.

The third critical relationship was with the United States. Japan and the United States were political allies and major trading partners, and were linked by mutual security concerns. The 1952 security treaty, several times amended, remained the cornerstone of Japanese defense planning. Until the 1980s Japan contributed only military bases. In recent decades Japan has moved toward more positive military cooperation—within the limits of its constantly reinterpreted and elastic "peace constitution." When terrorists struck at the United States in September 2001, Prime Minister Koizumi spoke out in support of the United States and against terrorism. The Diet passed new laws permitting the Self-Defense Force to play an active, noncombat role in a war zone in support of U.S. forces. In 2003 Japan sent troops to Iraq. In 2006 the Self-Defense Agency became a cabinet ministry. In an East Asia in which China, Russia, and the United States have atomic arsenals, and even North Korea a few A-bombs, Japanese feel increasingly vulnerable. If its trust in the U.S. "nuclear umbrella" should ever waver, Japan would become a nuclear power overnight.

China

The story of China after 1949 might begin with the four Ma's: Malthus, Marx, Ma Yinchu, and Mao Zedong. Malthus had claimed that population would expand geometrically, whereas food would increase only arithmetically. Marx rejected the Malthusian hypothesis, along with classical economics, as myths of the capitalist stage of history. Professor Ma Yinchu (1882–1982), the chancellor of Beijing University, published *New Principles on Chinese Population* in 1952, in which he argued that unchecked population growth would impede capital accumulation and depress living standards. Mao Zedong, faithfully following the teachings of Marx, purged Professor Ma and closed down population institutes at Chinese universities. What followed was a population increase from 550 million in 1949 to nearly a billion in 1981. Real growth occurred in the Chinese economy during the 1960s and 1970s, but extra mouths ate up the gains. In the face of this crisis, in 1981 the Chinese government adopted a national policy of one child per family. It recognized that the policy ran contrary to the deep-rooted Chinese sense of family but argued that without it, China's future would be bleak. Thereafter the increase slowed dramatically, but the population still crossed the 1.3 billion mark in 2005. Since the median age in China is low, the birthrate is high—despite the one-child policy. Population will peak, it is predicted, in 2030, and then very slowly decline.

•◄►•⎯Read the Document
China's One-Child Family Policy
(1970s) at **MyHistoryLab.com**

Soviet Period (1950–1960)

Civil war in China ended in 1949 as the last of Jiang Jieshi's troops fled to Taiwan. The People's Republic of China was proclaimed in October. The following year, China entered into an alliance with the Soviet Union. The decade that followed is often called the "Soviet period" because the Soviet model was adopted for the government, the army, the economy, and higher education.

The first step taken by the communist government was military consolidation. Even after the republic was proclaimed, Chinese armies continued to push outward, conquering vast areas with non-Chinese populations. Tibet, for example, was seized in 1950. Once subdued, the areas inhabited by Tibetans, Uighur Turks, Mongols, and other minorities were designated autonomous regions, but they were occupied by the Chinese army and were settled by a growing number of Chinese immigrants. Although members of the indigenous populations staffed their governments, the Chinese Communist Party exercised tight control.

Political consolidation followed. The most powerful elite was the Communist Party. Its members held the key levers of power in the government, army, and security forces. Mao was both party chairman and head of state. He ruled through the Standing Committee of the Political Bureau (Politburo) of the party's Central Committee. Below the Politburo were regional, provincial, and district committees with party cells in every village, factory, school, and govern-

ment office. The party expanded from 2.7 million members in 1947 to 17 million in 1961. Party members were exhorted to energize and enforce the local enactment of government policies.

Economic reconstruction began immediately. An attempt was made to integrate the industries in Manchuria and former treaty ports with the rest of China. Huge numbers of workers were mobilized to build new bridges, dams, roads, and railways. China's first five-year plan for economic development began in 1953. The Soviet Union sent financial aid as well as engineers and planners.

Rural society underwent two fundamental changes: land redistribution and collectivization. In the early 1950s, party cadres visited villages and held meetings at which landlords were denounced and forced to confess their crimes. Some were rehabilitated, others were sent to labor camps, and hundreds of thousands—some scholars estimate several million—were killed. Their holdings were redistributed to the landless, and local responsibilities formerly borne by landlord gentry were shifted to associations dominated by former tenant farmers. Then in 1955 and 1956, before the new landowners had time to put down roots as private landowners, all lands were seized by the state and collectivized. The timing was important: In the Soviet Union, collectivization had come six years after redistribution; it was resisted by the *kulaks*, who had had time to put down roots.

During the early 1950s, intellectuals and universities became targets for thought reform; the Chinese slang term was **brainwashing**. This involved the study of Marxism, group pressure to produce an atmosphere of insecurity and fear, self-examination, followed by confession, repentance, and reacceptance by society. The indoctrination strengthened the authority of the party. But beyond this was the optimistic belief that the inculcation of correct moral doctrines could mobilize human energies on behalf of the state—perhaps a belief with distant Confucian roots. In 1956 Mao felt that intellectuals had been adequately indoctrinated. Concerned that creativity might be stifled, he said in a speech, "Let the hundred flowers bloom"—a reference to the lively discourse among the many schools of philosophy in ancient Zhou China. To his surprise, intellectuals responded with a torrent of criticism that did not spare the Communist Party. Mao thereupon reversed his position, sending many leading writers and intellectuals to labor camps.

By the late 1950s, Mao was disappointed with the results of collectivization as it had developed during the first Five-Year Plan. In 1958 he scrapped the Soviet model in favor of a mass mobilization to unleash the productive energies of the people. He called it the **Great Leap Forward**. One slogan was "Hard work for a few years and happiness

A Closer Look

Trial of a Landlord

During the early 1950s, land redistribution followed the communist victory in China. Former landlords were put on trial for their crimes against the people.

Villagers who gather to watch the proceedings.

The village

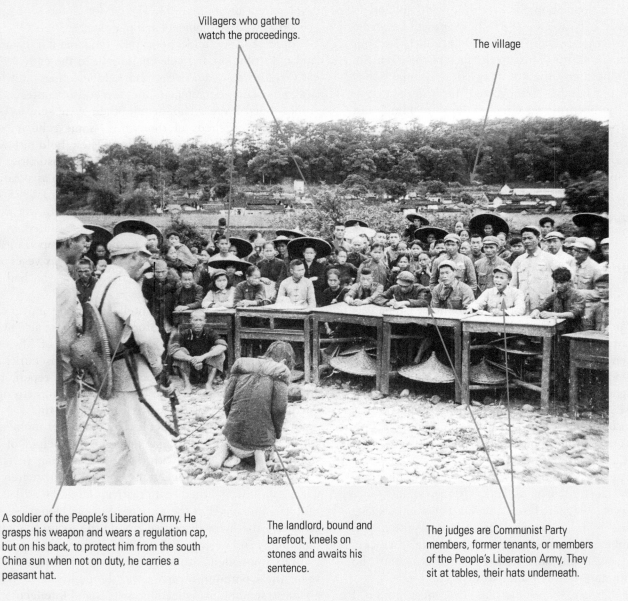

A soldier of the People's Liberation Army. He grasps his weapon and wears a regulation cap, but on his back, to protect him from the south China sun when not on duty, he carries a peasant hat.

The landlord, bound and barefoot, kneels on stones and awaits his sentence.

The judges are Communist Party members, former tenants, or members of the People's Liberation Army, They sit at tables, their hats underneath.

Questions

1. How would you distinguish between a judicial procedure and political theater?

2. Why are army representatives present at the trial?

 To examine this image in an interactive fashion, please go to **www.myhistorylab.com**

Performance during Cultural Revolution. Members of the Xiangyang Commune in Jiangsu province take part in the campaign to "Criticize Lin Biao and Confucius," one of the last large "campaigns" directed by members of the government in charge of the Cultural Revolution. Here, the commune's amateur troupe performs a ballad criticizing Confucius. The campaign began after the death of Lin Biao, who for a time was Mao Zedong's chosen successor but was later accused of attempting to seize power.

withdrew its engineers from China, and by 1963 the split was visible to the outside world. Each country deployed about a million troops along their mutual border. Had relations between the two communist giants been amicable, these troops, deployed elsewhere, might have changed the course of history in Southeast Asia and Eastern Europe. The Sino-Soviet split was the single most important development in postwar international politics.

The years between 1960 and 1965 saw conflicting trends. The utter failure of the Great Leap Forward led some Chinese leaders to turn away from Mao's reckless radicalism toward more moderate policies. Mao kept his position as the head of the party but was forced to give up his post as head of state to another veteran communist official. Yet even as the government moved toward realistic goals and stable bureaucratic management, General Lin Biao (1908–1971) reestablished within the army the party committees and procedures for ideological indoctrination that had lapsed after the failure of the Great Leap Forward. A new mass movement was also begun to transform education.

The Great Proletarian Cultural Revolution (1965–1976)

In 1965, Mao once again emerged to dominate Chinese politics. Mao the revolutionary had never been able to make the transition to Mao the ruler of an established state. When he looked at the Chinese Communist Party and the government bureaucracy, he saw a new privileged elite; when he looked at younger Chinese, he saw a generation with no experience of revolution. Mao feared that the Chinese revolution—his revolution—would end up as a Soviet-style bureaucratic communism run for the benefit of officials, so he called for a new revolution to create a truly egalitarian culture.

Obtaining army support, Mao urged students and teenaged youth to form bands of Red Guards. In the early feverish phase of the **Cultural Revolution**, the guards invoked Mao's sayings contained in the "Little Red Book" almost as holy scripture. Mass rallies were held. One rally in Beijing was attended by "millions" of youths, who then made "long marches" back to their home provinces to carry out Mao's program. Universities were shut down; student factions fought among themselves; teachers were beaten, imprisoned, and subjected to such extremes of humiliation that many committed suicide. Books and artworks were destroyed in a

for a thousand." Campaigns were organized to accomplish vast projects: iron smelters were built in "backyards," and instant industries were the order of the day. In the countryside, village-based collective farms gave way to communes of 30,000 persons or more. The results were disastrous. Homemade iron was unusable, instant industries failed, and agricultural production plummeted. Scholars estimate that between 1958 and 1962 as many as 20 to 30 million Chinese starved to death. To control the damage, communes were broken into production brigades in 1959, and two years later these were further broken into production teams of forty households. Even these actions did not overcome the ills of low incentives and collective responsibility; agricultural production fell through the 1970s.

((•—[Hear the **Audio**
Communist China 3
at **MyHistoryLab.com**

Sino-Soviet relations deteriorated during these years. Disputes arose over borders. China was dissatisfied with the level of Soviet aid. It was embarrassed by the Soviet debunking of Stalin's cult of personality, since within China Mao was still venerated as the "great helmsman." The Soviet Union, in turn, condemned the Great Leap Forward as leftist fanaticism and resented Mao's view of himself, after Stalin's death, as the foremost theoretician of world communism. In 1960, the Soviet Union halted economic aid and campaign against "the four olds." Stone Buddhas that had endured since the Song Dynasty were smashed or defaced. Things foreign also came under attack. Homes were ransacked for foreign books, and Chinese who had studied abroad were persecuted. Even the borrowing of foreign technology was denigrated as "sniffing after the farts of foreigners and calling them sweet." Red Guards attacked local party headquarters and beat to death persons they regarded as reactionaries, including some party cadres. High officials were purged. Revolutionary committees replaced the crippled apparatus of party and government. Chinese today recall these events as a species of mass hysteria that defies understanding.

Read the Document
Decision Concerning the Great Proletarian Cultural Revolution
at **MyHistoryLab.com**

Eventually Mao tired of the violence and near anarchy. In 1968 and 1969 he called in the army to take over the revolutionary committees. In 1969, a new Central Committee, composed largely of military men, was established, and Lin Biao was named as Mao's successor. As violence ended, millions of students and intellectuals were sent to the countryside to work on farms. In 1970 and 1971 revolutionary committees were reconstituted as party committees. Worsening relations with the Soviet Union also made China's leaders desire greater stability at home. In 1969, a pitched battle

See the Map
China in the Era of Revolution and Civil War
at **MyHistoryLab.com**

had broken out between Chinese and Russian troops over an island in the Ussuri River. After this encounter, the Chinese built bomb shelters in their main cities. It was just at this time that President Nixon began to withdraw U.S. troops from Vietnam. When he proposed a renewal of ties, China quickly responded. Nixon visited Beijing in 1972, opening a new era of diplomatic relations.

The second phase of the Cultural Revolution between 1969 and 1976 was moderate only in comparison with what had gone before. On farms and in factories, ideology was still seen as an adequate substitute for incentives. Universities reopened, but students were admitted by class background, not by examination. In 1971, Lin Biao was purged. According to the official account of his death, Lin had tried to kill Mao and seize the government, but when his coup failed, he died in a plane crash while attempting to escape to the Soviet Union. Lin's place was taken by the so-called Gang of Four, which included Mao's wife and was abetted by the aging Mao. Class struggle was revived, and an official campaign was launched attacking the rightist "political swindlers" Lin Biao and Confucius.

Hear the Audio
Communist China 4
at **MyHistoryLab.com**

China after Mao

Political Developments Mao's death in 1976 brought immediate changes. Within four weeks the Gang of Four and their radical supporters were arrested. In their place, Deng Xiaoping (1904–1997) emerged as the dominant figure in Chinese politics. Three times purged for rightist tendencies—once during the Cultural Revolution he was paraded around Beijing wearing a dunce cap—Deng was determined that such things not happen again. He ousted his enemies, rehabilitated those purged during the Cultural Revolution, and put his supporters in power. Portraits and statues of Mao were removed from most public places. After the lunacy of the Cultural Revolution, the establishment of a normal communist dictatorship came as a welcome relief. The people began to enjoy a measure of security and the prospect of better lives.

There arose, however, a tension between the determination of the ruling party to maintain its grip on power and its desire to obtain the benefits of some liberalization. The tension was most visible in China's intellectual life. The government's repudiation of the Cultural Revolution had led to an outpouring of stories, plays, and reports. In *Nightmare* by Xu Hui, the mother of a son killed during the Cultural Revolution asks, "Why? Why? Can anyone tell me why?" Liu Binyan wrote of corrupt officials who had "degenerated into parasitical insects that fed off the people's productivity and the socialist system." But criticism of Deng's rule was not allowed. Writers were regularly enjoined to be "led by the

Chronology

China Since 1949

1949	Communist victory; People's Republic of China established
1950	Sino-Soviet alliance; China occupies Tibet
1953	First Five-Year Plan
1958	Great Leap Forward
1960	Sino-Soviet split
1965–1976	Cultural Revolution
1972	Nixon visits Beijing
1976	Mao Zedong dies
1978–1997	Deng Xiaoping in power
1980–2007	China's economy grows at double-digit rate
1989	Tienanmen Square incident
2003	Hu Jintao becomes premier
2008	Beijing hosts Olympic games
2010	Chinese economy becomes second largest in the world

Communist Party and guided by Marx-Leninism." When a writer in 1983 overstepped the invisible line separating what was permissible from what was not, a short campaign was launched against "spiritual pollution." In 1985 and 1987 as well, the government organized campaigns against "capitalist thinking" and "bourgeois democracy."

Universities returned to normal in 1977. Entrance examinations were reinstituted, purged teachers were returned to their classrooms, and scientists and scholars were sent to study in Japan and the West. Students still spent one afternoon a week discussing party directives or the writings of Deng Xiaoping, but far more influential was the new openness within China and the growing contacts with the wider world as scholars returned from the West. Students became aware of the prosperity achieved by Japan, Hong Kong, and Taiwan. They began to demand greater freedoms and even political democracy. During the late 1980s, the ferment that marked Eastern Europe and the Soviet Union under Gorbachev also appeared in China: It was as if a new virus had entered the communist world.

Student demands came to a head in April and May of 1989, when hundreds of thousands of students, workers, and people from all walks of life demonstrated for democracy in Tiananmen Square in Beijing and in dozens of other cities. Hunger strikes were held. Students published prodemocracy newspapers. Banners proclaimed slogans, among them "Give us freedom or give us death." A 27-foot polystyrene-and-plaster Goddess of Democracy and Freedom was erected in the square. At first, government leaders could not agree on how to respond, but the Deng hardline faction won out and sent in tanks and troops. Hundreds of students were killed, and leaders who did not escape abroad were jailed. The event defined the political climate in China in the years that followed: No challenge to Communist Party rule was tolerated, though considerable freedom was allowed in other areas of life.

Deng stepped down in 1992 and Jiang Zemin, a generation younger, came to power. He argued, among other things, that the CCP must represent "the most advanced economic forces in society." One Chinese newspaper responded, not wholly inaccurately, with the headline "China's Communists Recruit Capitalist." Jiang stepped down in 2002 and Hu Jintao, born in 1944, became president of China. His policies are not unlike those of Deng and Jiang, but the China he governs has changed immensely.

●●●[Read the Document
Deng Xiaoping, on Introducing
Capitalist Principles to China
at **MyHistoryLab.com**

Economic Growth Deng, on taking power in 1978, repudiated the Maoist policies that had kept China poor. "To be rich is glorious," he said in a speech (or is said to have said), and he acknowledged that, "some must get rich first." In the decades after 1978, the results of Deng's policies demon-

Goddess of Democracy and Freedom. Student activists construct a "Goddess of Democracy and Freedom," taking the Statue of Liberty as their model. The goddess was in place in Tiananmen Square shortly before tanks drove students from the square in June 1989.

strated the superiority of market incentives to central planning. Other leaders flocked to his banner; in 1985, Hu Yaobang, the general secretary of the CCP, looked back at the years of Mao and stated that China "had wasted twenty years" on "radical leftist nonsense."

In villages the new policies established the family farm in place of collectives. Grain production grew from 300 to over 550 million tons between the early 1980s and 1997. A local leader commented, "When people work for themselves, they work better." To be sure, farm incomes, though improved, were still far below incomes of city dwellers.

The state sector, the glory of the Maoist command economy, underwent radical surgery. Most state-owned industries had run at a loss and had been a drain on China's state-run banks. Their workers enjoyed the security of the "iron rice bowl"—their basic needs were met but they were paid little and were given little incentive to work hard. The new economy did not totally eliminate the state sector. There were still

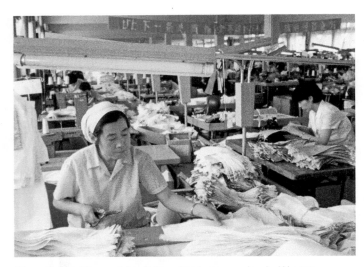

Cheap Labor. Wages at this Beijing shirt factory are low by Western standards but high by Chinese standards. This is not a sweatshop but a modern factory. Should Western nations leave the production of textiles to low-wage nations? What of steel or microelectronics?

five-year plans. "Strategic industries," such as the nuclear, military weaponry, oil, aviation, and shipbuilding, continued to be run by the government, but run more efficiently. The role of the state continued to be larger than in Japan, South Korea, and Taiwan—nations in which the state played a greater role than in the West. But most Chinese government enterprises were sold to private concerns. The new owners fired excess workers and turned to produce for national and international markets. During the 1990s, joint ventures with foreign firms also became increasingly prominent as investments poured in from Taiwan, Japan, South Korea, and the United States.

Olympics. Performers pass National Stadium, also known as the "Bird's Nest," during rehearsals for the opening ceremonies for the 2008 Olympic Games in Beijing. China's hosting of the Olympics was yet another confirmation of its status as a major player on the world stage.

The surge in new enterprises began in "special economic zones" along the border with Hong Kong and up the coast, but soon spread beyond these zones. Shanghai, with a population of more than 20 million (in 2010), became a city of skyscrapers and industrialists and the site of China's first stock exchange. Shandong and Manchuria in the northeast, attracting huge investments from abroad, achieved stunning growth. Growth gradually moved inland. Wuhan, a large city on the Yangtse that manufactured automobiles, averaged growth of 17 percent during the 1990s. In 2010 China became the largest automobile manufacturer in the world.

⊙ View the Image
Modern Hong Kong
at **MyHistoryLab.com**

Statistics reveal the magnitude of the Chinese achievement, as do Chinese goods that fill malls and supermarkets around the world. Trade rose from $100 billion in 1988 to $2,400 billion in 2008. The national product rose from $300 billion in 1980 to ten times that amount in 2010 (or a much higher figure if measured by purchasing power). In 2010, China passed Japan to become the second largest economy in the world. Per capita income has risen to a level that is ahead of India, Vietnam, and Indonesia, but still behind Thailand and Malaysia. In Japan, South Korea, and Taiwan, rapid growth ended when per capita incomes reached the $14,000 level. If that figure applies to China, growth may continue for several decades more.

China and the World The Cold War largely defined the first phase of China's foreign relations. The United States, Japan, South Korea, and U.S.-protected Taiwan were enemies. Other communist nations—the Soviet Union, North Korea, and North Vietnam—were allies. But then China broke with the Soviet Union in 1960 and remained hostile thereafter. It gave material aid to North Vietnam during the Vietnam War, but when traditional anti-Chinese sentiments resurfaced after the war, China briefly invaded Vietnam's northern provinces. Deng Xiaoping's comment was "Vietnam is a hooligan. We must teach it a lesson." Overall, China's foreign relations until after Mao's death in 1976 reflected the revolutionary tumult within.

A second phase of international relations, China as an "emerging nation," began in 1980. Its new market capitalism was coupled with an emphasis on export-led economic growth, which necessitated improved relations with the world's nations. The opening broadened as the Cold War drew to an end after 1989. China reestablished relations with Russia and Vietnam, and more importantly, improved relations with the United States, Japan, South Korea, Taiwan, and Europe.

Ties to the United States were complicated, despite the U.S. recognition of China in 1979. American military alliances with Japan and South Korea, its support of Taiwan, and its ties to the noncommunist nations of Southeast Asia continued to act as the main countervailing force to Chinese hegemony in the region. China resented this U.S. support for the independence of other East Asian nations within

Document   U.S. Foreign Policy: A Chinese Dissident's View

Wei Jingsheng, a Chinese advocate of democratic rights, was deported to the United States in late 1997. A year later, in an op-ed page essay in the *New York Times,* he criticized U.S. policy as pandering to Chinese tyranny. In October 2010 the Nobel Peace Prize was awared to Liu Xiaoho, who is serving an 11 year prison sentence for advocating human right in China. The Chinese government denounced the award of the prize to a "criminal".

■ *Should U.S. foreign policy be used to promote human rights even in poor countries with cultural traditions different from those in the West? Or should the United States avoid interference in the domestic politics of other nations and aim primarily at furthering American economic and security goals? What can foreign policy achieve? Where should the balance be struck?*

CHINA'S DIVERSIONARY TACTICS

One year ago, after 18 years in a Chinese prison, I was "released" and sent here. A Chinese official said that if I ever set foot in China again, I would immediately be returned to prison. . . .

The State Department, in a report last January, used my forced exile as evidence that China was taking "positive steps in human rights" and that "Chinese society continued to become more open." These "positive steps" led the United States and its allies to oppose condemnation of China at a meeting of the United Nations Commission on Human Rights in April. In the months that followed, President Clinton and other Western leaders traveled to China, trumpeting increased economic ties and muting criticism on human rights.

Thus, without fear of sanction, the Chinese Government intensified its repression in 1998. Once the leaders achieved their diplomatic victories, they turned to their main objective: the preservation of tyrannical power. This year, about 70 people are known to have been arrested. . . .

Li Peng, the speaker of the National People's Party Congress, declared recently, "If an organization's purpose is to promote a multiparty system in China and to negate the leadership prerogatives of the Chinese Communist Party, then it will not be permitted to exist."

This statement clearly shows that the Communist Party's primary objective is to sustain its tyranny, and to do so it must deny the people basic rights and freedoms. We must measure the leaders' progress on human rights not by the "release" of individuals but by the people's ability to speak, worship and assemble without official interference and persecution.

Source: Wei Jingsheng, "A Chinese Dissident's View" New York Times (Op-Ed) December 24, 1998. Copyright © 1998 Reprinted with permission of the author.

---

what it considered—in Middle Kingdom fashion—its own proper sphere of influence. Americans appreciated Chinese goods but criticized the extreme imbalance in trade: China's exports to the United States had increased from $5 billion to $296 billion between 1986 and 2009; but its imports from the United States increased only from $5 billion to $69 billion. The United States also protested the continuing Chinese piracy of hundreds of millions of dollars' worth of U.S. movies, computer software, and CDs each year, and was critical of Chinese human rights abuses. Despite disagreements, Chinese and American presidents regularly exchanged visits. In the World Trade Organization, the United Nations, and elsewhere, China slowly began to adapt to the standards of the larger international community. (See Document, "U.S. Foreign Policy: A Chinese Dissident's View.")

The third phase of foreign relations was China's emergence as a power to be reckoned with in the world. This phase began soon after the beginning of the twenty-first century, though it is difficult to give an exact date. Was it when China's per capita income doubled, or was it when its national product became greater than that of leading European states? Was it in 2003 when China began to cooperate with South Korea, Japan, Russia, and the United States to negotiate an end to North Korean nuclear weapons? Was it during the first decade of the new century when China began buying up natural resource companies in Africa, Australia, and elsewhere? Or should it be defined by China's purchase of submarines from Russia and the continued modernization of its military and nuclear weapons? Was it inaugurated by the 2008 Beijing Olympics, which were more extravagant than any Ringling Brothers circus? Or was it in 2010 when China's foreign currency reserves reached $2.6 trillion mark

See the Map
The Emergence of Modern China, 1919 to the Present
at **MyHistoryLab.com**

Reviewing the Troops in Hong Kong. Chinese President Hu Jintao inspects the People's Liberation Army garrison during a three-day visit to the Stonecutter's Naval Base in Hong Kong in 2007. Hu visited for three days to celebrate the tenth anniversary of Hong Kong's handover to Chinese rule.

and China produced more automobiles than any other nation? Taken together, these developments in mark China's advance to a new level.

Taiwan

Taiwan is a mountainous island less than 100 miles off the coast of central China. A little larger than Belgium or Massachusetts, it has a population of 23 million. Originally populated by aborigines, and then lightly settled by Chinese immigrants, it became a distant and backward part of the Qing Empire. In 1895, it became a Japanese colony as a spoil of the Sino-Japanese War. The Japanese found it easy to rule since the Taiwanese lacked a sense of national identity and were accustomed to rule by officials who came from across the seas and spoke a language they could not understand. (Standard Chinese and the Fujian dialect spoken by Taiwanese are mutually unintelligible.) The Japanese colonial government quickly suppressed opium and bandits and eradicated epidemic diseases. It built roads and railroads, reformed the land system, and introduced improvements in agriculture. Before 1895 education had been the privilege of a tiny elite; fifty years later, 71 percent of school-age children attended the "common schools" established by the Japanese. (In the Dutch East Indies and French Indochina the figure was about 10 or 15 percent.) Light industries were introduced, and during the 1930s, textiles, chemicals, ceramics, and machine tools were produced. Though mostly owned by Japanese and run in their interest, more benefits seem to have accrued to the local population than was the case in Korea, another Japanese colony.

Anticolonial feelings rose slowly. A few concessions were made during the 1920s, but after the war with China began in 1937, the Japanese reverted to strict controls and assimilationist policies. By 1945 the Taiwanese were happy to see the Japanese leave and welcomed GMD (Guomindang) officials as liberators. The mainland officials, however, viewed the Taiwanese as Japanese collaborators; they looted the economy and ruled harshly. When Taiwanese protested in February 1947, the GMD police put down the demonstrators and over several months killed almost 10,000 Taiwanese, many of them community leaders. By the time Jiang Jieshi (Chiang Kai-shek) and 2 million more military and civilian mainlanders fled to the island in 1949, its economy and society were in disarray. Mainlanders looked down on the Taiwanese; Taiwanese hated their new rulers and in private often compared them unfavorably to the Japanese.

From the 1950s onward three interdependent developments occurred: the economy grew, politics became democratic, and the relation to the Chinese mainland changed.

In managing the economy, the GMD, which had failed in China, succeeded in Taiwan. Its control of the island was complete, and the times were peaceful. It had restored order by the mid-1950s, and rapid growth followed. Heavy industries were put under state control; other former Japanese industries were sold to private parties. With the outbreak of the Korean War in 1950, U.S. aid became substantial. Foreign investment was welcomed. Light industries were followed by consumer electronics, steel, and petrochemicals and then by computers and semiconductors. Private industries led the way. By the late 1990s, Taiwan was the world's largest producer of monitors, keyboards, motherboards, and computer mice; it was second in notebook PCs

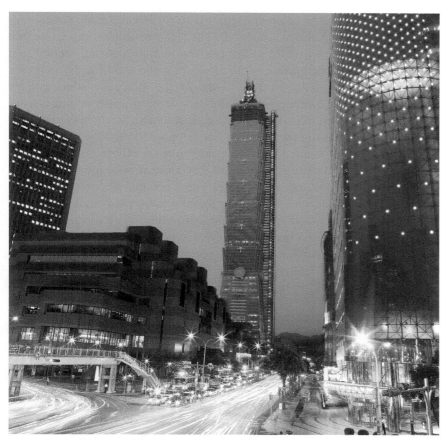

The World's Tallest Building. Evening traffic swirls around the Taipei 101, a building with 101 floors. At 1,671 feet, it was the only building in the world in 2004 to be over a half kilometer in height. The design was inspired by traditional Chinese architecture.

and fourth in integrated circuits. Many of these were actually manufactured in Taiwanese-owned plants in mainland China. By 2009, Taiwanese investments in China rose to $150 billion, and Chinese investments in Taiwan were permitted for the first time. Estimated Taiwanese GDP in 2009 was $360 billion (or as measured in purchasing power, $700 billion and a per capita income of $30,000).

The transition to democratic government in Taiwan was not unlike that in South Korea. For the first twenty years, the GMD government was a dictatorship. It ruled as it had on the mainland, banning opposition parties and enforcing martial law. It maintained that it was the legitimate government of all of China, and by control of the "central government" institutions (which it maintained in Taiwan), it dominated the "provincial government" (of Taiwan) in which Taiwanese were permitted to participate. Social changes began during the 1960s. Education advanced, with rising numbers entering universities. Taiwanese and mainlanders began to intermarry. As the economy advanced, a new middle class emerged, more concerned with economic well-being than it had been in

past history. Taiwanese entered the GMD and moved from provincial to central government posts. Jiang Jieshi died in 1975, a year earlier than Mao. Under his son Jiang Jingguo, who was president from 1978 to 1988, Taiwan inched toward representative government. In 1987, Jiang Jingguo ended martial law and permitted opposition parties to form.

After that, changes came quickly. In 1988 a native-born Taiwanese, who had risen to the top of the GMD, became president. In 1996, he was reelected in what he billed as "the first free election in 5,000 years of Chinese history." In 2000, another Taiwanese, the leader of an opposition party, became president in an election hailed by one scholar as "the first peaceful transition of power from one political party to another in Taiwanese history, and probably in all of Chinese history." He was reelected in 2004. A GMD candidate, Ma Jingjeou, won the most recent 2008 election. Ma was born in Hong Kong and educated at National Taiwan University, New York University, and Harvard. He campaigned on a platform of economic revitalization and better relations with China. Possibly his victory signaled the beginning of a two-party system in Taiwan.

Since 1949, Beijing has maintained that Taiwan is a province of China and has spoken of reclaiming the island by force. It held that its relation with the island was a matter of internal Chinese politics and refused ties with any nation maintaining diplomatic ties with Taiwan. From the outbreak of the Korean War in 1950 until 1979, Taiwan was a protégé of the United States, which, ignoring the mainland, supported Taiwan's claim to be the legitimate government of all of China and provided for the island's defense. But in 1979 the United States formally broke off relations with Taipei and recognized Beijing as the legitimate government of a China that included Taiwan. Nevertheless, the United States stressed that any reunion of China and Taiwan should be peaceful. It continued informal relations with Taiwan, and it continued to trade with it and sell it arms. Curiously, it was during the years of diplomatic limbo after the 1979 break that Taiwan's economy grew and its society became democratic.

At the onset of the twenty-first century, the status of Taiwan was still an issue. China was concerned that a democratically elected government gave Taiwan a claim to legitimacy in the eyes of the world. It worried that Taiwan's prosperity would make its peoples less willing to rejoin the mainland—a view lent credence by public opinion polls in

Taiwan. Occasionally it spoke of taking the island by force. But China was keenly aware that doing so would enormously disrupt China's world trade. China also knew that economic ties between Taiwan and China, and China's rising prosperity, might eventually make an invasion unnecessary. China is Taiwan's number one trading partner, and almost a million Taiwanese live in China. The United States watched, with some unease, the steady rise of Chinese military power. But as of 2010, all sides seemed content to leave the status of Taiwan to an indefinite future.

Korea

Korea and Vietnam, the other two countries in the East Asian zone of civilization, both became colonies: Korea, annexed by Japan in 1910; Vietnam, a part of French Indochina in 1883. In both countries, the imposition of colonialism on peoples with high indigenous cultures and a strong national identity engendered powerful anticolonial nationalisms. After World War II, both countries were divided into a communist north and a noncommunist south, Korea immediately and Vietnam years later. Both experienced civil war. In each case, the United States entered the conflicts to stem the spread of communism. Never before had the United States fought in countries about which it knew so little.

Korea as a Japanese Colony

The political, economic, and social ills of Choson Korea increased during the nineteenth century. As the century drew to a close, a three-cornered, imperialist rivalry arose among China, Japan, and Russia, with Korea as the prize. Japan won by defeating China in the Sino-Japanese War (1894–1895) and Russia in the Russo-Japanese War (1904–1905). Japan made Korea a protectorate in 1905 and annexed it in 1910.

Annexation was followed by efforts to make Korea a model colony. A land survey and land tax reform clarified land ownership. Public hygiene was enforced, infectious diseases dropped sharply, and the population grew from 14 million in 1910 to 24 million in 1940. Attendance at common schools increased from 20,000 in 1910 to 1.2 million in 1939, while attendance at higher common schools, girls' higher schools, and trade schools also rose. A new currency was issued and banks were established. As in Taiwan, huge investments were made in roads, railways, and telegraph lines. The 1920s saw further investments in hydroelectric power, fertilizer plants, and mining. Most large-scale industries were Japanese-owned, but Korean entrepreneurs began textile mills, shipping lines, and small industries. Even excluding mining and transport, employment in industry rose from 385,000 in 1932 to 1,322,000 in 1943.

The colonial transformation was not limited to economics. Koreans who studied at Japanese universities came into contact with the full range of political, social, literary, and artistic currents of the modern world and brought their new knowledge back to Korea. By the 1930s a modern culture was forming in Korea's cities. In sum, experiencing a truncated version of Meiji-type reforms, Korea became vastly different from what it had been in 1910.

Being a Japanese colony was nonetheless a hard road to modernity. The colonial government was authoritarian. Its goal was to make Korea into a subordinate part of Imperial Japan, and benefits to Koreans were incidental. Education was Japan-oriented, and instruction was given in Japanese. The land tax reform primarily benefited landowners. Japanese and Korean land companies bought up former crown lands, and tenancy rose from 42 percent in 1913 to 69 percent in 1945. The Japanese in Korea received better salaries, medical care, education, and jobs than their Korean counterparts. Whether in government, banking, or industry, Koreans were mainly relegated to the lower echelons. To be sure, this was the case in European colonies, but it rankled in Korea because Korea was an older culture and racially close to Japan. After 1937, the Japanese policy of "assimilation" grew even harsher: Koreans were pressured to adopt Japanese names, drafted to fight in Japan's wars, and sent to labor in factories in Japan. "Comfort women" were recruited, occasionally by force, to service Japanese troops. This bitter colonial legacy has only begun to subside in recent decades.

North and South

Upon Japan's defeat in 1945, Soviet troops entered the North; a month later U.S. forces occupied Korea south of the thirty-eighth parallel. Despite a promise of unification, two separate states developed. In the South, the United States initially aimed at the formation of a democratic, self-governing nation but settled for the anticommunist and authoritarian government of Syngman Rhee (1875–1965), a longtime nationalist leader whose party won the 1948 election. With Rhee as the Republic of Korea's first president, the United States formally ended its military governance of

◆●●─┤Read the Document
James F. Schnabel, from United
States Army in the Korean War
at **MyHistoryLab.com**

Korea. Many of Rhee's officials and officers had formerly served in the colonial government or the Japanese military. His government was strongly supported by conservative Koreans and by the million or so Koreans who fled from the North.

In the North, the Russians established a communist government under Kim Il Sung (1912–1994). Kim had worked with the Chinese communists during the 1930s and subsequently with the Soviet Union. When the South held elections in 1948, the North hurriedly followed suit, and the

Comfort Women. South Korean women, who were forced by the Japanese military to serve in brothels during World War II, protest near the Japanese embassy in Seoul, January 2003.

Map 32–2. The Korean War, 1950–1953.

Democratic People's Republic of Korea was established. Not a few of its officers and officials had fought on the communist side in the Chinese Civil War. At the end of 1948 the Soviet Union withdrew its troops from North Korea. During 1949 and early 1950 the United States withdrew most of its troops from the South, a part of a larger American disengagement from continental Asia after the communist victory in China. The words used at the time were "let the dust settle."

The Korean War and U.S. Involvement

In June 1950, North Korea invaded the South in an attempt to reunify Korea. Kim Il Sung, the North Korean leader, had received Stalin's permission for the invasion and a promise from Mao to send Chinese troops if the United States entered the war. He planned for a quick victory before the United States had time to react. But the Cold War had already begun in Europe, and the invasion, coming four months after the signing of the Sino-Soviet Alliance, was seen by the United States as an act of aggression by world communism. The United States rushed troops from Japan to South Korea and obtained United Nations backing. It also sent naval forces to the Taiwan Straits to protect Taiwan, and over the next several years, entered into military alliances with South Korea, Japan, Taiwan, the Philippines, and the noncommunist states of Southeast Asia. The Korean War was the catalyst for a major turn in postwar American foreign policy.

During the first months of the war, the unprepared American and South Korean forces were driven southward to a small "Pusan perimeter" on Korea's southeastern rim (see Map 32–2). But then, amphibious units led by the United Nations commander General Douglas MacArthur landed at Inchon in the middle of Korea's western coast and drove back the North Korean armies beyond the thirty-eighth parallel deep into North Korea. American policy shifted from the containment of communism to a rollback.

The UN forces in Korea were half American and two-fifths Korean; the rest were contingents from Britain, Australia, Turkey, and twelve other nations. In the final phase of the war, China sent in "volunteers" to rescue the beleaguered North Korean forces. Chinese troops pushed the overextended UN forces back to a line close to the thirty-eighth parallel. The war became stalemated in 1951 and ended with an armistice in July 1953. Thereafter the two Koreas maintained a hostile peace. Hundreds of thousands of troops guarded each side of the border. The 142,000 American casualties made the war the fourth largest in U.S. history.

South Korea: Growth and Democracy

After the armistice, two intertwined stories unfolded in South Korea: stunning economic growth and the rise of a democratic polity. Massive student demonstrations forced Rhee to retire in 1960. There followed twenty-seven years of rule by two generals. Park Chung-hee seized power in a military *coup d'état* in 1961. Shedding his uniform, he won a rigged election and became a civilian president. His rule was semiauthoritarian: Opposition parties were legal and active, but their leaders were often jailed. Students were able to mount protest demonstrations, which were routinely blocked by riot police and frequently tear-gassed. South Koreans could read noncommunist foreign books and magazines and travel abroad. In time, even Koreans who approved of Park's economic policies came to resent his police tactics. But when Park was assassinated by his intelligence chief in 1979, another general seized power, transformed himself into a civilian president, and ruled until 1987 in the pattern established by his predecessor.

At the inception of Park's rule, unemployment had been rife and poverty widespread. Both Park and his successor were determined to promote economic growth. Emphasizing science and technology, they supported business and swiftly expanded higher education. Management drew on skills learned during the colonial era; labor was disciplined, hardworking, and cheap. The United States gave large amounts of aid and provided an open market for Korean exports. The result was several decades of double-digit growth. Especially notable was the growth of **chaebol** such as

View the Image
South Korea Enters the U.S. Auto Market
at **MyHistoryLab.com**

Hyundai or Daewoo, which resembled the Mitsui or Mitsubishi *zaibatsu* of prewar Japan. The policies of the two leaders, and of their successors after 1987, were hugely successful. Korea's gross national product rose dramatically (see Figure 32–2).

With an average income in 2009 of $16,500 (with a purchasing power of $28,000), South Korea became a prosperous nation with one of the world's largest economies. Its voice in world affairs grew accordingly.

The second development during the twenty-odd years since 1987 was the rise of democracy. Ironically, the industrialization and urbanization during the rule by the two generals had created an affluent and educated middle class that was no longer willing to tolerate authoritarian rule. The presidential elections held at five-year intervals between 1987 and 2007 reflect a new consciousness within Korea. In 1987, a third ex-general was elected, but the election was free and fair. In 1992, a conservative politician with no ties to the military became president. He purged the generals who had supported the two previous presidents, replacing them with officers willing to work with party governments. He also launched investigations of his predecessors' finances. One reporter commented that corruption was as Korean as *kimchee* (a traditional dish of spicy, pickled cabbage), but the hundreds of millions of dollars in secret bank accounts uncovered by investigators astonished even the Koreans.

In 1997 and 2002, a deeper break with the past occurred when liberal leaders of opposition parties were elected as presidents. Both Kim Dae Jung and Roh Moo Hyun continued to emphasize economic growth. But also, unlike their predecessors, they attempted a rapprochement with North Korea. This was known as the "sunshine policy," which for a time had popular support. Koreans were patriotic and wanted to see their country reunited. The sunshine policy ultimately failed, when the North spurned South Korean initiatives. In 2007, in reaction to the failure, the conservative Lee Myung Bak was elected as president. Since then, tensions with the North have increased. But the principle that conservatives and liberals—both committed to the electoral process—may alternate in power appears to have been established within the South Korean polity.

North Korea

Japanese industries in colonial Korea were mainly in the North, which gave its postwar industrialization an early edge. North Korea's planned economy, however, was enclosed within a tightly sealed, authoritarian state, which stressed heavy industry, collectivized farms, and totally controlled education and the media. By the 1970s, its economy stagnated, and shortages of food, clothing, and necessities

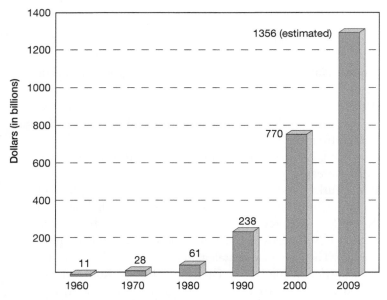

Figure 32–2 Growth of South Korean Gross Domestic Product, as Measured in Purchasing Power.

The Two Kims. South Korean President Kim Dae Jung traveled to Pyongyang in June 2000 to promote his "sunshine policy." As he departed he gave Kim Jong Il, the North Korean leader, a hug. When the North Korean leader failed to return his visit or to ease tensions, sunshine turned to rain and Kim Dae-jung's popularity sagged.

were chronic. During the 1990s and after the turn of the century, periods of famine were not uncommon.

The misery of the North Korean people was highlighted by the caviar and Mercedes Benz lifestyle of its leaders. The cult of personality surrounding "the great leader" Kim Il Sung went beyond that of even Stalin or Mao. The Korean Communist Party was Marxist-Leninist, but the kinship terminology used to describe the fatherly leader, the mother party, and the familial North Korean state gave the official state philosophy a Confucian tinge. Kim designated his son, "the beloved leader" Kim Jong Il (b. 1942), as his successor, and when the father died in 1994, the son became the leader of North Korea—the only instance of hereditary succession in a communist state.

The North Korean record was poor in every respect: It ran prison camps like those of the former Soviet Union. It kidnapped Japanese citizens, fired missiles into Japanese waters, and threatened Japan, saying that Tokyo would be reduced to "a sea of fire" if Japan continued its security arrangement with the United States. To obtain hard currency, it engaged in counterfeiting and drug smuggling. Increasingly isolated, and with a garrison state mentality, it used a Pakistani connection to import nuclear technology and develop its own atomic weapons. When charged with this in 2003, it first denied and then boasted of the development.

Early on, North Korea was backed by the Soviet Union and China, the latter asserting that their solidarity was "as close as lips and teeth." After the collapse of the Soviet

Union, however, Russia had little interest in its former ally. China continued to offer aid and trade. It liked the idea of North Korea as a buffer state. But it was put off by the North's poverty and radical eccentricity, by its unwillingness to follow the Chinese example, and by its cult of personality. China was more attracted by the economically vibrant South Korea, with which it established diplomatic relations in 1992. Since then, South Koreans have invested billions in China, and trade between the two nations has flourished; in 2010 South Korea was China's third most important export market.

Since 2003, the United States, China, Russia, South Korea, and Japan have tried to persuade North Korea to abandon its nuclear endeavors. Even China did not want a nuclear North Korea on its doorstep. But both China and South Korea with its "sunshine policy" were reluctant to apply pressure, fearing a North Korean collapse and a flood of refugees. In October 2006 North Korea detonated its first atomic bomb. This led China, North Korea's principal trading partner, to toughen its stance. The failure of the "sunshine policy" and the election of a conservative president made South Korea more willing to apply sanctions. As of early 2010, the future was unclear. All that can be said with certainty is that a small, isolated, bankrupt dictatorship has kept the attention of its larger neighbors for more than a decade.

●●─Read the Document
Famine in North Korea, 2002
at **MyHistoryLab.com**

Vietnam

The Colonial Backdrop

The Nguyen Dynasty that reunited Vietnam in 1802 was still vigorous in 1858, but was no match for France. France completed its conquest of Vietnam and Cambodia in 1883, formed the Indochinese Union in 1887, and added Laos to the Union in 1893.

Indochina was a classic example of colonial rule: a people of one race and culture, for the sake of economic benefits and national glory, controlling and exploiting a people of another race and culture in a far-off land. To obtain access to the country's natural resources, the French built harbors, roads, and a railway linking Saigon, Hanoi, and southern China. They established rubber plantations in the Mekong Delta and tea plantations in the highlands. They introduced modern mining technology for the extraction of coal and built breweries, rice and paper mills, and glass and cement factories. Large industries were dominated by the French, smaller enterprises by Vietnamese-Chinese. Workers were paid poorly. Vietnamese were mainly laborers, except for the few who became landlords. In the South, 3 percent of landowners owned 45 percent of the land and received 60 percent of the crop grown by their tenants. Although new irrigation works in the Mekong Delta quadrupled the area of rice fields, peasant consumption of rice declined. The skewed distribution of wealth meant that no indigenous middle class developed, apart from landlords and Chinese merchants whose commercial acumen was resented by Vietnamese. The French did little to educate the Vietnamese: In 1939, over 80 percent of the population was illiterate, possibly a higher percentage than in the early nineteenth century under the Nguyen.

In the early decades of French rule, the Vietnamese made futile attempts to restore the dynasty. In the early twentieth century, Vietnamese nationalists in exile in China, Japan, and France formed political parties. But when they tried to organize within Vietnam, the parties were suppressed and their leaders jailed or executed. Within Vietnam, only clandestine parties survived. The most skilled organizer of such parties was Ho Chi Minh (1892–1969), who had participated in the founding of the French Communist Party in 1920, studied in Moscow in 1923, and worked under the Comintern agent Mikhail Borodin in Canton in 1925. Ho founded the Revolutionary Youth League of Vietnam in 1925 and sent its cadres to China and the Soviet Union

Read the Document
Ho Chi Minh, "Equality!"
at **MyHistoryLab.com**

for training. He then founded the Indochinese Communist Party in 1930. When the Popular Front

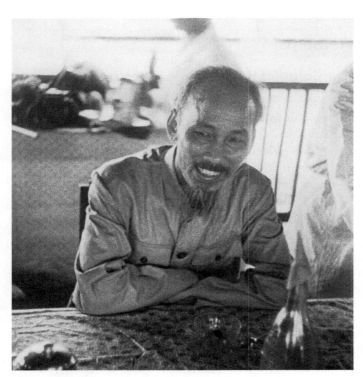

Ho Chi Minh (1892–1969). Ho became a communist in France in 1920, studied in Moscow, and founded the Indochinese Communist Party in 1930. He fought, in succession, against the Japanese, French, Americans, and South Vietnamese. He did not live to see the communist victory in 1975.

gained power in France (1936–1938), opposition parties were briefly tolerated in Vietnam and Ho's party was the strongest. After 1938 the French again suppressed all opposition groups. Shortly before the outbreak of the Pacific War, the Japanese occupied Vietnam. For their own convenience, until March 1945, they ruled through Vichy French puppets. Ho, who in 1941 had formed the **Viet Minh** (League for the Independence of Vietnam) as a popular front organization to resist the Japanese, proclaimed the Democratic Republic of Vietnam after Japan's defeat in 1945 and became the preeminent nationalist

Read the Document
Resolution Establishing the Viet Minh, 1941 at **MyHistoryLab.com**

leader in his country. There followed three cycles of war and three decades of peace.

The Anticolonial War

The first war lasted from 1946 to 1954. On one side was the Viet Minh, led by Ho. It was controlled by communists but included representatives of nationalist parties. On the other side were the French, who had reoccupied Vietnam immediately after the war, and their conservative Vietnamese allies. The French tried to legitimize their rule by setting up a puppet government in 1948 under Bao Dai, the last in the line of Nguyen emperors. From 1950, the French received American aid. But the French lost a major battle at Dien Bien Phu in 1954 and, with

Study and Review
Frantz Fanon and Ho Chi Minh Speak Out Against Imperialism at **MyHistoryLab.com**

it, the will to continue what critics at home called the "dirty war." They departed in defeat.

A conference at Geneva divided the country into a communist North and a noncommunist South. In the South, Ngo Dinh Diem, a nationalist leader who had not collaborated with the French, came to power and established the Republic of Viet-

Read the Document
Ho Chi Minh on Self-Determination (1954) at **MyHistoryLab.com**

nam. Much of his political support came from the 900,000 Vietnamese who fled from the North.

The Vietnam War

The second cycle of war, from 1959 to 1975, began with guerrilla attacks against Southern troops in the late 1950s. Some said these were a local response to Diem's suppression of his political enemies, while others, including North Vietnamese after the war, said they were directed from the North. Local incidents eventually turned into a full-scale war between the North and the South (see Map 32–3). The North received material aid but no "volunteers" from the Soviet Union and China. The United States sent troops to aid the South: 600 military advisers in 1961, 16,000 troops in 1963, 70,000 in 1965, and over half a million in 1969. Despite this massive support, South Vietnam—and the United States—lost the war. The reasons were several.

To explore this map further, go to
http://www.prenhall.com/craig_maps

Map 32–3. Vietnam and Its Southeast Asian Neighbors.
The map identifies important places during the war in Vietnam.

1. The South was difficult to govern. In comparison to the North, the region had been less deeply influenced by Chinese culture. It was ethnically diverse, containing Chinese, Cambodians, and Chams as well as Vietnamese. In religion, it was divided among several varieties of Buddhism, Catholicism, and two powerful "new religions," the Cao Dai in the eastern provinces and the Hoa Hao in the western provinces. The two millenarian sects possessed private armies, and though opposed to the communists, they stood apart from the South Vietnamese government, at times warring among themselves. Throughout this era, the inability of successive Southern governments to unify their fragmented society was a basic weakness in their struggles with the communist North.

2. All too often corrupt, the South Vietnamese government inspired little loyalty in its citizens.

3. Ho Chi Minh was a national hero to many South Vietnamese as well as to Northerners. Even noncommunists sometimes viewed the United States as the successor to the French and the communist guerrillas as fighting an anticolonial war.

4. Both communist guerrillas in the South and North Vietnamese troops fought better than the soldiers of the South Vietnamese government.

5. In the jungle terrain of Vietnam, the technological edge of the United States was blunted. A greater tonnage of bombs was dropped on supply trails in Cambodia than on Japan in World War II, yet supplies continued to flow south.

At the beginning, the U.S. government saw the war as part of its struggle against world communism. After the Sino-Soviet split, they perceived it as a war to halt the spread of Chinese communism. Few in the United States understood the depth of Vietnamese ambivalence toward China, which would resurface shortly after the war. As the war dragged on and casualties mounted, the American people turned against the war. When Richard Nixon became president, he called for the "Vietnamization" of the war and began to withdraw American troops. In January 1973, a ceasefire was arranged in Paris, and two months later the last U.S. troops left. Fighting broke out anew between North and South; South Vietnamese forces collapsed in 1975; the country was reunited under the Hanoi government in the North; Saigon was renamed Ho Chi Minh City.

After the war, few areas of the world were as devastated as Vietnam and its neighbors. After unifying the country, Hanoi sent thousands of those associated with the former South Vietnamese government to labor camps, collectivized agricultural lands, and in 1976 began a five-year plan for the economy. Several hundred thousand Vietnamese and ethnic Chinese fled by boat or across the Chinese border.

See the Map
The Vietnam War
at **MyHistoryLab.com**

War with Cambodia

Pol Pot (1926–1998) and his radical **Khmer Rouge** (Red Cambodia) came to power in Cambodia in 1975. During the next three years, he evacuated cities and towns, abolished money and trade, banned Buddhism, and executed or caused to die of starvation an estimated 1 million persons, roughly 15 percent of the Cambodian population. Schoolteachers and the educated were singled out as special targets. Vietnam was Cambodia's historical enemy, as China was Vietnam's. When Pol Pot purged the Khmer Rouge of pro-Vietnamese elements in 1978, Vietnam invaded and occupied most of Cambodia and set up a puppet government.

Skulls. A worker cleans a skull excavated from a mass grave in Cambodia. The Khmer Rouge, under Pol Pot, murdered about one-sixth of the Cambodian population. Doctors, teachers, and other educated people were targeted.

Cambodians accepted the government because they feared Pol Pot more than they hated Vietnam. But Vietnamese troops were unable to suppress Pol Pot's guerrilla forces completely.

The unified Vietnam of 1975 became an ally of the Soviet Union and gave the Soviets a naval base in return for economic, military, and diplomatic support. But relations with China soured. Vietnam feared Chinese domination and resented Nixon's visit to China in 1972, when American troops were still fighting on its soil. China, for its part, felt Vietnam had not duly appreciated its wartime aid, resented Vietnam's treatment of its ethnic Chinese, and feared Vietnam's close ties to the Soviet Union. In 1979, China decided to "teach Vietnam a lesson" and invaded four northern provinces. Seasoned Vietnamese troops repelled the invaders, but losses were heavy on both sides. For years thereafter China supported Pol Pot's guerrillas and occasionally shelled Vietnam's northern border.

Recent Developments

As if a kaleidocope had been shaken, the situation changed abruptly in the late 1980s. The collapse of the Soviet Union ended Vietnam's primary foreign relation. In 1989 Vietnam withdrew from its costly occupation of Cambodia in favor of a UN-sponsored government. Eight years later one faction, led by a pro-Vietnamese leader, took over the Cambodian government in a coup. His role was strengthened in 1998 when Pol Pot died and the Khmer Rouge collapsed.

Vietnam-Chinese relations improved, and China's landlocked province of Yunnan began using the Vietnamese port of Haiphong as an outlet for its products. In 1995, Vietnam joined the Association of Southeast Asian Nations (ASEAN), marking an important advance in its relations with its closest and richer neighbors, and it also reestablished diplomatic relations with the United States. As it moved toward "normal" relations with the rest of the world, Europeans and Americans began to take package tours to Vietnam, visiting scenic locales that only two decades earlier had been battle zones of a bitter war.

By the late 1990s, a "Chinese pattern" emerged in Vietnam. On the one hand, the communist government in Hanoi monopolized political power and controlled the army, police, and media. On the other, the leaders, aware that victories in wars were hollow as long as their people remained destitute, embraced capitalism as the road to growth. In place of collective agriculture, farmers were allowed to keep the rice they grew: Vietnam went from near starvation to become the world's second largest exporter of rice. Stock markets were established in Hanoi and Ho Chi Minh City. Taxes were kept low and a premium was put on education. Garment manufacturing, food processing, and the production of other consumer goods grew apace. Between 1991 and 2007, the economy averaged over 8 percent growth and received more offers of foreign investment than it could absorb. Taiwan and Singapore were the largest investors, but Intel, Nike, and other American companies were not far behind. Vietnam's exports to the United States in 2006 were nine times greater than its imports, a pattern not unlike that of China and the United States. By the turn of the millennium, shops in Vietnam were full of food and goods, when only a decade or so earlier there had been regional famines. During the first decade of the millennium, Vietnam experienced the second fastest economic growth in the world. South Vietnam was the engine of this economy. Even northern Vietnamese saw its openness, pluralism, and cosmopolitanism as attractive.

With a population of 87 million, Vietnam is one of the world's most densely populated nations. The government limits families to two children. Hanoi had a population of 130,000 in the 1930s and has 7 million today; Ho Chi Minh City (Saigon) rose from less than a million at the war's end in 1975 to 8 million today. As the economy grew, the gap between rural and urban widened. More than half of the population was born after 1975, and labor is still cheap. But conditions have improved immensely: In 1990, the national product was less than $10 billion; in 2010 it will reach $92 billion (or $258 billion in purchasing power), and per capita income has risen to $1,057, with a purchasing power of about $3,000. In short, Vietnam illustrates the trajectory common to all East Asian nations, except North Korea.

Summary

Japan. The U.S.-led occupation after World War II established a democratic government and set Japan on the way to its remarkable postwar prosperity. By the twenty-first century, Japan had the second largest economy in the world. Politically, Japan is a democracy with free elections. Socially, Japan has remained stable, with the world's highest longevity rate.

China. Communist rule was established in 1949. Until his death in 1976, Mao Zedong controlled China. Mao broke with the Soviet Union in the 1960s and launched the disastrous Cultural Revolution in 1965. After Mao's death, Deng Xiaoping opened China's economy to free-market reforms. The result has been surging economic growth and rising prosperity. Politically, the Communist Party has blocked any threat to its one-party rule. China has emerged as a world power.

Taiwan. The Nationalist Party (GMD) set up a separate state in Taiwan under U.S. protection after their defeat in the Chinese civil war in 1949. Since then Taiwan has moved from poverty to prosperity, from dictatorship to democracy. The Chinese government insists that Taiwan is a province of China. The United States agrees, but holds that only a peaceful reunification would be tolerable.

Korea. Postwar Korea was occupied by the Soviet Union in the north and the United States in the south. Two Koreas emerged. They fought the Korean War in 1950–1953. Since the war, South Korea has become democratic and prosperous, while North Korea is totalitarian and impoverished but has developed atomic weapons.

Vietnam. From the end of World War II until 1954, the Vietnamese fought French colonial rule. From 1959 to 1975, North Vietnam fought South Vietnam and the United States. North Vietnam's victory in 1975 reunified the country. Though its government remains a single-party dictatorship, Vietnam has recently embraced a market economy and begun substantial growth.

Key Terms

Article 9 of the No-War Constitution (p. 993)

brainwashing (p. 1001)

chaebol (p. 1012)

Cultural Revolution (p. 1003)

Great Leap Forward (p. 1001)

Khmer Rouge (p. 1015)

LDP (p. 994)

Viet Minh (p. 1014)

Review Questions

1. Is postwar Japan better understood as a return to the relative liberalism of the 1920s, or as a fresh start based on Occupation reforms? Why did the Occupation of Japan go so smoothly, in contrast, say, to the American occupation of Iraq?

2. Compare the trajectories of the Japanese and Chinese economies. In Japan, what factors ended double-digit growth? Will the same factors affect China in the near future?

3. Is China from 1949 until the death of Mao better understood as an outgrowth of its earlier history or as a communist state comparable, say, to the old Soviet Union? And to what country would you compare post-Deng China?

4. How did the precolonial and colonial eras of Korea and Vietnam shape their history after World War II? How did the Cold War shape their history?

5. If you were the U.S. secretary of state, what long-term China policy would you propose to the president? Where would Japan fit into your policy?

Note: *To learn more about the topics in this chapter, please turn to the Suggested Readings at the end of the book. For additional sources related to this chapter please see MyHistoryLab.com.*

myhistorylab Connections

Reinforce what you learned in this chapter by studying the many documents, images, maps, review tools, and videos available at **www.myhistorylab.com**.

Read and Review

✓●─[Study and Review **Chapter 32**

●●─[Read the Document *The Constitution of Japan (1947), p. 993*
China's One-Child Family Policy (1970s), p. 1001
Decision Concerning the Great Proletarian Cultural Revolution, p. 1004
Deng Xiaoping, on Introducing Capitalist Principles to China, p. 1005
James F. Schnabel, from United States Army in the Korean War, p. 1010
Famine in North Korea 2002, p. 1013
Ho Chi Minh, "Equality!", p. 1014
Resolution Establishing the Viet Minh, 1941, p. 1014
Ho Chi Minh on Self-Determination (1954), p. 1014

👁─[See the Map *Japan in 1945, p. 990*
The Emergence of Modern China, 1919 to the Present, p. 1007

◉─[View the Image *Japanese Technician Testing Equipment, p. 996*
Modern Hong Kong, p. 1006
South Korea Enters the U.S. Auto Market, p. 1012

((●─[Hear the Audio *Communist China 3, p. 1003*
Communist China 4, p. 1004

✓●─[Study and Review *Frantz Fanon and Ho Chi Minh Speak Out Against Imperialism, p. 1014*

Research and Explore

👁─[See the Map *China in the Era of Revolution and Civil War, p. 1004*

👁─[See the Map *The Vietnam War, p. 1015*

((●─[Hear the Audio

Hear the audio file for Chapter 32 at
www.myhistorylab.com.

33

Postcolonialism and Beyond: Latin America, Africa, Asia, and the Middle East

■ Beyond the Postcolonial Era

■ Latin America Since 1945

■ Postcolonial Africa

■ The Islamic Heartlands, from North Africa to Indonesia

■ The Postcolonial Middle East

Darfur, Western Sudan. Distraught Sudanese refugees wait at a food and clothing aid distribution point. The conflict, which began in February 2003, has killed as many as 400,000 people through violence, hunger, and disease. Some 2.5 million people have been displaced by the fighting.

THE DECADES AFTER WORLD WAR II SAW Europe eclipsed by the rise of two superpowers—the United States and the Soviet Union—and then the collapse of the Soviet Union and its subsequent displacement by China as the second superpower. Elsewhere in the world, especially in the industrializing regions, the postwar decades witnessed the end of Western colonialism and challenges to European and superpower imperialism. New nations emerged in Africa and Asia.

Two developments in Asia have particularly affected the entire world and will continue to do so for the foreseeable future. First, as explored in the previous chapter, Japan, and more recently China have emerged as major political and economic powers. Second, the rise of militant, politicized Islam as a result of developments in the postcolonial Middle East now presents a challenge to the status quo across much of the globe. The waning of imperial and colonial dominance of the many by the few and the emergence of new, powerful forces from the previous colonial world must, however, be set

Democratization, Globalization, and Terrorism

The World

Two remarkable political and economic developments have shaped our era: democratization and globalization.

Since 1970, on one continent or another, democratic political rights have expanded. Authoritarian regimes of both the right and the left have been reformed or collapsed. Dictatorships, military juntas, or one-party autocracies have begun to yield to more representative governments. Progress has not been uniform, but more and more people everywhere aspire to have a voice in how they are governed. This process of political change, usually termed democratization, involves expanding participation in political processes, as well as both orderly selection and succession of executive and legislative leaders through elections and establishment of viable civil societies. Many autocracies and authoritarian states still flourish, but more nations than ever before have seen democratic or semidemocratic forms of government instituted.

An unprecedented series of economic linkages, generally termed *globalization,* has paralleled the spread of more democratic institutions. This process has included the forging of new trade and manufacturing agreements, such as NAFTA, among leading industrial nations. Globalization has reduced trade barriers, including tariffs and other regulations hindering circulation of goods, services, and labor among nations. The emergence of worldwide trading and investment networks has led to consolidation of economic enterprises as owners of capital seek to locate their centers of production in the most advantageous labor and resource markets. The giant corporations of the United States, Europe, and Asia now operate in a multinational setting.

within a larger historical perspective. Since the 1500s, the various Asian, African, and Latin American regions of the globe had been drawn steadily into the European sphere of economic and political influence. Those areas to be treated here—Latin America, Africa, Central Asia, South and Southeast Asia, and the Middle East—were often conquered, exploited, and colonized by European powers. The period of colonialism that began in earnest in the seventeenth century was a fateful, but relatively brief, episode in world history. The last significant colonial territories gained their independence in the 1970s. ■

Beyond the Postcolonial Era

It may be argued that with the collapse of apartheid in South Africa, the fall of the Berlin Wall, and economic growth in India and China the postcolonial era has ended. It may, however, also be argued that lingering remnants of pre-1950s colonialism persist in many global regions today. Even with the global recession of 2008–2010, industrial

The End of Empire. A statue of Queen Victoria is removed from the front of the Supreme Court building in Georgetown, former capital of the British colony of Guyana, in February 1970, in preparation for the transition to independence.

Globalization's supporters contend that it will produce more goods and services at lower consumer cost than a highly regulated economy. Critics argue that globalization concentrates power in the hands of unregulated corporations and that governments have surrendered too much of their authority to regulate the economy, preserve the environment, and protect workers. Critics also believe that the new economic structures mean that poor nations, many of them the emerging nations discussed in this chapter, become poorer as rich nations become richer. Globalization rode the wave of prosperity that seems to have crested in the late 1990s. It remains to be seen what will occur in today's more difficult times.

The debate over globalization has made its admirers and detractors more aware of the vast, persistent areas of deep poverty around the world, especially in South and Central America, the Caribbean, Africa, and much of Asia—regions still struggling with the legacy of European colonialism. Most of these regions were impoverished even in the late nineteenth century by globalization when it was just beginning, but today's enormous prosperity in much of the Northern Hemisphere has made poorer regions more conscious of their poverty and, especially in Africa and the Middle East, ripe for political extremism. Among Muslims, such extremism has often been associated with political Islamism. The United States and Europe have become par-

ticular targets of those suffering from and opposed to globalization.

The economic, military, and diplomatic involvement of the United States and its European allies in other regions has led some to view them as imperial powers and even to use terrorist tactics against them. The overwhelming American support for the state of Israel, the festering Israeli-Palestinian conflict, and, most recently, the U.S. invasion of Iraq have also convinced many peoples, especially those in the Muslim world, that the United States especially is inimical to Islam. Within the United States and also around the world, debate continues over the future role of the United States and whether it can best protect its citizens' interests and world peace and prosperity through unilateral, preemptive invasions such as that of Iraq or through greater cooperation with international bodies such as the United Nations.

Focus Questions

- What are the arguments of the proponents and opponents of globalization?
- How has the legacy of European colonialism affected the Middle East, Asia, and Africa?
- Why has the United States moved ahead of even Europe as a prime target for terrorists?

nations have in the past decade experienced strong economic growth, much as in the early 1990s in East Asia. We have also seen new regional and transregional political alignments emerge; internal struggles to build political systems that encourage civil society and limit oligarchic or dictatorial power; and, most dramatically, the determination of radical Islamists to contest European and American political and economic global power.

After 1945 two distinct developments occurred in the world. The first—in a process generally termed **decolonization**—was the emergence of various parts of Africa and Asia from direct control by foreign powers and the reconstitution of these former colonial dependencies as independent states. Included in these states are India, Pakistan, most Arab states, the Latin American nations, and the new nations of Africa (see Map 33–1 on page 1022). Each newly independent African or Asian state has had typically to live within the colonial borders created by European colonial powers.

As decolonization proceeded and new nations established themselves with greater or lesser stability, their relationship to industrial European and Europeanized nations has undergone four stages. First, before the breakup of the Soviet Union, its rivalry with the United States manifested itself on every continent and added to this era's tensions

and turmoil. New emerging nations tended to develop under the patronage of one or the other superpower (or, less often, China). Artificially conceived, that bipolar division of the postcolonial world has ended.

((•—[Hear the **Audio**
Decolonization 1
at **MyHistoryLab.com**

Second, in the years since the Cold War's end and the Soviet Union's collapse, the character of the world economy in such areas as trade, investment, and resource allocation has engendered new economic, social, and cultural interdependencies, commonly termed **globalization**, that remain ill defined and troublesome, whether they relate to automobile production, oil reserves, trade restrictions, currency failures, or international debt.

Third, the ideas of civil society and participatory government, often symbolized by the democracies of the United States, Europe, Japan, and various Asian, African, and Latin American countries, have gained ground even where autocratic, authoritarian regimes have been the rule in government, at least since World War II.

In all three kinds of interaction, change has often outpaced peoples' and leaders' awareness of it. The world may look and feel different today from just thirty, let alone fifty, years ago, but the rhetoric of decolonization is still employed, though applied to different realities.

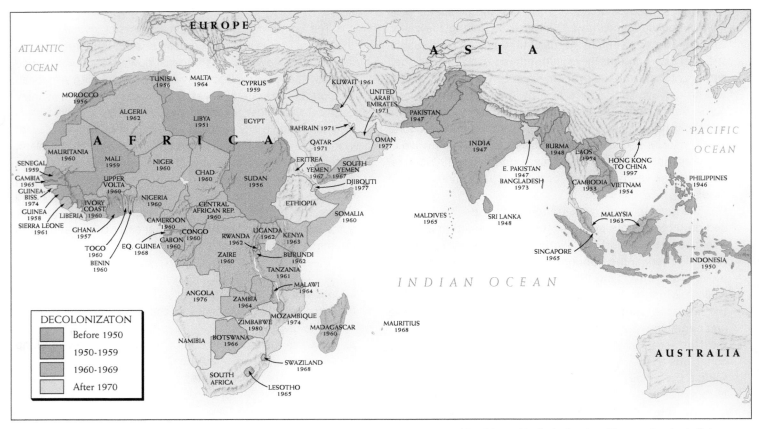

Map 33–1. **Decolonizaton since World War II.** Europe's rapid retreat from imperialism after World War II is graphically depicted on this map, showing half the globe—from Africa to the Pacific.

These stages of development seemed relatively steady and peaceful, but now have given way to a fourth, largely unanticipated, set of developments, in which forces of society, culture, and religion have asserted themselves in aggressive and dramatic ways, both regionally and internationally, around the globe. A central question today is whether to see the global variety of social, cultural, and religious traditions as creative or as divisive forces today and in the years ahead. One much-debated model for understanding the complex international scene today is that of "the West versus the Rest," in which the European and Europeanized world and its ethos are seen as the hope of the future, while all other social, religious, and cultural traditions are depicted as intrinsically opposed to European-style "modernity." In this model, the future is seen as involving potentially less conflict between nation states; instead a **clash of civilizations** will dominate world affairs.[1] This analysis pits Islamic, European and Eastern Orthodox Christian, Buddhist, Hindu, Confucian, and other religious, social, and cultural traditions of historical "civilizations" against one another in a resurgence of religious, social, ethnic, and cultural chauvinism that portends new bloodletting and international conflict. This analysis has found favor among some observers in the wake of international political developments following the terrorist attack of September 11, 2001, on the United States.

Other observers believe this analysis ignores the vast variety within every religious or cultural tradition and overstates the effects of religious resurgence and differences in values among the major human religiocultural traditions. They instead urge that much of the value of studying the varied world traditions and their modern representatives and derivatives is to develop a more nuanced view of the modern world as one in which many cultural, religious, and political traditions interact and compete, but in which people of all kinds can (and must) get along. Population control, the environment, political accommodation, food supply, public health, and the like thus become the foci of *shared* international concern and partnership. Although the history of the past century indicates it will not be easy, this argument holds that our common need for solutions to such transnational, planetwide problems must take precedence over vague, oversimplified "civilizational" differences.

---

[1]See Samuel P. Huntington, "The Clash of Civilizations?" *Foreign Affairs* 72, 3 (Summer 1993): pp. 22–49, and a vast array of articles around the world written in response to this provocative and simplistic piece. This article was followed by a whole book devoted to the so-called "Huntington thesis": *The Clash of Civilizations and the Remaking of World Order* (New York: 1996), in which Huntington somewhat refined his ideas.

However, if we seek to understand the larger global scene, we must recognize the persistent influence of history's great religious and moral traditions, however we evaluate that influence. In particular, Buddhist, Christian, and Islamic faith and values continue to claim the allegiance of major global sectors in not only Africa and Asia, but also Europe and the Americas. No longer can we assume that secular rationalism on the Western, post-Enlightenment model will easily monopolize ideology during the process of material modernization. Rather, we can expect a pluralistic global community in which diverse traditions have to coexist and learn from one another.

In the remainder of this chapter, we shall survey postcolonial political and economic developments in Latin America and from Africa across the southern half of Asia to Indonesia.

Latin America Since 1945

During the second half of the twentieth century and beyond, the nations of Latin America experienced divergent paths of political and economic change. Their leaders tried repeatedly to alleviate their people's dependence on the more developed portions of the globe. At best, these efforts produced mixed results; at worst, they led to repression and tragedy (see Map 33–2).

Before World War II the states of Latin America, as seen in Chapter 25, had been economically dependent on the United States and western Europe. Beginning in the 1950s a shift occurred in those dependent relationships without resulting in any significant change in the general

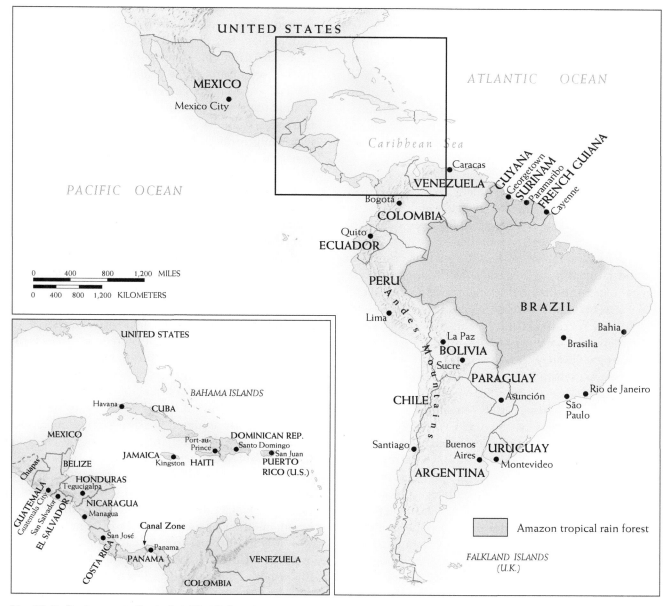

Map 33–2. Contemporary Central and South America.

situation of dependency. The United States loomed larger than ever; the influence of western Europe generally declined; the Soviet Union for a time came to play a far larger economic and political role. Economically and politically, Latin America, like so many other parts of the world, dwelled in the shadow of the rival Cold War superpowers and became an arena for confrontations between them.

The economic life of the region reflected those new relationships of dependence. Attempts were made to expand the industrial base and the agricultural production of the various national economies. Virtually all the financing came from U.S. and western European banks or from Soviet subsidies. Enormous debts were contracted to Western banks, and these debts made Latin American economies virtual prisoners to the fluctuations of world interest rates and the international banking community. Subsidies and special market arrangements with the Soviet Union made other Latin American nations no less dependent on outside economic forces. These shifting relationships, however, did not alter the underlying character of the national economies of most Latin American countries, which overwhelmingly remain exporters of agricultural commodities and mineral resources. The vast economic expansion that occurred in late twentieth-century Asia found no counterpart in Latin America.

What did occur was the rise of a major drug problem in the region. Since the 1970s, Latin America has shipped massive amounts of cocaine to the United States and Europe. In Colombia drug trafficking has produced forty years of political turmoil and civil war with tens of thousands of casualties. In recent years the problem of drug cartels has erupted in Mexico and resulted in very considerable local civil unrest. The desire to halt this drug trafficking has led to formal and informal intervention by the United States at one time or another in the affairs of several Latin American countries. These efforts have involved incentives to diversify local economies away from drug cultivation as well as providing arms to governments seeking to disrupt drug lords. The real question in Colombia, parts of Mexico, and other regions of the Andes is whether governments or drug cartels actually hold authority.

The social structures of the Latin American nations have become more complicated since World War II. A culture of poverty remains the dominant social characteristic of the area. (See Document, "Lourdes Arizpe Discusses the Silence of Peasant Women.") Even periods of economic boom, such as that fostered in Mexico by oil production in the late 1970s, proved brief and were almost inevitably followed by decline. Migration into the cities from the countryside has created tremendous urban overcrowding and slums inhabited by the desperately poor (see Figure 33–1). In many countries the standards of health and nutrition have fallen. The growth of service industries in the cities has also fostered the emergence of a professional, educated

Figure 33–1 Population of Major South American Cities, 1930–2006.

middle class, often possessed with a strong desire to imitate the affluent lifestyle of their social counterparts in the United States and western Europe. This new professional middle class has displayed little taste for radical politics, major social reform, or revolution which over the decades marked some parts of the region.

Political events in Latin America led to the establishment of authoritarian governments of both the left and the right and to a retreat from the ideal and model of parliamentary democracy. Only Mexico, Colombia, Venezuela, and Costa Rica remained parliamentary states throughout this period. Elsewhere, two paths of political development were followed. In Cuba and Nicaragua, and for a short time in Chile, revolutionary socialist governments with close ties to the Soviet Union were established. Elsewhere, often in response to the fear of revolution or communist activity, military governments held power for long periods, sometimes punctuated with brief interludes of civilian rule. Such were the situations in Chile, Brazil, Argentina, Paraguay, Bolivia, Peru, and Uruguay. Governments of both the left and the right engaged in repression, suspending civil liberties and arresting enemies.

These political changes fostered new roles for two traditional Latin American institutions: the military and the Roman Catholic Church. The armies of the various nations have played key political roles since the wars of independence, but toward the close of the twentieth century they frequently assumed the direct government of nations rather than use indirect influence. In the clash between the forces of social revolution and reaction, many Roman Catholic priests and bishops protested social and economic inequalities and attacked the repression of opposition forces. Certain Roman Catholic theologians combined traditional Christian ideas of concern for the poor with Marxist ideology to formulate what came to be known as a **liberation theology**. Generally speaking, the Vatican under both Pope John Paul II and Pope Benedict XVI has

◄┤Read the Document
Liberation Theology (1950s)
at **MyHistoryLab.com**

attacked this Latin American theological initiative, and as a result its impact has diminished.

Document

Lourdes Arizpe Discusses the Silence of Peasant Women

Lourdes Arizpe, a Mexican anthropologist, wrote extensively on the plight of peasant women in the 1970s. In this passage she discusses how the lives and history of Mexican peasant women are shrouded in silence. Though her remarks are directed toward the situation in Mexico, they may well apply to peasant women in other cultures as well.

■ *What are the factors that Arizpe cites as leading to the historical silence of peasant women? Why does she believe it is important for such women to learn to speak with their own voices? How do the stereotypes of Mexican peasant women both contribute to and arise from the silence? Why does she believe peasant women to be the most marginalized of all women?*

History has imposed a greater silence on peasant women than on any other social group. Perhaps it is the solitude of the plains or the obligatory circumspection of their gender or merely political repression, but circumstances combine to force them to live in a secret world. Doubtless there are those who would assert that their tie to nature leads them to express themselves with actions rather than words. But the male peasant lives in the natural world without being silenced.

Silence, when not deliberate (although, how can we be sure it isn't?) could be anger or wisdom or, simply, a gesture of dignity. When there is no one worth talking to, I stay silent. If someone doesn't want to recognize my existence, I stay silent. In the spectrum of invisibility that history has imposed on women, perhaps the most invisible of the invisibles have been the peasants.

When direct expression is not permitted, the possibility of knowledge is lost and we fill that disturbing vacuum with phantoms. It is therefore not surprising that the Mexican mentality is filled with myths and stereotypes about peasant women. There is the submissive Indian woman who is a product of condescending maternalism; the wild woman both fantasized about and feared by men; the brazen hussy of melodramatic soap operas; the faint-hearted but treacherous small-town woman invented by the urban mind. Silence is also created by everyone's desire to hear what they want to hear rather than listen to what women are trying to say.

Today it seems that everyone mouths concerns about peasant women without any sincere interest.

. . . What is important today is to create opportunities for peasant women to speak.

It is not that they have never spoken, only that their words have never been recognized. Because their words are discomforting when they denounce exploitation; disturbing when they display a deep understanding of the natural world not shared by their city sisters; strange when they describe an integrating vision of the universe; and because, being women's words, they are not important to androcentric [male-centered] history. Of all the marginalized peoples, peasant women are the most marginalized.

Source: Lourdes Arizpe, "Peasant Women and Silence," trans. by Laura Beard Milroy in *Women's Writing in Latin America: An Anthology,* by Sara Castro-Klarén, Sylvia Malloy, and Beatriz Sarlo. Copyright © 1992 by Westview Press. Reprinted by permission of Westview Press.

•◦•– Read the Document
Address before the Puebla Conference (1979)
at **MyHistoryLab.com**

During the last decade and a half, Latin America has changed significantly. Several nations, including Argentina, Chile, and Brazil, like the rest of the world, have moved toward democratization even while often facing serious economic turmoil. In a departure from earlier policies there has been a strong tendency throughout the continent to allow private markets rather than the state to address economic issues. Yet these changes have remained tenuous, as several nations have had difficulty paying their foreign debts and protecting the value of their currency. In most nations, the military keeps a watchful eye on democratic developments and remains apprehensive about disorder. The end of the Cold War brought to a close one source of external political challenge, but the internal social problems of these nations have continued to raise major difficulties for their governments. And as already noted, several nations have faced new sources of disorder in the post–Cold War era from powerful drug-producing cartels that have challenged the authority of governments.

The Turn to the Left in Latin American politics is represented by Hugo Chavez, who has oil wealth to fund his ambitions, and Evo Morales, the first indigenous president of Bolivia. Chavez assumed power in 1999, Morales in 2006.

Revolutionary Challenges

There were three major attempts among the nations of Latin America to establish genuinely revolutionary governments pursuing major social and economic change. They occurred in Cuba in 1959, in Chile in 1970, and in Nicaragua in 1979. Each of the four revolutionary initiatives involved some form of Marxist political organization, and each revolutionary government pursued a close relationship with the Soviet Union. All three revolutionary movements had immense symbolic importance not only in Latin America, but also anywhere the colonial influence of Europeans and the economic dominance of the United States once prevailed. The establishment of these governments provoked active resistance and intervention by the United States. In recent years leftist governments led by Hugo Chavez in Venezuela and Evo Morales in Bolivia have embraced policies reminiscent of those regimes including strong populist criticism of the United States, but they have not produced the regional impact of the earlier revolutionary governments.

The Cuban Revolution   Cuba had remained a colony of Spain until the Spanish-American War of 1898. Thereafter, it achieved independence within a sphere of U.S. influence, which took the form of economic domination and occasional military intervention. The fluctuating governments of the island had been both ineffective and corrupt. During the 1950s Fulgencio Batista (1901–1973), a dictator supported by the U.S. government, ruled Cuba.

Historically, Cuba had been politically restive. During the 1940s university student groups led antigovernment agitation. Among the students thus politicized in those years was Fidel Castro Ruz (b. 1926), the son of a wealthy landowner. On July 26, 1953, he and others attacked a government army barracks. The revolutionary movement that he thereafter came to lead in exile took its name from that date: the Twenty-Sixth of

July Movement. In 1956 Castro and a handful of followers set sail on a yacht from Mexico and landed in Cuba. They took refuge in the Sierra Maestra Mountains, from which they organized guerrilla attacks on Batista's supporters. By late 1958 Castro's forces were positioned to topple Batista, who fled Cuba on New Year's Day in 1959. By the middle of January, Castro had arrived in Havana as the revolutionary victor.

Castro undertook the most extensive and radical political, economic, and social reconstruction in recent Latin American history. He rejected parliamentary democracy and governed Cuba as a dictator. For approximately the first decade of the revolution he ruled in a personal manner; by the early 1970s, although Castro continued to dominate, executive power was vested in a council. The revolutionary government carried out major land redistribution. In some cases, groups of relatively small landowners were established. On other parts of the island, large state farms became the model.

The Cuban Revolution spurned an industrial economic model and concentrated on improving the agricultural sector. Despite an attempt to turn toward more mixed agriculture, the production of sugar kept its leading role, and the Cuban economy remained monocultural.

Efforts to expand sugar production were disappointing because too much was attempted too quickly by people who had had too little experience in raising and processing sugarcane. The sugar industry came to depend on large Soviet subsidies and on the Soviet bloc nations for its market. In that respect, the Cuban economy did not escape the cycle of external dependence.

Throughout the Cold War, Cuba assumed an importance far greater than its size might suggest. Shortly after achieving power, Castro aligned himself with the Cuban Communist Party and thereafter with the Soviet bloc. After 1959 it served as a center for the export of communist revolution throughout Latin America and, after it sent troops to Angola in the late

Fidel Castro, waving to cheering crowds acknowledging his triumph over the Batista regime on January 1, 1959.

1970s, in Africa as well. The United States, under both Republican and Democratic administrations, proved hostile toward Castro and toward the presence of a communist state less than 100 miles from the Florida mainland. In 1961 the United States and Cuban exiles launched the unsuccessful Bay of Pigs invasion. The close Cuban relationship to the Soviet Union prepared the ground for the missile crisis of 1962, generally regarded as the most dangerous incident of the entire Cold War. A key policy of the U.S. government, pursued with differing intensities and strategies under different administrations, was to prevent a second Cuba or communist-domi-nated state in Latin America. That goal led to direct and indirect intervention in other revolutionary situations and to support for authoritarian governments in Latin America that were dedicated to resisting Marxist revolution.

With the collapse of the Soviet Union and the end of the Cold War, the future of Castro's Cuba became uncertain, but the Castro government continued firmly in charge as a remarkably enduring authoritarian regime. Cuba remains the only state closely associated with the former Soviet bloc that has not experienced substantial political or economic reform. The subsidies that flowed from the Soviet Union to support the Cuban economy are no longer available, however, creating a shortage of everyday consumer goods. In 2006 Castro experienced serious problems with his health and disappeared from public sight. His brother Raul assumed the daily oversight of the government. Some observers believe Castro's death will see a collapse of the government; others believe that the bureaucracy Castro created may actually endure. It would appear that whatever transition occurs when Castro finally passes from the scene will be slower than once anticipated.

◆●▶ Read the Document
Fidel Castro, History Will Absolve Me, 1953 at **MyHistoryLab.com**

Chile   Until the 1970s Chile was the single most enduring model of parliamentary democracy in Latin America. It had experienced political turmoil and governments of the left and the right, but its parliamentary structures had remained in place. During the 1960s, however, as economic life became more difficult and class relationships deteriorated, Chilean politics became more polarized. Unemployment and labor unrest rose alarmingly. There was profound resentment of Chile's economic domination by large U.S. corporations.

The situation came to a head in 1970 when Salvador Allende (1908–1973), the candidate of the left-wing political coalition and a Marxist, was elected president with a plurality of the votes. His coalition did not control the Chilean congress, nor did it have the support of the military. For a few months the center and right-wing political groups took a watch-and-wait attitude. Allende nationalized some businesses. The congress blocked policies related to land redistribution, wage improvement, and resistance to foreign economic influence, so Allende began to expropriate foreign property, much of which belonged to U.S. corporations, by decree.

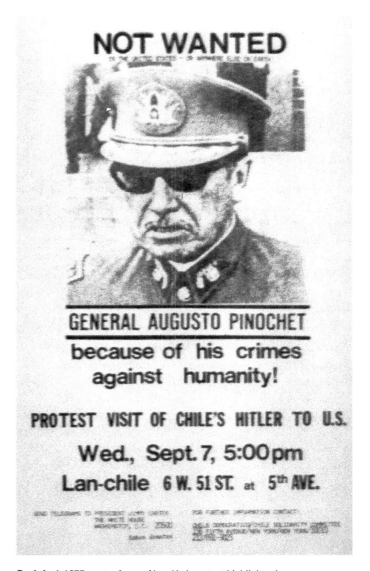

Pariah. A 1977 poster from a New York protest highlights the enormous international opposition to the policies of General Pinochet.

In the autumn of 1973 Allende found himself governing a nation in turmoil without significant domestic political support and with many foreign enemies. He proved unwilling to make significant political compromises. In the wake of strikes and disorder, the army became hostile. The Nixon administration actively supported the discontent within the Chilean army. In mid-September 1973 an army coup overthrew Allende, who was killed in the presidential palace. Chile's short-lived experiment in Marxist socialism ended.

Thereafter, for fifteen years Chile was governed by a military junta, whose most important member, General Augusto Pinochet (1915–2006), served as president. The military government pursued a close relationship with the United States and a policy of strong resistance to Marxism in the hemisphere. It also suggested a state-directed free-market economy and reversed the expropriations of the Allende years. After a brief period of economic improvement, inflation and unemployment resumed. The rule of the Chilean military was marked by harsh political repression.

In a referendum held in late 1988, Chileans rejected Pinochet's bid for another term as president. Democratization has been relatively smooth. Civilian governments have investigated the political repression of the Pinochet years and uncovered thousands of cases of torture and murder. The government nonetheless moved slowly, not wishing to provoke the army or revisit the most controversial era of the nation's history. In 1999, while in Great Britain for a medical consultation, General Pinochet was arrested when the government of Spain sought to extradite him to that country to stand trial for the disappearances of Spanish citizens under his rule. Pinochet was ultimately returned to Chile where he was judged too sick to stand trial. He died in 2006 and received no state funeral.

During the past two decades Chile has moved toward a more liberal constitutional government. During the first decade of the present century, politics in Chile were vigorously contested with peaceful changes between governments of the left and the right.

The Sandinista Revolution in Nicaragua In the summer of 1979 a Marxist guerrilla force, the **Sandinistas**, overthrew the corrupt dictatorship of the Somoza family in Nicaragua. The Somozas had governed Nicaragua more or less as their own personal preserve since the 1930s with moderate, but rarely enthusiastic, support from the United States. The Sandinistas established a collectivist government that pursued social and economic reform and reconstruction.

The government of the United States, particularly under the Reagan administration (1981–1989), was hostile to the Sandinistas. It provided both direct and indirect aid to the opposition guerrillas and criticized the Sandinistas. For the United States, the Sandinista government represented a Central American version of Castro's Cuba.

The rule of the Sandinistas came to a relatively quick end. In early 1990, after a negotiated peace settlement with the contras, they lost the presidential election to an opposition coalition that also captured control of the National Assembly. A floundering economy and U.S. aid had contributed to the electoral victory. Nicaraguans were also tired of the civil war that had shaken the country for a decade. The Sandinistas relinquished power peacefully, and a democratic government supported by the United States has remained in control despite persistent economic weaknesses.

Pursuit of Stability under the Threat of Revolution

Argentina In 1955 the Argentine army revolted against the excesses and corruption of the Perón dictatorship, and Juan Perón (1895–1974) went into exile. Two decades of economic stagnation and social unrest followed. Neither the

Read the Document
Juan Perón, excerpt from The Voice of Perón at **MyHistoryLab.com**

army nor the civilian political leaders could forge the kind of political coalition involving the working class that Perón had created. Nor could any of the post–Perón governments cope with unemployment and inflation. In 1973 Perón was recalled from exile in a desperate and futile attempt to restore the fragile stability of a generation earlier. He died about a year later.

By 1976 the army had undertaken direct rule. There was widespread repression; thousands of citizens simply disappeared, never to be heard of again. The leading army officers played something like a game of musical chairs as they moved in and out of an ever-changing ruling junta. In April 1982 General Leopoldo Galtieri (b. 1926), in an effort to score a political success, launched a disastrous invasion of the Islas Malvinas (Falkland Islands). Argentina was decisively defeated by Britain, and the military junta was thoroughly discredited.

In 1983 civilian rule was restored, and Argentina set out on the road to democratization. The major political figure responsible for this achievement was President Raul Alfonsín (b. 1927). Under his leadership, many of the former military figures responsible for the years of repression received prison sentences. Civilian courts took over the role formerly assigned to military tribunals. Alfonsín also sought to give greater political authority to the Argentine congress. In all respects Argentina has provided the most extensive example in Latin America of the restoration of democratic practices after military rule. Peaceful elections and transitions of governments have occurred for almost two decades. During the same era, however, the economic life of the nation has continued in a state of turmoil with no government being able to bring about stability of production and prices.

Brazil In 1964 the military assumed the direct government of Brazil and did not fully relinquish it until the mid-1980s. The military government stressed order and used repression to maintain it. The army itself, however, was divided about the wisdom of the military's move into the political realm. Many officers were concerned that the corruption of everyday politics would undermine the army reputation and sap its *esprit de corps*. They also feared that respect for the army would come to depend on its success in the political arena. Consequently, within the army itself, certain forces sought to restore a more nearly normal or democratic government. In 1985 civilian government returned under the military's watchful eye.

Read the Document
Brazil's Constitution of 1988 at **MyHistoryLab.com**

The military government fostered denationalized industrial development. Non-Brazilian corporations were invited to spearhead the drive toward industrialization. In this respect Brazil opted for an industrial model, but an industrialism guided and dominated from the outside. One result was the accumulation of a massive foreign debt, the servicing and repayment of which have become perhaps Brazil's most important national problem. The relative

Deforestation in the Amazon. A cut and burned section of trees on federal land in Brazil's Amazonian state of Para. The problems of deforestation, wood trafficking, habitat destruction, slave labor, land grabbing, and violence are all intertwined as colonization of the region accelerates.

success of the government's industrialization policy also made Brazil the major industrialized nation in Latin America, which has had a huge impact on the Brazilian rain forest. Subsidies and tax incentives have made the clearing of the Amazon rain forest especially profitable for large landholders involved in cattle ranching. By 1998, 12 percent of Brazil's rain forest had been cleared.

●◗●⌐Read the Document
Chico Mendes on the Rainforest
(1980s) at **MyHistoryLab.com**

The great question now is how the social changes wrought by industrialism, such as growing urbanization, will be able to receive political accommodation. In Brazil, as in Argentina, the economic and social pressures of the society have spawned conditions ripe for political agitation. It was just that possibility that in the past led so many citizens—within both the traditional and the new professional elites—to support authoritarian government.

The civilian government of President Fernando Collor de Mello that came to office in 1990, like numerous other governments in the region, advocated privatization. He and his advisers favored allowing market forces to stimulate growth. They also attempted to contain inflation. During 1992, however, President Collor was impeached by the Brazilian Senate on charges of corruption and using his office to enrich himself.

In 1995, Fernando Henrique Cardoso won the presidency and was later reelected to a second term. He pursued economic policies led by technocrats in hopes of achieving economic growth along with economic stability. By 2003, however, Brazil's economic growth had sharply slowed and required international assistance. In 2003 in the wake of the economic turmoil, Luiz Inácio Lula da Silva became the first person from a working-class background to achieve election to the Brazilian presidency. He was reelected in 2006. His administration combined socialist concern for social services along with an austere economic policy. Those policies set Brazil on a path of

sustained economic growth. Under his regime those workers at the bottom of the income scale have achieved greater improvement than their counterparts anywhere else in Latin America. Like the rest of the world, Brazil encountered difficulties in the recent economic slump, but has appeared to be regaining its footing with a significantly increasing growth rate.

Mexico Institutionally, Mexico has undergone relatively few political changes since World War II. In theory at least, the government continued to pursue the goals of the revolution. Power remained firmly in the control of the Partido Revolucionario Institucional (PRI), which until the late 1980s had maintained the appearance of stability.

Yet shifts had occurred under this apparently stable surface. The government retreated from some of the aims of the revolution and appeared conservative when compared to Marxist Cuba or Allende's Chile. In the early 1950s certain large landowners were exempted from the expropriation and redistribution of land. The Mexican government maintained open relations with Cuba and the other revolutionary regimes of Latin America but also resisted any intrusion of Marxist doctrines into Mexico. When necessary, it arrested political malcontents.

Mexico experienced an oil boom from 1977 to 1983. Oil revenues brought immense new wealth into the nation, but the world oil glut burst that bubble. The aftermath revealed the absence of any policy of stable growth. Like so many other states in the region, Mexico amassed large foreign debts and, in doing so, surrendered real economic independence.

In 1988 the PRI encountered a major challenge at the polls. Opposition candidates received much of the vote in a hotly contested election. Whether the election results were honestly reported may never be known. The PRI remained in power, but with the knowledge that it would not be able to dominate the political scene in the manner it had for over

Zapatistas. Named after the revolutionary hero Emiliano Zapata (depicted on the banner; see Chapter 25), the Zapatistas demanded rights for the impoverished Native American population of Mexico, especially in the southern state of Chiapas, where this photograph was taken in 1997.

A Closer Look

Mexican Farmers Protest the North American Free Trade Agreement

The North American Free Trade Agreement (1994), or NAFTA, was actually a series of agreements involving the United States, Canada, and Mexico. Its purpose was to remove trade barriers among these nations. In this respect it represented one of the early moves toward economic globalization, though it was restricted to North America. The free flow of agricultural commodities represented one of the chief goals of NAFTA. By 2008, agreements eliminated or phased out all agricultural tariffs between the United States and Mexico. The value of U.S. agricultural exports to Mexico rose significantly, having declined prior to the agreement. Farmers in Mexico often felt that the elimination of these tariffs worked to their disadvantage, with cheaper U.S. products replacing their products in the market. In January 2008, Mexican farmers riding their tractors protested the recent trade liberalization, which they argued opened Mexican markets to the importation of less expensive maize (corn) produced in the United States. Jobs had been lost in the Mexican agricultural sector because of the cheaper U.S. products—products made cheaper because of U.S. government subsidies to agriculture. Mexican government subsidies to agriculture had fallen in the same period. The farmers saw themselves as caught in a downward economic spiral.

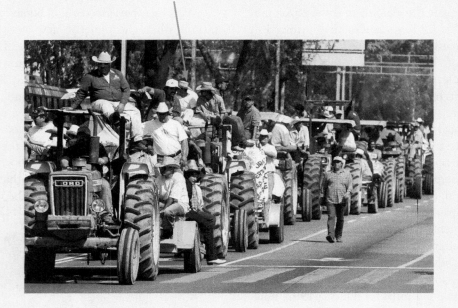

Questions

1. Even when tariffs and other trade barriers are lowered, how can other government policies place different economic sectors at a disadvantage? Why is agriculture especially vulnerable to such arrangements?

2. Why are Mexican farmers at a greater disadvantage in protesting policies that work to their detriment than unionized workers in manufacturing industries?

3. This picture illustrates the challenges faced by Mexican farmers. During the same period many U.S. manufacturers moved factories to Mexico, where wages are lower. How did this economic shift work to the disadvantage of U.S. wage earners in previously highly industrialized regions of the United States, such as Michigan and other parts of the Midwest?

4. What are the pros and cons of economic globalization?

half a century. Thereafter, the internal leadership of the party began to move toward greater decentralization in the way the party was run. The newly elected president, Carlos Salinas, moved rapidly to privatize economic enterprise. He also favored free-trade agreements. The most important of these agreements was the North American Free Trade Agreement (NAFTA), which created a vast free-trade area among Mexico, Canada, and the United States. Under Salinas's policies Mexico's economic growth rate became the best it had been in ten years. In 1991 Salinas came to a new accommodation with the Roman Catholic Church, thus moving away from the traditional anticlericalism that had characterized Mexican politics. By 1991 the PRI appeared to have regained its former political ascendancy.

The situation was largely a façade, however. Beginning in 1994 Mexico underwent a series of political shocks. Its government had to call out troops to quell armed rebellion in Chiapas. During the election of that year, the leading candidate of the PRI was assassinated, and party members were openly charged with complicity in the deed. Party corruption received increasing publicity. Early in 1995 Mexico suffered a major economic downturn, and the peso was sharply devalued. Only loans from the United States saved the economy. Ernesto Zedillo, elected president in 1994, blamed Salinas and his family for the situation, and Salinas went into exile abroad. Thereafter Mexico entered a period of political uncertainty and economic austerity; further unrest occurred in Chiapas. In the election of 2000 the PRI candidate for president lost to Vicente Fox of the National Action Party (PAN). For the first time in seventy years the PRI was out of power. The Fox presidency achieved less than had been expected. His term ended in late 2006 with a sharply contested election in which Felipe Calderon, also a PAN candidate, came into office with considerable opposition and controversy as the result of a very narrow electoral win. As for the PRI, it remains a party out of office and is deeply divided. Calderon has pursued policies of social conservatism tied to liberal economic policies. His administration has also been marked by expanding conflict between the state and the drug cartels.

Continuity and Change in Recent Latin American History

The most striking aspect of Latin America's history during the past six decades is its tragic continuity with its previous history. Revolution brought moderate social change, but at the price of authoritarian government, economic stagnation, and dependence on different foreign powers. Real independence has not been achieved. Throughout the region for much of the period, parliamentary democracy has been fragile at best; it was the first element of national life to be sacrificed to the conflicting goals of socialism, economic growth, or resistance to revolution.

The recent trends toward democratization and market economics may mark a break in that pattern, however. The region might well enjoy healthy economic growth if inflation can be contained and investment fostered. The challenge—difficult both politically and economically—will be to share the fruits of any new prosperity in a way that will prevent new political resentment and turmoil. Furthermore, as in the past, economic turmoil far from Latin America may have an adverse impact on its destiny. Each time such turmoil has occurred, the governments of Latin America have found themselves economically dependent on either the United States or European governments and bankers.

See the Map
Latin America, 2004
at **MyHistoryLab.com**

Postcolonial Africa

Modern Africa is marked by continuity between former, arbitrarily delineated colonial units and contemporary independent states.[2] Most modern African nations developed within colonial borders, just as their national capitals were formerly colonial capitals. Despite obvious reasons for such continuities, it is remarkable that colonial frontiers, which rarely mapped onto traditional tribal territories or indigenous states, should have managed to persist so consistently. If nationalism was a European export to the world, Africa provides striking examples of it as an attractive motive for supratribal and transregional state formation. The rise of African nationalism can be dated to the period between the two world wars, when previously fragmented or regional opposition to colonial

Prime Minister Kwame Nkrumah (center) waves to crowds of supporters on March 6, 1957, in celebration of Ghana's independence from Great Britain. Ghana was the first modern sub-Saharan country to gain independence.

---

[2]We are especially indebted to Roland Oliver, *The African Experience* (London, 1991), pp. 227–264, for many of the broader interpretations put forward in this section.

Document | The Pan-African Congress Demands Independence

For up to two centuries before World War II European powers had dominated or directly ruled large parts of Africa. Prior to the war, nationalist political movements emerged in a number of these colonial empires; afterward, they burgeoned throughout most of Africa. The costs of fighting the war left European powers with less wealth to govern colonies. Furthermore, colonialism was inconsistent with the principles of the victorious European Allies and the United States, now the dominant Western power.

In the following passage, representatives to the 1945 Fifth Pan-African Congress meeting in Manchester, England, make their demand for freedom.

■ *What are these African leaders' social and political goals? How did World War II help such goals to be voiced? Why did these leaders believe they were entitled to use force?*

DECLARATION TO THE COLONIAL POWERS

The delegates believe in peace. How could it be otherwise, when for centuries the African peoples have been the victims of violence and slavery? Yet if the Western world is still determined to rule mankind by force, then Africans, as a last resort, may have to appeal to force in the effort to achieve freedom, even if force destroys them and the world.

We are determined to be free. We want education. We want the right to earn a decent living; the right to express our thoughts and emotions, to adopt and create forms of beauty. We demand for Black Africa autonomy and independence so far and no further than it is possible in this One World for groups and peoples to rule themselves subject to inevitable world unity and federation.

We are not ashamed to have been an age-long patient people. We continue willingly to sacrifice and strive. But we are unwilling to starve any longer while doing the world's drudgery, in order to support by our poverty and ignorance a false aristocracy and a discarded imperialism.

We condemn the monopoly of capital and the rule of private wealth and industry for private profit alone. We welcome economic democracy as the only real democracy.

Therefore, we shall complain, appeal and arraign. We will make the world listen to the fact of our condition. We will fight in every way we can for freedom, democracy, and social betterment.

Source; Molefi Kete Asante and Abus S. Abarry, *African Intellectual Heritage: A Book of Sources* (Philadelphia: Temple University Press, 1996), pp. 520–521. © 1996 by Temple University. All Rights Reserved.

---

occupation began to be replaced by larger anti-imperialist movements. World War II proved a catalytic factor in African nationalism: Not only did Africa play an important role because of its natural and human resources, but also thousands of Africans were conscripted or volunteered to fight or labor abroad. Moreover, postwar Europe was largely disposed to give up colonial empires (see Chapter 31).

The Transition to Independence

The European "scramble for Africa" and colonization of Africa had occurred in the historical blink of an eye (see Chapters 26 and 28). Independence came almost as quickly. In 1950, only Egypt, Liberia, Ethiopia, and white-controlled South Africa were sovereign states. By 1980 no African territory (except two tiny Spanish holdings on the Moroccan coast) was ruled by a European state, although South Africa and Namibia continued to be white-dominated. African leaders, such as Kwame Nkrumah (1909–1972) in the Gold Coast (modern Ghana), Jomo Kenyatta (1893–1978) in Kenya, Julius Nyerere (1922–1999) in Tanganyika (later Tanzania), and Patrice Lumumba (1925–1961) in the Congo became symbols of African self-determination and independence. (See Document, "The Pan-African Congress Demands Independence.")

The actual transition from colonial administrative territories to independent nations was generally peaceful. However, the few cases of extended conflict with colonial powers involved ferocious battles. The most protracted and bloody wars of independence from European overlords were guerrilla struggles fought in French Algeria from 1955 to 1962; Portuguese Angola and Mozambique from 1961 to 1975; and the Belgian Congo (later Zaire, now the Democratic Republic of Congo), Northern Rhodesia (Zambia), and Southern Rhodesia (Zimbabwe) from 1960 to 1980. Violence was more likely in colonies with large European-settler populations (such as Algeria) or with lucrative exports of minerals or other resources (e.g., Congo).

In contrast to relatively peaceful colonial "handovers," ensuing internal conflicts in many newly independent states were often violent. Much of the instability in African states is a legacy of both the colonial powers' failure to prepare their colonial subjects for self-government and the haphazard nineteenth-century division of the continent into arbitrary colonial territories.

Before World War II, colonial powers largely assumed they would govern their African colonies indefinitely. Colonial administrators did not train an indigenous leadership or develop economic and governmental infrastructures that would allow successor states to function independently. No nascent state had enough educated and experienced African citizens to staff the administrative, economic, and social apparatuses of a sovereign nation, and this insured difficulties after independence. Corruption among new officials proved rife; military coups often provided the only stable governance available; attempts to implement planned economies on a socialist model often brought economic catastrophe; and ethnic and regional revolts created civil wars.

Most dangerous and costly to the new states were the separatist struggles, civil wars, and border wars between new states that followed the independence struggles. The Nigerian civil war of 1967–1970 was an especially bloody example (see below). Other new nations caught for periods in open warfare have been Morocco and the western Sahara; Libya and Chad; South African-held Namibia; Ethiopia and Eritrea; Kenya, Uganda, and Tanzania; Rwanda and Burundi; Somalia; Ethiopia and Somalia; and the Sudan. Strikingly, whatever the original goals of the parties involved, these conflicts universally served to ratify rather than repudiate postcolonial state divisions.

Every African state has had a different experience and history since World War II. Generally, however, the new independent African states have hardly been models. Thus far, with the notable exception of Zanzibar and Tanganyika uniting in the new state of Tanzania, any ideas of a union of nations have failed. Nevertheless, it is important to note that African polities did not revert to tiny tribal or regional political units.

As instances of African postcolonial national experience, the histories of four nations—Nigeria, South Africa, Congo, and Rwanda—provide closer looks at recent subSaharan African history.

◉ See the Map
Africa, 2004
at **MyHistoryLab.com**

Nigeria The modern Republic of Nigeria is the most populous state in Africa, with about 150 million inhabitants in 2009. Nigeria achieved independence from Britain in 1960 and ratified a constitution in 1964 that federated the three major provincial regions—the Eastern, Western, and Northern—under a national government based in Lagos, the for-

mer British administrative capital. Nigeria's largest ethnic and linguistic groups are from the same three regions: the Igbo (Eastern), Yoruba (Western), and Hausa and Fulani (Northern). Although their regional languages have been recognized since 1980 as acceptable for federal business, the official Nigerian language is English.

Nowhere was the aftermath of independence bloodier than in Nigeria, which was, at its inception, potentially the most powerful and successful state in independent Africa. The three-province federation soon proved unworkable, and a 1966 *coup d'état* brought a military government to power. Its leader himself was soon assassinated, and Lieutenant Colonel Yakubu Gawon (b. 1934) took over amid ethnic unrest that ended in massacres in late 1966. Gawon's government subdivided the three provinces into states, three each in the Western and Eastern Provinces and six in the Northern. In May 1967, the Eastern Province's assembly empowered its leader, Lieutenant Colonel Chukwuemeka Odumegwu Ojukwu (b. 1933), to form a new, independent state of Biafra out of the three Eastern-Province states. Ojukwu was an Igbo nationalist but aspired to control territory beyond those of the Igbos—in particular, that containing the important offshore oil reserves of the Eastern Province. Biafra was able to gain recognition from several African states; secure arms and support from France, South Africa, and Portugal; and develop successful worldwide propaganda depicting itself as a small, brave, largely Christian country fighting for survival against a hostile, oppressive, mostly Muslim central government.

The ensuing two and a half years saw a bloody civil war pit elements of independent Africa's best national army against each other. The larger federal forces slowly wore down the Biafrans. The estimated death toll soared above a million—the overwhelming majority Igbo civilians, mostly refugees dying of starvation—before the Biafrans surrendered in January 1970. In the end, Nigerians had purchased at great cost an increased sense of unity, along with a major role for the military in Nigerian politics. The struggle also contributed to the development of African diplomacy and international aid efforts in Africa.[3]

Gawon was overthrown by another military commander in 1975. Thereafter, Nigeria was plagued by political instability at the top, its leadership passing usually from one military ruler to another, except for the four-year Second Republic under President Shehu Usman Aliyu Shagari (b. 1925), a Fulani Muslim from the north, who was deposed by a military coup in 1983. A decade later, the military regime nullified the 1993 election of Yoruba leader Moshood Abiola as president. This debacle ended in a coup by General Sani Abacha, who instituted four years of repressive military rule, during which novelist and environmental activist Kenule "Ken" Saro-Wiwa (1941–1995) was executed.

---

[3]Oliver, *African Experience*, pp. 235–236.

Nobel laureate author Wole Soyinka (b. 1934) led public protests against the military government in 1994 and later went into exile, where in 1996 he helped found a seventeen-member National Liberation Council. Abacha died in June 1998 and was replaced by General Abubakar, who reversed some of Abacha's policies. Soyinka was able to return in October 1998 to a hero's welcome, and some political prisoners were released. Finally, military rule was replaced in 1999 by civilian government under an elected president, Olusegun Obasanjo, and a new constitution was ratified and implemented. Umaru Musa Yar'Adua succeeded Obasanjo as president in 2007 after an election widely viewed as tainted.

Today, Nigeria's future is still uncertain. Religious animosities and ethnic divisions continue. Serious pollution from oil spills in the Niger Delta, as well as major environmental degradation in most Nigerian cities are mounting unsolved problems. Despite its wealth, Nigeria and its development still suffer from corruption, lack of infrastructure, and mismanagement.

South Africa The radical separation of white from non-whites in all arenas of life endured as official government policy in South Africa for nearly fifty years. From the time the Afrikaner-led National Party (NP) assumed power in 1948, the Union of South Africa was governed under the avowedly racist policy of **apartheid** ("apartness"). Until the dismantling of this policy after 1991, the white minority (in 1991, 5.4 million persons) ran the country, maintaining economic and political control and privilege. Its 31 million blacks, 3.7 million "coloreds" (persons of mixed ancestry), and 1 million Indians were kept strictly segregated—treated, at best, as second-class citizens or, in the case of blacks, as noncitizens or even nonhumans. This system was maintained by repression, most visibly military and police action to quell dissent and enforce apartheid laws.

Watch the Video
Creating Apartheid in South Africa at MyHistoryLab.com

The history of apartheid and its passing was bloody and twisted, but finally triumphant. Partly because of worldwide opposition to apartheid, South Africa became increasingly isolated from the 1960s onward. Meanwhile, the rest of Africa—including other white-run states like Rhodesia (Zimbabwe)—progressed to majority, African rule. In 1961 South Africa withdrew from the British Commonwealth of Nations. In the 1960s and 1970s the government created three tiny "independent homelands" for blacks inside the country, allowing the white minority to treat blacks as immigrant "foreigners" in the parts of South Africa where most had to work. The international community refused to recognize these homelands, or "Bantustans." South Africa's isolation was further dramatized when two anti-apartheid black leaders, the Zulu chief Albert Luthuli (1898–1967) in 1960 and the Anglican bishop Desmond Tutu (b. 1931) in 1984, were awarded the Nobel Prize for their work against apartheid.

Apartheid. A police officer checks a black African's identification card, under the *apartheid* system's hated pass laws.

By 1978, as Pieter Botha (1916–2006) came to power, apartheid was failing: The homelands were economic and political catastrophes; the country was in an inflationary recession; skilled whites were emigrating; and with other colonial regimes yielding to majority, African rule, South Africa was becoming a pariah state. Threats from guerrilla forces prompted the government to send its troops on preemptive raids into neighboring countries. Botha's concessions on issues such as interracial marriage and public transportation segregation were not enough to calm the situation. Internal opposition and international pressure grew.

Beginning in 1986, many nations responded to Tutu's call and imposed economic sanctions against the government. Anti-apartheid movements in the United States and elsewhere convinced companies and individuals to liquidate investments in South Africa. Strikes by black workers in 1987 led the government to declare a state of emergency, but the resulting violence created widespread support among Western nations for a complete trade embargo. In June 1988 more than 2 million black workers went on strike to protest new repressive labor laws and a ban on political activity by trade unions and anti-apartheid groups. Finally, Botha resigned in August 1989.

In February 1990 the new president, F. W. de Klerk (b. 1936), began a series of landmark government actions: the ban on the African National Congress (ANC), the main anti-apartheid organization, was lifted; ANC leader Nelson Mandela was released after twenty-seven years' imprisonment; and the Separate Amenities Act, the legal basis for public

Nelson Mandela campaigning for the presidency of post-apartheid South Africa.

segregation, was repealed. In early 1991 de Klerk announced plans to repeal apartheid; in June the race registration law was repealed. In March 1992, in a whites-only referendum with over 85 percent voter turnout, 67.8 percent voted for constitutional equality for all races. De Klerk and Mandela, despite terrorist attempts from both black and white extremists, were able to bring their own and eighteen other parties to endorse a new interim constitution. For their leadership, Mandela and de Klerk shared the Nobel Peace Prize for 1993.

Read the Document

Nelson Mandela, from Freedom, Justice and Dignity for All South Africa at **MyHistoryLab.com**

Multiracial elections were held in April 1994, the ANC winning 63 percent of the vote, the NP 20 percent, and other parties the remainder. Mandela was elected president of what Tutu termed the Rainbow Nation, in honor of South Africa's racial and political diversity. The constitution of December 1996 provided a new structure for national governance. Meanwhile, the **Truth and Reconciliation Commission** (TRC), established in 1995, offered an unprecedented way to come to terms with the country's past: Rather than attempting to bring to legal justice the many perpetrators of human rights abuses during the apartheid era, the TRC offered amnesty in exchange for confessional testimony and provided victims a platform for detailing their losses. The TRC's premises were controversial—some victims of apartheid atrocities, for example, objected to their persecutors escaping punishment—but it is unlikely that any other mechanism could have generated a more comprehensive account of apartheid's abuses.

View the Image

Voters Waiting to Vote in South Africa's First Open Election, 1994 at **MyHistoryLab.com**

The governments of Thabo Mbeki (b. 1942), who succeeded Mandela in 1999, then Kgalema Motlanthe (b. 1949), who completed Mbeki's unfinished term in 2008–2009, and Jacob Zuma (b. 1942), the current president, have striven to deal with the major challenges that the country's 49 million citizens face. Despite substantial mineral resources and the highest GNP in Africa, South Africa's problems are immense:

one of the world's highest rates of HIV/AIDS infection (18.1 percent), from which 5,700,000 persons suffer (2007 estimate); high unemployment, poverty, and crime rates; extreme income inequalities; insufficient educational and economic infrastructure; woefully inadequate public services in much of the country; potentially severe potable-water supply problems; and difficulties fulfilling promises of a new era of socioeconomic progress, even with a functioning democratic government. Only time will tell how well the new democracy can handle these serious issues.

Congo European rule in Africa was nowhere benign, but it may have reached its nadir in the Congo Free State. In this personal fiefdom of Belgium's King Leopold II from 1885 to 1908, Africans were routinely mutilated or killed for offenses such as failing to meet local officials' quotas for rubber collection. As a Belgian colony thereafter, Congo fared only slightly better, and since independence in 1960 Congo has had a history infamous for ongoing atrocities.

The Republic of Congo was declared on June 30, 1960 with Patrice Lumumba (1925–1961) as prime minister and Joseph Kasavubu (1910–1969) as president. Lumumba and Kasavubu belonged to different parties, and almost immediately, the government began to factionalize. Two provinces, Katanga and South Kasai, separately attempted to secede. Kasavubu dismissed Lumumba from office. Lumumba resisted, and in the ensuing crisis the Congolese Army's chief of staff, Joseph-Désiré Mobutu (1930–1997), overthrew them both. Lumumba was assassinated in Katanga province in January 1961. Various presidents served brief terms until 1965, when Mobutu again seized power, this time with the backing of the U.S. Central Intelligence Agency. In the Cold War calculus, he was seen as a defense against African socialism, and this time he held power for over 30 years.

From 1967 to 1990, Mobutu outlawed all political parties except his own, the Popular Movement of the Revolution. He launched the *Authenticité* campaign to celebrate African culture by, among other measures, discouraging Western clothing, Africanizing place names (Congo became Zaire; Leopoldville, Kinshasa; and so on) and personal names (he became Mobutu Sese Seko Kuku Ngbendu Wa Za Banga, "The all-powerful warrior who, because of endurance and will to win, goes from conquest to conquest, leaving fire in his wake and arising from his enemies' blood and ashes like the Sun conquering the night"). As his new name suggests, he also developed a cult of personality. Mobutu's regime became increasingly corrupt and essentially a kleptocracy—he himself was rumored to be a multibillionaire.

Mobutu played his Cold War cards well, fostering close relationships with Western powers (particularly the United States) while formally proclaiming nonalignment. The end of the Cold War and Mobutu's failing health created an opening that opposition leaders quickly seized. Refugees from Rwanda's genocide further destabilized the country, and in 1996 insurgents supported by Rwanda, Uganda, Zambia, and Angola captured much of eastern Zaire in what is called the First Congo War. When Mobutu fled the country, most of these outsiders backed Laurent Kabila (1939–2001), and he was sworn in as president in the capital, Kinshasha, in May 1997. The country was renamed the Democratic Republic of the Congo (DRC).

Since 1998, what is called the Second Congo War, or even the African World War, has roiled the DRC. International alliances have been made and broken, ceasefires negotiated and violated. With some 5.4 million people killed, this has been the deadliest war anywhere since World War II. In eastern Congo, there continues not only widespread violence but a systematic war of rape and violence against women, called the worst in the world. In 2001, Kabila was assassinated; his son, Joseph Kabila, took office, and in 2006, in hotly contested, disputed elections, he was elected to the presidency.

The DRC is immense and possesses vast natural resources, especially valuable minerals. Nonetheless its future is wholly uncertain; fighting continues in the east especially, much infrastructure has been destroyed, and most citizens understandably mistrust their government.

Rwanda Rwanda is roughly one one-hundredth the size of the Democratic Republic of the Congo, but from 1994 the two countries' histories have been intertwined. Under Belgian administration, ethnicity in Ruanda-Urundi (today, Rwanda and Burundi) was determined by wealth: Since the minority Tutsi tribe already constituted the elite, anyone the Belgians deemed wealthy became a "Tutsi" and most others were designated as belonging to the largest preexisting ethnic group, the "Hutu." (There is also a significant minority population of Twa forest people, or "pygmies.") At independence in 1961, Rwanda and Burundi separated, and—despite the tradition of Tutsi monarchic rule—Rwanda became a republic with Hutu leadership.

Over the following decades, there were many border clashes between Rwanda, Burundi, and Uganda. Although this violence was usually labeled as Tutsi versus Hutu, there is no way to determine the extent to which ethnic animosities actually drove these conflicts, or how much ethnicity was a convenient cover for other agendas. In any case, on April 6, 1994, when a helicopter carrying the (Hutu) presidents of Rwanda and Burundi was shot down over Rwanda's capital, killing both, Tutsis were blamed. Interethnic civil war ensued. Over the following months, approximately 800,000 Tutsis and moderate Hutus were killed in a massive genocide. Then the Uganda-based, Tutsi-led Rwandan Patriotic Front (RPF) under Paul Kagame (b. 1957), took control of Rwanda with U.S. and U.K. support, and millions of Hutu refugees fled to Zaire. RPF and Ugandan forces pursued them into Zaire, an action that contributed to Mobutu's overthrow in 1997.

The Rwandan genocide sparked soul-searching, but little effective action, in the West. United Nations peacekeepers were

Rwandan refugees carry their belongings as they stream out of the Mugunga refugee camp in Zaire (Congo) back toward Rwanda, in the aftermath of the 1994 genocide.

●●▶ Read the Document
Alain Destexhe, excerpt from Rwanda and Genocide in the Twentieth Century at **MyHistoryLab.com**

in Rwanda when the genocide began, but the terms of their deployment prevented them from intervening. United States President Bill Clinton was harshly criticized for failing to take action; indeed, U.S. officials even avoided referring to events in Rwanda as "genocide" until late May 1994.

Following a period of transitional government, a new constitution was approved, and Paul Kagame (b. 1957) was elected president in 2003. Although Kagame has been criticized for stifling dissent and possible profiteering from world demand for "conflict mineral" resources found in Rwanda and Eastern Congo, his administration has been marked by some democratic as well as economic progress. Most observers believe that Rwanda has undergone an unexpected recovery, with average income tripling from 1999 to 2009 under a government that is more effective and possibly more honest than others in the region. In 2008 Rawanda became the first country with a majority of women elected to its legislature.

The African Future

Most African states have not achieved peace and prosperity. Some bloody conflicts or simply unbridled violence—most notably in eastern Congo and the Darfur region of Sudan—are still ongoing, their human consequences catastrophic and ultimate resolution unclear. However, the last half-century has seen radical change and development. Overall, prospects for future governmental stability have never been stronger.

Economic problems remain extremely threatening, but progress is being made after decades of failures. The heavy burdens of the past—be they regional rivalries, religious and linguistic divisions, major economic and social-policy mistakes in early independence, the corruption and violence that feed the outside world's demand for diamonds or critical metals, or the crippling experience of apartheid—still present formidable hurdles. Probably even more serious are the newer problems of public health, environmental degradation, social instability, and development with which almost all African nations have to contend as they strive to build better societies.

Health and Environment A variety of health and environmental challenges face Africa, the most notorious of which is **HIV/AIDS**. In late 2008, an estimated 22.4 million people in sub-Saharan Africa were living with HIV. There are significant regional variations in HIV infection rates: In general, rates are highest (over 20 percent of the adult population) in southern African nations, followed by East and central Africa,

●◆●▭Read the Document

Nelson Mandela, Closing Address at the 13th International AIDS Conference, July 2000 at **MyHistoryLab.com**

while rates are generally relatively lower (often under 5 percent) in West African nations (see Map 33–3). Governments have also varied tremendously in their responses to HIV/AIDS. Uganda, for example, embarked on an aggressive public education campaign in the 1990s, which seems to have helped reduce infection rates there. In contrast, in early 2000, South African President Mbeki publicly questioned whether HIV causes AIDS and made statements that contributed to an atmosphere of denial and shame surrounding HIV/AIDS in South Africa.

Other diseases, though less likely to capture headlines in the West, sicken or kill millions of Africans every year. The World Health Organization declared the prevalence of tuberculosis an emergency in Africa in 2005, and the situation has not improved since. Malaria and other tropical diseases reduce life expectancy, increase school and job absenteeism, and reduce economic productivity almost everywhere in Africa. Only very recently have significant

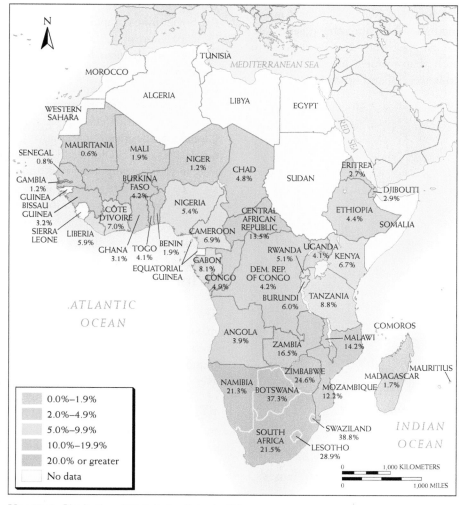

Map 33–3. Distribution of HIV Infection Rates in Africa.

See the Map
HIV Prevalence in Africa
at **MyHistoryLab.com**
global health initiatives, such as the Global Network for Neglected Tropical Diseases (established in 2006), begun to target Africa's interrelated health challenges.

African environmental challenges run the gamut from wildlife poaching to soil erosion to improper disposal of hazardous waste. Africans have been in the forefront of the environmental justice movement, with activists including Ken Saro-Wiwa (see above) and Nobel laureate Wangari Maathai, leader of Kenya's Green Belt Movement, building grass-roots environmental campaigns.

Social Change African society has changed rapidly during the postcolonial period, though many traditions endure. Rapid urbanization as a trend began in colonial times and continues to the present. The explosive growth of urban centers at the expense of rural areas has disrupted the continent's traditionally agrarian-based societies, age-old family and tribal allegiances, religious values, and sociopolitical systems. Migrants flock to cities in search of wage labor, but African urban economies have never grown as quickly as their populations; many cities harbor large slums where masses of people live in substandard housing, without plumbing and other essential infrastructure. In general, men have migrated from rural to urban areas more frequently than women, producing significant gender imbalances in both rural and urban areas.

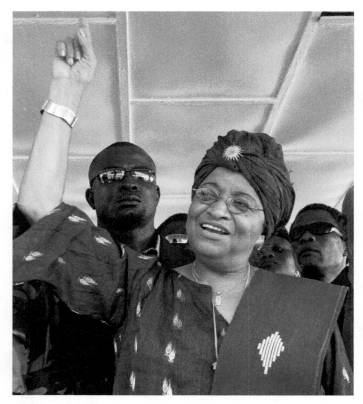

Ellen Sirleaf-Johnson was elected president of Liberia in 2005. She is the first woman elected to lead an African nation.

In a significant discontinuity with the colonial era, African women have been elected to many national offices. Women were active in anticolonial and anti-apartheid movements and took leadership roles in some postindependence rebellions (notably in Uganda), but it is only since the mid-1990s that women have been elected in growing numbers to national parliaments and other high offices. Ellen Sirleaf-Johnson, the first woman elected to lead an African nation, won the presidency of Liberia in 2005.

Population growth has been rapid throughout Africa, creating economic, social, and political challenges. Deaths from HIV/AIDS have created new population trends, such as the large numbers of "AIDS orphans"—children whose parents have been killed or incapacitated by disease.

Religion is an important force in the lives of most individual Africans and in the structures of African societies. Christianity and Islam both continue to gain converts. Evangelical Christianity, in particular, is growing rapidly.

Trade and Development

During the Cold War, one of the areas in which the West and the Soviet bloc competed was in dispensing development aid in Africa. Starting in the 1990s, trade has been emphasized as the best mechanism for improving African economies and standards of living. Under President Bill Clinton, for example, the United States encouraged private-sector trade and investment through the Partnership for Economic Growth and Opportunity in Africa. President Bush supported the African Global Competitiveness Initiative (AGCI) to build sub-Saharan Africa's capacity for trade and competitiveness. A factor of rapidly growing importance is trade with, and direct investment by, China. African economies still need to grow tremendously to meet their populations' needs.

The Islamic Heartlands, from North Africa to Indonesia

The lands today marked by Islamic culture and Muslim-majority populations or major Muslim minorities stretch from West Africa to the Philippines. More specifically, they are found in the Arab world from Morocco to Iraq and the Gulf; in West and East Africa; in the Balkans, the Turkish-speaking world of Turkey and the former Soviet Central Asian republics; in Persian-speaking Iran and Central Asia, in western China, and in South and Southeast Asia. The Muslims of the entire Arab world number only about 275 million. India, Bangladesh, Pakistan, and Indonesia have the four largest Muslim populations in the world, with about 156, 130, 171, and 207 million Muslims, respectively. The varied nations of this huge segment of the globe illustrate the many different ways in which Islamic allegiances manifest themselves and affect political life.

Document | A Modernist Muslim Poet's Eulogy for His Mother

The following is a poem drawn from the autobiography of Aziz Nesin, *That's How It Was but Not How It's Going to Be* (1966). Nesin (1915–1995) was a prolific Turkish writer, political commentator, and social critic who began writing in 1946 with a satirical weekly paper. The poem is a eulogy for his long-dead mother, a reflection on the deprivations she endured, and a determined promise to ensure women a better life in the future. It reflects the widespread feeling among secular modernists that one hallmark of modernity is the emancipation of women. The final two lines repeat the original Turkish title of Nesin's book.

■ *What is the impact of addressing the poem to his own mother rather than to some other woman? What specific things is Nesin criticizing?*

VOW TO MY MOTHER'S MEMORY

All mothers, the most beautiful of mothers,
You are the most beautiful of the beautiful,
At thirteen you married;
At fifteen you gave me birth.
You were twenty-six,
You died before you lived.
I owe you this heart overflowing with love.
I don't even have your picture;
It was a sin to have a photograph taken.
You saw neither movie, nor play.
Electricity, gas, water, stove,
Nor even a bedstead was found in your home.

You could never bathe in the sea,
You couldn't read nor write.
Your lovely eyes
Looked at the world from behind a black veil.
When you were twenty-six
You died, before you lived.
Henceforward, mothers will not die before they live.
That's how it was,
But not how it's going to be!

Source: Excerpts from *Istanbul Boy: The autobiography of Aziz Nesin, Part 1* by Aziz Nesin. Copyright © 1977 Reprinted by permission of the Center for Middle Eastern Studies, the University of Texas at Austin.

Turkey

Turkey stems from a modernist republican experiment that has attempted to create a democratic government and civil society despite struggles over the roles of the military, ethnicity, culture, and religion in both. The Turkish military has repeatedly deposed elected governments and supervised selection of new leadership. Economically, Turkey has had its difficulties, but along with Israel it is still the most economically advanced Middle Eastern country. In many ways, it is of all Muslim nations the most progressive in its range of tolerated interpretations of Islam, even though its current regime shows growing intolerance. With the creation of new Turkic-language states in post-Soviet Central Asia, Turkey is seeking to strengthen its ties with this underdeveloped part of the world and play a major role in its emergence. (See Document, "A Modernist Muslim Poet's Eulogy for His Mother.")

Geographically and culturally, Turkey belongs to both Europe and Asia. Istanbul, its main commercial and cultural center, is in continental Europe; its capital, Ankara, is in Asia Minor. In recent years, Turkey, long a member of NATO, has sought admission into the European Union, thus far without success. Turkey participates in European cultural and popular activities such as European soccer and the Eurovision song contest. Turkish membership in the EU is contested because many Europeans are skeptical of admitting a largely Muslim nation that also has a questionable human rights record as regards imprisonment of journalists and repression of freedom of speech, both of which have recently gotten worse. The longtime persecution of Turkey's 13 million Kurds (18 percent of the population) and ongoing Turkish denial of any Armenian genocide nearly a century ago remain problems for admission to the EU. Turkey's serious indebtedness to the International Money Fund has also worked against EU membership. In addition, various Islamist parties have emerged in Turkey and complicated the political landscape. It is unclear whether Turkey will align itself more with Europe, the Middle East, or Central Asia in the years ahead, even though it is making a strong effort to join Europe while reaching out to Central Asia.

✔●─ Study and Review
Soviet and Turkish Plans for Industrialization
at **MyHistoryLab.com**

Iran and Its Islamic Revolution

Iran was ruled as a monarchy from 1925 to 1941 by a former army commander, Reza Khan. He came to power through a British-supported military takeover and governed as Reza Shah with the ancient Persian name Pahlavi. Much like his contemporary, Atatürk (1881–1938), he attempted to introduce modernist economic, educational, and governmental reforms. He also tried to create a rich landlord and industrial class with few benefits for the pastoral, peasant, and urban classes. Reza Shah built a highly centralized autocracy, not a parliamentary state. His reforms differed from Atatürk's in that he did not have to deal with a battle-tested, well-armed military or an experienced and eager middle class, both of whom Atatürk had to placate to realize his social and industrialization projects.

By the time Russian and British forces deposed Reza Shah in 1941 and installed his son, Muhammad Reza, as shah, the activism of radical trade unionists and socialist-leaning intelligentsia had been crushed, and the power of Shi'ite religious leaders, or *ulama*, had been muted through the consolidation of a strong, centralized Pahlavi state. The son, much more than his father, sought to legitimize Pahlavi rule through linkage with pre-Islamic imperial Persia. He continued his father's secular and industrial state building from after World War II until 1978, with one interruption from 1951 to 1953. Those three years saw Muhammad Mosaddeq (1881–1967), after decades of parliamentary experience, become prime minister by successfully drawing together a broad coalition of workers, *bazari* merchants, religious leaders, intelligentsia, and government workers. They formed a political force, The National Front, which won the minds and hearts of Iranians with the nationalization of the British-owned Anglo-Iranian Oil Company in Abadan in 1951, which sent Iranians dancing into the streets of Tehran for days. Mossadeq's years as Iran's most popular prime minister came to an end, however, in August 1953 through a covert U.S. Central Intelligence Agency and British Military Intelligence *coup d'etat* called Operation Ajax. Though denied for decades, in the 1990s the United States quietly admitted to its part in the coup, thereby confirming Iranians' past suspicions and earning both the U.S. and Britain deep Iranian distrust.

Having clamped down on all opponents after the 1953 coup, in the 1960s Muhammad Reza Shah still faced two opposition groups, one led by educated secularists and the other by the *ulama*. Land reform and other Pahlavi "white revolutions" were opposed by both groups for different reasons, and the shah's heavy-handed, often brutal repression of any protest, including nonviolent marches, critical publications, and political meetings, forced the two groups to reassess the close association of the shah with the United States and the need for militant confrontation. While the *ulama* preferred continuing nonviolent opposition through the 1970s,

the middle- and upper-class professionals, including students, industrial workers, and leftists, opted for tactical, violent clashes with the regime and its U.S. ally. For all the modernizing military and economic buildup that the United States and the shah initiated, the gap between the extremely wealthy few and the extremely poor masses never narrowed. That fully half of Iran's 60-odd million inhabitants are Turkish, Kurdish, Arab, and other minorities did little to help Reza consolidate and strengthen his centralized monarchy.

Finally, in 1978 religious leaders and secularist revolutionaries joined forces to end the shah's long regime through a revolution engaging a wide spectrum of emotion, ideology, and secular as well as religious symbolism. What had begun as an Iranian Revolution ended up as an Islamic Revolution, so that in 1979 the new post-shah republic that emerged was not a secular but an Islamic one crafted under the guidance of the Shi'ite religious leader, Ayatollah Ruhollah Khomeini (1902–1989).

View the Image
Ayatollah Khomeini
at **MyHistoryLab.com**

Subsequent years brought protracted war with Iraq (1980–1988) and the institution of repressive, violent measures against enemies of the new regime not unlike those under the shah. Still, the new state—with religious leaders

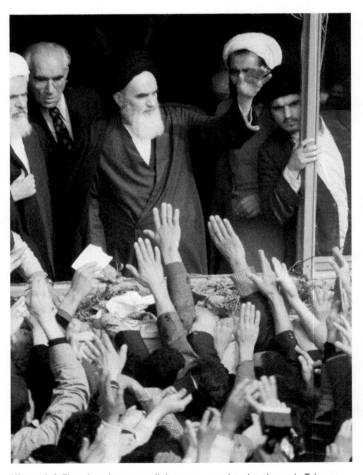

Khomeini. The triumphant ayatollah waves to a cheering throng in Tehran, Iran, in February 1979.

Iranian Nobel Prize Winner Shirin Ebadi at the Street Children's Home That She Founded in Tehran. Ebadi, on the right, was awarded the prestigious prize for her work in defending human rights. She was the first Muslim woman to be awarded a Nobel.

✓●—Study and Review
The Political Vision of Atatürk
and Khomeini
at **MyHistoryLab.com**

exercising an influence over politics not seen since sixteenth-century Safavid times—has survived. However, Khomeini and his successors, Hashemi Rafsanjani (b. 1934) and Ali Khameini (b. 1939), were not untainted by politics. They struggled to find a new formula for combining Muslim norms with contemporary *Realpolitik*, and this will continue to be a major challenge for their successors.

The immediate successor to Rafsanjani, Mohammad Khatami, was elected to the presidency in 1997, to the surprise of many, by a resounding majority in the first real national election since the 1979 revolution. Khatami, a moderate cleric as well as former minister of culture of liberal reputation, tried to steer a more moderate course. Many considered his election a key step in Iran's movement after its watershed revolution toward more stable government and more internationally engaged policies, particularly in the Middle Eastern and Indian Ocean sphere. The wide-ranging reforms that people expected from Khatami, however, failed to materialize. There have since been sporadic and unsuccessful student protests against the clerical leadership. In 2003, Shirin Ebadi, an Iranian lawyer, won the Nobel Peace Prize for her decades of dedicated work to improve the legal protections and status of women and children in Iran. Iran's Islamic leaders paid no attention to that singular honor for the first Muslim woman ever to receive such an international award. In 2005, Mahmud Ahmadinejad (b. 1956), a former *Basij,* or Youth Corps, officer, Iran–Iraq War veteran, and former mayor of Tehran, surprisingly defeated the veteran liberal religious politician and two-term Islamic Republic president, Ali Akbar Hashemi

Rafsanjani (b. 1956), introducing a new combination of bombast and simple talk to national and international politics. Consequently, the United States and its allies (particularly Israel) have wanted a regime change because of Iran's policies on nuclear energy and its alleged military involvement in the U.S. occupation of Iraq. Even with a new, less intervention-minded U.S. president in power since 2009, the future of Iran's international relations remains uncertain.

Afghanistan and the Former Soviet Republics

North of Iran, 40 million Central Asian Muslims predominate in the broad region that stretches across the south-central reaches of the former Soviet Union between the Crimea and China, in addition to 25 million or far more (data is conflicting) Chinese Muslims, concentrated in adjacent southwestern China. They have had to sustain their religious and intellectual traditions in the face of Russian and Chinese cultural, linguistic, and political imperialism. In the 1980s both Soviet and Chinese Muslims appeared to be asserting themselves. The 1979 Soviet occupation of Afghanistan, whose people had close ties to Soviet Muslims, reflected the potential importance of this movement. The phased withdrawal of Soviet forces from Afghanistan in 1988 looked surprisingly like the U.S. withdrawal from South Vietnam in 1974. It was soon followed by a much more momentous about-face with the dissolution of the Soviet Union in 1990 into many separate states, most of which remain loosely connected through the Commonwealth of Independent States (CIS). The CIS Central Asian republics include Kazakhstan, Kyrgyzstan, Tajikistan, Turkmenistan, and Uzbekistan, as well as the Caucasian republics of Armenia, Azerbaijan, Georgia, and Moldova. Suddenly the Islamic republics of the former Soviet Union found themselves effectively independent states, with little infrastructure to manage such a transition. The great challenge now is whether they can attain political viability without being destroyed by economic collapse or ethnic or regional conflict.

The Soviet invasion of Afghanistan produced a major unexpected result. Thousands of Muslims, mostly fundamentalist in outlook, came to Afghanistan to oust the Soviets and their Afghan puppets. Conservative Arab states and the United States supported this effort, which succeeded by the late 1980s. Conservative Arab states saw the Afghan War as an opportunity to resist expansion of Soviet influence in their territories and to divert the energies of their own religious extremists. The United States saw the Afghan War as another round in the Cold War. The militant Muslim fundamentalists saw it as a religious struggle against an impious non-Muslim power.

After the Soviets withdrew, a power vacuum existed for almost a decade. By 1998, however, extreme rigorist Muslims known as the *Taliban* seized control. They imposed their own literalist version of Islamic law, involving strict regimentation of women and public executions or mutilations for criminal offenses. The Taliban also allowed Muslim terrorist groups such as *al-Qa'ida* ("the base") to establish training camps in Afghanistan. The terrorists who attacked United States targets on September 11, 2001, came from these camps. As will be seen later in this chapter, one American response to those attacks was a military campaign against the Afghani Taliban government.

India

India, a largely Hindu state, and Pakistan, a largely Muslim state, gained independence in 1947 after the British agreed to partitioning the subcontinent between them. Much of their subsequent history has been one of mutual antagonism. This was born of Hindu-Muslim communal violence and the disputes over Kashmir and other areas accompanying Partition. The tragedy of the massive displacement of Muslims from the new India and of Hindus and Sikhs from the new Pakistan (about 8 million people in each case) was and remains immense for millions of families and individuals. The two states still have unresolved major differences, including conflicting claims to Kashmir. Their rivalry was exacerbated by a round of nuclear saber rattling begun by five Indian underground nuclear tests in May 1998 followed by similar Pakistani tests two weeks later. There have since been a number of crises between the two nations accompanied by fears of a nuclear exchange.

Bereft of its spiritual and material father, Mohandas Gandhi (1869–1948), after his assassination in 1948 by a Hindu fanatic, India has been led for most of its existence by leaders of Gandhi's Congress Party. First came Gandhi's follower and nationalist colleague, Jawaharlal Nehru (1889–1964), who developed India's theory of political neutrality vis-à-vis world alignments, notably that of the Cold War superpowers. Nehru's long leadership (1947–1964) carried India through the critical organizational period of early independence and Pakistani disputes, as well as a brief Himalayan border war with China in 1962. His secularist, reconciliatory policies reduced the communal hatreds, religious zealotry, and regional tensions of the postpartition era, and he also made progress in the economic development of the overpopulated, underdeveloped new nation. His government oversaw the nuts-and-bolts internal work of damping such potentially divisive movements as Sikh religious separatism and forging a national federation from states divided by religious, cultural, and political history as well as by language.

Read the Document

Jawaharlal Nehru, "Why India is Non-Aligned" (India), 1956 at **MyHistoryLab.com**

Hindu Militants. Hindu militants attack a Muslim mosque in Ayodhya, India, December 6, 1992. The razing of this mosque at the hands of a mob led by Hindu communalist extremists touched off a wave of Hindu-Muslim violence in India. The Hindus claimed the mosque, built some 500 years ago, occupied the site of what had originally been a Hindu temple and sought to have a new temple built once the mosque was cleared away.

In this era Hindi and English were declared national languages, and fourteen major regional languages, each associated with a state, were recognized for regional official use. Nehru's resolute opposition to caste privilege also helped improve citizens' equality beyond universal suffrage.

Nehru was succeeded by another Congress leader, Lal Bahadur Shastri (1904–1966), who saw India through a debilitating nine-month war and standoff with Pakistan in 1965. His successor was Nehru's daughter, Indira Gandhi (1917–1984; prime minister, 1966–1977, 1980–1984; not related to Mohandas Gandhi). She carried on most of her father's policies and similarly managed to steer a tricky neutral course during the Cold War and its East–West tensions. India's 1971 victory over Pakistan and the subsequent creation of Bangladesh to replace East Pakistan cemented for some years her often shaky political control; this war and the subsequent development, with Russian help, of an atomic bomb confirmed India as the major power in South Asia. However, her failure to reduce national poverty and improve general economic health soon overcame her postwar popularity. After her efforts to assume virtual dictatorial power in the face of calls for her resignation, in 1977 she and the Congress Party were ousted by the voters for three years. She was reelected prime minister in an amazing turnaround and served until her resolute efforts to quell Sikh separatism brought about her assassination in 1984 by two Sikhs from her own palace guard.

Indira Gandhi's son, Rajiv Gandhi (1944–1991), was elected prime minister after her, and his handling of the thorny Sikh issue was generally applauded. Indications that he and Prime Minister Bhutto might work together to resolve some of the old India–Pakistan hostilities were also promising. Charges of corruption in his government led to his party's temporary fall and the prime ministership of V. P. Singh (b. 1931), who also worked during his brief tenure to defuse Hindu–Sikh and Hindu–Muslim communal tensions. Singh's resignation gave Gandhi as leader of the Congress Party a chance in national and state elections in 1991, but during the campaign Gandhi was assassinated by a Sri Lankan Tamil suicide bomber. Because no party won the subsequent national vote, the leader of the Congress Party, P. V. Narasimha Rao, was asked to form a government. He and the Congress managed to make substantial economic progress and, despite failures such as the 1992 Hindu extremist attack on the Babri Mosque in Ayodhya, to keep the lid generally on communal and separatist problems, from Sikhs in the Punjab and Muslims in Kashmir and the south to Hindu extremists and Uttarakhand separatists in the Himalayas. In 1997, Vice President K. R. Narayanan, a former academic and foreign service officer, assumed the presidency. He and his party were displaced in 2004 by an unexpected Congress Party victory that brought Manmohan Singh, formerly finance minister (1991–1996) in as prime minister, a post he still retained in the 2009 general elections.

India's problems remain large. Poverty and disease, including plague outbursts, are serious. Separatist movements based on regional affinity such as that of the Tamils of the south, or religious affinity such as that of the Sikhs of the Punjab, have pulled at the unity of the state. Industrialization, agricultural modernization, and high-tech growth have recently made great strides, yet the neutralizing force of runaway population growth has yet to be countered sufficiently to ensure a brighter future for the masses. India's population in 2009 was about 1.15 billion, growing at nearly 2 percent per year. The increasing strength of militant Hindu nationalists and fundamentalists and new outbreaks of communal violence between Hindus and India's large Muslim minority pose serious threats to the country's political stability. As the world's largest functioning democracy, India will be an important model of representative government and pluralist society if it succeeds in staying together and reducing its harshest problems: overpopulation and mass poverty.

Pakistan and Bangladesh

The architect and first president of Pakistan, Muhammad Ali Jinnah (1876–1948), oversaw the creation of a Muslim state comprising the widely separated East and West Pakistan in the two predominantly Muslim areas of northwest India and East Bengal. New constitutions, war with India, religious-secularist ideological strife, repeated military rule, and consistent return to the ballot box have marked the often-baffling pendulum swings of the new nation in its first half century. In 1971 East Pakistan seceded and became the new Islamic nation of Bangladesh. Indian and Bangladeshi relations have been troubled since then. However, the main political divide in the subcontinent remains that between India and Pakistan.

●●●—**Read** the Document
Jinnah, the "Father" of Pakistan
at **MyHistoryLab.com**

Pakistan's groping efforts to create a fully Islamic society and to solve its massive economic problems have been hampered by periodic lapses into dictatorship. Such lapses are usually punctuated by bloodshed and military coups, the most recent being that which brought the military leader Zia ul-Haqq (1924–1988) to power in 1977. The elections of November 1988, following his death in a suspicious air crash, opened the door again to parliamentary rule.

The subsequent period of some twenty-two years have not seen Pakistan achieve any real stability under parliamentary rule. Benazir Bhutto (b. 1953), the daughter of the man whom Zia ul-Haqq had overthrown and executed, was elected prime minister following Zia's death, becoming the first female leader of a major Islamic state in the twentieth century. But her time in office was cut short by the president's dismissal of her government in August 1990; she was elected again in 1993, only to be deposed by the president on charges of corruption in 1996. The successor government did not last long, for in 1999, General Parviz Musharraf, Chief of Army Staff (a post he resigned in 2007), took over as president of Pakistan and governed with executive and legislative power for much of the time until his resignation under increasing protest in 2008. Benazir Bhutto had tried the previous year to win back her post as prime minister, only to be assassinated in December 2007. Upon Musharraf's resignation the following summer, her husband, Asif Ali Zardari was elected president in his stead in September 2008 and continues in this role today.

Of all Central Asian governments, that of Pakistan has confronted the most direct challenge from radical Islam. The presence of armed groups of Taliban or their sympathizers in west and northwest Pakistan continues to be a source of instability and threat for the Karachi government as well as Afghanistan's fragile situation. Whether Pakistan can move ahead with rebuilding truly representative parliamentary rule and achieve real stability unthreatened by constant challenges from Islamic extremists remains very much an open question.

Indonesia and Malaysia

The new East Indies state of Indonesia wars created in 1949 as a nominal republic succeeding the long Dutch and brief Japanese colonial dominions in the East Indies. The much smaller territory of Malaya received its independence from British colonial rule in 1957 as a federation under a rotating monarch; it was later joined by the states of Sarawak and Sabah in northern Borneo, forming the federation of Malaysia. Each of these two new sovereign states faces different challenges.

Indonesia, the largest Muslim country in the world (nearly 200 million of its estimated 241 million people are Muslim), is trying to achieve a consensus among its disparate and scattered parts. It must determine how Muslim religious faith is to be reconciled with secularist government. The overriding problem for Malaysia (population 26 million) has been the cleft between the largely Chinese (24 percent) and partly Indian (7 percent) non-Muslim minority on the one hand, and the largely Muslim majority of Malay and other indigenous peoples (60 percent) on the other. Both nations have rich cultural traditions and natural resources; it remains to be seen how each will choose to preserve them while meeting the demands of modern global politics and participation in the global economy. Not just the future of these two Asian states, but an important part of Islam's future as a global religiocultural tradition is at stake.

The Postcolonial Middle East

Today no other part of the world so dominates international concern and conflict as does the Middle East. The issues have arisen as a result of the French and British successor nations established in the region since World War I, the coming of the Jewish state of Israel and resulting Palestinian conflict, the rise of militant Islamists, and the recent military interventions and occupations by the United States in Iraq and Afghanistan.

Postcolonial Nations in the Middle East

The modern Middle East arose as a result of the collapse of the Ottoman Empire and the subsequent division of the region by France and Britain following the World War I Versailles Peace Conference. Those powers in effect carved out their own Middle Eastern colonial nations and protectorates. Saudi Arabia, Iraq, and Egypt became semi-independent states after World War I, and Lebanon and Syria were officially recognized as independent by France during World War II. In 1948 Britain abandoned its mandate government in Palestine; the United Nations recognized the state of Israel and established sixty U.N. Relief and Works Agency (UNRWA) Palestinian refugee camps in Gaza, the West Bank, Jordan, Lebanon, Syria, and Egypt. Another 4 million Palestinians live today in the Palestinian diaspora from Turkey to Texas, and seven regional wars and two internal uprisings (*Intifada*) have erupted so far involving Israel, with no end in sight as regional and international attempts to end the occupation of Palestinian lands continue today.

During the late 1940s and thereafter, other Arab states gained official political independence: Jordan in 1946; Libya in 1951; Morocco and Tunisia in 1956; Algeria in 1962; and, by 1971, Yemen, Oman, and the Arabian/Persian Gulf sheikhdoms. (See Map 33–4.)

As elsewhere in the industrializing world, these states have sought political self-determination amidst political instability and autocratic rule. All share the classical Arabic written language, but spoken colloquial dialects vary from region to region. Attempts to create pan-Arab alliances or federations have all failed primarily because the regional differences and political self-interests of elites have overcome shared social, cultural, and political realities. Still, the memory of these efforts to claim a regional, even pan-Arab, nationalism remains important to many.

In the wake of World War II, many of the foremost leaders of Arab nationalism, such as Gamal Abdel Nasser of Egypt (1918–1970), were sympathetic to socialism and the Soviet Union. Socialism was in part a European ideology, and Arab socialism was an adaptation of European concepts to conditions and traditions in the Middle East. Among both secular and religious middle-class supporters "Islamic socialism" had gained considerable support in the 1980s until discredited by the failures of their Arab, Turkish, Iranian, and Kurdish leaders. Soviet-style communism, however, was so overtly secular and antireligious that many Arab, Turkish, and Iranian Muslims were tentative, if not hostile, to their secular-minded contemporaries who embraced communist parties and trade union politics too readily.

Nationalism as "patriotism for the homeland" (e.g., "Egypt for Egyptians") remains the most important ideology from Morocco to India and thus has the broadest range of support from autocratic leaders, traditional monarchies, military juntas, and single-party dictatorships to regional factions, sectarian militias, and dissident groups. It is safe to say that no ideologies currently resonate more today than the feeling of "solidarity" among Arab, Turkish, Iranian, or Kurdish peoples, although religious allegiances are also strong. Social, political, and sectarian distinctions are determined not so much by shared political cultures as by access to wealth, income, land, and arms. Thus, the elites of oil-producing countries such as Syria, Iraq, Saudi Arabia, and the Gulf states with ready access to wealth, income, land, and arms act "nationalistically" when such actions serve their own interests, while regional and local elites with less access to wealth, income, land, and arms ally with the oil-producing "giants" as long as it serves their regional and local

Map 33–4 The Modern Middle East and the Distribution of Major Religious Communities. The inset shows Israel and the Occupied Territories.

interests and needs. All too often, the "giants" act in their own state and family interests in alliance with the United States and the European Union to guarantee their continued elite status, while regional and local elites are left to their own devices, frequently changing alliances, and responsive to their constituents' immediate needs for food, housing, education, and health care. Any attempt by a foreign power to intervene in, manipulate, or tinker with the delicate social, economic, political, and cultural alliances of the state, regional, and local elites carries great risks. These alliances shift quickly, are based on

historical as well as contemporary interests, and respond to a range of other needs unseen and little understood by any foreign power. Rising poverty, refugee displacement, urban crime, and social violence in the Middle East and North Africa during the past decades also affect the directions and redirections of local and regional alliances more often than not.

Arab governments, defining themselves in nationalistic terms, worked out arrangements with local Muslim authorities. For example, the Saudi royal family turned over its educational system to adherents of a rigorist, puritanical form of Islam called *Wahhabism* (see Chapter 26) while modernizing the country's infrastucture. The Egyptian government attempted to play different Islamic militant and professional groups off against one another. Most governments retained the support of prosperous, devout middle-class Muslims while doing little about the plight of the poor. In general, Muslim religious leaders were highly critical of the Soviet Union and its influence in the region. Consequently, for many in the Middle East today the memory of Arab nationalism and socialism remains the memory of deceptions, self-interest, and a failed quest for pan-Arab identity.

The Arab-Israeli Conflict

Nowhere in Middle East affairs has the influence of Europe and the superpowers been more sharply felt than in the 1948 creation of the state of Israel in the former British mandate territory of Palestine. This event was the achievement principally of the world Zionist movement founded in 1897 by Theodor Herzl (1860–1904) in Europe. The British Balfour Declaration of 1917, issued during World War I and thus reflecting British wartime goals, favored the establishment of a national homeland for the Jews in Palestine as long as "non-Jewish" rights were preserved. In 1920, however, there were only about 60,000 Jews and ten times that number of Muslim and Christian Arabs in Palestine. As some at the time, such as the American King-Crane Commission, foresaw and events would bear out, serious trouble lay ahead. (See Document, "The King-Crane Commission Report, August 28, 1919.") The Commission concluded that the Zionist program could not accomplish its goal of an independent state except by force.

The interwar years saw increasing Jewish colonies and growing clashes between Jews and Palestinians poorly mediated by the often wavering British policy. Immigration of Jews, largely from Eastern Europe, increased in the 1920s and 1930s until Britain tried in 1936 to restrict it severely in response to a Palestinian six-month General Strike. For the time being, European Jews escaping the Nazi Holocaust had to seek other refuge in other lands. It was not always easy. Because of the flood of immigrants wanting to enter the United States, a quota system was in effect, and Jewish immigrants faced many obstacles to entering. After the war the Zionist movement received a tremendous boost from Jews worldwide and from the Allied nations, who wanted to atone for the indescribable horror of the Holocaust by securing a refuge for Jews from around the world.

The concept of a return to the Holy Land had a long history in Judaism. However, translating the concept into the creation of a national state was difficult because for centuries the land, administered by the Ottoman Empire, had been the home of Arabic-speaking Palestinians, primarily

Holy City. Jews pray at the Wailing Wall in Jerusalem during Passover, immediately below the Dome of the Rock, Islam's third holiest site.
A. Ramey/PhotoEdit

Muslims, but also Christians and Jews, all of whom for most of the twentieth century were without a voice in the fate of their own land. The Palestinians have understandably not been able to accept that they should be displaced and persecuted, whether because of another people's historic religious attachment to the land or as reparation for Europe's sins against its Jews. On the other hand, especially in light of long-standing European anti-Semitic persecutions, European Jews themselves felt a desperate need for a Jewish homeland where they might be safe from persecution and to which Jews everywhere might flee from the anti-Semitism that still rears its ugly head around the globe. For over sixty years, displaced Palestinians and militant Israelis have continued to clash over the 1947 U.N. partition plan and the subsequent occupation of lands not approved by the United Nations but seized by Israeli military forces and Jewish colonists.

⊙ See the Map
The Partition of Palestine After World War II, 1948
at **MyHistoryLab.com**

Document

The King-Crane Commission Report, August 28, 1919

In the peace settlements following World War I it proved impossible to reconcile the claims of the Arabs, the Zionists, the British, and the French. American President Woodrow Wilson thus sent a fact-finding mission to the region to determine what the people there really wanted. The King-Crane Commission was headed by Henry C. King, the president of Oberlin College, and Charles R. Crane, a businessman and philanthropist. The commission spent several weeks in the Middle East meeting with representatives of the various ethnic, religious, and national communities. Although the commission's report had no influence on policy in the region, it is remarkable because it captured the uncertain political mood in the Middle East immediately following World War I. As the following section reveals, the United States was held in high regard in the region. The report also anticipated some of the problems relating to Arab-Jewish relations.

■ *What are some of the major political issues highlighted by the commission?*
Why did the commission find such a positive attitude toward the United States?

We recommend . . . serious modification of the extreme Zionist programme for Palestine of unlimited immigration of Jews, looking finally to making Palestine distinctly a Jewish state.

If, however, the strict terms of the Balfour Statement are adhered to, favouring the establishment in Palestine of a national home for the Jewish people, "it being clearly understood that nothing shall be done which may prejudice the civil and religious rights of existing non-Jewish communities in Palestine"—it can hardly be doubted that the extreme Zionist programme must be greatly modified. For a national home for the Jewish people is not equivalent to making Palestine into a Jewish State; nor can the erection of such a Jewish State be accomplished without the grave trespass upon the civil and religious rights of existing non-Jewish communities in Palestine. . . .

Then it is to be remembered that the non-Jewish population of Palestine—nearly nine-tenths of the whole—are emphatically against the entire Zionist programme. The tables show that there was no one thing upon which the population of Palestine was more agreed than upon this. To subject a people so minded to unlimited Jewish immigration, and to steady financial and social pressure to surrender the land, would be a gross violation of the principle just quoted, and of the people's rights, though it kept within the forms of law. It is to be noted also that the feeling against the Zionist programme is not confined to Palestine, but shared very generally by the people throughout Syria, as our conferences clearly showed. More than seventy-two percent—1.350 in all the petitions in the whole of Syria were directed against the Zionist programme. Only two requests—those for a united Syria and for independence had a larger support. . . .

In view of all these considerations, and with a deep sense of sympathy for the Jewish cause, the Commissioners feel bound to recommend that only a greatly reduced Zionist programme be attempted by the Peace Conference, and even that, only very gradually initiated. This would have to mean that Jewish immigration should be definitely limited, and that the project for making Palestine distinctly a Jewish commonwealth should be given up. . . . Nevertheless, upon the face of the returns, America was the first choice of 1,152 of the petitions presented—more than sixty percent—while no other Power had as much as fifteen per cent for first choice.

And the conferences showed that the people knew the grounds upon which they registered their choice for America. They declared that their choice was due to knowledge of America's record; the unselfish aims with which she had come into the War; the faith in her felt by multitudes of Syrians who had been in America; the spirit revealed in American educational institutions in Syria, especially the College in Beirut, with its well-known and constant encouragement of Syrian national sentiment; their belief that America had no territorial or colonial ambitions, and would willingly withdraw when the Syrian State was well established as her treatment both of Cuba and the Philippines seemed to them to illustrate; her genuinely democratic spirit; and her ample resources. From the point of view of the desires of the "people concerned," the Mandate should clearly go to America.

Source: (U.S. government)

In 1945 Britain found itself beset in Palestine by Jews seeking to settle there and by Jewish underground and terrorist organizations aiming to end British control, while Palestinian resistance had become increasingly violent. In 1947 the British washed their hands of Palestine, and the United Nations called for partition of the former mandate territory to create a Jewish state. The plan was 30 percent of arable land for Jews (who represented about 30 percent of the total population) and a Muslim/Christian Arab state of 70 percent of arable land (about 70 percent of the former Palestinian Mandate). Arab states refused to accept the U.N. resolution, but in May 1948 Jews in Palestine proclaimed the independent state of Israel anyway. This declaration led to the Israeli-Arab War of 1948–1949. In this war Syria, Iraq, Lebanon, Jordan, and Egypt attacked Israel with approximately 40,000 troops, but lost to the 92,000 Israeli forces, who were better armed, better trained, better connected with European countries, and more resolute. The combined Israeli forces not only occupied all the U.N.–proposed Israeli territory, but also seized a substantial portion of that designated by the U.N. for a Palestinian state. In addition to the plight of Palestinians subjected to Israeli rule or occupation, the creation of Israel also produced a massive Palestinian refugee problem that has yet to be resolved by anyone—the Arab nations, Israel, the United Nations, or other interested parties. Since 1948, nearly 75 percent of all Palestinians have been refugees from their homes and homeland. The wars or periods of open conflict of 1956, 1967, 1973, 1978–1982, 1987-1991, and 2006, as well as the two *Intifadas* (1987-1991, 2000-2005) only added more refugees to the original ones.

Since 1948 there has been, at best, an armed truce between Israel and its neighbors and, at worst, open warfare. The Arab nations and the Palestinian people displaced by the new state have generally not wanted to accept Israel's right to exist as a state, and Israel (with the support of the United States) has taken aggressive measures, often in defiance of world opinion and international law regarding the **occupied territories**, to ensure its survival. The most serious military confrontations were the Suez Crisis of 1956, when Israel (and briefly France and England) invaded the Sinai; the 1967 June war (often referred to as the "Six-Day War"), when Israel invaded and occupied the Sinai, the Golan Heights, and the West Bank (of the Jordan River); the October war of 1973, or the Yom Kippur war, when the Egyptians and Syrians staged a surprise attack on Israel in the Sinai and the Golan that ended in a standoff; the Israeli invasions of Lebanon in 1978, 1982, and 2006 to interdict or avenge anti-Israeli terrorist operations; and the recent 2009 Israeli invasion of Gaza.

Ever since the fall of 2000, the region has spiraled into an abyss of violence in the midst of the second Palestinian **Intifada**, or uprising (literally, "shaking off"), with repeated Israeli military assaults on towns and refugee camps in the West Bank and Gaza and regular Palestinian extremist suicide attacks on mainly Israeli civilian targets. Israel's highly provocative construction since 2000 of a massive 200+ mile "separation barrier" through the West Bank (adjudged a violation of international law by the International Court of Justice in 2004) is currently asserting Israeli control over still more Palestinian West-Bank territory, ostensibly in the name of increased Israeli security from suicide bombings. The United States' virtual pullback in the later Bush administration from serious effort at bringing either Israelis or Palestinians back into negotiations left the future of the region in still greater uncertainty. With a new American administration since 2009, some increased efforts at a return to negotiation have been made, but most recently (early 2010) the Israeli hard-line leader, Binyamin Natanyahu, has approved a new settlement in East Jerusalem in open defiance of the United States and world opinion.

Simultaneously, in a cycle of violence that has become familiar to us from Northern Ireland to Vietnam, the frustrations of an embattled Israel have made it increasingly ready to meet terrorist atrocities with preemptive military actions and violent reprisals, both at home and abroad. Israel has responded to extremist terrorist attacks and civilian resistance such as the Intifada in the occupied territories with air and commando raids on Arab states supporting Palestinian terrorism; with repressive, even punitive, measures against the Palestinian populations in the occupied territories; and with a hard-line stance against negotiation over the status of the territories seized in 1967.

Arab and some non-Arab states have been equally intransigent about recognizing Israel's right to exist, have supported guerrilla groups attacking Israel, and have refused until recently to deal directly with Israel to reach a long-term Middle East solution. Egypt was the first notable exception to this policy. In the late 1970s, under Gamal Abdel Nasser's successor, Anwar Sadat (1918–1981), and through the mediation of U.S. President Jimmy Carter (b. 1924), Egypt entered into direct negotiations with Israel's prime minister Menachem Begin (1913–1994). The two countries reached an agreement—the Camp David Accords—in 1978, and in 1979 signed a formal peace treaty. Sadat was assassinated in 1981 by Egyptian Muslim extremists, but the treaty has held up under his successor, Husni Mubarak (b. 1928).

Nonetheless, despite the Egyptian-Israeli accords, violence and political impasse—tragic, morally debilitating, and materially draining for all the peoples of the area—continued through the 1980s and 1990s and have only accelerated since 2000. Israeli military actions in the occupied territories and Gaza have been provoked by, but in turn have brought on more, Palestinian terrorist bombings in Israel and abroad.

Added to this bleak history and current struggle is the ugly legacy of hate instilled in many on both sides for decades. Arabs and even many Muslims outside the Arab world have come to label non-Israeli Jews, Israelis, and both religious and political Zionists as oppressors and enemies, making no distinctions among them. Many Israelis and many Jews around the world have similarly vilified all Arabs and Muslims. In some ways Arab-Israeli and Muslim-Jewish relations are at an all-time low, and it may require one or several generations to displace the prejudice, stereotyping, and hatred so long accumulated. The human crisis is far from over, even if peace were to arrive tomorrow.

Some events of recent years gave at least brief hope for an eventual resolution to the conflict. In 1991, in the wake of the Gulf War that followed Iraq's invasion of Kuwait, the parties to the Arab-Israeli conflict began peace negotiations. The negotiations ended with the 1993 Middle East Peace Agreement, also known as the Oslo Agreement, which raised hopes for a negotiated settlement and the creation of

Read the Document

Israel-PLO Declaration of Principles on Interim Self-Government Arrangements (1993) at **MyHistoryLab.com**

an independent Palestinian state alongside the Jewish state of Israel. However, little progress has been made since the 1993 agreement.

Jordan and Egypt did agree in 1994 to a peace treaty with Israel, but many other Arab states—Syria foremost—have not been willing to negotiate with Israel, and Israel has preferred to keep developing settlements and roads in such a way as to preclude any contiguous territory with which to form a viable Palestinian state. Extremists on both sides have tried to ensure the failure of the peace initiative. In early 1994 an American-born Israeli Jewish fanatic machine-gunned worshipers in a mosque in Hebron. In November 1995 another Jewish Israeli extremist assassinated Prime Minister Yitzhak Rabin for trying to make peace and to allow the eventual creation of even a circumscribed Palestinian state. Then, before the 1996 Israeli elections, called in the wake of Rabin's death, Palestinian extremists carried out a series of savage bombings on buses and in crowded shopping areas. The subsequent narrow victory in the elections of a Likud conservative hard-liner,

View the Image

Rabin and Arafat Shake Hands at the White House, 1993 at **MyHistoryLab.com**

Binyamin Netanyahu (b. 1949), over Rabin's Labor successor, Shimon Peres, cast new uncertainty on peace prospects for some time.

The leadership on both sides has proved unable to implement the ideals of the Oslo Agreement. The first Netanyahu regime repeatedly took hard-line stands and provocative actions such as expansion of Jewish West Bank settlements. To the latter end, new roads and building projects were implemented to divide further the Palestinian population in the territories. Other actions included curtailment of water supplies to Palestinian areas and declarations of Israel's determination to retain all of Jerusalem and much of the territories despite international censure. Nor was the Palestinian Authority created by the 1993 peace agreement any better. Under the leadership of Yasser Arafat (1929–2004), it grew steadily more corrupt, ineffec-

tive, and out of touch with its constituencies, and the suffering of the masses in the West Bank and Gaza in particular only grew worse after the agreement. Despite efforts of the Palestinian and Israeli security forces, Palestinian guerrillas of the extremist wing of the resistance organization Hamas found ways to kill Israelis—overwhelming civilians in daylight bombings, even during religious holidays such as Passover, in a sustained effort to torpedo the already shaky **peace process**. These terrorist attacks led Israel to seal its borders, resulting in the additional loss of 11 percent of West Bank Palestinian farmlands, a source of livelihood for thousands of Arabs in the occupied territories who normally work in Israel proper. This exacerbated the already dire plight of Gaza in particular, keeping thousands of Palestinian families in poverty and starvation and in turn feeding the agenda of extremist resistance groups.

The first Netanyahu era ended after a scandal involving the prime minister himself, and in March 2000, Ariel Sharon became prime minister. Sharon was the former army general charged with responsibility for the camp massacres by Christian militias operating in the 1982–1983 Israeli invasion of Lebanon. His administration was marked by escalating violence on both sides. Sharon, however, also proposed that Israel withdraw from Gaza and close Israeli settlements there, which proved controversial on both sides. His government also began the erection of the barrier fence separating Israeli and Palestinian territory. Arafat died in late 2004. His passing presented a new opportunity for negotiations with the Palestinians, now led by Mahmoud Abbas, who was elected to the Palestinian presidency in January 2005, but this opportunity was lost. Today, Netanyahu is again prime minister (since March 2009), and any resolution of the situation seems far away, not least because neither Abbas nor anyone from any Palestinian faction seems able or

See the Map

The Modern Middle East at **MyHistoryLab.com**

willing to come seriously to the negotiating table, even if Netanyahu were to change his antagonistic position.

Middle Eastern Oil

Arab and Iranian oil has been another significant factor in the region's modern history. Oil has been both blessing and curse for the Middle East. Ever since its discovery in Iran in 1908, but especially after Saudi Arabia's first oil production in 1939, the world demand for oil has climbed. In the mid-1970s, oil became a major bargaining chip in international diplomacy, one that the Arab and other oil-rich states—such as Venezuela, Nigeria, Iran, and Indonesia—used to their advantage. In Arab North Africa and especially Arabia and the Gulf, oil production and wealth have changed every aspect of life. Oil has propelled formerly peripheral countries of the Sahara or the Arabian deserts into major roles in interna-

Israeli Invasion of Gaza. Palestinian students view the ruins of the Islamic University in Gaza City, destroyed on December 29, 2008, during the 22-day offensive by Israel in Gaza.

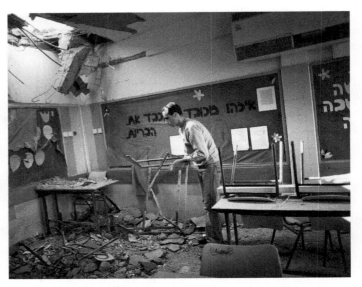

Palestinian Rocket Attack. An Israeli surveys the damage in a school classroom caused by a Palestinian rocket on December 31, 2008, in Beer Sheva, Israel.

tional banking and finance. Oil has also boosted the damaged Arab self-confidence after two centuries of European domination. A testimony to the global importance of Middle Eastern oil was the willingness of the United States and European nations to form a coalition with some Arab countries and commit massive forces to expel Iraq after its invasion of Kuwait in 1990. Although the economic benefits of oil are all too obvious, this resource has not necessarily had the corresponding political remuneration for people in the Middle East. Because of its importance to the world economy, Middle East oil has brought considerable foreign involvement, whether from Europe, the United States, or the former Soviet Union. This involvement has often been detrimental to regional political development. The most famous example is the 1953 CIA and British coup in Iran, which overthrew the popular government of Muhammad Mossadeq, who had sought to nationalize the Iranian oil industry. Nearly a half-century later, in 2000, then U.S. Secretary of State Madeline Albright apologized to the Iranian nation for the U.S. role in this coup and the negative effects it had on Iranian political development. Nevertheless, George W. Bush's subsequent invasion of Iraq in 2003 was arguably once again motivated in part by interest in Iraqi oil and Central Asian oil outlets.

The Rise of Militant Islamism

The increase in the global importance of the Middle East has coincided with a new round of Muslim efforts in the Middle East and elsewhere to revive pristine Muslim values and standards and reform the perceived evils and failures in Muslim societies. In the spirit of earlier Muslim resurgences such as those of the eighteenth century in India, Arabia, and Africa, many Muslims have sought to return to the "fundamentals" of Islamic life, faith, and society. They see

this as a means of rejuvenation, of social and economic as well as political justice, and of defense against the encroachment of foreign, usually Western secularist and materialist, values and norms. Indeed, a major new element in modern Muslim revivalism is its consciousness of responding to the destructive influence of Western-style "modernity" on the mores, values, and religious faith of Muslim peoples.

Much of the Islamists' appeal everywhere is their ability to address the needs of the underclasses in Middle Eastern, North African, and Asian cities and countries. Thus many Muslims around the world may generally agree with the social critique that these movements present, but they are most often not supportive of their militant solutions to current economic and cultural predicaments. Where governments of Muslim-majority countries have repeatedly failed to provide social services such as housing, medical care, education, and jobs, Islamist groups have succeeded under the banner of a just, moral Muslim societal ideal. While world, and especially U.S., journalists, focus only on the relatively small fringe groups of Islamist extremists, Muslims at the grass-roots level have seen major Islamist groups opposed to the authoritarian regimes under which they live providing social services long ignored or poorly delivered by the state.

Such Muslim fundamentalism—or, to give it a more correct name, "Islamist reformism"—motivated many of the revolutionaries who overthrew the shah in Iran in 1978. It is also seen in the Muslim Brethren movement in Egypt and elsewhere, in the Welfare Party in Turkey, and in other groups, from Morocco to the Persian Gulf, and outside the Middle East. Such Islamist groups see themselves as traditionalist, whether they are radical, conservative, or liberal—they feel they are upholding basic Muslim values and norms. The political acts of reformist groups range from revolution (Iran) to democratic participation (Turkey) to complete political quietism (the Tablighi international revivalist movement begun in Pakistan in the 1940s). Whether these movements will bring lasting change to Islamic societies is an open question for the Muslim world generally and the Middle East in particular. There is no question, however, of their present-day influence.

The Modern Middle Eastern Background

The background to this Islamist reform is the European expansion over much of the globe in just a few centuries. This expansion brought far more social and political change than religious or cultural change to the Islamic world. It saw the emergence globally of European-style nationalism and the nation-state idea; of post-Enlightenment ideals of individual liberties and rights and representative government; and of the concept of one's religious faith and affiliation as a private, "religious" matter and one's citizenship as a public, "secular" matter. Such ideas proved revolutionary, or at the least disruptive, in the Islamic world, especially in the past century.

The twentieth century in Islamic parts of the world presents a checkered history of autocratic governments generally at least as far removed from their citizenries as any of the medieval or premodern, often foreign (primarily Turkish) dynasties that had ruled Arab, Persian, Indian, or other regions of the Muslim-majority world. Experiments with European-style parliamentary government only rarely took hold in the Islamic world (or the rest of the Third World); nor did liberal democratic or Marxist-socialist ideologies prove viable for the long term. Even so, until recent decades, little political discourse in Islamic lands had given serious attention to specifically *Islamic* alternatives.

With the rise and postcolonial independence of many national states and the flourishing of diverse nationalisms, politics often became theoretically as well as actually divorced from Islamic religious tradition and its norms. This breach occurred in overt ways that it had not before, however large the actual gap always was between the religious ideals of government as guardian of the Shari'a order on the one hand and the political realities of power politics on the other. Where leaders had previously claimed Muslim faith and allegiance, some, such as the Arab nationalists of the post–World War I era, espoused secularism and ignored religion except as a political weapon.

In short, the recent past has seen no realization of an "ideal" Islamic state in which religious and political authority is conjoined. If anything, the gap has typically widened between Islamic ideals and political realities. Even in the current Islamic Republic of Iran there has been a clear division between political realities and religious standards. However sincerely the latter are claimed as the basis of state policy, no one can miss the frequent stretching of those stan-

dards to justify pragmatic political decisions. Nonetheless, the ideals championed in the Iranian Revolution proved a powerful counterweight to secular Persian nationalism.

When we consider Islamist movements of recent decades, we find that the calls for a congruence of religion and politics in the Islamic world trace less to some ideal Islamic model state or so-called **theocracy** than to a need for simple social and political justice, which Islam (or any of the other great religious traditions) has always demanded. The cries for a "jihad" (armed struggle) of Muslims are aimed less often outwardly than inwardly, less at foreign "devils" and more at domestic tyrants, corruption, and social and economic injustice. Indeed, perhaps the most internationally influential of all contemporary Islamic reform movements, that of the Tabligh-i Jama'at, is explicitly apolitical, looking to convert the individual of faith to true submission (*islam*) rather than lip service.

As for those avowedly political reform movements, be they activist but nonviolent (the majority) or extremist and violent (the minority), they feed upon the deep socioeconomic and political injustice that citizens of most Islamic countries (like most other Third World countries) have endured. Often they tie Western influence or support to unjust rule of their own countries. Such movements can go over the edge and end in extremism and terrorism. Osama Bin Laden, the dispossessed Saudi millionaire who has led his own violent movement, al-Qa'ida, from the 1990s to the present, stunned the world, and especially the United States, with suicide attacks using civilian airliners to destroy the World Trade Center towers and part of the Pentagon building on September 11, 2001. His motive was primarily revenge for the American military presence in Saudi Arabia, the American-led blockade of Iraq, and American support of Israel against the Palestinians. (See Document, "Jihad against Jews and Crusaders: World Islamic Front Statement, 1998.")

These carefully executed and destructive attacks led the United States into deeper military involvement in the Middle East and Central Asia. In October 2001, the United States attacked the Taliban government of Afghanistan, rapidly overthrowing it. The defeat of the Taliban destroyed al-Qa'ida's overt Afghan bases, but not its leadership, which appears to survive still, although it is dispersed and in hiding. Whether this military response to terrorism will eventually be successful remains to be seen, nearly nine years later. What is clearer, however, is that the ongoing "war on terrorism" is radically changing the security needs of the United States. The U.S. military is shifting many troops and bases previously located in western Europe and East Asia closer to the Middle East. It would appear that American troops will not soon leave this part of the world. The further U.S. intervention in 2003 in Iraq has even more deeply entangled the United States in Middle Eastern affairs.

Document

Jihad against Jews and Crusaders: World Islamic Front Statement, 1998

Osama Bin Laden is one of the leaders of the al–Qa'ida terrorist organization that was responsible for the attacks on September 11, 2001. He came from a privileged background in Saudi Arabia and eventually volunteered to fight the Soviet Union in Afghanistan in the 1980s. The success that Bin Laden and his associates had in driving out the Soviets convinced them that a similar "holy war" should be implemented elsewhere in the Islamic world. Their goal was to re-create an Islamic state to replace the debased, secular governments of the Middle East. Because a vast majority of Muslims do not agree with their political views and terrorist tactics, al- Qa'ida started increasingly to couch its rhetoric in xenophobic terms. Utilizing anti-American and anti-Semitic statements, Bin Laden and his followers hoped to grab the attention of Muslims around the world by highlighting prominent political problems in the region. In 1998, Bin Laden issued a legal proclamation, based on his questionable and invalid interpretation of Islamic faith, that called for the killing of Americans. When this proclamation was first issued, it did not garner considerable attention, nor did it inspire many Muslims around the world.

■ *On what religious authority does Bin Laden rest his claims? How does Bin Laden hope to ignite a mass revolution and support for his agenda?*

The Arabian Peninsula has never—since God made it flat, created its desert, and encircled it with seas—been stormed by any forces like the crusader armies spreading in it like locusts, eating its riches and wiping out its plantations. All this is happening at a time in which nations are attacking Muslims like people fighting over a plate of food. In the light of the grave situation and the lack of support,

we and you are obliged to discuss current events, and we should all agree on how to settle the matter.

No one argues today about three facts that are known to everyone; we will list them, in order to remind everyone:

First, for over seven years the United States has been occupying the lands of Islam in the holiest of places, the Arabian Peninsula, plundering its riches, dictating to its

Iraq: Intervention and Occupation

Modern Iraq was established by the British after World War I. For millennia, this area of Mesopotamia was home to powerful empires. More recently, it was part of the Ottoman Empire. Iraq as such had never been a distinct political unit and until 1921 was primarily a geographic term, referring to today's southern Iraq. Postwar imperial concern and the potential of oil motivated the British to oversee the creation of Iraq, which they felt would best protect their interests in the region. Given the disparate ethnic and religious groups in the country, the British could not identify a suitable leader within Iraq. Instead, they imported Faysal ibn Husayn, son of the Sharif of Mecca, and crowned him king of the Hashemite Monarchy of Iraq in 1921. Until 1958, the monarchy ruled Iraq with the help of British advisers. A consortium of foreign oil companies, largely British, dominated the Iraqi oil industry and the British army maintained military bases in Iraq.

Many Iraqis came to resent this foreign presence. A bloody *coup d'état* in 1958 under the leadership of Abd

al-Karim Qasem brought a violent end to the monarchy. By then, Iraqis had developed a sense of national identity and aversion to foreign involvement in Iraqi affairs. By 1979, the Ba'ath party was the dominant force in Iraqi politics. That year Saddam Hussein started his tyrannical reign. Shortly after he took power, he invaded Iran and initiated the bloody Iran–Iraq War (1980–1988). He also invaded and occupied Kuwait in 1990. An international military coalition under U.S. leadership drove the Iraqi army from Kuwait. During the 1990s, Iraq was an international pariah subjected to extensive economic sanctions monitored by the United Nations. The Iraqi government eventually expelled the U.N. inspectors in 1998, and the United Nations was unable to reinsert them for almost five years.

●●●-[Read the Document
Saddam Hussein's Invasion of Kuwait: (a) Saddam Hussein, "Victory Day" Speech; (b) Bishara A. Bahbah, "The Crisis in the Gulf: Why Iraq Invaded Kuwait" at **MyHistoryLab.com**

The United States adopted a policy of regime change in Iraq during the last years of the Clinton administration, though it did little to carry out that policy. In the wake of 9/11, rulers, humiliating its people, terrorizing its neighbors, and turning its bases in the Peninsula into a spearhead through which to fight the neighboring Muslim peoples.

If some people have in the past argued about the fact of the occupation, all the people of the Peninsula have now acknowledged it. The best proof of this is the Americans' continuing aggression against the Iraqi people using the Peninsula as a staging post, even though all its rulers are against their territories being used to that end, but they are helpless.

Second, despite the great devastation inflicted on the Iraqi people by the crusader-Zionist alliance, and despite the huge number of those killed, which has exceeded 1 million. . . despite all this, the Americans are once again trying to repeat the horrific massacres, as though they are not content with the protracted blockade imposed after the ferocious war or the fragmentation and devastation.

So here they come to annihilate what is left of this people and to humiliate their Muslim neighbors.

Third, if the Americans' aims behind these wars are religious and economic, the aim is also to serve the Jews' petty state and divert attention from its occupation of Jerusalem and murder of Muslims there. The best proof of this is their eagerness to destroy Iraq, the strongest neighboring Arab state, and their endeavor to fragment all the states of the region such as Iraq, Saudi Arabia, Egypt, and Sudan into paper statelets and through their disunion and weakness to guarantee Israel's survival and the continuation of the brutal crusade occupation of the Peninsula.

All these crimes and sins committed by the Americans are a clear declaration of war on Allah, his messenger, and Muslims. And ulema have throughout Islamic history unanimously agreed that the jihad is an individual duty. . . .

On that basis, and in compliance with Allah's order, we issue the following fatwa to all Muslims:

The ruling to kill the Americans and their allies—civilians and military—is an individual duty for every Muslim who can do it in any country in which it is possible to do it, in order to liberate the al-Aqsa Mosque and the holy mosque [Mecca] from their grip, and in order for their armies to move out of all the lands of Islam, defeated and unable to threaten any Muslim. This is in accordance with the words of Almighty Allah, "and fight the pagans all together as they fight you all together," and "fight them until there is no more tumult or oppression, and there prevail justice and faith in Allah."

This is in addition to the words of Almighty Allah: "And why should ye not fight in the cause of Allah and of those who, being weak, are ill-treated (and oppressed)?".women and children, whose cry is: "Our Lord, rescue us from this town, whose people are oppressors; and raise for us from thee one who will help!"

We—with God's help—call on every Muslim who believes in Allah and wishes to be rewarded to comply with God's order to kill the Americans and plunder their money wherever and whenever they find it. We also call on Muslim ulema, leaders, youths, and soldiers to launch the raid on Satan's U.S. troops and the devil's supporters allying with them, and to displace those who are behind them so that they may learn a lesson.

Source: (U.S. government translation)

---

however, the Bush administration decided to remove the government of Saddam Hussein and the threat of Iraqi weapons of mass destruction. During late 2002 and early 2003 the United States and British governments sought passage of a United Nations Security Council resolution requiring Iraq to disarm on its own or to face disarmament by military force. The efforts to obtain an effective resolution failed primarily because France and Russia threatened to veto the measure. In the face of the failure to pass a U.N. resolution, the United States, Great Britain, and Australia, backed by a coalition of over forty other nations, the "Coalition of the Willing," invaded Iraq in March 2003. After three weeks of fighting, the Coalition succeeded in removing Saddam Hussein's government from power. The announced goals of the invasion, in addition to toppling the Iraqi regime, were to destroy Iraq's capacity to manufacture or deploy weapons of mass destruction and to bring consensual government to the Iraqi people.

The invasion was undertaken with considerable international opposition, notably from France, Germany, and Russia. It also provoked large antiwar demonstrations in the United States and other parts of the world. The war has created strains within the European Union and NATO. It also marks a new era in relations between the United States and Europe as well as the rest of the world.

Currently, it remains difficult to ensure peace and stability in Iraq. Many Iraqis resisted the occupation by foreign forces, and historical factors militate against a unified government. The shocking lack of preparation by the Americans and their allies for dealing with the chaos of postwar Iraq exacerbated matters. The complete failure to find weapons of mass destruction in Iraq led to wide questioning of the real rationale for the war. The widespread destruction and suffering and the prolonged state of quasi-civil war that has only in the past year begun to diminish has left the American government open to criticism in the region and around the world.

Throughout Iraq an insurgency was launched against the Coalition forces and against Iraqis, particularly those in the security services, which had cooperated with the Coalition and

Suicide Bomb Explosion, Iraq 2010. Iraqi civilians help rescue teams remove rubble at the site of a suicide bomb explosion that targeted a restaurant in the center of Baghdad. In 2010, suicide bombings continue to occur at an alarming rate, wounding and killing scores of civilians.

the recently installed Iraqi government. In late January 2005, an election was held in Iraq under conditions of insurgent attacks to elect the Assembly that will write a new constitution. With voter turnout much higher than anticipated, the election did succeed. However, the challenges of securing ever-wider internal support for the construction of democratic processes still confront the shaky Iraqi government and American policy makers. A "surge" policy that increased the American troop presence in 2009 under new U.S. President Obama seems to have helped internal stability somewhat, and the recent elections of 2010, while in dispute, seem to hold promise of bringing a more democratic Iraqi government to power at the present time (March 2010). Internal violence has not ended, but a 2009 American plan for phased withdrawal of American troops (all combat units to be out by September 2010) seems to have some possibility of success in the coming year or two.

Summary

The Postcolonial World. Since 1945 European colonies have disappeared from Africa and Asia and have been replaced by independent and semi-independent states. These states have had to adjust their political and economic relations first to one or other of the superpowers during the Cold War and then, since the disappearance of the Soviet Union, to the United States especially.

Latin America. Most Latin American countries remain politically and economically dependent on the United States. Except in Cuba, no revolutionary movement has been able to overturn the traditional structure of Latin American society. Despite social and economic problems, Argentina and Brazil have managed to move from military rule to stable democratic, civilian government. In Mexico, the long dominance of the PRI ended in 2000.

Africa. Independent Africa has faced severe problems: arbitrary boundaries, disease, economic dependence, and political instability. While Nigeria has experienced ethnic and religious strife under a succession of military dictatorships, South Africa has emerged as a stable, multi-ethnic, but economically challenged democracy since the end of white rule in the 1990s. The challenge for Africa as a whole is to build truly civil societies and achieve economic health and political stability.

The Middle East. Oil and Arab objections to the creation of the State of Israel, and then Israel's occupation of Palestinian lands, have dominated the politics of the Middle East since the 1940s. While the possession of vast deposits of oil has made some Middle Eastern governments wealthy, it has not led to the creation of prosperous democratic societies. The existence of Israel and the consequent displacement of Palestinian Arabs have inflamed the Middle East for more than six decades. Although U.S. and European efforts to sponsor an Israeli-Palestinian peace have made some progress, the cycle of terror and retaliatory violence has persisted, and it is unclear whether a lasting peace between Israel and its neighbors can be achieved or a viable Palestinian state created.

Militant Islamists, though hardly a monolithic movement or majority among Muslims, have proved increasingly disruptive to a battle-scarred region and lands beyond. In the wake of the terrorist attacks of September 11, 2001, the United States overthrew the Taliban regime in Afghanistan and Saddam Hussein in Iraq. The United States finds itself increasingly embroiled in a chaotic and unstable region of the world, partly because of U.S. political and economic policies, and partly because of social, economic, and political inequities, poor national leadership, and continued weaknesses in family-dominated centralized states that plague the region.

Key Terms

apartheid (p. 1034)

clash of civilizations (p. 1022)

decolonization (p. 1021)

globalization (p. 1021)

HIV/AIDS (p. 1037)

Intifada (p. 1048)

liberation theology (p. 1024)

occupied territories (p. 1048)

peace process (p. 1049)

Sandinistas (p. 1028)

theocracy (p. 1051)

Truth and Reconciliation Commission (TRC) (p. 1035)

Review Questions

1. Are the nations of Latin America still economically dependent on the United States and western Europe? If so, why? How did the superpower rivalry of the Cold War affect Latin America? How successful has the worldwide trend toward democratization been in Latin America? Describe the transition from military rule to civilian democracy in Brazil, Argentina, and Chile. Has Mexico made a similar transition?

2. What factors contributed to decolonization in sub-Saharan Africa? What challenges did many newly independent states share? Has postcolonial Nigeria lived up to its potential? Why is Nigeria's record significant for Africa as a whole? Describe the apartheid regime in South Africa. Why was it dismantled in the 1990s? What problems does the Democratic Republic of the Congo face? What factors contributed to the 1994 genocide in Rwanda?

3. Compare and contrast the roles of social change, religion, and economics in Turkey, Iran, Pakistan, and Malaysia. How does the profound influence of Islam in this and other regions of the world suggest the power of religious traditions in modern politics and society? Compare the nationalization process and results in 1951 Iran and in 1956 Egypt.

4. What have been the major factors in the creation of the modern Middle East? How have interventions by European powers and the United States affected this region? Compare and contrast the roles of religion and nationalism in the Middle East.

5. Explain the origin and course of the Israeli-Palestinian conflict. What have been the major turning points? Have there been moments when the conflict might have reached a peaceful resolution?

6. Describe the origins and character of political and militant Islam. Why has it taken so radical a political course in the post–Iranian Revolution era (since 1979)? Why was the Soviet invasion of Afghanistan an important event in its development? Why has the United States become the primary target of militant Islamists?

Note: *To learn more about the topics in this chapter, please turn to the Suggested Readings at the end of the book. For additional sources related to this chapter please see MyHistoryLab.com*

myhistorylab Connections

Reinforce what you learned in this chapter by studying the many documents, images, maps, review tools, and videos available at **www.myhistorylab.com**.

Read and Review

✓●─ Study and Review   Chapter 33

●●─ Read the Document   *Liberation Theology (1950s), p. 1024*
Address before the Puebla Conference (1979), p. 1025
Fidel Castro, History Will Absolve Me, 1953, p. 1027
Juan Perón, excerpt from The Voice of Perón, p. 1028
Brazil's Constitution of 1988, p. 1028
Chico Mendes on the Rainforest (1980s), p. 1029
Nelson Mandela, from Freedom, Justice and Dignity for All
    South Africa, p. 1035
Alain Destexhe, excerpt from Rwanda and Genocide in the
    Twentieth Century, p. 1036
Nelson Mandela, Closing Address at the 13th International
    AIDS Conference, July 200, p. 1037
Jawaharlal Nehru, "Why India is Non-Aligned" (India),
    1956, p. 1042
Jinnah, the "Father" of Pakistan, p. 1043
Israel-PLO Declaration of Principles on Interim
    Self-Government Arrangements (1993), p. 1049
Saddam Hussein's Invasion of Kuwait: (a) Saddam Hussein,
    "Victory Day" Speech; (b) Bishara A. Bahbah, "The Crisis
    in the Gulf: Why Iraq Invaded Kuwait", p. 1052

●●─ See the Map   *Africa, 2004, p. 1033*
HIV Prevalence in Africa, p. 1038
The Partition of Palestine After World War II, 1948,
    p. 1046
The Modern Middle East, p. 1049

●●─ View the Image   *Voters Waiting to Vote in South Africa's*
First Open Election, 1994, p. 1035
Ayatollah Khomeini, p. 1040
Rabin and Arafat Shake Hands at the White House,
    1993, p. 1049

((●─ Hear the Audio   *Decolonization 1, p. 1021*

●●─ Watch the Video   *Creating Apartheid in South Africa,*
p. 1034

✓●─ Study and Review   *Soviet and Turkish Plans for*
Industrialization, p. 1039
The Political Vision of Atatürk and Khomeini, p. 1041

Research and Explore

●●─ See the Map   *Latin America, 2004, p. 1031*

●●─ See the Map   *Map Discovery: Palestine*

((●─ **Hear** the **Audio**

Hear the audio file for Chapter 33 at
www.myhistorylab.com.

Glossary

absolutism. Term applied to strong centralized continental monarchies that attempted to make royal power dominant over aristocracies and other regional authorities.

Acropolis. The religious and civic center of Athens. It is the site of the Parthenon.

Afrikaans. The new language, derived from Dutch, that evolved in the seventeenth- and eighteenth-century Cape Colony.

Afro-Asiatic. A language family that includes Semitic languages, Kushitic, and others.

agape. Meaning "love feast." A common meal that was part of the central ritual of early Christian worship.

agora. The Greek marketplace and civic center. It was the heart of the social life of the polis.

agricultural revolution. The innovations in farm production that began in the eighteenth century and led to a scientific and mechanized agriculture.

Ahura Mazda. Supreme god in ancient Iranian religion, especially in the religious system of the Iranian prophet Zoroaster (7th century–6th century B.C.). Ahura Mazda was worshiped by the Persian king Darius I (reigned 522 B.C.–486 B.C.) and his successors as the greatest of all gods and protector of the just king.

Aksum. A powerful Christianized trading state in the Ethiopian highlands.

Al-Andalus. The Arabic name given to those parts of the Iberian Peninsula governed by Muslims, or Moors, at various times between 711 and 1492.

amir/emir. An Islamic military commander.

Amitabha Buddha. The Buddhist Lord of the Western Paradise, or Pure Land.

Annam. The name given by the Chinese to modern-day Vietnam, meaning "peaceful" or "pacified South."

Anschluss. Meaning "union." The annexation of Austria by Germany in March 1938.

anti-Semitism. Prejudice, hostility, or legal discrimination against Jews.

apartheid. "Apartness," the term referring to racist policies enforced by the white-dominated regime that existed in South Africa from 1948 to 1992.

apostolic primacy. The doctrine that the popes are the direct successors to the Apostle Peter and as such are heads of the church.

appeasement. The Anglo-French policy of making concessions to Germany in the 1930s to avoid a crisis that would lead to war. It assumed that Germany had real grievances and Hitler's aims were limited and ultimately acceptable.

Areopagus. The governing council of Athens, originally open only to the nobility. It was named after the hill on which it met.

Arianism. The belief formulated by Arius of Alexandria (ca. 280–336 CE.) that Jesus was a created being, neither fully man nor fully God, but something in between.

aristocratic resurgence. Eighteenth-century aristocratic efforts to resist the expanding power of European monarchies.

Article 9 of the No-War Constitution. Article 9 of the Japanese Constitution not only forbids the use of force as a means to settling international disputes but also forbids Japan from maintaining an army, navy, or air force.

Aryans. The Indo-European speakers who invaded India and Iran in the second and first millennia B.C.E.

assignats. Government bonds based on the value of confiscated church lands issued during the early French Revolution.

Atman-Brahman. The unity of the Self (Atman) and the Infinite/Reality/Being/Universal (Brahman) in Indian religious thought.

Atomists. School of ancient Greek philosophy founded in the fifth century B.CE. by Leucippus of Miletus and Democritus of Abdera. It held that the world consists of innumerable, tiny, solid, indivisible, and unchangeable particles called atoms.

Augustus. The title given to Octavian in 27 B.CE. and borne thereafter by all Roman emperors.

Ausgleich. Meaning "compromise." The agreement between the Habsburg emperor and the Hungarians to give Hungary considerable administrative autonomy in 1867. It created the Dual Monarchy, or Austria-Hungary.

Austronesian. A widely dispersed language family with origins in the Pacific. Malagasy, spoken in Madagascar, is an Austronesian language.

Axis. The alliance between Nazi Germany and fascist Italy. Also called the Pact of Steel.

ayan. Ottoman notables.

ayatollah. A major Shi'ite religious leader.

Bakufu. "Tent government." The military regime that governed Japan under the shōguns.

Bantu. A large subgroup of the Niger-Congo language family; also, the people who speak Bantu languages.

bazaari. The Iranian commercial middle class.

bhakti. Hindu devotional movements.

bishop. Originally a person elected by early Christian congregations to lead them in worship and supervise their funds. In time, bishops became the religious and even political authorities for Christian communities within large geographical areas.

Black Death. The bubonic plague that killed millions of Europeans in the fourteenth century.

Black Legend. The argument that Spanish treatment of Native Americans was uniquely inhumane.

blitzkrieg. Meaning "lightning war." The German tactic early in World War II of employing fast-moving, massed armored columns supported by airpower to overwhelm the enemy.

bodhisattva. A "Buddha to be" who postpones his own nirvana until he has helped all other beings become enlightened.

Bolsheviks. Meaning the "majority." Term Lenin applied to his faction of the Russian Social Democratic Party. It became the Communist Party of the Soviet Union after the Russian Revolution.

Boxers. A nationalistic Chinese religious society that attacked foreigners and their encroachments on China in the late nineteenth century.

boyars. The Russian nobility.

Brahmanas. Texts dealing with the ritual application of the Vedas.

Bronze Age. The name given to the earliest civilized era, ca. 4000 to 1000 B.CE. The term reflects the importance of the metal bronze, a mixture of tin and copper, for the peoples of this age for use as weapons and tools.

caliphate. The true line of succession to Muhammad.

calpulli. The wards into which the Aztec capital, Tenochtitlán, was divided.

cantonments. The segregation of areas in which Europeans lived in British-ruled India from those areas inhabited by native Indians.

Cataract. A waterfall or steep rapids. Major cataracts on the Nile River are numbered.

Catholic. Meaning "universal." The body of belief held by most Christians enshrined within the church.

Catholic Emancipation. The grant of full political rights to Roman Catholics in Britain in 1829.

caudillo. Latin American strongman, or dictator, usually with strong ties to the military.

censor. Official of the Roman republic charged with conducting the census and compiling the lists of citizens and members of the Senate.

Censorate. The branch of the imperial Chinese government that acted as a watchdog, reporting instances of misgovernment directly to the emperor and remonstrating when it considered the emperor's behavior improper.

Chartism. The first large-scale European working-class political movement. It sought political reforms that would favor the interests of skilled British workers in the 1830s and 1840s.

chattel slavery. A form of slavery in which humans are owned as goods; the slave has no legal standing as a person and few, if any, rights.

chiaroscuro. The use of shading to enhance naturalness in painting and drawing.

chicha. A maize beer brewed by the *mamakuna* for the Inca elite.

civilization. A form of human culture marked by urbanism, metallurgy, and writing.

clash of civilizations. Political theory, most often identified with Harvard political scientist Samuel P. Huntington, which contends that conflict between the world's religiocultural traditions or "civilizations" increasingly dominates world affairs.

Cold War. The ideological and geographical struggle between the United States and its allies and the USSR and its allies that began after World War II and lasted until the dissolution of the USSR in 1989.

collectivization. The bedrock of Stalinist agriculture, which forced Russian peasants to give up their private farms and work as members of collectives, large agricultural units controlled by the state.

Columbian Exchange. Biological exchange of plants, animals, and diseases between the Americas and the rest of the world.

conquistadores. Meaning "conquerors." The Spanish conquerors of the New World.

Consulate. French government dominated by Napoleon from 1799 to 1804.

Convention. French radical legislative body from 1792 to 1794.

corvée. A French labor tax requiring peasants to work on roads, bridges, and canals.

Counter-Reformation. The sixteenth-century reform movement in the Roman Catholic Church in reaction to the Protestant Reformation.

Creoles. Persons of European descent who were born in the Spanish colonies.

Crusades. Religious wars directed by the church against infidels and heretics.

Cultural Revolution. A movement launched by Mao between 1965 and 1976 against the Soviet-style bureaucracy that had taken hold in China. It involved widespread disorder and violence.

culture. The ways of living built up by a group and passed on from one generation to another.

cuneiform. A writing system invented by the Sumerians that used a wedge-shaped stylus, or pointed tool, to write on wet clay tablets that were then baked or dried (*cuneus* means "wedge" in Latin). The writing was also cut into stone.

Curia. The papal government.

daimyo. Meaning "great name," these men were the most powerful feudal leaders in Japan from the tenth to the nineteenth century.

Daoism. A Chinese philosophy that teaches that wisdom lies in becoming one with the Tao, the "way," which is the creative principle of the universe.

dar-al-Islam. In Arabic, the "House of Submission," or Islamic world. There are many shades of meaning, ranging from a place where the government is under Muslim control to a place where individuals are free to practice Islamic beliefs.

debt peonage. A system that forces agricultural laborers (peons) to work and live on large estates (*haciendas*) until they have repaid their debts to the estate's owner.

Deccan. Large plateau with varying terrain that constitutes most of south central India.

deism. A belief in a rational God who had created the universe, but then allowed it to function without his interference according to the mechanisms of nature and a belief in rewards and punishments after death for human action.

Delian League. An alliance of Greek states under the leadership of Athens that was formed in 478–477 B.CE. to resist the Persians.

demesne. The part of a manor that was cultivated directly for the lord of the manor.

dependency theory. Theory that contends that after the states of Latin America achieved independence in the early to mid-nineteenth century, they remained economically and culturally dependent on Europe and later the United States.

devshirme. The system under the Ottoman Empire that required each province to furnish a levy of Christian boys who were raised as Muslims and became soldiers in the Ottoman army.

dharma. Moral law or duty.

Diet. The bicameral Japanese Parliament.

Diet of Worms. The meeting of the representative (diet) of the Holy Roman Empire presided over by the Emperor Charles V at the German city of Worms in 1521 at which Martin Luther was ordered to recant his ninety-five theses. Luther refused and was declared outlaw, although he was protected by the Elector of Saxony and other German princes.

diffusion. The spread of ideas, objects, or traits from one culture to another.

divine right of kings. The theory that monarchs are appointed by and answerable only to God.

Diwan. Arabic and Persian word used variously in Islamic contexts to mean (1) a book/collection of poetry; (2) in early Islam, the name-register of Muslims who had fought for Islam and were thus eligible to receive shares of booty; (3 a government department/office/ministry/high official.

domestic or putting-out system of textile production. Method of producing textiles in which agents furnished raw materials to households whose members spun them into thread and then wove cloth, which the agents then sold as finished products.

Duce. Meaning "leader." Mussolini's title as head of the Fascist Party.

Duma. The Russian Parliament, after the revolution of 1905.

dynastic cycle. The term used to describe the rise, decline, and fall of China's imperial dynasties.

ego. According to Freudian theory, the part of the mind that mediates between the impulses of the id and the asceticism of the superego and allows the personality to cope with the inner and outer demands of its existence.

empiricism. The use of experiment and observation derived from sensory evidence to construct scientific theory or philosophy of knowledge.

enclosures. The consolidation or fencing in of common lands by British landlords to increase production and achieve greater commercial profits. It also involved the reclamation of waste land and the consolidation of strips into block fields.

encomienda. The grant by the Spanish Crown to a colonist of the labor of a specific number of Indians for a set period of time.

Enlightenment. The eighteenth-century movement led by the *philosophes* that held that change and reform were both desirable through the application of reason and science.

Epicureans. School of philosophy founded by Epicurus of Athens (342–271 B.CE.). It sought to liberate people from fear of death and the supernatural by teaching that the gods took no interest in human affairs and that true happiness consisted in pleasure, which was defined as the absence of pain.

equestrians. Literally "cavalrymen" or "knights." In the earliest years of the Roman Republic, those who could afford to serve as mounted warriors.

Estado Novo. The "new state" based on political stability and economic and social progress supposedly established by the dictator Getulio Vargas after 1937.

Etruscans. A people of central Italy who exerted the most powerful external influence on the early Romans.

Eucharist. Meaning "thanksgiving." The celebration of the Lord's Supper. Considered the central ritual of worship by most Christians. Also called Holy Communion.

euro. The common currency created by the EEC in the late 1990s.

European Economic Community (EEC). The economic association formed by France, Germany, Italy, Belgium, the Netherlands, and Luxembourg in 1957. Also known as the Common Market.

European Union. The new name given to the EEC in 1993. It included most of the states of western Europe.

Fabians. British socialists in the late nineteenth and early twentieth centuries who sought to achieve socialism through gradual, peaceful, and democratic means.

family economy. The basic structure of production and consumption in preindustrial Europe.

fascism. Political movements that tend to be antidemocratic, anti-Marxist, antiparliamentary, and often anti-Semitic. Fascists were invariably nationalists and exhalted the nation over the individual. They supported the interests of the middle class and rejected the ideas of the French Revolution and nineteenth-century liberalism. The first Fascist regime was founded by Benito Mussolini (1883–1945) in Italy in the 1920s.

fealty. An oath of loyalty by a vassal to a lord, promising to perform specified services.

feudal society. The social, political, military, and economic system that prevailed in the Middle Ages and beyond in some parts of Europe.

fief. Land granted to a vassal in exchange for services, usually military.

Fourteen Points. President Woodrow Wilson's (1856–1924) idealistic war aims.

Führer. Meaning "leader." The title taken by Hitler when he became dictator of Germany.

gentry. In China, a largely urban, landowning class that represented local interests and functioned as quasi-bureaucrats under the magistrates.

ghazis. Warriors who carried Islam by force of arms to pagan groups.

ghettos. Separate communities in which Jews were required by law to live.

glasnost. Meaning "openness." The policy initiated by Mikhail Gorbachev in the 1980s of permitting open criticism of the policies of the Soviet Communist Party.

globalization. Term used to describe the increasing economic and cultural interdependence of societies around the world.

Glorious Revolution. The largely peaceful replacement of James II by William and Mary as English monarchs in 1688. It marked the beginning of constitutional monarchy in Britain.

Golden Horde. Name given to the Mongol rulers of Russia from 1240 to 1480.

Grand Mufti. The chief religious authority of the Ottoman Empire. Also called "the Shaykh of Islam."

Great Depression. A prolonged worldwide economic downturn that began in 1929 with the collapse of the New York Stock Exchange.

Great Leap Forward. Mao's disastrous attempt to modernize the Chinese economy in 1958.

Great Purges. The imprisonment and execution of millions of Soviet citizens by Stalin between 1934 and 1939.

Great Reform Bill (1832). A limited reform of the British House of Commons and an expansion of the electorate to include a wider variety of the propertied classes. It laid the groundwork for further orderly reforms within the British constitutional system.

Great Schism. The appearance of two and at times three rival popes between 1378 and 1415.

Great Trek. The migration between 1835 and 1847 of Boer pioneers (called *voortrekkers*) north from British-ruled Cape Colony to establish their own independent republics.

guild. An association of merchants or craftsmen that offered protection to its members and set rules for their work and products.

Guomingdang (GMD). China's Nationalist Party, founded by Sun Yat-sen.

hacienda. Large landed estates in Spanish America.

hadith. A report of a saying or action ascribed to Muhammad.

Hajj. The pilgrimage to Mecca that all Muslims are enjoined to perform at least once in their lifetime.

Harappan. Term used to describe the first civilization of the Indus Valley.

harem. The wives, concubines, female relatives, and servants in a Muslim household—usually confined to a section of a house or palace.

Hegira. The flight of Muhammad and his followers from Mecca to Medina in 622 CE. It marks the beginning of the Islamic calendar.

heliocentric theory. The theory, now universally accepted, that the earth and the other planets revolve around the sun. First proposed by Aristarchos of Samos (310–230 B.CE.).

Helots. Hereditary Spartan serfs.

heretics. People who publicly dissent from officially accepted dogma.

hieroglyphics. The complicated writing script of ancient Egypt. It combined picture writing with pictographs and sound signs. Hieroglyph means "sacred carvings" in Greek.

Hindu. Term applied to wide range of Indian religious communities or individuals who recognize the authority of the Vedas.

HIV/AIDS. Collection of symptoms and infections resulting from the specific damage to the immune system caused by the human immunodeficiency virus (HIV) in humans, and similar viruses in other species (SIV, FIV, etc.). The late stage of the condition leaves individuals susceptible to opportunistic infections and tumors. Although treatments for AIDS and HIV exist to decelerate the virus's progression, there is currently no known cure.

Holocaust. The Nazi extermination of millions of European Jews between 1940 and 1945. Also called the "final solution to the Jewish problem."

Holy Roman Empire. The revival of the old Roman Empire, based mainly in Germany and northern Italy, that endured from 870 to 1806.

home rule. The advocacy of a large measure of administrative autonomy for Ireland within the British Empire between the 1880s and 1914.

hoplite phalanx. The basic unit of Greek warfare in which infantrymen fought in close order, shield to shield, usually eight ranks deep.

Huguenots. French Calvinists.

humanism. The study of the Latin and Greek classics and of the Church Fathers both for their own sake and to promote a rebirth of ancient norms and values.

humanitas. The Roman name for a liberal arts education.

id. According to Freudian psychoanalysis, the part of the mind that consists of amoral, irrational, driving instincts for sexual gratification, aggression, and physical and sensual pleasure.

The *Iliad* and the *Odyssey*. The epic poems by Homer about the "Dark Age" heroes of Greece who fought at Troy. The poems were written down in the eighth century B.CE. after centuries of being sung by bards.

Il-khans. One of the four khananats within the Mongol Empire, comprising largely what is modern-day Iran.

imam. Islamic prayer leader.

impact of modernity. The effect of Western political, economic, and social ideas and institutions on traditional societies.

imperator. Under the Roman Republic, it was the title given to a victorious general. Under Augustus and his successors, it became the title of the ruler of Rome, meaning "emperor."

import substitution. The replacement of imported goods with those manufactured domestically.

Indirect Rule. The British practice of administering African colonies through indigenous political structures and leaders.

Indo-European. A widely distributed language group that includes most of the languages spoken in Europe, Persian, Sanskrit, and their derivatives.

Indo-Greeks. Bactrian rulers who broke away from the Seleucid Empire to found a state that combined elements of Greek and Indian civilizations.

indulgences. Remission of the temporal penalty of punishment in purgatory that remained after sins had been forgiven.

industrial revolution. Mechanization of the European economy that began in Britain in the second half of the eighteenth century.

intifadah. Literally, "shaking." Uprisings by the Palestinians against Israeli occupation.

Islam. Meaning "submission." The religion founded by the Prophet Muhammad.

Islamic fundamentalism. A misnomer widely used for any movement among Muslims to return to the "fundamentals" of Islamic faith, life, and society.

Italia Irredenta. Meaning "unredeemed Italy." Italian-speaking areas that had been left under Austrian rule at the time of the unification of Italy.

Jacobins. The radical republican party during the French Revolution that displaced the Girondins.

Jains. An Indian religious community that teaches compassion for all beings.

Janissaries. Elite Ottoman troops who were recruited through the ***devshirme***.

jatis. The many subgroups that make up the Hindu caste system.

jihad. "Struggle in the path of God." Although not necessarily implying violence, it is often interpreted to mean holy war in the name of Islam.

July Monarchy. The French regime set up after the overthrow of the Bourbons in July 1830.

Junkers. The noble landlords of Prussia.

junzi. The Confucian term for a person who behaves ethically, in harmony with the cosmic order.

Ka'ba. A black meteorite in the city of Mecca that became Islam's holiest shrine.

Kabuki. A realistic form of Japanese theater similar to English Elizabethan drama.

Kalahari. A large desert in southwestern Africa that partially isolates southern Africa from the rest of the continent.

kamikaze. "Divine winds" that sank a portion of the invading Mongol fleet in Japan in 1281.

karma. The Indian belief that every action has an inevitable effect. Good deeds bring good results; evil deeds have evil consequences.

Khmer Rouge. Meaning "Red Cambodia." The radical communist movement that ruled Cambodia from 1975 to 1978.

Khoisan. The language group spoken by the Khoikhoi, the San, and other peoples; also, the Khoikhoi and San peoples.

kleindeutsch. Meaning "small German." The argument that the German-speaking portions of the Habsburg Empire should be excluded from a united Germany.

Kristallnacht. Meaning "crystal night" because of the broken glass that littered German streets after the looting and destruction of Jewish homes, businesses, and synagogues across Germany on the orders of the Nazi Party in November 1938.

Kush. An ancient Nubian kingdom that in some periods dominated, and in others was dominated by, pharaonic Egypt.

La Reforma. The nineteenth-century Mexican liberal reform movement that opposed Santa Ana's dictatorship and sought to foster economic progress, civilian rule, and political stability. It was strongly anticlerical.

laissez-faire. French phrase meaning "allow to do." In economics, the doctrine of minimal government interference in the working of the economy.

latifundia. Large plantations for growing cash crops owned by wealthy Romans.

LDP. The Liberal Democratic Party. A conservative party that has dominated postwar Japanese politics.

League of Nations. The association of sovereign states set up after World War I to pursue common policies and avert international aggression.

Lebensraum. Meaning "living space," the Nazi plan to colonize and exploit Eastern Europe.

Legalism. The Chinese philosophical school that argued that a strong state was necessary in order to have a good society.

levée en masse. The French revolutionary conscription (1792) of all males into the army and the harnessing of the economy for war production.

liberalism. In the nineteenth century, support for representative government dominated by the propertied classes and minimal government interference in the economy.

liberation theology. The effort by certain Roman Catholic theologians to combine Marxism with traditional Christian concern for the poor.

Logos. Divine reason, or fire, which according to the Stoics, was the guiding principle in nature.

Long Count. A Mayan calendar that dated from a fixed point in the past.

Long March. The flight of the Chinese communists from their Nationalist foes to northwest China in 1934.

Luftwaffe. The German air force in World War II.

madrasa. An Islamic college of higher learning.

Maghreb. Literally, in Arabic, "place of sunset," or the west; refers to the northwest of Africa, and specifically what is now Morocco.

magi. A tribe from ancient Media, who, prior to the conquest of the Medes by the Achaemenid Empire in 550 B.C., were responsible for religious and funerary practices. The best known magi were the "Wise Men from the East" in the Bible.

Magna Carta. The "Great Charter" limiting royal power that the English nobility forced King John to sign in 1215.

Magna Graecia. Meaning "Great Greece" in Latin, it was the name given by the Romans to southern Italy and Sicily because there were so many Greek colonies in the region.

Magyars. The majority ethnic group in Hungary.

Mahabharata and Ramayana. The two classical Indian epics.

Mahayana. The "Great Vehicle" for salvation in Buddhism. It emphasized the Buddha's infinite compassion for all beings.

mamluk. Slave soldiers who converted to Islam, the mamluks eventually became a powerful military caste and even governed Egypt from 1250 to 1517.

manakuna. Inca women who lived privileged but celibate lives and had important economic and cultural roles.

Mandate of Heaven. The Chinese belief that Heaven entrusts or withdraws a ruler's or a dynasty's right to govern.

Manichaeism. A major dualistic ("good vs. evil") religious tradition that began in the third century C.E. with the teaching of the Persian prophet Mani (born in Babylonia, d. 276 C.E.).

Mannerism. A style of art in the mid- to late sixteenth century that permitted artists to express their own "manner" or feelings in contrast to the symmetry and simplicity of the art of the High Renaissance.

manor. Village farms owned by a lord.

mansa. Malian emperor, from Mandinka word meaning "king of kings."

marabout. In Sunni Islam as practiced in West Africa, a marabout is a spiritual leader, versed in the Koran, who often guides the personal lives of his followers.

Marshall Plan. The U.S. program, named after Secretary of State George C. Marshall, that provided economic aid to Europe after World War II.

Marxism. The theory of Karl Marx (1818–1883) and Friedrich Engels (1820–1895) that history is the result of class conflict, which will end in the inevitable triumph of the industrial proletariat over the bourgeoisie and the abolition of private property and social class.

Mau Mau. An uprising that began among the Kikuyu of the Kenya highlands and lasted through the 1950s. The British referred to it as the "Kenya Emergency."

Meiji Restoration. The overthrow of the Tokugawa *bakufu* in Japan in 1868 and the transfer, or "restoration," of power to the imperial government under the Emperor Meiji.

Mein Kampf. Meaning "My Struggle." Hitler's statement of his political program, published in 1924.

Mensheviks. Meaning the "minority." Term Lenin applied to the majority moderate faction of the Russian Social Democratic Party opposed to him and the Bolsheviks.

mercantilism. Term used to describe close government control of the economy that sought to maximize exports and accumulate as much precious metals as possible to enable the state to defend its economic and political interests.

Meroe. The capital city of the ancient Napatan Empire, which at one time rivaled Aksum.

Mesoamerica. The part of North America that extends from the central part of modern Mexico to Central America.

Mesopotamia. Modern Iraq. The land between the Tigris and Euphrates rivers where the first civilization appeared around 3000 B.CE.

Messiah. The redeemer whose coming Jews believed would establish the kingdom of God on earth. Christians considered Jesus to be the Messiah (Christ means Messiah in Greek).

mestizos. Persons of mixed Native American and European descent.

Mexica. The Aztecs name for themselves.

mfecane. A period of widespread warfare and chaos among Bantu peoples in east-central Africa during the early nineteenth century.

Middle Passage. The transatlantic crossing of ships carrying slaves from Africa to the Americas and Caribbean.

millets. Within the Ottoman Empire, ethnic communities that administered their own educational, charitable, and judicial affairs.

Minoan. The Bronze Age civilization that arose in Crete in the third and second millennia B.CE.

mita. The Inca system of forced labor in return for gifts and ritual entertainments.

Mitimaqs. Communities whom the Incas forced to settle in designated regions for strategic purposes.

mobilization. The placing of a country's military forces on a war footing.

Monophysite. Adhering to the dogma of the single, unitary nature of Christ (in opposition to the orthodox doctrine that Christ had two natures: human and divine).

Monotheism. The worship of one universal God.

Moors. The Spanish and Portuguese term for Muslims.

muezzin. The leader of a mosque's call to prayers.

Mughals. Descendants of the Mongols who established an Islamic empire in India in the sixteenth century with its capital at Delhi.

mujtahid. A Muslim religious scholar qualified to give legal interpretations.

mulattos. Persons of mixed African and European descent.

Mycenaean. The Bronze Age civilization of mainland Greece that was centered at Mycenae.

mystery religions. The cults of Isis, Mithras, and Osiris, which promised salvation to those initiated into the secret or "mystery" of their rites.

nacionalismo. A right-wing Argentine nationalist movement that arose in the 1930s and resembled European fascism.

nationalism. The belief that one is part of a nation, defined as a community with its own language, traditions, customs, and history that distinguish it from other nations and make it the primary focus of a person's loyalty and sense of identity.

National Studies. A Japanese intellectual tradition that emphasized native Japanese culture and institutions and rejected the influence of Chinese Confucianism.

natural selection. According to Darwin, the process in nature by which only the organisms best adapted to their environment tend to survive and transmit their genes, while those less adapted tend to be eliminated.

Nazis. The German Nationalist Socialist Party.

neocolonial economy. An economic relationship between a former colonial state and countries with more developed economies in which the former colony exports raw materials to and imports manufactured goods from the more developed nations.

Negritude. A movement begun among African students in 1930s Paris to celebrate African culture and thought.

Neo-Daoism. A revival of Daoist "mysterious learning" that flourished as a reaction against Confucianism during the Han Dynasty.

Neolithic Revolution. The shift beginning 10,000 years ago from hunter-gatherer societies to settled communities of farmers and artisans. Also called the Age of Agriculture, it witnessed the invention of farming, the domestication of plants and animals, and the develop-

ment of technologies such as pottery and weaving. "Neolithic" comes from the Greek words for "new stone."

New Economic Policy (NEP). A limited revival of capitalism, especially in light industry and agriculture, introduced by Lenin in 1921 to repair the damage inflicted on the Russian economy by the civil war and War Communism.

New Imperialism. The extension in the late nineteenth and early twentieth centuries of Western political and economic dominance to Asia, the Middle East, and Africa.

Nicene Creed. A statement of Christian belief, formulated by the council of Christian bishops at Nicaea in 324 CE., that rejected Arianism in favor of the doctrine that Christ is both fully human and fully divine.

Niger-Kongo. A language family that originated in the savannah and woodlands of west and south-central Africa.

Nilo-Saharan. A language family concentrated in the band between the Nile and Rift highlands of Morocco.

Nilotic Africa. The lands along the Nile River.

ninety-five theses. Document posted on the door of Castle Church in Wittenberg, Germany, on October 31, 1517, by Martin Luther protesting, among other things, the selling of indulgences.

Nirvana. Buddhist term for cessation of cause-and-effect (*karmic*) existence in the world of *Samsara.*

Nok. A west African Iron Age culture renowned for its artistry.

Nō play. A highly stylized form of Japanese drama in which the chorus provides the narrative line as in classical Greek plays.

oba. Title of the king of Benin.

obsidian. A hard volcanic glass that was widely used in Mesoamerica.

Occidental slave trade. The trade in slaves from Africa to the Islamic Mediterranean and Asia that predated the transatlantic slave trade.

occupied territories. Land occupied by Israel as a result of wars with its Arab neighbors in 1948–1949, 1967, and 1973.

Old Regime. Term applied to the pattern of social, political, and economic relationships and institutions that existed in Europe before the French Revolution.

orthodox. Meaning "holding the right opinions." Applied to the doctrines of the Catholic Church.

Ottoman Empire. The imperial Turkish state centered in Constantinople that ruled large parts of the Balkans, North Africa, and the Middle East until 1918.

padishah. Meaning "emperor." One of the titles of the Ottoman monarchs.

Paleolithic Age. The earliest period when stone tools were used, from about 1,000,000 to 10,000 B.CE. From the Greek meaning "old stone."

Pampas. The fertile South American lowlands that include the Argentine provinces of Buenos Aires, La Pampa, Santa Fe, and Córdoba, most of Uruguay, and the southernmost end of Brazil, Rio Grande do Sul, covering more than 750,000 km^2 (289,577 sq mi).

Panhellenic ("all-Greek"). The sense of cultural identity that all Greeks felt in common with each other.

pan-Islamism. The movement that advocates that the entire Muslim world should form a unified political and cultural entity.

Pan-Slavic movement. The movement to create a nation or federation that would embrace all the Slavic peoples of eastern Europe.

Papal States. Territory in central Italy ruled by the pope until 1870.

parlement. French regional court dominated by hereditary nobility. The most important was the Parlement of Paris, which claimed the right to register royal decrees before they could become law.

parliamentary monarchy. A state headed by a monarch but whose power is shared with a national representative body.

pastoralists. People whose way of life centers on the raising and herding of livestock; nomads.

patricians. The hereditary upper class of early Republican Rome.

peace process. Efforts, chiefly by the United States, to broker a peace between the State of Israel and the PLO.

Peloponnesian Wars. The protracted struggle between Athens and Sparta to dominate Greece between 465 and Athens' final defeat in 404 B.CE.

peninsulares. Native-born Spaniards who emigrated from Spain to settle in the Spanish colonies.

perestroika. Meaning "restructuring." The attempt in the 1980s to reform the Soviet government and economy.

Peronism. An authoritarian, nationalist movement founded in Argentina in the 1940s by the dictator Juan Perón.

pharaoh. The god-kings of ancient Egypt. The term originally meant "great house" or palace.

Pharisees. The group that was most strict in its adherence to Jewish law.

philosophes. The eighteenth-century writers and critics who forged the new attitudes favorable to change. They sought to apply reason and common sense to the institutions and societies of their day.

Phoenicians. The ancient inhabitants of modern Lebanon. A trading people, they established colonies throughout the Mediterranean.

pipiltin. Aztec bureaucrats and priests.

pirs. pir. Muslim holy man/spiritual master in sufi traditions.

plantation economy. The economic system stretching between Chesapeake Bay and Brazil that produced crops, especially sugar, cotton, and tobacco, using slave labor on large estates.

plebeians. The hereditary lower class of early Republican Rome.

plenitude of power. The teaching that the popes have power over all other bishops of the church.

pochteca. Aztec merchants.

pogroms. Organized riots against Jews in the Russian Empire.

polis. The basic Greek political unit. Usually, but incompletely, translated as "city-state," the Greeks thought of the *polis* as a community of citizens theoretically descended from a common ancestor.

political Islamism. Political movement that seeks to return to the fundamentals of Islamic life through rejuvenation of Muslim faith and society and the rejection of Western, materialist, and secularist values and norms.

polytheism. The worship of many gods.

Popular Front. A government of all left-wing parties that took power in France in 1936 to enact social and economic reforms.

populares. Roman politicians who sought to pursue a political career based on the support of the people rather than just the aristocracy.

positivism. The philosophy of Auguste Comte that science is the final, or positive, stage of human intellectual development because it involves exact descriptions of phenomena, without recourse to unobservable operative principles, such as gods or spirits.

Pragmatic Sanction. The legal basis negotiated by the Emperor Charles VI (r. 1711–1740) for the Habsburg succession through his daughter Maria Theresa (r. 1740–1780).

prazeros. Portuguese and mixed-race owners of large estates in the Zambezi Valley.

PRI. The Institutional Revolutionary Party, which emerged from the Mexican revolution of 1911 and governed Mexico until the end of the twentieth century.

Proletarianization. The process whereby independent artisans and factory workers lose control of the means of production and of the conduct of their own trades to the owners of capital.

Protectorate. A variation on colonial rule in which, at least in theory, exerts local authority over domestic issues.

Ptolemaic system. The pre-Copernican explanation of the universe, which placed the Earth at the center of the universe.

Punic Wars. Three wars between Rome and Carthage for dominance of the western Mediterranean that were fought from 264 B.CE. to 146 B.CE.

Pure Land Buddhism. A variety of Japanese Buddhism that maintains that only faith is necessary for salvation.

puritans. English Protestants who sought to "purify" the Church of England of any vestiges of Catholicism.

Qanun. Ottoman administrative law.

qasida. An Arabic poetic ode of praise, elegy, typically 60-100 lines, with a single end rhyme. Also used in other Islamic languages (Persian, Urdu, etc.).

Quechua. The Inca language.

quipu. Knotted string used by Andean peoples for record-keeping.

Qur'an. Meaning "a reciting." The Islamic scripture, which Muslims believe God revealed to the Prophet Muhammad.

racism. The pseudoscientific theory that biological features of race determine human character and worth.

raj. The years from 1858 to 1947 during which India was governed directly by the British Crown.

raja. An Indian king.

Ramadan. The month each year when Muslims must fast during daylight hours.

Reconquista. The Christian reconquest of Spain from the Muslims from 1000 to 1492.

Reformation. The sixteenth-century religious movement that sought to reform the Roman Catholic Church and led to the establishment of Protestantism.

regular clergy. Monks and nuns who belong to religious orders.

Reichstag. The German Parliament, which existed in various forms until 1945.

Reign of Terror. The period between the summer of 1793 and the end of July 1794 when the French revolutionary state used extensive executions and violence to defend the Revolution and suppress its alleged internal enemies.

relativity. Theory of physics, first expounded by Albert Einstein in 1905, in which time and space exist not separately, but rather as a combined continuum.

Renaissance. The revival of ancient learning and the supplanting of traditional religious beliefs by new secular and scientific values that began in Italy in the fourteenth and fifteenth centuries.

reparations. The requirement incorporated into the Versailles Treaty that Germany should pay for the cost of World War I.

repartimiento. A labor tax in Spanish America that required adult male Native Americans to devote a set number of days a year to Spanish economic enterprises.

revisionism. The advocacy among nineteenth-century German socialists of achieving a humane socialist society through the evolution of democratic institutions, not revolution.

SA. The Nazi parliamentary forces, or stormtroopers.

Sahara. The world's largest desert. It extends across Africa from the Atlantic to the eastern Sudan. Historically, the Sahara has hindered contact between the Mediterranean and sub-Saharan Africa.

Sahel. An area of steppe and semidesert that borders the Sahara.

samsara. The endless cycle of existence, of birth and rebirth.

samurai. Warrior class during Japan's feudal period.

Sandinistas. The Marxist guerrilla force that overthrew the Somoza dictatorship in Nicaragua in 1979.

sans-culottes. Meaning "without breeches." The lower-middle classes and artisans of Paris during the French Revolution.

satraps. Governors of provinces in the Persian Empire.

savannah. An area of open woodlands and grassy plains.

Schlieffen Plan. Germany's plan for achieving a quick victory in the West at the outbreak of World War I by invading France through Belgium and Luxembourg.

Scholasticism. Method of study based on logic and dialectic that dominated the medieval schools. It assumed that truth already existed; students had only to organize, elucidate, and defend knowledge learned from authoritative texts, especially those of Aristotle and the Church Fathers.

Scientific Revolution. The sweeping change in the scientific view of the universe that occurred in the West in the sixteenth and seventeenth centuries.

scramble for Africa. The late nineteenth-century takeover of most of Africa by European powers.

secular clergy. Parish clergy who did not belong to a religious order.

serfs. Peasants tied to the land they tilled.

Shahanshah. "King of kings," the title of the Persian ruler.

Shari'a. Islamic religious law.

sharifs. A term for leaders who are direct descendants of the Prophet Muhammad through his first grandson, Hasan ibn Ali.

shaykh. Arabic word for a tribal elder or Islamic scholar; can also be rendered as sheikh, sheik, or sheikh.

Shi'a. The major minority tradition of Islamic faith and practice, which became the majority tradition of Iran from the 16th century.

Shintō. "The way of the gods." The animistic worship of the forces of nature that is indigenous to Japan.

Shōgun. A military official who was the actual ruler of Japan in the emperor's name from the late 1100s until the mid-nineteenth century.

Silk Road. Trade route from China to the West that stretched across Central Asia.

Sophists. Professional teachers who emerged in Greece in the mid-fifth century B.CE. who were paid to teach techniques of rhetoric, dialectic, and argumentation.

soviets. Workers' and soldiers' councils formed in Russia during the Russian Revolution.

spinning jenny. A machine invented in England by James Hargreaves around 1765 to mass-produce thread.

SS. The chief security units of the Nazi state.

Steppe peoples. Nomadic tribespeople who dwelled on the Eurasian plains from eastern Europe to the borders of China and Iran. They frequently traded with or invaded more settled cultures.

Stoics. A philosophical school founded by Zeno of Citium (335–263 B.CE.) that taught that humans could be happy only with natural law.

streltsy. Professional troops who made up the Moscow garrison. They were suppressed by Peter the Great.

studia humanitatis. During the Renaissance, a liberal arts program of study that embraced grammar, rhetoric, poetry, history, philosophy, and politics.

stupa. A Buddhist shrine.

Sudan. The broad band of Sahel and savannah that crosses the African continent south of the Sahara.

suffragettes. British women who lobbied and agitated for the right to vote in the early twentieth century.

Sufi. Sufism is a mystic tradition within Islam that encompasses a diverse range of beliefs and practices dedicated to Divine love and the cultivation of the elements of the Divine within the individual human being. The chief aim of all Sufis is to let go of all notions of duality, including a conception of an individual self, and to realize the Divine unity.

sultans. Rulers who have almost complete sovereignty over a certain domain without claiming the title of caliph.

Sunna. Arabic word meaning "tradition".

Sunni. designates the majority religious tradition of Islam, or a single member of same..

superego. According to Freud, the part of the mind that embodies the external moral imperatives and expectations imposed on the personality by society and culture.

Swahili. A language and culture that developed from the interaction of native Africans and Arabs along the East African coast.

symposion. The carefully organized drinking party that was the center of Greek aristocratic social life. It featured games, songs, poetry, and even philosophical disputation.

syncretism. Blending or fusion of different systems of religious or philosophical beliefs.

Table of Ranks. An official hierarchy established by Peter the Great in imperial Russia that equated a person's social position and privileges with his rank in the state bureaucracy or army.

taille. The direct tax on the French peasantry.

Taiping rebellion. A nineteenth-century revolt against China's Manchu Dynasty that was inspired by quasi-Christian ideas and that led to enormous suffering and destruction before its collapse in 1868.

Tanzimat. Reform movement that started in 1839 in an attempt to bring the Ottoman Empire into the modern era.

Tennō. "Heavenly emperor." The official title of the emperor of Japan.

tetcutin. Subordinate Aztec lords.

tetrarchy. Diocletian's (r. 306–337 CE.) system for ruling the Roman Empire by four men with power divided territorially.

theocracy. A state ruled by religious leaders who claim to govern by divine authority.

Theravada. "The Way of the Elders." A school of Buddhism that emphasizes the monastic ideal.

Thermidorean Reaction. The reaction against the radicalism of the French Revolution that began in July 1794. Associated with the end of terror and establishment of the Directory.

Third Estate. The branch of the French Estates General representing all of the kingdom outside the nobility and the clergy.

three-field system. A medieval innovation that increased the amount of land under cultivation by leaving only one-third fallow in a given year.

tlatoani. An Aztec ruler.

transubstantiation. The doctrine that the entire substances of the bread and wine are changed in the Eucharist into the body and blood of Christ.

treaty ports. Chinese ports ruled by foreign consuls where foreigners enjoyed commercial privileges and immunity from Chinese laws.

Trekboers. White livestock farmers in Cape Colony.

tribunes. Roman officials who had to be plebeians and were elected by the plebeian assembly to protect plebeians from the arbitrary power of the magistrates.

Tripartite Pact. The alliance between Japan and Nazi Germany and Fascist Italy that was signed in 1940.

trypanosomiasis. Sleeping sickness; a parasitic disease that is transmitted by tsetse flies. If untreated, it is fatal both to humans and animals.

ulama. "Persons with correct knowledge." The Islamic scholarly elite who served a social function similar to the Christian clergy.

Umma. The Islamic community.

"unequal treaties." Those imposed on China, Japan, and other countries during the mid-19th-century; they involved extra-territoriality.

Upanishads. Indian religious texts dating largely to first half of the first millennium B.C.E., which began as commentary or elaboration on the Vedas and came to offer profound philosophical discussions important to the later Hindu traditions of India. The word means "sitting down near [a teacher]".

Urdu-Hindi. A language that combines Persian-Arabic and native Indian elements. Urdu is the Muslim version of the language. Hindi is the Hindu version.

uzama. An order of hereditary chiefs in Benin.

varnas. The four main classes that form the basis for Hindu caste relations.

vassal. A person granted an estate or cash payments in return for accepting the obligation to render services to a lord.

Vedas. The sacred texts of the ancient Aryan invaders of India. The Rig Vedas are the oldest materials in the Vedas.

vernacular. The everyday language spoken by the people, as opposed to languages such as Latin, Arabic or English that are a classical, literary, or administrative tongue used by upper and/or ruling classes.

Viet Minh. The communist-dominated popular front organization formed by Ho Chi Minh to establish an independent Vietnamese republic.

Wahhabis. Followers of Ibn Abd al-Wahhab (1703–1792) who sought to combat the excesses of popular and Sufi piety in Islam and looked to the Qur'an and the traditions of the Prophet as the sole authoritative guidance in religion.

War Communism. The economic policy adopted by the Bolsheviks during the Russian Civil War to seize the banks, heavy industry, railroads, and grain.

war guilt clause. Clause of the Versailles Treaty, which assigned responsibility for World War I solely to Germany.

water frame. A water-powered device invented by Richard Arkwright to produce a more durable cotton fabric. It led to the shift in the production of cotton textiles from households to factories.

Weimar Republic. The German democratic regime that existed between the end of World War I and Hitler's coming to power in 1933.

White Russians. Those Russians who opposed the Bolsheviks (the "Reds") in the Russian civil war of 1918–1921.

Works Progress Administration (WPA). New Deal program created by the Roosevelt administration in 1935 that provided relief for the unemployed in the industrial sector during the Great Depression in the United States.

yangban. Elite Korean families of the Choson period.

zaibatsu. Large industrial combines that came to dominate Japanese industry in the late nineteenth century.

Zen. A form of Buddhism, which taught that Buddha was only a man and exhorted each person to attain enlightenment by his or her own efforts.

Zionism. The movement to create a Jewish state in Palestine (the biblical Zion).

Zoroastrianism. A quasi-monotheistic Iranian religion founded by Zoroaster (ca. 628–551 B.CE.), who preached a message of moral reform and exhorted his followers to worship only Ahura Mazda, the Wise Lord.

Suggested Readings

Chapter 1

General Prehistory

P. Bogucki, The Origins of Human Society (1999). An excellent summary of recent scholarship on the earliest origins of human societies.

F. Bray, The Rice Economies: Technology and Development in Asian Societies (1986). Still the best authority on the origins of rice cultivation and its effect on the development of ancient Asia.

M. Ehrenberg, Women in Prehistory (1989). An account of the role of women in early times.

C. Freeman, Egypt, Greece and Rome: Civilizations of the Ancient Mediterranean (2004). Good comparative study of Egypt with Greece and Rome.

D.C. Johnson and M.R. Edey, Lucy: The Beginning of Mankind (1981). An account of the African origins of humans.

S.M. Nelson, ed., Ancient Queens: Archaeological Explorations (2003). Reassesses women rulers and female power in the ancient world.

S.M. Nelson and M. Rosen-Ayalon, In Pursuit of Gender: World-wide Archaeological Approaches (2002). Essays on gender and the archaeology of the ancient world.

D.L. Nichols and T.H. Charlton, eds., The Archaeology of City-States: Cross-cultural Approaches (1997). One of a growing body of books and essay collections employing cross-cultural and comparative approaches to world history and archaeology.

M. Oliphant, The Atlas of the Ancient World: Charting the Great Civilizations of the Past (1992). An excellent comprehensive atlas of the ancient world.

P.L. Shinnie, Ancient Nubia (1996). A study of the African state most influenced by Egyptian culture.

Near East

M.E. Auber, The Phoenicians and the West (1996). A new study of an important sea-going people who served as a conduit between East and West.

Ben-Tor, ed., The Archaeology of Ancient Israel (1992). A useful and up-to-date survey.

J. Bottéro, Everyday Life in Ancient Mesopotamia (2001). Interesting vignettes of ancient Mesopotamian life.

H. Crawford, Sumer and the Sumerians (1991). A discussion of the oldest Mesopotamian civilization.

I. Finkelstein and N.A. Silberman, The Bible Unearthed: Archaeology's New Vision of Ancient Israel and the Origin of Its Sacred Texts (2001). An interesting discussion of the insights of recent archaeological finds on the history of the Bible and ancient Israel.

G. Leick, Mesopotamia: The Invention of the City (2002). Good discussion of the urban history of ancient Mesopotamia.

J.N. Postgate, Early Mesopotamia (1992). An excellent study of Mesopotamian economy and society from the earliest times to about 1500 B.C.E., helpfully illustrated with drawings, photos, and translated documents.

D.B. Redford, Akhenaten (1987). A study of the controversial religious reformer.

W.F. Saggs, The Might That Was Assyria (1984). A history of the northern Mesopotamian Empire and a worthy companion to the author's account of the Babylonian Empire in the south.

M. Van de Mieroop, A History of the Ancient Near East, ca. 3000–323 B.C. (2004). An up-to-date comprehensive survey of ancient Near Eastern history.

India

D.P. Agrawal, The Archaeology of India (1982). A fine survey of the problems and data. Detailed, but with excellent summaries and brief discussions of major issues.

C. Chakraborty, Common Life in the Rigveda and Atharvaveda—An Account of the Folklore in the Vedic Period (1977). An interesting attempt to reconstruct everyday life in the Vedic period from the principal Vedic texts.

J.R. Mcintosh, A Peaceful Realm: The Rise and Fall of the Indus Civilization (2002). Discusses what archaeologists have managed to unearth so far regarding Harrapan civilization.

W.D. O'flaherty, The Rig Veda: An Anthology (1981). An excellent selection of Vedic texts in prosaic but very careful translation, with helpful notes on the texts.

J.E. Schwartzberg, ed., A Historical Atlas of South Asia (1978). The definitive reference work for historical geography. Includes chronological tables and substantive essays.

R. Thapar, Early India: From the Origins to A.D. 1300 (2003). A comprehensive introduction to the early history of India.

China

M. Loewe and E. Shaughnessy, eds., The Cambridge History of Ancient China: From the Origins of Civilization to 221 B.C. (1999). A comprehensive and authoritative history of ancient China.

K.C. Chang, The Archeology of Ancient China, 4th ed. (1986). The standard work on the subject.

K.C. Chang, Art, Myth, and Ritual: The Path to Political Authority in Ancient China (1984). A study of the relation between shamans, gods, agricultural production, and political authority during the Shang and Zhou dynasties.

N. Di Cosmo, Ancient China and Its Enemies: The Rise of Nomadic Power in East Asian History (2002). An excellent study of the relationship between China and nomadic peoples that was a powerful force in shaping Chinese and Central Asian history.

C.Y. Hsu, Western Chou Civilization (1988).

D.N. Keightley, The Origins of Chinese Civilization (1983).

M.E. Lewis, Sanctioned Violence in Early China (1990).

X.Q. Li, Eastern Zhou and Qin Civilizations (1986). Includes fresh interpretations based on archaeological finds.

Americas

R.L. Burger, Chavín and the Origins of Andean Civilization (1992). A lucid and detailed account of the rise of civilization in the Andes.

M.D. Coe and R. Koontz, Mexico: From the Olmecs to the Aztecs (2002). Good survey of ancient Mexico.

D. Drew, The Lost Chronicles of the Maya Kings (1999). Fine introduction to the history of Maya civilization.

V.W. Fitzhugh and A. Crowell, Crossroads of Continents: Cultures of Siberia and Alaska (1988). Covers the area where the immigration from Eurasia to the Americas began.

R. Ford, ed., Prehistoric Food Production in North America (1985). Examines the origins of agriculture in the Americas.

P.D. Hunt, Indian Agriculture in America: Prehistory to the Present (1987). Includes a discussion of preconquest agriculture.

A. Knight, Mexico: From the Beginning to the Spanish Conquest (2002). First of a three-volume comprehensive history of Mexico.

C. Morris and A. Von Hagen, The Inka Empire and Its Andean Origins (1993). An overview of Andean civilization with excellent illustrations.

M. Moseley, The Incas and Their Ancestors: The Archaeology of Ancient Peru (1992). An overview of Peruvian archaeology.

J.A. Sabloff, The New Archaeology and the Ancient Maya (1990). A lively account of recent research in Maya archaeology.

I. Silverblatt, Moon, Sun, and Witches: Gender Ideologies and Class in Inca and Colonial Peru (1987). A controversial but thought-provoking discussion of Incan ideas about gender.

Chapter 2

China

R. Bernstein, Ultimate Journey: Retracing the Path of an Ancient Buddhist Monk Who Crossed Asia in Search of Enlightenment (2001). Discusses the diffusion of Buddhism from India to China.

H.G. Creel, What Is Taoism? And Other Studies in Chinese Cultural History (1970).

W.T. de Bary et al., Sources of Chinese Tradition (1960). A reader in China's philosophical and historical literature. It should be consulted for the later periods as well as for the Zhou.

H. Fingarette, Confucius—The Secular as Sacred (1998).

Y.L. Fung, A Short History of Chinese Philosophy, ed. by D. Bodde (1948). A survey of Chinese philosophy from its origins down to recent times.

A. Graham, Disputers of the Tao (1989).

D. Hawkes, Ch'u Tz'u: The Songs of the South (1985).

D.C. Lau, trans., Lao-tzu, Tao Te Ching (1963).

D.C. Lau, trans., Confucius, The Analects (1979).

C. Li, ed., The Sage and the Second Sex: Confucianism, Ethics, and Gender (2000). A good introduction to gender and ethics in Confucian thought.

B.I. Schwartz, The World of Thought in Ancient China (1985).

A. Waley, Three Ways of Thought in Ancient China (1956). An easy yet sound introduction to Confucianism, Daoism, and Legalism.

A. Waley, The Book of Songs (1960).

B. Watson, trans., Basic Writings of Mo Tzu, Hsun Tzu, and Han Fei Tzu (1963).

B. Watson, trans., The Complete Works of Chuang Tzu (1968).

H. Welch, Taoism, The Parting of the Way (1967).

India

A.L. Basham, The Wonder That Was India, rev. ed. (1963). Still unsurpassed by more recent works. Chapter VII, "Religion," is a superb introduction to the Vedic Aryan, Brahmanic, Hindu, Jain, and Buddhist traditions of thought.

W.N. Brown, Man in the Universe: Some Continuities in Indian Thought (1970). A penetrating yet brief reflective summary of major patterns in Indian thinking.

W.T. de Bary et al., Sources of Indian Tradition (1958). 2 vols. Vol. I, From the Beginning to 1800, ed. and rev. by Ainslie T. Embree (1988). Excellent selections from a variety of Indian texts, with good introductions to chapters and individual selections.

P. Harvey, An Introduction to Buddhism (1990). Chapters 1–3 provide an excellent historical introduction.

T.J. Hopkins, The Hindu Religious Tradition (1971). A first-rate, thoughtful introduction to Hindu religious ideas and practice.

K. Klostermaier, Hinduism: A Short History (2000). A relatively compact survey of the history of Hinduism.

J.M. Koller, The Indian Way (1982). A useful, wide-ranging handbook of Indian thought and religion.

R.H. Robinson and W.L. Johnson, The Buddhist Religion, 3rd ed. (1982). An excellent first text on the Buddhist tradition, its thought and development.

R.C. Zaehner, Hinduism (1966). One of the best general introductions to central Indian religious and philosophical ideas.

Israel

A. Bach, ed., Women in the Hebrew Bible: A Reader (1999). Excellent introduction to the ways in which biblical scholars are exploring the role of women in the Bible.

Bright, A History of Israel (1968), 2nd ed. (1972). One of the standard scholarly introductions to biblical history and literature.

W.D. Davies and L. Finkelstein, eds., The Cambridge History of Judaism. Vol. I, Introduction: The Persian Period (1984). Excellent essays on diverse aspects of the exilic period and later.

J. Neusner, The Way of Torah: An Introduction to Judaism (1979). A sensitive introduction to the Judaic tradition and faith.

The Oxford History of the Biblical World, M. D. Coogan, ed. (1998).

Greece

The Cambridge Companion to Greek and Roman Philosophy, D. Sedley ed. (2003).

G.B. Kerferd, The Sophistic Movement (1981). An excellent description and analysis.

J. Lear, Aristotle: The Desire to Understand (1988). A brilliant yet comprehensible introduction to the work of the philosopher.

T.E. Rihil, Greek Science (1999). Good survey of Greek science incorporating recent reseach on the topic.

J.M. Robinson, An Introduction to Early Greek Philosophy (1968). A valuable collection of the main fragments and ancient testimony to the works of the early philosophers, with excellent commentary.

G. Vlastos, The Philosophy of Socrates (1971). A splendid collection of essays illuminating the problems presented by this remarkable man.

G. Vlastos, Platonic Studies, 2nd ed. (1981). A similar collection on the philosophy of Plato.

G. Vlastos, Socrates, Ironist and Moral Philosopher (1991). The results of a lifetime of study by the leading interpreter of Socrates in our time.

Comparative Studies

(Increasingly, world historians are looking at ancient civilizations in relationship to each other rather than as isolated entities to try to understand commonalities and differences in social and cultural development.)

W. Doniger, Splitting the Difference: Gender and Myth in Ancient Greece and India (1999).

G.E.R. Lloyd, The Ambitions of Curiosity: Understanding the World in Ancient Greece and China (2002).

G.E.R. Lloyd, The Way and the Word: Science and Medicine in Early China and Greece (2002).

T. McEvilley, The Shape of Ancient Thought: Comparative Studies of Greek and Indian Philosophies (2002).

Chapter 3

The Rise of Greek Civilization

P. Cartledge, The Spartans (2003). A readable account of this enigmatic people.

J. Chadwick, The Mycenaean World (1976). A readable account by a man who helped decipher Mycenaean writing.

R. Drews, The Coming of the Greeks (1988). A fine discussion of the Greeks' arrival as part of the movements of the Indo-European peoples.

J.V. Fine, The Ancient Greeks (1983). An excellent survey that discusses historical problems and the evidence that gives rise to them.

M.I. Finley, World of Odysseus, rev. ed. (1965). A fascinating attempt to reconstruct Homeric society.

P. Green, Xerxes at Salamis (1970). A lively and stimulating history of the Persian War.

D. Hamel, Trying Neaira (2003). A lively account of the events surrounding a famous jury trial that sheds interesting light on Athenian society in the fourth century B.C.E.

V.D. Hanson, The Western Way of War (1989). A brilliant and lively discussion of the rise and character of the hoplite phalanx and its influence on Greek society.

V.D. Hanson, The Other Greeks (1995). A revolutionary account of the Greek invention of the family farm and its centrality for the shaping of the polis.

D. Kagan, The Great Dialogue: A History of Greek Political Thought from Homer to Polybius (1965). A discussion of the relationship between the Greek historical experience and political theory.

W.K. Lacey, The Family in Ancient Greece (1984).

J.F. Lazenby, The Defense of Greece, 490–479 B.C. (1993). A new and valuable study of the Persian Wars.

J.F. McGlew, Tyranny and Political Culture in Ancient Greece (1993). A recent account of political developments in the Archaic period.

S.G. Miller, Ancient Greek Athletics (2004). The most complete and most useful account of the subject

O. Murray, Early Greece (1980). A lively and imaginative account of the early history of Greece to the end of the Persian War.

A.M. Snodgrass, The Dark Age of Greece (1972). A good examination of the archaeological evidence.

B.S. Strauss, The Battle of Salamis: The Naval Encounter That Saved Greece and Western Civilization (2004). A lively account of the major naval battle of the Persian Wars and its setting.

A.G. Woodhead, Greeks in the West (1962). An account of the Greek settlements in Italy and Sicily.

W.J. Woodhouse, Solon the Liberator (1965). A discussion of the great Athenian reformer.

Classical and Hellenistic Greece

W. Burkert, Greek Religion (1987). An excellent study by an outstanding student of the subject.

J.R. Lane Fox, Alexander the Great (1973). An imaginative account that does more than the usual justice to the Persian side of the problem.

Y. Garlan, Slavery in Ancient Greece (1988). An up-to-date survey.

P. Green, Alexander to Actium: The Historical Evolution of the Hellenistic Age (1990). A remarkable synthesis of political and cultural history.

C.D. Hamilton, Agesilaus and the Failure of Spartan Hegemony (1991). An excellent biography of the king who was the central figure in Sparta during its domination in the fourth century B.C.E.

N.G.L. Hammond, Philip of Macedon (1994). A new biography of the founder of the Macedonian Empire.

N.G.L. Hammond and G.T. Griffith, A History of Macedonia, Vol. 2, 550–336 B.C. (1979). A thorough account of Macedonian history that focuses on the careers of Philip and Alexander.

R. Just, Women in Athenian Law and Life (1988). An account of women's place in Athenian society.

D. Kagan, The Peloponnesian War (2003). A narrative history of the war.

B.M.W. Knox, The Heroic Temper: Studies in Sophoclean Tragedy (1964). A brilliant analysis of tragic heroism.

D.M. Lewis, Sparta and Persia (1977). A valuable discussion of relations between Sparta and Persia in the fifth and fourth centuries B.C.E.

A.A. Long, Hellenistic Philosophy: Stoics, Epicureans, Sceptics (1974). An account of Greek science in the Hellenistic and Roman periods.

R. Meiggs, The Athenian Empire (1972). A fine study of the rise and fall of the empire, making excellent use of inscriptions.

J.J. Pollitt, Art and Experience in Classical Greece (1972). A scholarly and entertaining study of the relationship between art and history in classical Greece, with excellent illustrations.

J.J. Pollitt, Art in the Hellenistic Age (1986). An extraordinary analysis that places the art in its historical and intellectual context.

E.W. Robinson, Ancient Greek Democracy (2004). A stimulating collection of ancient sources and modern interpretations.

D.M. Schaps, Economic Rights of Women in Ancient Greece (1981).

B.S. Strauss, Athens after the Peloponnesian War (1987). An excellent discussion of Athens' recovery and of the nature of Athenian society and politics in the fourth century B.C.E.

B.S. Strauss, Fathers and Sons in Athens (1993). An unusual synthesis of social, political, and intellectual history.

V. Tcherikover, Hellenistic Civilization and the Jews (1970). A fine study of the impact of Hellenism on the Jews.

G. Vlastos, Socrates, Ironist and Moral Philosopher (1991). The results of a lifetime of study by the leading interpreter of Socrates in our time.

Chapter 4

Iran

M. Boyce, Zoroastrians: Their Religious Beliefs and Practices (1979). A detailed survey by the current authority on Zoroastrian religious history, organized historically and based on extensive research. See Chapters 7–9.

M. Boyce, ed. and trans.,Textual Sources for the Study of Zoroastrianism (1984). Well-translated selections from a broad range of ancient Iranian materials and an important introduction that includes Boyce's arguments for a revision of the dates of Zoroaster's life (to between 1400 and 1200 B.C.E.).

J.M. Cook, The Persian Empire (1983). Survey of the Achaemenid period.

J. Curtis, Ancient Persia (1989). Excellent portfolio of photographs of artifacts and sites, with a clear historical survey of the arts and culture of ancient Iran.

W.D. Davies and L. Finklestein, ed., The Cambridge History of Judaism, Vol. 1, Introduction; "The Persian Period." Good articles on Iran and Iranian religion as well as Judaism.

J. Duchesne-Guillemin, trans., The Hymns of Zarathushtra, trans. by M. Henning (1952, 1963). The best short introduction to the original texts of the Zoroastrian hymns.

R.N. Frye, The Heritage of Persia (1963, 1966). A first-rate survey of Iranian history to Islamic times: readable but scholarly. Chapter 6 deals with the Sasanid era.

R. Ghirshman, Iran (1954). Good material on culture, society, and economy as well as politics and history.

R. Ghirshman, Persian Art: The Parthian and Sasanid Dynasties (1962). Superb photographs, and a very helpful glossary of places and names. The text is minimal.

W.W. Malandra, trans. and ed., An Introduction to Ancient Iranian Religion: Readings from the Avesta and Achaemenid Inscriptions (1983). Helpful especially for texts of inscriptions relevant to religion.

Geo Widengran, Mani and Manichaeism (1965). Still the standard introduction to Mani's life and the later spread and development of Manichaeism.

India

A.L. Basham, The Wonder That Was India, rev. ed. (1963). Excellent material on Mauryan religion, society, culture, and history.

A.L. Basham, ed., A Cultural History of India (1975). A fine collection of historical-survey essays by a variety of scholars. See Part I, "The Ancient Heritage" (Chapters 2–16).

N.N. Bhattacharyya, Ancient Indian History and Civilization: Trends and Perspectives (1988). Covers Mauryan and Gupta times as well as earlier periods, with chapters on political systems, cities and villages, ideology and religion, and art.

W.T. de Bary et al., comp., Sources of Indian Tradition, 2nd ed. (1958). Vol. I: From the Beginning to 1800, ed. and rev. by Ainslie T. Embree (1988). Excellent selections from a wide variety of Indian texts, with good introductions to chapters and selections.

S. Dutt, Buddhist Monks and Monasteries of India (1962). The standard work. See especially Chapters 3 ("Bhakti") and 4 ("Monasteries under the Gupta Kings").

D.G. Mandelbaum, Society in India (1972). 2 vols. The first two chapters in Volume I of this study of caste, family, and village relations are a good introduction to the caste system.

B. Rowland, The Art and Architecture of India: Buddhist/Hindu/Jain, 3rd rev. ed. (1970). The standard work, lucid and easy to read. Note Part Three, "Romano-Indian Art in North-West India and Central Asia." See also the excellent chapters on Sungan, Andhran, and other early Buddhist art (6–8, 14), the Gupta period (15), and the Hindu Renaissance (17–19).

V.A. Smith, ed., The Oxford History of India, 4th rev. ed. by Percival Spear et al. (1981), pp. 71–163. A dry, occasionally dated historical survey. Includes useful reference chronologies. See especially pp. 164–229 (the Gupta period and following era to the Muslim invasions).

R. Thapar, A History of India, Part I (1966), pp. 50–108. Three chapters that provide a basic survey of the period.

R. Thapar, Ashoka and the Decline of the Mauryans (1973). The standard treatment of Ashoka's reign. Three chapters cover the rise of mercantilism, the Gupta "classical pattern," and the southern dynasties to ca. 900 C.E.

S. Wolpert, A New History of India, 2nd ed. (1982). A basic survey history. Chapters 5 and 6 cover the Mauryans, Guptas, and Kushans.

P. Younger, Introduction to Indian Religious Thought (1972). A sensitive attempt to delineate classical concerns of classical Indian religious thought and culture.

Greek and Asian Dynasties

A.K. Narain, The Indo-Greeks (1957. Reprinted with corrections, 1962). The most comprehensive account of the complex history of the various kings and kingdoms.

F.E. Peters, The Harvest of Hellenism (1970), pp. 222–308. Helpful chapters on Greek rulers of the Eastern world from Seleucus to the last Indo-Greeks.

J.W. Sedlar, India and the Greek World: A Study in the Transmission of Culture (1980). A basic work that provides a good overview.

D. Sinor, ed., The Cambridge History of Early Inner Asia (1990). See especially Chapters 6 and 7.

Chapter 5

R. Bates, V.Y. Mudimbe, and Jean O'Barr, eds., Africa and the Disciplines (1993). Explores how knowledge of Africa has shaped various fields of scholarship. The essay on history by Steven Feierman is particularly relevant to this chapter.

P. Bohannan and P. Curtin, Africa and Africans, rev. ed. (1995). An enjoyable and enlightening discussion of African history and prehistory and of major African institutions (e.g., arts, family life, religion).

R. Bulliet, The Camel and the Wheel (1990). Explains why the camel was chosen over the wheel as a means of transport in the Sahara.

P. Curtin, On the Fringes of History: A Memoir (2005). An engaging autobiography by one of the pioneers in African Studies in the United States; explores what it means to be a historian in the modern world.

P. Curtin, S. Feiermann, L. Thompson, and J. Vansina, African History, rev. ed . (1995). The classic survey history, written by four of the leaders in the field.

T.R.H. Davenport and Christopher Saunders, South Africa: A Modern History, rev. ed. (2000). A comprehensive survey, beginning with coverage of prehistoric southern Africa, the Khoisan peoples, and the Bantu migrations.

B. Davidson, Africa in History, rev. ed. (1995). A sweeping history of the diverse parts of Africa, emphasizing cultural exchange within the continent and beyond.

C.A. Diop, Precolonial Black Africa (1988). A seminal work by the pioneering Afrocentric scholar; his conclusions are controversial, but his writings are always provocative.

P.A. Ebron, Performing Africa (2002). Analyzes the role of performance in the creation and global circulation of African history and identity.

P. Garlake, Early Art and Architecture of Africa (2002). Highlights the diversity and sophistication of early African art and discusses the social context in which it was created.

E. Gilbert and J. Reynolds, Africa in World History (2004). The best new survey of African history, placing it in a global context. In conversational prose, the authors attend to environmental factors in African history and emphasize the roles of Western

bias in shaping what we now know (and think we know) about Africa.

J. Iliffe, Africans: The History of a Continent (1995). A thematic survey of African history, from the paleontological record to the end of apartheid, with a focus on environment and demography.

E. Isichei, A History of Christianity in Africa: From Antiquity to the Present (1995). An amazing survey of Christianity's role on the African continent, from the time of Christ through European missionaries to the present popularity of Christian faith.

R. Oliver, The African Experience (1991). A masterly, balanced, and engaging sweep through African history.

I. Van Sertima, Black Women in Antiquity, rev. ed. (1988). From Lucy to Hatshepsut and beyond, essays explore the role and status of women in African societies of the past.

L. White et al., eds., African Words, African Voices: Critical Practices in Oral History (2001). A lively group of essays offer various perspectives on the uses of oral history in African research.

Chapter 6

From Republic to Empire

R. Baumann, Women and Politics in Ancient Rome (1995). A study of the role of women in Roman public life.

A.H. Bernstein, Tiberius Sempronius Gracchus: Tradition and Apostasy (1978). A new interpretation of Tiberius's place in Roman politics.

T.J. Cornell, The Beginnings of Rome: Italy and Rome from the Bronze Age to the Punic Wars, c. 1000–264 B.C. (1995). A consideration of the royal and early republican periods of Roman history.

T. Cornell and J. Matthews, Atlas of the Roman World (1982). Much more than the title indicates, this book presents a comprehensive view of the Roman world in its physical and cultural setting.

J-M. David, The Roman Conquest of Italy (1997). A good analysis of how Rome united Italy.

A. Goldsworthy, Roman Warfare (2002). A good military history of Rome.

A. Goldsworthy, In the Name of Rome: The Men Who Won the Roman Empire (2004). The story of Rome's greatest generals in the republican and imperial periods.

E.S. Gruen, Diaspora: Jews amidst Greeks and Romans (2002). A fine study of Jews in the Hellenistic and Roman world.

E.S. Gruen, The Hellenistic World and the Coming of Rome (1984). A new interpretation of Rome's conquest of the eastern Mediterranean.

W.V. Harris, War and Imperialism in Republican Rome, 327–70 B.C. (1975). An analysis of Roman attitudes and intentions concerning imperial expansion and war.

A. Keaveney, Rome and the Unification of Italy (1988). The story of how Rome organized its defeated opponents.

S. Lancel, Carthage, A History (1995). Includes a good account of Rome's dealings with Carthage.

J.F. Lazenby, Hannibal's War: A Military History of the Second Punic War (1978). A careful and thorough account.

F.G.B. Millar, The Crowd in Rome in the Late Republic (1999). A challenge to the view that only aristocrats counted in the late republic.

M. Pallottino, The Etruscans, 6th ed. (1974). Makes especially good use of archaeological evidence.

H.H. Scullard, A History of the Roman World, 753–146 B.C., 4th ed. (1980). An unusually fine narrative history with useful critical notes.

G. Williams, The Nature of Roman Poetry (1970). An unusually graceful and perceptive literary study.

Imperial Rome

W. Ball, Rome in the East: The Transformation of an Empire (2001). A thorough account of the influence of the East on Roman history.

T. Barnes, The New Empire of Diocletian and Constantine (1982).

K.R. Bradley, Slavery and Society at Rome (1994). A study of the role of slaves in Roman life.

P. Brown, The Rise of Western Christendom: Triumph and Diversity, 200–1000 (1996). A vivid picture of the spread of Christianity by a master of the field.

A. Ferrill, The Fall of the Roman Empire, The Military Explanation (1986). An interpretation that emphasizes the decline in the quality of the Roman army.

K. Galinsky, Augustan Culture (1996). A work that integrates art, literature, and politics.

A.H.M. Jones, The Later Roman Empire, 3 vols. (1964). A comprehensive study of the period.

D. Kagan, ed., The End of the Roman Empire: Decline or Transformation? 3rd ed. (1992). A collection of essays discussing the problem of the decline and fall of the Roman Empire.

J.E. Lendon, Empire of Honor, The Art of Government in the Roman World (1997). An original and path-breaking interpretation.

E.N. Luttwak, The Grand Strategy of the Roman Empire (1976). An original and fascinating analysis by a keen student of modern strategy.

R. MacMullen, Roman Social Relations, 50 B.C. to A.D. 284 (1981).

R. MacMullen, Corruption and the Decline of Rome (1988). A study that examines the importance of changes in ethical ideas and behavior.

R.W. Mathison, Roman Aristocrats in Barbarian Gaul: Strategies for Survival (1993). An unusual slant on the late empire.

J.F. Matthews, Laying Down the Law: A Study of the Theodosian Code (2000). A study of the importance of Roman law as a source for the understanding of Roman history and civilization.

W.A. Meeks, The Origins of Christian Morality: The First Two Centuries. An account of the shaping of Christianity in the Roman Empire.

F. Millar, The Emperor in the Roman World, 31 B.C.–A.D. 337 (1977). A study of Roman imperial government.

F. Millar, The Roman Empire and Its Neighbors, 2nd ed. (1981).

H.M.D. Parker, A History of the Roman World from A.D. 138 to 337 (1969). A good survey.

M.I. Rostovtzeff, Social and Economic History of the Roman Empire, 2nd ed. (1957). A masterpiece whose main thesis has been much disputed.

V. Rudich, Political Dissidence under Nero: The Price of Dissimulation (1993). A brilliant exposition of the lives and thoughts of political dissidents in the early empire.

E.T. Salmon, A History of the Roman World, 30 B.C. to A.D. 138 (1968). A good survey.

R. Syme, The Roman Revolution (1960). A brilliant study of Augustus, his supporters, and their rise to power.

R. Syme, The Augustan Aristocracy (1985). An examination of the new ruling class shaped by Augustus.

L.A. Thompson, Romans and Blacks (1989).

Chapter 7

D. Bodde, China's First Unifier (1938). A study of the Qin unification of China, viewed through the Legalist philosopher and statesman Li Si.

T.T. Ch'u, Law and Society in Traditional China (1961). Treats the sweep of Chinese history from 202 B.C.E. to 1911 C.E.

T.T. Ch'u, Han Social Structure (1972).

A. Cotterell, The First Emperor of China (1981). A study of the first Qin emperor.

R. Coulborn, Feudalism in History (1965). One chapter interestingly compares the quasi feudalism of the Zhou with that of the Six Dynasties period.

J.K. Fairbank, E.O. Reischauer, and A.M. Craig, East Asia: Tradition and Transformation (1989). A fairly detailed single-volume history covering China, Japan, and other countries in East Asia from antiquity to recent times.

J. Gernet, A History of Chinese Civilization (1982). A survey of Chinese history.

D.A. Graff and R. Higham, A Military History of China (2002).

C.Y. Hsu, Ancient China in Transition (1965). On social mobility during the Eastern Zhou era.

C.Y. Hsu, Han Agriculture (1980). A study of the agrarian economy of China during the Han Dynasty.

J. Levi, The Chinese Emperor (1987). A novel about the first Qin emperor based on scholarly sources.

M. Loewe, Everyday Life in Early Imperial China (1968). A social history of the Han Dynasty.

J. Needham, The Shorter Science and Civilization in China (1978). An abridgment of the multivolume work on the same subject with the same title—minus Shorter—by the same author.

S. Owen, ed., and Trans., An Anthology of Chinese Literature: Beginnings to 1911 (1996).

I. Robinet, Taoism: Growth of a Religion (1987).

M. Sullivan, The Arts of China (1967). An excellent survey history of Chinese art.

D. Twitchett and M. Loewe, eds., The Ch'in and Han Empires, 221 B.C.E.–C.E. 220 (1986). Vol. 1 of The Cambridge History of China.

Z. S. Wang, Han Civilization (1982).

B. Watson, Ssu-ma Ch'ien, Grand Historian of China (1958). A study of China's premier historian.

B. Watson, Records of the Grand Historian of China, Vols. 1 and 2 (1961). Selections from the Shiji by Sima Qian.

B. Watson, The Columbia Book of Chinese Poetry (1986).

F. Wood, The Silk Road: Two Thousand Years in the Heart of Asia (2003). A lively narrative combined with photographs and paintings.

A. Wright, Buddhism in Chinese History (1959).

Y.S. Yu, Trade and Expansion in Han China (1967). A study of economic relations between the Chinese and their neighbors.

Chapter 8

General

P. Bol, This Culture of Ours (1992). An insightful intellectual history of the Tang through the Song dynasties.

J. Cahill, Chinese Painting (1960). An excellent survey.

J.K. Fairbank and M. Goldman, China: A New History (1998). The summation of a lifetime engagement with Chinese history.

F.A. Kierman Jr., and J.K. Fairbank, eds., Chinese Ways in Warfare (1974). Chapters by different authors on the Chinese military experience from the Zhou to the Ming.

Sui and Tang

P.B. Ebrey, The Aristocratic Families of Early Imperial China (1978).

D. McMullen, State and Scholars in T'ang China (1988).

S. Owen, The Great Age of Chinese Poetry: The High T'ang (1980).

S. Owen, trans. and ed., An Anthology of Chinese Literature: Beginnings to 1911 (1996).

E.G. Pulleyblank, The Background of the Rebellion of An Lu-shan (1955). A study of the 755 rebellion that weakened the central authority of the Tang Dynasty.

E.O. Reischauer, Ennin's Travels in T'ang China (1955). China as seen through the eyes of a ninth-century Japanese Marco Polo.

E.H. Schafer, The Golden Peaches of Samarkand (1963). A study of Tang imagery.

So. Teiser, The Ghost Festival in Medieval China (1988). On Tang popular religion.

D. Twitchett, ed., The Cambridge History of China, Vol. III: Sui and T'ang China, 589–906 Part 1 (1979).

G. W. Wang, The Structure of Power in North China during the Five Dynasties (1963). A study of the interim period between the Tang and the Song dynasties.

A. F. Wright, The Sui Dynasty (1978).

Song

B. Birge, Women, Property, and Confucian Reaction in Song and Yuan China (960–1366) (2002). The rights of women to property—whether in the form of dowries or inheritances—were considerable during the Song but declined thereafter.

C.S. Chang and J. Smythe, South China in the Twelfth Century (1981). China as seen through the eyes of a twelfth-century Chinese poet, historian, and statesman.

E.L. Davis, Society and the Supernatural in Song China (2001).

J.W. Haeger, ed., Crisis and Prosperity in Song China (1975).

R. Hymes, Statesmen and Gentlemen (1987). On the transformation of officials into a local gentry elite during the twelfth and thirteenth centuries.

R. Hymes, Way and Byway: Taoism, Local Religion, and Models of Divinity in Sung and Modern China (2002).

M. Rossabi, China among Equals (1983). A study of the Liao, Qin, and Song empires and their relations.

W.M. Tu, Confucian Thought, Selfhood as Creative Transformation (1985).

K. Yoshikawa, An Introduction to Song Poetry, trans. by B. Watson (1967).

Yuan

T.T. Allsen, Mongol Imperialism (1987).

J.W. Dardess, Conquerors and Confucians: Aspects of Political Change in Late Yuan China (1973).

I. de Rachewiltz, Trans., The Secret History of the Mongols: A Mongolian Epic Chronicle of the Thirteenth Century (2003). A new translation of a key historical work on the life of Genghis.

H. Franke and D. Twitchett, eds., The Cambridge History of China, Vol. VI: Alien Regimes and Border States, 710–1368 (1994).

J.D. Langlois, China under Mongol Rule (1981).

R.Latham, trans., Travels of Marco Polo (1958).

H.D. Martin, The Rise of Chingis Khan and His Conquest of North China (1981).

D. Morgan, The Mongol Empire and Its Legacy (1999). Genghis, the several khanates, and the aftermath of empire.

P. Ratchnevsky, Genghis Khan, His Life and Legacy (1992). The rise to power of the Mongol leader, with a critical consideration of historical sources.

Chapter 9

M. Adolphson, The Gates of Power: Monks, Courtiers, and Warriors in Premodern Japan (2000). A new interpretation stressing the importance of temples in the political life of Heian and Kamakura Japan.

B.L. Batten, To the Ends of Japan: Premodern Frontiers, Boundaries, and Interactions. (2003). An interesting treatment of Heian Japan, topic by topic.

C. Blacker, The Catalpa Bow (1975). An insightful study of folk Shinto.

R. Borgen, Sugawara no Michizane and the Early Heian Court (1986). A study of a famous courtier and poet.

D.M. Brown, ed., The Cambridge History of Japan: Ancient Japan (1993). This series of six volumes sums up several decades of research on Japan.

D. Brown and E. Ishida, eds., The Future and the Past (1979). A translation of a history of Japan written in 1219.

The Cambridge History of Japan, D.M. Brown, ed.; Vol. 1, Ancient Japan, W. McCullough and D. H. Shively eds; Vol. 2, Heian Japan, K. Yamamura, ed. Vol. 3, Medieval Japan. Fine multi-author works.

M. Collcutt, Five Mountains (1980). A study of the monastic organization of medieval Zen.

T.D. Conlon, State of War: The Violent Order of Fourteenth Century Japan (2003). Compare Conlon's account with those of Souyri and Friday.

W.T. DeBary, D. Keene, G. Tanabe, and P. Varley, Comps., Sources of Japanese Tradition, 2nd ed. (2001).

P. Duus, Feudalism in Japan (1969). An easy survey of the subject.

W.W. Farris, Population, Disease, and Land in Early Japan, 645–900 (1985). An innovative reinterpretation of early history.

W.W. Farris, Heavenly Warriors: The Evolution of Japan's Military, 500–1300 (1992).

W.W. Farris, Sacred Texts and Buried Treasures (1998). Studies of Japan's prehistory and early history, based on recent Japanese research.

K.F. Friday, Samurai, Warfare and the State in Early Medieval Japan (2004). Weapons and warfare in Japan from the tenth to fourteenth centuries.

A.E. Goble, Go-Daigo's Revolution (1996). A provoking account of the 1331 revolt by an emperor who thought emperors should rule.

J.W. Hall, Government and Local Power in Japan, 500–1700: A Study Based on Bizen Province (1966). A splendid and insightful book.

J.W. Hall and T. Toyoda, Japan in the Muromachi Age (1977). Another collection of essays.

D. Keene, ed., Anthology of Japanese Literature from the Earliest Era to the Mid-Nineteenth Century (1955).

D. Keene, ed., Twenty Plays of the Nō Theatre (1970).

T. Lamarre, Uncovering Heian Japan: An Archeology of Sensation and Inscription (2000). The "archeology" in the title refers to digging into literature.

I.H. Levy, The Ten Thousand Leaves (1981). A fine translation of Japan's earliest collection of poetry.

J.P. Mass and W. Hauser, eds., The Bakufu in Japanese History (1985). Topics in Bakufu history from the twelfth to the nineteenth centuries.

I. Morris, trans., The Pillow Book of Sei Shōnagon (1967). Observations about the Heian court life by the Jane Austen of ancient Japan.

S. Murasaki, The Tale of Genji comparison of this translation with that of Seidensticker is instructive.

S. Murasaki, The Tale of Genji, trans. by E.G. Seidensticker (1976). The world's first novel and the greatest work of Japanese fiction.

R.J. Pearson et al., eds., Windows on the Japanese Past: Studies in Archaeology and Prehistory (1986).

D.L. Philippi, trans., Kojiki (1968). Japan's ancient myths.

J. Piggot, The Emergence of Japanese Kingship (1997).

E.O. Reischauer, Ennin's Diary, the Record of a Pilgrimage to China in Search of the Law and Ennin's Travels in T'ang China (1955).

E.O. Reischauer and A.M. Craig, Japan: Tradition and Transformation (1989). A more detailed work covering the sweep of Japanese history from the early beginnings through the 1980s.

H. Sato, Legends of the Samurai (1995). Excerpts from various tales and writings.

D.H. Shively and W.H. McCullough, eds., The Cambridge History of Japan: Heian Japan (1999).

D.T. Suzuki, Zen and Japanese Culture (1959).

H. Tonomura, Community and Commerce in Late Medieval Japan (1992).

R. Tsunoda, W.T. de Bary, and D. Keene, comps., Sources of the Japanese Tradition (1958). A collection of original religious, political, and philosophical writings from each period of Japanese history. The best reader. A new edition was published in 2005.

H.P. Varley, Imperial Restoration in Medieval Japan (1971). A study of the 1331 attempt by an emperor to restore imperial power.

A. Waley, trans., The Nō Plays of Japan (1957). Medieval dramas.

K. Yamamura, ed., Cambridge History of Japan: Medieval Japan (1990).

Chapter 10

O. Grabar, The Formation of Islamic Art (1973). A critical and creative interpretation of major themes in the development of distinctively Islamic forms of art and architecture.

A. Hourani, A History of the Arab Peoples (1991). A masterly survey of the Arabs down through the centuries and a clear picture of many aspects of Islamic history and culture that extend beyond the Arab world.

H. Kennedy, The Prophet and the Age of the Caliphates: The Islamic Near East from the Sixth to the Eleventh Century (1986). The best survey of early Islamic history.

I. Lapidus, A History of Islamic Societies (1988). A comprehensive overview of the rise and development of Islam all over the world.

F.E. Peters, Muhammad and the Origins of Islam (1994). A balanced analysis of the life of Muhammad.

F. Rahman, Major Themes of the Qur'an (1980). The best introduction to the basic ideas of the Qur'an and Islam, seen through the eyes of a perceptive Muslim modernist scholar.

F. Schuon, Understanding Islam (1994). Compares the Islamic worldview with Catholic Christianity. A dense, but intellectually stimulating, discussion.

M. Sells, Approaching the Qur'an. The Early Revelations (1999). A fine introduction and new translations of some of the more common earlier Qur'anic revelations.

B. Stowasser, Women in the Qur'an, Traditions and Interpretation (1994). An outstanding systematic study of statements regarding women in the Qur'an.

Chapter 11

K. Armstrong, Muhammad: A Biography of the Prophet (1992). Strong on religion.

R. Bartlett, The Making of Europe, 950–1350 (1992). A study of the way immigration and colonial conquest shaped the Europe we know.

M. Bloch, Feudal Society, Vols. 1 and 2, trans. by L. A. Manyon (1971). A classic on the topic and as an example of historical study.

C.B. Brown, Singing the Gospel: Lutheran Hymns and the Success of the Reformation (2005). Outstanding study of Luther's hymns for children.

C.M. Brand, Byzantium Confronts the West, 1180–1204 (1968). Analyzes the internal and external pressures that Byzantium experienced during this quarter-century time period.

P. Brown, Augustine of Hippo: A Biography (1967). Late antiquity seen through the biography of its greatest Christian thinker.

J.H. Burns, The Cambridge History of Medieval Political Thought c. 350–c. 1450 (1991). The best scan.

R.H.C. Davis, A History of Medieval Europe: From Constantine to St. Louis (1972). Unsurpassed in clarity.

N.M. El-Cheikh, Byzantium Viewed by the Arabs (2004). Examines the Arabic-Islamic view of Byzantium.

R. Fletcher, The Barbarian Conversion: From Paganism to Christianity (1998). Up-to-date survey.

J.B. Glubb, The Great Arab Conquests (1995). Jihadists.

G. Guglielmo, ed., The Byzantines (1997). Updates key issues.

D. Gutas, Greek Thought, Arabic Culture (1998). A comparative intellectual history.

G. Holmes, ed., The Oxford History of Medieval Europe (1992). Overviews of Roman and northern Europe during the "Dark Ages."

B.J. Kaplan, Divided by Faith: Religious Conflict and the Practice of Toleration in Early Modern Europe (2007). How the Reformation created religious toleration and sowed the seeds of religious pluralism.

B. Lewis, The Middle East: A Brief History of the Last 2,000 Years (1995).

A.E. Laiou and H. Maguire, eds., Byzantium, a World Civilization (1992). Examines the centrality of Byzantium's role in world history.

C. Mango, Byzantium: The Empire of New Rome (1980).

J. Martin, Medieval Russia 980–1584 (1995). A concise narrative history.

R. Mckitterick, ed., Carolingian Culture: Emulation and Innovation (1994). Fresh essays.

J.J. Norwich, Byzantium: The Decline and Fall (1995).

J.J. Norwich, Byzantium: The Apogee (1997). The whole story in two volulmes.

G. Ostrogorsky, History of the Byzantine State (1999). Traces the thousand-year course of the Byzantine Empire.

R.I. Page, Chronicles of the Vikings: Records, Memorials, and Myths (1995). Sources galore.

F. Robinson, ed., The Cambridge Illustrated History of the Islamic World (1996). Spectacular.

S. Runciman, Byzantine Civilization (1970). Succinct, comprehensive account by a master.

P. Sawyer, The Age of the Vikings (1962). Old but solid account.

C. Stephenson, Medieval Feudalism (1969). Excellent short summary and introduction.

L. White Jr., Medieval Technology and Social Change (1962). Often fascinating account of how primitive technology changed life.

D. Whitford, Reformation and Early Modern Europe: A Guide to Research (2008). A goldmine of information on all aspects of the Reformation.

H. Wolfram, The Roman Empire and Its Germanic Peoples (1997). Challenging, but most rewarding.

Chapter 12

The Islamic Heartlands

L. Ahmed, Women and Gender in Islam: Historical Roots of a Modern Debate (1992). A good historical survey of the status of women in Middle Eastern societies.

J. Berkey, The Formation of Islam: Religion and Society in the Near East, 600–1800 (2002). An interesting new synthesis focusing on political and religious trends.

C.E. Bosworth, The Islamic Dynasties: A Chronological and Genealogical Handbook (1967). A handy reference work for dynasties and families important to Islamic history in all periods and places.

M.A. Cook, Commanding Right and Forbidding Wrong in Islamic Thought (2001). A masterful analysis of the development of Islamic law.

P.K. Hitti, History of the Arabs, 8th ed. (1964). Still a useful English resource, largely for factual detail. See especially Part IV, "The Arabs in Europe: Spain and Sicily."

A. Hourani, A History of the Arab Peoples (1991). The newest survey history and the best, at least for the Arab Islamic world.

S.K. Jayyusi, ed., The Legacy of Muslim Spain, 2 vols. (1994). A comprehensive survey of the arts, politics, literature, and society by experts in various fields.

B. Lewis, ed., Islam and the Arab World (1976). A large-format, heavily illustrated volume with many excellent articles on diverse aspects of Islamic (not simply Arab, as the misleading title indicates) civilization through the premodern period.

D. Morgan, The Mongols (1986). A recent and readable survey history.

J.J. Saunders, A History of Medieval Islam (1965). A brief and simple, if sketchy, introductory survey of Islamic history to the Mongol invasions.

India

W.T. de Bary et al., comp., Sources of Indian Tradition, 2nd ed. (1958), Vol. I, From the Beginning to 1800, ed. and rev. by Ainslie T. Embree (1988). Excellent selections from a wide variety of Indian texts, with good introductions to chapters and individual selections.

S.M. Ikram, Muslim Civilization in India (1964). The best short survey history, covering the period 711 to 1857.

R.C. Majumdar, gen. ed., The History and Culture of the Indian People, Vol. VI, The Delhi Sultanate, 3rd ed. (1980). A comprehensive political and cultural account of the period in India.

F. Robinson, ed., The Cambridge History of India, Pakistan, Bangladesh, Sri Lanka, Nepal, Bhutan, and the Maldives (1989). A very helpful quick reference source with brief but well-done survey essays on a wide range of topics relevant to South Asian history down to the present.

A. Wink, Al-Hind: The Making of the Indo-Islamic World, Vol. 1 (1991). The first of five promising volumes to be devoted to the Indo-Islamic world's history. This volume treats the seventh to eleventh centuries.

Southeast Asia

L. Andaya, The World of Maluku: Eastern Indonesia in the Early Modern Period (1993). A comprehensive view of the formation of what is now Indonesia.

B.W. Andaya and L. Andaya, A History of Malaysia (1982). A good overview of Indonesia's smaller but critical northern neighbor.

J. Siegel, Shadow and Sound: The Historical Thought of a Sumatran People (1979). An excellent analysis tracing the relation between foreign influences and local practice.

Chapter 13

B.S. Bauer, The Development of the Inca State (1992). Emphasizes archaeological evidence over the Spanish chronicles in accounting for the emergence of the Inca Empire.

B. S. Bauer, Ancient Cuzco: Heartland of the Inca (2004). Exploration of the ramifications of late-twentieth-century archaeological explorations of the ancient Inca capital

K.O. Bruhns, Ancient South America (1994). A clear discussion of the archaeology and civilization of the region with emphasis on the Andes.

E. M. Brumfiel, The Aztec World (2008). A well-illustrated work.

R.L. Burger, Chavín and the Origins of Andean Civilization (1992). A detailed study of early Andean prehistory by one of the leading authorities on Chavín.

R. L. Burger, Machu Picchu: Unveiling the Mystery of the Incas (2008). The best study of this famous site.

I. Clendinnen, Aztecs: An Interpretation (1995). A classic exploration of the Aztec world.

B. Cobo and R. Hamilton, History of the Inca Empire, rev. ed. (1983). A seventeenth-century account, with a modern translation and interpretation.

M.D. Coe, Breaking the Maya Code (1992). The story of the remarkable achievement of deciphering the ancient Maya language.

M.D. Coe, Mexico from the Olmecs to the Aztecs (2008). A wide-ranging introductory discussion.

G. Conrad and A.A. Demarest, Religion and Empire: The Dynamics of Aztec and Inca Expansionism (1984). An interesting comparative study.

T. N. D'Altroy, The Incas (2004). A major study of all aspects of Inca civilization

A. Demarest, Ancient Maya: The Rise and Fall of a Rainforest Civilization (2004). Lively and engaged in recent scholarly debates.

S. T. Evans, Ancient Mexico & Central America: Archaeology and Culture History (2008). Now the best wide-ranging introduction.

S. Freidel, L. Schele, and J. Parker, Maya Cosmos: Three Thousand Years on the Shaman's Path (1995). The best account of the subject.

S.D. Gillespie, The Aztec Kings (1989).

R. Hassig, Aztec Warfare: Imperial Expansion and Political Control (1995). Explores the achievement of the Aztec Empire.

J. Hyslop, Inka Settlement Planning (1990). A detailed study.

M. León-Portilla, Fifteen Poets of the Aztec World (1992). An anthology of translations of Aztec poetry.

G. M. McEwan, The Incas: New Perspectives (2006). An excellent overview with fine reading lists for further exploration.

H. McKillop, The Ancient May: New Perspectives (2004). Clear presentations of recent research and debates.

M.E. Miller, The Art of Mesoamerica from Olmec to Aztec (2006). Most recent edition of a pioneering work.

C. Morris and A. Von Hagen, The Inka Empire and Its Andean Origins (1993). A clear overview of Andean prehistory by a leading authority. Beautifully illustrated.

M.E. Mosely, The Incas and Their Ancestors: The Archaeology of Peru (2001). Readable and thorough.

J.A. Sabloff, The Cities of Ancient Mexico (1989). Capsule summaries of ancient Mesoamerican cultures.

L. Schele and M.E. Miller, The Blood of Kings (1986). A rich and beautifully illustrated study of ancient Maya art and society.

H. Silverman, Andean Archaeology (2004). Overview of various Andean peoples.

M.E. Smith, The Aztecs (2002). Emphasizes impact of late-twentieth-century archaeological research.

R. Stone-Miller, Art of the Andes: From Chavin to Inca (2002). A well-illustrated overview.

Chapter 14

J. Abun-Nasr, A History of the Maghrib in the Islamic Period (1987). The most recent North African survey. Pages 59–247 are relevant to this chapter.

E.K. Akyeampong, ed., Themes in West Africa's History (2006). A wide-ranging collection of essays by leading scholars.

I. Battuta, N. King, and S. Hamdun, Ibn Battuta in Black Africa, rev. ed. (2005). Well-selected excerpts from Battuta's extensive journals.

P. Ben-Amos, Art, Innovation and Politics in Eighteenth-Century Benin (1999). Offers insights into the many levels of meaning and authority in Benin's artworks.

I. Berger, E.F. White, and C. Skidmore-Hess, Women in Sub-Saharan Africa: Restoring Women to History (1999). A valuable resource on the role of women in African history.

D. Birminham, Central Africa to 1870 (1981). Chapters from the Cambridge History of Africa that give a brief, lucid overview of developments in this region.

P. Bohannan and P. Curtin, Africa and Africans, rev. ed. (1995). Accessible, topical approach to African history, culture, society, politics, and economics.

P.D. Curtin, S. Feiermann, L. Thompson, and J. Vansina, African History, rev. ed. (1995). An older, but masterly survey. The relevant portions are Chapters 6–9.

B. Davidson, West Africa before the Colonial Era (1998). A typically readable survey by one of the great popularizers of African history.

R. Elphick, Kraal and Castle: Khoikhoi and the Founding of White South Africa (1977). An incisive, informative interpretation of the history of the Khoikhoi and their fateful interaction with European colonization.

R. Elphick and H. Giliomee, The Shaping of South African Society, 1652–1820 (1979). A superb, synthetic history of this crucial period.

J.D. Fage, A History of Africa, rev. ed., (2001). Still a readable survey history.

E. Gilbert and J. Reynolds, Africa in World History (2004). The best new survey of African history, placing it in a global context. See especially Chapters 6 and 7 on Islam, and Chapters 9 through 12 for the period leading to European colonization.

M. Hiskett, The Development of Islam in West Africa (1984). The standard survey study of the subject. Of the relevant sections (Chapters 1–10, 12, 15), that on Hausaland, which is treated only in passing in this text, is noteworthy.

M. Horton and J. Middleton, The Swahili (2000).

R.W. July, A History of the African People, 3rd ed. (1980). Chapters 3–6 treat Africa before about 1800 area by area; Chapter 7 deals with "The Coming of Europe."

N. Levtzion and R. Pouwels, eds. History of Islam in Africa (2000). A wide-ranging collection of essays.

N. Levtzion and D.T. Niani, eds., Africa from the Twelfth to the Sixteenth Century, UNESCO General History of Africa, Vol. IV (1984). Many survey articles cover the various regions and major states of Africa in the centuries noted in the title.

R. Oliver, The African Experience (1991). A masterly, balanced, and engaging survey, with outstanding syntheses and summaries of recent research.

C.A. Quinn and F. Quinn, Pride, Faith, and Fear: Islam in Sub-Saharan Africa (2005). A readable account of Islam in Africa, bringing the story up to the present.

D. Robinson, Muslim Societies in African History (2004). A comprehensive overview.

A.F.C. Ryder, Benin and the Europeans: 1485–1897 (1969). A basic study.

John K. Thornton, The Kingdom of Kongo: Civil War and Transition, 1641–1718 (1983). A detailed and perceptive analysis for those who wish to delve into Kongo state and society in the seventeenth century.

M. Wilson and L. Thompson, eds., The Oxford History of South Africa, Vol. I., South Africa to 1870 (1969). Relatively detailed, if occasionally dated, treatment.

Chapter 15

M. Brecht, Martin Luther: His Road to Reformation, 1483–1521 (1985). Best on young Luther.

C. Brown et al., Rembrandt: The Master and His Workshop (1991). A great master's art and influence.

R. Briggs, Witches and Neighbors: A History of European Witchcraft (1996). A readable introduction.

E. Duffy, The Stripping of the Altars (1992). Strongest argument yet that there was no deep Reformation in England.

H.O. Evennett, The Spirit of the Counter Reformation (1968). The continuity and independence of Catholic reform.

Hans-Jürgen Goertz, The Anabaptists (1996). Best treatment of minority Protestants.

O.P. Grell and A. Cunningham, Health Care and Poor Relief in Protestant Europe (1997). The civic side of the Reformation.

M. Holt, The French Wars of Religion, 1562–1629 (1995). Scholarly appreciation of religious side of the story.

J.C. Hutchison, Albrecht Durer (1990). The life behind the art.

H. Jedin, A History of the Council of Trent, Vols. 1, 2 (1957–1961). Comprehensive, detailed, and authoritative.

M. Kitchen, The Cambridge Illustrated History of Germany (1996). Comprehensive and accessible.

A. Kors and E. Peters, eds., European Witchcraft, 1100–1700 (1972). Classics of witch belief.

W. Maccaffrey, Elizabeth I (1993). Magisterial study.

G. Mattingly, The Armada (1959). A masterpiece, novel-like in style.

D. Mccolloch, The Reformation (2004). No stone unturned, with English emphasis.

H.A. Oberman, Luther: Man between God and Devil (1989). Authoritative biography.

J.W. O'Malley, The First Jesuits (1993). Extremely detailed account of the creation of the Society of Jesus and its original purposes.

S. Ozment, The Age of Reform, 1250–1550: An Intellectual and Religious History of Late Medieval and Reformation Europe (1980). Broad, lucid survey.

S. Ozment, When Fathers Ruled: Family Life in Reformation Europe (1983). Effort to portray the constructive side of Protestant thinking about family relationships.

S. Ozment, The Bürgermeister's Daughter: Scandal in a Sixteenth-Century German Town (1996). What a woman could do at law in the sixteenth century.

G. Parker, The Thirty Years' War (1984). Large, lucid survey.

J.H. Parry, The Age of Reconnaissance (1964). A comprehensive account of explorations from 1450 to 1650.

W. Prinz, Durer (1998). Latest biography of Germany's greatest painter.

J.J. Scarisbrick, Henry VIII (1968). The best account of Henry's reign.

G. Strauss, ed. and trans., Manifestations of Discontent in Germany on the Eve of the Reformation (1971). A rich collection of sources for both rural and urban scenes.

H. Wunder, *He Is the Sun, She Is the Moon: Women in Early Modern Germany* (1998). Best study of early modern women.

Chapter 16

J. Abun-Nasr, *A History of the Maghrib in the Islamic Period* (1987). The most recent North African survey. Pages 59–247 are relevant to this chapter.

D. Birmingham, *Central Africa to 1870* (1981). Chapters from the Cambridge History of Africa that give a brief, lucid overview of developments in this region.

P. Bohannan and P. Curtin, *Africa and Africans*, rev. ed. (1971). Accessible, topical approach to African history, culture, society, politics, and economics.

P.D. Curtin, S. Feiermann, L. Thompson, and J. Vansina, *African History* (1978). An older, but masterly survey. The relevant portions are Chapters 6–9.

R. Elphick, *Kraal and Castle: Khoikhoi and the Founding of White South Africa* (1977). An incisive, informative interpretation of the history of the Khoikhoi and their fateful interaction with European colonization.

R. Elphick and H. Giliomee, *The Shaping of South African Society, 1652–1820* (1979). A superb, synthetic history of this crucial period.

J.D. Fage, *A History of Africa* (1978). Still a readable survey history.

M. Hiskett, *The Development of Islam in West Africa* (1984). The standard survey study of the subject. Of the relevant sections (Chapters 1–10, 12, 15), that on Hausaland, which is treated only in passing in this text, is noteworthy.

R.W. July, *Precolonial Africa: An Economic and Social History* (1975). Chapter 10 gives an interesting overall picture of slaving in African history.

R.W. July, *A History of the African People*, 3rd ed. (1980). Chapters 3–6 treat Africa before about 1800 area by area; Chapter 7 deals with "The Coming of Europe."

I.M. Lewis, ed., *Islam in Tropical Africa* (1966), pp. 4–96. Lewis's introduction is one of the best brief summaries of the role of Islam in West Africa and the Sudan.

D.T. Niani, ed., *Africa from the Twelfth to the Sixteenth Century, UNESCO General History of Africa*, Vol. IV (1984). Many survey articles cover the various regions and major states of Africa in the centuries noted in the title.

R. Oliver, *The African Experience* (1991). A masterly, balanced, and engaging survey, with outstanding syntheses and summaries of recent research.

J.A. Rawley, *The Transatlantic Slave Trade: A History* (1981). Impressively documented, detailed, and well-presented survey history of the Atlantic trade; little focus on African dimensions.

A.F.C. Ryder, *Benin and the Europeans: 1485–1897* (1969). A basic study.

John K. Thornton, *The Kingdom of Kongo: Civil War and Transition, 1641–1718* (1983). A detailed and perceptive analysis for those who wish to delve into Kongo state and society in the seventeenth century.

M. Wilson and L. Thompson, eds., *The Oxford History of South Africa*, Vol. I., South Africa to 1870 (1969). Relatively detailed, if occasionally dated, treatment.

Chapter 17

R. Adorno, *The Polemics of Possession in Spanish American Narrative* (2008). An exploration of the rhetoric used by the Spanish to assure their holding of their American empire.

A.C. Bailey, *African Voices of the Atlantic Slave Trade: Beyond the Silence and the Shame* (2006). Delivers just what the title promises.

B. Bailyn, *Atlantic History: Concepts and Contours* (2005). An essential overview to this burgeoning area of historical inquiry, written by a leader in the field.

I. Berlin, *Many Thousands Gone: The First Two Centuries of Slavery in North America* (1998); *Generations of Captivity: A History of African American Slaves* (2003). Two volumes representing the most extensive and important recent treatment of slavery in North America; highlights the diversity of slave experiences.

R. Blackburn, *The Making of New World Slavery from the Baroque to the Modern 1492–1800* (1997). An extraordinary work.

V. Carretta, *Equiano, the African: The Biography of a Self-Made Man* (reprint 2007). Provides context and analysis of the renowned accounts of one-time slave Olaudah Equiano.

N.D. Cook, *Born to Die: Disease and New World Conquest, 1492–1650* (1998). A survey of the devastating impact of previously unknown diseases on the native populations of the Americas.

M.S. Creighton and L. Norling, eds. *Iron Men, Wooden Women: Gender and Seafaring in the Atlantic World, 1700–1920* (2006). Eye-opening accounts of life at sea, and how gender roles were shaped and challenged on the Atlantic.

P.D. Curtin, *The Atlantic Slave Trade: A Census* (1969). Remains a basic work.

P.D. Curtin, *The Rise and Fall of the Plantation Complex* (1998). Places the plantation economy in the context of world history.

D.B. Davis, *Inhuman Bondage: The Rise and Fall of Slavery in the New World* (2006). A splendid overview by a leading scholar.

J.H. Elliot, *Empires of the Atlantic World: Britain and Spain in America 1492–1830* (2006). A brilliant, accessible comparative.

D. Eltis, *The Rise of African Slavery in the Americas* (1999). Detailed discussion of the size and scope of the Atlantic market, with attention to the role of Africans on both sides of the Atlantic.

H.L. Gates Jr. and W.L. Andrews, eds., *Pioneers of the Black Atlantic: Five Slave Narratives from the Enlightenment, 1772–1815* (1998). An anthology of autobiographical accounts.

S. Gruzinski, *The Conquest of Mexico: The Incorporation of Indian Societies into the Western World, 16th–18th Centuries* (1993). Interprets the experience of Native Americans, from their own point of view, during the time of the Spanish conquest.

L. Hanke, *All Mankind Is One: A Study of the Disputation between Bartolome De Las Casas and Juan Gines De Sepulveda in 1550 on the Intellectual and Religious* (1994). A study of the Spanish debate over the humanity of Native Americans in the Spanish Empire.

R. Harms, The Diligent: A Voyage through the Worlds of the Slave Trade (2002). A powerful narrative of the voyage of a French slave trader.

J. Hemming, The Conquest of the Incas, rev. ed., (2003). A lucid account of the conquest of the Inca Empire and its aftermath.

J. Hemming, Red Gold: The Conquest of the Brazilian Native Americans, 1500–1760 (1978). A careful account with excellent bibliography.

H. Kamen, Empire: How Spain Became a World Power, 1492–1763 (2005). An excellent overview by a major scholar.

H. Klein, The Atlantic Slave Trade (1999). A synthesis of scholarly knowledge.

W. Klooster and A. Padula, The Atlantic World: Essays on Slavery, Migration, and Imagination (2004). Essays by leading scholars examine important aspects of the creation of a new way of living—and a new way of thinking about the world.

P.E. Lovejoy, Transformations in Slavery: A History of Slavery in Africa (2000). An important new evaluation of slavery as it was practiced within Africa, and its relation to the Islamic and transatlantic slave trades.

K. Macquarrie, The Last Days of the Incas (2007). A fast-moving popular account.

K. Mann, Rethinking the African Diaspora: The Making of a Black Atlantic World in the Bight of Benin and Brazil (2005). This analysis of the dynamics of human and cultural migration and exchange on the busiest route of the slave trade is a significant addition to Atlantic World scholarship.

P. Manning, Slavery and African Life: Occidental, Oriental, and African Slave Trades (1990). An admirably concise economic-historical synthesis of the evidence, with multiple tables and statistics to supplement the magisterial analysis.

A. Pagden, Lords of All the World: Ideologies of Empire in Spain, Britain, and France c. 1500–c. 1800 (1995). An effort to explain the imperial thinking of the major European powers.

S. Peabody and K. Grinberg, Slavery, Freedom, and the Law in the Atlantic World: A Brief History with Documents (2007). Examines the legal frameworks through which slavery was institutionalized, and documents the many ways people challenged slavery.

M. Rediker, The Slave Ship: A Human History (2007). A exploration of the harrowing experience of slave transportation across the Atlantic.

M. Rediker, Villains of all Nations: Atlantic Pirates in the Golden Age (2008). A serious historical treatment of the subject.

D.K. Richter, Facing East from Indian Country: A Native History of Early America, new ed. (2003). Uses the biographies of three Native Americans to offer a fresh perspective on North American history from the time of Columbus to the American Revolution.

M. Russell, Seven Myths of the Spanish Conquest (2003). Challenges many long-held views of the event.

S.B. Schwartz, All Can Be Saved: Religious Tolerance and Salvation in the Iberian Atlantic World (2009). The most important recent study of the social and religious life of the Spanish Empire.

S.B. Schwartz, ed., Tropical Babylons: Sugar and the Making of the Atlantic World, 1450–1680 (2003). A comprehensive examination of the role of sugar in the plantation economy.

S.E. Smallwood, Saltwater Slavery: A Middle Passage from Africa to American Diaspora (2008). An intimate examination of the experience and economy of the slave trade.

H. Thomas, Conquest: Montezuma, Cortés, and the Fall of Old Mexico (1993). A splendid modern narrative of the event, with careful attention to the character of the participants.

J. Thornton, Africa and Africans in the Making of the Atlantic World, 1400–1680 (1992). A discussion of the role of Africans in the emergence of the transatlantic economy.

N. Wachtel, The Vision of the Vanquished: The Spanish Conquest of Peru through Indian Eyes, 1530–1570 (1977). A presentation of the Incan experience of conquest.

C.A. Williams, Bridging the Early Modern Atlantic World (2009). Explores the cultural and ethnic diversity of the transatlantic economy.

Chapter 18

China

D. Bodde and C. Morris, Law in Imperial China (1967). Focuses on the Qing Dynasty (1644–1911).

T. Brook, The Confusions of Pleasure: Commerce and Culture in Ming China (1988).

C.S. Chang and S.L.H. Chang, Crisis and Transformation in Seventeenth-century China: Society, Culture, and Modernity (1992).

P. Crossley, Translucent Mirror: History and Identity in Qing Imperial Ideology (1999).

W.T. De Bary, Learning for One's Self: Essays on the Individual in Neo-Confucian Thought (1991). A useful corrective to the view that Confucianism is simply a social ideology.

M.C. Elliott, The Manchu Way: The Eight Banners and Ethnic Identity in Late Imperial China (2001). The latest word; compare to Crossley above.

M. Elvin, The Pattern of the Chinese Past: A Social and Economic Interpretation (1973). A controversial but stimulating interpretation of Chinese economic history in terms of technology. It brings in earlier periods as well as the Ming, Qing, and modern China.

J.K. Fairbank, ed., The Chinese World Order: Traditional China's Foreign Relations (1968). An examination of the Chinese tribute system and its varying applications.

H.L. Kahn, Monarchy in the Emperor's Eyes: Image and Reality in the Ch'ien-lung Reign (1971). A study of the Chinese court during the mid-Qing period.

P. Kuhn, Soulstealers: The Chinese Sorcery Scare of 1768 (1990).

Li Yu, The Carnal Prayer Mat, trans. by P. Hanan (1990).

F. Mote and D. Twitchett, eds., The Cambridge History of China: The Ming Dynasty 1368–1644, Vols. VI (1988) and VII (1998).

S. Naquin, Peking Temples and City Life, 1400–1900 (2000).

S. Naquin and E.S. Rawski, Chinese Society in the Eighteenth Century (1987).

J.B. Parsons, The Peasant Rebellions of the Late Ming Dynasty (1970).

P.C. Perdue, Exhausting the Earth, State and Peasant in Hunan, 1500–1850 (1987).

D.H. Perkins, Agricultural Development in China, 1368–1968 (1969).

E. Rawski, The Last Emperors: A Social History of Qing Imperial Institutions (1998).

M. Ricci, China in the Sixteenth Century: The Journals of Matthew Ricci, 1583–1610 (1953).

W. Rowe, Hankow (1984). A study of a city in late imperial China.

G.W. Skinner, The City in Late Imperial China (1977).

J.D. Spence, Ts'ao Yin and the K'ang-hsi Emperor: Bondservant and Master (1966). An excellent study of the early Qing court.

J.D. Spence, Emperor of China: A Self-Portrait of K'ang-hsi (1974). The title of this readable book does not adequately convey the extent of the author's contribution to the study of the early Qing emperor.

J.D. Spence, Treason by the Book (2001). An account of the legal workings of the authoritarian Qing state that reads like a detective story.

L.A. Struve, trans. and ed., Voices from the Ming-Qing Cataclysm (1993). A reader with translations of Chinese sources.

F. Wakeman, The Great Enterprise (1985). On the founding of the Manchu Dynasty.

Japan

M.E. Berry, Hideyoshi (1982). A study of the sixteenth-century unifier of Japan.

M.E. Berry, The Culture of Civil War in Kyoto (1994). On the Warring States era.

H. Bolitho, Treasures among Men: The Fudai Daimyo in Tokugawa Japan (1974). A study in depth.

H. Bolitho, Bereavement and Consolation: Testimonies from Tokugawa Japan (2003). Instances of how Tokugawa Japanese handled the death of a child.

C.R. Boxer, The Christian Century in Japan, 1549–1650 (1951).

The Cambridge History of Japan; Vol. 4, J.W. Hall, ed., Early Modern Japan (1991). A multi-author work.

M. Chikamatsu, Major Plays of Chikamatsu, trans. by D. Keene (1961).

R.P. Dore, Education in Tokugawa Japan (1965).

G.S. Elison, Deus Destroyed: The Image of Christianity in Early Modern Japan (1973). A brilliant study of the persecutions of Christianity during the early Tokugawa period.

J.W. Hall and M. Jansen, eds., Studies in the Institutional History of Early Modern Japan (1968). A collection of articles on Tokugawa institutions.

J.W. Hall, K. Nagahara, and K. Yamamura, eds., Japan before Tokugawa (1981).

S. Hanley, Everyday Things in Premodern Japan: The Hidden Legacy of Material Culture (1997).

H.S. Hibbett, The Floating World in Japanese Fiction (1959). An eminently readable study of early Tokugawa literature.

M. Jansen, ed., The Nineteenth Century, Vol. 5 in The Cambridge History of Japan (1989).

K. Katsu, Musui's Story, trans. by T. Craig (1988). The life and adventures of a boisterous, no-good samurai of the early nineteenth century. Eminently readable.

D. Keene, trans., Chushingura, the Treasury of Loyal Retainers (1971). The puppet play about the forty-seven men who took revenge on the enemy of their former lord.

O.G. Lidin, Tanegashima: The Arrival of Europe in Japan (2002). The impact of the musket and Europeans on sixteenth-century Japan.

M. Maruyama, Studies in the Intellectual History of Tokugawa Japan, trans. by M. Hane (1974). A seminal work in this field by one of modern Japan's greatest scholars.

J.L. McClain et al., Edo and Paris: Urban Life and the State in the Early Modern Era (1994). Comparison of city life and government role in the capitals of Tokugawa Japan and France.

K.W. Nakai, Shogunal Politics (1988). A brilliant study of Arai Hakuseki's conceptualization of Tokugawa government.

P. Nosco, ed., Confucianism and Tokugawa Culture (1984). A lively collection of essays.

H. Ooms, Tokugawa Village Practice: Class, Status, Power, Law (1996).

A. Ravina, Land and Lordship in Early Modern Japan (1999). A sociopolitical study of three Tokugawa domains.

I. Saikaku, The Japanese Family Storehouse, trans. by G.W. Sargent (1959). A lively novel about merchant life in seventeenth-century Japan.

G.B. Sansom, The Western World and Japan (1950).

J.A. Sawada, Confucian Values and Popular Zen (1993). A study of Shingaku, a popular Tokugawa religious sect.

C.D. Sheldon, The Rise of the Merchant Class in Tokugawa Japan (1958).

T.C. Smith, The Agrarian Origins of Modern Japan (1959). On the evolution of farming and rural social organization in Tokugawa Japan.

P.F. Souyri, The World Turned Upside Down: Medieval Japanese Society (2001). After a running start from the late Heian period, an analysis of the overthrow of lords by their vassals.

R.P. Toby, State and Diplomacy in Early Modern Japan: Asia in the Development of the Tokugawa Bakufu (1984).

C. Totman, Tokugawa Ieyasu: Shōgun (1983).

C. Totman, Green Archipelago, Forestry in Preindustrial Japan (1989).

H.P. Varley, The Ōnin War: History of Its Origins and Background with a Selective Translation of the Chronicle of Ōnin (1967).

K. Yamamura and S.B. Hanley, Economic and Demographic Change in Preindustrial Japan, 1600–1868 (1977).

Korea

T. Hatada, A History of Korea (1969).

W.E. Henthorn, A History of Korea (1971).

Ki-Baik Lee, A New History of Korea (1984).

P. Lee, Sourcebook of Korean Civilization, Vol. I (1993).

Vietnam

J. Buttinger, A Dragon Defiant, a Short History of Vietnam (1972).
Nguyen Du, The Tale of Kieu (1983).
N. Tarling, ed., The Cambridge History of Southeast Asia (1992).
K. Taylor, The Birth of Vietnam (1983).
A.B. Woodside, Vietnam and the Chinese Model (1988).

Chapter 19

R.C. Allen, The British Industrial Revolution in Global Perspective (2009). A much needed addition to the study of the industrial revolution.

F. Anderson, The Crucible of War: The Seven Years' War and the Fate of Empire in British North America, 1754–1766 (2000). A splendid narrative and analysis.

W. Beik, Louis XIV and Absolutism: A Brief Study with Documents (2000). An excellent collection by a major scholar of absolutism.

T. Blanning, The Pursuit of Glory: Europe 1648–1815 (2007). The best recent synthesis of the emergence of the modern European state system.

J. Blum, Lord and Peasant in Russia from the Ninth to the Nineteenth Century (1961). Remains a thorough and wide-ranging discussion.

P. Burke, The Fabrication of Louis XIV (1992). Examines the manner in which the public image of Louis XIV was forged in art.

J. Burnet, Gender, Work and Wages in Industrial Revolution Britain (2008). A major revisionist study of the wage structure for work by men and women.

P. Bushkovitch, Peter the Great: The Struggle for Power, 1671–1725 (2001). Replaces previous studies.

C. Clark, The Rise and Downfall of Prussia 1600-1947 (2006). A stunning survey.

L. Colley, Britons: Forging the Nation, 1707–1837 (1992) A major study of the making of British nationhood.

P. Deane, The First Industrial Revolution (1999). A well-balanced and systematic treatment.

J. De Vries, The Industrious Revolution: Consumer Behavior and the Household Economy, 1650 to the Present (2008). Discusses the rise of development through the psychology and actions of consumers, thus presenting an important new perspective.

W. Doyle, The Old European Order, 1660–1800 (1992). Remains a classic study.

D. Fraser, Frederick the Great: King of Prussia (2001) Excellent on both Frederick and eighteenth-century Prussia.

T. Harris, Restoration: Charles II and His Kingdom, 1660–1685 (2006). A major exploration of the tumultuous years of the restoration of the English monarchy after the civil war.

E. Hobsbawm, Industry and Empire: The Birth of the Industrial Revolution (1999). A survey by a major historian of the subject.

K. Honeyman, Women, Gender and Industrialization in England, 1700–1850 (2000). Emphasizes how certain work or economic roles became associated with either men or women.

O.H. Hufton, The Poor of Eighteenth-Century France, 1750–1789 (1975). A brilliant classic study of poverty and the family economy.

L. Hughes, Russia in the Age of Peter the Great (1998). An excellent account.

C.J. Ingrao, The Habsburg Monarchy, 1618–1815 (2000). The best recent survey.

D.I. Kertzer and M. Barbagli, The History of the European Family: Family Life in Early Modern Times, 1500–1709 (2001). A series of broad-ranging essays covering the entire Continent.

S. King and G. Timmons, Making Sense of the Industrial Revolution: English Economy and Society, 1700–1850 (2001). Examines the industrial revolution through the social institutions that brought it about and were changed by it.

M. Kishlansky, A Monarchy Transformed: Britain 1603–1714 (1996) An excellent synthesis.

A. Lossky, Louis XIV and the French Monarchy (1994). The most recent major analysis.

F.E. Manuel, The Broken Staff: Judaism through Christian Eyes (1992). An important discussion of Christian interpretations of Judaism.

M.A. Meyer, The Origins of the Modern Jew: Jewish Identity and European Culture in Germany, 1749–1824 (1967). A general introduction organized around individual case studies.

S. Pincus, 1688: The First Modern Revolution (2009). The most important recent study.

G. Treasure, *Louis XIV (2001). The best, most accessible recent study.*

D. Valenze, The First Industrial Woman (1995). An elegant work exploring the manner in which industrialization transformed the work of women.

J. West, Gunpower, Government, and War in the Mid-Eighteenth Century (1991). A study of how warfare touched much government of the day.

Chapter 20

S.S. Blair and J. Bloom, The Art and Architecture of Islam, 1250–1800 (1994). A fine survey of the period for all parts of the Islamic world.

R. Canfield, ed., Turko-Persia in Historical Perspctive (1991). A good general collection of essays.

K. Chelebi, The Balance of Truth (1957). A marvelous volume of essays and reflections by probably the major intellectual of Ottoman times.

W.T. de Bary et al., comp., Sources of Indian Tradition, 2nd ed. (1958), Vol. I, From the Beginning to 1800, ed. and rev. by Ainslie T. Embree (1988). Excellent selections from a wide variety of Indian texts, with good introductions to chapters and individual selections.

S. Faroqi, Towns and Townsmen of Ottoman Anatolia (1984). Examines the changing balances of economic power between the urban and rural areas.

C.H. Fleischer, Bureaucrat and Intellectual in the Ottoman Empire: The Historian Mustafa Ali (1541–1600) (1986). A major study of Ottoman intellectual history.

G. Hambly, Central Asia (1966). Excellent survey chapters (9–13) on the Chaghatay and Uzbek (Shaybanid) Turks.

R.S. Hattox, Coffee and Coffee-Houses: The Origins of a Social Beverage in the Medieval Near East (1985). A fascinating piece of social history.

M.G.S. Hodgson, The Gunpowder Empires and Modern Times, Vol. 3 of The Venture of Islam, 3 vols. (1974). Less ample than Vols. 1 and 2 of Hodgson's monumental history, but a thoughtful survey of the great post–1500 empires.

S.M. Ikram, Muslim Civilization in India (1964). Still the best short survey history, covering the period from 711 to 1857.

H. Inalcik, The Ottoman Empire: The Classical Age, 1300–1600 (1973). An excellent, if dated, survey with solid treatment of Ottoman social, religious, and political institutions.

H. Inalcik, An Economic and Social History of the Ottoman Empire, 1300–1914 (1994). A masterly survey by the dean of Ottoman studies today.

C. Kafadar, Between Two Worlds: The Construction of the Ottoman State (1995). A readable analysis of theories of Ottoman origins and early development.

N.R. Keddie, ed., Scholars, Saints, and Sufis: Muslim Religious Institutions in the Middle East since 1500 (1972). A collection of interesting articles well worth reading.

M. Mujeeb, The Indian Muslims (1967). The best cultural study of Islamic civilization in India as a whole, from its origins onward.

G. Necipoglu, Architecture, Ceremonial, and Power: The Topkapi Palace in the Fifteenth and Sixteenth Centuries (1991). A superb analysis of the symbolism of Ottoman power and authority.

L. Pierce, The Imperial Harem: Women and Sex in the Ottoman Empire (1993). Ground-breaking study on the role of women in the Ottoman Empire.

D. Quatarert, An Economic and Social History of the Ottoman Empire, 1300–1914 (1994). The authoritative account of Ottoman economy and society.

J. Richards, The Mughal Empire, Vol. 5 of The New Cambridge History of India (1993). A impressive synthesis of the varying interpretations of Mughal India.

S.A.A. Rizvi, The Wonder That Was India, Vol. II (1987). A sequel to Basham's original The Wonder That Was India; treats Mughal life, culture, and history from 1200 to 1700.

F. Robinson, Atlas of the Islamic World since 1500 (1982). Brief, excellent historical essays, color illustrations with detailed accompanying text, and chronological tables, as well as precise maps, make this a refreshing general reference work.

R. Savory, Iran under the Safavids (1980). A solid and readable survey.

S.J. Shaw, Empire of the Gazis: The Rise and Decline of the Ottoman Empire, 1280–1808, Vol. I of History of the Ottoman Empire and Modern Turkey (1976). A solid historical survey with excellent bibliographic essays for each chapter and a good index.

Chapter 21

D. Beales, Joseph II, 2 Vols. (1987, 2009). The best treatment in English of the life of Joseph II.

M. Biagioli, Galileo Courtier: The Practice of Science in the Culture of Absolutism (1993). A major revisionist work that emphasizes the role of the political setting in Galileo's career and thought.

D.D. Bien, The Calas Affair: Persecution, Toleration, and Heresy in Eighteenth-Century Toulouse (1960). Classic treatment of the famous case.

T.C.W. Blanning, The Culture of Power and the Power of Culture: Old Regime Europe 1660–1789 (2002). The strongest treatment of the relationship of eighteenth-century cultural changes and politics.

P. Blom, Enlightening the World: Encyclopedie, The Book That Changed the Course of History (2005). A lively, accessible introduction.

J. Buchan, Crowded with Genius: The Scottish Enlightenment (2003). A lively, accessible introduction.

J.A. Conner, Kepler's Witch: An Astronomer's Discovery of Cosmic Order amid Religious War, Political Intrigue, and the Heresy Trial of His Mother (2005). Fascinating account of Kepler's effort to vindicate his mother against charges of witchcraft.

L. Damrosch, Rousseau: Restless Genius (2007). The best recent biography.

R. Darnton, The Literary Underground of the Old Regime (1982). Classic essays on the world of printers, publishers, and booksellers.

P. Dear, Revolutionizing the Sciences: European Knowledge and Its Ambitions, 1500–1700 (2001). A broad-ranging study of both the ideas and institutions of the new science.

I. De Madariaga, Catherine the Great: A Short History (1990). A good brief biography.

M. Feingold, The Newtonian Moment: Isaac Newton and the Making of Modern Culture (2004). A superb, well-illustrated volume.

S. Gaukroger, The Emergence of a Scientific Culture: Science and the Shaping of Modernity (2007). A challenging book exploring the differing understanding of natural knowledge in early modern European culture.

S. Gaukroger, Francis Bacon and the Transformation of Early-Modern Philosophy (2001). An excellent, accessible introduction.

J. Gleixk, Isaac Newton (2003). The best brief biography.

D. Goodman, The Republic of Letters: A Cultural History of the French Enlightenment (1994). Concentrates on the role of salons.

J.L. Heilbron, The Sun in the Church: Cathedrals as Solar Observatories (2000). A remarkable study of the manner in which Roman Catholic cathedrals were used to make astsronomical observations and calculations.

C. Hesse, The Other Enlightenment: How French Women Became Modern (2004). Explores the manner in which French women authors created their own sphere of thought and cultural activity.

K.J. Howell, God's Two Books: Copernican Cosmology and Biblical Interpretation in Early Modern Science (2003). Best introduction to early modern issues of science and religion.

J. Melton, The Rise of the Public in Enlightenmen Europe (2001). A superb overview of the emergence of new institutions that made the expression of a broad public opinion possible in Europe.

C. A. Kors, Encyclopedia of the Enlightenment (2002). A major reference work on all of the chief intellectual themes of the era.

J. Marshall, John Locke, Toleration and Early Enlightenment Culture (2006). A magisterial, challenging survey of seventeenth-century arguments for and against toleration.

T. Munck, The Enlightenment: A Comparative Social History 1721–1794 (2000). A clear introduction to the social background that made possible the spread of Enlightenment thought.

S. Muthu, Enlightenment against Empire (2003) A study of philosophes who criticized the European empires of their day.

D. Outram, The Enlightenment (1995). An excellent brief introduction.

R. Peason, Voltaire Almighty: A Life in Pursuit of Freedom (2005). An accessible biography.

R. Porter, The Creation of the Modern World: The Untold Story of the British Enlightenment (2001). A superb, lively overview.

J. Repcheck, Copernicus' Secret: How the Scientific Revolution Began (2007). A highly accessible biography of Copernicus.

E. Rothchild, Economic Sentiments: Adam Smith, Condorcet, and the Enlightenment (2001). A sensitive account of Smith's thought and its relationship to the social questions of the day.

S. Shapin, The Scientific Revolution (1996). An important revisionist survey emphasizing social factors.

J. Sheehan, The Enlightenment Bible (2007). Explores the Enlightenment treatment of the Bible.

D. Sorkin, The Religious Enlightenment: Protestants, Jews, and Catholics from London to Vienna (2008). Argues that important Enlightenment figures sought to protect religion.

L. Steinbrügge, The Moral Sex: Woman's Nature in the French Enlightenment (1995). Emphasizes the conservative nature of Enlightenment thought on women.

P. Zagorin, How the Idea of Religious Toleration Came to the West (2003). An excellent exploration of the rise of toleration.

Chapter 22

D. Andress, The Terror: The Merciless War for Freedom in Revolutionary France (2006). The best recent survey of the reign of terror.

R. Anstey, The Atlantic Slave Trade and British Abolition, 1760–1810 (1975). A standard overview that emphasizes the role of religious factors.

B. Bailyn, The Ideological Origins of the American Revolution (1967). An important work illustrating the role of English radical thought in the perceptions of the American colonists.

K.M. Baker, Inventing the French Revolution: Essays on French Political Culture in the Eighteenth Century (1990). Important essays on political thought before and during the revolution.

K.M. Baker and C. Lucas, eds., The French Revolution and the Creation of Modern Political Culture, 3 vols. (1987). A splendid collection of important original articles on all aspects of politics during the revolution.

R.J. Barman, Brazil: The Forging of a Nation, 1798–1852 (1988). The best coverage of this period.

D. Bell, The First Total War: Napoleon's Europe and the Birth of Warfare as We Know It (2007). A consideration of the Napoleonic conflicts and the culture of warfare.

M. S. Bell, Toussaint Louverture: A Biography (2007). An outstanding new biography.

J.F. Bernard, Talleyrand: A Biography (1973). A useful account.

L. Bethell, The Cambridge History of Latin America, Vol. 3 (1985). Contains an extensive treatment of independence.

R. Blackburn, The Overthrow of Colonial Slavery, 1776–1848 (1988). A major discussion quite skeptical of the humanitarian interpretation.

J. Brooke, King George III (1972). The best biography.

R. Cobb, The People's Armies (1987). The major treatment in English of the revolutionary army.

O. Connelly, Napoleon's Satellite Kingdoms (1965). The rule of Napoleon and his family in Europe.

D.B. Davis, The Problem of Slavery in the Age of Revolution, 1770–1823 (1975). A transatlantic perspective on the issue.

W. Doyle, The Oxford History of the French Revolution (2003). A broad, complex narrative with an excellent bibliography.

L. Dubois, Avengers of the New World: The Story of the Haitian Revolution (2004). An analytic narrative likely to replace others.

P. Dwyer, Napoleon: The Path to Power, 1769–1799 (2008). A major study of the subject.

J. J. Ellis, His Excellency: George Washington (2004). A biography that explores the entire era of the American Revolution.

M. Glover, The Peninsular War, 1807–1814: A Concise Military History (1974). An interesting account of the military campaign that so drained Napoleon's resources in western Europe.

J. Godechot, The Counter-Revolution: Doctrine and Action, 1789–1804 (1971). An examination of opposition to the revolution.

A. Goodwin, The Friends of Liberty: The English Democratic Movement in the Age of the French Revolution (1979). A major work that explores the impact of the French Revolution on English radicalism.

L. Hunt, Politics, Culture, and Class in the French Revolution (1986). A series of essays that focus on the modes of expression of the revolutionary values and political ideas.

F. Kagan, The End of the old order: Napoleon and Europe, 1801–1805 (2006). A masterful narrative.

W.W. Kaufmann, British Policy and the Independence of Latin America, 1802–1828 (1951). A standard discussion of an important relationship.

E. Kennedy, A Cultural History of the French Revolution (1989). An important examination of the role of the arts, schools, clubs, and intellectual institutions.

M. Kennedy, The Jacobin Clubs in the French Revolution: The First Years (1982). A careful scrutiny of the organizations chiefly responsible for the radicalizing of the revolution.

M. Kennedy, The Jacobin Clubs in the French Revolution: The Middle Years (1988). A continuation of the previously listed study.

H. Kissinger, A World Restored: Metternich, Castlereagh and the Problems of Peace, 1812–1822 (1957). A provocative study by an author who became an American secretary of state.

G. Lefebvre, The Coming of the French Revolution (trans. 1947). A classic examination of the crisis of the French monarchy and the events of 1789.

G. Lefebvre, Napoleon, 2 vols., trans. by H. Stockhold (1969). The fullest and finest biography.

J. Lynch, Simon Bolivar: A Life (2006). Now the standard biography.

J. Lynch, The Spanish American Revolutions, 1808–1826 (1986). An excellent one-volume treatment.

P. Maier, American Scripture: Making the Declaration of Independence (1997). Stands as a major revision of our understanding of the Declaration.

S.E. Melzer and L.W. Rabine, eds., Rebel Daughters: Women and the French Revolution (1992). A collection of essays exploring various aspects of the role and image of women in the French Revolution.

M. Morris, The British Monarchy and the French Revolution (1998). Explores the manner in which the British monarchy saved itself from possible revolution.

R. Muir, Tactics and the Experience of Battle in the Age of Napoleon (1998). Examines the wars from the standpoint of the soldiers in combat.

H. Nicolson, The Congress of Vienna (1946). A good, readable account.

R.R. Palmer, Twelve Who Ruled: The Committee of Public Safety during the Terror (1941). A clear narrative and analysis of the policies and problems of the committee.

R.R. Palmer, The Age of the Democratic Revolution: A Political History of Europe and America, 1760–1800, 2 vols. (1959, 1964). An impressive survey of the political turmoil in the transatlantic world.

C. Proctor, Women, Equality, and the French Revolution (1990). An examination of how the ideas of the Enlightenment and the attitudes of revolutionaries affected the legal status of women.

A.J. Russell-Wood, ed., From Colony to Nation: Essays on the Independence of Brazil (1975). A series of important essays.

P. Schroeder, The Transformation of European Politics, 1763–1848 (1994). A fundamental treatment of the diplomacy of the era.

R. Scurr, Fatal Purity: Robespierre and the French Revolution (2007). A compelling analysis of a personality long difficult to understand.

A. Soboul, The Parisian Sans-Culottes and the French Revolution, 1793–94 (1964). The best work on the subject.

D.G. Sutherland, France, 1789–1825: Revolution and Counter-revolution (1986). A major synthesis based on recent scholarship in social history.

T. Tackett, Religion, Revolution, and Regional Culture in Eighteenth-Century France: The Ecclesiastical Oath of 1791 (1986). The most important study of this topic.

T. Tackett, Becoming a Revolutionary: The Deputies of the French National Assembly and the Emergence of a Revolutionary Culture (1789–1790) (1996). The best study of the early months of the revolution.

J.M. Thompson, Robespierre, 2 vols. (1935). The best biography.

D.K. Van Key, The Religious Origins of the French Revolution: From Calvin to the Civil Constitution, 1560–1791 (1996). Examines the manner in which debates within French Catholicism influenced the coming of the revolution.

M. Walzer, ed., Regicide and Revolution: Speeches at the Trial of Louis XVI (1974). An important and exceedingly interesting collection of documents with a useful introduction.

I. Woloch, The New Regime: Transformations of the French Civic Order, 1789–1820s (1994). An important overview of just what had and had not changed in France after the quarter century of revolution and war.

G. Wood, Empire of Liberty: A History of the Early Republic, 1789–1815 (2009) A major interpretation.

A. Zamoyski, Rites of Peace: The Fall of Napoleon and the Congress of Vienna (2007). A lively analysis and narrative.

Chapter 23

I. Berlin, Generations of Captivity: A History of African-American Slaves (2003). A major work.

P. Bew, Ireland: The Politics of Enmity 1789–2006 (2007). A major, new, outstanding survey of the sweep of modern Irish history.

D. Blackbourn, The Long Nineteenth Century: A History of Germany, 1780–1918 (1998). An outstanding survey.

D.G. Creighton, John A. MacDonald (1952, 1955). A major biography of the first Canadian prime minister.

D. Donald, Lincoln (1995). Now the standard biography.

R.B. Edgerton, Death or Glory: The Legacy of the Crimean War (2000). Multifaceted study of a badly mismanaged war that transformed many aspects of European domestic politics.

D.K. Goodwin, Team of Rivals: The Political Genius of Abraham Lincoln (2005). An accessible study of Lincoln's administration.

M. Holt, The Fate of Their Country: Politicians, Slavery Extension, and the Coming of the Civil War (2005). A brief introduction to the crucial decade of the 1850s in the United States.

M. Holt, The Rise and Fall of the American Whig Party: Jacksonian Politics and the Onset of the Civil War (2003). An extensive survey of the Jacksonian era.

R. Kee, The Green Flag: A History of Irish Nationalism (2001). A vast survey.

W. Lacquer, A History of Zionism (1989). The most extensive one-volume treatment.

M.B. Levinger, Enlightened Nationalism: The Transformation of Prussian Political Culture, 1806–1848 (2002). A major work.

J.M. McPherson, The Battle Cry of Freedom: The Civil War Era (1988). An excellent one-volume treatment.

D. Morton, A Short History of Canada (2001). Useful popular history.

J.P. Parry, The Rise and Fall of Liberal Government in Victorian Britain (1994). An outstanding study.

A. Plessis, The Rise and Fall of the Second Empire, 1852–1871 (1985). A useful survey of France under Napoleon III.

D.M. Potter, The Impending Crisis, 1848–1861 (1976) A penetrating study of the coming of the American Civil War.

L. Riall, Garibaldi: Invention of a Hero (2007). An exploration of a nationalist hero's reputation in his own day and later.

D. Shafer, The Paris Commune: French Politics, Culture, and Society at the Crossroads of the Revolutionary Tradition and Revolutionary Socialism (2005). Excellent in relating the Commune to previous and later revolutionary traditions.

A. Sked, Decline and Fall of the Habsburg Empire, 1815–1918 (2001). A major, accessible survey of a difficult subject.

A. Sked, Metternich and Austria: An Evaluation (2008). A thoughtful restoration of Metternich to the position of leading diplomat of his age.

D.M. Smith, Cavour (1984). An excellent biography.

C.P. Stacey, Canada and the Age of Conflict (1977, 1981). A study of Canadian foreign relations.

D. Wetzel, A Duel of Giants: Bismarck, Napoleon III, and the Origins of the Franco-Prussian War (2001). Broad study based on most recent scholarship.

Chapter 24

M. Adas, Machines as the Measure of Men: Science, Technology, and Ideologies of Western Dominance (1989). The best single volume on racial thinking and technological advances as forming ideologies of European colonial dominance.

A. Ascher and P.A. Stolypin, The Search for Stability in Late Imperial Russia (2000). A broad-ranging biography based on extensive research.

I. Berlin, Karl Marx: His Life and Environment, 4th ed. (1996). A classic volume that remains an excellent introduction.

P. Bowler, Evolution: The History of an Idea (2003). An outstanding survey.

Janet Browne, Charles Darwin, 2 vols. (2002). An eloquent, accessible biography.

J. Burrow, The Crisis of Reason: European Thought, 1848–1914 (2000). The best overview available.

A.D. Chandler Jr., The Visible Hand: Managerial Revolution in American Business (1977). Remains the best discussion of the innovative role of American business.

A. Clarke, The Struggle for the Breeches: Gender and the Making of the British Working Class (1995). An examination of the manner in which industrialization made problematical the relationships between men and women.

W. Cronin, Nature's Metropolis: Chicago and the Great West, 1848–1893 (1991). The best examination of any major American nineteenth-century city.

P. Gay, Freud: A Life for Our Time (1988). The new standard biography.

P. Gay, Modernism: The Lure of Heresy (2007). A broad interdisciplinary exploration.

R.F. Hamilton, Marxism, Revisionism, and Leninism: Explication, Assessment, and Commentary (2000). A contribution from the perspective of a historically minded sociologist.

S. Hahn, A Nation under Our Feet: Black Political Struggles in the Rural South from Slavery to the Great Migration (2003). A major synthesis.

A. Hourani, Arab Thought in the Liberal Age 1789–1939 (1967). A classic account, clearly written and accessible to the nonspecialist.

T. Hunt, Marx's General: The Revolutionary Life of Friedrich Engels (2009). A biography that also considers the general landscape of late nineteenth-century socialism.

D.I. Kertzer and M. Barbagli, eds., Family Life in the Long Nineteenth Century, 1789–1913: The History of the European Family (2002). Wide-ranging collection of essays.

J.T. Kloppenberg, Uncertain Victory: Social Democracy and Progressivism in European and American Thought (1986). An extremely important comparative study.

J. Köhler, Zarathustra's Secret: The Interior Life of Friedrich Nietzsche (2002). A controversial new biography.

L. Kolakowski, Main Currents of Marxism: Its Rise, Growth, and Dissolution, 3 vols. (1978). Especially good on the last years of the nineteenth century and the early years of the twentieth.

P. Krause, The Battle for Homestead, 1880–1892 (1992). Examines labor relations in the steel industry.

D. Landes, The Wealth and Poverty of Nations: Why Some Are So Rich and Some So Poor (1998). A major international discussion of the subject.

B. Lightman, Victorian Popularizers of Science: Designing Nature for New Audiences (2007). A study that adds numerous new dimensions to the subject.

G. Makari, Revolution in Mind: The Creation of Psychoanalysis (2008). A major, multidimensional survey.

M. McGerr, A Fierce Discontent: The Rise and Fall of the Progressive Moevement in America, 1870–1920 (2003). The best recent synthesis.

E. Morris, Theodore Rex (2002). Major survey of Theodore Roosevelt's presidency and personality.

A. Pais, Subtle Is the Lord: The Science and Life of Albert Einstein (1983). Remains the most accessible scientific biography.

J. Rendall, The Origins of Modern Feminism: Women in Britain, France and the United States, 1780–1860 (1985). A well-informed introduction.

R. Service, Lenin: A Biography (2002). Based on new sources and will no doubt become the standard biography.

R.M. Utley, The Indian Frontier and the American West, 1846–1890 (1984). A broad survey of the pressures of white civilization against Native Americans.

D. Vital, A People Apart: The Jews in Modern Europe, 1789–1939 (1999). A deeply informed survey.

Chapter 25

S. Arrom, The Women of Mexico City, 1790–1857 (1985). A pioneering study.

W. Baer, Brazilian Economy: Growth and Development (2007). An in-depth study of the subject.

L. Bethell, ed., The Cambridge History of Latin America, 8 vols. (1992). The single most authoritative coverage, with extensive bibliographical essays. This series has now been published in several smaller, nation-specific volumes edited by L. Bethell.

J.P. Brennan and M. Rougier, The Politics of National Capitalism: Peronism and the Argentine Bourgeoisie, 1946–1976 (2009). A challenging study of the relationship of Perón and business.

V. Bulmer-Thomas, The Economic History of Latin America since Independence (1994). Remains a major.

E.B. Burns, The Poverty of Progress: Latin America in the Nineteenth Century (1980). Remains a significant work arguing that the elites suppressed alternative modes of cultural and economic development.

D. Bushnell and N. Macaulay, The Emergence of Latin America in the Nineteenth Century (1994). A survey that examines the internal development of Latin America during the period.

R. Conrad, The Destruction of Brazilian Slavery, 1850–1889 (1971). Still a good survey of the most important problem in Brazil in the second half of the nineteenth century.

R. Conrad, World of Sorrow: The African Slave Trade to Brazil (1986). An excellent treatment of the subject.

N. Craske, Women and Politics in Latin America (1999). A useful overview.

E.V. Da Costa, The Brazilian Empire: Myths and Histories (1985). Essays that provide a thorough introduction to Brazil during the period of empire.

H.S. Ferns, Britain and Argentina in the Nineteenth Century (1968). Classic exploration of the intermeshing of the two economies.

M. Font, Coffee, Contention, and Change in the Making of Modern Brazil (1990). Extensive discussion of the problems of a single-commodity economy.

A. Gilly, The Mexican Revolution: A People's History (2005). Explores lesser known figures of the revolution.

R. Graham, Britain and the Onset of Modernization in Brazil (1968). Another study of British economic dominance.

S.H. Haber, Industry and Underdevelopment: The Industrialization of Mexico, 1890–1940 (1989). Examines the problem of industrialization before and after the revolution.

G. Hahner, Emancipating the Female Sex: The Struggle for Women's Rights in Brazil, 1850–1940 (1990). An extensive examination of a relatively understudied issue in Latin America.

C.H. Haring, Empire in Brazil: A New World Experiment with Monarchy (1958). Remains a useful overview.

J. Hemming, Amazon Frontier: The Defeat of the Brazilian Indians (1987). A brilliant survey of the experience of Native Americans in modern Brazil.

R.A. Humphreys, Latin America and the Second World War, 2 vols. (1981–1982). The standard work on the topic.

D. James, Resistance and Integration: Peronism and the Argentine Working Class, 1946–1976 (1994). Explores the complicated relationship of Perón and the working class over several decades.

M.B. Karush and O. Chamosa, The New Cultural History of Peronism: Power and Identity in Mid-Twentieth-Century Argentina (2010). Interdisciplinary collection of essays on the emergence of Peronism.

F. Katz, ed., Riot, Rebellion, and Revolution in Mexico: Social Base of Agrarian Violence, 1750–1940 (1988). Essays that put the violence of the revolution in a longer context.

F. Katz, The Life and Times of Pancho Villa (1998). An extensive critical biography

A. Knight, The Mexican Revolution, 2 vols. (1986). The best treatment of the subject.

C. M. MacLachlan, A History of Modern Brazil: The Past against the Future (2003). A basic brief introduction.

S. Mainwaring, The Catholic Church and Politics in Brazil, 1916–1985 (1986). An examination of a key institution in Brazilian life.

F. McLynn, Villa and Zapata: A History of the Mexican Revolution (2002). Examines the revolution through the lives and interrelationship of its two most important figures.

M. Morner, Adventurers and Proletarians: The Story of Migrants in Latin America (1985). Examines immigration to Latin America and migration within it.

A.D. Ortiz, Eva Perón: A Biography (1997) A biography of one of the most enigmatic figures of modern Latin America.

J. Page, Perón: A Biography (1983). The standard English treatment.

M. B. Plotkin, Manana Es San Perón: A Cultural History of Perón's Argentina (2003). Explores Argentina during the curious governance of Perón.

D. Rock, Politics in Argentina, 1890–1930: The Rise and Fall of Radicalism (2009). The major discussion of the Argentine Radical Party.

D. Rock, Argentina, 1516–1987: From Spanish Colonization to Alfonsin (1987). Now the standard survey.

D. Rock, ed., Latin America in the 1940s: War and Postwar Transitions (1994). Essays examining a very difficult decade for the continent.

R.M. Schneider, "Order and Progress": A Political History of Brazil (1991). A straightforward narrative with helpful notes for further reading.

R. Scott, The Abolition of Slavery and the Aftermath of Emancipation in Brazil (1988). A brief overview.

T.E. Skidmore, Black into White: Race and Nationality in Brazilian Thought (1993). Examines the role of racial theory in Brazil.

T.E. Skidmore, Politics in Brazil 1930–1964: An Experiment in Democracy (2007). An in-depth exploration of Brazilian politics before and after World War II.

S.J. Stein and B.H. Stein, The Colonial Heritage of Latin America: Essays on Economic Dependence in Perspective (1970). A classic statement of the dependence interpretation.

D. Tamarin, The Argentine Labor Movement, 1930–1945: A Study in the Origins of Perónism (1985). A useful introduction to a complex subject.

H.J. Wiarda, Politics and Social Change in Latin America: The Distinct Tradition (1974). Excellent essays that stress the ongoing role of Iberian traditions.

J.D. Wirth, ed., Latin American Oil Companies and the Politics of Energy (1985). A series of case studies.

J. Wolfe, Working Women, Working Men: São Paulo and the Rise of Brazil's Industrial Working Class, 1900–1955 (1993). Pays particular attention to the role of women.

J. Womack, Zapata and the Mexican Revolution (1968). A classic study.

Chapter 26

General Works

S. Cook, Colonial Encounters in the Age of High Imperialism (1996). A good introduction to the imperial enterprise in Africa and Asia.

D.K. Fieldhouse, The West and the Third World. Trade: Colonialism, Depedence and Development (1999). Addresses whether colonialism was detrimental or beneficial to colonized peoples.

D. Headrick, The Tentacles of Progress: Technology Transfer in the Age of Imperialism, 1850–1940 (1988). Discusses the roles of new methods of transportation (railroads, steamships), forms of expertise (doctors, botanists), and other types of "technology transfer" in European colonization, and post-independence development.

P. Hopkirk, The Great Game: The Struggle for Empire in Central Asia (1992). Focuses on the political and economic rivalries of the imperial powers.

India

A. Ahmad, Islamic Modernism in India and Pakistan, 1857–1964 (1967). The standard survey of Muslim thinkers and movements in India during the period.

C.A. Bayly, Indian Society and the Making of the British Empire, The New Cambridge History of India, II. 1 (1988). One of several major contributions of this author to the ongoing revision of our picture of modern Indian history since the eighteenth century.

A. Ghosh, In an Antique Land: History in the Guise of a Traveler's Tale (1992). An anthropologist traces the footsteps of a premodern slave traveling with his master from North Africa to India. A gripping tale of premodern life in the India Ocean basin and also of contemporary Egypt.

R. Guha, ed., Subaltern Studies: Writings on South Asian History and Society (1982). Essays on the colonial period that focus on the social, political, and economic history of "subaltern" groups and classes (hill tribes, peasants, etc.) rather than only the elites of India.

S.N. Hay, ed., "Modern India and Pakistan," Part VI of Wm. Theodore de Bary et al., eds., Sources of Indian Tradition, 2nd ed. (1988). A superb selection of primary-source documents, with brief introductions and helpful notes.

F. Robinson, ed., The Cambridge Encyclopedia of India, Pakistan, Bangladesh, Sri Lanka, Nepal, Bhutan, and the Maldives (1989). A fine collection of survey articles by various scholars, organized into topical chapters ranging from "Economies" to "Cultures."

Central Islamic Lands

W. Cleveland, A History of the Modern Middle East, 3rd ed. (2004). A balanced and well-organized overview of modern Middle Eastern history.

A. Dawisha, Arab Nationalism in the Twentieth Century, From Triumph to Despair (2003). A good overview of the development of Arab nationalism.

S. Deringil, The Well-Protected Domains: Ideology and the Legitimation of Power in the Ottoman Empire, 1876–1909 (1998). An impressive study on nationalism and reform in the Ottoman Empire.

J.J. Donahue and J.L. Esposito, eds., Islam in Transition: Muslim Perspectives (1982). An interesting selection of primary-source materials on Islamic thinking in this century.

D.F. Eickelman, Knowledge and Power in Morocco: The Education of a Twentieth-Century Notable (1985). A fascinating study of traditional Islamic education and society in the twentieth century through a social biography of a Moroccan religious scholar and judge.

A. Hourani, Arabic Thought in the Liberal Age, 1798–1939 (1967). The standard work, by which all subsequent scholarship on the topic is to be judged.

N.R. Keddie, An Islamic Response to Imperialism (1968). A brief study of al-Afghani, the great Muslim reformer, with translations of a number of his writings.

B. Lewis, The Emergence of Modern Turkey, 2nd ed. (1968). A concise but thorough history of the creation of the Turkish state, including nineteenth-century background.

J.O. Voll, Islam: Continuity and Change in the Modern World (1982). Chapters 1–6. An interpretive survey of the Islamic world since the eighteenth century. Its emphasis on eighteenth-century reform movements is especially noteworthy.

Africa

C. Achebe, Things Fall Apart (1959). Reading this classic novel may be the best way to get a profound sense of the ways African and European cultures interacted in the early colonial period.

D. Anderson, Histories of the Hanged: The Dirty War in Kenya and the End of Empire (2005). This account of the Kikuyu-led Mau Mau movement in Kenya emphasizes the way Mau Mau activities, and the British response, shaped and distorted Kenya's independence movement. (See also C. Elkins's Imperial Reckoning below.)

A.A. Boahen, Africa under Colonial Domination, 1880–1935 (1985). Vol. VII of the UNESCO General History of Africa.

Excellent chapters on various regions of Africa in the period. Chapters 3–10 detail African resistance to European colonial intrusion in diverse regions.

W. Cartey and M. Kilson, eds., The Africa Reader: Colonial Africa (1970). Original source materials give a vivid picture of African resistance to colonial powers, adaptation to foreign rule, and the emergence of the African masses as a political force.

P. Curtin, S. Feiermann, L. Thompson, and J. Vansina, African History (1978). The relevant portions are Chapters 10–20.

B. Davidson, Modern Africa: A Social and Political History (1989). A very useful survey of African history.

C. Elkins, Imperial Reckoning: The Untold Story of Britain's Gulag in Kenya (2004). The Pulitzer Prize–winning account of Britain's appalling response to the Mau Mau movement in colonial Kenya; while Elkins focuses on the British, D. Anderson in Histories of the Hanged (see above) emphasizes the Kenyan side of the story.

J.D. Fage, A History of Africa (1978). The relevant chapters, which give a particularly clear overview of the colonial period, are 12–16.

B. Freund, The Making of Contemporary Africa: The Development of African Society since 1800 (1984). A refreshingly direct synthetic discussion and survey that take an avowedly, but not reductive, materialist approach to interpretation.

E. Gilbert and J.T. Reynolds, Africa in World History: From Prehistory to the Present (2004). An engaging overview of the period, with attention to technology, economics, and ideologies, among other factors. See especially Chapters 13–15.

D. Headrick, Tools of Empire (1982). A provocative evaluation of the roles played by technology in the imperial venture.

A. Hochschild, King Leopold's Ghost: A Story of Greed, Terror, and Heroism in Colonial Africa (1998). A compelling, well-documented narrative of the atrocities committed in turn-of-the-twentieth-century Congo when it was held as the personal fiefdom of Belgium's monarch.

T. Pakenham, The Scramble for Africa (1991). An excellent analysis of the imperialist age in Africa.

A.D. Roberts, ed., The Colonial Moment in Africa: Essays on the Movement of Minds and Materials, 1900–1940 (1986). Chapters from The Cambridge History of Africa treating various aspects of the colonial period in Africa, including economics, politics, and religion.

Chapter 27

China

P.M. Coble, The Shanghai Capitalists and the Nationalist Government, 1927–1937 (1980).

L.E. Eastman, The Abortive Revolution: China under Nationalist Rule, 1927–1937 (1974).

L.E. Eastman, Seeds of Destruction: Nationalist China in War and Revolution, 1937–1949 (1984).

M. Elvin and G.W. Skinner, The Chinese City between Two Worlds (1974). A study of the late Qing and Republican eras.

J.W. Esherick, The Origins of the Boxer Rebellion (1987).

S. Et, China's Republican Revolution (1994).

J.K. Fairbank and M. Goldman, China, a New History (1998). A survey of the entire sweep of Chinese history; especially strong on the modern period.

J.K. Fairbank and D. Twitchett, eds., The Cambridge History of China. Like the premodern volumes in the same series, the volumes on modern China represent a survey of what is known. Volumes 10–15, which cover the history from the late Qing to the People's Republic, have been published, and the others will be available soon. The series is substantial. Each volume contains a comprehensive bibliography.

J. Fitzgerald, Awakening China: Politics, Culture, and Class in the Nationalist Revolution (1996).

C. Hao, Chinese Intellectuals in Crisis: Search for Order and Meaning, 1890–1911 (1987).

W.C. Kirby, ed., State and Economy in Republican China (2001).

P.A. Kuhn, Rebellion and Its Enemies in Late Imperial China: Militarization and Social Structure, 1796–1864 (1980). A study of how the Confucian gentry saved the Manchu Dynasty after the Taiping Rebellion.

P. Kuhn, Origins of the Modern Chinese State (2002).

J. Levenson, Liang Ch'i-ch'ao and the Mind of Modern China (1953). A classic study of a major Chinese reformer and thinker.

Lu Xun, Selected Works (1960). Novels, stories, and other writings by modern China's greatest writer.

S. Naquin, Peking: Temples and City Life, 1400–1900 (2000).

E.O. Reischauer, J.K. Fairbank, and A.M. Craig, East Asia: Tradition and Transformation (1989). A detailed text on East Asian history. Contains ample chapters on Japan and China and shorter chapters on Korea and Vietnam.

H.Z. Schiffrin, Sun Yat-sen, Reluctant Revolutionary (1980). A biography.

B.I. Schwartz, Chinese Communism and the Rise of Mao (1951). A classic study of Mao, his thought, and the Chinese Communist Party before 1949.

B.I. Schwartz, In Search of Wealth and Power: Yen Fu and the West (1964). A fine study of a late-nineteenth-century thinker who introduced Western ideas into China.

J.D. Spence, The Gate of Heavenly Peace: The Chinese and Their Revolution, 1895–1980 (1981). Historical reflections on twentieth-century China.

J.D. Spence, The Search for Modern China (1990). A thick text but well written.

M. Szonyi, Practicing Kinship: Lineage and Descent in Late Imperial China (2002).

S.Y. Teng and J.K. Fairbank, China's Response to the West (1954). A superb collection of translations from Chinese thinkers and political figures, with commentaries.

T.H. White and A. Jacoby, Thunder Out of China (1946). A view of China during World War II by two who were there.

Japan

G. Akita, Foundations of Constitutional Government in Modern Japan (1967). A study of Itō Hirobumi in the political process leading to the Meiji constitution.

G.C. Allen, A Short Economic History of Modern Japan (1958).

A.E. Barshay, The Social Sciences in Modern Japan: The Marxian and Modernist Traditions (2004). Different interpretations of history.

J.R. Bartholomew, The Formation of Science in Japan (1989). The pioneering English-language work on the subject.

W.G. Beasley, Japanese Imperialism, 1894–1945 (1987). Excellent short book on the subject.

G.M. Berger, Parties Out of Power in Japan, 1931–1941 (1977). An analysis of the condition of political parties during the militarist era.

G.L. Bernstein, ed., Recreating Japanese Women, 1600–1945 (1991).

The Cambridge History of Japan, The Nineteenth Century, M.B. Jansen, ed. (1989); The Twentieth Century, P. Duus, ed. (1988). Multi-author works.

A.M. Craig, Chōshū in the Meiji Restoration (2000). A study of the Chōshū domain, a Prussia of Japan, during the period 1840–1868.

A.M. Craig and D.H. Shively, eds., Personality in Japanese History (1970). An attempt to gauge the role of individuals and their personalities as factors explaining history.

P. Duus, Party Rivalry and Political Change in Taisho Japan (1968). A study of political change in Japan during the 1910s and 1920s.

P. Duus, The Abacus and the Sword: The Japanese Penetration of Korea, 1895–1910 (1995). A thoughtful analysis.

S. Ericson, The Sound of the Whistle: Railroads and the State in Meiji Japan (1996). An economic and social history of railroads, an engine of growth and popular symbol.

Y. Fukuzawa, Autobiography (1966). Japan's leading nineteenth-century thinker tells of his life and of the birth of modern Japan.

S. Garon, The State and Labor in Modern Japan (1987). A fine study of the subject.

C.N. Gluck, Japan's Modern Myths: Ideology in the Late Meiji Period (1988). A brilliant study of the complex weave of late Meiji thought.

A. Gordon, The Evolution of Labor Relations in Japan: Heavy Industry, 1853–1955 (1985). A seminal work.

B.R. Hackett, Yamagata Aritomo in the Rise of Modern Japan, 1932–1922 (1973). History as seen through the biography of a central figure.

I. Hall, Mori Arinori (1973). A biography of Japan's first minister of education.

T.R.H. Havens, The Valley of Darkness: The Japanese People and World War II (1978). Wartime society.

A. Iriye, After Imperialism: The Search for a New Order in the Far East, 1921–1931 (1965). (Also see other studies by this author.)

D.M.B. Jansen and G. Rozman, eds., Japan in Transition from Tokugawa to Meiji (1986). Contains fine essays.

W. Johnston, The Modern Epidemic: A History of Tuberculosis in Japan (1995). A social history of a disease.

D. Keene, ed., Modern Japanese Literature, An Anthology (1960). A collection of modern Japanese short stories and excerpts from novels.

Y.T. Matsusaka, The Making of Japanese Manchuria, 1904–1932 (2001). On railroad strategies in empire building.

J.W. Morley, ed., The China Quagmire (1983). A study of Japan's expansion on the continent between 1933 and 1941. (For diplomatic history, see also the many other works by this author.)

R.H. Myers and M.R. Peattie, eds., The Japanese Colonial Empire, 1895–1945 (1984).

T. Najita, Hara Kei in the Politics of Compromise, 1905–1915 (1967). A study of one of Japan's greatest party leaders.

K. Ohkawa and H. Rosovsky, Japanese Economic Growth: Trend Acceleration in the Twentieth Century (1973).

M. Ravina, The Last Samurai: The Life and Battles of Saigo Takamori (2004). Unlike the movie, this account of the Satsuma uprising is historical.

G. Shiba, Remembering Aizu (1999). A stirring autobiographical account of a samurai youth whose domain lost in the Meiji Restoration.

K. Smith, A Time of Crisis: The Great Depression and Rural Revitalization (2001). An intellectual history of village movements during the 1930s.

J.J. Stephan, Hawaii under the Rising Sun (1984). Japan's plans for rule in Hawaii.

R.H. Spector, Eagle against the Sun: The American War with Japan (1985). A narrative of World War II in the Pacific.

E.P. Tsurumi, Factory Girls: Women in the Thread Mills of Meiji Japan (1990). A sympathetic analysis of the key component of the Meiji labor force.

W. Wray, Mitsubishi and the N. Y. K., 1870–1914 (1984). The growth of a shipping zaibatsu, with analysis of business strategies, the role of government, and imperialist involvements.

Chapter 28

L. Albertini, The Origins of the War of 1914, 3 vols. (1952, 1957). Discursive but invaluable.

V.R. Berghahn, Germany and the Approach of War in 1914 (1973). A work similar in spirit to both of Fischer's (see below) but stressing the importance of Germany's naval program.

S.B. Fay, The Origins of the World War; 2 vols. (1928). The most influential of the revisionist accounts.

F. Fischer, Germany's Aims in the First World War (1967). An influential interpretation that stirred a great controversy in Germany and around the world by emphasizing Germany's role in bringing on the war.

D. Fromkin, Europe's Last Summer: Who Started the Great War in 1914? (2004). A lively account that fixes on the final crisis in July 1914.

J.N. Horne, Labour at War: France and Britain, 1914–1918 (1991). An examination of a major issue on the home fronts.

J. Keegan, The First World War (1999). A vivid and readable narrative.

P. Kennedy, The Rise of the Anglo-German Antagonism 1860–1914 (1980). An unusual and thorough analysis of the political, economic, and cultural roots of important diplomatic developments.

D.C.B. Lieven, Russia and the Origins of the First World War (1983). A good account of the forces that shaped Russian policy.

A. Mombauer, The Origins of the First World War. Controversies and Consensus (2002). A fascinating survey of the debate over the decades and the current state of the question.

R. Pipes, A Concise History of the Russian Revolution (1996). A one-volume version of a scholarly masterpiece.

Z. Steiner, Britain and the Origins of the First World War (1977). A perceptive and informed account of the way British foreign policy was made in the years before the war.

H. Strachan, The First World War (2004). A fine one-volume account of the war.

A.J.P. Taylor, The Struggle for Mastery in Europe, 1848–1918 (1954). Clever but controversial.

S.R. Williamson, Jr., Austria-Hungary and the Origins of the First World War (1991). A valuable study of a complex subject.

Chapter 29

W.S. Allen, The Nazi Seizure of Power: The Experience of a Single German Town, 1930–1935, rev. ed. (1984). A classic treatment of Nazism in a microcosmic setting.

A. Applebaum, Gulag: A History (2003). A superbly readable account of Stalin's system of persecution and resulting prison camps.

J. Barnard, Walter Reuther and the Rise of the Auto Workers (1983). A major introduction to the new American unions of the 1930s.

R.J. Bosworth, Mussolini (2002). A major new biography.

R.J.B. Bosworth, Mussolini's Italy: Life under the Fascist Dictatorship, 1915–1945 (2007) A broad-based study of both fascist politics and the impact of those politics on Italian life.

A. Brinkley, Voices of Protest: Huey Long, Father Coughlin, & the Great Depression (1983). An excellent study of Franklin Roosevelt's opponents.

M. Burleigh and W. Wipperman, The Racial State: Germany 1933–1945 (1991). Emphasizes the manner in which racial theory influenced numerous areas of policy.

R. Conquest, The Great Terror: Stalin's Purges of the Thirties (1968). Remains a major study.

B. Eichengreen, Golden Fetters: The Gold Standard and the Great Depression, 1919–1939 (1992). A remarkable study of the role of the gold standard in the economic policies of the interwar years.

R. Evans, The Coming of the Third Reich (2004) and The Third Reich in Power, 1933–1939 (2005) A superb narrative.

M.S. Fausold, The Presidency of Herbert Hoover (1985). An important treatment.

G. Feldman, The Great Disorder: Politics, Economics, and Society in the German Inflation, 1914–1924 (1993). The best work on the subject.

S. Fitzpatrick, Stalin's Peasants: Resistance and Survival in the Russian Village after Collectivization (1994). A pioneering study.

J.K. Galbraith, The Great Crash (1979). A well-known account by a leading economist.

R. Gellately, The Gestapo and German Society: Enforcing Racial Policy, 1933–1945 (1990). A discussion of how the police state supported Nazi racial policies.

R. Gellately and N. Stoltzfus, Social Outsiders in Nazi Germany (2001). Important essays on Nazi treatment of groups the party regarded as undesirables.

H.J. Gordon, Hitler and the Beer Hall Putsch (1972). An excellent account of the event and the political situation in the early Weimar Republic.

R. Hamilton, Who Voted for Hitler? (1982). An examination of voting patterns and sources of Nazi support.

P. Kenez, The Birth of the Propaganda State: Soviet Methods of Mass Mobilization, 1917–1929 (1985). An examination of the manner in which the communist government inculcated popular support.

D. Kennedy, Freedom from Fear: The American People in Depression and War, 1929–1945 (2001). The best one-volume study of the era.

B. Kent, The Spoils of War: The Politics, Economics, and Diplomacy of Reparations, 1918–1932 (1993). A comprehensive account of the intricacies of the reparations problem of the 1920s.

I. Kershaw, Hitler, 2 vols. (2001) Replaces all previous biographies.

D. Landes, The Unbound Prometheus: Technological Change and Industrial Development in Western Europe from 1750 to the Present (1969). Includes an excellent analysis of both the Great Depression and the few areas of economic growth.

W.E. Leuchtenburg, Franklin D. Roosevelt and the New Deal: 1932–1940 (2009). A superb one-volume treatment.

B. Lincoln, Red Victory: A History of the Russian Civil War (1989). An excellent narrative account.

D.J.K. Peukert, Inside Nazi Germany: Conformity, Opposition, and Racism in Everyday Life (1987). An excellent discussion of life under Nazi rule.

R. Pipes, The Unknown Lenin: From the Secret Archives (1996). A collection of previously unpublished documents that indicated the repressive character of Lenin's government.

P. Pulzer, Jews and the German State: The Political History of a Minority, 1848–1933 (1992). A detailed history by a major historian of European minorities.

L.J. Rupp, Mobilizing Women for War: German and America Propaganda, 1939–1945 (1978). Although concentrating on a later period, it includes an excellent discussion of general Nazi attitudes toward women.

R. Service, Stalin: A Biography (2005). The strongest of a host of recent biographical studies.

R. Service, Trotsky: A Biography (2009). A major new biography.

A. Solzhenitsyn, The Gulag Archipelago, 3 vols. (1974–1979). A major examination of the labor camps under Stalin by one of the most important late twentieth-century Russian writers.

A.J.P. Taylor, English History, 1914–1945 (1965). Lively and opinionated.

A. Tooze, The Wages of Destruction: The Making and Breaking of the Nazi Economy (2006). A wide-ranging, accessible study of the politics and ideology behind Nazi economic policy.

H.A. Turner Jr., German Big Business and the Rise of Hitler (1985). An important major study of the subject.

L. Yahil, The Holocaust: The Fate of European Jewry, 1932–1945 (1990). A major study of this fundamental subject in twentieth-century history.

Chapter 30

A. Adamthwaite, France and the Coming of the Second World War, 1936–1939 (1977). A careful account making good use of the French archives.

O. Bartov, Mirrors of Destruction: War, Genocide, and Modern Identity (2001). Remarkably penetrating essays.

E.R. Beck, Under the Bombs: The German Home Front, 1942–1945 (1986). An interesting examination of a generally unstudied subject.

P.M.H. Bell, The Origins of the Second World War in Europe, 3rd ed. (2007). A comprehensive study of the period and debates surrounding the European origins of World War II.

A. Beevor, The Spanish Civil War (2001). Particularly strong on the political issues.

C. Browning, The Origins of the Final Solution: The Evolution of the Nazi Jewish Policy (2004). The story of how Hitler's policy developed from discrimination to annihilation

A. Bullock, Hitler: A Study in Tyranny, rev. ed. (1964). A brilliant biography.

W.S. Churchill, The Second World War, 6 vols. (1948–1954). The memoirs of the great British leader.

A. Crozier, The Causes of the Second World War, 1997. An examination of what brought on the war.

R.B. Frank, Downfall: The End of the Imperial Japanese Empire (1998). A thorough, well-documented account of the last months of the Japanese Empire and the reasons for its surrender.

J.L. Gaddis, We Now Know: Rethinking Cold War History (1998). A fine account of the early years of the Cold War, making use of new evidence emerging since the collapse of the Soviet Union.

J.L. Gaddis, P.H. Gordon, E.May, eds., Cold War Statesmen Confront the Bomb: Nuclear Diplomacy since 1945 (1999). A collection of essays discussing the effect of atomic and nuclear weapons on diplomacy since World War II.

M. Gilbert, The Holocaust: A History of the Jews of Europe during the Second World War (1985). The best and most comprehensive treatment.

A. Iriye, Pearl Harbor and the Coming of the Pacific War (1999). Essays on how the Pacific war came about, including a selection of documents.

J. Keegan, The Second World War (1990). A lively and penetrating account by a master military historian.

I. Kershaw, Hitler: 1889–1936: Hubris (1999) and Hitler: 1936–1945: Nemesis (2001). An outstanding two-volume biography.

W.F. Kimball, Forged in War: Roosevelt, Churchill, and the Second World War (1998). A study of the collaboration between the two great leaders of the West based on a thorough knowledge of their correspondence.

W. Murray and A.R. Millett, A War to Be Won: Fighting the Second World War, (2000). A splendid account of the military operations in the war.

P. Neville, Hitler and Appeasement: The British Attempt to Prevent the Second World War (2005). A defense of the British appeasers of Hitler.

R. Overy, Why the Allies Won (1997). An anlysis of the reasons for the victory of the Allies, with special emphasis on technology.

N. Rich, Hitler War Aims, 2 vols. (1973–1974). The best study of the subject in English.

P. Wandycz, The Twilight of French Eastern Alliances, 1926–1936 (1988). A well-documented account of the diplomacy of central and eastern Europe in a crucial period.

G.L. Weinberg, A World at Arms: A Global History of World War II (1994). A thorough and excellent narrative account.

Chapter 31

B.S. Anderson and J.P. Pinsser, A History of Their Own: Women in Europe from Prehistory to the Present, Vol. 2 (1988). A broad-ranging survey.

R. Bernstein, Out of the Blue: The Story of September 11, 2001, from Jihad to Ground Zero (2002). An excellent account by a gifted journalist.

A. Brown, The Gorbachev Factor (1996). An important commentary by an English observer.

D. Calleo, Rethinking Europe's Future (2003). A daring book by an experienced commentator.

M. Cini, European Union Politics (2007). An authoritative guide.

J.F. Frieden, Global Capitalism: Its Fall and Rise in the Twentieth Century (2007). Background to the current financial crisis.

J.L. Gaddis, The Cold War: A New History (2006). An important overview.

D.J. Garrow, Bearing the Cross: Martin Luther King Jr. and the Southern Leadership Conference, 1955–1968 (1986). The best work on the subject.

M. I. Goldman, Petrostate: Putin, Power, and the New Russia (2008). A thoughtful, but critical analysis.

D. Halberstam, The Coldest Winter: America and the Korean War (2007). A superb narrative by a gifted journalist.

W. Hitchcock, Struggle for Europe: The Turbulent History of a Divided Continent, 1945–2002 (2003). The best overall narrative now available.

D. Kearns, Lyndon Johnson and the American Dream (1976). Remains a useful biography.

J. Keep, The Last of the Empires: A History of the Soviet Union, 1956–1991 (1995). A clear narrative.

M. Mandelbaum, The Ideas That Conquered the World: Peace, Democracy, and Free Markets (2002). An important analysis by a major commentator on international affairs.

J. Mann, The Rise of the Vulcans: The History of Bush's War Cabinet (2004). An account of the major foreign policy advisers behind the invasion of Iraq.

R. Mann, A Grand Delusion: America's Descent into Vietnam (2001). The best recent narrative.

J. McCormick, Understanding the European Union: A Concise Introduction (2002). Outlines the major features.

N. Naimark, Fires of Hatred: Ethnic Cleansing in Twentieth-Century Europe (2002). A remarkably sensitive treatment of a tragic subject.

T. R. Reid, The United States of Europe: The New Superpower and the End of American Supremacy (2004). A journalist's exploration of the impact of the European Union on American policy.

M.E. Sarotte, 1989: The Struggle to Create Post-Cold War Europe (2009). Explores paths taken and not taken at the time of the collapse of communism.

V. Sebestyen, Revolution 1989: The Fall of the Soviet Empire (2009). A masterful overview of the end of the Cold War Era.

L. Shevtsova, Russia—Lost in Transition: The Yelsin and Putin Legacies (2007). A major analysis and meditation on the past two decades.

R. Story, The Rise of Conservatism in America, 1945–2000: A Brief History with Documents (2007). A basic introductory overview.

M. Walker, The Cold War and the Making of the Modern World (1994). Remains a major survey.

Chapter 32

China

R. Baum, Burying Mao: Chinese Politics in the Age of Deng Xiaoping (1996).

A. Chan, R. Madsen, and J. Unger, Chen Village uunder Mao and Deng (1992).

J. Chang, Wild Swans: Three Daughters of China (1991). An intimate look at recent Chinese society through three generations of women. Immensely readable.

J. Feng, Ten Years of Madness: Oral Histories of China's Cultural Revolution (1996).

J. Fewsmith, China since Tiananmen: The Politics of Transition (2001). Focus is on the rise to power of Jiang Zemin and Chinese politics during the 1990s.

B.M. Frolic, Mao's People: Sixteen Portraits of Life in Revolutionary China (1987).

T. Gold, State and Society in the Taiwan Miracle (1986). The story of economic growth in postwar Taiwan.

M. Goldman, Sowing the Seeds of Democracy in China: Political Reform in the Deng Xiaoping Era (1994).

A. Iriye, China and Japan in the Global Setting (1992).

D.M. Lampton, Same Bed, Different Dreams: Managing U.S.–China Relations, 1989–2000 (2001).

H. Liang, Son of the Revolution (1983). An autobiographical account of a young man growing up in Mao's China.

K. Lieberthal, Governing China, from Revolution through Reform (2004).

B. Liu, People or Monsters? and Other Stories and Reportage from China After Mao (1983). Literary reflections on China.

R. MacFarquhar and J.K. Fairbank, eds., The Cambridge History of China, Vol. 14, Emergence of Revolutionary China (1987), and Vol. 15, Revolutions within the Chinese Revolution, 1966–1982 (1991).

L. Pan, Sons of the Yellow Emperor: A History of the Chinese Diaspora (1990). A pioneer study that treats not only Southeast Asia but the rest of the world as well.

M.R. Ristaino, Port of Last Resort: The Diaspora Communities of Shanghai (2001).

T. Saich, Governance and Politics of China (2004).

H. Wang, China's New Order (2003). Translation of a work by a Qinghua University professor, a liberal within the boundaries of what is permissible in China.

G. White, ed., In Search of Civil Society: Market Reform and Social Change in Contemporary China (1996).

M. Wolf, Revolution Postponed: Women in Contemporary China (1985).

Zhang X. and Sang Y., Chinese Lives: An Oral History of Contemporary China (1987).

Japan

A. Barshay, State and Intellectual in Imperial Japan (1988).

A. Barshay, The Social Sciences in Modern Japan (2007).

G.L. Bernstein, Haruko's World: A Japanese Farm Woman and Her Community (1983). A study of the changing life of a village woman in postwar Japan.

T. Bestor, Neighborhood Tokyo (1989). A portrait of contemporary urban life in Japan.

T. Bestor, Tsukiji (2003).

G.L. Curtis, The Logic of Japanese Politics: Leaders, Institutions, and the Limits of Change (1999).

G.L. Curtis, Policymaking in Japan: Defining the Role of Politicians (2002).

M.H. Cusumano, The Japanese Automobile Industry (1985). A neat study of the postwar business strategies of Toyota and Nissan.

W.T. DeBary, C. Gluck, and A. E. Tiedemann, Comps., Sources of the Japanese Tradition, 2nd ed. (2005).

R.P. Dore, Land Reform in Japan (1959). Another classic.

R.P. Dore, City Life in Japan (1999). A classic, reissued.

S. Garon, Molding Japanese Minds: The State in Everyday Life (1997).

S.M. Garon, The Evolution of Civil Society from Meiji to Heisei (2002). That is to say, from the mid-nineteenth century to the present day.

A. Gordon, ed., Postwar Japan as History (1993).

H. Hibbett, ed., Contemporary Japanese Literature: An Anthology of Fiction, Film, and Other Writing since 1945 (1977). Translations of postwar short stories.

Y. Kawabata, The Sound of the Mountain, trans. by E.G. Seidensticker (1970). Sensitive, moving novel by Nobel author.

J. Nathan, Sony, the Private Life (1999). A lively account of the human side of growth in the Sony Corporation.

D. Okimoto, Between MITI and the Market (1989). A discussion of the respective roles of government and private enterprise in Japan's postwar growth.

S. Pharr, Losing Face: Status Politics in Japan (1996).

E.F. Vogel, Japan as Number One: Lessons for America (1979). Though dated and somewhat sanguine, this remains an insightful classic.

Korea and Vietnam

B. Cumings, Korea: The Unknown War (1988).

B. Cumings, The Origins of the Korean War (Vol. 1, 1981; Vol. 2, 1991).

B. Cumings, The Two Koreas: On the Road to Reunification? (1990).

C.J. Eckert, Korea Old and New, A History (1990). The best short history of Korea, with extensive coverage of the postwar era.

C.J. Eckert, Offspring of Empire: The Koch'ang Kims and the Colonial Origins of Korean Capitalism, 1876–1945 (1991).

G.M.T. Kahin, Intervention: How America Became Involved in Vietnam (1986).

S. Karnow, Vietnam: A History, rev. ed., (1996).

L. Kendall, Shamans, Housewives, and Other Restless Spirits: Women in Korean Ritual and Life (1985).

K.B. Lee, A New History of Korea (1984). A translation by E. Wagner and others of an outstanding Korean work covering the full sweep of Korean history.

T. Li, Nguyen Cochinchina: South Vietnam in the Seventeenth and Eighteenth Centuries (1998).

D. Marr, Vietnam 1945: The Quest for Power (1995).

C.W. Sorensen, Over the Mountains Are Mountains (1988). How peasant households in Korea adapted to rapid industrialization.

A. Woodside, Vietnam and the Chinese Model (1988). Provides the background for Vietnam's relationship to China.

Chapter 33

General Works

P. Farmer, Pathologies of Power: Health, Human Rights, and the New War on the Poor (2003). Farmer, a physician, uses his experiences at Harvard and in the Caribbean to argue that inadequate health care in the Third World violates human rights and imperils us all.

J.H. Latham, Africa, Asia, and South America since 1800: A Bibliographic Guide (1995). A valuable tool for finding materials on the topics in this chapter.

S. Power, A Problem from Hell: America and the Age of Genocide (2002). A masterful analysis of genocides in the twentieth century (in Armenia, the Holocaust, the Khmer Rouge, Kurds, Rwanda, and Bosnia) and the U.S. response.

J.D. Sachs, The End of Poverty: Economic Possibilities for Our Time (2005). A renowned economist's plan to end extreme poverty around the world by 2025.

Latin America

S. Balfour, Castro (2008). A relatively brief survey of Castro's ability to hold power for half a century.

P. Brenner, A Contemporary Cuba Reader: Reinventing the Revolution (2007). A useful analysis of the developments in this century.

J. Dominguez and M. Shifter, Constructing Democratic Governance in Latin America (2008). Contains individual country studies.

G. W. Grayson, Mexico: Narco-Violence and a Failed State? (2009). Explores the impact of drug violence on Mexican politics.

G. Joseph et al., The Mexico Reader: History, Culture, Politics (2003). Excellent introduction to major issues.

P. Lowden, Moral Opposition to Authoritarian Rule in Chile (1996). A discussion of Chilean politics from the standpoint of human rights.

J. Preston and S. Dillon, Opening Mexico: The Making of a Democracy (2004). Excellent analysis of developments in Mexico prior to the outbreak of the drug wars.

H. Wiarda, Politics and Social Change in Latin America (2003). Attempts to examine the subject in light of long-standing historic trends in Latin America.

E. Williamson, The Penguin History of Latin America (2010). The best recent survey.

Africa

B. Davidson, Let Freedom Come (1978). Remains a thoughtful commentary of African independence.

P. Gourevitch, We Wish to Inform You that Tomorrow We Will Be Killed with Our Families (1999). An account of the Rwandan genocide that is beautifully written and almost unbearable to read.

J. Herbst, States and Power in Africa (2000). Relates current issues of African state-building to those before the colonial era.

R.W. July, A History of the African People, 5th ed. (1995). Provides a careful and clear survey of post–World War I history and consideration of nationalism.

N. Mandela, Long Walk to Freedom: The Autobiography of Nelson Mandela (1995). Autobiography of the African leader who transformed South Africa.

L. Thompson, A History of South Africa (2001). The best survey.

N. Van de Walle, African Economies and the Politics of Permanent Crisis, 1979–1999 (2001). Exploration of the difficulties of African economic development.

India and Pakistan

O.B. Jones, Pakistan: Eye of the Storm (2003). Best recent introduction.

R. Rashid, Taliban: Militant Islam, Oil and Fundamentalism in Central Asia (2001). Analysis of radical Isalmist regime in Afghanistan.

R.W. Stern, Changing India: Bourgeois Revolution on the Subcontinent (2003). Overview of forces now changing Indian society.

S. Wolpert, A New History of India (2003). The closing chapters of this fine survey history are particularly helpful in orienting the reader in postwar Indian history until the mid-1980s.

Islam and the Middle East

A. Ahmed, Discovering Islam: Making Sense of Muslim History and Society, rev. ed. (2003). An excellent and readable overview of Islamic–Western relations.

J. Esposito, The Islamic Threat: Myth or Reality, 2nd ed. (1992). A useful corrective to some of the polemics against Islam and Muslims today.

J.J. Esposito, ed., The Oxford Encyclopedia of Islam (1999). A thematic survey of Islamic history, particularly strong in the Modern Era.

D. Fromkin, A Peace to End All Peace: The Fall of the Ottoman Empire and the Creation of the Modern Middle East (2001). Very good on the impact of World War I on the region.

G. Fuller, The Future of Political Islam (2003). A very good overview of Islamist ideology by a former CIA staff member.

J. Keay, Sowing the Wind: The Seeds of Conflict in the Middle East (2003). A balanced account.

N.R. Keddie, Modern Iran: Roots and Results of Revolution (2003). Chapters 6–12 focus on Iran from 1941 through the first years of the 1978 revolution and provide a solid overview of history in this era.

G. Kepel, Jihad: The Trail of Political Islam (2002). An extensive treatment by a leading French scholar of the subject.

Credits

page 709: Image Works/Mary Evans Picture Library Ltd; page 709: Library of Congress; page 711: The Art Archive\Picture Desk, Inc./Kobal Collection; page 714: National Archives and Records Administration; page 717: Getty Images Inc. - Hulton Archive Photos; page 717: Getty Images Inc. - Hulton Archive Photos; page 719: Lady Elizabeth Thompson Butler (1846–1933), "The Roll Call: Calling the Roll after an Engagement, Crimea (unframed)". The Royal Collection © 2005, Her Majesty Queen Elizabeth II. Photo by SC. page 722: Art Resource/Bildarchiv Preussischer Kulturbesitz; page 728: Getty Images.

Chapter 24, page 731: "Parade of Tsarina's Meadow". Vsesoiuznyi Muzei A.S. Pushkina; page 734: Giuseppe Pellizza da Volpedo, "Il Quarto Stato" 1901. Oil on canvas, 283 cm × 550 cm. Photo by Marcello Saporetti. Galleria D'Arte Moderna, Milano. Copyright Comune di Milano; page 735: American Textile History Museum, Lowell, Mass; page 736: Edgar Degas (1834–1917), "The Bellelli Family" c. 1858-60. Musee d'Orsay, Paris, France. Photograph copyright Bridgeman-Giraudon/Art Resource, NY; page 739: Image Works/Mary Evans Picture Library Ltd; page 740: Reunion des Musees Nationaux/Art Resource, NY; page 741: Private Collection/Bridgeman Art Library; page 742: Opitz, George Emanuel. Dedication of a Synagogue in Alsace, c. 1820. The Jewish Museum, New York, NY, U.S.A.; page 743: The Granger Collection; page 744: Courtesy of the Library of Congress; page 747: UPI\CORBIS- NY; page 750: Soldiers fire on demonstrators infront of the Winter Palace on "Bloody Sunday", January 9, 1905. © Bildarchiv Preussischer Kulturbesitz/Art Resource, NY; page 752: The Denver Public Library, Western History Collection, Photographer J.B. Silvis, Call Number X-22221; page 754: Brown Brothers; page 756: Lewis W. Hine\Library of Congress; page 760: National History Museum, London, UK/Bridgeman Art Library; page 760: French Government Tourist Office; page 762: Clark University, Special Collections/Archives; page 763: Wikipedia, The Free Encyclopedia.

Chapter 25, page 766: Mexico City, 1942 (tempera on masonite) by Juan O'Gorman (1905-82) Museo de Arte Moderno, Mexico City, Mexico / Index / The Bridgeman Art Library Nationality / copyright status: Mexican / in copyright until 2058; page 771: Dagli Orti (A)\Picture Desk, Inc./Kobal Collection; page 773: CORBIS- NY; page 774: Guatemala Tourist Commission; page 776: CORBIS- NY; page 777: Courtesy of the Library of Congress; page 778: AP Wide World Photos; page 780: Edouard Manet (1832–1883), "The Execution of Emperor Maximilian of Mexico, June 19, 1867". Oil on canvas. Location: Staedtische Kunsthalle, Mannheim, Germany. Art Resource, NY; page 781: Private Collection/The Bridgeman Art Library; page 782: UPI\CORBIS- NY; page 785: The Granger Collection; page 788: UPI\CORBIS- NY.

Chapter 26, page 792: The Granger Collection, New York; page 796: Bristol City Museum and Art Gallery, UK/ The Bridgeman Art Library; page 798: [Photographer]/Hulton Archive/Getty Images; page 801: Margaret Bourke-White\Getty Images/Time Life Pictures; page 802: AP Wide World Photos; page 804: Courtesy of the Library of Congress; page 805: Bibliotheque des Arts Decoratifs, Paris, France/The Bridgeman Art Library; page 806: Chateau de Versailles, France/The Bridgeman Art Library; page 806: Illustrated London News of April 14, 1877. Mary Evans Picture Library Ltd. page 807: [Photographer]/Hulton Archive/Getty Images; page 810: Courtesy of the Library of Congress; page 811: Caravan with Ivory, French Congo, (now the Republic of the Congo). Robert Visser (1882–1894).

c. 1890–1900, postcard, collotype. Publisher unknown, c. 1900. Postcard 1912. Image No. EEPA 1985-140792. Eliot Elisofon Photographic Archives. National Museum of African Art, Smithsonian Institution; page 814: Getty Images Inc. - Hulton Archive Photos; page 815: Courtesy of the Library of Congress; page 815: National Archives of South Africa; page 817: Brown Brothers; page 818: © CORBIS All Rights Reserved; page 818: Getty Images Inc. - Hulton Archive Photos; page 822: Art Resource/Bildarchiv Preussischer Kulturbesitz; page 823: Courtesy of the Library of Congress. African and Middle Eastern Division; page 823: Tischler Fotografen\Photolibrary/Peter Arnold, Inc.

Chapter 27, page 824: Mita Arts Gallery CO., LTD; page 828: Courtesy United States Naval Academy Museum; page 831: Scala/Art Resource, NY; page 832: Adachi Ginko (active 1847–1894). View of the Issuance of the State Constitution in the State Chamber of the New Imperial Palace. Japan, Meiji period (1868–1912), March 2, 1889 (Meiji 22). Triptych of polychrome woodblock prints; ink and color on paper. The Metropolitan Museum of Art, Gift of Lincoln Kirstein, 1959 (JP3233-JP3225) Image © The Metropolitan Museum of Art/Art Resource, NY; page 833: ZUMA Press; page 834: Courtesy of the Library of Congress. Gift of Mrs. E. Crane Chadbourne; 1930; page 837: © Bettmann/CORBIS All Rights Reserved; page 840: National Archives and Records Administration; page 842: © CORBIS All Rights Reserved; page 843: CORBIS- NY; page 846: The Art Archive\Picture Desk, Inc./Kobal Collection; page 849: Library of Congress; page 850: © Burton Holmes / CORBIS All Rights Reserved; page 850: Private Collection/The Bridgeman Art Library; page 851: © CORBIS All Rights Reserved; page 856: IN/GEN/Camera Press\Retna Ltd; page 859: FPG\Getty Images Inc. - Hulton Archive Photos.

Chapter 28, page 863: Mary Evans Picture Library; page 868: Bettmann\CORBIS- NY; page 870: Anti-Slavery International; page 873: German Information Center; page 879: Brown Brothers; page 879: Brown Brothers; page 881: SPL\Photo Researchers, Inc.; page 881: National Archives and Records Administration; page 882: Photoprint by William Fox. Copyrighted by Underwood & Underwood. Courtesy of the Library of Congress; page 881: Hulton-Deutsch Collection/Corbis; page 885: Ria-Novosti\Sovfoto/Eastfoto; page 887: John Singer Sargent (1856–1925), "Gassed, an Oil Study". 1918-19 Oil on Canvas. Private Collection. Photo © Christie's Images. The Bridgeman Art Library; page 887: Art Resource/Bildarchiv Preussischer Kulturbesitz; page 888: CORBIS- NY.

Chapter 29, page 895: Art Resource/Bildarchiv Preussischer Kulturbesitz; page 898: Getty Images Inc. - Hulton Archive Photos; page 899: Gemalde von A. M. Gerassimow, "Lenin als Agitator." Bildarchiv Preussischer Kulturbesitz; page 900: AP Wide World Photos; page 901: Poster concerning the 1st 5 Year Plan with a photograph of Joseph Stalin 1879–1953), 'At the end of the Plan, the basis of collectivisation must be completed', 1932 (colour litho) by Klutchis (fl.1932). Deutsches Plakat Museum, Essen, Germany/Archives Charmet/The Bridgeman Art Library; page 903: Itar-Tass\Sovfoto/Eastfoto; page 905: AP Wide World Photos; page 908: Library of Congress; page 913: Art Resource/Bildarchiv Preussischer Kulturbesitz; page 914: Art Resource/Bildarchiv Preussischer Kulturbesitz; page 917: Art Resource/Bildarchiv Preussischer Kulturbesitz; page 918: Ball State University Libraries, Archives & Special Collections, W.A. Swift Photo Collection; page 919: UPI\CORBIS-

Index

A

Abbas I, Shah, 623–624
Abbasid Caliphate, 622
Abduh, Muhammad, 807
Abelard, Peter, 435–436
Abode of Islam, 631
Aboukir, 683
Absolute monarchy, 579
Absolutism, 490, 577, 580, 639, 646, 653, 660, 662–663, 665, 722, 805, G–1
Acheh sultans, 634
Acropolis, 420, G–1
Act of Settlement (1701), 578
Act of Succession, 475
Act of Supremacy, 475
Act of Uniformity, 475
Act of Union (1800), 707, 710
Acton, Lord, 726
The Advancement of Learning, 643
Affonso I, 416–417
Afghanistan, 1041–1042
Africa
Christian churches, 814
culture, 714–715
   industrial revolution, 601
   Muslim reform movements, 803
Africa (1800–1945)
   Catholic missionaries, 814–815
   Central, 811
   colonial rule and patterns of resistance, 817–818
   East, 811
   and European explorers, 814
   exploration and colonization, 813–817
   Islamic reform movement, 811–813
   nationalist movement, 818–819
   scramble for, 817
   Southern, 810–811
   West, 811
Africa, postcolonial era
   Congo, 1035–1036
   health and environment, 1037–1038
   HIV/AIDS, 1038
   Nigeria, 1032–1033
   religion, 1038
   Rwanda, 1036
   social changes, 1038
   South Africa, 1034–1035
   trade and development, 1038
Africa ca. 1000–1700
   Angola, 417
   Benin Kingdom, 412–414
   central, 415–417
   central Sudan empires, 411
   east, 417–419
   Egypt, 402
   Ghana, 404–405
   Gold Coast, 415
   Great Zimbabwe, 419
   impact of European arrival, 414–415

Islamic influence in sub-Saharan region, 402–404
   Kanem, 410–412
   Kanuri empire, 411
   Kongo Kingdom, 415–417
   Mali, 405–408
   north, 402
   Omanis of Zanzibar, 419
   Sahelian empires, 411
   Senegambia, 415
   Songhai kingdom, 408–410
   southern, 419–422
   Swahili culture and commerce, 417–419
   West African Forest Kingdoms, 412–414
   Yoruba kingdoms of Oyo and Ife, 412
Afrikaans, 422, G–1
Afro-Indian merchant, 632
Agricultural activity. *See also* Agricultural revolution; Family economy
   Americas, colonial, 513–514
   China, late imperial, 531–532
   farming societies, 654
   Japan, modern, 834
   Mali, 406
   Ming dynasty, 531–532
   nineteenth century, 732
   traditional European peasant society, 597
   Vietnam, 570
   Yangzi basin, 532
Agricultural revolution, 597–601, G–1
   open-field method, 599–600
   and population expansion, 600–601
   two-or three-field systems of rotation, 599
   village method, 599
Akbar the Great, 583, 626, 630
Al-Afghani, Jamal al-din, 763
Alawma, Idris, 411
Albanians, 703
Albert, King Charles, 720, 722
Albright, Madeline, 1050
Alexander I, Emperor, 684–685, 687
Alexander I, Tsar, 705
Alexander II, Tsar, 748
Alexander III, 748
Alexander VI, Pope, 452
Alexius I Comnenus, 427
Alfonsín, President Raul, 1028
Algarotti, Francesco, 645
Algeria, 814
Ali, Muhammad, 805–806
Alighieri, Dante, 450
Allende, Salvador, 1027
Allied Control Commission, 954
All Men Are Brothers, 545
Almagest, 639
Al-Maghili, Muhammad, 410
al-Qa'ida, 1042
   attacks, 1052
al-Wahhab, Ibn Abd, 803
American Civil War (1861–1865), 696, 798, 869

American Declaration of Independence (1776), 646
American investment capital, 897
American King-Crane Commission, 1046–1047
American Monroe Doctrine, 693
American National Academy of Sciences, 985
American Progressives, 758
American revolution. *See also* United States
   abolitionist movement, 715–717
   aids to rebels, 671
   chronology, 672
   coal and iron industries, 713
   cotton trade, 712, 714
   development of east–west railways, 713
   Missouri Compromise, 712, 715
   northern economic development, 712–713
   and political ideas of the American colonists, 669
   and prohibition of slavery, 712
   resistance to the imperial search for revenue, 668–669
   sectional conflict, 712–715
   slavery in south, 714–715
   Southern economy, 713–714
   textile production, 712
   trade routes development, 712–713
Americas, colonial. *See also* United States
   animals and agriculture, 513–514
   and Columbian Exchange, 511–514
   diseases, 511–514
   ecological transformations, 511–514
   exploitation, 503–504
   French and British colonies, 509–510
   influence of Anglican Church, 511
   on Roanoke Island, 510
   Seven Years' War (1756–1763), 591–592
Americas
antislavery movement, 715–717
industrial revolution, 601
Amida, 550
Amir/emir, 418, G–1
Anabaptism, 472
Anatolia, 614
Andropov, Yuri, 974
Anglo-Oriental College, Aligarh, 799
   Animal husbandry, Mali, 406
Anime, 999
Annam, 571, 618, G–1
Anschluss, 928, G–1
Anti-Comintern Pact, 842
Anti-French marriage alliances, 457
Anti-Semitism
   of Europe, 725–728, 778, 914
   of the Nazi Party, 914–915
Antoinette, Queen Marie, 675, 680
Apartheid laws, 1034
Appalachian Mountains, 670
Appeasement, 926–929
Arabs, 623
international trade networks of, 632

Arafat, Yasser, 1049
Arawak language, 462
Arbitrary taxation, 577
Archangel, 583
Architecture, Ottoman, 61
Argentina, 732, 774, 776–780
    expansion and growth, 777–778
    Nacionalismo, 778
    postcolonial era, 1028
Aristocratic resurgence, 594, 673, G–1
Aristotelianism, Islamic form of, 625
Aristotelian physics, 640
Aristotle, 639
Arizpe, Lourdes, 1033
Arkwright, Richard, 603–604
Arminius, Jacobus, 473
Arouet, François Marie, 647
Art
    Benin kingdom, 414
    Gothic, 442, 442, 451
    Great Zimbabwe civilization, *420*
    Ottomans, 619
    Renaissance Europe, 451–452
Article 9 of the No-War Constitution, 993, G–1
Articles of Confederation, 712
Aryans, 725, 915, G–1
Ashikaga, 530
Ashikaga daimyo, 547
Ashikaga lords, 547
Asia, 871
Asiento, 590
Asquith, Herbert, 741
Assignats, 676, G–1
Association of Southeast Asian Nations (ASEAN),
    1016
Atatürk, 1040
Atlantic Charter, 947
Auclert, Hubertine, 741
August 1991 coup, 978
Augustus, 441, 737, G–1
Augustus, Philip, 429
Ausgleich, 724, 728, G–1
Austerlitz, 684
Austin, Stephen F., 780
Australia, 732
Austria, 576, 660, 722
    hostility towards the Jewish community, 726
    Jewish communities in, 607
    political consolidation, 700
    political unity, 703
    Seven Weeks' War, 722
    war with Germany, 722
Austro-Hungarian Empire, 701
Authenticité campaign, 1035
Avanti, 905
Awadh, 794
Awrangzeb, 626–627
Axis powers, 445, 843, 924–925, 937–939, 948,
    G–1
Ayan, 619, G–1

B
Babur, 622
Backward peoples, 867
Bacon, Francis, 641–643
Badoglio, Marshal Pietro, 938
Bahadur, Teg, 627

Baien, Miura, 562
Bakufu system, 426, 530, 547, 551–555, 557, 561,
    564, 824–829, 844–845, G–1
Balfour Declaration (1917), 888
Banalities, 438
Bangladesh, 1043
Banto, Yamagata, 564
Bantu, 810
Barbarossa, Frederick, 429
Basho, 560
Basij, 1041
Bastille, fall of, 673
Batista, Fulgencio, 1026
Battle of Ayacucho (1824), 692
Battle of Nagashino (1575), 548
Battle of San Jacinto, 780
Battle of Stalingrad, 938
Battle of the Bulge, 939
Battle of the Nations, 686
Battle of Trafalgar, 684
Battle of Wagram, 685
Battles of Lexington and Concord (1775), 670
Bazaari, 805, 1040, G–2
Beauharnais, Josephine de, 685
Becquerel, Henri, 760
Beef, 773
Behaim, Martin, 462
Belgian Congo, 870–871
Belgium, 687
Belorussian Jews Petition, 607
Benin bronzes, 413
Benin Kingdom, 412–414
Bentinck, Governor General Lord William, 794
Berlin, 740
Berlin Academy of Sciences, 645
Berlin Decrees, 685
Berlin Wall, fall of, 1020
Bernadotte, French Marshal, 685
Bernard of Clairvaux, 429
Bernstein, Eduard, 747
Beyond Good and Evil, 761
Beza, Theodore, 483
Bhakti devotionalism, 629–630, G–2
Bishop, 473, 495, 579, 581, 583, 585, 674, 1034,
    G–2
Bhutto, Benazir, 1043
Bible, 439, 466–467, 495, 545
    relationship with science, 642
Bihzad, 625
Bill of Rights, 578
Biological determinism, 725
The Birth of Tragedy, 761
Black Death, 425, 444–446, 458, 485, G–2
Black Legend, 503, G–2
Black Sea peninsula, 718
"Bleeding Kansas," 715
Blitzkrieg, 941, G–2
Boccaccio, Giovanni, 445, 450
Bodhisattva, female, 550, G–2
Bohemia, 638, 660
Boleyn, Anne, 475
Bolívar, Simón, 691–692
Bolsheviks, 748–751, 763, 898–899, 904, 920,
    G–2
Bonaparte, Napoleon, 682, 804
    bloodiest battle of, 685

    coalition against, 686
    defeat at Waterloo, 687
    escape from Elba, 687
    The Hundred Days, 688
    marriage, 685
    organization of a Polish state, 685
    in Spain, 685
Boniface VIII, Pope, 447–448, *448*
Book of Common Prayer, 475
Borodin, Mikhail, 1014
Bosnia, 724, 983
Bosnia-Herzegovina, 983
Bossuet, bishop Jacques-Bénigne, 581, 583
Boston Tea Party, 670
Boulton, Matthew, 604
Bound ("lily") foot, 534
Bourbon family, 481
Boxers, 837, 852, G–2
Boyars, 583–585, G–2
Brahe, Tycho, 640
Brahmo Samaj, 796
Brainwashing, 1001
Brasília, 789
Brazil, 774
    collapse of the monarchy, 787
    colonial, 507–509
    economic problems and military coups,
        787–789
    postcolonial era, 1028–1029
    slavery issue, 785–786
Brazilian Communist Party, 788
Brazilian independence, 693
Brezhnev, Leonid, 973
Briand, Aristide, 910
British Broadcasting Company (BBC), 944
British East India Company, 543
British ministry of Lord North, 670
British North America Act of 1867, 718
British Raj, 797
British-Spanish commercial conflict, 590
Bronze Age, 570, G–2
Brüning, Heinrich, 912
Buddhism, 543, 630
    Indian Buddhist cultures of Burma, 613
    in South East Asia, 634
Buenos Aires, 776
Bukharin, Nikolai, 900
Bulgarians, 704
Buonarroti, Michelangelo, 451
Bureaucracy, 530–531
    China, late imperial, 536–537
    Ottoman Empire, 616–618
    Tokugawa era, 557
Burgundian empire, 444, 455
Bush, George W., 1050

C
Calas, Jean, 650
Calderon, Felipe, 1031
Calendar, 477
Caliphate, 612, 622, 807, 813, G–2
Calixtus II, Pope, 426
Calles, Plutarco Elías, 784
Calvin, John, 577
Calvinism, 472–473
Camacho, Manuel ávila, 784
Cambridge university, 708, 760

Camp David Accords, 1048
Campo Formio, 683
Canada Act of 1840, 718
Canadian revolution
    British North America Act of 1867, 718
    Canada Act of 1840, 718
    culture, 718
    first Reform Act (1832), 718
    parliamentary mode of government, 718
    relations with the United States, 717–718
    road to self-government, 718
Candide, 647
Cantonments, 798, G–2
Canton system, 543, 846
Cao Dai, 1015
Cape Colony, 815
Cape society, 422
Capetian dynasty, 441
Capitalism, Western, 530
Cárdenas, Lázaro, 784
Cardoso, Fernando Henrique, 1029
The Carnal Prayer Mat, 545
Carolingian renaissance, 450
Carpets, 625
Carranza, Venustiano, 783–784
Carter, President Jimmy, 1049
Casement, Roger, 871
Castle Church in Wittenberg, 468
Castlereagh, Viscount, 686
Cathedral of Notre Dame, 680
Catherine of Aragon, 457
Catherine the Great, 595, 607, 662–663, 662
Catholic Emancipation, 707–708, G–2
Catholic Emancipation Act, 708
Catholicism, 201–202, 592, 642, 649, 707, G–2
    Calvinism versus, 485
    Catholic League, 485
    Council of Trent, 476
    French, 581
    and Henry of Navarre, 481–482
    Ignatius of Loyola and, 475–476
    and Italian Fascist movement, 907
    laws against, 578
    under Louis XIV, 583
    Reformation, 475–476
    sources of reform, 475
    in Vietnam, 1015
Caudillos, 776, 779–780, G–2
Cavendish, Margaret, 644–645
Cavour, Count Camillo, 720, 722
Celestial Dynasty, 544
Censor, 536, 648, 657, G–2
Censorate, 536, 538, 573, G–2
Censorship, 707
Central Asian Islamic states, 630–632
Central Asian steppes, 614
Chaebol, 1012
Chaghatays, 630
Chaitanya, 630
Chamberlain, Austen, 910
Chamberlain, Houston Stewart, 725
Chamberlain, Joseph, 867
Chamberlain, Neville, 928
Chamber of Deputies, 707, 907
Champa kingdom, 570, 572
Cham state, 569
Changamire Shona dynasty, 421

Chapelier Law, 675
Charcoal, 604
Charcot, Jean-Martin, 761
Charles I, 577
Charles II, 578, 589, 646
Charles III, 689
Charles the Bold, 455
Charles V, Emperor, 454, 457, 474, 476
Charles VI, 587
Charles VIII, 453
Charles X, 706–707
Charter of the Nobility, 663
Chartism, 708, G–2
Charwoman, 736
Châtelet, Emilie du, 645
Chattel slavery, 438, 516, G–2
Chavez, Hugo, 1026
Chechen War, 979
Cheka, 899
Chelebi, Evliya, 619
Chelebi, Katib, 619
Chernenko, Constantin, 974
Chiaroscuro, 450, G–2
Chile, 774, 1027–1028
Chilean independence, 691
Chin, Fan, 546
China, 529
    attitudes toward outside civilizations, 531
    balance between centralization and
        decentralization, 576
    Chinese bureaucrats, virtues of, 531
    and environmental issues, 984–985
    industrial revolution, 601
    pattern of government, early, 530
    traditional society, 530
China, late imperial
    banking system, 533
    bureaucracy, 536–537
    cholera epidemic, 532
    civil service examinations, 534, 537, 544, 577
    commercial revolution, 532–534
    Confucianism, role of, 534
    contacts with the West, 543
    economy and commerce, 532–534
    education level, 538
    emperor, Ming–Qing times, 536
    gentry class, 537–538
    Grand Canal, 531
    Jesuit missionary, 543
    land and people, 531–532
    "law of avoidance," 537
    and Macartney mission for change, 544
    Ming dynasty, chronology, 539
    Ming–Qing foreign relations, 540–543
    pattern of Manchu rule, 538–540
    political system, 534–540
    pottery industry, during Ming–Qing times, 533,
        545
    property rights, 534
    Qing dynasty, chronology, 539
    scholar-gentry class, 531
    silk industry, 533
    silver import, 533
    Single Whip Reform, 533
    standard of living, 532
    "thin horse" business, 535
    urban growth, 534

    White Lotus Rebellion, 531, 540
    women, 534
China, modern
    borders, 850–851
    economic growth, 1005–1006
    Great Proletarian Cultural Revolution
        (1965–1976), 1003–1004
    May Fourth Movement, 854–855
    nationalist movement, 855–860
    Opium War, 844–846
    post Mao, 1004–1005
    rebellions against the Manchu, 846–848
    regional governments, 849
    and rest of the world, 1006–1007
    self-strengthening and decline (1874–1895),
        848–850
    Soviet Period (1950–1960), 1001
    and U.S. Foreign Policy, 1007
    Warlordism (1895–1926), 852–854
China Merchants Steam Navigation Company,
    850
Chinese Communist Party (CCP), 856–860
Chinese Neo-Confucianism, 531
Chittagong, 795
Choson Korea, 567–569
Christian doctrine of the Trinity, 578
Christian II, 473
Christianity
    anti-Islamic attitudes, 763
    in China, late imperial, 543
    ecclesiastical breakdown and revival, 447–448
    and European voyages, 462
    Great Schism and Conciliar Movement, 448
    hidden Christians, 550
    in Japan, 550
    and Jews, 434
    in Nubia, 412
    Peace of Augsburg, 474
    role in European unification, 960
    Scripture test, 472
    states of Maqurra and Alwa, 412
    superstition and enlightenment, 487–488
    and Thirty Years' War (1618–1648), 485–486
Christianity Not Mysterious, 649
Churchill, Winston, 944, 947–948, 953
Church of England, 577–578
Civil Code of 1804, 684
Civil Constitution of the Clergy, 676–677
Civilizations
    clash of, 1022
    of Southeast Asia, 569
Civil service examination, Chinese, 534, 537, 544,
    577
Civil society, 1021
Cixi, Empress Dowager, 849
Clash of civilizations, 1022, G–2
Clemenceau, Georges, 887
Clement VI, Pope, 468
Clement VII, 454
Clergy
    and Cluny reformers, 425
    fifteenth century, 478
    Middle Ages, 437–438
    and Protestant Reformation, 475
    and Reformation, 465
    role in witch hunting, 488
Clericis Laicos, 447

Clinton, President Bill, 1036
Clive, Robert, 592
Cluny reform movement, 425
"Coalition of the Willing," 1053
Cocoa, 773
Coffee, 773–774, 788
Coffeehouse, 621
Coke, 604
Cold War era, 482, 995, 1006, 1011, 1024–1027,
    1035, 1038, 1041–1042, 1054, G–2
  end of, 959
  events of 1956, 957–958
Collectivization, 899–902, 911, 1001, G–2
Colleges, 585
Colombia, 774
Colonial Assembly in Haiti, 689
Columbian Exchange, 463, 496, 511, 514, G–2
Columbus, Christopher, 457, 461
Commerce and economy
  in Islamic states, 632–634
  Europe, High Middle Ages, 433–434
Committee of Public Safety, 679
Common Market, 959
Common Sense, 670
Communism, 744
The Communist Manifesto, 744
Complutensian Polyglot Bible, 467
Compromise of 1867, 724
Concordat of Bologna, 452
The Condition of the Working Class in England,
    744
Confection, 734
Confederate States of America, 702, 704
Confederation of the Rhine, 684
Confucianism, 463, 529
  and similarity among east Asians, 529
  Tokugawa era, 561–562
  view of patriarchal society, 534
Congo, 810
Congress of Vienna, 686–689, 700
Conquistadores, 503, G–2
Conrad, Joseph, 871
Conservative Mexicans, 693
Constantine, 705
Constitutional Act of 1791, 717
Constitutional Convention (1787), 672
Constitutional Convention of 1788, 712
Constitutionalism, 725
Constitution of the Year II, 682
Constitution of the Year VII, 683
Consubstantiation, 472
Consulate in France (1799–1804), 683–684, 687,
    G–2
Consumer products of industrializing businesses,
    601
Continental Congress, 670
Continental System, 685
Continental war, 590
The Convention, 591, 672, 678–682, 704, 712,
    757, 761, 819, G–2
Convention of Westminster, 591
Convention People's Party in the Gold Coast, 819
Conversations on the Plurality of Worlds, 645
Copernican astronomy, 640
Copernicus, Nicolaus, 639
Cornwallis, Lord, 670
Corsica, 682

Cort, Henry, 604
Corvée, 594, G–2
Cotton, 532, 712–713, 834, 844
Cotton gin, 713
Council at Pisa, 448
Council of Elders, 682
Council of Mutual Assistance (COMECON), 955
Counter-Reformation, 457, 475, 477, 481, 485,
    501, 510, G–2
Counterrevolutionary Activity, 677–678
Count of Tilly, 485
Coup d'état (1958), 1052
Court Jews, 608
Court of Star Chamber, 457
Cranmer, Thomas, 475
Creole elite, 690, 692, 767, 775
Creole juntas, 691
Creole revolutionaries, 690
Creoles, 505, 690–693, G–2
Crimean War (1854–1856), 718–720, 804
Croatia, 983
Cromwell, Oliver, 577
Crown of Saint Stephen, 586
Crusades, 426–432, 441, 462–463, 468, 495, G–3
Cuba, 696, 774
Cuban Revolution, 1026–1027
Cult of the Supreme Being, 681
Cultural relativism, 639
Cultural traits, G–3
  British cultural imperialism, 795
  of east Asians, 529
  Ming–Qing, 544–546
  Ottoman society, 619–620
  Safavid dynasty, 625–626
Cunitz, Maria, 645
Curia, 448, 476, G–3
Czechoslovakia, 725, 954
Czechs, 703, 709, 724

D
Dadu, 629
Daewoo, 1012
Dahomey, 816
Daimyo, 547–550, 552–555, 557–558, 825–826,
    833, G–3
Daimyo castle, 548
Daimyo (dye-myoh) lords, 547–548, 553
D'Alembert, Jean le Rond, 647
D'Annunzio, Gabriele, 905
Dante's Divine Comedy, 639
Danube River, 664
Daoism, 543, 563, G–3
Daoist rites, 536
Dar-al-Islam, 402, G–3
Darwin's Theory of Natural Selection, 758–760
Da Silva, Luiz Inácio Lula, 1030
David, 451
Da Vinci, Leonardo, 451
Dawes Plan of 1924, 897
Dawud, Askia, 409
De Beauvoir, Simone, 968
Debt peonage, 505, 768, G–3
Decameron, 450
Deccan, 613, 626–627, G–3
Dechristianization of France, 680
De Cisneros, Francisco Jiménez, 467
Declaration of Female Independence, 704

Declaration of Pillnitz, 678
Declaration of Rights, Virginia, 673
Declaration of the Rights of Man and Citizen,
    673–674, 675, 704
Declaration of the Rights of Woman, 675, 676
Declaratory Act, 669
De Coligny, Gaspard, 481
Decolonization, 1021
Deferent, 639
De Gobineau, Arthur, 725
De Gouges, Olympe, 675, 679
Deism and the Enlightenment era, 649–650, 653,
    G–3
  God concept, 649–650
De Iturbide, Agustín, 693, 780
Delhi, 795
De Médicis, Catherine, 481
Democracy, 744
Democratic People's Republic of Korea, 1011
Democratic revolution, 530
De Montesquieu, Baron, 651–652
  belief in monarchy, 653
  influential ideas for France, 653
  The Spirit of the Laws, 653–654
Dependency theory, 768–769, G–3
De Rosas, Juan Manuel, 776
De San Martín, José, 691
De Santa Anna, Antonio López, 780
Descartes, René, 644
The Descent of Man, 760
Description of a New World, Called the Blazing
    World, 645
De Secondat, Charles Louis, 651
Despotism, 449
Dessalines, Jean-Jacques, 691, 695
De Urquiza, Justo José, 777
Devshirme, 617–618, G–3
Dialogues on the Two Chief Systems of the World,
    641
Díaz, Porfirio, 782
Dibbalemi, Mai Dunama, 411
Diderot, Denis, 647, 656
Diet, 831, 836–839, 841–844, G–3
Diet of Worms, 469–470
Diffusion, 469, G–3
Dingiswayo, king, 810
Discourse on the Moral Effects of the Arts and
    Sciences, 654
Discourse on the Origin of Inequality, 654
A Discussion of the Military Problems of a Maritime
    Nation, 564
Disraeli, Benjamin, 708–709, 758
Divine Comedy, 450
Divine right of kings, 490, 577, 579, 581, 583,
    G–3
  Divorce, nineteenth century, 736
  Diwan, 627, G–3
"Dollar Diplomacy," 775
Domestic or putting-out system, 603, G–3
Dominican (Jacobin) monastery, 678
Douglas, Stephen A., 715
Douglass, Frederick, 715
Dream analysis, 762
The Dream of the Red Chamber, 546
Dred Scott decision, 715
Drug Act (1906), 758
Dubcek, Alexander, 958

Duce, 905, G–3
Duke of York, 457
Duma, 751, G–3
Durrani, Ahmad Shah, 804
Dutch East India Company, 422
Duxiu, Chen, 855
Dyarchy, 539

E
Earl of Durham, 718
Earth, views about, 639–640
East Asia
    in late traditional era, 530
    premodern, 530
East Asia, modern, 990–991
    China, 846–860, 1000–1008
    Japan, 825–844, 990–1000
Eastern Christendom, 614
Eastern Europe (1989)
    Germany, 975
    Hungary, 975
    Poland, 975
    Velvet Revolution in Czechoslovakia, 975–977
    Violent Revolution in Romania, 977
East India Company, 670, 795–796
East–West summit, 959
The Economic Consequences of the Peace (1920), 891
Edict of Nantes, 482, 583
Edict of Worms, 470
Edo castle, 553
Edo establishments, 555
Education Act of 1870, 709
Edward IV, 457
Edward VI, 475
"Effective Suffrage—No Reelection," 782
Ego, 762, G–3
Egypt, 806, 869–870
Egyptian Feminist Union, 808
Egyptian-Israeli accords, 1049
Eiichi, Shibusawa, 833
Einstein, Albert, 761
Eisenstein, Serge, 946
Ekken, Kaibara, 556
Eleanor of Aquitaine, 441
Elements of the Philosophy of Newton, 647
Elizabeth I, 457, 484, 485
Elizabeth of Russia, Empress, 591
Elizabeth of York, 457
Emancipation crusade, 696
Emancipation Proclamation, 715
The Embossed Tea Kettle, 560
Émile, 658
Emmanuel II, Victor, 720, 722
Emmanuel III, King Victor, 905
"Emperor's Astronomy," *640*
Empirical induction method, 641, 643
Empiricism, 641–644, G–3
Enabling Act, 914
Enclosure of the land, 420, 599–600, G–3
Encomienda, 504–505, G–3
Encyclopedia, 647–649, 653
Engels, Friedrich, 744, 746
England, 577. *See also* Great Britain
    Act of Union in 1800, 707, 710
    chronology, 580
    during Elizabeth I (r. 1558–1603), 484

fifteenth century, 457
    industrial revolution, 602–605
    peace with France, 589
    political stability and economic prosperity
        during eighteenth century, 580
    political stability and economic prosperity of
        modern, 580
    population expansion in eighteenth century, 600
    power of the British monarchs, 580
    Reformation, 474–475
    relations with Spain, 484–485
    thirteenth century, 440–441
English Quakers, 694
Enlightened absolutism, 660–663
Enlightenment, 530, G–3
The Enlightenment era
    Catherine the Great, 662–663
    deism and, 649–650
    Encyclopedia, 647–649
    European, 638–639
    Joseph II of Austria, 660–662
    major publication dates of, 651
    and religion, 649–653
    and society, 653–660
    Voltaire, 647
    women in, 657–660
Enlightenment political thought, 639
Enlightenment writers, 639
Entente Cordiale, 874–876
Epicycles, 639
"E pur si muove", 641
Equal citizenship, 742
Erasmus, Desiderius, 467
Erfurt Program of 1891, 745
An Essay Concerning Human Understanding, 491, 645
Essay on the Inequality of the Human Races, 725
Estado Novo, 788, G–4
Eucharist, 438, 469, 472, 494, G–4
Eugenius IV, Pope, 448
Euro, 960, G–4
Europe, 1500–1650
    discovery of the Americas, 461–463
    European expansion, 462–463
    overseas expansion, 497–498
    Portuguese Voyages, 461–462
    sixteenth-century religious movement, 463–480
    Spanish Voyages, 462–463
    superstition and enlightenment, 487–491
    voyage to India, 461–462
    voyage to South Africa, 421
    Wars of Religion, 480–487
    writers and philosophers of, 488–491
Europe, during Great Depression era
    financial crises, 896–897
    and government policy, 898
    impact on agricultural commodities, 897–898
Europe, early modern
    absolutist political developments, 580
    agricultural revolution, 597–601
    aristocracy, 592–594
    artisans, 605–606
    bourgeoisie (middle class), 605
    cities, 605–606
    commercial success, 577
    dominance of, world, 576
    dominant states, 575

economic advances, 576
    English monarchy, 576–577, 592
    France, chronology, 583
    global commercial empires, 577
    Glorious Revolution, 578–580
    Habsburg empire, 586–587
    hierarchy and privilege, 592
    industrial revolution, 601
    Jewish communities, 606–608
    land and tillers, 594
    monarchy in France, 580–583
    parliamentary government in England,
        577–578
    patterns of preindustrial urbanization, 605
    peasants and serfs, 594–595
    political development, 576–577
    political stability and economic prosperity of
        Britain, 580
    political values in British Isles, 580
    Prussia, rise of, 587–588
    religion and arbitrary taxation conflict, 577
    Revolution of 1688, 578
    Romanov dynasty, 583
    Russia, 583–586
    urban class, 605–606
Europe, nineteenth century, 732
    capitalist production and competition, impacts,
        745
    class conflict, 744–745
    democracy and political parties, 744
    economic decline, 775
    English hand-loom weavers, 734
    entry of workers into a wage economy, 733
    factory workers and urban artisans, 733–735
    Jewish emancipation, 742–743
    labor migration, 733
    major cities, 734
    Marxism, 744–745
    modern thoughts, 758–763
    proletarian revolution, 745
    rules for laborers, 733
    socialism, 751
    trade unionism, 743
    working classes, 743–744
Europe, twentieth century
    creation of welfare states, 961–962
    feminism, 967
    migration of people, 963–965
    Muslim population, 966–967
    resistance to expansion, 962–963
    Thatcher Revolution, 963
    women, status of, 967
European Counter-Reformation, 457
European Economic Community, 959, G–4
European Enlightenment, 638–639
    critics of, 655–657
European family law, 736
European Free Trade Area, 959
European global expansionism, 615
European intellectual life, 644
European Jews, 608
European liberalism, 704–705
European nation-states, 701
European Recovery Program, 954
The European Settlement, 686–689
European Union (EU), 960, 1039, 1045, 1053,
    G–4

European warfare
   of the Austrian succession, 590–591
   eighteenth-century colonial arena, 590
   of Jenkins's Ear, 590
   of Louis XIV, 588–590
   Seven Years' War, 591–592
Eurozone region, 960
Evangelical Protestantism, 714
Evolutionary Socialism (1899), 747
Ewuare, King, 412

F

Fabians, 747, G–4
Fair Labor Standards Act of 1938, 919
Family economy, 595, 597, 602, 609–610, G–4
   post marriage, 597
   urban artisans and, 597
   women and, 597
Farm family, 595
Fasci di Combattimento, 905
Fascism, 841, 904–906, 921, G–4
Fascists' October march, 906
Fawcett, Millicent, 741
Ferdinand of Aragon, 452, 455–457
Ferdinand VII, 693
Feudal society, 444, 448, 454, 549, 562, G–4
Fief, 548, 552, 557, G–4
Finland, 954
First Continental Congress, 670
First Estate of the clergy, 672
First Ming emperor, 540
Fodio, Usman Dan, 803
Fontenelle, Bernard de, 645
Footbinding, 534, 534
Foot soldier revolution, 547–549
Forbidden Palace, 536
Ford, Henry, 918
Foundations of the Nineteenth Century, 725
Four-stage theory, 654
Four Treasures, 540
Fox, Vicente, 1031
France, 576–577, 638
   against Austria, 590
   early modern, chronology of history, 583
   empire in America, 590
   empire in southern Asia, 590
   in fifteenth century, 451–452, 455
   hostility towards the Jewish community, 726
   in India, 592
   invasion of Egypt, 683
   liberal monarchy, 707
   monarchy in, 580–583
   Montesquieu's influential ideas for, 653
   peace with England at Utrecht, 589
   political experiment, post World War I, 898
   political feminism, 741
   Popular Front Ministry, 898
   against Prussia, 591
   road construction, 594
   and settlement of eastern Europe, 687
   in thirteenth century, 441–442
   war with Great Britain, 683
   war with League of Augsburg, 588
   women, nineteenth century, 736
Francis I, King, 452, 469
Francis II, 678
Franco-Prussian War, 722–724

Franco-Russian alliance, 685
Frankfurt, 723
Franklin, Benjamin, 671
Frederick I Barbarossa, 442–444
Frederick II, Emperor, 444, 588
Frederick III, 485
Frederick IV, 485
Frederick the Great, 664
Freedom, 655
French and Indian War, 591
French Catholicism, 581
French Republic, 680
French revolution, 669
   chronology, 682
   Civil Constitution of the Clergy, 676–677
   Committee of Public Safety, 679
   Congress of Vienna and the European
     Settlement, 686–689
   Consulate in France (1799–1804), 683–684
   Convention and the Role of Sans-Culottes,
     678–679
   Counterrevolutionary activity, 677–678
   dechristianization of, 680
   Declaration of the Rights of Man and Citizen,
     673–674
   end of the Monarchy, 678
   Estates General Becomes the National
     Assembly, 672–673
   Fall of the Bastille, 673
   Great Fear and Surrender of Feudal Privileges,
     673
   Napoleonic era, 682–686
   Napoleon's Empire (1804–1814), 684–685
   period 1789, 672–675
   provincial uprisings, 680–681
   reconstruction of France, 675–678
   Reign of Terror and its aftermath, 679–682
   Republic of Virtue, 680
   second, 678–679
   social and political structure leading to, 674
   Society of Revolutionary Republican Women,
     679
   Thermidorian reaction, 682
   Wars of Liberation, 685–686
French Roman Catholic feminists, 741
French Wars of Religion (1562–1598)
   Guises versus Protestants, 481
   Henry IV's Edict of Nantes, 482
   rise to power of Henry of Navarre, 482
Freud, Sigmund, 761–762
Führer. *See* Hitler, Adolf
Fulbe (or Fulani), 811

G

Gabon, 696
Galicia, 664
Galilei, Galileo, 641, 644
Gallican liberties, 677
Gandhi, Indira, 1042
Gandhi, M.K., 795, 800–801, 1042
Gandhi, Rajiv, 1043
Gao rulers, 404
Garibaldi, Giuseppe, 720, 722
Garrison, William Lloyd, 715
The Genealogy of Morals, 761
Genetic theory, 725

Gentry class, 530–531, 534, 536–538, 544, 546,
   559, 573, 617, 669, 735, 827, 847–849, 852,
   854, 860, 1001, G–4
   late imperial China, 537–538
Geocentricism, 639
Geoffrin, Madame Marie-Thérse, 637
George, David Lloyd, 887
George I of England, King, 578
George III, 544, 592, 670
German clothing-making trades, 739
German national life, 725
German Reformation
   attack on indulgences, 468
   Hapsburg Charles I of Spain, election of,
     468–469
   and Imperial wars, 470
   justification by faith alone, 468
   Luther's stand on the Jews, 470
   Martin Luther's reform, 467–468, 473–474
   Martin Luther's religious teachings, 469–470
   and Peasants' Revolt, 470–471
   spread of, 470
German Roman Catholics, 742
German Social Democratic Party, 742, 961
German Weimar Republic, 907
   communism and Hitler, 913–914
   Constitution, 907
   depression and political deadlock, 912
   Hitler's early career, 908–910
   Hitler years, 912–915
   humiliations against, 907–908
   inflation impact, 907–908
   invasion of the Ruhr, 907–908
   Locarno Agreements, 910–912
   power of the Nazis, 912–915
   Stresemann years, 910
   women, status of, 915–916
Germany, 889
   anti-Semitism movement, 725–728
   Crusaders in, 428
   Erfurt Program of 1891, 745
   hostility towards the Jewish community, 726
   Middle Ages, 434, *443*, 444, 457
   Otto I, 425
   Peasants' Revolt, 470
   political consolidation, 700
   political experiment, post World War I, 907–916
   political feminism, 741
   political unity, 703
   Reformation, 465, 467–471
   revival of monarchies, 454
   Saint Maurice, 431
   Social Democratic Party (SPD), 745
   social democrats and revisionism, 745–747
   Thirty Years' War (1618–1648), 485–486
   trade unionism, 743
   unified, 702, 722–723
   women, nineteenth century, 736
Ghana, 811
Ghazis, 614, G–4
Ghettos, 608, 727, 742, G–4
Gibbon, Edward, 651
Girondists, 678–679, 681
Gladstone, William, 708–709, 758
Glasnost, 974, G–4
Global commercial empires, 577
Globalization, 1020–1021, 1030, G–4

Global Network for Neglected Tropical Diseases, 1038
"Globe Apple," 465
Glorious Revolution, 490, 578, 580, 608, G–4
God concept, 649–650, 759
   God images, Japanese, 550
Godwinsson, Harold, 440
Gokhale, G. K., 799
Golden Horde, 455, 542, G–4
The Golden Lotus, 545
Gomulka, Wladyslaw, 956
Gorbachev, Mikhail S., 959, 974
Gospel of Christian freedom, Luther's, 470
Goulert, President João, 789
Governments
   bakufu system, Tokugawa era, 551–552, 554
   Benin kingdom, 412
   Diet, 831–832
   Europe, High Middle Ages, 434
   Holy Roman Empire, 486
   Japan, modern, 991–993
   Kongo kingdom, 415
   during Ming–Qing times, 536–537
   of Nara and Heian Japan, 530
   Ottoman Empire, 616–618
   under Peter the Great, 585
   Safavid dynasty, 622
   Tokugawa era, 557
Grand Alliance, 589
Grand Army of Napoleon, 685
Grand Duchy of Warsaw, 685
Grand Duke Dimitri of Moscow, 455
Grand Inquisitor (1508), 467
Grand Mufti, 671, 807, G–4
Grand Secretaries, 536
Gravitational law, 644
Great Britain, 638, 679. *See also* England
   adultery, 736
   Education Act of 1870, 709
   and environmental issues, 984–985
   family law, 736
   Great Reform Bill (1832), 707–709
   independence movements in Latin America, 693
   Labour Party and Fabianism, 747
   political consolidation, 700
   political experiment, post World War I, 898
   Public Health Act of 1875, 709
   as strongest power, 700
   Thatcher Revolution, 963
   trade unionism, 743
   voting rights for women, 741
   war with France, 683
   women, nineteenth century, 736
Great Depression era, 755, 775, 790, 825, 836, 841, 843, 860, 895–896, 912, 916, 919–922, G–4
   United States, 918–920
Greater Learning for Women, 556
The Great Fear, 673
Great Leap Forward, 1001, 1003–1004, G–4
Great Northern War with Sweden, 584
Great Purges, 903–904, G–4
Great Reform Bill (1832), 707–709, G–4
Great Schism, 447–448, 454, 457–458, G–4
Great Trek of Boer *voortreker*, 810–811, 814, G–4
Greeks, 703

Greenhouse emissions, 986
Gregory VII, Pope, 426, 429
Gregory XI, Pope, 448
Gregory XII, Pope, 448
Grey, Earl, 708
Grey, Sir Edward, 876
Guilds, 447, 465, 505, 592, 606, 705, 734, G–4
Gulf of Finland, 584
Gulf Wars, 1049
Guomindang (GMD), 855–860, 1008–1009, 1017, G–4
Gutenberg, Johann, 466
Gutenberg Bible, 466

H
Habsburg Dynasty, 470
Habsburg Empire, 586–587, 631, 924
   home rule movement, 709
   Jews, 606
   nationalist unrest within, 724–725
   unrest within the, 724–725
Hacienda system, 505, 767, 772, 780, G–4
Haitian revolution, 667, 689–690
Hajj, 813, 823, G–5
Hamlet, 489
Han dynasty, 532
Hangu, 568
Hanlin Academy of China, 568
Hanoverians, 580, 723
Harding, Warren, 916
Harem, 536, 616, 618, 620, 651, G–5
Hastings, Warren, 795
Hawley-Smoot Tariff Act of 1930, 919
He, Zheng, 541
Heart of Darkness, 871
Heisenberg, Werner, 761
"He Kept Us Out of War!", 758
Heliocentric (sun-centered) model of earth, 640
Hemmed, 583
Hemp, 773
Henry I, 425
Henry III, 481–482
Henry IV of France, 482
Henry "the Navigator," Prince, 461
Henry V, Emperor, 426
Henry VI, 444, 457
Henry VII, 457
Henry VIII of England, King, 457
Heretics, 494, G–5
Hermit Kingdom, 531
Herzl, Theodor, 726–727, 1046
Hesse, 723
Hevelius, Elisabetha, 645
Hevelius, Johannes, 645
Hides, 773–774
Hideyoshi, Toyotomi, 547, 549, 551, 569
Hiroshima bombing, 941
Hitler, Adolf, 725, 908–910, 912–914, G–4
HIV/AIDS, 1035, 1037–1038, G–5
Hoa, Thanh, 571
Hobbes, Thomas, 490
Hobson, J. A., 865
Hohenstaufen Empire, 442–444
Hohenzollerns, 587–588
Holocaust, 725, 1046, G–5
Holstein, 722–723
Holy League at Marignano, 452

Holy Roman Empire, 442–443, 448, 455, *469*, 472, 481, 485–486, 586–587, 589, 684, 687, G–5
Holy Synod, 585
Holy War against the Muslim. *See* Crusades
Home Rule Bill, 709
Home rule movement, 703, 709–710, 799–801, G–5
Hongzhang, Li, 848–849
Hoover, Herbert, 897, 918
House of Commons, 580, 708, 709
House of Hanover, 589
House of Lancaster, 457
House of Peers, 840
House of York, 457
Hu, Butcher, 546
Hue Chinese institutions, 573
Hughes, Besançon, 481
Huguenot Henry of Navarre, 482
Huguenots, 481–482, 492, 583, G–5
Human beings dwelling, 655
Humanism, 449–450, 457, 467, G–5
Human nature, 646
Human societies, according to *four-stage theory*, 654
Hundred Years' War (1337–1453), 425, 444, 457
Hungarians, 703
Hungary, 724–725, 956
Hunnish Xiongnu Empire, 566
Husayn, Faysal ibn, 1052
Hussein, Saddam, 1053
Hussein, Tâhâ, 809
Hyundai, 1012

I
Ibn Battuta, 418
Ibn Sa'ud, Muhammad, 803
Id, 762, G–5
"Ideal" Islamic state, 1051
Ieyasu, Tokugawa, 547, 551
Ignatius of Loyola, 475
Il Popolo d'Italia, 905
Imams, 622, 625, 804, G–5
Impact of modernity, 793, G–5
Imperial Household Ministry, 831
Imperialism, 865
Imperialism and World War
   emergence of German empire, 872–876
   expansion of European power, 864–872
   religious, 867
Imperial Palace, 551
Import substitution, 775
India (1800–1945)
   British annexation policy, 794
   British-Indian relations, 795–798
   commercial supremacy of France and England, 577
   cultural relations between Britain and India, 797
   dispute over Kashmir between India and Pakistan, 801
   economic and social reforms (1828–1836), 794
   economic burdens on Indians, 798
   economic impact of Company rule, 794
   English-language curriculum in Indian schools, 797
   first half of nineteenth century, 793–795

India (*cont.*)
  Hindu–Muslim tensions, 799–801
  Hindu reform movement, 796–797
  Indian resistance, 798–800
  Islamic responses to declining power and
    independence, 802–803
  major personalities, 799
  under Marquess of Ripon, 798
  Muslim reform movements, 803
  post independence, 1042–1043
  Revolt of 1857, 798
Indianization of Southeast Asia, 569
Indirect Rule, 817, G–5
Indochinese Communist Party, 1014
Indonesia, 1044
Indulgence, 468, 474, 492, G–5
Industrial revolution, 530–531, 576, 601–602,
  605, 615, 714, 733, 735, 737, 744, G–5
Innocent III, Pope, 427, 432, 444
Inquiry into the Nature and Causes of the Wealth of
  Nations, 654
"Inserting the ornament" procedure, 535
Institutes of the Christian Religion, 473
Integralism, 788
Intifada, 1044, 1048, G–5
Intolerable Acts (1774), 670
Inuyama Castle, 547
Investiture Controversy, 426
Iqbal, Muhammad, 800
Iran, 804–805, 1040–1041
Iranian Islamic tradition, 625–626
Iran–Iraq War (1980–1988), 1052
Iraq, 810, 1052–1054
Ireland, 703
  Act of Union in 1800, 707, 710
  home rule movement, 709–710
Irigoyen, Hipólito, 778
"Irish problem," 703
Iron production, 604–605
Isabella of Castile, 455–457
Ishraqi school, 625, 626
Islam, G–5
  between 1450 and 1800, 614
  Christian critiques of, 651
  coffee-drinking bans, 621
  in Enlightenment thought, 651–653
  and late nineteenth-century European thoughts,
    763
  in modern world, 763
  Montagu's comments about, 652
  Muslim eclectic tendencies, 629
  in Songhai, 410
  spread of, 632
  in sub-Saharan region ca. 1000-1700, 402–404
  traditions of Aristotelianism and Platonism, 625
  in Vietnam, 569
Islam (1800–1945)
  Atatürk's major reforms, 807
  emulation of west, 805–807
  modernization of, 807–808
  Muslim reform movements in Africa, 803
  nationalist movements and, 809–810
  pan-Islamism, 807
  purification and revival of, 808
  responses to declining power and
    independence, 802–803
  Tanzimat reforms, 806–807

Wahhabi movement, 803
western political and economic encroachment,
  803–804
Western political ideology, culture, and
  technology, impact, 804–805
  and women, 808
Islamic civilization (1600), 612–613
Islamic Empires (1500–1800)
  Acheh, 634
  Anatolia, 614
  and arrival of Europeans, 632–634
  in Central Asia, 630–632
  control of Southern Seas, 632–634
  decline of Ottoman military and political power,
    621
  Mughal Empire, 626–630
  Ottoman Empire and Eastern Mediterranean
    World, 614–621
  reign of Süleyman, 618–621
  Safavid Dynasty, 622–626
  and Southern-Oceans trade, 632
  in Sumatra and Java, 634
Isma'il, Shah, 623
Isthmus of Panama, 775
Italia Irredenta, 883, G–5
Italian Fascist movement
  Chamber of Deputies, 907
  conception of the state, 904
  fascists in power, 906–907
  rise of Mussolini, 905–906
Italy, 638
  political consolidation, 700
  political experiment, post World War I, 904–907
  unified, 701, 720–722
Italy, Renaissance in, 448–453
  art, 451–452
  City-State, 449
  culture, 449
  despotism, 449
  education, 450
  French invasions and political decline, 452–453
  humanism, 449–450
  major political events, 454
  social conflicts, 449
  vernacular literature, 450
Ivan the Great, 455
Ivan the Terrible, 542, 583, 946
Ivory Coast, 816

J

Jacobins, 678–679, 681–682, G–5
Jains, 626, 799, G–5
James II, 578
James I of England, 577
James VI of Scotland, 577
Janissaries, 618, 806, G–6
Janissary corps, 806
Japan, 529, 851
  attitudes toward outside civilizations, 531
  balance between centralization and
    decentralization, 576
  culture, 550
  and environmental issues, 984–985
  Era of Unification, 549
  era of Warring States, 530
  exports to China, 549
  governments at Nara and Heian courts, 530

industrial revolution, 601
inheritance patterns, 548
Jesuit missionaries, 550
"late traditional," 547
modernization of, 711–712
political consolidation, 700
political history, 530
Portuguese merchants in, 549–550
resemblance with postfeudal Europe, 549
Tokugawa era, 550–564
traditional society, 530
Warring States era, 547–550
Japan, modern
  agricultural productivity, 834
  alliance with Germany against the Soviet Union,
    842
  Anglo-Japanese Alliance of 1902, 837
  banking system, 833, 836
  centralization of power, 829–831
  Choshu, 826
  chronology, 844
  collapse of *bakufu*-domain system, 825–826
  cotton textiles and railroads, 834
  Crisis in Manchuria, 840
  cultural shift, 827, 998–999
  decline of oligarchic control, 839
  democratization, 991–993
  economic growth, 832–836, 996–997
  economic institutions, 833
  export boom and military procurements, 836
  and Great Depression, 841
  Imperial (1890–1945), 836–843
  Japanese militarism and German Nazism,
    843–844
  liberalism, 839
  Manchuria, 840
  Meiji Constitution, 831–832
  Meiji era, 837–838
  Meiji Restoration (1868–1890), 827–832
  militarism and war (1927–1945), 840–843
  movement for a "union of court and camp," 826
  occupation reforms, 992–993
  political parties, 831, 993–996
  and the rest of the world, 1000
  rise of parties to power, 838–840
  Russo-Japanese agreement, 837
  Satsuma coup, 826
  society, 834, 998–999
  status of women, 998
  view of Western science and industry, 829
  and World War II, 842
The Japanese Family Storehouse, 561
Japanese pirate-traders, 549
Jenkins, Robert, 590
Jesuit missionaries
  in China, 531, 543
  in Japan, 550
Jewish communities
  in Austria, 607
  converted to Christianity, 608
  court Jews, 608
  establishment of a Jewish State, 727
  European Jews, 608, 726
  as finance capitalists, 726
  in Habsburg land, 606
  Jews from Spain, 608
  jihad against, 1052

and Joseph II, 662
in Ottoman society, 619
in Prussia, 607
in Russia, 607
Jewish emancipation
equal citizenship, 742
in Germany, 743
legal rights, 742–743
pogroms against Jews, 742
situation of European Jews, 742–743
status of political figures, 743
The Jewish State, 727
Jieshi, Jiang, 842, 856
Jihad, 411, 811–813, 1051–1052, G–6
Jinnah, Muhammad Ali, 800, 1043
Joao, 693
Joao VI, 693
John, King, 441
John XII, Pope, 425
Jong-Il, Kim, 1013
Jonson, Ben, 489
Jordan, 1049
Joseph, Francis, 724
Joseph II of Austria, Emperor, 660–662, 742
Josephinism, 662
Journées, 673
Juárez, Benito, 780–781
Julius II, Pope, 452, 468
July Monarchy, 707, *711*, G–6
Junkers, 588, G–6

K

Ka'ba, 823, G–6
Kabir, 629
Kabuki actors, 555, 561, 1000, G–6
Kadar, Janos, 957
Kaga daimyo, 558
Kagame, Paul, 1036
Kaiping Coal Mine, 849
Kalahari, 811, G–6
Kamikaze, 843, G–6
Kamakura *bakufu*, 530
Kanem, 410–412
Kangxi, Emperor, 539–540, 542, 576
Kano school, 559
Kansas, 732
Kansas-Nebraska Bill, 715
Kanuri Empire, 411
Kay, John, 603
Kemal, Mustafa, 807
Kemalism, 807
Kennedy, John F., 958
Kenyatta, Jomo, 795, 1032
Kepler, Johannes, 640
Keynes, John Maynard, 891
Khameini, Ali, 1041
Khan, Genghis, 630
Khan, Kublai, 540
Khan, Sayyid Ahmad, 799
Khatami, Mohammad, 1041
Khmer Rouge, 1015–1017, G–6
Khoikhoi people, 422
Khomeini, Ayatollah Ruholah, 1040
Kikuyu people, 818
Kimchee, 1012
King Lear, 489
Kinmochi, Saionji, 838

Kirch, Gottfried, 645
Kirov, Sergei, 904
Kiswahili, 417
Kleindeutsch, 722, G–6
Kômei, Katô, 839
Kongo Kingdom, 415–417
Koprülüs, 618
Korea, 529, 851, 956
Chinese principles of government, 566
Choson dynasty, 567–569
chronology of history, 568
comb-patterned pottery, 565
early history, 565–567
geography of, 565
Hunnish Xiongnu Empire, 566
invasions, 568
as Japanese colony, 1010
Koryo society, 566–567
modern, 1010–1013
Mongol incursions in, 567
North, 1010–1011, 1012–1013
population in the fifteenth century, 567
religion, 565–566
Silla rule, 566
South, 1012
Tungusic tribes of, 565
Korean War (1950), 1011
Koryo society, 566
Kowtow rite, 540–541
Koxinga state, 542
Kristallnacht, 915, G–6
Kronstadt, 899
Kropotkin, Peter, 854
Kruger, Paul, 875
Kubitschek, Juscelino, 789
Ku Klux Klan, 918
Kulaks, 901–902
Kwantung, 837
Kyoto Protocol on Climate Change, 985–986
Kyushu daimyo, 550

L

Lacombe, Claire, 679
La Frigiorique, 777
Lahore, 795
Laissezfaire economic thought and policy,
654–655, G–6
Landholdings
landlord power, 594
and Latin America, 767–769
Ottoman Empire, 617
Language and literature
Central Asian Islamic state, 632
East Asia, 559
of Europe, 702
Ming and Qing dynasties, 545–546
Ottoman Empire, 619
Portuguese influence in Japanese language, 550
Qianlong, Emperor, 540
Renaissance Europe, 449–450
Safavid dynasty, 625
Taino Indians, 462
Tokugawa era, 561
La Reforma, 780, G–6
Lateran Accord of February 1929, 907
Latifundia, 767, G–6
Latin America, 732

Argentina, 776–780
Brazil, 785–787
destruction of colonial trade monopolies, 773
economic crisis, post independence, 775
economic life, post independence, 767
economic resource management, post
independence, 773–774
exports, post independence, 774
immediate consequences of independence, 767
increased foreign ownership and influence, post
independence, 774–775
landholding, 767–769
Mexican independence, 780–784
Mexico, post independence, 767
political liberals, 705
political philosophies, 769–773
political stability, post independence, 775–776
social changes, post independence, 767
trade, post independence, 773
Latin American revolution
Bolívar, Simón, 691–692
Brazilian independence, 693
Chilean independence, 691
chronology, 694
de San Martín, José, 691
eighteenth-century developments, 689
in Haiti, 689–690
independence in New Spain, 692–693
on the South American continent, 690
Venezuela, liberation of, 691–692
Lausanne Conference (1932), 897
League of Augsburg, 588
League of Nations, 889, 916, 924, G–6
Lebanon, 810
Lebensraum, 924, 934, G–6
Le Dynasty, 571
Legislative Assembly, 680
Lenin, V. I., 744, 748–749, 865, 899
Leningrad Symphony, 946
Léon, Pauline, 679
Leopold I, 586
Leopold II, 662, 678, 816
Leo X, Pope, 468
Lessing, Gotthold, 651
"*L'état, c'est moi*," Louis XIV's declaration, 583
Letter Concerning Toleration, 645
Letters on the English, 647
Letter to the Grand Duchess Christiana, 642
Levée en masse, 679, G–6
Liberal Democratic Party (LDP), 994–995, G–6
Liberalism, 639, 677, 704–705, 727, G–6
in modern world, 705
relationship with nationalism, 705
Liberation theology, 1024, G–6
The Life of an Amorous Man, 561
The Life of an Amorous Woman, 561
Light-manufactured goods, 775
Lincoln, Abraham, 715
"Lincolnshire Ox," 600
Linguistic uniformity within European nations,
701
Lisbon Treaty, 960
Livingstone, David, 814
Llaneros (Venezuelan cowboys), 691
Lloyd-George, David, 758
Locke, John, 490–491, 579, 645–646, 655, 694
Loi, Le, 571

Lombard, Peter, 440
Long March of 6,000 miles, 857–858, 858, 1003, G–6
Louise, Archduchess Marie, 685
Louis IX, 441–442
Louis XI, 455
Louis XII, 453
Louis XIV, 463, 482, 553, 576, 578, 580–581, 584, 591
  alleged declaration, 583
  concept of royal authority, 583
  against the Dutch, 588
  wars of, 588–590
Louis XVI, 672–673, 677
Louis XVIII, 706
L'Ouverture, François-Dominique Toussaint, 689
Lucknow, 795
Ludendorff, General Erich, 910
Ludovico il Moro, 452
Lueger, Mayor Karl, 908
Luftwaffe, 932, 943, G–6
Lumumba, Patrice, 1035
Luther, Martin, 467
Lutheran reformations, 472

M
Mabiki, 559
MacArthur, General Douglas, 991, 1011
Macartney, Lord, 543
Macaulay, Lord, 797
Macbeth, 489
Mach, Ernst, 760
Machiavelli, Niccolò, 453–454, 453
A Madman's Diary, 854
Madrasa, 631, G–6
Magellan, Ferdinand, 463
Maghreb, 402
Magi, 431, G–6
Magna Carta, 430, 441, G–6
Magyars, 590, 725, G–6
Mahabharata, 569, G–6
Mahmud II, 802
Maize, 531
Malaysia, 1044
Mali, 405–408
Mamluks, 615, G–7
Manchu Dynasty, 542–543, 854
  banning of footbinding, 534
  pattern of rule, 538–540
Manchurian Chinese, 538
Mandate of Heaven, 562, G–7
Manga, 1000
Mannerism, 452, G–7
Mansa, 407
Marabouts, 409, 411, G–7
Marathas, 627
Marburg Colloquy, 472
March Revolution in Russia, 884–886
Marquess of Ripon, 798
Marriage>
  in early modern Europe, 478–480
and family economy, 597
Marshall, General George, 860, 954
Marshall Plan, 954, G–7
Martín, José de San, 775
Martin V, Pope, 448
Marx, Karl, 744, 746

Marxism, 745, G–7
Marxist-Leninist ideology, 899
Mary, 578
Masaryk, Jan, 954
Masaryk, Thomas, 954
The Mathematical Principles of Natural Philosophy, 644
Mauguet, Marie, 741
Mau Mau uprising, 818, G–7
Maurice, Saint, 431
Maximilian, Austrian Habsburg Archduke, 780
Maximilian I, Emperor, 457
May Fourth Movement, 854–855
Mazarin, Cardinal, 580
Mazorca (ear of corn) association, 776
Mazzini, Giuseppe, 703, 720
McKinley, William, 756
Meat Packing Act (1906), 758
Mechanical arts, 648
Medici pope Leo X, 452
Medvedev, Dmitri, 979
Mehmed II, 614, 616–617, 619
Meiji Restoration, 563, 712, 733, 827, 834–835, 844, G–7
Mein Kampf, 910, 924, G–7
Mekong Delta, 1013–1014
Melanchthon, Philip, 473
Mendel, Gregor, 759
Mensheviks, 749, G–7
Mercantilism, 499, 500, G–7
Mercantilist theory of economic exploitation, 498–499
Messiah, 494, G–7
Mesoamerica, 498, G–7
Mestizos, 690, 767, 771, 775, G–7
Mexican independence
  consequences, 780
  Díaz and dictatorship, 782
  foreign interventions, 780–782
  radical revolution, 782–784
Mexican Revolution of 1910, 776
Mexican War (1846–1848), 715
Mexicopostcolonial era, 1029–1030
post independence, 767
Mfecane, 810, G–7
Miao tribes, 532
Miao Wars, 532
Middle Ages, High
  the Crusades, 426–432
  Hohenstaufen Empire, 442–444
  investiture Struggle, 426
  medieval women, 439–440
  models of government, 434–436
  Order of Life, 436–439
  Otto I and revival of Empire, 425
  revival of Catholic church, 425–426
  rise of merchants, 433–434
  schools and universities, 434–435
  society, 436–439
  suppression of Muslim aggression, 427–430
  towns, 432–433
  traders and guilds, 433–434
  in western Europe, 426
Middle Ages, Late
  artisans, 447
  Black Death, 425, 444–447
  ecclesiastical breakdown and revival, 447–448

England, 457
  growth of national monarchies, 440–444
  Hundred Years' War (1337–1453), 425, 444
  Italy, Renaissance in, 448–453
  peasant revolt, 447
  revival of monarchies, 454–457
  Spain, 455–457
  trade guilds, 447
Middle East, 427
  slave trade, 515, 523
Middle East, post colonial
  Arab-Israeli conflict, 1046–1049
  Arab states, 1044
  Gulf War, 1049
  Iraq, 1052–1054
  Israeli-Arab War of 1948–1949, 1048
  Israeli invasion of Lebanon (1982–1983), 1049
  nationalism, 1044
  oil production, 1049–1050
  Palestinian terrorism, 1048
  rise of militant Islamism, 1050–1051
  state of Israel, 1044
  state of Palestine, 1044
  Suez Crisis of 1956, 1048
  U. S. invasion of Iraq, 1050
Middle East Peace Agreement. *See* Oslo Agreement
Middle Passage, 515, 522, 525, G–7
Milan Decree of 1807, 685
Military power/weaponry, Europe Late Middle Ages
Millets, 619, G–7
Minas Gerais, 787
Ming dynasty, 530, 567
  agricultural cash crops, 532
  and Confucianism, 534
  culture, 544–546
  emperors, 540
  foreign relations, 540–541
  good years of, 532
  landlord's holdings, 532
  literature, 545–546
Ming History, 539
Ming-Qing despotism, 531
Minh, Ho Chi, 1014–1015
Mirandola, Pico della, 452
Mita, 504–505, G–7
Mitsubishi *zaibatsu*, 1012
Mitsui, 1012
Mobilization, 823, 843, 1001, G–7
Mobutu, Joseph-Désiré, 1035
Modena, 720
Modernity, 1022
"Mohametan" Christian, 651
Molotov, Vyacheslav, 953
Mona Lisa painting, 452
Monarchies
  in England, 457
  growth of national, 440–441
  Pahlavi, 127
  revival of, 454–457
Mongol dynasty, 532
Mongol (or Tatar) rule, 455
Montagu, Lady Mary Wortley, 652
Montesquieu, 639
Montmorency-Châtillon family, 481
Moo Hyun, Roh, 1012

Moors, 419, 431, 456, 463, 501, G–7
Morales, Evo, 1026
Morel, E. D., 871
Morgan, J. P., 757
Moroccan Crisis, 876
Mossadeq, Muhammad, 1050
Mubarak, Husni, 1049
Muezzin, 405, 407, G–7
Mughals, 613–614, 623, 626–630, G–7
    Akbar's reign, 626
    Awrangzeb, 626–627
    chronology, 630
    Jahangir, 626
    origin, 626
    political decline, 627–629
    religious conservatism, 627
    religious developments, 629–630
    Shah Jahan, 626–627
    versus Sikhs and Marathas, 627
Muhammad, Prophet, 651
Muhammadanism, 651
Mujtahid, 804, G–7
Mulattos, 415, 689–690, 767, 771, 775–776, G–7
Multigeniture patterns, 548
Mumtaz, 627
Munich Agreement, 928–930
Murad IV, 618
Musa, Mansa, 407
Musharraf, General Parviz, 1043
Muskets, 548
Muslim Brotherhood in modern Egypt, 803
Mussolini, Benito, 905–907
Mutesa, King, 817
Mwene Mutapa kingdom, 420
Myung Bak, Lee, 1012

N

Nabrawi, Saize, 808
Nacionalismo, 778, G–8
Nacionalistas, 778
Nagy, Imre, 957
Na'ima, 619
Nanak, Guru, 627, 629
Napoleon I, 684
Napoleonic Code of law, 669, 684, 736
Napoleonic era, 682–686
    chronology, 687
Napoleon III, 711, 720, 723, 780
Napoleon's Empire (1804–1814), 684–685
Naqshbandiya, 630
Narayanan, K. R., 1043
The Narrow Road of Oku, 560
Nassau, 723
Nasser, President Gamal Abdel, 956
Nathan the Wise, 651
National Action Party (PAN), 1031
National Assembly, 673
National Constituent Assembly, 673, 675, 677
National Council of French Women (CNFF), 741
National Industrial Recovery Act (NIRA), 919
Nationalism in Europe, 700
    ideal of, 727
    political dangers of, 726
    relationship with liberalism, 705
    stirrings and impact on empires, 724–725
Nationalistic movements, during the nineteenth
    century, 701

Nationality, 703
National languages, 701
National Recovery Administration (NRA), 919
National Studies, 563–564, G–8
Nationhood, 701–702
Natural selection, 758–760, 855, G–8
Nazi program, 914
Nazis, 908, 912–917, G–8
Nazi-Soviet Pact, 930–931
Ndebele peoples, 871
Negritude, 818–819, G–8
Nehru, Jawaharlal, 799, 1042
Nelson, Admiral Horatio, 683
Nelson, Lord, 684
Neocolonial economy, 775, G–8
Neo-Confucianism, 567, 572
Neo-Platonists, 640
Nepalese Gurkhas, 795
Netanyahu, Binyamin, 1049
The Netherlands, 577, 687
Newcomen, Thomas, 604
New Deal years, 916–920
New Economic Policy (NEP), 899–900, G–8
New Principles on Chinese Population, 1001
New Spain, independence in, 692–693
Newton, Sir Isaac, 640, 643–644
New York stock market, 897
New Zealand, 732
Nguyen Dynasty, 572–573, 851, 1013–1014
Nicaraguans, 1028
Nicholas I, 705–706
Nicholas II, Tsar, 751
Nietzsche, Friedrich, 761
Nigeria, 810–811
Niger-Kongo, 407, G–8
Nilo-Saharan, 407, G–8
Nilotic Africa, 151, 158–163, 411, G–8
Ninety-five theses, 468, G–8
Ninth of Thermidor, 681
Nixon, Richard, 958
Nkrumah, Kwame, 819, 1032
Nobles, Middle Ages, 436–437
Noblewomen, 644–645
Nobunaga, Oda, 547
No drama, 285, 555, 559, 561
North Africa, 868–869
North America, nineteenth century
    European immigration to the United States,
        752–754
    labor unions, 754–755
    Progressives, 755
    social reforms, 755–756
North American Free Trade Agreement (NAFTA),
    1030–1031
North Atlantic Treaty Organization (NATO),
    955–956, 983–984, 1053
Northern Transatlantic Supremacy, 732–733
North Korea, 1010–1011
    growth and democracy, 1013
    relation with Japan, 1013
    "sunshine policy" of, 1013
The *Novum Organum*, 643
Nuclear Test Ban Treaty, 958
Nyamwezi, 811
Nyerere, Julius, 795

O

The Oath of the Horatii, 661
Oba, 412, 414, G–8
Obama, Barrack, 985
"Occidental" slave trade, 519–520, 522, G–8
Occupied territories, 1048, G–8
O'Connell, Daniel, 707
Odinga, Oginga, 819
O'Higgins, Bernardo, 691
Old Regime (*ancien régime*), 608, 684, G–8
    aristocracy, 592–594
    hierarchy and privilege, 592
    land and tillers, 594
    peasants and serfs, 594–595
Old Testament Christianity, 847
Oligarchs, 836
Omanis of Zanzibar, 419
On the Motion of Mars, 640
On the Origin of Species, 758, 760
On the Revolutions of the Heavenly Spheres,
    639–640
Open Door Policy (1899), 871
Operation Ajax, 1040
Opium War, 844–846
Oppenheimer, Samuel, 608
Ordinance of 1787, 712
Organic Articles of 1802, 683
Osaka Cotton Spinning Mill, 833
Osaka merchant house, 561
Oslo Agreement, 1049
Osmanlis, 614
Othello, 489
Otto I, 425
Ottoman Empire, 583–584, 600, 651, 683, 718,
    G–8
    administration under, 616–618
    army, 617–618
    art and architecture, 619
    on Balkan Peninsula, 614
    in Byzantine-Seljuk frontier, 614
    cavalry-gentry, 617–618
    chronology, 619
    conquest of Constantinople, 614
    control of *timar* lands, 617
    culture and society, 619–621
    decline of, 621
    economic developments, 618–619
    expansionist conquests of, 614
    Jewish communities, 619
    land holdings, 617
    literature, 619
    Orthodox Christians in, 621
    political and military developments, 618
    during Spanish Inquisition, 619
    under Süleyman, 615, 618
    territorial gains, 618
    versus Europe, 621
Ottoman-Safavid border wars, 623
Ottoman sovereignty, 615
Overman (übermensch), 761
Oxford university, 708, 738

P

Pact of the Littoral (1831), 776
Padishah, 615, G–8
Pagan kingdom, 569
Paine, Thomas, 670

Paintings, 549
    of Heiji wars, 548
    Ming Dynasty scroll painting, 532
    during Ming–Qing times, 545
    Mona Lisa, 450
    Safavid times, 625
    of a Shinto–river festival, 529
    Tokugawa, 560
    Woodblock print, 560
Pakistan, 1043
Palatine Calvinists, 485
Pampas, 777, G–8
Pan-African Congress, 1032
Panjab, 795
Panjabi Sikhs, 795
Pan-Islamism, 807, G–9
Pankhurst, Emmeline, 741
Papal States, 443, 449, 453, 486, G–9
Paraguay, 776
Paris, 678
    laboring populace of, 707
    rebellion against the Convention, 682
    sans-culottes of, 680
Paris club, 678, 681
Paris Commune, 678, 700
Parisians, 675
Paris Jacobin Club, 681
Paris settlement, 887–891
Parlement of Paris, 672
Parlements, 594, 653, 672, 674–675, G–9
Parliamentary monarchy in England, 577–578,
    G–9
Parma, 720
Parnell, Charles Stewart, 709–710
Partido Revolucionario Institucional (PRI), 784,
    1029–1030, G–9
Pascal, Blaise, 489
Pasha, Sa'd Zaghlul, 806
Pasha, Urabi, 806
Pashas, 804
Passover, 1049
Pastoralists, 421, G–9
Pastoral societies, 654
Paternalistic legislation, 705
Patriarch, 585
Paul III, Pope, 476
Pax Porfiriana, 782
Payne, Daniel A., 715
Peace of Augsburg (1555), 474, 485
Peace of Nijmegen (1678, 1679), 588
Peace of Nystad, 584
Peace of Westphalia (1648), 576, 587
Peace process, 1049, G–9
Peanuts, 531
Peasant household, 597
Peasant revolts, 595
Peasants, Middle Ages, 438–439
Pedro, 693
Peel, Robert, 707
Peninsulares, 505, 689–690, 767, G–9
Pensées, 489
The People's Will, 748
Pepper trade, 634
Perestroika, 974, G–9
Perón, Eva, 779
Perón, Juan, 778, 1028
Peronism, 778, G–9

Persian, 795
The Persian Letters, 651
Peru, 774
Peshawar, 795
Pessimism, 647
Peter III, Tsar, 591
Peter the Great, 542, 576, 595
    developing a navy, 584
    founding of Saint Petersburg, 584
    Great Northern War with Sweden, 584
    military establishment under, 584
    military strategies, 584
    radical administrative reforms, 584–585
    and Russian conquests, 584
    secular control of Church, 585
    son Aleksei, 584–585
    and Swedish institutions, 585
    Table of Ranks, 585
    taming of Streltsy and Boyars, 584
Petrarch, Francesco, 450
Philip, Archduke, 457
Philip II Augustus, 441
Philippe, Louise, 707, 711
Philip V of Spain, 589
Phillips, Captain Thomas, 524
Philosophes, 646–647, 649, 651, 653–654, 660,
    663, 690, 762, G–9
Philosophia Christi, 467
Philosophy of Tokugawa Japan, 561
Physical cosmology, 639
"Picture-treading" plaques, 551
Piedmont, 720, 721, 722
Pierre Patel the Elder, 582
Pinochet, General Augusto, 1027–1028
Pirs, 622, G–9
Pius VII, Pope, 683
Planck, Max, 761
Planetary positions, 639, 640
Plan of Ayala, 782
Plantation economy, 510, 517, 694, G–9
Plato, 640, 655
Platonism, Islamic form of, 625
Plekhanov, Georgii, 748
Podesta, 449
Poetry
    autobiography of Aziz Nesin, 1039
    Iqbal's, 808
    during Ming–Qing times, 545
    Ottoman, 619
    "The Slaves' Lament," 596
    Tokugawa era, 560
    during the Warring States period, 560
Pogroms, 427, 446, 742, 747, G–9
Poincaré, Henri, 760
Poland, 638
    communism and solidarity in, 973–974
    crises of 1956, 956
    nationhood, 702
    partition of, 664
    and settlement of eastern Europe, 687
Poles, 725
Polis, 655
Politburo, 904
Political consolidation, in the northern
    transatlantic world
    American Republic, 712–717
    Canada, 717–718

    creation of nations, 701
    economic goals of the liberals, 704–705
    European, 700, 709–712, 718–724
    nationalism in Europe, 700
    nationhood, 701–702
    nineteenth century, 701
    North America, 700
    political liberalism, 704–712
    racial theory and anti-semitism, 725–728
    regions of nationalistic pressure in Europe,
        703–704
    unrest of nationalities, 724–725
Political Islamism, 1021, G–9
Politique, 482
Polk, James, 780
Polo, Marco, 462
Polyglot Bible, 467
Popular Front, 898, 1014, G–9
Porcelains, 533, 625
Porteños, 776
Portugal and slave trade, 696
Portuguese pirate-traders, 550
Portuguese voyages, 461–462
Positivism, 771, 785, G–9
Postcolonial era
    Africa, 1030–1038
    Argentina, 1028
    Brazil, 1028–1029
    Chile, 1027–1028
    Cuba, 1026–1027
    developments after 1945, 1021
    Latin America, 1023–1030
    Mexico, 1029–1030
Pot, Pol, 1015–1016
Potato, 601
Potsdam, 948–949
Pottery industry of Europe, 545
Pragmatic Sanction, 467, 587–588, 590, G–9
Prazeros, 421, G–9
Predestination, concept of, 649
Primary intellectual inheritances, 637
Primogeniture patterns, 548
Principia Mathematica, 644
Principles of 1789, 704
Procurator general, 585
Progressives, 755–758
Prohibition Amendment of 1919, 918
Proletarianization, 733–734, G–9
Prosser, Gabriel, 695
Protectorate, 542, 806, 815–816, 851, 1010,
    1044, G–9
The Protestant Ethic and the Spirit of Capitalism,
    472
Protestant ethics, 530
Protestant House of Hanover in Germany, 578
Protestant Irishmen, 707
Protestant Reformation in England, 577
Protestants, 631, 642
    under Edward VI, 475
    Jesuit eyes Protestants, 476
    under Louis XIV, 583
    Peace of Augsburg, 474
    and Reformation, 465
    revocation of the Edict of Nantes, 583
    St. Bartholomew's Day Massacre of French,
        481, 483
    Theodore Beza's support, 483

Provincial Letters, 489
Prussia, 576, 587–588, 722, 723
    against France, 591
    invasion of Silesia, 590
    Jewish communities in, 607
    political unity, 703
    and settlement of eastern Europe, 687
Psychoanalysis, 761–762
Ptolemaic astronomy, 640
Ptolemaic system, 639–641, G–9
Public Health Act of 1875, 709
Public relations, 660
Pugachev, Emelyan, 595
Pugachev's Rebellion, 595–596
Pulguksa temple, 566
Pure Food (1906), 758
Pure Land Buddhist congregations, 549
Puritans, 577–578, G–10
Pusan perimeter, 1011
Putin, Vladimir, 979–980
Putting out system, in textiles, 534

Q

*Qadi*s, 408
Qajar regime, 805
Qanun, 616–617, G–10
Qanun-name (*"Lawbook"*), 616–617
Qasem, Abd al-Karim, 1052
Qianlong, Emperor, 539–540, 543
Qing dynasty, 530, 567
    culture, 544–546
    foreign relations, 542–543
    literature, 545–546
    during Qianlong, 540
Qizilbash ("Red Heads"), 622
Quadruple Alliance, 686, 688
Quaker communities, 694
Quebec Act (1774), 670, 717
Queen Christina of Sweden, 644
Queen of Scots, 485
Qur'an, 651, 803, G–10

R

Racism, 717, 725–728, 761, 771, 814, 817, 899,
    916, G–10
Racial thinking, 725–727
Radioactivity, 760–761
Raj, 795, G–10
Ramadan, 823, G–10
Ramananda, 629
Ramayana, 629
Rasputin, Grigori, 751
Raymond, Julian, 677
Reagan, President Ronald, 959
Realpolitik, 1041
Red Army, 899
Refactory clergy, 677
Reformation, the, 463–476, 530, 550
    achievements, 476–481
    and arranged marriages, 478
    Calvinism, 472–473
    Catholicism, 475–476
    and families, 479
    German, 467–471
    and later marriages, 478
    Peace of Augsburg, 474

postal systems and printing press, establishment
    of, 465–466
    Protestant, 465
    "Reformation Parliament," 475
    religion and society, 465
    secular administrative competency, 466
    Swiss, 472–473
    and wet nursing, 479
Reform Bill in Great Britain, 696
Refractory priests, 677
Regular clergy, 438
Reichstag, 745, 907, G–10
Reign of Terror and its aftermath, 679–682, G–10
Relativity, 761, G–10
Religions, of Southeast Asia, 634
Religious anti-Semitism, 726–728
Religious faith and practice. *See also* Buddhism;
    Christianity; Confucianism
    during epidemics, 445–446
    French wars (1562-1598), 482
    Reformation, impact of, 465–480
    Russia, 455
    in sixteenth-century life, 478
    Spain, 456–457
Religious pluralism, 639
The Renaissance, 425, 530, G–10
Renan, Ernest, 763
Repartimiento, 505, G–10
Reparations, 891, 896–897, 907, 910–911, G–10
Report on the Affairs of British North America, 718
Republic of Virtue, 680
Revisionism, 745–747, 912, G–10
Revolt of 1857, 795, 798
Revolution, meaning, 638
Revolutionary Youth League of Vietnam, 1014
Revolution-in-science metaphor, 638
Revolution of 1688, 578
Revolutions of 1848, 709–712
Reza, Muhammad, 1040
Rhee, Syngman, 1010
Rhineland Gazette, 744
Richard the Lion-Hearted, 429, 441
Río de la Plata, 776
Rivadavia, Bernardino, 776
Robespierre, 680–681
Rockefeller, John D., 757
Roehm, Captain Ernst, 909
Roentgen, Wilhelm, 760
Romagna, 720
Roman Catholic Church, 641–642, 662, 676, 683,
    778, 780, 907, 943, 960
Roman Catholicism, 650, 683, 707
The Romance of the Three Kingdoms, 545
Romanians, 704, 725
Romanov, Michael, 583
Rome–Berlin Axis Pact, 927
Romeo and Juliet, 489
Rommel, General Erwin, 933
Rônin, 555–557
Roosevelt, Theodore, 756–758, 837, 919,
    947–948
Rosie the Riveter, 944
Rousseau, Jean-Jacques, 654
Roy, Ram Mohan, 796
Royal absolutism, 662
Royal Society of London, 645
Royal Swiss guards, 678

Rural rebellions, 595
Russia, 576, 718. *See also* Soviet Union, post
    World War II
    as an active European power, 583
    autocracy of Nicholas I, 705–706
    birth of Bolshevism, 748–751
    Bloody Sunday, 750
    chronology, 586
    condition of the serfs, 595
    Decembrist Revolt of 1825, 705–706
    expansion (1689–1796), 664
    industrial development, nineteenth century,
        748–751
    Jewish emancipation, 742
    Jewish population, 607
    major dates in turn-of-the-century, 751
    March Revolution in, 884–886
    under Nicholas, 706
    nineteenth century, 731
    under Peter the Great, 583–585
    from Peter the Great through Catherine the
        Great, chronology, 664
    political experiment, post World War I, 898–904
    population expansion in eighteenth century, 600
    revolution of 1905 and its aftermath, 749–751
    Russo-Japanese agreement, 837
Russia, fifteenth century, 455
Russo-Japanese War of 1904–1905, 876, 1010
Rutherford, Ernest, 760
Ruz, Fidel Castro, 1026
Rwandan genocide, 1036

S

SA (*Sturm Abteilung*), 909, G–10
Sacrifice ceremonies, Benin kingdom, 412–414
Sadra, Mulla, 626
Safavid dynasty
    art, 625
    central rule, 622
    chronology, 625
    craft, 625
    culture and learning, 625–626
    decline of, 624–625
    literature, 625
    origin, 622–623
    Safavid-Shi'ite schism, 631
    wars with Ottoman, 623
Safavid Iran, 617–618
Sahara, 402–412, 415, 515–516, 810–811, 1030,
    1033, 1037–1038, 1049, G–10
Sahel, 403–404, 406, 408, 410–411, 415, 811,
    G–10
Saikaku, Ihara, 561
Saint Domingue, 695
Saint Helena, 688
Saint Petersburg, 584, 585
Saladin, 429
Salafiyya movement, 763
Salisbury, Lord, 709
Samurai, 547, 549, 831, G–10
Sandinista Revolution in Nicaragua, 1028, G–10
Sans-culottes, 678–680, 682, G–10
Sans-Culottes, Convention and the Role of,
    678–679
Sanskrit, 725, 795
São Paulo, 787
Sarajevo, 983

Saturday Evening Post, 944, 945
Scandinavia, 701
Scheidemann, Philipp, 891
Schleswig, 722–723, 723
Schlieffen Plan, 880, G–10
The Scholars, 546
Scholasticism, 434, 442, 544, G–10
Scholastic modes, of learning and thinking, 643
Scholastic philosophers, 643
Schuster, Morgan, 808
The Science of Mechanics, 760
Scientific revolution, 530, 637, G–10
    application of mathematics to scientific
        investigation, 641
    Bacon, Francis, 641–643
    Brahe, Tycho, 640
    complexity of, 638
    Copernicus, Nicolaus, 639–640
    empirical induction method, 641, 643
    Galilei, Galileo, 641
    influence on Western civilization, 643
    Kepler, Johannes, 640
    Locke, John, 645–646
    major figures in, 646
    political thought, 639
    and reappropriation of older knowledge, 638
    separated studies and crude laboratories, 638
    sixteenth and seventeenth centuries, 638
    and social activity, 638
    universe, concept, 639–641
    women and, 644–645
Scramble for Africa, 814–817, 867–868, 1032,
    G–10
Second Coalition, 683
Second Continental Congress, 670
Second Estate of the nobility, 672
Second Reform Act, 708
Secular clergy, 438, G–10
Secular values, 651
Seiyu-kai, Rikken, 837–838
Seiyûkai Party, 839
Sejong, King, 568
Selim I, 615
Selim III, 806
Seljuk institutions, 623
Seljuks of Rum, 614
Semana Trágica, 778
Seneca Falls Convention, 704
Senegal, 811
Senegambia, 415
Senghor, Leopold, 818–819
Sepoy Mutiny. *See* Revolt of 1857
September Massacres, 678
Serbo-Croatians, 725
Serbs, 703
Serfs, 433, 438, 446, 588, 594–596, 662, 692,
    748, 751, G–10
Servetus, Michael, 473
Seven Weeks' War, 722
Seven Years' War (1756–1763), 591–592, 667, 694
Shah, Qajar, 804
Shah, Reza, 1040
Shah Jahan, 626–627
Shakespeare, William, 489
Sha'rawi, Huda, 808
Sha'rawi's act, 808

Shari'a (religious law), 418, 616–617, 620, 812,
    822, 1051, G–10
Sharifs, 402, 418, 630, G–11
Shastri, Lal Bahadur, 1042
Shawls, 625
Shaybani, Muhammad, 630
Shaykh, 411, 628, G–11
Sheikhs, 622
Shi'ite imams, 622, 804
Shi'ite monarchy, 623
Shi'ite-Safavid schism, 631
Shi'ite sufi ideology, 622
Shi'ite-Sunni political competition, 630–632
Shi'ite *ulama*, 625
Shikai, Yuan, 852–853
Shivaji, 627
Shogun, Ashikaga, 549
Shona, 871
Shostakovich's Seventh Symphony, 946
Sierra Leone, 696
Sikh movement's militant reformism, 627
Sikhs, 627
Silk, 533, 833
Silk Road, 426, 615, 851, G–11
Singh, Gobind, 627
Singh, Manmohan, 1043
Singh, V. P., 1043
Single-track system, 991
Single Whip Reform, 533
Sino-Japanese War (1894–1895), 1010
Sino-Soviet Alliance, 1011
Sirhindi, Ahmad, 630
Six Articles of 1539, 475
Sixtus IV, Pope, 468
Slater, Samuel, 712
Slavery
    abolitionist movement, 715–717
    in Africa, 519–522
    Atlantic slave trade, 499
    colonial America, 515–518
    Haitian revolution, 689–690
    Kongo Empire, 417
    media of exchange, 521
    Oriental and Occidental slave trade, 519–520,
        522
    Pequots, 510
    plantation system of slave labor, 507, 519–520
    slave auction notice, 496
    slave populations in British colonies, 511
    slave ship *Brookes*, 525
    slave trade, Africa and Transatlantic, 518–526
    sources of the slaves for the transatlantic trade,
        522
    in Sudan, 519–520
    in sugar plantations of Brazil, 507–509
    transatlantic revolutions against, 693–696
    and women, 520, 523, 526
Slave trade, 577
    abolition of, 695–696
Slovenes, 703
Smith, Adam, 654
The Social Contract, 655
Social Darwinism, 725
"Social Gospel," 755
Socialism, 727, 748, 751
Social Revolutionary Party, 748
Social Security Administration, 920

Society, thoughts about, 655
Society of Jesus, 475
Society of Revolutionary Republican Women, 679
Socrates, 761
Solomon, Job Ben, 523
Solzhenitsyn, 973
Song dynasty, 533–534
Songhai kingdom, 408–410
Sons of Liberty, 669
So-seki, Natsume, 835
South Africa, 421–422, 871
Southern-seas trade centers, 632–634
South Korea, 1010–1011
    growth and democracy, 1012–1013
Soviets, 751, 1041–1042, 1052, G–11
Soviet Union, post World War II. *See also* Russia
    agricultural policy, 901–903
    Brezhnev Years, 973
    collapse of, 977–981
    collectivize farming, 901
    communism and solidarity in Poland, 973–974
    economic policy of War Communism, 899
    Five-Year Plans, 903
    under Gorbachev, 974
    Great Purges, 903–904
    Khrushchev Years, 972–973
    New Economic Policy, 899–900
    policy of collectivization, 901
    political murders and executions, 904
    rapid industrialization, 900–903
    right-wing versus left-wing faction, 900
    Russian invasion of Georgia, 981
    Stalin's policy against *kulak*, 901–902
Spain, 577
Spain, fifteenth century, 455–457
    commercial regulation and the flota system,
        505–507
    conquest of the Aztecs and the Incas, 500–501
    establishment of Spanish Empire, 500–502
    Roman Catholic Church in Spanish America,
        501–503
    varieties of economic activity, 503–505
Spanish-American War (1898), 732, 758, 864,
    1026
Spanish Creoles, 693
Spanish voyages, 462–463
Speer, Albert, 941
Spice Islands, 569, 613
Spinning jenny, 603, 605, G–11
The Spirit of the Laws, 651, 653–654, 694
Spiritual Exercises, 475
"Square Deal," 757
SS (*Schutzstaffel*), 914, G–11
St. Domingue (Haiti), 677
Stalin, Josef, 900, 946, 954
Stamp Act Congress (1765), 668, 671
Stanley, Henry Morton, 870
State of rest, 639
St. Bartholomew's Day Massacre of French
    Protestants, 482, 483
Steam engine, 604
Steam Navigation Company, 849
Steppes, of Central Asia, 614
Stewart, Robert, 686
Stolypin, P. A., 751
Stories from a Ming Collection and *The Courtesan's
    Jewel Box*, 545

Streltsy, 583–586, G–11
Stresemann, Gustav, 910
Stuart dynasty, 577
Studia humanitatis, 449, G–11
Studies in Hysteria, 762
Stupa, 566, G–11
The Subjection of Women, 741
Sudan, 402–412, 516, 520, 526, *613*, 763,
    811–813, 1019, *1022*, 1033, 1036, *1037*,
    1045, 1053, G–11
Suez Canal, 806, 870
    crises, 956–957
Suffragettes, 741, G–11
Sufi, 409, 621–622, 625, 628–632, 803, 807–808,
    812, 822–823, G–11
Sufi brotherhood, 623, 629–630
Sufi institution, 621
Sugar, 774
Sugar Act (1764), 668
Süleyman, 615
Süleymaniye Mosque in Istanbul, 617
Sultans, 419, 569, 623, 634, 806, G–11
Sundiata, King, 407
Sung, Kim II, 1010
Sun King, 581
Sunna, 410, G–11
Sunni Ottomans, 623, 631
Sunni sufi order in Azerbaijan, 622
Sunni Turkoman groups, 622
Superego, 762, G–11
Superstition and enlightenment, 487–491
Surrender of Feudal Privileges, 673
Swaraj, 799
Swadeshi, 801
Swahili, 417
Swahili, 403, 417–421, 811, 819, G–11
Sweet potatoes, 531
Swiss Reformation
    in Geneva, 472–473
    in Zurich, 472
Switzerland, 748
Syncretism, 410, G–11

T

Table of Ranks, 585–586, G–11
Tabula rasa, 645
Taft, William Howard, 758
Tahmasp I, 623
Taille, 447, 455, G–11
Taino Indians, 462
Taiping Rebellion, 717, 846–848, 854, G–11
Taipings, 847
Taiwan, 851, 1008–1010
Taj Mahal, 627
Takashi, Hara, 838
Taliban, 1042
Talleyrand, 687
Tallow, 774
Tang dynasty, 530, 566
Tanzimat, 802, 806–807, G–11
Tariqa, 622
Tehran meeting, 947
Temple of Reason, 680
Tennessee Valley Authority (TVA), 920
Test Act, 578
Tetzel, John, 468
Textile production, 602–604

Thatcher, Margaret, 963
Theocracy, 1051, G–11
Theory of race, 725
Theory of universal gravitation, 644
Theresa, Maria, 587, 662
Thermidorian reaction, 682, G–11
Third Estate, 672, G–11
Third Ming emperor, 540
Third Republic, 724
Third World countries, 564
Thomson, J. J., 760
Three-field system, 599, G–12
Thus Spake Zarathustra, 761
Tibetan lamas, 630
Tilak, B. G., 799
Time of Troubles, 583
Title of Protector of Peru, 691
Ti-yong reformism, 854
Togo, Admiral, 837
Toju, Nakae, 561
Tokugawa Confucianism, 561–562
Tokugawa economy, 832
Tokugawa era, 547
    bakufu system, 551–552, 554–557
    bureaucracy, 557
    chronology, 563
    culture, 559–560
    Dutch studies, 564
    economy, 559
    Edo establishments, 554
    eighteenth and early nineteenth centuries,
        555–559
    establishment of rule, 551–555
    "feudal" system of lord–vassal relationships, 562
    forty-seven *rônin*, 555–557
    government, 557
    Hideyoshi's rule, 551
    land holdings, 551
    poetry, 560
    political engineering and economic growth
        during the seventeenth century, 550–554
    reforms, 557
    Samurai loyalty, 562
    scholars, 563–564
    women, 556
Tokyo Imperial University, 839
Toland, John, 649, 651
Tong, Le Thanh, 571–572
Tories, 708
Toulon, 682
Transatlantic revolutions, 668–669
    abolition of slavery, 693–696
    in British Colonies in North America, 668–672
Transubstantiation, 472, 475–476, G–12
Treatise of Civil Government, 579
Treatise on Tolerance, 651
Treaty of Aix-la-Chapelle, 591
Treaty of Amiens, 683–684
Treaty of Basel of March 1795, 682
Treaty of Brest-Litovsk, 886
Treaty of Campo Formio, 682
Treaty of Chaumont, 686
Treaty of Hubertusburg (1763), 591
Treaty of Lunéville, 683
Treaty of Paris (1763), 592, 668, 717
Treaty of Paris (1783), 671
Treaty of Prague, 722

Treaty of Tilsit, 685
Treaty of Tordesillas, 507
Treaty of Utrecht (1713), 589–590
Treaty of Versailles, 891–892
Treaty of Westphalia (1648), 486
Treaty ports, 846, 847, 849–850, 856, 857, 1001,
    G–12
Trekboers, 421–422, G–12
Tribunes, 442, G–12
Tripartite Pact, 842–843, G–12
Tripitaka, 566
Triple Alliance (1873–1890), 872–874
Trotsky, Leon, 899, 900
Truth and Reconciliation Commission (TRC),
    1035
Tudor Dynasty, 457
Tuileries, palace of, 675
Tulasidas, 629
Turkey, 1039
Turkish Coffeehouse, *621*
Turkish dynasty. *See* Ottoman Empire
Turkish Embassy Letters, 652
Turkish women, 652
Turkoman Dynasty, 804
Turkoman tribesmen of eastern Anatolia, 622
Turner, Nat, 695
Tuscany, 720
Tutsi-led Rwandan Patriotic Front (RPF), 1036
Twenty-Sixth of July Movement, 1026
*Two Tactics of Social Democracy in the Bourgeois-
    Democratic Revolution*, 749
Two Treatises of Government, 645

U

Ukraine, 724, 901
Ulama, 617, 619, 624, 630, 653, 803, 1040, G–12
Ul-Haqq, Zia, 1043
Ulyanov, Vladimir Illich, 748
Umma, 805, 822, G–12
Unam Sanctam, 448
Unequal treaties, 830, 837, 846, 859, G–12
Unigeniture patterns, 548
Union of German Women's Organizations
    (BDFK), 741
United Automobile Workers, 920
United Mine Workers, 920
United States, 732
    American Progressives, 755–758
    child labor, 755–756
    and environmental issues, 984–985
    European immigration to, 752–754
    and Korean War, 1011
    New Deal, 916–920
    political consolidation, 700
    relationship between with Soviet Union post
        World War II, 952–955
    and Sandinistas, 1028
    and Vietnam War, 1014–1015
United States, twentieth century
    civil rights, 969
    Reagan administration, 971–972
    social programs, 970
    Truman and Eisenhower administrations,
        968–969
    Vietnam War and domestic turmoil, 970
    Watergate scandal, 970–971
Universe, concept of, 639–641, 644

University of Alcalá, 467
University of Padua, 641
University of Paris, 436
Upper Peru (Bolivia), 776
Urban II, Pope, 430
Urdu, 631
Uzama, 412, 414, G–12
Uzbek Turks, 622–623, 630

V

Vaccination, 652
Vaihinger, Hans, 760
Valois Dynasty, 470
Vargas, Getulio, 788
Vasa, Gustavus, 473
Vassal, 405–416, 437, 441, 454, 538, 540–541, 547–549, 551–554, G–12
Velvet Revolution in Czechoslovakia, 975–977
Venetian-Mameluk, 461
Venezuela, 691–692, 774
Vernacular, 422, 425, 440, 449–450, 466, 478, 797, G–12
Versailles, 582, 672, 675, 808
Versailles, palace at, 581–582
Versailles Treaty (1919), 905, 908–910, 916
Vespucci, Amerigo, 463
Victoria, Queen, 845
Vienna settlement, 689, 700
Viet Minh, 1014, G–12
Vietnam, 529, 851
    agricultural activity, 570
    anticolonial War, 1014
    Chinese control, 570–571
    chronology, 572
    civilization, 569
    civil service examinations, 572
    conquest of the Mekong Delta, 572
    cultural assimilation in, 569
    emigration of Chinese, 569
    Hindu-Buddhist Cambodian Empire, 570
    independent, 571
    influence of Chinese Buddhism, 569
    "the march to the south," 572
    Mekong Delta, conquest of, 572
    modern, 1013–1017
    Nguyen conquest of the north, 573
    Nguyen Dynasty, 572–573
    origin, 569–570
    position of women in, 572
    pottery, 570
    relations with China, 1016
    ruling families, 571
    unified, 1016
    War with Cambodia, 1015–1016
Vietnam War, 569, 1014–1015
Villa, Pancho, 782
A Vindication of the Rights of Woman, 660, 740
Vita Nuova, 450
Vladimir of Kiev, Prince, 455
Voltaire, 645, 647, 649–651
Von Bismarck, Otto, 722, 728, 745, 816, 868, 874
Von Papen, Franz, 912
Von Schleicher, General Kurt, 912
Von Tirpitz, Admiral Alfred, 875

W

Wafd, 806
Wagner Act of 1935, 919
Wahhabis, 763, 803, 808, 822, 828, 1046, G–12
Wakefield, Priscilla, 598
Wales, 600
Wallace, Alfred Russel, 759
Walpole, Robert, 580
War and Peace, 946
War Communism, 899, G–12
War of Jenkins's Ear (1731), 590
War of the American Revolution, 670
War of the Austrian Succession (1740–1748), 590–591, 660
War of the Spanish Succession (1701–1714), 589
Warring States era, 547, 555
    chronology, 549
    commercial growth of Kamakura and Ashikaga periods, 549
    content of trade, 549–550
    fiefs of aristocratic warriors, 549
    foot soldier revolution, 547–549
    foreign relations and trade, 549–550
    Jesuit missionaries, 550
    maritime expansion, 549–550
Warsaw Pact, 955–956
Wars of Liberation, 685–686
Washington, George, 670
Washington Conference, 840
Water frame, 603, G–12
Watt, James, 604
Watt steam engine, 604
The Wealth of Nations, 654, 694
Weber, Max, 530, 763
Weimar Republic, 742, 897, 907–912, G–12
Wellesley, Sir Arthur, 685
West, post World War II
    crises of 1956, 956–957
        NATO and the Warsaw Pact, 955–956
        relationship between the United States and the Soviet Union, 952–955
Western civilization, troubles of, 725
Western European unification, 959–960
Western science and the technology, 637
Western superiority, 725
Wet nursing, 479
Wheat, 773
White Lotus Rebellion, 531, 540
White Russians, 702, G–12
Whitney, Eli, 714
Wilberforce, William, 695–696
Wilkinson, John, 604
William I, Emperor, 588, 722, 745
William II, Emperor, 678, 745, 874, 876
William III, Frederick, 578, 687
William I of Prussia, 722
William IV, King, 708
William of Normandy, 440–441
William Pitt the Elder, 591
William Pitt the Younger, 684
William Prince of Orange, 578, 588
Williams, George Washington, 871
William the Silent, 578
Wilson, Woodrow, 758
Witches and witch hunting, 487–488
Wollstonecraft, Mary, 660
Women
    in the actions of the Parisian crowd, 675
    China, late imperial, 534
    Edo period, 556
    English versus Turkish, 652
    in the Enlightenment era, 657–660
    Europe, twentieth century, 967
    and family economy, 597
    Hakka, 534
    ideas of political liberalism, 704
    Japan, modern, 998
    in Nazi Germany, 915–916
    policies of exclusion from scientific endeavors, 645
    and reform in Middle East, 808
    Rousseau's view of, 659
    in Vietnam, 572
    in the world of Scientific Revolution, 644–645
Women, nineteenth century
    access to education, 737–738
    in Britain, 735–736
    chronology, 738
    concept of gender-determined roles, 735
    contraception and abortion, 737
    divorce, 736
    domestic division of labor, 735
    in domestic industries, 736
    in the early industrial revolution, 735–736
    employment patterns, 738–739
    family law, 736–737
    impact of the factory, 735
    late, 739–740
    new employment opportunities, 738–739
    obstacles to achieving equality, 740–741
    poverty, 736
    professional education, 737–738
    rise of political feminism, 740–742
    school teaching, 738
    secretarial and clerical jobs, 738–739
    sexual and reproductive rights, 737
    and social disabilities, 736–738
    in textile production, 735
    voting rights, 741
    withdrawal from labor force, 739
Women's Congress of Palestine, 808
Works Progress Administration (WPA), 920, G–12
Worldview
    Chinese, 534
    Confucianism, 534
    Newtonian, 649
World War I, 732, 760, 818
    assassination of Austrian Archduke Francis Ferdinand, 878
    Balkan Wars, 877–878
    Bosnian crisis, 877
    chronology, 879
    in East, 883–884
    end of, 886–891
    Germany and Austria's response to assassination, 878–879
    light manufacturing, 775
    period (1908–1914), 877
    at sea, 884
    second Moroccan crisis, 877
    settlement at Paris, 887–891
    strategies and stalemate (1914–1917), 880–884
    Triple Entente's response, 880
    and United States, 884

in West, 881–883
World War II, 775, 778, 789
   allied landings in Africa, Sicily, and Italy,
     937–938
   America's entry into the War, 937–938
   Battle of Britain, 932
   Battle of Stalingrad, 938
   cost of, 941
   coup in Austria, 928
   Czechoslovakia, 928
   defeat of Nazi Germany, 939–940
   destruction of Versailles, 924–925
   fall of the Japanese Empire, 940–941
   France, 943
   German attack on Russia, 933–934
   German Conquest of Europe, 931–932
   Germany, 941–943
   Great Britain, 943–944
   Hiroshima bombing, 941
   Hitler's racial theories and goals, 924
   Hitler's racism and Holocaust, 934–935
   Italian attack on Ethiopia, 925
   Japanese attack on United States, 935–937
   Munich Agreement, 928–930
   Nazi-Soviet Pact, 930–931
   peace preparations, 946–949
   Pearl Harbor, 935–937
   period (1933–1939), 924–931
   period (1939–1945), 931–941
   policy of appeasement, 926
   remilitarization of the Rhineland, 925–926
   Soviet Union, 944–946
   Spanish Civil War, 926–928
   strategic bombing, 938–939
   United States, 944
   use of atomic energy for military purposes, 941
Wudi, Emperor, 566

X
Xavier, Saint Francis, 550
Xiuquan, Hong, 847
X rays, 760

Y
Yalta meeting, 947–948
Yamagata, Prime Minister, 836
Yangban, 567–568, 573, G–12
Yaroslav the Wise, 455
Y Costilla, Miguel Hidalgo, 692
Yeltsin, Boris, 979
Yeni cheri, 617
Yohime, 558
Young Plan of 1929, 897, 911
Youwei, Kang, 852

Y Pavón, José María Morelos, 693
Yuanpei, Cai, 854
Yugoslavia, 725, 981–983
Yukichi, Fukuzawa, 564

Z
Zaibatsu, 826, 833, 841, 991, 1012, G–12
Zambia, 871
Zanj, 417
Zapata, Emiliano, 782
Zapatistas, 1030
Zardari, Asif Ali, 1043
Zedong, Mao, 545, 854, 857, 859
Zen Buddhism, 560
Zexu, Lin, 844
Zhongshan, Sun, 853
Zhou dynasty, 532
Zhou Rites, 847
Zhu Xi philosophy, 567
Zimbabwe, 871
Zionism, 726–727, 743, G–12
Zong, 695
Zongtang, Zuo, 851
Zulu nation and kingdom, 810, 871
Zulu war (1879), 818
Zwinglian reformations, 472